FOURTEENTH EDITION

SUBJECT & STRATEGY

A WRITER'S READER

PAUL ESCHHOLZ
University of Vermont

ALFRED ROSA
University of Vermont

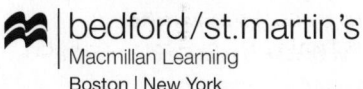

For Bedford/St. Martin's

Vice President, Editorial, Macmillan Learning Humanities: Edwin Hill
Editorial Director, English: Karen S. Henry
*Senior Publisher for Composition, Business and Technical Writing,
   Developmental Writing:* Leasa Burton
Executive Editor for Readers: John E. Sullivan III
Developmental Editor: Sherry Mooney
Assistant Editor: Jennifer Prince
Production Editor: Louis C. Bruno Jr.
Media Producer: Rand Thomas
Publishing Services Manager: Andrea Cava
Senior Production Supervisor: Robert Cherry
Executive Marketing Manager: Joy Fisher Williams
Project Management: Jouve
Photo Research Manager: Martha Friedman
Photo Researcher: Julie Tesser
Permissions Manager: Kalina K. Ingham
Text Permissions Researcher: Elaine Kosta
Senior Art Director: Anna Palchik
Text Design: Meryl Levavi
Cover Design: John Callahan
Cover Image: Andy Roberts/Getty Images
Composition: Jouve
Printing and Binding: LSC Communications

Copyright © 2017, 2014, 2011, 2009 by Bedford/St. Martin's

All rights reserved. No part of this book may be reproduced, stored in a retrieval system, or transmitted in any form or by any means, electronic, mechanical, photocopying, recording, or otherwise, except as may be expressly permitted by the applicable copyright statutes or in writing by the Publisher.

Manufactured in the United States of America.

1 0 9 8 7 6
f e d c b a

For information, write: Bedford/St. Martin's, 75 Arlington Street, Boston, MA 02116
   (617-399-4000)

ISBN 978-1-319-04015-4 (Student Edition)
ISBN 978-1-319-07550-7 (Instructor's Edition)

Acknowledgments

Text acknowledgments and copyrights appear at the back of the book on pages 776–79, which constitute an extension of the copyright page. Art acknowledgments and copyrights appear on the same page as the art selections they cover.

Preface for Instructors

SUBJECT & STRATEGY IS A READER FOR COLLEGE WRITERS. THE EIGHTY-TWO selections in this edition were chosen to entertain students and to contribute to their self-awareness and understanding of the world around them. Above all, however, we've brought together readings and thought-provoking apparatus to help students become better writers.

As its title suggests, *Subject & Strategy* places equal emphasis on the content and form of good writing. While all readers pay attention to content, far fewer notice the strategies—narration, description, illustration, process analysis, comparison and contrast, division and classification, definition, cause and effect analysis, and argumentation—that writers, artists, filmmakers, journalists, and storytellers use to organize their work and to make their subjects understandable and effective for a given audience. Because these strategies are such an essential element of the writer's craft, we have designed *Subject & Strategy* to help students understand what they are and how they work. Each print selection skillfully models the use of the strategies, while questions, writing prompts, visuals, and other pedagogy further support students in writing well-constructed essays of their own.

ENDURING FEATURES OF *SUBJECT & STRATEGY*

We continue to include the key features—developed and refined over thirteen previous editions—that have made *Subject & Strategy* a classic introductory text.

Timely, Teachable, and Diverse Readings

Eighty-two selections—sixty-nine professional selections and thirteen student essays—offer a broad spectrum of subjects, styles, and cultural points of view. The work of well-known writers—including Malcolm X, Maya Angelou, Bharati Mukherjee, Andrew Sullivan, and Isabel Allende—as well as emerging voices—including Nancy Armour, Roger Cohen, Derald Wing Sue, Alicia Ault, and Mindy Kaling—demonstrates for students the versatility and strengths of the different rhetorical strategies.

Thorough Coverage of the Reading and Writing Processes

Chapter 1, "Reading," discusses effective reading habits and illustrates attentive, analytical reading of essays and visuals using Cherokee Paul McDonald's "A View from the Bridge," Thomas L. Friedman's "My Favorite Teacher," a photograph of a street scene, and charts from the *Wall Street Journal* about bottled water consumption.

Chapter 2, "Writing," offers writing advice and provides a case study of a student paper in progress, which illustrates one student's writing process and shows what can be accomplished with careful, thoughtful revision.

Chapter 3, "Writers on Writing," showcases inspiration, insight, and advice on writing well from professional writers Russell Baker, Anne Lamott, Linda S. Flower, Susan Orlean, Stephen King, and Isabel Allende.

Detailed Introductions to Each Rhetorical Strategy

The introduction to each rhetorical chapter opens with an example of the strategy at work in everyday life and then examines its use in written texts, discusses the various purposes for which writers use the strategy, and offers advice on how to use it in various college disciplines. This discussion is followed by detailed advice on how to write an essay using the strategy, including guidelines on selecting topics, developing thesis statements, considering audiences, gathering evidence, and using other rhetorical strategies in support of the dominant strategy.

Annotated Student Essays

An annotated student essay appears in each rhetorical chapter, offering students realistic models for successfully incorporating a particular strategy into their own writing. Discussion questions follow each student essay, encouraging students to analyze and evaluate the overall effectiveness of the rhetorical strategies employed in the example.

Extensive Rhetorical Apparatus for Professional Essays

Numerous questions and prompts for thought, discussion, in-class activities, and writing accompany each professional essay:

- **Preparing to Read** prompts ask students to write about their own knowledge and/or experiences with the subject of each selection before they read.
- **Thinking Critically about the Text** prompts ask students to analyze, elaborate on, or take issue with a key aspect of each selection. From time to time, discussion questions and writing assignments ask students to revisit their responses to these prompts and reflect on them before moving ahead with more formal writing tasks.
- **Questions on Subject** focus students' attention on the content of each selection as well as on the author's purpose. These questions help students check their comprehension and provide a basis for classroom discussion.
- **Questions on Strategy** direct students to the various rhetorical strategies and writing techniques the writer has used. These questions encourage students to put themselves in the writer's place and to consider how they might employ the strategies in their own writing. In addition, questions in this section ask students to identify and analyze places where the author has used one or more rhetorical strategies to enhance or develop the essay's dominant strategy.
- **Questions on Diction and Vocabulary** emphasize the importance of diction, word choice, and verbal context.
- **Strategy in Action** activities accompanying each essay—usually requiring no more than ten to fifteen minutes of class time and designed for students to complete individually, in small groups, or as a class—allow students to apply their understanding of the strategies at work in a given selection.
- **Writing Suggestions** focus on the particular rhetorical strategy under discussion and/or explore the subject of the essay or a related topic.

End-of-Chapter Writing Suggestions

Writing suggestions at the end of each rhetorical chapter (Chapters 4 through 14) provide additional topics suitable to the strategy covered in each chapter. Select questions include **Writing with Sources** and **Writing in the Workplace** headings to offer practice in these skills. Many of the suggestions refer to particular selections or to multiple selections in the chapter. Instructors can use these writing suggestions to complement or substitute for the more focused writing topics that accompany individual selections.

Advice for Writing Researched Essays

Chapter 14, "Writing with Sources," helps students master this essential academic skill by offering sound, detailed advice on avoiding plagiarism and effectively integrating sources through quotation, summary, and paraphrase. The chapter also features four essays that integrate outside sources. Questions and prompts direct students' attention to how they can use sources persuasively in their own writing.

Chapter 15, "A Brief Guide to Researching and Documenting Essays," provides an overview of the research process, with a focus on finding, evaluating, and analyzing sources; taking notes; and documenting sources. MLA citation models following the 2016 *MLA Handbook* are provided for the most widely used types of sources, along with a sample documented student essay.

Editing Advice

Chapter 16, "Editing for Grammar, Punctuation, and Sentence Style," provides a concise guide to twelve of the most common writing challenges, from sentence run-ons and fragments to wordiness and lack of sentence variety.

Thematic Contents

Immediately after the main table of contents, a second table of contents groups the reading selections into general thematic categories, providing further opportunities for discussion and writing based on the content of individual selections.

Glossary of Rhetorical Terms

The glossary at the end of *Subject & Strategy* provides concise definitions of terms italicized in the text and called out in the questions that follow each reading selection.

NEW TO THIS EDITION OF *SUBJECT & STRATEGY*

Substantially updated for its fourteenth edition, *Subject & Strategy* combines the currency of a brand-new text with the effectiveness of a thoroughly class-tested one. Guided by comments and advice from instructors and students across the country who have used previous editions, we have made a number of meaningful changes to the text.

Engaging New Readings, Compelling Perspectives

Thirty-five readings—about 40 percent of this edition's selections—are new, including

- **Pulitzer Prize–winning author Junot Díaz**'s narrative reflection on fear and how it can become a state of being
- **Actress and author Mindy Kaling** on finding success and acceptance after high school
- **Best-selling writer Barbara Ehrenreich** on why displays of gratitude are so often self-serving
- **Three new annotated student essays** on learning a new skill, personality types, and growing hamburgers in a lab

A Fresh Take on Argument

To reflect the multiplicity of possible perspectives on any complex topic and to encourage students to consider arguments in a multifaceted, nuanced way, we offer the following two new argument clusters:

- *Race and Privilege: How to Address a System of Bias?* Author and researcher Derald Wing Sue, blogger J. Dowsett, and writer John Metta discuss the problem of institutional racism and where each sees both pitfalls and solutions.
- *Getting an Education: What's the Line between Comfort and Learning?* Journalist Jeffrey Zaslow, teaching assistant Siobhan Crowley, and author Greg Lukianoff, collaborating with social psychologist Jonathan Haidt, examine the tension between safety and intellectual growth on college campuses.

Stronger Support for Thematic Connections

An updated appendix of thematic writing assignments extends the thematic table of contents and provides support for cross-chapter connections. The list of key readings and chapter-opening images is organized into small groups and accompanied by writing prompts on such topics as the immigration experience, education, gender, nature, industrial food, inequality, innovation, crime and ethics, the power of language, privacy, and more.

Get the Most Out of Your Course with *Subject & Strategy*

Bedford/St. Martin's offers resources and format choices that help you and your students get even more out of your book and course. To learn more about or to order any of the following products, contact your Macmillan sales representative, e-mail sales support (**sales_support@bfwpub.com**), or search for *Subject & Strategy* at **macmillanlearning.com**.

Choose from Alternative Formats of *Subject & Strategy*

Bedford/St. Martin's offers a range of affordable formats, allowing students to choose the one that works best for them. For details about our e-book partners, visit **macmillanlearning.com/ebooks**.

Select Value Packages

Add value to your text by packaging one of the following resources with *Subject & Strategy*. To learn more about package options for any of the following products, contact your Bedford/St. Martin's sales representative or search for *Subject & Strategy* at **macmillanlearning.com**.

LaunchPad Solo for Readers and Writers offers instruction tailored to individual students' unique needs and features several innovative digital tools:

- **Reading comprehension quizzes.** A quiz is provided for every selection in *Subject & Strategy*.
- **Prebuilt units that support a learning arc.** Each unit includes a pre-test, multimedia instruction and assessment, help for multilingual writers, and a post-test that assesses what students have learned about critical reading, the writing process, using sources, grammar, style, and mechanics.
- **Video introductions.** Videos overview many unit topics and illustrate the concepts at hand.
- **Adaptive quizzing for targeted learning.** Most units include LearningCurve, game-like quizzing that focuses on the areas in which each student needs the most help.
- **The ability to monitor student progress.** Use the Gradebook to see which students are on track and which need additional help.

Writer's Help 2.0 is a powerful online writing resource that helps students find answers whether they are searching for writing advice on their own or as part of an assignment:

- **Reading comprehension quizzes.** A quiz is provided for every selection in *Subject & Strategy*.

- **Smart search.** Built on research with more than 1,600 student writers, the smart search in Writer's Help 2.0 provides reliable results even when students use novice terms such as *flow* and *unstuck*.
- **Trusted content from our best-selling handbooks.** Choose *Writer's Help 2.0, Hacker Version* or *Writer's Help 2.0, Lunsford Version,* and ensure that students have clear advice and examples for all of their writing questions.
- **Adaptive exercises that engage students.** Writer's Help 2.0 includes LearningCurve, game-like online quizzing that adapts to what students already know and helps them focus on what they need to learn.

Student access is packaged with *Subject & Strategy* at a significant discount. Contact your Bedford/St. Martin's sales representative to get a package ISBN. Students who rent a book or buy a used book can purchase access to Writer's Help 2.0 at **macmillanhighered.com/writershelp2**.

Instructors may request free access by registering as an instructor at **macmillanhighered.com/writershelp2**. For technical support, visit **macmillanlearning.com/getsupport**.

Portfolio Keeping, **Third Edition, by Nedra Reynolds and Elizabeth Davis**, provides all the information students need to use the portfolio method successfully in a writing course. *Portfolio Teaching*, a companion guide for instructors, provides the practical information instructors and writing program administrators need to use the portfolio method successfully in a writing course. To order *Portfolio Keeping* packaged with this text, contact your sales representative for a package ISBN.

Instructor Resources

You have a lot to do in your course. Bedford/St. Martin's wants to make it easy for you to find the support you need—and to get it quickly.

The Instructor's Manual for *Subject & Strategy* is available as a PDF that can be downloaded from the Bedford/St. Martin's online catalog. In addition to chapter overviews and teaching tips, the instructor's manual includes sample syllabi, answers to questions that appear in the book, and suggested classroom activities.

Join our community! Bedford/St. Martin's is part of the Macmillan English Community for professional resources, featuring Bedford *Bits*, our popular blog site offering new ideas for the composition classroom and composition teachers. Connect and converse with a growing team of Bedford authors and top scholars who blog on *Bits*: Andrea Lunsford, Nancy Sommers, Steve Bernhardt, Traci Gardner, Barclay Barrios, Jack Solomon, Susan Bernstein, Elizabeth Wardle, Doug Downs, Liz Losh, Jonathan Alexander, and Donna Winchell.

In addition, you'll find an expanding collection of resources that support your teaching:

- Sign up for webinars
- Download resources from our professional resource series that support your teaching
- Start a discussion
- Ask a question
- Follow your favorite members
- Review projects in the pipeline

Visit **community.macmillan.com** to join the conversation with your fellow teachers.

ACKNOWLEDGMENTS

We are gratified by the reception and use of the thirteen previous editions of *Subject & Strategy*. Composition teachers in hundreds of community colleges, liberal arts colleges, and universities have used the book. Many teachers responded to our detailed review questionnaire, thus helping tremendously in conceptualizing the improvements to this edition. We thank James Boswell, Harrisburg Area Community College; Kellie Cannon, Coastal Carolina Community College; Doris Coleman, California State University, Northridge; Maureen Connolly, Elmhurst College; Piera Fumagalli, Tseng College, California State University, Northridge; Christine Harvey Horning, Western Oregon University; Lance Hawvermale, Ranger College; Denise Lagos, Union County College; Shelley Mahoney, University of Manitoba; Barbara Millman, Fairleigh Dickinson University; Andralena Panczenko, Tseng College, California State University, Northridge; Lynn Reid, Fairleigh Dickinson University; Rose-Mary Rodrigues, Northwestern Connecticut Community College; Diane Sabatino, Johnson State College/Community College of Vermont; Eileen Sandlin, Northwood University; Judy Schmidt, Harrisburg Area Community College; Pam Solberg, Western Technical College; Dorothy Terry, Tougaloo College; and Kelly Terzaken, Coastal Carolina Community College.

Thanks go also to the Bedford/St. Martin's team: Sherry Mooney and Sarah Macomber, our development editors; Leasa Burton, Publisher for Composition and Business and Technical Writing; and Karen Henry, Editorial Director for English. We would also like to acknowledge Lou Bruno, Kevin Bradley, Joy Fisher Williams, and Jennifer Prince. Special thanks go to Sarah Federman for her assistance with developing the Instructor's Manual. We are also happy to recognize those students whose work appears in *Subject & Strategy* for their willingness to contribute their time and effort in writing and rewriting their essays: Katie Angeles, Barbara Bowman, Kevin Cunningham, Ria Foye-Edwards, Keith Eldred, Jake Jamieson, Paula Kersch, Laura LaPierre, Bill Peterson, Howard Solomon Jr., Kate Suarez, Courtney Sypher, and Jim Tassé. We are grateful to all of our writing students at the University of Vermont for their enthusiasm for writing and for their invaluable responses to materials included in this book. And we also thank our families for sharing in our commitment to quality teaching and textbook writing.

Finally, we thank each other. Since 1971 we have collaborated on many textbooks on language and writing, all of which have gone into multiple editions. With this fourteenth edition of *Subject & Strategy*, we enter more than forty-five years of working together. Ours must be one of the longest-running and most mutually satisfying writing partnerships in college textbook publishing. The journey has been invigorating and challenging as we have come to understand the complexities and joys of good writing and have sought new ways to help students become better writers.

PAUL ESCHHOLZ

ALFRED ROSA

Contents

Preface for Instructors   iii
Thematic Contents   xxxi

1 Reading 3

DEVELOPING AN EFFECTIVE READING PROCESS   3

Step 1: Prepare Yourself to Read the Selection   3
Step 2: Read the Selection   6
Step 3: Reread the Selection   6
Step 4: Annotate the Selection   7
- WHAT TO ANNOTATE IN A TEXT   7

An Example: Annotating Cherokee Paul McDonald's "A View from the Bridge"   8

Step 5: Analyze and Evaluate the Selection   10
- QUESTIONS FOR ANALYSIS AND EVALUATION   11

THE READING PROCESS IN ACTION: THOMAS L. FRIEDMAN'S "MY FAVORITE TEACHER"   12

ABOUT THE PHOTOGRAPHS AND VISUAL TEXTS IN THIS BOOK   15

THE READING-WRITING CONNECTION   19

Reading as a Writer   20

2 Writing 23

DEVELOPING AN EFFECTIVE WRITING PROCESS 23

Step 1: Understand Your Assignment 24
- DIRECTION WORDS 24
- FORMAL VERSUS INFORMAL WRITING 27
- QUESTIONS ABOUT AUDIENCE 27

Step 2: Gather Ideas and Formulate a Thesis 28
- WILL YOUR THESIS HOLD UP TO SCRUTINY? 31

Step 3: Organize and Write Your First Draft 31
- ORGANIZATIONAL STRATEGIES 31
- DETERMINING WHAT STRATEGIES TO USE WITH A SPECIFIC ASSIGNMENT 32
- DETERMINING WHAT STRATEGIES TO USE WITH AN OPEN ASSIGNMENT 33

Step 4: Revise Your Essay 35
- TIPS FOR REVISING YOUR DRAFT 35
- A BRIEF GUIDE TO PEER CRITIQUING 36
- QUESTIONS FOR REVISING THE LARGER ELEMENTS OF YOUR ESSAY 37
- QUESTIONS FOR WRITING BEGINNINGS AND ENDINGS 38
- QUESTIONS FOR REVISING SENTENCES 39

Step 5: Edit and Proofread Your Essay 39
- QUESTIONS TO ASK DURING EDITING AND PROOFREADING 39

A STUDENT ESSAY IN PROGRESS 40

Step 1: Keith's Assignment 40
Step 2: Keith's Ideas 40
Step 3: Keith's First Draft 41
Step 4: Keith's Revised Essay 42
Step 5: Keith's Edited Essay 44

Keith Eldred, *Secular Mantras* (student essay) 45

3 Writers on Writing — 49

Russell Baker, *Discovering the Power of My Words* 50
"And he started to read. My words! He was reading *my words* out loud to the entire class. What's more, the entire class was listening."

Anne Lamott, *Shitty First Drafts* 55
"All good writers write them. This is how they end up with good second drafts and terrific third drafts."

Linda S. Flower, *Writing for an Audience* 60
"A good piece of writing closes the gap between you and the reader."

Susan Orlean, *On Voice* 64
"The way you tell a story over dinner is true to who you are, whether that is deeply analytical or extremely witty."

Stephen King, *Reading to Write* 67
"If you want to be a writer, you must do two things above all others: read a lot and write a lot."

Isabel Allende, *Writing as an Act of Hope* 73
"Words came out like a violent torrent. I had thousands of untold words stuck in my chest, threatening to choke me."

4 Narration — 79

WHAT IS NARRATION? 79

NARRATION IN WRITTEN TEXTS 79

USING NARRATION AS A WRITING STRATEGY 81

USING NARRATION ACROSS THE DISCIPLINES 81

SAMPLE STUDENT ESSAY USING NARRATION AS A WRITING STRATEGY 82

    Laura LaPierre, *Why Are You Here?* (student essay) 83

SUGGESTIONS FOR USING NARRATION AS A WRITING STRATEGY 85

    Planning Your Narration Essay 85
    Organizing Your Narration Essay 88

Writing Your Narration Essay   88

Revising and Editing Your Narration Essay   90

- **QUESTIONS FOR REVISING AND EDITING: NARRATION**   90

Malcolm X, *Coming to an Awareness of Language*   92
"I saw that the best thing I could do was get hold of a dictionary — to study, to learn some words."

Junot Díaz, *The Terror*   98
"No sooner than that happened, my brother, who was one year older and my best friend and protector, was found to have leukemia, the kind that in those days had a real nasty habit of killing you."

David P. Bardeen, *Not Close Enough for Comfort*   104
"I had wanted to tell Will I was gay since I was twelve. As twins, we shared everything back then: clothes, gadgets, thoughts, secrets. Everything except this."

Barry Winston, *Stranger Than True*   110
"The next thing he remembers, he's waking up in a hospital room, hurting like hell, bandages and casts all over him, and somebody is telling him he's charged with manslaughter and DUI..."

Mindy Kaling, *Don't Peak in High School*   116
"What I've noticed is that almost no one who was a big star in high school is also a big star later in life. For us overlooked kids, it's so wonderfully *fair*."

WRITING SUGGESTIONS FOR NARRATION   122

5 Description   125

WHAT IS DESCRIPTION?   125

DESCRIPTION IN WRITTEN TEXTS   125

USING DESCRIPTION AS A WRITING STRATEGY   126

USING DESCRIPTION ACROSS THE DISCIPLINES   128

SAMPLE STUDENT ESSAY USING DESCRIPTION AS A WRITING STRATEGY 129

    Jim Tassé, *Trailcheck* (student essay) 129

SUGGESTIONS FOR USING DESCRIPTION AS A WRITING STRATEGY 132

    Planning Your Description Essay 132

    Organizing Your Description Essay 133

    Revising and Editing Your Description Essay 135

    • **QUESTIONS FOR REVISING AND EDITING: DESCRIPTION** 135

Jeannette Walls, *A Woman on the Street* 136
"I fretted about them, but I was embarrassed by them, too, and ashamed of myself for wearing pearls and living on Park Avenue while my parents were busy keeping warm and finding something to eat."

Robert Ramírez, *The Barrio* 141
"The barrio is a refuge from the harshness and the coldness of the Anglo world."

Helen MacDonald, *Hiding from Animals* 148
"There is a dubious satisfaction in the subterfuge of watching things that cannot see you, and it's deeply embedded in our culture."

Maya Angelou, *Sister Flowers* 154
"She acted just as refined as whitefolks in the movies and books and she was more beautiful, for none of them could have come near that warm color without looking gray by comparison."

Phyllis Korkki, *The Attachment that Still Makes Noise* 161
"But nothing, really, comes close to the satisfying clunk of a stapler: it's a sound that means work is getting done."

WRITING SUGGESTIONS FOR DESCRIPTION 168

6 Illustration 173

WHAT IS ILLUSTRATION? 173

ILLUSTRATION IN WRITTEN TEXTS 173

USING ILLUSTRATION AS A WRITING STRATEGY 175

USING ILLUSTRATION ACROSS THE DISCIPLINES 175

SAMPLE STUDENT ESSAY USING ILLUSTRATION AS A WRITING STRATEGY 176

> **Paula Kersch,** *Weight Management: More Than a Matter of Good Looks* (student essay) 177

SUGGESTIONS FOR USING ILLUSTRATION AS A WRITING STRATEGY 183

> Planning Your Illustration Essay 183
> Organizing Your Illustration Essay 185
> Revising and Editing Your Illustration Essay 186
> - **QUESTIONS FOR REVISING AND EDITING: ILLUSTRATION** 186

Natalie Goldberg, *Be Specific* 187
"Don't say 'fruit.' Tell what kind of fruit — 'It is a pomegranate.' Give things the dignity of their names."

Brent Crane, *For a More Creative Brain, Travel* 191
"Writers and thinkers have long felt the benefits of international travel."

Mitch Albom, *If You Had One Day with Someone Who's Gone* 196
"Have you ever lost someone you love and wanted one more conversation, one more day to make up for the time when you thought they would be here forever?"

Deborah Tannen, *How to Give Orders Like a Man* 202
"I challenge the assumption that talking in an indirect way necessarily reveals powerlessness, lack of self-confidence, or anything else about the character of the speaker."

Tim Kreider, *The "Busy" Trap* 213
"They're busy because of their own ambition or drive or anxiety, because they're addicted to busyness and dread what they might have to face in its absence."

WRITING SUGGESTIONS FOR ILLUSTRATION 219

7 Process Analysis 223

WHAT IS PROCESS ANALYSIS? 223

PROCESS ANALYSIS IN WRITTEN TEXTS 223

USING PROCESS ANALYSIS AS A WRITING STRATEGY 224

    Directional Process Analysis 224
    Informational Process Analysis 225
    Evaluative Process Analysis 226

USING PROCESS ANALYSIS ACROSS THE DISCIPLINES 226

SAMPLE STUDENT ESSAY USING PROCESS ANALYSIS AS A WRITING STRATEGY 227

    William Peterson, *Juggling Is Easier Than You Think* (student essay) 227

SUGGESTIONS FOR USING PROCESS ANALYSIS AS A WRITING STRATEGY 231

    Planning Your Process Analysis Essay 231
    Organizing and Writing Your Process Analysis Essay 231
    Revising and Editing Your Process Analysis Essay 232

- **QUESTIONS FOR REVISING AND EDITING: PROCESS ANALYSIS** 234

Mortimer Adler, *How to Mark a Book* 235
"Marking up a book is not an act of mutilation but of love."

Paul Roberts, *How to Say Nothing in 500 Words* 242
"You still have four hundred and sixty-eight [words] to go, and you've pretty well exhausted the subject."

Michael Pollan, *Eating Industrial Meat* 256
"If I stared at my steer hard enough, I could imagine the white lines of the butcher's chart dissecting his black hide: rump roast, flank steak, standing rib, tenderloin, brisket."

Alicia Ault, *How Do Spiders Make Their Webs?* 263
"Scientists have been trying for decades to decode exactly what gives the silk both strength and elasticity, but so far they have found only clues."

Nikki Giovanni, *Campus Racism 101* 268
"There are discomforts attached to attending predominantly white colleges, though no more so than living in a racist world."

WRITING SUGGESTIONS FOR PROCESS ANALYSIS 276

8 Comparison and Contrast — 281

WHAT ARE COMPARISON AND CONTRAST? 281

COMPARISON AND CONTRAST IN WRITTEN TEXTS 281

    Point-by-point Block Comparison   282

    Analogy: A Special Form of Comparison and Contrast   283

USING COMPARISON AND CONTRAST AS A WRITING STRATEGY 284

USING COMPARISON AND CONTRAST ACROSS THE DISCIPLINES 285

SAMPLE STUDENT ESSAY USING COMPARISON AND CONTRAST AS A WRITING STRATEGY 286

    Barbara Bowman, *Guns and Cameras* (student essay)   287

SUGGESTIONS FOR USING COMPARISON AND CONTRAST AS A WRITING STRATEGY 289

    Planning Your Comparison and Contrast Essay   289

    Organizing and Writing Your Comparison and Contrast Essay   291

    Revising and Editing Your Comparison and Contrast Essay   293

- **QUESTIONS FOR REVISING AND EDITING: COMPARISON AND CONTRAST**   293

Suzanne Britt, *Neat People vs. Sloppy People*   294
"I've finally figured out the difference between neat people and sloppy people. The distinction is, as always, moral."

James Hamblin, *Buy Experiences, Not Things*   299
"Minds tend to wander to dark, not whimsical, places. Unless that mind has something exciting to anticipate or sweet to remember."

Bharati Mukherjee, *Two Ways to Belong in America*   306
"America spoke to me — I married it — I embraced the demotion from expatriate aristocrat to immigrant nobody, surrendering those thousands of years of 'pure culture,' the saris, the delightfully accented English."

Andrew Vachss, *The Difference between "Sick" and "Evil"*   312
"Sickness is a condition. Evil is a behavior. Evil is always a matter of choice."

Bruce Catton, *Grant and Lee: A Study in Contrasts*   319
"They were two strong men, these oddly different generals, and they represented the strengths of two conflicting currents that, through them, had come into final collision."

WRITING SUGGESTIONS FOR COMPARISON AND CONTRAST   327

9 Division and Classification   331

WHAT ARE DIVISION AND CLASSIFICATION?   331

DIVISION AND CLASSIFICATION IN WRITTEN TEXTS   331

USING DIVISION AND CLASSIFICATION AS A WRITING STRATEGY   334

USING DIVISION AND CLASSIFICATION ACROSS THE DISCIPLINES   334

SAMPLE STUDENT ESSAY USING DIVISION AND CLASSIFICATION AS A WRITING STRATEGY   335

Katie Angeles, *The Forgotten Personality Type* (student essay)   336

SUGGESTIONS FOR USING DIVISION AND CLASSIFICATION AS A WRITING STRATEGY   339

Planning Your Division and Classification Essay   339

Organizing and Writing Your Division and Classification Essay   341

Revising and Editing Your Division and Classification Essay   343

- **QUESTIONS FOR REVISING AND EDITING: DIVISION AND CLASSIFICATION**   343

Deborah Tannen, *But What Do You Mean?*   344
"Women are often told they apologize too much."

Rosalind Wiseman, *The Queen Bee and Her Court*   353
"Our best politicians and diplomats couldn't do better than a teen girl does in understanding the social intrigue and political landscape that lead to power."

Judith Viorst, *The Truth about Lying*   367
"I'm willing to lie. But just as a last resort — the truth's always better."

Martin Luther King, Jr., *The Ways of Meeting Oppression* 374
"The problem is not a purely racial one, with Negroes set against whites. In the end, it's not a struggle between people at all, but a tension between justice and injustice."

Amy Tan, *Mother Tongue* 379
"I believed that her English reflected the quality of what she had to say."

WRITING SUGGESTIONS FOR DIVISION AND CLASSIFICATION 387

10 Definition 391

WHAT IS DEFINITION? 391

DEFINITION IN WRITTEN TEXTS 391

USING DEFINITION AS A WRITING STRATEGY 394

USING DEFINITION ACROSS THE DISCIPLINES 395

SAMPLE STUDENT ESSAY USING DEFINITION AS A WRITING STRATEGY 396

Howard Solomon, Jr., *Best Friends* (student essay) 396

SUGGESTIONS FOR USING DEFINITION AS A WRITING STRATEGY 399

Planning Your Definition Essay 400
Organizing and Writing Your Definition Essay 403
Revising and Editing Your Definition Essay 404

• QUESTIONS FOR REVISING AND EDITING: DEFINITION 406

Jo Goodwin Parker, *What Is Poverty?* 407
"Poverty is getting up every morning from a dirt- and illness-stained mattress. The sheets have long since been used for diapers. Poverty is living in a smell that never leaves."

G. Anthony Gorry, *Steal This MP3 File: What Is Theft?* 414
"In the case of digital music, where the material is disconnected from the physical moorings of conventional stores and copying is so easy, many of my students see matters differently."

Deborah M. Roffman, *What Does "Boys Will Be Boys" Really Mean?* 420
"It's not so much that the boy is always *being* bad — sometimes that sort of thing can seem so outrageous it's funny. It's the underlying assumption . . . that boys, by nature, are bad."

Ellen Goodman, *The Company Man* 427
"He worked like the Important People."

Barbara Ehrenreich, *The Selfish Side of Gratitude* 432
"But this holiday gratitude is all about you, and how you can feel better."

WRITING SUGGESTIONS FOR DEFINITION 437

11 Cause and Effect Analysis 441

WHAT IS CAUSE AND EFFECT ANALYSIS? 441

CAUSE AND EFFECT ANALYSIS IN WRITTEN TEXTS 441

USING CAUSE AND EFFECT ANALYSIS AS A WRITING STRATEGY 444

USING CAUSE AND EFFECT ANALYSIS ACROSS THE DISCIPLINES 445

SAMPLE STUDENT ESSAY USING CAUSE AND EFFECT ANALYSIS AS A WRITING STRATEGY 446

    Kevin Cunningham, *Gentrification* (student essay) 447

SUGGESTIONS FOR USING CAUSE AND EFFECT ANALYSIS AS A WRITING STRATEGY 449

    Planning Your Cause and Effect Analysis 449
    Organizing and Writing Your Cause and Effect Analysis 451
    Revising and Editing Your Cause and Effect Analysis 452
    • **QUESTIONS FOR REVISING AND EDITING: CAUSE AND EFFECT ANALYSIS** 453

Jon Katz, *How Boys Become Men* 455
"Men remember receiving little mercy as boys; maybe that's why it's sometimes difficult for them to show any."

Andrew Sullivan, *iPod World: The End of Society?* 460
"Even without the white wires, you can tell who they are. They walk down the street in their own MP3 cocoon, bumping into others, deaf to small social cues, shutting out anyone not in their bubble."

Michael Jonas, *The Downside of Diversity* 465
"Birds of different feathers may sometimes flock together, but they are also less likely to look out for one another."

Anahad O'Connor, *Coca-Cola Funds Scientists Who Shift Blame for Obesity Away from Bad Diets* 474
"Funding from the food industry is not uncommon in scientific research. But studies suggest that the funds tend to bias findings."

Deborah Cramer, *A Bird Whose Life Depends on a Crab* 481
"This has made a creature that survived the dinosaurs vital to modern medicine."

WRITING SUGGESTIONS FOR CAUSE AND EFFECT ANALYSIS 486

12 Argumentation 489

WHAT IS ARGUMENTATION? 489

ARGUMENT IN WRITTEN TEXTS 489

Persuasive and Logical Argument 490
Informational, or Exploratory, Argument 491
Focused Argument 491
Action-Oriented Argument 491
Quiet, or Subtle, Argument 492
Reconciliation Argument 492

USING ARGUMENTATION AS A WRITING STRATEGY 492

The Classical Appeals 493
Considering Audience 494
Argumentation and Other Rhetorical Strategies 494
Inductive and Deductive Reasoning 495

USING ARGUMENTATION ACROSS THE DISCIPLINES 497

SAMPLE STUDENT ESSAY USING ARGUMENTATION AS A WRITING STRATEGY   499

Kate Suarez, *Celebrity Obsession: Is It Healthy Behavior?* (student essay)   499

SUGGESTIONS FOR USING ARGUMENTATION AS A WRITING STRATEGY   502

Planning Your Argumentation Essay   503

Organizing and Writing Your Argumentation Essay   505

Revising and Editing Your Argumentation Essay   506

- **QUESTIONS FOR REVISING AND EDITING: ARGUMENTATION**   507

CLASSIC ARGUMENTS

Plato, *The Allegory of the Cave*   509
"To them, I said, the truth would be literally nothing but the shadows of the images."

Thomas Jefferson, *The Declaration of Independence*   518
"We hold these truths to be self-evident, that all men are created equal, that they are endowed by their Creator with certain unalienable Rights, that among these are Life, Liberty and the pursuit of Happiness."

Sojourner Truth, *Ain't I a Woman?*   525
"That man over there says that women need to be helped into carriages, and lifted over ditches, and to have the best place everywhere. Nobody ever helps me into carriages, or over mud-puddles, or gives me any best place!"

Henry David Thoreau, *Resistance to Civil Government*   528
"I ask for, not at once no government, but at *once* a better government."

Jonathan Swift, *A Modest Proposal*   548
"A young healthy child well nursed is at a year old most delicious, nourishing, and wholesome food, whether stewed, roasted, baked, or boiled..."

CONTEMPORARY ARGUMENTS

Richard Lederer, *The Case for Short Words*   558
"A lot of small words, more than you might think, can meet your needs with a strength, grace, and charm that large words do not have."

Nancy Armour, *You Shouldn't Get a Prize for Showing Up*   564
"If we're honest with ourselves, the trophies, ribbons and medals we hand out so willingly are more about us than the children getting them."

William Galston, *Telling Americans to Vote, Or Else* 568
"A democracy can't be strong if its citizenship is weak."

Roger Cohen, *The Organic Fable* 574
"The takeaway from the study could be summed up in two words: Organic, schmorganic."

ARGUMENT CLUSTER
Race and Privilege: How to Address a System of Bias? 579

John Metta, *I, Racist* 581
"You see, I don't talk about race with White people."

Derald Wing Sue, *Racial Microaggressions in Everyday Life: Is Subtle Bias Harmful?* 588
"Were we being overly sensitive, or was the flight attendant being racist?"

J. Dowsett, *What My Bike Has Taught Me about White Privilege* 594
"Privilege talk is not intended to make a moral assessment or a moral claim about the privileged at all. It is about systemic imbalance."

Making Connections: Writing and Discussion Suggestions on Race and Privilege 598

ARGUMENT CLUSTER
Getting an Education: What's the Line between Comfort and Learning? 600

Jeffrey Zaslow, *The Compliment Complex* 602
"A lot of today's young adults feel insecure if they're not regularly complimented."

Siobhan Crowley, *On the Subject of Trigger Warnings* 608
"I would hate for students to miss an opportunity to work through their trauma in my classroom, where I can mediate discussions to ensure that comments are not hurtful."

Greg Lukianoff and Jonathan Haidt, *The Coddling of the American Mind* 610
"According to the most basic tenets of psychology, helping people with anxiety disorders avoid the things they fear is misguided."

Making Connections: Writing and Discussion Suggestions on Getting an Education 623

WRITING SUGGESTIONS FOR ARGUMENTATION 626

13 Combining Strategies 631

WHAT DOES IT MEAN TO COMBINE STRATEGIES? 631

COMBINING STRATEGIES IN WRITTEN TEXTS 632

SAMPLE STUDENT ESSAY USING SUBJECTS AND STRATEGIES 633

> Ria Foye-Edwards, *The "Steaks" Are High* (student essay) 634

SUGGESTIONS FOR USING A COMBINATION OF STRATEGIES IN AN ESSAY 637

> Planning Your Combined Strategies Essay 637
> Organizing Your Combined Strategies Essay 638
> Revising and Editing Your Combined Strategies Essay 639
> - **QUESTIONS FOR REVISING AND EDITING: COMBINING STRATEGIES** 640

Lars Eighner, *On Dumpster Diving* 641
"I like the frankness of the word *scavenging*. I live from the refuse of others. I am a scavenger."

Michael White, *How to Reengineer Crops for the 21st Century* 646
"Unless we increase the world's capacity to grow food, the demand for food will outstrip supply in the next few decades."

Cooper Thompson, *Language Chauvinism: The Ugly American Revisited* 651
"No, I suspect they simply assumed that everyone here speaks English."

David Sedaris, *Me Talk Pretty One Day* 657
"That's the way they do it here – it's everybody into the language pool, sink or swim."

WRITING SUGGESTIONS FOR COMBINING STRATEGIES 664

14 Writing with Sources 667

WHAT DOES IT MEAN TO WRITE WITH SOURCES? 667

WRITING WITH SOURCES 667

LEARNING TO SUMMARIZE, PARAPHRASE, AND QUOTE FROM YOUR SOURCES 669

> Summarizing 669
> Paraphrasing 670
> Using Direct Quotation 671
> Using Direct Quotation with Summary or Paraphrase 672
> Integrating Borrowed Material into Your Text 673
> Synthesizing Several Sources to Deepen Your Discussion 674
>
> • **CHECKLIST FOR WRITING A SYNTHESIS** 677

AVOIDING PLAGIARISM 677

> Using Quotation Marks for Language Borrowed Directly 678
> Using Your Own Words and Word Order When Summarizing and Paraphrasing 679
>
> • **PREVENTING PLAGIARISM** 680

SAMPLE STUDENT ESSAY USING LIBRARY AND INTERNET SOURCES 681

> **Courtney Sypher,** *From Computer Cruelty to Campus Crime: Cyberbullying at College* (student essay) 682

Wayne Ellwood, *Bees: Why Are They Dying?* 687
"Where there is no nectar or pollen, there are no bees."

Nicola Freedman, *How Social Media Is Changing Hollywood* 695
"In the digitized world, the traditional model of Hollywood is crumbling."

Jake Jamieson, *The English-Only Movement: Can America Proscribe Language with a Clear Conscience?* (MLA model) 706
"Do we plan to allow everyone in this country the freedom of speech that we profess to cherish, or will we decide to reserve it only for those who speak English?"

15 A Brief Guide to Researching and Documenting Essays 717

ESTABLISHING A REALISTIC SCHEDULE 717

FINDING AND USING SOURCES 718

    Conducting Keyword Searches 720

    Using Subject Directories to Define and Develop Your Research Topic 722

EVALUATING YOUR SOURCES 722

ANALYZING YOUR SOURCES 724

DEVELOPING A WORKING BIBLIOGRAPHY FOR YOUR SOURCES 725

TAKING NOTES 727

DOCUMENTING SOURCES 728

    In-Text Citations 728

LIST OF WORKS CITED 730

16 Editing for Grammar, Punctuation, and Sentence Style 741

1 RUN-ONS: FUSED SENTENCES AND COMMA SPLICES 741

2 SENTENCE FRAGMENTS 742

3 COMMA FAULTS 743

4 SUBJECT-VERB AGREEMENT 745

5 UNCLEAR PRONOUN REFERENCES 746

6 PRONOUN-ANTECEDENT AGREEMENT 747

7 **DANGLING AND MISPLACED MODIFIERS** 749

8 **FAULTY PARALLELISM** 750

9 **WEAK NOUNS AND VERBS** 751

10 **SHIFTS IN VERB TENSE, MOOD, AND VOICE** 752

11 **WORDINESS** 753

12 **SENTENCE VARIETY** 755

Appendix: Thematic Writing Assignments   759
Glossary of Rhetorical Terms   764
Acknowledgments   775
Index   779

Thematic Contents

Discover more thematic connections as well as writing assignments in the appendix on pages 759–63.

CONTEMPORARY SOCIAL ISSUES

> **ARGUMENT CLUSTER:**
> **Race and Privilege** 579

> **ARGUMENT CLUSTER:**
> **Getting an Education** 600

Kevin Cunningham, *Gentrification* (student essay) 447

Barbara Ehrenreich, *The Selfish Side of Gratitude* 432

Michael Jonas, *The Downside of Diversity* 465

Anahad O'Connor, *Coca-Cola Funds Scientists Who Shift Blame for Obesity Away from Bad Diets* 474

Jo Goodwin Parker, *What Is Poverty?* 407

Michael Pollan, *Eating Industrial Meat* 256

Kate Suarez, *Celebrity Obsession: Is It Healthy Behavior?* (student essay) 499

Courtney Sypher, *From Computer Cruelty to Campus Crime: Cyberbullying at College* (student essay) 682

DISCOVERIES AND EPIPHANIES

Mindy Kaling, *Don't Peak in High School* 116

Malcolm X, *Coming to an Awareness of Language* 92

Cherokee Paul McDonald, *A View from the Bridge* 5

Plato, *The Allegory of the Cave* 509

David Sedaris, *Me Talk Pretty One Day* 657

Amy Tan, *Mother Tongue* 379

Barry Winston, *Stranger Than True* 110

EDUCATION

> ARGUMENT CLUSTER:
> Getting an Education 600

Mortimer Adler, *How to Mark a Book* 235

Russell Baker, *Discovering the Power of My Words* 50

Brent Crane, *For a More Creative Brain, Travel* 191

Thomas L. Friedman, *My Favorite Teacher* 12

Nikki Giovanni, *Campus Racism 101* 268

Stephen King, *Reading to Write* 67

Paul Roberts, *How to Say Nothing in 500 Words* 242

David Sedaris, *Me Talk Pretty One Day* 657

FAMILY AND RELATIONSHIPS

Mitch Albom, *If You Had One Day with Someone Who's Gone* 196

Maya Angelou, *Sister Flowers* 154

David P. Bardeen, *Not Close Enough for Comfort* 104

Ellen Goodman, *The Company Man* 427

Howard Solomon, Jr., *Best Friends* (student essay) 396

Amy Tan, *Mother Tongue* 379

Jeannette Walls, *A Woman on the Street* 136

GROWING UP

Maya Angelou, *Sister Flowers* 154

Junot Díaz, *The Terror* 98

Deborah M. Roffman, *What Does "Boys Will Be Boys" Really Mean?* 420

Rosalind Wiseman, *The Queen Bee and Her Court* 353

HISTORICAL PERSPECTIVES

Bruce Catton, *Grant and Lee: A Study in Contrasts* 319

Thomas Jefferson, *The Declaration of Independence* 518

Plato, *The Allegory of the Cave* 509

Jonathan Swift, *A Modest Proposal* 548

Sojourner Truth, *Ain't I a Woman?* 525

THE IMMIGRANT EXPERIENCE

Junot Díaz, *The Terror* 98

Jake Jamieson, *The English-Only Movement: Can America Proscribe Language with a Clear Conscience?* (MLA model) 706

Michael Jonas, *The Downside of Diversity* 465

Bharati Mukherjee, *Two Ways to Belong in America* 306

Robert Ramírez, *The Barrio* 141

Amy Tan, *Mother Tongue* 379

Cooper Thompson, *Language Chauvinism: The Ugly American Revisited* 651

MORAL VALUES

| ARGUMENT CLUSTER:
| Race and Privilege 579

Barbara Bowman, *Guns and Cameras* (student essay) 287

Barbara Ehrenreich, *The Selfish Side of Gratitude* 432

William Galston, *Telling Americans to Vote, Or Else*   568

Nikki Giovanni, *Campus Racism 101*   268

G. Anthony Gorry, *Steal This MP3 File: What Is Theft?*   414

Thomas Jefferson, *The Declaration of Independence*   518

Henry David Thoreau, *Resistance to Civil Government*   528

Andrew Vachss, *The Difference between "Sick" and "Evil"*   312

Judith Viorst, *The Truth about Lying*   367

Jeannette Walls, *A Woman on the Street*   136

THE NATURAL WORLD

Alicia Ault, *How Do Spiders Make Their Webs?*   263

Barbara Bowman, *Guns and Cameras* (student essay)   287

Deborah Cramer, *A Bird Whose Life Depends on a Crab*   481

Wayne Ellwood, *Bees: Why Are They Dying?*   687

Helen MacDonald, *Hiding from Animals*   148

Cherokee Paul McDonald, *A View from the Bridge*   5

Jim Tassé, *Trailcheck* (student essay)   129

PEER PRESSURE

Nicola Freedman, *How Social Media Is Changing Hollywood*   695

Mindy Kaling, *Don't Peak in High School*   116

Paula Kersch, *Weight Management: More Than a Matter of Good Looks* (student essay)   177

Tim Kreider, *The "Busy" Trap*   213

Deborah M. Roffman, *What Does "Boys Will Be Boys" Really Mean?*   420

Courtney Sypher, *From Computer Cruelty to Campus Crime: Cyberbullying at College* (student essay)   682

Rosalind Wiseman, *The Queen Bee and Her Court*   353

PEOPLE AND PERSONALITIES

Katie Angeles, *The Forgotten Personality Type* (student essay)   336

Suzanne Britt, *Neat People vs. Sloppy People*   294

Thomas L. Friedman, *My Favorite Teacher*   12

Ellen Goodman, *The Company Man*   427

Kate Suarez, *Celebrity Obsession: Is It Healthy Behavior?* (student essay)   499

Rosalind Wiseman, *The Queen Bee and Her Court*   353

THE POWER OF LANGUAGE

Russell Baker, *Discovering the Power of My Words*   50

Keith Eldred, *Secular Mantras* (student essay)   45

Jake Jamieson, *The English-Only Movement: Can America Proscribe Language with a Clear Conscience?* (MLA model)   706

Derald Wing Sue, *Racial Microaggressions in Everyday Life: Is Subtle Bias Harmful?*   588

Cooper Thompson, *Language Chauvinism: The Ugly American Revisited*   651

Malcolm X, *Coming to an Awareness of Language*   92

RACE IN AMERICA

> **ARGUMENT CLUSTER:**
> **Race and Privilege**   579

Nikki Giovanni, *Campus Racism 101*   268

Michael Jonas, *The Downside of Diversity*   465

Martin Luther King, Jr., *The Ways of Meeting Oppression*   374

Malcolm X, *Coming to an Awareness of Language*   92

Bharati Mukherjee, *Two Ways to Belong in America*   306

SENSE OF PLACE

Kevin Cunningham, *Gentrification* (student essay)   447

Plato, *The Allegory of the Cave*   509

Robert Ramírez, *The Barrio*   141

SENSE OF SELF

Katie Angeles, *The Forgotten Personality Type* (student essay)   336

David P. Bardeen, *Not Close Enough for Comfort*   104

Brent Crane, *For a More Creative Brain, Travel*   191

Mindy Kaling, *Don't Peak in High School*   116

Paula Kersch, *Weight Management: More Than a Matter of Good Looks* (student essay)   177

Tim Kreider, *The "Busy" Trap*   213

Laura LaPierre, *Why Are You Here?* (student essay)   83

Jeannette Walls, *A Woman on the Street*   136

TECHNOLOGY

Roger Cohen, *The Organic Fable*   574

Ria Foye-Edwards, *The "Steaks" Are High* (student essay)   634

Nicola Freedman, *How Social Media Is Changing Hollywood*   695

Andrew Sullivan, *iPod World: The End of Society?*   460

Courtney Sypher, *From Computer Cruelty to Campus Crime: Cyberbullying at College* (student essay)   682

Michael White, *How to Reengineer Crops for the 21st Century*   646

WOMEN AND MEN

David P. Bardeen, *Not Close Enough for Comfort*   104

Jon Katz, *How Boys Become Men*   455

Deborah M. Roffman, *What Does "Boys Will Be Boys" Really Mean?*   420

Deborah Tannen, *But What Do You Mean?* 344

Deborah Tannen, *How to Give Orders Like a Man* 202

Sojourner Truth, *Ain't I a Woman?* 525

THE WORLD OF WORK

Ellen Goodman, *The Company Man* 427

Deborah Tannen, *How to Give Orders Like a Man* 202

Jeffrey Zaslow, *The Compliment Complex* 602

WRITING ABOUT WRITING

Isabel Allende, *Writing as an Act of Hope* 73

Russell Baker, *Discovering the Power of My Words* 50

Linda S. Flower, *Writing for an Audience* 60

Natalie Goldberg, *Be Specific* 187

Stephen King, *Reading to Write* 67

Anne Lamott, *Shitty First Drafts* 55

Richard Lederer, *The Case for Short Words* 558

Susan Orlean, *On Voice* 64

Paul Roberts, *How to Say Nothing in 500 Words* 242

SUBJECT & STRATEGY
A WRITER'S READER

Joel Robison

CHAPTER 1

Reading

SUBJECT & STRATEGY PLACES EQUAL EMPHASIS ON CONTENT AND form—that is, on the *subject* of an essay and on the *strategies* an author uses to write it. All readers pay attention to content. Far fewer, however, notice form—the strategies authors use to organize their writing and the means they use to make it clear, logical, and effective.

When you learn to read actively and analytically, you come to appreciate the craftsmanship involved in writing—a writer's choice of an appropriate organizational strategy or strategies and his or her use of descriptive details, representative and persuasive examples, sentence variety, and clear, appropriate, vivid diction.

The image opposite—one of a series of surreal scenes conceived by photographer Joel Robison—seems quite whimsical for the way the man has collected or encountered many books along a remote riverbank. Yet it also underscores the very real importance of selecting just one book or essay at a time for attentive study and then carefully reflecting upon the encounter.

DEVELOPING AN EFFECTIVE READING PROCESS

Active, analytical reading requires, first of all, that you commit time and effort to it. Second, it requires that you try to take a positive interest in what you are reading, even if the subject matter is not immediately appealing. To help you get the most out of your reading, this chapter provides guidelines for an effective reading process.

Step 1: Prepare Yourself to Read the Selection

Instead of diving right into any given selection in *Subject & Strategy*, you need first to establish a context for what you will be reading. What's the essay about? What do you know about the author's background and reputation? Where was the essay first published? Who was the intended audience? And, finally, how much do you already know about the subject of the selection?

The materials that precede each selection in this book—the title, headnote, and Preparing to Read prompt—are intended to help you establish this context. From the *title* you often discover the writer's position on an issue or attitude toward the topic. The title can also give clues about the writer's intended audience and reasons for composing the piece.

Each *headnote* contains four essential elements:

1. A *photo* of the author lets you put a face to a name.
2. The *biographical information* provides details about the writer's life and work, as well as his or her reputation and authority to write on the subject.
3. The *publication information* for the selection tells you when the essay was published and where it first appeared. This information can also give you insight into the intended audience.
4. The *content and rhetorical highlights* of the selection preview the subject and point out key aspects of the writing strategies used by the author.

Finally, the Preparing to Read *journal prompt* encourages you to reflect and record your thoughts and opinions on the topic before you begin reading.

Carefully review the context-building materials on page 5 that accompany Cherokee Paul McDonald's "A View from the Bridge" to see how they can help you establish a context for the reading. The essay itself appears on pages 8–10.

DEVELOPING AN EFFECTIVE READING PROCESS | 5

A View from the Bridge

CHEROKEE PAUL MCDONALD

Title
Author
Headnote

Biographical information

A fiction writer and journalist, Cherokee Paul McDonald was raised and schooled in Fort Lauderdale, Florida. In 1970, he returned home from a tour of duty in Vietnam and joined the Fort Lauderdale Police Department, where he remained until 1980, when he resigned with the rank of sergeant. During this time, McDonald received a degree in criminal science from Broward Community College. He left the police department to become a writer and worked a number of odd jobs before publishing his first book, *The Patch*, in 1986. McDonald has said that almost all of his writing comes from his police work, and his common themes of justice, balance, and fairness reflect his life as part of the "thin blue line" (the police department). In 1991, he published *Blue Truth*, a memoir. His first novel, *Summer's Reason*, was released in 1994. His most recent book, *Into the Green: A Reconnaissance by Fire* (2001), is a memoir of his three years as an artillery forward observer in Vietnam.

Publication information

"A View from the Bridge" was originally published in *Sunshine*, a monthly magazine filled with uplifting short articles and stories, in 1990. The essay shows McDonald's usual expert handling of fish and fishermen, both in and out of water, and reminds us that things are not always as they seem. Notice his selective use of details to describe the young fisherman and the fish he has hooked on his line.

Content and rhetorical highlights

Preparing to Read

Journal prompt

The great American philosopher and naturalist Henry David Thoreau has written: "The question is not what you look at, but what you see." We've all had the experience of becoming numb to sights or experiences that once struck us with wonderment; but sometimes, with luck, something happens to renew our appreciation. Think of an example from your own experience. What are some ways we can retain or recover our appreciation of the remarkable things we have come to take for granted?

Courtesy of Simon Dearden

From reading these preliminary materials, what expectations do you have for "A View from the Bridge"? While McDonald's *title* does not give any specific indication of his topic, it does suggest that he will be writing about the view from a particular bridge and that what he sees is worth sharing with his readers. The *biographical note* reveals that McDonald, a Vietnam veteran and former police officer, is a fiction writer and journalist. The titles of his books suggest that much of his writing comes from his military and police work, where he developed important observational skills and sensitivity to people and the environment. From the *publication information* for the selection, you learn that the essay first appeared in 1990 in *Sunshine*, a monthly magazine with short, uplifting human-interest articles for a general readership. The *content and rhetorical highlights* advise you to look at how McDonald's knowledge about fish and fishing and his use of descriptive details help him paint a verbal picture of the young fisherman and the battle he has with the fish on his line. Finally, the *journal prompt* asks for your thoughts on why we become numb to experiences that once awed us. What, for you, is the difference between to "look at" and to "see," and how can we preserve our appreciation for the awesome things that we sometimes take for granted? After reading McDonald's essay, you can compare your reflections on "seeing" with what McDonald learned from his own experience with the boy who fished by the bridge.

Step 2: Read the Selection

Always read the selection at least twice, no matter how long it is. The first reading lets you get acquainted with the essay and get an overall sense of what the writer is saying and why. As you read, you may find yourself modifying the sense of the writer's message and purpose that you derived from the title, headnote, and your response to the writing prompt. Circle words you do not recognize so that you can look them up in a dictionary. Put a question mark alongside any passages that are not immediately clear. However, you will probably want to delay most of your annotating until a second reading so that your first reading can be fast, enabling you to concentrate on the larger issues of message and purpose.

Step 3: Reread the Selection

Your second reading should be quite different from your first. You will know what the essay is about, where it is going, and how it gets there; now you can relate the individual parts of the essay more accurately to the whole. Use your second reading to test your first impressions, developing and deepening your sense of how (and how well) the essay is written. Pay special attention to the author's purpose and means of achieving it. You can look for strategies of organization (see pages 31–32) and style and adapt them to your own work.

Step 4: Annotate the Selection

When you annotate a selection, you should do more than simply underline what you think are important points. It is easy to underline so much that the notations become meaningless, and it's common to forget why you underlined passages in the first place. Instead, as you read, write down your thoughts in the margins or on a separate piece of paper. Mark the selection's main point when you find it stated directly. Look for the strategy or strategies the author uses to explore and support that point and jot down this information. If you disagree with a statement or conclusion, object in the margin: "No!" If you feel skeptical, write "Why?" or "Explain." If you are impressed by an argument or turn of phrase, write "Good point!" Place vertical lines or a star in the margin to indicate especially important points.

> **What to Annotate in a Text**
>
> Here are some examples of what you may want to mark in a selection as you read:
> - Memorable statements or important points
> - Key terms or concepts
> - Central issues or themes
> - Examples that support a major point
> - Unfamiliar words
> - Questions you have about a point or passage
> - Your responses to a specific point or passage

Remember that there are no hard-and-fast rules for annotating elements. Choose a method of annotation that will make sense to you when you go back to recollect your thoughts and responses to the essay. Jot down whatever marginal notes come naturally to you. Most readers combine brief written responses with underlining, circling, highlighting, stars, or question marks.

Above all, don't let annotating become burdensome. A word or phrase is usually as good as a sentence. One helpful way to focus your annotations is to ask yourself questions such as those on page 11 while reading the selection a second time.

▶ An Example: Annotating Cherokee Paul McDonald's "A View from the Bridge"

Sets the scene

I was coming up on the little bridge in the Rio Vista neighborhood of Fort Lauderdale, deepening my stride and my breathing to negotiate the slight incline without altering my pace. And then, as I neared the crest, I saw the kid.

Nice description

He was a lumpy little guy with baggy shorts, a faded T-shirt and heavy sweat socks falling down over old sneakers.

Partially covering his shaggy blond hair was one of those blue baseball caps with gold braid on the bill and a sailfish patch sewn onto the peak. Covering his eyes and part of his face was a pair of those stupid-looking '50s-style wrap-around sunglasses.

Why "fumbling"?

He was fumbling with a beat-up rod and reel, and he had a little bait bucket by his feet. I puffed on by, glancing down into the empty bucket as I passed.

"Hey, mister! Would you help me, please?"

Jogger sounds irritated

The shrill voice penetrated my jogger's concentration, and I was determined to ignore it. But for some reason, I stopped.

With my hands on my hips and the sweat dripping from my nose I asked, "What do you want, kid?"

"Would you please help me find my shrimp? It's my last one and I've been getting bites and I know I can catch a fish if I can just find that shrimp. He jumped outta my hand as I was getting him from the bucket."

Shrimp is clearly visible, so why does kid ask for help?

Exasperated, I walked slowly back to the kid, and pointed.

"There's the damn shrimp by your left foot. You stopped me for *that*?"

As I said it, the kid reached down and trapped the shrimp.

Kid's polite

"Thanks a lot, mister," he said.

I watched as the kid dropped the baited hook down into the canal. Then I turned to start back down the bridge.

That's when the kid let out a "Hey! Hey!" and the prettiest tarpon I'd ever seen came almost six feet out of the water, twisting and turning as he fell through the air.

Dialogue enhances drama

"I got one!" the kid yelled as the fish hit the water with a loud splash and took off down the canal.

I watched the line being burned off the reel at an alarming rate. The kid's left hand held the crank while the extended fingers felt for the drag setting.

DEVELOPING AN EFFECTIVE READING PROCESS | 9

Jogger gets involved once kid hooks fish

"No, kid!" I shouted. "Leave the drag alone . . . just keep that damn rod tip up!"

Then I glanced at the reel and saw there were just a few loops of line left on the spool.

"Why don't you get yourself some decent equipment?" I said, but before the kid could answer I saw the line go slack.

"Ohhh, I lost him," the kid said. I saw the flash of silver as the fish turned.

Starts coaching kid

"Crank, kid, crank! You didn't lose him. He's coming back toward you. Bring in the slack!"

The kid cranked like mad, and a beautiful grin spread across his face.

"He's heading in for the pilings," I said. "Keep him out of those pilings!"

Impressive fish

The kid played it perfectly. When the fish made its play for the pilings, he kept just enough pressure on to force the fish out. When the water exploded and the silver missile hurled into the air, the kid kept the rod tip up and the line tight.

As the fish came to the surface and began a slow circle in the middle of the canal, I said, "Whooee, is that a nice fish or what?"

The kid didn't say anything, so I said, "Okay, move to the edge of the bridge and I'll climb down to the seawall and pull him out."

When I reached the seawall I pulled in the leader, leaving the fish lying on its side in the water.

"How's that?" I said.

Kid makes strange request

"Hey, mister, tell me what it looks like."

"Look down here and check him out," I said, "He's beautiful."

Wow!

But then I looked up into those stupid-looking sunglasses and it hit me. The kid was blind.

"Could you tell me what he looks like, mister?" he said again.

Jogger's new awareness makes him self-conscious

"Well, he's just under three, uh, he's about as long as one of your arms," I said. "I'd guess he goes about 15, 20 pounds. He's mostly silver, but the silver is somehow made up of *all* the colors, if you know what I mean." I stopped. "Do you know what I mean by colors?"

The kid nodded.

Drawing verbal picture

"Okay. He has all these big scales, like armor all over his body. They're silver too, and when he moves they sparkle. He has a strong body and a large powerful tail. He has big round eyes, bigger than a quarter, and a lower jaw that sticks out past the upper one and is very tough. His belly is almost white and his back is a gunmetal gray. When he jumped he came out of the water about six feet, and his scales caught the sun and flashed it all over the place."

By now the fish had righted itself, and I could see the bright-red gills as the gill plates opened and closed. I explained this to the kid, and then said, more to myself, "He's a beauty."

What a kid!

"Can you get him off the hook?" the kid asked. "I don't want to kill him."

I watched as the tarpon began to slowly swim away, tired but still alive.

By the time I got back up to the top of the bridge the kid had his line secured and his bait bucket in one hand.

He grinned and said, "Just in time. My mom drops me off here, and she'll be back to pick me up any minute."

He used the back of one hand to wipe his nose.

"Thanks for helping me catch that tarpon," he said, "and for helping me to see it."

Point of story — jogger's insight

I looked at him, shook my head, and said, "No, my friend, thank you for letting *me* see that fish."

I took off, but before I got far the kid yelled again.

"Hey, mister!"

I stopped.

Like his attitude!

"Someday I'm gonna catch a sailfish and a blue marlin and a giant tuna and *all* those big sportfish!"

As I looked into those sunglasses I knew he probably would. I wished I could be there when it happened.

Now that you have learned how to prepare yourself to read a selection, what to look for during a first and second reading, and what to annotate, it is time to move on to the next step: analyzing a text by asking yourself questions as you reread it.

Step 5: Analyze and Evaluate the Selection

As you continue to study the selection, analyze it for a deeper understanding and appreciation of the author's craft and try to evaluate its overall effectiveness as a piece of writing. Here are some questions you may find helpful as you start the process:

Questions for Analysis and Evaluation

1. What is the writer's topic?
2. What is the writer's main point or thesis?
3. What is the writer's purpose in writing?
4. What strategy or strategies does the writer use? *Where* and *how* does the writer use them?
5. Do the writer's strategies suit his or her subject and purpose? Why or why not?
6. How effective is the essay? Does the writer make his or her points clear and persuade the reader to accept them?

Each essay in *Subject & Strategy* is followed by study questions similar to these but specific to the essay. Some of the questions help you analyze the content, while others help you analyze the writer's use of the rhetorical strategies. In addition, there are questions about the writer's diction and style. As you read the essay a second time, look for details related to these questions and then answer the questions as fully as you can.

THE READING PROCESS IN ACTION: THOMAS L. FRIEDMAN'S "MY FAVORITE TEACHER"

To give you practice using the five-step reading process that we have just explored, we present an essay by Thomas L. Friedman, including the headnote material and the Preparing to Read prompt. Before you read Friedman's essay, think about the title, the biographical and rhetorical information in the headnote, and the Preparing to Read prompt. Make some notes of your expectations about the essay and write out a response to the prompt. Next, continue following the five-step process outlined in this chapter. As you read the essay for the first time, try not to stop; take it all in as if in one breath. The second time through, pause to annotate the text. Finally, using the questions listed above, analyze and evaluate the essay.

My Favorite Teacher

THOMAS L. FRIEDMAN

New York Times foreign affairs columnist Thomas L. Friedman was born in Minneapolis, Minnesota, in 1953. He graduated from Brandeis University in 1975 and received a Marshall Scholarship to pursue modern Middle East studies at St. Anthony's College, Oxford University, where he earned a master's degree. He has worked for the *New York Times* since 1981 — first in Lebanon, then in Israel, and since 1989 in Washington, D.C. He was awarded the Pulitzer Prize in 1983 and 1988 for his reporting and again in 2002 for his commentary. Friedman's 1989 bestseller *From Beirut to Jerusalem* received the National Book Award for nonfiction. His most recent books are *The World Is Flat: A Brief History of the Twenty-First Century* (2005), *Hot, Flat, and Crowded: Why We Need a Green Revolution — And How It Can Renew America* (2008), and *That Used to Be Us: How America Fell Behind in the World It Invented and How We Can Come Back* (2011), with Michael Mandelbaum. From 2013 to 2014, Friedman contributed to the climate change documentary series "Years of Living Dangerously."

In the following essay, which first appeared in the *New York Times* on January 9, 2001, Friedman pays tribute to his tenth-grade journalism teacher. As you read Friedman's profile of Hattie M. Steinberg, note the descriptive detail he selects to create the dominant impression of "a woman of clarity in an age of uncertainty."

Preparing to Read

If you had to name your three favorite teachers of all time, who would they be? Why do you consider each one a favorite? Which one, if any, are you likely to remember twenty-five years from now? Why?

Last Sunday's *New York Times Magazine* published its annual review of people who died last year who left a particular mark on the world. I am sure all readers have their own such list. I certainly do. Indeed, someone who made the most important difference in my life died last year — my high school journalism teacher, Hattie M. Steinberg.

I grew up in a small suburb of Minneapolis, and Hattie was the legendary journalism teacher at St. Louis Park High School, Room 313. I took her intro to journalism course in 10th grade, back in 1969, and have never needed, or taken, another course in journalism since. She was that good.

Hattie was a woman who believed that the secret for success in life was getting the fundamentals right. And boy, she pounded the fundamentals of journalism into her students—not simply how to write a lead or accurately transcribe a quote, but, more important, how to comport yourself in a professional way and to always do quality work. To this day, when I forget to wear a tie on assignment, I think of Hattie scolding me. I once interviewed an ad exec for our high school paper who used a four-letter word. We debated whether to run it. Hattie ruled yes. That ad man almost lost his job when it appeared. She wanted to teach us about consequences.

Hattie was the toughest teacher I ever had. After you took her journalism course in 10th grade, you tried out for the paper, *The Echo*, which she supervised. Competition was fierce. In 11th grade, I didn't quite come up to her writing standards, so she made me business manager, selling ads to the local pizza parlors. That year, though, she let me write one story. It was about an Israeli general who had been a hero in the Six-Day War, who was giving a lecture at the University of Minnesota. I covered his lecture and interviewed him briefly. His name was Ariel Sharon. First story I ever got published.

> The Internet can make you smarter, but it can't make you smart.

Those of us on the paper, and the yearbook that she also supervised, lived in Hattie's classroom. We hung out there before and after school. Now, you have to understand, Hattie was a single woman, nearing sixty at the time, and this was the 1960s. She was the polar opposite of "cool," but we hung around her classroom like it was a malt shop and she was Wolfman Jack. None of us could have articulated it then, but it was because we enjoyed being harangued by her, disciplined by her, and taught by her. She was a woman of clarity in an age of uncertainty.

We remained friends for thirty years, and she followed, bragged about, and critiqued every twist in my career. After she died, her friends sent me a pile of my stories that she had saved over the years. Indeed, her students were her family—only closer. Judy Harrington, one of Hattie's former students, remarked about other friends who were on Hattie's newspapers and yearbooks: "We all graduated forty-one years ago; and yet nearly each day in our lives something comes up—some mental image, some admonition that makes us think of Hattie."

Judy also told the story of one of Hattie's last birthday parties, when one man said he had to leave early to take his daughter somewhere. "Sit down," said Hattie. "You're not leaving yet. She can just be a little late."

That was my teacher! I sit up straight just thinkin' about her.

Among the fundamentals Hattie introduced me to was the *New York Times*. Every morning it was delivered to Room 313. I had never seen it before then. Real journalists, she taught us, start their day by reading the *Times* and columnists like Anthony Lewis and James Reston.

I have been thinking about Hattie a lot this year, not just because she died on July 31, but because the lessons she imparted seem so relevant now. We've just gone through this huge dot-com-Internet-globalization bubble—during which a lot of smart people got carried away and forgot the fundamentals of how you build a profitable company, a lasting portfolio, a nation state, or a thriving student. It turns out that the real secret of success in the information age is what it always was: fundamentals—reading, writing, and arithmetic; church, synagogue, and mosque; the rule of law and good governance.

The Internet can make you smarter, but it can't make you smart. It can extend your reach, but it will never tell you what to say at a P.T.A. meeting. These fundamentals cannot be downloaded. You can only upload them, the old-fashioned way, one by one, in places like Room 313 at St. Louis Park High. I only regret that I didn't write this column when the woman who taught me all that was still alive.

Once you have read and reread Friedman's essay, write your own answers to the six basic questions listed on page 11. Then compare your answers with those that follow.

1. **What is the writer's *topic*?**

    Friedman's topic is his high school journalism teacher, Hattie M. Steinberg; more broadly, his topic is the "secret for success in life," as taught to him by Steinberg.

2. **What is the writer's *main point* or *thesis*?**

    Friedman writes about Steinberg because she was "someone who made the most important difference in my life" (paragraph 1). His main point seems to be that "Hattie was a woman who believed that the secret for success in life was getting the fundamentals right" (3). Friedman learned this from Hattie and applied it to his own life. He firmly believes that "the real secret of success in the information age is what it always was: fundamentals" (10).

3. **What is the writer's *purpose* in writing?**

    Friedman's purpose is to memorialize Steinberg and to explain the importance of the fundamentals that she taught him more than forty years ago. He wants his readers to realize that there are no shortcuts or quick fixes on the road to success. Without the fundamentals, success often eludes people.

4. **What *strategy* or *strategies* does the writer use? *Where* and *how* does the writer use them?**

    Overall, Friedman uses the strategy of illustration, fleshing out his profile of Steinberg with specific examples of the fundamentals she instilled in her students (paragraphs 3 and 9). Friedman uses description as well to develop his profile of Steinberg. We learn that she was Friedman's "toughest teacher" (4), that she was "a single woman, nearing sixty at the time," that she was "the polar opposite of 'cool,'" and that she was "a woman of clarity in an age of uncertainty" (5). Finally, Friedman's brief narratives about an advertising executive, Ariel Sharon, Steinberg's classroom hangout, and one of the teacher's last birthday parties give readers insight into her personality by showing us what she was like instead of simply telling us.

5. **Do the writer's *strategies* suit his *subject* and *purpose*? Why or why not?**

   Friedman uses exemplification as a strategy to show why Steinberg had such a great impact on his life. Friedman knew that he was not telling Steinberg's story, or writing narration, as much as he was showing what a great teacher she was. Using examples of how Steinberg affected his life and molded his journalistic skills allows Friedman to introduce his teacher as well as to demonstrate her importance.

   In developing his portrait of Steinberg in this way, Friedman relies on the fundamentals of good journalism. When taken collectively, his examples create a poignant picture of this teacher. Steinberg would likely have been proud to see her former student demonstrating his journalistic skills in paying tribute to her.

6. **How effective is the essay? Does the writer make his points clear and persuade the reader to accept them?**

   Friedman's essay serves his purpose extremely well. He helps his readers visualize Steinberg and understand what she gave to each of her journalism students. In his concluding two paragraphs, Friedman shows us that Steinberg's message is as relevant today as it was more than forty years ago, in St. Louis Park High School, Room 313.

ABOUT THE PHOTOGRAPHS AND VISUAL TEXTS IN THIS BOOK

Subject & Strategy has a visual dimension to complement the many verbal texts. Each chapter opens with a visual text that provides insight into the chapter's writing strategy. In addition, we have illustrated at least one essay in each chapter with a photograph that captures one or more themes in the essay. Finally, we have included an assortment of visual texts in the activities that accompany each essay in *Subject & Strategy*. It is our hope that by adding this visual medium to the mix of written essays and text-based analytical activities and assignments, we can demonstrate not only another approach to themes and strategies but also how a different medium portrays these themes and strategies.

There's nothing unnatural or wrong about looking at a photograph and naming its subject or giving it a label. For example, summarizing the content of the photograph on page 17 is easy enough. We'd simply say, *"Here's a photograph of a man sitting in front of a store."*

The problem comes when we mistake *looking* for *seeing*. If we think we are seeing and truly perceiving but are only looking, we miss a lot. Our visual sense can become uncritical and nonchalant, perhaps even dismissive of what's going on in a photograph.

To reap the larger rewards, we need to move in more closely on an image. If we take a closer look, we will see all kinds of important details that we perhaps missed the first time around. We see elements in harmony as well as conflict. We see comparisons and contrasts. We see storytelling. We see process and change. We see highlights and shadows, foreground and background, light and dark, and a myriad of shades in between. There is movement—even in still photographs. There is tension and energy, peace and harmony, and line and texture. We see all this because we are seeing and not merely looking.

If we examine the photograph of the man again and truly *see* it, we might observe the following:

1. A man sits on a ledge that is low to the ground. He is likely traveling because he has two bags, one of which is so heavy that a wheeled cart is useful. Behind him is a store-window display with mannequins posed in various positions.
2. A casual observer might think the scene is in a mall, but closer observation reveals that the ledge is alongside an outdoor sidewalk. The glass of the store window reflects the activity of a busy urban street. We see the side of a bus and a set of handlebars reflected there. The man holds a cigarette in his right hand, evidence that he is outside.
3. The light square tiles of the sidewalk contrast with the round-edged, glossy dark ledge.
4. The man is not particularly meticulous about his appearance, unbothered by the street potentially dirtying his clothes. His white shirt is unbuttoned and rumpled. His athletic sneakers, loose-fitting camouflage jacket, and baseball cap suggest that he prioritizes comfort over style. The shadow on his cap indicates flexible, broken-in fabric. He may wear the hat often.
5. The man stares blankly ahead, uninterested in the goings-on outside the photograph. If he tried to observe the area in front of him, the cart's handle would obscure his view. His posture is rounded, and his arms rest on his knees. He seems tired. Perhaps it's late in the day or, if he has been traveling, it's been a complicated journey.

ABOUT THE PHOTOGRAPHS AND VISUAL TEXTS IN THIS BOOK | **17**

6. In contrast to the man's appearance and manner, the front-window display is formal and fashionable. We see decorative plant fronds in an ornate holder. Luxurious, fringed blankets and jacquard pillows rest on the right side of a squared, modern white bench. The headless, seated mannequin is styled with great care, dressed in skinny high heels, a short dress, and a three-buttoned jacket with a fur collar. The sharp angles of the mannequin's elbows strike a self-assured, confident pose.

Mark Henley/Panos Pictures

7. It's clear that the store carries upscale women's clothes and home furnishings. The clean, litter-free street suggests that the store may be in a well-kept area, perhaps catering to upscale shoppers.
8. The fact that both the mannequin and the man wear light, open jackets suggests a temperate, cool time of year. If we were to zoom on the window's text placard, we would see Chinese characters, suggesting that this scene is in a Chinese city.
9. The most striking thing about the photograph is the juxtaposition of the weary, casually dressed man with the formal and upscale mannequin in the store window. The man seems content to sit and smoke his cigarette, showing little interest in his surroundings. One wonders why he selected that particular spot.

Based on these detailed observations, we can begin to identify a number of themes at work in the photo: class and lifestyle differences, cultural contradictions, and the clash between concepts like work and leisure. Likewise, we can see that several rhetorical strategies are at work: comparison and contrast predominantly but also description and illustration.

Photographs are not the only visual texts that we encounter in our daily lives. Both in print and on the Internet, governments, organizations, and individuals present us with visual information in graphs, diagrams, flowcharts, and ads.

Consider the following graphic, which appeared in the *Wall Street Journal* in May 2015. During the height of the recession, consumer interest in bottled water dropped off, according to research done by Beverage Marketing Corporation.

Bubbling Up

Bottled water consumption in the U.S. has recovered from a slump during the recent recession. Nestlé says its biggest area for growth is within its home-delivery business.

Market share by volume

Brand	Share
Nestlé Waters	29.8%
Niagara	23.3%
Coke (Dasani)	5.8%
DS Waters	5.7%
Crystal Geyser	5.5%
Pepsi (Aquafina)	4.1%
Premium Waters	3.1%

Source: Beverage Marketing Corporation

THE WALL STREET JOURNAL.

Reprinted with permission of *The Wall Street Journal,* **Copyright © 2015 Dow Jones & Company, Inc. All Rights Reserved Worldwide. License number 3831540352289, 3831540138673.**

Before looking at the information in the graphic on page 18, consider whether you think bottled water will have made a recovery and whether you yourself ever buy bottled water. If so, do you prefer a specific brand? Now take the time to really see the graphic and write down observations about what you see.

What were you able to see communicated in this graphic? Here is what we observed:

1. The data is presented in two bar graphs. The first graph presents its data vertically, while the second is arranged horizontally. This gives the impression that the brands in the second graph make up the total 2014 consumption in the first graph.
2. The units in the first graph are presented as billions of gallons.
3. The units in the second graph are presented as percentages.
4. 2008 and 2009 are the first two years that consumption rates were lower than the year before. This must be the "slump" referred to in the text at the top of the graphic.
5. The images of bottled water on the right indicate that the 29.8% of market share held by Nestlé is made up of the sales from a variety of brands. It raises the question of whether the other companies have one brand or multiple brands.
6. Nestlé and Niagara together make up more than half of the bottled water market (53.1%).
7. If Nestle had 29.8% of the market share in 2014, then it sold over 2.98 billion gallons of water.

Similar close analysis of the other visuals in this book will enhance your understanding of how themes and strategies work in these visual texts. Practice in visual analysis will, in turn, add to your understanding of the reading selections. In reading, too, we need to train ourselves to pay close attention to catch all nuances and to be attuned to what is *not* expressed as well as to what is. By sharpening our observational skills, we penetrate to another level of meaning—a level not apparent to a casual reader. Finally, strengthening your ability to see and read deeply will also strengthen your ability to write. We need to see first, clearly and in detail, before we attempt, as writers, to find the appropriate words to help others see.

THE READING-WRITING CONNECTION

Reading and writing are two sides of the same coin. Active reading is one of the best ways to learn to write and to improve writing skills. By reading we can see how others have communicated their experiences, ideas, thoughts, and feelings in their writing. We can study how they have effectively used the various elements of the essay—thesis, organizational strategies, beginnings and endings, paragraphs, transitions, effective sentences, word choice, tone, and figurative language—to say what they wanted to say. By studying the style, technique, and rhetorical strategies of other writers—by reading, in effect, *as* writers—we learn how to write more effectively ourselves.

Reading as a Writer

What does it mean to read as a writer? Most of us have not been taught to read with a writer's eye, to ask why we like one piece of writing and not another. Likewise, most of us do not ask ourselves why one piece of writing is more believable or convincing than another. When you learn to read with a writer's eye, you begin to answer these important questions and, in the process, come to appreciate what is involved in selecting a subject.

At one level, reading stimulates your imagination by providing you with ideas on what to write about. After reading Thomas L. Friedman's "My Favorite Teacher," Malcolm X's "Coming to an Awareness of Language," David P. Bardeen's "Not Close Enough for Comfort," or Jeannette Walls's "A Woman on the Street," you might decide to write about a turning point in your life. Or, after reading Maya Angelou's "Sister Flowers" or Robert Ramírez's "The Barrio," you might be inspired to write about a person or place of similar personal significance to you.

Reading also provides you with information, ideas, and perspectives that can serve as jumping-off points for your own essays. For example, after reading Rosalind Wiseman's "The Queen Bee and Her Court," you might want to elaborate on what she has written, agreeing with her examples or generating better ones; qualify her argument or take issue with it; or use a variation of her classification scheme to discuss male relationships (i.e., "The King and His Court"). Similarly, if you wanted to write an essay in which you take a stand on an issue, you would find the essays on various controversies in the "Argumentation" chapter an invaluable resource.

Reading actively and analytically will also help you recognize effective writing and learn to emulate it. When you see, for example, how Deborah Tannen uses a strong thesis statement about the value of directness and indirectness in human communication to control the parts of her essay ("How to Give Orders Like a Man"), you can better appreciate the importance of having a clear thesis statement in your writing. When you see the way Andrew Sullivan ("iPod World: The End of Society?") uses transitions to link key phrases and important ideas so that readers can recognize how the parts of his essay are meant to flow together, you have a better idea of how to achieve such coherence in your writing. And when you see how Suzanne Britt ("Neat People vs. Sloppy People") uses a point-by-point organizational pattern to show the differences between neat and sloppy people, you see a powerful way in which you can organize an essay using the strategy of comparison and contrast.

Perhaps the most important reason to master the skill of reading like a writer is that, for everything you write, you will be your own first reader. How well you scrutinize your own drafts will affect how well you revise them, and revising well is crucial to writing well.

Alison J. Bechdel/*The New Yorker*, © Conde Nast

CHAPTER **2**

Writing

NOTHING IS MORE IMPORTANT TO YOUR SUCCESS IN SCHOOL AND IN THE workplace than learning to write well. You've heard it so often you've probably become numb to the advice. Let's ask the big question, however: Why is writing well so important? The simple answer is that no activity develops your ability to think better than writing does. Writing allows you to expand your thoughts and to "see" and reflect critically on what you think. In that sense, writing also involves its twin sister, reading. Small wonder, then, that employers in all fields are constantly looking for people who can read and write well. Simply put, employers want to hire and retain the best minds they can to further their business objectives, and the ability to read and write well is a strong indication of a good mind.

Moreover, in today's technology-driven economy, there is virtually no field of work that doesn't require clear, accurate, and direct expression in writing, whether it be writing cover letters and résumés, internal e-mails, self-appraisals, laboratory reports, contract bids, proposals, loan or grant applications, sales reports, market analyses, or any other document. Perhaps more than any other factor, your ability to organize your thoughts and clearly present them will affect your overall success on the job and in life.

College is a practical training ground for learning to write. In college, with the help of instructors, you will write essays, analyses, term papers, reports, reviews of research, critiques, and summaries. Take advantage of the opportunity college provides to develop your skills as a writer: What you learn now will be fundamental not only to your education but also to your later success.

DEVELOPING AN EFFECTIVE WRITING PROCESS

Writers cannot rely on inspiration alone to produce effective writing. Good writers follow a writing *process*: They analyze their assignment, gather ideas, draft, revise, edit, and proofread. Remember, however, that the writing process is rarely as simple and straightforward as this. Often the process is recursive, moving back and forth among different stages. Moreover, writing is personal—no two people go about it the same way. Consider this chapter's opening image, Alison Bechdel's depiction of her creative process, a mix of brainstorming, research, planning, writing, drawing, breaks, printing, distractions, and successes. As she would surely attest, writing well takes *time*. Still, it is nonetheless possible to describe basic guidelines for developing a writing process, thereby allowing you to devise your own reliable method for undertaking a writing task.

Step 1: Understand Your Assignment

A great deal of the writing you do in college will be in response to very specific assignments. Your American history professor, for example, may ask you to write a paper in which you explain the causes of the Spanish-American War or your environmental studies professor may ask you to report both pro and con arguments for hybrid city buses. It is important, therefore, that you understand exactly what your instructor is asking you to do. The best way to understand assignments such as these (or exam questions, for that matter) is to identify *subject* words (words that indicate the content of the assignment) and *direction* words (words that indicate your purpose or the writing strategy you should use). In the first example given above, the subject words are *Spanish-American War* and the direction word is *explain*. In the second example, the subject words are *hybrid city buses* and the direction word is *report*.

Most direction words are familiar to us, but we are not always sure how they differ from one another or exactly what they are asking us to do. The following list of direction words, along with explanations of what they call for, will help you analyze paper and exam assignments.

Direction Words

Analyze: take apart and examine closely

Argue: make a case for a particular position

Categorize: place into meaningful groups

Compare: look for differences; stress similarities

Contrast: look for similarities; stress differences

Critique: point out positive and negative features

Define: provide the meaning for a term or concept

Evaluate: judge according to some standard

Explain: make plain or comprehensible

Illustrate: show through examples

Interpret: explain the meaning of something

List: catalog or enumerate steps in a process
Outline: provide abbreviated structure for key elements
Prove: demonstrate truth through logic, fact, or example
Review: summarize key points
Synthesize: bring together or make connections among elements
Trace: delineate a sequence of events

FINDING A SUBJECT AREA AND FOCUSING ON A TOPIC. Although you will often be given specific assignments in your writing course, you may sometimes have the freedom to choose your subject matter and topic. In this case, begin by determining a broad subject that you like to think about and might enjoy writing about—a general subject like the Internet, popular culture, or foreign travel. Something you've recently read—one of the essays in *Subject & Strategy*, for example—may help bring particular subjects to mind. You might consider a subject related to your career ambitions—perhaps business, law, medicine, architecture, or computer programming. Another option is to list some subjects you enjoy discussing with friends: food, sports, television programs, or politics. Select several likely subjects and explore their potential. Your goal is to arrive at an appropriately narrowed topic.

Suppose, for example, you select as possible subject areas "farming" and "advertising." You could develop each according to the following chart:

Narrowing Subjects to Topics

SUBJECT		SUBJECT
farming	VERY GENERAL	advertising
farming in urban areas	LESS GENERAL	TV advertising
community gardens	GENERAL	TV advertising of food
laws covering community gardens	MORE SPECIFIC	TV advertising of cereals
permit process for community garden land	VERY SPECIFIC	TV advertising of high-fiber cereals
TOPIC		TOPIC

DETERMINING YOUR PURPOSE. All effective writing springs from a clear purpose. Most good writing seeks specifically to accomplish any one of the following three purposes:

- To express thoughts and feelings about life experiences
- To inform readers by explaining something about the world around them
- To persuade readers to adopt some belief or take some action

In *expressive writing*, or writing from experience, you put your thoughts and feelings before all other concerns. When Cherokee Paul McDonald reacts to watching a young boy fishing (Chapter 1), when Malcolm X shows his frustration at not having appropriate language to express himself (Chapter 4), and when Jeannette Walls describes seeing her homeless mother (Chapter 5), each one is writing from experience. In each case, the writer has clarified an important life experience and has conveyed what he or she learned from it.

Informative writing focuses on telling the reader something about the outside world. In informative writing, you report, explain, analyze, define, classify, compare, describe a process, or examine causes and effects. When Michael Pollan explains how the beef we eat travels from factory farms to our tables (Chapter 7) and when Deborah Tannen discusses examples of orders given and received in the workplace (Chapter 6), each one is writing to inform.

Argumentative writing seeks to influence readers' thinking and attitudes toward a subject and, in some cases, to move them to a particular course of action. Such persuasive writing uses logical reasoning, authoritative evidence, and testimony, and it sometimes includes emotionally charged language and examples. In writing their arguments, Richard Lederer uses numerous examples to show us the power of short words (Chapter 12), and Thomas Jefferson uses evidence and clearly expressed logic to argue that the fledgling American colonies are within their rights to break away from Britain (Chapter 12).

KNOWING YOUR AUDIENCE. The best writers always keep their audience in mind. Once they have decided on a topic and a purpose, writers present their material in a way that empathizes with their readers, addresses readers' difficulties and concerns, and appeals to their rational and emotional faculties. Based on knowledge of their audience, writers make conscious decisions on content, sentence structure, and word choice.

WRITING FOR AN ACADEMIC AUDIENCE. Academic writing most often employs the conventions of formal standard English, or the language of

Formal versus Informal Writing

Formal Writing	Informal Writing
Uses standard English, the language of public discourse typical of newspapers, magazines, books, and speeches	Uses nonstandard English, slang, colloquial expressions (*anyways, dude, freaked out*), and shorthand (*OMG, IMHO*)
Uses mostly third person	Uses first and second person most often
Avoids most abbreviations (*Professor, brothers, miles per gallon, Internet, digital video recorder*)	Uses abbreviations and acronyms (*Prof., bros., mpg, Net, DVR*)
Uses an impersonal tone (*The speaker took questions from the audience at the end of her lecture.*)	Uses an informal tone (*It was great the way she answered questions at the end of her talk.*)
Uses longer, more complex sentences	Uses shorter, simpler sentences
Adheres to the rules and conventions of proper grammar	Takes a casual approach to the rules and conventions of proper grammar

educated professionals. Rather than being heavy or stuffy, good academic writing is lively and engaging and holds the reader's attention by presenting interesting ideas supported with relevant facts, statistics, and detailed information. Informal writing, usually freer and simpler in form, is typically used in notes, journal entries, e-mail, text messages, instant messaging, and the like.

In order not to lessen the importance of your ideas and your credibility, be sure that informal writing does not carry over into your academic writing. Always keeping your audience and purpose in mind will help you achieve an appropriate style.

When you write, your audience might be an individual (your instructor), a group (the students in your class), a specialized group (art history majors), or a general readership (readers of your student newspaper). To help identify your audience, ask yourself the questions posed in the box below.

Questions about Audience

- Who are my readers? Are they a specialized or a general group?
- What do I know about my audience's age, gender, education, religious affiliation, economic status, and political views?

(continued on next page)

(continued from previous page)

- What does my audience know about my subject? Are they experts or novices?
- What does my audience need to know about my topic in order to understand my discussion of it?
- Will my audience be interested, open-minded, resistant, or hostile to what I have to say?
- Do I need to explain any specialized language so that my audience can understand my subject? Is there any language that I should avoid?
- What do I want my audience to do as a result of reading my essay?

Step 2: Gather Ideas and Formulate a Thesis

Ideas and information, facts and details lie at the heart of good prose. Ideas grow out of information; information supports ideas. Before you begin to draft, gather as many ideas as possible and as much information as you can about your topic in order to inform and stimulate your readers intellectually.

BRAINSTORMING. A good way to generate ideas and information about a topic is to *brainstorm*: Simply list everything you know about the topic, freely associating one idea with another. At this point, order is not important. Write quickly, but if you get stalled, reread what you have written; doing so will jog your mind in new directions. Keep your list handy so that you can add to it over the course of several days.

Here, for example, is a student's brainstorming list on why Martin Luther King, Jr.'s "I Have a Dream" speech is enduring. If you're not familiar with the speech, you can find video recordings online.

WHY "I HAVE A DREAM" IS MEMORABLE

- Delivered on steps of Lincoln Memorial during civil rights demonstration in Washington, D.C.; crowd of more than 200,000 people
- Repetition of "I have a dream"
- Allusions to the Bible, spirituals
- "Bad check" metaphor and other memorable figures of speech
- Echoes other great American writings—Declaration of Independence and Gettysburg Address
- Refers to various parts of the country and embraces all races and religions
- Sermon format
- Displays energy and passion

CLUSTERING. Clustering allows you to generate material and to sort it into meaningful groupings. Put your topic, or a key word or phrase about your topic, in the center of a sheet of paper and draw a circle around it. Draw four or five (or more) lines radiating out from this circle and jot down main ideas about your topic; draw circles around them as well. Repeat the process by drawing lines from the secondary circles and adding examples, details, and any questions you have.

Here is a student's cluster on television news programs:

RESEARCHING. You may want to supplement what you know about your topic with research. This does not necessarily mean formal library work or even online research. Firsthand observations and interviews with people knowledgeable about your topic are also forms of research. Whatever your form of research, take careful notes so you can accurately paraphrase an author or quote an interviewee.

REHEARSING IDEAS. Consider rehearsing what you are going to write by taking ten or fifteen minutes to talk your way through your paper with a roommate, friend, or family member. Rehearsing in this way may suit your personality and the way you think. Moreover, rehearsing may help you generate new ideas or find gaps in your research.

FORMULATING A THESIS. The thesis of an essay is its main idea, the major point the writer is trying to make.

A thesis should be:

- The most important point you make about your topic
- More general than the ideas and facts used to support it
- Focused enough to be covered in the space allotted for the essay

The thesis is often expressed in one or two sentences called a *thesis statement.* Here is an example of a thesis statement about television news programs:

> The so-called serious news programs are becoming too much like tabloid news shows in both their content and their presentation.

A thesis statement should not be a question but rather an assertion. If you find yourself writing a question for a thesis statement, answer the question first — this answer will be your thesis statement.

An effective strategy for developing a thesis statement is to begin by writing, "What I want to say is that . . ."

> *What I want to say is that* unless language barriers between patients and health care providers are bridged, many patients' lives in our most culturally diverse cities will be endangered.

Later you can delete the formulaic opening *What I want to say is that*, and you will be left with a thesis statement.

To determine whether your thesis is too general or too specific, think hard about how easy it will be to present data — that is, facts, statistics, names, examples or illustrations, and opinions of authorities — to support it. If you stray too far in either direction, your task will become much more difficult. A thesis statement that is too general will leave you overwhelmed by the number of issues you must address. For example, the statement "Malls have ruined the fabric of American life" would lead to the question "How?" To answer it, you would probably have to include information about traffic patterns, urban decay, environmental damage, economic studies, and so on. To cover all of this in the time and space you have for a typical college paper would mean taking shortcuts, and your paper would be ineffective. On the other hand, too specific a thesis statement will leave you with too little information to present. "The Big City Mall should not have been built because it reduced retail sales at existing Big City stores by 21.4 percent" does not leave you with any opportunity to develop an argument.

The thesis statement is usually presented near the beginning of the essay. One common practice in shorter college papers is to position the thesis statement as the final sentence of the first paragraph.

Will Your Thesis Hold Up to Scrutiny?

Once you have a possible thesis statement in mind for an essay, answer the following questions:

- Does my thesis statement take a clear position on an issue? If so, what is that position?
- Is my thesis the most important point I make about my topic?
- Is my thesis neither too general nor too specific? Will I be able to argue it in the time and space allotted?

Step 3: Organize and Write Your First Draft

There is nothing mysterious or difficult about the nine organizational strategies discussed in this book. In fact, you're familiar with most of them already. Whenever you tell a story, for example, you use the strategy *narration*. When you need to make a decision, you *compare and contrast* the things you must choose between. When you want to describe how to make a pizza, you use the *process analysis* strategy to figure out how to explain it. What might make these strategies seem unfamiliar, especially in writing, is that most people

Organizational* Strategies

Narration	Telling a story or giving an account of an event
Description	Presenting a picture in words
Illustration	Using examples to explain a point or an idea
Process analysis	Explaining how something is done or happens
Comparison and contrast	Demonstrating likenesses and differences
Division and classification	Breaking down a subject into its parts and placing them in appropriate categories
Definition	Explaining what something is
Cause and effect analysis	Explaining the causes of an event or the effects of an action
Argumentation	Using reason and logic to persuade

*Also known as *rhetorical* or *writing* strategies.

use them more or less intuitively. Sophisticated thinking and writing, however, do not come from simply using these strategies but rather from using them consciously and purposefully.

Writing strategies are not like blueprints or 3D printers that determine in advance exactly how the final product will be shaped. Rather, these strategies are flexible and versatile, with only a few fundamental rules or directions to define their shape—like the rules for basketball, chess, or other strategic games. Such directions leave plenty of room for imagination and variety. In addition, because these strategies are fundamental ways of thinking, they will help you in all stages of the writing process—from prewriting and the first draft through revising and editing your composition.

DETERMINING A STRATEGY FOR DEVELOPING YOUR ESSAY. Good essays often employ components of more than one strategy. In determining which strategies to use, the language of the writing assignment is very important. If a description is called for, if you need to examine causes and effects, or, as is often the case, if you are asked to argue for a position on an important issue, the language of the assignment will include key direction words and phrases

Determining What Strategies to Use with a Specific Assignment

Key Direction Words and Phrases	Suggested Writing Strategy
Give an account of; tell the story of; relate the events of	Narration
Describe; present a picture; discuss the details of	Description
Show; demonstrate; enumerate; discuss; give examples of	Illustration
Explain how something is done; explain how something works; explain what happens; analyze the steps	Process analysis
Compare; contrast; explain differences; explain similarities; evaluate	Comparison and contrast
Divide and classify; explain what the components are; analyze the parts of	Division and classification
Explain; define a person, place, or thing; give the meaning of	Definition
Explain causes; explain effects; give the reasons for; explain the consequences of	Cause and effect analysis
Argue for or against; make a case for or against; state your views on; persuade; convince; justify	Argumentation

that will indicate the primary strategy or strategies you should use in developing your essay.

In the chart on page 32, the first column lists some key direction words and phrases you may encounter in your writing assignments. The second column lists the strategy that is most likely called for by the use of those words.

Often in academic writing your instructor may not give you a specific assignment; instead, he or she may ask only that you write a paper of a specific length. In such cases, you are left to determine for yourself what strategy or strategies might best accomplish your purpose. If you are not given a specific assignment and are uncertain as to what strategy or strategies you should use in developing your essay, you might try the following four-step method:

Determining What Strategies to Use with an Open Assignment

1. State the main idea of your essay in a single phrase or sentence.
2. Restate the main idea as a question — in effect, the question your essay will answer.
3. Look closely at both the main idea and the question for key words or concepts that go with a particular strategy, just as you would when working with an assignment that specifies a topic.
4. Consider other strategies that would support your primary strategy.

CHOOSING STRATEGIES ACROSS THE DISCIPLINES. The following examples show how a student writing in different disciplines might decide what strategies to use.

American Literature

1. **MAIN IDEA:** John Updike relies on religion as a major theme in his fiction.
2. **QUESTION:** In what instances does John Updike use religion as a major theme?
3. **STRATEGY:** Illustration. The phrase "in what instances" suggests that it is necessary to show examples of where Updike uses the theme of religion to further his narrative purposes.
4. **SUPPORTING STRATEGIES:** Definition. What is meant by *religion* needs to be clear.

Biology

1. **MAIN IDEA:** Mitosis is the process by which cells divide.
2. **QUESTION:** How does the process of mitosis work?

3. **STRATEGY:** Process analysis. The words *how*, *process*, and *work* suggest a process analysis essay.
4. **SUPPORTING STRATEGIES:** Illustration. A good process analysis includes examples of each step in the process.

Political Science

1. **MAIN IDEA:** The threat of terrorism has changed the way people think about air travel.
2. **QUESTION:** What effects does terrorism have on air travel?
3. **STRATEGY:** Cause and effect. The phrase *what effects* asks for a list of the effects.
4. **SUPPORTING STRATEGIES:** Illustration. The best presentation of effects is through vivid examples.

These are just a few examples of how to decide on a writing strategy and supporting strategies that are suitable for your topic. In every case, your reading can guide you in recognizing the best plan to follow. In Chapter 13, you will learn more about combining strategies.

WRITING YOUR FIRST DRAFT. First drafts are exploratory and sometimes unpredictable. While writing your first draft, you may find yourself getting away from your original plan. What started as a definition essay may develop into a process analysis or an effort at argumentation. For example, a definition of *manners* could become an instructive process analysis on how to be a good host, or it could turn into an argument that respect is based on the ways people treat one another. A definition of *democracy* could evolve into a process analysis of how democracy works in the United States or into an argument for democratic forms of government.

If your draft is leaning toward a different strategy from the one you first envisioned, don't force yourself to revert to your original plan. Allow your inspiration to take you where it will. When you finish your draft, you can see whether the new strategy works better than the old one or whether it would be best to go back to your initial strategy. Use your first draft to explore your ideas; you will always have a chance to revise later.

It may also happen that, while writing your first draft, you run into a difficulty that prevents you from moving forward. For example, suppose you want to tell about something that happened to you, but you aren't certain whether you should be using the pronoun *I* so frequently. If you turn to the essays in Chapter 4 to see how authors of narrative essays handle this concern, you will find that it isn't necessarily a problem at all. For an account of a personal experience, it's perfectly acceptable to write *I* as often as you need to. Or suppose that after writing several pages describing someone you think is quite a character, you find that your draft seems flat and doesn't express how lively and funny the person really is. If you read the introduction to Chapter 5, you will learn that descriptions need lots of factual, concrete detail; the chapter selections give further proof of this. You suddenly realize that just such detail is what's missing from your draft.

If you do run into difficulties writing your first draft, don't worry or get upset. Even experienced writers run into problems at the beginning. Just try to keep going. Think about your topic and consider your details and what you want to say. You might even want to go back and look over your original brainstorming work for additional inspiration.

Step 4: Revise Your Essay

Once you have completed your first draft, set it aside awhile and do something else. When you are refreshed and again ready to give it your full attention, you are ready to revise.

Revision is a vital part of the writing process. It is not to be confused with editing or "cleaning up" a draft but should be regarded as a set of activities wherein a rough draft may be transformed into a polished essay that powerfully expresses your ideas. In fact, many writers believe that all writing is essentially *rewriting*. When you revise, you give yourself a chance to re-see how well you have captured your subject, to see what has worked and what still needs to be done.

In revising, you might need to reorganize your paragraphs or the sentences within some paragraphs, generate more information because you have too few examples, revise your thesis statement so that it better fits your argument, or find better transitions to bind your sentences and thoughts together. Many writers find revision not an arduous task but a very satisfying process because they are able to bring their work into sharper focus and give themselves a better chance of connecting with their audience. Best of all, when you revise, you are not staring at a blank page but rearranging the building blocks you have already created.

Tips for Revising Your Draft

- Triple-space your draft so that you can make changes more easily.
- Make revisions on a hard copy of your paper.
- Read your paper aloud, listening for parts that do not make sense.
- Have a fellow student read your essay and critique it.

The following sections offer proven techniques for initiating and carrying out one or more revisions of your developing essays.

TAKING ADVANTAGE OF PEER CRITIQUES. Peer critiquing is one of the best ways to encourage revision and improve your drafts. Peer critiquing is based on two ideas. The first is that by reading your writing aloud, you can determine for yourself where you need to make changes. Often writers say that when they read their work aloud, they themselves are bored or unclear about what they were trying to say. Revisions can follow very easily from such realizations. The second point is that peer critiquing requires an audience, one or more people who are listening to you read what you have written. By asking some simple but important questions, your listeners can verify that what you intended to say is what they heard. If some discrepancies occur,

---

A Brief Guide to Peer Critiquing

When critiquing someone else's work:

- Read the essay carefully. Read it to yourself first and, if possible, have the writer read it to you at the beginning of the session. Some flaws only become obvious when read aloud.
- Ask the writer to state his or her purpose for writing and to identify the thesis statement within the paper itself.
- Be positive but be honest. Never denigrate the paper's content or the writer's effort but do your best to identify how the writer can improve the paper through revision.
- Try to address the most important issues first. Think about the thesis and the organization of the paper before moving on to more specific topics like word choice.
- Do not be dismissive and do not dictate changes. Ask questions that encourage the writer to reconsider parts of the paper that you find confusing or ineffective.

When someone critiques your work:

- Give your reviewer a copy of your essay before your meeting, if possible.
- Listen carefully to your reviewer and try not to argue each issue. Record comments and evaluate them later.
- Do not get defensive or explain what you wanted to say if the reviewer misunderstands what you meant. Try to understand the reviewer's point of view and learn what you need to revise to clear up the misunderstanding.
- Consider every suggestion but use only the ones that make sense to you in your revision.
- Be sure to thank your reviewer for his or her effort on your behalf.

it's usually because you have not expressed yourself as well as you thought you have, and you need to revise. Typical problems are with the purpose for writing and the articulation of a thesis, with lesser problems concerning organization, evidence, and other paragraphs and sentences.

When you critique work with other students—yours or theirs—it is important to maximize the effectiveness and efficiency of the exercise. The tips outlined in the box on page 36 will help you get the most out of peer critiques.

REVISING THE LARGER ELEMENTS OF YOUR ESSAY. During revision, you should focus first on the larger issues of thesis, purpose, content, organization, and paragraph structure to make sure your writing says what you want it to say. One way to begin is to make an informal outline of your first draft—not as you planned it but as it actually came out. What does your outline tell you about the strategy you used? Does this strategy suit your purpose? Perhaps you meant to compare your two grandmothers, but you have not clearly shown their similarities and differences. Consequently, your draft is not one unified comparison and contrast essay but two descriptive essays spliced together.

Even if you are satisfied with the overall strategy of your draft, an outline can still help you make improvements. Perhaps your classification essay on types of college students is confusing because you create overlapping categories: foreign students, computer science majors, and athletes (a foreign student could, of course, be a computer science major, an athlete, or both). You may uncover a flaw in your organization, such as a lack of logic in an argument or faulty parallelism in a comparison and contrast. Now is the time to discover these problems and to fix them.

The following list of questions addresses the larger elements of your essay: thesis, purpose, organization, paragraphs, and evidence. Use it as a guide when reviewing your work as well as when reviewing the work of others during peer critique sessions.

Questions for Revising the Larger Elements of Your Essay

- Have I focused my **topic**?
- Does my **thesis statement** clearly identify my topic and make an assertion about it?
- Is the **writing strategy** I have chosen the best one for my purpose?
- Are my **paragraphs** adequately developed, and does each one support my thesis?
- Is my **beginning** effective in capturing my reader's interest and introducing my topic?

(continued on next page)

(continued from previous page)

- Is my **conclusion** effective? Does it grow naturally from what I've said in the rest of my essay?
- Have I accomplished my **purpose**?

WRITING BEGINNINGS AND ENDINGS. Beginnings and endings are very important to the effectiveness of an essay, but writing them can be daunting. Inexperienced writers often feel they must write their essays sequentially when, in fact, it is usually better to write both the beginning and the ending after you have completed most or all of the rest of your an essay. Once you see how your essay develops, you will know better how to capture the reader's attention and introduce the rest of the essay. As you work through the revision process, ask yourself the questions in the box below.

Questions for Writing Beginnings and Endings

- Does my introduction grab the reader's attention?
- Is my introduction confusing in any way? How well does it relate to the rest of the essay?
- If I state my thesis in the introduction, how effectively is it presented?
- Does my essay come to a logical conclusion, or does it seem to just stop?
- Does the conclusion relate well to the rest of the essay? Am I careful not to introduce topics or issues that I did not address in the essay?
- Does my conclusion underscore important aspects of the essay, or is it merely a mechanical rehashing of what I wrote earlier?

REVISING THE SMALLER ELEMENTS OF YOUR ESSAY. Once you have addressed the larger elements of your essay, you should turn your attention to the finer elements of sentence structure, word choice, and usage. The questions in the following box focus on these concerns.

If, after serious efforts at revision, you still find yourself dissatisfied with specific elements of your draft, look at some of the essays in *Subject & Strategy* to see how other writers have dealt with similar situations. For example, if you don't like the way the essay starts, find some beginnings you think are particularly effective. What characterizes those beginnings? If your paragraphs don't seem to flow into one another, examine how various writers use transitions. If you have lapsed into informal language, take a look at how other writers express themselves. If an example seems unconvincing, examine the way other writers include details, anecdotes, facts, and statistics to strengthen their illustrations.

Remember that the readings in this text are a resource for you as you write, as are the strategy chapter introductions, which outline the basic features of each strategy. In addition, the readings in Chapter 3, "Writers on Writing," will provide you with inspiration and advice to help you through the writing process.

Questions for Revising Sentences

- Do my sentences convey my thoughts clearly, and do they emphasize the most important parts of my thinking?
- Are all my sentences complete sentences?
- Are my sentences stylistically varied? Do I alter their pattern and rhythm for emphasis? Do I use some short sentences for dramatic effect?
- Are all my sentences written in the active voice?
- Do I use strong action verbs and concrete nouns?
- Is my diction fresh and forceful? Do I avoid wordiness?
- Have I achieved an appropriate degree of formality in my writing?
- Have I committed any errors in usage?

Step 5: Edit and Proofread Your Essay

During the *editing* stage, you check your writing for errors in grammar, punctuation, capitalization, spelling, and manuscript format. Chapter 16 of this book provides help for common problems with grammar, punctuation, and sentence style. A dictionary and a grammar handbook may be necessary for less common or more specific editing questions.

After editing, proofread your work carefully before turning it in. Though you may have used your computer's spell-checker, you might find that you have typed *their* instead of *there* or *form* instead of *from*. (A computer program won't know the difference, as long as you've spelled *some* word correctly.)

Questions to Ask during Editing and Proofreading

- Do I have any sentence fragments, comma splices, or run-on sentences?
- Have I used commas properly in all instances?
- Do my verbs agree in number with their antecedents?
- Do my pronouns clearly and correctly refer to their antecedents?
- Do any dangling or misplaced modifiers make my meaning unclear?
- Do I use parallel grammatical structures correctly in my sentences?

(continued on next page)

(continued from previous page)

- Have I used specific nouns and strong verbs wherever possible?
- Have I made any unnecessary shifts in person, tense, or number?
- Have I eliminated unnecessary words?
- Are my sentences appropriately varied and interesting?
- Have I checked for misspellings, mistakes in capitalization, commonly confused words like *its* and *it's*, and typos?
- Have I followed the prescribed guidelines for formatting my manuscript?

A STUDENT ESSAY IN PROGRESS

When he was a first-year student at the University of Vermont, Keith Eldred enrolled in Written Expression, an introductory writing course.

Step 1: Keith's Assignment

Near the middle of the semester, Keith's assignment was to write a three- to five-page definition essay. After reading the introduction to Chapter 10 in *Subject & Strategy* (pages 391–406) and the essays his instructor assigned from that chapter, Keith was ready to get to work.

Step 2: Keith's Ideas

Keith had already been introduced to the Hindu concept of the *mantra*, and he decided that he would like to explore this concept, narrowing his focus to the topic of mantras as they operate in the secular world. To get started, he decided to brainstorm. His brainstorming provided him with several examples of what he intended to call *secular mantras*; a dictionary definition of the word *mantra*; and the idea that a good starting point for his rough draft might be the story of "The Little Engine That Could." Here are the notes he jotted down:

> Mantra: "a mystical formula of invocation or incantation" (Webster's)
>
> Counting to ten when angry
>
> "Little Engine That Could" (possible beginning)
>
> "Let's Go Bulls" — action because crowd wants players to say it to themselves
>
> Swearing (not always a mantra)
>
> Tennis star — "Get serious!"
>
> "Come on, come on" (at traffic light)
>
> "Geronimo" "Ouch!"
>
> Hindu mythology

Step 3: Keith's First Draft

After mulling over his list, Keith began to organize his ideas with the following scratch outline:

1. Begin with story of "Little Engine That Could"
2. Talk about the magic of secular mantras
3. Dictionary definition and Hindu connections
4. Examples of individuals using mantras
5. Crowd chants as mantras — Bulls
6. Conclusion — talk about how you can't get through the day without using mantras

Based on this outline as well as what he learned from *Subject & Strategy* about definition as a writing strategy, Keith came up with the following first draft of his essay:

Secular Mantras: Magic Words
Keith Eldred

1   Do you remember "The Little Engine That Could"? If you recall, it's the story about the tiny locomotive that hauled the train over the mountain when the big, rugged locomotives wouldn't. Do you remember how the Little Engine strained and heaved and chugged "I think I can—I think I can—I think I can" until she reached the top of the mountain? That's a perfect example of a secular mantra in action.

2   A secular mantra (pronounced man-truh) is any word or group of words that helps a person use his or her energy. The key word here is "helps"—repeating a secular mantra doesn't *create* energy; it just makes it easier to channel a given amount. The Little Engine, for instance, obviously had the strength to pull the train up the mountain; apparently, she could have done it without saying a word. But we all know she wouldn't have been able to, any more than any one of us would be able to skydive the first time without yelling "Geronimo" or not exclaim "Ouch" if we touched a hot stove. Some words and phrases simply have a certain magic that makes a job easier or that makes us feel better when we repeat them. These are secular mantras.

3   It is because of their magical quality that these expressions are called "secular mantras" in the first place. A mantra (Sanskrit for "sacred counsel") is "a mystical formula of invocation or incantation" used in Hinduism (*Webster's*). According to Hindu mythology, Manu,

lawgiver and progenitor of humankind, created the first language by teaching people the thought-forms of objects and substances. "VAM," for example, is the thought-form of what we call "water." Mantras, groups of these ancient words, can summon any object or deity if they are miraculously revealed to a seer and properly repeated silently or vocally. Hindus use divine mantras to communicate with gods, acquire superhuman powers, cure diseases, and for many other purposes. Hence, everyday words that people concentrate on to help themselves accomplish tasks or cope with stress act as secular mantras.

All sorts of people use all sorts of secular mantras for all sorts of reasons. A father counts to 10 before saying anything when his son brings the car home dented. A tennis player faults and chides himself, "Get serious!" A frustrated mother pacing with her wailing baby mutters, "You'll have your own kids someday." A college student writhing before an exam instructs himself not to panic. A freshly grounded child glares at his mother's back and repeatedly promises never to speak to her again. Secular mantras are everywhere.

Usually, we use secular mantras to make ourselves walk faster or keep silent or do some other act. But we can also use them to influence the actions of other persons. Say, for instance, the Chicago Bulls are behind in the final minutes of a game. Ten thousand fans who want them to win scream, "Let's go, Bulls!" The Bulls are roused and win by 20 points. Chalk up the victory to the fans' secular mantra, which transferred their energy to the players on the court.

If you're not convinced of the power of secular mantras, try to complete a day without using any. Don't mutter anything to force yourself out of bed. Don't utter a sound when the water in the shower is cold. Don't grumble when the traffic lights are long. Don't speak to the computer when it's slow to boot up. And don't be surprised if you have an unusually long, painful, frustrating day.

Step 4: Keith's Revised Essay

Keith read his paper in a peer critique session with two of his fellow students who had the opportunity afterward to ask him questions about secular mantras, in particular. His classmates wrote what he gave as answers to their questions and presented him with their worksheets with those answers:

- Do a better job of defining *secular mantra*—expand it and be more specific—maybe tell what *secular mantras* are not.
- Get more examples, especially from everyday experience and TV.

- Don't eliminate background information about mantras.
- Thought Chicago Bulls example didn't work — keep or delete?
- Keep "The Little Engine That Could" example at the beginning of the draft.
- Write new conclusion — present conclusion doesn't follow from what you have written.

In subsequent drafts, Keith worked on each of the areas the students had suggested. While revising, he found it helpful to reread portions of the selections in Chapter 10. His reading led him to new insights about how to strengthen his essay. As he revised further, he found that he needed to make other unanticipated changes.

Keith revised his definitions of *mantra* and *secular mantra* to include the following meanings for the related *terms*:

Revised historical definition of mantra

Mantra means "sacred counsel" in Sanskrit and refers to a "mystical formula of invocation or incantation" used in Hinduism (*Webster's*). According to Hindu mythology, the god Manu created the first language by teaching humans the thought-form of every object and substance. "VAM," for example, was what he told them to call the stuff we call "water." But people altered or forgot most of Manu's thought-forms. Followers of Hinduism believe mantras, groups of these ancient words revealed anew by gods to seers, can summon specific objects or deities if they are properly repeated, silently or vocally. Hindus repeat mantras to gain superhuman powers, cure diseases, and for many other purposes. Sideshow fakirs chant "AUM" ("I agree" or "I accept") to become immune to pain when lying on beds of nails.

Expanded definition of secular mantra

Our "mantras" are "secular" because, unlike Hindus, we do not attribute them to gods. Instead, we borrow them from tradition or invent them to fit a situation, as the Little Engine did. They work not by divine power but because they help us, in a way, to govern transmissions along our central nervous systems.

Added explanation of how secular mantras work

Secular mantras give our brains a sort of dual signal-boosting and signal-damping capacity. The act of repeating them pushes messages, or impulses, with extra force along our nerves or interferes with incoming messages we would rather ignore. We can then perform actions more easily or

> cope with stress that might keep us from functioning the way we want to. We may even accomplish both tasks at once. A skydiver might yell "Geronimo," for example, both to amplify the signals telling his legs to jump and to drown out the ones warning him he's dizzy or scared.

He also rewrote the conclusion, adding yet more examples of secular mantras, this time drawn largely from television advertising. Finally, he made his conclusion more of a natural outgrowth of his thesis and purpose and thus a more fitting conclusion for his essay.

Sentence of examples moved from paragraph 4

Final sentence, which links to thesis and purpose, added

> You probably have favorite secular mantras already. Think about it. How many of us haven't uttered the following at least once: "Just do it"; "I'm lovin' it"; "Got milk?"; "Can you hear me now?"; or "Have it your way"? How about the phrases you mumble to yourself from your warm bed on chilly mornings? And those words you chant to ease your impatience when the traffic lights are endless? And the reminders you mutter so that you'll remember to buy bread at the store? If you're like most people, you'll agree that your life is much less painful and frustrating because of those magic words and phrases.

Step 5: Keith's Edited Essay

After expanding his definitions and strengthening his conclusion, as well as making other necessary revisions, Keith was now ready to edit his essay. His instructor told him to avoid the use of first- or second-person address in his essay and to correct sentences starting with coordinating conjunctions like *and* or *but*. In addition, he had to correct smaller but equally important errors in word choice, spelling, punctuation, and mechanics. He had put aside fixing such errors to make sure his essay had the appropriate content. Now he needed to make sure it was grammatically correct. For example, here is how he edited the first paragraph of his essay:

> That's
> ~~Do you~~ Rremember "The Little Engine That Could"? ~~If you recall, it's~~ ˬthe story about the tiny locomotive (o above a) that hauled the train over the mountain when the big, rugged locomotives (o above a) wouldn't. ~~Do you~~ Rremember how the Little Engine strained and heaved and chugged, "I think I can—I think I can—I think I can" until she reached the top of the mountain? That's a perfect example of a secular mantra in action.

By the deadline, Keith had written his essay, revised and edited it, printed it, proofread it one last time, and turned it in. Here is the final draft of his essay:

> ### Secular Mantras
> #### Keith Eldred
>
> 1. "The Little Engine That Could" is a story about a tiny locomotive that hauls a train over a mountain when the big, rugged locomotives refuse: The Little Engine strains and heaves and chugs, repeating "I think I can—I think I can—I think I can" until she reaches the top of the mountain. This refrain—"I think I can—I think I can"—is a perfect example of a secular mantra in action.
>
> 2. A secular mantra (pronounced "man-truh") is any word or group of words that focuses energy when consciously repeated. Most readers of this essay have already used a secular mantra today without realizing it. Some additional explanation is necessary, however, in order to understand what distinguishes a secular mantra from any other kind of phrase.
>
> 3. To be a secular mantra, a phrase must help the speaker focus and use energy. Thus, "I wish I were at home" is not a secular mantra if it's simply a passing thought. The same sentence becomes a secular mantra if, walking home on a cold day, a person repeats the sentence each time she takes a step, willing her feet to move in a steady, accelerated rhythm and take her quickly someplace warm. By the same token, every curse word a person mutters in order to

bear down on a job is a secular mantra, while every curse word that same person unthinkingly repeats is simple profanity.

It is important to understand, however, that secular mantras only help people use energy: They don't create it. The Little Engine, for instance, obviously had enough power to pull the train up the mountainside—she could have done it without a peep. Still, puffing "I think I can" clearly made her job easier, just as, say, chanting "left-right-left" makes marching in step easier for soldiers. Any such word or phrase that, purposefully uttered, helps a person perform something difficult qualifies as a secular mantra.

Why, though, use the term *secular mantra* to describe these phrases, rather than something else? *Mantra* means "sacred counsel" in Sanskrit and refers to a "mystical formula of invocation or incantation" used in Hinduism (*Webster's*). According to Hindu mythology, the god Manu created the first language by teaching humans the thought-form of every object and substance. VAM, for example, was what Manu taught humans to call "water." People unfortunately forgot or altered most of Manu's thought-forms, however. Followers of Hinduism believe that mantras, groups of these ancient words revealed anew by gods to seers, can summon specific objects or deities if they are properly repeated, silently or aloud. Hindus repeat mantras to gain superhuman powers, cure diseases, and for many other purposes. Sideshow fakirs chant *AUM* ("I agree" or "I accept") to become immune to pain when lying on a bed of nails.

The mantras that are the topic of this paper are called *secular* because Western culture does not claim that they are divine in origin; instead, they derive from tradition or are invented to fit a situation, as in the case of the Little Engine. In addition, most Westerners assume that they work not by divine power but through the mind-body connection, by helping govern transmissions along the central nervous system.

The Western, scientific explanation for the power of secular mantras runs something like this: Secular mantras give people's brains a sort of dual signal-boosting and signal-damping capacity. The act of repeating them pushes messages, or impulses, with extra force along the nerves or blocks incoming messages that would interfere with the task at hand. People repeating mantras are thus enabled to perform actions more easily or cope with stress that might keep them from functioning optimally. Mantras may even convey both benefits at once: A skydiver might yell "Geronimo!," for example, both to amplify the signals telling his legs to jump and to drown out the signals warning him he's dizzy or afraid.

Anyone can use words in this way to help accomplish a task. A father might count to ten to keep from bellowing when Junior returns the family car with a huge dent. A tennis player who tends to fault may shout "Get serious!" as he serves, to concentrate harder on controlling the ball. An exhausted new mother with her wailing baby can make her chore less painful by muttering, "Someday you'll do chores for me." Chanting "Grease cartridge" always cools this writer's temper because doing so once headed off a major confrontation with a friend while working on a cantankerous old Buick.

Most readers of this essay probably have favorite secular mantras already. Most people—at least those exposed in any way to contemporary popular culture—have at one point uttered one of the following: "Just do it"; "No worries"; "It's all good"; "I'm king of the world!!"; "We are the champions!"; or something similar. Many people have ritual phrases they mutter to get themselves to leave their warm beds on chilly mornings; others blurt out habitual phrases to help them get over impatience when traffic lights don't change or to help them endure a courtesy call to a neighbor they've never really liked. Most people, if they really think about it, will admit that the seeming magic of secular mantras has made their lives much less painful, less frustrating, and perhaps even a little more fun.

9

While it's not perfect, "Secular Mantras" is a fine essay of definition. Keith provides a clear explanation of the concept, offers numerous examples to illustrate it, and suggests how mantras work and how we use them. Keith's notes, rough draft, samples of revised and edited paragraphs, and final draft demonstrate how such effective writing is accomplished. By reading analytically—both his own writing and that of experienced writers—Keith came to understand the requirements of the strategy of definition. An honest and thorough appraisal of his rough draft led to thoughtful revisions, resulting in a strong and effective piece of writing.

Getty Images News/Getty Image

CHAPTER **3**

Writers on Writing

LIKE ANY OTHER CRAFT, WRITING INVOLVES LEARNING BASIC SKILLS AS well as more sophisticated techniques that can be refined and then shared among practitioners. Some of the most important lessons a student writer encounters may come from the experiences of other writers: suggestions, advice, cautions, corrections, encouragement. This chapter contains essays in which writers discuss their habits, difficulties, and judgments while they express both the joy of writing and the hard work it can entail. These writers deal with the full range of the writing process—from freeing the imagination in journal entries to correcting punctuation errors for the final draft. The advice they offer is pertinent and sound.

Sometimes, simply getting started can be a big challenge, but the more carefully you pay attention to your reading, surroundings, and reactions to your experiences, the easier it will be to transform your thoughts into written words. The photo opposite was taken in Tel Afar, Iraq, during an hourlong gun battle that stretched across the neighborhood. The man in the photo is a journalist practicing his craft in the midst of the chaos, using the stress of his surroundings to stimulate his work. Of course, good writing can spring from any subject. We often have an abundance of ideas before we even realize it. As Fyodor Dostoyevsky wrote, "But how could you live and have no story to tell?"

Discovering the Power of My Words

RUSSELL BAKER

Russell Baker has had a long and distinguished career as a newspaper reporter and columnist. He was born in Morrisonville, Virginia, in 1925 and enlisted in the Navy in 1943, after graduating from Johns Hopkins University. In 1947, he secured his first newspaper job, as a reporter for the *Baltimore Sun*, then moved to the *New York Times* in 1954, where he wrote the "Observer" column from 1962 to 1998. His incisive wit, by turns melancholic and sharp edged, is well represented in such quips as these: "Children rarely want to know who their parents were before they were parents, and when age finally stirs their curiosity, there is no parent left to tell them" and "Is fuel efficiency really what we need most desperately? I say that what we really need is a car that can be shot when it breaks down."

Yvonne Hemsey/Getty Images

Baker's columns have been collected in numerous books over the years. In 1979, he was awarded the Pulitzer Prize, journalism's highest award, as well as the George Polk Award for Commentary. Baker's memoir, *Growing Up* (1983), also received a Pulitzer. His autobiographical follow-up, *The Good Times*, was published in 1989. His other works include *Russell Baker's Book of American Humor* (1993); *Inventing the Truth: The Art and Craft of Memoir*, with William Zinsser and Jill Ker Conway (revised 1998); and *Looking Back* (2002), a collection of Baker's essays for *The New York Review of Books*. From 1993 to 2004 he hosted the distinguished PBS series *Exxon Mobil Masterpiece Theatre*.

The following selection is from *Growing Up*. As you read Baker's account of how he discovered the power of his own words, note particularly the joy he felt hearing his writing read aloud.

Preparing to Read

What has been your experience with writing teachers in school? Have any of them helped you become a better writer? What kind of writer do you consider yourself now — excellent, above average, good, below average? Why?

The notion of becoming a writer had flickered off and on in my head ... but it wasn't until my third year in high school that the possibility took hold. Until then I'd been bored by everything associated with English courses. I found English grammar dull and baffling. I hated the assignments to turn out "compositions," and went at them like heavy labor, turning out leaden, lackluster paragraphs that were agonies for teachers to read and for me to write. The classics thrust on me to read seemed as deadening as chloroform.

When our class was assigned to Mr. Fleagle for third-year English I anticipated another grim year in that dreariest of subjects. Mr. Fleagle was notorious among City students for dullness and inability to inspire. He was said to be stuffy, dull, and hopelessly out of date. To me he looked to be sixty or seventy and prim to a fault. He wore primly severe eyeglasses, his wavy hair was primly cut and primly combed. He wore prim vested suits with neckties blocked primly against the collar buttons of his primly starched white shirts. He had a primly pointed jaw, a primly straight nose, and a prim manner of speaking that was so correct, so gentlemanly, that he seemed a comic antique.

I anticipated a listless, unfruitful year with Mr. Fleagle and for a long time was not disappointed. We read *Macbeth*. Mr. Fleagle loved *Macbeth* and wanted us to love it, too, but he lacked the gift of infecting others with his own passion. He tried to convey the murderous ferocity of Lady Macbeth one day by reading aloud the passage that concludes

> . . . I have given suck, and know
> How tender 'tis to love the babe that milks me.
> I would, while it was smiling in my face,
> Have plucked my nipple from his boneless gums . . .

The idea of prim Mr. Fleagle plucking his nipple from boneless gums was too much for the class. We burst into gasps of irrepressible snickering. Mr. Fleagle stopped.

"There is nothing funny, boys, about giving suck to a babe. It is the— the very essence of motherhood, don't you see."

He constantly sprinkled his sentences with "don't you see." It wasn't a question but an exclamation of mild surprise at our ignorance. "Your pronoun needs an antecedent, don't you see," he would say, very primly. "The purpose of the Porter's scene, boys, is to provide comic relief from the horror, don't you see."

Late in the year we tackled the informal essay. "The essay, don't you see, is the . . ." My mind went numb. Of all forms of writing, none seemed so boring as the essay. Naturally we would have to write informal essays. Mr. Fleagle distributed a homework sheet offering us a choice of topics. None was quite so simpleminded as "What I Did on My Summer Vacation," but most seemed to be almost as dull. I took the list home and dawdled until the night before the essay was due. Sprawled on the sofa, I finally faced up to the grim task, took the list out of my notebook, and scanned it. The topic on which my eye stopped was "The Art of Eating Spaghetti."

This title produced an extraordinary sequence of mental images. Surging up from the depths of memory came a vivid recollection of a night in Belleville when all of us were seated around the supper table—Uncle Allen, my mother, Uncle Charlie, Doris, Uncle Hal—and Aunt Pat served spaghetti for supper. Spaghetti was an exotic treat in those days. Neither Doris nor I had ever eaten spaghetti, and none of the adults had enough experience to be good at it. All the good humor of Uncle Allen's house reawoke in my mind as I recalled the laughing arguments we had that night about the socially respectable method for moving spaghetti from plate to mouth.

Suddenly I wanted to write about that, about the warmth and good feeling of it, but I wanted to put it down simply for my own joy, not for Mr. Fleagle. It was a moment I wanted to recapture and hold for myself. I wanted to relive the pleasure of an evening at New Street. To write it as I wanted, however, would violate all the rules of formal composition I'd learned in school, and Mr. Fleagle would surely give it a failing grade. Never mind. I would write something else for Mr. Fleagle after I had written this thing for myself.

When I finished it the night was half gone and there was no time left to compose a proper, respectable essay for Mr. Fleagle. There was no choice next morning but to turn in my private reminiscence of Belleville. Two days passed before Mr. Fleagle returned the graded papers, and he returned everyone's but mine. I was bracing myself for a command to report to Mr. Fleagle immediately after school for discipline when I saw him lift my paper from his desk and rap for the class's attention.

"Now, boys," he said, "I want to read you an essay. This is titled 'The Art of Eating Spaghetti.'"

And he started to read. My words! He was reading *my words* out loud to the entire class. What's more, the entire class was listening. Listening attentively. Then somebody laughed, then the entire class was laughing, and not in contempt and ridicule, but with open-hearted enjoyment. Even Mr. Fleagle stopped two or three times to repress a small prim smile.

I did my best to avoid showing pleasure, but what I was feeling was pure ecstasy at this startling demonstration that my words had the power to make people laugh. In the eleventh grade, at the eleventh hour as it were, I had discovered a calling. It was the happiest moment of my entire school career. When Mr. Fleagle finished he put the final seal on my happiness by saying, "Now that, boys, is an essay, don't you see. It's—don't you see—it's of the very essence of the essay, don't you see. Congratulations, Mr. Baker."

For the first time, light shone on a possibility. It wasn't a very heartening possibility, to be sure. Writing couldn't lead to a job after high school, and it was hardly honest work, but Mr. Fleagle had opened a door for me. After that I ranked Mr. Fleagle among the finest teachers in the school.

Thinking Critically about the Text

In his opening paragraph, Baker states, "I hated the assignments to turn out 'compositions,' and went at them like heavy labor, turning out leaden, lackluster paragraphs that were agonies for teachers to read and for me to write." Have you ever had any assignments like these? How are such assignments different from Mr. Fleagle's assignment to write an informal essay about "The Art of Eating Spaghetti"? How do you think Baker would respond to the following cartoon about writing assignments?

"When writing your essays, I encourage you to think for yourselves while you express what I'd most agree with."

Matthew Henry Hall, www.matthewhenryhall.com

Discussing the Craft of Writing

1. How does Baker describe his teacher, Mr. Fleagle, in the second paragraph? What dominant impression does Baker create of this man? (Glossary: *Dominant Impression*)

2. Mr. Fleagle's homework assignment offered Baker and his classmates "a choice of topics." Is it important to have a "choice" of what you write about? Explain.

3. Once Baker's eye hits the topic of "The Art of Eating Spaghetti" on Mr. Fleagle's list, what happens? What triggers Baker's urge to write about the night his Aunt Pat served spaghetti for supper?

4. Why is Baker reluctant to submit his finished essay?

5. In paragraph 11, Baker states, "And he started to read. My words! He was reading *my words* out loud to the entire class. What's more, the entire class was listening. Listening attentively." Why do you suppose this episode was so memorable to Baker? What surprised him most about it?

6. What insights into the nature of writing does Baker's narrative offer? Explain.

Shitty First Drafts

ANNE LAMOTT

Born in San Francisco in 1954, Anne Lamott graduated from Goucher College in Baltimore and is the author of seven novels, including *Rosie* (1983), *All New People* (1989), *Blue Shoes* (2002), and *Imperfect Birds* (2010). She has also been a food reviewer for *California* magazine, a book reviewer for *Mademoiselle*, and a columnist for *Salon*. Her nonfiction books include *Operating Instructions: A Journal of My Son's First Year* (1993), in which she describes life as a single parent; *Traveling Mercies: Some Thoughts on Faith* (1999), in which she charts her journey toward faith in God; *Plan B: Further Thoughts on Faith* (2005); *Some Assembly Required: A Journal of My Son's First Son* (2012); *Help, Thanks, Wow: The Three Essential Prayers* (2012); and *Small Victories: Spotting Improvable Moments of Grace* (2014). Lamott has taught at the University of California–Davis, as well as at writing conferences around the country. Reflecting on the importance of writing and reading, Lamott has written, "Writing and reading decrease our sense of isolation. They deepen and widen and expand our sense of life: They feed the soul."

In the following selection, taken from Lamott's popular book about writing *Bird by Bird: Some Instructions on Writing and Life* (1994), she argues for the need to let go and write those "shitty first drafts" that lead to clarity and sometimes brilliance in subsequent drafts.

Preparing to Read

Many professional writers view first drafts as something they have to do before they can begin the real work of writing — revision. How do you view the writing of your first drafts? What patterns, if any, do you see in your writing behavior when working on them? Is the work liberating or restricting? Pleasant or unpleasant?

Now, practically even better news than that of short assignments is the idea of shitty first drafts. All good writers write them. This is how they end up with good second drafts and terrific third drafts. People tend to look at successful writers, writers who are getting their books published and maybe even doing well financially, and think that they sit down at their desks every morning feeling like a million dollars, feeling great about who they are and how much talent they have and what a great story they have to tell; that they take in a few deep breaths, push back their sleeves, roll their necks a few times to get all the cricks out, and dive in, typing fully formed passages as fast as a court reporter. But this is just the fantasy of the uninitiated. I know some very great writers, writers you love who write beautifully and have made a great deal of money, and not *one* of them sits down routinely feeling wildly enthusiastic and confident. Not one of them writes elegant first drafts. All right, one of them does, but we do not like her very much. We do not think that she has a rich inner life or that God likes her or can even stand her. (Although when I mentioned this to my priest friend Tom, he said you can safely assume you've created God in your own image when it turns out that God hates all the same people you do.)

> All good writers write them. This is how they end up with good second drafts and terrific third drafts.

Very few writers really know what they are doing until they've done it. Nor do they go about their business feeling dewy and thrilled. They do not type a few stiff warm-up sentences and then find themselves bounding along like huskies across the snow. One writer I know tells me that he sits down every morning and says to himself nicely, "It's not like you don't have a choice, because you do—you can either type or kill yourself." We all often feel like we are pulling teeth, even those writers whose prose ends up being the most natural and fluid. The right words and sentences just do not come pouring out like ticker tape most of the time. Now, Muriel Spark is said to have felt that she was taking dictation from God every morning—sitting there, one supposes, plugged into a Dictaphone, typing away, humming. But this is a very hostile and aggressive position. One might hope for bad things to rain down on a person like this.

For me and most of the other writers I know, writing is not rapturous. In fact, the only way I can get anything written at all is to write really, really shitty first drafts.

The first draft is the child's draft, where you let it all pour out and then let it romp all over the place, knowing that no one is going to see it and that you can shape it later. You just let this childlike part of you channel whatever voices and visions come through and onto the page. If one of the characters wants to say, "Well, so what, Mr. Poopy Pants?," you let her. No one is going to see it. If the kid wants to get into really sentimental, weepy, emotional territory, you let him. Just get it all down on paper, because there may be something great in those six crazy pages that you would never have gotten to by more rational, grown-up means. There may be something in the very last line of the very last paragraph on page six that you just love, that is so beautiful or wild that you now know what you're supposed to be writing about, more or less, or in what direction you might go—but there was no way to get to this without first getting through the first five and a half pages.

I used to write food reviews for *California* magazine before it folded. (My writing food reviews had nothing to do with the magazine folding, although every single review did cause a couple of canceled subscriptions. Some readers took umbrage at my comparing mounds of vegetable puree with various ex-presidents' brains.) These reviews always took two days to write. First I'd go to a restaurant several times with a few opinionated, articulate friends in tow. I'd sit there writing down everything anyone said that was at all interesting or funny. Then on the following Monday I'd sit down at my desk with my notes, and try to write the review. Even after I'd been doing this for years, panic would set in. I'd try to write a lead, but instead I'd write a couple of dreadful sentences, xx them out, try again, xx everything out, and then feel despair and worry settle on my chest like an X-ray apron. It's over, I'd think, calmly. I'm not going to be able to get the magic to work this time. I'm ruined. I'm through. I'm toast. Maybe, I'd think, I can get my old job back as a clerk-typist. But probably not. I'd get up and study my teeth in the mirror for a while. Then I'd stop, remember to breathe, make a few phone calls, hit the kitchen and chow down. Eventually I'd go back and sit down at my desk, and sigh for the next ten minutes. Finally I would pick up my one-inch picture frame, stare into it as if for the answer, and every time the answer would come: All I had to do was to write a really shitty first draft of, say, the opening paragraph. And no one was going to see it.

So I'd start writing without reining myself in. It was almost just typing, just making my fingers move. And the writing would be *terrible*. I'd write a lead paragraph that was a whole page, even though the entire review could only be three pages long, and then I'd start writing up descriptions of the food, one dish at a time, bird by bird, and the critics would be sitting on my shoulders, commenting like cartoon characters. They'd be pretending to snore, or rolling their eyes at my overwrought descriptions, no matter how hard I tried to tone those descriptions down, no matter how conscious I was of what a friend said to me gently in my early days of restaurant reviewing. "Annie," she said, "it is just a piece of *chicken*. It is just a bit of *cake*."

But because by then I had been writing for so long, I would eventually let myself trust the process — sort of, more or less. I'd write a first draft that was maybe twice as long as it should be, with a self-indulgent and boring beginning, stupefying descriptions of the meal, lots of quotes from my black-humored friends that made them sound more like the Manson girls than food lovers, and no ending to speak of. The whole thing would be so long and incoherent and hideous that for the rest of the day I'd obsess about getting creamed by a car before I could write a decent second draft.

I'd worry that people would read what I'd written and believe that the accident had really been a suicide, that I had panicked because my talent was waning and my mind was shot.

The next day, though, I'd sit down, go through it all with a colored pen, take out everything I possibly could, find a new lead somewhere on the second page, figure out a kicky place to end it, and then write a second draft. It always turned out fine, sometimes even funny and weird and helpful. I'd go over it one more time and mail it in.

Then, a month later, when it was time for another review, the whole process would start again, complete with the fears that people would find my first draft before I could rewrite it.

Almost all good writing begins with terrible first efforts. You need to start somewhere. Start by getting something—anything—down on paper. A friend of mine says that the first draft is the down draft—you just get it down. The second draft is the up draft—you fix it up. You try to say what you have to say more accurately. And the third draft is the dental draft, where you check every tooth, to see if it's loose or cramped or decayed, or even, God help us, healthy.

What I've learned to do when I sit down to work on a shitty first draft is to quiet the voices in my head. First there's the vinegar-lipped Reader Lady, who says primly, "Well, *that's* not very interesting, is it?" And there's the emaciated German male who writes these Orwellian memos detailing your thought crimes. And there are your parents, agonizing over your lack of loyalty and discretion; and there's William Burroughs, dozing off or shooting up because he finds you as bold and articulate as a houseplant; and so on. And there are also the dogs: let's not forget the dogs, the dogs in their pen who will surely hurtle and snarl their way out if you ever *stop* writing, because writing is, for some of us, the latch that keeps the door of the pen closed, keeps those crazy ravenous dogs contained.

Quieting these voices is at least half the battle I fight daily. But this is better than it used to be. It used to be 87 percent. Left to its own devices, my mind spends much of its time having conversations with people who aren't there. I walk along defending myself to people, or exchanging repartee with them, or rationalizing my behavior, or seducing them with gossip, or pretending I'm on their TV talk show or whatever. I speed or run an aging yellow light or don't come to a full stop, and one nanosecond later am explaining to imaginary cops exactly why I had to do what I did, or insisting that I did not in fact do it.

I happened to mention this to a hypnotist I saw many years ago, and he looked at me very nicely. At first I thought he was feeling around on the floor for the silent alarm button, but then he gave me the following exercise, which I still use to this day.

Close your eyes and get quiet for a minute, until the chatter starts up. Then isolate one of the voices and imagine the person speaking as a mouse. Pick it up by the tail and drop it into a mason jar. Then isolate another voice, pick it up by the tail, drop it in the jar. And so on. Drop in any high-maintenance parental units, drop in any contractors, lawyers, colleagues, children, anyone who is whining in your head. Then put the lid on, and watch all these mouse people clawing at the glass, jabbering away, trying to make you feel like shit because you won't do what they want — won't give them more money, won't be more successful, won't see them more often. Then imagine that there is a volume-control button on the bottle. Turn it all the way up for a minute, and listen to the stream of angry, neglected, guilt-mongering voices. Then turn it all the way down and watch the frantic mice lunge at the glass, trying to get to you. Leave it down, and get back to your shitty first draft.

A writer friend of mine suggests opening the jar and shooting them all in the head. But I think he's a little angry, and I'm sure nothing like this would ever occur to you.

Thinking Critically about the Text

What do you think of Lamott's use of the word *shitty* in her title and in the essay itself? Is it in keeping with her tone? (Glossary: *Tone*) Are you offended by the word? Explain. What would be lost or gained if she used a different word?

Discussing the Craft of Writing

1. Lamott says that the perception most people have of how writers work is different from the reality. She refers to this in paragraph 1 as the "fantasy of the uninitiated." What does she mean?

2. In paragraph 7, Lamott refers to a time when, through experience, she "eventually let [herself] trust the process — sort of, more or less." She is referring to the writing process, of course, but why "more or less"? Do you think her wariness is personal, or is she speaking for all writers? Explain.

3. From what Lamott has to say, is writing a first draft more about content or psychology? Do you agree when it comes to your own first drafts? Explain.

4. What is Lamott's thesis? (Glossary: *Thesis*)

5. Lamott adds humor to her argument for "shitty first drafts." Give some examples. Does her humor add to or detract from the points she makes? Explain.

6. In paragraph 5, Lamott narrates her experiences in writing a food review, during which she refers to an almost ritualistic set of behaviors. What is her purpose in telling her readers this story about her difficulties? (Glossary: *Purpose*) Is this information helpful? Explain.

Writing for an Audience

LINDA S. FLOWER

Linda S. Flower is a professor of English at Carnegie Mellon University, where she directed the Business Communication program for a number of years and is currently the director of the Center for the Study of Writing and Literacy. She has been a leading researcher on the composing process, and the results of her investigations shaped and informed her influential writing text *Problem-Solving Strategies for Writing in College and Community* (1997). Her other work includes *Talking Across Difference* (2004) and *Community Literacy and the Rhetoric of Public Engagement* (2008).

Courtesy of Linda Flower

In this selection, which is taken from *Problem-Solving Strategies*, Flower's focus is on audience — the people for whom we write. She believes that writers must establish a "common ground" between themselves and their readers that lessens their differences in knowledge, attitudes, and needs. Although we can never be certain who might read what we write, it is nevertheless important for us to have a target audience in mind. Many of the decisions that we make as writers are influenced by those real or imagined readers.

Preparing to Read

Imagine for a moment that you just received a speeding ticket for going sixty-five miles per hour in a thirty-mile-per-hour zone. How would you describe the episode to your best friend? To your parents? To the judge in court? Sketch out the three versions. What differences, if any, do you find in the three versions? Explain.

The goal of the writer is to create a momentary common ground between the reader and the writer. You want the reader to share your knowledge and your attitude toward that knowledge. Even if the reader eventually disagrees, you want him or her to be able for the moment to *see things as you see them*. A good piece of writing closes the gap between you and the reader.

ANALYZE YOUR AUDIENCE

The first step in closing that gap is to gauge the distance between the two of you. Imagine, for example, that you are a student writing your parents, who have always lived in New York City, about a wilderness survival expedition you want to go on over spring break. Sometimes obvious differences such as age or background will be important, but the critical differences for writers usually fall into three areas: the reader's *knowledge* about the topic; his or her *attitude* toward it; and his or her personal or professional *needs*. Because these differences often exist, good writers do more than simply express their meaning; they pinpoint the critical differences between themselves and their reader and design their writing to reduce those differences. Let us look at these areas in more detail.

Knowledge

This is usually the easiest difference to handle. What does your reader need to know? What are the main ideas you hope to teach? Does your reader have enough background knowledge to really understand you? If not, what would he or she have to learn?

Attitudes

When we say a person has knowledge, we usually refer to his conscious awareness of explicit facts and clearly defined concepts. This kind of knowledge can be easily written down or told to someone else. However, much of what we "know" is not held in this formal, explicit way. Instead it is held as an attitude or image—as a loose cluster of associations. For instance, my image of lakes includes associations many people would have, including fishing, water skiing, stalled outboards, and lots of kids catching night crawlers with flashlights. However, the most salient or powerful parts of my image, which strongly color my whole attitude toward lakes, are thoughts of cloudy skies, long rainy days, and feeling generally cold and damp. By contrast, one of my best friends has a very different cluster of associations: to him a lake means sun, swimming, sailing, and happily sitting on the end of a dock. Needless to say, our differing images cause us to react quite differently to a proposal that we visit a lake. Likewise, one reason people often find it difficult to discuss religion and politics is that terms such as "capitalism" conjure up radically different images.

> A good piece of writing closes the gap between you and the reader.

As you can see, a reader's image of a subject is often the source of attitudes and feelings that are unexpected and, at times, impervious to mere facts. A simple statement that seems quite persuasive to you, such as "Lake Wampago would be a great place to locate the new music camp," could have little impact on your reader if he or she simply doesn't visualize a lake as a "great place." In fact, many people accept uncritically any statement that fits in with their own attitudes—and reject, just as uncritically, anything that does not.

Whether your purpose is to persuade or simply to present your perspective, it helps to know the image and attitudes that your reader already holds. The more these differ from your own, the more you will have to do to make him or her *see* what you mean.

Needs

When writers discover a large gap between their own knowledge and attitudes and those of the reader, they usually try to change the reader in some way. Needs, however, are different. When you analyze a reader's needs, it is so that you, the writer, can adapt to him. If you ask a friend majoring in biology how to keep your fish tank from clouding, you don't want to hear a textbook recitation on the life processes of algae. You expect a friend to adapt his or her knowledge and tell you exactly how to solve your problem.

The ability to adapt your knowledge to the needs of the reader is often crucial to your success as a writer. This is especially true in writing done on a job. For example, as producer of a public affairs program for a television station, 80 percent of your time may be taken up planning the details of new shows, contacting guests, and scheduling the taping sessions. But when you write a program proposal to the station director, your job is to show how the program will fit into the cost guidelines, the FCC requirements for relevance, and the overall programming plan for the station. When you write that report, your role in the organization changes from producer to proposal writer. Why? Because your reader needs that information in order to make a decision. He may be *interested* in your scheduling problems and the specific content of the shows, but he *reads* your report because of his own needs as station director of the organization. He has to act.

In college, where the reader is also a teacher, the reader's needs are a little less concrete but just as important. Most papers are assigned as a way to teach something. So the real purpose of a paper may be for you to make connections between two historical periods, to discover for yourself the principle behind a laboratory experiment, or to develop and support your own interpretation of a novel. A good college paper doesn't just rehash the facts; it demonstrates what your reader, as a teacher, needs to know — that you are learning the thinking skills his or her course is trying to teach.

Effective writers are not simply expressing what they know, like a student madly filling up an examination bluebook. Instead they are *using* their knowledge: reorganizing, maybe even rethinking their ideas to meet the demands of an assignment or the needs of their reader.

Thinking Critically about the Text

What does Flower believe constitutes a "good college paper" (paragraph 9)? Do you agree? Why, or why not?

Discussing the Craft of Writing

1. How, according to Flower, does a competent writer achieve the goal of closing the gap between himself or herself and the reader? How does a writer determine what a reader's "personal or professional needs" (paragraph 2) are?

2. What, for Flower, is the difference between knowledge and attitude? Why is it important for writers to understand this difference?

3. In paragraph 4, Flower discusses the fact that many words have both positive and negative associations. How do you think words come to have associations? (Glossary: *Connotation/Denotation*) Consider, for example, such words as *home, anger, royalty, welfare, politician,* and *strawberry shortcake.*

4. Flower wrote this selection for college students. How well did she assess your needs as a member of this audience? Does Flower's use of language and examples show a sensitivity to her audience? Provide specific examples to support your view.

5. When using technical language in a paper on a subject you are familiar with, why is it important for you to know your audience? Explain. How could your classmates, friends, or parents help you?

On Voice

SUSAN ORLEAN

Susan Orlean writes the following about herself: "I'm an author, a staff writer for the *New Yorker*, a dog owner, a gardener, a parent, a frequent lecturer/speaker, an occasional teacher, a very occasional guest editor, a once-in-a-blue-moon movie inspiration, and doodler." She was born in Cleveland, Ohio, in 1955 and graduated from the University of Michigan before working on several newspapers and writing stories for the *New York Times*, *Esquire*, *Vogue*, *Spy*, and *Rolling Stone*. Her books include *The Orchid Thief* (made into the film *Adaptation*) (1998), *The Bullfighter Checks Her Makeup: My Encounters with Extraordinary People* (2001), and *Rin Tin Tin: The Life and the Legend* (2011). She has also edited such collections as *My Kind of Place: Travel Stories from a Woman Who's Been Everywhere* (2004) and *Best American Travel Writing 2007* (2007). Her most recent book, *The Floral Ghost*, is a collaboration with artist Philip Taaffe.

Amanda Edwards/FilmMagic/Getty Images

In "On Voice," taken from *Telling True Stories* (2007), an anthology of writings adapted from authors' presentations at the Neiman Conference on Narrative Nonfiction, Orlean tells us what voice is and explains how voice is created in writing.

Preparing to Read

Whenever you read aloud what you have written, you are better able to hear your writer's voice. If you have had that experience, what did you notice about your particular voice? Was it humorous, dark, witty, curt, drawn out, sarcastic, faint, bold, or did it reveal some other quality? What in your writing style do you think accounts for the impression it creates?

Developing a writer's voice is almost a process of unlearning, one analogous to children's painting. Young children often create fabulous paintings, only to be told after they start school that real houses don't look that way. At that point, most people lose their ability to be visually creative. Truly great painting retains some element of a child's emotional authenticity. Great writing does, too.

Self-analysis is crucial to developing a strong voice. *Who am I? Why do I write?* Your identity and your self-understanding become subliminal parts of your writer's voice—especially in long-form narrative writing. Imagine yourself telling friends about a story that excites you. Your friends follow the story even though it's not linear but circles back as you tell it.

The way you tell a story over dinner is true to who you are, whether that is deeply analytical or extremely witty. At such moments you aren't self-conscious, and you aren't thinking about your editor.

You can't invent a voice. And you can't imitate someone else's voice, though trying to can be a good exercise. It can lead you to begin to understand the *mechanisms* that convey the voice. Read your stories out loud so you can *hear* how you tell stories. As you read, ask yourself: *Does it sound real? Would I have said it that way?* If the answer to either question is no, you have done something wrong. I find that sometimes when I give readings of my published work, I skip parts that seem boring to me. Then I wonder, would it have been better to edit that out in the first place? When you read aloud, extraneous material falls away. Voice is — as the word itself tells us — the way a writer *talks*. You are *speaking* to your readers. Sometimes we think we have to come up with something clever, but cleverness for its own sake is rarely powerful.

> The way you tell a story over dinner is true to who you are, whether that is deeply analytical or extremely witty.

Pace, the sense of timing in a piece, is linked to voice. Pace determines whether attempts at humor will succeed. Change your story's pace to change the mood. Long sentences can slow down the reader. Short sentences race the reader through a scene. As you read your piece aloud, you hear how your readers will make their way through it. Then you can control that movement.

Word choice is another element of voice. When you make an analogy, it's not just to give the reader an image but to advance a larger idea or theme. Once I had a fight with an editor because I wanted to describe a basketball player's feet as "banana-shaped." My editor argued that feet can't really be banana-shaped. And, further, thinking about bananas takes the reader away from the subject: a person playing basketball. "You're giving the reader a ticket to the tropics," he said. I spent hours trying to find the right image to replace *banana*. Suddenly, it came to me: *pontoon*. His feet were pontoon-shaped; he floated over the basketball court. Analogies like these don't usually come as I am reporting. I have to sit at my desk and really work at finding the strongest image possible.

Another aspect of voice is taking on your characters' voices. Sometimes, immersed in my reporting, I find myself thinking in the same rhythm as someone I'm writing about. This is part of my temperament; I tend to become caught up in other worlds. As long as I don't slide into mimicry, it can help a piece of writing. You don't want to hijack someone's voice but draw inspiration from it. It is often a sign that you have submerged yourself deeply in a story, inhabiting it. I wrote half of "The American Man at Age Ten" in the voice of a boy. I stepped in and out of that persona throughout the story.

Soon after I started writing, I realized that I was crafty and could come up with gimmicks to make my work look jazzy. As I matured as a writer and gained more confidence, I began losing what I had mistakenly understood to be my style. I returned to something simpler. One watershed moment was the realization that my writing voice had circled back to something natural, intuitive, and instinctive.

Thinking Critically about the Text

In paragraph 1, Orlean writes, "Developing a writer's voice is almost a process of unlearning, one analogous to children's painting." How does she explain the analogy? Later, in paragraph 5, she writes, "When you make an analogy, it's not just to give the reader an image but to advance a larger idea or theme." How successful, in your opinion, has Orlean been in following her own advice about analogies?

Discussing the Craft of Writing

1. What, in your own words, is voice? Why is it important?
2. Why does Orlean say "self-analysis" is so important in developing one's voice? Can you illustrate this point from your own experience?
3. Why does reading aloud to a reader or an audience seem to reveal voice? Why do you think that reading to oneself does not accomplish the same goal?
4. Why is pacing so important in writing? Illustrate some instances in your own writing where pace makes a difference. How does a writer control pace?
5. What does Orlean's editor mean in paragraph 5 when he says to her, "'You're giving the reader a ticket to the tropics'"?
6. Is *voice* a different word for *style*? Explain.
7. Why do you think Orlean finds it important to define herself as she does in the headnote to this selection?

Reading to Write

STEPHEN KING

Born in 1947, Stephen King is a 1970 graduate of the University of Maine. He worked as a janitor in a knitting mill, a laundry worker, and a high school English teacher before he struck it big with his writing. Today, many people consider King's name synonymous with the macabre; he is, beyond dispute, the most successful writer of horror fiction today. He has written dozens of novels and hundreds of short stories, novellas, and screenplays, among other works. His books have sold well over 300 million copies worldwide, and many of his novels have been made into popular motion pictures, including *Stand by Me*, *Misery*, *The Green Mile*, and *Dreamcatcher*. His fiction, starting with *Carrie* in 1974, includes *Salem's Lot* (1975), *The Shining* (1977), *The Dead Zone* (1979), *Christine* (1983), *Pet Sematary* (1983), *The Girl Who Loved Tom Gordon* (1999), *From a Buick 8* (2002), *Everything's Eventual: Five Dark Tales* (2002), *11/22/63: A Novel* (2012), and *The Bazaar of Bad Dreams* (2015). Other works include *Danse Macabre* (1980), a nonfiction look at horror in the media, and *On Writing: A Memoir of the Craft* (2000).

BERTRAND LANGLOIS/AFP/Getty Images

In the following selection taken from *On Writing*, King discusses the importance of reading in learning to write. Reading, in his words, "offers you a constantly growing knowledge of what has been done and what hasn't, what is trite and what is fresh, what works and what just lies there dying (or dead) on the page."

Preparing to Read

In your opinion, are reading and writing connected in some way? If the two activities are related, what is the nature of that relationship? Do you have to be a reader to be a good writer, or is writing an activity that can be learned quite apart from reading?

If you want to be a writer, you must do two things above all others: Read a lot and write a lot. There's no way around these two things that I'm aware of, no shortcut.

I'm a slow reader, but I usually get through seventy or eighty books a year, mostly fiction. I don't read in order to study the craft; I read because I like to read. It's what I do at night, kicked back in my blue chair. Similarly, I don't read fiction to study the art of fiction, but simply because I like stories. Yet there is a learning process going on. Every book you pick up has its own lesson or lessons, and quite often the bad books have more to teach than the good ones.

When I was in the eighth grade, I happened upon a paperback novel by Murray Leinster, a science fiction pulp writer who did most of his work during the forties and fifties, when magazines like *Amazing Stories* paid a penny a word. I had read other books by Mr. Leinster, enough to know that the quality of his writing was uneven. This particular tale, which was about mining in the asteroid belt, was one of his less successful efforts. Only that's too kind. It was terrible, actually, a story populated by paper-thin characters and driven by outlandish plot developments. Worst of all (or so it seemed to me at the time), Leinster had fallen in love with the word *zestful*. Characters watched the approach of ore-bearing asteroids with *zestful smiles*. Characters sat down to supper aboard their mining ship with *zestful anticipation*. Near the end of the book, the hero swept the large-breasted, blonde heroine into a *zestful embrace*. For me, it was the literary equivalent of a smallpox vaccination: I have never, so far as I know, used the word *zestful* in a novel or a story. God willing, I never will.

> If you want to be a writer, you must do two things above all others: Read a lot and write a lot.

Asteroid Miners (which wasn't the title, but that's close enough) was an important book in my life as a reader. Almost everyone can remember losing his or her virginity, and most writers can remember the first book he/she put down thinking: *I can do better than this. Hell, I am doing better than this!* What could be more encouraging to the struggling writer than to realize his/her work is unquestionably better than that of someone who actually got paid for his/her stuff?

One learns most clearly what not to do by reading bad prose — one novel like *Asteroid Miners* (or *Valley of the Dolls*, *Flowers in the Attic*, and *The Bridges of Madison County*, to name just a few) is worth a semester at a good writing school, even with the superstar guest lecturers thrown in.

Good writing, on the other hand, teaches the learning writer about style, graceful narration, plot development, the creation of believable characters, and truth-telling. A novel like *The Grapes of Wrath* may fill a new writer with feelings of despair and good old-fashioned jealousy — "I'll never be able to write anything that good, not if I live to be a thousand" — but such feelings can also serve as a spur, goading the writer to work harder and aim higher. Being swept away by a combination of great story and great writing — of being flattened, in fact — is part of every writer's necessary formation. You cannot hope to sweep someone else away by the force of your writing until it has been done to you.

So we read to experience the mediocre and the outright rotten; such experience helps us to recognize those things when they begin to creep into our own work, and to steer clear of them. We also read in order to measure ourselves against the good and the great, to get a sense of all that can be done. And we read in order to experience different styles.

You may find yourself adopting a style you find particularly exciting, and there's nothing wrong with that. When I read Ray Bradbury as a kid, I wrote like Ray Bradbury—everything green and wondrous and seen through a lens smeared with the grease of nostalgia. When I read James M. Cain, everything I wrote came out clipped and stripped and hard-boiled. When I read Lovecraft, my prose became luxurious and Byzantine. I wrote stories in my teenage years where all these styles merged, creating a kind of hilarious stew. This sort of stylistic blending is a necessary part of developing one's own style, but it doesn't occur in a vacuum. You have to read widely, constantly refining (and redefining) your own work as you do so. It's hard for me to believe that people who read very little (or not at all in some cases) should presume to write and expect people to like what they have written, but I know it's true. If I had a nickel for every person who ever told me he/she wanted to become a writer but "didn't have time to read," I could buy myself a pretty good steak dinner. Can I be blunt on this subject? If you don't have time to read, you don't have the time (or the tools) to write. Simple as that.

Reading is the creative center of a writer's life. I take a book with me everywhere I go, and find there are all sorts of opportunities to dip in. The trick is to teach yourself to read in small sips as well as in long swallows. Waiting rooms were made for books—of course! But so are theater lobbies before the show, long and boring checkout lines, and everyone's favorite, the john. You can even read while you're driving, thanks to the audiobook revolution. Of the books I read each year, anywhere from six to a dozen are on tape. As for all the wonderful radio you will be missing, come on—how many times can you listen to Deep Purple sing "Highway Star"?

Reading at meals is considered rude in polite society, but if you expect to succeed as a writer, rudeness should be the second-to-least of your concerns. The least of all should be polite society and what it expects. If you intend to write as truthfully as you can, your days as a member of polite society are numbered, anyway.

Where else can you read? There's always the treadmill, or whatever you use down at the local health club to get aerobic. I try to spend an hour doing that every day, and I think I'd go mad without a good novel to keep me company. Most exercise facilities (at home as well as outside it) are now equipped with TVs, but TV—while working out or anywhere else—really is about the last thing an aspiring writer needs. If you feel you must have the news analyst blowhards on CNN while you exercise, or the stock market blowhards on MSNBC, or the sports blowhards on ESPN, it's time for you to question how serious you really are about becoming a writer. You must be prepared to do some serious turning inward toward the life of the imagination, and that means, I'm afraid, that Geraldo, Keith Olbermann, and Jay Leno must go. Reading takes time, and the glass teat takes too much of it.

Once weaned from the ephemeral craving for TV, most people will find they enjoy the time they spend reading. I'd like to suggest that turning off that endlessly quacking box is apt to improve the quality of your life as well as the quality of your writing. And how much of a sacrifice are we talking about here? How many *Frasier* and *ER* reruns does it take to make one American life complete? How many Richard Simmons infomercials? How many whiteboy/fatboy Beltway insiders on CNN? Oh man, don't get me started. Jerry-Springer-Dr.-Dre-Judge-Judy-Jerry-Falwell-Donny-and-Marie, I rest my case.

When my son Owen was seven or so, he fell in love with Bruce Springsteen's E Street Band, particularly with Clarence Clemons, the band's burly sax player. Owen decided he wanted to learn to play like Clarence. My wife and I were amused and delighted by this ambition. We were also hopeful, as any parent would be, that our kid would turn out to be talented, perhaps even some sort of prodigy. We got Owen a tenor saxophone for Christmas and lessons with Gordon Bowie, one of the local music men. Then we crossed our fingers and hoped for the best.

Seven months later I suggested to my wife that it was time to discontinue the sax lessons, if Owen concurred. Owen did, and with palpable relief—he hadn't wanted to say it himself, especially not after asking for the sax in the first place, but seven months had been long enough for him to realize that, while he might love Clarence Clemons's big sound, the saxophone was simply not for him—God had not given him that particular talent.

I knew, not because Owen stopped practicing, but because he was practicing only during the periods Mr. Bowie had set for him: half an hour after school four days a week, plus an hour on the weekends. Owen mastered the scales and the notes—nothing wrong with his memory, his lungs, or his eye-hand coordination—but we never heard him taking off, surprising himself with something new, blissing himself out. And as soon as his practice time was over, it was back into the case with the horn, and there it stayed until the next lesson or practice time. What this suggested to me was that when it came to the sax and my son, there was never going to be any real playtime; it was all going to be rehearsal. That's no good. If there's no joy in it, it's just no good. It's best to go on to some other area, where the deposits of talent may be richer and the fun quotient higher.

Talent renders the whole idea of rehearsal meaningless; when you find something at which you are talented, you do it (whatever *it* is) until your fingers bleed or your eyes are ready to fall out of your head. Even when no one is listening (or reading, or watching), every outing is a bravura performance, because you as the creator are happy. Perhaps even ecstatic. That goes for reading and writing as well as for playing a musical instrument, hitting a baseball, or running the four-forty. The sort of strenuous reading and writing program I advocate—four to six hours a day, every day—will not seem strenuous if you really enjoy doing these things and have an aptitude for them; in fact, you may be following such a program already. If you feel you need permission to do all the reading and writing your little heart desires, however, consider it hereby granted by yours truly.

The real importance of reading is that it creates an ease and intimacy with the process of writing; one comes to the country of the writer with one's papers and identification pretty much in order. Constant reading will pull you into a place (a mind-set, if you like the phrase) where you can write eagerly and without self-consciousness. It also offers you a constantly growing knowledge of what has been done and what hasn't, what is trite and what is fresh, what works and what just lies there dying (or dead) on the page. The more you read, the less apt you are to make a fool of yourself with your pen or word processor.

17

Thinking Critically about the Text

What does King mean when he writes that reading a bad novel is "worth a semester at a good writing school, even with the superstar guest lecturers thrown in" (paragraph 5)? Do you take his observation seriously? In your own words, what can one learn about writing by reading a bad novel? What can one learn by reading a good novel?

Discussing the Craft of Writing

1. In paragraph 3, King berates the author Murray Leinster for his repeated use of the word *zestful*. He says he himself has, as far as he knows, never used the word. Why do you suppose he doesn't like the word? Have you ever used it in your own writing? Explain. (Glossary: *Diction*)

2. In paragraph 7, King says that "we read in order to experience different styles." What examples does he use to support this statement? If you have learned from someone else's style, what exactly was it that you learned? (Glossary: *Evidence*)

3. Authors, especially those as famous as King, are very much sought after as guests on television shows, at writing conferences, and at celebrity and charity events. Why does King believe that it is incompatible for one to be both a member of polite society and an author? Do you agree with him? Why or why not?

4. King does not like TV. What does he find wrong with it, especially for writers?

5. Admittedly, not everyone who wants to write well also aspires to be a great novelist. What value, if any, does King's advice about reading and writing have for you as a college student? Explain.

6. How do you react to the following cartoon? What is a Klout score? Do you find the cartoon humorous? Why or why not? Do you think Stephen King would find it humorous?

"I'm sorry, Paige, but grades are based on the quality of the writing, not on your Klout score."

Matthew Diffee The New Yorker Collection/The Cartoon Bank

Writing as an Act of Hope

ISABEL ALLENDE

Writer and humanitarian Isabel Allende was born in 1942 and grew up in Santiago, Chile. As a young woman, she worked as a journalist, a television host, and an editor, and she co-founded the feminist magazine *Paula* in 1967. She also worked for the Food and Agriculture Organization of the United Nations in Santiago. In 1975, after the death of the president of Chile (a relative) and a related political coup, she emigrated with her family to Venezuela. Since 1988 Allende has lived near San Francisco, California. She has taught creative

DANIEL ROLAND/AFP/Getty Images

writing and literature at the University of California at Berkeley, Barnard College, and the University of Virginia. In 1996, she created the Isabel Allende Foundation, "dedicated to supporting programs that promote and preserve the fundamental rights of women and children to be empowered and protected."

Allende has published twenty-one books, including *The House of the Spirits* (1985); *Of Love and Shadows* (1987); *The Stories of Eva Luna* (1991); *Paula* (1995); *Daughter of Fortune* (1998); *My Invented Country* (2003); *Ines of my Soul* (2006); and *Maya's Notebook* (2013). Her most recent novel is *The Japanese Lover* (2015). Among her many awards are the Presidential Medal of Freedom; the Library of Congress Creative Achievement Award for Fiction; Before Columbus Foundation's American Book Award; PEN's Freedom to Write Award; membership in the Academy of Arts and Letters; and major international prizes in Chile, Germany, France, Mexico, Switzerland, Portugal, and the United Kingdom. This essay was published onIne in *Peace Review*, December 4, 2007.

Preparing to Read

Why do *you* write, other than to fulfill course assignments? You may not think of yourself as a writer, but consider that you probably write every day and that writing takes many forms: college and job applications, résumés, proposals, lists, texts, and e-mails, to name a few. What type of writing is easiest for you, and why do you think that is? What type is hardest, and why?

In every interview during the last few years I encountered two questions that forced me to define myself as a writer and as a human being: why do I write? And who do I write for? Tonight I will try to answer those questions. In 1981, in Caracas, I put a sheet of paper in my typewriter and wrote the first sentence of *The House of the Spirits*: "Barabbas came to us by sea." At that moment I didn't know why I was doing it, or for whom.

In fact, I assumed that no one would ever read it except my mother, who reads everything I write. I was not even conscious that I was writing a novel. I thought I was writing a letter—a spiritual letter to my grandfather, a formidable old patriarch[1], whom I loved dearly. He had reached almost one hundred years of age and decided that he was too tired to go on living, so he sat in his armchair and refused to drink or eat, calling for Death, who was kind enough to take him very soon.

I wanted to bid him farewell, but I couldn't go back to Chile, and I knew that calling him on the telephone was useless, so I began this letter. I wanted to tell him that he could go in peace because all his memories were with me. I had forgotten nothing. I had all his anecdotes, all the characters of the family, and to prove it I began writing the story of Rose, the fiancée my grandfather had had, who is called Rose the Beautiful in the book. She really existed; she's not a copy from Garcia Marquez, as some people have said.

For a year I wrote every night with no hesitation or plan. Words came out like a violent torrent. I had thousands of untold words stuck in my chest, threatening to choke me. The long silence of exile was turning me to stone; I needed to open a valve and let the river of secret words find a way out. At the end of that year there were five hundred pages on my table; it didn't look like a letter anymore. On the other hand, my grandfather had died long before, so the spiritual message had already reached him. So I thought, "Well, maybe in this way I can tell some other people about him, and about my country, and about my family and myself." So I just organized it a little bit, tied the manuscript with a pink ribbon for luck, and took it to some publishers.

The spirit of my grandmother was protecting the book from the very beginning, so it was refused everywhere in Venezuela. Nobody wanted it—it was too long; I was a woman; nobody knew me. So I sent it by mail to Spain, and the book was published there. It had reviews, and it was translated and distributed in other countries.

In the process of writing the anecdotes of the past, and recalling the emotions and pains of my fate, and telling part of the history of my country, I found that life became more comprehensible and the world more tolerable. I felt that my roots had been recovered and that during that patient exercise of daily writing I had also recovered my own soul. I felt at that time that writing was unavoidable—that I couldn't keep away from it. Writing is such a pleasure; it is always a private orgy, creating and recreating the world according to my own laws, fulfilling in those pages all my dreams and exorcising some of my demons.

---

[1] *patriarch*: a respected old man, especially one who is head of a family, clan, or tribe.

But that is a rather simple explanation. There are other reasons for writing.

Six years and three books have passed since The House of the Spirits. Many things have changed for me in that time. I can no longer pretend to be naive, or elude questions, or find refuge in irony. Now I am constantly confronted by my readers, and they can be very tough. It's not enough to write in a state of trance, overwhelmed by the desire to tell a story. One has to be responsible for each word, each idea. Be very careful: the written word cannot be erased. . . .

Maybe the most important reason for writing is to prevent the erosion of time, so that memories will not be blown away by the wind. Write to register history, and name each thing. Write what should not be forgotten. But then, why write novels? Probably because I come from Latin America, a land of crazy, illuminated people, of geological and political cataclysms—a land so large and profound, so beautiful and frightening, that only novels can describe its fascinating complexity. A novel is like a window, open to an infinite landscape. In a novel we can put all the interrogations, we can register the most extravagant, evil, obscene, incredible or magnificent facts—which, in Latin America, are not hyperbole, because that is the dimension of our reality. In a novel we can give an illusory order to chaos. We can find the key to the labyrinth of history. We can make excursions into the past, to try to understand the present and dream the future. In a novel we can use everything: testimony, chronicle, essay, fantasy, legend, poetry and other devices that might help us to decode the mysteries of our world and discover our true identity.

> "Words came out like a violent torrent. I had thousands of untold words stuck in my chest, threatening to choke me."

For a writer who nourishes himself or herself on images and passions, to be born in a fabulous continent is a privilege. In Latin America we don't have to stretch our imaginations. Critics in Europe and the United States often stare in disbelief at Latin American books, asking how the authors dare to invent those incredible lies of young women who fly to heaven wrapped in linen sheets; of black emperors who build fortresses with cement and the blood of emasculated bulls; of outlaws who die of hunger in the Amazon with bags full of emeralds on their backs; of ancient tyrants who order their mothers to be flogged naked in front of the troops and modern tyrants who order children to be tortured in front of their parents; of hurricanes and earthquakes that turn the world upside down; of revolutions made with machetes, bullets, poems and kisses; of hallucinating landscapes where reason is lost.

11 It is very hard to explain to critics that these things are not a product of our pathological[2] imaginations. They are written in our history; we can find them every day in our newspapers. We hear them in the streets; we suffer them frequently in our own lives. It is impossible to speak of Latin America without mentioning violence. We inhabit a land of terrible contrasts and we have to survive in times of great violence. Contrast and violence, two excellent ingredients for literature, although for us, citizens of that reality, life is always suspended from a very fragile thread.

12 The first, the most naked and visible form of violence, is the extreme poverty of the majority, in contrast with the extreme wealth of the very few. In my continent two opposite realities coexist. One is a legal face, more or less comprehensible and with a certain pretension to dignity and civilization. The other is a dark and tragic face, which we do not like to show but which is always threatening us. There is an apparent world and a real world—nice neighborhoods where blond children play on their bicycles and servants walk elegant dogs, and other neighborhoods, of slums and garbage, where dark children play naked with hungry mutts. There are offices of marble and steel where young executives discuss the stock market, and forgotten villages where people still live and die as they did in the Middle Ages. There is a world of fiction created by the official discourse, and another world of blood and pain and love, where we have struggled for centuries.

13 In Latin America we all survive on the borderline of those two realities. Our fragile democracies exist as long as they don't interfere with imperialist interests. Most of our republics are dependent on submissiveness. Our institutions and laws are inefficient. Our armed forces often act as mercenaries for a privileged social group that pays tribute to transnational enterprises. We are living in the worst economic, political and social crisis since the conquest of America by the Spaniards. There are hardly two or three leaders in the whole continent. Social inequality is greater every day, and to avoid an outburst of public rancor, repression also rises day by day. Crime, drugs, misery and ignorance are present in every Latin American country, and the military is an immediate threat to society and civil governments. We try to keep straight faces while our feet are stuck in a swamp of violence, exploitation, corruption, the terror of the state and the terrorism of those who take arms against the status quo. Our Latin America is also a land of hope and friendship and love. Writers navigate in these agitated waters. They don't live in ivory towers; they cannot remove themselves from this brutal reality. In such circumstances there is no time and no wish for narcissistic[3] literature. Very few of our writers contemplate

[2] *pathological*: adj. diseased; unhealthy.
[3] *narcissistic*: adj. pathologically self-centered; compulsively self-obsessed.

their navel in self-centered monologue. The majority want desperately to communicate.

I feel that writing is an act of hope, a sort of communion with our fellow men. The writer of good will carries a lamp to illuminate the dark corners. Only that, nothing more — a tiny beam of light to show some hidden aspect of reality, to help decipher and understand it and thus to initiate, if possible, a change in the conscience of some readers. This kind of writer is not seduced by the mermaid's voice of celebrity or tempted by exclusive literary circles. He has both feet planted firmly on the ground and walks hand in hand with the people in the streets. He knows that the lamp is very small and the shadows are immense. This makes him humble.

Thinking Critically about the Text

In paragraph 9, Allende writes "I come from Latin America, a land of crazy, illuminated people, of geological and political cataclysms." What did you know about Latin America before reading this essay, and what do you know now? What assumptions has Allende made about her readers' knowledge, and what details and context has she provided to help her audience understand her perspective?

Discussing the Craft of Writing

1. Allende offers several answers to the question "why do I write?" (paragraph 1). What are her reasons? Which ones resonate most with you, and why?

2. Allende writes that "the long silence of exile was turning me to stone" (4). What do you think she means by *the long silence of exile*? What is *exile*, and how might it make someone silent?

3. "Write to register history," Allende advises, "and name each thing. Write what should not be forgotten" (9). If you were following this advice, what would you write about, and why?

4. What insights into the nature of writing does Allende offer? Explain.

5. Paragraph 7 contains only two sentences: "But that is a rather simple explanation. There are other reasons for writing." How does this paragraph function in the larger context of Allende's essay?

6. Consider the metaphor Allende uses in her final paragraph: "The writer of good will carries a lamp to illuminate the dark corners.... He knows that the lamp is very small and the shadows are immense." What are these *dark corners* and *shadows* she speaks of?

LIFE IN THE WOODS

I WENT TO THE WOODS BECAUSE I WISHED TO LIVE DELIBERATELY.

I BROUGHT ALONG A FEW THINGS IN CASE I GOT BORED.

THERE I EXPERIENCED THE PROFOUND JOY OF SOLITUDE...

AND MADE SURE EVERYONE ELSE KNEW ABOUT IT.

#majestic

I MARCHED TO THE RHYTHMS OF NATURE, THE SOUNDS OF THE FOREST...

AND THE BEAT OF MY KILLER WILDERNESS PLAYLIST.

THE WOODS WERE FILLED WITH MANY WONDROUS CREATURES.

I TURNED THEM INTO MEMES.

CONDESCENDING OWL IS WISER THAN YOU

DEVIL SQUIRREL WANTS YOUR SOUL

CONFUSED GOOSE FLIES NORTH FOR WINTER

ALONE IN THE DARKNESS, I FOUND TRUE ILLUMINATION...

BY THE LIGHT OF MY EVER-GLOWING SCREENS.

Grant Snider, Incidental Comic

CHAPTER 4

Narration

WHAT IS NARRATION?

Whenever you recount an event or tell a story or an anecdote to illustrate an idea, you are using narration. In its broadest sense, narration includes any account of an event, or a series of events, presented in a logical sequence. The tremendous popularity in our culture of narrative forms like action movies, television dramas, celebrity gossip, graphic novels, and even the Facebook status update attests to the fact that nearly everyone loves a good story. Given a decent character and a good beginning, we all want to find out what happens next.

For one example of narration in popular culture, take a look at Grant Snider's "Life in the Woods," reproduced on the opposite page. Snider constructs his narrative with a series of pictures that provide snapshots of the narrator's experience in the woods. As we "read" the images and the accompanying text, we mentally fill in the gaps between panels to form a continuous progression of events, a story of the narrator's infatuation with the great outdoors. Starting with a purpose that echoes Thoreau's purpose in going to the woods in *Walden*, this totally contemporary narrator breaks with tradition and brings "along a few things in case [he gets] bored." Ironically, these electronic devices trivialize the narrator's appreciation for the solitude, the rhythms of nature, and the wondrous creatures he experienced.

NARRATION IN WRITTEN TEXTS

In the area of written texts, most of us associate narration with novels and short fiction. Narration is also useful and effective, however, in nonfiction writing, such as biography, autobiography, history, and news reporting. A good narrative essay provides a meaningful account of some significant event—anything from an account of recent U.S. involvement in the Middle East to a personal experience that gave you new insight about yourself or others. A narrative may present a straightforward message or moral, or it may make a more subtle point about us and the world we live in.

Consider, for example, the following narrative by E. J. Kahn, Jr. about the invention of Coca-Cola, as both a medicine and a soft drink, from his book *The Big Drink: The Story of Coca-Cola*.

Establishes context for narrative	In 1886—a year in which, as contemporary Coca-Cola officials like to point out, Conan Doyle unveiled Sherlock Holmes and France unveiled the Statue of Liberty—[John Styth] Pemberton unveiled a syrup that he called Coca-Cola. He had taken out the
Uses third-person point of view	wine and added a pinch of caffeine, and, when the end product tasted awful, had thrown in some extract of cola (or kola) nut and a
Organizes narrative chronologically, using time markers	few other oils, blending the mixture in a three-legged iron pot in his back yard and swishing it around with an oar. He distributed it to soda fountains in used beer bottles, and [his bookkeeper Frank M.] Robinson, with his flowing bookkeeper's script, presently devised a label on which "Coca-Cola" was written in the fashion that is still employed. Pemberton looked upon his concoction less as a refreshment than as a headache cure, especially for people whose throbbing temples could be traced to overindulgence. On a morning late in 1886, one such victim of the night before dragged himself into an
Focuses on the discovery that led to Coca-Cola's popularity as a soft drink	Atlanta drugstore and asked for a dollop of Coca-Cola. Druggists customarily stirred a teaspoonful of syrup into a glass of water, but in this instance the factotum on duty was too lazy to walk to the fresh-water tap, a couple of feet off. Instead, he mixed the syrup with some charged water, which was closer at hand. The suffering customer perked up almost at once, and word quickly spread that the best Coca-Cola was a fizzy one.

A good narrative essay, like the paragraph above, has four essential features. The first is *context*: The writer makes clear when the action happened, where it happened, and to whom. The second is *point of view*: The writer establishes and maintains a consistent relationship to the action, either as a participant or as a reporter looking on. The third is *selection of detail*: The writer carefully chooses what to include, focusing on actions and details that are most important to the story while playing down or even eliminating others. The fourth is *organization*: The writer arranges the events of the narrative in an appropriate sequence, often a strict chronology with a clear beginning, middle, and end.

As you read the selections in this chapter, watch for these features and for how each writer uses them to tell his or her story. Think about how each writer's choices affect the way you react to the selections.

USING NARRATION AS A WRITING STRATEGY

The most basic and most important purpose of narration is to share a meaningful experience with readers. Another important purpose of narration is to report and instruct—to give the facts, to tell what happened. Journalists and historians, in reporting events of the near and more distant past, provide us with information that we can use to form opinions about a current issue or to better understand the world around us. A biographer gives us another person's life as a document of an individual's past but also, perhaps, as a portrait of more general human potential. And naturalists recount the drama of encounters between predators and prey in the wild to remind us of the power of nature. We expect writers to make these narratives as objective as possible and to distinguish between facts and opinions.

Narration is often used in combination with one or more of the other rhetorical strategies. In an essay that is written primarily to explain a process—reading a book, for example—a writer might find it useful to tell a brief story or anecdote demonstrating an instance when the process worked especially well (Mortimer Adler, "How to Mark a Book," Chapter 7). In the same way, a writer attempting to define the term *poverty* might tell several stories to illustrate clearly the many facets of poverty (Jo Goodwin Parker, "What Is Poverty?" Chapter 10). Finally, a writer could use narrative examples to persuade—for example, to argue against handing out participation awards (Nancy Armour, "You Shouldn't Get a Prize for Showing Up," Chapter 12) or to demonstrate for readers the power and clarity of monosyllabic words (Richard Lederer, "The Case for Short Words," Chapter 12).

USING NARRATION ACROSS THE DISCIPLINES

When writing essays in the academic disciplines, you will have many opportunities to use the strategy of narration to both organize and strengthen the presentation of your ideas. To determine whether narration is the right strategy for you in a particular paper, use the guidelines described in Chapter 2 (Determining a Strategy for Developing Your Essay, pages 32–33). Consider the following examples, which illustrate how these guidelines work for typical college papers:

American History

1. **MAIN IDEA:** Although Abraham Lincoln was not the chief speaker at Gettysburg on November 19, 1863, the few remarks he made that day shaped the thinking of our nation as perhaps few other speeches have.
2. **QUESTION:** What happened at Gettysburg on November 19, 1863, that made Abraham Lincoln's speech so memorable and influential?

3. **STRATEGY:** Narration. The thrust of the main idea as well as the direction words *what happened* say "tell me the story," and what better way to tell what happened than to narrate the day's events?
4. **SUPPORTING STRATEGY:** Cause and effect analysis. The story and how it is narrated can be used to explain the impact of this speech on our nation's thinking.

Anthropology

1. **MAIN IDEA:** Food-gathering and religious activities account for a large portion of the daily lives of native peoples in rural Thailand.
2. **QUESTION:** What happens during a typical day or week in rural Thailand?
3. **STRATEGY:** Narration. The direction words in both the statement of the main idea (*account* and *daily*) and the question (*what happens*) cry out for a narration of what happens during any given day.
4. **SUPPORTING STRATEGY:** Illustration. The paper might benefit from specific examples of the various chores related to food gathering as well as examples of typical religious activities.

Life Science

1. **MAIN IDEA:** British bacteriologist Sir Alexander Fleming discovered penicillin quite by accident in 1928, and that discovery changed the world.
2. **QUESTION:** How did Fleming happen to discover penicillin, and why was this discovery so important?
3. **STRATEGY:** Narration. The direction words *how* and *did happen* call for the story of Fleming's accidental discovery of penicillin.
4. **SUPPORTING STRATEGY:** Argument. The claims that Fleming's discovery was *important* and *changed the world* suggest that the story needs to be both compelling and persuasive.

SAMPLE STUDENT ESSAY USING NARRATION AS A WRITING STRATEGY

After reading several personal narratives—David P. Bardeen's "Not Close Enough for Comfort" and Malcolm X's "Coming to an Awareness of Language" in particular—Laura LaPierre decided to write a narrative of her own. Only weeks prior to writing this essay Laura had received some very bad news. It was the experience of living with this news that she decided to write about. The writing was painful, and not everyone would feel comfortable with a similar task. Laura, however, welcomed the opportunity because she came to a more intimate understanding of her own fears and feelings as she moved from one draft to the next. What follows is the final draft of Laura's essay.

> **Why Are You Here?**
> Laura LaPierre
>
> *Title: asks central question*
>
> *Beginning: engages reader and establishes context — when, where, who*
>
> Balancing between a crutch on one side and an IV pole with wheels on the other, I dragged my stiff leg along the smooth, sterile floor of the hospital hall. All around me nurses, orderlies, and doctors bustled about, dodging well-meaning visitors laden with flowers and candy. The fluorescent lights glared down with a brightness so sharp that I squinted and thought that sunglasses might be in order. Sticking close to the wall, I rounded the corner and paused to rest for a moment. I breathed in the hot, antiseptic-smelling air which I had grown accustomed to and sighed angrily.
>
> *Details create image of harsh, unfriendly environment*
>
> *Point of view: first person*
>
> *Organization: straightforward and chronological*
>
> Tears of hurt and frustration pricked at the corner of my eyes as the now familiar pain seared my leg. I tugged my bath-robe closer around my shoulder and, hauling my IV pole with me, I continued down the hall. One, two—second door on the left, she had said. I opened the heavy metal door, entered, and realized that I must be a little early because no one else was there yet. After glancing at my watch, I sat down and looked around the room, noting with disgust the prevalence of beige: beige walls, beige ceiling, shiny beige floor tiles. A small cot stood in one corner with a beige bedspread, and in the opposite corner there was a sink, mirror, and beige waste basket. The only relief from the monotony was the circle of six or seven chairs where I sat. They were a vivid rust color and helped to brighten the dull room. The shades were drawn, and the lights were much dimmer than they had been in the hall. My eyes gradually relaxed as I waited.
>
> *Time reference maintains flow*
>
> *Descriptive details create dominant impression of an uninviting room*
>
> People began to drift in until five of the seats were filled. A nurse was the head of the odd-looking group. Three of us were attached by long tubes to IV poles, and then there was a social worker. The man to my left wore a slightly faded, royal
>
> *Details show that people in group are obviously ill, but specifics not revealed*

blue robe. He had a shock of unruly gray hair above an angular face with deeply sunken cheeks. His eyes were sunken, too, and glassy with pain. Yet he smiled and appeared untroubled by his IV pole.

Wearing a crisp white uniform and a pretty sweater, the nurse, a pleasant-looking woman in her late twenties, appeared friendly and sympathetic, though not to the point of being sappy. My impressions were confirmed as she began to speak.

"Okay. I guess we can begin. Welcome to our group, we meet every Monday at. . . ." She went on, but I wasn't paying attention anymore. I looked around the group and my eyes came to rest on the man sitting next to the nurse. In contrast to the other man's shriveled appearance, this man was robust. He was tall, with a protruding belly and a ruddy complexion. Unlike the other man, he seemed at war with his IV pole. He constantly fiddled with the tube and with the tape that held the needle in his arm. Eyes darting around the room, he nervously watched everyone.

I heard the nurse continue, "So, let's all introduce ourselves and tell why we are here." We went around the circle clockwise, starting with the nurse, and when we got to the social worker, I looked up and surveyed her while she talked. Aside from contributing to the beige monotony with her pants, she was agreeable both in appearance and disposition.

When it was my turn, I took a deep breath and with my voice quavering began, "My name is Laura and—"

"Hi, Laura!" interrupted the cheerful man on my left. I turned and smiled weakly at him.

Fighting back the tears, I continued, "And I have bone cancer."

> **Analyzing Laura LaPierre's Narration Essay:
> Questions for Discussion**
>
> 1. What context does Laura provide for her narrative? What else, if anything, would you have liked to know about the situation? What would have been lost had she told you more?
> 2. Laura tells her story in the first person. How would the narrative have changed had she used a third-person point of view?
> 3. For you, what details conveyed Laura's fear at being in the hospital? Are there places where she could have done more "showing" and less "telling"? Explain.
> 4. Laura uses a straightforward chronological organization for her narrative. Can you see any places where she might have used a flashback? What would have been the effect?
> 5. What meaning or importance do you think this experience holds for Laura?

SUGGESTIONS FOR USING NARRATION AS A WRITING STRATEGY

As you plan, write, and revise your narrative essay, be mindful of the writing process guidelines described in Chapter 2. Also, pay particular attention to the basic requirements and essential ingredients for this writing strategy.

▶ Planning Your Narration Essay

Planning is an essential part of writing a good narrative essay. You can save yourself a great deal of inconvenience by taking the time to think about the key components of your essay before you actually begin to write.

SELECT A TOPIC THAT HAS MEANING FOR YOU. In your writing course, you may have the freedom to choose the story you want to narrate, or your instructor may give you a list of topics from which to choose. Instead of jumping at the first topic that looks good, however, brainstorm a list of events that have had an impact on your life and that you could write about. Such a list might include your first blind date, catching frogs as a child, the death of a loved one, a trip to the Grand Canyon, or the breakup of a relationship.

As you narrow your options, look for an event or an incident that is particularly memorable. Memorable experiences are memorable for a reason; they offer us important insights into our lives. Such experiences are worth narrating because people want to read about them.

DETERMINE YOUR POINT AND PURPOSE. Before you begin writing, ask yourself why the experience you have chosen is meaningful. What did you learn from it? How are you different as a result of the experience? What has changed? Your narrative point (the meaning of your narrative) and purpose in writing will influence which events and details you include and which you leave out. Suppose, for example, you choose to write about how you learned to ride a bicycle. If you mean mainly to entertain, you will probably include a number of unusual incidents unique to your experience. If your purpose is mainly to report or inform, it will make more sense to concentrate on the kinds of details that are common to most people's experience. However, if your purpose is to tell your readers step-by-step how to ride a bicycle, you should use process analysis, a strategy used by writers whose purpose is to give directions for how something is done or to explain how something works (see Chapter 7).

The most successful narrative essays, however, do more than entertain or inform. While narratives do not ordinarily have a formal thesis statement, readers will more than likely expect your story to make a statement or to arrive at some meaningful conclusion—implied or explicit—about your experience. The student essay by Laura LaPierre, for example, shows how important it was for her to confront the reality of her bone cancer. In addressing her fears, she gains a measure of control over her life.

As you prepare to write, look for the significance in the story you want to tell—some broader, more instructive points it could make about the ways of the world. Learning to ride a bicycle may not suggest such points to you, and it may therefore not be a very good subject for your narrative essay. However, the subject does have possibilities. Here's one: Learning to master a difficult, even dangerous, but definitely useful skill like riding a bicycle is an important experience to have in life. Perhaps you can think of others. If, however, you do not know why you are telling the story and it seems pointless even to you, your readers will pick up on the ambivalence in your writing, and you should probably find another, more meaningful story to tell.

ESTABLISH A CONTEXT. Early in your essay, perhaps in the opening paragraphs, establish the context, or setting, of your story—the world within which the action took place:

When it happened—morning; afternoon; 11:37 on the dot; 1997; winter
Where it happened—in the street; at Chipotle; in Pocatello, Idaho
To whom it happened—to me; to my father; to the intern; to Teri Hopper

Without a clear context, your readers can easily get confused or even completely lost. And remember, readers respond well to specific contextual information because such details make them feel as if they are present, ready to witness the narrative.

CHOOSE THE MOST APPROPRIATE POINT OF VIEW. Consider what point of view to take in your narrative. Did you take part in the action? If so, it will seem most natural for you to use the first-person (*I, we*) point of view. On the other hand, if you weren't there at all and must rely on other sources for your information, you will probably choose the third-person (*he, she, it, they*) point of view, as did the author writing about the invention of Coca-Cola earlier in this chapter. However, if you were a witness to part or all of what happened but not a participant, then you will need to choose between the more immediate and subjective quality of the first person and the more distanced, objective effect of the third person. Whichever you choose, you should maintain the same point of view throughout your narrative.

GATHER DETAILS THAT "SHOW, DON'T TELL." When writing your essay, you will need enough detail about the action, the people involved, and the context to let your readers understand what is going on. Start collecting details by asking yourself the traditional reporter's questions:

- Who was involved?
- What happened?
- Where did it happen?
- When did it happen?
- Why did it happen?
- How did it happen?

Generate as many details as you can because you never know which ones will ensure that your essay *shows* and doesn't *tell* too much. For example, instead of telling readers that she dislikes being in the hospital, Laura LaPierre shows us what she sees, feels, hears, and smells and lets us draw our own conclusion about her state of mind.

As you write, you will want to select and emphasize details that support your point, serve your purpose, and show the reader what is happening. You should not, however, get so carried away with details that your readers become confused or bored by excess information: In good storytelling, deciding what to leave out can be as important as deciding what to include.

Organizing Your Narration Essay

IDENTIFY THE SEQUENCE OF EVENTS IN YOUR NARRATIVE. Storytellers tend to follow an old rule: Begin at the beginning, and go on till you come to the end; then stop. Chronological organization is natural in narration because it is a retelling of the original order of events; it is also easiest for the writer to manage and the reader to understand.

Some narratives, however, are organized using a technique called *flashback*: The writer may begin midway through the story, or even at the end, with an important or exciting event, then use flashbacks to fill in what happened earlier, leading up to that event. Some authors begin in the present and then use flashbacks to shift to the past to tell the story. Whatever organizational pattern you choose, words and phrases like "for a month," "afterward," and "three days earlier" will help you and your reader keep the sequence of events straight.

It may help you in organizing to jot down a quick outline before tackling the first draft of your narrative. Here's the outline that Laura LaPierre used to order the events in her narrative chronologically:

> Narration about my first group meeting at the hospital
>
> Point: At some point I had to confront the reality of my illness.
>
> Context: Hospital setting
>
> 1. Start slow walk down hospital hall attached to IV pole.
> 2. Sights, sounds, and smells of hospital hallway set scene.
> 3. Locate destination — first one to arrive for group meeting.
> 4. Describe "beige" meeting room.
> 5. Other patients arrive.
> 6. Young nurse leads our group meeting.
> 7. We start by introducing ourselves.
> 8. My turn — my moment of truth.

Such an outline can remind you of your point, your organization, and the emphasis you want when you write your first draft.

Writing Your Narration Essay

KEEP YOUR VERB TENSE CONSISTENT. Most narratives are in the past tense, and this is logical: They recount events that have already happened, even if very recently. But writers sometimes use the present tense to create an effect of immediacy, as if the events were happening as you read about them.

The important thing to remember is to be consistent. If you are recounting an event that has already occurred, use the past tense throughout. For an event in the present, use the present tense consistently. If you find yourself jumping from a present event to a past event, as in the case of a flashback, you will need to switch verb tenses to signal the change in time.

USE NARRATIVE TIME FOR EMPHASIS. The number of words or pages you devote to an event does not usually correspond to the number of minutes or hours the event took to happen. You may require several pages to recount an important or complex quarter of an hour but then pass over several hours or days in a sentence or two. Length has less to do with chronological time than with the amount of detail you include, and that's a function of the amount of emphasis you want to give to a particular incident.

USE TRANSITIONAL WORDS TO CLARIFY NARRATIVE SEQUENCE. Transitional words like *after, next, then, earlier, immediately,* and *finally* are useful, as they help your readers smoothly connect and understand the sequence of events that make up your narrative. Likewise, specific time marks like "on April 20," "two weeks earlier," and "in 2004" can indicate time shifts and can signal to readers how much time has elapsed between events.

Inexperienced writers sometimes overuse these words; this makes their writing style wordy and tiresome. Use these conventional transitions when you really need them, but when you don't—when your readers can follow your story without them—leave them out.

USE DIALOGUE TO BRING YOUR NARRATIVE TO LIFE. Having people in a narrative speak is a very effective way of showing rather than telling or summarizing what happened. Snippets of actual dialogue make a story come alive and feel immediate to the reader.

Consider this passage from an early draft of a student narrative:

> I hated having to call a garage, but I knew I couldn't do the work myself and I knew they'd rip me off. Besides, I had to get the car off the street before the police had it towed. I felt trapped without any choices.

Now compare this early draft with the revised draft below, in which the situation is revealed through dialogue.

> "University Gulf, Glen speaking. What can I do for ya?"
> "Yeah, my car broke down. I think it's the timing belt, and I was wondering if you could give me an estimate."
> "What kind of car is it?" asked Glen.
> "A Nissan Sentra."

"What year?"

"2008," I said, emphasizing the 8.

"Oh, those are a bitch to work on. Can ya hold on for a second?"

I knew what was coming before Glen came back on the line.

With dialogue, readers can hear the direct exchange between the car owner and the mechanic. You can use dialogue in your own writing to deliver a sense of immediacy to the reader.

Revising and Editing Your Narration Essay

When writing a narrative essay, it is often critical to find a fellow student or friend to read your draft. They will catch any missing details or inconsistencies in the narrative that you, being familiar or too close to material, might have missed. We include guidelines for peer review on page 36.

You will also want to ask yourself the questions below, and revisit Chapter 16, "Editing for Grammar, Punctuation, and Sentence Style" before you turn in a final draft.

Questions for Revising and Editing: Narration

1. Is my narrative well focused, or do I try to cover too great a period of time?
2. What is my reason for telling this story? Is that reason clearly stated or implied for readers?
3. Have I established a clear context for my readers? Is it clear when the action happened, where it happened, and to whom?
4. Have I used the most effective point of view to tell my story? How would my story be different had I used a different one?
5. Have I selected details that help readers understand what is going on in my narrative, or have I included unnecessary details that get in the way of what I'm trying to say? Do I give enough examples of the important events in my narrative?
6. Is the chronology of events in my narrative clear? Have I taken advantage of opportunities to add emphasis, drama, or suspense with flashbacks or other complications of the chronological organization?
7. Have I used transitional expressions or time markers to help readers follow the sequence of events in my narrative?
8. Have I employed dialogue in my narrative to reveal a situation, or have I told about or summarized the situation too much?

9. Have I avoided run-on sentences and comma splices? Have I used sentence fragments only deliberately to convey mood or tone?
10. Have I avoided other errors in grammar, punctuation, and mechanics? Is my sentence style as clear, smooth, and persuasive as possible?
11. Is the meaning of my narrative clear, or have I left my readers thinking, "So what?"

Coming to an Awareness of Language

MALCOLM X

Born Malcolm Little in Omaha, Nebraska, in 1925, Malcolm X rose from a world of street crime to become one of the most powerful and articulate African American leaders in the United States during the 1960s. On February 21, 1965, his life was cut short at age thirty-nine; he was shot and killed as he addressed an afternoon rally in Harlem. Malcolm X told his life story in *The Autobiography of Malcolm X* (1964), written with the assistance of *Roots* author Alex Haley. The book, a moving account of his life and his struggle for fulfillment, is still read by hundreds of thousands each year. In 1992, the life of this influential African American leader was reexamined in Spike Lee's film *Malcolm X*.

The following selection from *The Autobiography* refers to a period Malcolm X spent in federal prison. In the selection, Malcolm X explains how he was frustrated by his inability to express his ideas and how this frustration led him to a goal: acquiring the skills of reading and writing. Later he would say, "As I see it, the ability to read awoke inside me some long dormant craving to be mentally alive."

Preparing to Read

Our educational system places great emphasis on our having a large and varied vocabulary. Has anyone ever stressed to you the importance of developing a good vocabulary? What did you think when you heard this advice? In what ways can words be used as powerful tools? How would you judge your own vocabulary?

I've never been one for inaction. Everything I've ever felt strongly about, I've done something about. I guess that's why, unable to do anything else, I soon began writing to people I had known in the hustling world, such as Sammy the Pimp, John Hughes, the gambling house owner, the thief Jumpsteady, and several dope peddlers. I wrote them all about Allah and Islam and Mr. Elijah Muhammad. I had no idea where most of them lived. I addressed their letters in care of the Harlem or Roxbury bars and clubs where I'd known them.

I never got a single reply. The average hustler and criminal was too uneducated to write a letter. I have known many slick, sharp-looking hustlers, who would have you think they had an interest in Wall Street; privately, they would get someone else to read a letter if they received one. Besides, neither would I have replied to anyone writing me something as wild as "the white man is the devil."

What certainly went on the Harlem and Roxbury wires was that Detroit Red was going crazy in stir, or else he was trying some hype to shake up the warden's office.

During the years that I stayed in the Norfolk Prison Colony, never did any official directly say anything to me about those letters, although, of course, they all passed through the prison censorship. I'm sure, however, they monitored what I wrote to add to the files which every state and federal prison keeps on the conversion of Negro inmates by the teachings of Mr. Elijah Muhammad.

But at that time, I felt that the real reason was that the white man knew that he was the devil.

Later on, I even wrote to the Mayor of Boston, to the Governor of Massachusetts, and to Harry S. Truman. They never answered; they probably never even saw my letters. I handscratched to them how the white man's society was responsible for the black man's condition in this wilderness of North America.

It was because of my letters that I happened to stumble upon starting to acquire some kind of a homemade education.

I became increasingly frustrated at not being able to express what I wanted to convey in letters that I wrote, especially those to Mr. Elijah Muhammad. In the street, I had been the most articulate hustler out there—I had commanded attention when I said something. But now, trying to write simple English, I not only wasn't articulate, I wasn't even functional. How would I sound writing in slang, the way I would *say* it, something such as, "Look, daddy, let me pull your coat about a cat. Elijah Muhammad—"

Many who today hear me somewhere in person, or on television, or those who read something I've said, will think I went to school far beyond the eighth grade. This impression is due entirely to my prison studies.

It had really begun back in the Charlestown Prison, when Bimbi first made me feel envy of his stock of knowledge. Bimbi had always taken charge of any conversation he was in, and I had tried to emulate him. But every book I picked up had few sentences which didn't contain anywhere from one to nearly all of the words that might as well have been in Chinese. When I just skipped those words, of course, I really ended up with little idea of what the book said. So I had come to the Norfolk Prison Colony still going through only book-reading motions. Pretty soon, I would have quit even these motions, unless I had received the motivation that I did.

I saw that the best thing I could do was get hold of a dictionary—to study, to learn some words. I was lucky enough to reason also that I should try to improve my penmanship. It was sad. I couldn't even write in a straight line. It was both ideas together that moved me to request a dictionary along with some tablets and pencils from the Norfolk Prison Colony school.

I spent two days just riffling uncertainly through the dictionary's pages. I'd never realized so many words existed! I didn't know *which* words I needed to learn. Finally, just to start some kind of action, I began copying.

In my slow, painstaking, ragged handwriting, I copied into my tablet everything printed on that first page, down to the punctuation marks.

I believe it took me a day. Then, aloud, I read back, to myself, everything I'd written on the tablet. Over and over, aloud, to myself, I read my own handwriting.

I woke up the next morning, thinking about those words—immensely proud to realize that not only had I written so much at one time, but I'd written words that I never knew were in the world. Moreover, with a little effort, I also could remember what many of these words meant. I reviewed the words whose meanings I didn't remember. Funny thing, from the dictionary first page right now, that "aardvark" springs to my mind. The dictionary had a picture of it, a long-tailed, long-eared, burrowing African mammal, which lives off termites caught by sticking out its tongue as an anteater does for ants.

I was so fascinated that I went on—I copied the dictionary's next page. And the same experience came when I studied that. With every succeeding page, I also learned of people and places and events from history. Actually the dictionary is like a miniature encyclopedia. Finally the dictionary's A section had filled a whole tablet—and I went on into the B's. That was the way I started copying what eventually became the entire dictionary. It went a lot faster after so much practice helped me to pick up handwriting speed. Between what I wrote in my tablet, and writing letters, during the rest of my time in prison I would guess I wrote a million words.

I suppose it was inevitable that as my word-base broadened, I could for the first time pick up a book and read and now begin to understand what the book was saying. Anyone who has read a great deal can imagine the new world that opened. Let me tell you something: from then until I left that prison, in every free moment I had, if I was not reading in the library, I was reading on my bunk. You couldn't have gotten me out of books with a wedge. Between Mr. Muhammad's teachings, my correspondence, my visitors . . . and my reading of books, months passed without my even thinking about being imprisoned. In fact, up to then, I never had been so truly free in my life.

Thinking Critically about the Text

We are all to one degree or another prisoners of our own language. Sometimes we lack the ability to communicate as effectively as we would like. Why do you think this happens, and what do you think can be done to remedy it? How can improved language skills also improve a person's life?

Questions on Subject

1. In paragraph 8, Malcolm X refers to the difference between being "articulate" and being "functional" in his speaking and writing. What is the distinction he makes? In your opinion, is it a valid one?
2. Malcolm X offers two possible reasons for the warden's keeping track of African American inmates' conversion to the teachings of Elijah Muhammad. What are those two assertions, and what is their effect on the reader?
3. What is the nature of the freedom that Malcolm X refers to in the final sentence? In what sense can language be said to be liberating?

Questions on Strategy

1. Malcolm X narrates his experiences as a prisoner using the first-person *I*. Why is the first person particularly appropriate? What would be lost or gained had he narrated his story using the third-person pronoun *he*?
2. In the opening paragraph, Malcolm X refers to himself as a man of action and conviction. What details does he include to support this assertion?
3. Many people think of "vocabulary building" as learning strange, multisyllabic, difficult-to-spell words. But acquiring an effective vocabulary does not have to be so intimidating. How would you characterize Malcolm X's vocabulary in this narrative? Did you find his word choice suited to what he was trying to accomplish in this selection?
4. What is Malcolm X's narrative point in this selection? How do you know? What does he learn about himself as a result of this experience?
5. In reflecting on his years in prison, Malcolm X comes to an understanding of the events that caused him to reassess his life and take charge of his own education. Identify those events and discuss the changes that resulted from Malcolm X's actions. How does his inclusion of these causal links enhance the overall narrative? (Glossary: *Cause and Effect Analysis*)

Questions on Diction and Vocabulary

1. Although Malcolm X taught himself to be articulate in writing, we can still hear a street-savvy voice in his prose. Cite examples of his diction that convey a streetwise sound. (Glossary: *Diction*)

2. What do you do when you encounter new words in your reading? Do you skip those words as Malcolm X once did, do you take the time to look them up, or do you try to figure out their meanings from the context? Explain the strategies you use to determine the meaning of a word from its context. Can you think of other strategies?

3. Refer to a dictionary to determine the meanings of the following words as Malcolm X uses them in this selection: *hustler* (paragraph 2), *slick* (2), *hype* (3), *frustrated* (8), *emulate* (10), *riffling* (12), *inevitable* (17).

Narration in Action

Good narrative depends on a sense of continuity or flow, a logical ordering of events and ideas. The following sentences, which make up the first paragraph of E. B. White's essay "Once More to the Lake," have been rearranged. Place the sentences in what seems to be a coherent sequence based on such language signals as transitions, repeated words, pronouns, and temporal references. Be prepared to explain your reason for the placement of each sentence.

1. I have since become a salt-water man, but sometimes in summer there are days when the restlessness of the tides and the fearful cold of the sea water and the incessant wind that blows across the afternoon and into the evening make me wish for the placidity of a lake in the woods.

2. We all got ringworm from some kittens and had to rub Pond's Extract on our arms and legs night and morning, and my father rolled over in a canoe with all his clothes on; but outside of that the vacation was a success and from then on none of us ever thought there was any place in the world like that lake in Maine.

3. A few weeks ago this feeling got so strong I bought myself a couple of bass hooks and a spinner and returned to the lake where we used to go, for a week's fishing and to revisit old haunts.

4. One summer, along about 1904, my father rented a camp on a lake in Maine and took us all there for the month of August.

5. We returned summer after summer — always on August 1st for one month.

Writing Suggestions

1. Using Malcolm X's essay as a model, write a narrative about some goal you have set and achieved in which you were motivated by a strong inner conflict. What was the nature of your conflict? What feeling did it arouse in you, and how did the conflict help you to accomplish your goal?

2. **Writing with Sources.** Malcolm X solved the problems of his own near-illiteracy by carefully studying the dictionary. Would this be a practical solution to the national problem of illiteracy? In your experience, what does it mean to be literate? After investigating contemporary illiteracy in your college library or on the Internet, write a proposal on what can be done to promote literacy in this country. You might also consider what is being done now in your community. For models of and advice on integrating sources into your essay, see Chapters 14 and 15.

The Terror

JUNOT DÍAZ

Junot Díaz's writing focuses on Dominican culture and history and on the immigrant experience. Born in 1968 in the Dominican Republic, Díaz moved to New Jersey with his family at age six. He graduated from Rutgers University, working as a dishwasher and gas station attendant and delivering pool tables to help pay his way through school. After college, he served as an editorial assistant at Rutgers University Press and then went on to earn his MFA from Cornell University in 2005. Currently, he is a professor of writing at Massachusetts Institute of Technology and fiction editor at the *Boston Review*.

Photo by D Dipasupil/FilmMagic/Getty Images

Díaz's books include the short story collection *Drown* (1995), the Pulitzer Prize–winning *The Brief Wondrous Life of Oscar Wao* (2007), and *This Is How You Lose Her* (2012). Some of his many awards include a MacArthur "Genius" Fellowship, the National Book Critics Circle Award, and the PEN/O.Henry Award. All of his books have been national bestsellers. Díaz is also co-founder of Vona Voices, an organization whose goal "is to develop emerging writers of color through programs and workshops taught by established writers of color."

This essay appeared in the July 2015 *New York Times Magazine*, in an issue focused on the theme of mental health. As you read, pay close attention to the way Díaz uses language to convey his emotions and to reflect on his experience.

Preparing to Read

What books were powerful to you when you were in middle school, and why? How did they, or any one book in particular, influence your actions and behavior?

I got jumped at a pretty bad time in my life. Not that there's ever a *good* time. 1

What I mean is that I was already deep in the vulnerability matrix. 2
I had just entered seventh grade, was at peak adolescent craziness and, to make matters worse, was dealing with a new middle school whose dreary white middle-class bigotry was cutting the heart out of me. I wasn't two periods into my first day before a classmate called me a "sand nigger," as if it were no big deal. Someone else asked me if my family ate dogs every day or only once in a while. By my third month, that school had me feeling like the poorest, ugliest immigrant freak in the universe.

My home life was equally trying. My father abandoned the family the year before, plunging our household into poverty. No sooner than that happened, my brother, who was one year older and my best friend and protector, was found to have leukemia, the kind that in those days had a real nasty habit of killing you. One day he was sprawled on our front stoop in London Terrace holding court, and the next he was up in Newark, 40 pounds lighter and barely able to piss under his own power, looking as if he were one bad cold away from the grave.

I didn't know what to do with myself. I tried to be agreeable, to make friends, but that didn't work so hot; mostly I just slouched in my seat, hating my clothes and my glasses and my face. Sometimes I wrote my brother letters. Made it sound as though I were having a great time at school — a ball.

And then came the beat-down. Not at school, as I would have expected, but on the other side of the neighborhood. At the hands and feet of these three brothers I dimly knew. The youngest was my age, and on the day in question we had a spat over something — I can't remember what. I do remember pushing him down hard onto the sidewalk and laughing about it, and the kid running off in tears, swearing he was going to kill me. Then the scene in my head jumps, and the next thing I know, the kid comes back with his two older brothers, and I'm getting my face punched in. The older brothers held me down and let the younger brother punch me all he wanted. I cried out for my brother, but he was in Beth Israel Hospital, saving no one. I remember one of the older ones saying, "Hit him in the *teeth*."

As these things go, it wasn't too bad. I didn't actually lose any teeth or break any limbs or misplace an eye. Afterward, I even managed to limp home. My mother was at the hospital, so no one noticed that I had gotten stomped. Even took my blackened eye to classes the next day, but because my assailants attended another school, I didn't have to tell the truth. I said, "It happened in karate."

My first real beat-down, and I was furious and ashamed, but above all else I was afraid. Afraid of my assailants. Afraid they would corner me again. Afraid of a second beat-down. Afraid and afraid and afraid. Eventually the bruises and the rage faded, but not the fear. The fear remained. An awful withering dread that coiled around my bowels—that followed me into my dreams. ("Hit him in the *teeth*.") I guess I should have told someone, but I was too humiliated. And besides, my No. 1 confidant, my brother, wasn't available.

So I locked up the whole miserable affair deep inside. I thought that would help, but avoidance only seemed to give it more strength.

Without even thinking about it, I started doing everything I could to duck the brothers. I shunned their part of the neighborhood. I started looking around buildings to make sure the coast was clear. I stayed in the apartment a lot more, reading three, four books a week. And whenever I saw the brothers, together or individually—in a car, on a bike, on foot—the fear would spike through me so powerfully that I felt as though I was going to lose my mind. In *Dune*, a novel I adored in those days, Frank Herbert observed that "Fear is the mind-killer," and let me tell you, my man knows of what he speaks. When the brothers appeared, I couldn't think for nothing. I would drop whatever I was doing and *get away*, and it was only later, after I calmed down, that I would realize what I had done.

The brothers didn't pursue me. They would jeer at me and occasionally throw rocks, but even if they weren't chasing me in the flesh, they sure were chasing me in spirit. After these encounters, I would be a mess for days: depressed, irritable, hypervigilant, ashamed. I hated these brothers from the bottom of my heart, but even more than them, I hated myself for my cowardice.

Before that attack, I had felt fear plenty of times—which poor immigrant kid hasn't?—but after my beating, *I became afraid*. And at any age, that is a dismal place to be.

Given all the other crap I was facing, my adolescence was never going to win any awards. But sometimes I like to think that if that beat-down didn't happen, I might have had an easier time of it. Maybe a whole bunch of other awfulness would not have happened. But who can really know? In the end, the fear become another burden I had to shoulder—like having a sick brother or brown skin in a white school.

Took me until I was a sophomore in high school—yes, that long—before I finally found it in me to start facing my terror. By then, my older brother was in remission and wearing a wig to hide his baldness. Maybe his improbable survival was what gave me courage, or maybe it was all the Robert Cormier I was reading—his young heroes were always asking themselves, "Do I dare disturb the universe?" before ultimately deciding that yes, they did dare. Whatever it was, one day I found myself fleeing from a sighting of the brothers, and suddenly I was brought up short by an appalling vision: me running away forever.

I forced myself to stop. I forced myself to turn toward them, and it felt as if the whole world was turning with me. I couldn't make myself walk toward them, I could barely even look at them, so I settled for standing still. As the brothers approached, the ground started tilting out from under me. One of them scowled.

And then, without a word, they walked past.

Thinking Critically about the Text

Were you ever bullied, either emotionally or physically? Remember the circumstances and how you felt. Did you alter any of your routines to try to avoid whoever was bothering you, and were you successful? Did you have a protector (as Díaz described his brother to be before he got sick) you could rely on? How and when did the bullying stop?

Questions on Subject

1. Why do Díaz's classmates call him names and ask him if his family eats dogs?
2. Why do you think Díaz wrote to his brother making "it sound as though I were having a great time" (paragraph 4)? Why would he lie?
3. In paragraph 11, Díaz writes that he "had felt fear plenty of times" but that "after my beating, *I became afraid*." What is the difference between feeling fear and being afraid? Provide examples from your own life to support your answer.
4. Díaz quotes the writer Robert Cormier's heroes, who ask themselves "Do I dare disturb the universe?" (paragraph 13). Does Díaz think he disturbed the universe in the course of this story, and if so, how?

Questions on Strategy

1. Díaz's essay opens dramatically: "I got jumped at a pretty bad time in my life." But instead of narrating the details of his beating immediately, he provides three paragraphs of background, or context, first. Why do you think he delays telling readers about the actual beating? How would the essay be different if he had described the beating in the first paragraph?
2. Díaz tells his story from the first-person point of view. What would have been lost or gained had he used the third-person point of view? (Glossary: *Point of View*)
3. Díaz shares just a few details to make us understand how sick his brother is. What details does he use, and why are they powerful?
4. In paragraph 5, Díaz switches from past to present tense for one sentence: "Then the scene in my head jumps, and the next thing I know, the kid comes

back with his two older brothers, and I'm getting my face punched in." What is the effect of this shift in tense?

5. What time markers does Díaz use to help him organize his narrative? Locate and list as many as you can. How do they help the reader understand Díaz's story, both in the past and in the present? (Glossary: *Sequence*)

6. Explain how Díaz uses sentence fragments in his narrative. What effect do these sometimes short, incomplete sentences have on you?

Questions on Diction and Vocabulary

1. In paragraph 2, Díaz writes that he was "already deep in the vulnerability matrix." What do you think he means by this phrase?

2. Díaz uses a mix of formal and informal language; for example, contrast the phrases "I wasn't two periods into my first day before" (paragraph 2) with "that didn't work so hot" (4). Find additional examples of both types of language. What is the effect of using these styles that seem to conflict?

3. Refer to a dictionary to determine the meaning of the following words as Díaz uses them in this selection: *bigotry* (paragraph 2), *leukemia* (3), *hypervigilant* (10), *remission* (13).

Narration in Action

Write your birth date at the top of a piece of paper and the date you're doing this activity at the bottom. In between, fill in any significant dates you can think of. There are no rules about what to record, as long as each event has some importance to you. Some possible entries might be:

- the first day of preschool or kindergarten
- accomplishing something important (such as reading a book, learning to swim, teaching someone something, winning an award or a race)
- the birth of a younger sibling or a niece or nephew
- moving to a new home or new school
- learning to drive

Once your list is finished, add details about each event. As you do so, you'll notice that you're already comfortable with some of the key elements of narrative: context, organization, and details.

Writing Suggestions

1. Think of a time you were deeply frightened of something or someone. If you have moved past that fear, try to explain how you did so. What inspiration or combination of circumstances helped you find the courage you needed to

stop being afraid? If you are still afraid, what strategies do you use to cope? What do you think might help you find the courage to move past your fear? Using Díaz's narrative as a model, write an essay about an event related to this fear. Be sure to establish a context for this event, select meaningful details, and consider how you want to organize those details.

2. Most people have some experience of feeling like an outsider; it might be because you don't look like your classmates or neighbors, or you might feel you don't fit in for other reasons, such as having had different experiences or having different values. Or all of these things might be true. Write an essay about a time when you, like Díaz, felt like a "freak" or hated your "face." Describe how you felt and explore why you felt this way. Were you able to manage these feelings, make friends, and do well in school? Or did isolation and unhappiness affect your social life and school performance? How did you get through this period, and would you handle things differently today?

Not Close Enough for Comfort

DAVID P. BARDEEN

David P. Bardeen was born in 1974 in New Haven, Connecticut, and grew up in Seattle, Washington. He graduated cum laude from Harvard University in 1996 and then worked for J. P. Morgan & Co. as an investment banking analyst. In 2002, he received his J.D. from the New York University School of Law, where he was the managing editor of the school's *Law Review*. After graduation, he joined the law firm Cleary, Gottlieb, Steen & Hamilton and became a member of the New York Bar. Bardeen is proficient in Spanish, and his practice focuses on international business transactions involving clients in Latin America. A freelance writer on a variety of topics, he is also active with Immigration Equality, a national organization fighting for equality for lesbian, gay, bisexual, transgender, and HIV-positive immigrants.

In the following article, which appeared in the *New York Times Magazine* on February 29, 2004, Bardeen tells the story of a lunch meeting at which he reveals a secret to his twin brother, a secret that had derailed their relationship for almost fifteen years.

Preparing to Read

Recall a time when a parent, sibling, friend, teacher, or some other person close to you kept a secret from you. How did the secret affect your relationship? How did you feel once the secret was revealed? How has the relationship fared since?

I had wanted to tell Will I was gay since I was twelve. As twins, we shared everything back then: clothes, gadgets, thoughts, secrets. Everything except this. So when we met for lunch more than a year ago, I thought that finally coming out to him would close the distance that had grown between us. When we were kids, we created our own language, whispering to each other as our bewildered parents looked on. Now, at twenty-eight, we had never been further apart.

I asked him about his recent trip. He asked me about work. Short questions. One-word answers. Then an awkward pause.

Will was one of the last to know. Partly it was his fault. He is hard to pin down for brunch or a drink, and this was not the sort of conversation I wanted to have over the phone. I had actually been trying to tell him for more than a month, but he kept canceling at the last minute — a friend was in town, he'd met a girl.

But part of me was relieved. This was the talk I had feared the most. Coming out is, in an unforgiving sense, an admission of fraud. Fraud against yourself primarily, but also fraud against your family and friends. So, once I resolved to tell my secret, I confessed to my most recent "victims" first. I told my friends from law school—those I had met just a few years earlier and deceived the least—then I worked back through college to the handful of high-school friends I still keep in touch with.

Keeping my sexuality from my parents had always seemed permissible, so our sit-down chat did not stress me out as much as it might have. We all mislead our parents. "I'm too sick for school today." "No, I wasn't drinking." "Yes, Mom, I'm fine. Don't worry about me." That deception is understood and, in some sense, expected. But twins expect complete transparency, however romantic the notion.

> I had wanted to tell Will I was gay since I was twelve. As twins, we shared everything back then: clothes, gadgets, thoughts, secrets. Everything except this.

Although our lives unfolded along parallel tracks—we went to college together, both moved to New York and had many of the same friends—Will and I quietly drifted apart. When he moved abroad for a year, we lost touch almost entirely. Our mother and father didn't think this was strange, because like many parents of twins, they wanted us to follow divergent paths. But friends were baffled when we began to rely on third parties for updates on each other's lives. "How's Will?" someone would ask. "You tell me," I would respond. One mutual friend, sick of playing the intermediary, once sent me an e-mail message with a carbon copy to Will. "Dave, meet Will, your twin," it said. "Will, let me introduce you to Dave."

Now, here we were, at lunch, just the two of us. "There's something I've been meaning to tell you," I said. "I'm gay." I looked at him closely, at the edges of his mouth, the wrinkles around his eyes, for some hint of what he was thinking.

"O.K.," he said evenly.

"I've been meaning to tell you for a while," I said.

"Uh-huh." He asked me a few questions but seemed slightly uneasy, as if he wasn't sure he wanted to hear the answers. Do Mom and Dad know? Are you seeing anyone? How long have you known you were gay? I hesitated.

I've known since I was young, and to some degree, I thought Will had always known. How else to explain my adolescent melancholy, my withdrawal, the silence when the subject changed to girls, sex, and who was hot. As a teenager I watched, as if from a distance, as my demeanor went from outspoken to sullen. I had assumed, in the self-centered way kids often do, that everyone noticed this change—and that my brother had guessed the reason. To be fair, he asked me once in our twenties, after I had ended yet another brief relationship with a woman. "Of course I'm not gay," I told him, as if the notion were absurd.

"How long have you known?" he asked again. 12

"About fifteen years," I said. Will looked away. 13

Food arrived. We ate and talked about other things. Mom, Dad, the mayor, and the weather. We asked for the check and agreed to get together again soon. No big questions, no heart to heart. Just disclosure, explanation, follow-up, conclusion. But what could I expect? I had shut him out for so long that I suppose ultimately he gave up. Telling my brother I was gay hadn't made us close, as I had naively hoped it would; instead it underscored just how much we had strayed apart. 14

As we left the restaurant, I felt the urge to apologize, not for being gay, of course, but for the years I'd kept him in the dark, for his being among the last to know. He hailed a cab. It stopped. He stepped inside, the door still open. 15

"I'm sorry," I said. 16

He smiled. "No, I think it's great." 17

A nice gesture. Supportive. But I think he misunderstood. 18

A year later, we are still only creeping toward the intimacy everyone expects us to have. Although we live three blocks away from each other, I can't say we see each other every week or even every two weeks. But with any luck, next year, I'll be the one updating our mutual friends on Will's life. 19

Thinking Critically about the Text

How do you think Will felt when David announced that he was gay? Do you think Will had any clue about David's sexual orientation? What in Will's response to David's announcement led you to this conclusion? Why do you think it has been so difficult for them to recapture the "intimacy everyone expects [them] to have" (paragraph 19) in the year following David's coming out to Will?

Questions on Subject

1. Why do you suppose Bardeen chose to keep his sexual orientation a secret from his brother? Why was this particular "coming out" so difficult? Was Bardeen realistic in thinking that "Will had always known" (paragraph 11) that he was gay?

2. What does Bardeen mean when he says, "But twins expect complete transparency, however romantic the notion" (paragraph 5)?

3. Why does Bardeen feel the need to apologize to his brother as they part? Do you think his brother understood the meaning of the apology? Why or why not?

4. What do you think Bardeen had hoped would happen after he confided his secret to his brother? Was this hope unrealistic?

5. How does Bardeen feel his secret harmed his relationship with his brother? How does he seem to think the relationship will heal?

Questions on Strategy

1. Bardeen narrates his coming out using the first-person pronoun *I*. (Glossary: *Point of View*) Why is the first person particularly appropriate for telling a story such as this one? Explain.

2. How has Bardeen organized his narrative? (Glossary: *Organization*) In paragraphs 3 through 6, Bardeen uses flashbacks to give readers a context for his relationship with his twin. What would have been lost or gained had he begun his essay with paragraphs 3 through 6?

3. During the lunch-meeting part of the narrative (paragraphs 7–17), Bardeen uses dialogue. (Glossary: *Dialogue*) What does he gain by doing this? Why do you suppose he uses dialogue sparingly elsewhere?

4. Bardeen uses a number of short sentences and deliberate sentence fragments. What effect do these have on you? Why do you suppose he uses some sentence fragments instead of complete sentences?

5. Bardeen's title plays on the old saying "too close for comfort." What does his title suggest to you? (Glossary: *Title*) How effectively does it capture the essence of his relationship with his brother? Explain.

6. In paragraphs 6 and 11, Bardeen uses comparison and contrast to highlight the similarities and differences between himself and Will. (Glossary: *Comparison and Contrast*) Which did you find more interesting and revealing — the similarities or differences? Why?

Questions on Diction and Vocabulary

1. How would you describe Bardeen's voice in this narrative? How is that voice established? What, if anything, does Bardeen's diction tell you about him as a person? (Glossary: *Diction*) Explain.

2. Bardeen says that "[c]oming out is, in an unforgiving sense, an admission of fraud" (paragraph 4). Why do you suppose he uses the word *fraud* to describe

how he felt about his coming out? What does he mean when he says "in an unforgiving sense"? What other words might he have used instead of *fraud*?

3. Refer to a dictionary to determine the meanings of the following words as Bardeen uses them in this selection: *baffled* (paragraph 6), *melancholy* (11), *demeanor* (11), *sullen* (11), *intimacy* (19).

Narration in Action

Beginning at the beginning and ending at the end is not the only way to tell a story. Think of the individual incidents or events in a story that you would like to tell or perhaps one that you are already working on. Don't write the story itself; simply make a list of the events that you need to include. Be sure to identify at least six to ten key events in your story. Start by listing the events in chronological order. (See student outline on page 84.) Now play with the arrangement of those events; try to develop one or two alternative sequences that include the use of flashback. Using your list of events, discuss with other class members how flashback can improve the dramatic impact of your narrative.

Writing Suggestions

1. Using your Preparing to Read response for this selection, write an essay about a secret you once had and how it affected relationships with those close to you. What exactly was your secret? Why did you decide to keep this information secret? How did you feel while you kept your secret? What happened when you revealed your secret? What insights into secrets do you have as a result of this experience?

2. In paragraph 4, Bardeen states, "So, once I resolved to tell my secret, I confessed to my most recent 'victims' first. I told my friends from law school — those I had met just a few years earlier and deceived the least — then I worked back through college to the handful of high-school friends I still keep in touch with." Write an essay in which you compare and contrast your level of honesty among your friends or a larger community and your level of honesty among your family or people with whom you are very close. (Glossary: *Comparison and Contrast*) Are there secrets you would be more likely to share with one group than another? If so, how would you classify those secrets? (Glossary: *Classification; Division*) Do you think it is easier to be honest with people who do or do not know you very well? Why?

3. The "coming out" photograph below was taken at a gay pride festival in 2012. How do you "read" this photograph? (For a discussion of how to analyze photographs and other visual texts, see pages 15–19.) How do you interpret the message on her T-shirt? How do her expression and her surroundings impact your reading of this photo? Using Bardeen's essay, this photograph, and your own observations and experiences, write an essay about the mixed feelings and emotions as well as the potential misunderstandings attendant on "coming out."

© Ed Simons/Alamy Stock Photo

Stranger Than True

BARRY WINSTON

Barry Winston is a practicing attorney in Chapel Hill, North Carolina. He was born in New York City in 1934 and served in the Marine Corps from 1953 to 1955. He later graduated from the University of North Carolina, from which he also received his law degree. His specialty is criminal law. He was admitted to the North Carolina Bar in 1961 and for almost over fifty years has been an active defense lawyer. He is listed in the *Bar Register of Preeminent Lawyers*.

"Stranger Than True" was published in *Harper's* magazine in December 1986. In the story, Winston recounts his experience defending a young college graduate accused of driving while under the influence of alcohol and causing his sister's death. The story is characterized by Winston's energetic and strong voice. In commenting on his use of narrative detail, Winston says, "I could have made it twice as long, but it wouldn't have been as good a story." What do you think he meant by this comment?

Preparing to Read

The American judicial system works on the basis of the presumption of innocence. In short, you are innocent until proven guilty. But what about a situation in which all the evidence seems to point to a person's guilt? What's the purpose of a trial in such a case?

Let me tell you a story. A true story. The court records are all there if anyone wants to check. It's three years ago. I'm sitting in my office, staring out the window, when I get a call from a lawyer I hardly know. Tax lawyer. Some kid is in trouble and would I be interested in helping him out? He's charged with manslaughter, a felony, and driving under the influence. I tell him sure, have the kid call me. 1

So the kid calls and makes an appointment to see me. He's a nice kid, fresh out of college, and he's come down here to spend some time with his older sister, who's in med school. One day she tells him they're invited to a cookout with some friends of hers. She's going directly from class, and he's going to take her car and meet her there. It's way out in the country, but he gets there before she does, introduces himself around, and pops a beer. She shows up after a while and he pops another beer. Then he eats a hamburger and drinks a third beer. At some point his sister says, "Well, it's about time to go," and they head for the car. 2

And, the kid tells me, sitting there in my office, the next thing he remembers, he's waking up in a hospital room, hurting like hell, bandages and casts all over him, and somebody is telling him he's charged with manslaughter and DUI because he wrecked his sister's car, killed her in the 3 process, and blew fourteen on the Breathalyzer. I ask him what the hell he means by "the next thing he remembers," and he looks me straight in the eye and says he can't remember anything from the time they leave the cookout until he wakes up in the hospital. He tells me the doctors say he has post-retrograde amnesia. I say of course I believe him, but I'm worried about finding a judge who'll believe him.

> The next thing he remembers, he's waking up in a hospital room, hurting like hell, bandages and casts all over him, and somebody is telling him he's charged with manslaughter and DUI . . .

I agree to represent him and send somebody for a copy of the wreck report. It says there are four witnesses: a couple in a car going the other way who passed the kid and his sister just before their car ran off the road, the guy whose front yard they landed in, and the trooper who investigated. I call the guy whose yard they ended up in. He isn't home. I leave word. Then I call the couple. The wife agrees to come in the next day with her husband. While I'm talking to her, the first guy calls. I call him back, introduce myself, tell him I'm representing the kid and need to talk to him about the accident. He hems and haws and I figure he's one of those people who think it's against the law to talk to defense lawyers. I say the D.A. will tell him it's O.K. to talk to me, but he doesn't have to. I give him the name and number of the D.A. and he says he'll call me back.

Then I go out and hunt up the trooper. He tells me the whole story. The kid and his sister are coming into town on Smith Level Road, after it turns from fifty-five to forty-five. The Thornes — the couple — are heading out of town. They say this sports car passes them, going the other way, right after that bad turn just south of the new subdivision. They say it's going like a striped-ass ape, at least sixty-five or seventy. Mrs. Thorne turns around to look and Mr. Thorne watches in the rearview mirror. They both see the same thing: halfway into the curve, the car runs off the road on the right, whips back onto the road, spins, runs off on the left, and disappears. They turn around in the first driveway they come to and start back, both terrified of what they're going to find. By this time, Trooper Johnson says, the guy whose front yard the car has ended up in has pulled the kid and his sister out of the wreck and started CPR on the girl. Turns out he's an emergency medical technician. Holloway, that's his name. Johnson tells me that Holloway says he's sitting in his front room, watching television, when he hears a hell of a crash in his yard. He runs outside and finds the car flipped over, and so he pulls the kid out from the driver's side, the girl from the other side. She dies in his arms.

And that, says Trooper Johnson, is that. The kid's blood/alcohol content was fourteen, he was going way too fast, *and* the girl is dead. He had to charge him. It's a shame, he seems a nice kid, it was his own sister and all, but what the hell can he do, right?

The next day the Thornes come in, and they confirm everything Johnson said. By now things are looking not so hot for my client, and I'm thinking it's about time to have a little chat with the D.A. But Holloway still hasn't called me back, so I call him. Not home. Leave word. No call. I wait a couple of days and call again. Finally I get him on the phone. He's very agitated, and won't talk to me except to say that he doesn't have to talk to me.

I know I better look for a deal, so I go to the D.A. He's very sympathetic. But. There's only so far you can get on sympathy. A young woman is dead, promising career cut short, all because somebody has too much to drink and drives. The kid has to pay. Not, the D.A. says, with jail time. But he's got to plead guilty to two misdemeanors: death by vehicle and driving under the influence. That means probation, a big fine. Several thousand dollars. Still, it's hard for me to criticize the D.A. After all, he's probably going to have the MADD mothers all over him because of reducing the felony to a misdemeanor.

On the day of the trial, I get to court a few minutes early. There are the Thornes and Trooper Johnson, and someone I assume is Holloway. Sure enough, when this guy sees me, he comes over and introduces himself and starts right in: "I just want you to know how serious all this drinking and driving really is," he says. "If those young people hadn't been drinking and driving that night, that poor young girl would be alive today." Now, I'm trying to hold my temper when I spot the D.A. I bolt across the room, grab him by the arm, and say, "We gotta talk. Why the hell have you got all those people here? That jerk Holloway. Surely to God you're not going to call him as a witness. This is a guilty plea! My client's parents are sitting out there. You don't need to put them through a dog-and-pony show."

The D.A. looks at me and says, "Man, I'm sorry, but in a case like this, I gotta put on witnesses. Weird Wally is on the bench. If I try to go without witnesses, he might throw me out."

The D.A. calls his first witness. Trooper Johnson identifies himself, tells about being called to the scene of the accident, and describes what he found when he got there and what everybody told him. After he finishes, the judge looks at me. "No questions," I say. Then the D.A. calls Holloway. He describes the noise, running out of the house, the upside-down car in his yard, pulling my client out of the window on the left side of the car and then going around to the other side for the girl. When he gets to this part, he really hits his stride. He describes, in minute detail, the injuries he saw and what he did to try and save her life. And then he tells, breath by breath, how she died in his arms.

The D.A. says, "No further questions, your Honor." The judge looks at me. I shake my head, and he says to Holloway, "You may step down."

One of those awful silences hangs there, and nothing happens for a minute. Holloway doesn't move. Then he looks at me, and at the D.A., and then at the judge. He says, "Can I say something else, your Honor?"

All my bells are ringing at once, and my gut is screaming at me, Object! Object! I'm trying to decide in three quarters of a second whether it'll be worse to listen to a lecture on the evils of drink from this jerk Holloway or piss off the judge by objecting. But all I say is, "No objections, your Honor." The judge smiles at me, then at Holloway, and says, "Very well, Mr. Holloway. What did you wish to say?"

It all comes out in a rush. "Well, you see, your Honor," Holloway says, "it was just like I told Trooper Johnson. It all happened so fast. I heard the noise, and I came running out, and it was night, and I was excited, and the next morning, when I had a chance to think about it, I figured out what had happened, but by then I'd already told Trooper Johnson and I didn't know what to do, but you see, the car, it was upside down, and I did pull that boy out of the left-hand window, but don't you see, the car was upside down, and if you turned it over on its wheels like it's supposed to be, the left-hand side is really on the right-hand side, and your Honor, that boy wasn't driving that car at all. It was the girl that was driving, and when I had a chance to think about it the next morning, I realized that I'd told Trooper Johnson wrong, and I was scared and I didn't know what to do, and that's why" — and now he's looking right at me — "why I wouldn't talk to you."

Naturally, the defendant is allowed to withdraw his guilty plea. The charges are dismissed and the kid and his parents and I go into one of the back rooms in the courthouse and sit there looking at one another for a while. Finally, we recover enough to mumble some Oh my Gods and Thank yous and You're welcomes. And that's why I can stand to represent somebody when I know he's guilty.

Thinking Critically about the Text

Much abuse is heaped on lawyers who defend clients whose guilt seems obvious. How does Winston's story help explain why lawyers need to defend "guilty" clients?

Questions on Subject

1. Why does the D.A. bring in witnesses for a case that has been plea-bargained? What is ironic about that decision? (Glossary: *Irony*)

2. Why was Holloway reluctant to be interviewed by Winston about what he saw and did in the aftermath of the accident? What might he have been afraid of?
3. Why did Holloway finally ask to speak to the court? Why do you suppose Winston chose not to object to Holloway's request?
4. What do you think is the point of Winston's narrative?

Questions on Strategy

1. Winston establishes the context for his story in the first three paragraphs. What basic information does he give readers?
2. What details does Winston choose to include in the story? Why does he include them? Is there other information that you would like to have had? Why do you suppose Winston chose to omit that information?
3. Explain how Winston uses sentence variety to pace his narrative. What effect do his short sentences and sentence fragments have on you?
4. What does Winston gain as a writer by telling us that this is "a true story," one that we can check out in the court records?
5. During the courtroom scene (paragraphs 9–15), Winston relies heavily on dialogue. (Glossary: *Dialogue*) What does he gain by using dialogue? Why do you suppose he uses dialogue sparingly in the other parts of his narrative?
6. How does Winston use description to differentiate the four witnesses to the accident? (Glossary: *Description*) Why is it important for him to give his readers some idea of their differing characters?

Questions on Diction and Vocabulary

1. How would you characterize Winston's voice in this story? How is that voice established? (Glossary: *Voice*)
2. What, if anything, does Winston's diction tell you about Winston himself? (Glossary: *Diction*) What effect does his diction have on the tone of his narrative? (Glossary: *Tone*)
3. Refer to a dictionary to determine the meanings of the following words as Winston uses them in this selection: *felony* (paragraph 1), *agitated* (7), *misdemeanor* (8), *probation* (8), *bolt* (9).

Narration in Action

Effective narration uses strong verbs and clear, vivid description. Newspaper writers, because they must concisely and vividly evoke everyday events, are acutely aware of the need for effective narration. It is not enough for them to say that the city council discussed the resolution, the tornado happened, or the team won; they must choose language that efficiently brings the discussion, the weather, and the game to life. For this reason, verbs such as *argued, tore, destroyed, buried, trounced*, and the like are common in the headlines of our local papers, and great care is taken to ensure that meaning is conveyed efficiently but accurately.

Sometimes these efforts go astray. As an exercise in both using and editing for strong verbs, consider the following real newspaper headlines — headlines that should have been reconsidered before the paper went to press. First, identify the source of the unintended humor in each headline. Then — as illustrated in the sample below — rewrite the headline using effective narration techniques.

> Sample headline: Red Tape Holds Up New Bridges
> Edited headline: Red Tape ~~Holds Up~~ Bureaucratic Delays New Bridges

New Study of Obesity Looks for Larger Test Group

Kids Make Nutritious Snacks

Local High School Dropouts Cut in Half

Hospitals Sued by 7 Foot Doctors

Police Begin Campaign to Run Down Jaywalkers

Typhoon Rips Through Cemetery: Hundreds Dead

Juvenile Court to Try Shooting Defendant

If Strike Isn't Settled Quickly, It May Last Awhile

Writing Suggestions

1. "Stranger Than True" is a first-person narrative told from the defense lawyer's point of view. Imagine that you are a newspaper reporter covering this case. What changes would you have to make in Winston's narrative to make it a news story? Make a list of the changes you would have to make and then rewrite the story.

2. Holloway's revelation in the courtroom catches everyone by surprise. Analyze the chain of events in the accident and the assumptions that people made based on the accounts of those events. After reading the introduction to Chapter 11, "Cause and Effect Analysis," write a cause and effect essay in which you explain some of the possible reasons Holloway's confession is so unexpected. (Glossary: *Cause and Effect Analysis*)

//
Don't Peak in High School

MINDY KALING

Actor, writer, and producer Mindy Kaling was born in Cambridge, Massachusetts, in 1979. Kaling graduated from Dartmouth College, where she studied playwriting and classics. From 2004 to 2013, Kaling wrote for the television comedy *The Office*, on which she also played the character Kelly Kapoor. She received an Emmy nomination for one of the episodes she wrote. Since 2012, she has been the creator, producer, writer, and star of the television situation comedy *The Mindy Project*, the first television situation comedy to star an Indian American character. Her films include *The 40 Year Old Virgin* (2005), *This Is the End* (2013), and the animated comedies *Despicable Me* (2010) and *Inside Out* (2015).

Vivien Killilea/Getty Images for SCAD

Kaling has written two books, *Is Everyone Hanging Out Without Me? (and Other Concerns)* (2011) and *Why Not Me?* (2015); both were on the *New York Times* bestseller list. Her work has been recognized numerous times by the Screen Actors Guild, Critics' Choice Television Awards, Asian Excellence Awards, and Satellite Awards, among others.

This selection is from *Is Everyone Hanging Out Without Me? (and Other Concerns)*, in which Kaling also shares the following observations: "Writing, at its heart, is a solitary pursuit, designed to make people depressoids, drug addicts, misanthropes, and antisocial weirdos."

Preparing to Read

How did you feel about your high school experience? Were you well known for something, such as being class president, valedictorian, or captain of a team? If not, did it matter to you that you weren't well known? Now, in college, are you pursuing the same interests you had in high school? What aspects of your high school experience seem most important?

Sometimes teenage girls ask me for advice about what they should be doing if they want a career like mine one day. There are basically two ways to get where I am: (1) learn a provocative dance and put it on YouTube; (2) convince your parents to move to Orlando and homeschool you until you get cast on a kids' show, *or* do what I did, which is (3) stay in school and be a respectful and hard-working wallflower, and go to an accredited non-online university.

Teenage girls, please don't worry about being super popular in high school, or being the best actress in high school, or the best athlete.

Not only do people not care about any of that the second you graduate, but when you get older, if you reference your successes in high school too much, it actually makes you look kind of pitiful, like some babbling old Tennessee Williams character with nothing else going on in her current life. What I've noticed is that almost no one who was a big star in high school is also big star later in life. For us overlooked kids, it's so wonderfully *fair*.

I was never the lead in the play. I don't think I went to a single party with alcohol at it. No one offered me pot. It wasn't until I was sixteen that I even knew marijuana and pot were the same thing. I didn't even learn this from a cool friend; I gleaned it from a syndicated episode of *21 Jump Street*. My parents didn't let me do social things on weeknights because weeknights were for homework, and *maybe* an episode of *The X-Files* if I was being a good kid (*X-Files* was on Friday night), and *on extremely rare occasions* I could watch *Seinfeld* (Thursday, a school night), if I had just aced my PSATs or something.

It is easy to freak out as a sensitive teenager. I always felt I was missing out because of the way the high school experience was dramatized in television and song. For every realistic *My So-Called Life*, there were ten *90210*s or *Party of Five*s, where a twenty-something Luke Perry was supposed to be just a typical guy at your high school. If Luke Perry had gone to my high school, everybody would have thought, "What's the deal with this brooding greaser? Is he a narc?" But that's who Hollywood put forth as "just a dude at your high school."

In the genre of "making you feel like you're not having an awesome American high school experience," the worst offender is actually a song: John Cougar Mellencamp's "Jack and Diane." It's one of those songs—like Eric Clapton's "Tears in Heaven"—that everyone knows all the words to without ever having chosen to learn them. I've seen people get incredibly pumped when this song comes on; I once witnessed a couple request it four times in a row at Johnny Rockets and belt it while loudly clapping their hands above their heads, so apparently it is an anthem of some people's youth. I think across America, as I type this, there are high school couples who strive to be like Jack and Diane from that song. Just hangin' out after school, makin' out at the Tastee Freez, sneakin' beers into their cars, without a care in the world. Just two popular, idle, all-American white kids, having a blast.

The world created in "Jack and Diane" is maybe okay-charming because, like, all right, that kid Jack is going to get shipped off to Vietnam and there was going to be a whole part two of the story when he returned as some traumatized, disillusioned vet. The song is only interesting to me as the dreamy first act to a much more interesting *Born on the Fourth of July*–type story.

As it is, I guess I find "Jack and Diane" a little disgusting.

As a child of immigrant professionals, I can't help but notice the wasteful frivolity of it all. Why are these kids not home doing their homework? Why aren't they setting the table for dinner or helping out around the house? Who allows their kids to hang out in parking lots? Isn't that loitering?

I wish there was a song called "Nguyen and Ari," a little ditty about a hardworking Vietnamese girl who helps her parents with the franchised Holiday Inn they run, and does homework in the lobby, and Ari, a hardworking Jewish boy who does volunteer work at his grandmother's old-age home, and they meet after school at Princeton Review. They help each other study for the SATs and different AP courses, and then, after months of studying, and mountains of flashcards, they kiss chastely upon hearing the news that they both got into their top college choices. This is a song teens need to inadvertently memorize. Now that's a song I'd request at Johnny Rockets!

In high school, I had fun in my academic clubs, watching movies with my girlfriends, learning Latin, having long, protracted, unrequited crushes on older guys who didn't know me, and yes, hanging out with my family. I liked hanging out with my family! Later, when you're grown up, you realize you never get to hang out with your family. You pretty much have only eighteen years to spend with them full time, and that's it. So, yeah, it all added up to a happy, memorable time. Even though I was never a star.

Because I was largely overlooked at school, I watched everyone like an observant weirdo, not unlike Eugene Levy's character Dr. Allan Pearl in *Waiting for Guffman*, who "sat next to the class clown, and studied him." But I did that with everyone. It has helped me so much as a writer; you have no idea.

I just want ambitious teenagers to know it is totally fine to be quiet, observant kids. Besides being a delight to your parents, you will find you have plenty of time later to catch up. So many people I work with—famous actors, accomplished writers—were overlooked in high school. Be like Allan Pearl. Sit next to the class clown and study him. Then grow up, take everything you learned, and get paid to be a real-life clown, unlike whatever unexciting thing the actual high school class clown is doing now.

The chorus of "Jack and Diane" is: *Oh yeah, life goes on, long after the thrill of living is gone.*

Are you kidding me? The thrill of living was *high school*? Come on, Mr. Cougar Mellencamp. Get a life.

Thinking Critically about the Text

Kaling wants ambitious teenagers "to know it is totally fine to be quiet, observant kids" (paragraph 12). Does this match the messages you get from your peers? From your parents? From the media, such as advertising, movies, and television? How do your answers help explain why Kaling may have written this essay?

Questions on Subject

1. How does Mindy Kaling describe her childhood? Does she think her parents were overly strict or that they did not provide enough supervision? Did she enjoy her classes and school activities?

2. In her second sentence, Kaling writes, "There are basically two ways to get where I am." She then goes on to list not two but *three* possibilities. Do you think Kaling is bad at simple addition, or is there some other reason these numbers don't match?

3. Kaling calls herself an "overlooked" kid (see paragraphs 1 and 11). What does she mean by *overlooked*, and why is this an important part of her story?

4. What is the main point of Kaling's narrative, and where does she state it? (Glossary: *Thesis*)

Questions on Strategy

1. Kaling establishes the context for this essay in her first sentence, noting that she is sometimes asked for advice on how to get started in comedy. But there is a larger context, as well. What is it, and where do you find that information?

2. How has Kaling organized her narrative? Note that only one paragraph (3) is written entirely in the past tense. Why do you think Kaling devotes such a small portion of her essay to recounting her own experiences in high school? (Glossary: *Strategy*)

3. Kaling uses the strategy of illustration throughout her essay. Why do you think she uses so many examples from fictional television shows and songs? (Glossary: *Example*)

4. What details does Kaling use that show, rather than tell, what high school was like for her? Why does she include them? Is there other information you would have liked to have known? If so, why do you think Kaling did not include this information?

Questions on Diction and Vocabulary

1. Kaling combines fairly sophisticated vocabulary (*protracted, traumatized, disillusioned, inadvertently*) with informal language (*super, freaked, pumped, weirdo*). What tone does this create in the selection? How might the tone be different if she had used only sophisticated, or only informal, diction? (Glossary: *Tone*)

2. At the beginning of paragraph 2, Kaling writes, "Teenage girls, please don't worry..." and in her last paragraph she writes, "Come on, Mr. Cougar Mellencamp." What is the effect of directly addressing these imagined readers? Does she really think Mr. Cougar Mellencamp is reading this essay?

3. Kaling writes, "As it is, I guess I find 'Jack and Diane' a little disgusting" (paragraph 7). Why do you think she uses the words *guess* and *little* in this sentence? What do they add to the sentence?

4. Refer to a dictionary to determine the meanings of the following words as Kaling uses them in this selection: *gleaned* (3), *anthem* (5), *loitering* (8), *franchised* (9), *unrequited* (10).

Narration in Action

Kaling references many writers, musicians, and television shows that her intended audience, teenage girls, may not be familiar with because they originated in the 1980s, 1990s, or even the 1940s. Make a list of all these artists and shows. Next, with a show of hands, find out how many of your classmates:

- have seen (or read) at least one play by Tennessee Williams
- have seen at least one episode of *My So-Called Life*, *21 Jump Street*, *The X-Files*, *Seinfeld*, *Beverly Hills 90210*, *Party of Five*
- know the lyrics to John Cougar Mellencamp's "Jack and Diane" and Eric Clapton's "Tears in Heaven"
- have seen the movies *Born on the Fourth of July* or *Waiting for Guffman*

Select the five artists, songs, or shows with which your class as a whole is *least* familiar. Discuss how Kaling makes these references effective for readers who have *not* watched or listened to them. Are there references that are not effective for you or your classmates? If so, why aren't they effective? Suggest other references that might have been more effective and explain why.

Writing Suggestions

1. Using this essay as a model and your Preparing to Read prompt as a starting point, write an essay about something you have learned since finishing high school. Be sure to establish a context for the information you want to share, to carefully select details that best illustrate your story, and to organize the details so that the story is most effective.

2. Write an essay disagreeing with Kaling's advice that "it is totally fine to be quiet, observant kids." Argue that she is oversimplifying the issue and that there are disadvantages to being a "hardworking wallflower" (paragraph 1) who doesn't "do social things on weeknights" (3) and who focuses on homework and spending time with family. What might such a student be missing?

Are there alternatives to sneaking beers and making out in cars? Are there constructive ways to spend your time other than, or in addition to, doing homework and obeying your parents? Are there benefits to making those choices instead?

3. Think of a well-known song or show that you've never liked because you think it presents an unrealistic or trivial view of some aspect of the world. Write an essay explaining why you find the song or show objectionable. Be sure to use specific detail from the song or show to argue your point.

WRITING SUGGESTIONS FOR NARRATION

1. Using Malcolm X's, David P. Bardeen's, or Mindy Kaling's essay as a model, narrate an experience that gave you a new awareness of yourself. Use enough telling detail in your narrative to help your reader visualize your experience and understand its significance for you. You may find the following suggestions helpful in choosing an experience to narrate in the first person:

    a. my greatest success or failure
    b. my most embarrassing moment
    c. my happiest moment
    d. a truly frightening experience
    e. an experience that, in my eyes, turned a hero or an idol into an ordinary person
    f. an experience that turned an ordinary person I know into one of my heroes
    g. the experience that was the most important turning point in my life

2. Each of us can tell of an experience that has been unusually significant in teaching us about our relationship to society or to life's institutions — schools, social or service organizations, religious groups, government. Think about your past and identify one experience that has been especially important for you in this way. After you have considered this event's significance, write an essay recounting it. In preparing to write your narrative, you might benefit from reading J. Dowsett's account of how a commonplace action raised his awareness in "What My Bike Has Taught Me about White Privilege" (page 594–97). To bring your experience into focus and to help you decide what to include in your essay, ask yourself: Why is this experience important to me? What details are necessary for me to re-create the experience in an interesting and engaging way? How can my narrative be most effectively organized? What point of view will work best?

3. While growing up, we have all done something we know we should not have done. Sometimes we have gotten away with our transgressions, sometimes not. Sometimes our actions have no repercussions; sometimes they have very serious ones. Tell the story of one of your escapades and explain why you have remembered it so well.

4. Many people love to tell stories (that is, they use narration) to illustrate an abstract point, to bring an idea down to a personal level, or to render an idea memorable. Often, the telling of such stories can be entertaining as well as instructive. Think about a belief or position that you hold dear (e.g., every individual deserves respect, recycling matters, voluntarism creates community, people need artistic outlets, nature renews the individual) and try to capture that belief in a sentence or two. Then, narrate a story that illustrates your belief or position.

5. **Writing with Sources.** As a way of gaining experience with third-person narration, write an article intended for your school or community newspaper in which you report on what happened at one of the following:
   a. the visit of a state or national figure to your campus or community
   b. a dormitory meeting
   c. a current event of local, state, or national significance
   d. an important sports event
   e. a current research project of one of your professors
   f. a campus gathering or performance
   g. an important development at a local business or at your place of employment

   You may find it helpful to read the third-person narrative about the invention of Coca-Cola (page 80) before starting to write your own narrative. In order to provide context for your article, consider interviewing one or more people involved and/or doing some background research on the object of your narrative. For models of and advice on integrating sources in your essay, see Chapters 14 and 15.

6. Take some time to study Grant Snider's "Life in the Woods," reproduced at the beginning of this chapter (page 78).
   a. Take a few minutes to describe what's going on in this illustration. Who is the character? Where is he or she? What happens? Next, consider how you know this. What aspects of the narrative are conveyed by written elements? What parts are conveyed by visual elements only?
   b. Write a short paper in which you discuss what you discovered about the differences between visual and written narratives.

7. **Writing with Sources.** Consider broadening and deepening your exploration of the differences between visual and written narratives by reading what others have to say about using visuals to convey meaning. (One good source for such discussion is Scott McCloud's *Understanding Comics*.) Alternatively, consider writing a paper in which you compare and contrast two genres (graphic novels and films, perhaps) used with a single work or two examples from the same genre (for instance, Gene Luen Yang's *American Born Chinese* and Marjane Satrapi's *Persepolis*, two graphic novels). For models of and advice on integrating sources in your essay, see Chapters 14 and 15.

8. **Writing in the Workplace.** Imagine that you will be attending a national sales conference, representing the office where you work. For one of the opening small-group sessions, you have been asked to prepare a three- to five-minute narrative in which you tell a revealing story about yourself as a way of introducing yourself to the group. What is it that you think others would be interested in knowing about you?

Library of Congress, Prints & Photographs Division, FSA/OWI Collection, LC-USF34-013407-C

CHAPTER 5

Description

WHAT IS DESCRIPTION?

DESCRIBING SOMETHING WITH WORDS IS OFTEN COMPARED TO PAINTING a verbal picture. Both verbal description (like a magazine article profiling a celebrity) and visual description (like a photograph, painting, or drawing accompanying the article) seek to transform fleeting perceptions into lasting images—through words in the case of an article and pixels, paints, or pencils in the case of a photograph, painting, or drawing. Both verbal and visual descriptions enable us to imaginatively experience the subject using some or all of our five senses. Both kinds of description convey information about a subject, telling us something we didn't know before. Both can convey a dominant impression of the subject. And, finally, both verbal and visual descriptions can be classed as objective or subjective, depending on how much they reveal the perspective of the person doing the describing.

The photograph opposite—one of a series of portraits of Ella Watson, a custodial worker in a federal government building, taken by Gordon Parks in August 1942—is a good example of description conveyed through strictly visual cues, principally lighting and composition (the arrangement of the flag, mop, and broom, with an unsmiling Watson at the center).

DESCRIPTION IN WRITTEN TEXTS

Description is a key element in many kinds of written texts. Consider, for example, the following description by Bernd Heinrich from his book *One Man's Owl* (1987). In this selection, Heinrich describes trekking through the woods in search of owls. First, try to see, hear, smell, and feel the scene he describes: Form the jigsaw puzzle of words and details into a complete experience. Once you've accomplished this, define the dominant impression Heinrich creates.

Sets the scene with description of landscape	By mid-March in Vermont, the snow from the winter storms has already become crusty as the first midday thaws refreeze during the cold nights. A solid white cap compacts the snow, and you can walk on it without breaking through to your waist. The maple sap is starting to run on warm days, and one's blood quickens.
Describes sights and sounds of birds in early spring	Spring is just around the corner, and the birds act as if they know. The hairy and downy woodpeckers drum on dry branches and on the loose flakes of maple bark, and purple finches sing merrily from the spruces. This year the reedy voices of the pine siskins can be heard everywhere on the ridge where the hemlocks grow, as can the chickadees' two-note, plaintive song. Down in the bog, the first red-winged blackbirds have just returned, and they can be heard yodeling from the tops of dry cattails. Flocks of rusty blackbirds fly over in long skeins, heading north.
Reveals his position and relies on auditory details as night approaches	From where I stand at the edge of the woods overlooking Shelburne Bog, I feel a slight breeze and hear a moaning gust sweeping through the forest behind me. It is getting dark. There are eery creaking and scraping noises. Inside the pine forest it is becoming black, pitch black. The songbirds are silent. Only the sound of the wind can be heard above the distant honks of Canada geese flying below the now starry skies. Suddenly I hear a booming hollow "hoo-hoo-*hoo*-hoo—." The deep resonating hoot can send a chill down any spine, as indeed it has done to peoples of many cultures. But I know what the sound is, and it gives me great pleasure.

Heinrich could have described the scene with far fewer words, but that description would likely not have conveyed his dominant impression—one of comfort with his natural surroundings. Heinrich reads the landscape with subtle insight; he knows all the different birds and understands their springtime habits. The reader can imagine the smile on Heinrich's face when he hears the call of the owl.

USING DESCRIPTION AS A WRITING STRATEGY

Writers often use the strategy of description to inform—to provide readers with specific data. You may need to describe the results of a chemical reaction for a lab report, the style of a Renaissance painting for an art history term paper, the physical capabilities and limitations of a stroke patient for a case study, or the acting of Charlize Theron in a movie you want your friends to see. Such descriptions will sometimes be scientifically objective, sometimes intensely impressionistic. The approach you use will depend on the subject itself, the information you want to communicate about it, and the format in which the description appears.

Another important use of description is to create a mood or atmosphere or even to convey your own views—to develop a *dominant impression*. Jeannette Walls uses the strategy of description to capture her sense of overlapping memories, her confused understanding of her mother:

> Mom stood fifteen feet away. She had tied rags around her shoulders to keep out the spring chill and was picking through the trash while her dog, a black-and-white terrier mix, played at her feet. Mom's gestures were all familiar—the way she tilted her head and thrust out her lower lip when studying items of potential value that she'd hoisted out of the Dumpster, the way her eyes widened with childish glee when she found something she liked. Her long hair was streaked with gray, tangled and matted, and her eyes had sunk deep into their sockets, but still she reminded me of the mom she'd been when I was a kid, swan-diving off cliffs and painting in the desert and reading Shakespeare aloud. Her cheekbones were still high and strong, but the skin was parched and ruddy from all those winters and summers exposed to the elements. To the people walking by, she probably looked like any of the thousands of homeless people in New York City.

Each of the descriptions in this chapter is distinguished by the strong dominant impression the writer creates.

There are essentially two types of description: objective and subjective. *Objective description* is as factual as possible, emphasizing the actual qualities of the subject being described while subordinating the writer's personal responses. For example, a witness to a mugging would try to give authorities a precise, objective description of the assailant, unaffected by emotional responses, so that a positive identification could be made. In the excerpt from his book, Bernd Heinrich objectively describes what he sees: "The hairy and downy woodpeckers drum on dry branches and on the loose flakes of maple bark, and purple finches sing merrily from the spruces."

Subjective or *impressionistic description*, on the other hand, conveys the writer's personal opinion or impression of the object, often in language rich in modifiers and figures of speech. A food critic describing a memorable meal would inevitably write about it impressionistically, using colorful or highly subjective language. (In fact, relatively few words in English can describe the subtleties of smell and taste in neutral terms.) In "A Woman on the Street," Jeannette Walls uses objective and subjective description techniques to capture a picture of her mother and what she sees as her dilemma.

Notice that with objective description, it is usually the person, place, or thing being described that stands out, whereas with subjective description the response of the person doing the describing is the most prominent feature. Most topics, however, lend themselves to both objective and subjective description, depending on the writer's purpose. You could write, for example, that you had "exactly four weeks" to finish a history term paper (objective) or that you had "all the time in the world" or "an outrageously short amount of time" (subjective). Each type of description can be accurate and useful in its own way.

Although descriptive writing can stand alone, and often does, it is also used with other types of writing. In a narrative, for example, descriptions provide the context for the story—and make the characters, settings, and events come alive. Description may also help to define an unusual object or animal, such as a giraffe, or to clarify the steps of a process, such as diagnosing an illness. Wherever it is used, good description creates vivid and specific pictures that clarify, create a mood, and build a dominant impression.

USING DESCRIPTION ACROSS THE DISCIPLINES

When writing essays in the academic disciplines, you will have many opportunities to use the strategy of description to both organize and strengthen the presentation of your ideas. To determine whether description is the right strategy for you in a particular paper, review the guidelines in Chapter 2 (Determining a Strategy for Developing Your Essay, pages 32–33). Consider the following examples:

History

1. **MAIN IDEA:** Roman medicine, while primitive in some ways, was in general very advanced.
2. **QUESTION:** What primitive beliefs and advanced thinking characterize Roman medicine?
3. **STRATEGY:** Description. The direction word *characterize* signals the need to describe Roman medical practices and beliefs.
4. **SUPPORTING STRATEGY:** Comparison and contrast might be used to set off Roman practices and beliefs from those in later periods of history.

Chemistry

1. **MAIN IDEA:** The chemical ingredients in acid rain are harmful to humans and the environment.
2. **QUESTION:** What are the components of acid rain?
3. **STRATEGY:** Description. The direction word *components* suggests the need for a description of acid rain, including as it does sulfuric acid, carbon monoxide, carbon dioxide, chlorofluorocarbons, and nitric acid.
4. **SUPPORTING STRATEGY:** Cause and effect might be used to show the harm caused by acid rain. Process analysis might be used to explain how acid rain develops.

Psychology

1. **MAIN IDEA:** Law enforcement officers who are under abnormal stress manifest certain symptoms.
2. **QUESTION:** What comprises the symptoms?
3. **STRATEGY:** Description. The direction word *comprises* suggests the need for a picture or description of the *symptoms*.
4. **SUPPORTING STRATEGY:** Comparison and contrast might be used to differentiate those officers suffering from stress. Process analysis might be used to explain how to carry out an examination to identify the symptoms of stress. Argumentation might be used to indicate the need for programs to test for excessive stress on the job.

SAMPLE STUDENT ESSAY USING DESCRIPTION AS A WRITING STRATEGY

Jim Tassé wrote the following essay while he was a student at the University of Vermont, where he majored in English and religion. Tassé hopes to teach eventually, perhaps at the college level, but his most immediate interests include biking and singing with a rock band. As his essay "Trailcheck" reveals, Tassé is an enthusiastic skier. His experience working on ski patrol during winter breaks provided him with the subject for a striking description.

Trailcheck
Jim Tassé

Context — early morning in January and preparations for Trailcheck

At a quarter to eight in the morning, the sharp cold of the midwinter night still hangs in the air of Smuggler's Notch. At the base of Madonna Mountain, we stamp our feet and turn up our collars while waiting for Dan to get the chairlift running. Trailcheck always begins with this cold, sleepy wait—but it can continue in many different ways. The ski patrol has to make this first run every morning to assess the trail conditions before the mountain opens—and you never know what to expect on top of the Mad Dog, Madonna Mountain. Sometimes we take our first run down the sweet, light powder that fell the night before; sometimes we have to ski the rock-hard boilerplate ice that formed when yesterday's mush froze. But there's always the cold—the dank, bleary cold of 8 a.m. in January.

Description of Trailcheck begins with explanation of what it is

Use of present tense gives immediacy to the description

I adjust my first-aid belt and heft my backpack up a little higher, cinching it tight. I shiver, and pull my hat down a bit

1

2

lower. I am sleepy, cold, and impatient. Dan's finally got the lift running, and the first two patrollers, Chuck and Ken, get on. Three more chairs get filled, and then there's me. Looks like I'm riding up alone. The chairlift jars me a little more awake as it hits the back of my boots. I sit down and am scooped into the air.

It's a cold ride up, and I snuggle my chin deep into my parka. The bumps of the chair going over the lift-tower rollers help keep me awake. Trees piled high and heavy with snow move silently past. Every so often, in sudden randomness, a branch lets go a slide and the air fills with snow dust as the avalanche crashes from branch to branch, finally landing with a soft thud on the ground. Snow dances in the air with kaleidoscopic colors, shining in the early daylight.

I imagine what it would have been like on the mountain on a similar day three hundred years ago. A day like this would have been just as beautiful, or maybe even more so—the silent mountain, all trees and cold and sunshine, with no men and no lifts. I think of the days when the fog rolls out of the notch, and the wind blows cold and damp, and the trees are close and dark in the mist, and I try to imagine how terrifyingly wild the mountain would have been centuries ago, before the white man came and installed the chairlift that takes me to the top so easily. I think how difficult it would have been to climb through the thick untamed forest that bristles out of the mountain's flanks, and I am glad I don't have to walk up Madonna this sleepy-eyed morning.

I watch the woods pass, looking for the trails of small animals scrolled around the trees. Skiing should be nice with all the new snow. Arriving at the top, I throw up the safety bar, tip my skis up, make contact, stand, and ski clear of the lift. The view from the mountaintop is incredible. I can see over the slopes of Stowe, where another patrol is running trail-check just as we are. Across the state, Mt. Washington hangs above the horizon like a mirage. Back toward Burlington, I can see the frozen lake sprawling like a white desert.

I toss my backpack full of lunch and books to Marty, who's going into the patrol shack to get the stove fired up. I stretch my legs a little as we share small talk, waiting for the mountain captain to say we can go down. I tighten my boots. Finally, Ken's radio crackles out the word, and I pull down my goggles and pole forward.

SAMPLE STUDENT ESSAY USING DESCRIPTION AS A WRITING STRATEGY

Opening sentence and two fragments following signal the end of the ride and the beginning of the Trailcheck

Wake up! The first run of the day. Trailcheck. Today the run is heaven—eight inches of light dry powder. My turns are relaxed giant slaloms that leave neat S's in the snow behind me. No need to worry about ice or rocks—the snow covers everything with an airy cushion that we float on, fly on, our skis barely on the ground. We split up at the first intersection, and I bear to the left, down the Glades. My skis gently hiss as they break the powder, splitting the snow like a boat on calm water. I blast through deep drifts of snow, sending gouts and geysers of snow up around me. The air sparkles with snow, breaking the light into flecks of color.

Strong action verbs bring the description alive

Contrast enhances description of the Trailcheck

What a day! Some mornings I ride up in fifteen-below-zero cold, only to ski down icy hardpack on which no new snow has fallen for days. There are rocks and other hazards to be noted and later marked with bamboo poles so skiers don't hit them. Fallen branches must be cleared from the trail. On days like that, when the snow is lousy and I have to worry about rocks gouging the bottoms of the skis, trail-check is work—cold, necessary work done too early in the morning. But when the run is like today, the suffering is worthwhile.

Dominant impression of ecstatic playfulness emerges

I yelp with pleasure as I launch myself off a knoll and gently land in the soft whiteness, blasting down a chute of untracked powder that empties out into a flatter run. I can hear the other patroller whooping and yelling with me in the distance. Turns are effortless; a tiny shift of weight and the skis respond like wings. I come over the next pitch, moving fast, and my skis hit an unseen patch of ice; my tails slide, too late to get the edge in, and POOF! I tumble into the snow in an explosion of snow dust. For a second I lie panting. Then I wallow in ecstasy, scooping the handfuls of powder over myself, the sweet light snow tingling in the air. After a moment I hop up and continue down, sluicing the S-turns on the whipped-cream powder.

Concluding comment sums up the writer's experience in one word

Reaching the patrol room, I click off my skis and stamp the snow from myself. No longer do I feel the night's cold breath in the air—just the sting of the melting snow on my face. Ken looks at me as I drip and glisten over my trail report, and asks: "Good run, Jim?"

I grin at him and say, "Beau-ti-ful!"

> **Analyzing Jim Tassé's Description Essay: Questions for Discussion**
>
> 1. How does Tassé support his dominant impression in this essay?
> 2. How does Tassé *show* that the mountain is beautiful rather than simply *say* that it is?
> 3. How and where does Tassé indicate the importance of a trailcheck?

SUGGESTIONS FOR USING DESCRIPTION AS A WRITING STRATEGY

As you plan, write, and revise your essay of description, be mindful of the writing process guidelines described in Chapter 2. Pay particular attention to the basic requirements and essential ingredients of this writing strategy.

▸ Planning Your Description Essay

Planning is an essential part of writing a good description essay. You can save yourself a great deal of work by taking the time to think about key building blocks of your essay before you actually begin to write.

DETERMINE A PURPOSE. Begin by determining your purpose: Are you trying to inform, express your emotions, persuade, or entertain? While it is not necessary, or even desirable, to state your purpose explicitly, it is necessary that you have one that your readers recognize. If your readers do not see a purpose in your writing, they may be tempted to respond by asking, "So what?" Making your reason for writing clear in the first place will help you avoid this pitfall.

USE DESCRIPTION IN THE SERVICE OF AN IDEA. Your readers will want to know why you chose to describe what you did. You should always write description with a thesis in mind, an idea you want to convey to your readers. For example, you might describe a canoe trip as one of both serenity and exhilarating danger, which for you symbolize the contrasting aspects of nature. In his essay "A View from the Bridge" (see pages 8–10), Cherokee Paul McDonald uses description in the service of an idea, and that idea is description itself: McDonald needs to describe a fish so that a blind boy can "see" it. In the process of describing, the author comes to an epiphany: The act of describing the fish brings him closer to the essence of it. He realizes then that he has received from the boy more than he has given.

SHOW, DON'T TELL: USE SPECIFIC NOUNS AND ACTION VERBS. Inexperienced writers often believe that adjectives and adverbs are the basis for effective descriptions. They're right in one sense, but not wholly so. Although

Diagram: central node "talk" connected to: yell, sputter, declaim, gossip, gab, utter, scream, whisper, speak, spill, confer, babble, harangue, blab, lisp, lecture.

strong adjectives and adverbs are crucial, description also depends on well-chosen nouns and verbs. *Vehicle* is not nearly as descriptive as something more specific—*Jeep, snowmobile,* or *Honda Civic.* Similarly, the verb *talk* does far less to describe the *way* something is said than do any of a host of possible substitutes (see the diagram above). The more specific and strong you make your nouns and verbs, the more lively and interesting your descriptions will be.

When you have difficulty thinking of specific action nouns and verbs to use, reach for a thesaurus—but only if you are sure you can discern the best word for your purpose. Most word-processing programs have a thesaurus utility, and there are many reasonable versions online as well. A thesaurus will help you keep your descriptions from getting repetitive and will be invaluable when you need to find a specific word with just the right meaning.

▶ Organizing Your Description Essay

CREATE A DOMINANT IMPRESSION. After generating as many details as possible describing your subject, reread them and select those that will be most helpful in developing a dominant impression. Suppose that you wish to depict the hospital emergency room as a place of great tension. You will then naturally choose details to reinforce that sense of tension: the worried looks on the faces of a couple sitting in the corner, the quick movements of the medical staff as they tend to a patient on a wheeled stretcher, the urgent whisperings of two interns out in the hallway, the incessant paging of Dr. Thomas. If the dominant impression you want to create is of the emergency room's sterility, however, you will choose different details: the smell of disinfectant, the spotless white uniforms of the staff members, the stainless steel tables and chairs, the gleaming instruments the nurse hands to the physician.

ORGANIZE YOUR DETAILS TO CREATE A VIVID PICTURE. Once you have decided which details to include and which to leave out, you need to arrange your details in an order that serves your purpose and is easy for the reader to follow.

In describing some subjects, it might make sense to imagine what the reader would experience first. A description of an emergency room, for example, could begin at the entrance, move through the waiting area, pass the registration desk, and proceed into the treatment cubicles. A description of a restaurant kitchen might conjure up the smells and sounds that escape through the swinging doors even before moving on to the first glimpse inside the kitchen.

Other patterns of organization include moving from general to specific, from smallest to largest, from least to most important, or from the usual to the unusual. Keep in mind that the last details you present will probably stay in the reader's mind the longest and that the first details will also have special force.

Before you begin your first draft, you may find it useful to sketch out an outline of your description. Here's a sample outline for Bernd Heinrich's description of his trek through the late winter landscape in search of owls (page 126):

Description of Shelburne Bog

Dominant impression: Comfort with the natural surroundings

Paragraph 1: Snow-crusted landscape in mid-March

Paragraph 2: Activity and sounds of the birds (e.g., woodpeckers, finches, chickadees, and red-winged blackbirds) described from the edge of the woods

Paragraph 3: Activity and sounds inside the pine forest behind the speaker, culminating with the familiar call of the owl

Such an outline can remind you of the dominant impression you want to create and can suggest which specific details may be most useful to you.

Revising and Editing Your Description Essay

As the author, you are familiar with the scenes, people, or items you are describing. It might be helpful to find a fellow classmate to read your draft, to ensure that they can vividly 'see' whatever you are describing through your writing. The guidelines on page 36 will help to guide their review, just as the tips on the twelve common writing problems in Chapter 16 will help you in your own self-review.

> **Questions for Revising and Editing: Description**
>
> 1. Do I have a clear purpose for my description? Have I answered the "so what" question?
> 2. Is the subject of my description interesting and relevant to my audience?
> 3. What senses have I chosen to use to describe it? For example, what does it look like, sound like, or smell like? Does it have a texture or taste that is important to mention?
> 4. Which details must I include in my essay? Which are irrelevant or distracting to my purpose and should be discarded?
> 5. Have I achieved the dominant impression I wish to leave with my audience?
> 6. Does the organization I have chosen for my essay make it easy for the reader to follow my description?
> 7. How carefully have I chosen my descriptive words? Are my nouns and verbs strong and specific?
> 8. Have I used figurative language, if appropriate, to further strengthen my description?
> 9. Does my paper contain any errors in grammar, punctuation, or mechanics? Is my sentence style as clear, smooth, and persuasive as possible?

A Woman on the Street

JEANNETTE WALLS

Jeannette Walls was born in 1960 in Phoenix, Arizona, and later moved with her family to San Francisco, California, to Battle Mountain, Nevada, and to Welch, West Virginia. At age seventeen she entered Barnard College in New York City, and she graduated with honors in 1984. After college she interned and then became a reporter for the *Phoenix*, a small newspaper in Brooklyn, New York. Walls is best known for her gossip reporting on "The Scoop" on MSNBC (1998–2007) and for *The Glass Castle* (2005), a memoir of her childhood years growing up in a nomadic, and at times homeless, family. *The Glass Castle* remained on the *New York Times* bestseller list for more than 200 weeks, sold over 2.5 million copies, was translated into twenty-two languages, and has been optioned as a movie by Paramount. Walls has written three other books, *Dish: The Inside Story on the World of Gossip* (2000), *Half-Broke Horses: A True-Life Novel* (2009), and *The Silver Star* (2013).

Photo by Andrew Testa/REX/Newscom

In "A Woman on the Street," the first chapter of *The Glass Castle*, Walls describes a chance sighting of her mother scavenging in a Dumpster in New York City and a subsequent meeting to try to help "improve" her mother's homeless life.

Preparing to Read

Do you ever wonder about the homeless, their lives before becoming homeless, and their beliefs and values? Does the way we think about the homeless depend mostly on how we describe them, or are there real aspects of their lives that support our impressions? If you know someone who is homeless, what qualities does that person possess that others might not know?

I was sitting in a taxi, wondering if I had overdressed for the evening, when I looked out the window and saw Mom rooting through a Dumpster. It was just after dark. A blustery March wind whipped the steam coming out of the manholes, and people hurried along the sidewalks with their collars turned up. I was stuck in traffic two blocks from the party where I was heading.

Mom stood fifteen feet away. She had tied rags around her shoulders to keep out the spring chill and was picking through the trash while her dog, a black-and-white terrier mix, played at her feet. Mom's gestures were all familiar—the way she tilted her head and thrust out her lower lip when studying items of potential value that she'd hoisted out of the Dumpster, the way her eyes widened with childish glee when she found something she liked. Her long hair was streaked with gray, tangled and matted, and her eyes had sunk deep into their sockets, but still she reminded me of the mom she'd been when I was a kid, swan-diving off cliffs and painting in the desert and reading Shakespeare aloud. Her cheekbones were still high and strong, but the skin was parched and ruddy from all those winters and summers exposed to the elements. To the people walking by, she probably looked like any of the thousands of homeless people in New York City.

It had been months since I laid eyes on Mom, and when she looked up, I was overcome with panic that she'd see me and call out my name, and that someone on the way to the same party would spot us together and Mom would introduce herself and my secret would be out.

I slid down in the seat and asked the driver to turn around and take me home to Park Avenue.

The taxi pulled up in front of my building, the doorman held the door for me, and the elevator man took me up to my floor. My husband was working late, as he did most nights, and the apartment was silent except for the click of my heels on the polished wood floor. I was still rattled from seeing Mom, the unexpectedness of coming across her, the sight of her rooting happily through the Dumpster. I put some Vivaldi on, hoping the music would settle me down.

I looked around the room. There were the turn-of-the-century bronze- and-silver vases and the old books with worn leather spines that I'd collected at flea markets. There were the Georgian maps I'd had framed, the Persian rugs, and the overstuffed leather armchair I liked to sink into at the end of the day. I'd tried to make a home for myself here, tried to turn the apartment into the sort of place where the person I wanted to be would live. But I could never enjoy the room without worrying about Mom and Dad huddled on a sidewalk grate somewhere. I fretted about them, but I was embarrassed by them, too, and ashamed of myself for wearing pearls and living on Park Avenue while my parents were busy keeping warm and finding something to eat.

What could I do? I'd tried to help them countless times, but Dad would insist they didn't need anything, and Mom would ask for something silly, like a perfume atomizer or a membership in a health club. They said that they were living the way they wanted to.

After ducking down in the taxi so Mom wouldn't see me, I hated myself—hated my antiques, my clothes, and my apartment. I had to do something, so I called a friend of Mom's and left a message. It was our system of staying in touch. It always took Mom a few days to get back to me, but when I heard from her, she sounded, as always, cheerful and casual, as though we'd had lunch the day before. I told her I wanted to see her and suggested she drop by the apartment, but she wanted to go to a restaurant. She loved eating out, so we agreed to meet for lunch at her favorite Chinese restaurant.

Mom was sitting at a booth, studying the menu, when I arrived. She'd made an effort to fix herself up. She wore a bulky gray sweater with only a few light stains, and black leather men's shoes. She'd washed her face, but her neck and temples were still dark with grime.

She waved enthusiastically when she saw me. "It's my baby girl!" she called out. I kissed her cheek. Mom had dumped all the plastic packets of soy sauce and duck sauce and hot-and-spicy mustard from the table into her purse. Now she emptied a wooden bowl of dried noodles into it as well. "A little snack for later on," she explained.

We ordered. Mom chose the Seafood Delight. "You know how I love my seafood," she said.

She started talking about Picasso. She'd seen a retrospective of his work and decided he was hugely overrated. All the cubist stuff was gimmicky, as far as she was concerned. He hadn't really done anything worthwhile after his Rose Period.

"I'm worried about you," I said. "Tell me what I can do to help."

Her smile faded. "What makes you think I need your help?"

"I'm not rich," I said. "But I have some money. Tell me what it is you need."

She thought for a moment. "I could use an electrolysis treatment."

"Be serious."

"I am serious. If a woman looks good, she feels good."

"Come on, Mom." I felt my shoulders tightening up, the way they invariably did during these conversations. "I'm talking about something that could help you change your life, make it better."

"You want to help me change my life?" Mom asked. "I'm fine. You're the one who needs help. Your values are all confused."

"Mom, I saw you picking through trash in the East Village a few days ago."

"Well, people in this country are too wasteful. It's my way of recycling." She took a bite of her Seafood Delight. "Why didn't you say hello?"

"I was too ashamed, Mom. I hid."

Mom pointed her chopsticks at me. "You see?" she said. "Right there. That's exactly what I'm saying. You're way too easily embarrassed. Your father and I are who we are. Accept it."

"And what am I supposed to tell people about my parents?"

"Just tell the truth," Mom said. "That's simple enough."

Thinking Critically about the Text

"A Woman on the Street" is a description of Walls's mother, but if you reflect on what she has written, you soon realize that the essay is equally about her as a daughter. Explain how Walls is able to "turn the tables" on herself, as it were.

Questions on Subject

1. Do you think Walls's mother is happy? Why or why not?
2. Do you think Walls herself is happy? Why or why not?
3. Is Walls's mother against material possessions? How do you know?
4. Why do you suppose Walls's mother refuses to go to her daughter's apartment?
5. In the end, what point is her mother trying to make Walls understand? What does she mean when she says to her daughter, "I'm fine. You're the one that needs help. Your values are all confused" (paragraph 20)? Are Walls's values confused? Explain.

Questions on Strategy

1. How does Walls describe her mother? What details does she reveal about her?
2. How does Walls describe herself? What details does she reveal about herself?
3. How does Walls use comparison and contrast in this selection? (Glossary: *Comparison and Contrast*)
4. Is Walls's essay arranged inductively or deductively? Explain. (Glossary: *Deduction*; *Induction*)
5. In your opinion, is Walls a reliable narrator? What evidence does she present to indicate that she is or is not telling the story truthfully to the best of her ability?
6. Why do you think Walls makes paragraph 4 a single sentence?

Questions on Diction and Vocabulary

1. Walls uses certain words and phrases to quickly draw distinctions between the life her mother is leading and the life she herself is leading. Point out a half dozen of those terms and phrases and explain how they work as a kind of descriptive shorthand.

2. In paragraph 16, is Walls's mother being straightforward or ironic when she says that she would like "an electrolysis treatment"? How do you know? (Glossary: *Irony*)

3. What do you think about Walls's title for this selection? Do you think it is the best title? Can you offer some alternatives that you think would work better? (Glossary: *Title*)

Description in Action

Think about your topic — the person, place, thought, or concept that lies at the center of your descriptive essay. Make a list of all the details that you could gather about it using your five senses, as well as those that simply come to mind when you consider your topic. Determine a dominant impression that you would like to create and then choose from your list the details that will best help you form it. Your instructor may wish to have you and your classmates go over your lists together and discuss how effective your choices will be in building dominant impressions.

Writing Suggestions

1. In paragraph 6, Walls says of her own apartment, "I tried to make a home for myself here, tried to turn the apartment into the sort of place where the person I wanted to be would live." Write an essay in which you consider the idea that homelessness might be as much a state of mind as a physical reality. In other words, does one have to be without a home to be homeless? Can one be homeless living in a wonderful house with all its creature comforts? What is it that makes a person have a sense of belonging, and a sense of warmth, comfort, safety, and satisfaction? Describe that life.

2. Walls's writing demonstrates that a writer need not include a lot of details to paint a picture, only the ones that will do the job. For example, she describes her own apartment in the first three sentences of paragraph 6 in a very revealing way. Describe your own room, whether at school or at home, using a minimum of details to convey a sense of the place in the manner that you want your reader to know it. Start with a list of all the objects that might be included and then winnow the list to the most telling and essential details for your purpose. Finally, be sure to make your description not an exercise in selectivity and brevity alone but one which, like Walls's essay, is part of a narrative that relies on your description to make your story work.

The Barrio

ROBERT RAMÍREZ

Robert Ramírez was born in 1949 and was raised in Edinburg, Texas, near the Mexican border. He graduated from the University of Texas–Pan American and then worked in several communications-related jobs before joining KGBT-TV in Harlingen, Texas, where he was an anchor. He then moved to finance and worked for a time in banking and as a development officer responsible for alumni fund-raising for his alma mater.

Ramírez's knowledge of the barrio allows him to paint an affectionate portrait of barrio life that nevertheless has a hard edge. His barrio is colorful but not romantic, and his description raises important societal issues as it describes the vibrant community. "The Barrio" was originally published in *Pain and Promise: The Chicano Today* (1972), edited by Edward Simmen.

Courtesy of Robert Ramirez

Preparing to Read

Describe the neighborhood in which you grew up or the most memorable neighborhood you have encountered. Did you like it? Why or why not? How strong was the sense of community between neighbors? How did it contrast with other neighborhoods nearby?

1   The train, its metal wheels squealing as they spin along the silvery tracks, rolls slower now. Through the gaps between the cars blinks a streetlamp, and this pulsing light on a barrio streetcorner beats slower, like a weary heartbeat, until the train shudders to a halt, the light goes out, and the barrio is deep asleep.

2   Throughout Aztlán (the Nahuatl term meaning "land to the north"), trains grumble along the edges of a sleeping people. From Lower California, through the blistering Southwest, down the Rio Grande to the muddy Gulf, the darkness and mystery of dreams engulf communities fenced off by railroads, canals, and expressways. Paradoxical communities, isolated from the rest of the town by concrete columned monuments of progress, yet stranded in the past. They are surrounded by change. It eludes their reach, in their own backyards, and the people, unable and unwilling to see the future, or even touch the present, perpetuate the past.

3   Leaning from the expressway or jolting across the tracks, one enters a different physical world permeated by a different attitude. The physical dimensions are impressive. It is a large section of town which extends for

fifteen blocks north and south along the tracks, and then advances eastward, thinning into nothingness beyond the city limits. Within the invisible (yet sensible) walls of the barrio are many, many people living in too few houses. The homes, however, are much more numerous than on the outside.

Members of the barrio describe the entire area as their home. It is a home, but it is more than this. The barrio is a refuge from the harshness and the coldness of the Anglo world. It is a forced refuge. The leprous people are isolated from the rest of the community and contained in their section of town. The stoical pariahs of the barrio accept their fate, and from the angry seeds of rejection grow the flowers of closeness between outcasts, not the thorns of bitterness and the mad desire to flee. There is no want to escape, for the feeling of the barrio is known only to its inhabitants, and the material needs of life can also be found here.

> The barrio is a refuge from the harshness and the coldness of the Anglo world.

The *tortillería* fires up its machinery three times a day, producing steaming, round, flat slices of barrio bread. In the winter, the warmth of the tortilla factory is a wool *sarape* in the chilly morning hours, but in the summer, it unbearably toasts every noontime customer.

The *panadería* sends its sweet messenger aroma down the dimly lit street, announcing the arrival of fresh, hot sugary *pan dulce.*

The small corner grocery serves the meal-to-meal needs of customers, and the owner, a part of the neighborhood, willingly gives credit to people unable to pay cash for foodstuffs.

The barbershop is a living room with hydraulic chairs, radio, and television, where old friends meet and speak of life as their salted hair falls aimlessly about them.

The pool hall is a junior level country club where 'chucos, strangers in their own land, get together to shoot pool and rap, while veterans, unaware of the cracking, popping balls on the green felt, complacently play dominoes beneath rudely hung *Playboy* foldouts.

The *cantina* is the night spot of the barrio. It is the country club and the den where the rites of puberty are enacted. Here the young become men. It is in the taverns that the young dude shows his *machismo* through the quantity of beer he can hold, the stories of *rucas* he has had, and his willingness and ability to defend his image against hardened and scarred old lions.

No, there is no frantic wish to flee. It would be absurd to leave the familiar and nervously step into the strange and cold Anglo community when the needs of the Chicano can be met in the barrio.

The barrio is closeness. From the family living unit, familial relationships stretch out to immediate neighbors, down the block, around the corner, and to all parts of the barrio. The feeling of family, a rare and treasurable sentiment, pervades and accounts for the inability of the people to leave. The barrio is this attitude manifested on the countenances of the people, on the faces of their homes, and in the gaiety of their gardens.

The color-splashed homes arrest your eyes, arouse your curiosity, and make you wonder what life scenes are being played out in them. The flimsy, brightly colored, wood-frame houses ignore no neon-brilliant color. Houses trimmed in orange, chartreuse, lime-green, yellow, and mixtures of these and other hues beckon the beholder to reflect on the peculiarity of each home. Passing through this land is refreshing like Brubeck, not narcotizing like revolting rows of similar houses, which neither offend nor please.

In the evenings, the porches and front yards are occupied with men calmly talking over the noise of children playing baseball in the unpaved extension of the living room, while the women cook supper or gossip with female neighbors as they water their *jardines*. The gardens mutely echo the expressive verses of the colorful houses. The denseness of multicolored plants and trees gives the house the appearance of an oasis or a tropical island hideaway, sheltered from the rest of the world.

Fences are common in the barrio, but they are fences and not the walls of the Anglo community. On the western side of town, the high wooden fences between houses are thick, impenetrable walls, built to keep the neighbors at bay. In the barrio, the fences may be rusty, wire contraptions or thick green shrubs. In either case you can see through them and feel no sense of intrusion when you cross them.

Many lower-income families of the barrio manage to maintain a comfortable standard of living through the communal action of family members who contribute their wages to the head of the family. Economic need creates interdependence and closeness. Small barefooted boys sell papers on cool, dark Sunday mornings, deny themselves pleasantries, and give their earnings to *mamá*. The older the child, the greater the responsibility to help the head of the household provide for the rest of the family.

There are those, too, who for a number of reasons have not achieved a relative sense of financial security. Perhaps it results from too many children too soon, but it is the homes of these people and their situation that numbs rather than charms. Their houses, aged and bent, oozing children, are fissures in the horn of plenty. Their wooden homes may have brick-pattern asbestos tile on the outer walls, but the tile is not convincing.

Unable to pay city taxes or incapable of influencing the city to live up to its duty to serve all the citizens, the poorer barrio families remain trapped in the nineteenth century and survive as best they can. The backyards have well-worn paths to the outhouses, which sit near the alley. Running water is considered a luxury in some parts of the barrio. Decent drainage is usually unknown, and when it rains, the water stands for days, an incubator of health hazards and an avoidable nuisance. Streets, costly to pave, remain rough, rocky trails. Tires do not last long, and the constant rattling and shaking grind away a car's life and spread dust through screen windows.

The houses and their *jardines*, the jollity of the people in an adverse world, the brightly feathered alarm clock pecking away at supper and cautiously eyeing the children playing nearby, produce a mystifying sensation at finding the noble savage alive in the twentieth century. It is easy to look at the positive qualities of life in the barrio, and look at them with a distantly envious feeling. One wishes to experience the feelings of the barrio and not the hardships. Remembering the illness, the hunger, the feeling of time running out on you, the walls, both real and imagined, reflecting on living in the past, one finds his envy becoming more elusive, until it has vanished altogether.

Back now beyond the tracks, the train creaks and groans, the cars jostle each other down the track, and as the light begins its pulsing, the barrio, with all its meanings, greets a new dawn with yawns and restless stretchings.

Thinking Critically about the Text

Does Ramírez's essay leave you with a positive or negative image of the barrio? Is it a place you would like to live, visit, or avoid? Explain your answer.

Questions on Subject

1. Based on Ramírez's essay, what is the barrio? Why do you think that Ramírez uses the image of the train to introduce and close his essay about the barrio?

2. Why do you think Ramírez refers to the barrios of the Southwest as "paradoxical communities" (paragraph 2)?

3. In paragraph 4, Ramírez states that residents consider the barrio something more than a home. What does he mean? In what ways is it more than just a place where they live?

4. Why are the color schemes of the houses in the barrio striking? How do they contrast with houses in other areas of town? (Glossary: *Comparison and Contrast*)

5. Many of the barrio residents are able to achieve financial security. How are they able to do this? What is life like for those who cannot?

Questions on Strategy

1. Explain Ramírez's use of the imagery of walls and fences to describe a sense of cultural isolation. What might this imagery symbolize?

2. Ramírez uses several metaphors throughout his essay. (Glossary: *Figures of Speech*) Identify them and discuss how they contribute to the essay.

3. Ramírez begins his essay with a relatively positive picture of the barrio but ends on a more disheartening note. (Glossary: *Beginnings/Endings*) Why has he organized his essay this way? What might the effect have been if he had reversed the images?

4. Ramírez goes into detail about the many groups living in the barrio. How does his subtle use of division and classification add to his description of the barrio? (Glossary: *Classification; Division*) In what ways do the groups he identifies contribute to the unity of life in the barrio?

5. Ramírez invokes such warm images of the barrio that his statement that its inhabitants do not wish to leave seems benign. In the end, however, it has a somewhat ominous ring. How does the description of the barrio have two components, one good and one bad? What are the two sides of the barrio's embrace for the residents?

Questions on Diction and Vocabulary

1. Ramírez uses Spanish phrases throughout his essay. Why do you suppose he uses them? What is their effect on the reader? He also uses the words *home*, *refuge*, *family*, and *closeness*. In what ways, if any, are they essential to his purpose? (Glossary: *Purpose*)

2. Ramírez calls barrio residents "the leprous people" (paragraph 4). What does the word *leprous* connote in the context of this essay? (Glossary: *Connotation/Denotation*) Why do you think Ramírez chose to use such a strong word to communicate the segregation of the community?

3. In paragraph 6, Ramírez uses personification when he calls the aroma of freshly baked sweet rolls a "messenger" who announces the arrival of the baked goods. Cite other words or phrases that Ramírez uses to give human characteristics to the barrio.

Description in Action

1. Using action verbs can make a major difference in the quality of your writing. Review a draft of a descriptive essay that you have written and look for at least three weak verbs — verbs that do not add very much descriptive punch — and make a list of at least three alternatives you could use in place of each one. Be sure that the meaning of each of your alternative action verbs supports your meaning and fits the context in which you use it.

2. Examine the photo on this page carefully. Based on the visual details in the photograph, what can you say about the community? Which details suggest the area's ethnicity and socioeconomic status? What can you say about the pace of life as depicted in the photograph? From what you see, is this an appealing neighborhood, in your judgment? How does this scene differ from the portrait of a barrio that Ramírez paints in his essay?

TIM SLOAN/AFP/Getty Images

Writing Suggestions

1. Ramírez frames his essay with the image of a train rumbling past the sleeping residents. Using Ramírez's essay as a model, write a descriptive essay about the place you currently live and use a metaphorical image to frame your essay. (Glossary: *Figures of Speech*) What image is both a part of where you live and an effective metaphor for it?

2. Write a comparison and contrast essay in which you compare where you live now with another residence. (Glossary: *Comparison and Contrast*) Where are you more comfortable? What about your current surroundings do you like? What do you dislike? How does it compare with your hometown, your first apartment, or another place you have lived? If and when you move on, where do you hope to go?

Hiding from Animals

HELEN MACDONALD

Writer, naturalist, and historian Helen Macdonald was born in 1970 in the town of Chertsey, England. After studying biology at the University of Cambridge, she worked in falcon research and conservation in Wales and the Arab Emirates and as a professional falconer. She has been a research fellow at Jesus College, Cambridge and a lecturer at the Department of History and Philosophy of Science at the University of Cambridge. Her most recent book, the international bestseller *H Is for Hawk*, part memoir and part biography of the naturalist T.H. White, was named one of the best books of the year by the *New York Times*, NPR, *The Oprah Magazine*, and *Slate*, among others. Macdonald's other books include *Falcon* (2006) and *Shaler's Fish* (2016), a collection of poems.

Anthony Harvey/Getty Images

Macdonald currently lives near Newmarket with her parrot Birdoole. She writes a monthly column, "On Nature," for the *New York Times*, where the essay below originally appeared on July 14, 2015. In a recent interview, she noted, "There's been a renaissance in nature writing in the U.K. over the last few years, and I'm delighted to be part of it, though saddened that much of what we are all writing about is fast disappearing or already gone. It's hard not to be elegiac when faced with the raw facts of biodiversity decline in Europe over the last few decades." As you read, consider this statement and notice what words and strategies Macdonald uses to create this elegiac tone.

Preparing to Read

How do you feel about nature? Do you enjoy spending time in the outdoors? If so, do you prefer activities like running and hiking, or are you more drawn to sitting still and observing? Either way, describe how these activities make you feel. If you don't like nature, describe those feelings: do you feel bored, uncomfortable, or frightened?

I'm walking beside a hedge of tangled dog roses in a nature preserve in eastern England, toward a hide, a building whose purpose is to make me disappear. This one is a rustic box with bench seats and narrow slits in the wall. Half-hidden by branches, it looks like a small, weather-beaten wooden shed. I've made myself disappear in hides for as long as I can remember; structures like this are found in nature preserves all over the world, and they seem as natural here as trees and open water. Even so, a familiar, nervous apprehension flares up as I reach for the door, so I pause for a few seconds before opening it and walk inside, where the air is hot and dark and smells of dust and wood preservative.

Alone, I sit on a bench and lower a wooden window blind to make a bright rectangle in the darkness; as my eyes adjust, I can see through it to a shallow lagoon under cumulus clouds. I scan the scene with binoculars, ticking off species—three shoveler ducks, two little egrets, a common tern—but my mind is elsewhere, puzzling over that odd sense of apprehension, trying to work out what causes it.

Perhaps it is partly the knowledge that wildlife hides are not innocent of history. They evolved from photographic blinds, which in turn were based on structures designed to put people closer to animals in order to kill them: duck blinds, deer stands, tree platforms for shooting big cats. Hunters have shaped modern nature appreciation in myriad unacknowledged ways, even down to the tactics used to bring animals into view. As hunters bait deer and decoy ducks, so preserve managers create shallow feeding pools that concentrate wading birds near hides, or set up feeding stations for wary nocturnal mammals. In the Highlands of Scotland, one celebrated hide gives visitors a 95 percent chance of seeing rare pine martens—lithe, tree-climbing predators—munching on piles of peanuts.

What you see from hides is supposed to be true reality: animals behaving perfectly naturally because they do not know they are being observed. But turning yourself into a pair of eyes in a darkened box distances you from the all-encompassing landscape around the hide, reinforcing a divide between human and natural worlds, encouraging us to think that animals and plants should be looked at, not interacted with. Sometimes the window in front of me resembles nothing so much as a television screen.

To witness wild animals behaving naturally, you don't need to be invisible. As scientists studying meerkats and chimps have shown, with time you can habituate them to your presence. But hiding is a habit that is hard to break. There is a dubious satisfaction in the subterfuge of watching things that cannot see you, and it's deeply embedded in our culture. When wild animals unexpectedly appear close by and seem unbothered by our presence, we can feel as flustered and unsure about how to behave as teenagers at a dance.

Two years ago, I was walking with my friend Christina through a park in a small English town when characters I've only ever seen in bird hides began to appear: camouflage-clad photographers with 300-millimeter lenses and expressions of urgent concentration. We looked to where the cameras were pointed, and were astonished. Three meters away, two of

Britain's most elusive mammals were swimming in the shallow river running through the park. Otters! They didn't seem to see us; they certainly didn't care.

Their wet flanks gleamed like tar as they rolled in the water. They broke the surface to crunch fish in their sharp white teeth, showering droplets from their stiff whiskers, then slipped back beneath the surface to swim down the river, the photographers chasing them like paparazzi and intermittently running backward because the lenses they'd brought were the wrong ones for such close views. It was thrilling. We followed the otters downstream and stopped by a woman with a toddler and a baby in a stroller, who were watching them, too. She told me she loved these otters. They were part of her town. Part of her local community. They'd eaten all the expensive carp from the fishpond in the big house, she said, amused. Then she tilted her head at the photographers. "Aren't they weird?" she asked. Outside the hide, they looked faintly ridiculous, so accustomed to their binoculars, camouflage and high-zoom lenses that they felt compelled to use them even when they were unnecessary.

Hides are places designed for watching wildlife, but they are equally rewarding places to watch people who watch wildlife and to study their strange social behavior. One reason I hesitated before entering the little hide is that I was worried there would be other people in it: Walking into a crowded hide is rather like arriving late at a live theatrical performance and trying to find your seat. There are unspoken rules in hides. As in a theater or a library, you are required to be silent, or to speak in a low murmur. Some rules are to prevent animals' detecting your presence—a general prohibition on telephone calls, slamming the door, extending hands out the window. But others are more curious, stemming from a particular problem: Your job in a hide is to pretend you are not there, and when there is more than one person in the hide, the sense of disembodiment that the trick relies on is threatened. Regular visitors to hides often solve this conundrum spatially. When she started visiting hides for the first time, my friend Christina wondered why people chose to sit at the far edges, leaving the seats with the best view unoccupied. "I thought it was self-sacrificing English etiquette," she said, "before I realized that people sat at the far sides of the hide because they wanted to be as far from everyone else as possible."

In the hide, there is a constant monitoring of others' expertise as the inhabitants listen to one another's muttered conversations about the things outside—and it can be agonizing when they get things wrong. I remember the chill in the air one spring day in Suffolk after a man confidently told his companion that what he was watching was a water vole. Everyone else in the hide knew this lumbering creature with a long tail was a large brown rat. No one said anything. One man coughed. Another snorted. The tension was unbearable. With true British reserve, no one was comfortable correcting his mistake and lessening him in the eyes of his friend. A few people couldn't bear the atmosphere and left the hide. It is always a relief when you open a hide door and find you are alone.

The uses of hides are as various as their inhabitants. You can sit with a camera hoping for the perfect shot of a passing marsh hawk or owl. You can sit with a proficient naturalist and hear whispered identification tips, or use it as a place to sit down midway through a long walk. Most people sit and scan the view with binoculars for a few minutes before deciding there is nothing of sufficient interest or rarity to keep them there. But there is another kind of hide-watching that I am increasingly learning to love. It is when you embrace the possibility that you will see little or nothing of interest. You literally wait and see. Sitting in the dark for an hour or two and looking at the world through a hole in a wall requires a meditative patience. You have given yourself time to watch clouds drift from one side of the sky to the other and cast moving shadows across 90 minutes of open water. A sleeping snipe, its long bill tucked into pale-tipped scapular feathers and its body pressed against rushes striped with patterns of light and shade, wakes, raises its wings and stretches. A heron as motionless as a marble statue for minutes on end makes a cobra-strike to catch a fish. The longer you sit there, the more you become abstracted from this place, and yet fixed to it. The sudden appearance of a deer at the lake's shore, or a flight of ducks tipping and whiffling down to splash on sunlit water, becomes treasure, through the simple fact of the passing of time.

Thinking Critically about the Text

What is Macdonald's purpose in writing this essay? How does she engage readers who may not already be especially interested in the natural world?

Questions on Subject

1. What is a *hide*? What is a *photographic blind*? What are the purposes of these structures?

2. "I've made myself disappear in hides for as long as I can remember," Macdonald writes in her first paragraph. What is she disappearing from?

3. In paragraph 4, Macdonald says this about her experience in a hide: "Sometimes the window in front of me resembles nothing so much as a television screen." What conflict is she suggesting here?

4. What are the unspoken rules in hides (paragraph 8)? Why do these rules exist?

5. Macdonald discusses several types of hiding in this essay. List as many as you can find.

Questions on Strategy

1. Macdonald writes from the first person point of view. Why do you think she chose this perspective? (Glossary: *Point of View*)
2. What is Macdonald's thesis, and where do you find it stated? (Glossary: *Thesis*)
3. In paragraphs 6 and 7, Macdonald narrates an experience she had with her friend Christina. Where else does she use narrative in the essay, and what does it accomplish?
4. Where does Macdonald use comparison in the essay, and what is the purpose of these comparisons? How do they help readers better understand her subject? (Glossary: *Comparison/Contrast*)
5. Macdonald begins the essay feeling apprehension (paragraph 1) but ends it describing what she sees as "treasure" (10). How would the essay be different if she had begun by describing the beauty and peace she experiences in the blind? (Glossary: *Beginnings/Endings*)

Questions on Diction and Vocabulary

1. Macdonald uses several phrases that suggest magic in this essay, including "a building whose purpose is to make me disappear" (paragraph 1) and "turning yourself into a pair of eyes in a darkened box" (4). How do these phrases contribute to the dominant impression she is trying to create? (Glossary: *Figurative Language*)
2. In paragraph 6, Macdonald mentions "camouflage-clad photographers with 300-millimeter lenses and expressions of urgent concentration." What is her attitude toward photographers and how they interact with nature? Where in the essay do you see evidence of this attitude?
3. The last sentence of the essay includes the word *whiffling*. Did you know this word before reading this essay, and if not, were you able to determine its meaning from context? Find any other words in the essay you don't know and look up their meanings.

Description in Action

Macdonald mentions many species in this essay. But she only describes otters, a snipe, and a heron in detail. What do these detailed descriptions add to her essay? Pick one of the other species she mentions, such as deer, meerkats, rats, or owls. Write a description of one of these creatures. Would adding this description change the power of the essay? Why or why not?

Writing Suggestions

1. In paragraph 9, Macdonald tells of overhearing a man incorrectly identify an animal, writing that "no one was comfortable correcting his mistake and lessening him in the eyes of his friend." Recall a time when you witnessed someone speak as an authority but get the facts wrong. Did you correct that person? Why or why not? Write an essay describing the circumstances and the attitudes of everyone present. Be sure to use specific details to help your readers understand how you felt and how you imagine the speaker and onlookers must have felt.

2. Describe something that you love to watch. It could be creatures in nature or nature itself, as in Macdonald's essay. It could be a specific sport, or ballet, or children in a playground, or the flames of a campfire, or the construction of a building. Write an essay in which you explore why you enjoy watching this activity or thing. Use Macdonald's essay as a model to examine both your own motivations and the risks and rewards involved. Use sensory details and strong verbs to create your dominant impression.

Sister Flowers

MAYA ANGELOU

Best-selling author and poet Maya Angelou (1928–2014) was an educator, historian, actress, playwright, civil rights activist, producer, and director. She is best known as the author of *I Know Why the Caged Bird Sings* (1970), the first book in a series that constitutes her autobiography, and for "On the Pulse of the Morning," a characteristically optimistic poem on the need for personal and national renewal that she read at President Clinton's inauguration in 1993. Starting with her beginnings in St. Louis in 1928, Angelou's autobiography presents a joyful triumph over hardships that test her courage and threaten her spirit. It includes the titles *All God's Children Need Traveling Shoes* (1986), *Wouldn't Take Anything for My Journey Now* (1993), and *Heart of a Woman* (1997). The sixth book in the series, *A Song Flung Up to Heaven*, was published in 2002. Angelou reflects on her often difficult relationship with her mother in *Mom & Me & Mom* (2013). Several volumes of her poetry were collected in *Complete Collected Poems of Maya Angelou* in 1994.

© Syracuse Newspapers/Frank Ordonez/The Image Works

In the following excerpt from *I Know Why the Caged Bird Sings*, Angelou describes a family friend who had a major impact on her early life. As you read, notice the way Angelou describes Sister Flowers's physical presence, her stately manners, and the guidance she offered her as a youngster.

Preparing to Read

Think about a major crisis you have had to face. Was there someone who came to your aid, offering solid advice and comforting support? How would you describe that person? What physical and personality traits characterize that person?

1   For nearly a year [after I was raped], I sopped around the house, the Store, the school, and the church, like an old biscuit, dirty and inedible. Then I met, or rather got to know, the lady who threw me my first life line.

2   Mrs. Bertha Flowers was the aristocrat of Black Stamps. She had the grace of control to appear warm in the coldest weather, and on the Arkansas summer days it seemed she had a private breeze which swirled around, cooling her. She was thin without the taut look of wiry people, and her printed voile dresses and flowered hats were as right for her as denim overalls for a farmer. She was our side's answer to the richest white woman in town.

Her skin was a rich black that would have peeled like a plum if snagged, but then no one would have thought of getting close enough to Mrs. Flowers to ruffle her dress, let alone snag her skin. She didn't encourage familiarity. She wore gloves too.

I don't think I ever saw Mrs. Flowers laugh, but she smiled often. A slow widening of her thin black lips to show even, small white teeth, then the slow effortless closing. When she chose to smile on me, I always wanted to thank her. The action was so graceful and inclusively benign.

She was one of the few gentlewomen I have ever known, and has remained throughout my life the measure of what a human being can be.

Momma had a strange relationship with her. Most often when she passed on the road in front of the Store, she spoke to Momma in that soft yet carrying voice, "Good day, Mrs. Henderson." Momma responded with "How you, Sister Flowers?"

Mrs. Flowers didn't belong to our church, nor was she Momma's familiar. Why on earth did she insist on calling her Sister Flowers? Shame made me want to hide my face. Mrs. Flowers deserved better than to be called Sister. Then, Momma left out the verb. Why not ask, "How *are* you, *Mrs.* Flowers?" With the unbalanced passion of the young, I hated her for showing her ignorance to Mrs. Flowers. It didn't occur to me for many years that they were as alike as sisters, separated only by formal education.

Although I was upset, neither of the women was in the least shaken by what I thought an unceremonious greeting. Mrs. Flowers would continue her easy gait up the hill to her little bungalow, and Momma kept on shelling peas or doing whatever had brought her to the front porch.

Occasionally, though, Mrs. Flowers would drift off the road and down to the Store and Momma would say to me, "Sister, you go on and play." As she left I would hear the beginning of an intimate conversation. Momma persistently using the wrong verb, or none at all.

"Brother and Sister Wilcox is sho'ly the meanest—" "Is," Momma? "Is"? Oh, please, not "is," Momma, for two or more. But they talked, and from the side of the building where I waited for the ground to open up and swallow me, I heard the soft-voiced Mrs. Flowers and the textured voice of my grandmother merging and melting. They were interrupted from time to time by giggles that must have come from Mrs. Flowers (Momma never giggled in her life). Then she was gone.

She appealed to me because she was like people I had never met personally. Like women in English novels who walked the moors (whatever they were) with their loyal dogs racing at a respectful distance. Like the women who sat in front of roaring fireplaces, drinking tea incessantly from silver trays full of scones and crumpets. Women who walked over the "heath" and read morocco-bound books and had two last names divided by a hyphen. It would be safe to say that she made me proud to be Negro, just by being herself.

She acted just as refined as whitefolks in the movies and books and she was more beautiful, for none of them could have come near that warm color without looking gray by comparison.

It was fortunate that I never saw her in the company of powhitefolks. For since they tend to think of their whiteness as an evenizer, I'm certain that I would have had to hear her spoken to commonly as Bertha, and my image of her would have been shattered like the unmendable Humpty-Dumpty.

One summer afternoon, sweet-milk fresh in my memory, she stopped at the Store to buy provisions. Another Negro woman of her health and age would have been expected to carry the paper sacks home in one hand, but Momma said, "Sister Flowers, I'll send Bailey up to your house with these things."

She smiled that slow dragging smile, "Thank you, Mrs. Henderson. I'd prefer Marguerite, though." My name was beautiful when she said it. "I've been meaning to talk to her, anyway." They gave each other age-group looks.

Momma said, "Well, that's all right then. Sister, go and change your dress. You going to Sister Flowers's."

The chifforobe was a maze. What on earth did one put on to go to Mrs. Flowers's house? I knew I shouldn't put on a Sunday dress. It might be sacrilegious. Certainly not a house dress, since I was already wearing a fresh one. I chose a school dress, naturally. It was formal without suggesting that going to Mrs. Flowers's house was equivalent to attending church.

I trusted myself back into the Store.

"Now, don't you look nice." I had chosen the right thing, for once. . . .

There was a little path beside the rocky road, and Mrs. Flowers walked in front swinging her arms and picking her way over the stones.

She said, without turning her head, to me, "I hear you're doing very good school work, Marguerite, but that it's all written. The teachers report that they have trouble getting you to talk in class." We passed the triangular farm on our left and the path widened to allow us to walk together. I hung back in the separate unasked and unanswerable questions.

"Come and walk along with me, Marguerite." I couldn't have refused even if I wanted to. She pronounced my name so nicely. Or more correctly, she spoke each word with such clarity that I was certain a foreigner who didn't understand English could have understood her.

"Now no one is going to make you talk—possibly no one can. But bear in mind, language is man's way of communicating with his fellow man and it is language alone which separates him from the lower animals." That was a totally new idea to me, and I would need time to think about it.

"Your grandmother says you read a lot. Every chance you get. That's good, but not good enough. Words mean more than what is set down on paper. It takes the human voice to infuse them with the shades of deeper meaning."

I memorized the part about the human voice infusing words. It seemed so valid and poetic.

She said she was going to give me some books and that I not only must read them, I must read them aloud. She suggested that I try to make a sentence sound in as many different ways as possible.

"I'll accept no excuse if you return a book to me that has been badly handled." My imagination boggled at the punishment I would deserve if in fact I did abuse a book of Mrs. Flowers's. Death would be too kind and brief.

The odors in the house surprised me. Somehow I had never connected Mrs. Flowers with food or eating or any other common experience of common people. There must have been an outhouse, too, but my mind never recorded it.

The sweet scent of vanilla had met us as she opened the door.

"I made tea cookies this morning. You see, I had planned to invite you for cookies and lemonade so we could have this little chat. The lemonade is in the icebox."

It followed that Mrs. Flowers would have ice on an ordinary day, when most families in our town bought ice late on Saturdays only a few times during the summer to be used in the wooden ice-cream freezers.

She took the bags from me and disappeared through the kitchen door. I looked around the room that I had never in my wildest fantasies imagined I would see. Browned photographs leered or threatened from the walls and the white, freshly done curtains pushed against themselves and against the wind. I wanted to gobble up the room entire and take it to Bailey, who would help me analyze and enjoy it.

"Have a seat, Marguerite. Over there by the table." She carried a platter covered with a tea towel. Although she warned that she hadn't tried her hand at baking sweets for some time, I was certain that like everything else about her the cookies would be perfect.

They were flat round wafers, slightly browned on the edges and butter-yellow in the center. With the cold lemonade they were sufficient for childhood's lifelong diet. Remembering my manners, I took nice little lady-like bites off the edges. She said she had made them expressly for me and that she had a few in the kitchen that I could take home to my brother. So

I jammed one whole cake in my mouth and the rough crumbs scratched the insides of my jaws, and if I hadn't had to swallow, it would have been a dream come true.

As I ate she began the first of what we later called "my lessons in living." She said that I must always be intolerant of ignorance but understanding of illiteracy. That some people, unable to go to school, were more educated and even more intelligent than college professors. She encouraged me to listen carefully to what country people called mother wit. That in those homely sayings was couched the collective wisdom of generations.

When I finished the cookies she brushed off the table and brought a thick, small book from the bookcase. I had read *A Tale of Two Cities* and found it up to my standards as a romantic novel. She opened the first page and I heard poetry for the first time in my life.

"It was the best of times and the worst of times . . ." Her voice slid in and curved down through and over the words. She was nearly singing. I wanted to look at the pages. Were they the same that I had read? Or were there notes, music, lined on the pages, as in a hymn book? Her sounds began cascading gently. I knew from listening to a thousand preachers that she was nearing the end of her reading, and I hadn't really heard, heard to understand, a single word.

"How do you like that?"

It occurred to me that she expected a response. The sweet vanilla flavor was still on my tongue and her reading was a wonder in my ears. I had to speak.

I said, "Yes, ma'am." It was the least I could do, but it was the most also.

"There's one more thing. Take this book of poems and memorize one for me. Next time you pay me a visit, I want you to recite."

I have tried often to search behind the sophistication of years for the enchantment I so easily found in those gifts. The essence escapes but its aura remains. To be allowed, no, invited, into the private lives of strangers, and to share their joys and fears, was a chance to exchange the Southern bitter wormwood for a cup of mead with Beowulf or a hot cup of tea and milk with Oliver Twist. When I said aloud, "It is a far, far better thing that I do, than I have ever done . . ." tears of love filled my eyes at my selflessness.

On that first day, I ran down the hill and into the road (few cars ever came along it) and had the good sense to stop running before I reached the Store.

I was liked, and what a difference it made. I was respected not as Mrs. Henderson's grandchild or Bailey's sister but for just being Marguerite Johnson.

Childhood's logic never asks to be proved (all conclusions are absolute). I didn't question why Mrs. Flowers had singled me out for attention, nor did it occur to me that Momma might have asked her to give me a little talking to. All I cared about was that she had made tea cookies for *me* and read to *me* from her favorite book. It was enough to prove that she liked me.

Thinking Critically about the Text

In paragraph 44, Marguerite indicates how important it was for her to be respected and liked for "just being Marguerite Johnson." Why do you suppose she, in particular, feels that way? Why is it important for anyone to feel that way?

Questions on Subject

1. What is Angelou's main point in describing Sister Flowers? Why was Sister Flowers so important to her?
2. What does Angelou mean when she writes that Sister Flowers did not "encourage familiarity" (paragraph 3)?
3. Why does Sister Flowers think that reading is "good, but not good enough" for Marguerite (paragraph 24)?
4. What revelations about race relations in her community growing up does Angelou impart in this selection? What do those revelations add to the point Angelou is trying to make?
5. Why is being liked by Sister Flowers important to Marguerite?

Questions on Strategy

1. What dominant impression of Sister Flowers does Angelou create in this selection? (Glossary: *Dominant Impression*)
2. To which of the reader's senses does Angelou appeal in describing Sister Flowers? To which senses does she appeal in describing Sister Flowers's house?
3. At the end of her description of Sister Flowers, Angelou implies that at the time it did not occur to her that Sister Flowers might have been asked to give her "a little talking to" (paragraph 45). What clues in the description suggest that Momma asked Sister Flowers to befriend and draw out Marguerite? Why do you suppose Momma didn't take on that task herself?
4. Why does Angelou have her younger self imagine the conversations that Momma and Sister Flowers have on several occasions instead of reporting them directly (paragraph 10)?
5. Comment on Angelou's reference to the issue of subject–verb agreement in paragraph 10. Does Momma need to use standard grammar to be understood? Why is Marguerite — who rarely speaks — so embarrassed?

Questions on Diction and Vocabulary

1. Angelou uses figures of speech in paragraphs 1 and 3. Explain how they work and what they add to her description of herself and Sister Flowers. (Glossary: *Figures of Speech*)
2. How do Momma and Sister Flowers differ in their manner of speaking? What annoys Marguerite about the way Momma speaks? Does Momma's speech annoy Sister Flowers? Why or why not?
3. What do you think Sister Flowers means when she tells Marguerite that "words mean more than what is set down on paper" (paragraph 24)? Why is it important for Sister Flowers to tell Marguerite about this difference between reading and speaking?

Description in Action

One of the best ways to make a description memorable is to use figurative language such as a simile (making a comparison using *like* or *as*) or a metaphor (making a comparison without the use of *like* or *as*). Create a simile or metaphor that would be helpful in describing each item in the following list. To illustrate the activity, the first one has been completed for you.

1. a skyscraper: The skyscraper sparkled like a huge glass needle.
2. a large explosion:
3. a crowded bus:
4. a pillow:
5. a narrow alley:
6. a thick milkshake:
7. hot sun:
8. a dull knife:

Writing Suggestions

1. Sister Flowers is an excellent example of a person with grace, charm, spirit, intelligence, generosity, and high-mindedness — personality traits we ourselves might aspire to possess or admire in someone else. Describe someone you know who has similar personality traits and try to imagine what might account for such traits. Can such qualities be learned from a role model? Can they be taught in the abstract?
2. Review your response to the Preparing to Read prompt for this selection. How would you describe the person who came along at just the right time to help you when you were having a personal crisis? Write a description of that person's physical and character traits. Be sure to select the details of your description carefully so that you create a dominant impression rather than simply offer a series of loosely related descriptive details.

The Attachment that Still Makes Noise

PHYLLIS KORKKI

Phyllis Korkki is the assignment editor for the *New York Times* Sunday Business section. She writes about work–life balance, job hunting, older workers, telecommuting, and related subjects. Previously, she worked as a copy editor at *The Pioneer Press*, a newspaper in St. Paul, Minnesota. She is the author of the book *The Big Thing: How to Complete Your Creative Project Even if You're a Lazy, Self-Doubting Procrastinator Like Me* (2016), which is "a meditation on the importance of self-expression and purpose."

    The essay below first appeared in the *New York Times* on March 23, 2013, and considers the importance of tangible objects in an increasingly digital world.

Preparing to Read

What associations, if any, do you have with staplers? If none, think of another piece of mechanical office equipment you might see every day. Have you ever given this item any thought? If not, why do you think that is?

MyLoupe/UIG via Getty Images

1 Do you have a stapler?

2   If you do, maybe it's a little dusty in this age of PDFs. Or maybe it's been missing for a while, after someone borrowed it and never brought it back. Or maybe you've affixed your name to your stapler with a piece of clear tape, so your co-workers know: you take this stapler, you die.

Even as data moves to computers and the cloud, staplers continue to help people keep it together. On the computer, we can file copies in folders and send messages to mailboxes. We can cut, copy and paste text and files. But which computer activity is similar to stapling? Sure, there's the paper-clip icon that attaches documents to e-mail. But nothing, really, comes close to the satisfying ka-chunk of a stapler: it's a sound that means work is getting done.

Paper receipts are supposed to be on their way out, but they continue to flutter their way through restaurants, stores and doctors' offices. Staplers are there, attaching the receipt to the business card, the return receipt to the original receipt, the merchant copy to the bill, the receipt to the takeout bag.

If you have a stapler, the odds are fairly good that it was made by Swingline. Other companies, including Stanley-Bostitch, along with OfficeMax and Staples, also make staplers. But Swingline, now owned by Acco Brands, has long been the market leader.

Acco, based in suburban Chicago, sounds like the perfect name for a faceless conglomerate from the era of "The Man in the Gray Flannel Suit." But it actually has a sterling office products pedigree—it is short for the American Clip Company, a manufacturer of paper clips founded by Fred J. Kline of Queens at the turn of the 20th century.

Signs at Swingline's old plant in Queens came down in 1999.

Queens was once the center of the paper-fastening universe. In 1925, it was where Jack Linsky founded the Parrot Speed Fastener Company, later renamed Swingline. For years, the bright red sign of his Swingline factory was a beacon to Queens residents as they drove across the Queensboro Bridge from Manhattan.

Stapling devices have existed since at the least the French court of Louis XV. But before Mr. Linsky's time, staples generally had to be laboriously loaded, one by one, into the rear of the stapler. Mr. Linsky helped revolutionize stapling by creating an easy way to fill the devices under a horizontal cap. He found an adhesive that could attach staples in rows so that they stayed together in a metal magazine until they were pushed out and bent individually to grip their paper quarry.

Swingline promised to make office work easy. In a newspaper ad from the 1940s, a young woman—presumably a secretary—loads a stapler and says: "Now we're in the groove, boss! That Swingline Stapler loads quicker, works slicker because of its open, trouble-free channel."

> But nothing, really, comes close to the satisfying ka-chunk of a stapler: it's a sound that means work is getting done.

But Mr. Linsky wasn't satisfied to serve only the office market; he helped increase demand for staplers by emphasizing their handiness in other tasks, like tacking shelf paper, fastening paper around sandwiches and constructing party hats. ("Swingline does the darnedest things!" another ad boasted.) He also expanded the business by making specialized staplers for carpeting, roofing and auto upholstery.

In 1970, Mr. Linsky sold Swingline to American Brands, and in the next decade Acco merged into Swingline. Amid the manufacturing crisis of the 1990s, American Brands closed the Swingline factory in Queens and moved its manufacturing to Mexico; nearly 500 New York workers lost their jobs, and the Swingline sign came down. Now most staplers are produced in Asia.

Swingline made Mr. Linsky very rich. He and his wife, Belle, were philanthropists and art collectors who once owned one of the largest collections of Fabergé eggs in America. Jack died in 1980, and in 1982 Belle donated a collection of the couple's European art, then worth $60 million, to the Metropolitan Museum of Art.

Staplers generally don't rise to the level of prized collectibles, which is why a Swingline's role as an object of obsession was so funny in the 1999 cult comedy "Office Space."

In the film, a mumbling, superwide-eyed character named Milton becomes desperate after his red Swingline stapler is taken away during a frenzy of cost-cutting and downsizing at a soulless I.T. company.

You might assume that this stapler, not only cherished but central to the plot of "Office Space," was a brilliant product placement move. In fact, Swingline had no hand in the story line. It had long stopped making that type of red stapler, and a black Swingline was painted red by the filmmakers.

At first, Swingline executives weren't sure they liked being associated with such a dark parody of corporate life. But in 2002, recognizing the value of its pop-culture star turn, it released its Rio Red collectors edition 747 stapler. The company bills it "as the star of any office space."

Staplers come in a range of colors, shapes and sizes and can vary in their staple capacity and in the number of sheets they can puncture. The ideal stapler is a perfect melding of heft and lightness that can accommodate either in-the-air or on-the-desk fastening.

Staplers are still such a fact of everyday life that we've lost sight of what a triumph of manufacturing they are. They can bend metal—no batteries or electricity required. They are similar to guns in that they contain magazines meant to be filled with metal objects that you load and release.

A Swingline stapler is designed to be "a fusion of form and function," says Chris Cunningham, global design director at Acco, which owns the brand.

"The engineering of a stapler is not fully appreciated," said Mike Parrish, director of product development for Acco Brands. Under the cap of a stapler, a pusher connected to a spring forces the row of staples forward. A special blade drives the first staple through a slot at the front of the magazine. A metal square with indentations at the edge of the open part of the base, called the anvil, helps bend the staple so it can grip the paper. The bottom of the completed staple is known as the clinch, and the top is the crown.

Without just the right alignment in the stapler, and the proper adhesive level and tensile strength in the row of staples, this delicate operation could go awry. You could end up with a jam (as with a gun), or an incomplete clinch (and maybe a bloody finger).

A Swingline stapler is designed to be "a fusion of form and function," said Chris Cunningham, global design director for Acco. The design of a traditional model is meant to look streamlined, he added, and so robust and durable that even if the whole building burned down, one senses that the stapler would still be there.

Industrywide, sales of desktop and hand-held staplers (nonelectric) totaled $80.3 million in 2012, up 3 percent from the previous year, according to NPD, the market research firm. Sales of office products in general rose after a decline amid the recession.

Robert Keller, the departing C.E.O. of Acco Brands (he will remain as executive chairman), started his career at I.B.M. in the 1970s, when experts were predicting that paperless offices were just around the corner. Well, here he is, four decades later, leading a huge office products company with paper and staplers as its core products.

But Mr. Keller knows full well that computers will continue to eat into the business; that's why Acco is aggressively expanding into global markets where technology is not as entrenched.

Time is a big threat to the stapler industry, and to office products in general. More people who grew up with staplers are going to retire and die. And the younger generation just isn't as attached to staplers, said Lora Morsovillo, president of office supplies for NPD.

But there's hope, she said, if stapler makers look at their products as decorative objects. "The growth is coming from uniqueness and personalization," especially in home offices, she said. She puts staplers in the same general category as tape dispensers, and, she noted, there's a tape dispenser out there in the shape of a stiletto heel.

Swingline has yet to produce a stiletto stapler, but it recently introduced a line of fashion staplers with bright colors and decorations. On the whole, though, staplers have been "drab and dreary," maintained Randy Nicolau, the chief executive of Poppin, a new e-commerce company that aims to turn products like staplers, notebooks, pens, pen cups, trays and calculators into jewelry for your desk.

The bright colors of Poppin staplers are in sync with Poppin's image as a fashion company.

Poppin's open-plan office is bright with the colors of its coordinated products, including white, black, yellow, orange, red, pink, purple, two shades of blue (aqua and "pool") and lime green. "We consider ourselves to be a fashion company before anything else," Mr. Nicolau said.

The company also cares about function, said Jeff Miller, vice president of product design. But in addition to making a product that performs well, Mr. Miller said, he seeks to create sleek, concise forms, and modular sizes — so that the stapler on your desk, for example, matches up with the tape dispenser.

The company's staplers are made overseas, but its headquarters are in Manhattan, across the East River from where Jack Linsky once set up shop. The stylish staplers sold by Poppin look much different from the utilitarian ones Mr. Linsky once made, but some things haven't changed. The staplers still have a magazine, a spring, a pusher and an anvil, and they still make a satisfying metallic sound when you press down on them, signaling that work has been done.

Thinking Critically about the Text

"Paper receipts are supposed to be on their way out," Korkki writes in paragraph 4. Do you think paper receipts will disappear? What other paper objects might become obsolete? Is that a good or bad thing, and why?

Questions on Subject

1. Are you familiar with what Korkki calls "the satisfying ka-chunk" of the stapler? Do you think her description is accurate? Explain. If not, describe the sound in your own words.
2. Korkki writes that staplers make "a sound that means work is getting done" (paragraph 3). When you hear someone use a stapler, is this what you think? If not, why? What sounds do you associate with work getting done? What actions do they accompany?
3. The author calls staplers "a triumph of manufacturing" (19). What do you think she means by this? How are staplers a triumph, and what have they triumphed over?
4. Korkki writes that "Time is a big threat to the stapler industry" (27). What does she mean? In what way is the industry threatened?

Questions on Strategy

1. Why do you think Korkki opens her essay with a question? What is the effect of doing so?
2. Korkki refers to two movies in this essay: *The Man in the Gray Flannel Suit* (paragraph 6) and *Office Space* (14). The first was made in 1956; the second in 1999. Are you familiar with either movie? If not, does that interfere with your understanding the essay? Why do you think Korkki refers to these two films, knowing full well her readers may not have seen them? (Glossary: *Allusion*)
3. In paragraph 18, Korkki writes that staplers "are similar to guns." How are they similar to guns? How are they different? Do you find this comparison useful? Why or why not? (Glossary: *Comparison and Contrast*)
4. The author quotes a number of professionals associated with creating and marketing staplers. Where in the essay does she do this, and why? What is the effect of using experts to share their opinions and explanations about staplers? (Glossary: *Evidence*)

Questions on Diction and Vocabulary

1. Korkki threads her essay with some very dramatic statements, including "you take this stapler, you die" (paragraph 2) and "to look . . . so robust and durable that even if the whole building burned down, one senses that the stapler would still be there" (23). What is the tone of these statements and how do they function in the essay? (Glossary: *Tone*)
2. Refer to a dictionary to determine the meanings of the following words as they are used in this essay: *conglomerate* (paragraph 6), *pedigree* (6), *quarry* (9), *philanthropists* (13), *parody* (17), *melding* (19), *heft* (19), *tensile* (22), *robust* (23), *entrenched* (26), *modular* (32).

Description in Action

Brainstorm a list of sounds you find enjoyable. Next, come up with at least ten words and phrases to describe each one. Some possibilities to consider:

- A bat hitting a baseball or a hockey stick hitting the puck
- Fingers tapping very quickly on a keyboard
- A train whistle or a fog horn
- Snow squeaking under boots
- Autumn leaves as you walk through them
- The sound of a match lighting

Writing Suggestions

1. Think of a sound that you find especially satisfying; feel free to use the classroom activity above as a starting point. Write an essay exploring this sound. Be sure to set the scene and use sensory details to create a dominant impression. Try to appeal to all five senses: sight, sound, taste, touch, and smell.

2. In paragraph 28, Korkki mentions that "there's a tape dispenser out there in the shape of a stiletto heel." Think of a product you've encountered that is designed to look like something entirely different than what it is. Or, if you've never seen such a product, invent one. Describe the item in detail and analyze its effectiveness. What was it designed to do? Does its appearance affect its ability to do that job or serve that purpose? Would you buy such a product, and why or why not? Consider the relationship between form and function. Is this product a good idea or a waste of time and resources?

3. Write an essay about the history of some item people use every day. Research original and intermediate versions and analyze the evolution of the product. Some possibilities might include pencil sharpeners, thermometers, or food processors. Consider manual, electric, and digital versions. What was gained and what was lost in each iteration? Use concrete details to describe each version of the item, including what it feels like, looks like, sounds like, and, if relevant, smells like. (Pencil shavings, for instance, have a very distinct smell.)

WRITING SUGGESTIONS FOR DESCRIPTION

1. Most description is predominantly visual; that is, it appeals to our sense of sight. Good description, however, often goes beyond the visual; it appeals as well to one or more of the other senses — hearing, smell, taste, and touch. One way to heighten your awareness of these other senses is to purposefully deemphasize the visual impressions you receive. For example, while standing on a busy street corner, sitting in a classroom, or shopping in a supermarket, carefully note what you hear, smell, taste, or feel. (It may help if you close your eyes to eliminate visual distractions as you carry out this experiment.) Use these sense impressions to write a brief description of the street corner, the classroom, the supermarket, or another spot of your choosing.

2. Select one of the following topics and write an objective description of it. Remember that your task in writing an objective description is to inform the reader about the object, not to convey to the reader the mood or feeling that the object evokes in you.

    a. a pine tree
    b. a café
    c. a dictionary
    d. a fast-food restaurant
    e. a basketball
    f. the layout of your campus
    g. a movie theater
    h. your room

3. Select one of the following places and write a multiparagraph description that captures your subjective sense impressions of that particular place.

    a. a busy doctor's office
    b. a bakery
    c. a dorm room
    d. a factory
    e. a gas station
    f. a cafeteria
    g. a farmers' market
    h. a locker room
    i. a bank
    j. a library

4. At college you have the opportunity to meet many new people, students as well as teachers. In a letter to someone back home, describe one of your new acquaintances. Try to capture the essence of the person you chose and to explain why this person stands out from all the other people you have met at school.

5. The readings in this chapter on description focus on people (Jeannette Walls and her mother, Sister Flowers), places (a barrio), and things (a stapler). Write an essay in which you compare and contrast any two of these readings. Here are some questions to get you started:

    a. If you choose to write about the selections that describe people, ask yourself what features of those people the authors concentrate on. What features do they leave out or downplay? Which person do you get to know best, and why?

b. If you choose to write about a selection focusing on a place or a thing, ask yourself what techniques are employed that contribute to a better understanding or appreciation of the place or thing. What is the dominant impression the author portrays?

c. If you choose to compare or contrast two different subjects (a person with a place, for instance), consider how the descriptions might be reversed. Could the description of a person also apply to a place or a thing? How are the adjectives similar? How is the imagery different?

6. McDonald's "A View from the Bridge" on pages 8–10 and the *Calvin and Hobbes* cartoon on page 170 are just two "fish stories" in the long and rich tradition of that genre. In their own ways, both the essay and the cartoon play on the ironic notion that fishing is a quiet sport but one in which the unexpected frequently occurs. (Glossary: *Irony*)

For the narrator in McDonald's story, there is the revelation of the difference between merely looking and truly seeing. For Calvin, there is that sudden splash in the water (this time, alas, not the sign of a great catch). Write an essay in which you tell a descriptive "fish story" of your own, one that reveals a larger, significant truth or life lesson. Pay particular attention to the pattern of organization you choose, and be sure to revise your essay to tighten up your use of the pattern. If possible, incorporate some elements of surprise as well.

7. **Writing with Sources.** Writers of description often rely on factual information to make their writing more substantial and interesting. Using facts, statistics, or other information found online or in your college library, write an essay describing one of the people, places, or things in the following list. Be sure that you focus your description, that you have a purpose for your description, and that you present your facts in an interesting manner.

   a. the Statue of Liberty
   b. Adele
   c. the Grand Canyon
   d. the Great Wall of China
   e. Hillary Rodham Clinton
   f. LeBron James
   g. the Tower of London
   h. the sun
   i. Disney World
   j. the Hubble Space Telescope
   k. Ruth Bader Ginsburg
   l. a local landmark

   For models of and advice on integrating sources in your essay, see Chapters 14 and 15.

8. **Writing with Sources.** As a way of getting to know your campus, select a building, statue, sculpture, or other familiar landmark and research it. What is its significance or meaning to your college or university? Are there any

ceremonies or rituals associated with the object? What are its distinctive or unusual features? When was it erected? Who sponsored it? Is it currently being used as originally intended? Once you have completed your research, write a description of your subject in which you create a dominant impression of your landmark's importance to the campus community.

CALVIN AND HOBBES © 1986 Watterson. Reprinted with permission of UNIVERSAL UCLICK. All rights reserved.

    You and your classmates may wish to turn this particular assignment into a collaborative class project: the compilation of a booklet of essays that introduces readers to the unique physical and historic features of your campus. To avoid duplication, the class should make a list of campus landmarks, and each student should sign up for the one that he or she would like to write about. For models of and advice on integrating sources in your essay, see Chapters 14 and 15.

9. **Writing with Sources.** Study the photograph by Gordon Parks that appears at the beginning of this chapter (page 124). First, respond to the photograph, answering the following questions: What does the image convey to you? How would you characterize the figure of the woman, the presence of the American flag and the broom and mop? Do you see any significance in how the woman and the inanimate objects are positioned in the photograph?

    Next, do some research on Parks's work. (You might start by searching for the Library of Congress's online exhibit entitled "Ella Watson, U.S. Government Charwoman.") Be sure to find out why the photo is commonly called *American Gothic*. What is its connection to American painter Grant Wood's iconic painting of the same name? In what ways is Parks's photograph a parody of or commentary on Wood's painting?

    Finally, write an essay describing the photograph and discussing its history and the message you think Parks means to convey. For models of and advice on integrating sources in your essay, see Chapters 14 and 15.

10. **Writing in the Workplace.** You are working for your local weekly newspaper, and your boss has assigned you to do a profile of a local celebrity for a series on getting to know important people in the community. Interview your subject and describe the person both objectively and subjectively, telling of the person's background and achievements so as to make lively reading for the average weekly newspaper reader. What special qualities do you detect in your subject? What contributions has the person made to the community? What weaknesses has the person overcome? What triumphs has your subject achieved? What stands out for you about your subject, and what is it that readers will most want to know about this community figure?

Rick McKee, Courtesy of Cagle Cartoons

CHAPTER **6**

Illustration

WHAT IS ILLUSTRATION?

THE STRATEGY OF ILLUSTRATION USES EXAMPLES—FACTS, OPINIONS, samples, and anecdotes or stories—to make a general observation, assertion, or claim more vivid, understandable, and persuasive. We use examples all the time in everyday life to make our points clearer. How often have we asked for or given an example or two when something was not evident or clear?

The cartoon on the opposite page uses the strategy of illustration to fill the graduate's speech bubble with current buzzwords of political correctness, offering them as examples of what the student learned while in college. The cartoonist uses these examples to invite the reader to critique both the out of touch, aging father and the socially aware but combative son. The irony is that each term the son uses is meant to signify his open-mindedness and acceptance of others, yet each usage further distances father and son and undermines their ability to communicate.

ILLUSTRATION IN WRITTEN TEXTS

In the following paragraph from "Wandering through Winter," notice how naturalist Edwin Way Teale uses examples to illustrate his generalization that "country people" have many superstitions about how harsh the coming winter will be:

Topic sentence about weather superstitions frames entire paragraph	In the folklore of the country, numerous superstitions relate to winter weather. Back-country farmers examine their husks—the thicker the husk, the colder the winter. They watch the acorn crop—the more acorns, the more severe the season. They observe where white-faced hornets place their paper nests—the higher they are, the deeper will be the snow. They examine the size and shape and color of the spleens of butchered hogs for clues to the severity of the season. They keep track of the blooming of the dogwood in the spring—the more abundant the blooms, the more bitter the cold

173

Series of examples amplify and clarify topic sentence

in January. When chipmunks carry their tails high and squirrels have heavier fur, the superstitious gird themselves for a long, hard winter. Without any specific basis, a wider-than-usual black band on a woolly-bear caterpillar is accepted as a sign that winter will arrive early and stay late. Even the way a cat sits beside the stove carries its message to the credulous. According to the belief once widely held in the Ozarks, a cat sitting with its tail to the fire indicates very cold weather is on the way.

Teale uses nine separate examples to illustrate and explain his topic sentence about weather-related superstitions. These examples both demonstrate his knowledge of folk traditions and entertain us. As readers, we come away from Teale's paragraph thinking that he is an authority on his subject.

Teale's examples are a series of related but varied illustrations of his main point. Sometimes, however, just one sustained example can be equally effective if the example is representative and the writer develops it well. Here is one such example by basketball legend Bill Russell from his autobiographical *Second Wind*:

Topic sentence focuses on athletes slipping into a new gear

Extended example of Bob Beamon's record-shattering day exemplifies topic sentence

Example illustrates that even Beamon did not anticipate his own performance

Every champion athlete has a moment when everything goes so perfectly for him he slips into a gear that he didn't know was there. It's easy to spot that perfect moment in a sport like track. I remember watching the 1968 Olympics in Mexico City, where the world record in the long jump was just under 27 feet. Then Bob Beamon flew down the chute and leaped out over the pit in a majestic jump that I have seen replayed many times. There was an awed silence when the announcer said that Beamon's jump measured 29 feet 2¼ inches. Generally world records are broken by fractions of inches, but Beamon had exceeded the existing record by more than two feet. On learning what he had done, Beamon slumped down on the ground and cried. Most viewers' image of Beamon ends with the picture of him weeping on the ground, but in fact he got up and took some more jumps that day. I like to think that he did so because he had jumped for so long at his best that *even then* he didn't know what might come out of him. At the end of the day he wanted to be absolutely sure that he'd had his perfect day.

Few readers have experienced that "extra gear" that Russell describes, so he illustrates what he means with a single, extended example—in this case, an anecdote that gives substance to the idea he wants his readers to understand. Russell's example of Bob Beamon's record-breaking jump is not only concrete and specific, it is also memorable because it so aptly captures the essence of his topic sentence about athletic perfection. Without this extended example, Russell's claim that every great athlete "slips into a gear that he didn't know was there" would simply be a hollow statement.

USING ILLUSTRATION AS A WRITING STRATEGY

Illustrating a point with examples serves several purposes for writers. First, examples make writing more vivid and interesting. Writing that consists of loosely strung together generalizations is lifeless and difficult to read, regardless of the believability of the generalizations or our willingness to accept them. Good writers try to provide just the right kind and number of examples to make their ideas clear and convincing. For example, an essay about television bloopers will be dull and pointless without some examples of on-screen blunders—accidents, pratfalls, and "tips of the slongue," as one writer calls them. Likewise, a more serious essay on the dangers of drunk driving will have more impact if it is illustrated with descriptive examples of the victims' suffering and the grief of their family members and friends.

Writers also use illustration to explain or clarify their ideas. All readers want specific information and feel that it is the writer's responsibility to provide it. Even if readers can provide examples themselves, they want to see what kind of evidence the writer can present. In an essay on political leadership for a history or political science class, for instance, the assertion "Successful leaders are often a product of their times" will certainly require further explanation. Such explanation could be provided effectively through examples: Franklin D. Roosevelt, Winston Churchill, Corazon Aquino, and Nelson Mandela all rose to power because their people were looking for leadership in a time of national crisis. Keep in mind, however, that the use of these specific examples paints a different picture of the term "successful leaders" than a different set of examples would; unlike leaders like Joseph Stalin, Adolf Hitler, and Benito Mussolini, who rose to power under similar circumstances, the first group of leaders exercised their power in the interest of the people.

Illustration is so useful and versatile a strategy that it is found in many different kinds of writing, such as reports, cover letters, editorials, applications, proposals, law briefs, and reviews. In fact, there is hardly an essay in this book that does not use illustration in one way or another.

USING ILLUSTRATION ACROSS THE DISCIPLINES

When writing essays in the academic disciplines, you will have many opportunities to use the strategy of illustration to both organize and strengthen the presentation of your ideas. To determine whether illustration is the right strategy for you in a particular paper, review the guidelines described in Chapter 2 (Determining a Strategy for Developing Your Essay, pages 32–33). Consider the following examples.

American Literature

1. **MAIN IDEA:** Mark Twain uses irony to speak out against racism in *The Adventures of Huckleberry Finn*.
2. **QUESTION:** Where does Mark Twain use irony to combat racism in *The Adventures of Huckleberry Finn*?
3. **STRATEGY:** Illustration. The direction words *uses* and *where* say "show me," and what better way to show than with solid, representative examples from the novel of Twain's use of irony to speak out against racism?
4. **SUPPORTING STRATEGY:** Argument. The examples can be used to argue in favor of a particular interpretation of Twain's work.

Criminal Justice

1. **MAIN IDEA:** America's criminal justice system neglects the families of capital offenders.
2. **QUESTION:** How has America's criminal justice system neglected the families of capital offenders?
3. **STRATEGY:** Illustration. Both the statement of the main idea and the question cry out for proof or evidence, and the best evidence would be a series of examples of the claimed neglect.
4. **SUPPORTING STRATEGY:** Process analysis. The paper might conclude with a possible remedy or solution—a step-by-step process for eliminating the current neglect.

Biology

1. **MAIN IDEA:** Cloning and other biotechnical discoveries give rise to serious moral and ethical issues that need our attention.
2. **QUESTION:** What are some of the moral and ethical issues raised by recent biotechnical discoveries that we need to address?
3. **STRATEGY:** Illustration. The direction words *what* and *some* call for examples of the moral and ethical issues raised by biotechnical discoveries.
4. **SUPPORTING STRATEGY:** Argument. The direction word *need* suggests that the examples should be both compelling and persuasive so that readers will want to address these issues.

SAMPLE STUDENT ESSAY USING ILLUSTRATION AS A WRITING STRATEGY

Diets and dieting fascinated Paula Kersch, especially because she and her friends were constantly trying out the popular plans. Eventually, however, Paula began wondering: If these diets really worked, why were people always looking for new ones to try? She also wondered if these diets posed any real risks, especially when she started thinking about the more extreme ones. She made a list of the various diets she and her friends had tried and then did some research on the Internet to see what she could learn about them. On the basis of what she discovered, she developed the following thesis: "If Americans knew more about the risks that accompany trendy diets and the seriousness of our obesity problem, perhaps they would not look for a quick fix but instead would adopt a weight-management plan that would help them achieve the desired results without compromising their health and their pocketbooks."

Before drafting her essay, Paula familiarized herself with the materials found in Chapter 14, "Writing with Sources," and Chapter 15, "A Brief Guide to Researching and Documenting Essays." What follows is the final draft of her essay. Notice how she uses examples of specific diet plans to explain her key points.

Title introduces paper topic

Weight Management: More Than
a Matter of Good Looks
Paula Kersch

Beginning engages reader by referring to common experience and observation

Americans are obsessed with their weight. Most Americans consider themselves in need of some type of diet, and, whether they're looking to lose those extra holiday pounds or the accumulation of a lifetime, there's plenty of help out there. Bookstore owners often stock an entire section with the latest diet books, and a quick search of the Internet reveals over 250 trendy diets that are currently in vogue. This help is there because dieting is big business in America. In fact, the U.S. Centers for Disease Control and Prevention reported in 2008 that "the dieting industry earned 55 billion dollars in 2006" (*Latest*). At the same time, most experts agree that fad diets don't work (Katz, "Pandemic"). Some estimate that a full 95% of fad diets fail (Hulse).

Thesis announces essay's focus: trendy diets can be dangerous

In the face of the staggering failure rate for most fad diets, why do these quick-loss plans remain so popular? If Americans knew more about the risks that accompany trendy diets and the seriousness of our obesity problem, perhaps they would not be so quick to look for a quick fix but instead would adopt a weight-management plan that would help them achieve the desired results without compromising their health and their pocketbooks.

Most of the currently popular quick-weight-loss schemes appeal to Americans' desire for instant

1

2

3

gratification. Who wants to look forward to a year of losing a pound or less a week? Most of these diets fall into one of several categories: (1) fasts and detox cleanses, (2) plans that emphasize one food group while eliminating or minimizing others, and (3) diet pills and supplements. All of these crash-dieting methods produce results. People who try them lose pounds quickly just as the ads promise—the South Beach Diet boasts seven pounds in seven days and Dr. Simeons' HCG Weight Loss Protocol, thirty-four pounds in forty-three days. Sadly, however, virtually all dieters compromise their health and gain back the weight they lose—and then some.

People have been using water and juice fasts and cleanses since biblical times for both spiritual and physical reasons. Most regimens last only a few days, resulting in the rapid loss of five to seven pounds in some cases. The popular Master Cleanse—also known as the Lemonade Diet—developed by Stanley Burroughs in 1941 recommends a slightly longer fourteen-day program to achieve the desired detoxification and diet results (Ogunnaike). Because humans can go without food for longer periods of time if they have water, this regimen is not necessarily dangerous. However, some people push fasts and cleanses to unhealthy extremes. Even apart from the health risks, these extremes often fail to produce the desired long-term weight-loss results.

Although there is a technical difference between fasting and starving, metabolically the human body does not differentiate between the two. When a person fasts, the body has to rely on burning its own reserves for energy. Because the body does not know when its next meal might be coming, the body lowers its metabolism in order to conserve fuel, thus slowing weight loss. Also, while fasting may produce lost pounds on the scale, usually it is not the fat loss most dieters aim for. Short-term fasts result in large water losses, which are almost immediately regained once the fast is broken.

The longer a fast or cleanse continues, the greater the serious risk for muscle damage in the body because the body is not getting the nutrients it needs. Additionally, people are at risk of gaining even more weight than they lost after coming off a fast because their bodies will still be functioning at a slower metabolic rate, allowing more rapid weight gain on fewer calories. Repeated fasting can permanently alter the body's base metabolic rate.

One does not have to be a nutritionist to understand that if people eat only foods from one food group and do not eat any from others, their bodies will not be able to function correctly. Over the years there have been a number of high-protein low-carb diets that promise quick weight loss by emphasizing foods high in protein, while excluding most carbohydrates. The infamous Last-Chance Diet of the 1970s, with its emphasis on a liquid-protein drink and the exclusion of all other food, led to numerous heart attacks and over sixty deaths among users. The Atkins Diet, an enormously popular diet first developed in the 1970s and later updated in *Dr. Atkins's New Diet Revolution*, is another prime example of a diet that excludes large groups of foods. Meat and fat are emphasized to the exclusion of other foods, making the diet high in cholesterol. Neither medically sound nor nutritionally safe, this diet results in a rapid and dangerous drop in weight.

In spite of the fact that this and other low-carb diets—like the currently popular Dr. Arthur Agatston's *The South Beach Diet Supercharged* and *Dr. Gott's No Flour, No Sugar Diet*—can compromise a person's health, many people continue to follow these diets to shed their excess pounds. These and other trendy diets that emphasize single foods or food groups, like the Cabbage Soup Diet, the Grapefruit Diet, and the Apple Cider Vinegar Diet, have all been debunked as unhealthy and unrealistic solutions to a very real problem.

America's search for a quick, easy solution to the weight problem is perhaps epitomized best in the popularity of diet pills and supplements. In years gone by dieters have used thyroid hormone injections, amphetamines, and fen-phen—a combination of fenfluramine or dexfenfluramine and phentermine—among other things. In September 1997, however, manufacturers took the "fen" drugs off the market at the request of the Food and Drug Administration (FDA) because fen-phen was linked to heart valve damage and death (Kolata). In May of 2009, the FDA recalled Hydroxycut, a popular dietary supplement containing ephedra, which caused liver damage.

Nevertheless, the search for a magic bullet to combat excess weight continues, motivated by the public's desire for more attractive and healthy bodies and corporate America's pursuit of unimaginable profits if they are able to hit on the right formula. In June of 2008, GlaxoSmithKline first marketed Alli (pronounced "ally," as in supporter or friend), an over-the-counter version of the prescription-strength Xenical, an FDA-approved fat blocker. When used as recommended, Alli promises to increase weight loss by up to 50% over what might normally be lost by most people following a healthy diet and a regular exercise program. (Alli is not intended as a stand-alone solution for someone with a nutritionally unhealthy diet and no exercise regimen.)

Example explores promise of diet pill Alli in detail

The FDA recommends that Alli not be used by children or for longer than two consecutive years—considerable restrictions. Alli also has some annoying side effects, among them "excessive flatulence, oily bowel movements, which can be difficult to control, and anal leakage" (Baldwin). Some may find these side effects minor deterrents, but others may not be willing to endure the embarrassment and inconvenience associated with them. Some critics allege that while Alli blocks the absorption of some fats, it may also block some important vitamins and minerals. Dr. Sidney Wolfe, director of Public Citizen's Health Research Group in Washington, DC, sees no reason to take Alli because "there are demonstrable short-term risks and no possibility of long-term benefit" (qtd. in Mann).

Discusses the drawbacks of using Alli

Quotation from medical authority supports reservations about using Alli

It is obvious from even this cursory examination of trendy dieting practices that "get-thin-quick" schemes typically offer little more than empty promises. According to experts, the key to real weight loss is not dieting: The best results come from long-term changes in lifestyle habits. Weight control is best achieved with commonsense eating, consisting of foods high in nutrition and low in fat and sugar, in conjunction with regular exercise. While this kind of weight control cannot offer fast results, it usually proves successful where diets ultimately fail. Here's why.

Weight management introduced as healthy alternative to "get-thin-quick" schemes

Losing weight in a healthy manner is a slow process. Most nutritionists suggest that a sensible goal is 2–4 pounds per month. When a person follows a sustainable eating and exercise program, that person's body will naturally start to slim down over time. Eating a well-balanced diet with foods from the four food groups gives the body all the essentials it needs. The high amounts of fiber in fruits, vegetables, and whole grains make the stomach feel full and satisfied.

Emphasis on eating well-balanced diet and exercising regularly

When the body receives the nutrients it needs, it functions better as well. It is common knowledge that depression, migraine headaches, and lethargy are often triggered by overindulgence or nutritional deficiencies. Once moderation is achieved and any deficiencies eliminated, ailments tend to disappear (United States, *Nutrition*).

Many trendy diets do not advocate exercise; some even claim that exercise is unnecessary. But working out is an essential ingredient in any good weight-management program. Exercise tones up the body and gives people more energy and a sense of well-being. Moderate exercise such as rapid walking can rev up the metabolism and help the body burn calories more efficiently. Regular exercise has the additional benefit of increasing over time the body's base metabolic rate so that more food may be eaten with no weight gain (United States, *Physical*).

Trendy dieting as practiced during the past two decades just has not worked. Fasting, one-food-group dieting, and diet pills and supplements often do more harm than good in terms of nutrition and general well-being. As a society, Americans must face the obesity problem head-on. If we do not, the consequences will be dire. Dr. David L. Katz, nutrition and weight-control expert and director of the Yale Prevention Research Center, warns that "by 2018 more than 100 million Americans will be obese, and we will be spending roughly $340 billion annually on obesity, a tripling of current levels that are already breaking the bank" ("Compelling" 3B). Long-term weight-management programs that incorporate healthy lifestyle habits offer a real solution where trendy diets fail. When overweight Americans forsake the lure of quick weight loss and understand all the negative aspects associated with these trendy diets, they will begin to get a handle on what they must do to tackle their weight problems.

Works Cited

Baldwin, Donovan. "Pros and Cons of the New Alli Diet Pill." *SearchWarp.com*, 20 June 2007, searchwarp.com/swa224916.htm.

Hulse, Dean. "Fad Diets Popular but Have Major-League Failure Rate." *News for North Dakotans*, Agriculture Communication, North Dakota State U, 8 July 1999, www.ext.nodak.edu/extnews/newsrelease/1999/070899/04faddie.htm.

See pages 730–38 for more models of MLA entries

Katz, David L. "The Compelling Case for Obesity Control." *Naples Daily News*, 3 Jan. 2010, p. B1+.

---. "Pandemic Obesity and the Contagion of Nutritional Nonsense." *Public Health Review*, vol. 31 no. 1, 2003, pp. 33–44.

Kolata, Gina. "Companies Recall 2 Top Diet Drugs at F.D.A.'s Urging." *The New York Times*, 16 Sept. 1997, www.nytimes.com/1997/09/16/ /diet-drug-recall.html?hp&action=second-column-region&region=top-news& r=0. Accessed 8 Feb. 2010.

"Latest CDC Data Show More Americans Report Being Obese." *Centers for Disease Control and Prevention*, US Department of Health and Human Services / Centers for Disease Control and Prevention, 17 July 2008, www.cdc.gov/media/pressrel/2008/r080717.htm.

Mann, Denise. "All about Alli, the Weight Loss Pill." *WebMD*, 2007, www.webmd.com/diet/obesity/weight-loss-prescription-weight-loss-alli.

"Nutrition for Everyone." *Centers for Disease Control and Prevention*, US Department of Health and Human Services / Centers for Disease Control and Prevention,14 Sept. 2009, www.cdc.gov/nutrition/general.

Ogunnaike, Lola. "I Heard It through the Diet Grapevine." *The New York Times*, 10 Dec. 2006, www.nytimes.com/2006/12/10/fashion/10cleanse.html?_r=1.

"Physical Activity for Everyone." *Centers for Disease Control and Prevention*, US Department of Health and Human Services / Centers for Disease Control and Prevention, 14 Sept. 2009, www.cdc.gov/physicalactivity/success/index.htm.

Analyzing Paula Kersch's Illustration Essay: Questions for Discussion

1. What points do Paula's examples illustrate or support?
2. Are her examples relevant and representative? Explain why or why not. What examples of your own can you think of to illustrate her points?
3. Which examples did you find most effective? Least effective? Why?
4. Paula used outside sources in her essay. What did these sources add to the essay?
5. How does Paula conclude her essay? In what ways is her conclusion connected to her beginning? Explain.

SUGGESTIONS FOR USING ILLUSTRATION AS A WRITING STRATEGY

As you plan, write, and revise your illustration essay, be mindful of the writing process guidelines described in Chapter 2 (see pages 23–47). Also, pay particular attention to the basic requirements and essential ingredients for this writing strategy.

▶ Planning Your Illustration Essay

Planning is an essential part of writing a good illustration essay. You can save yourself a great deal of effort by taking the time to think about the key building blocks of your essay before you actually begin to write.

FOCUS ON YOUR THESIS OR MAIN IDEA. Begin by thinking of how you can make your ideas clearer and more persuasive by illustrating them with examples—facts, anecdotes, and specific details. Once you have established your thesis—the main point that you will develop in your essay—you should find examples that add clarity, color, and authority.

Consider the following thesis:

> Americans are a pain-conscious people who would rather get rid of pain than seek and cure its root causes.

This assertion is broad; it cries out for evidence or support. You could make it stronger and more meaningful through illustration. You might, for example, point to the sheer number of over-the-counter painkillers available and the different types of pain they address, or you might cite specific situations in which people you know have gone to a drugstore instead of to a doctor. In addition, you might cite sales figures for painkillers in the United States and compare them with sales figures in other countries.

GATHER MORE EXAMPLES THAN YOU CAN USE. Before you begin to write, bring together as many examples as you can that are related to your subject—more than you can possibly use. An example may be anything from a fact or a statistic to an anecdote or a story; it may be stated in a few words—"India's population is now approaching 1.3 billion people"—or it may go on for several pages of elaborate description or explanation.

The kinds of examples you look for and where you look for them will depend, of course, on your subject and the point you want to make about it. If you plan to write about all the quirky, fascinating people who make up your family, you can gather your examples without leaving your room: descriptions of their habits and clothing, stories about their strange adventures, facts about their backgrounds, quotations from their conversations. If, however, you are writing an essay on book censorship in American public schools, you will need to do research in the library or on the Internet and read many sources to supply yourself with examples. Your essay might include accounts drawn from newspapers; statistics published by professional organizations; judicial opinions on censorship; and interviews with school board members, parents, publishers, and even the authors whose work has been pulled off library shelves or kept out of the classroom. The range of sources and the variety of examples are limited only by your imagination and the time you can spend on research. For models of and advice on integrating sources in your essay, see Chapters 14 and 15.

Collecting an abundance of examples will allow you to choose the strongest and most representative ones for your essay, not merely the first ones that come to mind. Having enough material will also make it less likely that you will have to stop mid-draft and hunt for additional examples, losing the rhythm of your work or the thread of your ideas. Moreover, the more examples you gather, the more you will learn about your subject and the easier it will be to write about it with authority.

CHOOSE RELEVANT EXAMPLES. You must make sure that your examples are relevant. Do they clarify and support the points you want to make? Suppose the main point of your planned essay is that censorship currently runs rampant in American public education. A newspaper story about the banning of *The Catcher in the Rye* and *The Merchant of Venice* from the local high school's English curriculum would clearly be relevant because it concerns book censorship at a public school. The fact that James Joyce's novel *Ulysses* was once banned as obscene and then vindicated in a famous trial, although a landmark case of censorship in American history, has nothing to do with book censorship in contemporary public schools. While the case of *Ulysses* might be a useful example for other discussions of censorship, it would not be relevant to your essay.

Sometimes more than one of your examples will be relevant. In such cases, choose the examples that are most closely related to your thesis. If you were working on an essay on how Americans cope with pain, a statistic indicating the sales of a particular drug in a given year might be useful; however, a statistic showing that over the past ten years painkiller sales in America have increased more rapidly than the population has would be directly relevant to the idea that Americans are a pain-conscious people and would therefore be a more effective example. Examples may be interesting in and of themselves, but they only come alive when they illustrate and link important ideas that you are trying to promote.

BE SURE YOUR EXAMPLES ARE REPRESENTATIVE. Besides being relevant, your examples should also be representative—that is, they should be typical of the main point or concept, indicative of a larger pattern rather than an uncommon or isolated occurrence. In the essay on pain referred to earlier, figures showing how many people use aspirin, and for what purposes, would be representative because aspirin is the most widely used painkiller in America. Statistics about a newly developed barbiturate (a highly specialized kind of painkiller) might show a tremendous increase in its use, but the example would not be representative because not many people use barbiturates. Giving the barbiturate example might even cause readers to wonder why aspirin, which is better known, was not used as an example.

If, while working on the censorship paper, you found reports on a dozen quiet administrative hearings and orderly court cases, but only one report of a sensational incident in which books were actually burned in a school parking lot, the latter incident, however dramatic, is clearly not a representative example. You might want to mention the book burning in your essay as an extreme example, but you should not present it as typical.

What if your examples do not support your point? Perhaps you have missed some important information and need to look further. It may be, though, that the problem is with the point itself. For example, suppose you intend your censorship paper to illustrate the following thesis: "Book censorship has seriously influenced American public education." While researching your topic, however, you have not found very many examples in which specific books were actually censored or banned outright. In fact, most attempts at censorship were ultimately prevented or overturned in the courts. You might then have to revise your original thesis: "Although there have been many well-publicized attempts to censor books in public schools, actual censorship is relatively rare and less of a problem than is commonly thought."

▶ Organizing Your Illustration Essay

SEQUENCE YOUR EXAMPLES LOGICALLY. It is important to arrange your examples in an order that serves your purpose, is easy for readers to follow, and will have maximum effect. Some possible patterns of organization include chronological order and spatial order. Others include moving from broad examples to personal examples, as in Tim Kreider's "The 'Busy' Trap" (pages 213–16), or from briefer examples to a longer, central illustration, as in Deborah Tannen's "How to Give Orders Like a Man" (pages 202–10). Or you may hit on an order that "feels right" to you, as Edwin Way Teale did in his paragraph about winter superstitions (pages 173–74).

How many examples you include depends, of course, on the length and nature of the assignment. Before starting the first draft, you may find it helpful to work out your organization in a rough outline, using only enough words so that you can tell which example each entry refers to.

USE TRANSITIONS. While it is important to give the presentation of your examples an inherent logic, it is also important to link your examples to the topic sentences in your paragraphs and, indeed, to the thesis of your entire essay by using transitional words and expressions such as *for example, for instance, therefore, afterward, in other words, next,* and *finally*. Such structural devices will make the sequencing of the examples easy to follow.

▶ Revising and Editing Your Illustration Essay

You may find it particularly helpful to share the drafts of your essays with other students in your writing class. One of our students commented, "In total, I probably wrote five or six different versions of this essay. I shared them with members of the class, and their comments were extremely insightful. I remember one student's question in particular because she really got me to focus on the problems with fad diets. The students also helped me to see where I needed examples to explain what I was talking about. The very first draft that I wrote is completely different from the one I submitted in class." To maximize the effectiveness of peer conferences, utilize the suggestions on page 36. Feedback from these conferences often provides one or more places where you can start writing. Then, review Chapter 16 and the questions below to give your essay its final polish.

Questions for Revising and Editing: Illustration

1. Is my topic well focused?
2. Does my thesis statement clearly identify my topic and make an assertion about it?
3. Are my examples well chosen to support my thesis? Are there other examples that might work better?
4. Are my examples representative? That is, are they typical of the main point or concept rather than bizarre or atypical?
5. Do I have enough examples to be convincing? Do I have too many examples?
6. Have I developed my examples in enough detail to be clear to readers?
7. Have I organized my examples in some logical pattern, and is that pattern clear to readers?
8. Does the essay accomplish my purpose?
9. Are my topic sentences strong? Are my paragraphs unified?
10. Does my paper contain any errors in grammar, punctuation, or mechanics? Is my sentence style as clear, smooth, and persuasive as possible?

Be Specific

NATALIE GOLDBERG

Author Natalie Goldberg has made a specialty of writing about writing. Her first and best-known work, *Writing Down the Bones: Freeing the Writer Within*, was published in 1986. Goldberg's advice to would-be writers is, on the one hand, practical and pithy; on the other, it is almost mystical in its call to know and appreciate the world. In a 2007 interview with Shara Stewart for *Ascent* magazine, Goldberg remarked that "[w]riting and Zen for me are completely interconnected. The relationship is seamless for me. . . . Writing is a practice for me, like someone else would do sitting or walking. Writing is a true spiritual practice." "Be Specific," the excerpt that appears below, is representative of the book as a whole. Amid widespread acclaim for the book, one critic commented, "Goldberg teaches us not only how to write better, but how to live better." *Writing Down the Bones* was followed by four more books about writing: *Wild Mind: Living the Writer's Life* (1990), *Living Color: A Writer Paints Her World* (1996), *Thunder and Lightning: Cracking Open the Writer's Craft* (2000), and *The Essential Writer's Notebook* (2001). Goldberg has also written fiction; her first novel, *Banana Rose*, was published in 1994. Her most recent books are *Old Friend from Far Away: The Practice of Writing Memoir* (2008), *The True Secret of Writing: Connecting Life with Language* (2013), and *The Great Spring* (2016), a collection of personal stories.

Notice the way in which Goldberg demonstrates her advice to be specific in the following selection.

Preparing to Read

Suppose someone says to you, "I walked in the woods." What do you envision? Write down what you see in your mind's eye. Now suppose someone says, "I walked in the redwood forest." Again, write what you see. What's different about your two descriptions, and why?

Be specific. Don't say "fruit." Tell what kind of fruit — "It is a pomegranate." Give things the dignity of their names. Just as with human beings, it is rude to say, "Hey, girl, get in line." That "girl" has a name. (As a matter of fact, if she's at least twenty years old, she's a woman, not a "girl" at all.) Things, too, have names. It is much better to say "the geranium in the window" than "the flower in the window." "Geranium" — that one word gives us a much more specific picture. It penetrates more deeply into the beingness of that flower.

It immediately gives us the scene by the window — red petals, green circular leaves, all straining toward sunlight.

> Don't say "fruit." Tell what kind of fruit — "It is a pomegranate." Give things the dignity of their names.

About ten years ago I decided I had to learn the names of plants and flowers in my environment. I bought a book on them and walked down the tree-lined streets of Boulder, examining leaf, bark, and seed, trying to match them up with their descriptions and names in the book. Maple, elm, oak, locust. I usually tried to cheat by asking people working in their yards the names of the flowers and trees growing there. I was amazed how few people had any idea of the names of the live beings inhabiting their little plot of land.

When we know the name of something, it brings us closer to the ground. It takes the blur out of our mind; it connects us to the earth. If I walk down the street and see "dogwood," "forsythia," I feel more friendly toward the environment. I am noticing what is around me and can name it. It makes me more awake.

If you read the poems of William Carlos Williams, you will see how specific he is about plants, trees, flowers — chicory, daisy, locust, poplar, quince, primrose, black-eyed Susan, lilacs — each has its own integrity. Williams says, "Write what's in front of your nose." It's good for us to know what is in front of our noses. Not just "daisy," but how the flower is in the season we are looking at it — "The dayseye hugging the earth / in August . . . brownedged, / green and pointed scales / armor his yellow."[1] Continue to hone your awareness: to the name, to the month, to the day, and finally to the moment.

Williams also says: "No idea, but in things." Study what is "in front of your nose." By saying "geranium" instead of "flower," you are penetrating more deeply into the present and being there. The closer we can get to what's in front of our nose, the more it can teach us everything. "To see the World in a Grain of Sand, and a heaven in a Wild Flower . . ."[2]

In writing groups and classes, too, it is good to quickly learn the names of all the other group members. It helps to ground you in the group and make you more attentive to each other's work.

Learn the names of everything: birds, cheese, tractors, cars, buildings. A writer is all at once everything — an architect, French cook, farmer — and at the same time, a writer is none of these things.

---

[1] William Carlos Williams, "Daisy," in *The Collected Earlier Poems* (New York: New Directions, 1938).
[2] William Blake, "The Auguries of Innocence."

Thinking Critically about the Text

Natalie Goldberg found that she wasn't the only one in her neighborhood who didn't know the names of local trees and flowers. Would you be able to name many? How might you go about learning them? (Consider why Goldberg says it was "cheating" to ask people the names of their flowers and trees.) What would you gain by knowing them?

Questions on Subject

1. In paragraphs 3, 5, and 6, Goldberg cites a number of advantages to be gained by knowing the names of things. Review these advantages. What are they? Do they ring true?
2. Throughout the essay, Goldberg instructs readers to be specific and to be aware of the world around them. Of what besides names are the readers advised to be aware? Why?

Questions on Strategy

1. How does Goldberg "specifically" follow the advice she gives writers in this essay?
2. Goldberg makes several lists of the names of things. What purpose do these lists serve? How does she use these specifics to illustrate her point?
3. What specific audience is Goldberg addressing in this essay? (Glossary: *Audience*) How do you know?
4. The strategies of definition and illustration are closely intertwined in this essay; to name a thing precisely, after all, is to take the first step in defining it. (Glossary: *Definition*) What central concept is defined by Goldberg's many illustrations of naming? How might a writer use illustration to make definitions richer and more meaningful?

Questions on Diction and Vocabulary

1. Goldberg says that to name an object gives it dignity (paragraph 1) and integrity (4). What does she mean in each case?
2. In paragraph 1, Goldberg writes, "It [the word *geranium*] penetrates more deeply into the beingness of that flower." The word *beingness* does not appear in the dictionary. Where does it come from? Why does Goldberg use it, and what does she mean by her statement?
3. In his poem "Daisy," quoted in paragraph 4, William Carlos Williams calls the flower "dayseye." How does this spelling reinforce the central idea of the paragraph? Of the essay as a whole?
4. Refer to a dictionary to determine the meanings of the following words as Goldberg uses them in this selection: *pomegranate* (paragraph 1), *integrity* (4).

Illustration in Action

Specific examples are always more effective and convincing than general ones. A useful exercise in learning to be specific is to see the words we use for people, places, objects, and ideas as being positioned somewhere on a continuum of specificity. In the following chart, notice how the words become more specific as you move from left to right:

More General	General	Specific	More Specific
Organism	Reptile	Snake	Coral snake
Food	Sandwich	Corned beef sandwich	Reuben

Fill in the missing part for each of the following lists:

More General	General	Specific	More Specific
Writing instrument		Fountain pen	Waterman fountain pen
Vehicle	Car		1958 Chevrolet Impala
Book	Reference book	Dictionary	
American		Navaho	Laguna Pueblo
	Oral medicine	Gel capsule	Tylenol Gel Caps
School	High school	Technical high school	

Writing Suggestions

1. Write a brief essay advising your readers of something they should do. Title your essay, as Goldberg does, with a directive ("Be Specific"). Tell your readers how they can improve their lives by taking your advice and give strong examples of the behavior you are recommending.

2. Goldberg likes William Carlos Williams's statement "No idea, but in things" (paragraph 5). Using this line as both a title and a thesis, write your own argument for the use of the specific over the general in a certain field — journalism, history, political science, biology, or literature, for example. (Glossary: *Argument*) Be sure to support your argument with relevant, representative examples.

For a More Creative Brain, Travel

BRENT CRANE

Brent Crane, a journalist and photographer, holds degrees in international affairs and Chinese studies from the University of Colorado at Boulder and engaged in Chinese language and ethnic studies at Yunnan Nationalities University in China. He is a features reporter for the *Phnom Penh Post* in Cambodia and has written for a wide variety of print and online venues, including the *Atlantic*, the *Guardian*, the *Telegraph*, the *Diplomat*, *World Affairs*, *Narratively*, *Vice*, *Condé Nast Traveler*, and *Outside* magazine. When he isn't writing or taking photographs (and sometimes when he is), he enjoys hiking, fishing, skiing, and playing guitar.

In the following essay, first published in the *Atlantic* in March 2015, Crane suggests a link between travel and creativity. Notice how he uses examples to establish this link.

Preparing to Read

Think about your own travel experiences. Travel to other states, cities, and even neighborhoods counts. How would you characterize these experiences? Which were most valuable, and why?

There are plenty of things to be gained from going abroad: new friends, new experiences, new stories.

But living in another country may come with a less noticeable benefit, too: Some scientists say it can also make you more creative.

Writers and thinkers have long felt the creative benefits of international travel. Ernest Hemingway, for example, drew inspiration for much of his work from his time in Spain and France. Aldous Huxley, the author of *Brave New World*, moved from the U.K. to the U.S. in his 40s to branch out into screenwriting. Mark Twain, who sailed around the coast of the Mediterranean in 1869, wrote in his travelogue *Innocents Abroad* that travel is "fatal to prejudice, bigotry, and narrow-mindedness."

In recent years, psychologists and neuroscientists have begun examining more closely what many people have already learned anecdotally: that spending time abroad may have the potential to affect mental change. In general, creativity is related to neuroplasticity, or how the brain is wired. Neural pathways are influenced by environment and habit, meaning they're also sensitive to change: New sounds, smells, language, tastes, sensations, and sights spark different synapses in the brain and may have the potential to revitalize the mind.

"Foreign experiences increase both cognitive flexibility and depth and integrativeness of thought, the ability to make deep connections between disparate forms," says Adam Galinsky, a professor at Columbia Business School and the author of numerous studies on the connection between creativity and international travel. Cognitive flexibility is the mind's ability to jump between different ideas, a key component of creativity. But it's not just about *being* abroad, Galinsky says: "The key, critical process is multicultural engagement, immersion, and adaptation. Someone who lives abroad and doesn't engage with the local culture will likely get less of a creative boost than someone who travels abroad and really engages in the local environment." In other words, going to Cancun for a week on spring break probably won't make a person any more creative. But going to Cancun and living with local fishermen might.

Writers and thinkers have long felt the creative benefits of international travel.

In Galinsky's latest study, published last month in the *Academy of Management Journal*, he and three other researchers examined the experiences of the creative directors of 270 high-end fashion houses. Combing through 11 years' worth of fashion lines, Galinsky and his team searched for links between the creative directors' experience working abroad and the fashion houses' "creative innovations," or the degree "to which final, implemented products or services are novel and useful from the standpoint of external audiences." The level of creativity of a given product was rated by a pool of trade journalists and independent buyers. Sure enough, the researchers found a clear correlation between time spent abroad and creative output: The brands whose creative directors had lived and worked in other countries produced more consistently creative fashion lines than those whose directors had not.

The researchers also found that the more countries the executives had lived in, the more creative the lines tended to be—but only up to a point. Those who had lived and worked in more than three countries, the study found, still tended to show higher levels of creativity than those who hadn't worked abroad at all, but less creativity than their peers who had worked in a smaller number of foreign countries. The authors hypothesized that those who had lived in too many countries hadn't been able to properly immerse themselves culturally; they were bouncing around too much. "It gets back to this idea of a deeper level of learning that's necessary for these effects to occur," Galinsky says.

Cultural distance, or how different a foreign culture is from one's own, may also play a role: Surprisingly, Galinsky and his colleagues found that living someplace with a larger cultural distance was often associated with lower creativity than living in a more familiar culture. The reason for that, they hypothesized, was that an especially different culture might come with a bigger intimidation factor, which may discourage people from immersing themselves in it—and no immersion, they explained, could mean none of the cognitive changes associated with living in another country.

Traveling may have other brain benefits, too. Mary Helen Immordino-Yang, an associate professor of education and psychology at the University of Southern California, says that cross-cultural experiences have the potential to strengthen a person's sense of self. "What a lot of psychological research has shown now is that the ability to engage with people from different backgrounds than yourself, and the ability to get out of your own social comfort zone, is helping you to build a strong and acculturated sense of your own self," she says. "Our ability to differentiate our own beliefs and values . . . is tied up in the richness of the cultural experiences that we have had."

Cross-cultural experiences have the potential to pull people out of their cultural bubbles, and in doing so, can increase their sense of connection with people from backgrounds different than their own. "We found that when people had experiences traveling to other countries it increased what's called generalized trust, or their general faith in humanity," Galinsky says. "When we engage in other cultures, we start to have experience with different people and recognize that most people treat you in similar ways. That produces an increase in trust."

This trust may play an important role in enhancing creative function. In a 2012 study out of Tel Aviv University, researchers found that people who "believe that racial groups have fixed underlying essences"—beliefs the authors termed "essentialist views"—performed significantly worse in creative tests than those who saw cultural and racial divisions as arbitrary and malleable. "This categorical mindset induces a habitual closed-mindedness that transcends the social domain and hampers creativity," the study authors wrote. In other words, those who put people in boxes had trouble thinking *outside* the box.

Of course, although a new country is an easy way to leave a "social comfort zone," the cultural engagement associated with cognitive change doesn't have to happen abroad. If a plane ticket isn't an option, maybe try taking the subway to a new neighborhood. Sometimes, the research suggests, all that's needed for a creative boost is a fresh cultural scene.

Thinking Critically about the Text

Crane uses several detailed examples to explore the relationship between travel and creativity. Have you thought about this relationship before? If so, did this essay give you new insights? If not, does the connection between these ideas resonate with you?

Questions on Subject

1. What *is* creativity? Is the concept defined in the essay, and if so, where? If not, try to devise a definition based on the content of this essay.
2. In paragraph 5, Crane writes about immersing oneself in another culture. What is immersion, and why does Crane think it's important?
3. "Cross-cultural experiences have the potential to pull people out of their cultural bubbles," Crane writes in paragraph 10. What do you think he means by a "cultural bubble"? How might you describe your own cultural bubble?
4. In paragraph 10, Crane quotes the researcher Adam Galinsky explaining that people gain "a general faith in humanity" from traveling to other countries. Based on your own experience and what you know about the world, do you agree with this idea?

Questions on Strategy

1. What is the thesis or main idea of Crane's essay, and where does he present it? (Glossary: *Thesis*)
2. In paragraph 3, Crane introduces his first examples, the writers Hemingway, Huxley, and Twain. Have you read these writers? What do you know about them? Why do you think he presents these examples first? (Glossary: *Examples*)
3. What other examples does Crane use, and are they all relevant and representative? Should any be deleted or expanded? Explain.
4. How has Crane organized his essay? Are examples sequenced logically?
5. How does Crane use transitions to move from one example to the next? (Glossary: *Transitions*)

Questions on Diction and Vocabulary

1. How would you describe Crane's diction in this essay? Is the amount of scientific language he uses right for a general reader? Where does he use this language, and why do you think he does so?
2. Refer to a dictionary to determine the meanings of the following words as they are used in this essay: *anecdotally* (paragraph 4), *neural* (4), *synapses* (4), *cognitive* (5), *disparate* (5), *correlation* (6), *hypothesized* (7), *acculturated* (9), *categorical* (11), *hamper* (11).

Illustration in Action

Crane ends paragraph 10 with Adam Galinsky's statement that "When we engage in other cultures, we start to have experience with different people and recognize that most people treat you in similar ways. That produces an increase in trust." Brainstorm about what the word *culture* means in this context. Make a list of "other cultures" you have engaged in, share it with your classmates, and discuss whether each of you experienced an "increase in trust."

Writing Suggestions

1. Crane writes "New sounds, smells, language, tastes, sensations, and sights spark different synapses in the brain and may have the potential to revitalize the mind" (paragraph 4). Have any of these things ever sparked your creativity? If not, what does? Perhaps it's a scientific or mathematical challenge, or music or art or spending time in the natural world. Write an essay exploring a time you experienced a boost in creativity. Be sure to explain the circumstances and use detailed, relevant examples to illustrate your story.

2. In paragraph 9, Crane cites a professor talking about the value of getting "out of your social comfort zone." Write an essay about a time you stepped outside your social comfort zone. What were the circumstances? How did you feel? What, if anything, did you learn? Use examples and details that will help your readers understand and share your experience.

If You Had One Day with Someone Who's Gone

MITCH ALBOM

Journalist and author Mitch Albom was born in Passaic, New Jersey, in 1958. He earned a degree in sociology from Brandeis University in 1979 and master's degrees in journalism and business administration from Columbia University in 1981 and 1982. Starting in 1985, after working for newspapers in New York and Florida, Albom landed a staff position at the *Detroit Free Press*, where he writes a regular sports column. Over the years he has earned a loyal following of Detroit sports fans both as a columnist and as a host of radio and television sports talk shows. His reputation as a sportswriter blossomed with the publication of *The Live Albom: The Best of Detroit Free Press Sports* (1988–1995), four volumes of his sports column. With the University of Michigan's legendary football coach Bo Schembechler, he wrote *Bo: The Bo Schembechler Story* (1989) and, when Michigan won the national championship in basketball, he authored *Fab Five: Basketball, Trash Talk, and the American Dream* (1993). But it was the publication of *Tuesdays with Morrie: An Old Man, a Young Man, and Life's Greatest Lesson* (1997), the story of Albom's weekly visits with his former sociology professor Morrie Schwartz, that catapulted Albom onto the national stage. Albom followed this work of nonfiction with *Have a Little Faith: A True Story* (2009) and the novels *The Five People You Meet in Heaven* (2003), *The Time Keeper* (2012), and *The First Phone Call from Heaven* (2014), all of which have been national bestsellers. His most recent novel, *The Magic Strings of Frankie Presto* came out in 2015.

In "If You Had One Day with Someone Who's Gone," an essay first published in *Parade* magazine on September 17, 2006, Albom uses the illustrative stories of five people to find out what they would do if they were granted one more day with a loved one. His examples led him to a surprising life lesson.

Preparing to Read

Have you ever lost or become disconnected from someone you loved or were close to — a family member or childhood friend? What were the circumstances that separated you? What would you most like to do with this person if you could be reconnected for a whole day?

Her world shattered in a telephone call. My mother was fifteen years old. "Your father is dead," her aunt told her.

Dead? How could he be dead? Hadn't she seen him the night before, when she kissed him goodnight? Hadn't he given her two new words to look up in the dictionary? Dead?

"You're a liar," my mother said.

But it wasn't a lie. Her father, my grandfather, had collapsed that morning from a massive heart attack. No final hugs. No goodbye. Just a phone call. And he was gone.

Have you ever lost someone you love and wanted one more conversation, one more day to make up for the time when you thought they would be here forever? I wrote that sentence as part of a new novel. Only after I finished did I realize that, my whole life, I had wondered this question of my mother.

So, finally, I asked her.

"One more day with my father?" she said. Her voice seemed to tumble back into some strange, misty place. It had been six decades since their last day together. Murray had wanted his little girl, Rhoda, to be a doctor. He had wanted her to stay single and go to medical school. But after his death, my mother had to survive. She had to look after a younger brother and a depressed mother. She finished high school and married the first boy she ever dated. She never finished college.

"I guess, if I saw my father again, I would first apologize for not becoming a doctor," she answered. "But I would say that I became a different kind of doctor, someone who helped the family whenever they had problems.

"My father was my pal, and I would tell him I missed having a pal around the house after he was gone. I would tell him that my mother lived a long life and was comfortable at the end. And I would show him my family—his grandchildren and his great-grandchildren—of which I am the proudest. I hope he'd be proud of me, too."

My mother admitted that she cried when she first saw the movie *Ghost*, where Patrick Swayze "comes back to life" for a few minutes to be with his girlfriend. She couldn't help but wish for time like that with her father. I began to pose this scenario to other people—friends, colleagues, readers. How would they spend a day with a departed loved one? Their responses said a lot about what we long for.

Almost everyone wanted to once again "tell them how much I loved them"—even though these were people they had loved their whole lives on Earth.

Others wanted to relive little things. Michael Carroll, from San Antonio, Texas, wrote that he and his departed father "would head for the racetrack, then off to Dad's favorite hamburger place to eat and chat about old times."

Cathy Koncurat of Bel Air, Maryland, imagined a reunion with her best friend, who died after mysteriously falling into an icy river. People had always wondered what happened. "But if I had one more day with her, those questions wouldn't be important. Instead, I'd like to spend it the way we did when we were girls—shopping, seeing a movie, getting our hair done."

Some might say, "That's such an ordinary day."

Maybe that's the point.

Rabbi Gerald Wolpe has spent nearly fifty years on the pulpit and is a senior fellow at the University of Pennsylvania's Center for Bioethics. Yet, at some moment every day, he is an eleven-year-old boy who lost his dad to a sudden heart attack in 1938.

"My father is a prisoner of my memory," he said. "Would he even recognize me today?" Rabbi Wolpe can still picture the man, a former vaudevillian, taking him to Boston Braves baseball games or singing him a bedtime prayer.

Help me always do the right
Bless me every day and night.

If granted one more day, Rabbi Wolpe said, he "would share the good and the bad. My father needed to know things. For example, as a boy, he threw a snowball at his brother and hit him between the eyes. His brother went blind. My father went to his death feeling guilty for that.

"But we now know his brother suffered an illness that made him susceptible to losing his vision. I would want to say, 'Dad, look. It wasn't your fault.'"

At funerals, Rabbi Wolpe often hears mourners lament missed moments: "I never apologized. My last words were in anger. *If only I could have one more chance.*"

Maury De Young, a pastor in Kentwood, Michigan, hears similar things in his church. But De Young can sadly relate. His own son, Derrick, was killed in a car accident a few years ago, at age sixteen, the night before his big football game. There was no advance notice. No chance for goodbye.

"If I had one more day with him?" De Young said, wistfully. "I'd start it off with a long, long hug. Then we'd go for a walk, maybe to our cottage in the woods."

De Young had gone to those woods after Derrick's death. He'd sat under a tree and wept. His faith had carried him through. And it eases his pain now, he said, "because I know Derrick is in heaven."

Still, there are questions. Derrick's football number was 42. The day after his accident, his team, with heavy hearts, won a playoff game by scoring 42 points. And the next week, the team won the state title by scoring—yes—42 points.

"I'd like to ask my son," De Young whispered, "if he had something to do with that."

We often fantasize about a perfect day—something exotic and far away. But when it comes to those we miss, we desperately want one more familiar meal, even one more argument. What does this teach us? That the ordinary is precious. That the normal day is a treasure.

Think about it. When you haven't seen a loved one in a long time, the first few hours of catching up feel like a giddy gift, don't they? That's the gift we wish for when we can't catch up anymore. That feeling of connection. It could be a bedside chat, a walk in the woods, even a few words from the dictionary.

I asked my mother if she still recalled those two words her father had assigned her on the last night of his life.

"Oh, yes," she said quickly. "They were 'detrimental' and 'inculcate.' I'll never forget them."

Then she sighed, yearning for a day she didn't have and words she never used. And it made me want to savor every day with her even more.

Thinking Critically about the Text

Albom shares with us the stories of five people who lost a loved one. In each case, the loss was sudden and unexpected. How did the suddenness of the loss affect each of the survivors? In what ways do you think sudden loss is different from losing someone to a terminal illness or old age? Explain.

Questions on Subject

1. Why did Albom's mother cry when she first viewed the movie *Ghost*?
2. When asked how they would spend a day with a departed loved one — if that were possible — how did people respond? What life lesson does Albom draw from these responses in his conclusion?
3. What do you think Rabbi Wolpe meant when he said, "My father is a prisoner of my memory" (paragraph 17)?
4. What does it say about Albom's mother and the relationship she had with her father when it's revealed that she still remembers the two vocabulary words her father gave her the night before he died six decades ago? Explain.

Questions on Strategy

1. Albom opens his essay with the story of his mother losing her father when she was fifteen years old. How effective did you find this beginning? How is Albom's conclusion connected to this beginning? (Glossary: *Beginnings/Endings*)

2. Paragraph 5 starts with the rhetorical question "Have you ever lost someone you love and wanted one more conversation, one more day to make up for the time when you thought they would be here forever?" (Glossary: *Rhetorical Question*) How does this question function in the context of Albom's essay?

3. How did Albom find the examples he uses in this essay? In what ways are Albom's examples both relevant and representative?

4. Albom often repeats key words or ideas to make the transition from one paragraph to the next. Identify several places where he has done this particularly well. What other transitional devices or expressions does he use? (Glossary: *Transitions*)

5. Why do you suppose Albom uses several one-sentence paragraphs? What would be lost had he tacked the sentence "So, finally, I asked her" (paragraph 6) on the end of the previous paragraph?

Questions on Diction and Vocabulary

1. Albom lets most of the people in his examples speak for themselves. What does he gain by letting people tell their own stories instead of telling us what they said? Explain.

2. What, if anything, does Albom's diction tell you about Albom himself? (Glossary: *Diction*) Do you think Albom's diction and tone are appropriate for his subject? (Glossary: *Tone*) Explain.

3. Refer to a dictionary to determine the meanings of the following words as Albom uses them in this selection: *scenario* (paragraph 10), *vaudevillian* (17), *lament* (20), *wistfully* (22), *giddy* (27), *detrimental* (29), *inculcate* (29).

Illustration in Action

Suppose you are writing an essay about the career choices that members of your extended family have made to see what trends or influences you could discover. Using your own extended family (great-grandparents, grandparents, parents, aunts and uncles, siblings) as potential material, make several lists of examples — for instance, one for family members who worked in agriculture, a second for those who worked in education, a third for those who worked at an office job, a fourth for those who worked in the service sector, and a fifth for those who worked in the medical or legal fields. Reflect on the ways you could use these examples in an essay.

Writing Suggestions

1. Has someone close to you — a parent, grandparent, relative, or friend — died, or has someone moved away whom you would like to see again, if only for a day? Write an essay in which you first tell us something about your

relationship with the person you are missing and then describe what you would do with that person for one whole day.

2. What do you value most about your relationships with family members? Do you have a special relationship with one particular parent, sibling, aunt or uncle, or grandparent? How would you describe the relationship you have with this person? What specifically do you get from him or her? Write an essay about your relationship with this family member, using relevant and representative examples to illustrate why you value having the person in your life.

How to Give Orders Like a Man

DEBORAH TANNEN

Deborah Tannen, professor of linguistics at Georgetown University, was born in 1945 in Brooklyn, New York. Tannen received her B.A. in English from the State University of New York at Binghamton in 1966 and taught English in Greece until 1968. She then earned an M.A. in English literature from Wayne State University in 1970. While pursuing her Ph.D. in linguistics at the University of California–Berkeley, she received several prizes for her poetry and short fiction. Her work has appeared in *New York*, *Vogue*, and the *New York Times Magazine*. In addition, she has authored three best-selling books on how people communicate: *You Just Don't Understand* (1990), *That's Not What I Meant* (1991), and *Talking from Nine to Five* (1994). The success of these books attests to the public's interest in language, especially when it pertains to gender differences. Tannen's other books include *The Argument Culture: Stopping America's War of Words* (1998), *You're Wearing* That? *Mothers and Daughters in Conversation* (2006), and most recently *You Were Always Mom's Favorite: Sisters in Conversation throughout Their Lives* (2009). Her research led Tannen to conclude that "in some ways, siblings and especially sisters are more influential in your childhood than your parents."

Courtesy of Deborah Tannen

In this essay, first published in the *New York Times Magazine* in August 1994, Tannen looks at the variety of ways in which orders are given and received. Interestingly, she concludes that, contrary to popular belief, directness is not necessarily logical or effective and indirectness is not necessarily manipulative or insecure.

Preparing to Read

Write about a time in your life when you were ordered to do something. Who gave you the order—a friend, a parent, maybe a teacher or coach? Did the person's relationship to you affect how you carried out the order? Did it make a difference to you whether the order giver was male or female? Why?

A university president was expecting a visit from a member of the board of trustees. When her secretary buzzed to tell her that the board member had arrived, she left her office and entered the reception area to greet him. Before ushering him into her office, she handed her secretary a sheet of paper and said: "I've just finished drafting this letter. Do you think you could type it right away? I'd like to get it out before lunch. And would you please do me a favor and hold all calls while I'm meeting with Mr. Smith?"

When they sat down behind the closed door of her office, Mr. Smith began by telling her that he thought she had spoken inappropriately to her secretary. "Don't forget," he said. "*You're* the president!"

Putting aside the question of the appropriateness of his admonishing the president on her way of speaking, it is revealing—and representative of many Americans' assumptions—that the indirect way in which the university president told her secretary what to do struck him as self-deprecating. He took it as evidence that she didn't think she had the right to make demands of her secretary. He probably thought he was giving her a needed pep talk, bolstering her self-confidence.

I challenge the assumption that talking in an indirect way necessarily reveals powerlessness, lack of self-confidence, or anything else about the character of the speaker. Indirectness is a fundamental element in human communication. It is also one of the elements that varies most from one culture to another, and one that can cause confusion and misunderstanding when speakers have different habits with regard to using it. I also want to dispel the assumption that American women tend to be more indirect than American men. Women and men are both indirect, but in addition to differences associated with their backgrounds—regional, ethnic, and class—they tend to be indirect in different situations and in different ways.

At work, we need to get others to do things, and we all have different ways of accomplishing this. Any individual's ways will vary depending on who is being addressed—a boss, a peer, or a subordinate. At one extreme are bald commands. At the other are requests so indirect that they don't sound like requests at all, but are just a statement of need or a description of a situation. People with direct styles of asking others to do things perceive indirect requests—if they perceive them as requests at all—as manipulative. But this is often just a way of blaming others for our discomfort with their styles.

The indirect style is no more manipulative than making a telephone call, asking "Is Rachel there?" and expecting whoever answers the phone to put Rachel on. Only a child is likely to answer "Yes" and continue holding the phone—not out of orneriness but because of inexperience with the conventional meaning of the question. (A mischievous adult might do it to tease.) Those who feel that indirect orders are illogical or manipulative do not recognize the conventional nature of indirect requests.

Issuing orders indirectly can be the prerogative of those in power. Imagine, for example, a master who says "It's cold in here" and expects a servant to make a move to close a window, while a servant who says the same thing is not likely to see his employer rise to correct the situation and make him more comfortable. Indeed, a Frenchman raised in Brittany tells me that his family never gave bald commands to their servants but always communicated orders in indirect and highly polite ways. This pattern renders less surprising the finding of David Bellinger and Jean Berko Gleason that fathers' speech to their young children had a higher incidence than mothers' of both direct imperatives like "Turn the bolt with the wrench" *and* indirect orders like "The wheel is going to fall off."

The use of indirectness can hardly be understood without the cross-cultural perspective. Many Americans find it self-evident that directness is logical and aligned with power while indirectness is akin to dishonesty and reflects subservience. But for speakers raised in most of the world's cultures, varieties of indirectness are the norm in communication. This is the pattern found by a Japanese sociolinguist, Kunihiko Harada, in his analysis of a conversation he recorded between a Japanese boss and a subordinate.

The markers of superior status were clear. One speaker was a Japanese man in his late 40s who managed the local branch of a Japanese private school in the United States. His conversational partner was a Japanese American woman in her early 20s who worked at the school. By virtue of his job, his age, and his native fluency in the language being taught, the man was in the superior position. Yet when he addressed the woman, he frequently used polite language and almost always used indirectness. For example, he had tried and failed to find a photography store that would make a black-and-white print from a color negative for a brochure they were producing. He let her know that he wanted her to take over the task by stating the situation and allowed her to volunteer to do it: (This is a translation of the Japanese conversation.)

> On this matter, that, that, on the leaflet? This photo, I'm thinking of changing it to black-and-white and making it clearer. . . . I went to a photo shop and asked them. They said they didn't do black-and-white. I asked if they knew any place that did. They said they didn't know. They weren't very helpful, but anyway, a place must be found, the negative brought to it, the picture developed.

Harada observes, "Given the fact that there are some duties to be performed and that there are two parties present, the subordinate is supposed to assume that those are his or her obligation." It was precisely because of his higher status that the boss was free to choose whether to speak formally or informally, to assert his power or to play it down and build rapport—an option not available to the subordinate, who would have seemed cheeky if she had chosen a style that enhanced friendliness and closeness.

The same pattern was found by a Chinese sociolinguist, Yuling Pan, in a meeting of officials involved in a neighborhood youth program. All spoke in ways that reflected their place in the hierarchy. A subordinate addressing a superior always spoke in a deferential way, but a superior addressing a subordinate could either be authoritarian, demonstrating his power, or friendly, establishing rapport. The ones in power had the option of choosing which style to use. In this spirit, I have been told by people who prefer their bosses to give orders indirectly that those who issue bald commands must be pretty insecure; otherwise why would they have to bolster their egos by throwing their weight around?

I am not inclined to accept that those who give orders directly are really insecure and powerless, any more than I want to accept that judgment of those who give indirect orders. The conclusion to be drawn is that ways of talking should not be taken as obvious evidence of inner psychological states like insecurity or lack of confidence. Considering the many influences on conversational style, individuals have a wide range of ways of getting things done and expressing their emotional states. Personality characteristics like insecurity cannot be linked to ways of speaking in an automatic, self-evident way.

Those who expect orders to be given indirectly are offended when they come unadorned. One woman said that when her boss gives her instructions, she feels she should click her heels, salute, and say "Yes, boss!" His directions strike her as so imperious as to border on the militaristic. Yet I received a letter from a man telling me that indirect orders were a fundamental part of his military training. He wrote:

> Many years ago, when I was in the Navy, I was training to be a radio technician. One class I was in was taught by a chief radioman, a regular Navy man who had been to sea, and who was then in his third hitch. The students, about twenty of us, were fresh out of boot camp, with no sea duty and little knowledge of real Navy life. One day in class the chief said it was hot in the room. The students didn't react, except perhaps to nod in agreement. The chief repeated himself: "It's hot in this room." Again there was no reaction from the students.
>
> Then the chief explained. He wasn't looking for agreement or discussion from us. When he said that the room was hot, he expected us to do something about it—like opening the window. He tried it one more time, and this time all of us left our workbenches and headed for the windows. We had learned. And we had many opportunities to apply what we had learned.

This letter especially intrigued me because "It's cold in here" is the standard sentence used by linguists to illustrate an indirect way of getting someone to do something—as I used it earlier. In this example, it is the very obviousness and rigidity of the military hierarchy that makes the statement of a problem sufficient to trigger corrective action on the part of subordinates.

A man who had worked at the Pentagon reinforced the view that the burden of interpretation is on subordinates in the military—and he noticed the difference when he moved to a position in the private sector. He was frustrated when he'd say to his new secretary, for example, "Do we have a list of invitees?" and be told, "I don't know; we probably do" rather than "I'll get it for you." Indeed, he explained, at the Pentagon, such a question would likely be heard as a reproach that the list was not already on his desk.

The suggestion that indirectness is associated with the military must come as a surprise to many. But everyone is indirect, meaning more than is put into words and deriving meaning from words that are never actually said. It's a matter of where, when, and how we each tend to be indirect and look for hidden meanings. But indirectness has a built-in liability. There is a risk that the other will either miss or choose to ignore your meaning.

On January 13, 1982, a freezing cold, snowy day in Washington, Air Florida Flight 90 took off from National Airport, but could not get the lift it needed to keep climbing. It crashed into a bridge linking Washington to the state of Virginia and plunged into the Potomac. Of the seventy-nine people on board, all but five perished, many floundering and drowning in the icy water while horror-stricken bystanders watched helplessly from the river's edge and millions more watched, aghast, on their television screens. Experts later concluded that the plane had waited too long after deicing to take off. Fresh buildup of ice on the wings and engine brought the plane down. How could the pilot and co-pilot have made such a blunder? Didn't at least one of them realize it was dangerous to take off under these conditions?

Charlotte Linde, a linguist at the Institute for Research on Learning in Palo Alto, California, has studied the "black box" recordings of cockpit conversations that preceded crashes as well as tape recordings of conversations that took place among crews during flight simulations in which problems were presented. Among the black box conversations she studied was the one between the pilot and co-pilot just before the Air Florida crash. The pilot, it turned out, had little experience flying in icy weather. The co-pilot had a bit more, and it became heartbreakingly clear on analysis that he had tried to warn the pilot, but he did so indirectly.

The co-pilot repeatedly called attention to the bad weather and to ice building up on other planes:

> Co-pilot: Look how the ice is just hanging on his, ah, back, back there, see that?
> . . .
> Co-pilot: See all those icicles on the back there and everything?
> Captain: Yeah.

He expressed concern early on about the long waiting time between deicing:

> Co-pilot: Boy, this is a, this is a losing battle here on trying to deice those things, it [gives] you a false feeling of security, that's all that does.

Shortly after they were given clearance to take off, he again expressed concern:

> Co-pilot: Let's check these tops again since we been setting here awhile.
> Captain: I think we get to go here in a minute.

When they were about to take off, the co-pilot called attention to the engine instrument readings, which were not normal:

> Co-pilot: That don't seem right, does it? [three-second pause] Ah, that's not right. . . .
> Captain: Yes, it is, there's eighty.
> Co-pilot: Naw, I don't think that's right. [seven-second pause] Ah, maybe it is.
> Captain: Hundred and twenty.
> Co-pilot: I don't know.

The takeoff proceeded, and thirty-seven seconds later the pilot and co-pilot exchanged their last words.

The co-pilot had repeatedly called the pilot's attention to dangerous conditions but did not directly suggest they abort the takeoff. In Linde's judgment, he was expressing his concern indirectly, and the captain didn't pick up on it—with tragic results.

That the co-pilot was trying to warn the captain indirectly is supported by evidence from another airline accident—a relatively minor one—investigated by Linde that also involved the unsuccessful use of indirectness.

On July 9, 1978, Allegheny Airlines Flight 453 was landing at Monroe County Airport in Rochester, when it overran the runway by 728 feet. Everyone survived. This meant that the captain and co-pilot could be interviewed. It turned out that the plane had been flying too fast for a safe landing. The captain should have realized this and flown around a second time, decreasing his speed before trying to land. The captain said he simply had not been aware that he was going too fast. But the co-pilot told interviewers that he "tried to warn the captain in subtle ways, like mentioning the possibility of a tail wind and the slowness of flap extension." His exact words were recorded in the black box. The crosshatches indicate words deleted by the National Transportation Safety Board and were probably expletives:

> Co-pilot: Yeah, it looks like you got a tail wind here.
> Captain: Yeah.
> [?]: Yeah [it] moves awfully # slow.
> Co-pilot: Yeah the # flaps are slower than a #.
> Captain: We'll make it, gonna have to add power.
> Co-pilot: I know.

The co-pilot thought the captain would understand that if there was a tail wind, it would result in the plane going too fast, and if the flaps were slow, they would be inadequate to break the speed sufficiently for a safe landing. He thought the captain would then correct for the error by not trying to land. But the captain said he didn't interpret the co-pilot's remarks to mean they were going too fast.

Linde believes it is not a coincidence that the people being indirect in these conversations were the co-pilots. In her analyses of flight-crew conversations she found it was typical for the speech of subordinates to be more mitigated—polite, tentative, or indirect. She also found that topics broached in a mitigated way were more likely to fail, and that captains were more likely to ignore hints from their crew members than the other way around. These findings are evidence that not only can indirectness and other forms of mitigation be misunderstood, but they are also easier to ignore.

In the Air Florida case, it is doubtful that the captain did not realize what the co-pilot was suggesting when he said, "Let's check these tops again since we been setting here awhile" (though it seems safe to assume he did not realize the gravity of the co-pilot's concern). But the indirectness of the co-pilot's phrasing certainly made it easier for the pilot to ignore it. In this sense, the captain's response, "I think we get to go here in a minute," was an indirect way of saying, "I'd rather not." In view of these patterns, the flight crews of some airlines are now given training to express their concerns, even to superiors, in more direct ways.

The conclusion that people should learn to express themselves more directly has a ring of truth to it—especially for Americans. But direct communication is not necessarily always preferable. If more direct expression is better communication, then the most direct-speaking crews should be the best ones. Linde was surprised to find in her research that crews that used the most mitigated speech were often judged the best crews. As part of the study of talk among cockpit crews in flight simulations, the trainers observed and rated the performances of the simulation crews. The crews they rated top in performance had a higher rate of mitigation than crews they judged to be poor.

This finding seems at odds with the role played by indirectness in the examples of crashes that we just saw. Linde concluded that since every utterance functions on two levels—the referential (what it says) and the relational (what it implies about the speaker's relationships), crews that attend to the relational level will be better crews. A similar explanation was suggested by Kunihiko Harada. He believes that the secret of successful communication lies not in teaching subordinates to be more direct, but in teaching higher-ups to be more sensitive to indirect meaning. In other words, the crashes resulted not only because the co-pilots tried to alert the captains to danger indirectly but also because the captains were not attuned to the co-pilots' hints. What made for successful performance among the best crews might have been the ability—or willingness—of listeners to pick up on hints, just as members of families or longstanding couples come to understand each other's meaning without anyone being particularly explicit.

It is not surprising that a Japanese sociolinguist came up with this explanation; what he described is the Japanese system, by which good communication is believed to take place when meaning is gleaned without being stated directly—or at all.

While Americans believe that "the squeaky wheel gets the grease" (so it's best to speak up), the Japanese say, "The nail that sticks out gets hammered back in" (so it's best to remain silent if you don't want to be hit on the head). Many Japanese scholars writing in English have tried to explain to bewildered Americans the ethics of a culture in which silence is often given greater value than speech, and ideas are believed to be best communicated without being explicitly stated. Key concepts in Japanese give a flavor of the attitudes toward language that they reveal—and set in relief the strategies that Americans encounter at work when talking to other Americans.

Takie Sugiyama Lebra, a Japanese-born anthropologist, explains that one of the most basic values in Japanese culture is *omoiyari*, which she translates as "empathy." Because of *omoiyari*, it should not be necessary to state one's meaning explicitly; people should be able to sense each other's meaning intuitively. Lebra explains that it is typical for a Japanese speaker to let sentences trail off rather than complete them because expressing ideas before knowing how they will be received seems intrusive. "Only an insensitive, uncouth person needs a direct, verbal, complete message," Lebra says.

Sasshi, the anticipation of another's message through insightful guesswork, is considered an indication of maturity.

Considering the value placed on direct communication by Americans in general, and especially by American businesspeople, it is easy to imagine that many American readers may scoff at such conversational habits. But the success of Japanese businesses makes it impossible to continue to maintain that there is anything inherently inefficient about such conversational conventions. With indirectness, as with all aspects of conversational style, our own habitual style seems to make sense—seems polite, right, and good. The light cast by the habits and assumptions of another culture can help us see our way to the flexibility and respect for other styles that is the only best way of speaking.

Thinking Critically about the Text

In her essay, Tannen states that "indirectness is a fundamental element in human communication" (paragraph 4). Do you agree with Tannen on this point? What does she mean when she says that it is just as important to notice what we do not say as what we actually say?

Questions on Subject

1. How does Tannen define indirect speech? What does she see as the built-in liability of indirect speech? Do you see comparable liability inherent in direct speech?
2. Tannen doesn't contest a finding that fathers had a higher incidence of both direct imperatives and indirect orders than mothers did. How does she interpret these results?
3. Why do you think Tannen doesn't tell her audience how to deal with an insecure boss?
4. Why is it typical for Japanese speakers to let their sentences trail off?

Questions on Strategy

1. What is Tannen's thesis, and where does she present it? (Glossary: *Thesis*)
2. Tannen mostly uses examples in which men give direct orders. In what ways do these examples support her thesis?
3. For what audience has Tannen written this essay? Does this help to explain why she focuses primarily on indirect communication? Why or why not? (Glossary: *Audience*)

4. Tannen gives two examples of flight accidents that resulted from indirect speech, yet she then explains that top-performing flight teams used indirect speech more often than poorly performing teams. How do these seemingly contradictory examples support the author's argument?

5. Explain how Tannen uses comparison and contrast to document the assertion that "indirectness is a fundamental element in human communication. It is also one of the elements that varies most from one culture to another, and one that can cause confusion and misunderstanding when speakers have different habits with regard to using it" (paragraph 4). (Glossary: *Comparison and Contrast*) How does this strategy enhance or support the dominant strategy of illustration in the essay?

Questions on Diction and Vocabulary

1. In paragraph 13, what irony does Tannen point out in the popular understanding of the word *militaristic*? (Glossary: *Irony*)

2. How would you describe Tannen's diction in this essay? (Glossary: *Diction*) Does she ever get too scientific for the general reader? If so, where do you think her language gets too technical? Why do you think she uses such language?

3. Refer to a dictionary to determine the meanings of the following words as Tannen uses them in this selection: *admonishing* (paragraph 3), *self-deprecating* (3), *manipulative* (5), *prerogative* (7), *subservience* (8), *cheeky* (10), *deferential* (11), *imperious* (13), *liability* (16), *mitigated* (28), *broached* (28), *gleaned* (32), *relief* (33), *empathy* (34).

Illustration in Action

Once you have established what examples you will use in a paper, you need to decide how you will organize them. Here are some major patterns of organization you may want to use:

- Chronological (oldest to newest or the reverse)
- Spatial (top to bottom, left to right, inside to outside, and so forth)
- Most familiar to least familiar or the reverse
- Easiest to most difficult to comprehend
- Easiest to most difficult to accept or carry out
- According to similarities or differences

Use one or more of these patterns to organize the examples in the paper you are currently working on or to organize the lists of examples of career choice in your extended family that you generated for the classroom activity accompanying the Albom essay on page 200.

Writing Suggestions

1. Tannen concludes that "the light cast by the habits and assumptions of another culture can help us see our way to the flexibility and respect for other styles that is the only best way of speaking" (paragraph 36). Write an essay in which you use concrete examples from your own experience, observation, or readings to agree or disagree with her conclusion.

2. Write an essay comparing the command styles of two people — either people you know or fictional characters. You might consider your parents, professors, coaches, television characters, or characters from movies or novels. What conclusions can you draw from your analysis? (Glossary: *Comparison and Contrast*) Illustrate your essay with clear examples of the two command styles.

The "Busy" Trap

TIM KREIDER

Tim Kreider was born in Baltimore in 1967, went to Johns Hopkins University, and worked primarily as a cartoonist until 2009. His strip "The Pain — When Will It End?" ran in the Baltimore *City Paper* and other alternative publications for 12 years. His writing has appeared in a wide variety of publications and online venues, including the *New York Times*, the *Baltimore Sun*, *Al Jazeera*, the *Huffington Post*, the *New Yorker*'s "Page-Turner" blog, *Film Quarterly*, *Men's Journal*, and *Modern Farmer*. He has published three collections of cartoons and a collection of essays, *We Learn Nothing* (2012).

Noah Sheppard

He divides his time between Brooklyn and a cabin in Maryland, referred to in this essay as an "Undisclosed Location." In a "self-interview" Kreider did for the website *The Nervous Breakdown*, he describes his work as follows: "I'm not an especially brilliant thinker or keen observer of the human condition or a great prose stylist; my only meager strength as a writer is to be as honest as I can." This essay was originally published in the *New York Times*'s "Anxiety" blog in 2015. As you read, watch how Kreider uses examples to make his point about what it really means when people claim to be "too busy" and what we can do about it.

Preparing to Read

Do you consider yourself too busy, or do you think you've struck a good balance of work and relaxation in your life? If you feel too busy, do you have any ideas about how to solve this problem?

If you live in America in the 21st century you've probably had to listen to a lot of people tell you how busy they are. It's become the default response when you ask anyone how they're doing: "Busy!" "*So* busy." "*Crazy* busy." It is, pretty obviously, a boast disguised as a complaint. And the stock response is a kind of congratulation: "That's a good problem to have," or "Better than the opposite."

Notice it isn't generally people pulling back-to-back shifts in the I.C.U. or commuting by bus to three minimum-wage jobs who tell you how busy they are; what those people are is not busy but *tired. Exhausted. Dead on their feet.* It's almost always people whose lamented busyness is purely self-imposed: work and obligations they've taken on voluntarily, classes and activities they've "encouraged" their kids to participate in. They're busy because of their own ambition or drive or anxiety, because they're addicted to busyness and dread what they might have to face in its absence.

Almost everyone I know is busy. They feel anxious and guilty when they aren't either working or doing something to promote their work. They schedule in time with friends the way students with 4.0 G.P.A.'s make sure to sign up for community service because it looks good on their college applications. I recently wrote a friend to ask if he wanted to do something this week, and he answered that he didn't have a lot of time but if something was going on to let him know and maybe he could ditch work for a few hours. I wanted to clarify that my question had not been a preliminary heads-up to some future invitation; this was the invitation. But his busyness was like some vast churning noise through which he was shouting out at me, and I gave up trying to shout back over it.

> They're busy because of their own ambition or drive or anxiety, because they're addicted to busyness and dread what they might have to face in its absence.

Even *children* are busy now, scheduled down to the half-hour with classes and extracurricular activities. They come home at the end of the day as tired as grown-ups. I was a member of the latchkey generation and had three hours of totally unstructured, largely unsupervised time every afternoon, time I used to do everything from surfing the World Book Encyclopedia to making animated films to getting together with friends in the woods to chuck dirt clods directly into one another's eyes, all of which provided me with important skills and insights that remain valuable to this day. Those free hours became the model for how I wanted to live the rest of my life.

The present hysteria is not a necessary or inevitable condition of life; it's something we've chosen, if only by our acquiescence to it. Not long ago I Skyped with a friend who was driven out of the city by high rent and now has an artist's residency in a small town in the south of France. She described herself as happy and relaxed for the first time in years. She still gets her work done, but it doesn't consume her entire day and brain. She says it feels like college—she has a big circle of friends who all go out to the cafe together every night. She has a boyfriend again. (She once ruefully summarized dating in New York: "Everyone's too busy and everyone thinks they can do better.") What she had mistakenly assumed was her personality—driven, cranky, anxious and sad—turned out to be a deformative effect of her environment. It's not as if any of us wants to live like this, any more than any one person wants to be part of a traffic jam or stadium trampling or the hierarchy of cruelty in high school—it's something we collectively force one another to do.

Busyness serves as a kind of existential reassurance, a hedge against emptiness; obviously your life cannot possibly be silly or trivial or meaningless if you are so busy, completely booked, in demand every hour of the day. I once knew a woman who interned at a magazine where she wasn't allowed to take lunch hours out, lest she be urgently needed for some reason. This was an entertainment magazine whose raison d'être was obviated when "menu" buttons appeared on remotes, so it's hard to see this pretense of indispensability as anything other than a form of institutional self-delusion. More and more people in this country no longer make or do anything tangible; if your job wasn't performed by a cat or a boa constrictor in a Richard Scarry book I'm not sure I believe it's necessary. I can't help but wonder whether all this histrionic exhaustion isn't a way of covering up the fact that most of what we do doesn't matter.

I am not busy. I am the laziest ambitious person I know. Like most writers, I feel like a reprobate who does not deserve to live on any day that I do not write, but I also feel that four or five hours is enough to earn my stay on the planet for one more day. On the best ordinary days of my life, I write in the morning, go for a long bike ride and run errands in the afternoon, and in the evening I see friends, read or watch a movie. This, it seems to me, is a sane and pleasant pace for a day. And if you call me up and ask whether I won't maybe blow off work and check out the new American Wing at the Met or ogle girls in Central Park or just drink chilled pink minty cocktails all day long, I will say, what time?

But just in the last few months, I've insidiously started, because of professional obligations, to become busy. For the first time I was able to tell people, with a straight face, that I was "too busy" to do this or that thing they wanted me to do. I could see why people enjoy this complaint; it makes you feel important, sought-after and put-upon. Except that I hate actually being busy. Every morning my in-box was full of e-mails asking me to do things I did not want to do or presenting me with problems that I now had to solve. It got more and more intolerable until finally I fled town to the Undisclosed Location from which I'm writing this.

Here I am largely unmolested by obligations. There is no TV. To check e-mail I have to drive to the library. I go a week at a time without seeing anyone I know. I've remembered about buttercups, stink bugs and the stars. I read. And I'm finally getting some real writing done for the first time in months. It's hard to find anything to say about life without immersing yourself in the world, but it's also just about impossible to figure out what it might be, or how best to say it, without getting the hell out of it again.

Idleness is not just a vacation, an indulgence or a vice; it is as indispensable to the brain as vitamin D is to the body, and deprived of it we suffer a mental affliction as disfiguring as rickets. The space and quiet that idleness provides is a necessary condition for standing back from life and seeing it whole, for making unexpected connections and waiting for the wild summer lightning strikes of inspiration—it is, paradoxically, necessary to getting any work done. "Idle dreaming is often of the essence of what we do," wrote Thomas Pynchon in his essay on sloth. Archimedes' "Eureka" in the bath, Newton's apple, Jekyll & Hyde and the benzene ring: history is full of stories of inspirations that come in idle moments and dreams. It almost makes you wonder whether loafers, goldbricks and no-accounts aren't responsible for more of the world's great ideas, inventions and masterpieces than the hardworking.

"The goal of the future is full unemployment, so we can play. That's why we have to destroy the present politico-economic system." This may sound like the pronouncement of some bong-smoking anarchist, but it was actually Arthur C. Clarke, who found time between scuba diving and pinball games to write "Childhood's End" and think up communications satellites. My old colleague Ted Rall recently wrote a column proposing that we divorce income from work and give each citizen a guaranteed paycheck, which sounds like the kind of lunatic notion that'll be considered a basic human right in about a century, like abolition, universal suffrage and eight-hour workdays. The Puritans turned work into a virtue, evidently forgetting that God invented it as a punishment.

Perhaps the world would soon slide to ruin if everyone behaved as I do. But I would suggest that an ideal human life lies somewhere between my own defiant indolence and the rest of the world's endless frenetic hustle. My role is just to be a bad influence, the kid standing outside the classroom window making faces at you at your desk, urging you to just this once make some excuse and get out of there, come outside and play. My own resolute idleness has mostly been a luxury rather than a virtue, but I did make a conscious decision, a long time ago, to choose time over money, since I've always understood that the best investment of my limited time on earth was to spend it with people I love. I suppose it's possible I'll lie on my deathbed regretting that I didn't work harder and say everything I had to say, but I think what I'll really wish is that I could have one more beer with Chris, another long talk with Megan, one last good hard laugh with Boyd. Life is too short to be busy.

Thinking Critically about the Text

"Almost everyone I know is busy," Kreider writes. "They feel anxious and guilty when they aren't either working or doing something to promote their work" (paragraph 3). Does this accurately describe people you know, and if so, do you think they should feel and behave differently? Or do you think they have good reasons to work all the time?

Questions on Subject

1. Kreider writes that people who complain about being busy "dread what they might have to face" (paragraph 2) in the absence of busyness. What does he think they might have to face if they weren't so busy?

2. Kreider says that as a child, his daily hours of free time after school "provided him with important skills and insights that remain valuable to this day" (4). What skills and insights do you think he is talking about?

3. In paragraph 9, Kreider writes "I'm finally getting some real writing done for the first time in months." What do you think he means by "real writing"? What has been keeping him from doing this real writing? How does this statement connect to the overall message of his essay? Do you think he would count this essay as "real writing"?

4. In his final paragraph, Kreider writes that his "role is just to be a bad influence, . . . urging you to just this once make some excuse and get out of there, come outside and play" (12). Does he literally consider himself a "bad" influence? Explain. (Glossary: *Irony*)

Questions on Strategy

1. How does Kreider use comparison in paragraph 2, and what is the effect of this comparison?

2. Kreider uses a simile at the end of paragraph 3 (Glossary: *Figures of Speech*), describing his friend's busyness as "some vast churning noise through which he was shouting at me." Where else does he use figurative language, and to what effect?

3. Who is Kreider's audience, and how do you know? Pay special attention to the first sentence in paragraph 2 and the last sentence in paragraph 7. (Glossary: *Audience*)

4. Consider the examples Kreider provides in the second half of paragraph 10: Thomas Pynchon, Archimedes, Newton, and Jekyll & Hyde. (Glossary: *Allusion*) Do you understand all of these references? Would more information have been helpful here, or can you infer their importance from the surrounding context?

Questions on Diction and Vocabulary

1. Kreider uses the term *raison d'être* in paragraph 6. What is the effect of using this French idiom? (Glossary: *Idiom*)

2. In paragraph 5, Kreider says of a friend, "What she had mistakenly assumed was her personality — driven, cranky, anxious, and sad — turned out to be a deformative effect of her environment." What does *deformative* mean, in this context, and what is its effect on the reader?

3. Kreider states that in what he calls his "Undisclosed Location," he is "largely unmolested by obligations" (paragraph 8). What obligations is he talking about? And what is the effect of using the verb *unmolested* instead of *bothered* or *interrupted*? Why do you think he made this choice?

4. Refer to a dictionary to determine the meanings of the following words as Kreider uses them in this selection: *acquiescence* (5), *existential* (6), *obviated* (6), *histrionic* (6), *reprobate* (7), *insidiously* (8), *rickets* (10), *indolence* (12), *frenetic* (12), *resolute* (12).

Illustration in Action

Make a chart with seven columns, one for each day of the week, and twenty-four rows, one for each hour of the day. To the best of your memory, fill in what you did every hour this past week. Are there activities you don't want to be doing? Are there some things you must do but could do more quickly? Are there things you can eliminate altogether? Finally, are there things you want to be doing that are not represented in the chart? Now create a revised chart, illustrating your ideal way to spend these hours. Consider whether your ideal schedule seems possible. Is there a reasonable compromise you could reach, making some, if not all, of these changes?

Writing Suggestions

1. "More and more people in this country no longer make or do anything tangible," Kreider writes in paragraph 6. "I can't help but wonder whether all this histrionic exhaustion isn't a way of covering up the fact that most of what we do doesn't matter." What relationship is Kreider suggesting between making or doing something "tangible" and whether what we do matters? Do you believe that work must be tangible in order to matter? What does it mean for work to be tangible? Does the product have to be something physical we can pick up or handle in some way, something concrete we can use? What other kinds of work are there? Write an essay about the kinds of work that you think matter, making sure to provide examples of both the jobs in question and the impact they make.

2. In paragraph 9, Kreider writes that in his "Undisclosed Location," he has no TV or easy access to e-mail and he goes "a week at a time without seeing anyone" he knows. Does this scenario appeal to you? Why or why not? What might you gain by not watching television or using the Internet and by spending most of your time alone? What would you lose? Write an essay exploring how such a setting might be physically and psychologically healthy for you, or alternatively, write about how such a setting might be detrimental to your physical and psychological well-being. Illustrate your essay with detailed examples of how your life would improve, or be worse, under these circumstances.

WRITING SUGGESTIONS FOR ILLUSTRATION

1. Write an essay on one of the following statements, using examples to illustrate your ideas. You should be able to draw some of your examples from personal experience and firsthand observations.

    a. The latest trend is usually ridiculous.
    b. Television has produced a number of "classic" programs.
    c. Every college campus has its own unique slang terms.
    d. All good teachers (*or* doctors, secretaries, auto mechanics, sales representatives) have certain traits in common.
    e. Reality television is an accurate (*or* inaccurate) reflection of our society.
    f. Good literature always teaches us something about our humanity.
    g. Grades are not always a good indication of what has been learned.
    h. Recycling starts with the individual.

2. College students are not often given credit for the community volunteer work they do. Write a letter to the editor of your local newspaper in which you demonstrate, with several extended examples, the beneficial impact that you and your fellow students have had on the community.

3. How do advertisers portray older people in their advertisements? Based on your analysis of some real ads, how fair are advertisers to senior citizens? What tactics do advertisers use to sell their products to senior citizens? Write an essay in which you use actual ads to illustrate two or three such tactics.

4. Most students would agree that in order to be happy and "well adjusted," people need to learn how to relieve stress and to relax. What strategies do you and your friends use to relax? What have been the benefits of these relaxation techniques for you? Write an article for the school newspaper in which you give examples of several of these techniques and encourage your fellow students to try them.

5. The Internet has profoundly altered the way people around the world communicate and share information. One area in which significant change is especially evident is education. While having so much information at your fingertips can be exciting, such technology is not without problems. What are the advantages and disadvantages of using technology in the classroom? Write an essay in which you analyze the educational value (or the temptation for distraction) inherent in bringing technology into the classroom. Document your assessment with specific examples.

6. Some people think it's important to look their best and, therefore, give careful attention to the clothing they wear. Others do not seem to care. How much stock do you put in the old saying "Clothes make the person"? Use examples of the people on your own campus or in your community to argue your position.

7. **Writing with Sources.** Write an essay on one of the following statements, using examples to illustrate your ideas. Draw your examples from a variety of sources: your library's print and Internet resources, interviews, and information gathered from lectures and the media. As you plan your essay, consider whether you will want to use a series of short examples or one or more extended examples.

   a. Much has been (*or* should still be) done to eliminate barriers for the physically disabled.
   b. Nature's oddities are numerous.
   c. Throughout history, dire predictions have been made about the end of the world.
   d. The past predictions of science fiction are today's realities.
   e. The world has not seen an absence of warfare since World War II.
   f. Young executives have developed many innovative management strategies.
   g. A great work of art may come out of an artist's most difficult period.
   h. Genius is 10 percent talent and 90 percent hard work.

   For models of and advice on integrating sources in your essay, see Chapters 14 and 15.

8. **Writing with Sources.** Take some time to study the cartoon that opens this chapter (page 172). What's going on in the illustration? How much of what's going on is conveyed by the written text, and how much by the visual text? How effective do you find the visual? Do some research online or in the argument chapter of this book (pages 579–625) about the topic of microaggressions and safe spaces. Then, write an essay responding to the comic and incorporating information from your sources to support your point.

   Before starting your research and drafting your essay, you will find it helpful to become familiar with Chapter 14, "Writing with Sources," and Chapter 15, "A Brief Guide to Researching and Documenting Essays."

9. **Writing in the Workplace.** Your boss at your internship asks you to evaluate one aspect of the company's operation (customer service, advertising/promotion, internal communications, employee morale, community service, etc.). After selecting an aspect of the company you wish to evaluate and talking with customers and/or other employees, write a memo to your boss in which you use examples to document your findings.

HOW PASTRIES BECOME PLASTIC

Food waste
Muffins, pastries, cakes and breads collected from bakeries

+

Fungus
Added to the starchy food to break down chemical bonds

Bacteria
Added to the sugars to produce other chemicals

+

Sugars and a nitrogen compound
Released after fungus enzymes digest the food waste

Succinic acid
One of a few versatile ingredients created by the bacteria

=

Bioplastics
Formed using succinic acid (among other chemicals) and used to make eco-friendly laundry-detergent bottles, car parts and more

Heather Jones

CHAPTER 7

Process Analysis

WHAT IS PROCESS ANALYSIS?

THE STRATEGY OF PROCESS ANALYSIS INVOLVES SEPARATING AN EVENT, an operation, or a cycle of development into distinct steps, describing each step precisely, and arranging the steps in their proper order.

Whenever you explain how something occurs or how it can (and should) be done—how plants create oxygen, how to make ice cream, or merely how to get to your house—you are using process analysis. Recipes are a form of process analysis; so are the instruction and assembly manuals for the many technological devices we use around the house; and so are posters telling us what to do in case of fire, choking, or other emergency. The graphically illustrated explanation on the opposite page is a little different, however. Showing the process whereby stale and unused baked goods collected from bakeries are turned into plastics, it's not a directional process analysis but an informational one. Rather than provide a recipe for how specifically to make it happen, the presentation explains how the process is carried out.

PROCESS ANALYSIS IN WRITTEN TEXTS

Each year, thousands of books and articles tell us how to make home repairs, how to lose weight and get physically fit, how to improve our memories, how to play better tennis, how to manage our money. They try to satisfy our curiosity about how television shows are made, how jet airplanes work, and how monkeys, bees, or whales find food. People simply want to know how things work and how to do things for themselves, so it's not surprising that process analysis is one of the most widespread and popular forms of writing today.

Here is a process analysis written by Bernard Gladstone to explain how to light a fire in a fireplace:

First sentence establishes purpose: how to build a fire in a fireplace	Though "experts" differ as to the best technique to follow when building a fire, one generally accepted method consists of first laying a generous amount of crumpled newspaper on the hearth between

223

[First paragraph takes us through six steps: the result is a wood-and-paper structure]

the andirons. Kindling wood is then spread generously over this layer of newspaper and one of the thickest logs is placed across the back of the andirons. This should be as close to the back of the fireplace as possible, but not quite touching it. A second log is then placed an inch or so in front of this, and a few additional sticks of kindling are laid across these two. A third log is then placed on top to form a sort of pyramid with air space between all logs so that flames can lick freely up between them.

[Next three paragraphs present three common mistakes]

A mistake frequently made is in building the fire too far forward so that the rear wall of the fireplace does not get properly heated. A heated back wall helps increase the draft and tends to suck smoke and flames rearward with less chance of sparks or smoke spurting out into the room.

Another common mistake often made by the inexperienced fire-tender is to try to build a fire with only one or two logs, instead of using at least three. A single log is difficult to ignite properly, and even two logs do not provide an efficient bed with adequate fuel burning capacity.

Use of too many logs, on the other hand, is also a common fault and can prove hazardous. Building too big a fire can create more smoke and draft than the chimney can safely handle, increasing the possibility of sparks or smoke being thrown out into the room. For best results, the homeowner should start with three medium-sized logs as described above, then add additional logs as needed if the fire is to be kept burning.

[Conclusion reinforces his directions for building a fire]

USING PROCESS ANALYSIS AS A WRITING STRATEGY

Process analysis resembles narration because both strategies present a series of events occurring over time. But a narration is the story of how things happened in a particular way, during one particular period of time; process analysis relates how things always happen—or always should happen—in essentially the same way time after time.

There are essentially two major reasons for writing a process analysis: to give directions, known as *directional process analysis*, and to inform, known as *informational process analysis*. Writers often combine one of these reasons with other rhetorical strategies to evaluate the process in question; this is known as *evaluative process analysis*. Let's take a look at each of these forms more closely.

▶ Directional Process Analysis

Writers use directional process analysis to provide readers with the necessary steps to achieve a desired result. The directions may be as simple as the instructions on a frozen-food package ("Heat in microwave on high for six to eight minutes. Rotate one-quarter turn halfway through cooking time, stir, and serve") or as complex as the operator's manual for a personal computer. Mortimer Adler proposes a method for getting the most out of reading in his essay "How to Mark a Book." First he compares what he sees as the "two ways in which one can own a book" and classifies book lovers into three categories. Then he presents his directions for how one should make marginal comments to get the most out of a book. In a brief selection on pages 223–224, Bernard Gladstone explains step-by-step how to build a fire in a fireplace. No matter their length or complexity, however, all directions have the same purpose: to guide the reader through a clear and logically ordered series of steps toward a particular goal.

▶ Informational Process Analysis

This strategy deals not with processes that readers are able to perform for themselves but with processes that readers are curious about or would like to understand better: how presidents are elected, how plants reproduce, how an elevator works, how the brain processes and generates language. In the following selection from *Lives around Us*, Alan Devoe explains what happens to an animal when it goes into hibernation:

>   When the temperature of the September days falls below 50 degrees or so, the woodchuck becomes too drowsy to come forth from his burrow in the chilly dusk to forage. He remains in the deep nest-chamber, lethargic, hardly moving. Gradually, with the passing of hours or days, his coarse-furred body curls into a semicircle, like a fetus, nose-tip touching tail. The small legs are tucked in, the hand-like clawed forefeet folded. The woodchuck has become a compact ball. Presently the temperature of his body begins to fall.
>   In normal life the woodchuck's temperature, though fluctuant, averages about 97 degrees. Now, as he lies tight-curled in a ball with the winter sleep stealing over him, this body heat drops ten degrees, twenty degrees, thirty. Finally, by the time the snow is on the ground and the woodchuck's winter dormancy has become complete, his temperature is only 38 or 40. With the falling of the body heat there is a slowing of his heartbeat and his respiration. In normal life he breathes thirty or forty times each minute; when he is excited, as many as a hundred times. Now he breathes slower and slower: ten times a minute, five times a minute, once a minute, and at last only ten or twelve times in an hour. His heartbeat is a twentieth of normal. He has entered fully into the oblivion of hibernation.

The process Devoe describes is natural to woodchucks but not to humans, so obviously he cannot be giving instructions. Rather, he has created an informational process analysis to help us understand what happens during the remarkable process of hibernation. Using transitional expressions and time markers, Devoe shows us that the process lasts for weeks, even months.

He connects the progress of hibernation with changes in the weather because the woodchuck's body responds to the dropping temperature as autumn sets in rather than to the passage of specific periods of time.

Evaluative Process Analysis

People often want to understand processes in order to evaluate and improve them by making them simpler, quicker, safer, or more efficient. They may also wish to analyze processes to understand them more deeply or accurately. For instance, in explaining how to build a fire in a fireplace, Bernard Gladstone presents three common mistakes to avoid when trying to make a fire.

USING PROCESS ANALYSIS ACROSS THE DISCIPLINES

When writing essays in the academic disciplines, you will have many opportunities to use the strategy of process analysis to both organize and strengthen the presentation of your ideas. To determine whether process analysis is the right strategy for you in a particular paper, review the guidelines described in Chapter 2 (Determining a Strategy for Developing Your Essay, pages 32–33). Consider the following examples:

Psychology

1. **MAIN IDEA:** Most people go through a predictable grief process when a friend or loved one dies.
2. **QUESTION:** What are the steps in the grieving process?
3. **STRATEGY:** Process analysis. The word *steps* signals the need to list the stages of the grieving process.
4. **SUPPORTING STRATEGY:** Description. Each step might be described and be accompanied by descriptions of the subject's behavior throughout the process.

Biology

1. **MAIN IDEA:** Human blood samples can be tested to determine their blood groups.
2. **QUESTION:** What steps are followed in typing human blood?
3. **STRATEGY:** Process analysis. The word *steps* suggests a sequence of activities that is to be followed in testing blood.
4. **SUPPORTING STRATEGY:** Comparison and contrast; Classification. Comparison and contrast might be used to differentiate blood characteristics and chemistry. Classification might be used to place samples in various categories.

Anthropology

1. **MAIN IDEA:** Anthropologists use several main methods for gathering their data.
2. **QUESTION:** How do anthropologists go about collecting data?
3. **STRATEGY:** Process analysis. The words *how do* and *go about* suggest process analysis.
4. **SUPPORTING STRATEGY:** Illustration and argumentation. Illustration can give examples of particular data and how it is collected. Argumentation might support one method over others.

SAMPLE STUDENT ESSAY USING PROCESS ANALYSIS AS A WRITING STRATEGY

William Peterson grew up in New Hartford, New York. After graduating from the University of Vermont, where he majored in business, Bill took some time to follow his interests in golfing and skiing before pursuing his career in the advertising and marketing industry. In this informative and playful essay, he explains the three-step process of juggling. In addition, he tells of some of the problems readers may encounter and gives sound advice on how to deal with each separate one.

Juggling Is Easier Than You Think
William Peterson

Context-setting introduction invites reader to learn how to juggle

The first time I went to the circus I was fascinated by the jugglers, clowns, and acrobats who juggled everything from bowling pins and burning batons to sharp swords. I never thought of myself as a juggler, however, until that night in college when I watched some comedian on "Saturday Night Live" telling jokes while nonchalantly juggling. When his act ended I went out to my garage and started to experiment with some tennis balls. At first, I felt helpless after tossing and chasing the balls for what seemed like countless hours. However, I actually did start to learn how to juggle. To my surprise I discovered that juggling is much easier than it had at first appeared. If you'd like to learn how to juggle, I recommend that you find some tennis balls or lacrosse balls and continue reading.

Transition links to next section

1

First step in process is introduced: the simple toss	Step one is the simple toss. Stand erect and hold one ball in your right hand. Carefully toss the ball up to approximately an inch above your head and to about half an arm's length in front of you. The ball should arch from your right hand across to your left. This step should now be repeated, starting with your left hand and tossing to your right. Be sure that the ball reaches the same height and distance from you and is not simply passed from your left hand to your right. Keep tossing the ball back and forth until you have become thoroughly disgusted with this step. If you have practiced this toss enough, we can now call this step "the perfect toss." If it is not quite perfect, then you have not become disgusted enough with the step. We'll assume that you've perfected it. Now you're ready to take a little breather and move on.
Recommendation is given to practice first step until it is perfected	
Writer labels step one as "the perfect toss"	
Transition links to next section	Step two is the toss and return. Get back on your feet and this time hold a ball in each hand. Take a deep breath and make a perfect toss with the ball in your right hand. As that ball reaches its peak make another perfect toss with the ball in your left hand. The second ball should end up passing under the first one and reaching approximately the same height. When the second ball peaks, you should be grabbing—or already have grabbed, depending on timing—the first ball. The second ball should then gently drop into your awaiting right hand. If it was not that easy, then don't worry about the "gently" bit. Most people do not achieve perfection at first. Step two is the key factor in becoming a good juggler and should be practiced at least five times as much as step one.
Writer describes the second step in process: the toss and return	
Writer emphasizes the need to practice step two	
A helpful suggestion is provided	Don't deceive yourself after a few successful completions. This maneuver really must be perfected before step three can be approached. As a way to improve dexterity, you should try several tosses and returns starting with your left hand. Let's call step two "the exchange." You're now ready for another well-deserved breather before you proceed.
Writer labels step two as "the exchange"	
Writer labels third step in process: "addition of a third ball"	Ready or not, here it goes. Step three is merely a continuum of "the exchange" with the addition of a third ball. Don't worry if you are confused—I will explain. Get back up again, and now hold two balls in your right hand and one in your left. Make a perfect toss with one of the balls in your right hand and then an exchange with the one in your left hand. The ball coming from your left hand should now be exchanged with the, as of now, unused ball in your right hand. This process should be continued until you find yourself reaching under nearby chairs for bouncing tennis balls. It is true that many persons' backs and legs become sore when learning how to

juggle because they've been picking up balls that they've inadvertently tossed around the room. Try practicing over a bed; you won't have to reach down so far. Don't get too upset if things aren't going well; you're probably keeping the same pace as everyone else at this stage. You're certainly doing better than I was because you've had me as a teacher.

Transitional paragraph links to next section

Don't worry, this teacher is not going to leave you stranded with hours of repetition of the basic steps. I am sure that you have already run into some basic problems. I will now try to relate some of my beginner's troubles and some of the best solutions you can try for them.

Writer discusses problem one and its solutions

Problem one, you are getting nowhere after the simple toss. This requires a basic improvement of hand to eye coordination. Solution one is to just go back and practice the simple toss again and again. Unfortunately, this becomes quite boring. Solution two is not as tedious and involves quite a bit more skill. Try juggling two balls in one hand. Some people show me this when I ask them if they can juggle—they're not fooling anyone. Real juggling is what you're here to learn. First try circular juggling in one hand. This involves tosses similar to "the perfect toss." They differ in that the balls go half as far towards the opposite hand, are tossed and grabbed by the same hand, and end up making their own circles (as opposed to going up and down in upside down V's like exchanges). Then try juggling the balls in the same line style. I think this is harder. You have to keep two balls traveling in their own vertical paths (the balls should go as high as they do in a "perfect toss") with only one hand. I think this is harder than the circular style because my hands normally tend to make little circles when I juggle.

Writer discusses problem two and its solution

Problem two, you can make exchanges but you just can't accomplish step three. The best solution to this is to just continue practicing step two, but now add a twist. As soon as the first ball is caught by the left hand in our step two, throw it back up in another perfect toss for another exchange. Continue this and increase speed up to the point where two balls just don't seem like enough. You should now be ready to add the third ball and accomplish what you couldn't before—real juggling.

Writer discusses problem three and its solutions

Problem three, you have become the "runaway juggler." This means you can successfully achieve numerous exchanges but you're always chasing after balls tossed too far in front of you. The first solution is to stand in front of a wall. This causes you to end up catching a couple of balls bouncing off the wall or else you'll end up consciously keeping your tosses in closer to your body. The second solution is you put your back up against a wall. This will tend to make you toss in closer to yourself because you will be restricted to keeping your back up against the wall. This solution can work, but more often than not you'll find yourself watching balls fly across the room in front of you! I've told you about the back-on-the-wall method because some people find it effective. As you can tell, I don't.

Step 1   Step 2   Step 3

Writer concludes with a visual presentation of three-step process

Juggling is a simple three-step process. Following my routine is the easiest way to get from being a spastic ball chaser to an accomplished juggler. Patience and coordination are really not required. The only requirements are a few tennis balls, the ability to follow some basic instructions, and the time to have some fun.

Next time you're out with friends and conversation lags, you just might be surprised where your new-found juggling skills will take you.

Analyzing Bill Peterson's Process Analysis Essay: Questions for Discussion

1. Peterson uses personal experience as the basis for his essay. How do his experiences learning to juggle help the reader, who is presumably playing the role of novice juggler?

2. Successful juggling depends on successfully tying together a series of basic steps, so the transitions in the above essay are extremely important. Identify what Peterson does to create smooth transitions between the steps, which are presented in a series of paragraphs.

3. Peterson presents the whole process of learning to juggle before presenting common problems. Why does he address the problems after the fact? How does this organization help his readers reach their goal?

SUGGESTIONS FOR USING PROCESS ANALYSIS AS A WRITING STRATEGY

As you plan and revise your process analysis essay, be mindful of the writing guidelines described in Chapter 2. Pay particular attention to the basic requirements and essential ingredients of this strategy.

▶ Planning Your Process Analysis Essay

KNOW THE PROCESS YOU ARE WRITING ABOUT. Be sure that you have more than a vague or general grasp of the process you are writing about: Make sure you can analyze it fully, from beginning to end. You can sometimes convince yourself that you understand an entire process when, in fact, your understanding is somewhat superficial. If you do outside research, it's a good idea to read explanations by several authorities on the subject. If you were analyzing the process by which children learn language, for example, you wouldn't want to rely on only one expert's account. Turning to more than one account reinforces your understanding of key points in the process, and it also points out various ways the process is performed; you may want to consider these alternatives in your writing.

HAVE A CLEAR PURPOSE. Giving directions for administering cardiopulmonary resuscitation and explaining how the El Niño phenomenon unfolds are worthy purposes for writing a process analysis paper. Many process analysis papers go beyond these fundamental purposes, however. They lay out processes to evaluate them, to suggest alternative steps, to point out shortcomings in generally accepted practices, and to suggest improvements. In short, process analysis papers are frequently persuasive or argumentative. Be sure to decide what you want your writing to do before you begin.

▶ Organizing and Writing Your Process Analysis Essay

ORGANIZE THE PROCESS INTO STEPS. As much as possible, make each step a simple and well-defined action, preferably a single action. To guide yourself in doing so, write a scratch outline listing the steps. Here, for example, is an outline of Bernard Gladstone's directions for building a fire.

Process Analysis of Building a Fire in a Fireplace
1. Put down crumpled newspaper.
2. Lay kindling.
3. Place back log near rear wall but not touching.

4. Place next log an inch forward from the first one.
5. Bridge logs with kindling.
6. Place third log on top of kindling bridge.

Next, check your outline to make sure that the steps are in the right order and that none has been omitted. Then analyze your outline more carefully. Are any steps so complex that they need to be described in some detail—or perhaps divided into more steps? Will you need to explain the purpose of a certain step because the reason for it is not obvious? Especially in an informational process analysis, two steps may take place at the same time; perhaps they are performed by different people or different parts of the body. Does your outline make this clear? (One solution is to assign both steps the same number but divide them into substeps by labeling one of them "A" and the other "B.") When you feel certain that the steps of the process are complete and correct, ask yourself two more questions. Will the reader need any other information to understand the process—definitions of unusual terms, for example, or descriptions of special equipment? Should you anticipate common mistakes or misunderstandings and discuss them, as Gladstone does? If so, be sure to add an appropriate note or two to your scratch outline as a reminder.

USE TRANSITIONS TO LINK THE STEPS. Transitional words and phrases like *then, next, after doing this,* and *during the summer months* can both emphasize and clarify the sequence of steps in your process analysis. The same is true of sequence markers like *first, second, third,* and so on. Devoe uses such words to make clear which stages in the hibernation process are simultaneous and which are not; Gladstone includes an occasional *first* or *then* to alert us to shifts from one step to the next.

▶ Revising and Editing Your Process Analysis Essay

ENERGIZE YOUR WRITING: USE THE ACTIVE VOICE AND STRONG ACTION VERBS. Writers prefer the active voice because it stresses the doer of an action, is lively and emphatic, and uses strong descriptive verbs. The passive voice, on the other hand, stresses what was done rather than who did it and uses forms of the weak verb *to be.*

active   The coaches analyzed the game film, and the fullback decided to rededicate herself to playing defense.

passive   A game film analysis was performed by the coaches, and a rededication to playing defense was decided on by the fullback.

Sometimes, however, the doer of an action is unknown or less important than the recipient of an action. In this case, it is acceptable to use the passive voice.

> The Earth's moon was formed more than 4 billion years ago.

When you revise your drafts, scan your sentences for passive constructions and weak verbs. Put your sentences into the active voice and find strong action verbs to replace weak verbs. Instead of the weak verb *run*, use *fly, gallop, hustle, jog, race, rush, scamper, scoot, scramble, tear,* or *trot,* for example. Instead of the weak verb *say,* you could use *declare, express, muse, mutter, pronounce, report, respond, recite, reply, snarl,* or *utter.* Whenever possible, avoid forms of the verb *to be* (*is, are, was, were, will be, should be*), which are weak and nondescriptive. Here are some other common weak verbs you should replace with strong action verbs in your writing:

have, had, has	do	determine
make	use	become
concern	get	go
reflect	involve	appear
provide		

USE CONSISTENT VERB TENSE. A verb's tense indicates when an action is taking place: some time in the past, right now, or in the future. Using verb tense consistently helps your readers understand time changes in your writing. Inconsistent verb tenses — or *shifts* — within a sentence confuse readers and are especially noticeable in narration and process analysis writing, which are sequence — and time — oriented. Generally, you should write in the past or present tense and maintain that tense throughout your sentence.

> **inconsistent** I mixed the eggs and sugar and then add the flour.

Mixed is past tense; *add* is present tense.

> **corrected** I mix the eggs and sugar and then add the flour.

The sentence is now consistently in the present tense. The sentence can also be revised to be consistently in the past tense.

> **corrected** I mixed the eggs and sugar and then added the flour.

Here's another example:

> **inconsistent** The painter studied the scene and pulls a fan brush decisively from her cup.

Studied is past tense, indicating an action that has already taken place; *pulls* is present tense, indicating an action taking place now.

corrected   The painter studies the scene and pulls a fan brush decisively from her cup.

corrected   The painter studied the scene and pulled a fan brush decisively from her cup.

After you are confident that you have selected strong verbs in a consistent tense, consider sharing your draft with others to get some additional feedback. Page 36 will give you some helpful guidelines for peer review, and the box below will help to steer your own self-critique.

> **Questions for Revising and Editing: Process Analysis**
>
> 1. Do I have a thorough knowledge of the process I chose to write about?
> 2. Have I clearly informed readers about how to perform the process (directional process analysis), or have I explained how a process occurs (informational process analysis)? Does my choice reflect the overall purpose of my process analysis paper?
> 3. Have I divided the process into clear, readily understandable steps?
> 4. Did I pay particular attention to transitional words to take readers from one step to the next?
> 5. Are all my sentences in the active voice? Have I used strong action verbs?
> 6. Is my tense consistent?
> 7. Have I succeeded in tailoring my diction to my audience's familiarity with the subject?
> 8. Are my pronoun antecedents clear?
> 9. How did readers of my draft respond to my essay? Did they find any confusing passages or any missing steps?
> 10. Have I avoided errors in grammar, punctuation, and mechanics? Is my sentence style as clear, smooth, and persuasive as possible?

How to Mark a Book

MORTIMER ADLER

Writer, editor, and educator Mortimer Adler (1902–2001) was born in New York City. A high school dropout, Adler completed the undergraduate program at Columbia University in three years, but he did not graduate because he refused to take the mandatory swimming test. Adler is recognized for his editorial work on the *Encyclopaedia Britannica* and for his leadership of the Great Books Program at the University of Chicago, where adults from all walks of life gathered twice a month to read and discuss the classics.

In the following essay, which first appeared in the *Saturday Review of Literature* in 1940, Adler offers a timeless lesson: He explains how to take full ownership of a book by marking it up, by making it "a part of yourself."

Preparing to Read

When you read a book that you must understand thoroughly and remember for a class or for your own purposes, what techniques do you use to help understand what you are reading? What helps you remember important parts of the book and improve your understanding of what the author is saying?

You know you have to read "between the lines" to get the most out of anything. I want to persuade you to do something equally important in the course of your reading. I want to persuade you to "write between the lines." Unless you do, you are not likely to do the most efficient kind of reading.

I contend, quite bluntly, that marking up a book is not an act of mutilation but of love.

You shouldn't mark up a book which isn't yours. Librarians (or your friends) who lend you books expect you to keep them clean, and you should. If you decide that I am right about the usefulness of marking books, you will have to buy them. Most of the world's great books are available today in reprint editions.

There are two ways in which one can own a book. The first is the property right you establish by paying for it, just as you pay for clothes and furniture. But this act of purchase is only the prelude to possession. Full ownership comes only when you have made it a part of yourself, and the best way to make yourself a part of it is by writing in it. An illustration may make the point clear. You buy a beefsteak and transfer it from the butcher's icebox to your own. But you do not own the beefsteak in the most important sense until you consume it and get it into your bloodstream. I am arguing that books, too, must be absorbed in your bloodstream to do you any good.

Confusion about what it means to *own* a book leads people to a false reverence for paper, binding, and type—a respect for the physical thing—the craft of the printer rather than the genius of the author. They forget that it is possible for a man to acquire the idea, to possess the beauty, which a great book contains, without staking his claim by pasting his bookplate inside the cover. Having a fine library doesn't prove that its owner has a mind enriched by books; it proves nothing more than that he, his father, or his wife, was rich enough to buy them.

> Marking up a book is not an act of mutilation but of love.

There are three kinds of book owners. The first has all the standard sets and best-sellers—unread, untouched. (This deluded individual owns woodpulp and ink, not books.) The second has a great many books—a few of them read through, most of them dipped into, but all of them as clean and shiny as the day they were bought. (This person would probably like to make books his own, but is restrained by a false respect for their physical appearance.) The third has a few books or many—every one of them dog-eared and dilapidated, shaken and loosened by continual use, marked and scribbled in from front to back. (This man owns books.)

Is it false respect, you may ask, to preserve intact and unblemished a beautifully printed book, an elegantly bound edition? Of course not. I'd no more scribble all over a first edition of *Paradise Lost* than I'd give my baby a set of crayons and an original Rembrandt! I wouldn't mark up a painting or a statue. Its soul, so to speak, is inseparable from its body. And the beauty of a rare edition or of a richly manufactured volume is like that of a painting or a statue.

But the soul of a book *can* be separated from its body. A book is more like the score of a piece of music than it is like a painting. No great musician confuses a symphony with the printed sheets of music. Arturo Toscanini reveres Brahms, but Toscanini's score of the C-minor Symphony is so thoroughly marked up that no one but the maestro himself can read it. The reason why a great conductor makes notations on his musical scores—marks them up again and again each time he returns to study them—is the reason why you should mark your books. If your respect for magnificent binding or typography gets in the way, buy yourself a cheap edition and pay your respects to the author.

Why is marking up a book indispensable to reading? First, it keeps you awake. (And I don't mean merely conscious; I mean wide awake.) In the second place, reading, if it is active, is thinking, and thinking tends to express itself in words, spoken or written. The marked book is usually the thought-through book. Finally, writing helps you remember the thoughts you had, or the thoughts the author expressed. Let me develop these three points.

If reading is to accomplish anything more than passing time, it must be active. You can't let your eyes glide across the lines of a book and come up with an understanding of what you have read. Now an ordinary piece of light fiction, like say, *Gone with the Wind*, doesn't require the most active kind of reading. The books you read for pleasure can be read in a state of relaxation, and nothing is lost. But a great book, rich in ideas and beauty, a book that raises and tries to answer great fundamental questions, demands the most active reading of which you are capable. You don't absorb the ideas of John Dewey[1] the way you absorb the crooning of Mr. Vallee.[2] You have to reach for them. That you cannot do while you're asleep.

If, when you've finished reading a book, the pages are filled with your notes, you know that you read actively. The most famous active reader of great books I know is President Hutchins, of the University of Chicago. He also has the hardest schedule of business activities of any man I know. He invariably reads with a pencil, and sometimes, when he picks up a book and pencil in the evening, he finds himself, instead of making intelligent notes, drawing what he calls "caviar factories" on the margins. When that happens, he puts the book down. He knows he's too tired to read, and he's just wasting time.

But, you may ask, why is writing necessary? Well, the physical act of writing, with your own hand, brings words and sentences more sharply before your mind and preserves them better in your memory. To set down your reaction to important words and sentences you have read, and the questions they have raised in your mind, is to preserve those reactions and sharpen those questions.

Even if you wrote on a scratch pad, and threw the paper away when you had finished writing, your grasp of the book would be surer. But you don't have to throw the paper away. The margins (top and bottom, as well as side), the end-papers, the very space between the lines, are all available. They aren't sacred. And, best of all, your marks and notes become an integral part of the book and stay there forever. You can pick up the book the following week or year, and there are all your points of agreement,

---

[1] John Dewey (1859–1952) was an educational philosopher who had a profound influence on learning through experimentation. — Eds.
[2] Rudy Vallee (1901–1986) was a popular singer of the 1920s and '30s, famous for his crooning high notes. — Eds.

disagreement, doubt, and inquiry. It's like resuming an interrupted conversation with the advantage of being able to pick up where you left off.

And that is exactly what reading a book should be: a conversation between you and the author. Presumably he knows more about the subject than you do; naturally, you'll have the proper humility as you approach him. But don't let anybody tell you that a reader is supposed to be solely on the receiving end. Understanding is a two-way operation; learning doesn't consist in being an empty receptacle. The learner has to question himself and question the teacher. He even has to argue with the teacher, once he understands what the teacher is saying. And marking a book is literally an expression of your differences, or agreements of opinion, with the author.

There are all kinds of devices for marking a book intelligently and fruitfully. Here's the way I do it:

1. *Underlining:* of major points, of important or forceful statements.

2. *Vertical lines at the margin:* to emphasize a statement already underlined.

3. *Star, asterisk, or other doo-dad at the margin:* to be used sparingly, to emphasize the ten or twenty most important statements in the book. (You may want to fold the bottom corner of each page on which you use such marks. It won't hurt the sturdy paper on which most modern books are printed, and you will be able to take the book off the shelf at any time and, by opening it at the folded-corner page, refresh your recollection of the book.)

4. *Numbers in the margin:* to indicate the sequence of points the author makes in developing a single argument.

5. *Numbers of other pages in the margin:* to indicate where else in the book the author made points relevant to the point marked; to tie up the ideas in a book, which, though they may be separated by many pages, belong together.

6. *Circling:* of key words or phrases.

7. *Writing in the margin, or at the top or bottom of the page, for the sake of:* recording questions (and perhaps answers) which a passage raised in your mind; reducing a complicated discussion to a simple statement; recording the sequence of major points right through the book. I use the end-papers at the back of the book to make a personal index of the author's points in the order of their appearance.

The front end-papers are, to me, the most important. Some people reserve them for a fancy bookplate. I reserve them for fancy thinking. After I have finished reading the book and making my personal index on the back end-papers, I turn to the front and try to outline the book, not page by page, or point by point (I've already done that at the back), but as an integrated structure, with a basic unity and an order of parts. This outline is, to me, the measure of my understanding of the work.

If you're a die-hard anti-book-marker, you may object that the margins, the space between the lines, and the end-papers don't give you room enough. All right. How about using a scratch pad slightly smaller than the page-size of the book—so that the edges of the sheets won't protrude? Make your index, outlines, and even your notes on the pad, and then insert these sheets permanently inside the front and back covers of the book.

Or, you may say that this business of marking books is going to slow up your reading. It probably will. That's one of the reasons for doing it. Most of us have been taken in by the notion that speed of reading is a measure of our intelligence. There is no such thing as the right speed for intelligent reading. Some things should be read quickly and effortlessly, and some should be read slowly and even laboriously. The sign of intelligence in reading is the ability to read different things differently according to their worth. In the case of good books, the point is not to see how many of them you can get through, but rather how many can get through you— how many you can make your own. A few friends are better than a thousand acquaintances. If this be your aim, as it should be, you will not be impatient if it takes more time and effort to read a great book than it does a newspaper.

You may have one final objection to marking books. You can't lend them to your friends because nobody else can read them without being distracted by your notes. Furthermore, you won't want to lend them because a marked copy is a kind of intellectual diary, and lending it is almost like giving your mind away.

If your friend wishes to read your *Plutarch's Lives*, *Shakespeare*, or *The Federalist Papers*, tell him gently but firmly to buy a copy. You will lend him your car or your coat—but your books are as much a part of you as your head or your heart.

Thinking Critically about the Text

After you have read Adler's essay, compare your answer to the Preparing to Read prompt with Adler's guidelines for reading. What are the most significant differences between Adler's guidelines and your own? How can you better make the books you read part of yourself?

Questions on Subject

1. What are the three kinds of book owners Adler identifies? What are their differences?
2. According to Adler, why is marking up a book indispensable to reading? Do you agree with his three arguments? (Glossary: *Argument*) Why or why not?

3. What does Adler mean when he writes "the soul of a book *can* be separated from its body" (paragraph 8)? Is the separation a good thing? Explain.

4. Adler says that reading a book should be a conversation between the reader and the author. What characteristics does he say the conversation should have? How does marking a book help in carrying on and preserving the conversation?

5. What kinds of devices do you use for "marking a book intelligently and fruitfully" (paragraph 15)? How useful do you find these devices?

Questions on Strategy

1. In the first paragraph, Adler writes, "I want to persuade you to do something equally important in the course of your reading. I want to persuade you to 'write between the lines.'" What assumptions does Adler make about his audience when he chooses to use the parallel structure of "I want to persuade you . . ."? (Glossary: *Audience; Parallelism*) Is stating his intention so blatantly an effective way of presenting his argument? (Glossary: *Argument*) Why or why not?

2. Adler expresses himself very clearly throughout the essay, and his topic sentences are carefully crafted. (Glossary: *Topic Sentence*) Reread the topic sentences for paragraphs 3–6 and identify how each introduces the main idea for the paragraph and unifies it.

3. Throughout the essay, Adler provides the reader with a number of verbal cues ("There are two ways," "Let me develop these three points"). What do these verbal cues indicate about the organizational connections of the essay? (Glossary: *Organization*) Explain how Adler's organization creates an essay that logically follows from sentence to sentence and from paragraph to paragraph.

4. Summarize in your own words Adler's process analysis about how one should mark a book. Explain how Adler's process analysis is also an argument for the correct way to read. (Glossary: *Argument*)

5. Adler's process analysis is also a description of an event or a sequence of events (how to read). Does he claim that his recommended reading process will aid the reader's understanding, increase the reader's interest, or both?

Questions on Diction and Vocabulary

1. Adler makes an analogy that links reading books with the statement "A few friends are better than a thousand acquaintances" (paragraph 25). (Glossary: *Analogy*) Explain how this analogy works. Why is this analogy important to Adler's overall argument?

2. Throughout the essay, Adler uses the personal pronoun *I* to describe his reading experience. (Glossary: *Point of View*) How does this personalized voice help or hinder the explanation of the process of reading?

3. What does Adler mean by the phrase "active reading"?

Process Analysis in Action

This exercise requires that you work in pairs. Draw a simple geometric design, such as the one below, without letting your partner see your drawing.

With the finished design in front of you, write a set of directions that will allow your partner to reproduce it accurately. Before writing your directions, ask yourself how you will convey the context for your instructions, where you will begin, and how what you write may help your partner or lead your partner astray. As your partner attempts to draw the design from your instructions, do not offer any verbal advice. Let your directions speak for themselves. Once you have finished, compare your drawing to the one your partner has produced. Discuss the results with your partner and, if time allows, with the entire class.

Writing Suggestions

1. Write a directional process analysis in which you present your techniques for getting the most enjoyment out of a common activity. For example, perhaps you have a set routine you follow for spending an evening watching television — preparing popcorn, checking what's on, clearing off the coffee table, finding the remote control, settling into your favorite chair, and so on. Choose from the following topics or select one of your own:

    a. how to listen to music
    b. how to eat an ice-cream cone
    c. how to reduce stress
    d. how to wash a dog

2. Adler devotes a large portion of his essay to persuading his audience that marking books is a worthwhile task. (Glossary: *Persuasion*) Write an essay in which you instruct your audience about how to do something they do not necessarily wish to do or they do not think they need to do. For instance, before explaining how to buy the best robot vacuum, you may need to convince readers that they *should* buy a robot vacuum. Write your directional process analysis after making a convincing argument for the validity of the process you wish to present. (Glossary: *Argument*)

How to Say Nothing in 500 Words

PAUL ROBERTS

Paul Roberts (1917–1967) was a linguist, a teacher, and a writer at San Jose State College from 1946 to 1960 and at Cornell University from 1962 to 1964. His books on writing, including *English Syntax* (1954) and *Patterns of English* (1956), have helped generations of high school and college students become better writers.

"How to Say Nothing in 500 Words" is taken from his best-known book, *Understanding English* (1958). Although written almost sixty years ago, the essay is still relevant for student writers today. Good writing, Roberts tells us, is not simply a matter of filling up a page; rather, the words have to hold the reader's interest, and they must say something. In this essay, Roberts uses lively prose and a step-by-step process to guide the student from the blank page to the finished essay. His bag of writing strategies holds good advice for anyone who wants to write well.

Preparing to Read

How do you feel about writing? Do you find writing difficult? What are some of your most memorable experiences with writing in school or during your free time? How have these experiences affected your current attitude toward writing? Explain.

NOTHING ABOUT SOMETHING

It's Friday afternoon, and you have almost survived another week of classes. You are just looking forward dreamily to the weekend when the English instructor says: "For Monday you will turn in a five-hundred-word composition on college football."

Well, that puts a good big hole in the weekend. You don't have any strong views on college football one way or the other. You get rather excited during the season and go to all the home games and find it rather more fun than not. On the other hand, the class has been reading Robert Hutchins in the anthology and perhaps Shaw's "Eighty-Yard Run," and from the class discussion you have got the idea that the instructor thinks college football is for the birds. You are no fool, you. You can figure out what side to take.

After dinner you get out the portable typewriter that you got for high school graduation. You might as well get it over with and enjoy Saturday and Sunday. Five hundred words is about two double-spaced pages with normal margins. You put in a sheet of paper, think up a title, and you're off:

Why College Football Should Be Abolished

College football should be abolished because it's bad for the school and also bad for the players. The players are so busy practicing that they don't have any time for their studies.

This, you feel, is a mighty good start. The only trouble is that it's only thirty-two words. You still have four hundred and sixty-eight to go, and you've pretty well exhausted the subject. It comes to you that you do your best thinking in the morning, so you put away the typewriter and go to the movies. But the next morning you have to do your washing and some math problems, and in the afternoon you go to the game. The English instructor turns up too, and you wonder if you've taken the right side after all. Saturday night you have a date, and Sunday morning you have to go to church. (You shouldn't let English assignments interfere with your religion.) What with one thing and another, it's ten o'clock Sunday night before you get out the typewriter again. You make a pot of coffee and start to fill out your views on college football. Put a little meat on the bones.

> You still have four hundred and sixty-eight [words] to go, and you've pretty well exhausted the subject

Why College Football Should Be Abolished

In my opinion, it seems to me that college football should be abolished. The reason why I think this to be true is because I feel that football is bad for the colleges in nearly every respect. As Robert Hutchins says in his article in our anthology in which he discusses college football, it would be better if the colleges had race horses and had races with one another, because then the horses would not have to attend classes. I firmly agree with Mr. Hutchins on this point, and I am sure that many other students would agree too.

One reason why it seems to me that college football is bad is that it has become too commercial. In the olden times when people played football just for the fun of it, maybe college football was all right, but they do not play football just for the fun of it now as they used to in the old days. Nowadays college football is what you might call a big business. Maybe this is not true at all schools, and I don't think it is especially true here at State, but certainly this is the case at most colleges and universities in America nowadays, as Mr. Hutchins points out in his very interesting article. Actually the coaches and alumni go around to the high schools and offer the high school stars large salaries to come to their colleges and play football for them. There was one case where a high school star was offered a convertible if he would play football for a certain college.

Another reason for abolishing college football is that it is bad for the players. They do not have time to get a college education, because they are so busy playing football. A football player has to practice every afternoon from three to six, and then he is so tired that he can't concentrate on his studies. He just feels like dropping off to sleep after dinner, and then the next day he goes to his classes without having studied and maybe he fails the test.

(Good ripe stuff so far, but you're still a hundred and fifty-one words from home. One more push.)

Also I think college football is bad for the colleges and the universities because not very many students get to participate in it. Out of a college of ten thousand students only seventy-five or a hundred play football, if that many. Football is what you might call a spectator sport. That means that most people go to watch it but do not play it themselves.

(Four hundred and fifteen. Well, you still have the conclusion, and when you retype it, you can make the margins a little wider.)

These are the reasons why I agree with Mr. Hutchins that college football should be abolished in American colleges and universities.

On Monday you turn it in, moderately hopeful, and on Friday it comes back marked "weak in content" and sporting a big D.

This essay is exaggerated a little, not much. The English instructor will recognize it as reasonably typical of what an assignment on college football will bring in. He knows that nearly half of the class will contrive in five hundred words to say that college football is too commercial and bad for the players. Most of the other half will inform him that college football builds character and prepares one for life and brings prestige to the school. As he reads paper after paper all saying the same thing in almost the same words, all bloodless, five hundred words dripping out of nothing, he wonders how he allowed himself to get trapped into teaching English when he might have had a happy and interesting life as an electrician or a confidence man.

Well, you may ask, what can you do about it? The subject is one on which you have few convictions and little information. Can you be expected to make a dull subject interesting? As a matter of fact, this is precisely what you are expected to do. This is the writer's essential task. All subjects, except sex, are dull until somebody makes them interesting. The writer's job is to find the argument, the approach, the angle, the wording that will take the reader with him. This is seldom easy, and it is particularly hard in subjects that have been much discussed: College Football, Fraternities, Popular Music, Is Chivalry Dead?, and the like. You will feel that there is nothing you can do with such subjects except repeat the old bromides. But there are some things you can do which will make your papers, if not throbbingly alive, at least less insufferably tedious than they might otherwise be.

AVOID THE OBVIOUS CONTENT

Say the assignment is college football. Say that you've decided to be against it. Begin by putting down the arguments that come to your mind: it is too commercial, it takes the students' minds off their studies, it is hard on the players, it makes the university a kind of circus instead of an intellectual center, for most schools it is financially ruinous. Can you think of any more arguments just off hand? All right. Now when you write your paper, *make sure that you don't use any of the material on this list*. If these are the points that leap to your mind, they will leap to everyone else's too, and whether you get a C or a D may depend on whether the instructor reads your paper early when he is fresh and tolerant or late, when the sentence "In my opinion, college football has become too commercial," inexorably repeated, has brought him to the brink of lunacy.

Be against college football for some reason or reasons of your own. If they are keen and perceptive ones, that's splendid. But even if they are trivial or foolish or indefensible, you are still ahead so long as they are not everybody else's reasons too. Be against it because the colleges don't spend enough money on it to make it worthwhile, because it is bad for the characters of spectators, because the players are forced to attend classes, because the football stars hog all the beautiful women, because it competes with baseball and is therefore un-American and possibly Communist inspired. There are lots of more or less unused reasons for being against college football.

Sometimes it is a good idea to sum up and dispose of the trite and conventional points before going on to your own. This has the advantage of indicating to the reader that you are going to be neither trite nor conventional. Something like this:

> We are often told that college football should be abolished because it has become too commercial or because it is bad for the players. These arguments are no doubt very cogent, but they don't really go to the heart of the matter.

Then you go to the heart of the matter.

TAKE THE LESS USUAL SIDE

One rather simple way of getting interest into your paper is to take the side of the argument that most of the citizens will want to avoid. If the assignment is an essay on dogs, you can, if you choose, explain that dogs are faithful and lovable companions, intelligent, useful as guardians of the house and protectors of children, indispensable in police work—in short, when all is said and done, man's best friends. Or you can suggest that those big brown eyes conceal, more often than not, a vacuity of mind and an inconstancy of purpose; that the dogs you have known most intimately have been mangy, ill-tempered brutes, incapable of instruction; and that only your nobility of mind and fear of arrest prevent you from kicking the flea-ridden animals when you pass them on the street.

Naturally, personal convictions will sometimes dictate your approach. If the assigned subject is "Is Methodism Rewarding to the Individual?" and you are a pious Methodist, you have really no choice. But few assigned subjects, if any, will fall in this category. Most of them will lie in broad areas of discussion with much to be said on both sides. They are intellectual exercises and it is legitimate to argue now one way and now another, as debaters do in similar circumstances. Always take the side that looks to you hardest, least defensible. It will almost always turn out to be easier to write interestingly on that side.

This general advice applies where you have a choice of subjects. If you are to choose among "The Value of Fraternities" and "My Favorite High School Teacher" and "What I Think about Beetles," by all means plump for the beetles. By the time the instructor gets to your paper, he will be up to his ears in tedious tales about the French teacher at Bloombury High and assertions about how fraternities build character and prepare one for life. Your views on beetles, whatever they are, are bound to be a refreshing change.

Don't worry too much about figuring out what the instructor thinks about the subject so that you can cuddle up with him. Chances are his views are no stronger than yours. If he does have convictions and you oppose them, his problem is to keep from grading you higher than you deserve in order to show he is not biased. This doesn't mean that you should always cantankerously dissent from what the instructor says; that gets tiresome too. And if the subject assigned is "My Pet Peeve," do not begin, "My pet peeve is the English instructor who assigns papers on 'my pet peeve.'" This was still funny during the War of 1812, but it has sort of lost its edge since then. It is in general good manners to avoid personalities.

SLIP OUT OF ABSTRACTION

If you will study the essay on college football . . . you will perceive that one reason for its appalling dullness is that it never gets down to particulars. It is just a series of not very glittering generalities: "football is bad for the colleges," "it has become too commercial," "football is a big business," "it is bad for the players," and so on. Such round phrases thudding against the reader's brain are unlikely to convince him, though they may well render him unconscious.

If you want the reader to believe that college football is bad for the players, you have to do more than say so. You have to display the evil. Take your roommate, Alfred Simkins, the second-string center. Picture poor old

Alfy coming home from football practice every evening, bruised and aching, agonizingly tired, scarcely able to shovel the mashed potatoes into his mouth. Let us see him staggering up to the room, getting out his econ textbook, peering desperately at it with his good eye, falling asleep and failing the test in the morning. Let us share his unbearable tension as Saturday draws near. Will he fail, be demoted, lose his monthly allowance, be forced to return to the coal mines? And if he succeeds, what will be his reward? Perhaps a slight ripple of applause when the third-string center replaces him, a moment of elation in the locker room if the team wins, of despair if it loses. What will he look back on when he graduates from college? Toil and torn ligaments. And what will be his future? He is not good enough for pro football, and he is too obscure and weak in econ to succeed in stocks and bonds. College football is tearing the heart from Alfy Simkins and, when it finishes with him, will callously toss aside the shattered hulk.

This is no doubt a weak enough argument for the abolition of college football, but it is a sight better than saying, in three or four variations, that college football (in your opinion) is bad for the players.

Look at the work of any professional writer and notice how constantly he is moving from the generality, the abstract statement, to the concrete example, the facts and figures, the illustration. If he is writing on juvenile delinquency, he does not just tell you that juveniles are (it seems to him) delinquent and that (in his opinion) something should be done about it. He shows you juveniles being delinquent, tearing up movie theatres in Buffalo, stabbing high school principals in Dallas, smoking marijuana in Palo Alto. And more than likely he is moving toward some specific remedy, not just a general wringing of the hands.

It is no doubt possible to be *too* concrete, too illustrative or anecdotal, but few inexperienced writers err this way. For most the soundest advice is to be seeking always for the picture, to be always turning general remarks into seeable examples. Don't say, "Sororities teach girls the social graces." Say, "Sorority life teaches a girl how to carry on a conversation while pouring tea, without sloshing the tea into the saucer." Don't say, "I like certain kinds of popular music very much." Say, "Whenever I hear Gerber Spinklittle play 'Mississippi Man' on the trombone, my socks creep up my ankles."

GET RID OF OBVIOUS PADDING

The student toiling away at his weekly English theme is too often tormented by a figure: five hundred words. How, he asks himself, is he to achieve this staggering total? Obviously by never using one word when he can somehow work in ten.

He is therefore seldom content with a plain statement like "Fast driving is dangerous." This has only four words in it. He takes thought, and the sentence becomes:

> In my opinion, fast driving is dangerous.

Better, but he can do better still:

> In my opinion, fast driving would seem to be rather dangerous.

If he is really adept, it may come out:

> In my humble opinion, though I do not claim to be an expert on this complicated subject, fast driving, in most circumstances, would seem to be rather dangerous in many respects, or at least so it would seem to me.

Thus four words have been turned into forty, and not an iota of content has been added.

Now this is a way to go about reaching five hundred words, and if you are content with a D grade, it is as good a way as any. But if you aim higher, you must work differently. Instead of stuffing your sentences with straw, you must try steadily to get rid of the padding, to make your sentences lean and tough. If you are really working at it, your first draft will greatly exceed the required total, and then you will work it down, thus:

> It is thought in some quarters that fraternities do not contribute as much as might be expected to campus life.
> Some people think that fraternities contribute little to campus life.
> The average doctor who practices in small towns or in the country must toil night and day to heal the sick.
> Most country doctors work long hours.
>
> When I was a little girl, I suffered from shyness and embarrassment in the presence of others.
> I was a shy little girl.
> It is absolutely necessary for the person employed as a marine fireman to give the matter of steam pressure his undivided attention at all times.
> The fireman has to keep his eye on the steam gauge.

You may ask how you can arrive at five hundred words at this rate. Simply. You dig up more real content. Instead of taking a couple of obvious points off the surface of the topic and then circling warily around them for six paragraphs, you work in and explore, figure out the details. You illustrate. You say that fast driving is dangerous, and then you prove it. How long does it take to stop a car at forty and at eighty? How far can you see at night? What happens when a tire blows? What happens in a head-on collision at fifty miles an hour? Pretty soon your paper will be full of broken glass and blood and headless torsos, and reaching five hundred words will not really be a problem.

CALL A FOOL A FOOL

Some of the padding in freshman themes is to be blamed not on anxiety about the word minimum but on excessive timidity. The student writes, "In my opinion, the principal of my high school acted in ways that I believe every unbiased person would have to call foolish." This isn't exactly what he means. What he means is, "My high school principal was a fool." If he was a fool, call him a fool. Hedging the thing about with "in-my-opinion's" and "it-seems-to-me's" and "as-I-see-it's" and "at-least-from-my-point-of-view's" gains you nothing. Delete these phrases whenever they creep into your paper.

The student's tendency to hedge stems from a modesty that in other circumstances would be commendable. He is, he realizes, young and inexperienced, and he half suspects that he is dopey and fuzzy-minded beyond the average. Probably only too true. But it doesn't help to announce your incompetence six times in every paragraph. Decide what you want to say and say it as vigorously as possible, without apology and in plain words.

Linguistic diffidence can take various forms. One is what we call *euphemism*. This is the tendency to call a spade "a certain garden implement" or women's underwear "unmentionables." It is stronger in some eras than others and in some people than others but it always operates more or less in subjects that are touchy or taboo: death, sex, madness, and so on. Thus we shrink from saying, "He died last night" but say instead, "passed away," "left us," "joined his Maker," "went to his reward." Or we try to take off the tension with a lighter cliché: "kicked the bucket," "cashed in his chips," "handed in his dinner pail." We have found all sorts of ways to avoid saying *mad*: "mentally ill," "touched," "not quite right upstairs," "feeble-minded," "innocent," "simple," "off his trolley," "not in his right mind." Even such a now plain word as *insane* began as a euphemism with the meaning "not healthy."

Modern science, particularly psychology, contributes many polysyllables in which we can wrap our thoughts and blunt their force. To many writers there is no such thing as a bad schoolboy. Schoolboys are maladjusted or unoriented or misunderstood or in need of guidance or lacking in continued success toward satisfactory integration of the personality as a social unit, but they are never bad. Psychology no doubt makes us better men or women, more sympathetic and tolerant, but it doesn't make writing any easier. Had Shakespeare been confronted with psychology, "To be or not to be" might have come out, "To continue as a social unit or not to do so. That is the personality problem. Whether 'tis a better sign of integration at the conscious level to display a psychic tolerance toward the maladjustments and repressions induced by one's lack of orientation in one's environment or—" But Hamlet would never have finished the soliloquy.

Writing in the modern world, you cannot altogether avoid modern jargon. Nor, in an effort to get away from euphemism, should you salt your paper with four-letter words. But you can do much if you will mount guard against those roundabout phrases, those echoing polysyllables that tend to slip into your writing to rob it of its crispness and force.

BEWARE OF THE PAT EXPRESSION

Other things being equal, avoid phrases like "other things being equal." Those sentences that come to you whole, or in two or three doughy lumps, are sure to be bad sentences. They are no creation of yours but pieces of common thought floating in the community soup.

Pat expressions are hard, often impossible, to avoid, because they come too easily to be noticed and seem too necessary to be dispensed with. No writer avoids them altogether, but good writers avoid them more often than poor writers.

By "pat expressions" we mean such tags as "to all practical intents and purposes," "the pure and simple truth," "from where I sit," "the time of his life," "to the ends of the earth," "in the twinkling of an eye," "as sure as you're born," "over my dead body," "under cover of darkness," "took the easy way out," "when all is said and done," "told him time and time again," "parted the best of friends," "stand up and be counted," "gave him the best years of her life," "worked her fingers to the bone." Like other clichés, these expressions were once forceful. Now we should use them only when we can't possibly think of anything else.

Some pat expressions stand like a wall between the writer and thought. Such a one is "the American way of life." Many student writers feel that when they have said that something accords with the American way of life or does not they have exhausted the subject. Actually, they have stopped at the highest level of abstraction. The American way of life is the complicated set of bonds between a hundred and eighty million ways. All of us know this when we think about it, but the tag phrase too often keeps us from thinking about it.

So with many another phrase dear to the politician: "this great land of ours," "the man in the street," "our national heritage." These may prove our patriotism or give a clue to our political beliefs, but otherwise they add nothing to the paper except words.

COLORFUL WORDS

The writer builds with words, and no builder uses a raw material more slippery and elusive and treacherous. A writer's work is a constant struggle to get the right word in the right place, to find that particular word that will convey his meaning exactly, that will persuade the reader or soothe him or startle or amuse him. He never succeeds altogether—sometimes he feels that he scarcely succeeds at all—but such successes as he has are what make the thing worth doing.

There is no book of rules for this game. One progresses through everlasting experiment on the basis of ever-widening experience. There are few useful generalizations that one can make about words as words, but there are perhaps a few.

Some words are what we call "colorful." By this we mean that they are calculated to produce a picture or induce an emotion. They are dressy instead of plain, specific instead of general, loud instead of soft. Thus, in place of "Her heart beat," we may write "Her heart *pounded, throbbed, fluttered, danced.*" Instead of "He sat in his chair," we may say, "He *lounged, sprawled, coiled.*" Instead of "It was hot," we may say, "It was *blistering, sultry, muggy, suffocating, steamy, wilting.*"

However, it should not be supposed that the fancy word is always better. Often it is as well to write "Her heart beat" or "It was hot" if that is all it did or all it was. Ages differ in how they like their prose. The nineteenth century liked it rich and smoky. The twentieth has usually preferred it lean and cool. The twentieth-century writer, like all writers, is forever seeking the exact word, but he is wary of sounding feverish. He tends to pitch it low, to understate it, to throw it away. He knows that if he gets too colorful, the audience is likely to giggle.

See how this strikes you: "As the rich, golden glow of the sunset died away along the eternal western hills, Angela's limpid blue eyes looked softly and trustingly into Montague's flashing brown ones, and her heart pounded like a drum in time with the joyous song surging in her soul." Some people like that sort of thing, but most modern readers would say, "Good grief," and turn on the television.

COLORED WORDS

Some words we would call not so much colorful as colored—that is, loaded with associations, good or bad. All words—except perhaps structure words—have associations of some sort. We have said that the meaning of a word is the sum of the contexts in which it occurs. When we hear a word, we hear with it an echo of all the situations in which we have heard it before.

In some words, these echoes are obvious and discussable. The word *mother*, for example, has, for most people, agreeable associations. When you hear *mother* you probably think of home, safety, love, food, and various other pleasant things. If one writes, "She was like a mother to me," he gets an effect which he would not get in "She was like an aunt to me." The advertiser makes use of the associations of *mother* by working it in when he talks about his product. The politician works it in when he talks about himself.

So also with such words as *home, liberty, fireside, contentment, patriot, tenderness, sacrifice, childlike, manly, bluff, limpid*. All of these words are loaded with favorable associations that would be rather hard to indicate in a straightforward definition. There is more than a literal difference between "They sat around the fireside" and "They sat around the stove." They might have been equally warm and happy around the stove, but *fireside* suggests leisure, grace, quiet tradition, congenial company, and *stove* does not.

Conversely, some words have bad associations. *Mother* suggests pleasant things, but *mother-in-law* does not. Many mothers-in-law are heroically lovable and some mothers drink gin all day and beat their children insensible, but these facts of life are beside the point. The thing is that *mother* sounds good and *mother-in-law* does not.

Or consider the word *intellectual*. This would seem to be a complimentary term, but in point of fact it is not, for it has picked up associations of impracticality and ineffectuality and general dopiness. So also with such words as *liberal, reactionary, Communist, Socialist, capitalist, radical, schoolteacher, truck driver, undertaker, operator, salesman, huckster, speculator*. These convey meanings on the literal level, but beyond that—sometimes, in some places—they convey contempt on the part of the speaker.

The question of whether to use loaded words or not depends on what is being written. The scientist, the scholar, try to avoid them; for the poet, the advertising writer, the public speaker, they are standard equipment. But every writer should take care that they do not substitute for thought. If you write, "Anyone who thinks that is nothing but a Socialist (or Communist or capitalist)" you have said nothing except that you don't like people who think that, and such remarks are effective only with the most naïve readers. It is always a bad mistake to think your readers more naïve than they really are.

COLORLESS WORDS

But probably most student writers come to grief not with words that are colorful or those that are colored but with those that have no color at all. A pet example is *nice*, a word we would find it hard to dispense with in casual conversation but which is no longer capable of adding much to a description. Colorless words are those of such general meaning that in a particular sentence they mean nothing. Slang adjectives, like *cool* ("That's real cool.") tend to explode all over the language. They are applied to everything, lose their original force, and quickly die.

Beware also of nouns of very general meaning, like *circumstances, cases, instances, aspects, factors, relationships, attitudes, eventualities,* etc. In most circumstances you will find that those cases of writing which contain too many instances of words like these will in this and other aspects have factors leading to unsatisfactory relationships with the reader resulting in unfavorable attitudes on his part and perhaps other eventualities, like a grade of D. Notice also what *etc.* means. It means "I'd like to make this list longer, but I can't think of any more examples."

Thinking Critically about the Text

In this essay, Roberts points out certain features, positive and negative, found in the work of many writers. Does your writing exhibit any of these features? How would you rate your writing with respect to each of these features?

Questions on Subject

1. What, for you, is the most important advice Roberts has to offer?
2. According to Roberts, what is the job of the writer? Why, in particular, is it difficult for college students to do this job well? Discuss how your college experience leads you to agree or disagree with Roberts.
3. The author offers several "tricks" or techniques of good writing in his essay. What are they? Do you find them more useful than other techniques? Explain.
4. If, according to Roberts, a good writer never uses unnecessary words, then what are the legitimate ways a student can reach the goal of the five-hundred-word essay?
5. According to Roberts, how has modern psychology made it more difficult to write well?

Questions on Strategy

1. What is Roberts's thesis in this essay? (Glossary: *Thesis*)

2. Make a scratch outline of Roberts's essay. What are the similarities between his organization of material and the process analysis he outlines for students? (Glossary: *Organization*) Explain.

3. What kind of information does the title of Roberts's essay lead you to expect? (Glossary: *Title*) Does the author deliver what the title promises? Why do you think he chose this title?

4. What are Roberts's main points? How do his examples help him explain and clarify his main points? (Glossary: *Illustration*)

5. Roberts's writing style is well suited to his student audience; he includes examples that would be familiar to many students. How would you describe his writing style? What are some of the ways he uses narration and illustration to make the process analysis easy to follow? (Glossary: *Illustration; Narration*)

Questions on Diction and Vocabulary

1. Roberts wrote this essay almost sixty years ago, and at some points the facts he cites indicate this: For example, he gives the population of the United States as 180 million (paragraph 36), whereas today it is nearly 320 million. Is there anything in his diction or word choice that makes Roberts's writing seem dated, or does it sound contemporary? Choose examples from the text to support your answer. (Glossary: *Diction*)

2. What does Roberts mean by "colorful words," "colored words," and "colorless words"?

3. What is Roberts's tone in this essay? What words does he use to create this tone? Explain how the tone affects you as a reader. (Glossary: *Tone*)

Process Analysis in Action

Before class, find a how-to article that interests you at the Web site www.wikihow.com. Bring a copy of the article to class and be prepared to discuss why you think the article is incomplete or inaccurate and how you might revise it.

Writing Suggestions

1. In paragraph 20, Roberts explains how a brief but good essay on college football might be written. He obeys a major rule of good writing — show, don't tell. Thus, instead of a dry string of words, his brief "essay" uses humor, exaggeration, and concrete details to breathe life into the football player. Review

Roberts's strategies for good writing. Then choose one of the dull topics he suggests or one of your own, and following the steps he lays out, write a five-hundred-word essay.

2. Roberts's essay was first published in 1958 — before personal computers and word processing programs became ubiquitous. Write an essay in which you compare and contrast the process of writing an essay on a typewriter or by hand and on a computer. (Glossary: *Comparison and Contrast*) How is the process similar? How is it different? What equipment and supplies does each require? Which do you prefer? Why?

Eating Industrial Meat

MICHAEL POLLAN

Writer, journalist, and educator Michael Pollan was born in 1955 and grew up on Long Island. In 1977 he graduated from Bennington College. He attended Mansfield College, Oxford University, and received a master's in English from Columbia University in 1981. Running throughout Pollan's work is the belief that eating is our most deeply significant interaction with the natural world. His award-winning nonfiction books include *Second Nature: A Gardener's Education* (1991), *A Place of My Own: The Education of an Amateur Builder* (1997), *The Omnivore's Dilemma: A Natural History of Four Meals* (2006), and *Cooked: A Natural History of Transformation* (2013). Since 1987 Pollan has been a contributing writer to the *New York Times Magazine*, and his articles on various food-related topics have appeared in *Esquire, Harper's, Gourmet, Condé Nast Traveler, Mother Jones,* and *Vogue*. He has taught at the University of Pittsburgh and the University of Wisconsin and is currently the John S. and James L. Knight Professor of Journalism at the University of California–Berkeley, where he directs the Knight Program in Science and Environmental Journalism.

Courtesy of Ken Light

In the following selection, excerpted from *The Omnivore's Dilemma*, Pollan examines the process of bringing beef to market. His focus is one steer in particular, number 534, as it's being held in a feedlot in Kansas to gain weight before being slaughtered. As you read, pay special attention to the far-ranging connections and implications of what he's learned about the way we have industrialized cattle farming in this country.

Preparing to Read

Reflect on the origins of the food you eat. Do you know where it comes from? Do you have any sense of how it is farmed or manufactured? If you are a meat eater, do you ever think about what the creatures you eat have themselves eaten? If you know very little about the origins of the food you eat, does that lack of knowledge affect you?

My first impression of pen 63, where my steer [534] is spending his last five months, was, *Not a bad little piece of real estate, all considered.* The pen is far enough from the feed mill to be fairly quiet and it has a water view of what I thought was a pond or reservoir until I noticed the brown scum. The body of water is what is known, in the geography of CAFOs,[1] as a manure

---
[1] Concentrated animal feeding operations — Eds.

lagoon. I asked the feedlot manager why they didn't just spray the liquefied manure on neighboring farms. The farmers don't want it, he explained. The nitrogen and phosphorus levels are so high that spraying the crops would kill them. He didn't say that feedlot wastes also contain heavy metals and hormone residues, persistent chemicals that end up in waterways downstream, where scientists have found fish and amphibians exhibiting abnormal sex characteristics. CAFOs like Poky transform what at the proper scale would be a precious source of fertility—cow manure—into toxic waste.

The pen 534 lives in is surprisingly spacious, about the size of a hockey rink, with a concrete feed bunk along the road, and a fresh water trough out back. I climbed over the railing and joined the ninety steers, which, en masse, retreated a few lumbering steps, and then stopped to see what I would do.

I had on the same carrot-colored sweater I'd worn to the ranch in South Dakota, hoping to elicit some glint of recognition from my steer. I couldn't find him at first; all the faces staring at me were either completely black or bore an unfamiliar pattern of white marks. And then I spotted him—the three white blazes—way off in the back. As I gingerly stepped toward him the quietly shuffling mass of black cowhide between us parted, and there stood 534 and I, staring dumbly at one another. Glint of recognition? None, none whatsoever. I told myself not to take it personally; 534 and his pen mates have been bred for their marbling, after all, not their ability to form attachments.

I noticed that 534's eyes looked a little bloodshot. Dr. Metzin had told me that some animals are irritated by feedlot dust. The problem is especially serious in the summer months, when the animals kick up clouds of the stuff and workers have to spray the pens with water to keep it down. I had to remind myself that this is not ordinary dirt dust, inasmuch as the dirt in a feedyard is not ordinary dirt; no, this is fecal dust. But apart from the air quality, how did feedlot life seem to be agreeing with 534? I don't know enough about the emotional life of a steer to say with confidence that 534 was miserable, bored, or indifferent, but I would not say he looked happy.

He's clearly eating well, though. My steer had put on a couple hundred pounds since we'd last met, and he looked it: thicker across the shoulder and round as a barrel through the middle. He carried himself more like a steer now than a calf, even though his first birthday was still two months away. Dr. Metzin complimented me on his size and conformation. "That's a handsome-looking beef you got there." (Shucks.)

If I stared at my steer hard enough, I could imagine the white lines of the butcher's chart dissecting his black hide: rump roast, flank steak, standing rib, tenderloin, brisket. One way of looking at 534—the feedlot way, the industrial way—was as a most impressive machine for turning number 2 field corn into cuts of beef. Every day between now and his slaughter in six months, 534 will convert thirty-two pounds of feed into four pounds of gain—new muscle, fat, and bone. This at least is how 534 appears in the computer program I'd seen at the mill: the ratio of feed to gain that determines his efficiency. (Compared to other food animals, cattle are terribly inefficient: The ratio of feed to flesh in chicken, the most efficient animal by this measure, is two pounds of corn to one of meat, which is why chicken costs less than beef.) Poky Feeders is indeed a factory, transforming—as fast as bovinely possible—cheap raw materials into a less cheap finished product, through the mechanism of bovine metabolism.

> If I stared at my steer hard enough, I could imagine the white lines of the butcher's chart dissecting his black hide: rump roast, flank steak, standing rib, tenderloin, brisket.

Yet metaphors of the factory and the machine obscure as much as they reveal about the creature standing before me. He has, of course, another, quite different identity—as an animal, I mean, connected as all animals must be to certain other animals and plants and microbes, as well as to the earth and the sun. He's a link in a food chain, a thread in a far-reaching web of ecological relationships. Looked at from this perspective, everything going on in this cattle pen appears quite different, and not nearly as far removed from our world as this manure-encrusted patch of ground here in Nowhere, Kansas, might suggest.

For one thing, the health of these animals is inextricably linked to our own by that web of relationships. The unnaturally rich diet of corn that undermines a steer's health fattens his flesh in a way that undermines the health of the humans who will eat it. The antibiotics these animals consume with their corn at this very moment are selecting, in their gut and wherever else in the environment they end up, for new strains of resistant bacteria that will someday infect us and withstand the drugs we depend on to treat that infection. We inhabit the same microbial ecosystem as the animals we eat, and whatever happens in it also happens to us.

Then there's the deep pile of manure on which I stand, in which 534 sleeps. We don't know much about the hormones in it—where they will end up, or what they might do once they get there—but we do know something about the bacteria, which can find their way from the manure on the ground to his hide and from there into our hamburgers. The speed at which these animals will be slaughtered and processed—four hundred an hour at the plant where 534 will go—means that sooner or later some of the manure caked on these hides gets into the meat we eat. One of the bacteria that almost certainly resides in the manure I'm standing in is particularly lethal to humans. *Escherichia coli* 0157:H7 is a relatively new strain of the common intestinal bacteria (no one had seen it before 1980) that thrives in feedlot cattle, 40 percent of which carry it in their gut. Ingesting as few as ten of these microbes can cause a fatal infection; they produce a toxin that destroys human kidneys.

Most of the microbes that reside in the gut of a cow and find their way into our food get killed off by the strong acids in our stomachs, since they evolved to live in the neutral pH environment of the rumen. But the rumen of a corn-fed feedlot steer is nearly as acidic as our own stomachs, and in this new, man-made environment new acid-resistant strains of *E. coli*, of which 0157:H7 is one, have evolved—yet another creature recruited by nature to absorb the excess biomass coming off the Farm Belt. The problem with these bugs is that they can shake off the acid bath in our stomachs—and then go on to kill us. By acidifying the rumen with corn we've broken down one of our food chain's most important barriers to infection. Yet another solution turned into a problem.

We've recently discovered that this process of acidification can be reversed, and that doing so can greatly diminish the threat from *E. coli* 0157:H7. Jim Russell, a USDA microbiologist on the faculty at Cornell, has found that switching a cow's diet from corn to grass or hay for a few days prior to slaughter reduces the population of *E. coli* 0157:H7 in the animal's gut by as much as 80 percent. But such a solution (*Grass?!*) is considered wildly impractical by the cattle industry and (therefore) by the USDA. Their preferred solution for dealing with bacterial contamination is irradiation—essentially, to try to sterilize the manure getting into the meat.

So much comes back to corn, this cheap feed that turns out in so many ways to be not cheap at all. While I stood in pen 63 a dump truck pulled up alongside the feed bunk and released a golden stream of feed. The black mass of cowhide moved toward the trough for lunch. The $1.60 a day I'm paying for three meals a day here is a bargain only by the narrowest of calculations. It doesn't take into account, for example, the cost to the public health of antibiotic resistance or food poisoning by *E. coli* 0157:H7. It doesn't take into account the cost to taxpayers of the farm subsidies that keep Poky's raw materials cheap. And it certainly doesn't take into account all the many environmental costs incurred by cheap corn.

I stood alongside 534 as he lowered his big head into the stream of fresh grain. How absurd, I thought, the two of us standing hock-deep in manure in this godforsaken place, overlooking a manure lagoon in the middle of nowhere somewhere in Kansas. Godforsaken perhaps, and yet not apart, I realized, as I thought of the other places connected to this place by the river of commodity corn. Follow the corn from this bunk back to the fields where it grows and I'd find myself back in the middle of that 125,000-mile-square monoculture, under a steady rain of pesticide and fertilizer. Keep going, and I could follow the nitrogen runoff from that fertilizer all the way down the Mississippi into the Gulf of Mexico, adding its poison to an eight-thousand-square-mile zone so starved of oxygen nothing but algae can live in it. And then go farther still, follow the fertilizer (and the diesel fuel and the petrochemical pesticides) needed to grow the corn all the way to the oil fields of the Persian Gulf.

14 I don't have a sufficiently vivid imagination to look at my steer and see a barrel of oil, but petroleum is one of the most important ingredients in the production of modern meat, and the Persian Gulf is surely a link in the food chain that passes through this (or any) feedlot. Steer 534 started his life part of a food chain that derived all of its energy from the sun, which nourished the grasses that nourished him and his mother. When 534 moved from ranch to feedlot, from grass to corn, he joined an industrial food chain powered by fossil fuel—and therefore defended by the U.S. military, another never-counted cost of cheap food. (One-fifth of America's petroleum consumption goes to producing and transporting our food.) After I got home from Kansas, I asked an economist who specializes in agriculture and energy if it might be possible to calculate precisely how much petroleum it will take to grow my steer to slaughter weight. Assuming 534 continues to eat twenty-five pounds of corn a day and reaches a weight of twelve hundred pounds, he will have consumed in his lifetime the equivalent of thirty-five gallons of oil—nearly a barrel.

15 So this is what commodity corn can do to a cow: industrialize the miracle of nature that is a ruminant, taking this sunlight- and prairie grass-powered organism and turning it into the last thing we need: another fossil fuel machine. This one, however, is able to suffer.

16 Standing there in the pen alongside my steer, I couldn't imagine ever wanting to eat the flesh of one of these protein machines. Hungry was the last thing I felt. Yet I'm sure that after enough time goes by, and the stink of this place is gone from my nostrils, I will eat feedlot beef again. Eating industrial meat takes an almost heroic act of not knowing or, now, forgetting. But I left Poky determined to follow this meat to a meal on a table somewhere, to see this food chain at least that far. I was curious to know what feedlot beef would taste like now, if I could taste the corn or even, since taste is as much a matter of what's in the head as it is about molecules dancing on the tongue, some hint of the petroleum. "You are what you eat" is a truism hard to argue with, and yet it is, as a visit to a feedlot suggests, incomplete, for you are what what you eat eats, too. And what we are, or have become, is not just meat but number 2 corn and oil.

Thinking Critically about the Text

Pollan writes at the beginning of his essay that his first impression of the feedlot was that it was *"Not a bad little piece of real estate, all considered."* What facts undermine his first impression?

Questions on Subject

1. Why don't farmers want the liquefied manure from feedlots? What does that fact tell you about industrialized beef?
2. A butcher might look at 534 as an array of cuts of meat. Identify some of the other perspectives by which farm animals such as 534 are viewed.
3. What discoveries have been made regarding reversing the acidification of the rumen of steers? Explain how it works.
4. Why do the cattle industry and the USDA find feeding grass to cattle impractical?
5. Why does the cheap corn fed to cows turn out to be not cheap after all, according to Pollan?

Questions on Strategy

1. How does Pollan organize his essay? (Glossary: *Organization*) Explain why his organization seems most appropriate for his subject.
2. Explain the process by which bacteria enter cattle and end up in the hamburgers we eat. Does Pollan leave you with any questions or missing steps?
3. Explain the process by which a natural barrier to infection is diminished by feeding corn to cows. How does Pollan simplify this technical process?
4. How has Pollan used transitions to move from paragraph to paragraph in his essay? (Glossary: *Transitions*) Cite several examples and explain how they work.
5. How does Pollan connect what's happening to 534 to the oil fields of the Persian Gulf?

Questions on Diction and Vocabulary

1. In paragraph 3, Pollan writes, "534 and his pen mates have been bred for their marbling, after all, not their ability to form attachments." What does he mean by *marbling*?
2. Pollan ends paragraph 5 with "(Shucks)." How are we meant to interpret that expression? (Glossary: *Irony*)
3. What does Pollan mean when he writes in paragraph 7, "Yet metaphors of the factory and the machine obscure as much as they reveal about the creature standing before me." (Glossary: *Figures of Speech*)

Process Analysis in Action

Most do-it-yourself jobs require that you follow a set process to achieve the best results. Make a list of the steps involved in accomplishing one of the following household tasks:

   a. baking chocolate chip cookies
   b. transplanting a plant
   c. packing a suitcase
   d. mowing a lawn
   e. washing a pile of dirty towels

Compare your list with those of other students who focused on the same task. How do the lists differ? What could be improved?

Writing Suggestions

1. In an essay, write, as Pollan does, about the web of interconnectedness among processes that might at first seem unrelated. Pollan writes, for example, about the unintended consequences that arise when we pursue food-production practices and processes that run counter to the laws of nature. For your essay, consider an entirely different arena — the world of the Internet, for example, and the unintended consequences of our pursuit of maximum technological connectivity.

2. **Writing with Sources.** Pollan focuses his attention on the processes by which we raise cattle and bring them to market. By explaining those processes as they are carried out by the large industrial meat producers, he intends to provide us with information we need in order to make decisions about our economy, our environment, and our health. Do some research on other areas of food production — fruit growing or milk production, for example — and explain the processes involved. Write an essay in which you describe what the implications of the process might be for our economy, environment, or health. For models of and advice on integrating sources in your essay, see Chapters 14 and 15.

How Do Spiders Make Their Webs?

ALICIA AULT

Journalist Alicia Ault graduated from Boston University and later earned a CASE journalism fellowship to study at the University of Pittsburgh's School of Medicine. Ault specializes in science, medicine, and health policy, covering everything from the Affordable Care Act to the National Institutes of Health and the Food and Drug Administration. She also writes about art, business, real estate, food, and adventure sports, including races in Borneo, Patagonia, and the Sierra Nevada mountains. She worked as associate editor for Frontline Medical Communications and has written for the *New York Times*, the *Washington Post*, the *Wall Street Journal*, Reuters, *Wired*, the *Miami Herald*, *Science*, *Nature*, the Discovery Channel, and Sirius Radio. Ault now divides her time between Washington, D.C., and New Orleans.

Ault is currently a contributing writer for both Medscape Medical News and Smithsonian.com, where she writes the "Ask Smithsonian" column. This essay appeared in that column in December 2015. Here Ault explores how spiders do what they do and what scientists might accomplish with that knowledge.

Preparing to Read

Is there a process, natural or otherwise, that has always intrigued you? Perhaps you wonder how a tadpole turns into a frog, or how the electoral college works, or how a wireless router transmits a signal. Consider what you know about the process and where you might turn to learn more.

Spiders are skillful engineers, gifted with amazing planning skills and a material that allows them to precisely design rigorous and functional webs.

The material—spider silk—has chemical properties that make it lustrous, strong and light. It's stronger than steel and has impressive tensile strength, meaning it can be stretched a lot before it snaps. Scientists have been trying for decades to decode exactly what gives the silk both strength and elasticity, but so far they have found only clues.

Any individual spider can make up to seven different types of silk, but most generally make four to five kinds, says Jonathan Coddington, director of the Global Genome Initiative and senior scientist at the Smithsonian's National Museum of Natural History.

Spiders use their silk for several purposes, including web-building. That diversity is not hard to imagine, given that Earth hosts 45,749 species of spiders, according to the World Spider Catalog. The number is changing constantly with the frequent discovery of new species.

Why build webs? They serve as "pretty much offense and defense," says Coddington. "If you're going to live in a web, it's going to be a defensive structure," he says, noting that vibrations in the strands can alert the spiders to predators. Webs are also used to catch prey, says Coddington, whose research has focused in part on spider evolution and taxonomy.

> Scientists have been trying for decades to decode exactly what gives the silk both strength and elasticity, but so far they have found only clues.

Sometimes spiders eat their own webs when they are done with them, as a way to replenish the silk supply.

Spider silk is made of connected protein chains that help make it strong, along with unconnected areas that give it flexibility. It is produced in internal glands, moving from a soluble form to a hardened form and then spun into fiber by the spinnerets on the spider's abdomen.

Spiders' multiple spinnerets and eight legs come in handy for web-building. The architecture of a web is very species-specific, says Coddington. "If you show me a web, I can tell you what spider made it," he says, adding that spiders "are opinionated" about where they will make a web. Some might be at home in the bottom of a paper cup, while others wouldn't touch that space.

Most web-building happens under the cover of darkness.

The typical orb weaver spider (the group that's most familiar to Americans) will build a planar orb web, suspended by seven guy lines attached to leaves, twigs, rocks, telephone poles or other surfaces. Hanging from a leaf or some other object, the spider must get its silk from that point to the other surfaces.

The spider starts by pulling silk from a gland with its fourth leg. The opposite fourth leg is used to pull out multiple strands of silk from about 20 additional silk glands, creating a balloon-like structure. The spider sits patiently, knowing that eventually a warm breeze will take up the balloon, which carries away the first line of silk.

Eventually the balloon's trailing silk strand snags — and, like an angler with a fish on the line, the spider can feel the hit. It tugs to make sure the silk strand is truly attached, then it pulls out new silk and attaches the strand to whatever it is perched on and starts gathering up the snagged strand, pulling itself towards the endpoint, all the while laying out new silk behind it.

That new silk is the first planar line. The spider may do this 20 times, creating a network of dry (not sticky) silk lines arcing in all directions.

The spider then has to determine which of those lines constitute seven good attachment points—they must be in a plane and "distributed usefully around the circle the web will occupy," says Coddington. The spider cuts away the 13 lines that it won't use. "Now that you have the seven attachments you need, you no longer need to touch the ground, leaves, twigs, anything . . . you are in your own, arguably solipsistic, world."

Then the spider starts to spin its web, a relatively simple and predictable process. It begins at the outside and works its way in, attaching segment by segment with its legs, creating concentric circles and ending with a center spiral of sticky silk that traps much-needed prey—all the energy invested in making the web depletes protein stores.

The sticky stuff merely immobilizes the prey. The coup de grâce comes from the spider's jaws. "Most spiders attack with their teeth," says Coddington. "They just wade in and bite the thing to death." That's a risky proposition, though, because the prey might not be entirely stuck.

A few families of spiders have developed an alternative mode of offense: the sticky-silk wrap attack. Those spiders lay a strand of sticky silk across the ground. When an insect crosses, the vibration alerts the spider, which then attacks, flicking lines of sticky, strong silk around the insect and wrapping it up until it is fully immobilized. The spider then moves in for the death bite. But this is more of a rarity than a rule in the spider world.

Many researchers are studying spider behavior and spider silk in the hopes of some day being able to farm the material or perhaps replicate it through genetic engineering. The silk could be used, for instance, to increase the strength of body armor, or to create skin grafts. "That would be a great thing for the human race," says Coddington.

A handful of companies are currently invested in spider silk, including Ann Arbor, Michigan–based Kraig Biocraft Laboratories, a Swedish biotech firm, Spiber Technologies, and a German company, AMSilk, which says it has genetically engineered a protein that is similar to spider silk that is currently being used in shampoos and other cosmetics.

Thinking Critically about the Text

Ault mentions two possible uses for spider silk: body armor and skin grafts. Based on the information provided in this article, can you think of other potential uses for spider silk?

Questions on Subject

1. What purposes do spider webs serve? Where do you find this information?
2. What are the qualities of spider silk? Why do scientists consider it valuable?
3. Paragraph 4 begins "Spiders use their silk for several purposes, including web-building." What other purposes do spiders use their silk for?
4. Paragraph 9 consists of one sentence "Most web-building happens under the cover of darkness." Why do you think Ault includes this information? What significance does it have?

Questions on Strategy

1. What is Ault's purpose in this essay? Where is it stated? (Glossary: *Purpose*)
2. Who is Ault's audience for this essay, and how do you know? (Glossary: *Audience*)
3. Ault relies heavily on description. What dominant impression does she create of spiders and of their webs? Locate the details she uses to do this.
4. In your own words, summarize the steps a spider takes to build a web.
5. How many experts has Ault cited in this essay? Is her research adequate and convincing? Would you like to have heard from additional scientists? Why or why not? (Glossary: *Evidence*)
6. How is this selection organized? What transitional expressions and time markers are used to help create a logical flow of ideas?

Questions on Diction and Vocabulary

1. How would you describe Ault's tone in this essay? Is she serious, conversational, awestruck, or matter of fact? What words and phrases lead you to this conclusion? (Glossary: *Tone*)
2. Why do you think Ault uses the simile "like an angler with a fish on the line" (paragraph 12) to describe part of the web-building process? What is the effect of this phrase on the reader? (Glossary: *Figures of Speech*)
3. Refer to a dictionary to determine the meanings of the following words as they are used in this selection: *lustrous* (paragraph 1), *taxonomy* (5), *replenish* (6), *soluble* (7), *planar* (10), *solipsistic* (13), *concentric* (14), *depletes* (14), *coup de grâce* (15).

Process Analysis in Action

Draw the process Ault describes in paragraphs 10–15. You don't need to be an artist for this activity: the spider can be an oval with 8 lines representing legs. Create at least one image for each paragraph; you'll probably need several images for the more complex steps. Work in pencil so you can adjust your drawing as you proceed. Does the act of drawing the process help you more clearly understand it? Why do you think that is?

Writing Suggestions

1. Ault tells us that researchers hope they may one day be able to "replicate [spider silk] through genetic engineering" (paragraph 17). According to the Union of Concerned Scientists, "Genetic engineering is a set of technologies used to change the genetic makeup of cells, including the transfer of genes within and across species boundaries to produce improved or novel organisms." Both genetically modified food and human genetic engineering are highly controversial. What do you know about genetic engineering, and how do you feel about it? Are the uses mentioned in this article (strengthening body armor and skin grafts) legitimate? What concerns do you have about genetic engineering? Write an essay exploring the pros and cons of genetic engineering, providing detailed examples to support your claims.

2. **Writing with Sources.** Using the Preparing to Read prompt as a starting point, select a process you'd like to research. Search both print and online resources and write an informational process analysis on your topic. Be sure to identify each step in the process and to use transitional expressions and time markers to create a logical, unified essay.

Campus Racism 101

NIKKI GIOVANNI

Yolanda Cornelia "Nikki" Giovanni was born in Knoxville, Tennessee, in 1943 and raised in Ohio. After graduating from Fisk University, she organized the Black Arts Festival in Cincinnati and then entered graduate school at the University of Pennsylvania. Her first book of poetry, *Black Feeling, Black Talk*, was published in 1968 and began a lifetime of writing that reflects on the African American identity. Recent books of poetry include the anthologies *Selected Poems of Nikki Giovanni* (1996), *Blues for All the Changes: New Poems* (1999), *Quilting the Black-Eyed Pea: Poems and Not Quite Poems* (2002), *Acolytes: Poems* (2007), *Bicycles: Love Poems* (2009), and *Chasing Utopia: A Hybrid* (2013). Her honors include the Langston Hughes Award for Distinguished Contributions to Arts and Letters in 1996, seven NAACP Image awards, and Woman of the Year awards from several magazines, including *Essence, Mademoiselle*, and *Ladies' Home Journal*. She is currently professor of English and Gloria D. Smith Professor of Black Studies at Virginia Tech.

The following selection, taken from her nonfiction work *Racism 101*, instructs black students about how to succeed at predominantly white colleges.

Preparing to Read

How would you characterize race relations at your school? How much do white and minority students interact, and what, in your experience, is the tone of those interactions? What is being done within the institution to address any problems or to foster greater respect and understanding?

There is a bumper sticker that reads: TOO BAD IGNORANCE ISN'T PAINFUL. I like that. But ignorance is. We just seldom attribute the pain to it or even recognize it when we see it. Like the postcard on my corkboard. It shows a young man in a very hip jacket smoking a cigarette. In the background is a high school with the American flag waving. The caption says: "Too cool for school. Yet too stupid for the real world." Out of the mouth of the young man is a bubble enclosing the words "Maybe I'll start a band." There could be a postcard showing a jock in a uniform saying, "I don't need school. I'm going to the NFL or NBA." Or one showing a young man or woman studying and a group of young people saying, "So you want to be white." Or something equally demeaning. We need to quit it.

I am a professor of English at Virginia Tech. I've been here for four years, though for only two years with academic rank. I am tenured, which means I have a teaching position for life, a rarity on a predominantly white campus. Whether from malice or ignorance, people who think I should be at a predominantly Black institution will ask, "Why are you at Tech?" Because it's here. And so are Black students. But even if Black students weren't here, it's painfully obvious that this nation and this world cannot allow white students to go through higher education without interacting with Blacks in authoritative positions. It is equally clear that predominantly Black colleges cannot accommodate the numbers of Black students who want and need an education.

Is it difficult to attend a predominantly white college? Compared with what? Being passed over for promotion because you lack credentials? Being turned down for jobs because you are not college-educated? Joining the armed forces or going to jail because you cannot find an alternative to the streets? Let's have a little perspective here. Where can you go and what can you do that frees you from interacting with the white American mentality? You're going to interact; the only question is, will you be in some control of yourself and your actions, or will you be controlled by others? I'm going to recommend self-control.

What's the difference between prison and college? They both prescribe your behavior for a given period of time. They both allow you to read books and develop your writing. They both give you time alone to think and time with your peers to talk about issues. But four years of prison doesn't give you a passport to greater opportunities. Most likely that time only gives you greater knowledge of how to get back in. Four years of college gives you an opportunity not only to lift yourself but to serve your people effectively. What's the difference when you are called nigger in college from when you are called nigger in prison? In college you can, though I admit with effort, follow procedures to have those students who called you nigger kicked out or suspended. You can bring issues to public attention without risking your life. But mostly, college is and always has been the future. We, neither less nor more than other people, need knowledge. There are discomforts attached to attending predominantly white colleges, though no more so than living in a racist world. Here are some rules to follow that may help:

There are discomforts attached to attending predominantly white colleges, though no more so than living in a racist world.

Go to class. No matter how you feel. No matter how you think the professor feels about you. It's important to have a consistent presence in the classroom. If nothing else, the professor will know you care enough and are serious enough to be there.

Meet your professors. Extend your hand (give a firm handshake) and tell them your name. Ask them what you need to do to make an A. You may never make an A, but you have put them on notice that you are serious about getting good grades.

Do assignments on time. Typed or computer-generated. You have the syllabus. Follow it, and turn those papers in. If for some reason you can't complete an assignment on time, let your professor know before it is due and work out a new due date — then meet it.

Go back to see your professor. Tell him or her your name again. If an assignment received less than an A, ask why, and find out what you need to do to improve the next assignment.

Yes, your professor is busy. So are you. So are your parents who are working to pay or help with your tuition. Ask early what you need to do if you feel you are starting to get into academic trouble. Do not wait until you are failing.

Understand that there will be professors who do not like you; there may even be professors who are racist or sexist or both. You must discriminate among your professors to see who will give you the help you need. You may not simply say, "They are all against me." They aren't. They mostly don't care. Since you are the one who wants to be educated, find the people who want to help.

Don't defeat yourself. Cultivate your friends. Know your enemies. You cannot undo hundreds of years of prejudicial thinking. Think for yourself and speak up. Raise your hand in class. Say what you believe no matter how awkward you may think it sounds. You will improve in your articulation and confidence.

Participate in some campus activity. Join the newspaper staff. Run for office. Join a dorm council. Do something that involves you on campus. You are going to be there for four years, so let your presence be known, if not felt.

You will inevitably run into some white classmates who are troubling because they often say stupid things, ask stupid questions — and expect an answer. Here are some comebacks to some of the most common inquiries and comments:

Q: What's it like to grow up in a ghetto?
A: I don't know.

Q: (from the teacher) Can you give us the Black perspective on Toni Morrison, Huck Finn, slavery, Martin Luther King Jr., and others?
A: I can give you *my* perspective. (Do not take the burden of 22 million people on your shoulders. Remind everyone that you are an individual, and don't speak for the race or any other individual within it.)

Q: Why do all the Black people sit together in the dining hall?
A: Why do all the white students sit together?

Q: Why should there be an African American studies course?
A: Because white Americans have not adequately studied the contributions of Africans and African Americans. Both Black and white students need to know our total common history.

Q: Why are there so many scholarships for "minority" students?
A: Because they wouldn't give my great-grandparents their forty acres and the mule.

Q: How can whites understand Black history, culture, literature, and so forth?
A: The same way we understand white history, culture, literature, and so forth. That is why we're in school: to learn.

Q: Should whites take African American studies courses?
A: Of course. We take white-studies courses, though the universities don't call them that.

Comment: When I see groups of Black people on campus, it's really intimidating.
Comeback: I understand what you mean. I'm frightened when I see white students congregating.

Comment: It's not fair. It's easier for you guys to get into college than for other people.
Comeback: If it's so easy, why aren't there more of us?

Comment: It's not our fault that America is the way it is.
Comeback: It's not our fault, either, but both of us have a responsibility to make changes.

It's really very simple. Educational progress is a national concern; education is a private one. Your job is not to educate white people; it is to obtain an education. If you take the racial world on your shoulders, you will not get the job done. Deal with yourself as an individual worthy of respect, and make everyone else deal with you the same way. College is a little like playing grown-up. Practice what you want to be. You have been telling your parents you are grown. Now is your chance to act like it.

Thinking Critically about the Text

Giovanni concludes her essay by pointing out the nature of the "job" black students have undertaken, focusing on what it does *not* involve for them. For you, does the "job" of being a student involve more than just getting an education? If so, what other priorities do you have, and what additional challenges do they present? If not, explain your situation. How well are you able to put other things aside to achieve your educational goals?

Questions on Subject

1. Who is Giovanni's audience? When does the intended audience first become clear? (Glossary: *Audience*)
2. Why does Giovanni dismiss the notion that it is difficult being a black student at a predominantly white college? What contexts does she use to support her contention?
3. The rules Giovanni presents to help black students succeed at white colleges offer a lot of sound advice for any student at any college. Why does Giovanni use what could be considered general information in her essay?
4. On what topic does Giovanni provide sample questions and answers for her readers? Why is the topic important to her readers?

Questions on Strategy

1. What is Giovanni arguing for in this essay? (Glossary: *Argument*) What is her thesis? (Glossary: *Thesis*)
2. Giovanni begins her essay with staccato rhythm. Short sentences appear throughout the essay, but they are emphasized in the beginning. (Glossary: *Beginnings/Endings*) Reread paragraph 1. What does Giovanni accomplish with her rapid-fire delivery? Why is it appropriate for the subject matter?
3. What does Giovanni gain by including her short personal narrative in paragraph 2? (Glossary: *Narration*) Why is it necessary to know her personal history and current situation?
4. After beginning her essay with straight prose, Giovanni uses a list with full explanations and a series of Q&A examples to outline strategies to help black students cope at predominantly white colleges. Why did Giovanni use these techniques to convey her material? How might they add to the usefulness of the essay for the reader?
5. What does Giovanni mean when she says, "Educational progress is a national concern; education is a private one" (paragraph 34)? What is the difference between "educational progress" and "education"? In what ways is this point important to her purpose? (Glossary: *Purpose*)

Questions on Diction and Vocabulary

1. How did you first react to Giovanni's title, "Campus Racism 101"? What did it connote to you? (Glossary: *Connotation/Denotation*) After reading the essay, do you think the title is appropriate? Explain your answer.

2. Giovanni uses the word *stupid* on two occasions. The first use (paragraph 1), "too stupid for the real world," provides a context for how she views the word, while the second characterizes what white students sometimes ask or say to black students. The second use (paragraph 13) is a little jarring — often these days the characterization is softened to "insensitive" or "thoughtless." The use of *stupid* implies a more active ignorance on the part of the questioner. What does Giovanni gain by using the word? Do you think it is meant to be pejorative toward the white students? Explain your answer.

3. How would you describe the author's tone in this essay? (Glossary: *Tone*) Is it angry, firm, moderate, instructional, or something else? Explain.

Process Analysis in Action

After finishing the first draft of your process analysis essay, have someone else in your writing class read it. If you are writing a directional analysis, ask your reader to follow the instructions and then tell you whether he or she was able to understand each step and, if possible, perform it satisfactorily. Was the desired result achieved? If not, examine your process step by step, looking for errors and omissions that would explain the unsatisfactory result.

Writing Suggestions

1. What specific strategies do you employ to do well in your classes? Do you ask the professor what is needed for an A and make sure you attend every class, as Giovanni suggests in her essay? Do you take meticulous notes, study every day, just cram the night before exams, or have a lucky shirt for test days? Write a process analysis in which you present your method for success in school in a way that others could emulate, should they so choose.

2. In Giovanni's Q&A section, she replies to the question "Why are there so many scholarships for 'minority' students?" with the answer "Because they wouldn't give my great-grandparents their forty acres and the mule" (paragraphs 22–23). Write an argumentative essay in which you react to both Giovanni's answer and the situation as a whole. Do you think qualified minority students should receive preferential treatment for admissions and financial aid? If you argue no, what other strategies would you support to address the current educational inequities between whites and blacks?

3. **Writing with Sources.** The battle over education rights became one of the most important components of the civil rights movement and led to some of the most contentious showdowns. The photograph below shows James Meredith as he attempts to become the first African American to enter the University of Mississippi on October 1, 1962. His efforts resulted in riots that caused two deaths and 160 injuries. Meredith graduated from Ole Miss in 1964 and then went on to Columbia University and earned a degree in law.

What evidence of determination do you see on the faces and in the body language of both those who wished to keep James Meredith from entering the

© Flip Schulke/CORBIS

university and those who were his supporters? What do you learn from the posture and expression of Meredith himself? Notice that the photograph reveals a sort of mirror image, with the opposing sides reflecting each other's confrontational attitudes.

Research the background and precipitating circumstances of Meredith's admittance to the University of Mississippi and write an essay explaining the process he went through to make his case heard and accepted by authorities in the civil rights movement, the federal government, the state of Mississippi, and the university. You might also research the Black Lives Matter movement and student protests on college campuses to make an argument about current tensions surrounding race and higher education. For models of and advice on integrating sources in your essay, see Chapters 14 and 15.

WRITING SUGGESTIONS FOR PROCESS ANALYSIS

1. Write a directional or evaluative process analysis on one of the following topics:

   a. how to write a blog
   b. how to adjust bicycle brakes
   c. how to save photos you take on your smartphone
   d. how to throw a party
   e. how to add, drop, or change a course
   f. how to play a particular card game
   g. how to wash a sweater
   h. how to cook in a dorm
   i. how to select a major course of study
   j. how to safely dispose of old electronics
   k. how to rent an apartment
   l. how to develop confidence
   m. how to wrap a present
   n. how to change the oil in a car

2. Think about your favorite pastime or activity. Write an essay in which you explain one or more of the processes you follow in participating in that activity. For example, if basketball is your hobby, how do you go about making a layup? If you are a photographer, how do you develop and print a picture following traditional methods? If you are an actor, how do you go about learning your lines? If cooking is your passion, how do you get ready to prepare a particular dish? Do you follow standard procedures, or do you personalize the process in some way?

3. All college students have to register for courses each term. What is the registration process like at your college? Do you find any part of the process unnecessarily frustrating or annoying? In a letter to your campus newspaper or an appropriate administrator, evaluate your school's current registration procedure and offer suggestions for making the process more efficient and pleasurable.

4. Writing to a person who is a computer novice, explain how to do a Web search. Be sure to define key terms and to illustrate the steps in your process with screen shots of search directories and search results.

5. Based on an idea similar to the one contained in the cartoon below, write a humorous process analysis essay with the thesis "Nothing is ever as simple as it looks."

"And that's how you make a peanut butter sandwich."

Tom Cheney/The New Yorker Collection/The Cartoon Bank

6. **Writing with Sources.** Do some research and then write an informational or evaluative process analysis on one of the following topics:
   a. how your heart functions
   b. how a U.S. president is elected
   c. how ice cream is made
   d. how a volcano erupts
   e. how the human circulatory system works
   f. how a camera works
   g. how an atomic bomb or reactor works
   h. how a refrigerator works
   i. how a recession occurs

   For models of and advice on integrating sources in your essay, see Chapters 14 and 15.

7. **Writing with Sources.** Although each of us hopes never to be in a natural disaster such as an earthquake or a major flood, many of us have been or could be, and it is important that people know what to do. Do some research on the topic and then write an essay in which you explain the steps that a person should follow to protect life and property during and in the aftermath of a particular natural disaster. For models of and advice on integrating sources in your essay, see Chapters 14 and 15.

8. **Writing with Sources.** If you are scientifically minded or simply want to know more about evolution, research some subprocesses that contribute to the evolutionary process, using books, journals, articles, videos, and online resources. Some of the subprocesses that you may want to pursue include adaptation, selection, divergence, genetic drift, natural selection, mutation, and bipedalism. Consider an educated, general-interest reader to be your audience, so be sure to define technical terms. For models of and advice on integrating sources in your essay, see Chapters 14 and 15.

9. **Writing with Sources.** The opening illustration for this chapter on page 222 is an informational process analysis about how baked goods are recycled into plastics. Do some research in your library or online and write a set of detailed directions for carrying out that process. You will need to explain how to get the ingredients, how much of each ingredient is needed, and the types of required equipment and machinery, as well as explicit directions for carrying out the process. As with any other good set of directions, you need not only to say what to do but also what not to do. Mention where the process can go wrong at every point and what the components and ingredients should look like at each step. For models of and advice on integrating sources in your essay, see Chapters 14 and 15.

10. **Writing in the Workplace.** You have just been hired to be the person in charge of small gift giving for a local nonprofit organization. Among your various responsibilities is the writing of letters of acknowledgment for gifts to the organization. Prepare several letters thanking donors and explaining how their contributions will be used. One should be a general letter suitable for most donors. The second letter should be one in which the donor makes the gift in memory of someone and wants that person's family to be notified of the gift. You will need to make up a name for your organization, a fictitious name for the donor, and one for the person in whose memory the gift is being made. Before starting to draft your letter, think about what needs to be said in each situation. Also be sure to carefully consider the tone of your letter in each case.

d-l-b/Getty Images

CHAPTER 8

Comparison and Contrast

WHAT ARE COMPARISON AND CONTRAST?

A COMPARISON PRESENTS TWO OR MORE SUBJECTS (PEOPLE, IDEAS, OR objects), considers them together, and shows in what ways they are alike; a contrast shows how they differ. These two perspectives, apparently in contradiction to each other, actually work so often in conjunction that they are commonly considered a single strategy, called *comparison and contrast* or simply *comparison* for short.

Comparison and contrast are so much a part of daily life that we are often not aware of using them. Whenever you make a choice—what to wear, where to eat, what college to attend, what career to pursue—you implicitly use comparison and contrast to evaluate your options and arrive at your decision.

The graphic on the opposite page uses visual comparison and contrast to clearly demonstrate the rapidly advancing technology of telephones. Points of comparison can be found in the size of the phones, the relative mobility of the phones, and the activities that can be accomplished (though this one requires some knowledge on the part of the viewer). We can see that technology has become increasingly mobile and streamlined. In what ways has telephone technology remained the same? In what other ways is it different than it used to be? Are there any other details you think the artist should have captured?

COMPARISON AND CONTRAST IN WRITTEN TEXTS

The strategy of comparison and contrast is most commonly used in writing when the subjects under discussion belong to the same class or general category: four makes of car, for example, or two candidates for Senate. (See Chapter 9, "Division and Classification," for a more complete discussion of classes.) Such subjects are said to be *comparable*, or to have a strong basis for comparison.

281

Point-by-Point and Block Comparison

There are two basic ways to organize comparison and contrast essays. In the first, *point-by-point comparison*, the author starts by comparing both subjects in terms of a particular point, moves on to a second point and compares both subjects, moves on to a third point, and so on. The other way to organize a comparison is called *block comparison.* In this pattern, the information about one subject is gathered into a block, which is followed by a block of comparable information about the second subject.

Each pattern of comparison has advantages and disadvantages. Point-by-point comparison allows the reader to grasp fairly easily the specific points of comparison the author is making; it may be harder, though, to pull together the details and convey a distinct impression of what each subject is like. The block comparison guarantees that each subject will receive a more unified discussion; however, the points of comparison between them may be less clear.

The first of the following two annotated passages illustrates a point-by-point comparison. This selection, a comparison of President Franklin Roosevelt and his vice-presidential running mate Harry Truman of Missouri, is from historian David McCullough's Pulitzer Prize–winning biography *Truman* (1992):

Point-by-point comparison identifies central similarities	Both were men of exceptional determination, with great reserves of personal courage and cheerfulness. They were alike, too, in their enjoyment of people. (The human race, Truman once told a reporter, was an "excellent outfit.") Each had an active sense of humor and was inclined to be dubious of those who did not. But Roosevelt, who loved stories, loved also to laugh at his own, while Truman was more
Point-by-point contrast introduces several differences	of a listener and laughed best when somebody else told "a good one." Roosevelt enjoyed flattery, Truman was made uneasy by it. Roosevelt loved the subtleties of human relations. He was a master of the circuitous solution to problems, of the pleasing if ambiguous answer to difficult questions. He was sensitive to nuances in a way Harry Truman never was and never would be. Truman, with his rural Missouri background, and partly, too, because of the limits of his
Development of key difference	education, was inclined to see things in far simpler terms, as right or wrong, wise or foolish. He dealt little in abstractions. His answers to questions, even complicated questions, were nearly always direct and assured, plainly said, and followed often by a conclusive "And that's all there is to it," an old Missouri expression, when in truth there may have been a great deal more "to it."

Point-by-point comparison and contrast of each man's life struggles and experiences

Each of them had been tested by his own painful struggle, Roosevelt with crippling polio, Truman with debt, failure, obscurity, and the heavy stigma of the Pendergasts. Roosevelt liked to quote the admonition of his old headmaster at Groton, Dr. Endicott Peabody: "Things in life will not always run smoothly. Sometimes we will be rising toward the heights—then all will seem to reverse itself and start downward. The great fact to remember is that the trend of civilization is forever upward. . . ." Assuredly Truman would have subscribed to the same vision. They were two optimists at heart, each in his way faithful to the old creed of human progress. But there had been nothing in Roosevelt's experience like the night young Harry held the lantern as his mother underwent surgery, nothing like the Argonne, or Truman's desperate fight for political survival in 1940.

In the following example from *Harper's* magazine, Otto Friedrich uses a block format to contrast a newspaper story with a newsmagazine story:

Subjects of comparison: Newspaper story and magazine story belong to the same class

There is an essential difference between a news story, as understood by a newspaperman or a wire-service writer, and a newsmagazine story. The chief purpose of the conventional news story is to tell what happened. It starts with the most important information and continues into increasingly inconsequential details, not only because the reader may not read beyond the first paragraph, but because an editor working on galley proofs a few minutes before press time likes to be able to cut freely from the end of the story.

Block comparison: Each paragraph deals with one type of story

A newsmagazine is very different. It is written to be read consecutively from beginning to end, and each of its stories is designed, following the critical theories of Edgar Allan Poe, to create one emotional effect. The news, what happened that week, may be told in the beginning, the middle, or the end; for the purpose is not to throw information at the reader but to seduce him into reading the whole story, and into accepting the dramatic (and often political) point being made.

In this selection, Friedrich has two purposes: to offer information that explains the differences between a newspaper story and a newsmagazine story and to persuade readers that magazine stories tend to be more biased than newspaper stories.

▶ Analogy: A Special Form of Comparison and Contrast

When the subject under discussion is unfamiliar, complex, or abstract, the resourceful writer may use a special form of comparison called *analogy* to help readers understand the difficult subject. Whereas most comparisons analyze items within the same class, analogies compare two largely dissimilar subjects to look for illuminating similarities. In addition, while the typical comparison seeks to illuminate specific features of both subjects, the primary purpose of analogy is to clarify one subject that is complex or unfamiliar by pointing out its similarities to a more familiar or concrete subject.

If, for example, your purpose were to explain the craft of fiction writing, you might note its similarities to the craft of carpentry. In this case, you would be drawing an analogy because the two subjects clearly belong to different classes. You would be using the concrete work of the carpenter to help readers understand the more abstract work of the novelist. You can use analogy in one or two paragraphs to clarify a particular aspect of the larger topic, or you can use it as the organizational strategy for an entire essay.

In the following example from *The Mysterious Sky* (1960), observe how Lester Del Rey explains the functions of Earth's atmosphere (a subject that people have difficulty with because they can't "see" it) by making an analogy to an ordinary window:

> The atmosphere of Earth acts like any window in serving two very important functions. It lets light in and it permits us to look out. It also serves as a shield to keep out dangerous or uncomfortable things. A normal glazed window lets us keep our houses warm by keeping out cold air, and it prevents rain, dirt, and unwelcome insects and animals from coming in. As we have already seen, Earth's atmospheric window also helps to keep our planet at a comfortable temperature by holding back radiated heat and protecting us from dangerous levels of ultraviolet light.

You'll notice that Del Rey's analogy establishes no direct relationship between the subjects under comparison. The analogy is effective precisely because it enables the reader to visualize the atmosphere, which is unobservable, by comparing it to something quite different—a window—that is familiar and concrete.

USING COMPARISON AND CONTRAST AS A WRITING STRATEGY

To compare one thing or idea with another, to discover the similarities and differences between them, is one of the most basic human strategies for learning, evaluating, and making decisions. Because it serves so many fundamental purposes, comparison and contrast is a particularly useful strategy for the writer. It may be the primary mode for essay writers who seek to educate or persuade the reader; to evaluate things, people, or events; and to differentiate between apparently similar subjects or to reconcile the differences between dissimilar ones.

Comparison and contrast may be combined readily with other writing strategies and often serve to sharpen, clarify, and add interest to essays written in a different primary mode. For example, an essay of argumentation gains credibility when the writer contrasts desirable and undesirable reasons or examples. In the Declaration of Independence (pages 518–21), Thomas Jefferson effectively contrasts the actual behavior of the English king with the ideals of a democratic society. In "The Downside of Diversity" (pages 465–71), Michael Jonas examines the results of a recent study finding that diverse communities have less civic engagement than homogeneous communities. Likewise, Richard Lederer, in "The Case for Short Words" (pages 558–61), uses comparison and contrast to showcase the virtues of one-syllable words when measured against their multisyllabic counterparts.

Many descriptive essays rely heavily on comparison and contrast; one of the most effective ways to describe any person, place, or thing is to show how it is like another model of the same class and how it differs. Robert Ramírez ("The Barrio," pages 141–44) describes his Hispanic neighborhood as contrasted with "the harshness and the coldness of the Anglo world." Definition is also clarified and enriched by the use of comparison and contrast. Virtually all the essays in Chapter 10 employ comparison and contrast to enhance and refine the definitions being developed.

USING COMPARISON AND CONTRAST ACROSS THE DISCIPLINES

When writing essays in the academic disciplines, you will have many opportunities to use the strategy of comparison and contrast to both organize and strengthen the presentation of your ideas. To determine whether comparison and contrast is the right strategy for you in a particular paper, review the guidelines described in Chapter 2 (Determining a Strategy for Developing Your Essay, pages 32–33). Consider the following examples:

Music

1. **MAIN IDEA:** The music of the Romantic period sharply contrasts with the music of the earlier Classical period.
2. **QUESTION:** What are the key differences between the music of the Romantic and the Classical periods?
3. **STRATEGY:** Comparison and contrast. The direction words *contrasts* and *differences* call for a discussion distinguishing characteristics of the two periods in music history.
4. **SUPPORTING STRATEGIES:** Definition and illustration. It might be helpful to define the key terms *Romanticism* and *Classicism* and to

illustrate each of the differences with examples from representative Romantic composers (Brahms, Chopin, Schubert, and Tchaikovsky) and Classical composers (Beethoven, Haydn, and Mozart).

Political Science

1. **MAIN IDEA:** Though very different people, Winston Churchill and Franklin D. Roosevelt shared many larger-than-life leadership qualities during World War II, a period of doubt and crisis.
2. **QUESTION:** What are the similarities between Winston Churchill and Franklin D. Roosevelt as world leaders?
3. **STRATEGY:** Comparison and contrast. The direction words *shared* and *similarities* require a discussion of the leadership traits displayed by both men.
4. **SUPPORTING STRATEGY:** Definition. It might prove helpful to define *leader* and/or *leadership* to establish a context for this comparison.

Physics

1. **MAIN IDEA:** Compare and contrast the three classes of levers—simple machines used to amplify force.
2. **QUESTION:** What are the similarities and differences among the three classes of levers?
3. **STRATEGY:** Comparison and contrast. The direction words *compare, contrast, similarities*, and *differences* say it all.
4. **SUPPORTING STRATEGY:** Illustration. Readers will certainly appreciate familiar examples—pliers, nutcrackers, and tongs—of the three classes of levers, examples that both clarify and emphasize the similarities and differences.

SAMPLE STUDENT ESSAY USING COMPARISON AND CONTRAST AS A WRITING STRATEGY

A studio art major from Pittsburgh, Pennsylvania, Barbara Bowman has a special interest in photography. In her writing courses, Bowman has discovered many similarities between the writing process and the process that an artist follows. Her essay "Guns and Cameras," however, explores similarities of another kind: those between hunting with a gun and hunting with a camera.

Guns and Cameras
Barbara Bowman

With a growing number of animals heading toward extinction and with the idea of protecting such animals on game reserves increasing in popularity, photographic safaris are replacing hunting safaris. This may seem odd because of the obvious differences between guns and cameras. Shooting is aggressive, photography is passive; shooting eliminates, photography preserves. However, some hunters are willing to trade their guns for cameras because of similarities in the way the equipment is used, as well as in the relationship among equipment, user, and "prey."

The hunter has a deep interest in the apparatus he uses to kill his prey. He carries various types of guns, different kinds of ammunition, and special sights and telescopes to increase his chances of success. He knows the mechanics of his guns and understands how and why they work. This fascination with the hardware of his sport is practical—it helps him achieve his goal—but it frequently becomes an end, almost a hobby in itself.

Not until the very end of the long process of stalking an animal does a game hunter use his gun. First he enters into the animal's world. He studies his prey, its habitat, its daily habits, its watering holes and feeding areas, its migration patterns, its enemies and allies, its diet and food chain. Eventually the hunter himself becomes animal-like, instinctively sensing the habits and moves of his prey. Of course, this instinct gives the hunter a better chance of killing the animal; he knows where and when he will get the best shot. But it gives him more than that. Hunting is not just pulling the trigger and killing the prey. Much of it is a multifaceted and ritualistic identification with nature.

After the kill, the hunter can do a number of things with his trophy. He can sell the meat or eat it himself. He can hang the animal's head on the wall or lay its hide on the floor or even sell these objects. But any of these uses is a luxury, and its cost is high. An animal has been destroyed; a life has been eliminated.

Like the hunter, the photographer has a great interest in the tools he uses. He carries various types of cameras, lenses, and film to help him get the picture he wants. He

Point A: equipment — understands the way cameras work, the uses of telephoto and micro lenses, and often the technical procedures of printing and developing. Of course, the time and interest a photographer invests in these mechanical aspects of his art allow him to capture and produce the image he wants. But as with the hunter, these mechanics can and often do become fascinating in themselves.

Point B: stalking — The wildlife photographer also needs to stalk his "prey" with knowledge and skill in order to get an accurate "shot." Like the hunter, he has to understand the animal's patterns, characteristics, and habitat; he must become animal-like in order to succeed. And like the hunter's, his pursuit is much more prolonged and complicated than the shot itself. The stalking processes are almost identical and give many of the same satisfactions. 6

Point C: the result — The successful photographer also has something tangible to show for his efforts. A still picture of an animal can be displayed in a home, a gallery, a shop; it can be printed in a publication, as a postcard, or as a poster. In fact, a single photograph can be used in all these ways at once; it can be reproduced countless times. And despite all these ways of using his "trophies," the photographer continues to preserve his prey. 7

Conclusion: The two activities are similar and give the same satisfaction, so why kill? — Photography is obviously the less violent and to many the more acceptable method for obtaining a trophy of a wild animal. People no longer need to hunt in order to feed or clothe themselves, and hunting for "sport" seems to be barbaric. Luckily, the excitement of pursuing an animal, learning its habits and patterns, outsmarting it on its own level, and finally "getting" it can all be done with a camera. So why use guns? 8

Analyzing Barbara Bowman's Comparison and Contrast Essay: Questions for Discussion

1. What is Bowman's thesis in this essay?
2. What are her main points of comparison between hunting with a gun and hunting with a camera?
3. How has Bowman organized her comparison? Why do you suppose she decided on this option? Explain.
4. How else could she have organized her essay? Would this alternative organization have been as effective as the one she used? Explain.
5. How does Bowman conclude her essay? In what ways is her conclusion a reflection of her thesis?

SUGGESTIONS FOR USING COMPARISON AND CONTRAST AS A WRITING STRATEGY

As you plan, write, and revise your comparison and contrast essay, be mindful of the writing process guidelines described in Chapter 2 (see pages 23–40). Also, pay particular attention to the basic requirements and essential ingredients for this writing strategy.

▶ Planning Your Comparison and Contrast Essay

Planning is an essential part of writing a good comparison and contrast essay. You can save yourself a great deal of aggravation by taking the time to think about the key components of your essay before you actually begin to write.

Many college assignments ask you to use the strategy of comparison and contrast. As you read an assignment, look for one or more of the words that suggest the use of this strategy. When you are asked to identify the *similarities* and *differences* between two items, you should use comparison and contrast. Other assignments might ask you to determine which of two options is *better* or to select the *best* solution to a particular problem. Again, the strategy of comparison and contrast will help you make this evaluation and arrive at a sound, logical conclusion.

As you start planning and writing a comparison and contrast essay, keep in mind the basic requirements of this writing strategy.

COMPARE SUBJECTS FROM THE SAME CLASS. Remember that the subjects of your comparison should be in the same class or general category so that you can establish a clear basis for comparison. (There are any number of possible classes, such as particular types of persons, places, and things, as well as occupations, activities, philosophies, points in history, and even concepts and ideas.) If your subject is difficult, complex, or unobservable, you may find that analogy, a special form of comparison, is the most effective strategy to explain that subject. Remember, also, that if the similarities and differences between the subjects are too obvious, your reader is certain to lose interest quickly.

DETERMINE YOUR PURPOSE AND FOCUS ON IT. Suppose you choose to compare and contrast solar energy with wind energy. It is clear that both are members of the same class—energy—so there is a basis for comparing them; there also seem to be enough interesting differences to make a comparison and contrast possible. But before going any further, you must ask yourself why you want to compare and contrast these particular subjects.

What audience do you seek to address? Do you want to inform, to emphasize, to explain, to evaluate, to persuade? Do you have more than one purpose? Whatever your purpose, it will influence the content and organization of your comparison.

In comparing and contrasting solar and wind energy, you will certainly provide factual information, and you will probably also want to evaluate the two energy sources to determine whether either is a practical means of producing energy. You may also want to persuade your readers that one technology is superior to the other.

FORMULATE A THESIS STATEMENT. Once you have your purpose clearly in mind, formulate a preliminary thesis statement. At this early stage in the writing process, the thesis statement is not cast in stone; you may well want to modify it later on, as a result of research and further consideration of your subject. A preliminary thesis statement has two functions: First, it fixes your direction so that you will be less tempted to stray into byways while doing research and writing drafts; second, establishing the central point of the essay makes it easier for you to gather supporting material and to organize your essay.

Suppose, for example, that you live in the Champlain Valley of Vermont, one of the cloudiest areas of the country, where the wind whistles along the corridor between the Green Mountains and the Adirondacks. If you were exploring possible alternative energy sources for the area, your purpose might be to persuade readers of a local environmental journal that wind is preferable to sun as a source of energy for this region. The thesis statement for this essay will certainly differ from that of a writer for a national newsmagazine whose goal is to offer general information about alternative energy sources to a broad readership.

CHOOSE THE POINTS OF COMPARISON. *Points of comparison* are the qualities and features of your subjects on which you base your comparison. For some comparisons, you will find the information you need in your own head; for others, you will have to search for information in the library or on the Internet.

At this stage, if you know only a little about the subjects of your comparison, you may have only a few hazy ideas for points of comparison. Perhaps wind energy means no more to you than an image of giant windmills lined up on a California ridge, and solar energy brings to mind only the reflective, glassy roof on a Colorado ski lodge. Even so, it is possible to list points of comparison that will be relevant to your subjects and your purpose. Here, for example, are important points of comparison in considering energy sources:

Cost

Efficiency

Convenience

Environmental impact

A tentative list of points will help you by suggesting the kind of information you need to gather for your comparison and contrast. You should always remain alert, however, for other factors you may not have thought of. For example, as you conduct research, you may find that maintenance requirements are another important factor in considering energy systems, and thus you might add that point to your list.

▶ Organizing and Writing Your Comparison and Contrast Essay

CHOOSE AN ORGANIZATIONAL PATTERN THAT FITS YOUR MATERIAL. Once you have gathered the necessary information, you should decide which organizational pattern, block or point-by-point, will best serve your purpose. In deciding which pattern to use, you may find it helpful to jot down a scratch outline before beginning your draft.

Block organization works best when the two objects of comparison are relatively straightforward and when the points of comparison are rather general, are few in number, and can be stated succinctly. As a scratch outline illustrates, block organization makes for a unified discussion of each object, which can help your readers understand the information you have for them:

Block Organization

BLOCK ONE   **Solar Energy**
  Point 1. Cost
  Point 2. Efficiency
  Point 3. Convenience
  Point 4. Maintenance requirements
  Point 5. Environmental impact

BLOCK TWO   **Wind Energy**
  Point 1. Cost
  Point 2. Efficiency
  Point 3. Convenience
  Point 4. Maintenance requirements
  Point 5. Environmental impact

If your essay will be more than two or three pages long, however, block organization may be a poor choice: By the time your readers come to your discussion of the costs of wind energy, they may well have forgotten what you had to say about solar energy costs several pages earlier. In this case, you would do better to use point-by-point organization:

Point-by-Point Organization

POINT ONE   **Cost**
   Subject 1. Solar energy
   Subject 2. Wind energy

POINT TWO   **Efficiency**
   Subject 1. Solar energy
   Subject 2. Wind energy

POINT THREE   **Convenience**
   Subject 1. Solar energy
   Subject 2. Wind energy

POINT FOUR   **Maintenance Requirements**
   Subject 1. Solar energy
   Subject 2. Wind energy

POINT FIVE   **Environmental Impact**
   Subject 1. Solar energy
   Subject 2. Wind energy

USE PARALLEL CONSTRUCTIONS FOR EMPHASIS. Use parallel grammatical structures to emphasize the similarities and differences between the items being compared. Parallelism is the repetition of word order or grammatical form either within a single sentence or in several sentences that develop the same central idea. As a rhetorical device, parallel structure can aid coherence and add emphasis. Franklin Roosevelt's famous Depression-era statement "I see one-third of a nation *ill-housed, ill-clad,* and *ill-nourished*" illustrates effective parallelism. Look for opportunities to use parallel constructions with (1) paired items or items in a series, (2) correlative conjunctions, and (3) the words *as* or *than.*

DRAW A CONCLUSION FROM YOUR COMPARISON. Only after you have gathered your information and made your comparisons will you be ready to decide on a conclusion. When drawing your essay to its conclusion, remember your purpose in writing, the claim made in your thesis statement, and your audience and emphasis.

Perhaps, having presented information about both technologies, your comparison shows that solar and wind energy are both feasible, with solar energy having a slight edge on most points. If your purpose has been evaluation for a general audience, you might conclude, "Both solar and wind energy are practical alternatives to conventional energy sources." If you asserted in your thesis statement that one of the technologies is superior to the other, your comparison will support a more persuasive conclusion. For the general audience, you might say, "While both solar and wind energy are practical technologies, solar energy now seems the better investment." However, for a readership made up of residents of the cloudy Champlain Valley, you might conclude, "While both solar and wind energy are practical technologies, wind energy makes more economic sense for investors in northwest Vermont."

▶ Revising and Editing Your Comparison and Contrast Essay

Careful re-reading, or even reading aloud to yourself, will help you to catch missing or unequal points of comparison. You may also want to ask a friend or fellow students to read through your draft, using the guidelines presented on page 36. A fresh pair of eyes is always helpful, and they may give you a head start in catching grammatical inconsistencies (see Chapter 16) as well.

**Questions for Revising and Editing:
Comparison and Contrast**

1. Are the subjects of my comparison comparable; that is, do they belong to the same class of items (for example, two cars, two advertisements, two landscape paintings) so that there is a clear basis for comparison?
2. Are there any complex or abstract concepts that might be clarified by using an analogy?
3. Is the purpose of my comparison clearly stated?
4. Have I presented a clear thesis statement?
5. Have I chosen my points of comparison well? Have I avoided obvious points of comparison, concentrating instead on similarities between obviously different items or differences between essentially similar items?
6. Have I developed my points of comparison in sufficient detail so that my readers can appreciate my thinking?
7. Have I chosen the best pattern — block or point-by-point — to organize my information?
8. Have I drawn a conclusion that is in line with my thesis and purpose?
9. Have I used parallel constructions correctly in my sentences?
10. Have I avoided other errors in grammar, punctuation, and mechanics? Is my sentence style as clear, smooth, and persuasive as possible?

Neat People vs. Sloppy People

SUZANNE BRITT

Born in Winston-Salem, North Carolina, Suzanne Britt now makes her home in Raleigh. She graduated from Salem College and Washington University, where she received an M.A. in English. A poet and essayist, Britt has been a columnist for the Raleigh *News and Observer* and *Stars and Stripes*, European edition. Her work appears regularly in *North Carolina Gardens and Homes*, the *New York Times*, *Newsweek*, and the *Boston Globe*. Her essays have been collected in two books, *Skinny People Are Dull and Crunchy Like Carrots* (1982) and *Show and Tell* (1983). She is the author of *A Writer's Rhetoric* (1988), a college textbook, and *Images: A Centennial Journey* (1991), a history of Meredith College, the small independent women's college in Raleigh where Britt teaches English and continues to write.

The following essay was taken from *Show and Tell*, a book Britt humorously describes as a report on her journey into "the awful cave of self: You shout your name and voices come back in exultant response, telling you their names." Here, mingling humor with a touch of seriousness, Britt examines the differences between neat and sloppy people and gives us some insights about several important personality traits.

Preparing to Read

Many people in our society are fond of comparing people, places, and things. Often, these comparisons are premature and even damaging. Consider the ways people judge others based on clothes, appearance, or hearsay. Write about a time in your life when you made such a comparison about someone or something. Did your initial judgment hold up? If not, why did it change?

I've finally figured out the difference between neat people and sloppy people. The distinction is, as always, moral. Neat people are lazier and meaner than sloppy people.

Sloppy people, you see, are not really sloppy. Their sloppiness is merely the unfortunate consequence of their extreme moral rectitude. Sloppy people carry in their mind's eye a heavenly vision, a precise plan, that is so stupendous, so perfect, it can't be achieved in this world or the next.

Sloppy people live in Never-Never Land. Someday is their métier.[1] Someday they are planning to alphabetize all their books and set up home

---

[1] Activity or work for which a person is especially suited. — Eds.

catalogs. Someday they will go through their wardrobes and mark certain items for tentative mending and certain items for passing on to relatives of similar shape and size. Someday sloppy people will make family scrapbooks into which they will put newspaper clippings, postcards, locks of hair, and the dried corsage from their senior prom. Someday they will file everything on the surface of their desks, including the cash receipts from coffee purchases at the snack shop. Someday they will sit down and read all the back issues of *The New Yorker*.

> I've finally figured out the difference between neat people and sloppy people. The distinction is, as always, moral.

For all these noble reasons and more, sloppy people never get neat. They aim too high and wide. They save everything, planning someday to file, order, and straighten out the world. But while these ambitious plans take clearer and clearer shape in their heads, the books spill from the shelves onto the floor, the clothes pile up in the hamper and closet, the family mementos accumulate in every drawer, the surface of the desk is buried under mounds of paper and the unread magazines threaten to reach the ceiling.

Sloppy people can't bear to part with anything. They give loving attention to every detail. When sloppy people say they're going to tackle the surface of the desk, they really mean it. Not a paper will go unturned; not a rubber band will go unboxed. Four hours or two weeks into the excavation, the desk looks exactly the same, primarily because the sloppy person is meticulously creating new piles of papers with new headings and scrupulously stopping to read all of the old book catalogs before he throws them away. A neat person would just bulldoze the desk.

Neat people are bums and clods at heart. They have cavalier attitudes toward possessions, including family heirlooms. Everything is just another dust-catcher to them. If anything collects dust, it's got to go and that's that. Neat people will toy with the idea of throwing the children out of the house just to cut down on the clutter.

Neat people don't care about process. They like results. What they want to do is get the whole thing over with so they can sit down and watch the rasslin' on TV. Neat people operate on two unvarying principles: Never handle any item twice, and throw everything away.

The only thing messy in a neat person's house is the trash can. The minute something comes to a neat person's hand, he will look at it, try to decide if it has immediate use and, finding none, throw it in the trash.

Neat people are especially vicious with mail. They never go through their mail unless they are standing directly over a trash can. If the trash can is beside the mailbox, even better. All ads, catalogs, pleas for charitable contributions, church bulletins, and money-saving coupons go straight into the trash can without being opened. All letters from home, postcards from Europe, bills, and paychecks are opened, immediately responded to, then dropped in the trash can. Neat people keep their receipts only for tax purposes. That's it. No sentimental salvaging of birthday cards or the last letter a dying relative ever wrote. Into the trash it goes.

Neat people place neatness above everything, even economics. They are incredibly wasteful. Neat people throw away several toys every time they walk through the den. I knew a neat person once who threw away a perfectly good dish drainer because it had mold on it. The drainer was too much trouble to wash. And neat people sell their furniture when they move. They will sell a La-Z-Boy recliner while you are reclining in it.

Neat people are no good to borrow from. Neat people buy everything in expensive little single portions. They get their flour and sugar in two-pound bags. They wouldn't consider clipping a coupon, saving a leftover, reusing plastic nondairy whipped cream containers, or rinsing off tin foil and draping it over the unmoldy dish drainer. You can never borrow a neat person's newspaper to see what's playing at the movies. Neat people have the paper all wadded up and in the trash by 7:05 A.M.

Neat people cut a clean swath through the organic as well as the inorganic world. People, animals, and things are all one to them. They are so insensitive. After they've finished with the pantry, the medicine cabinet, and the attic, they will throw out the red geranium (too many leaves), sell the dog (too many fleas), and send the children off to boarding school (too many scuff marks on the hardwood floors).

Thinking Critically about the Text

Suzanne Britt reduces people to two types: sloppy and neat. What does she see as the defining characteristics of each type? Do you consider yourself a sloppy or a neat person? Perhaps you are neither. If this is the case, make up your own category and explain why Britt's categories are not broad enough.

Questions on Subject

1. Why do you suppose Britt characterizes the distinction between sloppy and neat people as a "moral" one (paragraph 1)? What is she really poking fun at with this reference? (Glossary: *Irony*)

2. In your own words, what is the "heavenly vision," the "precise plan," Britt refers to in paragraph 2? How does Britt use this idea to explain why sloppy people can never be neat?

3. Exaggeration, as Britt uses it, is only effective if it is based on some shared idea of the truth. What commonly understood ideas about sloppy and neat people does Britt rely on? Do you agree with her? Why or why not?

Questions on Strategy

1. Note Britt's use of transitions as she moves from trait to trait. (Glossary: *Transitions*) How well does she use transitions to achieve unity in her essay? Explain.

2. One of the ways Britt achieves a sense of the ridiculous in her essay is to switch the commonly accepted attributes of sloppy and neat people. Cite examples of this technique and discuss the ways in which it adds to her essay. What does it reveal to the reader about her purpose in writing the essay? (Glossary: *Purpose*)

3. Britt uses block comparison to point out the differences between sloppy and neat people. Make a side-by-side list of the traits of sloppy and neat people. After reviewing your list, determine any ways in which sloppy and neat people may be similar. Why do you suppose Britt does not include any of the ways in which they are the same?

4. Why do you think Britt has chosen to use a block comparison? What would have been gained or lost had she used a point-by-point system of contrast?

5. Throughout the essay, Britt uses numerous examples to show the differences between sloppy and neat people. (Glossary: *Illustration*) Cite five examples that Britt uses to exemplify these points. How effective do you find Britt's use of examples? What do they add to her comparison and contrast essay?

Questions on Diction and Vocabulary

1. Cite examples of Britt's diction that indicate her change of **tone** when she is talking about either sloppy or neat people. (Glossary: *Diction; Tone*)

2. How would you characterize Britt's vocabulary in the essay — easy or difficult? What does her choice of vocabulary say about her intended audience? In which places does Britt use precise word choice to particularly good effect?

3. Refer to a dictionary to determine the meanings of the following words as Britt uses them in this selection: *rectitude* (paragraph 2), *tentative* (3), *meticulously* (5), *heirlooms* (6), *salvaging* (9), *swath* (12).

Comparison and Contrast in Action

Using the sample outlines on pages 291–92 as models, prepare both block and point-by-point outlines for one of the following topics:

1. dogs and cats as pets
2. print media and electronic media
3. an economy car and a luxury car
4. your local newspaper and the *New York Times*
5. a high school teacher and a college teacher

Explain any advantages of one organizational plan over the other.

Writing Suggestions

1. Write an essay in which you describe yourself as either sloppy or neat. In what ways does your behavior compare or contrast with the traits Britt offers? You may follow Britt's definition of sloppy and neat, or you may come up with your own.

2. Take some time to reflect on a relationship in your life — perhaps one with a friend, a family member, or a teacher. Write an essay in which you describe what it is about you and that other person that makes the relationship work. You may find it helpful to think of a relationship that doesn't work to better understand why the relationship you're writing about does work. What discoveries about yourself did you make while working on this essay? Explain.

Buy Experiences, Not Things

JAMES HAMBLIN

James Hamblin, a health writer and senior editor at *The Atlantic* magazine, was born in 1983, though he is often compared with fictional doctor Doogie Houser because of his youthful appearance. Trained as a physician at UCLA, he left his radiology residency during his third year because he "felt very removed from patient care" and pursued another interest: improvisational and standup comedy. He has since combined both passions in his writing, on Twitter, and in the video series "If Our Bodies Could Talk," produced by *The Atlantic* and subtitled "Off-beat Perspectives on Health Topics from Dr. James Hamblin."

The Atlantic

His work has also appeared in print in the *New York Times*, *Politico* magazine, and *New York* magazine and online at *Mental_Floss* and the *Awl*. He received a Yale University Poynter Fellowship in journalism; he was a finalist in the 2013 Webby awards for Best Web Personality, and BuzzFeed named him "the most delightful MD ever."

In an interview with *Columbia Journalism Review*'s Anna Clark, Hamblin says, "I want to tell good stories and to be the person that shows that these things are complex. Not to oversimplify, make false promises, or scare people." Consider this goal as you read Hamblin's discussion of experiential and material purchases.

Preparing to Read

What makes you happy and why? Have you given much thought to this question before now? Do you think there's more than one kind of happiness?

Forty-seven percent of the time, the average mind is wandering. It wanders about a third of the time while a person is reading, talking with other people, or taking care of children. It wanders 10 percent of the time, even, during sex. And that wandering, according to psychologist Matthew Killingsworth, is not good for well-being. A mind belongs in one place. During his training at Harvard, Killingsworth compiled those numbers and built a scientific case for every cliché about *living in the moment*. In a 2010 *Science* paper co-authored with psychology professor Daniel Gilbert, the two wrote that "a wandering mind is an unhappy mind."

For Killingsworth, happiness is in the content of moment-to-moment experiences. Nothing material is intrinsically valuable, except in whatever promise of happiness it carries. Satisfaction in owning a thing does not have to come during the moment it's acquired, of course. It can come as anticipation or nostalgic longing. Overall, though, the achievement of the human brain to contemplate events past and future at great, tedious length has, these psychologists believe, come at the expense of happiness. Minds tend to wander to dark, not whimsical, places. Unless that mind has something exciting to anticipate or sweet to remember.

> Minds tend to wander to dark, not whimsical, places. Unless that mind has something exciting to anticipate or sweet to remember.

Over the past decade, an abundance of psychology research has shown that experiences bring people more happiness than do possessions. The idea that experiential purchases are more satisfying than material purchases has long been the domain of Cornell psychology professor Thomas Gilovich. Since 2003, he has been trying to figure out exactly how and why experiential purchases are so much better than material purchases. In the journal *Psychological Science* last month, Gilovich and Killingsworth, along with Cornell doctoral candidate Amit Kumar, expanded on the current understanding that spending money on experiences "provide[s] more enduring happiness." They looked specifically at anticipation as a driver of that happiness; whether the benefit of spending money on an experience accrues before the purchase has been made, in addition to after. And, yes, it does.

Essentially, when you can't live in a moment, they say, it's best to live in anticipation of an experience. Experiential purchases like trips, concerts, movies, et cetera, tend to trump material purchases because the utility of buying anything really starts accruing before you buy it.

Mean Self-Report Ratings

Data from: Kumar et al., *Psychological Science/The Atlantic*

Waiting for an experience apparently elicits more happiness and excitement than waiting for a material good (and more "pleasantness" too—an eerie metric). By contrast, waiting for a possession is more likely fraught with impatience than anticipation. "You can think about waiting for a delicious meal at a nice restaurant or looking forward to a vacation," Kumar told me, "and how different that feels from waiting for, say, your pre-ordered iPhone to arrive. Or when the two-day shipping on Amazon Prime doesn't seem fast enough."

Gilovich's prior work has shown that experiences tend to make people happier because they are less likely to measure the value of their experiences by comparing them to those of others. For example, Gilbert and company note in their new paper, many people are unsure if they would rather have a high salary that is lower than that of their peers, or a lower salary that is higher than that of their peers. With an experiential good like vacation, that dilemma doesn't hold. Would you rather have two weeks of vacation when your peers only get one? Or four weeks when your peers get eight? People choose four weeks with little hesitation.

Experiential purchases are also more associated with identity, connection, and social behavior. Looking back on purchases made, experiences make people happier than do possessions. It's kind of counter to the logic that if you pay for an experience, like a vacation, it will be over and gone; but if you buy a tangible thing, a couch, at least you'll have it for a long time. Actually most of us have a pretty intense capacity for tolerance, or hedonic adaptation, where we stop appreciating things to which we're constantly exposed. iPhones, clothes, couches, et cetera, just become background. They deteriorate or become obsolete. It's the fleetingness of experiential purchases that endears us to them. Either they're not around long enough to become imperfect, or they are imperfect, but our memories and stories of them get sweet with time. Even a bad experience becomes a good story.

When it rains through a beach vacation, as Kumar put it, "People will say, well, you know, we stayed in and we played board games and it was a great family bonding experience or something." Even if it was negative in the moment, it becomes positive after the fact. That's a lot harder to do with material purchases because they're right there in front of you. "When my Macbook has the colorful pinwheel show up," he said, "I can't say, well, at least my computer is malfunctioning!"

"At least my computer and I get to spend more time together because it's working so slowly," I offered.

"Yes, exactly."

"Maybe we should destroy our material possessions at their peak, so they will live on in an idealized state in our memories?"

"I don't know if I'd go that far," he said. "The possibility of making material purchases more experiential is sort of interesting."

That means making purchasing an experience, which is terrible marketing-speak, but in practical terms might mean buying something on a special occasion or on vacation or while wearing a truly unique hat. Or tying that purchase to subsequent social interaction. Buy this and you can talk about buying it, and people will talk about you because you have it.

"Turns out people don't like hearing about other people's possessions very much," Kumar said, "but they do like hearing about that time you saw Vampire Weekend."

I can't imagine ever wanting to hear about someone seeing Vampire Weekend, but I get the point. Reasonable people are just more likely to talk about their experiential purchases than their material purchases. It's a nidus for social connection. ("What did you do this weekend?" "Well! I'm so glad you asked. . . .")

The most interesting part of the new research, to Kumar, was the part that "implies that there might be notable real-world consequences to this study." It involved analysis of news stories about people waiting in long lines to make a consumer transaction. Those waiting for experiences were in better moods than those waiting for material goods. "You read these stories about people rioting, pepper-spraying, treating each other badly when they have to wait," he said. It turns out, those sorts of stories are much more likely to occur when people are waiting to acquire a possession than an experience. When people are waiting to get concert tickets or in line at a new food truck, their moods tend to be much more positive.

Even a bad experience becomes a good story.

"There are actually instances of positivity when people are waiting for experiences," Kumar said, like talking to other people in the concert line about what songs Vampire Weekend might play. So there is opportunity to connect with other people. "We know that social interaction is one of the most important determinants of human happiness, so if people are talking with each other, being nice to one another in the line, it's going to be a lot more pleasant experience than if they're being mean to each other which is what's (more) likely to happen when people are waiting for material goods."

Research has also found that people tend to be more generous to others when they've just thought about an experiential purchase as opposed to a material purchase. They're also more likely to pursue social activities. So, buying those plane tickets is good for *society*. (Of course, maximal good to society and personal happiness comes from pursuing not happiness but meaning. All of this behavioral economics-happiness research probably assumes you've already given away 99 percent of your income to things bigger than yourself, and there's just a very modest amount left to maximally utilize.)

What is it about the nature of imagining experiential purchases that's different from thinking about future material purchases? The most interesting hypothesis is that you can imagine all sorts of possibilities for what an experience is going to be. "That's what's fun," Kumar said. "It could turn out a whole host of ways." With a material possession, you kind of know what you're going to get. Instead of whetting your appetite by imagining various outcomes, Kumar put it, people sort of think, *Just give it to me now*.

It could turn out that to get the maximum utility out of an experiential purchase, it's really best to plan far in advance. Savoring future consumption for days, weeks, years only makes the experience more valuable. It definitely trumps impulse buying, where that anticipation is completely squandered. (Never impulse-buy anything ever.)

That sort of benefit would likely be a lot stronger in an optimistic person as opposed to a pessimistic person. Some people hate surprises. Some people don't anticipate experiences because they dwell on what could—no, will—go wrong. But we needn't dwell in their heads. Everyone can decide on the right mix of material and experiential consumption to maximize their well-being. The broader implications, according to Gilovich in a press statement, are that "well-being can be advanced by providing infrastructure that affords experiences, such as parks, trails, and beaches, as much as it does material consumption." Or at least the promise of that infrastructure, so we can all look forward to using it. And when our minds wander, that's where they'll go.

Thinking Critically about the Text

According to Hamblin, Daniel Gilbert's research revealed that "many people are unsure if they would rather have a high salary that is lower than that of their peers, or a lower salary that is higher than that of their peers" (paragraph 6). Which would you rather have, and why? Does your choice support Hamblin's thesis?

Questions on Subject

1. Hamblin begins his essay with a statistic: "Forty-seven percent of the time, the average mind is wandering." Why is this statistic important? What does it have to do with Hamblin's overall message?

2. What is Hamblin's thesis in this selection? Where does he present it? (Glossary: *Thesis*)

3. In paragraph 3, Hamblin writes that researchers "looked specifically at anticipation as a driver of that happiness." What do you think he means by this? How can anticipation lead to happiness?

4. Hamblin writes "waiting for a possession is more likely fraught with impatience than anticipation" (paragraph 5). What is the difference between *impatience* and *anticipation*, in your own words? (Glossary: *Connotation/Denotation*)

Questions on Strategy

1. What is Hamblin's purpose in writing this essay?
2. How has Hamblin organized his essay? Is it block comparison, point-by-point, or a combination of both? Would an alternative organization have been equally effective? (Glossary: *Organization*)
3. What does the graph add to this essay? Why do you think Hamblin included it?
4. Consider the use of dialogue in paragraphs 9–12 and 14–15. Why do you think Hamblin chose to use dialogue here? How would the essay be different if Hamblin had summarized these exchanges rather than quoting them? (Glossary: *Dialogue*)
5. Hamblin relies heavily on examples in this essay. Are all his examples relevant and representative? Explain.

Questions on Diction and Vocabulary

1. How would you characterize Hamblin's vocabulary in this essay? What does his vocabulary say about his intended audience? Cite specific words and phrases to support your answer.
2. Hamblin ends paragraph 3 with the brief sentence "And, yes, it does." How does this sentence differ from the other sentences in this paragraph, and what is the effect of this shift in tone and style?
3. Refer to a dictionary to determine the meanings of the following words as Hamblin uses them in this selection: *intrinsically* (paragraph 2), *nostalgic* (2), *whimsical* (2), *accrues* (3), *elicits* (5), *metric* (5), *fraught* (5), *dilemma* (6), *hedonic* (7), *nidus* (15), *hypothesis* (20), *squandered* (21).

Comparison and Contrast in Action

Make a list of at least ten *experiences* you look forward to having, large and small. These might range from the mundane (having your second cup of coffee this morning or watching your favorite show tonight) to the ambitious and profound (hiking the Appalachian trail, earning a Ph.D., becoming a parent). Next, make a list of at least ten *things* you look forward to having: perhaps a coffeemaker to make that coffee, a new pair of hiking boots, the next-generation smart phone, or a house. Now, rank each group in order of how much you want each entry. Finally, combine your lists, placing whatever you want most at the top and working your way to what seems least important. Do you have more experiences or more things near the top of your list? Are you surprised by the results?

Writing Suggestions

1. Have you ever made an impulse purchase? What were the circumstances, and what did you buy? Did it live up to your expectations? Write an essay exploring your motivations behind the purchase, the reward or pleasure it has given you, and whether you agree with Hamblin that one should "never impulse-buy anything ever" (paragraph 21).

2. Using the classroom activity and your response to the Preparing to Read prompt as a springboard, write an essay comparing an experience you hope to have with a material thing you hope to have. First, determine your purpose: You may want to value either the experience or the thing as better or more important, or you may want to say they are of equal importance. Next, examine both similarities and differences and decide whether block organization or point-by-point organization will be most effective. Finally, make sure to draw a conclusion from your comparison.

3. In paragraph 8, Hamblin writes: "When it rains through a beach vacation, as Kumar put it, 'People will say, well, you know, we stayed in and we played board games and it was a great family bonding experience or something.' Even if it was negative in the moment, it becomes positive after the fact." Do you have a similar story? If so, write a narrative about that experience, showing both the positive and negative aspects. If not, write about an experience you were looking forward to that turned out to be a bad experience. What happened? Why do you think you weren't able to turn that experience into a good story? Does the reason have anything to do with the relative value of experience versus things?

Two Ways to Belong in America

BHARATI MUKHERJEE

The prominent Indian American writer and university professor Bharati Mukherjee was born into a wealthy family in Calcutta (now Kolkata), India, in 1940. Shortly after India gained its independence, her family relocated to England. In the 1950s, she returned to India, where she earned her bachelor's degree at the University of Calcutta in 1959 and a master's degree from the University of Baroda in 1961. Later she pursued her long-held desire to become a writer by earning a master of fine arts degree at the University of Iowa and eventually a doctorate in English and comparative literature. After marrying an American, Clark Blaise, she moved with her husband to Canada, where they lived for fourteen years until legislation there against South Asians led them to move back to the United States.

Reagan Louie

Before joining the faculty at the University of California–Berkeley, Mukherjee taught at McGill University, Skidmore College, Queens College, and the City University of New York. Currently her work centers on writing and the theme of immigration, particularly as it concerns women, immigration policy, and cultural alienation. With her husband, she has authored *Days and Nights in Calcutta* (1977) and *The Sorrow and the Terror: The Haunting Legacy of the Air India Tragedy* (1987). In addition, she has published eight novels, including *The Tiger's Daughter* (1971), *Jasmine* (1989), *The Holder of the World* (1993), and *Miss New India* (2011); two collections of short stories, *Darkness* (1985) and *The Middleman and Other Stories* (1988), for which she won the National Book Critics Circle Award; and two works of nonfiction, *Political Culture and Leadership in India* (1991) and *Regionalism in Indian Perspective* (1992).

The following essay was first published in the *New York Times* in 1996, in response to new legislation championed by then–vice president Al Gore, which provided for expedited routes to citizenship for legal immigrants living in the United States. As you read Mukherjee's essay, notice the way she has organized the contrasting views she and her sister have toward various aspects of living as either a legal immigrant or a citizen.

Preparing to Read

The word *immigrant* has many connotations. What associations does the word have for you? If you were to move to another country, how do you think it would feel to be considered an immigrant? If you are considered an immigrant now, what has been your experience since arriving in this country?

This is a tale of two sisters from Calcutta, Mira and Bharati, who have lived in the United States for some thirty-five years, but who find themselves on different sides in the current debate over the status of immigrants. I am an American citizen and she is not. I am moved that thousands of long-term residents are finally taking the oath of citizenship. She is not.

Mira arrived in Detroit in 1960 to study child psychology and preschool education. I followed her a year later to study creative writing at the University of Iowa. When we left India, we were almost identical in appearance and attitude. We dressed alike, in saris; we expressed identical views on politics, social issues, love, and marriage in the same Calcutta convent-school accent. We would endure our two years in America, secure our degrees, then return to India to marry the grooms of our father's choosing.

Instead, Mira married an Indian student in 1962 who was getting his business administration degree at Wayne State University. They soon acquired the labor certifications necessary for the green card of hassle-free residence and employment.

Mira still lives in Detroit, works in the Southfield, Michigan, school system, and has become nationally recognized for her contributions in the fields of preschool education and parent–teacher relationships. After thirty-six years as a legal immigrant in this country, she clings passionately to her Indian citizenship and hopes to go home to India when she retires.

In Iowa City in 1963, I married a fellow student, an American of Canadian parentage. Because of the accident of his North Dakota birth, I bypassed labor-certification requirements and the race-related "quota" system that favored the applicant's country of origin over his or her merit. I was prepared for (and even welcomed) the emotional strain that came with marrying outside my ethnic community. In thirty-three years of marriage, we have lived in every part of North America. By choosing a husband who was not my father's selection, I was opting for fluidity, self-invention, blue jeans, and T-shirts, and renouncing three thousand years (at least) of caste-observant, "pure culture" marriage in the Mukherjee family. My books have often been read as unapologetic (and in some quarters overenthusiastic) texts for cultural and psychological "mongrelization." It's a word I celebrate.

Mira and I have stayed sisterly close by phone. In our regular Sunday morning conversations, we are unguardedly affectionate. I am her only blood relative on this continent. We expect to see each other through the looming crises of aging and ill health without being asked. Long before Vice President Gore's "Citizenship USA" drive, we'd had our polite arguments over the ethics of retaining an overseas citizenship while expecting the permanent protection and economic benefits that come with living and working in America.

Like well-raised sisters, we never said what was really on our minds, but we probably pitied one another. She, for the lack of structure in my life, the erasure of Indianness, the absence of an unvarying daily core. I, for the narrowness of her perspective, her uninvolvement with the mythic depths or the superficial pop culture of this society. But, now, with the scapegoating of "aliens" (documented or illegal) on the increase, and the targeting of long-term legal immigrants like Mira for new scrutiny and new self-consciousness, she and I find ourselves unable to maintain the same polite discretion. We were always unacknowledged adversaries, and we are now, more than ever, sisters.

"I feel used," Mira raged on the phone the other night. "I feel manipulated and discarded. This is such an unfair way to treat a person who was invited to stay and work here because of her talent. My employer went to the INS and petitioned for the labor certification. For over thirty years, I've invested my creativity and professional skills into the improvement of *this* country's preschool system. I've obeyed all the rules, I've paid my taxes, I love my work, I love my students, I love the friends I've made. How dare America now change its rules in midstream? If America wants to make new rules curtailing benefits of legal immigrants, they should apply only to immigrants who arrive after those rules are already in place."

To my ears, it sounded like the description of a long-enduring, comfortable yet loveless marriage, without risk or recklessness. Have we the right to demand, and to expect, that we be loved? (That, to me, is the subtext of the arguments by immigration advocates.) My sister is an expatriate, professionally generous and creative, socially courteous and gracious, and that's as far as her Americanization can go. She is here to maintain an identity, not to transform it.

I asked her if she would follow the example of others who have decided to become citizens because of the anti-immigration bills in Congress. And here, she surprised me. "If America wants to play the manipulative game, I'll play it, too," she snapped. "I'll become a U.S. citizen for now, then change back to Indian when I'm ready to go home. I feel some kind of irrational attachment to India that I don't to America. Until all this hysteria against legal immigrants, I was totally happy. Having my green card meant I could visit any place in the world I wanted to and then come back to a job that's satisfying and that I do very well."

In one family, from two sisters alike as peas in a pod, there could not be a wider divergence of immigrant experience. America spoke to me—I married it—I embraced the demotion from expatriate aristocrat to immigrant nobody, surrendering those thousands of years of "pure culture," the saris, the delightfully accented English. She retained them all. Which of us is the freak?

Mira's voice, I realize, is the voice not just of the immigrant South Asian community but of an immigrant community of the millions who have stayed rooted in one job, one city, one house, one ancestral culture, one cuisine, for the entirety of their productive years. She speaks for greater numbers than I possibly can. Only the fluency of her English and the anger, rather than fear, born of confidence from her education, differentiate her from the seamstresses, the domestics, the technicians, the shop owners, the millions of hardworking but effectively silenced documented immigrants as well as their less fortunate "illegal" brothers and sisters.

> I embraced the demotion from expatriate aristocrat to immigrant nobody, surrendering those thousands of years of "pure culture," the saris, the delightfully accented English.

Nearly twenty years ago, when I was living in my husband's ancestral homeland of Canada, I was always well-employed but never allowed to feel part of the local Quebec or larger Canadian society. Then, through a Green Paper that invited a national referendum on the unwanted side effects of "nontraditional" immigration, the government officially turned against its immigrant communities, particularly those from South Asia.

I felt then the same sense of betrayal that Mira feels now. I will never forget the pain of that sudden turning, and the casual racist outbursts the Green Paper elicited. That sense of betrayal had its desired effect and drove me, and thousands like me, from the country.

Mira and I differ, however, in the ways in which we hope to interact with the country that we have chosen to live in. She is happier to live in America as an expatriate Indian than as an immigrant American. I need to feel like a part of the community I have adopted (as I tried to feel in Canada as well). I need to put roots down, to vote and make the difference that I can. The price that the immigrant willingly pays, and that the exile avoids, is the trauma of self-transformation.

Thinking Critically about the Text

What do you think Mukherjee's sister means when she says in paragraph 10, "If America wants to play the manipulative game, I'll play it, too"? How do you react to her plans? Explain.

Questions on Subject

1. What is Mukherjee's thesis? (Glossary: *Thesis*) Where does she present it?
2. What arguments does Mukherjee make for becoming an American citizen? What arguments does her sister make for retaining Indian citizenship?
3. Why do you think Mukherjee's sister feels "used" by attempts to change American laws regarding benefits for legal noncitizens?
4. At the end of paragraph 11, Mukherjee asks a question. How does she answer it? How would you answer it?
5. What does Mukherjee mean when she says, "The price that the immigrant willingly pays, and that the exile avoids, is the trauma of self-transformation" (paragraph 15)?
6. In your eyes, did one sister make the right decision? Explain.

Questions on Strategy

1. How has Mukherjee organized her essay? Is it block comparison, point-by-point comparison, or some combination of the two?
2. Why is the pattern of organization that Mukherjee uses appropriate for her subject and purpose? (Glossary: *Purpose; Subject*)
3. Mukherjee chooses to let her sister, Mira, speak for herself in this essay. What do you think would have been lost had Mukherjee simply reported what Mira felt and believed? Explain.

Questions on Diction and Vocabulary

1. Mukherjee uses the word *mongrelization* in paragraph 5. What do you think she means by this word, and why does she "celebrate" it?
2. Mukherjee uses quotation marks around a number of words — "quota" (paragraph 5), "pure culture" (5, 11), "aliens" (7), "illegal" (12), "nontraditional" (13). What does she gain by using the quotation marks?
3. How does Mukherjee use marriage to describe the essential differences between Mira's and her relationship to America?
4. Refer to a dictionary to determine the meanings of the following words as Mukherjee uses them in this selection: *caste* (paragraph 5), *ethics* (6), *scapegoating* (7), *subtext* (9), *expatriate* (15).

Comparison and Contrast in Action

Consider the cartoon below.

How is it possible for two people with similar backgrounds to have completely different views about something? And why are we so fascinated by differences when we were expecting similarities or by similarities when we were expecting differences? Explain.

"Conversation? I thought we were just meeting for coffee."
Michael Maslin/The New Yorker Collection/The Cartoon Bank

Writing Suggestions

1. Mukherjee writes about her relationship with her sister, saying, "[W]e never said what was really on our minds, but we probably pitied one another" (paragraph 7). Such differences are often played out on a larger scale when immigrants who assimilate into American life are confronted by those who choose to retain their ethnic identity; these tensions can lead to name-calling and even aggressive prejudice within immigrant communities. Write an essay about an ethnic or cultural community you are familiar with, comparing and contrasting lifestyle choices its members make as they try to find a comfortable place in American society.

2. Mukherjee presents her sister's reasons for not becoming a citizen and supports them with statements that her sister has made. Imagine that you are Mira Mukherjee. Write a counterargument to the argument presented by Bharati, giving your reasons for remaining an Indian citizen. Remember that you have already broken with tradition by marrying a man not of your "father's choosing" and that the "trauma of self-transformation" that Bharati raises in the conclusion of her essay is much deeper and more complicated than she has represented it to be. Can you say that you are holding to tradition when you are not? Can you engage in a challenging self-transformation if it is not genuinely motivated?

The Difference between "Sick" and "Evil"

ANDREW VACHSS

Andrew Vachss, attorney and author, was born in New York City in 1942. Before graduating from the New England School of Law in 1975, Vachss held a number of positions all related to child protection, ranging from a New York City social services caseworker to director of a maximum-security prison for aggressive violent juvenile offenders. As a lawyer, he exclusively represents children and youths and serves as a child protection consultant. Vachss has written more than twenty-five novels, three collections of short stories, three plays, and two works of nonfiction. He is perhaps best known as the author of the award-winning Burke series of hard-boiled crime mysteries. Vachss lectures widely on issues relating to child protection and has written for *Esquire*, *Playboy*, the *New York Times*, and *Parade* among others. For more information, see http://www.vachss.com.

AP Photo Mark Lennihan

In the following article, which first appeared in *Parade* on July 14, 2002, Andrew Vachss issues a call to action to protect America's children in the wake of the so-called "pedophile priest" scandal. Here he asks the fundamental question: "Are those who abuse their positions of trust to prey upon children — a category certainly not limited to those in religious orders — sick . . . or are they evil?" To answer this question, Vachss believes that we need to establish a clear understanding of the differences between the words *sick* and *evil*, two words that the public often uses synonymously.

Preparing to Read

How do you define *evil*? What kinds of behavior or things do you use the word *evil* to describe? Identify several historical figures whom you consider evil and briefly describe what makes them evil.

The shock waves caused by the recent exposures of so-called "pedophile priests" have reverberated throughout America. But beneath our anger and revulsion, a fundamental question pulsates: Are those who abuse their positions of trust to prey upon children—a category certainly not limited to those in religious orders—sick . . . or are they evil?

We need the answer to that fundamental question. Because, without the truth, we cannot act. And until we act, nothing will change.

My job is protecting children. It has taken me from big cities to rural outposts, from ghettos to penthouses, and from courtrooms to genocidal battlefields. But whatever the venue, the truth remains constant: Some humans intentionally hurt children. They commit unspeakable acts—for their pleasure, their profit, or both.

Many people who hear of my cases against humans who rape, torture, and package children for sale or rent immediately respond with, "That's sick!" Crimes against children seem so grotesquely abnormal that the most obvious explanation is that the perpetrator must be mentally ill—helpless in the grip of a force beyond his or her control.

But that very natural reaction has, inadvertently, created a special category of "blameless predator." That confusion of "sick" with "sickening" is the single greatest barrier to our primary biological and ethical mandate: the protection of our children.

> Sickness is a condition. Evil is a behavior. Evil is always a matter of choice.

The difference between sick and evil cannot be dismissed with facile eye-of-the-beholder rhetoric. There are specific criteria we can employ to give us the answers in every case, every time.

Some of those answers are self-evident and beyond dispute: A mother who puts her baby in the oven because she hears voices commanding her to bake the devil out of the child's spirit is sick; and a mother who sells or rents her baby to child pornographers is evil. But most cases of child sexual abuse—especially those whose "nonviolent" perpetrators come from within the child's circle of trust—seem, on their surface, to be far more complex.

That complexity is an illusion. The truth is as simple as it is terrifying:

Sickness is a condition.

Evil is a behavior.

Evil is always a matter of choice. Evil is not thought; it is conduct. And that conduct is always volitional.

And just as evil is always a choice, sickness is always the absence of choice. Sickness happens. Evil is inflicted.

Until we perceive the difference clearly, we will continue to give aid and comfort to our most pernicious enemies. We, as a society, decide whether something is sick or evil. Either decision confers an obligation upon us. Sickness should be treated. Evil must be fought.

If a person has desires or fantasies about sexually exploiting children, that individual may be sick. (Indeed, if such desires are disturbing, as opposed to gratifying, to the individual, there may even be a "cure.") But if the individual chooses to act upon those feelings, that conduct is evil. People are not what they think; they are what they do.

Our society distrusts the term *evil*. It has an almost biblical ring to it—something we believe in (or not), but never actually understand. We prefer scientific-sounding terms, such as *sociopath*. But sociopathy is not a mental condition; it is a specific cluster of behaviors. The diagnosis is only made from actual criminal conduct.

No reputable psychiatrist claims to be able to cure a sociopath—or, for that matter, a predatory pedophile. Even the most optimistic professionals do not aim to change such a person's thoughts and feelings. What they hope is that the predator can learn self-control, leading to a change in behavior.

Such hopes ignore the inescapable fact that the overwhelming majority of those who prey upon children don't want to change their behavior—they want only to minimize the consequences of being caught at it.

In the animal kingdom, there is a food chain—predators and prey. But among humans, there is no such natural order. Among our species, predators select themselves for that role.

Psychology has given us many insights of great value. But it has also clouded our vision with euphemisms. To say a person suffers from the "disease" of pedophilia is to absolve the predator of responsibility for his behavior.

Imagine if an attorney, defending someone accused of committing a dozen holdups, told the jury his poor client was suffering from "armed-robberia." That jury would decide that the only crazy person in the courtroom was the lawyer.

When a perpetrator claims to be sick, the *timing* of that claim is critical to discovering the truth. Predatory pedophiles carefully insinuate themselves into positions of trust. They select their prey and approach cautiously. Gradually, sometimes over a period of years, they gain greater control over their victims. Eventually, they leave dozens of permanently damaged children in their wake.

But only when they are caught do predatory pedophiles declare themselves to be sick. And the higher the victim count, the sicker (and, therefore less responsible), they claim to be.

In too many cases, a veil of secrecy and protection then descends. The predator's own organization appoints itself judge and jury. The perpetrator is deemed sick, and sent off for in-house "treatment." The truth is never made public. And when some secret tribunal decides a cure has been achieved, the perpetrator's rights and privileges are restored, and he or she is given a new assignment.

In fact, such privileged predators actually are assisted. They enter new communities with the blessing of their own organization, their history and propensities kept secret. As a direct result, unsuspecting parents entrust their children to them. Inevitably, the predator eventually resumes his or her conduct and preys upon children again. And when that conduct comes to light, the claim of "sickness" re-emerges as well.

Too often, our society contorts itself to excuse such predators. We are so eager to call those who sexually abuse children "sick," so quick to understand their demons. Why? Because sickness not only offers the possibility of finding a cure but also assures us that the predator didn't really mean it. After all, it is human nature to try to understand inhuman conduct.

Conversely, the concept of evil terrifies us. The idea that some humans *choose* to prey upon our children is frightening, and their demonstrated skill at camouflage only heightens this fear.

For some, the question, "Does evil exist?" is philosophical. But for those who have confronted or been victimized by predatory pedophiles, there is no question at all. We are what we do.

Just as conduct is a choice, so is our present helplessness. We may be powerless to change the arrogance of those who believe they alone should have the power to decide whether predatory pedophiles are "sick," or when they are "cured." But, as with the perpetrators themselves, we do have the power to change their behavior.

In every state, laws designate certain professions that regularly come into contact with children—such as teachers, doctors, social workers, and day-care employees—as "mandated reporters." Such personnel are required to report reasonable suspicion of child abuse when it comes to their attention. Failure to do so is a crime.

Until now, we have exempted religious organizations from mandated-reporter laws. Recent events have proven the catastrophic consequences of this exemption. We must demand—now—that our legislators close this pathway to evil.

A predatory pedophile who is recycled into an unsuspecting community enters it cloaked with a protection no other sex offender enjoys. If members of religious orders were mandated reporters, we would not have to rely on their good-faith belief that a predator is cured. We could make our own informed decisions on this most vital issue.

Modifying the law in this way would not interfere with priest–penitent privileges: When child victims or their parents disclose abuse, they are not confessing, they are crying for help. Neither confidentiality nor religious freedom would in any way be compromised by mandatory reporting.

Changing the laws so that religious orders join the ranks of mandated reporters is the right thing to do. And the time is right now.

Thinking Critically about the Text

Vachss believes that "our society distrusts the term *evil*" (paragraph 15). Do you agree? Why is the concept of evil such a difficult one to understand when it comes to human behavior?

Questions on Subject

1. What question does Vachss ask in his opening paragraph? Why does he believe that it is important for us to find an answer?
2. What for Vachss is the essential difference between "sick" and "evil"? What criteria does he offer to help his readers understand the difference? How does the public's confusion with "sick" and "sickening" muddy the waters?
3. What does Vachss mean when he says that "psychology has given us many insights of great value. But it has also clouded our vision with euphemisms" (paragraph 19)?
4. Why does Vachss believe that the "timing" of one's claim to be sick is critical to uncovering the truth (paragraph 21)?
5. Why does Vachss believe that people are so willing to call sex offenders sick instead of evil? Do you agree? What is the danger of letting evil pass as a sickness?
6. What action does Vachss want his readers to take after reading his article? Did you find Vachss's argument compelling? Why or why not?

Questions on Strategy

1. What is Vachss's thesis, and where is it stated? (Glossary: *Thesis*)
2. What experience or expertise qualifies Vachss to write about this subject?
3. What is Vachss's purpose in writing this essay? (Glossary: *Purpose*) How do you know?
4. How does Vachss develop the essential differences between "sick" and "evil" in paragraphs 6 through 14? How effectively does he use examples to illustrate these differences? (Glossary: *Illustration*)
5. In paragraph 20, Vachss uses the analogy of a lawyer defending a robber to give his readers insight into the "'disease' of pedophilia" presented in the previous paragraph. How effective or convincing do you find his analogy? (Glossary: *Analogy*)
6. Why do you suppose Vachss devotes so much space to discussing the concept of "evil" when he discusses evil behavior?

Questions on Diction and Vocabulary

1. Vachss adds interest and vitality to his opening two sentences with the strong action verbs *reverberated* and *pulsates*. (Glossary: *Verb*) Identify other strong

verbs that Vachss uses and explain what they add to the appeal of his writing.

2. In paragraph 5, Vachss uses the oxymoron "blameless predator" as a label for perpetrators who are somehow excused by society for their crimes because they are mentally ill. How did you react when you first read about the blameless predators we have inadvertently created? What does Vachss find inherently wrong about the concept of a predator who is deemed blameless? Explain.

3. Refer to a dictionary to determine the meanings of the following words as Vachss uses them in this selection: *revulsion* (paragraph 1), *venue* (3), *mandate* (5), *facile* (6), *pernicious* (13), *sociopath* (15), *insinuate* (21), *propensities* (24).

Comparison and Contrast in Action

After reviewing the discussion of analogy in the introduction to this chapter (pages 283–84) and Vachss's analogy in paragraphs 18–20, create an analogy to explain one of the following:

1. your relationship with one of your teachers or coaches
2. the essence of a game that you enjoy playing
3. a scientific or sociological principle or idea
4. a creative activity such as writing, weaving, painting, or composing music

Share your analogy with other members of your class and discuss how well the analogies work.

Writing Suggestions

1. As Vachss demonstrates in his discussion of "sick" and "evil," important decisions and actions hinge on establishing a clear understanding of the similarities and/or differences in the terminology that we use. Using his essay as a model, write an essay in which you compare and contrast one of the following pairs of terms or a pair of your own choosing:

smart and intelligent	professional and amateur	normal and abnormal
weird and eccentric	manager and leader	public and private

2. What is your position on capital punishment? Who has the right to take the life of another? Ideally, knowing what the punishment will be should deter people from doing the wrong thing in the first place, but does the death penalty really act as a deterrent? Are certain punishments more effective as deterrents than others? In this context, consider the message in the cartoon below, which highlights the great irony that is inherent in capital punishment. Write an essay in which you compare and contrast the arguments for and against the death penalty.

"Maybe this will teach you that it's morally wrong to kill people!"

CartoonStock.com

3. **Writing with Sources.** For more than four decades, lawyer Andrew Vachss has advocated for children victimized by adult predators. His article in *Parade* on July 14, 2002, was written in response to the handling of the so-called pedophile priests in America. However, as Vachss points out, there are other instances of people who intentionally hurt children, people who "rape, torture, and package children for sale or rent." In your library or online, research one such case that has recently been in the news. What was the nature of the crime against the children? Would you label the perpetrator "sick" or "evil"? Why? How was the perpetrator of the crime punished? Do you agree with the way the perpetrator was handled? Write an essay in which you report your findings. For models of and advice on integrating sources in your essay, see Chapters 14 and 15.

Grant and Lee: A Study in Contrasts

BRUCE CATTON

Arguably the most prolific and popular Civil War historian, Bruce Catton (1899–1978) was born in Petoskey, Michigan, and attended Oberlin College. Early in his career, Catton worked as a reporter for various newspapers, among them the *Cleveland Plain Dealer.* His interest in history led him to write about the Civil War. His books on the subject include *Mr. Lincoln's Army* (1951), *Glory Road* (1952), *A Stillness at Appomattox* (1953), *This Hallowed Ground* (1956), *The Coming Fury* (1961), *Never Call Retreat* (1965), and *Gettysburg: The Final Fury* (1974). Catton won both the Pulitzer Prize and the National Book Award in 1954. A fellow historian once wrote, "There is a near-magic power of imagination in Catton's work that seem[s] to project him physically into the battlefields, along the dusty roads, and to the campfires of another age."

Hank Walker/The LIFE Picture Collection/Getty Images

The following selection was included in *The American Story*, a collection of historical essays edited by Earl Schenck Miers. In this essay, Catton considers "two great Americans, Grant and Lee — very different, yet under everything very much alike."

Preparing to Read

What do you know about America's Civil War and the roles played by Ulysses S. Grant and Robert E. Lee in that monumental struggle? For you, what does each of these men represent? Do you consider either of them to be an American hero? Explain.

When Ulysses S. Grant and Robert E. Lee met in the parlor of a modest house at Appomattox Court House, Virginia, on April 9, 1865, to work out the terms for the surrender of Lee's Army of Northern Virginia, a great chapter in American life came to a close, and a great new chapter began.

These men were bringing the Civil War to its virtual finish. To be sure, other armies had yet to surrender, and for a few days the fugitive Confederate government would struggle desperately and vainly, trying to find some way to go on living now that its chief support was gone. But in effect it was all over when Grant and Lee signed the papers. And the little room where they wrote out the terms was the scene of one of the poignant, dramatic contrasts in American history.

They were two strong men, these oddly different generals, and they represented the strengths of two conflicting currents that, through them, had come into final collision.

Back of Robert E. Lee was the notion that the old aristocratic concept might somehow survive and be dominant in American life.

Lee was tidewater Virginia, and in his background were family, culture, and tradition ... the age of chivalry transplanted to a New World which was making its own legends and its own myths. He embodied a way of life that had come down through the age of knighthood and the English country squire. America was a land that was beginning all over again, dedicated to nothing much more complicated than the rather hazy belief that all men had equal rights and should have an equal chance in the world. In such a land Lee stood for the feeling that it was somehow of advantage to human society to have a pronounced inequality in the social structure. There should be a leisure class, backed by ownership of land; in turn, society itself should be keyed to the land as the chief source of wealth and influence. It would bring forth (according to this ideal) a class of men with a strong sense of obligation to the community; men who lived not to gain advantage for themselves, but to meet the solemn obligations which had been laid on them by the very fact that they were privileged. From them the country would get its leadership; to them it could look for the higher

Robert E. Lee
National Archives and Records Administration

values — of thought, of conduct, of personal deportment — to give it strength and value.

Lee embodied the noblest elements of this aristocratic ideal. Through him, the landed nobility justified itself. For four years, the Southern states had fought a desperate war to uphold the ideals for which Lee stood. In the end, it almost seemed as if the Confederacy fought for Lee; as if he himself was the Confederacy . . . the best thing that the way of life for which the Confederacy stood could ever have to offer. He had passed into legend before Appomattox. Thousands of tired, underfed, poorly clothed Confederate soldiers, long since past the simple enthusiasm of the early days of the struggle, somehow considered Lee the symbol of everything for which they had been willing to die. But they could not quite put this feeling into words. If the Lost Cause, sanctified by so much heroism and so many deaths, had a living justification, its justification was General Lee.

> They were two strong men, these oddly different generals, and they represented the strengths of two conflicting currents that, through them, had come into final collision.

Grant, the son of a tanner on the Western frontier, was everything Lee was not. He had come up the hard way and embodied nothing in particular except the eternal toughness and sinewy fiber of the men who grew up beyond the mountains. He was one of a body of men who owed reverence and obeisance to no one, who were self-reliant to a fault, who cared hardly anything for the past but who had a sharp eye for the future.

These frontier men were the precise opposite of the tidewater aristocrats. Back of them, in the great surge that had taken people over the Alleghenies and into the opening Western country, there was a deep, implicit dissatisfaction with a past that had settled into grooves. They stood for democracy, not from any reasoned conclusion about the proper ordering of human society, but simply because they had grown up in the middle of democracy and knew how it worked. Their society might have privileges, but they would be privileges each man had won for himself. Forms and patterns meant nothing. No man was born to anything, except perhaps to a chance to show how far he could rise. Life was competition.

Yet along with this feeling had come a deep sense of belonging to a national community. The Westerner who developed a farm, opened a shop, or set up in business as a trader, could hope to prosper only as his own community prospered — and his community ran from the Atlantic to the Pacific and from Canada down to Mexico. If the land was settled, with

Ulysses S. Grant
National Archives and Records Administration

towns and highways and accessible markets, he could better himself. He saw his fate in terms of the nation's own destiny. As its horizons expanded, so did his. He had, in other words, an acute dollars-and-cents stake in the continued growth and development of his country.

And that, perhaps, is where the contrast between Grant and Lee becomes most striking. The Virginia aristocrat, inevitably, saw himself in relation to his own region. He lived in a static society which could endure almost anything except change. Instinctively, his first loyalty would go to the locality in which that society existed. He would fight to the limit of endurance to defend it, because in defending it he was defending everything that gave his own life its deepest meaning.

The Westerner, on the other hand, would fight with an equal tenacity for the broader concept of society. He fought so because everything he lived by was tied to growth, expansion and a constantly widening horizon. What he lived by would survive or fall with the nation itself. He could not possibly stand by unmoved in the face of an attempt to destroy the Union.

He would combat it with everything he had, because he could only see it as an effort to cut the ground out from under his feet.

So Grant and Lee were in complete contrast, representing two diametrically opposed elements in American life. Grant was the modern man emerging; beyond him, ready to come on the stage, was the great age of steel and machinery, of crowded cities and a restless burgeoning vitality. Lee might have ridden down from the old age of chivalry, lance in hand, silken banner fluttering over his head. Each man was the perfect champion of his cause, drawing both his strengths and his weaknesses from the people he led.

Yet it was not all contrast, after all. Different as they were—in background, in personality, in underlying aspiration—these two great soldiers had much in common. Under everything else, they were marvelous fighters. Furthermore, their fighting qualities were really very much alike.

Each man had, to begin with, the great virtue of utter tenacity and fidelity. Grant fought his way down the Mississippi Valley in spite of acute personal discouragement and profound military handicaps. Lee hung on in the trenches at Petersburg after hope itself had died. In each man there was an indomitable quality . . . the born fighter's refusal to give up as long as he can still remain on his feet and lift his two fists.

Daring and resourcefulness they had, too; the ability to think faster and move faster than the enemy. These were the qualities which gave Lee the dazzling campaigns of Second Manassas and Chancellorsville and won Vicksburg for Grant.

Lastly, and perhaps greatest of all, there was the ability, at the end, to turn quickly from war to peace once the fighting was over. Out of the way these two men behaved at Appomattox came the possibility of a peace of reconciliation. It was a possibility not wholly realized, in the years to come, but which did, in the end, help the two sections to become one nation again . . . after a war whose bitterness might have seemed to make such a reunion wholly impossible. No part of either man's life became him more than the part he played in their brief meeting in the McLean house at Appomattox. Their behavior there put all succeeding generations of Americans in their debt. Two great Americans, Grant and Lee—very different, yet under everything very much alike. Their encounter at Appomattox was one of the great moments of American history.

Thinking Critically about the Text

Catton concludes with the claim that Grant and Lee's "encounter at Appomattox was one of the great moments of American history" (paragraph 16). How does Catton prepare readers for this claim? What, for Catton, do these two Civil War generals represent, and what does he see as the implications for the country of Lee's surrender?

Questions on Subject

1. In paragraphs 10–12, Catton discusses what he considers to be the most striking contrast between Grant and Lee. What is that difference?
2. List the similarities that Catton sees between Grant and Lee. Which similarity does Catton believe is most important? Why?
3. What attitudes and ideas does Catton describe to support his view that the culture of tidewater Virginia was a throwback to the "age of chivalry" (paragraph 5)?
4. Catton says that Grant was "the modern man emerging" (paragraph 12). How does he support that statement? Do you agree?

Questions on Strategy

1. What would have been lost had Catton looked at the similarities between Grant and Lee before looking at the differences? Would anything have been gained?
2. How does Catton organize the body of his essay (paragraphs 3–16)? When answering this question, you may find it helpful to summarize the point of comparison in each paragraph and to label whether the paragraph concerns Lee, Grant, or both. (Glossary: *Organization*)
3. Catton makes clear transitions between paragraphs. Identify the transitional devices he uses to lead readers from one paragraph to the next throughout the essay. As a reader, how do these transitions help you? (Glossary: *Transitions*) Explain.
4. How does Catton use both description and cause and effect analysis to enhance his comparison and contrast of Grant and Lee? In what ways does description serve to sharpen the differences between these generals? How does Catton use cause and effect analysis to explain their respective natures? Cite several examples of Catton's use of each strategy to illustrate your answer. (Glossary: *Cause and Effect Analysis; Description*)

Questions on Diction and Vocabulary

1. Identify at least two metaphors that Catton uses and explain what each contributes to his comparison. (Glossary: *Figures of Speech*)
2. Refer to a dictionary to determine the meanings of the following words as Catton uses them in this selection: *poignant* (paragraph 2), *chivalry* (5), *sanctified* (6), *sinewy* (7), *obeisance* (7), *tidewater* (8), *tenacity* (11), *aspiration* (13).

Comparison and Contrast in Action

Carefully read the following paragraphs from Stephen E. Ambrose's book *Crazy Horse and Custer: The Parallel Lives of Two American Warriors* (1975) and then answer the questions that follow.

> It was bravery, above and beyond all other qualities, that Custer and Crazy Horse had in common. Each man was an outstanding warrior in war-mad societies. Thousands upon thousands of Custer's fellow whites had as much opportunity as he did to demonstrate their courage, just as all of Crazy Horse's associates had countless opportunities to show that they equaled him in bravery. But no white warrior, save his younger brother, Tom, could outdo Custer, just as no Indian warrior, save his younger brother, Little Hawk, could outdo Crazy Horse. And for both white and red societies, no masculine virtue was more admired than bravery. To survive, both societies felt they had to have men willing to put their lives on the line. For men who were willing to do so, no reward was too great, even though there were vast differences in the way each society honored its heroes.
>
> Beyond their bravery, Custer and Crazy Horse were individualists, each standing out from the crowd in his separate way. Custer wore outlandish uniforms, let his hair fall in long, flowing golden locks across his shoulders, surrounded himself with pet animals and admirers, and in general did all he could to draw attention to himself. Crazy Horse's individualism pushed him in the opposite direction — he wore a single feather in his hair when going into battle, rather than a war bonnet. Custer's vast energy set him apart from most of his fellows; the Sioux distinguished Crazy Horse from other warriors because of Crazy Horse's quietness and introspection. Both men lived in societies in which drugs, especially alcohol, were widely used, but neither Custer nor Crazy Horse drank. Most of all, of course, each man stood out in battle as a great risk taker.

What is Ambrose's point in these two paragraphs? How does he use comparison and contrast to make this point? How has he organized his paragraphs?

Writing Suggestions

1. Catton gives readers few details of the physical appearance of Grant and Lee, but the portraits that accompany this essay do show us what these men looked like. (For a discussion of how to analyze photographs and other visual texts, see pages 15–19.) Write a brief essay in which you compare and contrast the men you see in the portraits. How closely does your assessment of each general match the "picture" Catton presents in his essay? How would you describe the appearance — both dress and posture — of these two generals? What details in the photographs are most telling for you? Explain why. In what ways can Grant and Lee be said to represent the way of life associated with the side each commanded? Explain.

2. In the persons of Grant and Lee, Catton sees the "final collision" (paragraph 3) between two ways of living and thinking — the "age of steel and machinery" (12) conquering the "age of chivalry" (5). Today, more than 150 years after the conclusion to the Civil War, what do you see as the dominant ways of living and thinking in the current "age of information"? Do today's lifestyles appear to be on a collision course with one another, or do you think they can coexist? Write an essay in which you present your position and defend it using appropriate examples.

3. **Writing with Sources.** Write an essay in which you compare and contrast two world leaders, sports figures, or celebrities whose careers have at some point crossed in a dramatic or decisive way. Examples include Hillary Rodham Clinton and Bernie Sanders; Ronald Reagan and Mikhail Gorbachev; Serena Williams and Maria Sharapova; Brad Pitt and Angelina Jolie; Marilyn Monroe and Joe DiMaggio. Use library resources and the Internet to research your two famous people. For models of and advice on integrating sources in your essay, see Chapters 14 and 15.

WRITING SUGGESTIONS FOR COMPARISON AND CONTRAST

1. Write an essay in which you compare and contrast two objects, people, or events to show at least one of the following:
   a. their important differences
   b. their significant similarities
   c. their relative value
   d. their distinctive qualities

2. Select a topic from the list that follows. Write an essay using comparison and contrast as your primary means of development. Be sure that your essay has a definite purpose and a clear direction.
   a. two television situation comedies
   b. two types of summer employment
   c. two people who display different attitudes toward responsibility
   d. two restaurants
   e. two courses in the same subject area
   f. two friends who exemplify different lifestyles
   g. two video streaming services
   h. two attitudes toward death

3. Use one of the following "before and after" situations as the basis for an essay of comparison and contrast:
   a. before and after an examination
   b. before and after seeing a movie
   c. before and after reading an important book
   d. before and after a big meal
   e. before and after a long trip

4. Most of us have seen something important in our lives — a person, place, or thing — undergo a significant change, either in the subject itself or in our own perception of it. Write an essay comparing and contrasting the person, place, or thing before and after the change. There are many possibilities to consider. Perhaps a bucolic vista of open fields has become a shopping mall; perhaps a favorite athletic team has gone from glory to shame; perhaps a loved one has been altered by decisions, events, or illness.

5. Interview a professor who has taught for many years at your college or university. Ask the professor to compare and contrast the college as it was when he or she first taught there with the way it is now; encourage reminiscence and evaluation. Combine strategies of description, comparison and contrast, and possibly definition as you write your essay. (Glossary: *Definition; Description*)

6. **Writing with Sources.** Five of the essays in this book deal, more or less directly, with issues related to the definition, achievement, or nature of manhood in America. The essays are "How to Give Orders Like a Man" (page 202) by Deborah Tannen; "Grant and Lee: A Study in Contrasts" by Bruce Catton (page 319); "What Does 'Boys Will Be Boys' Really Mean?" by Deborah M. Roffman (page 420); and "How Boys Become Men" by Jon Katz (page 455). Read these essays and discuss with classmates the broad issues they raise. Choose one aspect of the topic of particular interest to you and study the three or four essays that seem to bear most directly on this topic. Write an essay in which you compare, contrast, and evaluate the assertions in these essays. For models of and advice on integrating sources in your essay, see Chapters 14 and 15.

7. **Writing in the Workplace.** Imagine that you were recently hired to work in a small insurance business that employs five people. Your boss asks you to research and make a recommendation about the purchase of a new printer or copier for the office. Explore different office machines online or visit an office equipment store and talk with a salesperson about what printers or copiers might be appropriate for a five-person office. Decide which two or three printers or copiers best fill the bill and then write a memo to your boss in which you compare and contrast the features of the top candidates, concluding with your recommendation of which model to purchase. In addition to research at retail outlets, you might find it helpful to visit the Web sites of different manufacturers to learn the specifications and capabilities of each machine. For models of and advice on integrating sources in your essay, see Chapters 14 and 15.

Smithsonian National Museum of Natural History

Second Floor

- Backyard Dinos
- Korea Gallery
- FossilLab
- IMAX Theater (Exit)
- Last American Dinosaurs
- Gems and Minerals Store
- Research Wings (Staff access only)
- Mummies
- Bones
- Geology
- Live Insect Zoo
- Live Butterfly Pavilion
- Hope Diamond
- Gems and Minerals

First Floor

- Human Origins
- Ocean Hall
- Q?rius jr.
- African Voices
- IMAX Theater (Entrance)
- Research Wings (Staff access only)
- Mammals
- Rotunda
- National Fossil Hall (Closed for renovation)
- Mammals Store
- Entrance from National Mall

Ground Floor

- Entrance from Constitution Avenue / Accessible Entrance
- Q?rius
- T.rex Skull
- Atrium Café
- Café Natural
- Family Store
- Gallery Store
- Research Wings (Staff access only)
- Baird Auditorium
- Birds of DC

North

SPECIAL EXHIBITIONS
1. Into Africa — Second Floor
2. Wilderness Forever — Second Floor
3. Nature's Best Photography — Second Floor
4. Life in One Cubic Foot — First Floor
5. Mali Mud Masons — First Floor
6. Iceland Revealed — First Floor
7. Color in a New Light — Ground Floor

INTENSIVE INTERACTIVES
- Live Butterflies and Plants — Second Floor
- Q?rius Designed for teens — Ground Floor
- Q?rius jr. Ages 9 and under — First Floor

ANIMALS & ECOSYSTEMS
- Bones — Second Floor
- Live Insect Zoo — Second Floor
- Mammals — First Floor
- Ocean Hall — First Floor
- Birds of DC — Ground Floor

DINOSAURS AND FOSSILS
- National Fossil Hall — Closed for renovation
- Backyard Dinos — Second Floor
- The Last American Dinosaurs — Second Floor
- FossilLab — Second Floor
- T.rex Skull — Ground Floor

EARTH SCIENCES
- Gems and Minerals — Second Floor
- Hope Diamond — Second Floor
- Geology — Second Floor

HUMAN DIVERSITY
- Korea Gallery — Second Floor
- Mummies — Second Floor
- African Voices — First Floor
- Human Origins — First Floor

AMENITIES
- Stores
- Tickets
- Dining
- ATM

FACILITIES
- Accessible
- Elevator
- Escalator
- First Aid
- Information Desk
- Locker Storage
- Pay Phone
- Restrooms
- Security Office
- Stairs

Staff Access Only — 2nd Floor / 1st Floor / Ground Floor

National Mall — Constitution Avenue

Jennifer Renteria/Samir Bitar; Smithsonian Institution

CHAPTER 9

Division and Classification

WHAT ARE DIVISION AND CLASSIFICATION?

LIKE COMPARISON AND CONTRAST, DIVISION AND CLASSIFICATION ARE separate yet closely related operations. Division involves breaking down a single large unit into smaller subunits or separating a group of items into discrete categories. Classification, on the other hand, entails placing individual items into established categories. Division, then, takes apart, whereas classification groups together. But even though the two processes can operate separately, they tend to be used together.

The floor plan of the National Museum of Natural History (opposite) illustrates division and classification at work. The museum has divided its three floors into sections and further divided those sections between exhibits and staff-only research space. The layout of the exhibits suggests how different categories relate to one another. For instance, the butterfly pavilion is located in an area dedicated to bugs and insects. Visitors to the museum can quickly glance at the floor plan, get a simplified understanding of the natural world, and learn where to go to see representative examples of a particular class of objects from that world. The principles of division and classification have provided an easy way for museumgoers to make sense out of what would otherwise be an overwhelming conglomeration of objects.

DIVISION AND CLASSIFICATION IN WRITTEN TEXTS

In writing, division can be the most effective method for making sense of one large, complex, or multifaceted entity. Consider, for example, the following passage from E. B. White's *Here Is New York,* in which he discusses New Yorkers and their city:

Division into categories occurs in opening sentence	There are roughly three New Yorks. There is, first, the New York of the man or woman who was born here, who takes the city for granted and accepts its size and its turbulence as natural and inevitable. Second, there is the New York of the commuter—the city

331

Author explains the nature of people in each category

that is devoured by locusts each day and spat out each night. Third, there is the New York of the person who was born somewhere else and came to New York in quest of something. Of these three trembling cities the greatest is the last — the city of final destination, the city that is a goal. It is this third city that accounts for New York's highstrung disposition, its poetical deportment, its dedication to the arts, and its incomparable achievements. Commuters give the city its tidal restlessness; natives give it solidarity and continuity; but the settlers give it passion. And whether it is a farmer arriving from Italy to set up a small grocery store in a slum, or a young girl arriving from a small town in Mississippi to escape the indignity of being observed by her neighbors, or a boy arriving from the Corn Belt with a manuscript in his suitcase and a pain in his heart, it makes no difference: each embraces New York with the intense excitement of first love, each absorbs New York with the fresh eyes of an adventurer, each generates heat and light to dwarf the Consolidated Edison Company.

In his opening sentences, White suggests a principle for dividing the population of New York, establishing his three categories on the basis of a person's relationship to the city. There is the New York of the native, the New York of the commuter, and the New York of the immigrant. White's divisions help him make a point about the character of New York City, depicting its restlessness, its solidarity, and its passion.

In contrast to breaking a large idea into parts, classification can be used to draw connections between disparate elements based on a common category — such as price, for example. Often, classification is used in conjunction with another rhetorical strategy, such as comparison and contrast. Consider, for example, how in the following passage from Toni Cade Bambara's "The Lesson" she classifies a toy in F.A.O. Schwarz and other items in the thirty-five-dollar category to compare the relative values of things in the life of two girls, Sylvia and Sugar.

Classification used along with comparison and contrast

Me and Sugar at the back of the train watchin the tracks whizzin by large then small then getting gobbled up in the dark. I'm thinkin about this tricky toy I saw in the store. A clown that somersaults on a bar then does chin-ups just cause you yank lightly at his leg. Cost $35. I could see me askin my mother for a $35 birthday clown. "You wanna who that costs what?" she'd say, cocking her head to the side to get a better view of the hole in my head. Thirty-five dollars could buy new bunk beds for Juniot and Gretchen's boy. Thirty-five dollars and the whole household could go visit Grand-daddy Nelson in the country. Thirty-five dollars would pay for the rent and the piano bill, too. Who are these people that spend that much for performing clowns and $1000 for toy sailboats? What kinda work they do and how they live and how come we ain't in on it?

Another example may help clarify how division and classification work hand in hand. Suppose a sociologist wants to determine whether the socioeconomic status of the people in a particular neighborhood has any influence on their voting behavior. Having decided on her purpose, the sociologist chooses as her subject the fifteen families living on Maple Street. Her goal then becomes to group these families in a way that will be relevant to her purpose: (1) according to socioeconomic status (low-income earners, middle-income earners, and high-income earners) and (2) according to voting behavior (voters and nonvoters).

In confidential interviews with each family, the sociologist begins to classify each family according to her established categories. Her work leads her to construct the following diagram, which allows her to visualize her division and classification system and its essential components: the subject, her bases or principles of division, the subclasses or categories that derive from these principles, and her conclusion.

Purpose: To study the relationship between socioeconomic status and voting behavior

[**Subject**] The 15 families on Maple Street

Subclasses: (based on family income)

Low Income (under $35,000)	Middle Income ($35,000–$90,000)	High Income (over $90,000)
Bowman	Reilly	Rigby
Packer	Santana	Kretz
Eells	Lane	Wagner
Weiss	Pfeffer	
Murray	Halstead	
Nadel		
Sikorski		

Subclasses: (based on voting behavior)

Non-voting	Voting	Non-voting	Voting	Non-voting	Voting
Bowman		Lane	Reilly	Wagner	Rigby
Packer			Santana		Kretz
Eells			Pfeffer		
Weiss			Halstead		
Murray					
Nadel					
Sikorski					

Conclusion: On Maple Street there seems to be a relationship between socioeconomic status and voting behavior: The low-income families are nonvoters.

USING DIVISION AND CLASSIFICATION AS A WRITING STRATEGY

As the work of the Maple Street sociologist shows, division and classification are used primarily to demonstrate a particular point about the subject under discussion. In a paper about the emphasis a television network places on reaching various audiences, you could begin by dividing prime-time programming into suitable subclasses: shows primarily for adults, shows for families, shows for children, and so forth. You could then classify each of that network's programs into one of these categories, analyze this data, and draw your conclusions about which audiences the network tries hardest to reach.

Another purpose of division and classification is to help writers and readers make choices. A voter may classify politicians on the basis of their attitudes toward nuclear energy or abortion; the technology magazine *Wired* classifies smartphones on the basis of available memory, screen size, processor speed, camera pixels, and carrier availability; high school seniors classify colleges and universities on the basis of prestige, geographic location, programs available, and tuition fees. In such cases, division and classification have an absolutely practical end: making a decision about whom to vote for, which smartphone to buy, and where to apply for admission to college.

Finally, writers use division and classification as a basic organizational strategy to bring a sense of order to a large amorphous whole. As you'll see later in this chapter, for example, Rosalind Wiseman's system of classification in "The Queen Bee and Her Court" establishes seven categories of roles played by young girls in school cliques to help us better understand how those cliques function.

USING DIVISION AND CLASSIFICATION ACROSS THE DISCIPLINES

When writing essays in the academic disciplines, you will have many opportunities to use the strategy of division and classification to both organize and strengthen the presentation of your ideas. To determine whether division and classification is the right strategy to use in a particular paper, review the guidelines described in Chapter 2 (Determining a Strategy for Developing Your Essay, pages 32–33). Consider the following examples:

Earth Sciences
1. **MAIN IDEA:** Pollution is a far-reaching and unwieldy subject.
2. **QUESTION:** On what basis can we divide pollution into its various categories, and what examples of pollution can we place into each category?

3. **STRATEGY:** Division and classification. This strategy involves two activities: dividing into categories and placing items in their appropriate categories. The word *divide* signals the need to separate pollution into manageable groupings. The word *examples* and the phrase *place into each category* signal the need to classify types of pollution into appropriate categories.
4. **SUPPORTING STRATEGY:** Argumentation is often used to support both the rationale for categorization and classification itself.

Education

1. **MAIN IDEA:** Children's learning disabilities fall into three major groups.
2. **QUESTION:** What are the major types of learning disabilities into which children fall?
3. **STRATEGY:** Division and classification. The words *major types* suggest the need to divide learning problems into major categories. The words *fall into* suggest that every learning disability can be classified into one of the three categories.
4. **SUPPORTING STRATEGY:** Argumentation could be used to persuade readers that the categories of problems discussed are major and to persuade them that a knowledge of these three major types of problems can be useful to teachers and parents in helping a child.

Political Science

1. **MAIN IDEA:** There are four types of U.S. presidents.
2. **QUESTION:** On what basis or bases do we group U.S. presidents?
3. **STRATEGY:** Division and classification. The words *basis* and *bases* signal the need to establish criteria for dividing all our presidents. The word *group* suggests the need to classify the presidents according to the established groupings.
4. **SUPPORTING STRATEGY:** Illustration can be used to provide examples of various presidents.

SAMPLE STUDENT ESSAY USING DIVISION AND CLASSIFICATION AS A WRITING STRATEGY

In the following essay, student Katie Angeles explores and defines a range of personality types, focusing on the phlegmatic personality in the context of three other personality types: sanguine, melancholic, and choleric. By establishing and placing people into these categories and supporting her claims with research, Angeles helps us see the personality types more clearly. In addition, she challenges some preconceptions we may have had about them.

The Forgotten Personality Type
Katie Angeles

[Margin note: Division into categories occurs in second, third, and fourth sentences]

The next time you're at a party or any other type of social gathering, look around. Some people are telling stories and making everyone laugh, others are making sure everything is running smoothly and perfectly, and a few individuals are the bold ones who liven things up and "get the party started." These are the obvious personalities—the "life of the party," the "busy bee," and the "leader." Personality experts call these personalities sanguine (the popular one), the melancholic (the perfect one), and choleric (the powerful one). However, there's one personality that's not so easy to spot, and therefore is usually forgotten—the peaceful phlegmatic.

[Margin note: Thesis: The phlegmatic personality is easy to overlook]

[Margin note: Author introduces history of the concept of personality types]

What makes people the way they are? Why do some people command the spotlight, while others are experts at fading into the background? Personality types were first identified around 400 BC, when the Greek physician Hippocrates noticed that people not only looked different, but also acted differently. He believed that each person's personality type was related to a particular body fluid they had in excess: yellow bile, black bile, blood, or phlegm. These were classified as the "four humors" (Funder 203). Around AD 149, a Greek physiologist named Galen built on Hippocrates's theory, stating that sanguines had an excess amount of yellow bile, melancholics had extra black bile, cholerics had more blood than others, and phlegmatics had an extraordinary amount of phlegm (Littauer 16). In later years, more theories evolved—American scientist William Sheldon believed that personality was related to body type, while people in India said that metabolic body type contributed to the way people behave (Funder 373). Ultimately, these theories were proven incorrect; but we still recognize different personality types. Today, what do we think determines personality?

As *Time* magazine reported on January 15, 1996, D4DR, a gene that regulates dopamine, is usually found in people who are risk takers (Toufexis par. 2). However, researchers suspected that the gene itself wasn't the only cause of risk-taking and that other genes, as well as upbringing, contributed to this phenomenon (Toufexis par. 3). At the time the report appeared, people were worried that parents would use prenatal testing to weed out certain genes that invoked undesirable personality traits (Toufexis par. 6). Since all personalities have their good and bad sides, this would have been a controversial development. Thankfully, parents are not yet able to test for their child's future personality.

Point-by-point comparison of birth order

Moreover, we know that even though people may be born with a certain personality, the way they are brought up can also contribute to how they relate to others later in life. For example, birth order has been shown to affect personality type (Franco par. 1). Firstborn children tend to be choleric since they have the job of leading their siblings; middle children are usually phlegmatic since they're in a prime negotiating spot; and the youngest are generally sanguine because they're used to being spoiled (Franco par. 2–4). Parents can also influence the way a child's personality turns out.

Point-by-point comparison of weaknesses

Each personality type has its strength, but a strength taken to an extreme can become a weakness. While sanguines love to talk, sometimes they may talk too much. Although cholerics are born leaders, they may use their influence in negative ways. Melancholics are perfectionists, but they may prefer being right to being happy, and phlegmatics tend to be easygoing and agreeable, but they may be too passive and have a fear of conflict. Their laid-back attitude can be very frustrating to the most fast-paced personalities, such as cholerics and melancholics.

Paragraph devoted entirely to the essay's main topic: phlegmatics

Phlegmatic people can be hard to notice because they're usually not doing anything to call attention to themselves. While the sanguines are talking and loving life, the cholerics are getting things done, and the melancholics are taking care of the little details, the phlegmatics distinguish themselves by simply being laid-back and easygoing. Even though phlegmatic people tend to fly under the radar, it's very noticeable when they're not around, because they are the peacemakers of the world and the glue that holds everyone together. They are low-maintenance, adaptable, even-keeled, calm, cool, and collected individuals. They are usually reserved, yet they love being around people, and they have a knack for saying the right thing at the right time. Phlegmatics also work well under pressure. However, they hate change, they avoid taking risks, they are extremely stubborn, and it's very hard to get them motivated or excited, which can translate into laziness (Littauer 21). Aside from these traits, the phlegmatic's characteristics are hard to define, because phlegmatics tend to adopt the traits of either the sanguine personality or the melancholy personality.

Examples of how personality types may be combined

Most people are a combination of personalities—they have a dominant and a secondary personality that combine the traits of the personalities. For example, some phlegmatics are phlegmatic-sanguine, making them more talkative, while others are phlegmatic-melancholy, causing them to be more introverted. It's not possible to be phlegmatic-choleric, since phlegmatics avoid conflict and cholerics are fueled by it (Littauer 24, 25). People who try to resist their natural personality type can wind up unhappy, since they are trying to be someone they are not.

All personalities have emotional needs. The sanguine needs attention, affection, approval, and activity; the melancholic needs space, support, silence, and stability; the choleric needs action, appreciation, leadership, and control; and the phlegmatic needs peace, self-worth, and significance (Littauer 22). If people don't have their emotional needs met, their worst sides tend to emerge. For example, if a phlegmatic, easygoing, type B personality is in a family of all cholerics, or "go-getter," type A personalities, the phlegmatics may find themselves masking their true personality in order to survive. This can be very draining for phlegmatics, and sooner or later, their negative side will emerge.

Phlegmatics are very adaptable—they get along with everyone because they are able to meet the emotional needs of all the individual personalities. They listen to the sanguine, they follow the choleric, and they support the melancholic. In return, the sanguine entertains them, the choleric motivates them, and the melancholic listens to them. However, if phlegmatics feel like they're being taken for granted, they will become resentful. Since they have an innate need for peace, they won't say anything, and people won't know that there's a problem (Littauer 125).

Conclusion: The purpose and usefulness of the classification is explained

Even though phlegmatics are often overlooked, they have a lot to contribute with their ability to work under pressure, their diplomatic skill, and their contagious contentment. So the next time you're checking out personalities at a party, try looking for the phlegmatic first. The forgotten personality might just be the most interesting person in the room.

Works Cited

Franco, Virginia. "Siblings Birth Order and Personality Types." *Essortment*. Pagewise, 2002. il.essortment.com/birthordersibl_rbay.htm.

Funder, D.C. *The Personality Puzzle*. 2nd ed. W.W. Norton, 2001.
Littauer, Florence. *Personality Plus for Couples: Understanding Yourself and the One You Love*. Baker Publishing Group, 2001.
Toufexis, Anastasia. "What Makes Them Do It." *Time*, 15 Jan 1996, www.time.com/time/magazine/article/0,9171,983955,00.html.

Analyzing Katie Angeles' Division and Classification Essay: Questions for Discussion

1. What categories does Angeles use to classify her subject? What are the distinguishing characteristics of each category? Does she do a good job making distinctions between her categories?
2. How has Angeles organized the categories in her essay? Is the organization effective? If not, what changes might improve it?
3. Are the categories Angeles presents complete? Does she account for all personality types, or are there types she has not considered?
4. Why does Angeles include paragraph three, about the relationship between genes and personality?
5. Does Angeles remain focused on her subject and stay within the limits of her categories throughout the essay?

SUGGESTIONS FOR USING DIVISION AND CLASSIFICATION AS A WRITING STRATEGY

As you plan, write, and revise your division and classification essay, be mindful of the writing process guidelines described in Chapter 2. Pay particular attention to the basic requirements and essential ingredients of this writing strategy.

▶ **Planning Your Division and Classification Essay**

Planning is an essential part of writing a good division and classification essay. You can save yourself a great deal of trouble by taking the time to think about the key building blocks of your essay before you actually begin to write.

DETERMINE YOUR PURPOSE AND FOCUS ON IT. The principle you use to divide your subject into categories depends on your larger purpose. It is crucial, then, that you determine a clear purpose for your division and classification before you begin to examine your subject in detail. For example, in studying the student body at your school, you might have any number of purposes, such as discovering how much time your classmates spend in the library during the week, explaining how financial aid is distributed, discussing the most popular movies or music on campus, or describing styles of dorm-room decor. The categories into which you divide the student body will vary according to your purpose.

Let's say, for example, that you are in charge of writing an editorial for your school newspaper that will make people aware of how they might reduce the amount of trash going to the landfill. Having established your purpose, your next task might be to identify the different ways objects could be handled to avoid sending them to the landfill. For instance, you might decide that there are four basic ways to prevent things from ending up in the trash. Then, you could establish a sequence or an order of importance in which they should be addressed. Your first draft might start something like the following:

> Over the course of the last semester, more trash was removed from our campus than in any semester in history. But was it all trash that had to go to the landfill? For example, many of us love to wear fleece vests, but did you know that they are made from recycled plastic bottles? Much of what is considered trash need not go to the landfill at all. There are four ways we can prevent trash from being sent to the landfill. I call them the four R's. First, we can all reduce the amount of individually packaged goods that we send to the landfill by buying frequently used items in family-size or bulk containers. Next, we can reuse those containers, as well as other items, either for their original purpose or for another. Be creative. After a while, though, things will wear out after repeated use. Then it's a good time to try to restore them. If that, too, can no longer be done, then they should be recycled. Only after these options have failed should items be considered "real" trash and be removed to the landfill. Using the four R's—Reduce, Reuse, Restore, Recycle—we can reduce the amount of trash our campus sends to the landfill every semester.

This introduction clearly expresses the purpose of the editorial: to change readers' behavior regarding the amount of "trash" they throw out.

As this example shows, classification and division can be used to persuade readers toward or away from certain types of actions. As we will see in the essay "The Ways of Meeting Oppression" later in this chapter, Martin Luther King, Jr., by identifying three categories of protest, is able to cite historical precedents to argue against violent forms of protest and in favor of nonviolent ones. (Argumentation, one of the most powerful rhetorical modes, will be explained in detail in Chapter 12.)

FORMULATE A THESIS STATEMENT. When writing a division and classification essay, be sure that your thesis statement clearly presents the categories that you will be using to make your point. Here is an example from this chapter:

- *"Because girls' social hierarchies are complicated, I'm going to take you through a general breakdown of the different positions in the clique."* This thesis statement is from Rosalind Wiseman's "The Queen Bee and Her Court" (page 354). From this opening statement, the reader knows exactly what Wiseman intends to discuss and how.

When you begin to formulate your thesis statement, keep this example in mind. You could also look for other examples of thesis statements in the essays throughout this book. As you begin to develop your thesis statement, ask yourself the following questions: "What is my point?" "What categories will be most useful in making my point?" If you can't answer these questions, write down some ideas and try to determine your main point from these ideas.

Once you have settled on an idea, go back to the two questions above and write down your answers to them. Then combine the answers into a single thesis statement. (Your thesis statement does not necessarily have to be one sentence; making it one sentence, though, can be an effective way of focusing both your point and your categories.)

▶ Organizing and Writing Your Division and Classification Essay

ESTABLISH VALID CATEGORIES. When establishing categories, make sure that they meet three criteria:

- *The categories must be appropriate to your purpose.* In determining the factors affecting financial aid distribution among students at a particular school, you might consider family income, academic major, and athletic participation, but obviously you would not consider style of dress or preferred brand of toothpaste.
- *The categories must be consistent and mutually exclusive.* For example, dividing the student body into the classes men, women, and athletes would be illogical because athletes can be either male or female.

Instead, you could divide the student body into male athletes, female athletes, male nonathletes, and female nonathletes.

- *The categories must be complete, and they must account for all the members or aspects of your subject.* In dividing the student body according to place of birth, it would be inaccurate to consider only states in the United States; such a division would not account for foreign students or citizens born outside the country.

You may often find that a diagram (such as the one of families on Maple Street, shown on page 333), a chart, or a table can help you visualize your organization and help you make sure that your categories are appropriate, mutually exclusive, and complete.

Division and classification essays, when sensibly planned, can generally be organized with little trouble; an essay's chief divisions will reflect the classes into which you have divided the subject. A scratch outline can help you see those divisions and plan your presentation. For example, here is an outline of student Katie Angeles's essay "The Forgotten Personality Type" about how one personality type gets lost among all the others:

Four Personality Types:

1. Sanguine
    a. Popular
    b. "Life of the party"
    c. yellow bile

2. Melancholic
    a. Perfect
    b. "Busy bee"
    c. black bile

3. Choleric
    a. Powerful
    b. "Leader"
    c. blood

4. Phlegmatic
    a. Peaceful
    b. "Forgotten"
    c. phlegm

Such an outline clearly reveals the essay's overall structure.

STATE YOUR CONCLUSION. Your essay's purpose will determine the kinds of conclusions you reach. For example, a study of the student body of your college might show that 35 percent of male athletes are receiving scholarships, compared with 20 percent of female athletes, 15 percent of male nonathletes, and 10 percent of female nonathletes. These facts could provide a conclusion in themselves, or they might be the basis for a more controversial assertion about your school's athletic program. A study of dorm-room decor might conclude with the observation that juniors and seniors tend to have more elaborate rooms than first-year students. Your conclusion will depend on the way you work back and forth between the various classes you establish and the individual items available for you to classify.

▶ Revising and Editing Your Division and Classification Essay

Revision is best done by asking yourself (and others) key questions about what you have written. Along with the questions in the box below, try reading your essay aloud or asking a classmate to read through your writing, following the guidelines on page 36. If you or your classmate find any problems that you cannot think of a solution for, take a look at Chapter 16, which offers help for twelve common writing problems.

**Questions for Revising and Editing:
Division and Classification**

1. Is my subject a coherent entity that readily lends itself to analysis by division and classification?
2. Does the manner in which I divide my subject into categories help me achieve my purpose in writing the essay?
3. Does my thesis statement clearly identify the number and type of categories I will be using in my essay?
4. Do I stay focused on my subject and stay within the limits of my categories throughout my essay?
5. Do my categories meet the following three criteria: Are they appropriate to my purpose, consistent and mutually exclusive, and complete?
6. Have I organized my essay in a way that makes it easy for the reader to understand my categories and how they relate to my purpose?
7. Are there other rhetorical strategies that I can use to help achieve my purpose?
8. Is my use of headings and subheadings consistent? Could I use headings and subheadings to clarify the organization of my essay?
9. Does my paper contain any errors in grammar, punctuation, or mechanics? Is my sentence style as clear, smooth, and persuasive as possible?

But What Do You Mean?

DEBORAH TANNEN

Deborah Tannen, University Professor of linguistics at Georgetown University, was born in 1945 in Brooklyn, New York. Tannen received a bachelor's degree in English from the State University of New York at Binghamton in 1966 and taught English in Greece until 1968. She then earned a master's in English literature from Wayne State University in 1970. While pursuing her doctorate in linguistics at the University of California — Berkeley, she received several prizes for her poetry and short fiction. Her work has appeared in the *New York Times*, *Newsweek*, *Time*, the *Washington Post*, the *Harvard Business Review*, and *Politico*, among other places. In addition, she has authored three best-selling books on how people communicate: *You Just Don't Understand: Women and Men in Conversation* (1990), *That's Not What I Meant: How Conversational Style Makes or Breaks Relationships* (1991), and *Talking from Nine to Five: Women and Men at Work* (1994). The success of these books attests to the public's interest in language, especially when it pertains to gender differences. Tannen's other books include *I Only Say This Because I Love You: Talking to Your Parents, Partners, Sibs, and Kids When You're All Adults* (2002), *You're Wearing That? Mothers and Daughters in Conversation* (2006), and, most recently, *You Were Always Mom's Favorite: Sisters in Conversation throughout Their Lives* (2009).

In this essay, adapted from her book *Talking from Nine to Five*, Tannen looks at the differences between the ways men and women communicate. Interestingly, she concludes that, contrary to popular belief, directness is not necessarily logical or effective, and indirectness is not necessarily manipulative or insecure.

Courtesy of Deborah Tannen

Preparing to Read

How would you describe your communication style overall? Consider whether there are certain phrases you use often and whether you use statements more than questions or vice versa. Ask your friends and family members as well as relying on your own memory.

Conversation is a ritual. We say things that seem obviously the thing to say, without thinking of the literal meaning of our words, any more than we expect the question "How are you?" to call forth a detailed account of aches and pains.

Unfortunately, women and men often have different ideas about what's appropriate, different ways of speaking. Many of the conversational rituals common among women are designed to take the other person's feelings into account, while many of the conversational rituals common among men are designed to maintain the one-up position, or at least avoid appearing one-down. As a result, when men and women interact—especially at work—it's often women who are at the disadvantage. Because women are not trying to avoid the one-down position, that is unfortunately where they may end up.

Here, the biggest areas of miscommunication.

1. Apologies

Women are often told they apologize too much. The reason they're told to stop doing it is that, to many men, apologizing seems synonymous with putting oneself down. But there are many times when "I'm sorry" isn't self-deprecating, or even an apology; it's an automatic way of keeping both speakers on an equal footing. For example, a well-known columnist once interviewed me and gave me her phone number in case I needed to call her back. I misplaced the number and had to go through the newspaper's main switchboard. When our conversation was winding down and we'd both made ending-type remarks, I added, "Oh, I almost forgot—I lost your direct number, can I get it again?" "Oh, I'm sorry," she came back instantly, even though she had done nothing wrong and *I* was the one who'd lost the number. But I understood she wasn't really apologizing; she was just automatically reassuring me she had no intention of denying me her number.

> Women are often told they apologize too much.

Even when "I'm sorry" *is* an apology, women often assume it will be the first step in a two-step ritual: I say "I'm sorry" and take half the blame, then you take the other half. At work, it might go something like this:

A: When you typed this letter, you missed this phrase I inserted.

B: Oh, I'm sorry. I'll fix it.

A: Well, I wrote it so small it was easy to miss.

When both parties share blame, it's a mutual face-saving device. But if one person, usually the woman, utters frequent apologies and the other doesn't, she ends up looking as if she's taking the blame for mishaps that aren't her fault. When she's only partially to blame, she looks entirely in the wrong.

I recently sat in on a meeting at an insurance company where the sole woman, Helen, said "I'm sorry" or "I apologize" repeatedly. At one point she said, "I'm thinking out loud. I apologize." Yet the meeting was intended to be an informal brainstorming session, and *everyone* was thinking out loud.

The reason Helen's apologies stood out was that she was the only person in the room making so many. And the reason I was concerned was that Helen felt the annual bonus she had received was unfair. When I interviewed her colleagues, they said that Helen was one of the best and most productive workers—yet she got one of the smallest bonuses. Although the problem might have been outright sexism, I suspect her speech style, which differs from that of her male colleagues, masks her competence.

Unfortunately, not apologizing can have its price too. Since so many women use ritual apologies, those who don't may be seen as hard-edged. What's important is to be aware of how often you say you're sorry (and why), and to monitor your speech based on the reaction you get.

2. Criticism

A woman who cowrote a report with a male colleague was hurt when she read a rough draft to him and he leapt into a critical response—"Oh, that's too dry! You have to make it snappier!" She herself would have been more likely to say, "That's a really good start. Of course, you'll want to make it a little snappier when you revise."

Whether criticism is given straight or softened is often a matter of convention. In general, women use more softeners. I noticed this difference when talking to an editor about an essay I'd written. While going over changes she wanted to make, she said, "There's one more thing. I know you may not agree with me. The reason I noticed the problem is that your other points are so lucid and elegant." She went on hedging for several more sentences until I put her out of her misery: "Do you want to cut that part?" I asked—and of course she did. But I appreciated her tentativeness. In contrast, another editor (a man) I once called summarily rejected my idea for an article by barking, "Call me when you have something new to say."

Those who are used to ways of talking that soften the impact of criticism may find it hard to deal with the right-between-the-eyes style. It has its own logic, however, and neither style is intrinsically better. People who prefer criticism given straight are operating on an assumption that feelings aren't involved: "Here's the dope. I know you're good; you can take it."

3. Thank-Yous

A woman manager I know starts meetings by thanking everyone for coming, even though it's clearly their job to do so. Her "thank-you" is simply a ritual.

A novelist received a fax from an assistant in her publisher's office; it contained suggested catalog copy for her book. She immediately faxed him her suggested changes and said, "Thanks for running this by me," even though her contract gave her the right to approve all copy. When she thanked the assistant, she fully expected him to reciprocate: "Thanks for giving me such a quick response." Instead, he said, "You're welcome." Suddenly, rather than an equal exchange of pleasantries, she found herself positioned as the recipient of a favor. This made her feel like responding, "Thanks for nothing!"

Many women use "thanks" as an automatic conversation starter and closer; there's nothing literally to say thank you for. Like many rituals typical of women's conversation, it depends on the goodwill of the other to restore the balance. When the other speaker doesn't reciprocate, a woman may feel like someone on a seesaw whose partner abandoned his end. Instead of balancing in the air, she has plopped to the ground, wondering how she got there.

4. Fighting

Many men expect the discussion of ideas to be a ritual fight — explored through verbal opposition. They state their ideas in the strongest possible terms, thinking that if there are weaknesses someone will point them out, and by trying to argue against those objections, they will see how well their ideas hold up.

Those who expect their own ideas to be challenged will respond to another's ideas by trying to poke holes and find weak links — as a way *of helping*. The logic is that when you are challenged you will rise to the occasion: Adrenaline makes your mind sharper; you get ideas and insights you would not have thought of without the spur of battle.

But many women take this approach as a personal attack. Worse, they find it impossible to do their best work in such a contentious environment. If you're not used to ritual fighting, you begin to hear criticism of your ideas as soon as they are formed. Rather than making you think more clearly, it makes you doubt what you know. When you state your ideas, you hedge in order to fend off potential attacks. Ironically, this is more likely to *invite* attack because it makes you look weak.

Although you may never enjoy verbal sparring, some women find it helpful to learn how to do it. An engineer who was the only woman among four men in a small company found that as soon as she learned to argue she was accepted and taken seriously. A doctor attending a hospital staff meeting made a similar discovery. She was becoming more and more angry with a male colleague who'd loudly disagreed with a point she'd made. Her better judgment told her to hold her tongue, to avoid making an enemy of this powerful senior colleague. But finally she couldn't hold it in any longer, and she rose to her feet and delivered an impassioned attack on his position. She sat down in a panic, certain she had permanently damaged her relationship with him.

To her amazement, he came up to her afterward and said, "That was a great rebuttal. I'm really impressed. Let's go out for a beer after work and hash out our approaches to this problem."

5. Praise

A manager I'll call Lester had been on his new job six months when he heard that the women reporting to him were deeply dissatisfied. When he talked to them about it, their feelings erupted; two said they were on the verge of quitting because he didn't appreciate their work, and they didn't want to wait to be fired. Lester was dumbfounded: He believed they were doing a fine job. Surely, he thought, he had said nothing to give them the impression he didn't like their work. And indeed he hadn't. That was the problem. He had said *nothing*—and the women assumed he was following the adage "If you can't say something nice, don't say anything." He thought he was showing confidence in them by leaving them alone.

Men and women have different habits in regard to giving praise. For example, Deirdre and her colleague William both gave presentations at a conference. Afterward, Deirdre told William, "That was a great talk!" He thanked her. Then she asked, "What did you think of mine?" and he gave her a lengthy and detailed critique. She found it uncomfortable to listen to his comments. But she assured herself that he meant well, and that his honesty was a signal that she, too, should be honest when he asked for a critique of his performance. As a matter of fact, she had noticed quite a few ways in which he could have improved his presentation. But she never got a chance to tell him because he never asked—and she felt put down. The worst part was that it seemed she had only herself to blame, since she *had* asked what he thought of her talk.

But had she really asked for his critique? The truth is, when she asked for his opinion, she was expecting a compliment, which she felt was more or less required following anyone's talk. When he responded with criticism, she figured, "Oh, he's playing 'Let's critique each other'"—not a game she'd initiated, but one which she was willing to play. Had she realized he was going to criticize her and not ask her to reciprocate, she would never have asked in the first place.

It would be easy to assume that Deirdre was insecure, whether she was fishing for a compliment or soliciting a critique. But she was simply talking automatically, performing one of the many conversational rituals that allow us to get through the day. William may have sincerely misunderstood Deirdre's intention — or may have been unable to pass up a chance to one-up her when given the opportunity.

6. Complaints

"Troubles talk" can be a way to establish rapport with a colleague. You complain about a problem (which shows that you are just folks) and the other person responds with a similar problem (which puts you on equal footing). But while such commiserating is common among women, men are likely to hear it as a request to *solve* the problem.

One woman told me she would frequently initiate what she thought would be pleasant complaint-airing sessions at work. She'd talk about situations that bothered her just to talk about them, maybe to understand them better. But her male office mate would quickly tell her how she could improve the situation. This left her feeling condescended to and frustrated. She was delighted to see this very impasse in a section in my book *You Just Don't Understand,* and showed it to him. "Oh," he said, "I see the problem. How can we solve it?" Then they both laughed, because it had happened again: He short-circuited the detailed discussion she'd hoped for and cut to the chase of finding a solution.

Sometimes the consequences of complaining are more serious: A man might take a woman's lighthearted griping literally, and she can get a reputation as a chronic malcontent. Furthermore, she may be seen as not up to solving the problems that arise on the job.

7. Jokes

I heard a man call in to a talk show and say, "I've worked for two women and neither one had a sense of humor. You know, when you work with men, there's a lot of joking and teasing." The show's host and the guest (both women) took his comment at face value and assumed the women this man worked for were humorless. The guest said, "Isn't it sad that women don't feel comfortable enough with authority to see the humor?" The host said, "Maybe when more women are in authority roles, they'll be more comfortable with power." But although the women this man worked for *may* have taken themselves too seriously, it's just as likely that they each had a terrific sense of humor, but maybe the humor wasn't the type he was used to. They may have been like the woman who wrote to me: "When I'm with men, my wit or cleverness seems inappropriate (or lost!) so I don't bother. When I'm with my women friends, however, there's no hold on puns or cracks and my humor is fully appreciated."

The types of humor women and men tend to prefer differ. Research has shown that the most common form of humor among men is razzing, teasing, and mock-hostile attacks, while among women it's self-mocking. Women often mistake men's teasing as genuinely hostile. Men often mistake women's mock self-deprecation as truly putting themselves down.

Women have told me they were taken more seriously when they learned to joke the way the guys did. For example, a teacher who went to a national conference with seven other teachers (mostly women) and a group of administrators (mostly men) was annoyed that the administrators always found reasons to leave boring seminars, while the teachers felt they had to stay and take notes. One evening, when the group met at a bar in the hotel, the principal asked her how one such seminar had turned out. She retorted, "As soon as you left, it got much better." He laughed out loud at her response. The playful insult appealed to the men—but there was a trade-off. The women seemed to back off from her after this. (Perhaps they were put off by her using joking to align herself with the bosses.)

There is no "right" way to talk. When problems arise, the culprit may be style differences—and *all* styles will at times fail with others who don't share or understand them, just as English won't do you much good if you try to speak to someone who knows only French. If you want to get your message across, it's not a question of being "right"; it's a question of using language that's shared—or at least understood.

Thinking Critically about the Text

Do you agree with Tannen that "there is no 'right' way to talk" (paragraph 31)? Or do you think there are principles that should be followed no matter what the context? Are certain words or behaviors or styles always appropriate or, conversely, always inappropriate?

Questions on Subject

1. What is Tannen's thesis, and where do you find it? (Glossary: *Thesis*)
2. Into what categories does Tannen divide communication? Is her classification complete, or do you believe there are categories she has missed? If so, what are they?
3. In paragraph 4, Tannen cites an example from her own experience, explaining that a woman "wasn't really apologizing; she was just automatically reassuring

me she had no intention of denying me her number." Does Tannen's analysis seem accurate to you? What else might this woman have meant, in this context?

4. In paragraph 24, Tannen describes someone as "simply talking automatically, performing one of the many conversational rituals that allow us to get through the day." What do you think she means by this? How do conversational rituals help us get through the day?

Questions on Strategy

1. What is Tannen's purpose in this essay? Where is it stated? (Glossary: *Purpose*)
2. The title of this essay is "But What Do You Mean?" Why do you think Tannen chose to use a question rather than a statement as her title? What is its effect?
3. Where does Tannen use comparison in this essay? Who or what does she compare, and how do these comparisons support her thesis? (Glossary: *Comparison and Contrast*)
4. Tannen relies heavily on illustration in this essay. Are all her examples effective? Are there any you would drop? Which resonate most with you? Are there other types of evidence that might have made her essay stronger? (Glossary: *Illustration*)
5. How does Tannen organize her categories? Do you find this organization effective? (Glossary: *Organization*)

Questions on Diction and Vocabulary

1. How would you describe Tannen's diction in this essay? What words and phrases lead you to this conclusion? (Glossary: *Diction*)
2. Refer to a dictionary to determine the meanings of the following words as Tannen uses them in this selection: *self-deprecating* (paragraph 4), *convention* (11), *tentativeness* (11), *intrinsically* (12), *reciprocate* (14), *adrenaline* (17), *rebuttal* (20), *soliciting* (24), *rapport* (25), *malcontent* (27).

Division and Classification in Action

Imagine that you have the opportunity to meet the authors of this text. What would you like to tell them about the book's strengths and weaknesses? Consider the chapter introductions, model essays, questions surrounding the essays, and anything else you'd like to comment on. Make a chart with three columns, labeled, from left to right, "Part of Book," "Direct Comment," and "Indirect Comment." Now fill in your chart, crafting two different versions of each comment you'd like to share with the authors. In column 2, try to be as concise as possible. In column 3, try to be as considerate and sensitive as you can.

Writing Suggestions

1. Using your answer to the Preparing to Read prompt as a starting point, write an essay describing your communication style. Do you think you express yourself well, or do you often feel misunderstood? Analyze your own communication strengths and weaknesses, using examples of real conversations you've had. Consider each of Tannen's seven categories: apologies, criticism, thank-yous, fighting, praise, complaints, and jokes. Which do you employ, and how well do they work? How might you alter your communication style to make it more effective or successful?

2. Think of a time you received what Tannen calls "softened" criticism and a time you received direct, abrupt criticism, perhaps from your parents or at school or at work. To which kind did you respond better? Why do you think that's the case? Write an essay comparing these episodes. Describe the contexts and be sure to use dialogue to illustrate your points.

3. In paragraph 15, Tannen writes that "many rituals typical of women's conversation" depend on "the goodwill of the other [speaker] to restore the balance." Do you believe this only happens to women, or are there other circumstances in which this dynamic is likely to occur? Write an essay about a time you expected "an equal exchange of pleasantries" (paragraph 15) but were shut down. Use narration, description, and illustration to depict the circumstances and tell your story.

The Queen Bee and Her Court

ROSALIND WISEMAN

Rosalind Wiseman has had only one job since graduating from Occidental College in Los Angeles in 1988—to help communities shift the way we think about children and teens' emotional and physical wellbeing. As a teacher, thought leader, author, and media spokesperson on bullying, ethical leadership, the use of social media, and media literacy, she is in constant dialogue and collaboration with educators, parents, children, and teens.

Rosalind is the author of *Queen Bees and Wannabes: Helping Your Daughter Survive Cliques, Gossip, Boyfriends, and the New Realities of Girl World*—the groundbreaking, best-selling book that was the basis for the movie *Mean Girls*. Her latest book, *Masterminds & Wingmen: Helping Our Boys Cope with Schoolyard Power, Locker-Room Tests, Girlfriends, and the New Rules of Boy World* was published in September 2013. In addition, she wrote a free companion e-book for high school boys, entitled *The Guide: Managing Douchebags, Recruiting Wingmen, and Attracting Who You Want* and a school edition entitled, *The Guide: Managing Jerks, Recruiting Wingmen, and Attracting Who You Want.*

National media regularly depends on Rosalind as the expert on ethical leadership, media literacy and bullying prevention. She has been profiled in *The New York Times, People, Los Angeles Times, Chicago Tribune, The Washington Post,* and *USA Today.* She is a frequent guest on *The Today Show, Anderson Cooper 360, CNN, Good Morning America, Al Jazeera,* and *NPR* affiliates throughout the country.

In 2011, she was one of the principal speakers at the White House Summit on Bullying. Other audiences have included the American School Counselors Association, International Chiefs of Police, American Association of School Administrators, and countless schools throughout the US and abroad. She is a consultant for Cartoon Network's Speak Up, Stop Bullying Campaign and an advisor to the US Department of Health and Human Services' Substance Abuse and Mental Health Administration.

In "The Queen Bee and Her Court," an excerpt from *Queen Bee and Wannabes,* 3rd edition, Wiseman divides and classifies young schoolgirls into various hierarchical social classes dominated by the "Queen Bee."

Preparing to Read

How did the various cliques work in your elementary school and high school? What roles did you play within those cliques?

We need to give girls credit for the sophistication of their social structures. Our best politicians and diplomats can't match a girl who understands the social intrigue and political landscape that lead to power. Cliques are sophisticated, complex, and multilayered, and every girl has a role within them. However, positions in cliques aren't static. A girl can lose her position to another girl, and she can move up and down the social hierarchy. The reality is that few girls are stuck in one role, and they can often have moments of being something else or a combination. Here are the different roles that your daughter and her friends might play:

Queen Bee	Pleaser/Wannabe
Sidekick	Torn Bystander
Banker	Target
Messenger	Champion

Because girls' social hierarchies are complicated, I'm going to take you through a general breakdown of the different positions in the clique. But putting labels on girls' behavior can be tricky—and counterproductive. No one, girls included, likes other people to label them. I came up with these characterizations as a way for girls and the people who care about them to identify why a girl acts a specific way when she's in a group, and help them understand the possible consequences. Ideally, a label should be something a person decides to pick and associate with herself—even if there are negative things connected to that label. Likewise, a person should be able to take off a label when it no longer feels right to them.

Girls aren't unique. Every one of us has interacted in various kinds of groups since we were children, so we have all learned ways to operate within them. We may not be thinking about it, but we all learn to constantly assess our social power and influence throughout our lives. For girls, think of it this way: Everyone, even the girl with the highest social status, has moments in her life of trying to please someone with more power. But what's important to notice is that the roles emerge in full force when there's conflict in the group, or when someone in the group is abusing their power. Instantaneously, each person's role emerges. The behavior behind these roles is in the girls' programming.

But girls can change their roles or play different roles in different environments. A girl may act like a Queen Bee at school but be a Pleaser on her soccer or basketball team. A Queen Bee can have a Champion moment. A Champion can get into such a tough situation that she acts more like a Torn Bystander. Also, your daughter doesn't have to be in the "popular" group to play a role within her group of friends. So if and when you talk to your daughter, or any girl, about cliques, encourage her to come up with her own names and create roles she thinks I've missed. If you can answer yes to the majority of items for each role, you've identified a pattern of behavior that could connect to the girl you're reading this for. Now let's break down what those these roles are.

THE QUEEN BEE

Through a combination of charisma, force, money, looks, will, and social intelligence, this girl reigns supreme over the other girls and weakens their friendships with others, thereby strengthening her own power and influence. Never underestimate her power over other girls (and boys as well). She can and will silence her peers with a look and then turn around and be incredibly nice. But the bottom line is you're on her side or else — you are with her or against her.

> She will do anything to have control. She will humiliate you in front of your whole grade, just if you are getting a little attention from boys, even if the boys are just your friends. —KELLY, FOURTEEN

Your Daughter Is a Queen Bee If . . .

- Her friends do what she wants them to do.
- She isn't intimidated by other girls in her class.
- She complains about other people copying her, never leaving her alone, or being too sensitive.
- When she's hanging out in a group, she's in the center. When she moves, they follow.
- She can argue or charm anyone down, including friends, peers, teachers, and parents.
- She can make another girl feel "anointed" by declaring her a special friend.
- She's strategically affectionate. For example, she sees two girls in her group, one she's pleased with and one she isn't. When she greets them, she'll throw her arms around one and insist that they sit together and barely say anything to the other.
- She won't (or is reluctant to) take responsibility when she hurts someone's feelings.
- If she thinks she's been wronged, she feels she has the right to seek revenge and will do so.

> She thinks she's better than everyone else. She's in control, intimidating, smart, caring, and has the power to make others feel good or bad. She'll make stuff up about people and everyone will believe her. —ANNE, FIFTEEN

If you have a sinking feeling in your stomach because you're recognizing your daughter in what I've written above, that's a good thing — it just doesn't feel like it. If you are thinking, "How can my daughter already be a Queen Bee at the age of seven?" it's absolutely possible. Seeing it now means you have a better chance of addressing it.

What Does She Gain by Being a Queen Bee?

She feels power and control over her environment. She's the center of attention, and people pay homage to her.

What Does She Lose by Being a Queen Bee?

Her friendships are defined by power, not mutual support, trust, or care. She can be cynical about her friendships with both boys and girls. She may easily feel that she can't admit to anyone when she's in over her head because her reputation dictates that she always has everything and everyone under control.

I want to share with you an experience I had in a middle school. It resonates with me because it's not often that I come across Queen Bees who admit their fall from power. I'd just finished an assembly with the sixth grade when the counselor asked me if I could talk to a couple of girls. I looked over in the corner to see two beautiful girls with stick-straight brown hair, button-down shirts, plaid skirts, and Ugg boots throwing furtive glances in my direction.

"Hi, girls, what's up?" I said.

Both girls scanned the room anxiously. The smaller one pushed her long bangs out of her face. "OK, we were in this clique with four other girls, but they kicked both of us out. They now talk bad about us and have code words for my name. It's really bad . . ." She looked away, obviously trying not to cry. "When I try to talk to any of them, they just walk away and whisper to each other and laugh."

The other girl broke in, "We've tried to talk to them. But they just throw it back in our face. I know we used to be the Queen Bees, but now I cry every night. And I know the school didn't like us in the group because sometimes I guess we were mean to people. Now . . . I guess I know what it feels like. . . . I guess they were never my friends."

For twenty minutes we talked candidly. One admitted that she had "a serious problem wanting to know everyone's business all the time." They knew they'd abused their power, and that their victims weren't sympathetic to their plight. I left them with a plan based on the idea that this could be a life-changing moment for both of them. Could they learn from this and use their dynamic, powerful personalities for good? Would they remember what it felt like to be excluded and betrayed, and speak out when it was happening to someone else?

But my other reason for sharing this experience is that a lot of people love to see Queen Bees brought down. Of course, we need to hold the Queen Bees accountable for wielding their power unethically, but we also need to be there to catch them when they fall. Remember, they're still girls. What I want you to take away from this is the understanding that even Queen Bees experience the negative effects of cliques.

If you find out that your daughter has been acting like a Queen Bee, you can't let your anger get the best of you. She can see that you're angry. She can see that you're disappointed. She can even see that her behavior contradicts what you stand for, but you need to come across as wanting to know why it was so important to her to act this way. And if you've just finished this section and thought, "Well, I'd rather have a Queen Bee than a pushover," check yourself. I don't want your daughter to be a pushover either, but we need girls who are effective leaders who don't want to crush others.

THE SIDEKICK

She's the lieutenant or second in command—the girl who's closest to the Queen Bee and will back her no matter what because her power depends on the confidence she gets from the Queen Bee. Together they appear to other girls as an impenetrable force. They commonly bully and silence other girls to advance their own agenda. The Queen Bee and Sidekick are usually the first to focus on boys. The difference between the two is that if you separate the Sidekick from the Queen Bee, the Sidekick can alter her behavior for the better, while the Queen Bee would be more likely to find another Sidekick and begin again. On the other hand, sometimes a Sidekick can stage a coup against the Queen Bee and take over her position.

Your Daughter Is a Sidekick If . . .

- She's jealous of someone else being friends with the Queen Bee.
- The Queen Bee is your daughter's authority figure, not you.
- She feels like it's just the two of them and everyone else is a Wannabe (see the Pleaser/Wannabe section).
- You think her best friend pushes her around.

> She notices everything about the Queen Bee. She will do everything the Queen Bee says and wants to be her. She lies for the Queen Bee, but she isn't as pretty as the Queen Bee. —MADELINE, FOURTEEN

What Does She Gain by Being a Sidekick?

A Sidekick has power over other girls that she wouldn't have without the Queen Bee. She has a close friend who makes her feel popular and included.

What Does She Lose by Being a Sidekick?

If she's with the Queen Bee too long, she may forget she ever had her own opinion. Her sense of self and identity is entirely formed around her alliance with another girl.

THE BANKER

Information about other people is currency in Girl World—whoever has the most information has the most power. I call that girl the "Banker." She creates chaos by banking information about girls in her social sphere and dispensing it at strategic intervals.

For instance, if a girl has said something negative about another girl, the Banker will casually mention it to someone in conversation because she knows it's going to cause a conflict and strengthen her status as someone in the know. She can get girls to trust her because when she pumps them for information it doesn't seem like gossip; instead, she does it in an innocent, "I'm trying to be there for you" kind of way.

> Her power lies in getting girls to confide in her. Once they figure out she can't be trusted, it's too late because she already has information on them, and in order to keep her from revealing things, girls will be nice to her.
> —Leigh, seventeen

The Banker can be as powerful as the Queen Bee, but it's easy to mistake her for the Messenger, the next in line in the hierarchy. The Banker is usually really cute, quiet, and withdrawn in front of adults. This is the girl who sneaks under adult radar all the time because she seems so harmless.

Your Daughter Is a Banker If . . .

- She is extremely secretive.
- She thinks in complex, strategic ways.
- She seems to be friends with everyone; some girls even treat her like a pet.
- She's rarely the subject of fights.
- She's rarely excluded from the group.

> She's the switchboard operator for all the gossip. —Tessa, eighteen

What Does She Gain by Being a Banker?

She gets to create drama. The Banker is confusing to other girls because she seems harmless yet everyone is afraid of her. People come to her for advice and affirmation.

What Does She Lose by Being a Banker?

Once other girls figure out what she's doing, they don't trust her. With her utilitarian mind-set, she can forget to look to other girls as a trusted resource. If girls do organize against her, it can be really hurtful and unsettling because she's never been on that end of it.

> The girls can't oust the Banker from the clique because she has information on everyone and could make or break reputations based on the information she knows. —CHARLOTTE, FIFTEEN

THE MESSENGER

The Messenger also trades personal information and gossip about others; however, she differs from the Banker in that she wants to prove her usefulness to the other girls in the group. She rationalizes her behavior by saying that she wants to help the girls get along better or reconcile. By doing this, she hopes to gain recognition and social power. Parents can easily misread their daughter if she's the Messenger, because they see her peacemaking efforts as being entirely altruistic.

Your Daughter Is a Messenger If . . .

- She lives for drama, and she's obvious about it.
- She loves to "help" people out when they are in fights, which most parents describe as "just wanting everyone to get along."
- When a conflict arises between girls, it's all she thinks about.
- She gets an adrenaline rush from being in the middle of a conflict (but it looks to unsuspecting adults as if her only motivation is caring too much, wanting everyone to get along, and trying to make peace).
- She feels better about herself when other girls come to her for help.

What Does She Gain by Being a Messenger?

She feels valued, because friendships will be made or broken based on her involvement.

What Does She Lose by Being a Messenger?

Her position is precarious. Others can easily turn on her, especially if she gets information wrong (which she inevitably will because it's too hard to keep all the details right) or if others deny what she's claimed. She can be easily used, manipulated, and then discarded when no longer useful.

THE PLEASER/WANNABE

This person will do almost anything to be in the group or gain favor from the Queen Bee or the Sidekick. She often observes and imitates their behavior, clothes, and interests but never feels completely in the group—that's why she's always proving her loyalty to the more powerful girls. As a result, she can give up what's important to her and/or what she enjoys. She constantly anticipates what people want from her but doesn't ask herself what she wants in return.

Your Daughter Is a Pleaser/Wannabe If . . .

- Other girls' opinions and wants are more important than her own.
- Her opinions on dress, style, friends, and "in" celebrities constantly change according to what the Queen Bee does and says.
- She has trouble developing personal boundaries and communicating them to others.
- She can't tell the difference between what she wants and what the group wants.
- She's desperate to have the "right" look (clothes, hair, and so forth).
- She'll stop doing things she likes because she fears the clique's disapproval.
- She avoids conflicts. Her common response when asked her opinion is, "Whatever you want, doesn't matter to me."

What Does She Gain by Being a Pleaser/Wannabe?

She has the feeling that she belongs.

What Does She Lose by Being a Pleaser/Wannabe?

Frankly, almost all girls and women have moments of being the Pleaser. Because girls are rewarded for being "nice," pleasing behavior is reinforced because it is socially condoned. Therefore, it's really hard to see when a girl is sacrificing her personal boundaries. As a result, many pleasers have low self-esteem from sacrificing their needs and judgment. Pleasers often assume that the more they please, the more liked they will be, or positively recognized for their actions. But, ironically, that's not true. Instead, the more Pleasers accommodate, the worse people treat them.

> She thinks she belongs, but the Queen Bee and the Sidekick are just using her; she'll lose all her friends, then the Queen Bee and her Sidekick will destroy her reputation. Don't be a Pleaser/Wannabe if you can help it.
> —Trinity, sixteen

THE TORN BYSTANDER

She doesn't want to go against the more powerful people in the group and usually convinces herself not to challenge them. She wants to help the Target, the next in line, but she is not sure how, or thinks it won't make a difference. She may rationalize her own silence or apologize for others' behavior.

Your Daughter Is a Torn Bystander If . . .

- She's always finding herself in situations where she has to choose between friends.
- She tries to accommodate everyone.
- She's not good at saying no to her friends.
- She wants everyone "to get along."
- She can't imagine standing up to anyone she has a conflict with; she goes along to get along.

> She's confused and insecure because her reputation is over if she doesn't stick with the Queen Bee, but she can be really cool when she's alone.
> —Anne, thirteen

What Does She Gain by Being a Torn Bystander?

Her silence buys her acceptance into the group. In high-social-status groups, that also means she has increased access to popularity, high social status herself, and boys.

What Does She Lose by Being a Torn Bystander?

Her fear of the Queen Bee or other girls in power can be so terrifying that she never learns to take a stand. She can't imagine having the personal power to do it. So she's smart enough to know something's wrong but feels incapable of exerting any influence over the situation.

THE TARGET

She's the girl who gets set up by the other girls to be humiliated, made fun of, and/or excluded. Targets are assumed to be out of the clique. Although this is sometimes true, it's not always the case. A girl in the clique not only can be targeted by another girl in the group, but it's often a strategy to reinforce the power dynamics between the girls. Often the social hierarchy of the clique is maintained precisely by having someone clearly at the bottom of the social ladder. Girls who are consistently targeted tend to be perceived to be trying too hard, or are targeted because their style of dress, behavior, or personal background is outside the norms acceptable to the clique.

Your Daughter Is a Target If . . .

- She may be very rule oriented and inflexible or anxious.
- She feels helpless to stop the girls' behavior.
- She feels she has no allies. No one will back her up.
- She may struggle to read people's social cues.
- She can mask her hurt by rejecting people first, saying she doesn't like anyone.

This role can be harder to figure out than you would think, and your daughter may be too embarrassed to tell you. She might admit she feels excluded, or she might just withdraw from you and "not want to talk about it." That's why I'll discuss how to talk with your daughter in the next chapter.

> Targets don't want to tell their parents because they don't want their parents to think they're a loser or a nobody. —JENNIFER, SIXTEEN

What Does She Gain by Being a Target?

This may seem like an odd question, but being a Target can have some hidden benefits. There's nothing like being targeted to teach your daughter about empathy and understanding for people who are bullied and/or discriminated against. Being a Target can also give her objectivity. She can see the costs of fitting in and decide she's better off outside the clique because at least she can be true to herself and/or find good friends who like her for who she is, not for her social standing. Remember the girl who wrote that she was in the loser clique but at least she knew her friends were true friends? A lot of girls don't have that security. But in general, the benefits of having these experiences usually become clear to girls as they get older. In the meantime, being the Target can be excruciating. At the least, it doesn't seem like a very good trade-off for being made fun of now.

What Does She Lose by Being a Target?

She can feel helpless in the face of other girls' cruelty. She feels ashamed of being rejected by the other girls because of who she is. She'll be tempted to change herself in order to fit in. She feels vulnerable and unable to affect the outcome of her situation. She could become so anxious that she can't concentrate on schoolwork.

> If a girl's stuck in a degrading clique, it's the same as when she's later in a bad relationship. She doesn't expect to be treated any better. —ELLEN, FIFTEEN

THE CHAMPION

> In every girl there is a Champion who wants to get out. —JOANNA, SEVENTEEN

In the first edition, I called these people the "Floaters," but I don't think that was a clear enough definition—and way too many people insisted to me that their daughter was one. So now, I'm calling this person the "Champion." But it's not like this person is walking around all the time being the Champion. The main goal of this book is to help your daughter have more Champion moments at every age. She can take criticism, doesn't make people choose friends, and doesn't blow off someone for a better offer. She has friends in different groups and doesn't treat people differently when groups are together. She can and will stand up to the Queen Bee in a way that treats them both with dignity.

You can usually spot this girl because she doesn't associate with only one clique. She has friends in different groups but can move freely among them (but remember, so did the Banker who wrote to me in the beginning of the chapter).

Your Daughter Is a Champion If . . .

- She doesn't want to exclude people; you aren't always having fights with her about spending time with people she considers "losers."
- Her friends are comfortable around her and don't seem intimidated; she's not "winning" all the conversations.
- She's not exclusively tied to one group of friends.
- She can and is willing to bring another person into a group of friends.

What Does She Lose by Being a Champion?

Being a Champion is more complicated than it looks. A parent wrote me the following about her own childhood. I bet a lot of Champions can relate to her experiences.

> I was widely respected and liked. I could float among the groups with ease, could stick up for anyone at will (and usually did). But I never belonged to anything in particular, and that is true of all floaters. Also, those girls that do stick by their principles and behave admirably during junior high school are respected, but generally shunned. I was particularly prized as a foul-weather friend, because I was kind, practical, and always kept people's secrets; but when things were going well, I was not particularly needed. What the floater learns is that she is, and probably has to be, an island unto herself. That she has the backbone to live by her principles, but that this will come at a price. I feel like being a responsible, well-respected floater left me cut adrift and a little bit old before my time. —ELLE

Our goal is to have more Champion moments—in all of our lives, not just those of our daughters. Think of it this way: If your daughter has a moment of being the Banker, the Messenger, or even the Queen Bee, and you can face it with integrity and honesty—that is your Champion moment.

Thinking Critically about the Text

How real for you is the social classification system that Wiseman establishes in this selection? If you are a woman, where would you place your younger self in the hierarchy? Do you think a similar classification would work for boys? What about students who don't identify with a particular gender? How might they fit into this classification?

Questions on Subject

1. What characteristics does the Queen Bee possess, according to Wiseman? Would you add or subtract any characteristics? Explain.
2. Throughout her essay, Wiseman includes quotes from young girls, offering their own accounts of the characters. How effective do you find these quotations? What do they add, if anything, to Wiseman's classification system?
3. For every character type, Wiseman includes a formulaic set of questions: "What does she gain by being an *X*?" and "What does she lose by being an *X*?" Why do you suppose she uses that formula? (Glossary: *Cause and Effect Analysis*)
4. Wiseman states that each character in the hierarchy gains from her position — even the Target. Do you agree? Explain.
5. What explanation does Wiseman give for the development of cliques? (Glossary: *Cause and Effect Analysis*)

Questions on Strategy

1. What does Wiseman mean when she writes that "cliques are sophisticated, complex, and multilayered, and every girl has a role within them" (paragraph 1)? Is this statement her thesis? (Glossary: *Thesis*)
2. What does Wiseman hope to gain when she advises that "when you talk to your daughter about cliques, encourage her to come up with her own names and create roles she thinks I've missed" (paragraph 4)? Why is her advice a useful strategy, given her subject and audience? (Glossary: *Audience; Subject*)
3. Into what classes does Wiseman divide all young girls?
4. Explain how Wiseman has organized her essay. (Glossary: *Organization*) Is that organizational pattern effective? Explain.
5. Wiseman's division and classification is supported by her use of definition, illustration, and comparison and contrast. (Glossary: *Comparison and Contrast; Definition; Illustration*) How do these supporting strategies strengthen her essay?

Questions on Diction and Vocabulary

1. How effective is Wiseman's title? (Glossary: *Title*) How effective are the names she gives each class? Would you change any of those names? If so, why?
2. What is Wiseman's attitude toward cliques? (Glossary: *Attitude*) What in her diction indicates that attitude? (Glossary: *Diction*)
3. Refer to a dictionary to determine the meanings of the following words as Wiseman uses them in this selection: *clique* (paragraph 1), *anointed* (7), *cynical* (11), *agenda* (19), *utilitarian* (30), *oust* (31), *precarious* (41), *rationalize* (35).

Division and Classification in Action

Think about how you might classify people within one of the following groups:

athletes

commuters

college students

Compare your method of classification with the method used by others in your class who chose the same category. What conclusions can you draw from the differences?

Writing Suggestions

1. Rosalind Wiseman offers her classification system for the roles that young girls play in cliques. But what about boys' cliques? Write a classification essay in which you divide and classify schoolboys on the basis of their behavioral characteristics and the roles they play within cliques. Model your organization on Wiseman's, modify her design, or create an entirely new approach.

2. What about parents? Can we classify them into some recognizable and meaningful classes and subclasses? Jim Fay of the Love and Logic Institute in Golden, Colorado, thinks so. He classifies parents into three groups: the Consultant who "provides guidance," the Helicopter "who hovers over children and rescues them from the hostile world in which they live," and the Drill Sergeant "who commands and directs the lives of children." Think about your parents and talk to your friends, the students in your class, and others to gather opinions about the various parenting approaches. Use the information to write an essay in which you classify parents. Be sure to define each class clearly and provide examples of their behavior. (Glossary: *Definition; Illustration*)

3. The photograph below depicts a common scene of a group of girls sitting, talking, and passing the time together. How do you "read" this photograph? What might the girls' facial expressions, body language, hairstyles, and dress tell you about them as individuals? As members of the group? What does their configuration on the steps tell you about their roles in the group? Write an essay in which you analyze the photograph and speculate about this group of girls and the dynamics that may hold them together as well as separate them.

© Stefanie Felix

The Truth about Lying

JUDITH VIORST

Judith Viorst, poet, journalist, author of children's books, and novelist, was born in 1931. She has chronicled her life in such books as *It's Hard to Be Hip Over Thirty and Other Tragedies of Married Life* (1968), *How Did I Get to Be Forty and Other Atrocities* (1976), and *When Did I Stop Being Twenty and Other Injustices: Selected Prose from Single to Mid-Life* (1987). In 1981, she went back to school, taking courses at the Washington Psychoanalytic Institute. This study, along with her personal experience of psychoanalysis, helped to inspire *Necessary Losses* (1986), a popular and critical success. Combining theory, poetry, interviews, and anecdotes, Viorst approaches personal growth as a shedding of illusions. She is also the author of the acclaimed children's book *Alexander and the Terrible, Horrible, No Good, Very Bad Day*.

Brendan Smialowski/The New York Times/Redux

In this essay, first published in the March 1981 issue of *Redbook*, the author approaches lying with delicacy and candor as she carefully classifies the different types of lies we all encounter.

Preparing to Read

Lying happens every day in our society, whether it is a politician hiding behind a subtly worded statement or a guest fibbing to a host about the quality of a meal. What, for you, constitutes lying? Are all lies the same? In other words, are there different degrees or types of lying?

I've been wanting to write on a subject that intrigues and challenges me: the subject of lying. I've found it very difficult to do. Everyone I've talked to has a quite intense and personal but often rather intolerant point of view about what we can—and can never *never*—tell lies about. I've finally reached the conclusion that I can't present any ultimate conclusions, for too many people would promptly disagree. Instead, I'd like to present a series of moral puzzles, all concerned with lying. I'll tell you what I think about them. Do you agree?

SOCIAL LIES

Most of the people I've talked with say that they find social lying acceptable and necessary. They think it's the civilized way for folks to behave. Without these little white lies, they say, our relationships would be short and brutish and nasty. It's arrogant, they say, to insist on being so incorruptible and so brave that you cause other people unnecessary embarrassment or pain by compulsively assailing them with your honesty. I basically agree. What about you?

Will you say to people, when it simply isn't true, "I like your new hairdo," "You're looking much better," "It's so nice to see you," "I had a wonderful time"?

Will you praise hideous presents and homely kids?

Will you decline invitations with "We're busy that night—so sorry we can't come," when the truth is you'd rather stay home than dine with the So-and-sos?

And even though, as I do, you may prefer the polite evasion of "You really cooked up a storm" instead of "The soup"—which tastes like warmed-over coffee—"is wonderful," will you, if you must, proclaim it wonderful?

There's one man I know who absolutely refuses to tell social lies. "I can't play that game," he says; "I'm simply not made that way." And his answer to the argument that saying nice things to someone doesn't cost anything is, "Yes, it does—it destroys your credibility." Now, he won't, unsolicited, offer his views on the painting you just bought, but you don't ask his frank opinion unless you want *frank*, and his silence at those moments when the rest of us liars are muttering, "Isn't it lovely?" is, for the most part, eloquent enough. My friend does not indulge in what he calls "flattery, false praise, and mellifluous comments." When others tell fibs he will not go along. He says that social lying is lying, that little white lies are still lies. And he feels that telling lies is morally wrong. What about you?

PEACE-KEEPING LIES

Many people tell peace-keeping lies; lies designed to avoid irritation or argument; lies designed to shelter the liar from possible blame or pain; lies (or so it is rationalized) designed to keep trouble at bay without hurting anyone.

I tell these lies at times, and yet I always feel they're wrong. I understand why we tell them, but still they feel wrong. And whenever I lie so that someone won't disapprove of me or think less of me or holler at me, I feel I'm a bit of a coward, I feel I'm dodging responsibility, I feel . . . guilty. What about you?

Do you, when you're late for a date because you overslept, say that you're late because you got caught in a traffic jam?

Do you, when you forget to call a friend, say that you called several times but the line was busy?

Do you, when you didn't remember that it was your father's birthday, say that his present must be delayed in the mail?

And when you're planning a weekend in New York City and you're not in the mood to visit your mother, who lives there, do you conceal—with a lie, if you must — the fact that you'll be in New York? Or do you have the courage — or is it the cruelty? — to say, "I'll be in New York, but sorry — I don't plan on seeing you"?

(Dave and his wife Elaine have two quite different points of view on this very subject. He calls her a coward. She says she's being wise. He says she must assert her right to visit New York sometimes and not see her mother. To which she always patiently replies: "Why should we have useless fights? My mother's too old to change. We get along much better when I lie to her.")

Finally, do you keep the peace by telling your husband lies on the subject of money? Do you reduce what you really paid for your shoes? And in general do you find yourself ready, willing and able to lie to him when you make absurd mistakes or lose or break things?

"I used to have a romantic idea that part of intimacy was confessing every dumb thing that you did to your husband. But after a couple of years of that," says Laura, "have I changed my mind!"

And having changed her mind, she finds herself telling peace-keeping lies. And yes, I tell them, too. What about you?

PROTECTIVE LIES

Protective lies are lies folks tell — often quite serious lies — because they're convinced that the truth would be too damaging. They lie because they feel there are certain human values that supersede the wrong of having lied. They lie, not for personal gain, but because they believe it's for the good of the person they're lying to. They lie to those they love, to those who trust them most of all, on the grounds that breaking this trust is justified.

They may lie to their children on money or marital matters.

They may lie to the dying about the state of their health.

They may lie about adultery, and not — or so they insist — to save their own hide, but to save the heart and the pride of the men they are married to.

They may lie to their closest friend because the truth about her talents or son or psyche would be — or so they insist — utterly devastating.

I sometimes tell such lies, but I'm aware that it's quite presumptuous to claim I know what's best for others to know. That's called playing God. That's called manipulation and control. And we never can be sure, once we start to juggle lies, just where they'll land, exactly where they'll roll.

And furthermore, we may find ourselves lying in order to back up the lies that are backing up the lie we initially told.

And furthermore — let's be honest — if conditions were reversed, we certainly wouldn't want anyone lying to us.

Yet, having said all that, I still believe that there are times when protective lies must nonetheless be told. What about you?

If your Dad had a very bad heart and you had to tell him some bad family news, which would you choose: to tell him the truth or lie?

If your former husband failed to send his monthly child-support check and in other ways behaved like a total rat, would you allow your children — who believed he was simply wonderful — to continue to believe that he was wonderful?

If your dearly beloved brother selected a wife whom you deeply disliked, would you reveal your feelings or would you fake it?

And if you were asked, after making love, "And how was that for you?" would you reply, if it wasn't too good, "Not too good"?

Now, some would call a sex lie unimportant, little more than social lying, a simple act of courtesy that makes all human intercourse run smoothly. And some would say all sex lies are bad news and unacceptably protective. Because, says Ruth, "a man with an ego that fragile doesn't need your lies — he needs a psychiatrist." Still others feel that sex lies are indeed protective lies, more serious than simple social lying, and yet at times they tell them on the grounds that when it comes to matters sexual, everybody's ego is somewhat fragile.

"If most of the time things go well in sex," says Sue, "I think you're allowed to dissemble when they don't. I can't believe it's good to say, 'Last night was four stars, darling, but tonight's performance rates only a half.'"

I'm inclined to agree with Sue. What about you?

TRUST-KEEPING LIES

Another group of lies are trust-keeping lies, lies that involve triangulation, with *A* (that's you) telling lies to *B* on behalf of *C* (whose trust you'd promised to keep). Most people concede that once you've agreed not to betray a friend's confidence, you can't betray it, even if you must lie. But I've talked with people who don't want you telling them anything that they might be called on to lie about.

"I don't tell lies for myself," says Fran, "and I don't want to have to tell them for other people." Which means, she agrees, that if her best friend is having an affair, she absolutely doesn't want to know about it.

"Are you saying," her best friend asks, "that if I went off with a lover and I asked you to tell my husband I'd been with you, that you wouldn't lie for me, that you'd betray me?"

Fran is very pained but very adamant. "I wouldn't want to betray you, so . . . don't ask me."

Fran's best friend is shocked. What about you?

Do you believe you can have close friends if you're not prepared to receive their deepest secrets?

Do you believe you must always lie for your friends?

Do you believe, if your friend tells a secret that turns out to be quite immoral or illegal, that once you've promised to keep it, you must keep it?

And what if your friend were your boss—if you were perhaps one of the President's men—would you betray or lie for him over, say, Watergate?

As you can see, these issues get terribly sticky.

It's my belief that once we've promised to keep a trust, we must tell lies to keep it. I also believe that we can't tell Watergate lies. And if these two statements strike you as quite contradictory, you're right—they're quite contradictory. But for now they're the best I can do. What about you?

Some say that truth will out and thus you might as well tell the truth. Some say you can't regain the trust that lies lose. Some say that even though the truth may never be revealed, our lies pervert and damage our relationships. Some say . . . well, here's what some of them have to say.

"I'm a coward," says Grace, "about telling close people important, difficult truths. I find that I'm unable to carry it off. And so if something is bothering me, it keeps building up inside till I end up just not seeing them anymore."

"I lie to my husband on sexual things, but I'm furious," says Joyce, "that he's too insensitive to know I'm lying."

"I suffer most from the misconception that children can't take the truth," says Emily. "But I'm starting to see that what's harder and more damaging for them is being told lies, is not being told the truth."

"I'm afraid," says Joan, "that we often wind up feeling a bit of contempt for the people we lie to."

And then there are those who have no talent for lying.

"Over the years, I tried to lie," a friend of mine explained, "but I always got found out and I always got punished. I guess I gave myself away because I feel guilty about any kind of lying. It looks as if I'm stuck with telling the truth."

> "I'm willing to lie. But just as a last resort — the truth's always better."

For those of us, however, who are good at telling lies, for those of us who lie and don't get caught, the question of whether or not to lie can be a hard and serious moral problem. I liked the remark of a friend of mine who said, "I'm willing to lie. But just as a last resort—the truth's always better."

"Because," he explained, "though others may completely accept the lie I'm telling, I don't."

I tend to feel that way, too.

What about you?

Thinking Critically about the Text

The title of the essay plays with the relationship between lies and the truth. Viorst discusses lies that help to conceal the truth, but she's quick to point out that not all lies are malicious. Look at her subsections about "protective lies" (paragraphs 18–33) and "trust-keeping lies" (34–44). Do you think these lies are necessary, or would it be easier to tell the truth? Explain.

Questions on Subject

1. Why is Viorst wary of giving advice on the subject of lying?
2. Viorst admits to contradicting herself in her section on "trust-keeping lies." Where else do you see her contradicting herself?
3. In telling a "protective lie," what assumption about the person hearing the lie does Viorst make? Would you make the same assumption? Why or why not?
4. What's the difference between a "peace-keeping lie" and a "protective lie"?

Questions on Strategy

1. Into what main categories does Viorst divide lying? Do you agree with her division, or do some of her categories seem to overlap? Explain.
2. Viorst recognizes that many people have steadfast views on lying. What accommodations does she make for this audience? (Glossary: *Audience*) How does she challenge this audience?
3. There are at least two parties involved in a lie — the liar and the listener. How much significance does the author give to each of these parties? How does she make the distinction?
4. Viorst presents the reader with a series of examples or moral puzzles. How do these puzzles encourage further thought on the subject of lying? Are they successful? Why or why not?
5. Viorst chooses an unconventional way to conclude her essay, by showing different people's opinions of lying. What do you think she's doing in this last section, beginning in paragraph 45? Does this ending intensify any of the points she has made? Explain. (Glossary: *Beginnings/Endings*)
6. Viorst wants us to see that a lie is not a lie is not a lie is not a lie (i.e., that not all lies are the same). To clarify the various types of lies, she uses division and classification. She also uses illustration to show the reasons people lie. (Glossary: *Illustration*) Using several of the examples that work best for you, discuss how Viorst's use of illustration strengthens and enhances her classification.

Questions on Diction and Vocabulary

1. How would you characterize Viorst's diction in this essay? (Glossary: *Diction*) Consider the essay's subject and audience. (Glossary: *Audience; Subject*) Cite specific examples of her word choices to support your conclusions.

2. Refer to a dictionary to determine the meanings of the following words as Viorst uses them in this selection: *mellifluous* (paragraph 7), *supersede* (18), *dissemble* (32).

Division and Classification in Action

Consider the following classes of items:

movies

college professors

social sciences

roommates

professional sports

Determine at least two principles of division that could be used for each class. Then write a paragraph or two in which you classify one of the groups of items according to a single principle of division. For example, in discussing crime, one could use the seriousness of the crime or the type of crime as principles of division. If the seriousness of the crime were used, this might yield two categories: felonies and misdemeanors. If the types of crime were used, this would yield categories such as burglary, murder, arson, fraud, rape, and drug dealing.

Writing Suggestions

1. Viorst wrote this essay for *Redbook*, which is usually considered a women's magazine. If you were writing this essay for a male audience, would you change the examples? If so, how would you change them? If not, why not? Do you think men are more likely to tell lies of a certain category? Explain. Write an essay in which you discuss whether men and women share similar perspectives about lying. (Glossary: *Comparison and Contrast*)

2. Write an essay on the subject of friends, using division and classification. How many different types of friends do you recognize? On what basis do you differentiate them? Are some friends more important, more useful, more intimate, more convenient, more trustworthy, more reliable, more supportive, more lasting than others? Are you more willing to share your most personal thoughts and feelings with some friends than with others? Be sure to establish a context for why you are writing about friends and putting forth an essay that divides and classifies them. Conclude with an insightful statement drawn from your thesis, the division and classification you establish, and the examples you provide.

The Ways of Meeting Oppression

MARTIN LUTHER KING, JR.

Martin Luther King, Jr. (1929–1968) was the son of a Baptist minister. Ordained at age eighteen, King went on to study at Morehouse College, Crozer Theological Seminary, Boston University, and Chicago Theological Seminary. He came to prominence in 1955 in Montgomery, Alabama, when he led a successful boycott against the city's segregated bus system. A powerful orator and writer, King went on to become the leading spokesperson for the civil rights movement during the 1950s and 1960s. In 1964, he was awarded the Nobel Peace Prize for his policy of nonviolent resistance to racial injustice, a policy that he explains in the following selection. King was assassinated in April 1968 after speaking at a rally in Memphis, Tennessee.

© Flip Schulke/CORBIS

This selection is excerpted from the book *Stride toward Freedom* (1958). Notice how King classifies the three ways oppressed people throughout history have reacted to their oppressors and how his organization prepares the reader for his conclusion.

Preparing to Read

Summarize what you know about the civil rights movement of the late 1950s and early 1960s. What were the goals of the movement? What tactics did its leaders use? How successful were those tactics? How did this movement change American society?

Oppressed people deal with their oppression in three characteristic ways. One way is acquiescence: The oppressed resign themselves to their doom. They tacitly adjust themselves to oppression, and thereby become conditioned to it. In every movement toward freedom some of the oppressed prefer to remain oppressed. Almost 2,800 years ago Moses set out to lead the children of Israel from the slavery of Egypt to the freedom of the promised land. He soon discovered that slaves do not always welcome their deliverers. They become accustomed to being slaves. They would rather bear those ills they have, as Shakespeare pointed out, than flee to others that they know not of. They prefer the "fleshpots of Egypt" to the ordeals of emancipation.

There is such a thing as the freedom of exhaustion. Some people are so worn down by the yoke of oppression that they give up. A few years ago in the slum areas of Atlanta, a Negro guitarist used to sing almost daily: "Been down so long that down don't bother me." This is the type of negative freedom and resignation that often engulfs the life of the oppressed.

But this is not the way out. To accept passively an unjust system is to cooperate with that system; thereby the oppressed become as evil as the oppressor. Noncooperation with evil is as much a moral obligation as is cooperation with good. The oppressed must never allow the conscience of the oppressor to slumber. Religion reminds every man that he is his brother's keeper. To accept injustice or segregation passively is to say to the oppressor that his actions are morally right. It is a way of allowing his conscience to fall asleep. At this moment the oppressed fails to be his brother's keeper. So acquiescence—while often the easier way—is not the moral way. It is the way of the coward. The Negro cannot win the respect of his oppressor by acquiescing; he merely increases the oppressor's arrogance and contempt. Acquiescence is interpreted as proof of the Negro's inferiority. The Negro cannot win the respect of the white people of the south or the peoples of the world if he is willing to sell the future of his children for his personal and immediate comfort and safety.

> The problem is not a purely racial one, with Negroes set against whites. In the end, it's not a struggle between people at all, but a tension between justice and injustice.

A second way that oppressed people sometimes deal with oppression is to resort to physical violence and corroding hatred. Violence often brings about momentary results. Nations have frequently won their independence in battle. But in spite of temporary victories, violence never brings permanent peace. It solves no social problem; it merely creates new and more complicated ones.

Violence as a way of achieving racial justice is both impractical and immoral. It is impractical because it is a descending spiral ending in destruction for all. The old law of an eye for an eye leaves everybody blind. It is immoral because it seeks to humiliate the opponent rather than win his understanding; it seeks to annihilate rather than to convert. Violence is immoral because it thrives on hatred rather than love. It destroys community and makes brotherhood impossible. It leaves society in monologue rather than dialogue. Violence ends by defeating itself. It creates bitterness in the survivors and brutality in the destroyers. A voice echoes through time saying to every potential Peter, "Put up your sword." History is cluttered with the wreckage of nations that failed to follow this command.

If the American Negro and other victims of oppression succumb to the temptation of using violence in the struggle for freedom, future generations will be the recipients of a desolate night of bitterness, and our chief legacy to them will be an endless reign of meaningless chaos. Violence is not the way.

The third way open to oppressed people in their quest for freedom is the way of nonviolent resistance. Like the synthesis in Hegelian philosophy, the principle of nonviolent resistance seeks to reconcile the truths of two opposites—the acquiescence and violence—while avoiding the extremes and immoralities of both. The nonviolent resister agrees with the person who acquiesces that one should not be physically aggressive toward his opponent; but he balances the equation by agreeing with the person of violence that evil must be resisted. He avoids the nonresistance of the former and the violent resistance of the latter. With nonviolent resistance, no individual or group need submit to any wrong, nor need anyone resort to violence in order to right a wrong.

It seems to me that this is the method that must guide the actions of the Negro in the present crisis in race relations. Through nonviolent resistance the Negro will be able to rise to the noble height of opposing the unjust system while loving the perpetrators of the system. The Negro must work passionately and unrelentingly for full stature as a citizen, but he must not use inferior methods to gain it. He must never come to terms with falsehood, malice, hate, or destruction.

Nonviolent resistance makes it possible for the Negro to remain in the South and struggle for his rights. The Negro's problem will not be solved by running away. He cannot listen to the glib suggestion of those who would urge him to migrate en masse to other sections of the country. By grasping his great opportunity in the South he can make a lasting contribution to the moral strength of the nation and set a sublime example of courage for generations yet unborn.

By nonviolent resistance, the Negro can also enlist all men of good will in his struggle for equality. The problem is not a purely racial one, with Negroes set against whites. In the end, it is not a struggle between people at all, but a tension between justice and injustice. Nonviolent resistance is not aimed against oppressors but against oppression. Under its banner consciences, not racial groups, are enlisted.

Thinking Critically about the Text

Find the definition of *oppress* or *oppression* in a dictionary. Exactly what does King mean when he speaks of people being "oppressed" in the South in twentieth-century America? Do you think that people are still being oppressed in America today? Explain.

Questions on Subject

1. What does King mean by the phrase "freedom of exhaustion" (paragraph 2)? Why is he scathing in his assessment of people who succumb to such a condition in response to oppression?
2. According to King, what is the role of religion in the battle against oppression?
3. Why does King advocate the avoidance of violence in fighting oppression, despite the short-term success violence often achieves for the victors? How do such victories affect the future?
4. According to King, how does nonviolent resistance transform a racial issue into one of conscience?

Questions on Strategy

1. King's essay is easy to read and understand, and everything in it relates to his purpose. (Glossary: *Purpose*) What is that purpose? Summarize how each paragraph supports his purpose. How does the essay's organization help King achieve his purpose? (Glossary: *Organization*)
2. King says that "nonviolent resistance is not aimed against oppressors but against oppression" (paragraph 10). What does he mean by this? Why does he deflect anger and resentment away from a concrete example, the oppressors, to an abstract concept, oppression? (Glossary: *Concrete/Abstract*) How does this choice support his purpose? (Glossary: *Purpose*)
3. King evokes the names of Moses, Shakespeare, and Hegel in his essay. What does this tell you about his intended audience? (Glossary: *Audience*) Why does King address the audience in this way?
4. King uses division and classification to help argue his point in this essay. What other rhetorical strategies does King use? How does each strategy, including division and classification and argument, contribute to the effectiveness of the essay?

Questions on Diction and Vocabulary

1. In his discussion about overcoming oppression with violence, King says that "future generations will be the recipients of a desolate night of bitterness" (paragraph 6). What image do his words evoke for you? Why do you think he chooses to use a striking metaphor here instead of a less poetic statement? (Glossary: *Figures of Speech*)
2. King urges Negroes to avoid "falsehood, malice, hate, or destruction" (paragraph 8) in their quest to gain full stature as citizens. How does each of these terms relate to his earlier argument about avoiding violence? How does each enhance or add new meaning to his earlier argument?

3. Refer to a dictionary to determine the meanings of the following words as King uses them in this selection: *acquiescence* (paragraph 1), *tacitly* (1), *yoke* (2), *perpetrators* (8), *glib* (9), *sublime* (9).

Division and Classification in Action

Be prepared to discuss in class why you believe division and classification are important strategies or ways of thinking in everyday life. Explain, for example, how useful the two complementary strategies are for you as you go shopping in the supermarket for items on your shopping list or look for particular textbooks in your college bookstore.

Writing Suggestions

1. Write a division and classification essay in which you follow King's model. Identify three methods that you can use to achieve a goal, such as studying for a test, applying to graduate school, or interviewing for a job. Choose one method to advocate; then frame your essay so that the division and classification strategy helps you make your point.

2. Toward the end of his essay, King states, "By grasping his great opportunity in the South [the Negro] can make a lasting contribution to the moral strength of the nation and set a sublime example of courage for generations yet unborn" (paragraph 9). With your classmates, discuss whether the movement that King led achieved its goal of solving many of the underlying racial tensions and inequities in the United States. In terms of equality, what has happened in the United States since King's famous "I Have a Dream" speech? Write a paper in which you argue for or against the idea that King's "dream" is alive and well. (Glossary: *Argument*)

Mother Tongue

AMY TAN

Amy Tan was born in Oakland, California, in 1952, to Chinese immigrant parents. After studying English and linguistics at San Jose State University, she earned her M.A. in linguistics and worked as a language development specialist for children with developmental disabilities. After a stint as a business writer, she turned to fiction. Her first book, *The Joy Luck Club* (1989), became a bestseller and was nominated for the National Book Award and the National Book Critics Circle Award, and it was selected for the National Endowment for the Arts' Big Read program. Her other books include the novels *The Kitchen God's Wife* (1991), *The Bonesetter's Daughter* (2000), and *The Valley of Amazement* (2013), and the children's books *The Moon Lady* (1992) and *The Chinese Siamese Cat* (1994); the latter was adapted into an internationally popular television series for children. Her work has appeared in *The New Yorker*, the *Atlantic*, *Grand Street*, *National Geographic*, and other publications and has been translated into 35 languages.

Mireya Acierto/Getty Images

"Mother Tongue" first appeared in the *Threepenny Review* and was reprinted in *The Best American Essays* (1991). In this essay, Tan examines the way context shapes how we use and understand language. As you read, notice the different categories she creates and how she illustrates them.

Preparing to Read

Think about the different languages you know. Perhaps English was not the first language you spoke, or maybe you grew up with a family who spoke another language. Even if the only language you know is English, do you speak more than one kind of English? Are there things you say at home that you would say differently at school or at work? Are there things you say to your friends that you wouldn't say at home? Do you consciously adjust how you speak in different circumstances, or do you think this happens naturally?

I am not a scholar of English or literature. I cannot give you much more than personal opinions on the English language and its variations in this country or others.

I am a writer. And by that definition, I am someone who has always loved language. I am fascinated by language in daily life. I spend a great deal of my time thinking about the power of language—the way it can evoke an emotion, a visual image, a complex idea, or a simple truth. Language is the tool of my trade. And I use them all—all the Englishes I grew up with.

Recently, I was made keenly aware of the different Englishes I do use. I was giving a talk to a large group of people, the same talk I had already given to half a dozen other groups. The nature of the talk was about my writing, my life, and my book, *The Joy Luck Club*. The talk was going along well enough, until I remembered one major difference that made the whole talk sound wrong. My mother was in the room. And it was perhaps the first time she had heard me give a lengthy speech, using the kind of English I have never used with her. I was saying things like "The intersection of memory upon imagination" and "There is an aspect of my fiction that relates to thus-and-thus"—a speech filled with carefully wrought grammatical phrases, burdened, it suddenly seemed to me, with nominalized forms, past perfect tenses, conditional phrases, all the forms of standard English that I had learned in school and through books, the forms of English I did not use at home with my mother.

Just last week, I was walking down the street with my mother, and I again found myself conscious of the English I was using, the English I do use with her. We were talking about the price of new and used furniture and I heard myself saying this: "Not waste money that way." My husband was with us as well, and he didn't notice any switch in my English. And then I realized why. It's because over the twenty years we've been together I've often used that same kind of English with him, and sometimes he even uses it with me. It has become our language of intimacy, a different sort of English that relates to family talk, the language I grew up with.

So you'll have some idea of what this family talk I heard sounds like, I'll quote what my mother said during a recent conversation which I videotaped and then transcribed. During this conversation, my mother was talking about a political gangster in Shanghai who had the same last name as her family's, Du, and how the gangster in his early years wanted to be adopted by her family, which was rich by comparison. Later, the gangster became more powerful, far richer than my mother's family, and one day showed up at my mother's wedding to pay his respects. Here's what she said in part:

"Du Yusong having business like fruit stand. Like off the street kind. He is Du like Du Zong—but not Tsung-ming Island people. The local people call putong, the river east side, he belong to that side local people. That man want to ask Du Zong father take him in like become own family. Du Zong father wasn't look down on him, but didn't take seriously, until that man big like become a mafia. Now important person, very hard to inviting him. Chinese way, came only to show respect, don't stay for dinner. Respect for making big celebration, he shows up. Mean gives lots of respect. Chinese custom. Chinese social life that way. If too important won't have to stay too long. He come to my wedding. I didn't see, I heard it. I gone to boy's side, they have YMCA dinner. Chinese age I was nineteen."

You should know that my mother's expressive command of English belies how much she actually understands. She reads the *Forbes* report, listens to *Wall Street Week*, converses daily with her stockbroker, reads all of Shirley MacLaine's books with ease—all kinds of things I can't begin to understand. Yet some of my friends tell me they understand 50 percent of what my mother says. Some say they understand 80 to 90 percent. Some say they understand none of it, as if she were speaking pure Chinese. But to me, my mother's English is perfectly clear, perfectly natural. It's my mother tongue. Her language, as I hear it, is vivid, direct, full of observation and imagery. That was the language that helped shape the way I saw things, expressed things, made sense of the world.

Lately, I've been giving more thought to the kind of English my mother speaks. Like others, I have described it to people as "broken" or "fractured" English. But I wince when I say that. It has always bothered me that I can think of no other way to describe it other than "broken," as if it were damaged and needed to be fixed, as if it lacked a certain wholeness and soundness. I've heard other terms used, "limited English," for example. But they seem just as bad, as if everything is limited, including people's perceptions of the limited English speaker.

I know this for a fact, because when I was growing up, my mother's "limited" English limited *my* perception of her. I was ashamed of her English. I believed that her English reflected the quality of what she had to say. That is, because she expressed them imperfectly her thoughts were imperfect. And I had plenty of empirical evidence to support me: the fact that people in department stores, at banks, and at restaurants did not take her seriously, did not give her good service, pretended not to understand her, or even acted as if they did not hear her.

> **I believed that her English reflected the quality of what she had to say.**

My mother has long realized the limitations of her English as well. When I was fifteen, she used to have me call people on the phone to pretend I was she. In this guise, I was forced to ask for information or even to complain and yell at people who had been rude to her. One time it was a call to her stockbroker in New York. She had cashed out her small portfolio and it just so happened we were going to go to New York the next week, our very first trip outside California. I had to get on the phone and say in an adolescent voice that was not very convincing, "This is Mrs. Tan."

And my mother was standing in the back whispering loudly, "Why he don't send me check, already two weeks late. So mad he lie to me, losing me money."

And then I said in perfect English, "Yes, I'm getting rather concerned. You had agreed to send the check two weeks ago, but it hasn't arrived."

Then she began to talk more loudly. "What he want, I come to New York tell him front of his boss, you cheating me?" And I was trying to calm her down, make her be quiet, while telling the stockbroker, "I can't tolerate any more excuses. If I don't receive the check immediately, I am going to have to speak to your manager when I'm in New York next week." And sure enough, the following week there we were in front of this astonished stockbroker, and I was sitting there red-faced and quiet, and my mother, the real Mrs. Tan, was shouting at his boss in her impeccable broken English.

We used a similar routine just five days ago, for a situation that was far less humorous. My mother had gone to the hospital for an appointment, to find out about a benign brain tumor a CAT scan had revealed a month ago. She said she had spoken very good English, her best English, no mistakes. Still, she said, the hospital did not apologize when they said they had lost the CAT scan and she had come for nothing. She said they did not seem to have any sympathy when she told them she was anxious to know the exact diagnosis, since her husband and son had both died of brain tumors. She said they would not give her any more information until the next time and she would have to make another appointment for that. So she said she would not leave until the doctor called her daughter. She wouldn't budge. And when the doctor finally called her daughter, me, who spoke in perfect English—lo and behold—we had assurances the CAT scan would be found, promises that a conference call on Monday would be held, and apologies for any suffering my mother had gone through for a most regrettable mistake.

I think my mother's English almost had an effect on limiting my possibilities in life as well. Sociologists and linguists probably will tell you that a person's developing language skills are more influenced by peers. But I do think that the language spoken in the family, especially in immigrant families which are more insular, plays a large role in shaping the language of the child. And I believe that it affected my results on achievement tests, IQ tests, and the SAT. While my English skills were never judged as poor, compared to math, English could not be considered my strong suit. In grade school I did moderately well, getting perhaps B's, sometimes B-pluses, in English and scoring perhaps in the sixtieth or seventieth percentile on achievement tests. But those scores were not good enough to override the opinion that my true abilities lay in math and science, because in those areas I achieved A's and scored in the ninetieth percentile or higher.

This was understandable. Math is precise; there is only one correct answer. Whereas, for me at least, the answers on English tests were always a judgment call, a matter of opinion and personal experience. Those tests were constructed around items like fill-in-the-blank sentence completion, such as "Even though Tom was ____, Mary thought he was ____." And the correct answer always seemed to be the most bland combinations of thoughts, for example, "Even though Tom was shy, Mary thought he was charming," with the grammatical structure "even though" limiting the correct answer to some sort of semantic opposites, so you wouldn't get answers like, "Even though Tom was foolish, Mary thought he was ridiculous." Well, according to my mother, there were very few limitations as to what Tom could have been and what Mary might have thought of him. So I never did well on tests like that.

The same was true with word analogies, pairs of words in which you were supposed to find some sort of logical, semantic relationship — for example, "*Sunset* is to *nightfall* as ____ is to ____." And here you would be presented with a list of four possible pairs, one of which showed the same kind of relationship: *red* is to *stoplight*, *bus* is to *arrival*, *chills* is to *fever*, *yawn* is to *boring*. Well, I could never think that way. I knew what the tests were asking, but I could not block out of my mind the images already created by the first pair, "*sunset* is to *nightfall*" — and I would see a burst of colors against a darkening sky, the moon rising, the lowering of a curtain of stars. And all the other pairs of words — red, bus, stoplight, boring — just threw up a mass of confusing images, making it impossible for me to sort out something as logical as saying: "A sunset precedes nightfall" is the same as "a chill precedes a fever." The only way I would have gotten that answer right would have been to imagine an associative situation, for example, my being disobedient and staying out past sunset, catching a chill at night, which turns into feverish pneumonia as punishment, which indeed did happen to me.

I have been thinking about all this lately, about my mother's English, about achievement tests. Because lately I've been asked, as a writer, why there are not more Asian Americans represented in American literature. Why are there few Asian Americans enrolled in creative writing programs? Why do so many Chinese students go into engineering? Well, these are broad sociological questions I can't begin to answer. But I have noticed in surveys — in fact, just last week — that Asian students, as a whole, always do significantly better on math achievement tests than in English. And this makes me think that there are other Asian-American students whose English spoken in the home might also be described as "broken" or "limited." And perhaps they also have teachers who are steering them away from writing and into math and science, which is what happened to me.

Fortunately, I happen to be rebellious in nature and enjoy the challenge of disproving assumptions made about me. I became an English major my first year in college, after being enrolled as pre-med. I started writing nonfiction as a freelancer the week after I was told by my former boss that writing was my worst skill and I should hone my talents toward account management.

But it wasn't until 1985 that I finally began to write fiction. And at first I wrote using what I thought to be wittily crafted sentences, sentences that would finally prove I had mastery over the English language. Here's an example from the first draft of a story that later made its way into *The Joy Luck Club*, but without this line: "That was my mental quandary in its nascent state." A terrible line, which I can barely pronounce.

Fortunately, for reasons I won't get into today, I later decided I should envision a reader for the stories I would write. And the reader I decided upon was my mother, because these were stories about mothers. So with this reader in mind—and in fact she did read my early drafts—I began to write stories using all the Englishes I grew up with: the English I spoke to my mother, which for lack of a better term might be described as "simple"; the English she used with me, which for lack of a better term might be described as "broken"; my translation of her Chinese, which could certainly be described as "watered down"; and what I imagined to be her translation of her Chinese if she could speak in perfect English, her internal language, and for that I sought to preserve the essence, but neither an English nor a Chinese structure. I wanted to capture what language ability tests can never reveal: her intent, her passion, her imagery, the rhythms of her speech, and the nature of her thoughts.

Apart from what any critic had to say about my writing, I knew I had succeeded where it counted when my mother finished reading my book and gave me her verdict: "So easy to read."

Thinking Critically about the Text

Tan writes that she "succeeded where it counted when my mother finished reading my book and gave me her verdict: 'So easy to read'" (paragraph 22). If someone told you this about your own writing, would you feel you had succeeded? What are your goals for your writing? Do you want it to be easy to read, no matter what? Are there types of writing that should be difficult?

Questions on Subject

1. What is the main idea of Tan's essay, and where do you find it? (Glossary: *Thesis*)
2. What are the different Englishes Tan examines in this essay? Define each one, using evidence from the essay to support your answer.
3. In paragraph 9, Tan writes that as a child, she was "ashamed of" her mother's English. Why did she feel this way? Now, as an adult, does she feel the same way?
4. Tan writes that in school, she did better in math than in English because "math is precise; there is only one correct answer." Do you agree with her that the answers on English tests are "always a judgment call, a matter of opinion and personal experience" (paragraph 15)? Why or why not?

Questions on Strategy

1. What is Tan's purpose in this essay? Where is it stated? (Glossary: *Purpose*)
2. Tan uses definition in the first two paragraphs of her essay. How does she define herself, and where does she use negative definition?
3. Tan provides many examples of spoken language in this essay — both her own and her mother's. Are all her examples effective? Which did you find most powerful? (Glossary: *Examples*)
4. In paragraph 6, Tan shares a story her mother told, recording the exact words her mother used. Could you follow what Tan's mother said? Do you think you would have been able to understand it as well without Tan's explanation in the preceding paragraph? Why do you think Tan included paragraph 6? (Glossary: *Dialogue*)
5. Tan hears her mother's language as "vivid, direct, full of observation and imagery" (paragraph 7). Yet she spends much of the essay discussing the limitations of her mother's English. How does this apparent contradiction contribute to the overall message of Tan's essay?
6. In paragraph 21, Tan writes that she envisioned her mother as "a reader for the stories I would write." Who do you think she envisions as the reader of this selection? Where do you find evidence to support your answer?

Questions on Diction and Vocabulary

1. How would you describe Tan's diction in this essay? What words and phrases lead you to that conclusion?
2. Refer to a dictionary to determine the meanings of the following words as Tan uses them in this selection: *nominalized* (paragraph 4), *belies* (7), *empirical* (9), *guise* (10), *insular* (15), *semantic* (16), *associative* (17), *quandary* (20), *nascent* (20).

Division and Classification in Action

Categorize the kinds of television programs you watch or the kinds of music you listen to. Think not only of classes but also of subclasses. For example, you may claim that the only types of programs you watch are documentaries, situation comedies, and sports, but within the sports category you realize you watch only NFL games and not college games. Perhaps you watch basketball, but only college games and not NBA games. By looking at subclasses as well as classes, you will come to a much more detailed understanding of your viewing or listening habits.

Writing Suggestions

1. Using the Preparing to Read prompt as a springboard, write an essay in which you create a classification system for the different types of language you use. Consider the language you use with your family, your friends, your teachers, and at work. Remember that there may be subclasses, such as different parts of your family (your siblings versus your parents or grandparents) or different groups of friends (your school friends versus your neighborhood friends). How and why do your languages differ? Have you ever felt ignored or invisible because you are being misunderstood? Have you ever dismissed someone because you couldn't understand them or they couldn't understand you? Be sure to provide examples, with dialogue, to illustrate your understanding of the way you use, and react to, your different types of language.

2. Writers use division and classification to generate new ways of understanding topics, and some use it to revisit subjects of lasting interest on which they wish to offer fresh insights. Select a topic for your essay and then decide which approach you want to take. If you think you're devising an original classification, do some research first to see whether others have, in fact, already written on the same topic. Note, for example, that much has already been written about types of love, types of war, types of lies, types of students, types of humor, types of bosses, types of poetry, and types of cars. If you are writing a classification that has been treated before, you will want to learn all you can about the way other writers have already treated this subject. Naturally, you will want to offer fresh ideas rather than simply offering examples of what others have already found to be true.

WRITING SUGGESTIONS FOR DIVISION AND CLASSIFICATION

1. To write a meaningful classification essay, you must analyze a body of unorganized material and arrange it for a particular purpose. (Glossary: *Purpose*) For example, to identify for a buyer the most economical cars currently on the market, you might initially determine which cars can be purchased for under $25,000 and which cost between $25,000 and $35,000. Then, using a second basis of selection — fuel economy — you could determine which cars have the best mileage within each price range.

    Select one of the following subjects and write a classification essay. Be sure that your purpose is clearly explained and that your bases of selection are chosen and ordered in accordance with your purpose.

    a. attitudes toward physical fitness
    b. reasons for going to college
    c. attitudes toward the religious or spiritual side of life
    d. choosing a hobby
    e. college professors
    f. local restaurants
    g. choosing a career
    h. college courses
    i. recreational activities
    j. ways of financing a college education
    k. parties or other social events

2. We sometimes resist classifying other people because doing so can seem like "pigeonholing" or stereotyping individuals unfairly. In an essay, compare and contrast two or more ways of classifying people, including at least one that you would call legitimate and one that you would call misleading. (Glossary: *Comparison and Contrast*) What conclusions can you draw about the difference between useful classifications and damaging stereotypes?

3. Use division and classification to explain your school or town. What categories might you use? Would you divide your subject into different types of people? Would you classify people by their spending habits? What are the other ways in which you might explain your school or town? What other rhetorical strategies might you incorporate to strengthen your presentation? You might want to look at the Web site of your school or town to find out what categories it uses to present itself.

4. The cartoon below, created by Bernard Schoenbaum, first appeared in *The New Yorker* on September 19, 1994.

© Bernard Schoenbaum/The New Yorker/The Cartoon Bank

While it's meant to be amusing, the cartoon's classification of books according to the reader's attention span does provide more than a moment's comic relief: Readers usually do prefer certain types of books, from more to less challenging, depending on what they hope to achieve by reading. Write an essay in which you divide and classify book readers according to a system of your own devising.

5. **Writing with Sources.** Do some research on the last presidential election or another political campaign that interests you. Reread or watch online major news coverage of the last days of the election and identify at least three qualities that were mentioned most often for the two final contenders. What categories or classes do these qualities belong to? Write an essay in which you discuss how this division and classification of the candidates' qualities might have contributed to the winner's victory. Also consider who did the dividing: Was it the media? The public? For models of and advice on integrating sources in your essay, see Chapters 14 and 15.

6. **Writing with Sources.** The opening illustration for this chapter on page 330 is an excerpt of a floor plan from the National Museum of Natural History, a part of the Smithsonian Institution. Search "Floor Plans of the Smithsonian National Museum of Natural History" online to examine the full version, which is color-coded and

also contains a key to the meaning of each icon. Then, using the terms "museum floor plan," search online for other, similarly formatted layouts. Consider museums that you've visited in the past or museums you hope to visit in the future. Look at a few different plans and then select one with exhibit categories that interest you. Brainstorm a list of things that might appear in each category and write a paragraph about why those items would be a good fit for the museum's overall purpose, focus, and audience. Be sure to reference specific parts of your floor plan in your explanation. For models of and advice on integrating sources in your essay, see Chapters 14 and 15.

7. **Writing in the Workplace.** You are starting a new business, either a nonprofit charitable organization in which you are looking for donors or a for-profit business for which you need customers. Develop a fund-raising plan or a marketing plan in which you divide and classify your potential donors and customers. Be sure that your plan identifies the classes and subclasses of donors and customers that would maximize your desired outcome. When classifying, consider such demographics as age, sex, income, race, ethnicity, location, and likely proficiency with social media.

Espresso
[ess-press-oh]

Espresso Macchiato
[ess-press-oh mock-e-ah-toe]

Espresso con Panna
[ess-press-oh kon pawn-nah]

Caffé Latte
[caf-ay lah-tey]

Flat White

Cafe Breve
[caf-ay brev-ay]

Cappuccino
[kap-oo-chee-noh]

Caffé Mocha
[caf-ay moh-kuh]

Americano
[uh-mer-i-kan-oh]

Lokesh Dhakar

CHAPTER **10**

Definition

WHAT IS DEFINITION?

IF YOU HAVE EVER USED A DICTIONARY, YOU ARE ALREADY FAMILIAR with the concept of definition. The job of explaining the meanings of words and phrases is not limited to the dictionary alone, however: We use definition all the time in our everyday lives to make our points clearer. How often have you been asked what you mean when a word or phrase you're using is ambiguous, unusual, or simply unfamiliar to your listener? We can only communicate with one another clearly and effectively when we all define the words we use in the same way—and that is not always easy.

Visuals can come to our aid in definition, as the chart on the opposite page shows. While we could certainly define the various coffee drinks using words alone, the illustration gives a quick, at-a-glance indication of their basic components. A chart like this one displayed at a specialty coffee shop would reduce ambiguity in ordering.

DEFINITION IN WRITTEN TEXTS

Unlike the relative proportions of coffee, milk, and water in various coffee drinks, understanding and explaining complex concepts is often impossible without using precise, detailed, verbal definitions. These definitions can take on many different forms, depending, in part, on the purpose of the definition and on what is being defined.

For example, let's look at how Robert Keith Miller attempts to define *discrimination* in his essay called "Discrimination Is a Virtue," which first appeared in *Newsweek*:

> We have a word in English which means "the ability to tell differences." That word is *discrimination*. But within the last [sixty] years, this word has been so frequently misused that an entire generation has grown up believing that "discrimination" means "racism." People are always proclaiming that

"discrimination" is something that should be done away with. Should that ever happen, it would prove to be our undoing.

Discrimination means discernment; it means the ability to perceive the truth, to use good judgment and to profit accordingly. The *Oxford English Dictionary* traces this meaning of the word back to 1648 and demonstrates that for the next 300 years, "discrimination" was a virtue, not a vice. Thus, when a character in a nineteenth-century novel makes a happy marriage, Dickens has another character remark, "It does credit to your discrimination that you should have found such a very excellent young woman."

Of course, "the ability to tell differences" assumes that differences exist, and this is unsettling for a culture obsessed with the notion of equality. The contemporary belief that discrimination is a vice stems from the compound "discriminate against." What we need to remember, however, is that some things deserve to be judged harshly: We should not leave our kingdoms to the selfish and the wicked.

Discrimination is wrong only when someone or something is discriminated against because of prejudice. But to use the word in that sense, as so many people do, is to destroy its true meaning. If you discriminate against something because of general preconceptions rather than particular insights, then you are not discriminating—bias has clouded the clarity of vision that discrimination demands.

How does Miller define *discrimination*? He mainly uses a technique called *extended definition*, a definition that requires a full discussion. This is only one of many types of definition that you could use to explain what a word or an idea means to you. The following paragraphs identify and explain several other types.

A *formal definition*—a definition such as that found in a dictionary—explains the meaning of a word by assigning it to a class and then differentiating it from other members of that class.

TERM		CLASS	DIFFERENTIATION
Music	is	sound	made by voices or instruments and characterized by melody, harmony, or rhythm.

Note how crucial the differentiation is here: There are many sounds—from the roar of a passing jet airplane to the fizz of soda in a glass—that must be excluded for the definition to be precise and useful. Dictionary entries often follow the class-differentiation pattern of the formal definition.

A *synonymous definition* explains a word by pairing it with another word of similar but perhaps more limited meaning:

Music is melody.

Synonymous definition is almost never as precise as formal definition because few words share exactly the same meaning. But when the word being defined is reasonably familiar and somewhat broad, a well-chosen synonym can provide readers with a surer sense of its meaning in context.

A *negative definition* explains a word by saying what it does not mean.

> Music is not silence, and it is not noise.

Such a definition must obviously be incomplete: There are sounds that are neither silence nor noise and yet are not music—quiet conversation, for example. But specifying what something is *not* often helps to clarify other statements about what it is.

An *etymological definition* also seldom stands alone, but by tracing a word's origins it helps readers understand its meaning. *Etymology* itself is defined as the study of the history of a linguistic form—the history of words.

> Music is descended from the Greek word *mousikē*, meaning literally "the art of the Muse."

The Muses, according to Greek mythology, were deities and the sources of inspiration in the arts. Thus the etymology suggests why we think of music as an art and as the product of inspiration. Etymological definitions often reveal surprising sources that suggest new ways of looking at ideas or objects.

A *stipulative definition* is a definition invented by a writer to convey a special or unexpected sense of an existing and often familiar word.

> Music is a language, but a language of the intangible, a kind of soul-language.   —EDWARD MACDOWELL
>
> Music is the arithmetic of sounds.   —CLAUDE DEBUSSY

Although these two examples seem to disagree with each other, and perhaps also with your idea of what music is, note that neither is arbitrary. (That is, neither assigns to the word *music* a completely foreign meaning, as Humpty Dumpty did in *Through the Looking-Glass*, when he defined *glory* as "a nice knock-down argument.") The stipulative definitions by MacDowell and Debussy help explain each composer's conception of the subject and can lead, of course, to further elaboration. Stipulative definitions almost always provide the basis for a more complex discussion. These definitions are often the subjects of an extended definition.

Extended definition, like the definition of *discrimination* given by Robert Keith Miller on pages 391–92, is used when a word, or the idea it stands for, requires more than a sentence of explanation. *Extended definition* may employ any of the definition techniques mentioned above, as well as the strategies discussed in other chapters. For example, an extended definition of music might provide *examples*, ranging from African drumming to a Bach fugue to a Bruce Springsteen song, to develop a fuller and more vivid sense of what music is. A writer might *describe* music in detail by showing its characteristic features, or explain the *process* of composing music, or *compare and contrast* music with language (according to MacDowell's stipulative definition) or arithmetic (according to Debussy's). Each of these strategies helps make the meaning of a writer's words and ideas clear.

In his extended definition of the word *discrimination*, Miller uses a very brief formal definition of *discrimination* [term]: "the ability [class] to tell differences [differentiation]." He then offers a negative definition (discrimination is not racism) and a synonymous definition (discrimination is discernment). Next he cites the entry in a great historical dictionary of English to support his claim, and he quotes an example to illustrate his definition. He concludes by contrasting the word *discrimination* with the compound "discriminate against." Each of these techniques helps make the case that the most precise meaning of *discrimination* is in direct opposition to its common usage today.

USING DEFINITION AS A WRITING STRATEGY

Since most readers have dictionaries, it might seem that writers would hardly ever have to define their terms using formal definitions. In fact, writers don't necessarily do so all the time, even when using an unusual word like *tergiversation*, which few readers have in their active vocabularies; if readers don't know it, the reasoning goes, let them look it up. But there are times when a formal definition is quite necessary. One of these times is when a writer uses a word so specialized or so new that it simply won't be in dictionaries; another is when a writer must use a number of unfamiliar technical terms within only a few sentences. Also, when a word has several different meanings or may mean different things to different people, writers often state exactly the sense in which they are using the word. In each of these cases, definition serves the purpose of achieving clarity.

But writers also sometimes use definition, particularly extended definition, to explain the essential nature of the things and ideas they write about. For example, consider E. B. White's definition of *democracy*, which first appeared in *The New Yorker* on July 3, 1943:

> We received a letter from the Writers' War Board the other day asking for a statement on "The Meaning of Democracy." It presumably is our duty to comply with such a request, and it is certainly our pleasure.
>
> Surely the Board knows what democracy is. It is the line that forms on the right. It is the *don't* in "don't shove." It is the hole in the stuffed shirt

through which the sawdust slowly trickles; it is the dent in the high hat. Democracy is the recurrent suspicion that more than half of the people are right more than half of the time. It is the feeling of privacy in the voting booths, the feeling of communion in the libraries, the feeling of vitality everywhere. Democracy is a letter to the editor. Democracy is the score at the beginning of the ninth. It is an idea which hasn't been disproved yet, a song the words of which have not gone bad. It's the mustard on the hot dog and the cream in the rationed coffee. Democracy is a request from a War Board, in the middle of a morning in the middle of a war, wanting to know what democracy is.

Such writing goes beyond answering the question "What does _____ mean exactly?" to tackle the much broader and deeper question "What is _____, and what does it represent?"

Although exploring a term and what it represents is often the primary object of such a definition, sometimes writers go beyond giving a formal definition; they also use extended definitions to make persuasive points. Take the Miller essay, for example (pages 391–92). The subject of Miller's extended definition is clearly the word *discrimination*. His purpose, however, is less immediately obvious. At first it appears that he wants only to explain what the word means. But by the third sentence he is distinguishing what it does not mean, and at the end it's clear he's trying to persuade readers to use the word correctly and thus to discriminate more sharply and justly themselves.

USING DEFINITION ACROSS THE DISCIPLINES

When writing essays in the academic disciplines, you will have many opportunities to use the strategy of definition to both organize and strengthen the presentation of your ideas. To determine whether definition is the right strategy for you in a particular paper, use the guidelines described in Chapter 2 (Determining a Strategy for Developing Your Essay, pages 32–33). Consider the following examples:

Philosophy

1. **MAIN IDEA:** A person of integrity is more than just an honest person.
2. **QUESTION:** What does it mean to have *integrity*?
3. **STRATEGY:** Definition. The direction words *mean* and *is more than* call for a complete explanation of the meaning of the word *integrity*.
4. **SUPPORTING STRATEGY:** Comparison and contrast. To clarify the definition of *integrity*, it might be helpful to differentiate a person of integrity from a moral person or an ethical person.

Economics

1. **MAIN IDEA:** One way to understand the swings in the U.S. economy is to know the meaning of inflation.
2. **QUESTION:** What is inflation?
3. **STRATEGY:** Definition. The direction words *meaning* and *is* point us toward the strategy of definition; the word *inflation* needs to be explained.
4. **SUPPORTING STRATEGY:** Cause and effect analysis. In explaining the meaning of *inflation*, it would be interesting to explore economic factors that cause inflation as well as the effects of inflation on the economy.

Astronomy

1. **MAIN IDEA:** With the demotion of Pluto from planet to "dwarf planet" or plutoid, astronomers have given new attention to the definition of *planet*.
2. **QUESTION:** What is a planet?
3. **STRATEGY:** Definition. The direction words *definition* and *is* call for an extended definition of the word *planet*. For clarification purposes, it would be helpful to define *asteroid* as well.
4. **SUPPORTING STRATEGIES:** Illustration; cause and effect analysis. The definition of *planet* could be supported with several concrete examples of planets as well as an explanation of why astronomers thought a new definition was necessary.

SAMPLE STUDENT ESSAY USING DEFINITION AS A WRITING STRATEGY

Originally a native of New York City, Howard Solomon, Jr. studied in France as part of the American Field Services Intercultural Program in high school, and he majored in French at the University of Vermont. Solomon's other interests include foreign affairs, languages, photography, and cycling; in his wildest dreams, he imagines becoming an international lawyer. For the following essay, Solomon interviewed twenty students in his dormitory, collecting information and opinions that he eventually brought together with his own experiences to develop a definition of *best friends*.

Best Friends
Howard Solomon, Jr.

Introduction: brief definition of *best friend* — Best friends, even when they are not a part of people's day-to-day lives, are essential to their well-being. They supply the companionship, help, security, and love that

Purpose: in defining *best friend*, writer comes to new understanding of self and relationships	all people need. It is not easy to put into words exactly what a best friend is, because the matter is so personal. People can benefit, however, from thinking about their best friends—who they are, what characteristics they share, and why they are so important—in order to gain a better understanding of themselves and their relationships.
Organization: sequence of interview questions	When interviewed for their opinions about the qualities they most valued in their own best friends, twenty people in a University of Vermont dormitory agreed on three traits: reciprocity, honesty, and love. Reciprocity means that one
3-part answer to question 1: What qualities do you value in a best friend?	can always rely on a best friend in times of need. A favor doesn't necessarily have to be returned, but best friends will return it anyway, because they want to. Best friends are willing to help each other for the sake of helping and not just for
Defines reciprocity between best friends	personal gain. One woman interviewed said that life seemed more secure because she knew her best friend was there if she ever needed help.
Defines honesty between best friends	Honesty in a best friendship is the sharing of feelings openly and without reserve. All people interviewed said they could rely on their best friends as confidants: They could share problems with their best friends and ask for advice. They also felt that, even if best friends were critical of each other, they would never be hurtful or spiteful.
Describes feelings of love between best friends	Love is probably the most important quality of a best friend relationship, according to the interview group. They very much prized the affection and enjoyment they felt in the company of their best friends. One man described it as a "gut reaction," and all said it was a different feeling from being with other friends. Private jokes, looks, and gestures create personal communication between best friends that is at a very high level—many times one person knows what the other is thinking without anything being said. The specifics differ, but almost everyone agreed that a special feeling exists, which is best described as love.
Answers to question 2: Who can be a best friend?	When asked who could be a best friend and who could not, most of those interviewed stated that it was impossible for parents, other relatives, and people of the opposite sex (especially husbands or wives) to be best friends. One woman said such people were "too inhibitive." Only two of those interviewed, both of whom were men, disagree—each had
Interprets informants' responses	a female best friend. However, they seem to be an exception. Most of the people interviewed thought that their best

friends were not demanding, while relatives and partners of the opposite sex can be very demanding.

To the question of how many best friends one can have, about half of the sample responded that it is possible to have several best friends, although very few people can do so; others said it was possible to have only a very few best friends; and still others felt they could have just one. It was interesting to see how ideas varied on this question. Although best friends may be no less special for one person than another, people do define the concept differently.

Regarding how long it takes to become best friends and how long the relationship lasts, all were in agreement. "It is a long hard process which takes a lot of time," one woman explained. "It isn't something that can happen overnight," suggested another. One man said, "You usually know the person very well before you consider him your best friend. In fact you know everything about him, his bad points as well as his good points, so there is little likelihood that you can come into conflict with him." In addition, everyone thought that once a person has become a best friend, he or she remains so for the rest of one's life.

During the course of the interviews one important and unexpected difference emerged between men and women. The men all said that a best friend usually possessed one quality that stood out above all others—an easygoing manner or humor or sympathy, for example. One of them said that he looked not for loyalty but for honesty, for someone who was truthful, because it was so rare to find this quality in anyone. The women, however, all responded that they looked for a well-rounded person who had many good qualities. One woman said that a person who had just one good quality and not several would be "too boring to associate with." If this difference holds true beyond my sample, it means that men and women have quite different definitions of their best friends.

On a personal note, I have always wondered why my own best friends were so important to me; it wasn't until recently that something happened to make me really understand my relationship with them. My father died, and this was a crisis for me. Most of my friends gave me their condolences, but my best friends did more than that: They actually supported me. They called long distance to see how I was and what I needed, to try to help me work out my problems, or simply to

> talk. Two of my best friends even took time from their spring break and, along with two other best friends, attended my father's memorial service. None of my other friends came. Since then, these are the only people who have continued to worry about me and talk to me about my father. I know that whenever I need someone they will be there and willing to help me. I know also that whenever they need help I will be ready to do the same for them.
>
> Yet, like the people I interviewed, I don't value my best friends just for what they do for me. I simply enjoy their company more than anyone else's. We talk, joke, play sports, and do all kinds of things when we are together. I never feel ill at ease with them, even after we've been apart for a while. As with virtually all of those I interviewed, the most important thing for me about best friends is the knowledge that I am never alone, that there are others in the world who care about my well-being as much as I do about theirs. Viewed in this light, having a best friend seems more like a necessity than it does a luxury reserved for the lucky few.

Conclusion: personal definition of best friend

Thesis

10

Analyzing Howard Solomon, Jr.'s Definition Essay: Questions for Discussion

1. How does Solomon define *best friend* in his opening paragraph?
2. According to the people Solomon surveyed, what three qualities are valued most in a best friend?
3. Which of these qualities is considered the most important? Why?
4. How do men's and women's definitions of *best friend* differ? Do you agree with Solomon's interviewees?
5. In what ways do Solomon's interviews enhance his own definition of *best friend*?
6. In the final analysis, why does Solomon think people value their best friends so much?

SUGGESTIONS FOR USING DEFINITION AS A WRITING STRATEGY

As you plan, write, and revise your definition essay, be mindful of the writing process guidelines described in Chapter 2. Also, pay particular attention to the basic requirements and essential ingredients for this writing strategy.

▸ Planning Your Definition Essay

Planning is an essential part of writing a good definition essay. You can save yourself a great deal of work by taking the time to think about the key components of your essay before you actually begin to write.

DETERMINE YOUR PURPOSE. Whatever your subject, make sure you have a clear sense of your purpose. Why are you writing a definition? If it's only to explain what a word or phrase means, you'll probably run out of things to say in a few sentences, or you'll find that a good dictionary has already said them for you. An effective extended definition should attempt to explain the essential nature of a thing or an idea, whether it be *photosynthesis* or *spring fever* or *Republicanism* or *prison* or *common sense*.

Often the challenge of writing a paper using the rhetorical strategy of definition is in getting your audience to understand your particular perception of the term or idea you are trying to define and explain. Take, for example, the following selection from a student essay. For many years, the citizens of Quebec, one of Canada's ten provinces, have been debating and voting on the issue of secession from Canada. At the core of this volatile issue is the essential question of Canadian identity. As you will see from the student's introduction, the Quebecois define Canadian identity very differently from the way other Canadians define it.

Quebecois Are Canadians

The peaceful formation of Canada as an independent nation has led to the current identity crisis in Quebec. The Quebecois perceive themselves to be different from all other Canadians because of their French ancestry and their unique history as both rulers and minorities in Canada. In an attempt to create a unified Canada the government has tried to establish a common Canadian culture through the building of a transcontinental railroad, a nationalized medical system, a national arts program, a national agenda, and the required use of both French and English in all publications and on all signs. As the twenty-first century begins, however, Canadians, especially the Quebecois, continue to grapple with the issue of what it means to be a Canadian, and unless some consensus can be reached on the definition of the Canadian identity, Quebec's attempt to secede from Canada may succeed.

This introductory paragraph establishes the need to define the terms *Canadians* and *Quebecois*. The emphasis on these two terms implies that another rhetorical strategy—comparison and contrast—will likely come into play. The writer might go on to use other strategies, such as description or illustration, to highlight common characteristics or differences between the Canadians and Quebecois. Judging from the title, it is clear that an argument will be made that Quebecois are Canadians.

When you decide on your topic, consider an idea or a term that you would like to clarify or explain to someone. For example, Howard Solomon, Jr. hit on the idea of defining what a best friend is. He recalls that "a friend of mine had become a best friend, and I was trying to figure out what had happened, what was different. So I decided to explore what was on my mind." At the beginning, you should have at least a general idea of what your subject means to you, as well as a sense of the audience you are writing your definition for and the impact you want your definition to achieve. The following advice will guide you as you plan and draft your essay.

FORMULATE A THESIS STATEMENT. A strong, clear thesis statement is critical in any essay. When writing an essay using extended definition, you should formulate a thesis statement that states clearly both the word or idea that you want to define or explain and the way in which you are going to present your thoughts. Here are two examples from this chapter.

> **thesis** We have a word in English which means "the ability to tell differences." That word is *discrimination*. But within the last [sixty] years, this word has been so frequently misused that an entire generation has grown up believing that "discrimination" means "racism."
>
> [Robert Keith Miller's thesis statement tells us that he will be discussing the word *discrimination* and how it is not the same as racism.]
>
> **thesis** As the twenty-first century begins, however, Canadians, especially the Quebecois, continue to grapple with the issue of what it means to be a Canadian, and unless some consensus can be reached on the definition of the Canadian identity, Quebec's attempt to secede from Canada may succeed.
>
> [The student writer makes it clear that the identity of both the Canadians and the Quebecois will be defined. The thesis statement also conveys a sense of the urgency of discussing these definitions and the possible consequences.]

As you begin to develop your thesis statement, ask yourself, "What is my point?" Next, ask yourself, "What types of definitions will be most useful in making my point?" If you can't answer these questions yet, write down some ideas and try to determine your main point from these ideas.

Once you have settled on an idea, go back to the two questions above and write down your answers to them. Then combine the answers into a single-sentence thesis statement. Your eventual thesis statement does not have to be one sentence, but this exercise can help you focus your point.

CONSIDER YOUR AUDIENCE. What do your readers know? If you're an economics major in an undergraduate writing course, you can safely assume that you know economics as a subject better than most of your readers do, and so you will have to explain even very basic terms and ideas. If, however, you're writing a paper for your course in econometrics, your most important reader—the one who grades your paper—won't even slow down at your references to *monetary aggregates* and *Philips curves*—provided, of course, that you use the terms correctly, showing that you know what they mean.

CHOOSE A TYPE OF DEFINITION THAT FITS YOUR SUBJECT. How you choose to develop your definition depends on your subject, your purpose, and your readers. Many inexperienced writers believe that any extended definition, no matter what the subject, should begin with a formal "dictionary" definition. This is not necessarily so; you will find that few of the essays in this chapter include formal definitions.

Instead, their authors assume that their readers have dictionaries and know how to use them. If, however, you think your readers do require a formal definition at some point, don't simply quote from a dictionary. Unless you have some very good reason for doing otherwise, put the definition into your own words—words that suit your approach and the probable readers of your essay. (Certainly, in an essay about photosynthesis, nonscientists would be baffled by an opening such as this: "The dictionary defines *photosynthesis* as 'the process by which chlorophyll-containing cells in green plants convert incident light to chemical energy and synthesize organic compounds from inorganic compounds, especially carbohydrates from carbon dioxide and water, with the simultaneous release of oxygen.' ") There's another advantage to using your own words: You won't have to write "The dictionary defines . . ." or "According to *Webster's* . . ."; stock phrases like these almost immediately put the reader's mind to sleep.

Certain concepts, such as *liberalism* and *discrimination*, lend themselves to different interpretations, depending on the writer's point of view. While readers may agree in general about what such subjects mean, there will be much disagreement over particulars and therefore room for you to propose and defend your own definitions.

Solomon remembers the difficulties he had getting started with his essay on best friends:

> The first draft I wrote was nothing. I tried to get a start with the dictionary definition, but it didn't help—it just put into two words what really needs hundreds of words to explain, and the words it used had to be defined, too. My teacher suggested I might get going better if I talked about my topic with other people. I decided to make it semiformal, so I made up a list of a few specific questions—five questions—and went to twenty people I knew and asked them questions like, "What qualities do your best friends have?" and "What are some of the things they've done for you?" I took notes on the answers, and I was surprised when so many of them agreed. It isn't a scientific sampling, but the results helped me get started.

▶ Organizing and Writing Your Definition Essay

DEVELOP AN ORGANIZATIONAL PLAN. Once you have gathered all the information you will need for your extended definition essay, you will want to settle on an organizational plan that suits your purpose and your materials. If you want to show that one definition of *family* is better than others, for example, you might want to lead with the definitions you plan to discard and end with the one you want your readers to accept.

Howard Solomon, Jr. can trace several distinct stages that his paper went through before he settled on the plan of organizing his examples around the items on his interview questionnaire:

> Doing this paper showed me that writing isn't all that easy. Boy, I went through so many drafts—adding some things, taking out some things, reorganizing. At one point half the paper was a definition of *friends*, so I could contrast them with the definition of *best friends*. That wasn't necessary. Then the personal stuff came in late. In fact, my father died after I'd begun writing the paper, so that paragraph came in almost last of all. On the next-to-last draft everything was there, but it was put together in a sort of random way—not completely random, one idea would lead to the next and then the next—but there was a lot of circling around. My teacher pointed this out and suggested I outline what I'd written and work on the outline. So I tried it, and I saw what the problem was and what I had to do. It was just a matter of getting my examples into an order that corresponded to my interview questions.

USE OTHER RHETORICAL STRATEGIES TO SUPPORT YOUR DEFINITION. Although definition can be used effectively as a separate rhetorical strategy, it is generally used alongside other writing strategies. Photosynthesis, for example, is a natural process, so one logical strategy for defining it would be *process analysis*; readers who know little about biology may better understand photosynthesis if you draw an *analogy* with the eating and breathing of human beings. *Common sense* is an abstract concept, so its meaning could certainly be *illustrated* with concrete *examples*; in addition, its special nature might emerge more sharply through *comparison and contrast* with other ways of thinking. To define a salt marsh, you might choose a typical marsh and *describe* it. To define economic inflation or a particular disease, you might discuss its *causes and effects*. In the end, only one requirement limits your choice of supporting strategy: The strategy must help you define your term.

As you read the essays in this chapter, consider all of the writing strategies that the authors have used to support their definitions. Solomon, for example, builds his definition essay around the many examples he garnered from his interviews with other students and from his own personal experiences. As you read the other essays and note the supporting strategies authors use when defining their subjects, ask yourself the following: How do you think these other strategies have added to or changed the style of the essay? Are there strategies that you might have added or taken out? What strategies, if any, do you think you might use to strengthen your definition essay?

▶ Revising and Editing Your Definition Essay

Begin your revision by reading aloud what you have written. This will help you to hear any lapses in the logical flow of thought and makes it easier to catch any words that have been accidentally left out. Once you have caught any major errors, use Chapter 16 along with the guidelines and questions below to help you make your corrections.

SELECT WORDS THAT ACCURATELY DENOTE AND CONNOTE WHAT YOU WANT TO SAY. The *denotation* of a word is its literal meaning or dictionary definition. Most of the time you will have no trouble with denotation, but problems can occur when words are close in meaning or sound a lot alike.

accept	*v.*, to receive
except	*prep.*, to exclude
affect	*v.*, to influence
effect	*n.*, the result; *v.*, to produce, bring into existence
anecdote	*n.*, a short narrative
antidote	*n.*, a medicine for countering effects of poison
coarse	*adj.*, rough; crude
course	*n.*, a route, a program of instruction

disinterested	*adj.*, free of self-interest or bias
uninterested	*adj.*, without interest
eminent	*adj.*, outstanding, as in reputation
immanent	*adj.*, remaining within, inherent
imminent	*adj.*, about to happen
principal	*n.*, a school official; in finance, a capital sum; *adj.*, most important
principle	*n.*, a basic law or rule of conduct
than	*conj.*, used in comparisons
then	*adv.*, at that time

Consult a dictionary if you are not sure you are using the correct word.

Words have connotative values as well as denotative meanings. *Connotations* are the associations or emotional overtones that words have acquired. For example, the word *hostage* denotes a person who is given or held as security for the fulfillment of certain conditions or terms, but it connotes images of suffering, loneliness, torture, fear, deprivation, starvation, or anxiety, as well as other images based on our individual associations. Because many words in English are synonyms or have the same meanings—*strength, potency, force,* and *might* all denote "power"—your task as a writer in any given situation is to choose the word with the connotations that best suit your purpose.

USE SPECIFIC AND CONCRETE WORDS. Words can be classified as relatively general or specific, abstract or concrete. *General words* name groups or classes of objects, qualities, or actions. *Specific words* name individual objects, qualities, or actions within a class or group. For example, *dessert* is more specific than *food* but more general than *pie*, and *pie* is more general than *blueberry pie*.

Abstract words refer to ideas, concepts, qualities, and conditions—*love, anger, beauty, youth, wisdom, honesty, patriotism,* and *liberty*, for example. *Concrete words*, on the other hand, name things you can see, hear, taste, touch, or smell. *Corn bread, rocking chair, sailboat, nitrogen, computer, rain, horse,* and *coffee* are all concrete words.

General and abstract words generally fail to create in the reader's mind the kind of vivid responses that concrete, specific words do, as Natalie Goldberg memorably notes on pages 187–88. Always question the words you choose. Notice how Jo Goodwin Parker uses concrete, specific diction in the opening sentences of many paragraphs in her essay "What Is Poverty?" to paint a powerful verbal picture of what poverty is:

> Poverty is getting up every morning from a dirt- and illness-stained mattress. . . .
> Poverty is being tired. . . .

Poverty is dirt....
Poverty is staying up all night on cold nights to watch the fire, knowing one spark on the newspaper covering the walls means your sleeping children die in flames. —Jo Goodwin Parker, "What Is Poverty?" pages 407–11

Collectively, these specific and concrete words create a memorable definition of the abstraction *poverty*.

QUESTION YOUR OWN WORK WHILE REVISING AND EDITING. Revision is best done by asking yourself key questions about what you have written. Begin by reading, preferably aloud, what you have written. Reading aloud forces you to pay attention to every single word, and you are more likely to catch lapses in the logical flow of thought. After you have read your paper through, answer the following questions for revising and editing, and make the necessary changes.

Questions for Revising and Editing: Definition

1. Have I selected a subject in which there is some controversy or at least a difference of opinion about the definitions of key words?
2. Is the purpose of my definition clearly stated?
3. Have I presented a clear thesis statement?
4. Have I considered my audience? Do I oversimplify material for knowledgeable people or complicate material for beginners?
5. Have I used the types of definitions (*formal definition, synonymous definition, negative definition, etymological definition, stipulative definition,* and *extended definition*) that are most useful in making my point?
6. Is my definition essay easy to follow? That is, is there a clear organizational principle (chronological or logical, for example)?
7. Have I used other rhetorical strategies — such as illustration, comparison and contrast, and cause and effect analysis — as needed and appropriate to enhance my definition?
8. Does my conclusion stem logically from my thesis statement and purpose?
9. Have I used precise language to convey my meaning? Have I used words that are specific and concrete?
10. Have I avoided errors in grammar, punctuation, and mechanics? Is my sentence style as clear, smooth, and persuasive as possible?

What Is Poverty?

JO GOODWIN PARKER

Everything we know about Jo Goodwin Parker comes from the account of professor George Henderson, who received the following essay from Parker while he was compiling a selection of readings intended for future educators planning to teach in rural communities. This selection, which Henderson subsequently included in *America's Other Children: Public Schools Outside Suburbs* (1971), has been identified as the text of a speech given in De Land, Florida, on December 27, 1965. Although Henderson has not shared any biographical information about the author, it may be useful to consider her identity. While Parker may be who she claims to be — one of the rural poor who eke out a difficult living just beyond view of America's middle-class majority — it is also possible that she is instead a spokesperson for these individuals, families, and communities, writing not from her own experience but from long and sympathetic observation. In either case, her definition of *poverty* is so detailed and forceful that it conveys, even to those who have never known it, the nature of poverty.

Preparing to Read

What does it mean to you to be poor? What do you see as some of the effects of poverty on people?

You ask me what is poverty? Listen to me. Here I am, dirty, smelly, and with no "proper" underwear on and with the stench of my rotting teeth near you. I will tell you. Listen to me. Listen without pity. I cannot use your pity. Listen with understanding. Put yourself in my dirty, worn-out, ill-fitting shoes, and hear me.

Poverty is getting up every morning from a dirt- and illness-stained mattress. The sheets have long since been used for diapers. Poverty is living in a smell that never leaves. This is a smell of urine, sour milk, and spoiling food sometimes joined with the strong smell of long-cooked onions. Onions are cheap. If you have smelled this smell, you did not know how it came. It is the smell of the outdoor privy. It is the smell of young children who cannot walk the long dark way in the night. It is the smell of the mattresses where years of "accidents" have happened. It is the smell of the milk which has gone sour because the refrigerator long has not worked, and it costs money to get it fixed. It is the smell of rotting garbage. I could bury it, but where is the shovel? Shovels cost money.

Poverty is being tired. I have always been tired. They told me at the hospital when the last baby came that I had chronic anemia caused from poor diet, a bad case of worms, and that I needed a corrective operation.

I listened politely—the poor are always polite. The poor always listen. They don't say that there is no money for iron pills, or better food, or worm medicine. The idea of an operation is frightening and costs so much that, if I had dared, I would have laughed. Who takes care of my children? Recovery from an operation takes a long time. I have three children. When I left them with "Granny" the last time I had a job, I came home to find the baby covered with fly specks, and a diaper that had not been changed since I left. When the dried diaper came off, bits of my baby's flesh came with it. My other child was playing with a sharp bit of broken glass, and my oldest was playing alone at the edge of a lake. I made twenty-two dollars a week, and a good nursery school costs twenty dollars a week for three children. I quit my job.

Poverty is getting up every morning from a dirt- and illness-stained mattress. The sheets have long since been used for diapers. Poverty is living in a smell that never leaves.

Poverty is dirt. You say in your clean clothes coming from your clean house, "Anybody can be clean." Let me explain about housekeeping with no money. For breakfast I give my children grits with no oleo or cornbread without eggs and oleo. This does not use up many dishes. What dishes there are, I wash in cold water and with no soap. Even the cheapest soap has to be saved for the baby's diapers. Look at my hands, so cracked and red. Once I saved for two months to buy a jar of Vaseline for my hands and the baby's diaper rash. When I had saved enough, I went to buy it and the price had gone up two cents. The baby and I suffered on. I have to decide every day if I can bear to put my cracked, sore hands into the cold water and strong soap. But you ask, why not hot water? Fuel costs money. If you have a wood fire it costs money. If you burn electricity, it costs money. Hot water is a luxury. I do not have luxuries. I know you will be surprised when I tell you how young I am. I look so much older. My back has been bent over the wash tubs for so long, I cannot remember when I ever did anything else. Every night I wash every stitch my school-age child has on and just hope her clothes will be dry by morning.

Poverty is staying up all night on cold nights to watch the fire, knowing one spark on the newspaper covering the walls means your sleeping children die in flames. In summer poverty is watching gnats and flies devour your baby's tears when he cries. The screens are torn and you pay so little rent you know they will never be fixed. Poverty means insects in your food, in your nose, in your eyes, and crawling over you when you sleep. Poverty is hoping it never rains because diapers won't dry when it rains and soon you are using newspapers. Poverty is seeing your children forever with runny noses. Paper handkerchiefs cost money and all your rags you need for other things. Even more costly are antihistamines. Poverty is cooking without food and cleaning without soap.

Poverty is asking for help. Have you ever had to ask for help, knowing your children will suffer unless you get it? Think about asking for a loan from a relative, if this is the only way you can imagine asking for help. I will tell you how it feels. You find out where the office is that you are supposed to visit. You circle that block four or five times. Thinking of your children, you go in. Everyone is very busy. Finally, someone comes out and you tell her that you need help. That never is the person you need to see. You go see another person, and after spilling the whole shame of your poverty all over the desk between you, you find that this isn't the right office after all—you must repeat the whole process, and it never is any easier at the next place.

You have asked for help, and after all it has a cost. You are again told to wait. You are told why, but you don't really hear because of the red cloud of shame and the rising black cloud of despair.

Poverty is remembering. It is remembering quitting school in junior high because "nice" children had been so cruel about my clothes and my smell. The attendance officer came. My mother told him I was pregnant. I wasn't but she thought that I could get a job and help out. I had jobs off and on, but never long enough to learn anything. Mostly I remember being married. I was so young then. I am still young. For a time, we had all the things you have. There was a little house in another town, with hot water and everything. Then my husband lost his job. There was unemployment insurance for a while and what few jobs I could get. Soon, all our nice things were repossessed and we moved back here. I was pregnant then. This house didn't look so bad when we first moved in. Every week it gets worse. Nothing is ever fixed. We now had no money. There were a few odd jobs for my husband, but everything went for food then, as it does now. I don't know how we lived through three years and three babies, but we did. I'll tell you something, after the last baby I destroyed my marriage. It had been a good one, but could you keep on bringing children in this dirt? Did you ever think how much it costs for any kind of birth control? I knew my husband was leaving the day he left, but there were no good-byes between us. I hope he has been able to climb out of this mess somewhere. He never could hope with us to drag him down.

That's when I asked for help. When I got it, you know how much it was? It was, and is, seventy-eight dollars a month for the four of us; that is all I ever can get. Now you know why there is no soap, no needles and thread, no hot water, no aspirin, no worm medicine, no hand cream, no shampoo. None of these things forever and ever and ever. So that you can see clearly, I pay twenty dollars a month rent, and most of the rest goes for food. For grits and cornmeal, and rice and milk and beans. I try my best to use only the minimum electricity. If I use more, there is that much less for food.

Poverty is looking into a black future. Your children won't play with my boys. They will turn to other boys who steal to get what they want. I can already see them behind the bars of their prison instead of behind the bars of my poverty. Or they will turn to the freedom of alcohol or drugs, and find themselves enslaved. And my daughter? At best, there is for her a life like mine.

But you say to me, there are schools. Yes, there are schools. My children have no extra books, no magazines, no extra pencils, or crayons, or paper and the most important of all, they do not have health. They have worms, they have infections, they have pinkeye all summer. They do not sleep well on the floor, or with me in my one bed. They do not suffer from hunger, my seventy-eight dollars keeps us alive, but they do suffer from malnutrition. Oh yes, I do remember what I was taught about health in school. It doesn't do much good. In some places there is a surplus commodities program. Not here. The county said it cost too much. There is a school lunch program. But I have two children who will already be damaged by the time they get to school.

But, you say to me, there are health clinics. Yes, there are health clinics and they are in the towns. I live out here eight miles from town. I can walk that far (even if it is sixteen miles both ways), but can my little children? My neighbor will take me when he goes; but he expects to get paid, *one way or another*. I bet you know my neighbor. He is that large man who spends his time at the gas station, the barbershop, and the corner store complaining about the government spending money on the immoral mothers of illegitimate children.

Poverty is an acid that drips on pride until all pride is worn away. Poverty is a chisel that chips on honor until honor is worn away. Some of you say that you would do *something* in my situation, and maybe you would, for the first week or the first month, but for year after year after year?

Even the poor can dream. A dream of a time when there is money. Money for the right kinds of food, for worm medicine, for iron pills, for toothbrushes, for hand cream, for a hammer and nails and a bit of screening, for a shovel, for a bit of paint, for some sheeting, for needles and thread. Money to pay *in money* for a trip to town. And, oh, money for hot water and money for soap. A dream of when asking for help does not eat away the last bit of pride. When the office you visit is as nice as the offices of other governmental agencies, when there are enough workers to help you quickly, when workers do not quit in defeat and despair. When you have to tell your story to only one person, and that person can send you for other help and you don't have to prove your poverty over and over and over again.

I have come out of my despair to tell you this. Remember I did not come from another place or another time. Others like me are all around you. Look at us with an angry heart, anger that will help you help me. Anger that will let you tell of me. The poor are always silent. Can you be silent, too?

Thinking Critically about the Text

Throughout the essay, Parker describes the feelings and emotions associated with her poverty. Have you ever witnessed or observed people in Parker's situation? What was your reaction?

Questions on Subject

1. Why didn't Parker have the operation that was recommended for her? Why did she quit her job?
2. In Parker's view, what makes asking for help such a difficult and painful experience? What compels her to do so anyway?
3. Why did Parker's husband leave her? How does she justify her attitude toward his leaving? (Glossary: *Attitude*)
4. In paragraph 12, Parker says the following about a neighbor giving her a ride to the nearest health clinic: "My neighbor will take me when he goes; but he expects to get paid, *one way or another*. I bet you know my neighbor." What is she implying in these sentences and in the rest of the paragraph?
5. What are the chances that the dreams described in paragraph 14 will come true? What do you think Parker would say?

Questions on Strategy

1. What is Parker's purpose in defining poverty as she does? (Glossary: *Purpose*) Why has she cast her essay in the form of an extended definition? What effect does this have on the reader?
2. What techniques of definition does Parker use? What is missing that you would expect to find in a more general and impersonal definition of poverty? Why does Parker leave out such information?
3. Parker repeats words and phrases throughout this essay. Choose several examples and explain their impact on you. (Glossary: *Coherence*)
4. In depicting poverty, Parker uses description to create vivid verbal pictures, and she illustrates the various aspects of poverty with examples drawn from

her experience. (Glossary: *Description; Illustration*) What are the most striking details she uses? How do you account for the emotional impact of the details and images she has selected? In what ways do description and illustration enhance her definition of poverty?

Questions on Diction and Vocabulary

1. Although her essay is written for the most part in simple, straightforward language, Parker does make use of an occasional striking figure of speech. (Glossary: *Figures of Speech*) Identify at least three such figures — you might begin with those in paragraph 13 (for example, "Poverty is an acid") — and explain their effect on the reader.

2. In paragraph 10, Parker states that "poverty is looking into a black future." How does this language characterize her children's future?

3. How would you characterize Parker's tone and her style? (Glossary: *Style; Tone*) How do you respond to her use of the pronoun *you*? Point to specific examples of her diction and descriptions as support for your view. (Glossary: *Diction*)

4. Refer to a dictionary to determine the meanings of the following words as Parker uses them in this selection: *chronic* (paragraph 3), *anemia* (3), *grits* (4), *oleo* (4), *antihistamines* (5).

Definition in Action

Without consulting a dictionary, try writing a formal definition for one of the following terms by putting it in a class and then differentiating it from other words in the class. (See page 392 for a discussion of formal definitions together with examples.)

tortilla chips	trombone
psychology	*Making of a Murderer*
robin	Catholicism
anger	secretary

Once you have completed your definition, compare it with the definition found in a dictionary. What conclusions can you draw? Explain.

Writing Suggestions

1. Using Parker's essay as a model, write an extended definition of a topic about which you have some expertise. Choose as your subject a particular environment (suburbia, the inner city, a dormitory, a shared living area), a way of living (as the child of divorce, as a person with a disability, as a working student), or a topic of your own choosing. If you prefer, you can adopt a persona instead of writing from your own perspective.

2. **Writing with Sources.** Write a proposal or a plan of action that will make people aware of poverty or some other social problem in your community. How do you define the problem? What needs to be done to increase awareness of it? What practical steps would you propose be undertaken once the public is made aware of the situation? You will likely need to do some research in the library or online in order to garner support for your proposal. For models of and advice on integrating sources in your essay, see Chapters 14 and 15.

Steal This MP3 File: What Is Theft?

G. ANTHONY GORRY

G. Anthony Gorry is a medical educator and information technology specialist. He received his B.S. from Yale University in 1962 and pursued graduate study at the University of California–Berkeley, where he earned his M.S. in chemical engineering in 1963, and at the Massachusetts Institute of Technology (MIT), where he received his Ph.D. in computer science in 1967. Gorry has taught at MIT and Baylor College of Medicine and is currently the Friedkin Professor of Management and a professor of computer science at Rice University. He is the author of numerous journal articles on management information systems and problem identification. Since 1997 he has served as a director for Ore Pharmaceutical Holdings, Inc.

Courtesy of T. Anthony Gorry

In the following article, which first appeared in the *Chronicle of Higher Education* on May 23, 2003, Gorry recounts an experience he had in one of his information technology courses in order to demonstrate how technology might be shaping the attitudes of today's youth. He senses that the meaning of *theft* may be shifting in our ever-changing world.

Preparing to Read

What for you constitutes theft? Do you recall ever having stolen anything? Did you get caught? Did you have to return the item or make restitution? How did you feel about the incident at the time? How do you feel about it now?

Sometimes when my students don't see life the way I do, I recall the complaint from *Bye Bye Birdie*, "What's the matter with kids today?" Then I remember that the "kids" in my class are children of the information age. In large part, technology has made them what they are, shaping their world and what they know. For my students, the advance of technology is expected, but for me, it remains both remarkable and somewhat unsettling.

In one course I teach, the students and I explore the effects of information technology on society. Our different perspectives on technology lead to engaging and challenging discussions that reveal some of the ways in which technology is shaping the attitudes of young people. An example is our discussion of intellectual property in the information age, of crucial importance to the entertainment business.

In recent years, many users of the Internet have launched an assault on the music business. Armed with tools for "ripping" music from compact discs and setting it "free" in cyberspace, they can disseminate online countless copies of a digitally encoded song. Music companies, along with some artists, have tried to stop this perceived pillaging of intellectual property by legal and technical means. The industry has had some success with legal actions against companies that provide the infrastructure for file sharing, but enthusiasm for sharing music is growing, and new file-sharing services continue to appear.

The Recording Industry Association of America ... filed lawsuits against four college students, seeking huge damages for "an emporium of music piracy" run on campus networks. However, the industry settled those lawsuits less than a week after a federal judge in California ruled against the association in another case, affirming that two of the Internet's most popular music-swapping services are not responsible for copyright infringements by their users. (In the settlement, the students admitted no wrongdoing but agreed to pay amounts ranging from $12,000 to $17,500 in annual installments over several years and to shut down their file-sharing systems.)

> In the case of digital music, where the material is disconnected from the physical moorings of conventional stores and copying is so easy, many of my students see matters differently.

With so many Internet users currently sharing music, legal maneuvers alone seem unlikely to protect the industry's way of doing business. Therefore, the music industry has turned to the technology itself, seeking to create media that cannot be copied or can be copied only in prescribed circumstances. Finding the right technology for such a defense, however, is not easy. Defensive technology must not prevent legitimate uses of the media by customers, yet it must somehow ward off attacks by those seeking to "liberate" the content to the Internet. And each announcement of a defensive technology spurs development of means to circumvent it.

In apparent frustration, some companies have introduced defective copies of their music into the file-sharing environment of the Internet, hoping to discourage widespread downloading of music. But so far, the industry's multifaceted defense has failed. Sales of CDs continue to decline. And now video ripping and sharing has emerged on the Internet, threatening to upset another industry in the same way.

Music companies might have more success if they focused on the users instead of the courts and technology. When they characterize file sharing as theft, they overlook the interplay of technology and behavior that has altered the very idea of theft, at least among young people. I got a clear demonstration of that change in a class discussion that began with the matter of a stolen book.

During the '60s, I was a graduate student at a university where student activism had raised tensions on and around the campus. In the midst of debates, demonstrations, and protests, a football player was caught leaving the campus store with a book he had not bought. Because he was well known, his misadventure made the school newspaper. What seemed to be a simple case of theft, however, took on greater significance. A number of groups with little connection to athletics rose to his defense, claiming that he had been entrapped: The university required that he have the book, the publisher charged an unfairly high price, and the bookstore put the book right in front of him, tempting him to steal it. So who could blame him?

Well, my students could. They thought it was clear that he had stolen the book. But an MP3 file played from my laptop evoked a different response. Had I stolen the song? Not really, because a student had given me the file as a gift. Well, was that file stolen property? Was it like the book stolen from the campus bookstore so many years ago? No again, because it was a copy, not the original, which presumably was with the student. But then what should we make of the typical admonition on compact-disc covers that unauthorized duplication is illegal? Surely the MP3 file was a duplication of the original. To what extent is copying stealing?

The readings for the class amply demonstrated the complexity of the legal, technical, and economic issues surrounding intellectual property in the information age and gave the students much to talk about. Some students argued that existing regulations are simply inadequate at a time when all information "wants to be free" and when liberating technology is at hand. Others pointed to differences in the economics of the music and book businesses. In the end, the students who saw theft in the removal of the book back in the '60s did not see stealing in the unauthorized copying of music. For me, that was the most memorable aspect of the class because it illustrates how technology affects what we take to be moral behavior.

The technology of copying is closely related to the idea of theft. For example, my students would not take books from a store, but they do not consider photocopying a few pages of a book to be theft. They would not copy an entire book, however, perhaps because they vaguely acknowledge intellectual-property rights but probably more because copying would be cumbersome and time-consuming. They would buy the book instead. In that case, the very awkwardness of the copying aligns their actions with moral guidelines and legal standards.

But in the case of digital music, where the material is disconnected from the physical moorings of conventional stores and copying is so easy, many of my students see matters differently. They freely copy and share music. And they copy and share software, even though such copying is often illegal. If their books were digital and thus could be copied with comparable ease, they most likely would copy and share them.

Of course, the Digital Millennium Copyright Act, along with other laws, prohibits such copying. So we could just say that theft is theft, and complain with the song, "Why can't they be like we were, perfect in every way? . . . Oh, what's the matter with kids today?" But had we had the same digital technology when we were young, we probably would have engaged in the same copying and sharing of software, digital music, and video that are so common among students today. We should not confuse lack of tools with righteousness.

The music industry would be foolish to put its faith in new protective schemes and devices alone. Protective technology cannot undo the changes that previous technology has caused. Should the industry aggressively pursue legal defenses like the suits against the four college students? Such highly publicized actions may be legally sound and may even slow music sharing in certain settings, but they cannot stop the transformation of the music business. The technology of sharing is too widespread, and my students (and their younger siblings) no longer agree with the music companies about right and wrong. Even some of the companies with big stakes in recorded music seem to have recognized that lawsuits and technical defenses won't work. Sony, for example, sells computers with "ripping and burning" capabilities, MP3 players, and other devices that gain much of their appeal from music sharing. And the AOL part of AOL Time Warner is promoting its new broadband service for faster downloads, which many people will use to share music sold by the Warner part of the company.

The lesson from my classroom is that digital technology has unalterably changed the way a growing number of customers think about recorded music. If the music industry is to prosper, it must change, too—perhaps offering repositories of digital music for downloading (like Apple's . . . iTunes Music Store), gaining revenue from the scope and quality of its holdings, and from a variety of new products and relationships, as yet largely undefined. Such a transformation will be excruciating for the industry, requiring the abandonment of previously profitable business practices with no certain prospect of success. So it is not surprising that the industry has responded aggressively, with strong legal actions, to the spread of file sharing. But by that response, the industry is risking its relationship with a vital segment of its market. Treating customers like thieves is a certain recipe for failure.

Thinking Critically about the Text

Where do you stand on file sharing? Like Gorry's students, do you freely copy and share music or software? Do you consider all such sharing acceptable, or is there some point where it turns into theft? Explain.

Questions on Subject

1. What is intellectual property, and how is it different from other types of property?
2. How has the music industry tried to stop "music piracy" on the Internet? How successful have those efforts been?
3. Do you think the football player caught leaving the campus store with a book was guilty of stealing, or are you persuaded by the argument that "he had been entrapped" (paragraph 8)? Explain.
4. What does Gorry mean when he says that "the technology of copying is closely related to the idea of theft" (paragraph 11)?
5. What advice do Gorry and his students have for the music industry? Is this advice realistic? Explain. What suggestions would you like to add?

Questions on Strategy

1. What is Gorry's thesis, and where is it stated? (Glossary: *Thesis*)
2. Gorry's purpose is to show that there has recently been a shift in what the Internet generation believes constitutes theft. (Glossary: *Purpose*) How well does he accomplish his purpose?
3. What examples does Gorry use to develop his definition of theft? (Glossary: *Illustration*) How does he use these examples to illustrate the shift in meaning that he believes has occurred?
4. With what authority does Gorry write on the subjects of intellectual property, technology, and theft?
5. Gorry uses lyrics from the movie *Bye Bye Birdie* to introduce his essay and start his conclusion. (Glossary: *Beginnings/Endings*) Are these just gimmicky quotations, or do they contribute to the substance of Gorry's essay?
6. Gorry ends paragraph 8 with the question "So who could blame him?" and then begins paragraph 9 with the response "Well, my students could," thus making a smooth transition from one paragraph to the next. (Glossary: *Transitions*) What other transitional devices does Gorry use to add coherence to his essay? (Glossary: *Coherence*)

Questions on Diction and Vocabulary

1. Who is Gorry's intended audience? (Glossary: *Audience*) To whom does the pronoun *we* in paragraph 13 refer? What other evidence in Gorry's diction do you find to support your conclusion about his audience?
2. How would you describe Gorry's diction — formal, objective, conversational, jargon-filled? (Glossary: *Technical Language*) Point out specific words and phrases that led you to this conclusion.
3. Refer to a dictionary to determine the meanings of the following words as Gorry uses them in this selection: *disseminate* (paragraph 3), *encoded* (3), *emporium* (4), *infringements* (4), *repositories* (15).

Definition in Action

Definitions are often dependent on one's perspective, as Gorry illustrates with the word *theft* in his essay. Discuss with your classmates other words or terms — such as *success, failure, wealth, poverty, cheap, expensive, happiness, loneliness, want, need* — whose definitions often are dependent on one's perspective. Write brief definitions for several of these words from your perspective. Share your definitions with other members of your class. What differences in perspective, if any, are apparent in the definitions?

Writing Suggestions

1. Although it is not always immediately apparent, English is constantly changing because it is a living language. New words come into the lexicon, and others become obsolete. Some words, like *theft*, change over time to reflect society's thinking and behavior. Another word whose definition has ignited recent debate is *immigrant*. Using Gorry's essay as a model, write a paper in which you define a word whose meaning has changed over the past decade.
2. Gorry is very aware of how information technology is shaping our attitudes about the world. We're living at a time when digital technology makes it not only possible but also surprisingly easy to copy and share software, music, e-books, and video. Gorry does not condemn such behavior out of hand; instead, he warns that "we should not confuse lack of tools with righteousness" (paragraph 13). Write an essay in which you explore some of the ways today's technology has shaped your attitudes, especially as it "affects what we take to be moral behavior" (10). Be sure to support your key points with examples from your own reading or experience. (Glossary: *Illustration*)

What Does "Boys Will Be Boys" Really Mean?

DEBORAH M. ROFFMAN

A nationally certified sexuality and family life educator, Deborah M. Roffman was born in 1948 in Baltimore, Maryland. She graduated from Goucher College in 1968 and later received an M.S. in community health education from Towson University. Since 1975, Roffman has worked with scores of public and private schools on curriculum, faculty development, and parent education issues. Her work in health and sex education has been featured in the *New York Times, Baltimore Sun, Chicago Tribune, Los Angeles Times, Education Week,* and *Parents* magazine. A former associate editor of the *Journal of Sex Education and Therapy*, she has appeared on an HBO special on parenting, on National Public Radio, on *The Early Show*, and on *The O'Reilly Factor*. In 2001 Roffman published her first book, *Sex and Sensibility: The Thinking Parent's Guide to Talking Sense about Sex*, followed in 2002 by *But How'd I Get in There in the First Place? Talking to Your Young Children about Sex*. Of the latter book, one reviewer wrote, "Roffman is a powerful advocate for children, understanding that in a society that gives confusing and exploitative messages about sexuality, children are desperate for communication from the caring adults in their lives." Her most recent book is *Talk to Me First: Everything You Need to Know to Become Your Kids' "Go-To" Person about Sex* (2012). Currently Roffman lives in Baltimore, where she teaches human sexuality education in grades 4 through 12.

The following essay was first published in the *Washington Post* on February 5, 2006. Roffman reports that the reaction to this article was overwhelming. "Many people thanked me for underscoring the point that boys and men are also treated disrespectfully in our culture and in some ways even more disrespectfully than girls and women, because of the gender-role stereotyping that defines them in even animalistic terms." Here she takes a common expression — "boys will be boys" — and asks us to think about what it really means and how that message affects boys in our society. Her conclusions will surprise those who have come to take the meaning of the expression for granted.

Courtesy of Deborah Roffman

Preparing to Read

When you hear the expression "boys will be boys," what comes to mind? What traits or characteristics about boys and men does the expression imply for you?

Three of my seventh-grade students asked the other week if we might view a recent episode of the Fox TV cartoon show *Family Guy* in our human sexuality class. It's about reproduction, they said, and besides, it's funny. Not having seen it, I said I'd have to check it out.

Well, there must be something wrong with my sense of humor because most of the episode made me want to alternately scream and cry.

It centers on Stewie, a sexist, foul-mouthed preschooler who hates his mother, fantasizes killing her off in violent ways, and wants to prevent his parents from making a new baby—until he realizes that he might get to have a sibling as nasty as he is. Then he starts encouraging his parents' lovemaking. At one point he peers into their room and tells his dad to "Give it to her good, old man." When his father leaves the bed he orders him to "Come here this instant you fat [expletive] and do her!"

Of course I know that this is farce, but I announced the next day that no, we wouldn't be taking class time to view the episode, titled "Emission Impossible." When I asked my students why they thought that was, they guessed: The language? The women dressed like "bimbos"? The implied sexual acts? The mistreatment of the mother?

> It's not so much that the boy is always *being* bad — sometimes that sort of thing can seem so outrageous it's funny. It's the underlying assumption . . . that boys, by nature, are bad.

Nope, nope, nope, I replied. I didn't love any of that, either, but it was the less obvious images and messages that got my attention, the ones that kids your age *are* less likely to notice. It's not so much that the boy is always *being* bad—sometimes that sort of thing can seem so outrageous it's funny. It's the underlying assumption in the show, and often in our society, that boys, by nature, are bad.

I said I thought the "boys will be bad" message of the show was a terribly disrespectful one, and I wouldn't use my classroom in any way to reinforce it. It was a good moment: Recognizing for the first time the irony that maybe it was they who were really being demeaned, some of the boys got mad, even indignant.

You can hear and see evidence of this long-standing folk "wisdom" about boys almost everywhere, from the gender-typed assumptions people make about young boys to the resigned attitude or blind eye adults so often turn to disrespectful or insensitive male behavior. Two years ago, when Justin Timberlake grabbed at Janet Jackson's breast during the Super Bowl halftime, he got a free pass while she was excoriated. As the mother of two sons and teacher of thousands of boys, the reaction to that incident made me furious, but perhaps not for the reason you may think: I understood it paradoxically as a twisted kind of compliment to women and a hidden and powerful indictment of men. Is the female in such instances the only one from whom we think we can expect responsible behavior?

That incident and so many others explain why, no matter how demeaning today's culture may seem toward girls and women, I've always understood it to be fundamentally more disrespectful of boys and men — a point that escapes many of us because we typically think of men as always having the upper hand.

Consider, though, what "boys will be boys" thinking implies about the true nature of boys. I often ask groups of adults or students what inherent traits or characteristics the expression implies. The answers typically are astonishingly negative: Boys are messy, immature, and selfish; hormone-driven and insensitive; irresponsible and troublemaking; rebellious, rude, aggressive, and disrespectful — even violent, predatory, and animal-like.

Is this a window into what we truly think, at least unconsciously, of the male of the species? Is it possible that deep inside we really think they simply can't be expected to do any better than this? How else to explain the very low bar we continue to set for their behavior, particularly when it comes to girls, women, and sex? At a talk I gave recently, a woman in the audience asked, only half in jest, "Is it okay to instruct my daughters that when it comes to sex, teenage boys are animals?" Do we stop to think how easily these kinds of remarks can become self-fulfilling prophecies or permission-giving of the worst kind?

Thanks to popular culture, unfortunately, it only gets worse. Not too long ago, I confiscated a hat from a student's head that read, "I'm a Pimp." This once-derogatory term is a complimentary handle these days for boys whom girls consider "hot." I asked the boy whether he would wear a hat that said "I'm a Rapist." Totally offended, he looked at me as if I had three heads. "Duh," I said. "Do you have any idea what real pimps do to keep their 'girls' in line?" Yet the term — like "slut" for girls — has been glamorized and legitimized by TV, movies, and popular music to such an extent that kids now bandy it about freely.

Just as fish don't know they're in water, young people today, who've been swimming all their formative years in the cesspool that is American popular culture, are often maddeningly incapable of seeing how none of this is in their social, sexual, or personal best interest.

Adults I work with tend to be a lot less clueless. They are sick and tired of watching the advertising and entertainment industries shamelessly pimp the increasingly naked bodies of American women and girls to sell everything from Internet service to floor tiles (I've got the ads to prove it).

Yet from my perspective, these same adults aren't nearly as clued in about how destructive these ubiquitous images and messages can be for boys. It, too, often takes patient coaching for them to see "boys will be boys" for what it is—an insidious and long-neglected character issue: People who think of and treat others as objects, in any way, are not kind, decent people. It's bad enough that boys are being trained by the culture to think that behaving in these ways is "cool"; it's outrageous and much more disturbing that many of the immediate adults in their lives can't see it, and may even buy into it.

The "boys will be bad" stereotype no doubt derives from a time when men were the exclusively entitled gender: Many did behave badly, simply because they could. (Interestingly, that's pretty much how Bill Clinton in hindsight ultimately explained his poor behavior in the Lewinsky affair.) For today's boys, however, the low expectations set for them socially and sexually have less to do with any real entitlement than with the blinders we wear to these antiquated and degrading gender myths.

I think, too, that the staying power of these myths has to do with the fact that as stereotypes go, they can be remarkably invisible. I've long asked students to bring in print advertisements using sex to sell products or showing people as sex objects. No surprise that in the vast majority of ads I receive, women are the focus, not men.

And yet, as I try to teach my students, there's always at least one invisible man present—looking at the advertisement. The messages being delivered to and/or about him are equally if not more powerful.

In one of my least favorite examples, a magazine ad for a video game (brought to me by a sixth-grade boy) depicts a highly sexualized woman with a dominatrix air brandishing a weapon. The heading reads, "Bet you'd like to get your hands on these!," meaning her breasts, er, the game controllers. And the man or boy not in the picture but looking on? The ad implies that he's just another low-life guy who lives and breathes to ogle and grab every large-breasted woman he sees.

Many boys I've talked with are pretty savvy about the permission-giving that "boys will be bad" affords and use it to their advantage in their relationships with adults. "Well, they really don't expect as much from us as they do from girls," said one tenth-grade boy. "It makes it easier to get away with a lot of stuff."

Others play it sexually to their advantage, knowing that in a system where boys are expected to want sex but not necessarily to be responsible about it, the girl will probably face the consequences if anything happens. As long as girls can still be called sluts, the sexual double standard—and its lack of accountability for boys—will rule.

Most boys I know are grateful when they finally get clued in to all this. A fifth-grade boy once told me that the worst insult anyone could possibly give him would be to call him a girl. When I walked him through what he seemed to be saying—that girls are inferior to him—he was suddenly ashamed that he could have thought such a thing. "I'm a better person than that," he said.

Just as we've adjusted the bar for girls in academics and athletics, we need to let boys know that, in the sexual and social arenas, we've been shortchanging them by setting the bar so low. We need to explain why the notion that "boys will be boys" embodies a bogus and ultimately corrupting set of expectations that are unacceptable.

We'll know we've succeeded when girls and boys better recognize sexual and social mistreatment and become angry and personally offended whenever anyone dares use the word *slut* against any girl, call any boy a *pimp*, or suggest that anyone reduce themselves or others to a sexual object.

We'll also know when boys call one another more often on disrespectful behavior, instead of being congratulatory, because they will have the self-respect and confidence that comes with being held to and holding themselves to high standards.

Thinking Critically about the Text

Why is it important that Roffman ask her readers to think about what the expression "boys will be boys" really means? What does she think the expression means? What does she mean when she says, "We need to explain why the notion that 'boys will be boys' embodies a bogus and ultimately corrupting set of expectations that are unacceptable" (paragraph 22)?

Questions on Subject

1. Why did Roffman's students think she did not want to show the episode of *Family Guy* in class? How does she respond to their answers? What about the show does Roffman find objectionable?

2. How did some of the boys react when Roffman revealed her reason for not viewing the show in class? In what ways was it "a good moment" (paragraph 6)?

3. In paragraph 7, Roffman uses the now infamous Justin Timberlake and Janet Jackson "wardrobe malfunction" incident during the Super Bowl halftime festivities as an example of "this longstanding folk 'wisdom' about boys." In what ways does she find this episode demeaning and disrespectful of boys and men? Do you agree?

4. What about America's advertising and entertainment industries does Roffman find objectionable? What does she find disturbing about adult responses to the images and messages in so much current advertising and entertainment?

5. What does Roffman see as the source of the "boys will be bad" stereotype? Why does she believe this stereotype has such staying power?

Questions on Strategy

1. Roffman opens her essay with an anecdote about seventh-graders asking to view and discuss an episode of *Family Guy* in their human sexuality class. How effective did you find this introduction? (Glossary: *Beginnings/Endings*)

2. What is Roffman's purpose in writing this essay? (Glossary: *Purpose*)

3. In paragraph 10, Roffman asks a series of questions. How do these questions function in the context of her essay? How did you answer these questions when you first read them?

4. Identify the analogy that Roffman uses in paragraph 12. (Glossary: *Analogy*) How does this strategy help her explain the plight of today's young people? Explain.

Questions on Diction and Vocabulary

1. Who is Roffman's intended audience? (Glossary: *Audience*) To whom do the pronouns *you* in paragraph 7 and *us* and *we* in paragraph 8 refer? What other evidence in Roffman's diction do you find to support your conclusion about her audience?

2. In paragraph 9, Roffman lists the negative traits and characteristics of boys suggested by the expression "boys will be boys." What connotations do you associate with each of the descriptors? (Glossary: *Connotation/Denotation*) What order, if any, do you see in her list? Explain.

3. Refer to a dictionary to determine the meanings of the following words as Roffman uses them in this selection: *sibling* (paragraph 3), *expletive* (3), *farce* (4), *irony* (6), *excoriated* (7), *paradoxically* (7), *bandy* (11), *cesspool* (12), *ubiquitous* (14), *insidious* (14).

Definition in Action

Consider the following *Grand Avenue* strip by Steve Breen and Mike Thompson.

GRAND AVENUE © 2009 Steve Breen and Mike Thompson. Reprinted by permission of UNIVERSAL UCLICK for UFS. All rights reserved.

What insights into the nature of definition does the cartoon give you? If you were asked to help Michael, what advice or suggestions would you give him?

Writing Suggestions

1. When discussing people, we often resort to personality labels to identify or define them — *leader, procrastinator, workaholic, obsessive-compulsive, liar, addict, athlete, genius, mentor,* and so on. But such labels can be misleading because one person's idea of what a leader or a workaholic is doesn't necessarily match another person's idea. Write an essay in which you explain the defining characteristics for one of these personality types or for one personality type of your own choosing. Be sure to use examples to illustrate each of the defining characteristics.

2. **Writing with Sources.** In analyzing "print advertisements using sex to sell products or showing people as sex objects" (paragraph 16), Roffman recounts how she and her students discovered that, while most of the ads focused on women, "there's always at least one invisible man present — looking at the advertisement" (17). They conclude that what these ads say or imply about this invisible man is not very flattering. Collect several print advertisements that use sex to promote products or show women or men as sex objects and analyze one of them. What insights, if any, do these advertisements offer about how popular culture portrays and defines both men and women? How do you think Roffman would interpret or analyze your advertisement? Write a paper in which you report your findings and conclusions. For models of and advice on integrating sources in your essay, see Chapters 14 and 15.

The Company Man

ELLEN GOODMAN

Journalist, public speaker, and commentator Ellen Goodman was born in Newton, Massachusetts, in 1941. After graduating from Radcliffe College, she worked as a researcher at *Newsweek* magazine and a reporter at the *Detroit Free Press*. She next moved to the *Boston Globe*, where she wrote an extremely popular and widely syndicated column for over 30 years. In 1980, Goodman won the Pulitzer Prize for Distinguished Commentary. Other awards include the American Society of Newspaper Editors Distinguished Writing Award, the Hubert H. Humphrey Civil Rights Award from the Leadership Conference on Civil Rights, the President's Award by the National Women's Political Caucus, a Nieman Fellowship at Harvard, and the Ernie Pyle Award for Lifetime Achievement from the National Society of Newspaper columnists. Her books include *Paper Trail: Common Sense in Uncommon Times* (2004), *I Know Just What You Mean: The Power of Friendship in Women's Lives* (2000), *Close to Home* (1979), and *Value Judgments* (1993). In 2012, Goodman founded The Conversation Project, "a public health campaign that aims to change the way people talk about, and prepare for, death — across the nation and beyond."

In this selection, published in her collection *Close to Home*, Goodman chronicles a man's work history, defining a certain type of person and a certain type of career. As you read, pay close attention to the way she uses repetition to reinforce her meaning.

Preparing to Read

What is your concept of a good job? What career path are you interested in? Do you imagine it will involve sacrifices and, if so, what kind? If not, how do you hope to accomplish your professional goals?

He worked himself to death, finally and precisely, at 3:00 a.m. Sunday morning.

The obituary didn't say that, of course. It said that he died of a coronary thrombosis — I think that was it — but everyone among his friends and acquaintances knew it instantly. He was a perfect Type A, a workaholic, a classic, they said to each other and shook their heads — and thought for five or ten minutes about the way they lived.

This man who worked himself to death finally and precisely at 3:00 a.m. Sunday morning — on his day off — was fifty-one years old and a vice-president. He was, however, one of six vice-presidents, and one of three who might conceivably—if the president died or retired soon enough—have moved to the top spot. Phil knew that.

He worked six days a week, five of them until eight or nine at night, during a time when his own company had begun the four-day week for everyone but the executives. He worked like the Important People. He had no outside "extracurricular interests," unless, of course, you think about a monthly golf game that way. To Phil, it was work. He always ate egg salad sandwiches at his desk. He was, of course, overweight, by twenty or twenty-five pounds. He thought it was okay, though, because he didn't smoke.

He worked like the Important People.

On Saturdays, Phil wore a sports jacket to the office instead of a suit, because it was the weekend.

He had a lot of people working for him, maybe sixty, and most of them liked him most of the time. Three of them will be seriously considered for his job. The obituary didn't mention that.

But it did list his "survivors" quite accurately. He is survived by his wife, Helen, forty-eight years old, a good woman of no particular marketable skills, who worked in an office before marrying and mothering. She had, according to her daughter, given up trying to compete with his work years ago, when the children were small. A company friend said, "I know how much you will miss him." And she answered, "I already have."

"Missing him all those years," she must have given up part of herself which had cared too much for the man. She would be "well taken care of."

His "dearly beloved" eldest of the "dearly beloved" children is a hard-working executive in a manufacturing firm down South. In the day and a half before the funeral, he went around the neighborhood researching his father, asking the neighbors what he was like. They were embarrassed.

His second child is a girl, who is twenty-four and newly married. She lives near her mother and they are close, but whenever she was alone with her father, in a car driving somewhere, they had nothing to say to each other.

The youngest is twenty, a boy, a high-school graduate who has spent the last couple of years, like a lot of his friends, doing enough odd jobs to stay in grass and food. He was the one who tried to grab at his father, and tried to mean enough to him to keep the man at home. He was his father's favorite. Over the last two years, Phil stayed up nights worrying about the boy.

The boy once said, "my father and I only board here."

At the funeral, the sixty-year-old company president told the forty-eight-year-old widow that the fifty-one-year-old deceased had meant much to the company and would be missed and would be hard to replace. The widow didn't look him in the eye. She was afraid he would read her bitterness and, after all, she would need him to straighten out her finances—the stock options and all that.

Phil was overweight and nervous and worked too hard. If he wasn't at the office, he was worried about it. Phil was a Type A, a heart-attack natural. You could have picked him out in a minute from a lineup.

So when he finally worked himself to death, at precisely 3:00 a.m. Sunday morning, no one was really surprised.

By 5:00 p.m. the afternoon of the funeral, the company president had begun, discreetly of course, with care and taste, to make inquiries about his replacement. One of three men. He asked around: "Who's been working the hardest?"

Thinking Critically about the Text

Goodman tells us that Phil was "overweight, by twenty or twenty-five pounds. He thought it was okay, though, because he didn't smoke" (paragraph 4). Why do you think she includes these details? Is Phil's employer in any way responsible for Phil's being overweight? Was Phil responsible for knowing the risks of being overweight, or stressed, whether or not he smoked? Do you think social values and expectations contributed to Phil's death?

Questions on Subject

1. What is a Type A personality? Where does Goodman define this phrase?
2. What does Goodman mean when she writes that Phil "worked himself to death"? How did his job as an executive who sat at a desk cause him to die at 3 a.m. on a Sunday when he was not even at the office? (Glossary: *Cause and Effect Analysis*)
3. According to Goodman, why did Phil work as hard as he did? Are there other explanations you can imagine?
4. Goodman tells us Phil was an executive but does not tell us what he actually did, what kind of job he had. Why do you think Goodman did not include Phil's specific profession?

Questions on Strategy

1. What is Goodman's purpose in this essay? How do you know? (Glossary: *Purpose*)
2. Why do you think Goodman waits till the end of her third paragraph to use the name of the man she is writing about (Phil)? What is the effect of referring to him as "he" or "the man" until that point? (Glossary: *Organization*)
3. What examples does Goodman use to support her main idea? Make a list and then describe the overall picture they paint. (Glossary: *Evidence*)

4. Goodman uses quotation marks around several words and phrases in this essay: *"extracurricular interests"* (paragraph 4), *"survivors"* (7), and *"dearly beloved"* (9). Why do you think she does this, and how does it affect you as a reader?

5. How would you describe Goodman's tone in this selection? What words and phrases support your answer? (Glossary: *Tone*)

6. Goodman uses a lot of numbers in this essay: For example, Phil was one of "six vice presidents" (paragraph 3); "maybe sixty" people worked for him (6), and "the sixty-year-old company president told the forty-eight-year-old widow that the fifty-one-year-old deceased . . . would be hard to replace" (13). What do all these numbers add to the selection?

Questions on Diction and Vocabulary

1. Describing her subject, Goodman repeats the phrase "worked himself to death, finally and precisely, at 3:00 a.m. Sunday morning" (see paragraphs 1, 3, and 15). Where else does she use repetition in this selection? What is the effect of this repetition on the reader? (Glossary: *Strategy*)

2. Would you describe Goodman's diction as being formal or informal? Point to word choices that support your conclusion.

3. Refer to a dictionary to determine the meanings of the following words as Goodman uses them in this selection: *thrombosis* (paragraph 2), *conceivably* (3), *discreetly* (16).

Definition in Action

Write your own obituary, focusing on how you would like to be remembered. You are defining your future self, imagining your future, so there are no limits on what you can include. Consider interests and causes, talents and accomplishments, as well as people upon whom you've had an impact, whether individual family members and friends or the larger public.

Writing Suggestions

1. In the last sentence of Goodman's essay, Phil's boss begins to think about Phil's replacement, wondering " 'Who's been working the hardest?' " In your experience and with what you've witnessed of the world so far, does working hard usually lead to a promotion? Are there other factors or qualities that seem to make a difference, and if so, what are they? Consider personality, communication skills, connections, creativity, and any other factors you can think of. Write an essay explaining your own theory about when and why people should be promoted, using concrete examples from your own life and the lives of varied professionals.

2. **Writing with Sources.** Does working extremely hard and striving to excel *require* neglecting one's mental and physical health? Research the connection between the Type A personality and stress, and write an essay reporting your findings. What strategies and attitudes can be used to help manage stress, and how effective are they? What other precautions can highly driven and competitive people take to ensure their well-being? Be sure to consult scholarly scientific resources (for example, the *New England Journal of Medicine,* the American Psychological Association, or the Centers for Disease Control and Prevention) as well as popular journals. Also consider field research; you might interview some highly successful professionals to learn their perspectives on this issue. For models of and advice on integrating sources into your essay, see Chapters 14 and 15.

The Selfish Side of Gratitude

BARBARA EHRENREICH

Writer and activist Barbara Ehrenreich was born in Butte, Montana, in 1941. After studying chemistry and physics at Reed College and earning her Ph.D. in cellular immunology from Rockefeller University, she turned her research and investigative skills to writing. Focusing on science, health policy, and labor issues, she wrote columns for *Time*, *Ms*, and *Mother Jones* and articles for *Harper's*, *The Atlantic Monthly*, *Esquire*, the *New York Times Magazine*, the *Washington Post Magazine*, and many other publications. She is the author of 21 books, including the best-selling *Bright-Sided: How Positive Thinking Is Undermining America* (2009), *Bait and Switch: The (Futile) Pursuit of the American Dream* (2005), *Nickeled and Dimed: On Not Getting By in America* (2001), and, most recently, *Living with a Wild God: An Unbeliever's Search for the Truth about Everything* (2014). Ehrenreich's many awards include a Guggenheim Fellowship, the Ford Foundation award, and the Puffin/Nation Prize for Creative Citizenship. In 2011, she founded the Economic Hardship Reporting Project, which promotes "cutting edge journalism about poverty by recruiting journalists (very often poor themselves), helping them define their projects, and raising money to pay them for their work."

Phil Velasquez/Chicago Tribune/ MCT via Getty Images

In this article, which appeared as an op-ed in the *New York Times* on December 31, 2015, Ehrenreich examines the concept of gratitude. Notice how she uses quotations to build and support her argument.

Preparing to Read

Do you believe in "mind over matter"? Can you think of a time when you were able to feel better about a negative situation by adopting a positive attitude? If so, think about your process: What did you do to make yourself feel better? If not, what *do* you do when you need to feel better?

This holiday season, there was something in the air that was even more inescapable than the scent of pumpkin spice: gratitude.

In November, NPR issued a number of brief exhortations to cultivate gratitude, culminating in an hourlong special on the "science of gratitude," narrated by Susan Sarandon. Writers in *Time* magazine, the *New York Times* and *Scientific American* recommended it as a surefire ticket to happiness and even better health. Robert Emmons, a psychology professor at the University of California, Davis, who studies the "science of gratitude," argues that it leads to a stronger immune system and lower blood pressure, as well as "more joy and pleasure."

It's good to express our thanks, of course, to those who deserve recognition. But this holiday gratitude is all about you, and how you can feel better.

Gratitude is hardly a fresh face on the self-improvement scene. By the turn of the century, Oprah Winfrey and other motivational figures were promoting an "attitude of gratitude." Martin Seligman, the father of "positive psychology," which is often enlisted to provide some sort of scientific basis for "positive thinking," has been offering instruction in gratitude for more than a decade. In the logic of positive self-improvement, anything that feels good—from scenic walks to family gatherings to expressing gratitude—is worth repeating.

Positive thinking was in part undone by its own silliness, glaringly displayed in the 2006 best seller "The Secret," which announced that you could have anything, like the expensive necklace you'd been coveting, simply by "visualizing" it in your possession.

The financial crash of 2008 further dimmed the luster of positive thinking, which had done so much to lure would-be homeowners and predatory mortgage lenders into a frenzy. This left the self-improvement field open to more cautious stances, like mindfulness and resilience and—for those who could still muster it—gratitude.

Gratitude is at least potentially more prosocial than the alternative self-improvement techniques. You have to be grateful to *someone*, who could be an invisible God, but might as well be a friend, mentor or family member. The gratitude literature often advises loving, human interactions: writing a "gratitude letter" to a helpful colleague, for example, or taking time to tell a family member how wonderful they are. These are good things to do, in a moral sense, and the new gratitude gurus are here to tell us that they also *feel* good.

But is gratitude always appropriate? The answer depends on who's giving it and who's getting it or, very commonly in our divided society, how much of the wealth gap it's expected to bridge. Suppose you were an $8-an-hour Walmart employee who saw her base pay elevated this year, by company fiat, to $9 an hour. Should you be grateful to the Waltons, who are the richest family in America? Or to Walmart's chief executive, whose annual base pay is close to $1 million and whose home sits on nearly 100 acres of land in Bentonville, Ark.? Grateful people have been habitually dismissed as "chumps," and in this hypothetical case, the term would seem to apply.

Perhaps it's no surprise that gratitude's rise to self-help celebrity status owes a lot to the conservative-leaning John Templeton Foundation. At the start of this decade, the foundation, which promotes free-market capitalism, gave $5.6 million to Dr. Emmons, the gratitude researcher. It also funded a $3 million initiative called Expanding the Science and Practice of Gratitude through the Greater Good Science Center at the University of California, Berkeley, which co-produced the special that aired on NPR. The foundation does not fund projects to directly improve the lives of poor individuals, but it has spent a great deal, through efforts like these, to improve their attitudes.

It's a safe guess, though, that most of the people targeted by gratitude exhortations actually have something to be grateful for, such as Janice Kaplan, the author of the memoir "The Gratitude Diaries," who spent a year appreciating her high-earning husband and successful grown children. And it is here that the pro-social promise of gratitude begins to dim. True, saying "thank you" is widely encouraged, but much of the gratitude advice involves no communication or interaction of any kind.

Consider this, from a yoga instructor on CNN.com: "Cultivate your sense of gratitude by incorporating giving thanks into a personal morning ritual such as writing in a gratitude journal, repeating an affirmation or practicing a meditation. It could even be as simple as writing what you give thanks for on a sticky note and posting it on your mirror or computer. To help you establish a daily routine, create a 'thankfulness' reminder on your phone or computer to pop up every morning and prompt you."

Who is interacting here? "You" and "you."

The *Harvard Mental Health Letter* begins its list of gratitude interventions with the advice that you should send a thank-you letter as often as once a month, but all the other suggested exercises can be undertaken without human contact: "thank someone mentally," "keep a gratitude journal," "count your blessings," "meditate" and, for those who are so inclined, "pray."

So it's possible to achieve the recommended levels of gratitude without spending a penny or uttering a word. All you have to do is to generate, within yourself, the good feelings associated with gratitude, and then bask in its warm, comforting glow. If there is any loving involved in this, it is self-love, and the current hoopla around gratitude is a celebration of onanism.

Yet there is a need for more gratitude, especially from those who have a roof over their heads and food on their table. Only it should be a more vigorous and inclusive sort of gratitude than what is being urged on us now. Who picked the lettuce in the fields, processed the standing rib roast, drove these products to the stores, stacked them on the supermarket shelves and, of course, prepared them and brought them to the table? Saying grace to an abstract God is an evasion; there are crowds, whole communities of actual people, many of them with aching backs and tenuous finances, who made the meal possible.

The real challenge of gratitude lies in figuring out how to express our debt to them, whether through generous tips or, say, by supporting their demands for decent pay and better working conditions. But now we're not talking about gratitude, we're talking about a far more muscular impulse—and this is, to use the old-fashioned term, "solidarity"—which may involve getting up off the yoga mat.

Thinking Critically about the Text

What is your definition of gratitude? Is it reflected in Ehrenreich's essay, and if so, where? If not, draft your definition, using either a formal, synonymous, negative, or etymological definition.

Questions on Subject

1. According to the studies and research Ehrenreich cites, what are the benefits of gratitude? List as many as you can.

2. How does Ehrenreich define gratitude? Where do you find this definition?

3. In paragraph 8, Ehrenreich asks "But is gratitude always appropriate?" Why do you think she asks this? Under what circumstances does she suggest it might be inappropriate?

4. What does Ehrenreich mean by "the pro-social promise" of gratitude (paragraph 10)? Why does she think gratitude has to be pro-social to be valuable?

5. What does Ehrenreich want her readers to do instead of expressing gratitude? (Glossary: *Persuasion*)

Questions on Strategy

1. Ehrenreich opens her essay with the sentence "This holiday season, there was something in the air that was even more inescapable than the scent of pumpkin spice: gratitude." What relationship is she suggesting between pumpkin spice and gratitude by placing these two nouns side-by-side? (Glossary: *Comparison and Contrast*)

2. What is Ehrenreich's purpose in this article? How do you know? (Glossary: *Purpose*)

3. How does Ehrenreich use illustration in this essay? Are all her examples effective? Are there any you would drop? Which resonate most with you? Are there other types of evidence that might have made her essay stronger? (Glossary: *Evidence*)

4. How has Ehrenreich organized her essay? Are examples sequenced logically? Is there a logical flow of ideas? (Glossary: *Organization*)

5. Ehrenreich uses quotation marks around each of the following phrases: *"science of gratitude"* (paragraph 2), *"positive psychology"* (4), and *"positive thinking"* (4). Why do you think she uses quotation marks here? What is the effect of doing so?

Questions on Diction and Vocabulary

1. How would you describe Ehrenreich's tone in this article? Is it respectful, even-handed, condescending, dismissive, or something else? What words and phrases lead you to this conclusion? (Glossary: *Tone*)
2. Refer to a dictionary to determine the meanings of the following words as Ehrenreich uses them in this selection: *exhortations* (paragraph 2), *cultivate* (2), *speculative* (6), *stances* (6), *resilience* (6), *fiat* (8), *hypothetical* (8), *initiative* (9), *affirmation* (11), *hoopla* (14), *onanism* (14), *tenuous* (15), *solidarity* (16).

Definition in Action

Make a chart with four columns and brainstorm a list of the things you are grateful for. You might think about people (such as family members, friends, colleagues), circumstances (your job, your upbringing, your school), and things (your home, your computer, your car). In the first column, enter each of the items you appreciate. In the second column, state how you "got" this thing. (Were you born into it? Was it a gift? Did you earn it in some way?) In the third column, write a phrase or sentence about *why* you are grateful: How does this person, situation, or item make your life better? Why is it of value? Use the last column to say whether you'd like to acknowledge each item and, if so, how you'd like to do that. Finally, consider what you have learned about your own definition of gratitude from this exercise. Is there a simple relationship between how you "get" something and how you feel about it? Can you simultaneously feel gratitude and not be content? Is there more than one way to show gratitude?

Writing Suggestions

1. Using your response to the Preparing to Read prompt as a starting point, tell the story of a time when adopting a positive attitude has helped you through a difficult time or situation. Consider such challenges as failing an exam or a course; losing something you really wanted, such as an important game, a role in a play, or a job; breaking up with your significant other; or the illness or death of a loved one. If positive thinking did not help you manage this challenge, what did? Either way, do you think that your strategy for coping with this difficulty would necessarily work for anyone else? Why or why not?
2. Ehrenreich writes that "saying grace to an abstract God is an evasion; there are crowds, whole communities of actual people, many of them with aching backs and tenuous finances, who made the meal possible" (paragraph 15). Do you agree with her perspective about who should be thanked? Does it have to be *either* God *or* human workers? Write an essay arguing that there are two different kinds of "gratitude" being discussed here and write definitions for each kind to demonstrate how they are different.

WRITING SUGGESTIONS FOR DEFINITION

1. Some of the most pressing social issues in American life today are further complicated by imprecise definitions of critical terms. Various medical cases, for example, have brought worldwide attention to the legal and medical definitions of the word *death*. Debates continue about the meanings of other controversial words, such as these:

   a. values
   b. alcoholism
   c. cheating
   d. kidnapping
   e. lying
   f. censorship
   g. remedial
   h. insanity
   i. forgiveness
   j. sex
   k. success
   l. happiness
   m. life
   n. equality

   Select one of these words and write an essay in which you discuss not only the definition of the term but also the problems associated with defining it.

2. Write an essay in which you define one of the words listed below by telling not only what it is but also what it is *not*. (For example, one could say that "poetry is that which cannot be expressed in any other way.") Remember, however, that defining by negation does not relieve you of the responsibility of defining the term in other ways as well.

   a. intelligence
   b. leadership
   c. patriotism
   d. wealth
   e. failure
   f. family
   g. loyalty
   h. selflessness
   i. creativity
   j. humor

3. Consider the sample introduction to the essay defining Quebecois and Canadian identity (page 400). Think about your school, town, or country's identity. How would you define its essential character? Choose a place that is important in your life and write an essay defining its character and significance to you.

4. **Writing with Sources.** Karl Marx defined *capitalism* as an economic system in which the bourgeois owners of the means of production exploit the proletariat for their own selfish gain. How would you define *capitalism*? Write an essay defining *capitalism* that includes all six types of definition: formal, synonymous, negative, etymological, stipulative, and extended. Do some research in the

library or online to help with your definitions. For models of and advice on integrating sources in your essay, see Chapters 14 and 15.

5. The opening visual for this chapter on page 390 defines various types of coffee drinks using a highly graphic style. Visual definitions can be an excellent complement to text-only definitions because our brains are often able to process them more quickly. Using the coffee-drinks image as a model, create a coherent set of visual definitions for types of pasta. Search online or in your library or supermarket to find the names of six to twelve different pasta shapes or doughs. You may want to combine a few select words with your images to clearly distinguish what your illustration represents, as was done in the coffee-drinks image. To create your visual, either sketch by hand or use photo and graphics applications, keeping in mind that simple visuals often have greater resonance with viewers. Once your visual definitions are complete, write a paragraph explaining what your visual would uniquely add to a set of more traditional, text-only definitions. In what ways might the images affect your choice of pasta to purchase, prepare, or eat?

6. **Writing with Sources.** In discussing the power of labels that define identity, psychiatrist Thomas Szasz once wrote:

   The struggle for definition is veritably the struggle for life itself. In the typical western two men fight desperately for the possession of a gun that has been thrown to the ground: Whoever reaches the weapon first, shoots and lives; his adversary is shot and dies. In ordinary life, the struggle is not for guns but for words: Whoever first defines the situation is the victor; his adversary, the victim. . . . In short, he who first seizes the word imposes reality on the other; he who defines thus dominates and lives; and he who is defined is subjugated and may be killed. — From *The Second Sin*

   Take some time to think about words like *gay*, *retarded*, or *jock*, whose meaning in our culture has become contested — that is, challenged by some who are offended by the way(s) in which those words are used. (For information on campaigns that attempt to educate the public on these issues, see www.glsen.org and r-word.org.) What other defining labels have you encountered or observed? After doing some research in your library as well as on the Internet, write an essay in which you explore the power of labels to define. For models of and advice on integrating sources in your essay, see Chapters 14 and 15.

7. **Writing in the Workplace.** One pressing social issue facing all-women's colleges today is the question of how to define the term *female* when considering student applications. Some colleges, such as Smith, have changed their acceptance criteria to include transgender students who currently (or used to) identify as female, while other women's colleges are still sorting out what

definitions they will accept. Suppose for a minute that you are a dean in the admissions office at one of these schools, preparing for a meeting to set the guidelines for your applicant pool. In preparation for your meeting, write a definition essay to explain your understanding of female and what it means with regard to acceptance at your school. To make your definition clearer to your reader, you might consider employing one or more of the other methods, which will almost certainly include classification and might benefit from the inclusion of a relevant narrative.

WHERE
DID ALL THE MONEY GO ?

Easy Credit
Growing foreign capital fueled a demand for new investment, in turn creating easy credit.

↓

Housing Boom
Easy credit meant more people could buy houses. The increased demand drove house prices up.

↓

Mortgage Securitization
Mortgage-backed securities (MBS's) grew in demand on the stock market. Virtually all mortgages were securitized and traded. Banks could take old loans off their balance sheets and acquire new ones (making money on the fees).

↓

Market Saturation
The easy credit allowed everyone who wanted a house to get one. MBS's still were in high demand as "safe bets."

↓

Lowered Loan Standards
Lenders had to find a way to create yet more loans, so they lowered the requirements for who could get one. The loans were quickly sold off, so the lender did not bear any risk in the case of a default. It did not matter whom they were lending to or whether the money would be repaid. The lenders and brokers just collected their fees and created the MBS's for the market demand.

Global Economic Downturn
Lack of credit caused a mad cycle of stock selloffs, bankruptcies, cutbacks, higher unemployment, lower spending & production. The global economy shrunk. There was less money to go around.

↑

Credit Crisis
Toxic assets, toxic companies, and panic virtually stopped global lending. Some lenders ceased out of fear: scared that they would never get their money back. Others (such as major banks) could no longer afford to lend. They had lost too much capital and had nothing to lend out.

↑

Subprime Crisis
Throughout the housing boom, the financial market operated with the assumption that house prices would not fall. Assets that were thought to be safe were only safe because they were backed by houses of increasing value. When the prices did fall, the entire system was turned on its head.

↑

House Prices Fall
The average household income did not increase as house prices soared. Even with the easy loans, people could not afford houses anymore and stopped buying. More houses were still being built so the supply kept growing, but the demand dropped. House prices fell. Drastically.

Emilia Klimiuk

CHAPTER **11**

Cause and Effect Analysis

WHAT IS CAUSE AND EFFECT ANALYSIS?

PEOPLE EXHIBIT THEIR NATURAL CURIOSITY ABOUT THE WORLD BY asking questions. These questions represent a fundamental human need to find out how things work. Whenever a question asks *why*, answering it will require discovering a *cause* or a series of causes for a particular *effect*; whenever a question asks *what if*, its answer will point out the effect or effects that can result from a particular cause. Cause and effect analysis, then, explores the relationship between events or circumstances and the outcomes that result from them.

The illustration opposite is an excerpt from an analysis that attempts to explain a persistent question people had about the economic woes in the United States during the Great Recession: Where did all the money go? The complex causal chain that "turned our country's pockets inside out" is represented with a combination of text and graphics explaining that easy credit, the initial cause, led to a chain of events culminating in the global economic downturn, with its multitude of disastrous consequences that Americans and others around the world are still feeling in many aspects of their lives.

CAUSE AND EFFECT ANALYSIS IN WRITTEN TEXTS

You will have frequent opportunity to use cause and effect analysis in your college writing. For example, a history instructor might ask you to explain the causes of the Six-Day War between Israel and its neighbors. In a paper for an American literature course, you might try to determine why *Huckleberry Finn* has sparked so much controversy in a number of schools and communities. On an environmental studies exam, you might have to speculate about the long-term effects acid rain will have on the ecology of northeastern Canada and the United States. Demonstrating an understanding of cause and effect is crucial to the process of learning.

One common use of the strategy is for the writer to identify a particular causal agent or circumstance and then discuss the consequences or effects it has had or may have. In the following passage from *Telephone* by John Brooks, it is clear from the first sentence that the author is primarily concerned with the effects that the telephone has had or may have had on modern life:

<small>First sentence establishes purpose in the form of a question</small>

What has the telephone done to us, or for us, in the hundred years of its existence? A few effects suggest themselves at once. It has saved lives by getting rapid word of illness, injury, or famine from remote places. By joining with the elevator to make possible the multistory residence or office building, it has made possible — for better or worse — the modern city. By bringing about a quantum leap in the speed and ease with which information moves from place to place, it has greatly accelerated the rate of scientific and technological change and growth in industry. Beyond doubt it has crippled if not killed the ancient art of letter writing. It has made living alone possible for persons with normal social impulses; by so doing, it has played a role in one of the greatest social changes of this century, the breakup of the multigenerational household. It has made the waging of war chillingly more efficient than formerly. Perhaps (though not provably) it has prevented wars that might have arisen out of international misunderstanding caused by written communication. Or perhaps — again not provably — by magnifying and extending irrational personal conflicts based on voice contact, it has caused wars. Certainly it has extended the scope of human conflicts, since it impartially disseminates the useful knowledge of scientists and the babble of bores, the affection of the affectionate and the malice of the malicious.

<small>A series of effects with the telephone as cause</small>

The bulk of Brooks's paragraph is devoted to answering the very question he poses in his opening sentence: "What has the telephone done to us, or for us, in the hundred years of its existence?" Notice that even though many of the effects Brooks discusses are verifiable or probable, he is willing to admit that he is speculating about those effects that he cannot prove.

A second common use of the strategy is to reverse the forms by first examining the effect; the writer describes an important event or problem (effect) and then examines the possible reasons (causes) for it. For example, experts might trace the causes of poverty to any or all of the following: poor education, a nonprogressive tax system, declining commitment to social services, inflation, discrimination, or even the welfare system that is designed to help those most in need.

A third use of the strategy is for the writer to explore a complex causal chain. In this selection from his book *The Politics of Energy*, Barry

Commoner examines the series of malfunctions that led to the near disaster at the Three Mile Island nuclear facility in Harrisburg, Pennsylvania:

> On March 28, 1979, at 3:53 a.m., a pump at the Harrisburg plant failed. Because the pump failed, the reactor's heat was not drawn off in the heat exchanger and the very hot water in the primary loop overheated. The pressure in the loop increased, opening a release valve that was supposed to counteract such an event. But the valve stuck open and the primary loop system lost so much water (which ended up as a highly radioactive pool, six feet deep, on the floor of the reactor building) that it was unable to carry off all the heat generated within the reactor core. Under these circumstances, the intense heat held within the reactor could, in theory, melt its fuel rods, and the resulting "meltdown" could then carry a hugely radioactive mass through the floor of the reactor. The reactor's emergency cooling system, which is designed to prevent this disaster, was then automatically activated, but when it was, apparently, turned off too soon, some of the fuel rods overheated. This produced a bubble of hydrogen gas at the top of the reactor. (The hydrogen is dissolved in the water in order to react with oxygen that is produced when the intense reactor radiation splits water molecules into their atomic constituents. When heated, the dissolved hydrogen bubbles out of the solution.) This bubble blocked the flow of cooling water so that despite the action of the emergency cooling system the reactor core was again in danger of melting down. Another danger was that the gas might contain enough oxygen to cause an explosion that could rupture the huge containers that surround the reactor and release a deadly cloud of radioactive material into the surrounding countryside. Working desperately, technicians were able to gradually reduce the size of the gas bubble using a special apparatus brought in from the atomic laboratory at Oak Ridge, Tennessee, and the danger of a catastrophic release of radioactive materials subsided. But the sealed-off plant was now so radioactive that no one could enter it for many months—or, according to some observers, for years—without being exposed to a lethal dose of radiation.

Tracing a causal chain, as Commoner does here, is similar to narration. The writer must organize the events sequentially to show clearly how each event leads to the next.

In a causal chain, an initial cause brings about a particular effect, which in turn becomes the immediate cause of a further effect, and so on, bringing about a series of effects that also act as new causes. The so-called domino effect is a good illustration of the idea of a causal chain; the simple tipping over of a domino (initial cause) can result in the toppling of any number of dominoes down the line (series of effects). For example, before a salesperson approaches an important client about a big sale, she prepares extensively for the meeting (initial cause). Her preparation causes her to impress the client (effect A), which guarantees her the big sale (effect B), which in turn results in her promotion to district sales manager (effect C). The sale she made is the most immediate and most obvious cause of her promotion, but it is possible to trace the chain back to its more essential cause: her hard work preparing for the meeting.

While the ultimate purpose of cause and effect analysis may seem simple—to know or to understand why something happens—determining causes and effects is often a thought-provoking and complex strategy. One reason for this complexity is that some causes are less obvious than others. *Immediate causes* are readily apparent because they are closest in time to the effect; the immediate cause of a flood, for example, may be the collapse of a dam. However, *remote causes* may be just as important, even though they are not as apparent and are perhaps even hidden. The remote (and, in fact, primary) cause of the flood might have been an engineering error or the use of substandard building materials or the failure of personnel to relieve the pressure on the dam caused by unseasonably heavy rains. In many cases, it is necessary to look beyond the most immediate causes to discover the true underlying sources of an event.

A second reason for the complexity of this strategy is the difficulty of distinguishing between possible and actual causes, as well as between possible and actual effects. An upset stomach may be caused by spoiled food, but it may also be caused by overeating, by flu, by nervousness, by pregnancy, or by a combination of factors. Similarly, an increase in the cost of electricity may have multiple effects: higher profits for utility companies, fewer sales of electrical appliances, higher prices for other products that depend on electricity in their manufacture, and even the development of alternative sources of energy. Making reasonable choices among the various possibilities requires thought and care.

USING CAUSE AND EFFECT ANALYSIS AS A WRITING STRATEGY

Writers may use cause and effect analysis for three essential purposes: to inform, to speculate, and to argue. Most commonly, they will want to inform—to help their readers understand some identifiable fact. A state wildlife biologist, for example, might wish to tell the public about the effects severe winter weather has had on the state's deer herds. Similarly, in a newsletter, a member of Congress might explain to his or her constituency the reasons changes are being made in the Social Security system.

Cause and effect analysis may also allow writers to speculate—to consider what might be or what might have been. To satisfy the board of trustees, for example, a university treasurer might discuss the impact an increase in tuition will have on the school's budget. A columnist for *People* magazine might speculate about the reasons for a new singer's sudden popularity. Similarly, pollsters estimate the effects that various voter groups will have on future elections, and historians evaluate how the current presidency will continue to influence American government in the coming decades.

Finally, cause and effect analysis provides an excellent basis from which to argue a given position or point of view. An editorial writer, for example, could argue that bringing a professional basketball team into the area would have many positive effects on the local economy and on the community as a whole.

USING CAUSE AND EFFECT ANALYSIS ACROSS THE DISCIPLINES

When writing essays in the academic disciplines, you will have many opportunities to use the strategy of cause and effect analysis to both organize and strengthen the presentation of your ideas. To determine whether cause and effect analysis is the right strategy for you in a particular paper, use the guidelines described in Chapter 2 (Determining a Strategy for Developing Your Essay, pages 32–33). Consider the following examples:

Native American History

1. **MAIN IDEA:** Treaties between Native American groups and the U.S. government had various negative effects on the Native Americans involved.
2. **QUESTION:** What have been some of the most harmful results for Native Americans of treaties between Native American groups and the U.S. government?
3. **STRATEGY:** Cause and effect analysis. The word *results* signals that this study needs to examine the harmful effects of the provisions of the treaties.
4. **SUPPORTING STRATEGY:** Illustration. Examples need to be given of both treaties and their consequences.

Nutrition

1. **MAIN IDEA:** A major factor to be considered when examining why people suffer from poor nutrition is poverty.
2. **QUESTION:** What is the relationship between poverty and nutrition?

3. **STRATEGY:** Cause and effect analysis. The word *relationship* signals a linkage between poverty and nutrition. The writer has to determine what is meant by poverty and poor nutrition in this country or in the countries examined.
4. **SUPPORTING STRATEGY:** Definition. Precise definitions will first be necessary in order for the writer to make valid judgments concerning the causal relationship in question.

Nursing

1. **MAIN IDEA:** Alzheimer's disease is the progressive loss of brain nerve cells, causing gradual loss of memory, concentration, understanding, and in some cases sanity.
2. **QUESTION:** What role does the overproduction of a protein that destroys nerve cells play in the development of Alzheimer's disease, and what causes the overproduction in the first place?
3. **STRATEGY:** Cause and effect analysis. The words *role*, *play*, and *causes* signal that the issue here is determining and explaining how Alzheimer's disease originates.
4. **SUPPORTING STRATEGY:** Process analysis. Describing how Alzheimer's operates will be essential to making the reader understand its causes and effects.

SAMPLE STUDENT ESSAY USING CAUSE AND EFFECT ANALYSIS AS A WRITING STRATEGY

Born in Brooklyn, New York, Kevin Cunningham spent most of his life in Flemington, New Jersey. While enrolled in the mechanical engineering program at the University of Vermont, Cunningham shared an apartment near the Burlington waterfront with several other students. There he became interested in the effects that upscale real estate development — or gentrification — would have on his neighborhood. Such development is not unique to Burlington; it is common in the older sections of cities across the country. After gathering information for his essay by talking with people who live in the neighborhood, Cunningham found it useful to discuss both the causes and the effects of gentrification in his well-unified essay.

Gentrification
Kevin Cunningham

Epigraph sets the theme

> I went back to Ohio, and my city was gone....
> —Chrissie Hynde, of the Pretenders

Thesis

My city is in Vermont, not Ohio, but soon my city might be gone, too. Or maybe it's I who will be gone. My street, Lakeview Terrace, lies unobtrusively in the old northwest part of Burlington and is notable, as its name suggests, for spectacular views of Lake Champlain framed by the Adirondacks. It's not that the neighborhood is going to seed, though—quite the contrary. Recently it has been discovered, and now it is on the verge of being gentrified. For some of us who live here, that's bad.

Well-organized and unified paragraph: describes life cycle of city neighborhoods

Cities are often assigned human characteristics, one of which is a life cycle: They have a birth, a youth, a middle age, and an old age. A neighborhood is built and settled by young, vibrant people, proud of their sturdy new homes. Together, residents and houses mature, as families grow larger and extensions get built on. Eventually, though, the neighborhood begins to show its age. Buildings sag a little, houses aren't repainted as quickly, and maintenance slips. The neighborhood may grow poorer, as the young and upwardly mobile find new jobs and move away, while the older and less successful inhabitants remain.

Decay, renewal, or redevelopment awaits aging neighborhoods

One of three fates awaits the aging neighborhood. Decay may continue until the neighborhood becomes a slum. It may face urban renewal, with old buildings being razed and ugly, new apartment houses taking their place. Finally, it may undergo redevelopment, in which government encourages the upgrading of existing housing stock by offering low-interest loans or outright grants. This last possibility would mean that the original character of the neighborhood may be retained or restored, allowing the city to keep part of its identity.

Organization: example of Hoboken, New Jersey

Effects of redevelopment on Hoboken

An example of redevelopment at its best is Hoboken, New Jersey. In the early 1970s Hoboken was a dying city, with rundown housing and many abandoned buildings. However, low-interest loans enabled some younger residents to begin to refurbish their homes, and soon the area began to show signs of renewed vigor. Outsiders moved in and rebuilt some of the abandoned houses. Today, whole blocks have been restored, and neighborhood life is active again.

The city does well, too, because property values are higher and so are property taxes. There, at least for my neighborhood, is the rub.

Lakeview Terrace is a demographic potpourri of students and families, young professionals and elderly retirees, homeowners and renters. It's a quiet street where kids can play safely and the neighbors know each other. Most of the houses are fairly old and look it, but already some redevelopment has begun. Recently, several old houses were bought by a real estate company, rebuilt, and sold as condominiums; the new residents drive BMWs and keep to themselves. The house where I live is owned by a young professional couple—he's an architect—and they have renovated the place to what it must have looked like when it was new. They did a nice job, too. These two kinds of development are the main forms of gentrification, and so far they have done no real harm.

The city is about to start a major property tax reappraisal, however. Because of the renovations, the houses on Lakeview Terrace are currently worth more than they used to be; soon there will be a big jump in property taxes. That's when a lot of people will be hurt—possibly even evicted from their own neighborhood.

Clem is a retired General Electric employee who has lived on Lakeview for over thirty years and who owns his home. About three years ago some condos were built on the lot next door, which didn't please Clem—he says they just don't fit in. With higher property taxes, however, it may be Clem who no longer fits in. At the very least, since he's on a fixed income, he will have to make sacrifices in order to stay. Ryan works as a mailman and also owns his Lakeview Terrace home, which is across the street from the houses that were converted into condos: same cause, same effect.

Then there are those who rent. As landlords have to pay higher property taxes, they will naturally raise rents at least as much (and maybe more, if they've spent money on renovations of their own). Some renters won't be able to afford the increase and will have to leave. "Some renters" almost certainly includes me, as well as others who have lived on Lakeview Terrace much longer than I have. In fact, the exodus has already begun, with the people who were displaced by the condo conversions.

> | Conclusion
> |
> |
> |
> |
> | Restatement
> | of thesis
>
> Of course, many people would consider what's happening on Lakeview Terrace a genuine improvement in every way, resulting not only in better-looking houses but also in a better class of people. I dispute that. The new people may be more affluent than those they displace, but certainly not "better," not by any standard that matters. Gentrification may do wonders for a neighborhood's aesthetics, but it certainly can be hard on its soul.   9

Analyzing Kevin Cunningham's Cause and Effect Analysis: Questions for Discussion

1. According to Cunningham, in what way are cities like humans? What does he describe as the three possible outcomes for aging neighborhoods?

2. Cunningham presents this causal chain: Redevelopment (cause) increases property values (effect), which in turn increases property taxes upon reassessment by the city (effect), which leads to the displacement of poorer residents (effect). What other effects of redevelopment can you think of?

3. Cunningham decries the gentrification of his neighborhood, but a neighborhood descending into disrepair is not a desirable alternative. What do you think Cunningham would like to see happen on Lakeview Terrace? How can a neighborhood fend off decay while still maintaining its "soul"?

4. Would the essay have benefited if Cunningham had proposed and speculated about a viable alternative to gentrification? Explain.

SUGGESTIONS FOR USING CAUSE AND EFFECT ANALYSIS AS A WRITING STRATEGY

As you plan, write, and revise your cause and effect analysis, be mindful of the writing process guidelines described in Chapter 2. Pay particular attention to the basic requirements and essential ingredients of this writing strategy.

▶ Planning Your Cause and Effect Analysis

ESTABLISH YOUR FOCUS. Decide whether your essay will propose causes, talk about effects, or analyze both causes and effects. Any research you do and any questions you ask will depend on how you wish to concentrate your attention. For example, let's say that as a reporter for the school paper, you are writing a story about a fire that destroyed an apartment building in the neighborhood, killing four people. In planning your story, you might focus on the cause of the fire: Was there more than one cause? Was carelessness to blame? Was the fire of suspicious origin? You might focus on the effects of the fire: How much damage was done to the building? How many people were left homeless? What was the impact on the families of the four victims? Or you might cover both the reasons for this tragic event and its ultimate effects, setting up a sort of causal chain. Such focus is crucial as you gather information. For example, student Kevin Cunningham decided early on that he wanted to explore what would happen to his neighborhood (the effects) if gentrification continued.

DETERMINE YOUR PURPOSE. Once you begin to draft your essay and as you continue to refine it, make sure your purpose is clear. Do you wish your cause and effect analysis to be primarily informative, speculative, or argumentative? An informative essay allows readers to say, "I learned something from this. I didn't know that the fire was caused by faulty wiring." A speculative essay suggests to readers new possibilities: "That never occurred to me before. The apartment house could indeed be replaced by an office building." An argumentative essay convinces readers that some sort of action should be taken: "I have to agree: Fire inspections should occur more regularly in our neighborhood." In his essay on gentrification, Cunningham uses cause and effect analysis to question the value of redevelopment by examining what it does to the soul of a neighborhood. Whatever your purpose, be sure to provide the information necessary to carry it through.

FORMULATE A THESIS STATEMENT. Every essay needs a strong, clear thesis statement. When you are writing an essay using cause and effect, your thesis statement should clearly present either a cause and its effect(s) or an effect and its cause(s). As a third approach, your essay could focus on a complex causal chain of events. Here are a few examples from this chapter:

- *"What has the telephone done to us, or for us, in the hundred years of its existence?"* (page 442) This opening sentence signals that the essay will explore the effects of a single cause, the telephone.
- *"On March 28, 1979, at 3:53 a.m., a pump at the Harrisburg plant failed."* (page 443) Here, the pump failure introduces a causal chain of events leading to the disaster at Three Mile Island.
- *"Recently [our neighborhood] has been discovered, and now it is on the verge of being gentrified. For some of us who live here, that's bad."* (page 447) The first sentence asserts how one trend followed another, while the second gives the author's opinion of those trends.

When you begin to formulate your thesis statement, keep these examples in mind. You can find other examples of thesis statements in the essays throughout this book. As you begin to develop your thesis statement, ask yourself, "What is my point?" Next, ask yourself, "What approach to a cause and effect essay will be most useful in making my point?" If you can't answer these questions yet, write down some ideas and try to determine your main point from those ideas.

▶ Organizing and Writing Your Cause and Effect Analysis

AVOID OVERSIMPLIFICATION AND ERRORS OF LOGIC. Sound and thoughtful reasoning, while present in all good writing, is central to any analysis of cause and effect. Writers of convincing cause and effect analysis must examine their material objectively and develop their essays carefully, taking into account any potential objections that readers might raise. Therefore, do not jump to conclusions or let your prejudices interfere with the logic of your interpretation or the completeness of your presentation. In gathering information for his essay, Kevin Cunningham discovered that he had to distinguish between cause and effect and mere coincidence:

> You have to know your subject, and you have to be honest. For example, my downstairs neighbors moved out last month because the rent was raised. Somebody who didn't know the situation might say, "See? Gentrification." But that wasn't the reason—it's that heating costs went up. This is New England, and we had a cold winter; gentrification had nothing to do with it. It's something that is just beginning to happen, and it's going to have a big effect, but we haven't actually felt many of the effects here yet.

Be sure that you do not oversimplify the cause and effect relationship you are writing about. A good working assumption is that most important matters cannot be traced to a single verifiable cause; similarly, a cause or set of causes rarely produces a single isolated effect. To be believable, your analysis of your topic must demonstrate a thorough understanding of the surrounding circumstances; readers are unlikely to be convinced by single-minded determination to show one particular connection. For example, someone writing about how the passage of a tough new crime bill (cause) has led to a decrease in arrests in a particular area (effect) will have little credibility unless other possible causes—socioeconomic conditions, seasonal fluctuations in crime, the size and budget of the police force, and so on—are also examined and taken into account. Of course, to achieve coherence, you will want to emphasize the important causes or the most significant effects. Just be careful not to lose your reader's trust by insisting on an oversimplified "X leads to Y" relationship.

The other common problem in cause and effect analysis is lack of evidence in establishing a cause or an effect. This error is known as the "after this, therefore because of this" fallacy (in Latin, *post hoc, ergo propter hoc*). In attempting to discover an explanation for a particular event or circumstance, a writer may point to something that merely preceded it in time, assuming a causal connection where none has in fact been proven. For example, if you have dinner out one evening and the next day come down with stomach cramps, you may blame your illness on the restaurant where you ate the night before; you do so without justification, however, if your only proof is the fact that you ate there beforehand. More evidence would be required to establish a causal relationship. The *post hoc, ergo propter hoc* fallacy is often harmlessly foolish ("I failed the exam because I lost my lucky key chain"). It can, however, lead writers into serious errors of judgment and blind them to more reasonable explanations of cause and effect. And, like oversimplification, such mistakes in logic can undercut a reader's confidence. Make sure that the causal relationships you cite are, in fact, based on demonstrable evidence and not merely on a temporal connection.

USE OTHER RHETORICAL STRATEGIES. Although cause and effect analysis can be used effectively as a separate writing strategy, it is more common for essays to combine different strategies. For example, in an essay about a soccer team's victories, you might use comparison and contrast to highlight the differences between the team's play in two losses and in five victories. Narration from interviews might also be used to add interest and color. An essay about the Internet might incorporate the strategy of argumentation as well as definition to defend the openness and effectiveness of the Internet. The argument could analyze exactly how the benefits outweigh the drawbacks, while definition could be used to focus the subject matter to better achieve your purpose. By combining strategies, you can gain both clarity and forcefulness in your writing.

Be aware, however, that you must always keep the purpose of your essay and the tone you wish to adopt in the front of your mind when combining strategies. Without careful planning, using more than one rhetorical strategy can alter both the direction and the tone of your essay in ways that detract from, rather than contribute to, your ability to achieve your purpose.

As you read the essays in this chapter, consider all of the writing strategies the authors have used to support their cause and effect analysis. How have these other strategies added to or changed the style of the essay? Are there strategies that you might have added or taken out? What strategies, if any, do you think you might use to strengthen your cause and effect essay?

▶ Revising and Editing Your Cause and Effect Analysis

SELECT WORDS THAT STRIKE A BALANCED TONE. Be careful to neither overstate nor understate your position. Avoid exaggerations like "there can be no question" and "the evidence speaks for itself." Such diction is usually annoying and undermines your interpretation. Instead, allow your analysis of the facts to convince readers of the cause and effect relationship you wish to suggest. At the same time, no analytical writer convinces by continually understating or qualifying information with words and phrases such as *it seems that, perhaps, maybe, I think, sometimes, most often, nearly always,* or *in my opinion.* While it may be your intention to appear reasonable, overusing such qualifying words can make you sound unclear or indecisive, and it renders your analysis less convincing. Present your case forcefully, but do so honestly and sensibly.

QUESTION YOUR OWN WORK WHILE REVISING AND EDITING. Revision is best done by asking yourself key questions about what you have written. Begin by reading, preferably aloud, what you have written. Reading aloud forces you to pay attention to every word, and you are more likely to catch lapses in the logic. After you have read your paper through, answer the questions for revising and editing below and on the following page, and make the necessary changes.

SHARE YOUR DRAFT WITH OTHERS. Ask a fellow student to look over your draft. Have them tell you what they think is the point of your analysis, and whether your causal relationship seems reasonable. The guidelines on page 36 will help make the peer review more effective. After getting feedback from a classmate, answer the questions in the box below and see Chapter 16 for advice on solving common writing problems.

Questions for Revising and Editing: Cause and Effect Analysis

1. Why do I want to use cause and effect analysis: to inform, to speculate, or to argue? Does my analysis help me achieve my purpose?
2. Is my topic manageable for the essay I wish to write? Have I effectively established my focus?
3. Does my thesis statement clearly state either the cause and its effects or the effect and its causes?
4. Have I identified the nature of my cause and effect scenario? Is there a causal chain? Have I identified immediate and remote causes? Have I distinguished between possible and actual causes and effects?
5. Have I been able to avoid oversimplifying the cause and effect relationship I am writing about? Are there any errors in my logic?
6. Is my tone balanced, neither overstating nor understating my position?
7. Is there another rhetorical strategy that I can use with cause and effect analysis to assist me in achieving my purpose? If so, have I been able to implement it with care so that I have not altered either the direction or the tone of my essay?

(continued on next page)

(continued from previous page)

8. Have I taken every opportunity to use words and phrases that signal cause and effect relationships?
9. Have I used *affect* and *effect* properly?
10. Have I avoided the phrase *the reason is because*?
11. Have I avoided errors in grammar, punctuation, and mechanics? Is my sentence style as clear, smooth, and persuasive as possible?

How Boys Become Men

JON KATZ

Journalist and novelist Jon Katz was born in 1947. He writes with a keen understanding of life in contemporary suburban America. Each of his four mystery novels is a volume in the Suburban Detective Mystery series: *The Family Stalker* (1994), *Death by Station Wagon* (1994), *The Father's Club* (1996), and *The Last Housewife* (1996). The best known of these novels, *The Last Housewife*, won critical praise for its insights into the pressures and conflicts experienced by young professional couples in their efforts to achieve the American dream. Katz is also the author of *Media Rants: Postpolitics in the Digital Nation* (1997), a collection of his newspaper columns dealing primarily with the role and influence of the media in the public life of modern America; *Virtuous Reality: How Americans Surrendered Discussion of Moral Values to Opportunists, Nitwits, and Blockheads Like William Bennett* (1998); and *Geeks: How Two Lost Boys Rode the Internet Out of Idaho* (2000). *The Second Chance Dog: A Love Story*, which he wrote in 2013, continues his recent focus on writing fiction and nonfiction about dogs.

James Lattanzo

In the following essay, first published in January 1993 in *Glamour*, Katz explains why many men appear to be insensitive.

Preparing to Read

How important are childhood experiences to the development of identity? How do the rituals of the playground, the slumber party, and the neighborhood gang help mold us as men and women? Write about one or two examples from your own experience.

Two nine-year-old boys, neighbors and friends, were walking home from school. The one in the bright blue windbreaker was laughing and swinging a heavy-looking book bag toward the head of his friend, who kept ducking and stepping back. "What's the matter?" asked the kid with the bag, whooshing it over his head. "You chicken?"

His friend stopped, stood still, and braced himself. The bag slammed into the side of his face, the thump audible all the way across the street where I stood watching. The impact knocked him to the ground, where he lay mildly stunned for a second. Then he struggled up, rubbing the side of his head. "See?" he said proudly. "I'm no chicken."

No. A chicken would probably have had the sense to get out of the way. This boy was already well on the road to becoming a *man*, having learned one of the central ethics of his gender: Experience pain rather than show fear.

Women tend to see men as a giant problem in need of solution. They tell us that we're remote and uncommunicative, that we need to demonstrate less machismo and more commitment, more humanity. But if you don't understand something about boys, you can't understand why men are the way we are, why we find it so difficult to make friends or to acknowledge our fears and problems.

Boys live in a world with its own Code of Conduct, a set of ruthless, unspoken, and unyielding rules:

> Don't be a goody-goody.
> Never rat. If your parents ask about bruises, shrug.
> Never admit fear. Ride the roller coaster, join the fistfight, do what you have to do. Asking for help is for sissies.
> Empathy is for nerds. You can help your best buddy, under certain circumstances. Everyone else is on his own.
> Never discuss anything of substance with anybody. Grunt, shrug, dump on teachers, laugh at wimps, talk about comic books. Anything else is risky.

Boys are rewarded for throwing hard. Most other activities—reading, befriending girls, or just thinking—are considered weird. And if there's one thing boys don't want to be, it's weird.

More than anything else, boys are supposed to learn how to handle themselves. I remember the bitter fifth-grade conflict I touched off by elbowing aside a bigger boy named Barry and seizing the cafeteria's last carton of chocolate milk. Teased for getting aced out by a wimp, he had to reclaim his place in the pack. Our fistfight, at recess, ended with my knees buckling and my lip bleeding while my friends, sympathetic but out of range, watched resignedly.

When I got home, my mother took one look at my swollen face and screamed. I wouldn't tell her anything, but when my father got home I cracked and confessed, pleading with them to do nothing. Instead, they called Barry's parents, who restricted his television for a week.

The following morning, Barry and six of his pals stepped out from behind a stand of trees. "It's the rat," said Barry.

I bled a little more. *Rat* was scrawled in crayon across my desk.

They were waiting for me after school for a number of afternoons to follow. I tried varying my routes and avoiding bushes and hedges. It usually didn't work.

I was as ashamed for telling as I was frightened. "You did ask for it," said my best friend. Frontier Justice has nothing on Boy Justice.

In panic, I appealed to a cousin who was several years older. He followed me home from school, and when Barry's gang surrounded me, he came barreling toward us. "Stay away from my cousin," he shouted, "or I'll kill you."

After they were gone, however, my cousin could barely stop laughing. "You were afraid of *them*?" he howled. "They barely came up to my waist."

Men remember receiving little mercy as boys; maybe that's why it's sometimes difficult for them to show any.

> **Women tend to see men as a giant problem in need of solution.**

"I know lots of men who had happy childhoods, but none who have happy memories of the way other boys treated them," says a friend. "It's a macho marathon from third grade up, when you start butting each other in the stomach."

"The thing is," adds another friend, "you learn early on to hide what you feel. It's never safe to say, 'I'm scared.' My girlfriend asks me why I don't talk more about what I'm feeling. I've gotten better at it, but it will *never* come naturally."

You don't need to be a shrink to see how the lessons boys learn affect their behavior as men. Men are being asked, more and more, to show sensitivity, but they dread the very word. They struggle to build their increasingly uncertain work lives but will deny they're in trouble. They want love, affection, and support but don't know how to ask for them. They hide their weaknesses and fears from all, even those they care for. They've learned to be wary of intervening when they see others in trouble. They often still balk at being stigmatized as weird.

Some men get shocked into sensitivity—when they lose their jobs, their wives, or their lovers. Others learn it through a strong marriage, or through their own children.

It may be a long while, however, before male culture evolves to the point that boys can learn more from one another than how to hit curve balls. Last month, walking my dog past the playground near my house, I saw three boys encircling a fourth, laughing and pushing him. He was skinny and rumpled, and he looked frightened. One boy knelt behind him while another pushed him from the front, a trick familiar to any former boy. He fell backward.

When the others ran off, he brushed the dirt off his elbows and walked toward the swings. His eyes were moist and he was struggling for control.

"Hi," I said through the chain-link fence. "How ya doing?"

"Fine," he said quickly, kicking his legs out and beginning his swing.

Thinking Critically about the Text

Do you agree with Katz that men in general are less communicative, less sensitive, and less sympathetic in their behavior than women? Why or why not? Where does "Boy Justice" originate?

Questions on Subject

1. Why, according to Katz, do "women tend to see men as a giant problem in need of solution" (paragraph 4)?
2. In paragraph 3, Katz states that one of the "central ethics" of his gender is "Experience pain rather than show fear." Would you agree with Katz?
3. What is it that boys are supposed to learn "more than anything else" (paragraph 7)? What do you think girls are supposed to learn more than anything else?
4. In paragraph 12, what does Katz mean when he says, "Frontier Justice has nothing on Boy Justice"?
5. How, according to Katz, do some men finally achieve sensitivity? Can you think of other softening influences on adult males?

Questions on Strategy

1. This essay was originally published in *Glamour* magazine. Can you find any places where Katz addresses himself specifically to an audience of young women? Where? (Glossary: *Audience*)
2. Early in the essay, Katz refers to men as "we," but later he refers to men as "they." What is the purpose of this change?
3. Notice that in paragraphs 16 and 17, Katz quotes two friends on the nature of male development. Why is the location of these quotes crucial to the structure of the essay?
4. Katz illustrates his thesis with three anecdotes. Identify each of them. Where in the essay is each located? How do they differ? How does each enhance the author's message? (Glossary: *Narration*)
5. What irony is expressed by the boy's answer "Fine" in paragraph 23? (Glossary: *Irony*)

Questions on Diction and Vocabulary

1. In paragraph 3, Katz identifies what he describes as "one of the central ethics" of his gender. Why does he call it an ethic rather than a rule?
2. What connotations do the words *chicken* and *weird* have for you? (Glossary: *Connotation/Denotation*)
3. Are you familiar with the word *rat* as Katz uses it? What does it mean? Check your dictionary for what it says about *rat* as a noun and as a verb.

Cause and Effect Analysis in Action

Think about what might be necessary to write an essay similar to Katz's that explores how children grow to adulthood in a specific country (for instance, "How Americans Become Adults"). If we assume, as Katz does, that who we are is the product of our early experiences, what aspects of national cultures might shape us? How might they do so? Share your thoughts with others in your class.

Writing Suggestions

1. Write an essay patterned on "How Boys Become Men," showing the causes and effects surrounding females growing up in American culture. In preparing to write, it may be helpful to review your response to the Preparing to Read prompt as well as ideas generated by the Cause and Effect Analysis in Action activity for this selection. You might come to the conclusion that women do not have a standard way of growing up; you could also write a cause and effect essay supporting this idea. Either way, be sure to include convincing examples.

2. **Writing with Sources.** The subject of the differences between men and women perpetually spawns discussion and debate, and a spate of widely read books have commented seriously on relationship issues. Read one of these books. (*Men Are from Mars, Women Are from Venus* by John Gray and *You Just Don't Understand* by Deborah Tannen are good examples.) Write a review presenting and evaluating the major thesis of the book you have chosen. What issues make male–female relations so problematic? What can be done to bridge the "gender gap" that so many experts, books, and teachers struggle to explain? For models of and advice on integrating sources in your essay, see Chapters 14 and 15.

iPod World: The End of Society?

ANDREW SULLIVAN

Andrew Sullivan was born in 1963 in South Godstone, Surrey, England, to Irish parents. He earned his B.A. degree in modern history at Magdalene College, Oxford, and his master's degree and Ph.D. in government at Harvard. Sullivan began his career in journalism at the *New Republic* and later wrote for the *New York Times Magazine*. A gay, Catholic, conservative, and often controversial commentator, Sullivan has made history as a blogger. His *The Daily Dish* blog became popular post–9/11 and received more than 50,000 hits a day by 2005. He moved the blog to the *Atlantic* in 2007, and then again to *The Daily Beast* in 2011, before moving it to a reader-supported stand-alone site in 2013. He retired from blogging in 2015. Sullivan has written several books: *Virtually Normal: An Argument about Homosexuality* (1995); *Love Undetectable: Notes on Friendship, Sex, and Survival* (1998); and *The Conservative Soul: How We Lost It, How to Get It Back* (2006).

Peter Kramer/Getty Images for TFF

In "iPod World: The End of Society?" which was first published in the *New York Times Magazine* on February 20, 2005, Sullivan examines the effects, both positive and negative, of the proliferation of iPods in our society.

Preparing to Read

If you are an iPod owner, what is attractive to you about the device? What does it allow you to do? What does it prevent you from having to do? Do you feel any sense of isolation when using your iPod? Do you think that your use of an iPod represents anything unique in our history? If so, what? If you do not have an iPod, what has prevented you from entering "iPod World"?

I was visiting New York City last week and noticed something I'd never thought I'd say about the big city. Yes, nightlife is pretty much dead (and I'm in no way the first to notice that). But daylife—that insane mishmash of yells, chatter, clatter, hustle, and chutzpah that makes New York the urban equivalent of methamphetamine—was also a little different. It was just a little quieter. Yes, the suburbanization of Manhattan is now far-gone, its downtown a Disney-like string of malls, riverside parks, and pretty upper-middle-class villages. But there was something else as well. And as I looked across the throngs on the pavements, I began to see why. There were little white wires hanging down from their ears, tucked

1

into pockets or purses or jackets. The eyes were a little vacant. Each was in his or her own little musical world, walking to their own soundtrack, stars in their own music video, almost oblivious to the world around them. These are the iPod people.

Even without the white wires, you can tell who they are. They walk down the street in their own MP3 cocoon, bumping into others, deaf to small social cues, shutting out anyone not in their bubble. Every now and again, some start unconsciously emitting strange tuneless squawks, like a badly-tuned radio, and their fingers snap or their arms twitch to some strange soundless rhythm. When others say, "Excuse me," there's no response. "Hi." Ditto. It's strange to be among so many people and hear so little. Except that each one is hearing so much.

Yes, I might as well fess up. I'm one of them. I witnessed the glazed New York looks through my own glazed pupils, my own white wires peeping out of my eardrums. I joined the cult a few years ago: the sect of the little white box worshippers. Every now and again, I go to church — those huge, luminous Apple stores, pews in the rear, the clerics in their monastic uniforms all bustling around, or sitting behind the "Genius Bars," like priests waiting to hear confessions. Others began, like I did, with a Walkman — and then another kind of clunkier MP3 player. But the sleekness of the iPod won me over. Unlike previous models, it actually gave me my entire musical collection to rearrange as I saw fit — on the fly, in my pocket. What was once an occasional musical diversion became a compulsive obsession. Now I have my iTunes in my iMac for my iPod in my iWorld. It's Narcissus's heaven: We've finally put the "i" into Me.

And, like all addictive cults, it's spreading. There are now 22 million iPod owners in the United States and Apple is now becoming a mass market company for the first time. Walk through any U.S. airport these days, and you will see person after person gliding through the social ether as if on autopilot. Get on a subway, and you're surrounded by a bunch of Stepford commuters, all sealed off from each other, staring into mid-space as if anesthetized by technology. Don't ask, don't tell, don't overhear, don't observe. Just tune in and tune out.

It wouldn't be so worrisome if it weren't part of something even bigger. Americans are beginning to narrowcast their own lives. You get your news from your favorite blogs, the ones that won't challenge your own view of the world. You tune in to a paid satellite radio service that also aims directly at a small market—for New Age fanatics, or liberal talk, or Christian rock. Television is all cable. Culture is all subculture. Your cell phones can receive e-mail feeds of your favorite blogger's latest thoughts—seconds after he has posted them—or sports scores for your own team, or stock quotes of just your portfolio. Technology has given us finally a universe entirely for ourselves—where the serendipity of meeting a new stranger, or hearing a piece of music we would never choose for ourselves, or an opinion that might actually force us to change our mind about something are all effectively banished. Atomization by little white boxes and cell phones. Society without the social. Others who are chosen—not met at random.

Human beings have never lived like this before. Yes, we have always had homes or retreats or places where we went to relax or unwind or shut the world out. But we didn't walk around the world like hermit crabs with our isolation surgically attached. Music in particular was once the preserve of the living room or the concert hall. It was sometimes solitary but it was primarily a shared experience, something that brought people together, gave them the comfort of knowing that others too understood the pleasure of that Brahms symphony or that Beatles album.

But music is as atomized now as living is. And it's also secret. That bloke next to you on the bus could be listening to heavy metal or Gregorian chant. You'll never know. And so, bit by bit, you'll never really know him. And by his very white wires, he is indicating he doesn't really want to know you.

What do we get from this? The awareness of more music, more often. The chance to slip away for a while from everydayness, to give our lives our own sound track, to still the monotony of the commute, to listen more closely and carefully to music that can lift you up and keep you going. We become masters of our own interests, more connected to people like us over the Internet, more instantly in touch with anything we want or need or think we want and think we need. Ever tried a stairmaster in silence? And why not listen to a Haydn trio while in line at Tesco?

But what are we missing? That hilarious shard of an overheard conversation that stays with you all day; the child whose chatter on the sidewalk takes you back to your own early memories; birdsong; weather; accents; the laughter of others; and those thoughts that come not by filling your head with selected diversion, but by allowing your mind to wander aimlessly through the regular background noise of human and mechanical life. External stimulation can crowd out the interior mind. Even the boredom that we flee has its uses. We are forced to find our own means to overcome it. And so we enrich our life from within, rather than from the static of white wires.

It's hard to give up, though, isn't it? Not so long ago, I was on a trip   10
and realized I had left my iPod behind. Panic. But then something else. I
noticed the rhythms of others again, the sound of the airplane, the opinions of the cabby, the small social cues that had been obscured before. I
noticed how others related to each other. And I felt just a little bit connected again. And a little more aware. Try it. There's a world out there.
And it has a sound track all its own.

Thinking Critically about the Text

Sullivan's title asks whether "iPod World" represents the end of society. Do you think Sullivan answers his own question? If so, how and where in the text does he do so? If not, why might Sullivan have left the question for us to answer? Explain.

Questions on Subject

1. What is Sullivan's thesis in this essay? (Glossary: *Thesis*)
2. What does Sullivan see as the benefits of iPod World? What does he see as the drawbacks?
3. What does Sullivan mean when he writes in paragraph 5, "Culture is all subculture"?
4. What suggestion does Sullivan make at the conclusion of his essay? Is his suggestion an appropriate conclusion for his essay? (Glossary: *Beginnings/Endings*)

Questions on Strategy

1. What particular features of the iPod lead to the effects Sullivan points out?
2. In paragraph 3, Sullivan equates iPod World to a cult or religion. How does his analogy work? (Glossary: *Analogy*)
3. Sullivan writes in paragraph 6, "Human beings have never lived like this before." How does he use comparison and contrast to help make his point? (Glossary: *Comparison and Contrast*)
4. Cite several examples where Sullivan uses irony in his essay. (Glossary: *Irony*) To what effect does he use this rhetorical device?
5. In his final paragraph, Sullivan gives us a brief example of cause and effect at work. What happens when he forgets to take his iPod on a trip?

Questions on Diction and Vocabulary

1. Reread paragraph 7. If you didn't already know that Sullivan was an Englishman, would you be able to tell from his diction in this paragraph? Explain.
2. Sullivan uses the words *atomization* (paragraph 5) and *atomized* (7). What does he mean by their use, and why do these words work so well for him?

3. How would you characterize Sullivan's style in this essay? Is it formal or informal, chatty or preachy, journalistic or academic, or something else? Support your answer with examples from the text. (Glossary: *Style*)

Cause and Effect Analysis in Action

In preparation for a classroom discussion, use your iPod or other MP3 player for a morning as you go about your daily campus activities. In the afternoon, do not use the device at all. Make a brief list of the effects of both using and not using the device as a prompt for your later classroom discussion. If you don't have an iPod or other music player, try working in your room with music playing.

Writing Suggestions

1. Study the photo below. It is one of a series of poster advertisements for the iPod on which someone has written an interpretation of the meaning of the *i* in *iPod*. Write an argument for or against the idea expressed in the handwritten comment: "The *i* stands for ISOLATION." Feel free to use the ideas and statements that Andrew Sullivan uses in his essay as prompts, quotations, and evidence in your own work but do not simply parrot what Sullivan has to say. Reach out in new and creative ways to express the causal relationship between the iPod and isolation.

2. Every time a new technological advance is made and then widely accepted — telephone, radio, television, video, DVDs, cell phones, and similar devices — some people decry the innovation as the end of society as we know it. Write an essay in which you argue either that the iPod is just such a device or that it is different from the others in significant ways. Be sure to include clear explanations that are based in cause and effect analysis.

3. An underlying concern, and perhaps a theme, in Sullivan's essay is that music plays a vital role in our sense of well-being. Each person with an iPod plays, in effect, a personally programmed and designed sound track for his or her life. Write an essay in which you examine music as a cause in your life and the way it affects you.

Staci Schwartz/stacipop.com

The Downside of Diversity

MICHAEL JONAS

Michael Jonas, who has been a journalist since the early 1980s, is executive editor of *CommonWealth* magazine, a quarterly focused on politics, ideas, and civic life in Massachusetts. Jonas was born in 1959 in Ann Arbor, Michigan, and received his B.A. in history from Hampshire College in 1981. Before joining the *CommonWealth* staff in 2001, Jonas was a contributing writer for the magazine. His cover story for *CommonWealth*'s Fall 1999 issue on youth antiviolence workers was selected for a PASS (Prevention for a Safer Society) Award from the National Council on Crime and Delinquency. His 2009 article on the centralization of power in the Massachusetts House of Representatives won an award for commentary and analysis from Capitolbeat, the national organization of state capitol reporters and editors.

Mary Beth Meehan

In the following article, first published August 5, 2007, on Boston.com, the Web presence of the *Boston Globe*, Jonas reports on a Harvard political scientist who finds that diversity hurts civic life. "Be fearless in your willingness to probe difficult questions and write uncomfortable truths," comments Jonas. "Not only do I hope my article does this, but it is, in many ways, what Robert Putnam, the Harvard scholar whose study I write about, confronted himself in publishing research results that are at odds with what he would have hoped to find."

Preparing to Read

Do you think that people who live in ethnically diverse communities demonstrate stronger or weaker civic engagement and interconnectedness than people who live in homogeneous communities? What are your reasons for thinking as you do?

It has become increasingly popular to speak of racial and ethnic diversity as a civic strength. From multicultural festivals to pronouncements from political leaders, the message is the same: Our differences make us stronger.

But a massive new study, based on detailed interviews of nearly 30,000 people across America, has concluded just the opposite. Harvard political scientist Robert Putnam—famous for *Bowling Alone*, his 2000 book on declining civic engagement—has found that the greater the diversity in a community, the fewer people vote and the less they volunteer, the less they give to charity and work on community projects. In the most diverse communities, neighbors trust one another about half as much as they do in the most homogeneous settings. The study, the largest ever on civic engagement in America, found that virtually all measures of civic health are lower in more diverse settings.

"The extent of the effect is shocking," says Scott Page, a University of Michigan political scientist.

The study comes at a time when the future of the American melting pot is the focus of intense political debate, from immigration to race-based admissions to schools, and it poses challenges to advocates on all sides of the issues. The study is already being cited by some conservatives as proof of the harm large-scale immigration causes to the nation's social fabric. But with demographic trends already pushing the nation inexorably toward greater diversity, the real question may yet lie ahead: how to handle the unsettling social changes that Putnam's research predicts.

"We can't ignore the findings," says Ali Noorani, executive director of the Massachusetts Immigrant and Refugee Advocacy Coalition. "The big question we have to ask ourselves is, what do we do about it; what are the next steps?"

The study is part of a fascinating new portrait of diversity emerging from recent scholarship. Diversity, it shows, makes us uncomfortable — but discomfort, it turns out, isn't always a bad thing. Unease with differences helps explain why teams of engineers from different cultures may be ideally suited to solve a vexing problem. Culture clashes can produce a dynamic give-and-take, generating a solution that may have eluded a group of people with more similar backgrounds and approaches. At the same time, though, Putnam's work adds to a growing body of research indicating that more diverse populations seem to extend themselves less on behalf of collective needs and goals.

His findings on the downsides of diversity have also posed a challenge for Putnam, a liberal academic whose own values put him squarely in the prodiversity camp. Suddenly finding himself the bearer of bad news, Putnam has struggled with how to present his work. He gathered the initial raw data in 2000 and issued a press release the following year outlining the results. He then spent several years testing other possible explanations.

When he finally published a detailed scholarly analysis in June in the journal *Scandinavian Political Studies*, he faced criticism for straying from data into advocacy. His paper argues strongly that the negative effects of diversity can be remedied and says history suggests that ethnic diversity may eventually fade as a sharp line of social demarcation.

"Having aligned himself with the central planners intent on sustaining such social engineering, Putnam concludes the facts with a stern pep talk," wrote conservative commentator Ilana Mercer, in a recent *Orange County Register* op-ed titled "Greater diversity equals more misery."

Putnam has long staked out ground as both a researcher and a civic player, someone willing to describe social problems and then have a hand in addressing them. He says social science should be "simultaneously rigorous and relevant," meeting high research standards while also "speaking to concerns of our fellow citizens." But on a topic as charged as ethnicity and race, Putnam worries that many people hear only what they want to.

"It would be unfortunate if a politically correct progressivism were to deny the reality of the challenge to social solidarity posed by diversity," he writes in the new report. "It would be equally unfortunate if an ahistorical and ethnocentric conservatism were to deny that addressing that challenge is both feasible and desirable."

Putnam is the nation's premier guru of civic engagement. After studying civic life in Italy in the 1970s and 1980s, Putnam turned his attention to the United States, publishing an influential journal article on civic engagement in 1995 that he expanded five years later into the best-selling *Bowling Alone*. The book sounded a national wake-up call on what Putnam called a sharp drop in civic connections among Americans. It won him audiences with presidents Bill Clinton and George W. Bush and made him one of the country's best-known social scientists.

> Birds of different feathers may sometimes flock together, but they are also less likely to look out for one another.

Putnam claims the United States has experienced a pronounced decline in *social capital*, a term he helped popularize. Social capital refers to the social networks—whether friendships or religious congregations or neighborhood associations—that he says are key indicators of civic well-being. When social capital is high, says Putnam, communities are better places to live. Neighborhoods are safer; people are healthier; and more citizens vote.

The results of his new study come from a survey Putnam directed among residents in forty-one U.S. communities, including Boston. Residents were sorted into the four principal categories used by the U.S. Census: black, white, Hispanic, and Asian. They were asked how much they trusted their neighbors and those of each racial category and questioned about a long list of civic attitudes and practices, including their views on local government, their involvement in community projects, and their friendships. What emerged in more diverse communities was a bleak picture of civic desolation, affecting everything from political engagement to the state of social ties.

Putnam knew he had provocative findings on his hands. He worried about coming under some of the same liberal attacks that greeted Daniel Patrick Moynihan's landmark 1965 report on the social costs associated with the breakdown of the black family. There is always the risk of being pilloried as the bearer of "an inconvenient truth," says Putnam.

After releasing the initial results in 2001, Putnam says he spent time "kicking the tires really hard" to be sure the study had it right. Putnam realized, for instance, that more diverse communities tended to be larger, have greater income ranges, higher crime rates, and more mobility among their residents—all factors that could depress social capital independent of any impact ethnic diversity might have.

"People would say, 'I bet you forgot about X,'" Putnam says of the string of suggestions from colleagues. "There were twenty or thirty Xs."

But even after statistically taking them all into account, the connection remained strong: Higher diversity meant lower social capital. In his findings, Putnam writes that those in more diverse communities tend to "distrust their neighbors, regardless of the color of their skin, to withdraw even from close friends, to expect the worst from their community and its leaders, to volunteer less, give less to charity and work on community projects less often, to register to vote less, to agitate for social reform more but have less faith that they can actually make a difference, and to huddle unhappily in front of the television."

"People living in ethnically diverse settings appear to 'hunker down'—that is, to pull in like a turtle," Putnam writes.

In documenting that hunkering down, Putnam challenged the two dominant schools of thought on ethnic and racial diversity, the "contact" theory and the "conflict" theory. Under the contact theory, more time spent with those of other backgrounds leads to greater understanding and harmony between groups. Under the conflict theory, that proximity produces tension and discord.

Putnam's findings reject both theories. In more diverse communities, he says, there were neither great bonds formed across group lines nor heightened ethnic tensions, but a general civic malaise. And in perhaps the most surprising result of all, levels of trust were not only lower between groups in more diverse settings, but even among members of the same group.

"Diversity, at least in the short run," he writes, "seems to bring out the turtle in all of us."

The overall findings may be jarring during a time when it's become commonplace to sing the praises of diverse communities, but researchers in the field say they shouldn't be.

"It's an important addition to a growing body of evidence on the challenges created by diversity," says Harvard economist Edward Glaeser.

In a recent study, Glaeser and colleague Alberto Alesina demonstrated that roughly half the difference in social welfare spending between the

United States and Europe—Europe spends far more—can be attributed to the greater ethnic diversity of the U.S. population. Glaeser says lower national social welfare spending in the United States is a "macro" version of the decreased civic engagement Putnam found in more diverse communities within the country.

Economists Matthew Kahn of UCLA and Dora Costa of MIT reviewed fifteen recent studies in a 2003 paper, all of which linked diversity with lower levels of social capital. Greater ethnic diversity was linked, for example, to lower school funding, census response rates, and trust in others. Kahn and Costa's own research documented higher desertion rates in the Civil War among Union Army soldiers serving in companies whose soldiers varied more by age, occupation, and birthplace.

Birds of different feathers may sometimes flock together, but they are also less likely to look out for one another. "Everyone is a little self-conscious that this is not politically correct stuff," says Kahn.

So how to explain New York, London, Rio de Janeiro, Los Angeles—the great melting-pot cities that drive the world's creative and financial economies?

The image of civic lassitude dragging down more diverse communities is at odds with the vigor often associated with urban centers, where ethnic diversity is greatest. It turns out there is a flip side to the discomfort diversity can cause. If ethnic diversity, at least in the short run, is a liability for social connectedness, a parallel line of emerging research suggests it can be a big asset when it comes to driving productivity and innovation. In high-skill workplace settings, says Scott Page, the University of Michigan political scientist, the different ways of thinking among people from different cultures can be a boon.

"Because they see the world and think about the world differently than you, that's challenging," says Page, author of *The Difference: How the Power of Diversity Creates Better Groups, Firms, Schools, and Societies.* "But by hanging out with people different than you, you're likely to get more insights. Diverse teams tend to be more productive."

In other words, those in more diverse communities may do more bowling alone, but the creative tensions unleashed by those differences in the workplace may vault those same places to the cutting edge of the economy and of creative culture.

Page calls it the "diversity paradox." He thinks the contrasting positive and negative effects of diversity can coexist in communities, but "there's got to be a limit." If civic engagement falls off too far, he says, it's easy to imagine the positive effects of diversity beginning to wane as well. "That's what's unsettling about his findings," Page says of Putnam's new work.

Meanwhile, by drawing a portrait of civic engagement in which more homogeneous communities seem much healthier, some of Putnam's worst fears about how his results could be used have been realized. A stream of conservative commentary has begun—from places like the Manhattan Institute and the *American Conservative*—highlighting the harm the study suggests will come from large-scale immigration. But Putnam says he's also received hundreds of complimentary e-mails laced with bigoted language. "It certainly is not pleasant when David Duke's Web site hails me as the guy who found out racism is good," he says.

In the final quarter of his paper, Putnam puts the diversity challenge in a broader context by describing how social identity can change over time. Experience shows that social divisions can eventually give way to "more encompassing identities" that create a "new, more capacious sense of 'we,' " he writes.

Growing up in the 1950s in a small midwestern town, Putnam knew the religion of virtually every member of his high school graduating class because, he says, such information was crucial to the question of "who was a possible mate or date." The importance of marrying within one's faith, he says, has largely faded since then, at least among many mainline Protestants, Catholics, and Jews.

While acknowledging that racial and ethnic divisions may prove more stubborn, Putnam argues that such examples bode well for the long-term prospects for social capital in a multiethnic America.

In his paper, Putnam cites the work done by Page and others, and uses it to help frame his conclusion that increasing diversity in America is not only inevitable, but ultimately valuable and enriching. As for smoothing over the divisions that hinder civic engagement, Putnam argues that Americans can help that process along through targeted efforts. He suggests expanding support for English-language instruction and investing in community centers and other places that allow for "meaningful interaction across ethnic lines."

Some critics have found his prescriptions underwhelming. And in offering ideas for mitigating his findings, Putnam has drawn scorn for stepping out of the role of dispassionate researcher. "You're just supposed to tell your peers what you found," says John Leo, senior fellow at the Manhattan Institute, a conservative think tank. "I don't expect academics to fret about these matters."

But fretting about the state of American civic health is exactly what Putnam has spent more than a decade doing. While continuing to research questions involving social capital, he has directed the Saguaro Seminar, a project he started at Harvard's Kennedy School of Government that promotes efforts throughout the country to increase civic connections in communities.

"Social scientists are both scientists and citizens," says Alan Wolfe, director of the Boisi Center for Religion and American Public Life at

Boston College, who sees nothing wrong in Putnam's efforts to affect some of the phenomena he studies.

Wolfe says what is unusual is that Putnam has published findings as a social scientist that are not the ones he would have wished for as a civic leader. There are plenty of social scientists, says Wolfe, who never produce research results at odds with their own worldview.

"The problem too often," says Wolfe, "is people are never uncomfortable about their findings."

Thinking Critically about the Text

If ethnic diversity seems to be a liability, at least in the short term, why does Putnam think it's "ultimately valuable and enriching" (paragraph 37)?

Questions on Subject

1. What are the effects of greater social diversity that Putnam's research reveals? What's being lost and gained? How serious are the losses, as Putnam sees them?

2. Putnam coined the term *social capital*. What does he mean by the term? (Glossary: *Definition*)

3. Why did Putnam worry about the effects that his research might have on his fellow social scientists and on the public at large?

4. What evidence related to the world's most vibrant cities seems to contradict the findings in Putnam's study? (Glossary: *Evidence*)

5. What are Putnam's suggestions for increasing social capital within diverse ethnic communities? Do you think those efforts are worthwhile? Why or why not?

Questions on Strategy

1. How does cause and effect work in Jonas's essay? Does it work only on the level of diversity and its effects?

2. In paragraph 38, conservative think-tank fellow John Leo is scornful of Putnam's role as an advocate for diversity. Do you agree with Leo's criticism of Putnam? Why or why not?

3. Jonas uses a number of very short, one- or two-sentence paragraphs. Examine several of them and explain why you think he uses them. Could Jonas have combined these short paragraphs with other paragraphs? Explain.

4. Examine Jonas's essay for examples of his use of outside authorities and evidence. How have these outside sources helped him to provide perspective on the issues he discusses? (Glossary: *Evidence*)

5. Is Jonas objective about the results and implications of Putnam's research, or does he reveal his own attitude about them? (Glossary: *Attitude*) Explain.

Questions on Diction and Vocabulary

1. One of Putnam's earlier works was *Bowling Alone*, a book that studied the gradual change from earlier decades in American culture, in which bowling was a very social activity, to more recent times, in which bowling has become an activity primarily engaged in by solitary individuals. Why was that metaphor a good one for the loss of social capital he wrote about? (Glossary: *Figures of Speech*)

2. Putnam says in paragraph 19 that "people living in ethnically diverse settings appear to 'hunker down' — that is, to pull in like a turtle." What figure of speech does his statement contain, and what does it mean? (Glossary: *Figures of Speech*)

Cause and Effect Analysis in Action

Determining causes and effects requires careful thought. Establishing a causal chain of events is no less demanding, but it can also bring clarity and understanding to many complex issues. Consider the following example involving the H1N1 virus, or swine flu:

> **ultimate cause** According to the Centers for Disease Control (CDC), this virus was originally referred to as "swine flu" because laboratory testing showed that many of the genes in this new virus were very similar to influenza viruses that normally occur in pigs (swine) in North America. But further study has shown that this new virus is very different from what normally circulates in North American pigs. It has two genes from flu viruses that normally circulate in pigs in Europe and Asia and bird (avian) genes and human genes. Scientists call this a "quadruple reassortant" virus.
>
> **immediate cause** Contact with surfaces that have the flu virus on them and then touching the mouth or nose or eyes
>
> **effect** Influenza (fever, cough, sore throat, runny or stuffy nose, body aches, headache, chills and fatigue, possible vomiting and diarrhea)
>
> **effect** Possible death; possible pandemic

Develop a causal chain for each of the cause and effect pairs listed below. Then mix two of the pairs (for example, develop a causal chain for vacation/anxiety). Be prepared to discuss your answers with the class.

terror/alert   making a speech/anxiety
vacation/relaxation   climate change/technological innovation

Writing Suggestions

1. In the note that precedes this selection, Jonas suggests that you "be fearless in your willingness to probe difficult questions and write uncomfortable truths." Write an essay in which you examine more deeply the implications of Jonas's advice. Why does he consider it good and necessary advice to follow? What might be the difficult-to-deal-with effects of following that advice?

2. Write an essay in which you examine your own ideas about diversity at all levels. What do you think are its benefits and its negative aspects? How might we as Americans work to achieve more social integration and understanding? In thinking about your topic, you might want to consider the lessons that American history has taught us about how waves of immigrants gradually learned to live in mutually beneficial settings. Consider as well the measures that have been taken legally, socially, economically, and in other ways to maintain respect for diversity as well as social cohesion.

Coca-Cola Funds Scientists Who Shift Blame for Obesity Away from Bad Diets

ANAHAD O'CONNOR

Anahad O'Connor was born the second youngest in a family of seven children in New York City in 1981. As a high school senior, he was selected as a *New York Times* College Scholar, and he went on to receive a bachelor's degree in psychology from Yale University. He began his writing career at the *New York Times* in 2003, writing for the weekly Tuesday science section. Since then, he has expanded his coverage to include politics, metropolitan and breaking news, and consistent contributions to the paper's Health and Wellness blog. He is the author of four books, including *Never Shower in a Thunderstorm: Surprising Facts and Misleading Myths about Our Health and the World We Live In* (2007) and, most recently, *Lose It! The Personalized Weight Loss Revolution* (2010).

This article appeared on the *New York Times* Health and Wellness blog on August 9, 2015. Consider the cause that Coca-Cola is addressing for obesity. Does O'Connor agree with the company's assessment? How does he make his case, and what other causes — and potential effects — does he bring to the reader's attention?

Preparing to Read

What is your relationship with your weight? Has a doctor ever advised you to lose or gain weight? Have you tried to address the issues with diet, exercise, or a combination of the two? How successful have you been? If you have always maintained a healthy weight, why do you think that is the case?

Coca-Cola, the world's largest producer of sugary beverages, is backing a new "science-based" solution to the obesity crisis: To maintain a healthy weight, get more exercise and worry less about cutting calories. [1]

The beverage giant has teamed up with influential scientists who are advancing this message in medical journals, at conferences and through social media. To help the scientists get the word out, Coke has provided financial and logistical support to a new nonprofit organization called the Global Energy Balance Network, which promotes the argument that weight-conscious Americans are overly fixated on how much they eat and drink while not paying enough attention to exercise. [2]

"Most of the focus in the popular media and in the scientific press is, 'Oh they're eating too much, eating too much, eating too much' — blaming fast food, blaming sugary drinks and so on," the group's vice president, Steven N. Blair, an exercise scientist, says in a recent video announcing the [3] new organization. "And there's really virtually no compelling evidence that that, in fact, is the cause."

Health experts say this message is misleading and part of an effort by Coke to deflect criticism about the role sugary drinks have played in the spread of obesity and Type 2 diabetes. They contend that the company is using the new group to convince the public that physical activity can offset a bad diet despite evidence that exercise has only minimal impact on weight compared with what people consume.

> Funding from the food industry is not uncommon in scientific research. But studies suggest that the funds tend to bias findings.

This clash over the science of obesity comes in a period of rising efforts to tax sugary drinks, remove them from schools and stop companies from marketing them to children. In the last two decades, consumption of full-calorie sodas by the average American has dropped by 25 percent.

"Coca-Cola's sales are slipping, and there's this huge political and public backlash against soda, with every major city trying to do something to curb consumption," said Michele Simon, a public health lawyer. "This is a direct response to the ways that the company is losing. They're desperate to stop the bleeding."

Coke has made a substantial investment in the new nonprofit. In response to requests based on state open records laws, two universities that employ leaders of the Global Energy Balance Network disclosed that Coke had donated $1.5 million last year to start the organization.

Since 2008, the company has also provided close to $4 million in funding for various projects to two of the organization's founding members: Blair, a professor at the University of South Carolina whose research over the past 25 years has formed much of the basis of federal guidelines on physical activity, and Gregory A. Hand, dean of the West Virginia University School of Public Health.

Records show that the network's website, gebn.org, is registered to Coca-Cola headquarters in Atlanta, and the company is also listed as the site's administrator. The group's president, James O. Hill, a professor at the University of Colorado School of Medicine, said Coke had registered the website because the network's members did not know how.

"They're not running the show," he said. "We're running the show."

Coca-Cola's public relations department repeatedly declined requests for an interview with its chief scientific officer, Rhona Applebaum. In a statement, the company said it had a long history of supporting scientific research related to its beverages and topics such as energy balance.

"We partner with some of the foremost experts in the fields of nutrition and physical activity," the statement said. "It's important to us that the researchers we work with share their own views and scientific findings, regardless of the outcome, and are transparent and open about our funding."

Blair and other scientists affiliated with the group said that Coke had no control over its work or message and that they saw no problem with the company's support because they had been transparent about it.

But as of last week, the group's Twitter and Facebook pages, which promote physical activity as a solution to chronic disease and obesity while remaining largely silent on the role of food and nutrition, made no mention of Coca-Cola's financial support. The group's website also omitted mention of Coke's backing until Yoni Freedhoff, an obesity expert at the University of Ottawa, wrote to the organization to inquire about its funding. Blair said this was an oversight that had been quickly corrected.

"As soon as we discovered that we didn't have not only Coca-Cola but other funding sources on the website, we put it on there," Blair said. "Does that make us totally corrupt in everything we do?"

Funding from the food industry is not uncommon in scientific research. But studies suggest that the funds tend to bias findings. A recent analysis of beverage studies, published in the journal *PLOS Medicine*, found that those funded by Coca-Cola, PepsiCo, the American Beverage Association and the sugar industry were five times more likely to find no link between sugary drinks and weight gain than studies whose authors reported no financial conflicts.

The group says there is "strong evidence" that the key to preventing weight gain is not reducing food intake — as many public health experts recommend — "but maintaining an active lifestyle and eating more calories." To back up this contention, the group provides links on its website to two research papers, each of which contains this footnote: "The publication of this article was supported by The Coca-Cola Company."

Hill said he had sought money from Coke to start the nonprofit because there was no funding available from his university. The group's website says it is also supported by a few universities and ShareWIK Media Group, a producer of videos about health. Hill said that he had also received a commitment of help from General Mills, as well as promises of support from other businesses, which had not formally confirmed their offers.

He said he believed public health authorities could more easily change the way people eat by working with the food industry instead of against it.

On its website, the group recommends combining greater exercise and food intake because, Hill said, " 'Eat less' has never been a message that's been effective. The message should be 'Move more and eat smarter.' "

He emphasized that weight loss involved a combination of complex factors and that his group's goal was not to play down the role of diet or to portray obesity as solely a problem of inadequate exercise.

"If we are out there saying it's all about physical activity and it's not about food, then we deserve criticism," he said. "But I think we haven't done that."

While people can lose weight in several ways, many studies suggest that those who keep it off for good consume fewer calories. Growing evidence also suggests that maintaining weight loss is easier when people limit their intake of high glycemic foods such as sugary drinks and other refined carbohydrates, which sharply raise blood sugar.

Physical activity is important and certainly helps, experts say. But studies show that exercise increases appetite, causing people to consume more calories. Exercise also expends far fewer calories than most people think. A 12-ounce can of Coca-Cola, for example, contains 140 calories and roughly 10 teaspoons of sugar. "It takes 3 miles of walking to offset that one can of Coke," said Barry M. Popkin, a professor of global nutrition at the University of North Carolina at Chapel Hill.

Kelly D. Brownell, dean of the Sanford School of Public Policy at Duke University, said that as a business, Coke "focused on pushing a lot of calories in, but then their philanthropy is focused on the calories out part, the exercise."

In recent years, Coke has donated money to build fitness centers in more than 100 schools across the country. It sponsors a program called "Exercise is Medicine" to encourage doctors to prescribe physical activity to patients. And when Chicago's City Council proposed a soda tax in 2012 to help address the city's obesity problem, Coca-Cola donated $3 million to establish fitness programs in more than 60 of the city's community centers.

The initiative to tax soda ultimately failed.

"Reversing the obesity trend won't happen overnight," Coca-Cola said in an ad for its Chicago exercise initiative. "But for thousands of families in Chicago, it starts now, with the next pushup, a single situp or a jumping jack."

Thinking Critically about the Text

O'Connor points out that the scientists backed by Coca-Cola "promote physical activity as a solution to chronic disease and obesity while remaining largely silent on the role of food and nutrition" (14). Why does he feel this message is misleading and potentially harmful? Do you agree? Why or why not?

Questions on Subject

1. Explain the title of O'Connor's article: "Coca-Cola Funds Scientists Who Shift Blame for Obesity Away from Bad Diets." How does this title prepare the reader for the argument that is to follow? Be specific.
2. What does O'Connor think is the main cause of obesity?
3. O'Connor says that "Coke has provided financial and logistical support" (paragraph 2) to Global Energy Balance Network. According to O'Connor, what is the mission of this network, and why is Coca-Cola's support relevant?
4. What is the "clash over the science of obesity" mentioned in paragraph 5?
5. O'Connor writes that "In recent years, Coke has donated money to build fitness centers in more than 100 schools across the country" (paragraph 26). What does this have to do with the "Exercise is Medicine" campaign and Coke's financing Global Energy Balance Network?

Questions on Strategy

1. How does O'Connor use cause and effect analysis in his essay? Cite several examples.
2. Who is O'Connor's audience, and how do you know? (Glossary: *Audience*)
3. O'Connor ends the fifteenth paragraph with a citation from Global Energy Balance Network's vice president Steven N. Blair: "Does that [neglecting to list Coca-Cola as a sponsor, allegedly by accident] make us totally corrupt in everything we do?" How would O'Connor answer this question? How can you tell? What is the stylistic effect of including this interrogative in the text?
4. According to O'Connor, how might Coca-Cola's prescription for fighting obesity ("To maintain a healthy weight, get more exercise and worry less about cutting calories") ultimately serve the soda company's interests? How do you know?
5. Characterize O'Connor's use of quotations. Select three of the quotations O'Connor uses, from three different sources. Determine what purpose they serve in developing his argument by analyzing how he integrates them into the piece.
6. What evidence does O'Connor cite to support his thesis? Is his research adequate and convincing? Would you like to have heard from additional experts? (Glossary: *Evidence*)

Questions on Diction and Vocabulary

1. The essay begins with this sentence: "Coca-Cola, the world's largest producer of sugary beverages, is backing a new 'science-based' solution to the obesity crisis." Notice how O'Connor's ideas are organized and presented through syntax — including word choice, parentheticals, scare quotes, etc. Describe the first impression that this opening affords the reader. What might the shape of this sentence suggest about O'Connor's position? (Glossary: *Syntax*)

2. Refer to a dictionary to determine the meanings of the following words as O'Connor uses them in this selection: *fixated* (paragraph 2), *misleading* (4), *deflect* (4), *backlash* (6), *transparent* (12, 13), *omitted* (14), *oversight* (14), *corrupt* (15), *bias* (16), *key* (17), *glycemic* (23), *philanthropy* (25).

3. Note the strand of related words in paragraph 15: *silent, no mention, omitted*. How would you name or categorize this strand of words? How do they contribute to the main idea of this paragraph? Subsequently, how does the main idea of this paragraph advance the article's thesis?

Cause and Effect Analysis in Action

In preparation for writing a cause and effect analysis, list at least two effects on society and two effects on personal behavior for one of the following: television talk shows, online shopping, all-sports channels, reality television programs, television advertising, Internet advertising, fast food, or another item of your choosing. For example, a cell phone could be said to have the following effects:

Society

- Fewer highway fatalities due to quicker response to accidents
- Expansion of the economy

Personal Behavior

- Higher personal phone bills
- Risks to users, other drivers, and pedestrians' safety

Writing Suggestions

1. Write a cause and effect analysis on one of the following topics or on one of your own choosing. Consider the causal claims that might have led to one of the following situations:

   - a ban on bottled water in your community
   - a car that won't start
   - an increase in voter participation in local elections
   - the approval of hydraulic fracturing (fracking) in your state
   - the crash of the real estate market in 2008

What questions need to be asked and answered? For example, if math scores on standardized tests have improved recently in your local high school, was it the school board, the parents, the teachers, the students, or someone else who asked for changes to be made? Was more time allotted to the teaching of math? Were new teaching materials provided? What other causes might have been in play, and in what order might they have occurred? Make sure to do research as needed to support your claims.

2. Select a favorite movie, story, or novel and write a cause and effect essay about some key aspect of the plot. What happens in this story, and why? Does a main character accomplish a goal, or die, or change in some way? How did this character end up where he or she does at the end of the story? Consider both immediate and remote causes and be careful not to oversimplify. Be sure to come up with a minimum of two reasons for any claim you make and provide evidence from the story for each of your reasons.

A Bird Whose Life Depends on a Crab

DEBORAH CRAMER

Deborah Cramer, who holds degrees from Wellesley College, Middlebury College, and the Massachusetts Institute of Technology, writes and lectures about science and the environment. She is the author of three books: *Great Waters: An Atlantic Passage* (2002), *Smithsonian Ocean: Our Water, Our World* (2008), and *The Narrow Edge: A Tiny Bird, an Ancient Crab, and an Epic Journey* (2016), which received the 2016 Reed Award for Environmental Writing. Her work has also appeared in the *New York Times,* the *Boston Globe,* and *Wellesley* magazine. She lives in Gloucester, Massachusetts, serves on the advisory council of the Stellwagen Bank National Marine Sanctuary, and is currently a visiting scholar at the Massachusetts Institute of Technology.

Shawn Henry

Interestingly, Cramer "disliked science as a kid. But when she grew up, she moved to a home on the edge of a salt marsh, and soon she was captivated by what was happening in her own backyard." This essay, published in the *New York Times* in late 2013, embraces that newfound appreciation. In it, Cramer describes the relationship between crabs, birds, and the humans who have threatened them both.

Preparing to Read

Why is it important to save animals and plants from extinction? Are there justifications for diminishing *any* population — for example, if that population can be used for medical research to benefit human beings?

Horseshoe crabs have been around for 475 million years, making them among earth's oldest animals. They emerge from waters along the Eastern Seaboard during the high tides of full and new moons each May and June to spawn and lay their eggs on sandy beaches. The world's largest population is concentrated in the Delaware Bay off the coasts of New Jersey and Delaware.

Arriving not far behind the crabs are thousands of small russet-colored shorebirds, known as red knots. They show up just in time to feast on the abundance of crab eggs before resuming their 9,300-mile journey from Tierra del Fuego to the Canadian Arctic. More than half of the red knots along the Western Atlantic flyway converge at this crucial springtime refueling stop, our own avian Serengeti.

But the number of horseshoe crabs has declined over the years. We'd been catching too many to use as bait to snag other sea creatures. That has meant trouble not only for red knots, whose numbers in the Delaware Bay have plummeted by 70 percent since the early 1980s, but for us.

Just as the red knots depend on crabs for food, we depend on them for their blood, which is exquisitely sensitive to bacterial toxins that can cause illness or death in humans. This has made a creature that survived the dinosaurs vital to modern medicine. The biomedical industry uses crab blood to create a clotting agent to test for bacterial contamination in an array of drugs and medical devices—from vaccines to intravenous medicines, heart stents and artificial hips.

The demand for these crabs has been a factor in the decline of the red knot, *Calidris canutus rufa*, whose numbers have dwindled to the point that the United States Fish and Wildlife Service recently proposed designating the bird as threatened, or likely to become in danger of extinction. If the red knot is so designated following the public comment period that ends on Friday, the government would develop a plan for the bird's recovery.

This could involve further protecting the crab, now used by commercial fishermen as bait for eel and whelk. The Atlantic States Marine Fisheries Commission, which regulates fishing along the coast, began restricting crab catches in 2000, and last year linked future harvest levels to recovery goals for the red knot.

Tougher action is required. The number of horseshoe crabs has stabilized in the Delaware Bay, but despite a moratorium imposed by New Jersey on crab harvesting by the bait industry, their population does not appear to be increasing. Meanwhile, since 2007, the number of crabs that die each year after being collected for their blood has exceeded the number recommended by the commission's management plan.

The biomedical industry catches crabs, extracts some of their blood and releases most of them back to the water. Many die as a result. Last year, the commission estimated that 15 percent, or 79,800, died—40 percent more than its suggested threshold of 57,500 crabs. Recent studies suggest that the mortality from the biomedical catch could range from 20 to 30 percent. The industry says it is much lower.

Demand for horseshoe crab blood is only likely to increase as worldwide demand for medical devices and drugs continues to rise. The biomedical industry's catch has increased by 85 percent since 2004. Industry representatives have agreed to discuss with the commission how to reduce mortality.

Looking ahead, other threats also loom both for the red knot and horseshoe crab. The sea is becoming increasingly acidic as we pump more and more carbon dioxide into the atmosphere, and this is stunting the growth of tiny clams and mussels eaten by both crabs and shorebirds.

The red knot is the first bird proposed for inclusion on the endangered species list whose troubles are primarily a result of climate change. Erosion and storm surges are likely to become more intense as the climate warms and the seas rise, threatening the beaches where crabs spawn and shorebirds feed. Last year, Hurricane Sandy wiped out 70 percent of the Delaware Bay's best horseshoe crab spawning beaches, requiring restoration.

Biologists also worry that changes in the climate could affect the red knot's Arctic breeding grounds and also result in "asynchronies" or mismatches in the timing of the bird's migratory cycle and the availability of food along its round-trip of more than 18,000 miles.

We need to address threats to the red knots before another storm or a bad spawning season for crabs pushes the birds closer to extinction. Regulators can begin by reducing horseshoe crab mortality in the biomedical industry. The rest of us can protect what is left of our coast by curbing development and insisting on aggressive reductions of greenhouse gas emissions. As seas rise and storms become more intense, we're not the only ones with something precious to lose.

Thinking Critically about the Text

Do you agree, based on the evidence provided in this essay, that the red knot's decline is the result of climate change? What about all the causes mentioned in paragraphs 1 through 9?

Questions on Subject

1. What is Cramer's thesis, and where do you find it? (Glossary: *Thesis*)
2. Why are horseshoe crabs valuable? Name as many reasons as you can.
3. What is the Western Atlantic flyway (paragraph 2)? How do you know?
4. What threats are faced by horseshoe crab and red knot bird populations?

Questions on Strategy

1. What is Cramer's purpose in this essay? Where is it stated? What does she want her readers to do? (Glossary: *Purpose*)

2. Is Cramer writing for a scientific or a general audience? How do you know? (Glossary: *Audience*)

3. Do you feel that Cramer uses a lot of technical language to make her point? If so, find two or three examples and make sure that you understand the definitions. If not, find two or three examples of how she uses approachable language to explain complex ideas.

4. What evidence does Cramer cite to support her thesis? Is her research adequate and convincing? Would you like to have heard from additional experts? (Glossary: *Evidence*)

5. How would you describe Cramer's tone in this selection? What words and phrases lead you to this conclusion? (Glossary: *Tone*)

6. Cramer uses a lot of numbers in this essay, such as 475 million (paragraph 1), 9,300-mile journey (2), 70 percent (3), 79,800 (8), and 85 percent (9). What do all these numbers add to the selection?

Questions on Diction and Vocabulary

1. Cramer uses strong verbs, such as *snag* and *plummeted*, both in paragraph 3. What other strong verbs can you locate? What is their effect on the reader?

2. Refer to a dictionary to determine the meanings of the following words as Cramer uses them in this selection: *spawn* (paragraph 1), *russet* (2), *abundance* (2), *converge* (2), *exquisitely* (4), *toxins* (4), *intravenous* (4), *dwindled* (5), *whelk* (6), *moratorium* (7), *mortality* (8), *migratory* (12).

Cause and Effect Analysis in Action

As a class, brainstorm all the species — animal and plant — you can think of that are endangered. Next, come up with at least two possible reasons each one might be threatened. What reasons come up most frequently? Do you think the reasons you cite are accurate, or would you need to do some research to be sure?

Writing Suggestions

1. "The red knot is the first bird proposed for inclusion on the endangered species list whose troubles are primarily a result of climate change" (paragraph 11). Name another species you believe to be endangered because of climate change. Make your case in a cause and effect essay modeled on Cramer's. Consider both immediate and remote causes and be careful not to oversimplify. Be sure to come up with a minimum of two reasons for any claim you make and provide evidence from Cramer's essay or outside sources for each of your reasons.

2. Write an essay in which you argue, as Cramer does, that climate change is a problem. Of particular importance will be how you handle the question of the alarming increase in natural disasters globally. Has the rate of disasters been increasing, decreasing, or stable over the past 500 years? If the rate is changing, what accounts for the change? What, if anything, changes if we look at the fluctuations in climate over the life of the planet? Does that additional research alter the concerns about climate change?

WRITING SUGGESTIONS FOR CAUSE AND EFFECT ANALYSIS

1. Write an essay in which you analyze the most significant reasons for your decision to attend college. You may wish to discuss your family background, your high school experience, people and events that influenced your decision, and your goals in college as well as in later life.

2. It is interesting to think of ourselves in terms of the influences that have caused us to be who we are. Write an essay in which you discuss two or three of what you consider the most important influences on your life. Following are some areas you may wish to consider in planning and writing your paper:

    a. a parent
    b. a book or movie
    c. a member of the clergy
    d. a teacher
    e. a friend
    f. a hero
    g. a coach
    h. your neighborhood
    i. your ethnic background

3. Write an essay about a recent achievement of yours or about an important achievement in your community. Explain the causes of this success. Look at all of the underlying elements involved in the accomplishment and explain how you selected the one main cause or the causal chain that led to the achievement. To do this, you will probably want to use the rhetorical strategy of comparison and contrast. You might also use exemplification and process analysis to explain the connection between your cause and its effect.

4. **Writing with Sources.** Decisions often involve cause and effect relationships; that is, a person usually weighs the possible results of an action before deciding to act. Write an essay in which you consider the possible effects that would result from one decision or another in one of the following controversies. You will need to do some research in the library or online to support your conclusions.

    a. taxing cars on the basis of fuel consumption
    b. requiring an ethics course in college
    c. mandatory licensing of handguns

d. cloning humans

   e. abolishing grades for college courses

   f. raising the minimum wage

   For models of and advice on integrating sources in your essay, see Chapters 14 and 15.

5. **Writing with Sources.** Review the graphic that opens this chapter (page 440). Take any one of the topics in the causal chain put forth in the graphic — for example, the housing boom, mortgage securitization, subprime crisis, or global economic downturn — and write an essay in which you dig deeper into the topic, exploring further causes and effects. For example, what caused "easy credit" to become available? How did foreign investors infuse our financial institutions with money? In examining mortgage securitization further, what did banks do that destabilized the mortgage system as we know it? What checks and balances or regulations did the government provide in this area of banking? Why did they fail? What causes (immediate and ultimate), effects, and causal chains do you see in the events?

   For any of these topics you will need to do further research in print and online sources to understand and report on your findings. For models of and advice on integrating sources in your essay, see Chapters 14 and 15.

6. **Writing in the Workplace.** A position paper gives advice on an issue and may incorporate any combination of the different development methods you're studying in this book. Most likely, however, it will place the greatest emphasis on cause and effect analysis and argumentation. The purpose of a position paper is to make a case for a way of regarding a topic and for taking action on it. Rather than a review of research that explores all that's been said about a topic or issue, or an essay that allows you to show your own thinking about it, the position paper presents a question, considers the pros and cons of various courses of action, and makes a recommendation that the author thinks is best.

   Say that you are an executive at the Javro Coffee Roasters Company, and the board of directors is interested in moving toward a fair-trade business model. Fair trade means selling coffee from beans that are raised on environmentally sustainable plantations, where workers are paid according to a fair and equitable wage scale, and where all business transactions are transparent and ethical. At the board's request, write a position paper on the feasibility of pursuing the fair-trade model, the pros and cons of the approach, and your recommendation about whether Javro should adopt it.

I AM NOT A RUG

As few as 3,890 wild tigers remain. Poaching for their skins, bones and other parts is the greatest immediate threat to their survival.

Find out what you can do to stop wildlife crime.

WWF | STOP WILDLIFE CRIME | IT'S DEAD SERIOUS

worldwildlife.org/wildlifecrime

2014 WWF-US Stop Wildlife Crime PSA

CHAPTER **12**

Argumentation

WHAT IS ARGUMENTATION?

THE WORD *ARGUMENT* PROBABLY FIRST BRINGS TO MIND DISAGREEMENTS and disputes. Occasionally, such disputes are constructive. More often, though, disputes like these are inconclusive and result only in anger over your opponent's stubbornness or in the frustration of realizing that you have failed to make your position understood.

Reasoned argument is something else again entirely. In reasoned argument, we attempt to convince listeners or readers to agree with a particular point of view, to make a particular decision, or to pursue a particular course of action. Such arguments involve the presentation of well-chosen evidence and the artful control of language or other persuasive tools. Arguments need not be written to be effective, however; oral argument, if well planned and well delivered, can be equally effective, as can primarily visual arguments.

For an example of argument that combines text and visuals, consider the antipoaching public service advertisement on the opposite page. This ad, created by the World Wildlife Fund, uses a photograph and an emphatic text headline to make its argument: The lives of tigers matter, and it's not right to hunt and kill them in order to turn their bodies into commodities. The declarative headline ("I Am . . .") personifies the tiger, reminding viewers that each animal has a unique personality. Ultimately, the ad encourages viewers to be responsible, thoughtful, and respectful consumers who refuse to perpetuate the cycle of wildlife crime.

ARGUMENT IN WRITTEN TEXTS

Written arguments must be carefully planned. The writer must settle in advance on a specific thesis or proposition rather than grope toward one, as in a dispute. There is a greater need for organization, for choosing the most effective types of evidence from all that are available, and for determining the strategies of rhetoric, language, and style that will best suit the argument's subject, purpose, thesis, and effect on the intended audience.

Most strong arguments are constructed around an effective thesis statement. Take, for example, the following opening to the essay "The Case for Short Words" by Richard Lederer (558):

> **Thesis statement**
>
> When you speak and write, there is no law that says you have to use big words. Short words are as good as long ones, and short, old words—like *sun* and *grass* and *home*—are best of all. A lot of small words, more than you might think, can meet your needs with a strength, grace, and charm that large words do not have.
>
> **Several examples support the thesis**
>
> Big words can make the way dark for those who read what you write and hear what you say. Small words cast their clear light on big things—night and day, love and hate, war and peace, and life and death. Big words at times seem strange to the eye and the ear and the mind and the heart. Small words are the ones we seem to have known from the time we were born, like the hearth fire that warms the home.

Note how Lederer uses examples to support his thesis statement. When you read the whole essay, you will want to check whether Lederer's argument is well reasoned and carefully organized. You will also want to check that his argument is logical and persuasive. A strong argument will have all of these qualities.

▶ Persuasive and Logical Argument

Most people who specialize in the study of argument identify two essential categories: persuasion and logic.

Persuasive argument relies primarily on appeals to emotion, to the subconscious, even to bias and prejudice. These appeals involve diction, slanting, figurative language, analogy, rhythmic patterns of speech, and a tone that encourages a positive, active response. Examples of persuasive argument are found in the claims of advertisers and in the speech making of politicians and social activists.

Logical argument, on the other hand, appeals primarily to the mind—to the audience's intellectual faculties, understanding, and knowledge. Such appeals depend on the reasoned movement from assertion to evidence to conclusion and on an almost mathematical system of proof and counterproof. Logical argument, unlike persuasion, does not normally impel its audience to action. Logical argument is commonly found in scientific or philosophical articles, in legal decisions, and in technical proposals.

Most arguments, however, are neither purely persuasive nor purely logical in nature. A well-written newspaper editorial that supports a controversial piece of legislation or that proposes a solution to a local problem, for example, will rest on a logical arrangement of assertions and evidence but will employ striking diction and other persuasive patterns of language to make it more effective. Thus the kinds of appeals a writer emphasizes depend on the nature of the topic, the thesis or proposition of the argument, the various kinds of support (e.g., evidence, opinions, examples, facts, statistics) offered, and a thoughtful consideration of the audience. Knowing the differences between persuasive and logical arguments is, then, essential in learning both to read and to write arguments.

Some additional types of arguments that are helpful in expanding your understanding of this strategy are described below.

▶ Informational, or Exploratory, Argument

It is often useful to provide a comprehensive review of the various facets of an issue. This is done to inform an audience, especially one that may not understand why the issue is controversial in the first place, and to help that audience take a position. The writer of this type of argument does not take a position but aims, instead, to render the positions taken by the various sides in accurate and clear language. Your instructors may occasionally call for this kind of argumentative writing as a way of teaching you to explore the complexity of a particular issue.

▶ Focused Argument

This kind of argument has only one objective: to change the audience's mind about a controversial issue. An example of this kind of argument is Nancy Armour's "You Shouldn't Get a Prize for Showing Up," which argues firmly against the notion of participation awards and points out the negative precedent they establish. Being comprehensive or taking the broad view is not the objective here. If opposing viewpoints are considered, it is usually to show their inadequacies and thereby to strengthen the writer's own position. This kind of argument is what we usually think of when we think of traditional argument.

▶ Action-Oriented Argument

This type of argument is highly persuasive and attempts to accomplish a specific task. This is the loud car salesperson on your television, the over-the-top subscription solicitation in your mail, the vote-for-me-because-I-am-the-only-candidate-who-can-lower-your-taxes type of argument. The language is emotionally charged, and buzzwords designed to arouse the emotions of the audience may even be used, along with such propaganda devices as glittering generalities (broad, sweeping statements) and bandwagonism ("Everyone else is voting for me—don't be left out").

▶ Quiet, or Subtle, Argument

Some arguments do not immediately appear to the audience to be arguments at all. They set out to be informative and objective, but when closely examined, they reveal that the author has consciously, or perhaps subconsciously, shaped and slanted the evidence in such a manner as to favor a particular position. Such shaping may be the result of choices in diction that bend the audience to the writer's perspective, or they may be the result of decisions not to include certain types of evidence while admitting others. Such arguments can, of course, be quite convincing, as there are always those who distrust obvious efforts to convince them, preferring to make their own decisions on the issues. This kind of argument is perhaps best demonstrated by Plato in "The Allegory of the Cave." Allegories are a valuable strategy in gently leading readers to a perspective, as Plato does by sharing a story of men trapped in a cave to make a larger point about awareness.

▶ Reconciliation Argument

Increasingly popular today is a form of argument in which the writer attempts to explore all facets of an issue to find common ground or areas of agreement. Of course, one way of viewing that common ground is to see it as a new argumentative thrust, a new assertion, about which there may yet be more debate. The object, nevertheless, is to lessen stridency and the hardening of positions and to mediate opposing views into a rational and, where appropriate, even practical outcome. Martin Luther King, Jr.'s speech "I Have a Dream" is perhaps the greatest example of a reconciliation argument of the past century.

USING ARGUMENTATION AS A WRITING STRATEGY

Reasoned arguments are limited to assertions about which there is a legitimate and recognized difference of opinion. It is unlikely that anyone will ever need to convince a reader that falling in love is a rare and intense experience, that crime rates should be reduced, or that computers are changing the world. Not everyone would agree, however, that women experience love more intensely than men do, that the death penalty reduces the incidence of crime, or that computers are changing the world for the worse; these assertions are arguable and admit differing perspectives. Similarly, a leading heart specialist might argue in a popular magazine that too many doctors are advising patients to have pacemakers implanted when they are not necessary; the editorial writer for a small-town newspaper could urge that a local agency supplying food to poor families be given a larger percentage of the town's budget; and in a lengthy and complex book, a foreign-policy specialist might attempt to prove that the current administration exhibits no consistent policy in its relationship with other countries and that the State Department needs to be overhauled.

No matter what forum it uses and no matter what its structure, an argument has as its chief purpose the detailed setting forth of a particular point of view and the rebuttal of any opposing views.

▶ The Classical Appeals

Classical thinkers believed that there are three key components in all rhetorical situations or attempts to communicate: the *speaker* (and, for us, the *writer*) who comments about a *subject* to an *audience*. For purposes of discussion, we can isolate each of these three entities, but in actual rhetorical situations, they are inseparable, each inextricably tied to and influencing the other two. The ancients also recognized the importance of qualities attached to each of these components that are especially significant in the case of argumentation: *ethos*, which is related to the speaker; *logos*, which is related to the subject; and *pathos*, which is related to the audience. Let's look a little closer at each of these.

Ethos (Greek for "character") has to do with the authority, the credibility, and, to a certain extent, the morals of the speaker or writer. In other words, *ethos* is the speaker's character as perceived by the audience, often based on shared values. Aristotle and Cicero, classical rhetoricians, believed that it was important for the speaker to be credible and to argue for a worthwhile cause. Putting one's argumentative skills in the service of a questionable cause was simply not acceptable. But how did one establish credibility? Sometimes it was gained through achievements outside the rhetorical arena — that is, the speaker had experience with an issue, had argued the subject before, and had been judged to be sincere and honest.

In the case of your own writing, establishing such credentials is not always possible, so you will need to be more concerned than usual with presenting your argument reasonably, sincerely, and in language untainted by excessive emotionalism. Finally, it is well worth remembering that you should always show respect for your audience in your writing.

Logos (Greek for "word"), related as it is to the subject, is the effective presentation of the argument itself. It refers to the speaker's grasp of the subject—his or her knowledge. Is the thesis or claim a worthwhile one? Is it logical, consistent, and well buttressed by supporting evidence? Is the evidence itself factual, reliable, and convincing? Finally, is the argument so thoughtfully organized and so clearly presented that it has an impact on the audience and could change opinions? Indeed, this aspect of argumentation is the most difficult to accomplish but is, at the same time, the most rewarding.

Pathos (Greek for "emotion") has the most to do with the audience. The essential question is, How does the speaker or writer present an argument or a persuasive essay to maximize its appeal for a given audience? One way, of course, is to appeal to the audience's emotions through the artful and strategic use of well-crafted language. Certain buzzwords, slanted diction, or emotionally loaded language may become either rallying cries or causes of resentment in an argument.

▶ Considering Audience

It is worth remembering at this point that you can never be certain who your audience is; readers range along a spectrum from extremely friendly and sympathetic to extremely hostile and resistant, with a myriad of possibilities in between. A friendly audience will welcome new information and support the writer's position; a hostile audience will look for just the opposite—flaws in logic and examples of dishonest manipulation. With many arguments, there is the potential for a considerable audience of interested parties who are uncommitted. If the targeted audience is judged to be friendly, the writer needs to be logical but should feel free to use emotional appeals. If the audience is thought to be hostile, the *logos* must be the writer's immediate concern, and the language should be straightforward and objective. The greatest caution, subtlety, and critical thinking must be applied to the attempt to win over an uncommitted audience.

▶ Argumentation and Other Rhetorical Strategies

In general, writers of argument are interested in explaining aspects of a subject as well as in advocating a particular view. Consequently, they frequently use the other rhetorical strategies in supportive roles. In your efforts to argue convincingly, you may find it necessary to define, to compare and contrast, to analyze causes and effects, to classify, to describe, and to narrate. (For more information on the use of other strategies in argumentation, see Use Other Rhetorical Strategies, page 506.) Nevertheless, it is the writer's attempt to convince, not explain, that is of primary importance in an argumentative essay. In this respect, it is helpful to know that there are two basic patterns of thinking and of presenting our thoughts that are followed in argumentation: *induction* and *deduction*.

Inductive and Deductive Reasoning

Inductive reasoning moves from a set of specific examples to a general statement or principle. As long as the evidence is accurate, pertinent, complete, and sufficient to represent the assertion, the conclusion of an inductive argument can be regarded as valid; if, however, you can spot inaccuracies in the evidence or can point to contrary evidence, you have good reason to doubt the assertion as it stands. Inductive reasoning is the most common of argumentative structures.

Deductive reasoning, more formal and complex than inductive reasoning, moves from an overall premise, rule, or generalization to a more specific conclusion. Deductive logic follows the pattern of the *syllogism*, a simple three-part argument consisting of a major premise, a minor premise, and a conclusion. For example, notice how the following syllogism works:

a. All humans are mortal. (*Major premise*)
b. Catalina is a human. (*Minor premise*)
c. Catalina is mortal. (*Conclusion*)

The conclusion here is true because both premises are true, and the logic of the syllogism is valid.

Obviously, a syllogism fails to work if either of the premises is untrue, as in this example:

a. All living creatures are mammals. (*Major premise*)
b. A lobster is a living creature. (*Minor premise*)
c. A lobster is a mammal. (*Conclusion*)

The problem is immediately apparent. The major premise is obviously false: There are many living creatures that are not mammals, and a lobster happens to be one of them. Consequently, the conclusion is invalid.

Syllogisms, however, can fail even if both premises are objectively true. Such failures occur most often when the arguer jumps to a conclusion without taking into account obvious exceptions, as in this example:

a. All college students read books. (*Major premise*)
b. Larry reads books. (*Minor premise*)
c. Larry is a college student. (*Conclusion*)

Both of the premises in this syllogism are true, but the syllogism is invalid because it does not take into account that other people besides college students read books. The problem is in the way the major premise has been interpreted: If the minor premise were instead "Larry is a college student," then the valid conclusion "Larry reads books" would logically follow.

It is fairly easy to see the problems in a deductive argument when its premises and conclusion are rendered in the form of a syllogism. It is often more difficult to see errors in logic when the argument is presented discursively, or within the context of a long essay. If you can reduce the argument to its syllogistic form, however, you will have much less difficulty testing its validity. Similarly, if you can isolate and examine out of context the evidence provided to support an inductive assertion, you can more readily evaluate the written inductive argument.

Consider this excerpt from "The Draft: Why the Country Needs It," an article by James Fallows that first appeared in the *Atlantic* in 1980:

> The Vietnam draft was unfair racially, economically, educationally. By every one of those measures, the volunteer Army is less representative still. Libertarians argue that military service should be a matter of choice, but the plain fact is that service in the volunteer force is too frequently dictated by economics. Army enlisted ranks E1 through E4, the privates and corporals, the cannon fodder, the ones who will fight and die, are 36 percent black now. By the Army's own projections, they will be 42 percent black in three years. When other "minorities" are taken into account, we will have, for the first time, an army whose fighting members are mainly "nonmajority," or more bluntly, a black and brown army defending a mainly white nation. The military has been an avenue of opportunity of many young blacks. They may well be first-class fighting men. They do not represent the nation.
>
> Such a selective sharing of the burden has destructive spiritual effects in a nation based on the democratic creed. But its practical implications can be quite as grave. The effect of a fair, representative draft is to hold the public hostage to the consequences of its decisions, much as the children's presence in the public schools focuses parents' attention on the quality of the schools. If the citizens are willing to countenance a decision that means that someone's child may die, they may contemplate more deeply if there is the possibility that the child will be theirs. Indeed, I would like to extend this principle even further. Young men of nineteen are rightly suspicious of the congressmen and columnists who urge them to the fore. I wish there were a practical way to resurrect provisions of the amended Selective Service Act of 1940, which raised the draft age to forty-four. Such a gesture might symbolize the desire to offset the historic injustice of the Vietnam draft, as well as suggest the possibility that, when a bellicose columnist recommends dispatching the American forces to Pakistan, he might also realize that he could end up as a gunner in a tank.

Here Fallows presents an inductive argument against the volunteer army and in favor of reinstating a draft. His argument can be summarized as follows:

Assertion: The volunteer army is racially and economically unfair.

Evidence: He points to the disproportionate percentage of blacks in the army, as well as to projections indicating that, within three years of the article's publication, more than half of the army's fighting members would be nonwhite.

Conclusion: "Such a selective sharing of the burden has destructive spiritual effects in a nation based on the democratic creed." Not until there is a fair, representative draft will the powerful majority be held accountable for any decision to go to war.

Fallows's inductive scheme here is, in fact, very effective. The evidence is convincing, and the conclusion is strong. But his argument also depends on a more complicated deductive syllogism:

a. The democratic ideal requires equal representation in the responsibilities of citizenship. (*Major premise*)

b. Military service is a responsibility of citizenship. (*Minor premise*)

c. The democratic ideal requires equal representation in military service. (*Conclusion*)

To attack Fallows's argument, it would be necessary to deny one of his premises.

Fallows also employs a number of other persuasive techniques, including an analogy: "The effect of a fair, representative draft is to hold the public hostage to the consequences of its decisions, much as the children's presence in the public schools focuses parents' attention on the quality of the schools." The use of such an analogy proves nothing, but it can force readers to reconsider their viewpoint and can make them more open-minded. The same is true of Fallows's almost entirely unserious suggestion about raising the draft age to forty-four. Like most writers, Fallows uses persuasive arguments to complement his more important logical ones.

USING ARGUMENTATION ACROSS THE DISCIPLINES

When writing essays in the academic disciplines, you will have many opportunities to use the strategy of argumentation to both organize and strengthen the presentation of your ideas. To determine whether argumentation is the right strategy for you in a particular paper, use the guidelines described in

Chapter 2 (Determining a Strategy for Developing Your Essay, pages 32–33). Consider the following examples, which illustrate how this four-step method works for typical college papers:

Ethics

1. **MAIN IDEA:** Suicide as an end-of-life option.
2. **QUESTION:** Should a person be allowed to end his or her life when no longer able to maintain an acceptable quality of life?
3. **STRATEGY:** Argumentation. The question "Should a person be allowed" triggers a pro/con argument. The writer argues for or against laws that allow physician-assisted suicide, for example.
4. **SUPPORTING STRATEGY:** Definition should be used to clarify what is meant by the expression "quality of life." Cause and effect analysis should be used to determine, for example, at what point a person has lost a desirable "quality of life."

Environmental Studies

1. **MAIN IDEA:** The burning of fossil fuels is creating greenhouse gas emissions that are, in turn, causing global warming.
2. **QUESTION:** What can we do to reduce emissions from the burning of fossil fuels?
3. **STRATEGY:** Argumentation. The question "What can we do?" suggests an answer in the form of an argument. The writer might want to argue for higher taxes on fossil fuels or for the installation of smokestack scrubbers.
4. **SUPPORTING STRATEGY:** Cause and effect analysis will be necessary to show how burning fossil fuels increases greenhouse emissions and how higher taxes and smokestack scrubbers will work to reduce harmful gases.

Biology

1. **MAIN IDEA:** The use of animals in biomedical research is crucial.
2. **QUESTION:** Should there be a ban on the use of animals in biomedical research?
3. **STRATEGY:** Argumentation. The word *should* signals a pro/con debate: Animals should/should not be used in biomedical research.
4. **SUPPORTING STRATEGY:** Comparison and contrast might be used to help make the case that alternatives to the use of animals are better/worse than using animals.

SAMPLE STUDENT ESSAY USING ARGUMENTATION AS A WRITING STRATEGY

Student Kate Suarez begins her argumentation essay by questioning what she refers to as her "newest obsession," celebrity comings and goings. She was worried about how her fascination with celebrities might be affecting her character. Might it be "unhealthy"? she asks. In attempting to answer her question, she considers arguments both pro and con, supported by evidence from outside experts, before stating her own thesis at the conclusion of her essay: "We can use celebrities to see both ourselves and our communities just a bit clearer."

Celebrity Obsession: Is It Healthy Behavior?
Kate Suarez

Title hints at writer's position

Celebrities are my newest obsession. I've always perused photos of young Hollywood stars, but lately I check tabloid blogs three times a day. I forward photos of young actresses in studded heels to friends, asking, *Can I pull this off?* Each "Get It for Less" guide is my ticket to instant celebrity style. To say that my time would be better spent studying the *New York Times* and catching up on current events misses the point that celebrity culture is its own full world of events. Still, with it taking over so much of my day, I find myself wondering whether an obsession with celebrity—or even a passing interest—might be unhealthy.

Writer explains personal experience

Writer identifies central question: Is celebrity obsession harmful or healthy?

It's easy to let sensationalized celebrity stories dominate our everyday conversations. In a recent blog post in the *Huffington Post*, *Celebrity, Inc.* author Jo Piazza blamed our constant stream of celebrity news for our false sense of closeness to celebrities. Even though they're technically strangers to us, we're incredibly comfortable chatting about and sharing their tweets, Facebook posts, and *TMZ* controversies. However, those chats can come at the expense of real interpersonal connections with those around us. Rather than sharing our own thoughts or feelings, we talk about our favorite celebrities as though they are close acquaintances or friends, which distracts us from our own experiences and gets in the way of knowing the people in our lives.

First argument: celebrity worship is practiced at expense of real-life experiences

Yet defenders of celebrity culture maintain that this casual conversation fosters a feeling of national closeness. They suggest that it doesn't matter what we're talking about,

Counterargument: the unifying force of celebrity worship can be beneficial

> *Writer cites source to support idea that celebrity worship is a unifying force*

just that we're talking about the same thing. Older, traditional forms of entertainment like movies, books, plays, and television shows have become so numerous that we're all watching and reading different things. In contrast, the narrow focus of celebrity news means that we all share the same knowledge. Neal Gabler, author of *Life: The Movie: How Entertainment Conquered Reality*, calls celebrities "America's modern denominators," explaining,

> as disparate and stratified as Americans are, practically all of them seem to share an intense engagement, or at the very least an acquaintance, with the sagas of Jon and Kate or Brad and Angelina or Jennifer and whomever, which is oddly comforting (2).

Whether the story is love lost or found, the breakdown of a career, or even a death, sharing the same emotions unifies us. When a pop icon like Michael Jackson dies, everyone has something to say, and we listen to each other. It's real dialogue, and it's an exercise in communication that helps us tackle more serious social or political issues. We're reminded that we're all in this together.

> *Rejection of counterargument: writer cites source to support idea that flaunting togetherness is not sincere and leads us into false beliefs and emulation*

Critics of celebrity don't deny this aspect of community building, but they do wonder how much sincerity is behind it. The average consumer might downplay the influence of celebrities on her life, but Piazza counters that our consumption of celebrity news has exceeded a healthy level. Consuming so much celebrity news tricks us into false belief and emulation, both psychologically and economically:

> Our obsession has gone beyond mere escapism. The noise that celebrities create in our brains is helping to turn us into zombies who look to celebrities as role models and often blindly follow their advice (1).

We are seduced by the glitz and glamour of each celebrity narrative, often failing to understand that beyond the headlines and online ads, much of what we view as celebrity "real life" is constructed and fake. In fact, celebrities' very public status guarantees that everything they eat, drink, wear, and drive is on display, making them desirable company spokespeople. Companies are willing to pay for that kind of automatic attention and audience, and celebrities are happy for the increased exposure and additional cash. This makes the promoted product irrelevant, except to the consumer audience that is all too ready to imitate a celebrity's buying habits. Thus, when we make decisions motivated by celebrity endorsements, we might literally be buying into a personal choice fantasy—no one is getting something they really want, but everyone is getting something for it. In the case of celebrities, it's money. In the case of companies, it's exposure. In the case of us, it's the illusion that we're just like our favorite stars.

This puts the responsibility on us to be mindful of our celebrity habits, but it doesn't discredit celebrity itself. Salon.com advice columnist Cary Tennis insists that our hunger for more is valuable: "It is natural for us to be transfixed by these characters because we are thirsty for magic. We are not satisfied with our earthly existence, nor should we be" (2). Furthermore, admiring celebrities gives us an opportunity to learn more about ourselves: "What do your likes and dislikes of various celebrities say about you as a person, your aspirations, your secret hopes, your values?" he asks (2). If we think critically about the celebrity stories that appeal to us, we learn a lot about our fears and ambitions.

Karen Sternheimer, author of *Celebrity Culture and the American Dream*, agrees that celebrity culture helps form our values in a positive way. A professor of sociology, Sternheimer writes that without the shared experiences stimulated by celebrity culture, we'd miss a key aspect of our moral development: "Talking about celebrities, whether we express admiration, sympathy, or condemnation for them, offers us a framework through which to construct our social selves" (5). For example, we might erringly rationalize our own bad behavior by pointing to celebrities who behave similarly. By contrast, outrage over a celebrity's illegal drug use signals that we won't tolerate that behavior. Or, by harshly criticizing a celebrity's cheating scandal, we might position our values above those in the situation. On a personal level, evaluating celebrity behavior encourages self-discovery about what we do and don't find acceptable; on a pop culture level, such judgments set up a moral framework for long-term social bonds.

Although celebrity news might at first seem trivial, it's clear that its effects can be lasting and serious. We must maintain a healthy balance between sharing our own stories and those of our idols, and we must be skeptical about what reporters and advertisements claim as facts about celebrities' lives. At the same time, we can and should take advantage of those shared stories as a way to learn more about ourselves and others. A bit of aspiration will motivate us to work harder in our own lives, and a bit of comparison can help us clarify what we really want out of them. In this way, we can use celebrities to see both ourselves and our communities just a bit clearer.

Works Cited

Gabler, Neal. "The Greatest Show on Earth." *The Daily Beast*, 11 Dec. 2009, www.thedailybeast.com/articles/2009/12/11/the-greatest-show-on-earth.html.

Piazza, Jo. "Americans Have an Unhealthy Obsession with Celebrities." *The Huffington Post*, 28 March 2012, www.huffingtonpost.com/jo-piazza/americans-unhealthy-obsession-with-celebrities_b_1385405.html.

Sternheimer, Karen. *Celebrity Culture and the American Dream: Stardom and Social Mobility*. Routledge, 2011.

Tennis, Cary. "Why Am I Obsessed with Celebrity Gossip?" *Salon*, 6 Jan. 2006, www.salon.com/2006/01/06/celebrities_3/.

Analyzing Kate Suarez's Argumentation Essay: Questions for Discussion

1. In paragraph 3, Suarez claims that when we talk about celebrities, it "helps us tackle more serious social and political issues." Can you offer some ways in which this statement is true?
2. In paragraph 4, Suarez claims that in our purchases, "we make decisions motivated by celebrity endorsements." Have you ever been so influenced? Did you feel you were somehow manipulated, or did you regard your decisions as relatively harmless ones?
3. How might you define a celebrity? Do you count prominent politicians or athletes? Why or why not? How does this definition impact your perception of Suarez's argument?
4. What observations and insights regarding celebrity obsessions can you add to Suarez's argument?

SUGGESTIONS FOR USING ARGUMENTATION AS A WRITING STRATEGY

As you plan, write, and revise your argumentation essay, be mindful of the writing process guidelines described in Chapter 2. Pay particular attention to the basic requirements and essential ingredients of this writing strategy.

▶ Planning Your Argumentation Essay

Writing an argument can be very rewarding. By its nature, an argument must be carefully reasoned and thoughtfully structured to have maximum effect. In other words, the *logos* of the argument must be carefully tended. Allow yourself, therefore, enough time to think about your thesis, to gather the evidence you need, and to draft, revise, edit, and proofread your essay. Sloppy thinking, confused expression, and poor organization will be immediately evident to your reader and will make for weaker arguments.

For example, you might be given an assignment in your history class to write a paper explaining what you think was the main cause of the Civil War. How would you approach this topic? First, it would help to assemble a number of possible interpretations of the causes of the Civil War and to examine them closely. Once you have determined what you consider to be the main cause, you will need to develop points that support your position. Then you will need to explain why you did not choose other possibilities, and you will have to assemble reasons that refute them. For instance, you might write an opening similar to this example:

> The Fugitive Slave Act Forced the North to Go to War
>
> While the start of the Civil War can be attributed to many factors—states' rights, slavery, a clash between antithetical economic systems, and westward expansion—the final straw for the North was the Fugitive Slave Act. This act, more than any other single element of disagreement between the North and the South, forced the North into a position in which the only option was to fight.
> Certainly, slavery and the clash over open lands in the West contributed to the growing tensions between the two sides, as did the economically incompatible systems of production—plantation and manufacture—but the Fugitive Slave Act required the North either to actively support slavery or to run the risk of becoming a criminal in defiance of it. The North chose not to support the Fugitive Slave Act and was openly angered by the idea that it should be required to do so by law. This anger and open defiance led directly to the Civil War.

In these opening paragraphs, the author states the main argument for the cause of the Civil War and sets up, in addition, the possible alternatives to this view. The points outlined in the introduction would lead, one by one, to a logical argument asserting that the Fugitive Slave Act was responsible for the onset of the Civil War and refuting the other interpretations.

This introduction is mainly a logical argument. As mentioned earlier, writers often use persuasive, or emotional, arguments along with logical ones. Persuasive arguments focus on issues that appeal to people's subconscious or emotional nature, along with their logical powers and intellectual understanding. Such arguments rely on powerful and charged language, and they appeal to the emotions. Persuasive arguments can be especially effective but should not be used without a strong logical backing. Indeed, this is the only way to use emotional persuasion ethically. Emotional persuasion, when not in support of a logical point, can be dangerous in that it can make an illogical point sound appealing to a listener or reader.

DETERMINE YOUR THESIS OR PROPOSITION. Begin by determining a topic that interests you and about which there is some significant difference of opinion or about which you have a number of questions. Find out what's in the news, what people are talking about, what authors and instructors are emphasizing as important intellectual arguments. As you pursue your research, consider what assertion you can make about the topic you chose. The more specific this thesis or proposition, the more directed your research can become and the more focused your ultimate argument will be. While researching your topic, however, be aware that the information may point you in new directions. Don't hesitate at any point to modify or even reject an initial or preliminary thesis as continued research warrants.

A thesis can be placed anywhere in an argument, but it is probably best while learning to write arguments to place the statement of your controlling idea somewhere near the beginning of your composition. Explain the importance of the thesis and make clear to your reader that you share a common concern or interest in this issue. You may wish to state your central assertion directly in your first or second paragraph so that there is no possibility for your reader to be confused about your position. You may also wish to lead with a particularly striking piece of evidence to capture your reader's interest.

CONSIDER YOUR AUDIENCE. It is well worth remembering that in no other type of writing is the question of audience more important than in argumentation. Here again, the *ethos* and *pathos* aspects of argumentation come into play. The tone you establish, the type of diction you choose, the kinds of evidence you select to buttress your assertions, and indeed the organizational pattern you design and follow will all influence your audience's perception of your trustworthiness and believability. If you make good judgments about the nature of your audience, respect its knowledge of the subject, and correctly envision whether it is likely to be hostile, neutral, complacent, or receptive, you will be able to tailor the various aspects of your argument appropriately.

GATHER SUPPORTING EVIDENCE. For each point of your argument, be sure to provide appropriate and sufficient supporting evidence: verifiable facts and statistics, illustrative examples and narratives, or quotations from authorities. Don't overwhelm your reader with evidence but don't skimp either; it is important to demonstrate your command of the topic and your control of the thesis by choosing carefully from all the evidence at your disposal. If there are strong arguments on both sides of the issue, you will need to take this into account while making your choices. (See the Consider Refutations to Your Argument section below.)

▶ Organizing and Writing Your Argumentation Essay

CHOOSE AN ORGANIZATIONAL PATTERN. Once you think that you have sufficient evidence to make your assertion convincing, consider how best to organize your argument. To some extent, your organization will depend on your method of reasoning: inductive, deductive, or a combination of the two. For example, is it necessary to establish a major premise before moving on to discuss a minor premise? Should most of your evidence precede or follow your direct statement of an assertion? Will induction work better with the particular audience you have targeted?

As you present your primary points, you may find it effective to move from those that are least important to those that are most important or from those that are least familiar to those that are most familiar. A scratch outline can help, but it is often the case that a writer's most crucial revisions in an argument involve rearranging its components into a sharper, more coherent order. It is often difficult to tell what that order should be until the revision stage of the writing process.

CONSIDER REFUTATIONS TO YOUR ARGUMENT. As you proceed with your argument, you may wish to take into account well-known and significant opposing arguments. To ignore them would be to suggest to your readers any one of the following: You don't know about them, you know about them and are obviously and unfairly weighting the argument in your favor, or you know about them and have no reasonable answers to them. Grant the validity of the opposing argument or refute it, but respect your readers' intelligence by addressing the problems. Your readers will in turn respect you for doing so.

To avoid weakening your thesis, you must be very clear in your thinking and presentation. It must remain apparent to your readers why your argument is superior to opposing points of view. If you feel that you cannot introduce opposing arguments because they will weaken rather than strengthen your thesis, you should probably reassess your thesis and the supporting evidence.

USE OTHER RHETORICAL STRATEGIES. Although argument is one of the most powerful single rhetorical strategies, it is almost always strengthened by incorporating other strategies. In every professional selection in this chapter, you will find a number of rhetorical strategies at work.

Combining strategies is probably not something you want to think about when you first try to write an argument. Instead, let the strategies develop naturally as you organize, draft, and revise your essay. As you develop your argument essay, use the following chart as a reminder of what the eight strategies covered previously can do for you.

Strategies for Development	
Narration	Telling a story or giving an account of an event
Description	Presenting a picture in words
Illustration	Using examples to explain a point or an idea
Process analysis	Explaining how something is done or happens
Comparison and contrast	Demonstrating likenesses and differences
Division and classification	Separating a subject into its parts and placing them in appropriate categories
Definition	Explaining what something is or means
Cause and effect analysis	Explaining why something happens or the ramifications of an action

As you draft your essay, look for places where you can use the above strategies to strengthen your argument. For example, do you need a more convincing example, a term defined, a process explained, or the likely effects of an action detailed?

CONCLUDE FORCEFULLY. In the conclusion of your essay, be sure to restate your position in different language, at least briefly. Besides persuading your reader to accept your point of view, you may also want to encourage some specific course of action. Above all, your conclusion should not introduce new information that may surprise your reader; it should seem to follow naturally, almost seamlessly, from the series of points that have been carefully established in the body of the essay.

▶ Revising and Editing Your Argumentation Essay

AVOID FAULTY REASONING. Have someone read your argument, checking sentences for errors in judgment and reasoning. Sometimes others can see easily what you can't because you are so intimately tied to your assertion.

Review the following list of errors in reasoning and make sure you have not committed any of them:

Oversimplification—a foolishly simple solution to what is clearly a complex problem. *The reason we have a balance-of-trade deficit is that other countries make better products than we do.*

Hasty generalization—in inductive reasoning, a generalization that is based on too little evidence or on evidence that is not representative. *It was the best movie I saw this year, and so it should get an Academy Award.*

Post hoc, ergo propter hoc ("after this, therefore because of this")—confusing chance or coincidence with causation. The fact that one event comes after another does not necessarily mean that the first event caused the second. *Every time I wear my orange Syracuse sweater to a game, we win.*

Begging the question—assuming in a premise something that needs to be proven. *Parking fines work because they keep people from parking illegally.*

False analogy—making a misleading analogy between logically connected ideas. *Of course he'll make a fine coach. He was an all-star basketball player.*

Either/or thinking—seeing only two alternatives when there may in fact be other possibilities. *Either you love your job or you hate it.*

Non sequitur ("it does not follow")—an inference or conclusion that is not clearly related to the established premises or evidence. *She is very sincere; she must know what she is talking about.*

Name-calling—linking a person to a negative idea or symbol. The hope is that by invoking the name, the user will elicit a negative reaction without the necessary evidence. *Senator Jones is a bleeding heart.*

Questions for Revising and Editing: Argumentation

1. Is my thesis or proposition focused? Do I state my thesis well?
2. Assess the different kinds of arguments. Am I using the right technique to argue my thesis? Does my strategy fit my subject matter and audience?
3. Does my presentation include enough evidence to support my thesis? Do I acknowledge opposing points of view in a way that strengthens, rather than weakens, my argument?
4. Have I chosen an appropriate organizational pattern that makes it easy to support my thesis?
5. Have I avoided faulty reasoning within my essay? Have I had a friend read the essay to help me find problems in my logic?

(continued on next page)

(continued from previous page)

6. Is my conclusion forceful and effective?
7. Have I thought about or attempted to combine rhetorical strategies to strengthen my argument? If so, is the combination of strategies effective? If not, what strategy or strategies would help my argument?
8. Have I used a variety of sentences to enliven my writing? Have I avoided wordiness?
9. Have I avoided errors in grammar, punctuation, and mechanics?

CLASSIC ARGUMENTS

The Allegory of the Cave

PLATO

Plato is believed to have been born around 428 BCE in Greece. He was a pivotal philosopher and founded the Academy in Athens. Plato studied under Socrates, and Aristotle was one of Plato's many students. Among his more famous works are *The Republic* and *Laws*.

The selection below is from *The Republic* and makes a case about the nature of reality.

Hulton Archive/Getty Images

Preparing to Read

Consider how your five senses contribute to your understanding of the world around you. Which sense is the one you rely on the most heavily? Sight? Sound? Touch? Have you ever felt that your senses were deceiving you? If so, what steps did you take to confirm your understanding of the situation?

And now, I said, let me show in a figure how far our nature is enlightened or unenlightened:—Behold! human beings living in an underground den, which has a mouth open towards the light and reaching all along the den; here they have been from their childhood, and have their legs and necks chained so that they cannot move, and can only see before them, being prevented by the chains from turning round their heads. Above and behind them a fire is blazing at a distance, and between the fire and the prisoners there is a raised way; and you will see, if you look, a low wall built along the way, like the screen which marionette players have in front of them, over which they show the puppets.

I see.

And do you see, I said, men passing along the wall carrying all sorts of vessels, and statues and figures of animals made of wood and stone and various materials, which appear over the wall? Some of them are talking, others silent.

You have shown me a strange image, and they are strange prisoners.

Like ourselves, I replied; and they see only their own shadows, or the shadows of one another, which the fire throws on the opposite wall of the cave?

True, he said; how could they see anything but the shadows if they were never allowed to move their heads?

And of the objects which are being carried in like manner they would only see the shadows?

Yes, he said.

And if they were able to converse with one another, would they not suppose that they were naming what was actually before them?

Very true.

And suppose further that the prison had an echo which came from the other side, would they not be sure to fancy when one of the passers-by spoke that the voice which they heard came from the passing shadow?

No question, he replied.

To them, I said, the truth would be literally nothing but the shadows of the images.

That is certain.

And now look again, and see what will naturally follow if the prisoners are released and disabused of their error. At first, when any of them is liberated and compelled suddenly to stand up and turn his neck round and walk and look towards the light, he will suffer sharp pains; the glare will distress him, and he will be unable to see the realities of which in his former state he had seen the shadows; and then conceive someone saying to him, that what he saw before was an illusion, but that now, when he is approaching nearer to being and his eye is turned towards more real existence, he has a clearer vision—what will be his reply? And you may further imagine that his instructor is pointing to the objects as they pass and requiring him to name them,—will he not be perplexed? Will he not fancy that the shadows which he formerly saw are truer than the objects which are now shown to him?

To them, I said, the truth would be literally nothing but the shadows of the images.

Far truer.

And if he is compelled to look straight at the light, will he not have a pain in his eyes which will make him turn away to take refuge in the objects of vision which he can see, and which he will conceive to be in reality clearer than the things which are now being shown to him?

True, he said.

And suppose once more, that he is reluctantly dragged up a steep and rugged ascent, and held fast until he is forced into the presence of the sun himself, is he not likely to be pained and irritated? When he approaches the light his eyes will be dazzled, and he will not be able to see anything at all of what are now called realities.

Not all in a moment, he said.

He will require to grow accustomed to the sight of the upper world. And first he will see the shadows best, next the reflections of men and other objects in the water, and then the objects themselves; then he will gaze upon the light of the moon and the stars and the spangled heaven; and he will see the sky and the stars by night better than the sun or the light of the sun by day?

Certainly.

Last of all he will be able to see the sun, and not mere reflections of him in the water, but he will see him in his own proper place, and not in another; and he will contemplate him as he is.

Certainly.

He will then proceed to argue that this is he who gives the season and the years, and is the guardian of all that is in the visible world, and in a certain way the cause of all things which he and his fellows have been accustomed to behold?

Clearly, he said, he would first see the sun and then reason about him.

And when he remembered his old habitation, and the wisdom of the den and his fellow prisoners, do you not suppose that he would felicitate himself on the change, and pity them?

Certainly, he would.

And if they were in the habit of conferring honors among themselves on those who were quickest to observe the passing shadows and to remark which of them went before, and which followed after, and which were together; and who were therefore best able to draw conclusions as to the future, do you think that he would care for such honors and glories, or envy the possessors of them? Would he not say with Homer, Better to be the poor servant of a poor master, and to endure anything, rather than think as they do and live after their manner?

Yes, he said, I think that he would rather suffer anything than entertain these false notions and live in this miserable manner.

Imagine once more, I said, such an one coming suddenly out of the sun to be replaced in his old situation; would he not be certain to have his eyes full of darkness?

To be sure, he said.

And if there were a contest, and he had to compete in measuring the shadows with the prisoners who had never moved out of the den, while his sight was still weak, and before his eyes had become steady (and the time which would be needed to acquire this new habit of sight might be very considerable), would he not be ridiculous? Men would say of him that up he went and down he came without his eyes; and that it was better not even to think of ascending; and if any one tried to loose another and lead him up to the light, let them only catch the offender, and they would put him to death.

No question, he said.

This entire allegory, I said, you may now append, dear Glaucon, to the previous argument; the prison house is the world of sight, the light of the fire is the sun, and you will not misapprehend me if you interpret the journey upwards to be the ascent of the soul into the intellectual world according to my poor belief, which, at your desire, I have expressed—whether rightly or wrongly God knows. But, whether true or false, my opinion is that in the world of knowledge the idea of good appears last of all, and is seen only with an effort; and, when seen, is also inferred to be the universal author of all things beautiful and right, parent of light and of the lord of light in this visible world, and the immediate source of reason and truth in the intellectual; and that this is the power upon which he who would act rationally either in public or private life must have his eye fixed.

I agree, he said, as far as I am able to understand you.

Moreover, I said, you must not wonder that those who attain to this beatific vision are unwilling to descend to human affairs; for their souls are ever hastening into the upper world where they desire to dwell; which desire of theirs is very natural, if our allegory may be trusted.

Yes, very natural.

And is there anything surprising in one who passes from divine contemplations to the evil state of man, misbehaving himself in a ridiculous manner; if, while his eyes are blinking and before he has become accustomed to the surrounding darkness, he is compelled to fight in courts of law, or in other places, about the images or the shadows of images of justice, and is endeavoring to meet the conceptions of those who have never yet seen absolute justice?

Anything but surprising, he replied.

Anyone who has common sense will remember that the bewilderments of the eyes are of two kinds, and arise from two causes, either from coming out of the light or from going into the light, which is true of the mind's eye, quite as much as of the bodily eye; and he who remembers this when he sees anyone whose vision is perplexed and weak, will not be too ready to laugh; he will first ask whether that soul of man has come out of the brighter life, and is unable to see because unaccustomed to the dark, or having turned from darkness to the day is dazzled by excess of light. And he will count the one happy in his condition and state of being, and he will pity the other; or, if he have a mind to laugh at the soul which comes from below into the light, there will be more reason in this than in the laugh which greets him who returns from above out of the light into the den.

That, he said, is a very just distinction.

But then, if I am right, certain professors of education must be wrong when they say that they can put a knowledge into the soul which was not there before, like sight into blind eyes.

They undoubtedly say this, he replied.

Whereas, our argument shows that the power and capacity of learning exists in the soul already; and that just as the eye was unable to turn from darkness to light without the whole body, so too the instrument of knowledge can only by the movement of the whole soul be turned from the world of becoming into that of being, and learn by degrees to endure the sight of being, and of the brightest and best of being, or in other words, of the good.

Very true.

And must there not be some art which will effect conversion in the easiest and quickest manner; not implanting the faculty of sight, for that exists already, but has been turned in the wrong direction, and is looking away from the truth?

Yes, he said, such an art may be presumed.

And whereas the other so-called virtues of the soul seem to be akin to bodily qualities, for even when they are not originally innate they can be implanted later by habit and exercise, the virtue of wisdom more than anything else contains a divine element which always remains, and by this conversion is rendered useful and profitable; or, on the other hand, hurtful and useless. Did you never observe the narrow intelligence flashing from the keen eye of a clever rogue—how eager he is, how clearly his paltry soul sees the way to his end; he is the reverse of blind, but his keen eyesight is forced into the service of evil, and he is mischievous in proportion to his cleverness?

Very true, he said.

But what if there had been a circumcision of such natures in the days of their youth; and they had been severed from those sensual pleasures, such as eating and drinking, which, like leaden weights, were attached to them at their birth, and which drag them down and turn the vision of their souls upon the things that are below—if, I say, they had been released from these impediments and turned in the opposite direction, the very same faculty in them would have seen the truth as keenly as they see what their eyes are turned to now.

Very likely.

Yes, I said; and there is another thing which is likely, or rather a necessary inference from what has preceded, that neither the uneducated and uninformed of the truth, nor yet those who never make an end of their education, will be able ministers of State; not the former, because they have no single aim of duty which is the rule of all their actions, private as well as public; nor the latter, because they will not act at all except upon compulsion, fancying that they are already dwelling apart in the islands of the blessed.

Very true, he replied.

Then, I said, the business of us who are the founders of the State will be to compel the best minds to attain that knowledge which we have already shown to be the greatest of all—they must continue to ascend until they arrive at the good; but when they have ascended and seen enough we must not allow them to do as they do now.

What do you mean?

I mean that they remain in the upper world: but this must not be allowed; they must be made to descend again among the prisoners in the den, and partake of their labors and honors, whether they are worth having or not.

But is not this unjust? he said; ought we to give them a worse life, when they might have a better?

You have again forgotten, my friend, I said, the intention of the legislator, who did not aim at making any one class in the State happy above the rest; the happiness was to be in the whole State, and he held the citizens together by persuasion and necessity, making them benefactors of the State, and therefore benefactors of one another; to this end he created them, not to please themselves, but to be his instruments in binding up the State.

True, he said, I had forgotten.

Observe, Glaucon, that there will be no injustice in compelling our philosophers to have a care and providence of others; we shall explain to them that in other States, men of their class are not obliged to share in the toils of politics: and this is reasonable, for they grow up at their own sweet will, and the government would rather not have them. Being self-taught, they cannot be expected to show any gratitude for a culture which they have never received. But we have brought you into the world to be rulers of the hive, kings of yourselves and of the other citizens, and have educated you far better and more perfectly than they have been educated, and you are better able to share in the double duty. Wherefore each of you, when his turn comes, must go down to the general underground abode, and get the habit of seeing in the dark. When you have acquired the habit, you will see ten thousand times better than the inhabitants of the den, and you will know what the several images are, and what they represent, because you have seen the beautiful and just and good in their truth. And thus our State, which is also yours, will be a reality, and not a dream only, and will be administered in a spirit unlike that of other States, in which men fight with one another about shadows only and are distracted in the struggle for power, which in their eyes is a great good. Whereas the truth is that the State in which the rulers are most reluctant to govern is always the best and most quietly governed, and the State in which they are most eager, the worst.

Quite true, he replied.

And will our pupils, when they hear this, refuse to take their turn at the toils of State, when they are allowed to spend the greater part of their time with one another in the heavenly light?

Impossible, he answered; for they are just men, and the commands which we impose upon them are just; there can be no doubt that every one of them will take office as a stern necessity, and not after the fashion of our present rulers of State.

Yes, my friend, I said; and there lies the point. You must contrive for your future rulers another and a better life than that of a ruler, and then you may have a well-ordered State; for only in the State which offers this, will they rule who are truly rich, not in silver and gold, but in virtue and wisdom, which are the true blessings of life. Whereas if they go to the administration of public affairs, poor and hungering after their own private advantage, thinking that hence they are to snatch the chief good, order there can never be; for they will be fighting about office, and the civil and domestic broils which thus arise will be the ruin of the rulers themselves and of the whole State.

Most true, he replied.

And the only life which looks down upon the life of political ambition is that of true philosophy. Do you know of any other?

Indeed, I do not, he said.

Thinking Critically about the Text

Why do you think that Plato chose to use an allegory to make his argument about perception and reality? How would trying to write his theory in plain language have made it harder to understand? How would doing so have simplified your understanding?

Questions on Subject

1. Before presenting his allegory, Plato says that it will show how far human nature is enlightened or unenlightened. Do you think Plato has done so? In the context of this piece, do you find human nature enlightened or unenlightened?

2. Why is it significant that Plato has set his allegory in a prison? What is the impact of this metaphor? (Glossary: *Metaphor*)

3. In paragraph 35, Plato explicitly defines the elements of his allegory. Using your own words, how would you explain what his allegory means?
4. How does Plato believe that philosophy and politics are related?
5. Plato concludes that the highest aspiration a person can have is to be a true philosopher. Do you agree? Why or why not?

Questions on Strategy

1. What is Plato's thesis? (Glossary: *Thesis*) Does he ever state it explicitly? Does he have more than one?
2. Plato makes several allusions, including one to Homer, the blind poet credited with creating *The Iliad* and *The Odyssey*. What does this allusion contribute for you as a reader? What significance might it have had for Plato's contemporaries? (Glossary: *Allusion*)
3. Portions of this essay follow the strategy of process analysis, showing a series of events for the hypothetical prisoners. (Glossary: *Process Analysis*) What other strategies does Plato use to support his argument?
4. Plato presents his argument as a conversation between himself and Glaucon, his brother. (Glossary: *Dialogue*) How does this contribute to the pacing of his argument? Does it make it easier or harder to follow?
5. How does Plato support his claim that philosophers and politicians have a responsibility to share their knowledge for the good of the State?

Questions on Diction and Vocabulary

1. Throughout the piece, Plato repeats the words "True," "Certainly," and "Very true." Does this continual confirmation contribute to the persuasiveness of Plato's writing? Why or why not?
2. Plato identifies himself as a philosopher, and his argument is a purely philosophical one. Use a dictionary to look up the term *philosopher*. Then, using the references in the library or on the Web, explore the history of the term. How has the meaning changed since Plato used it? How is the meaning the same?

Argumentation in Action

One of Plato's most famous teachers was Socrates, for whom the Socratic method is named. This method of argumentation involves asking and answering questions to help develop a student's critical thinking skills. In groups of three, begin with a broad question from the list below and take turns asking and answering questions until you have narrowed it down to a useful argumentative thesis.

1. Is fracking good or bad for the environment?
2. Does democracy work?

3. Should everyone study a foreign language?
4. Why does courtesy matter?
5. Is philosophy still a useful field of study?

Writing Suggestions

1. An allegory is defined as a text that can be interpreted as having an unstated meaning. Select a topic or an idea about which you feel strongly and create an allegory of your own to highlight an important facet of the issue. Some potential topics include how elections are conducted in the United States and how to get a job. When creating your allegory, don't lose track of your central argument and keep in mind that your symbolism does not need to be complicated.

2. **Writing with Sources.** Do some research into the role of a politician in ancient Greece and make a case for how politicians today should emulate the values or practices of those in ancient Greece. Alternatively, argue that politics today is conducted in a more ethical or practical manner. How will you define the role of the politician? What are politicians' obligations to society? To themselves? For models of and advice on integrating sources, see Chapters 14 and 15.

The Declaration of Independence

THOMAS JEFFERSON

President, governor, statesman, diplomat, lawyer, architect, philosopher, thinker, and writer, Thomas Jefferson (1743–1826) is one of the most important figures in U.S. history. He was born in Albemarle County, Virginia, and attended the College of William and Mary. After being admitted to law practice in 1767, he began a long and illustrious career of public service to the colonies and, later, the new republic.

Library of Congress

Jefferson drafted the Declaration of Independence in 1776. Although it was revised by Benjamin Franklin and his colleagues in the Continental Congress, in its sound logic and forceful, direct style, the document retains the unmistakable qualities of Jefferson's prose.

Preparing to Read

What, for you, is the meaning of democracy? Where do your ideas about democracy come from?

When in the course of human events, it becomes necessary for one people to dissolve the political bonds which have connected them with another, and to assume among the Powers of the earth, the separate and equal station to which the Laws of Nature and of Nature's God entitle them, a decent respect to the opinions of mankind requires that they should declare the causes which impel them to the separation.

We hold these truths to be self-evident, that all men are created equal, that they are endowed by their Creator with certain unalienable Rights, that among these are Life, Liberty and the pursuit of Happiness.—That to secure these rights, Governments are instituted among Men, deriving their just powers from the consent of the governed,—That whenever any Form of Government becomes destructive of these ends, it is the Right of the People to alter or to abolish it, and to institute new Government, laying its foundation on such principles and organizing its powers in such form, as to them shall seem most likely to effect their Safety and Happiness. Prudence, indeed, will dictate that Governments long established should not be changed for light and transient causes; and accordingly all experience hath shewn, that mankind are more disposed to suffer, while evils are sufferable, than to right themselves by abolishing the forms to which they are accustomed. But when a long train of abuses and usurpations, pursuing invariably the same Object evinces a design to reduce them under absolute Despotism, it is their right, it is their duty, to throw off such Government, and to provide new Guards for their future security.—Such has been the patient sufferance of these Colonies; and such is now the necessity which constrains them to alter their former Systems of Government. The history of the present King of Great Britain is a history of repeated injuries and usurpations, all having in direct object the establishment of an absolute Tyranny over these States. To prove this, let Facts be submitted to a candid world.

He has refused his Assent to Laws, the most wholesome and necessary for the public good.

> We hold these truths to be self-evident, that all men are created equal, that they are endowed by their Creator with certain unalienable Rights, that among these are Life, Liberty and the pursuit of Happiness.

He has forbidden his Governors to pass Laws of immediate and pressing importance, unless suspended in their operation till his Assent should be obtained; and when so suspended, he has utterly neglected to attend to them.

He has refused to pass other Laws for the accommodation of large districts of people, unless those people would relinquish the right of Representation in the Legislature, a right inestimable to them and formidable to tyrants only.

He has called together legislative bodies at places unusual, uncomfortable, and distant from the depository of their public Records, for the sole purpose of fatiguing them into compliance with his measures.

He has dissolved Representative Houses repeatedly, for opposing with manly firmness his invasions on the rights of the people.

He has refused for a long time, after such dissolutions, to cause others to be elected; whereby the Legislative powers, incapable of Annihilation, have returned to the People at large for their exercise; the State remaining in the mean time exposed to all the dangers of invasion from without, and convulsions within.

He has endeavoured to prevent the population of these States; for that purpose obstructing the Laws of Naturalization of Foreigners; refusing to pass others to encourage their migration hither, and raising the conditions of new Appropriations of Lands.

He has obstructed the Administration of Justice, by refusing his Assent to Laws for establishing Judiciary Powers.

He has made Judges dependent on his Will alone, for the tenure of their offices, and the amount and payment of their salaries.

He has erected a multitude of New Offices, and sent hither swarms of Officers to harass our People, and eat out their substance.

He has kept among us, in times of peace, Standing Armies without the Consent of our legislatures.

He has affected to render the Military independent of and superior to the Civil power.

He has combined with others to subject us to a jurisdiction foreign to our constitution, and unacknowledged by our laws; giving his Assent to their Acts of pretended Legislation:

For quartering large bodies of armed troops among us:

For protecting them, by a mock Trial, from punishment for any Murders which they should commit on the Inhabitants of these States:

For cutting off our Trade with all parts of the world:

For imposing Taxes on us without our Consent:

For depriving us in many cases, of the benefits of Trial by Jury:

For transporting us beyond Seas to be tried for pretended offenses:

For abolishing the free System of English Laws in a neighbouring Province, establishing therein an Arbitrary government, and enlarging its Boundaries so as to render it at once an example and fit instrument for introducing the same absolute rule into these Colonies:

For taking away our Charters, abolishing our most valuable Laws, and altering fundamentally the Forms of our Governments:

For suspending our own Legislatures, and declaring themselves invested with power to legislate for us in all cases whatsoever.

He has abdicated Government here, by declaring us out of his Protection and waging War against us.

He has plundered our seas, ravaged our Coasts, burnt our towns, and destroyed the lives of our people.

He is at this time transporting large Armies of foreign Mercenaries to compleat works of death, desolation and tyranny already begun with circumstances of Cruelty & perfidy scarcely paralleled in the most barbarous ages, and totally unworthy the Head of a civilized nation.

He has constrained our fellow Citizens taken Captive on the high Seas to bear Arms against their Country, to become the executioners of their friends and Brethren, or to fall themselves by their Hands.

He has excited domestic insurrections amongst us, and has endeavoured to bring on the inhabitants of our frontiers, the merciless Indian Savages, whose known rule of warfare, is an undistinguished destruction of all ages, sexes and conditions.

In every stage of these Oppressions We Have Petitioned for Redress in the most humble terms: Our repeated Petitions have been answered only by repeated injury. A Prince, whose character is thus marked by every act which may define a Tyrant, is unfit to be the ruler of a free people.

Nor have We been wanting in attention to our Brittish brethren. We have warned them from time to time of attempts by their legislature to extend an unwarrantable jurisdiction over us. We have reminded them of the circumstances of our emigration and settlement here. We have appealed to their native justice and magnanimity, and we have conjured them by the ties of our common kindred to disavow these usurpations, which, would inevitably interrupt our connections and correspondence. They too have been deaf to the voice of justice and of consanguinity. We must, therefore, acquiesce in the necessity, which denounces our Separation, and hold them, as we hold the rest of mankind, Enemies in War, in Peace Friends.

We, therefore, the Representatives of the united States of America, in General Congress, Assembled, appealing to the Supreme Judge of the world for the rectitude of our intentions, do, in the Name, and by Authority of the good People of these Colonies, solemnly publish and declare, That these United Colonies are, and of Right ought to be Free and Independent States; that they are Absolved from all Allegiance to the British Crown, and that all political connection between them and the State of Great Britain, is and ought to be totally dissolved; and that as Free and Independent States, they have full Power to levy War, conclude Peace, contract Alliances, establish Commerce, and to do all other Acts and Things which Independent States may of right do. And for the support of this Declaration, with a firm reliance on the protection of divine Providence, we mutually pledge to each other our Lives, our Fortunes and our sacred Honor.

Thinking Critically about the Text

Why do you think the Declaration of Independence is still such a powerful and important document more than two hundred years after it was written? Do any parts of it seem more memorable than others? Did any part surprise you in this reading?

Questions on Subject

1. Where, according to Jefferson, do rulers get their authority? What does Jefferson believe is the purpose of government?
2. What argument does the Declaration of Independence make for overthrowing any unacceptable government? What assumptions underlie this argument?

3. In paragraphs 3–29, Jefferson lists the many ways King George has wronged the colonists. Which of these "injuries and usurpations" (paragraph 2) do you feel are just cause for the colonists to declare their independence?

4. According to the Declaration of Independence, how did the colonists try to persuade the English king to rule more justly?

5. What are the specific declarations that Jefferson makes in his final paragraph?

Questions on Strategy

1. The Declaration of Independence is a deductive argument; it is therefore possible to present it in the form of a syllogism. What are the major premise, the minor premise, and the conclusion of Jefferson's argument? (Glossary: *Syllogism*)

2. In paragraph 2, Jefferson presents certain "self-evident" truths. What are these truths, and how are they related to the intent of his argument?

3. The list of charges against the king is given as evidence in support of Jefferson's minor premise. Does he offer any evidence in support of his major premise? Why or why not? (Glossary: *Evidence*)

4. What organizational pattern do you see in the list of grievances in paragraphs 3–29? (Glossary: *Organization*) Describe the cumulative effect of this list on you as a reader.

5. Explain how Jefferson uses cause and effect thinking to justify the colonists' argument in declaring their independence. (Glossary: *Cause and Effect Analysis*)

Questions on Diction and Vocabulary

1. Who is Jefferson's audience, and in what tone does he address this audience? Discuss why this tone is or isn't appropriate for this document. (Glossary: *Audience*)

2. Is the language of the Declaration of Independence coolly reasonable or emotional, or does it change from one to the other? Give examples to support your answer.

3. Paraphrase the following excerpt and comment on Jefferson's diction and syntax: "They too have been deaf to the voice of justice and of consanguinity. We must, therefore, acquiesce in the necessity, which denounces our Separation, and hold them, as we hold the rest of mankind, Enemies in War, in Peace Friends" (paragraph 31). Describe the author's tone in these two sentences. (Glossary: *Diction; Tone*)

Argumentation in Action

Use the following test, developed by William V. Haney, to determine your ability to analyze accurately evidence that is presented to you. After completing Haney's test, discuss your answers with other members of your class and then compare them to the correct answers printed at the bottom of page 524.

THE UNCRITICAL INFERENCE TEST

Directions

1. You will read a brief story. Assume that all of the information presented in the story is definitely accurate and true. Read the story carefully. You may refer back to the story whenever you wish.

2. You will then read statements about the story. Answer them in numerical order. *Do not go back* to fill in answers or to change answers. This will only distort your test score.

3. After you read each statement carefully, determine whether the statement is:

    a. "T" — meaning: On the basis of the information presented in the story the statement is *definitely true*.

    b. "F" — meaning: On the basis of the information presented in the story the statement is *definitely false*.

    c. "?" — The statement *may* be true (or false) but on the basis of the information presented in the story you cannot be definitely certain. (If any part of the statement is doubtful, mark the statement "?".)

4. Indicate your answer by circling either "T" or "F" or "?" opposite the statement.

The Story

Babe Smith has been killed. Police have rounded up six suspects, all of whom are known gangsters. All of them are known to have been near the scene of the killing at the approximate time that it occurred. All had substantial motives for wanting Smith killed. However, one of these suspected gangsters, Slinky Sam, has positively been cleared of guilt.

Statements about the Story

1. Slinky Sam is known to have been near the scene of the killing of Babe Smith.   T   F   ?
2. All six of the rounded-up gangsters were known to have been near the scene of the murder.   T   F   ?
3. Only Slinky Sam has been cleared of guilt.   T   F   ?
4. All six of the rounded-up suspects were near the scene of Smith's killing at the approximate time that it took place.   T   F   ?
5. The police do not know who killed Smith.   T   F   ?
6. All six suspects are known to have been near the scene of the foul deed.   T   F   ?
7. Smith's murderer did not confess of his own free will.   T   F   ?
8. Slinky Sam was not cleared of guilt.   T   F   ?
9. It is known that the six suspects were in the vicinity of the cold-blooded assassination.   T   F   ?

Writing Suggestions

1. To some people, the Declaration of Independence still accurately reflects America's political philosophy and way of life; to others, it does not. What is your position on this issue? Discuss your analysis of the Declaration of Independence's contemporary relevance, and try to persuade others to accept your position.

2. **Writing with Sources.** How does a monarchy differ from American democracy? Write an essay in which you compare and contrast a particular monarchy and the presidency. How are they similar? You might also consider comparing the presidency with the British monarchy of 1776. Do some research online or in the library to support your analysis. For models of and advice on integrating sources in your essay, see Chapters 14 and 15.

ANSWERS: 1. T 2. ? 3. ? 4. T 5. ? 6. ? 7. ? 8. F 9. ?

Ain't I a Woman?

SOJOURNER TRUTH

Sojourner Truth was born into slavery and named Isabella in Ulster County, New York, in 1797. After her escape from slavery in 1827, she went to New York City and underwent a profound religious transformation. She worked as a domestic servant, and as an evangelist she tried to reform prostitutes. Adopting the name Sojourner Truth in 1843, she became a traveling preacher and abolitionist, frequently appearing with Frederick Douglass. Although she never learned to write, Truth's compelling presence gripped her audience as she spoke eloquently about emancipation and women's rights. After the Civil War and until her death in 1883, she worked to provide education and employment for emancipated slaves.

Library of Congress

At the Women's Rights Convention in Akron, Ohio, in May 1851, Truth extemporaneously delivered the following speech to a nearly all-white audience. The version we reprint was transcribed by Elizabeth Cady Stanton.

Preparing to Read

What comes to mind when you hear the word *speech*? Have you ever attended a rally or convention and heard speeches given on behalf of a social cause or political issue? What were your impressions of the speakers and their speeches?

Well, children, where there is so much racket there must be something out of kilter. I think that 'twixt the Negroes of the South and the women of the North, all talking about rights, the white men will be in a fix pretty soon. But what's all this here talking about?

That man over there says that women need to be helped into carriages, and lifted over ditches, and to have the best place everywhere. Nobody ever helps me into carriages, or over mud-puddles, or gives me any best place! And ain't I a woman? Look at me! Look at my arm! I have ploughed and planted, and gathered into barns, and no man could head me! And ain't I a woman? I could work as much and eat as much as a man—when I could get it—and bear the lash as well! And ain't I a woman? I have borne thirteen children, and seen them most all sold off to slavery, and when I cried out with my mother's grief, none but Jesus heard me! And ain't I a woman?

Then they talk about this thing in the head; what's this they call it? [Intellect, someone whispers.] That's it, honey. What's that got to do with women's rights or negro's rights? If my cup won't hold but a pint, and yours holds a quart, wouldn't you be mean not to let me have my little half-measure full?

> Nobody ever helps me into carriages, or over mud-puddles, or gives me any best place!

Then that little man in black there, he says women can't have as much rights as men, 'cause Christ wasn't a woman! Where did your Christ come from? Where did your Christ come from? From God and a woman! Man had nothing to do with Him.

If the first woman God ever made was strong enough to turn the world upside down all alone, these women together ought to be able to turn it back, and get it right side up again! And now they is asking to do it, the men better let them.

Obliged to you for hearing me, and now old Sojourner ain't got nothing more to say.

Thinking Critically about the Text

What are your immediate impressions of Truth's speech? Now take a minute to read her speech again, this time aloud. What are your impressions now? Are they different, and if so, how and why? What aspects of her speech are memorable?

Questions on Subject

1. What does Truth mean when she says "Where there is so much racket there must be something out of kilter" (paragraph 1)? Why does Truth believe that white men are going to find themselves in a "fix" (1)?
2. What does Truth put forth as her "credentials" as a woman?
3. How does Truth counter the argument that "women can't have as much rights as men, 'cause Christ wasn't a woman" (paragraph 4)?

Questions on Strategy

1. What is Truth's purpose in this essay? (Glossary: *Purpose*) Why is it important for her to define what a woman is for her audience? (Glossary: *Audience*)
2. How does Truth use the comments of "that man over there" (paragraph 2) and "that little man in black" (4) to help her establish her definition of *woman*?
3. What, for you, is the effect of Truth's repetition of the question "And ain't I a woman?" four times? (Glossary: *Rhetorical Question*) What other questions does she ask? Why do you suppose Truth doesn't provide answers to the questions in paragraph 3 but does for the question in paragraph 4?

4. How would you characterize Truth's tone in this speech? (Glossary: *Tone*) What phrases in the speech suggest that tone to you?

5. Explain how Truth uses comparison and contrast to help establish her definition of *woman*, especially in paragraph 2. (Glossary: *Comparison and Contrast*)

Questions on Diction and Vocabulary

1. How would you describe Truth's diction in this speech? What does her diction reveal about her character and background?

2. Refer to a dictionary to determine the meanings of the following words as Truth uses them in this selection: *kilter* (paragraph 1), *ditches* (2), *intellect* (3), *obliged* (6).

Argumentation in Action

In a letter to the editor of the *New York Times*, Nancy Stevens, president of a small New York City advertising agency, argues against using the word *guys* to address women. She believes that the "use of *guy* to mean 'person' is so insidious that I'll bet most women don't notice they are being called 'guys,' or, if they do, find it somehow flattering to be one of them." Do you find such usage objectionable? Why or why not? How is the use of *guy* to mean "person" different from using *gal* to mean "person"? How do you think Truth would react to the use of the word *guys* to refer to women? What light does your dictionary shed on this issue of definition?

Writing Suggestions

1. Sojourner Truth spoke out against the injustice she saw around her. In arguing for the rights of women, she found it helpful to define *woman* in order to make her point. What social cause do you find most compelling today? Human rights? Climate change? Domestic abuse? Alcoholism? Gay marriage? Racism? Select an issue about which you have strong feelings. Now carefully identify all key terms that you must define before arguing your position. Write an essay in which you use definition to make your point convincingly.

2. Sojourner Truth's speech holds out hope for the future. She envisions a future in which women join together to take charge and "turn [the world] back, and get it right side up again" (paragraph 5). What she envisioned has, to some extent, come to pass. For example, today the distinction between "women's work" and "men's work" has blurred or even vanished in some fields. Write an essay in which you speculate about how Truth would react to the world as we know it. What do you think would please her? What would disappoint her? What do you think she would want to change about our society? Explain your reasoning.

Resistance to Civil Government

HENRY DAVID THOREAU

Henry David Thoreau (1817–1862) was one of the leaders of the transcendentalist movement in the United States. Born in Concord, Massachusetts, he studied at Harvard College, though apocryphal legend is that he refused to pay the fee for his diploma. This story is believable, given Thoreau's active philosophies of simple living and civil disobedience. He was also a fervent abolitionist. An author, poet, and philosopher, he is best known for his book *Walden*.

The essay below, "Resistance to Civil Government" is also known by the title "Civil Disobedience." The essay was based on a lecture given by Thoreau at the Concord Lyceum and first appeared in print in 1849.

DeAgostini/Getty Images

Preparing to Read

How do you feel about the government? Do you think it should take a more active role in the lives of its citizens, or do you agree with Thoreau that "that government is best which governs least"? Would you ever go to jail because of that conviction, as Thoreau did?

I heartily accept the motto—"That government is best which governs least," and I should like to see it acted up to more rapidly and systematically. Carried out, it finally amounts to this, which also I believe—"That government is best which governs not at all"; and when men are prepared for it, that will be the kind of government which they will have. Government is at best but an expedient; but most governments are usually, and all governments are sometimes, inexpedient. The objections which have been brought against a standing army, and they are many and weighty, and deserve to prevail, may also at last be brought against a standing government. The standing army is only an arm of the standing government. The government itself, which is only the mode which the people have chosen to execute their will, is equally liable to be abused and perverted before the people can act through it. Witness the present Mexican war, the work of comparatively a few individuals using the standing government as their tool; for in the outset the people would not have consented to this measure.

This American government—what is it but a tradition, a recent one, endeavoring to transmit itself unimpaired to posterity but each instant losing some of its integrity? It has not the vitality and force of a single living man; for a single man can bend it to his will. It is a sort of wooden gun to the people themselves. But it is not the less necessary for this; for the people must have some complicated machinery or other, and hear its din, to satisfy that idea of government which they have. Governments show thus how successfully men can be imposed on, even impose on themselves, for their own advantage. It is excellent, we must all allow. Yet this government never of itself furthered any enterprise but by the alacrity with which it got out of its way. *It* does not keep the country free. *It* does not settle the West. *It* does not educate. The character inherent in the American people has done all that has been accomplished; and it would have done somewhat more if the government had not sometimes got in its way. For government is an expedient by which men would fain succeed in letting one another alone; and, as has been said, when it is most expedient the governed are most let alone by it. Trade and commerce, if they were not made of India-rubber, would never manage to bounce over the obstacles which legislators are continually putting in their way; and, if one were to judge these men wholly by the effects of their actions and not partly by their intentions, they would deserve to be classed and punished with those mischievous persons who put obstructions on the railroads.

But to speak practically and as a citizen, unlike those who call themselves no-government men, I ask for, not at once no government, but *at once* a better government. Let every man make known what kind of government would command his respect, and that will be one step toward obtaining it.

> **I ask for, not at once no government, but *at once* a better government.**

After all, the practical reason why, when the power is once in the hands of the people, a majority are permitted, and for a long period continue, to rule is not because they are most likely to be in the right, nor because this seems fairest to the minority but because they are physically the strongest. But a government in which the majority rule in all cases cannot be based on justice, even as far as men understand it. Can there not be a government in which majorities do not virtually decide right and wrong but conscience?—in which majorities decide only those questions to which the rule of expediency is applicable? Must the citizen ever for a moment, or in the least degree, resign his conscience to the legislator? Why has every man a conscience then? I think that we should be men first and subjects afterward. It is not desirable to cultivate a respect for the law, so much as for the right. The only obligation which I have a right to assume is to do at any time what I think right. It is truly enough said that a corporation has no conscience; but a corporation of conscientious men is a corporation *with* a conscience. Law never made men a whit more just; and, by means of their respect for it, even the well-disposed are daily made the agents of injustice. A common and natural result of an undue respect for law is that you may see a file of soldiers, colonel, captain, corporal, privates, powder-monkeys, and all, marching in admirable order over hill and dale to the wars, against their wills, ay, against their common sense and consciences, which makes it very steep marching indeed and produces a palpitation of the heart. They have no doubt that it is a damnable business in which they are concerned; they are all peaceably inclined. Now, what are they? Men at all? or small movable forts and magazines at the service of some unscrupulous man in power? Visit the Navy-Yard, and behold a marine, such a man as an American government can make, or such as it can make a man with its black arts — a mere shadow and reminiscence of humanity, a man laid out alive and standing, and already, as one may say, buried under arms with funeral accompaniments, though it may be—

> Not a drum was heard, not a funeral note,
> As his corse to the rampart we hurried;
> Not a soldier discharged his farewell shot
> O'er the grave where our hero we buried.

The mass of men serve the state thus, not as men mainly, but as machines, with their bodies. They are the standing army, and the militia, jailers, constables, posse comitatus, &c. In most cases there is no free exercise whatever of the judgment or of the moral sense; but they put themselves on a level with wood and earth and stones; and wooden men can perhaps be manufactured that will serve the purpose as well. Such command no more respect than men of straw or a lump of dirt. They have the same sort of worth only as horses and dogs. Yet such as these even are commonly esteemed good citizens. Others — as most legislators, politicians, lawyers, ministers, and office-holders — serve the state chiefly with their heads; and, as they rarely make any moral distinctions, they are as likely to serve the Devil, without *intending* it, as God. A very few, as heroes, patriots, martyrs, reformers in the great sense, and *men*, serve the state with their consciences also and so necessarily resist it for the most part; and they are commonly treated as enemies by it. A wise man will only be useful as a man and will not submit to be "clay" and "stop a hole to keep the wind away," but leave that office to his dust at least:

> I am too high-born to be propertied,
> To be a secondary at control,
> Or useful serving-man and instrument
> To any sovereign state throughout the world.

He who gives himself entirely to his fellow-men appears to them useless and selfish; but he who gives himself partially to them is pronounced a benefactor and philanthropist.

How does it become a man to behave toward this American government today? I answer, that he cannot without disgrace be associated with it. I cannot for an instant recognize that political organization as *my* government which is the *slave's* government also.

All men recognize the right of revolution; that is, the right to refuse allegiance to, and to resist the government when its tyranny or its inefficiency are great and unendurable. But almost all say that such is not the case now. But such was the case, they think, in the Revolution of '75. If one were to tell me that this was a bad government because it taxed certain foreign commodities brought to its ports, it is most probable that I should not make an ado about it, for I can do without them. All machines have their friction; and possibly this does enough good to counterbalance the evil. At any rate, it is a great evil to make a stir about it. But when the friction comes to have its machine, and oppression and robbery are organized, I say let us not have such a machine any longer. In other words, when a sixth of the population of a nation which has undertaken to be the refuge of liberty are slaves, and a whole country is unjustly overrun and conquered by a foreign army and subjected to military law, I think that it is not too soon for honest men to rebel and revolutionize. What makes this duty the more urgent is the fact that the country so overrun is not our own, but ours is the invading army.

Paley, a common authority with many on moral questions, in his chapter on the "Duty of Submission to Civil Government," resolves all civil obligation into expediency; and he proceeds to say, "that so long as the interest of the whole society requires it, that is, so long as the established government cannot be resisted or charged without public inconveniency, it is the will of God that the established government be obeyed, and no longer.... This principle being admitted, the justice of every particular case of resistance is reduced to a computation of the quantity of the danger and grievance on the one side, and of the probability and expense of redressing it on the other." Of this, he says, every man shall judge for himself. But Paley appears never to have contemplated those cases to which the rule of expediency does not apply, in which a people, as well as an individual, must do justice, cost what it may. If I have unjustly wrested a plank from a drowning man, I must restore it to him though I drown myself. This, according to Paley, would be inconvenient. But he that would save his life, in such a case, shall lose it. This people must cease to hold slaves and to make war on Mexico, though it cost them their existence as a people.

In their practice, nations agree with Paley; but does anyone think that Massachusetts does exactly what is right at the present crisis?

> A drab of state, a cloth-o'-silver slut,
> To have her train borne up, and her soul trail in the dirt.

Practically speaking, the opponents to a reform in Massachusetts are not a hundred thousand politicians at the South but a hundred thousand merchants and farmers here, who are more interested in commerce and agriculture than they are in humanity, and are not prepared to do justice to the slave and to Mexico, cost what it may. I quarrel not with far-off foes but with those who, near at home, co-operate with, and do the bidding of, those far away, and without whom the latter would be harmless. We are accustomed to say that the mass of men are unprepared; but improvement is slow because the few are not materially wiser or better than the many. It is not so important that many should be as good as you as that there be some absolute goodness somewhere; for that will leaven the whole lump. There are thousands who are in opinion opposed to slavery and to the war who yet in effect do nothing to put an end to them; who, esteeming themselves children of Washington and Franklin, sit down with their hands in their pockets and say that they know not what to do, and do nothing; who even postpone the question of freedom to the question of free trade, and quietly read the prices-current along with the latest advices from Mexico after dinner and, it may be, fall asleep over them both. What is the price-current of an honest man and patriot today? They hesitate and they regret and sometimes they petition; but they do nothing in earnest and with effect. They will wait, well-disposed, for others to remedy the evil, that they may no longer have it to regret. At most, they give only a cheap vote, and a feeble countenance and God-speed, to the right, as it goes by them. There are nine hundred and ninety-nine patrons of virtue to one virtuous man. But it is easier to deal with the real possessor of a thing than with the temporary guardian of it.

All voting is a sort of gaming, like checkers or backgammon, with a slight moral tinge to it, a playing with right and wrong, with moral questions; and betting naturally accompanies it. The character of the voters is not staked. I cast my vote, perchance, as I think right; but I am not vitally concerned that that right should prevail. I am willing to leave it to the majority. Its obligation, therefore, never exceeds that of expediency. Even voting *for the right* is *doing* nothing for it. It is only expressing to men feebly your desire that it should prevail. A wise man will not leave the right to the mercy of chance, nor wish it to prevail through the power of the majority. There is but little virtue in the action of masses of men. When the majority shall at length vote for the abolition of slavery, it will be because they are indifferent to slavery, or because there is but little slavery left to be abolished by their vote. *They* will then be the only slaves. Only *his* vote can hasten the abolition of slavery who asserts his own freedom by his vote.

I hear of a convention to be held at Baltimore, or elsewhere, for the selection of a candidate for the Presidency, made up chiefly of editors, and men who are politicians by profession; but I think, what is it to any independent, intelligent, and respectable man what decision they may come to? Shall we not have the advantage of his wisdom and honesty nevertheless? Can we not count upon some independent votes? Are there not many individuals in the country who do not attend conventions? But no: I find that the responsible man, so called, has immediately drifted from his position, and despairs of his country when his country has more reason to despair of him. He forthwith adopts one of the candidates thus selected as the only *available* one, thus proving that he is himself *available* for any purposes of the demagogue. His vote is of no more worth than that of any unprincipled foreigner or hireling native who may have been bought. O for a man who is a *man* and, as my neighbor says has a bone in his back which you cannot pass your hand through! Our statistics are at fault: the population has been returned too large. How many *men* are there to a square thousand miles in this country? Hardly one. Does not America offer any inducement for men to settle here? The American has dwindled into an Odd Fellow—one who may be known by the development of his organ of gregariousness and a manifest lack of intellect and cheerful self-reliance; whose first and chief concern, on coming into the world, is to see that the Almshouses are in good repair; and, before yet he has lawfully donned the virile garb, to collect a fund for the support of the widows and orphans that may be; who, in short, ventures to live only by the aid of the Mutual Insurance Company, which has promised to bury him decently.

It is not a man's duty, as a matter of course, to devote himself to the eradication of any, even the most enormous wrong; he may still properly have other concerns to engage him; but it is his duty, at least, to wash his hands of it and, if he gives it no thought longer, not to give it practically his support. If I devote myself to other pursuits and contemplations, I must first see, at least, that I do not pursue them sitting upon another man's shoulders. I must get off him first, that he may pursue his contemplations too. See what gross inconsistency is tolerated. I have heard some of my townsmen say, "I should like to have them order me out to help put down an insurrection of the slaves, or to march to Mexico—see if I would go"; and yet these very men have each directly by their allegiance and so indirectly, at least, by their money, furnished a substitute. The soldier is applauded who refuses to serve in an unjust war by those who do not refuse to sustain the unjust government which makes the war; is applauded by those whose own act and authority he disregards and sets at naught; as if the State were penitent to that degree that it hired one to scourge it while it sinned, but not to that degree that it left off sinning for a moment. Thus, under the name of Order and Civil Government, we are all made at last to pay homage to and support our own meanness. After the first blush of sin comes its indifference; and from immoral it becomes, as it were, *un*moral, and not quite unnecessary to that life which we have made.

The broadest and most prevalent error requires the most disinterested virtue to sustain it. The slight reproach to which the virtue of patriotism is commonly liable, the noble are most likely to incur. Those who, while they disapprove of the character and measures of a government, yield to it their allegiance and support, are undoubtedly its most conscientious supporters, and so frequently the most serious obstacles to reform. Some are petitioning the State to dissolve the Union, to disregard the requisitions of the President. Why do they not dissolve it themselves—the union between themselves and the State—and refuse to pay their quota into its treasury? Do not they stand in the same relation to the State that the State does to the Union? And have not the same reasons prevented the State from resisting the Union which have prevented them from resisting the State?

How can a man be satisfied to entertain an opinion merely, and enjoy *it*? Is there any enjoyment in it if his opinion is that he is aggrieved? If you are cheated out of a single dollar by your neighbor, you do not rest satisfied with knowing that you are cheated, or with saying that you are cheated, or even with petitioning him to pay you your due; but you take effectual steps at once to obtain the full amount and see that you are never cheated again. Action from principle, the perception and the performance of right, changes things and relations; it is essentially revolutionary and does not consist wholly with anything which was. It not only divides states and churches, it divides families; ay, it divides the *individual*, separating the diabolical in him from the divine.

Unjust laws exist: shall we be content to obey them, or shall we endeavor to amend them and obey them until we have succeeded, or shall we transgress them at once? Men generally, under such a government as this, think that they ought to wait until they have persuaded the majority to alter them. They think that if they should resist the remedy would be worse than the evil. *It* makes it worse. Why is it not more apt to anticipate and provide for reform? Why does it not cherish its wise minority? Why does it cry and resist before it is hurt? Why does it not encourage its citizens to be on the alert to point out its faults and *do* better than it would have them? Why does it always crucify Christ and excommunicate Copernicus and Luther and pronounce Washington and Franklin rebels?

One would think that a deliberate and practical denial of its authority was the only offense never contemplated by government; else why has it not assigned its definite, its suitable and proportionate penalty? If a man who has no property refuses but once to earn nine shillings for the State, he is put in prison for a period unlimited by any law that I know, and determined only by the discretion of those who placed him there; but if he should steal ninety times nine shillings from the State, he is soon permitted to go at large again.

If the injustice is part of the necessary friction of the machine of government, let it go, let it go: perchance it will wear smooth — certainly the machine will wear out. If the injustice has a spring or a pulley or a rope or a crank exclusively for itself, then perhaps you may consider whether the remedy will not be worse than the evil; but if it is of such a nature that it requires you to be the agent of injustice to another, then I say break the law. Let your life be a counter friction to stop the machine. What I have to do is to see, at any rate, that I do not lend myself to the wrong which I condemn.

As for adopting the ways which the State has provided for remedying the evil, I know not of such ways. They take too much time, and a man's life will be gone. I have other affairs to attend to. I came into this world, not chiefly to make this a good place to live in, but to live in it, be it good or bad. A man has not everything to do, but something; and because he cannot do *everything*, it is not necessary that he should do *something* wrong. It is not my business to be petitioning the Governor or the Legislature any more than it is theirs to petition me; and if they should not hear my petition what should I do then? But in this case the State has provided no way: its very Constitution is the evil. This may seem to be harsh and stubborn and unconciliatory; but it is to treat with the utmost kindness and consideration the only spirit that can appreciate or deserves it. So is all change for the better, like birth and death, which convulse the body.

I do not hesitate to say that those who call themselves Abolitionists should at once effectually withdraw their support, both in person and property, from the government of Massachusetts, and not wait till they constitute a majority of one before they suffer the right to prevail through them. I think that it is enough if they have God on their side, without waiting for that other one. Moreover, any man more right than his neighbors constitutes a majority of one already.

21 I meet this American government or its representative, the State government, directly and face to face once a year—no more—in the person of its tax-gatherer; this is the only mode in which a man situated as I am necessarily meets it; and it then says distinctly, Recognize me; and the simplest, the most effectual and, in the present posture of affairs, the indispensablest mode of treating with it on this head, of expressing your little satisfaction with and love for it, is to deny it then. My civil neighbor, the tax-gatherer, is the very man I have to deal with—for it is, after all, with men and not with parchment that I quarrel—and he has voluntarily chosen to be an agent of the government. How shall he ever know well what he is and does as an officer of the government, or as a man, until he is obliged to consider whether he shall treat me, his neighbor, for whom he has respect, as a neighbor and well-disposed man, or as a maniac and disturber of the peace, and see if he can get over this obstruction to his neighborliness without a ruder and more impetuous thought or speech corresponding with his action. I know this well, that if one thousand, if one hundred, if ten men whom I could name—if ten *honest* men only—ay, if *one* HONEST man in this State of Massachusetts, *ceasing to hold slaves*, were actually to withdraw from this copartnership and be locked up in the county jail therefor, it would be the abolition of slavery in America. For it matters not how small the beginning may seem to be: what is once well done is done forever. But we love better to talk about it: that we say is our mission. Reform keeps many scores of newspapers in its service but not one man. If my esteemed neighbor, the State's ambassador, who will devote his days to the settlement of the question of human rights in the Council Chamber, instead of being threatened with the prisons of Carolina, were to sit down the prisoner of Massachusetts, that State which is so anxious to foist the sin of slavery upon her sister—though at present she can discover only an act of inhospitality to be the ground of a quarrel with her—the Legislature would not wholly waive the subject the following winter.

22 Under a government which imprisons any unjustly, the true place for a just man is also a prison. The proper place today, the only place which Massachusetts has provided for her freer and less desponding spirits is in her prisons, to be put out and locked out of the State by her own act, as they have already put themselves out by their principles. It is there that the fugitive slave and the Mexican prisoner on parole and the Indian come to plead the wrongs of his race should find them; on that separate but more free and honorable ground where the State places those who are not *with* her but *against* her—the only house in a slave State in which a free man can abide with honor. If any think that their influence would be lost there, and their voices no longer afflict the ear of the State, that they would not be as an enemy within its walls, they do not know by how much truth is

stronger than error, nor how much more eloquently and effectively he can combat injustice who has experienced a little in his own person. Cast your whole vote, not a strip of paper merely, but your whole influence. A minority is powerless while it conforms to the majority; it is not even a minority then; but it is irresistible when it clogs by its whole weight. If the alternative is to keep all just men in prison or give up war and slavery, the State will not hesitate which to choose. If a thousand men were not to pay their tax-bills this year, that would not be a violent bloody measure, as it would be to pay them, and enable the State to commit violence and shed innocent blood. This is, in fact, the definition of a peaceable revolution, if any such is possible. If the tax-gatherer or any other public officer asks me, as one has done, "But what shall I do?" my answer is, "If you really wish to do anything, resign your office." When the subject has refused allegiance and the officer has resigned his office, then the revolution is accomplished. But even suppose blood should flow. Is there not a sort of blood shed when the conscience is wounded? Through this wound a man's real manhood and immortality flow out, and he bleeds to an everlasting death. I see this blood flowing now.

I have contemplated the imprisonment of the offender rather than the seizure of his goods — though both will serve the same purpose — because they who assert the purest right, and consequently are most dangerous to a corrupt State, commonly have not spent much time in accumulating property. To such the State renders comparatively small service, and a slight tax is wont to appear exorbitant, particularly if they are obliged to earn it by special labor with their hands. If there were one who lived wholly without the use of money, the State itself would hesitate to demand it of him. But the rich man — not to make any invidious comparison — is always sold to the institution which makes him rich. Absolutely speaking, the more money, the less virtue; for money comes between a man and his objects and obtains them for him; and it was certainly no great virtue to obtain it. It puts to rest many questions which he would otherwise be taxed to answer; while the only new question which it puts is the hard but superfluous one, how to spend it. Thus his moral ground is taken from under his feet. The opportunities of living are diminished in proportion as what are called the "means" are increased. The best thing a man can do for his culture when he is rich is to endeavor to carry out those schemes which he entertained when he was poor. Christ answered the Herodians according to their condition. "Show me the tribute-money," said he — and one took a penny out of his pocket — if you use money which has the image of Caesar on it, and which he has made current and valuable, that is, if *you are men of the State* and gladly enjoy the advantages of Caesar's government, then pay him back some of his own when he demands it; "Render therefore to Caesar that which is Caesar's, and to God those things which are God's"—leaving them no wiser than before as to which was which; for they did not wish to know.

When I converse with the freest of my neighbors, I perceive that whatever they may say about the magnitude and seriousness of the question, and their regard for the public tranquillity, the long and the short of the matter is that they cannot spare the protection of the existing government, and they dread the consequences to their property and families of disobedience to it. For my own part, I should not like to think that I ever rely on the protection of the State. But if I deny the authority of the State when it presents its tax-bill, it will soon take and waste all my property and so harass me and my children without end. This is hard. This makes it impossible for a man to live honestly, and at the same time comfortably, in outward respects. It will not be worth the while to accumulate property; that would be sure to go again. You must hire or squat somewhere and raise but a small crop and eat that soon. You must live within yourself and depend upon yourself always tucked up and ready for a start, and not have many affairs. A man may grow rich in Turkey even, if he will be in all respects a good subject of the Turkish government. Confucius said: "If a state is governed by the principles of reason, poverty and misery are subjects of shame; if a state is not governed by the principles of reason, riches and honors are the subjects of shame." No; until I want the protection of Massachusetts to be extended to me in some distant Southern port, where my liberty is endangered, or until I am bent solely on building up an estate at home by peaceful enterprise, I can afford to refuse allegiance to Massachusetts and her right to my property and life. It costs me less in every sense to incur the penalty of disobedience to the State than it would to obey. I should feel as if I were worth less in that case.

Some years ago the State met me in behalf of the Church and commanded me to pay a certain sum toward the support of a clergyman whose preaching my father attended, but never I myself. "Pay," it said, "or be locked up in the jail." I declined to pay. But, unfortunately, another man saw fit to pay it. I did not see why the schoolmaster should be taxed to support the priest, and not the priest the schoolmaster; for I was not the State's schoolmaster, but I supported myself by voluntary subscription. I did not see why the lyceum should not present its tax-bill and have the State to back its demand, as well as the Church. However, at the request of the selectmen, I condescended to make some such statement as this in writing:—"Know all men by these presents, that I, Henry Thoreau, do not wish to be regarded as a member of any incorporated society which I have not joined." This I gave to the town clerk; and he has it. The State, having thus learned that I did not wish to be regarded as a member of that church, has never made a like demand on me since; though it said that it must adhere to its original presumption that time. If I had known how to name them, I should then have signed off in detail from all the societies which I never signed on to; but I did not know where to find a complete list.

I have paid no poll-tax for six years. I was put into a jail once on this account, for one night; and, as I stood considering the walls of solid stone, two or three feet thick, the door of wood and iron, a foot thick, and the iron grating which strained the light, I could not help being struck with the foolishness of that institution which treated me as if I were mere flesh and blood and bones, to be locked up. I wondered that it should have concluded at length that this was the best use it could put me to and had never thought to avail itself of my services in some way. I saw that if there was a wall of stone between me and my townsmen, there was a still more difficult one to climb or break through before they could get to be as free as I was. I did not for a moment feel confined, and the walls seemed a great waste of stone and mortar. I felt as if I alone of all my townsmen had paid my tax. They plainly did not know how to treat me but behaved like persons who are underbred. In every threat and in every compliment there was a blunder; for they thought that my chief desire was to stand on the other side of that stone wall. I could not but smile to see how industriously they locked the door on my meditations, which followed them out again without let or hindrance, and *they* were really all that was dangerous. As they could not reach me, they had resolved to punish my body; just as boys, if they cannot come at some person against whom they have a spite, will abuse his dog. I saw that the State was half-witted, that it was timid as a lone woman with her silver spoons, and that it did not know its friends from its foes, and I lost all my remaining respect for it and pitied it.

Thus the State never intentionally confronts a man's sense, intellectual or moral, but only his body, his senses. It is not armed with superior wit or honesty but with superior physical strength. I was not born to be forced. I will breathe after my own fashion. Let us see who is the strongest. What force has a multitude? They only can force me who obey a higher law than I. They force me to become like themselves. I do not hear of *men* being *forced* to live this way or that by masses of men. What sort of life were that to live? When I meet a government which says to me, "Your money or your life," why should I be in haste to give it my money? It may be in a great strait and not know what to do: I cannot help that. It must help itself; do as I do. It is not worth the while to snivel about it. I am not responsible for the successful working of the machinery of society. I am not the son of the engineer. I perceive that, when an acorn and a chestnut fall side by side, the one does not remain inert to make way for the other, but both obey their own laws and spring and grow and flourish as best they can till one, perchance, overshadows and destroys the other. If a plant cannot live according to its nature, it dies; and so a man.

28 The night in prison was novel and interesting enough. The prisoners in their shirt-sleeves were enjoying a chat and the evening air in the doorway when I entered. But the jailer said, "Come, boys, it is time to lock up"; and so they dispersed, and I heard the sound of their steps returning into the hollow apartments. My room-mate was introduced to me by the jailer as "a first-rate fellow and a clever man." When the door was locked, he showed me where to hang my hat and how he managed matters there. The rooms were whitewashed once a month; and this one, at least, was the whitest, most simply furnished, and probably the neatest apartment in the town. He naturally wanted to know where I came from and what brought me there; and when I had told him, I asked him in my turn how he came there, presuming him to be an honest man, of course; and, as the world goes, I believe he was. "Why," said he, "they accuse me of burning a barn; but I never did it." As near as I could discover, he had probably gone to bed in a barn when drunk and smoked his pipe there; and so a barn burnt. He had the reputation of being a clever man, had been there some three months waiting for his trial to come on, and would have to wait as much longer; but he was quite domesticated and contented, since he got his board for nothing and thought that he was well treated.

29 He occupied one window, and I the other; and I saw that if one stayed there long, his principal business would be to look out the window. I had soon read all the tracts that were left there and examined where former prisoners had broken out and where a grate had been sawed off and heard the history of the various occupants of that room; for I found that even here there was a history and a gossip which never circulated beyond the walls of the jail. Probably this is the only house in the town where verses are composed, which afterward printed in a circular form but not published. I was shown quite a long list of verses which were composed by some young men who had been detected in an attempt to escape, who avenged themselves by signing them.

30 I pumped my fellow-prisoner as dry as I could, for fear I should never see him again; but at length he showed me which was my bed and left me to blow out the lamp.

31 It was like travelling into a far country, such as I had never expected to behold, to lie there for one night. It seemed to me that I never had heard the town-clock strike before, nor the evening sounds of the village; for we slept with the windows open, which were inside the grating. It was to see my native village in the light of the Middle Ages, and our Concord was turned into a Rhine stream, and visions of knights and castles passed before me. They were the voices of old burghers that I heard in the streets. I was

an involuntary spectator and auditor of whatever was done and said in the kitchen of the adjacent village-inn — a wholly new and rare experience to me. It was a closer view of my native town. I was fairly inside of it. I never had seen its institutions before. This is one of its peculiar institutions; for it is a shire town. I began to comprehend what its inhabitants were about.

In the morning our breakfasts were put through the hole in the door, in small oblong-square tin pans, made to fit, and holding a pint of chocolate, with brown bread and an iron spoon. When they called for the vessels again, I was green enough to return what bread I had left; but my comrade seized it and said that I should lay that up for lunch or dinner. Soon after he was let out to work at haying in a neighboring field, whither he went every day, and would not be back till noon; so he bade me good-day, saying that he doubted if he should see me again.

When I came out of prison — for someone interfered and paid that tax — I did not perceive that great changes had taken place on the common, such as he observed who went in a youth and emerged a tottering and gray-headed man; and yet a change had to my eyes come over the scene — the town and State and country — greater than any that mere time could effect. I saw yet more distinctly the State in which I lived. I saw to what extent the people among whom I lived could be trusted as good neighbors and friends; that their friendship was for summer weather only; that they did not greatly propose to do right; that they were a distinct race from me by their prejudices and superstitions, as the Chinamen and Malays are; that, in their sacrifices to humanity, they ran no risks, not even to their property; that, after all, they were not so noble but they treated the thief as he had treated them and hoped, by a certain outward observance and a few prayers, and by walking in a particular straight though useless path from time to time, to save their souls. This may be to judge my neighbors harshly; for I believe that many of them are not aware that they have such an institution as the jail in their village.

It was formerly the custom in our village, when a poor debtor came out of jail, for his acquaintances to salute him, looking through their fingers, which were crossed to represent the grating of a jail window, "How do ye do?" My neighbors did not thus salute me but first looked at me and then at one another as if I had returned from a long journey. I was put into jail as I was going to the shoemaker's to get a shoe which was mended. When I was let out the next morning I proceeded to finish my errand, and having put on my mended shoe, joined a huckleberry party who were impatient to put themselves under my conduct; and in half an hour — for the horse was soon tackled — was in the midst of a huckleberry field on one of our highest hills two miles off, and then the State was nowhere to be seen.

This is the whole history of "My Prisons."

I have never declined paying the highway tax, because I am as desirous of being a good neighbor as I am of being a bad subject; and as for supporting schools I am doing my part to educate my fellow countrymen now. It is for no particular item in the tax-bill that I refuse to pay it. I simply wish to refuse allegiance to the State, to withdraw and stand aloof from it effectually. I do not care to trace the course of my dollar, if I could, till it buys a man or a musket to shoot one with—the dollar is innocent—but I am concerned to trace the effects of my allegiance. In fact, I quietly declare war with the State, after my fashion, though I will still make what use and get what advantage of her I can, as is usual in such cases.

If others pay the tax which is demanded of me from a sympathy with the State, they do but what they have already done in their own case, or rather they abet injustice to a greater extent than the State requires. If they pay the tax from a mistaken interest in the individual taxed, to save his property, or prevent his going to jail, it is because they have not considered wisely how far they let their private feelings interfere with the public good.

This, then, is my position at present. But one cannot be too much on his guard in such a case, lest his action be biased by obstinacy or an undue regard for the opinions of men. Let him see that he does only what belongs to himself and to the hour.

I think sometimes, Why, this people mean well; they are only ignorant; they would do better if they knew how: why give your neighbors this pain to treat you as they are not inclined to? But I think again, this is no reason why I should do as they do or permit others to suffer much greater pain of a different kind. Again, I sometimes say to myself, When many millions of men, without heat, without ill will, without personal feeling of any kind, demand of you a few shillings only, without the possibility, such is their constitution, of retracting or altering their present demand, and without the possibility, on your side, of appeal to any other millions, why expose yourself to this overwhelming brute force? You do not resist cold and hunger, the winds and the waves, thus obstinately; you quietly submit to a thousand similar necessities. You do not put your head into the fire. But just in proportion as I regard this as not wholly a brute force but partly a human force, and consider that I have relations to those millions as to so many millions of men, and not of mere brute or inanimate things, I see that appeal is possible, first and instantaneously, from them to the Maker of them, and secondly, from them to themselves. But if I put my head deliberately into the fire, there is no appeal to fire or to the Maker of fire, and I have only myself to blame. If I could convince myself that I have any right to be satisfied with men as they are, and to treat them accordingly, and not according, in some respects, to my requisitions and expectations of what they and I ought to be, then, like a good Mussulman and fatalist, I should endeavor to be satisfied with things as they are and say it is the will of God. And, above all, there is this difference between resisting this and a purely brute or natural force, that I can resist this with some effect; but I cannot expect, like Orpheus, to change the nature of the rocks and trees and beasts.

I do not wish to quarrel with any man or nation. I do not wish to split hairs, to make fine distinctions, or set myself up as better than my neighbors. I seek rather, I may say, even an excuse for conforming to the laws of the land. I am but too ready to conform to them. Indeed, I have reason to suspect myself on this head; and each year, as the tax-gatherer comes round, I find myself disposed to review the acts and position of the general and State governments, and the spirit of the people, to discover a pretext for conformity.

> We must affect our country as our parents;
> And if at any time we alienate
> Our love or industry from doing it honor,
> We must respect effects and teach the soul
> Matter of conscience and religion,
> And not desire of rule or benefit.

I believe that the State will soon be able to take all my work of this sort out of my hands, and then I shall be no better a patriot than my fellow-countrymen. Seen from a lower point of view, the Constitution, with all its faults, is very good; the law and the courts are very respectable; even this State and this American government are, in many respects, very admirable and rare things, to be thankful for, such as a great many have described them; but seen from a point of view a little higher, they are what I have described them; seen from a higher still, and the highest, who shall say what they are, or that they are worth looking at or thinking of at all?

However, the government does not concern me much, and I shall bestow the fewest possible thoughts on it. It is not many moments that I live under a government, even in this world. If a man is thought-free, fancy-free, imagination-free, that which *is not* never for a long time appearing *to be* to him, unwise rulers or reformers cannot fatally interrupt him.

I know that most men think differently from myself; but those whose lives are by profession devoted to the study of these or kindred subjects content me as little as any. Statesmen and legislators, standing so completely within the institution, never distinctly and nakedly behold it. They speak of moving society but have no resting-place without it. They may be men of a certain experience and discrimination and have no doubt invented ingenious and even useful systems, for which we sincerely thank them; but all their wit and usefulness lie within certain not very wide limits. They are wont to forget that the world is not governed by policy and expediency. Webster never goes behind government and so cannot speak with authority about it. His words are wisdom to those legislators who contemplate no essential reform in the existing government; but for thinkers, and those who legislate for all time, he never once glances at the subject. I know of those whose serene and wise speculations on this theme would soon reveal the limits of his mind's range and hospitality. Yet, compared with the cheap professions of most reformers, and the still cheaper wisdom and eloquence of politicians in general, his are almost the only sensible and valuable words, and we thank Heaven for him. Comparatively, he is always strong, original, and, above all, practical. Still his quality is not wisdom but prudence. The lawyer's truth is not Truth but consistency, or a consistent expediency. Truth is always in harmony with herself and is not concerned chiefly to reveal the justice that may consist with wrong-doing. He well deserves to be called, as he has been called, the Defender of the Constitution. There are really no blows to be given by him but defensive ones. He is not a leader but a follower. His leaders are the men of '87. "I have never made an effort," he says, "and never propose to make an effort; I have never countenanced an effort, and never mean to countenance an effort, to disturb the arrangement as originally made, by which the various States came into the Union." Still thinking of the sanction which the Constitution gives to slavery, he says, "Because it was a part of the original compact—let it stand." Notwithstanding his special acuteness and ability, he is unable to take a fact out of its merely political relations and behold it as it lies absolutely to be disposed of by the intellect—what, for instance, it behooves a man to do here in America today with regard to slavery but ventures, or is driven, to make some such desperate answer as the following, while professing to speak absolutely, and as a private man—from which what new and singular code of social duties might be inferred? "The manner," says he, "in which the governments of those States where slavery exists are to regulate it, is for their own consideration, under their responsibility to their constituents, to the general laws of propriety, humanity, and justice, and to God. Associations formed elsewhere, springing from a feeling of humanity, or any other cause, have nothing whatever to do with it. They have never received any encouragement from me, and they never will."

They who know of no purer sources of truth, who have traced up its stream no higher, stand, and wisely stand, by the Bible and the Constitution, and drink at it there with reverence and humility; but they who behold where it comes trickling into this lake or that pool gird up their loins once more and continue their pilgrimage toward its fountain-head.

44 No man with a genius for legislation has appeared in America. They are rare in the history of the world. There are orators, politicians, and eloquent men by the thousand; but the speaker has not yet opened his mouth to speak who is capable of settling the much-vexed questions of the day. We love eloquence for its own sake and not for any truth which it may utter or any heroism it may inspire. Our legislators have not yet learned the comparative value of free-trade and of freedom, of union, and of rectitude, to a nation. They have no genius or talent for comparatively humble questions of taxation and finance, commerce and manufacturers and agriculture. If we were left solely to the wordy wit of legislators in Congress for our guidance, uncorrected by the seasonable experience and the effectual complaints of the people, America would not long retain her rank among the nations. For eighteen hundred years, though perchance I have no right to say it, the New Testament has been written; yet where is the legislator who has wisdom and practical talent enough to avail himself of the light which it sheds on the science of legislation?

45 The authority of government, even such as I am willing to submit to—for I will cheerfully obey those who know and can do better than I, and in many things even those who neither know nor can do so well—is still an impure one: to be strictly just, it must have the sanction and consent of the governed. It can have no pure right over my person and property but what I concede to it. The progress from an absolute to a limited monarchy, from a limited monarchy to a democracy, is a progress toward a true respect for the individual. Even the Chinese philosopher was wise enough to regard the individual as the basis of the empire. Is a democracy such as we know it the last improvement possible in government? Is it not possible to take a step further towards recognizing and organizing the rights of man? There will never be a really free and enlightened State until the State comes to recognize the individual as a higher and independent power, from which all its own power and authority are derived, and treats him accordingly. I please myself with imagining a State at last which can afford to be just to all men and to treat the individual with respect as a neighbor; which even would not think it inconsistent with its own repose if a few were to live aloof from it, not meddling with it, nor embraced by it, who fulfilled all the duties of neighbors and fellow-men. A State which bore this kind of fruit and suffered it to drop off as fast as it ripened would prepare the way for a still more perfect and glorious State, which also I have imagined but not yet anywhere seen.

Thinking Critically about the Text

In his essay, Thoreau does not push back against every aspect of the government. He mentions his willingness to pay "the highway tax" and "supporting schools" to prove that he does see some value in the government. How does

Thoreau distinguish between the positive and negative contributions of government? Do you notice any patterns to his choices?

Questions on Subject

1. What distinction does Thoreau make between the State and the individual? What does he see as the responsibilities of each?
2. What action does Thoreau claim will lead to "the abolition of slavery in America" (paragraph 21)? Does this seem reasonable to you, or is Thoreau exaggerating? How does this point contribute to his overall argument?
3. Throughout his essay, Thoreau's friends and neighbors persist in paying taxes on his behalf, or in bailing him out of prison. Why does he include these details in his argument? What point is he making about his neighbors, himself, and the State?
4. Thoreau says that "the State never intentionally confronts a man's sense, intellectual or moral, but only his body, his senses" (27). What evidence does he use to support this claim?
5. What are the characteristics of the "still more perfect and glorious State" that Thoreau has imagined (45)?

Questions on Strategy

1. "Resistance to Civil Government" is written in the first person. Do you think it would be more or less effective in the third person? Why or why not?
2. Rather than listing particular branches or offices of government, Thoreau argues against the failings of "the State." How does this contribute to the coherence and impact of his concerns? (Glossary: *Coherence*)
3. Thoreau quotes a number of other writers and poets, including Shakespeare and the Bible. How do these quotes contribute to Thoreau's *ethos* as a writer? (Glossary: *Ethos*) Select one quotation and explain why it might have been included.
4. In paragraph 10, Thoreau makes an analogy between voting and playing games like checkers or backgammon. (Glossary: *Analogy*) Why is this an apt comparison? How does it contribute to his overall thesis?
5. In paragraph 20, Thoreau discusses "those who call themselves Abolitionists." What distinction is he making? Why is it important?

Questions on Diction and Vocabulary

1. Throughout his essay, Thoreau uses italics to add emphasis. Find some examples from the text and make a case for how they make Thoreau a more or less effective writer.

2. Thoreau makes frequent use of semicolons to separate related ideas, a tactic that results in longer-than-usual sentences. How does this choice contribute to your sense of Thoreau's style? (Glossary: *Style*) How does it impact your ability to understand his message?

Argumentation in Action

An excellent way to gain some experience in formulating an argumentative position on an issue, and perhaps to establish a thesis, is to engage in a debate with someone who is on the other side of the question. When we listen to arguments and think of refutations and counterarguments, we have a chance to rehearse and revise our position before it is put in written form.

To try this out, adapt Thoreau's arguments about the purpose and size of government. Divide the class into pro and con sides — those for a larger, more active government and those in favor of a smaller, more hands-off approach. Each side should elect a spokesperson to present its arguments before the class. Finally, have the class make some estimate of the success of each side in (1) articulating its position, (2) presenting ideas and evidence to support that position, and (3) convincing the audience of its position. The exercise should give you a good idea of the kind of work that's involved in preparing a written argument.

Writing Suggestions

1. **Writing with Sources.** Thoreau, and "Resistance to Civil Government" in particular, have inspired many other great writers, including Martin Luther King, Jr. (p. 374) and Mahatma Gandhi. Research some of their more famous speeches and essays and write an essay arguing that their work was influenced by this essay. Don't forget to cite specific examples, and to review Chapters 14 and 15 for models of and advice on integrating sources into your essay.

2. **Writing in the Workplace.** Like Thoreau, you may also encounter institutional practices that you find concerning. In a future workplace, it will be your responsibility to report such practices to your supervisor or human resources officer. This can often be an uncomfortable process, and you will want to state your case firmly and rigorously.

   Say that you are a recent hire at a consulting firm. In the past several months, you have noticed that one of your colleagues is consistently granting the most prestigious projects only to his close friends, often overlooking those who are more qualified. Draft a letter to your supervisor or to the human resources department, arguing against this unfair practice. Be sure to keep a reasoned tone, anticipate counterarguments, and cite specific examples.

A Modest Proposal

JONATHAN SWIFT

One of the world's great satirists, Jonathan Swift was born in 1667 to English parents in Dublin, Ireland, and was educated at Trinity College. When his early efforts at a literary career in England met no success, he returned to Ireland in 1694 and was ordained an Anglican clergyman. From 1713 until his death in 1745, he was dean of Dublin's St. Patrick's Cathedral. A prolific chronicler of human folly, Swift is best known as the author of *Gulliver's Travels* and of the work included here, "A Modest Proposal."

Beinecke Rare Book and Manuscript Library

In the 1720s Ireland had suffered several famines, but the English gentry, who owned most of the land, did nothing to alleviate the suffering of tenant farmers and their families; nor would the English government intervene. A number of pamphlets were circulated proposing solutions to the Irish problem.

"A Modest Proposal," published anonymously in 1729, was Swift's ironic contribution to the discussion.

Preparing to Read

Satire is a literary and dramatic art form wherein the shortcomings, foibles, abuses, and idiocies of both people and institutions are accented and held up for ridicule in order to shame their perpetrators into reforming themselves. Perhaps the very easiest way to see satire around us today is in the work of our political cartoonists. Think of individuals and institutions both here and abroad who today might make good subjects for satire.

> FOR PREVENTING THE CHILDREN OF POOR PEOPLE IN IRELAND
> FROM BEING A BURDEN TO THEIR PARENTS OR COUNTRY, AND
> FOR MAKING THEM BENEFICIAL TO THE PUBLIC

It is a melancholy object to those who walk through this great town[1] or travel in the country, when they see the streets, the roads, and cabin doors, crowded with beggars of the female sex, followed by three, four, or six children, all in rags and importuning every passenger for an alms. These mothers, instead of being able to work for their honest livelihood, are forced to employ all their time in strolling to beg sustenance for their helpless infants, who, as they grow up, either turn thieves for want of work,

---

[1]Dublin.—ED.

or leave their dear native country to fight for the Pretender in Spain, or sell themselves to the Barbadoes.[2]

I think it is agreed by all parties that this prodigious number of children in the arms, or on the backs, or at the heels of their mothers, and frequently of their fathers, is in the present deplorable state of the kingdom a very great additional grievance; and therefore whoever could find out a fair, cheap, and easy method of making these children sound, useful members of the commonwealth would deserve so well of the public as to have his statue set up for a preserver of the nation.

But my intention is very far from being confined to provide only for the children of professed beggars; it is of a much greater extent, and shall take in the whole number of infants at a certain age who are born of parents in effect as little able to support them as those who demand our charity in the streets.

As to my own part, having turned my thoughts for many years upon this important subject, and maturely weighed the several schemes of other projectors,[3] I have always found them grossly mistaken in their computation. It is true, a child just dropped from its dam may be supported by her milk for a solar year, with little other nourishment; at most not above the value of two shillings, which the mother may certainly get, or the value in scraps, by her lawful occupation of begging; and it is exactly at one year old that I propose to provide for them in such a manner as instead of being a charge upon their parents or the parish, or wanting food and raiment for the rest of their lives, they shall on the contrary contribute to the feeding, and partly to the clothing, of many thousands.

There is likewise another great advantage in my scheme, that it will prevent those voluntary abortions, and that horrid practice of women murdering their bastard children, alas, too frequent among us, sacrificing the poor innocent babes, I doubt, more to avoid the expense than the shame, which would move tears and pity in the most savage and inhuman breast.

The number of souls in this kingdom[4] being usually reckoned one million and a half, of these I calculate there may be about two hundred thousand couples whose wives are breeders; from which number I subtract thirty thousand couples who are able to maintain their own children, although I apprehend there cannot be so many under the present distresses of the kingdom; but this being granted, there will remain an hundred and

---

[2]Many Irish Catholics were loyal to James Stuart, a claimant (or "pretender") to the English crown, and followed him into exile. Others, stricken by poverty, sold themselves into virtual slavery in order to escape to British colonies (like Barbados) in the New World.—ED.
[3]Proposers of solutions.—ED.
[4]Ireland.—ED.

seventy thousand breeders. I again subtract fifty thousand for those women who miscarry, or whose children die by accident or disease within the year. There only remain an hundred and twenty thousand children of poor parents annually born. The question therefore is, how this number shall be reared and provided for, which, as I have already said, under the present situation of affairs, is utterly impossible by all the methods hitherto proposed. For we can neither employ them in handicraft or agriculture; we neither build houses (I mean in the country) nor cultivate land. They can very seldom pick up a livelihood by stealing till they arrive at six years old, except where they are of towardly parts;[5] although I confess they learn the rudiments much earlier, during which time they can however be looked upon only as probationers, as I have been informed by a principal gentleman in the county of Cavan, who protested to me that he never knew above one or two instances under the age of six, even in a part of the kingdom so renowned for the quickest proficiency in that art.

I am assured by our merchants that a boy or a girl before twelve years old is no salable commodity; and even when they come to this age they will not yield above three pounds, or three pounds and half a crown at most on the Exchange; which cannot turn to account either to the parents or the kingdom, the charge of nutriment and rags having been at least four times that value.

I shall now therefore humbly propose my own thoughts, which I hope will not be liable to the least objection.

I have been assured by a very knowing American of my acquaintance in London, that a young healthy child well nursed is at a year old a most delicious, nourishing, and wholesome food, whether stewed, roasted, baked, or boiled; and I make no doubt that it will equally serve in a fricassee or a ragout.[6]

I do therefore humbly offer it to public consideration that of the hundred and twenty thousand children, already computed, twenty thousand may be reserved for breed, whereof only one fourth part to be males, which is more than we allow to sheep, black cattle, or swine; and my reason is that these children are seldom the fruits of marriage, a circumstance not much regarded by our savages, therefore one male will be sufficient to serve four females. That the remaining hundred thousand may at a year old be offered

---

[5]Or "advanced for their age." —ED.
[6]Types of stews. —ED.

in sale to the persons of quality and fortune through the kingdom, always advising the mother to let them suck plentifully in the last month, so as to render them plump and fat for a good table. A child will make two dishes at an entertainment for friends; and when the family dines alone, the fore or hind quarter will make a reasonable dish, and seasoned with a little pepper or salt will be very good boiled on the fourth day, especially in winter.

I have reckoned upon a medium that a child just born will weigh twelve pounds, and in a solar year if tolerably nursed increaseth to twenty-eight pounds.

I grant this food will be somewhat dear, and therefore very proper for landlords, who, as they have already devoured most of the parents, seem to have the best title to the children.

Infant's flesh will be in season throughout the year, but more plentiful in March, and a little before and after. For we are told by a grave author, an eminent French physician,[7] that fish being a prolific diet, there are more children born in Roman Catholic countries about nine months after Lent than at any other season; therefore, reckoning a year after Lent, the markets will be more glutted than usual, because the number of popish infants is at least three to one in this kingdom; and therefore it will have one other collateral advantage, by lessening the number of papists among us.

I have already computed the charge of nursing a beggar's child (in which list I reckon all cottagers, laborers, and four fifths of the farmers) to be about two shillings per annum, rags included; and I believe no gentleman would repine to give ten shillings for the carcass of a good fat child, which, as I have said, will make four dishes of excellent nutritive meat, when he hath only some particular friend or his own family to dine with him. Thus the squire will learn to be a good landlord, and grow popular among the tenants; the mother will have eight shillings net profit, and be fit for work till she produces another child.

Those who are more thrifty (as I must confess the times require) may flay the carcass; the skin of which artificially[8] dressed will make admirable gloves for ladies, and summer boots for fine gentlemen.

As to our city of Dublin, shambles[9] may be appointed for this purpose in the most convenient parts of it, and butchers we may be assured will not be wanting; although I rather recommend buying the children alive, and dressing them hot from the knife as we do roasting pigs.

A very worthy person, a true lover of his country, and whose virtues I highly esteem, was lately pleased in discoursing on this matter to offer a

---

[7]François Rabelais (c. 1494–1553), a French satirist—not at all "grave"—whom Swift admired for his broad humor and sharp wit.—ED.
[8]Skillfully, artfully.—ED.
[9]Slaughterhouses.—ED.

refinement upon my scheme. He said that many gentlemen of this kingdom, having of late destroyed their deer, he conceived that the want of venison might be well supplied by the bodies of young lads and maidens, not exceeding fourteen years of age nor under twelve, so great a number of both sexes in every county being now ready to starve for want of work and service; and these to be disposed of by their parents, if alive, or otherwise by their nearest relations. But with due deference to so excellent a friend and so deserving a patriot, I cannot be altogether in his sentiments; for as to the males, my American acquaintance assured me from frequent experience that their flesh was generally tough and lean, like that of our schoolboys, by continual exercise, and their taste disagreeable; and to fatten them would not answer the charge. Then as to the females, it would, I think with humble submission, be a loss to the public, because they soon would become breeders themselves: and besides, it is not improbable that some scrupulous people might be apt to censure such a practice (although indeed very unjustly) as a little bordering upon cruelty; which, I confess, hath always been with me the strongest objection against any project, how well soever intended.

But in order to justify my friend, he confessed that this expedient was put into his head by the famous Psalmanazar,[10] a native of the island Formosa, who came from thence to London above twenty years ago, and in conversation told my friend that in his country when any young person happened to be put to death, the executioner sold the carcass to persons of quality as a prime dainty; and that in his time the body of a plump girl of fifteen, who was crucified for an attempt to poison the emperor, was sold to his Imperial Majesty's prime minister of state, and other great mandarins of the court, in joints from the gibbet, at four hundred crowns. Neither indeed can I deny that if the same use were made of several plump young girls in this town, who without one single groat to their fortunes cannot stir abroad without a chair, and appear at the playhouse and assemblies in foreign fineries which they never will pay for, the kingdom would not be the worse.

Some persons of a desponding spirit are in great concern about that vast number of poor people who are aged, diseased, or maimed, and I have been desired to employ my thoughts what course may be taken to ease the nation of so grievous an encumbrance. But I am not in the least pain upon that matter, because it is very well known that they are every day dying and rotting by cold and famine, and filth and vermin, as fast as can be reasonably expected. And as to the younger laborers, they are now in almost as hopeful a condition. They cannot get work, and consequently pine away

---

[10] George Psalmanazar (c. 1679–1763), a French imposter who fooled London society with his tales of human sacrifice and cannibalism on Formosa. —ED.

for want of nourishment to a degree that if at any time they are accidentally hired to common labor, they have not strength to perform it; and thus the country and themselves are happily delivered from the evils to come.

I have too long digressed, and therefore shall return to my subject. I think the advantages by the proposal which I have made are obvious and many, as well as of the highest importance.

For first, as I have already observed, it would greatly lessen the number of Papists, with whom we are yearly overrun, being the principal breeders of the nation as well as our most dangerous enemies; and who stay at home on purpose to deliver the kingdom to the Pretender, hoping to take their advantage by the absence of so many good Protestants, who have chosen rather to leave their country than stay at home and pay tithes against their conscience to an Episcopal curate.

Secondly, the poorer tenants will have something valuable of their own, which by law may be made liable to distress,[11] and help to pay their landlord's rent, their corn and cattle being already seized and money a thing unknown.

Thirdly, whereas the maintenance of an hundred thousand children, from two years old and upwards, cannot be computed at less than ten shillings a piece per annum, the nation's stock will be thereby increased fifty thousand pounds per annum, besides the profit of a new dish introduced to the tables of all gentlemen of fortune in the kingdom who have any refinement in taste. And the money will circulate among ourselves, the goods being entirely of our own growth and manufacture.

Fourthly, the constant breeders, besides the gain of eight shillings sterling per annum by the sale of their children, will be rid of the charge of maintaining them after the first year.

Fifthly, this food would likewise bring great custom to taverns, where the vintners will certainly be so prudent as to procure the best receipts for dressing it to perfection, and consequently have their houses frequented by all the fine gentlemen, who justly value themselves upon their knowledge in good eating; and a skillful cook, who understands how to oblige his guests, will contrive to make it as expensive as they please.

Sixthly, this would be a great inducement to marriage, which all wise nations have either encouraged by rewards or enforced by laws and penalties. It would increase the care and tenderness of mothers toward their children, when they were sure of a settlement for life to the poor babes, provided in some sort by the public, to their annual profit instead of expense. We should see an honest emulation among the married women, which of them could bring the fattest child to the market. Men would

---

[11]Subject to seizure by creditors. —ED.

become as fond of their wives during the time of their pregnancy as they are now of their mares in foal, their cows in calf, or sows when they are ready to farrow; nor offer to beat or kick them (as is too frequent a practice) for fear of a miscarriage.

Many other advantages might be enumerated. For instance, the addition of some thousand carcasses in our exportation of barreled beef, the propagation of swine's flesh, and improvement in the art of making good bacon, so much wanted among us by the great destruction of pigs, too frequent at our tables, which are no way comparable in taste or magnificence to a well-grown, fat, yearling child, which roasted whole will make a considerable figure at a lord mayor's feast or any other public entertainment. But this and many others I omit, being studious of brevity.

Supposing that one thousand families in this city would be constant customers for infants' flesh, besides others who might have it at merry meetings, particularly weddings and christenings, I compute that Dublin would take off annually about twenty thousand carcasses, and the rest of the kingdom (where probably they will be sold somewhat cheaper) the remaining eighty thousand.

I can think of no one objection that will possibly be raised against this proposal, unless it should be urged that the number of people will be thereby much lessened in the kingdom. This I freely own, and it was indeed one principal design in offering it to the world. I desire the reader will observe, that I calculate my remedy for this one individual kingdom of Ireland and for no other that ever was, is, or I think ever can be upon earth. Therefore let no man talk to me of other expedients: of taxing our absentees at five shillings a pound: of using neither clothes nor household furniture except what is of our own growth and manufacture: of utterly rejecting the materials and instruments that promote foreign luxury: of curing the expensiveness of pride, vanity, idleness, and gaming in our women: of introducing a vein of parsimony, prudence, and temperance: of learning to love our country, in the want of which we differ even from Laplanders and the inhabitants of Topinamhoo:[12] of quitting our animosities and factions, nor acting any longer like the Jews, who were murdering one another at the very moment their city was taken:[13] of being a little cautious not to sell our country and conscience for nothing: of teaching landlords to have at least one degree of mercy toward their tenants: lastly, of putting a spirit of honesty, industry, and skill into our shopkeepers; who, if a resolution could

---

[12]In other words, even from Laplanders who love their icy tundra and primitive Brazilian tribes who love their jungle.—ED.
[13]Swift refers to the Roman siege of Jerusalem in A.D. 70; the inhabitants lost the city because they dissolved into violent factions.—ED.

now be taken to buy only our native goods, would immediately unite to cheat and exact upon us in the price, the measure, and the goodness, nor could ever yet be brought to make one fair proposal of just dealing, though often and earnestly invited to it.

Therefore I repeat, let no man talk to me of these and the like expedients, till he hath at least some glimpse of hope that there will ever be some hearty and sincere attempt to put them in practice.

But as to myself, having been wearied out for many years with offering vain, idle, visionary thoughts, and at length utterly despairing of success, I fortunately fell upon this proposal, which, as it is wholly new, so it hath something solid and real, of no expense and little trouble, full in our own power, and whereby we can incur no danger in disobliging England. For this kind of commodity will not bear exportation, the flesh being of too tender a consistence to admit a long continuance in salt, although perhaps I could name a country which would be glad to eat up our whole nation without it.

After all, I am not so violently bent upon my own opinion as to reject any offer proposed by wise men, which shall be found equally innocent, cheap, easy, and effectual. But before something of that kind shall be advanced in contradiction to my scheme, and offering a better, I desire the author or authors will be pleased maturely to consider two points. First, as things now stand, how they will be able to find food and raiment for an hundred thousand useless mouths and backs. And secondly, there being a round million of creatures in human figure throughout this kingdom, whose sole subsistence put into a common stock would leave them in debt two millions of pounds sterling, adding those who are beggars by profession to the bulk of farmers, cottagers, and laborers, with their wives and children who are beggars in effect; I desire those politicians who dislike my overture, and may perhaps be so bold to attempt an answer, that they will first ask the parents of these mortals whether they would not at this day think it a great happiness to have been sold for food at a year old in the manner I prescribe, and thereby have avoided such a perpetual scene of misfortunes as they have since gone through by the oppression of landlords, the impossibility of paying rent without money or trade, the want of common sustenance, with neither house nor clothes to cover them from the inclemencies of the weather, and the most inevitable prospect of entailing the like or greater miseries upon their breed forever.

I profess, in the sincerity of my heart, that I have not the least personal interest in endeavoring to promote this necessary work, having no other motive than the public good of my country, by advancing our trade, providing for infants, relieving the poor, and giving some pleasure to the rich. I have no children by which I can propose to get a single penny; the youngest being nine years old, and my wife past childbearing.

Thinking Critically about the Text

Satire often has a "stealth quality" about it; that is, the audience for it often does not realize at first that the author of the satire is not being serious. At some point in the satire the audience usually catches on and then begins to see the larger issue at the center of the satire. At what point in your reading did you begin to catch on to Swift's technique and larger, more important, message?

Questions on Subject

1. What problem is being addressed in this essay? Describe the specific solution being proposed. What are the proposal's "advantages" (paragraph 20)?

2. What "other expedients" (paragraph 29) are dismissed as "vain, idle, visionary thoughts" (31)? What do paragraphs 29 through 31 tell you about Swift's purpose? (Glossary: *Purpose*)

3. Describe the "author" of the proposal. Why does Swift choose such a character to present this plan? When can you detect Swift's own voice coming through?

4. What is the meaning and the significance of the title? (Glossary: *Title*)

5. In paragraph 2, Swift talks of making Ireland's "children sound, useful members of the commonwealth." In what way is this statement ironic? Cite several other examples of Swift's irony. (Glossary: *Irony*)

Questions on Strategy

1. Toward what belief and/or action is Swift attempting to persuade his readers? How does he go about doing so? For example, did you feel a sense of outrage at any point in the essay? Did you feel that the essay was humorous at any point? If so, where and why?

2. What is the effect of the first paragraph of the essay? How does it serve to introduce the proposal? (Glossary: *Beginnings/Endings*)

3. What strategies does Swift use in this essay to make his proposer sound like an authority? Explain how this sense of authority relates to Swift's real purpose.

4. In what ways can the argument presented in this essay be seen as logical? What is the effect, for example, of the complicated calculations in paragraph 6?

5. What strategies, in addition to argumentation, does Swift use to develop his satire? Cite examples to support your answer. (Glossary: *Argument*)

Questions on Diction and Vocabulary

1. It is not easy to summarize Swift's tone in a single word, but how would you describe the overall tone he establishes? Point to specific passages in the essay where you find his language particularly effective.

2. What is Swift's intent in using the term *modest*? (Glossary: *Purpose*)

3. In paragraph 6, Swift refers to women as "breeders." In terms of his proposal, why is the diction appropriate? (Glossary: *Diction*) Cite other examples of such diction used to describe the poor people of Ireland.

Subjects and Strategies in Action

Imagine that you will write a satire based on the model of Swift's "A Modest Proposal." Think in terms of attacking the foolish thinking or absurdity of a situation you find on the national, state, or local level and how your satire will get people to think about that issue in productive ways. What additional strategies might you employ to accomplish your satire? Discuss your possible approaches to this assignment with other members of your class.

Writing Suggestions

1. **Writing with Sources.** Write a modest proposal of your own to solve a difficult social or political problem of the present day or, on a smaller scale, a problem you see facing your school or community. Do some research on your topic in the library or online. For models of and advice on integrating sources in your essay, see Chapters 14 and 15.

2. **Writing with Sources.** What is the most effective way to bring about social change and to influence societal attitudes? Would Swift's methods work today, or would they have to be significantly modified? Concentrating on the sorts of changes you have witnessed over the last ten years, write an essay in which you describe how best to influence public opinion. Do some research on your topic in the library or online. For models of and advice on integrating sources in your essay, see Chapters 14 and 15.

CONTEMPORARY ARGUMENTS

The Case for Short Words

RICHARD LEDERER

Born in 1938, Richard Lederer has been a lifelong student of language. He holds degrees from Haverford College, Harvard University, and the University of New Hampshire. For twenty-seven years he taught English at St. Paul's School in Concord, New Hampshire. Anyone who has read one of his more than thirty books will understand why he has been referred to as "Conan the Grammarian" and "America's wittiest verbalist." Lederer loves language and enjoys writing about its richness and usage by Americans. His books include *Anguished English* (1987), *Crazy English* (1989), *Adventures of a Verbivore* (1994), *Nothing Risque, Nothing Gained* (1995), *A Man of My Words: Reflections on the English Language* (2003), and *Word Wizard: Super Bloopers, Rich Reflections, and Other Acts of Word Magic* (2006). In addition to writing books, Lederer pens a weekly syndicated column called "Lederer on Language" for the San Diego *Union-Tribune*, which appears both in print and online. He has been the "Grammar Grappler" for *Writer's Digest*, the language commentator for National Public Radio, and the founding cohost of *A Way with Words*, a weekly radio program out of San Diego, California.

Courtesy of Richard Lederer

In the following selection, a chapter from *The Miracle of Language* (1990), Lederer sings the praises of short words and reminds us that well-chosen monosyllabic words can be a writer's best friends because they are functional and often pack a powerful punch. Note the clever way in which he uses short words throughout the essay to support his argument.

Preparing to Read

Find a paragraph you like in a book that you have enjoyed reading. What is it that appeals to you? What did the author do to make the writing so appealing? Do you like the vocabulary, the flow of the words, the imagery it presents, or something else?

When you speak and write, there is no law that says you have to use big words. Short words are as good as long ones, and short, old words—like *sun* and *grass* and *home*—are best of all. A lot of small words, more than you might think, can meet your needs with a strength, grace, and charm that large words do not have.

Big words can make the way dark for those who read what you write and hear what you say. Small words cast their clear light on big things — night and day, love and hate, war and peace, and life and death. Big words at times seem strange to the eye and the ear and the mind and the heart. Small words are the ones we seem to have known from the time we were born, like the hearth fire that warms the home.

Short words are bright like sparks that glow in the night, prompt like the dawn that greets the day, sharp like the blade of a knife, hot like salt tears that scald the cheek, quick like moths that flit from flame to flame, and terse like the dart and sting of a bee.

Here is a sound rule: Use small, old words where you can. If a long word says just what you want to say, do not fear to use it. But know that our tongue is rich in crisp, brisk, swift, short words. Make them the spine and the heart of what you speak and write. Short words are like fast friends. They will not let you down.

> A lot of small words, more than you might think, can meet your needs with a strength, grace, and charm that large words do not have.

The title of this chapter and the four paragraphs that you have just read are wrought entirely of words of one syllable. In setting myself this task, I did not feel especially cabined, cribbed, or confined. In fact, the structure helped me to focus on the power of the message I was trying to put across.

One study shows that twenty words account for twenty-five percent of all spoken English words, and all twenty are monosyllabic. In order of frequency they are: *I, you, the, a, to, is, it, that, of, and, in, what, he, this, have, do, she, not, on,* and *they.* Other studies indicate that the fifty most common words in written English are each made of a single syllable.

For centuries our finest poets and orators have recognized and employed the power of small words to make a straight point between two minds. A great many of our proverbs punch home their points with pithy monosyllables: "Where there's a will, there's a way," "A stitch in time saves nine," "Spare the rod and spoil the child," "A bird in the hand is worth two in the bush."

Nobody used the short word more skillfully than William Shakespeare, whose dying King Lear laments:

> And my poor fool is hang'd! No, no, no life!
> Why should a dog, a horse, a rat have life,

> And thou no breath at all? . . .
> Do you see this? Look on her; look, her lips.
> Look there, look there!

Shakespeare's contemporaries made the King James Bible a centerpiece of short words — "And God said, Let there be light: and there was light. And God saw the light, that it was good." The descendants of such mighty lines live on in the twentieth century. When asked to explain his policy to Parliament, Winston Churchill responded with these ringing monosyllables: "I will say: It is to wage war, by sea, land, and air, with all our might and with all the strength that God can give us." In his "Death of the Hired Man" Robert Frost observes that "Home is the place where, when you have to go there, / They have to take you in." And William H. Johnson uses ten two-letter words to explain his secret of success: "If it is to be, / It is up to me."

You don't have to be a great author, statesman, or philosopher to tap the energy and eloquence of small words. Each winter I ask my ninth graders at St. Paul's School to write a composition composed entirely of one-syllable words. My students greet my request with obligatory moans and groans, but, when they return to class with their essays, most feel that, with the pressure to produce high-sounding polysyllables relieved, they have created some of their most powerful and luminous prose. Here are submissions from two of my ninth graders:

> What can you say to a boy who has left home? You can say that he has done wrong, but he does not care. He has left home so that he will not have to deal with what you say. He wants to go as far as he can. He will do what he wants to do.
>
> This boy does not want to be forced to go to church, to comb his hair, or to be on time. A good time for this boy does not lie in your reach, for what you have he does not want. He dreams of ripped jeans, shorts with no starch, and old socks.
>
> So now this boy is on a bus to a place he dreams of, a place with no rules. This boy now walks a strange street, his long hair blown back by the wind. He wears no coat or tie, just jeans and an old shirt. He hates your world, and he has left it.
>
> —CHARLES SHAFFER

> For a long time we cruised by the coast and at last came to a wide bay past the curve of a hill, at the end of which lay a small town. Our long boat ride at an end, we all stretched and stood up to watch as the boat nosed its way in.
>
> The town climbed up the hill that rose from the shore, a space in front of it left bare for the port. Each house was a clean white with sky blue or grey trim; in front of each one was a small yard, edged by a white stone wall strewn with green vines.

As the town basked in the heat of noon, not a thing stirred in the streets or by the shore. The sun beat down on the sea, the land, and the back of our necks, so that, in spite of the breeze that made the vines sway, we all wished we could hide from the glare in a cool, white house. But, as there was no one to help dock the boat, we had to stand and wait.

At last the head of the crew leaped from the side and strode to a large house on the right. He shoved the door wide, poked his head through the gloom, and roared with a fierce voice. Five or six men came out, and soon the port was loud with the clank of chains and creak of planks as the men caught ropes thrown by the crew, pulled them taut, and tied them to posts. Then they set up a rough plank so we could cross from the deck to the shore. We all made for the large house while the crew watched, glad to be rid of us.

—CELIA WREN

You, too, can tap into the vitality and vigor of compact expression. Take a suggestion from the highway department. At the boundaries of your speech and prose place a sign that reads "Caution: Small Words at Work."

Thinking Critically about the Text

Reread a piece of writing you turned in earlier this year for any class. Analyze your choice of words and describe your writing vocabulary. Did you follow Lederer's admonition to use short words whenever they are appropriate, or did you tend to use longer, more important-sounding words? Is Lederer's essay likely to change the way you write papers in the future? Why or why not?

Questions on Subject

1. What rule does Lederer present for writing? What does he do to demonstrate the feasibility of this rule?

2. Lederer states that the twenty words that account for a quarter of all spoken English words are monosyllabic. So are the fifty most common written words. Why, then, do you think Lederer felt it was necessary to argue that people should use them? Who is his audience? (Glossary: *Audience*)

3. How do his students react to the assignment he gives them requiring short words? How do their essays turn out? What does the assignment teach them?

4. In paragraph 10, Lederer refers to the relief his students feel when released from "the pressure to produce high-sounding polysyllables." Where does this pressure come from? How does it relate to the central purpose of his essay?

5. What sort of impact do you think Lederer's argument will have on your own writing? What about how you read the writing of others? Explain.

Questions on Strategy

1. As you read Lederer's essay for the first time, were you surprised by his announcement in paragraph 5 that the preceding four paragraphs contained only single-syllable words? If not, when were you first aware of what he was doing? What does Lederer's strategy tell you about small words?

2. Lederer starts using multisyllabic words when discussing the process of writing with single-syllable words. Why do you think he abandons his single-syllable presentation? Does it diminish the strength of his argument? Explain.

3. Lederer provides two long examples of writing by his own students. What does he accomplish by using these examples along with ones from famous authors? (Glossary: *Illustration*)

4. Lederer illustrates his argument with examples from several prominent authors as well as from students. (Glossary: *Illustration*) Which of these examples did you find the most effective? Why? Provide an example from your own reading that you think is effective in illustrating Lederer's argument.

5. How does Lederer's final paragraph serve to close the essay effectively? (Glossary: *Beginnings/Endings*)

Questions on Diction and Vocabulary

1. Lederer uses similes to help the reader form associations and images with short words. (Glossary: *Figures of Speech*) What are some of these similes? Do you find the similes effective in the context of Lederer's argument? Explain.

2. In paragraph 9, Lederer uses such terms as *mighty* and *ringing monosyllables* to describe the passages he gives as examples. Do you think such descriptions are appropriate? Why do you think he includes them?

3. Carefully analyze the two student essays that Lederer presents. In particular, circle all the main verbs that each student uses. (Glossary: *Verb*) What, if anything, do these verbs have in common? What conclusions can you draw about verbs and strong, powerful writing?

Argumentation in Action

One strategy in developing a strong argument that most people find convincing is illustration. As Lederer demonstrates, an array of examples, both brief and extended, has a remarkable ability to convince readers of the truth of a proposition. While it is possible to argue a case with one specific example that is both appropriate and representative, most writers find that a varied set of examples often makes a more convincing case. Therefore, it is important to identify your examples before starting to write.

As an exercise in argumentation, choose one of the following position statements:

a. More parking spaces should be provided on campus for students.
b. Capital punishment is a relatively ineffective deterrent to crime.
c. More computer stations should be provided on campus for students.
d. In-state residency requirements for tuition are unfair at my school.

Make a list of the examples — types of information and evidence — you would need to write an argumentative essay on the topic you choose. Indicate where and how you might obtain this information. Finally, share your list of examples with other students in your class who chose the same topic.

Writing Suggestions

1. People tend to avoid single-syllable words because they are afraid they will look inadequate and that their writing will lack sophistication. Are there situations in which demonstrating command of a large vocabulary is desirable? If you answer yes, present one situation and argue that the overuse of short words in that situation is potentially detrimental. If you answer no, defend your reasoning. How can the use of short words convey the necessary style and sophistication in all situations?

2. Advertising is an industry that depends on efficient, high-impact words. Choose ten advertising slogans and three jingles that you find effective. Consider phrases that are widely recognized even after their advertising cycle, such as "Just Do It" and "Think Different." Analyze the ratio of short to long words in the slogans and jingles, and write an essay in which you present your findings. What is the percentage of short words? Argue that the percentage supports or contradicts Lederer's contention that short words are often best for high-impact communicating.

You Shouldn't Get a Prize for Showing Up

NANCY ARMOUR

Nancy Armour began her career as the Associated Press correspondent in South Bend, Indiana, before moving to Chicago and making a name for herself as a sports writer. In two consecutive years, 2006 and 2007, Armour won the Will Grimsley Award for Outstanding Body of Work. She is currently writing for the USA Today Sports Media group, where she regularly covers major events such as the Olympics and the World Cup.

In the following article, published in *USA Today Sports* in August 2015, Armour points out the long-term consequences of what she calls "youth sports trophy culture."

Preparing to Read

Did you ever receive a participation award growing up? Did it make you feel accomplished, or did you dismiss it as meaningless? Do you think these sorts of awards made a lasting impression on you or anyone you know?

Life isn't always fair.

You can work your hardest, try your best, expend every ounce of energy you have and sometimes things just don't work out the way you hoped or imagined. That's just the way things go.

Yet somewhere along the way, someone had the misguided notion that kids should live in a la-la land where everything is perfect, there are no hardships or heartbreaks, and you get a shiny trophy or a pretty blue ribbon just for being you.

There's time enough to get acquainted with reality, the thinking goes. In the meantime, children should be praised and encouraged, reminded at every turn how wonderful they are.

No wonder study after study has shown that millennials, the first of the trophy generations, are stressed out and depressed. They were sold a bill of goods when they were kids, and discovering that the harsh realities of life apply to them, too, had to have been like a punch to the gut.

Pittsburgh Steelers linebacker James Harrison may be the last person you want to take life lessons from, given his history of violence on and off the field. But his announcement Sunday that he was giving back his 8- and 6-year-old son's "participation" trophies because they hadn't earned them was dead on, and that message shouldn't be discounted simply because he was the one delivering it.

"While I am very proud of my boys for everything they do and will encourage them till the day I die, these trophies will be given back until they EARN a real trophy," Harrison said in a post on Instagram. "I'm sorry I'm not sorry for believing that everything in life should be earned and I'm not about to raise two boys to be men by making them believe that they are entitled to something just because they tried their best."

Amen.

Everybody-gets-a-trophy proponents say children should be rewarded for their efforts, that the prizes give kids incentive to always try their best and persevere. But isn't that what the orange slices and cookies are for? By handing out trophies and medals at every turn, it actually sends the *opposite* message, essentially telling kids it's enough just to show up.

Why should a kid strive to improve or put in the extra effort when he or she is treated no differently than the kid who sits in the outfield picking dandelions? Or, as NFL MVP Kurt Warner said on Twitter on Monday, "They don't let kids pass classes 4 just showing up!"

"The whole idea is to protect that kid and, ultimately, it's a huge disservice. What kids need is skill-building. Help them do what they're doing and do it better," said Ashley Merryman, co-author of *Top Dog: The Science of Winning and Losing*.

If we're honest with ourselves, the trophies, ribbons and medals we hand out so willingly are more about us than the children getting them.

"The benefit of competition isn't actually winning. The benefit is improving," Merryman added. "When you're constantly giving a kid a trophy for everything they're doing, you're saying, 'I don't care about improvement. I don't care that you're learning from your mistakes. All we expect is that you're always a winner.'"

And if you've taken a peek at any 9-year-old's room recently, you'll see how much those precious trophies and ribbons really mean. Most are either coated in dust or buried in the back of a closet.

If we're honest with ourselves, the trophies, ribbons and medals we hand out so willingly are more about us than the children getting them. It's affirmation that our kids are as wonderful as we think they are. It's also a way to fool ourselves into thinking that we're sheltering them, at least temporarily, from the cold, cruel world.

But real life is hard, and no amount of trophies can shield kids from the disappointments and challenges they'll eventually face.

"I like kids. I want them to be happy and do well," said Merryman, who has mentored Olympic athletes. "But I'd much rather have a 6-year-old cry because he didn't get a medal than have a 26-year-old lose it because they realized they weren't as special as they thought they were."

Learning the true values of hard work, perseverance and resilience, that's the real reward. All other trophies pale in comparison.

Thinking Critically about the Text

Armour anticipated that readers might refute her argument on the grounds that linebacker James Harrison is not an ideal role model. How does she address this potential concern? Do you think her position is reasonable? What does the inclusion of Harrison's announcement contribute to her argument?

Questions on Subject

1. According to Armour, what is the central problem with participation trophies? Where does she state her thesis? (Glossary: *Thesis*)

2. Where does Armour address the views of those in favor of participation awards? What does she identify as the reasoning behind this practice?

3. In paragraph 5, Armour calls millennials "the first of the trophy generations" and characterizes them as stressed out and depressed. Does she provide sufficient evidence for this claim? Why or why not?

4. The author suggests in paragraph 14 that the participation trophies are actually for adults rather than children. Why does she think so? What does she believe that adults get out of giving awards to their children?

Questions on Strategy

1. The article begins with the declarative sentence "Life isn't always fair." (Glossary: *Beginnings/Endings*) How does this trope set the tone for Armour's entire argument? (Glossary: *Tone*)

2. Armour says that millennials were "sold a bill of goods" when they were children (paragraph 5). What does she mean by this? How does her use of this metaphor contribute to her argument?

3. In paragraph 16, the author quotes Ashley Merryman, the co-author of a book on winning and losing. What does this quotation add to her argument? (Glossary: *Figures of Speech*)

4. Paragraph 8 consists of only a single word, "Amen." Why might Armour have chosen to let this word stand alone, rather than including it at the end of the previous paragraph?

5. After pointing out the potential harm of participation trophies, Armour adds that most nine-year-olds don't actually value them anyway (13). How does this statement contribute to her thesis? How might it weaken her argument?

Questions on Diction and Vocabulary

1. Armour includes a quote by linebacker James Harrison, saying "I'm sorry I'm not sorry" (paragraph 7). How does this slang impact your perception of Harrison? (Glossary: *Slang*)

2. Although Armour is making a serious point, her tone is casual. Do you think it is appropriate for her usual audience, given that she is a sports writer? Identify language in her piece that would need to be changed to turn this into an academic argument.

3. Use a dictionary to look up the following words as they are used in the reading: *proponents* (9), *incentive* (9), *affirmation* (14), *resilience* (17)

Argumentation in Action

It can be challenging to make an argument using sources that might not have the best reputations, as Armour did in quoting James Harrison. Generally, it is advisable to simply find a source with stronger appeal to *ethos*, but occasionally you may encounter important quotes or evidence that come from controversial sources. Select some quotes from a source that others might view as suspect (for instance, a convict speaking on prison reform or a discredited politician) and brainstorm ways to incorporate their message without weakening your argument. If you get stuck, revisit Armour's article and note how she addresses the flaws in her source directly and supplements Harrison's quotes with a tweet from NFL MVP Kurt Warner.

Writing Suggestions

1. Armour is primarily a sports writer, and she examines the issue of participation awards through the lens of athletics. Select another activity where participation might be rewarded, such as learning in a classroom or entering a costume contest or a painting contest. Do you think Armour's argument is valid in the activity you have chosen? Write a brief paper arguing why or why not.

2. **Writing from Sources.** Football has recently come under fire for causing brain damage in players, and doctors have expressed concerns that even children and young adults who play football in school are at risk. Do some research into concussions caused by sports and write a paper arguing for or against dramatic changes in youth athletics.

Telling Americans to Vote, or Else

WILLIAM GALSTON

William Galston (born in 1946) served as a sergeant in the Marine Corps before receiving his Ph.D. from the University of Chicago in 1973. He taught government at the University of Texas before becoming a policy advisor under President Clinton. He is the author of eight books on politics and governance, including *The Practice of Liberal Pluralism* (2004) and *Public Matters* (2005). He has also written numerous articles and has a weekly column in the *Wall Street Journal*.

The article below first appeared in the *New York Times* in November 2011. Galston lays out a series of arguments in favor of mandatory voting. He points to the success of similar programs in Australia and other countries and suggests that a mandatory vote might be the remedy to the increasingly polarized politics in the United States.

Preparing to Read

Did you vote in the last presidential election? Have you ever voted in a local election? Do you see an increase in the polarization of American politics? How would you solve the problem of poor voter turnout?

Jury duty is mandatory; why not voting? The idea seems vaguely un-American. Maybe so, but it's neither unusual nor undemocratic. And it would ease the intense partisan polarization that weakens our capacity for self-government and public trust in our governing institutions.

Thirty-one countries have some form of mandatory voting, according to the International Institute for Democracy and Electoral Assistance. The list includes nine members of the Organization for Economic Cooperation and Development and two-thirds of the Latin American nations. More than half back up the legal requirement with an enforcement mechanism, while the rest are content to rely on the moral force of the law.

Despite the prevalence of mandatory voting in so many democracies, it's easy to dismiss the practice as a form of statism that couldn't work in America's individualistic and libertarian political culture. But consider Australia, whose political culture is closer to that of the United States than that of any other English-speaking country. Alarmed by a decline in voter turnout to less than 60 percent in 1922, Australia adopted mandatory voting in 1924, backed by small fines (roughly the size of traffic tickets) for nonvoting, rising with repeated acts of nonparticipation. The law established permissible reasons for not voting, like illness and foreign travel, and allows citizens who faced fines for not voting to defend themselves.

The results were remarkable. In the 1925 election, the first held under the new law, turnout soared to 91 percent. In recent elections, it has hovered around 95 percent. The law also changed civic norms. Australians are more likely than before to see voting as an obligation. The negative side effects many feared did not materialize. For example, the percentage of ballots intentionally spoiled or completed randomly as acts of resistance remained on the order of 2 to 3 percent.

Proponents offer three reasons in favor of mandatory voting. The first is straightforwardly civic. A democracy can't be strong if its citizenship is weak. And right now American citizenship is attenuated—strong on rights, weak on responsibilities. There is less and less that being a citizen requires of us, especially after the abolition of the draft. Requiring people to vote in national elections once every two years would reinforce the principle of reciprocity at the heart of citizenship.

> A democracy can't be strong if its citizenship is weak.

The second argument for mandatory voting is democratic. Ideally, a democracy will take into account the interests and views of all citizens. But if some regularly vote while others don't, officials are likely to give greater weight to participants. This might not matter much if nonparticipants were evenly distributed through the population. But political scientists have long known that they aren't. People with lower levels of income and education are less likely to vote, as are young adults and recent first-generation immigrants.

Changes in our political system have magnified these disparities. During the 1950s and '60s, when turnout rates were much higher, political parties reached out to citizens year-round. At the local level these parties, which reformers often criticized as "machines," connected even citizens of modest means and limited education with neighborhood institutions and gave them a sense of participation in national politics as well. (In its heyday, organized labor reinforced these effects.) But in the absence of these more organic forms of political mobilization, the second-best option is a top-down mechanism of universal mobilization.

Mandatory voting would tend to even out disparities stemming from income, education and age, enhancing our system's inclusiveness. It is true, as some object, that an enforcement mechanism would impose greater burdens on those with fewer resources. But this makes it all the more likely that these citizens would respond by going to the polls, and they would stand to gain far more than the cost of a traffic ticket.

The third argument for mandatory voting goes to the heart of our current ills. Our low turnout rate pushes American politics toward increased polarization. The reason is that hard-core partisans are more likely to dominate lower-turnout elections, while those who are less fervent about specific issues and less attached to political organizations tend not to participate at levels proportional to their share of the electorate.

A distinctive feature of our constitutional system—elections that are quadrennial for president but biennial for the House of Representatives—magnifies these effects. It's bad enough that only three-fifths of the electorate turns out to determine the next president, but much worse that only two-fifths of our citizens vote in House elections two years later. If events combine to energize one part of the political spectrum and dishearten the other, a relatively small portion of the electorate can shift the system out of all proportion to its numbers.

Some observers are comfortable with this asymmetry. But if you think that today's intensely polarized politics impedes governance and exacerbates mistrust—and that is what most Americans firmly (and in my view rightly) believe—then you should be willing to consider reforms that would strengthen the forces of conciliation.

Imagine our politics with laws and civic norms that yield near-universal voting. Campaigns could devote far less money to costly, labor-intensive get-out-the-vote efforts. Media gurus wouldn't have the same incentive to drive down turnout with negative advertising. Candidates would know that they must do more than mobilize their bases with red-meat rhetoric on hot-button issues. Such a system would improve not only electoral politics but also the legislative process. Rather than focusing on symbolic gestures whose major purpose is to agitate partisans, Congress might actually roll up its sleeves and tackle the serious, complex issues it ignores.

The United States is not Australia, of course, and there's no guarantee that the similarity of our political cultures would produce equivalent political results. For example, reforms of general elections would leave untouched the distortions generated by party primaries in which small numbers of voters can shape the choices for the entire electorate. And the United States Constitution gives the states enormous power over voting procedures. Mandating voting nationwide would go counter to our traditions (and perhaps our Constitution) and would encounter strong state opposition. Instead, a half-dozen states from parts of the country with different civic traditions should experiment with the practice, and observers—journalists, social scientists, citizens' groups and elected officials—would monitor the consequences.

We don't know what the outcome would be. But one thing is clear: If we do nothing and allow a politics of passion to define the bounds of the electorate, as it has for much of the last four decades, the prospect for a less polarized, more effective political system that enjoys the trust and confidence of the people is not bright.

Thinking Critically about the Text

Galston believes that voting should be mandatory nationwide, even though he acknowledges that this is likely to go against the Constitution. Why does he feel that voting is of such great importance? What type of argument is he making, and how does he support it?

Questions on Subject

1. What does Galston mean when he says that America is "strong on rights, weak on responsibilities" (paragraph 5).
2. What three arguments does Galston present in favor of mandatory voting?
3. Where does Galston address opposing arguments? Does he make any rebuttal? How would you address the concerns he raises?
4. Galston wrote this essay in 2011, a year in which there were no major elections occurring. Why, given Galston's argument, was his piece still immediately relevant?
5. How does Galston think that mandatory voting would benefit citizens who have fewer resources?

Questions on Strategy

1. The title for this piece, "Telling Americans to Vote, or Else," is effective at capturing the attention of readers. (Glossary: *Title*) How does the tone of the title relate to the tone of the article itself? (Glossary: *Tone*) Why might Galston have made this choice?
2. The article opens with a brief comparison between voting and jury duty. What is the impact of this comparison? Why is it located at the beginning? (Glossary: *Beginnings/Endings*)
3. Throughout the article, Galston compares the success of the Australian voting laws with a projection of how those same laws would play out in the United States. (Glossary: *Comparison and Contrast*) What is the effect of this comparison? Why is it convincing?

4. Galston labels the three central arguments for mandatory voting. How do these transitions help you to follow his argument? (Glossary: *Transitions*) How might they be improved?

Questions on Diction and Vocabulary

1. Based on the terms and language that Galston uses, who do you believe is the target audience for his article? What specific words or strategies support your answer?
2. Use a dictionary to determine the meanings of the following words as Galston uses them in this selection: *prevalence* (paragraph 3), *libertarian* (3), *attenuated* (5), *reciprocity* (5), *disparities* (7), *mobilization* (7), *quadrennial* (10), *biennial* (10), *electorate* (10), *asymmetry* (11).

Argumentation in Action

Organizing your argument effectively can be the key to persuading your audience. Depending on the complexity of the argument you are making, as well as your audience, you could present the same set of information and order it in different ways. Suppose, for example, you wanted to make the case that fracking is harmful to the environment. You could present the risks from least hazardous to most hazardous, or you could describe the process of hydraulic fracturing, noting areas for concern along the way.

In order to see how this works, first make a list of supporting details on the topic of your choice. Then organize them according to any two of the following principles:

> Best to worst
> By process
> Least important to most important
> Simplest to most complicated
> General to specific

Writing Suggestions

1. **Writing from Sources.** Visit the website for the International Institute for Democracy and Electoral Assistance (www.idea.int). Spend some time on the site, exploring the trending news. Select a region or topic that interests you and write an exploratory argument on the subject. Don't forget to cite any facts that are not common knowledge. For advice on integrating sources in your essay, see Chapters 14 and 15.
2. **Writing in the Workplace.** Imagine that you are working on a political campaign. You are in charge of writing scripts for the call center that the volunteers will use when they contact potential voters. You will need to write two

scripts. The first will be for voters who are believed to be in favor of your candidate. This script should encourage the person to vote, inform him or her of the date of the election, and provide advice on registering in the area. The second should be aimed at voters who may be neutral or hostile. This script should offer evidence on why your candidate is preferable and list some quick responses to frequently asked questions your volunteers may receive. Remember that people are often impatient on the phone so be concise in delivering your information.

The Organic Fable

ROGER COHEN

Roger Cohen was born in London in 1955. He received his master's degrees in history and French in 1977 from Oxford University before moving to Paris to teach English. While there, he became a contributor to *Paris Metro*. In 1983, Cohen began writing for the *Wall Street Journal* in Rome, before being transferred to Beirut. He became a foreign correspondent for the *New York Times* in 1990, covering the Bosnian War and winning the Burger Human Rights Award for a piece on a Serbian-run concentration camp. He currently writes a biweekly column for the *New York Times* and has written a number of books, including, most recently, *The Girl from Human Street: Ghosts of Memory in a Jewish Family* (2015).

Gilbert Carrasquillo/FilmMagic

In "The Organic Fable," an op-ed that first appeared in the *New York Times* on September 6, 2012, Cohen compares the realities of organic food with the romanticized marketing messages. He concludes that while there are some benefits to the concept of organic eating, the practice is not sustainable on a global level.

Preparing to Read

Where do you buy your food? Does it come mostly from a dining hall, a grocery store, or a specialty store? Why do you choose that location: convenience, cost, quality, or a combination of those reasons? What qualities in a store or brand would make you willing to pay more for its food?

LONDON—At some point—perhaps it was gazing at a Le Pain Quotidien menu offering an "organic baker's basket served with organic butter, organic jam and organic spread" as well as seasonally organic orange juice—I found I just could not stomach the "O" word or what it stood for any longer.

Organic has long since become an ideology, the romantic back-to-nature obsession of an upper middle class able to afford it and oblivious, in their affluent narcissism, to the challenge of feeding a planet whose population will surge to 9 billion before the middle of the century and whose poor will get a lot more nutrients from the two regular carrots they can buy for the price of one organic carrot.

An effective form of premium branding rather than a science, a slogan rather than better nutrition, "organic" has oozed over the menus, markets and malls of the world's upscale neighborhood at a remarkable pace. In

2010, according to the Organic Trade Association, organic food and drink sales totaled $26.7 billion in the United States, or about 4 percent of the overall market, having grown steadily since 2000. The British organic market is also large; menus like to mention that bacon comes from pampered pigs at the Happy Hog farm down the road.

In the midst of the fad few questions have been asked. But the fact is that buying organic baby food, a growing sector, is like paying to send your child to private school: It is a class-driven decision that demonstrates how much you love your offspring but whose overall impact on society is debatable.

So I cheered this week when Stanford University concluded, after examining four decades of research, that fruits and vegetables labeled organic are, on average, no more nutritious than their cheaper conventional counterparts. The study also found that organic meats offered no obvious health advantages. And it found that organic food was not less likely to be contaminated by dangerous bacteria like E.coli.

> The takeaway from the study could be summed up in two words: Organic, schmorganic.

The takeaway from the study could be summed up in two words: Organic, schmorganic. That's been my feeling for a while.

Now let me say three nice things about the organic phenomenon. The first is that it reflects a growing awareness about diet that has spurred quality, small-scale local farming that had been at risk of disappearance.

The second is that even if it's not better for you, organic farming is probably better for the environment because less soil, flora and fauna are contaminated by chemicals (although of course, without fertilizers, you have to use more land to grow the same amount of produce or feed the same amount of livestock). So this is food that is better ecologically even if it is not better nutritionally.

The third is that the word organic—unlike other feel-good descriptions of food like "natural"—actually means something. Certification procedures in both the United States and Britain are strict. In the United States, organic food must meet standards ensuring that genetic engineering, synthetic fertilizers, sewage and irradiation were not used in the food's production. It must also be produced using methods that, according to the Department of Agriculture, "foster cycling of resources, promote ecological balance and conserve biodiversity."

Still, the organic ideology is an elitist, pseudoscientific indulgence shot through with hype. There is a niche for it, if you can afford to shop at Whole Foods, but the future is nonorganic.

To feed a planet of 9 billion people, we are going to need high yields not low yields; we are going to need genetically modified crops; we are going to need pesticides and fertilizers and other elements of the industrialized food processes that have led mankind to be better fed and live longer than at any time in history.

Logically, the organic movement should favor genetically modified produce. If you cannot use pesticides or fertilizers, you might at least want to modify your crops so they are more resilient and plentiful. But that would go against the ideology and romance of a movement that says: We are for nature, everyone else is against nature.

I'd rather be against nature and have more people better fed. I'd rather be serious about the world's needs. And I trust the monitoring agencies that ensure pesticides are used at safe levels—a trust the Stanford study found to be justified.

Martin Orbach, the co-founder and program director of the Abergavenny Food Festival in Britain, owns a company called Shepherds that produces a superb sheep's milk ice-cream sold at a store in Hay-on-Wye. It has a cult following at the Hay literary festival and beyond. Journalists, Orbach told me, regularly report that they have eaten an "organic sheep's milk ice cream."

The only catch is this is not true. "We have never said it's organic because it would be illegal for us to do so," Orbach said. "But it fits with the story of a small sheep's milk ice-cream maker."

Organic is a fable of the pampered parts of the planet—romantic and comforting. Now, thanks to Stanford researchers, we know just how replete with myth the "O" fable is.

Thinking Critically about the Text

If Cohen is correct, and the benefits of organic food are largely a myth, what do you think it would take to convince others to stop purchasing specifically organic food? What does Cohen believe is the potential impact if this trend continues?

Questions on Subject

1. What type of argument is Cohen making? (See pages 490–92 for a discussion of the different types of argument.) How do you know?
2. In paragraph 4, what does Cohen mean by "a class-driven decision"?
3. Cohen describes the term *organic* as "an effective form of premium branding rather than a science" (paragraph 3). What does he mean? How does this idea support his thesis?
4. Why does Cohen say that the organic movement will not "favor genetically modified produce" (paragraph 12)? Why does he believe it should?

5. What does Cohen mean when he says that he would rather be "against nature and have more people better fed" (paragraph 10). Why is this a potentially controversial statement, given his likely readership?

Questions on Strategy

1. Where does Cohen state his thesis? (Glossary: *Thesis*) Why do you think he expresses it as he does?

2. Find moments in the piece where Cohen incorporates quotes from outside sources. Select three and explain how they contribute to Cohen's argument.

3. Cohen's argument begins and ends with "O" standing in place of the word organic. What does this decision imply about Cohen's stance on the word? How do you know? (Glossary: *Beginnings/Endings*)

4. Why, after agreeing with a Stanford University study that organic food is not any better, does Cohen go on to "say three nice things about the organic phenomenon" (paragraph 7)?

5. Cohen is actually making two connected arguments in his essay: that organic food is not any better for you and that we need pesticides and other chemicals to grow enough food to feed the world. How does Cohen connect these two ideas? Does he spend more time on either argument, or does he spend equal time on both?

Questions on Diction and Vocabulary

1. What does Cohen mean in paragraph 6 when he says "Organic, schmorganic"? Given that his other word choices are generally more academic, what is the impact of this break in tone? (Glossary: *Tone*)

2. In the context of this essay, why is *pseudoscientific* an apt term (paragraph 10)?

3. What are high and low yields (paragraph 11)? Consult a dictionary if you're unsure.

Argumentation in Action

In the process of arguing against organic foods, Cohen makes an argument about what the term *organic* actually means, particularly in terms of the health of consumers. Write your own definition of one of the food-related words below and explain how the term is more complicated — or means something different — than most people realize.

Artisanal	Light	Natural
Free	Local	Sustainable
Lean		

Writing Suggestions

1. Write a rebuttal addressing Cohen's points and arguing for the importance of having an organic food option.

2. **Writing from Sources.** One of the benefits Cohen mentions for organic food is the resurgence of small-scale local farms. Do some research into this sort of farm and make an argument for or against the need to develop more of them. What are the benefits of local farms? What are the benefits of large, corporate food organizations? Which benefits, in your opinion, are the most important? For models of and advice on integrating sources in your essay, see Chapters 14 and 15.

ARGUMENT CLUSTER

Race and Privilege: How to Address a System of Bias?

Intolerance and racism have sadly been a part of the United States since it was established a few centuries ago. As a society, we have celebrated movement toward equality, holding up leaders of the civil rights movement as the social heroes they were. And, as a society, we have felt the shame and regret of our many missteps. Social scientists are coming to realize, however, that the problem of racism does not have clear, obvious definitions and boundaries. In 1999, an investigation was made into the brutal, racially motivated murder of Stephen Lawrence, a resident of London. The public investigation into his death revealed an as-yet-undefined threat: institutional racism. This is a form of discrimination practiced not by individuals but openly or subtly by political entities, organizations, and companies.

Although the term *institutional racism* was first recognized and defined in England, it has been embraced by social scientists in the United States as a valuable tool for understanding—and hopefully counteracting—this pervasive and damaging prejudice. Research at Teachers College, Columbia University led Derald Wing Sue to classify some of what scholars in the field term *microaggressions*, or "the brief and everyday slights, insults, indignities and denigrating messages sent to people of color by well-intentioned White people who are unaware of the hidden messages being communicated" (see Sue's essay "Racial Microaggressions in Everyday Life: Is Subtle Bias Harmful?" later in this chapter). Sue goes on to note that these actions are not a part of conscious behaviors and hopes that by raising awareness and making "the 'invisible' visible," this subtle form of racism might be eradicated.

All of the authors in this cluster attempt to delve beyond the obvious expressions of racism in our society to explore the subtle aggressions and systematic disadvantages that are so divisive, and all of them do so with an eye toward both self-improvement and creating a culture of change. John Metta explains why he hesitates to talk about race with "White people" and shares his resolution to speak up in the future in "I, Racist." In "What My Bike Has Taught Me about White Privilege," J. Dowsett makes a compelling analogy between being a biker in a world designed for automobiles and being a minority when legal and social structures protect the majority view. Finally, author and professor Derald Wing Sue shares some of his research into microaggressions and pledges to continue to pursue the many unanswered questions that remain.

Preparing to Read

What role does race play in your life? Is it something that impacts you on a daily basis or something that you seldom consider? Do you think it's possible to address the subtle biases and institutional prejudices that plague our society? How might we do so? Is awareness enough of a first step, as some of the authors in this cluster propose? How does social change happen?

I, Racist

JOHN METTA

John Metta studied anthropology and geology at the College of Charleston before earning master's degrees in ecological engineering and resource geography. A programmer and integrations specialist in the software industry, he has also worked as a teacher, cook, clerk, and park ranger. His work has appeared in the *San Francisco Chronicle*, the *Huffington Post*, Al Jazeera, and Medium.

Jessica Metta

Metta describes this selection as "the text of 'a sermon' he gave" to an all-white audience at the Bethel Congregational Church of Christ. He began with this quote from Chimamanda Ngozi Adichie's *Americanah*:

> The only reason you say that race was not an issue is because you wish it was not. We all wish it was not. But it's a lie. I came from a country where race was not an issue; I did not think of myself as black and I only became black when I came to America. When you are black in America and you fall in love with a white person, race doesn't matter when you're alone together because it's just you and your love. But the minute you step outside, race matters. But we don't talk about it. We don't even tell our white partners the small things that piss us off and the things we wish they understood better, because we're worried they will say we're overreacting, or we're being too sensitive. And we don't want them to say, Look how far we've come, just forty years ago it would have been illegal for us to even be a couple blah blah blah, because you know what we're thinking when they say that? We're thinking why the fuck should it ever have been illegal anyway? But we don't say any of this stuff. We let it pile up inside our heads and when we come to nice liberal dinners like this, we say that race doesn't matter because that's what we're supposed to say, to keep our nice liberal friends comfortable. It's true. I speak from experience.

Consider how this quotation relates to Metta's argument.

1   A couple weeks ago, I was debating what I was going to talk about in this sermon. I told Pastor Kelly Ryan I had great reservations talking about the one topic that I think about every single day.

2   Then, a terrorist massacred nine innocent people in a church that I went to, in a city that I still think of as home. At that point, I knew that despite any misgivings, I needed to talk about race.

3   You see, I don't talk about race with White people.

To illustrate why, I'll tell a story:

It was probably about 15 years ago when a conversation took place between my aunt, who is White and lives in New York State, and my sister, who is Black and lives in North Carolina. This conversation can be distilled to a single sentence, said by my Black sister:

"The only difference between people in the North and people in the South is that down here, at least people are honest about being racist."

> You see, I don't talk about race with White people.

There was a lot more to that conversation, obviously, but I suggest that it can be distilled into that one sentence because it has been, by my White aunt. Over a decade later, this sentence is still what she talks about. It has become the single most important aspect of my aunt's relationship with my Black family. She is still hurt by the suggestion that people in New York, that she, a northerner, a liberal, a good person who has Black family members, is a racist.

This perfectly illustrates why I don't talk about race with White people. Even — or rather, especially — my own family.

I love my aunt. She's actually my favorite aunt, and believe me, I have *a lot* of awesome aunts to choose from. But the facts are actually quite in my sister's favor on this one.

New York State is one of the most segregated states in the country. Buffalo, New York, where my aunt lives, is one of the 10 most segregated school systems in the country. The racial inequality of the area she inhabits is so bad that it has been the subject of reports by the Civil Rights Action Network and the NAACP.

Those, however, are facts that my aunt does not need to know. She does not need to live with the racial segregation and oppression of her home. As a white person with upward mobility, she has continued to improve her situation. She moved out of the area I grew up in — she moved to an area with better schools. She doesn't have to experience racism, and so it is not real to her.

Nor does it dawn on her that the very fact that she moved away from an increasingly Black neighborhood to live in a White suburb might itself be a aspect of racism. She doesn't need to realize that "better schools" exclusively means "whiter schools."

I don't talk about race with White people because I have so often seen it go nowhere. When I was younger, I thought it was because all white people are racist. Recently, I've begun to understand that it's more nuanced than that.

To understand, you have to know that Black people think in terms of Black *people*.

We don't see a shooting of an innocent Black child in another state as something separate from us because we know viscerally that it could be our child, our parent, or us, that is shot.

The shooting of Walter Scott in North Charleston resonated with me because Walter Scott was portrayed in the media as a deadbeat and a criminal—but when you look at the facts about the actual man, he was nearly indistinguishable from my own father.

Racism affects us directly because the fact that it happened at a geographically remote location or to another Black person is only a coincidence, an accident. It could just as easily happen to us—right here, right now.

Black people think in terms of *we* because we live in a society where the social and political structures interact with us *as Black people*.

White people do not think in terms of *we*. White people have the privilege to interact with the social and political structures of our society *as individuals*. You are "you," I am "one of them." Whites are often not directly affected by racial oppression even in their own community, so what does not affect them locally has little chance of affecting them regionally or nationally. They have no need, nor often any real desire, to think in terms of a group. They are supported by the system, and so are mostly unaffected by it.

What they are affected by are attacks on their own character. To my aunt, the suggestion that "people in The North are racist" is an attack on her *as a racist*. She is unable to differentiate her participation *within* a racist system (upwardly mobile, not racially profiled, able to move to White suburbs, etc.) from an accusation that she, individually, is *a racist*. Without being able to make that differentiation, White people in general decide to vigorously defend their own personal non-racism, or point out that it doesn't exist because they don't see it.

The result of this is an incessantly repeating argument where a Black person says "Racism still exists. It is real," and a white person argues "You're wrong, I'm not racist at all. I don't even see any racism." My aunt's immediate response is not "that is wrong, we should do better." No, her response is self-protection: "That's not my fault, I didn't do anything. You are wrong."

Racism is not slavery. As President Obama said, it's not avoiding the use of the word Nigger. Racism is not white water fountains and the back of the bus. Martin Luther King did not end racism. Racism is a cop severing the spine of an innocent man. It is a 12 year old child being shot for playing with a toy gun in a state where it is legal to openly carry firearms.

But racism is even more subtle than that. It's more nuanced. Racism is the fact that "White" means "normal" and that anything else is different. Racism is our acceptance of an all white Lord of the Rings cast because of "historical accuracy," ignoring the fact that this is a world with an *entirely fictionalized history*.

Even when we make shit up, we want it to be white.

And racism is the fact that we all *accept* that it *is* white. Benedict Cumberbatch playing Khan in Star Trek. Khan, who is from India. Is there anyone Whiter than Benedict fucking Cumberbatch? What? They needed a "less racial" cast because they already had the Black Uhura character?

That is racism. Once you let yourself see it, it's there all the time.

Black children learn this when their parents give them "The Talk." When they are sat down at the age of 5 or so and told that their best friend's father is not sick, and not in a bad mood—he just doesn't want his son playing with you. Black children grow up early to life in The Matrix. We're not given a choice of the red or blue pill. Most white people, like my aunt, never have to choose. The system was made for White people, so White people don't have to think about living in it.

But we can't point this out.

Living every single day with institutionalized racism and then having to argue its very existence, is tiring, and saddening, and angering. Yet if we express any emotion while talking about it, we're tone policed, told we're being angry. In fact, a key element in any racial argument in America is the Angry Black person, and racial discussions shut down when that person speaks. The Angry Black person invalidates any arguments about racism because they are "just being overly sensitive," or "too emotional," or— playing the race card. Or even worse, we're told that *we* are being racist. (Does any intelligent person actually believe a systematically oppressed demographic has the ability to oppress those in power?)

But here is the irony, here's the thing that all the angry Black people know, and no calmly debating White people want to admit: The entire discussion of race in America centers around the protection of White feelings.

Ask any Black person and they'll tell you the same thing. The reality of thousands of innocent people raped, shot, imprisoned, and systematically disenfranchised are less important than the suggestion that a single White person might be complicit in a racist system.

This is the country we live in. Millions of Black lives are valued less than a single White person's hurt feelings.

White people and Black people are not having a discussion about race. Black people, thinking as a group, are talking about *living in a racist system*. White people, thinking as individuals, refuse to talk about "I, racist" and instead protect their own individual and personal goodness. In doing so, they reject the existence of racism.

But arguing about personal non-racism is missing the point.

Despite what the Charleston Massacre makes things look like, people are dying not because individuals are racist, but because individuals are helping support a racist system by wanting to protect their own non-racist self beliefs.

People are dying because we are supporting a racist system that justifies White people killing Black people.

We see this in how one Muslim killer is Islamic terror; how one Mexican thief points to the need for border security; in one innocent, unarmed Black man shot in the back by a cop, then sullied in the media as a thug and criminal.

And in the way a white racist in a state that still flies the confederate flag is seen as "troubling" and "unnerving." In the way people "can't understand why he would do such a thing."

A white person smoking pot is a "hippie" and a Black person doing it is a "criminal." It's evident in the school to prison pipeline and the fact that there are close to 20 people of color in prison for every white person.

There's a headline from *The Independent* that sums this up quite nicely: "Charleston shooting: Black and Muslim killers are 'terrorists' and 'thugs'. Why are white shooters called 'mentally ill'?"

I'm gonna read that again: "Black and Muslim killers are 'terrorists' and 'thugs'. Why are white shooters called 'mentally ill'?"

Did you catch that? It's beautifully subtle. This is an article talking specifically about the different way we treat people of color in this nation and even in this article's headline, the white people are "shooters" and the Black and Muslim people are "killers."

Even when we're talking about racism, we're using racist language to make people of color look dangerous and make White people come out as not so bad.

Just let that sink in for a minute, then ask yourself why Black people are angry when they talk about race.

The reality of America is that White people are fundamentally good, and so when a white person commits a crime, it is a sign that they, *as an individual*, are bad. Their actions as a person are not indicative of any broader social construct. Even the fact that America has a growing number of violent hate groups, populated mostly by white men, and that nearly *all* serial killers are white men can not shadow the fundamental truth of white male goodness. In fact, we like White serial killers so much, we make mini-series about them.

White people are good as a whole, and only act badly as individuals.

People of color, especially Black people (but boy we can talk about "The Mexicans" in this community) are seen as fundamentally bad. There might be a good one—and we are always quick to point them out to our friends, show them off as our Academy Award for "Best Non-Racist in a White Role"—but when we see a bad one, it's just proof that the rest are, as a rule, bad.

This, all of this, expectation, treatment, thought, the underlying social system that puts White in the position of Normal and good, and Black in the position of "other" and "bad," all of this, is racism.

And White people, every single one of you, are complicit in this racism because *you benefit directly from it.*

This is why I don't like the story of the good samaritan. Everyone likes to think of themselves as the person who sees someone beaten and bloodied and helps him out.

That's too easy.

If I could re-write that story, I'd rewrite it from the perspective of Black America. What if the person wasn't beaten and bloody? What if it wasn't so obvious? What if they were just systematically challenged in a thousand small ways *that actually made it easier for you to succeed in life*?

Would you be so quick to help then?

Or would you, like most White people, stay silent and let it happen?

Here's what I want to say to you: Racism is so deeply embedded in this country not because of the racist right-wing radicals who practice it openly, it exists because of the silence and hurt feelings of liberal America.

That's what I want to say, but really, I can't. I can't say that because I've spent my life not talking about race to White people. In a big way, it's my fault. Racism exists because I, as a Black person, don't challenge you to look at it.

Racism exists because I, not you, am silent.

But I'm caught in the perfect Catch 22, because when I start pointing out racism, I become the Angry Black Person, and the discussion shuts down again. So I'm stuck.

All the Black voices in the world speaking about racism all the time do not move White people to think about it—but one White John Stewart talking about Charleston has a whole lot of White people talking about it. That's the world we live in. Black people can't change it while White people are silent and deaf to our words.

White people are in a position of power in this country *because of racism.* The question is: Are they brave enough to use that power to speak against the system that gave it to them?

So I'm asking you to help me. Notice this. Speak up. Don't let it slide. Don't stand watching in silence. Help build a world where it never gets to the point where the Samaritan has to see someone bloodied and broken.

As for me, I will no longer be silent.

I'm going to *try* to speak kindly, and softly, but that's gonna be hard. Because it's getting harder and harder for me to think about the protection of White people's feelings when White people don't seem to care at all about the loss of so many Black lives.

Thinking Critically

After reading this selection, do you better understand why minorities are often angry or frustrated when talking about race? How closely do your own experiences match those of Metta?

Examining the Issue

1. Metta writes, "I had great reservations talking about the one topic that I think about every single day" (paragraph 1). What is this topic, and why might someone feel this way? Why wouldn't someone want to talk about a topic he thinks about all the time?
2. Do you believe you are complicit in racism? Explain.
3. Do you agree that "the entire discussion of race in America centers around the protection of White feelings"?
4. What does "tone policed" (29) mean?
5. Metta writes that "Black people think in terms of *we*" and "White people do not think in terms of *we*" (18 and 19). Do these statements match your experience? Have you ever thought of yourself as part of a "we" because of the color of your skin, your ethnicity, your religion, your sexual orientation, or for any other reason? Do you have the option of defining yourself as belonging to more than one group?
6. Where does Metta use definition in this essay?
7. Metta writes that the fact that his aunt "moved away from an increasingly Black neighborhood to live in a White suburb might itself be an aspect of racism" (12). What do you think he means by this?
8. Why does Metta believe that racism exists?

Racial Microaggressions in Everyday Life: Is Subtle Bias Harmful?

DERALD WING SUE

Derald Wing Sue is a professor at Columbia University, where he teaches psychology and education courses. He has written extensively on race, including articles in *American Psychologist* and *Cultural Diversity and Ethnic Minority Psychology*. He published his first book, *Counseling the Culturally Diverse: Theory and Practice* in 1981 and has since published more than a half dozen others, including the textbook *Understanding Abnormal Behavior*, which went into its tenth edition in 2013. In 1996, Sue served on the President's Advisory Board on Race under President Bill Clinton.

The exploration below was published as a blog post on PsychologyToday.com in October 2010. In it, Sue addresses the question of whether subconscious racial discrimination — even in its most subtle forms — is harmful.

Not too long ago, I (Asian American) boarded a small plane with an African American colleague in the early hours of the morning. As there were few passengers, the flight attendant told us to sit anywhere, so we choose seats near the front of the plane and across the aisle from one another.

At the last minute, three White men entered the plane and took seats in front of us. Just before takeoff, the flight attendant, who is White, asked if we would mind moving to the back of the aircraft to better balance the plane's weight. We grudgingly complied but felt singled out as passengers of color in being told to "move to the back of the bus." When we expressed these feelings to the attendant, she indignantly denied the charge, became defensive, stated that her intent was to ensure the flight's safety, and wanted to give us some privacy.

Since we had entered the plane first, I asked why she did not ask the White men to move instead of us. She became indignant, stated that we had misunderstood her intentions, claimed she did not see "color," suggested that we were being "oversensitive," and refused to talk about the matter any further.

Were we being overly sensitive, or was the flight attendant being racist? That is a question that people of color are constantly faced with in their day-to-day interactions with well-intentioned White folks who experience themselves as good, moral, and decent human beings.

THE COMMON EXPERIENCE OF RACIAL MICROAGGRESSIONS

Such incidents have become a common-place experience for many people of color because they seem to occur constantly in our daily lives.

- When a White couple (man and woman) passes a Black man on the sidewalk, the woman automatically clutches her purse more tightly, while the White man checks for his wallet in the back pocket. (Hidden Message: Blacks are prone to crime and up to no good.)
- A third generation Asian American is complimented by a taxi cab driver for speaking such good English. (Hidden Message: Asian Americans are perceived as perpetual aliens in their own country and not "real Americans.")
- Police stop a Latino male driver for no apparent reason but to subtly check his driver's license to determine immigration status. (Hidden message: Latinas/os are illegal aliens.)
- American Indian students at the University of Illinois see Native American symbols and mascots—exemplified by Chief Illiniwek dancing and whooping fiercely during football games. (Hidden Message: American Indians are savages, blood-thirsty, and their culture and traditions are demeaned.)

Were we being overly sensitive, or was the flight attendant being racist?

In our 8-year research at Teachers College, Columbia University, we have found that these racial microaggressions may on the surface appear like a compliment or seem quite innocent and harmless, but nevertheless, they contain what we call demeaning meta-communications or hidden messages.

WHAT ARE RACIAL MICROAGGRESSIONS?

The term racial microaggressions, was first coined by psychiatrist Chester Pierce, MD, in the 1970s. But the concept is also rooted in the work of Jack Dovidio, Ph.D. (Yale University) and Samuel Gaertner, Ph.D. (University of Delaware) in their formulation of aversive racism—many well-intentioned Whites consciously believe in and profess equality, but unconsciously act in a racist manner, particularly in ambiguous situations.

Racial microaggressions are the brief and everyday slights, insults, indignities and denigrating messages sent to people of color by well-intentioned

White people who are unaware of the hidden messages being communicated. These messages may be sent verbally ("You speak good English."), nonverbally (clutching one's purse more tightly) or environmentally (symbols like the confederate flag or using American Indian mascots). Such communications are usually outside the level of conscious awareness of perpetrators. In the case of the flight attendant, I am sure that she believed she was acting with the best of intentions and probably felt aghast that someone would accuse her of such a horrendous act.

Our research and those of many social psychologists suggest that most people, like the flight attendant, harbor unconscious biases and prejudices that leak out in many interpersonal situations and decision points. In other words, the attendant was acting with bias — she just didn't know it. Getting perpetrators to realize that they are acting in a biased manner is a monumental task because (a) on a conscious level they see themselves as fair minded individuals who would never consciously discriminate, (b) they are genuinely not aware of their biases, and (c) their self image of being "a good moral human being" is assailed if they realize and acknowledge that they possess biased thoughts, attitudes and feelings that harm people of color.

To better understand the type and range of these incidents, my research team and other researchers are exploring the manifestation, dynamics and impact of microaggressions. We have begun documenting how African Americans, Asian Americans, American Indians and Latina(o) Americans who receive these everyday psychological slings and arrows experience an erosion of their mental health, job performance, classroom learning, the quality of social experience, and ultimately their standard of living.

CLASSIFYING MICROAGGRESSIONS

In my book, *Racial Microaggressions in Everyday Life: Race, Gender and Sexual Orientation* (John Wiley & Sons, 2010), I summarize research conducted at Teachers College, Columbia University which led us to propose a classification of racial microaggressions. Three types of current racial transgressions were described:

- Microassaults: Conscious and intentional discriminatory actions: using racial epithets, displaying White supremacist symbols — swastikas, or preventing one's son or daughter from dating outside of their race.
- Microinsults: Verbal, nonverbal, and environmental communications that subtly convey rudeness and insensitivity that demean a person's racial heritage or identity. An example is an employee who asks a co-worker of color how he/she got his/her job, implying he/she may have landed it through an affirmative action or quota system.

- Microinvalidations: Communications that subtly exclude negate or nullify the thoughts, feelings, or experiential reality of a person of color. For instance, White people often ask Latinos where they were born, conveying the message that they are perpetual foreigners in their own land.

Our research suggests that microinsults and microvalidiations are potentially more harmful because of their invisibility, which puts people of color in a psychological bind: While people of color may feel insulted, they are often uncertain why, and perpetrators are unaware that anything has happened and are not aware they have been offensive. For people of color, they are caught in a Catch-22. If they question the perpetrator, as in the case of the flight attendant, denials are likely to follow. Indeed, they may be labeled "oversensitive" or even "paranoid." If they choose not to confront perpetrators, the turmoil stews and percolates in the psyche of the person, taking a huge emotional toll. In other words, they are damned if they do and damned if they don't.

Note that the denials by perpetrators are usually not conscious attempts to deceive; they honestly believe they have done no wrong. Microaggressions hold their power because they are invisible, and therefore they don't allow Whites to see that their actions and attitudes may be discriminatory. Therein lays the dilemma. The person of color is left to question what actually happened. The result is confusion, anger and an overall draining of energy.

Ironically, some research and testimony from people of color indicate they are better able to handle overt, conscious and deliberate acts of racism than the unconscious, subtle and less obvious forms. That is because there is no guesswork involved in overt forms of racism.

HARMFUL IMPACT

Many racial microaggressions are so subtle that neither target nor perpetrator may entirely understand what is happening. The invisibility of racial microaggressions may be more harmful to people of color than hate crimes or the overt and deliberate acts of White supremacists such as the Klan and Skinheads. Studies support the fact that people of color frequently experience microaggressions, that it is a continuing reality in their day-to-day interactions with friends, neighbors, co-workers, teachers, and employers in academic, social and public settings.

They are often made to feel excluded, untrustworthy, second-class citizens, and abnormal. People of color often describe the terrible feeling of being watched suspiciously in stores, that any slipup they make would negatively impact every person of color, that they felt pressured to represent the group in positive ways, and that they feel trapped in a stereotype. The burden of constant vigilance drains and saps psychological and spiritual energies of targets and contributes to chronic fatigue and a feeling of racial frustration and anger.

Space does not allow me to elaborate the harmful impact of racial microaggressions, but I summarize what the research literature reveals. Although they may appear like insignificant slights, or banal and trivial in nature, studies reveal that racial microaggressions have powerful detrimental consequences to people of color. They have been found to: (a) assail the mental health of recipients, (b) create a hostile and invalidating work or campus climate, (c) perpetuate stereotype threat, (d) create physical health problems, (e) saturate the broader society with cues that signal devaluation of social group identities, (f) lower work productivity and problem solving abilities, and (g) be partially responsible for creating inequities in education, employment and health care.

FUTURE BLOGS

I realize that I have left many questions unanswered with this posting, but my research team and I plan to continue updating our findings for readers to consider. For readers who desire a more thorough understanding of microaggressions, I recommend two major sources on the topic published this year (2010): *Microaggressions in Everyday Life: Race, Gender, and Sexual Orientation* and *Microaggressions and Marginality: Manifestation, Dynamics and Impact*. Both can be accessed through the John Wiley & Sons, publisher's website.

Future blogs will deal with questions such as: How do people of color cope with the daily onslaught of racial microaggressions? Are some coping strategies better than others? How do we help perpetrators to become aware of microaggressions? What are the best ways to prevent them at an individual, institutional and societal level? Do other socially marginalized groups like women, LGBTs, those with disabilities, and religious minorities experience microaggressions? In what ways are they similar or different? Is it possible for any of us to be born and raised in the United States without inheriting the racial, gender and sexual orientation biases of our ancestors? Are you personally a racist, sexist, or heterosexist? What is the best way for the average U.S. citizen to overcome these biases?

The first step in eliminating microaggressions is to make the "invisible" visible. I realize how controversial topics of race and racism, gender and sexism and sexual orientation and heterosexism push emotional hot buttons in all of us. I am hopeful that our blogs will stimulate discussion, debate, self-reflection, and helpful dialogue directed at increasing mutual respect and understanding of the multiple social identities we all possess.

Thinking Critically about the Text

Sue writes in his final sentence of his hope that his work will "stimulate discussion, debate, self-reflection, and helpful dialogue." Do you think these things are sufficient to address the concerns he raises about microaggressions? What are some of the questions that Sue acknowledges he has left unanswered (paragraph 18)?

Examining the Issue

1. What is a microaggression? Why does Sue find microinvalidations concerning?
2. Why does Sue reiterate throughout his piece that microaggressions are unconscious actions? How does this strengthen or weaken his argument?
3. Compare and contrast the three types of "racial transgressions" Sue identifies. How are they similar? How are they different? What is most significant about the differences?
4. Why does Sue believe that microinsults and microinvalidations have the potential to be more harmful than microassaults?
5. Sue opens his piece with a brief narrative of his own experience. (Glossary: *Narration*) How does this contribute to his argument?
6. Why does Sue include the history of the term *microaggression* in paragraph 7?
7. Why does Sue call microaggressions both *brief* and *everyday* (paragraph 8)?

What My Bike Has Taught Me about White Privilege

J. DOWSETT

J. Dowsett blogs about a variety of issues, from race and the media to church politics. He attempts to create a space for dialogue with his personal blog, A Little More Sauce, and tries to "think deeply and Christianly about the problems we're confronted with in the (post)modern world" and how those problems might be overcome.

Elizabeth Silky

Dowsett's post, the first of two on this topic, first appeared on his WordPress blog on August 20, 2014. It has since garnered more than 1,100 comments as visitors to the site struggle to express the same questions and concerns addressed by all the authors in this cluster.

The phrase "white privilege" is one that rubs a lot of white people the wrong way. It can trigger something in them that shuts down conversation or at least makes them very defensive. (Especially those who grew up relatively less privileged than other folks around them). And I've seen more than once where this happens and the next move in the conversation is for the person who brought up white privilege to say, "The reason you're getting defensive is because you're feeling the discomfort of having your privilege exposed."

I'm sure that's true sometimes. And I'm sure there are a lot of people, white and otherwise, who can attest to a kind of a-ha moment or paradigm shift where they "got" what privilege means and they did realize they had been getting defensive because they were uncomfortable at having their privilege exposed. But I would guess that more often than not, the frustration and the shutting down is about something else. It comes from the fact that nobody wants to be a racist. And the move "you only think that because you're looking at this from the perspective of privilege" or the more terse and confrontational "check your privilege!" kind of sound like an accusation that someone is a racist (if they don't already understand privilege). And the phrase "white privilege" kind of sounds like, "You are a racist and there's nothing you can do about it because you were born that way."

And if this were what "white privilege" meant—which it is not—defensiveness and frustration would be the appropriate response. But privilege talk is not intended to make a moral assessment or a moral claim about the privileged at all. It is about systemic imbalance. It is about injustices that have arisen because of the history of racism that birthed the way things are now. It's not saying, "You're a bad person because you're white." It's saying, "The system is skewed in ways that you maybe haven't realized or had to think about precisely because it's skewed in YOUR favor."

> Privilege talk is not intended to make a moral assessment or a moral claim about the privileged at all. It is about systemic imbalance.

I am white. So I have not experienced racial privilege from the "under" side firsthand. But my children (and a lot of other people I love) are not white. And so I care about privilege and what it means for racial justice in our country. And one experience I have had firsthand, which has helped me to understand privilege and listen to privilege talk without feeling defensive, is riding my bike.

Now, I know, it sounds a little goofy at first. But stick with me. Because I think that this analogy might help some white people understand privilege talk without feeling like they're having their character attacked.

About five years ago I decide to start riding my bike as my primary mode of transportation. As in, on the street, in traffic. Which is enjoyable for a number of reasons (exercise, wind in yer face, the cool feeling of going fast, etc.) But the thing is, I don't live in Portland or Minneapolis. I live in the capital city of the epicenter of the auto industry: Lansing, MI. This is not, by any stretch, a bike-friendly town. And often, it is down-right dangerous to be a bike commuter here.

Now sometimes it's dangerous for me because people in cars are just blatantly a**holes to me. If I am in the road—where I legally belong—people will yell at me to get on the sidewalk. If I am on the sidewalk—which is sometimes the safest place to be—people will yell at me to get on the road. People in cars think it's funny to roll down their window and yell something right when they get beside me. Or to splash me on purpose. People I have never met are angry at me for just being on a bike in "their" road and they let me know with colorful language and other acts of aggression.

I can imagine that for people of color life in a white-majority context feels a bit like being on a bicycle in midst of traffic. They have the right to be on the road, and laws on the books to make it equitable, but that doesn't change the fact that they are on a bike in a world made for cars. Experiencing this when I'm on my bike in traffic has helped me to understand what privilege talk is really about.

Now most people in cars are not intentionally aggressive toward me. But even if all the jerks had their licenses revoked tomorrow, the road would still be a dangerous place for me. Because the whole transportation infrastructure privileges the automobile. It is born out of a history rooted in the auto industry that took for granted that everyone should use a car as their mode of transportation. It was not built to be convenient or economical or safe for me.

And so people in cars—nice, non-aggressive people—put me in danger all the time because they see the road from the privileged perspective of a car. E.g., I ride on the right side of the right lane. Some people fail to change lanes to pass me (as they would for another car) or even give me a wide berth. Some people fly by just inches from me not realizing how scary/dangerous that is for me (like if I were to swerve to miss some roadkill just as they pass). These folks aren't aggressive or hostile toward me, but they don't realize that a pothole or a build up of gravel or a broken bottle, which they haven't given me enough room to avoid—because in a car they don't need to be aware of these things—could send me flying from my bike or cost me a bent rim or a flat tire.

So the semi driver who rushes past throwing gravel in my face in his hot wake isn't necessarily a bad guy. He could be sitting in his cab listening to Christian radio and thinking about nice things he can do for his wife. But the fact that "the system" allows him to do those things instead of being mindful of me is a privilege he has that I don't. (I have to be hyper-aware of him.)

This is what privilege is about. Like drivers, nice, non-aggressive white people can move in the world without thinking about the "potholes" or the "gravel" that people of color have to navigate, or how things that they do—not intending to hurt or endanger anyone—might actually be making life more difficult or more dangerous for a person of color.

Nice, non-aggressive drivers that don't do anything at all to endanger me are still privileged to pull out of their driveway each morning and know that there are roads that go all the way to their destination. They don't have to wonder if there are bike lanes and what route they will take to stay safe. In the winter, they can be certain that the snow will be plowed out of their lane into my lane and not the other way around.

And it's not just the fact that the whole transportation infrastructure is built around the car. It's the law, which is poorly enforced when cyclists are hit by cars, the fact that gas is subsidized by the government and bike tires aren't, and just the general mindset of a culture that is in love with cars after a hundred years of propaganda and still thinks that bikes are toys for kids and triathletes.

So when I say the semi driver is privileged, it isn't a way of calling him a bad person or a man-slaughterer or saying he didn't really earn his truck, but just a way of acknowledging all that—infrastructure, laws, government, culture—and the fact that if he and I get in a collision, I will probably die and he will just have to clean the blood off of his bumper. In the same way, talking about *racial* privilege isn't a way of telling white people they are bad people or racists or that they didn't really earn what they have.

It's a way of trying to make visible the fact that the system is not neutral, it is not a level-playing field, it's not the same experience for everyone. There are biases and imbalances and injustices built into the warp and woof of our culture. (The recent events in Ferguson, MO should be evidence enough). Not because you personally are a racist, but because the system has a history and was built around this category "race" and that's not going to go away overnight (or even in 100 years). To go back to my analogy: Bike lanes are relatively new, and still just kind of an appendage on a system that is inherently car-centric.

So—white readers—the next time someone drops the p-word, try to remember they aren't calling you a racist or saying you didn't really earn your college degree, they just want you to try to empathize with how scary it is to be on a bike sometimes (metaphorically speaking).

One last thing: Now, I know what it is like to be a white person engaged in racial reconciliation or justice work and to feel like privilege language is being used to silence you or to feel frustrated that you are genuinely trying to be a part of the solution not the problem but every time you open your mouth someone says, "Check you privilege." (I.e., even though privilege language doesn't mean "You are one of the bad guys," some people do use it that way.) So if you'll permit me to get a few more miles out of this bike analogy (ya see what I did there?), I think it can help encourage white folks who have felt that frustration to stay engaged and stay humble.

I have a lot of "conversations" with drivers. Now, rationally, I know that most drivers are not jerks. But I have a long and consistent history of bad experiences with drivers and so, when I've already been honked at or yelled at that day, or when I've read a blog post about a fellow cyclist who's been mowed down by a careless driver, it's hard for me to stay civil.

But when I'm not so civil with a "privileged" driver, it's not because I hate him/her, or think s/he is evil. It's because it's the third time that day I got some gravel in the face. So try to remember that even if you don't feel like a "semi driver," a person of color might be experiencing you the way a person on a bike experiences being passed by a semi. Even if you're listening to Christian radio.

Thinking Critically about the Text

Discuss the "a-ha" moment Dowsett describes when people recognize their own privilege. Have you had one of these moments? What prompted it?

Examining the Issue

1. What is Dowsett's thesis? (Glossary: *Thesis*) Where does he state it?
2. In paragraphs 2 and 3, Dowsett makes a definitional argument about the term "white privilege." According to Dowsett, what does it mean? What does it not mean?
3. What illustrating examples does Dowsett provide for his mistreatment at the hands of drivers? (Glossary: *Illustration*)
4. Why do well-intentioned people in cars put Dowsett in danger?
5. Why does Dowsett consider the semi driver privileged?
6. How does Dowsett connect his biking analogy to race?
7. What does Dowsett mean in paragraph 17 by "the p-word"?
8. What other types of privilege might be explained using Dowsett's analogy? How might each of us find ourselves being "semi-drivers"?

MAKING CONNECTIONS

Writing and Discussion Suggestions on Race and Privilege

1. Each of the authors in this cluster addresses an aspect of privilege. Combining the thoughts of all three authors, write your own brief definition of the term. How is your definition similar to that of each of the authors in this cluster? How does it differ?
2. Both John Metta and Derald Wing Sue use the term *Catch-22*, a reference to the book by Joseph Heller. (Glossary: *Allusion*) Explain the concept of a Catch-22. What does this reference add to Metta's and Sue's arguments?
3. In "What My Bike Has Taught Me about White Privilege," J. Dowsett compares the experience of riding a bike to the experience of being a minority in the United States. How is this an effective argumentative strategy? What other analogies might serve this same purpose? Create your own extended analogy and explain how it serves to illustrate the minority experience. (Glossary: *Analogy*)
4. Derald Wing Sue argues that subtle instances of racial aggression are potentially more damaging than overt racism. Use examples from your own life to support or refute this claim.
5. How might companies — like the airline in Derald Wing Sue's piece — help to address our current systems of racial bias? What types of training or guidelines would help employees to better interact with the public? Might this be more difficult in some industries than in others?

6. **Writing with Sources.** Write a letter to your state or local representative with suggestions for raising public awareness of institutional racism. Use information and arguments from the three essays in this cluster as well as articles and books you find on the Internet and in the library to help build a case for why this is necessary. For models of and advice on integrating sources in your essay, see Chapters 14 and 15.

7. In the following cluster, authors Greg Lukianoff and Jonathan Haidt argue strongly against concepts such as microaggressions. Read their essay on the topic and evaluate each piece in terms of its effectiveness. Do you find one reading more convincing than another? Why or why not?

8. **Writing with Sources.** Do some research online or in your school library about racially motivated violence, such as the riots in Ferguson, Missouri, mentioned in J. Dowsett's piece. Have there been more of these incidents in the past five years than in prior decades, or have there been fewer? Do you think such incidents may have been prompted, in some way, by the more subtle forms of racism addressed in this chapter? Why or why not? Be sure to cite specific examples and integrate material from your sources. For models of and advice on integrating sources in your essay, see Chapters 14 and 15.

ARGUMENT CLUSTER

Getting an Education: What's the Line between Comfort and Learning?

The free speech movement first began on a college campus in the 1960s, when students gathered to protest at the University of California–Berkeley. After the school placed a ban on certain public political displays, students staged a sit-in and, although the event was peaceful, nearly 800 students were arrested. The conversations that this movement started—conversations about what is acceptable and what is offensive, what is done in the name of learning and what is hurtful to both students and instructors—have continued to grow and spread, bringing us to the most recent manifestation of the debate: What is the line between comfort and learning?

As you'll see from the readings in this chapter, this is a contentious question, one that has moved beyond the bounds of colleges and universities into workplaces, religious creeds, and even the science used to study our brains and how we use them. Jeffrey Zaslow, in his piece "The Compliment Complex," points out the scarcity of praise that previous generations received in the workplace; as one professional put it, "If you weren't getting yelled at, you felt like that was praise." Today, many major companies, including Bank of America and Hallmark, dedicate significant resources to training managers to provide the positive reinforcement they feel the younger generation needs. This praise is often given whether it is earned or not, leading to resentment from older colleagues and diminished potential for improvement. Lack of growth is also a concern for educators who see a similar need for continual praise of their students.

On many campuses, demands are being made to create "safe spaces" and remove students from the possibility of facing mental or emotional discomfort. "Trigger warnings" are meant to prevent a student from accidentally stumbling across content that might cause them to have painful flashbacks or experience traumatic emotions. Critics worry that these measures will make students close-minded and give them excuses for not stepping outside their comfort zones or facing difficult but important issues. How, they ask, can our society address serious social evils if we are not even willing to learn about them? Advocates of trigger warnings seek to protect students who may already have experienced trauma and to prevent other students from facing the many racist, homophobic, or otherwise offensive elements of much of the educational canon. These include instances of sexual violence in literature and discussions of social philosophy written by known anti-Semites.

The authors in this cluster approach the question from three separate angles. Jeffrey Zaslow's "The Compliment Complex" opens the discussion by exploring the impact of excessive compliments in the workplace and how the emotional needs of a generation are redefining corporate structures. Next, in "On the Subject of Trigger Warnings," teaching assistant Siobhan Crowley questions whether students will miss out on critical material in their efforts to avoid triggers and offers her classroom as a place for working through traumatic experiences in a safe environment.

Finally, Greg Lukianoff, the president and CEO of the Foundation for Individual Rights in Education, joined up with Jonathan Haidt, a professor and social psychologist, to examine the issue from a health perspective, identifying "common cognitive disorders" in the current movement for safe spaces and trigger warnings at colleges. These authors warn that colleges and universities need to tone down on outrage and recommit to "follow[ing] truth wherever it may lead."

Preparing to Read

You may disagree with some, or even all, of the writers in this cluster, but the questions they raise are fundamental ones. What is free speech, and what is hate speech? Who gets to make the decision about which is which? Are some forms of discomfort or trauma healing necessary, or should students be protected from ideas that conflict with their foundational beliefs? Where do we draw the line?

The Compliment Complex

JEFFREY ZASLOW

Jeffrey Zaslow (1958–2012) was a bestselling author and columnist. He graduated from Carnegie Mellon with a degree in creative writing in 1980. Zaslow began as a journalist at the *Wall Street Journal* in 1983 and replaced Ann Landers at the *Chicago Sun-Times* in 1987. In 2008, he received the Distinguished Column Writing Award from the New York Newspaper Publishers Association and published the book he is best known for, *The Last Lecture*, which he co-authored with Carnegie Mellon professor Randy Pausch. His other books include *The Girls from Ames* (2009), *Gabby: A Story of Courage and Hope* (2011), and *The Magi Room: A Story about the Love We Wish for Our Daughters* (2012). Zaslow was killed in a car accident in 2012.

Steve Kagan/The LIFE Images Collection/Getty Images

This essay first appeared as a column in the *Wall Street Journal* in April 2007. In it, Zaslow points out the flaws in "the culture of praise" that has sprung up in America. This "praise inflation," he worries, has created a culture that needs "instant feedback" that is detrimental to work and doesn't make anyone any happier.

You, You, You—you really are special, you are! You've got everything going for you. You're attractive, witty, brilliant. "Gifted" is the word that comes to mind.

Childhood in recent decades has been defined by such stroking—by parents who see their job as building self-esteem, by soccer coaches who give every player a trophy, by schools that used to name one "student of the month" and these days name 40.

Now, as this greatest generation grows up, the culture of praise is reaching deeply into the adult world. Bosses, professors and mates are feeling the need to lavish praise on young adults, particularly twenty-somethings, or else see them wither under an unfamiliar compliment deficit.

Employers are dishing out kudos to workers for little more than showing up. Corporations including Lands' End and Bank of America are hiring consultants to teach managers how to compliment employees using email, prize packages and public displays of appreciation. The 1,000-employee Scooter Store Inc., a power-wheelchair and scooter firm in New Braunfels, Texas, has a staff "celebrations assistant" whose job it is to throw confetti—25 pounds a week—at employees. She also passes out 100 to 500 celebratory helium balloons a week. The Container Store, Inc. estimates that one of its 4,000 employees receives praise every 20 seconds, through such efforts as its "Celebration Voice Mailboxes."

Certainly, there are benefits to building confidence and showing attention. But some researchers suggest that inappropriate kudos are turning too many adults into narcissistic praise-junkies. The upshot: A lot of today's young adults feel insecure if they're not regularly complimented.

America's praise fixation has economic, labor and social ramifications. Adults who were overpraised as children are apt to be narcissistic at work and in personal relationships, says Jean Twenge, a psychology professor at San Diego State University. Narcissists aren't good at basking in other people's glory, which makes for problematic marriages and work relationships, she says.

Her research suggests that young adults today are more self-centered than previous generations. For a multiuniversity study released this year, 16,475 college students took the standardized narcissistic personality inventory, responding to such statements as "I think I am a special person." Students' scores have risen steadily since the test was first offered in 1982. The average college student in 2006 was 30% more narcissistic than the average student in 1982.

PRAISE INFLATION

Employers say the praise culture can help them with job retention, and marriage counselors say couples often benefit by keeping praise a constant part of their interactions. But in the process, people's positive traits can be exaggerated until the words feel meaningless. "There's a runaway inflation of everyday speech," warns Linda Sapadin, a psychologist in Valley Stream, N.Y. These days, she says, it's an insult unless you describe a pretty girl as "drop-dead gorgeous" or a smart person as "a genius." "And no one wants to be told they live in a nice house," says Dr. Sapadin. "'Nice' was once sufficient. That was a good word. Now it's a put-down."

The Gottman Institute, a relationship-research and training firm in Seattle, tells clients that a key to marital happiness is if couples make at least five times as many positive statements to and about each other as negative ones. Meanwhile, products are being marketed to help families make praise a part of their daily routines. For $32.95, families can buy the "You Are Special Today Red Plate," and then select one worthy person each meal to eat off the dish.

But many young married people today, who grew up being told regularly that they were special, can end up distrusting compliments from their spouses. Judy Neary, a relationship therapist in Alexandria, Va., says it's common for her clients to say things like: "I tell her she's beautiful all the time, and she doesn't believe it." Ms. Neary suspects: "There's a lot of insecurity, with people wondering, 'Is it really true?'"

"Young married people who've been very praised in their childhoods, particularly, need praise to both their child side and their adult side," adds Dolores Walker, a psychotherapist and attorney specializing in divorce mediation in New York.

Employers are finding ways to adjust. Sure, there are still plenty of surly managers who offer little or no positive feedback, but many withholders are now joining America's praise parade to hold on to young workers. They're being taught by employee-retention consultants such as Mark Holmes, who encourages employers to give away baseball bats with engravings ("Thanks for a home-run job") or to write notes to employees' kids ("Thanks for letting dad work here. He's terrific!")

Bob Nelson, billed as "the Guru of Thank You," counsels 80 to 100 companies a year on praise issues. He has done presentations for managers of companies such as Walt Disney Co. and Hallmark Cards, Inc., explaining how different generations have different expectations. As he sees it, those over age 60 tend to like formal awards, presented publicly. But they're more laid back about needing praise, and more apt to say: "Yes, I get recognition every week. It's called a paycheck." Baby boomers, Mr. Nelson finds, often prefer being praised with more self-indulgent treats such as free massages for women and high-tech gadgets for men.

Workers under 40, he says, require far more stroking. They often like "trendy, name-brand merchandise" as rewards, but they also want near-constant feedback. "It's not enough to give praise only when they're exceptional, because for years they've been getting praise just for showing up," he says.

Mr. Nelson advises bosses: If a young worker has been chronically late for work and then starts arriving on time, commend him. "You need to recognize improvement. That might seem silly to older generations, but today, you have to do these things to get the performances you want," he says. Casey Priest, marketing vice president for Container Store, agrees. "When you set an expectation and an employee starts to meet it, absolutely praise them for it," she says.

Sixty-year-old David Foster, a partner at Washington, D.C., law firm Miller & Chevalier, is making greater efforts to compliment young associates—to tell them they're talented, hard-working and valued. It's not a natural impulse for him. When he was a young lawyer, he says, "If you weren't getting yelled at, you felt like that was praise."

But at a retreat a couple of years ago, the firm's 120 lawyers reached an understanding. Younger associates complained that they were frustrated; after working hard on a brief and handing it in, they'd receive no praise. The partners promised to improve "intergenerational communication." Mr. Foster says he feels for younger associates, given their upbringings. "When they're not getting feedback, it makes them very nervous."

MODERN PRESSURES

Some younger lawyers are able to articulate the dynamics behind this. "When we were young, we were motivated by being told we could do anything if we believed in ourselves. So we respond well to positive feedback," explains 34-year-old Karin Crump, president of the 25,000-member Texas Young Lawyers Association.

Scott Atwood, president-elect of the Young Lawyers Division of the Florida Bar, argues that the yearning for positive input from superiors is more likely due to heightened pressure to perform in today's demanding firms. "It has created a culture where you have to have instant feedback or you'll fail," he says.

In fact, throughout history, younger generations have wanted praise from their elders. As Napoleon said: "A soldier will fight long and hard for a bit of colored ribbon." But when it comes to praise today, "Gen Xers and Gen Yers don't just say they want it. They are also saying they require it," says Chip Toth, an executive coach based in Denver. How do young workers say they're not getting enough? "They leave," says Mr. Toth.

Many companies are proud of their creative praise programs. Since 2004, the 4,100-employee Bronson Healthcare Group in Kalamazoo, Mich., has required all of its managers to write at least 48 thank-you or praise notes to underlings every year.

Universal Studios Orlando, with 13,000 employees, has a program in which managers give out "Applause Notes," praising employees for work well done. Universal workers can also give each other peer-to-peer "S.A.Y. It!" cards, which stand for "Someone Appreciates You!" The notes are redeemed for free movie tickets or other gifts.

Bank of America has several formal rewards programs for its 200,000 employees, allowing those who receive praise to select from 2,000 gifts. "We also encourage managers to start every meeting with informal recognition," says Kevin Cronin, senior vice president of recognition and rewards. The company strives to be sensitive. When new employees are hired, managers are instructed to get a sense of how they like to be praised.

"Some prefer it in public, some like it one-on-one in an office," says Mr. Cronin.

NO MORE RED PENS

Some young adults are consciously calibrating their dependence on praise. In New York, Web-developer Mia Eaton, 32, admits that she loves being complimented. But she feels like she's living on the border between a twentysomething generation that requires overpraise and a thirtysomething generation that is less addicted to it. She recalls the pre-Paris Hilton, pre-reality-TV era, when people were famous—and applauded—for their achievements, she says. When she tries to explain this to younger colleagues, "they don't get it. I feel like I'm hurting their feelings because they don't understand the difference."

Young adults aren't always eager for clear-eyed feedback after getting mostly "atta-boys" and "atta-girls" all their lives, says John Sloop, a professor of rhetorical and cultural studies at Vanderbilt University. Another issue: To win tenure, professors often need to receive positive evaluations from students. So if professors want students to like them, "to a large extent, critical comments [of students] have to be couched in praise," Prof. Sloop says. He has attended seminars designed to help professors learn techniques of supportive criticism. "We were told to throw away our red pens so we don't intimidate students."

At the Wharton School of the University of Pennsylvania, marketing consultant Steve Smolinsky teaches students in their late 20s who've left the corporate world to get M.B.A. degrees. He and his colleagues feel handcuffed by the language of self-esteem, he says. "You have to tell students, 'It's not as good as you can do. You're really smart, and can do better.'"

Mr. Smolinsky enjoys giving praise when it's warranted, he says, "but there needs to be a flip side. When people are lousy, they need to be told that." He notices that his students often disregard his harsher comments. "They'll say, 'Yeah, well . . .' I don't believe they really hear it."

In the end, ego-stroking may feel good, but it doesn't lead to happiness, says Prof. Twenge, the narcissism researcher, who has written a book titled "Generation Me: Why Today's Young Americans Are More Confident, Assertive, Entitled—and More Miserable than Ever Before." She would like to declare a moratorium on "meaningless, baseless praise," which often starts in nursery school. She is unimpressed with self-esteem preschool ditties, such as the one set to the tune of "Frère Jacques": "I am special/I am special/ Look at me . . ."

For now, companies like the Scooter Store continue handing out the helium balloons. Katie Lynch, 22, is the firm's "celebrations assistant," charged with throwing confetti, filling balloons and showing up at employees' desks to offer high-fives. "They all love it," she says, especially younger workers who "seem to need that pat on the back. They don't want to go unnoticed."

Ms. Lynch also has an urge to be praised. At the end of a long, hard day of celebrating others, she says she appreciates when her manager, Burton De La Garza, gives her a high-five or compliments her with a cell-phone text message.

"I'll just text her a quick note—'you were phenomenal today,'" says Mr. De La Garza, "She thrives on that. We wanted to find what works for her, because she's completely averse to confetti."

Thinking Critically about the Text

Zaslow shines a light on a cultural shift toward excessive compliments, arguing that they created a high-pressure, low-achievement culture. Is it concerning that it is contrasted with a culture where "if you weren't getting yelled at, you felt like that was praise"? Why do you think Zaslow presents two extremes?

Examining the Issue

1. What is Zaslow's thesis? Where does he state it?
2. How effective is Zaslow in describing the ways in which excessive compliments are becoming normal in the workplace? How does he use illustration to build his case?
3. Why does Zaslow see excessive compliments as a generational issue?
4. In paragraph 15 Zaslow quotes Bob Nelson as saying, "You need to recognize improvement." Why does Zaslow seem to find this unreasonable in the larger context?
5. Why does Zaslow think that excessive praise creates "heightened pressure" (paragraph 19)?
6. What academic concern does Zaslow point out in paragraph 25? Why is this a problem?
7. Zaslow concludes by quoting De La Garza. What is the irony inherent in saying that the "celebrations assistant" is "completely averse to confetti" (31)? (Glossary: *Irony*)

On the Subject of Trigger Warnings

SIOBHAN CROWLEY

Siobhan Crowley is a teaching assistant who has requested that her school remain anonymous. She is currently pursuing her Master's in English literature and teaches first-year writing and literature. She grew up in rural Missouri.

The essay below was written in response to a call for writing on the topic of education and safe spaces. In it, Crowley expresses her mixed feelings about avoiding triggering issues in her own classroom.

A college president at a Midwestern school recently took issue with the idea of "triggers" and "safe zones." He remarked vividly that his school "is not a daycare. [It] is a university." While I can appreciate the snarkiness of his comments, and the frustration with yet another roadblock to effectively teaching students, I have to disagree with his stance that there is anything infantile about dealing with triggering experiences. The trauma involved can be very real, and I think student concerns need to be met with serious reflection. I have concerns, however, over whether they can be met with equally serious action, if not for the reasons that a certain president mentions.

Let's start with the easy part of the argument: If a student has experiences that impede their ability to approach certain subject matter, then allowances absolutely need to be made. Alternative assignments might be created, for instance, or a student might be excused from multiple class sessions. Final tests might be adapted for the one or two students who have come privately to express their inability to address certain topics.

From there, however, the question gets more difficult. Let's say you study literature. Or sociology. And you can't read certain selections because the idea of imperialism or slavery is a trigger for you. Or the concept of sexual assault is a trigger for you. So you don't study *Huckleberry Finn* or *Othello* or read Marx or chunks of Weber. And then you go out into the world to use your degree and you have these glaring blind spots. You won't have been prepared adequately in the field you said you studied. Let's say you want to be a teacher (as many TAs in English go on to do). Are you going to *not* teach *Romeo and Juliet* because someone in your family committed suicide? Or not teach *Huck Finn* because you can't address the issue of race? That would be a criminal neglect to students who need to learn this material, if only so that they can address *exactly these issues*. Will your papers ever be accepted in a sociological journal if you skip obvious references to canon theorists?

I appreciate the validity of trigger-warnings and other accommodations as a theory, but I think that they can only apply to non-major courses. Someone majoring in math certainly doesn't need to know *Othello* (though they might benefit from doing so). But someone who majors in English really ought to. Not even *Othello* specifically, but you just can't get away from race or sexual violence, or suicide, or any triggering issue in literature because these are the very meat of what authors are trying to address.

The other concern, of course, is that great literature is great *because* it tackles these painful topics. *Beloved* and *Sula* were difficult books to read, but there is power in tapping into that artistic expression of pain. Power that I worry my students will need when they leave school behind and enter a culture that does not make the allowances that college professors can make. A world full of triggering episodes. I would hate for students to miss an opportunity to work through their trauma in my classroom, where I can mediate discussions to ensure that comments are not hurtful. Particularly if that student makes me aware of their fears and I can work with them in conjunction with a university counselor. There is so much to be gained from the study of literature, including the ability to address and mediate the very triggering issues that students want to avoid. It makes me sad to think that students will blindly turn away from that power and that opportunity. Even for the very best of reasons.

Thinking Critically about the Text

This message was written by a graduate student and teaching assistant at a four-year college. How do you think Crowley's teaching experience has influenced her stance on trigger warnings? Do you think that experience strengthens or undermines her perspective?

Examining the Issue

1. What is Crowley's thesis? (Glossary: *Thesis*) Where is it stated?

2. Crowley identifies two central concerns with not teaching triggering content. What are they?

3. On the basis of what authority does Crowley make her argument? Does her position make you more or less likely to be convinced by her argument?

4. What distinction does Crowley make between majors and non-majors? Why is it important to her argument?

5. In paragraph 5, Crowley mentions the "power in tapping into artistic expressions of pain." What do you think that power might be? Do you agree with Crowley that it exists?

6. In paragraph 4, Crowley mentions that a math major does not need to understand *Othello* to pursue their degree. Why might triggering topics be less likely to occur in some subjects than others? Can you think of any other majors where triggers are unlikely to be a concern? What majors might be particularly problematic?

7. How effective is the author's conclusion?

The Coddling of the American Mind

GREG LUKIANOFF AND JONATHAN HAIDT

Greg Lukianoff received his law degree from Stanford Law School and was a practicing lawyer in California before joining the Foundation for Individual Rights in Education, of which he is the president and CEO. He has been published extensively, including in the *Wall Street Journal*, the *New York Times*, *Time*, and *Forbes*. He is frequently a guest on a variety of news programs, including C-SPAN's *Washington Journal* and NBC's *Today Show*.

Jonathan Haidt received his Ph.D. in psychology from the University of Pennsylvania before working as a professor at the University of Virginia. He has written a number of books, including *The Happiness Hypothesis: Finding Modern Truth in Ancient Wisdom* (2009) and *The Righteous Mind: Why Good People Are Divided by Politics and Religion* (2012). He is currently the Thomas Cooley professor of ethical leadership at the NYU-Stern School of Business.

In the article below, Lukianoff and Haidt explain the dangers they see in trigger warnings and the rise of initiatives to protect the emotional well-being of students on college campuses. These initiatives, they feel, are harmful both to education and to mental health.

Something strange is happening at America's colleges and universities. A movement is arising, undirected and driven largely by students, to scrub campuses clean of words, ideas, and subjects that might cause discomfort or give offense. Last December, Jeannie Suk wrote in an online article for *The New Yorker* about law students asking her fellow professors at Harvard not to teach rape law—or, in one case, even use the word *violate* (as in "that violates the law") lest it cause students distress. In February, Laura Kipnis, a professor at Northwestern University, wrote an essay in *The Chronicle of Higher Education* describing a new campus politics of sexual paranoia—and was then subjected to a long investigation after students who were offended by the article and by a tweet she'd sent filed Title IX complaints against her. In June, a professor protecting himself with a pseudonym wrote an essay for Vox describing how gingerly he now has to teach. "I'm a Liberal Professor, and My Liberal Students Terrify Me," the headline said. A number of popular comedians, including Chris Rock, have stopped performing on college campuses. Jerry Seinfeld and Bill Maher have publicly condemned the oversensitivity of college students, saying too many of them can't take a joke.

Two terms have risen quickly from obscurity into common campus parlance. *Microaggressions* are small actions or word choices that seem on their face to have no malicious intent but that are thought of as a kind of violence nonetheless. For example, by some campus guidelines, it is a microaggression to ask an Asian American or Latino American "Where were you born?," because this implies that he or she is not a real American. *Trigger warnings* are alerts that professors are expected to issue if something in a course might cause a strong emotional response. For example, some students have called for warnings that Chinua Achebe's *Things Fall Apart* describes racial violence and that F. Scott Fitzgerald's *The Great Gatsby* portrays misogyny and physical abuse, so that students who have been previously victimized by racism or domestic violence can choose to avoid these works, which they believe might "trigger" a recurrence of past trauma.

Some recent campus actions border on the surreal. In April, at Brandeis University, the Asian American student association sought to raise awareness of microaggressions against Asians through an installation on the steps of an academic hall. The installation gave examples of microaggressions such as "Aren't you supposed to be good at math?" and "I'm colorblind! I don't see race." But a backlash arose among other Asian American students, who felt that the display itself was a microaggression. The association removed the installation, and its president wrote an e-mail to the entire student body apologizing to anyone who was "triggered or hurt by the content of the microaggressions."

This new climate is slowly being institutionalized, and is affecting what can be said in the classroom, even as a basis for discussion. During the 2014–15 school year, for instance, the deans and department chairs at the 10 University of California system schools were presented by administrators at faculty leader-training sessions with examples of microaggressions. The list of offensive statements included: "America is the land of opportunity" and "I believe the most qualified person should get the job."

The press has typically described these developments as a resurgence of political correctness. That's partly right, although there are important differences between what's happening now and what happened in the 1980s and '90s. That movement sought to restrict speech (specifically hate speech aimed at marginalized groups), but it also challenged the literary, philosophical, and historical canon, seeking to widen it by including more-diverse perspectives. The current movement is largely about emotional well-being. More than the last, it presumes an extraordinary fragility of the collegiate psyche, and therefore elevates the goal of protecting students from psychological harm. The ultimate aim, it seems, is to turn campuses into "safe spaces" where young adults are shielded from words and ideas that make some uncomfortable. And more than the last, this movement seeks to punish anyone who interferes with that aim, even accidentally. You might call this impulse *vindictive protectiveness.* It is creating a culture in which everyone must think twice before speaking up, lest they face charges of insensitivity, aggression, or worse.

We have been studying this development for a while now, with rising alarm. (Greg Lukianoff is a constitutional lawyer and the president and CEO of the Foundation for Individual Rights in Education, which defends free speech and academic freedom on campus, and has advocated for students and faculty involved in many of the incidents this article describes; Jonathan Haidt is a social psychologist who studies the American culture wars.) The dangers that these trends pose to scholarship and to the quality of American universities are significant; we could write a whole essay detailing them. But in this essay we focus on a different question: What are the effects of this new protectiveness *on the students themselves*? Does it benefit the people it is supposed to help? What exactly are students learning when they spend four years or more in a community that polices unintentional slights, places warning labels on works of classic literature, and in many other ways conveys the sense that words can be forms of violence that require strict control by campus authorities, who are expected to act as both protectors and prosecutors?

There's a saying common in education circles: Don't teach students *what* to think; teach them *how* to think. The idea goes back at least as far as Socrates. Today, what we call the Socratic method is a way of teaching that fosters critical thinking, in part by encouraging students to question their own unexamined beliefs, as well as the received wisdom of those around them. Such questioning sometimes leads to discomfort, and even to anger, on the way to understanding.

But vindictive protectiveness teaches students to think in a very different way. It prepares them poorly for professional life, which often demands intellectual engagement with people and ideas one might find uncongenial or wrong. The harm may be more immediate, too. A campus culture devoted to policing speech and punishing speakers is likely to engender patterns of thought that are surprisingly similar to those long identified by cognitive behavioral therapists as causes of depression and anxiety. The new protectiveness may be teaching students to think pathologically.

HOW DID WE GET HERE?

It's difficult to know exactly why vindictive protectiveness has burst forth so powerfully in the past few years. The phenomenon may be related to recent changes in the interpretation of federal antidiscrimination statutes (about which more later). But the answer probably involves generational shifts as well. Childhood itself has changed greatly during the past generation. Many Baby Boomers and Gen Xers can remember riding their bicycles around their hometowns, unchaperoned by adults, by the time they were 8 or 9 years old. In the hours after school, kids were expected to occupy themselves, getting into minor scrapes and learning from their experiences. But "free range" childhood became less common in the 1980s. The surge in crime from the '60s through the early '90s made Baby Boomer parents more protective than their own parents had been. Stories of abducted children appeared more frequently in the news, and in 1984, images of them began showing up on milk cartons. In response, many parents pulled in the reins and worked harder to keep their children safe.

The flight to safety also happened at school. Dangerous play structures were removed from playgrounds; peanut butter was banned from student lunches. After the 1999 Columbine massacre in Colorado, many schools cracked down on bullying, implementing "zero tolerance" policies. In a variety of ways, children born after 1980—the Millennials—got a consistent message from adults: life is dangerous, but adults will do everything in their power to protect you from harm, not just from strangers but from one another as well.

These same children grew up in a culture that was (and still is) becoming more politically polarized. Republicans and Democrats have never particularly liked each other, but survey data going back to the 1970s show that on average, their mutual dislike used to be surprisingly mild. Negative feelings have grown steadily stronger, however, particularly since the early 2000s. Political scientists call this process "affective partisan polarization," and it is a very serious problem for any democracy. As each side increasingly demonizes the other, compromise becomes more difficult. A recent study shows that implicit or unconscious biases are now at least as strong across political parties as they are across races.

So it's not hard to imagine why students arriving on campus today might be more desirous of protection and more hostile toward ideological opponents than in generations past. This hostility, and the self-righteousness fueled by strong partisan emotions, can be expected to add force to any moral crusade. A principle of moral psychology is that "morality binds and blinds." Part of what we do when we make moral judgments is express allegiance to a team. But that can interfere with our ability to think critically. Acknowledging that the other side's viewpoint has any merit is risky — your teammates may see you as a traitor.

Social media makes it extraordinarily easy to join crusades, express solidarity and outrage, and shun traitors. Facebook was founded in 2004, and since 2006 it has allowed children as young as 13 to join. This means that the first wave of students who spent all their teen years using Facebook reached college in 2011, and graduated from college only this year.

These first true "social-media natives" may be different from members of previous generations in how they go about sharing their moral judgments and supporting one another in moral campaigns and conflicts. We find much to like about these trends; young people today are engaged with one another, with news stories, and with prosocial endeavors to a greater degree than when the dominant technology was television. But social media has also fundamentally shifted the balance of power in relationships between students and faculty; the latter increasingly fear what students might do to their reputations and careers by stirring up online mobs against them.

We do not mean to imply simple causation, but rates of mental illness in young adults have been rising, both on campus and off, in recent decades. Some portion of the increase is surely due to better diagnosis and greater willingness to seek help, but most experts seem to agree that some portion of the trend is real. Nearly all of the campus mental-health directors surveyed in 2013 by the American College Counseling Association reported that the number of students with severe psychological problems was rising at their schools. The rate of emotional distress reported by students themselves is also high, and rising. In a 2014 survey by the American College Health Association, 54 percent of college students surveyed said that they had "felt overwhelming anxiety" in the past 12 months, up from 49 percent in the same survey just five years earlier. Students seem to be reporting more emotional crises; many seem fragile, and this has surely changed the way university faculty and administrators interact with them. The question is whether some of those changes might be doing more harm than good.

THE THINKING CURE

For millennia, philosophers have understood that we don't see life as it is; we see a version distorted by our hopes, fears, and other attachments. The Buddha said, "Our life is the creation of our mind." Marcus Aurelius said, "Life itself is but what you deem it." The quest for wisdom in many traditions begins with this insight. Early Buddhists and the Stoics, for example, developed practices for reducing attachments, thinking more clearly, and finding release from the emotional torments of normal mental life.

Cognitive behavioral therapy is a modern embodiment of this ancient wisdom. It is the most extensively studied nonpharmaceutical treatment of mental illness, and is used widely to treat depression, anxiety disorders, eating disorders, and addiction. It can even be of help to schizophrenics. No other form of psychotherapy has been shown to work for a broader range of problems. Studies have generally found that it is as effective as antidepressant drugs (such as Prozac) in the treatment of anxiety and depression. The therapy is relatively quick and easy to learn; after a few months of training, many patients can do it on their own. Unlike drugs, cognitive behavioral therapy keeps working long after treatment is stopped, because it teaches thinking skills that people can continue to use.

The goal is to minimize distorted thinking and see the world more accurately. You start by learning the names of the dozen or so most common cognitive distortions (such as overgeneralizing, discounting positives, and emotional reasoning). Each time you notice yourself falling prey to one of them, you name it, describe the facts of the situation, consider alternative interpretations, and then choose an interpretation of events more in line with those facts. Your emotions follow your new interpretation. In time, this process becomes automatic. When people improve their mental hygiene in this way—when they free themselves from the repetitive irrational thoughts that had previously filled so much of their consciousness—they become less depressed, anxious, and angry.

The parallel to formal education is clear: cognitive behavioral therapy teaches good critical-thinking skills, the sort that educators have striven for so long to impart. By almost any definition, critical thinking requires grounding one's beliefs in evidence rather than in emotion or desire, and learning how to search for and evaluate evidence that might contradict one's initial hypothesis. But does campus life today foster critical thinking? Or does it coax students to think in more-distorted ways?

Let's look at recent trends in higher education in light of the distortions that cognitive behavioral therapy identifies. We will draw the names and descriptions of these distortions from David D. Burns's popular book *Feeling Good*, as well as from the second edition of *Treatment Plans and Interventions for Depression and Anxiety Disorders*, by Robert L. Leahy, Stephen J. F. Holland, and Lata K. McGinn.

HIGHER EDUCATION'S EMBRACE OF "EMOTIONAL REASONING"

Burns defines *emotional reasoning* as assuming "that your negative emotions necessarily reflect the way things really are: 'I feel it, therefore it must be true.'" Leahy, Holland, and McGinn define it as letting "your feelings guide your interpretation of reality." But, of course, subjective feelings are not always trustworthy guides; unrestrained, they can cause people to lash out at others who have done nothing wrong. Therapy often involves talking yourself down from the idea that each of your emotional responses represents something true or important.

Emotional reasoning dominates many campus debates and discussions. A claim that someone's words are "offensive" is not just an expression of one's own subjective feeling of offendedness. It is, rather, a public charge that the speaker has done something objectively wrong. It is a demand that the speaker apologize or be punished by some authority for committing an offense.

There have always been some people who believe they have a right not to be offended. Yet throughout American history—from the Victorian era to the free-speech activism of the 1960s and '70s—radicals have pushed boundaries and mocked prevailing sensibilities. Sometime in the 1980s, however, college campuses began to focus on preventing offensive speech, especially speech that might be hurtful to women or minority groups. The sentiment underpinning this goal was laudable, but it quickly produced some absurd results.

Among the most famous early examples was the so-called water-buffalo incident at the University of Pennsylvania. In 1993, the university charged an Israeli-born student with racial harassment after he yelled "Shut up, you water buffalo!" to a crowd of black sorority women that was making noise at night outside his dorm-room window. Many scholars and pundits at the time could not see how the term *water buffalo* (a rough translation of a Hebrew insult for a thoughtless or rowdy person) was a racial slur against African Americans, and as a result, the case became international news.

Claims of a right not to be offended have continued to arise since then, and universities have continued to privilege them. In a particularly egregious 2008 case, for instance, Indiana University–Purdue University at Indianapolis found a white student guilty of racial harassment for reading a book titled *Notre Dame vs. the Klan*. The book honored student opposition to the Ku Klux Klan when it marched on Notre Dame in 1924. Nonetheless, the picture of a Klan rally on the book's cover offended at least one of the student's co-workers (he was a janitor as well as a student), and that was enough for a guilty finding by the university's Affirmative Action Office.

These examples may seem extreme, but the reasoning behind them has become more commonplace on campus in recent years. Last year, at the University of St. Thomas, in Minnesota, an event called Hump Day, which would have allowed people to pet a camel, was abruptly canceled.

Students had created a Facebook group where they protested the event for animal cruelty, for being a waste of money, and for being insensitive to people from the Middle East. The inspiration for the camel had almost certainly come from a popular TV commercial in which a camel saunters around an office on a Wednesday, celebrating "hump day"; it was devoid of any reference to Middle Eastern peoples. Nevertheless, the group organizing the event announced on its Facebook page that the event would be canceled because the "program [was] dividing people and would make for an uncomfortable and possibly unsafe environment."

Because there is a broad ban in academic circles on "blaming the victim," it is generally considered unacceptable to question the reasonableness (let alone the sincerity) of someone's emotional state, particularly if those emotions are linked to one's group identity. The thin argument "I'm offended" becomes an unbeatable trump card. This leads to what Jonathan Rauch, a contributing editor at this magazine, calls the "offendedness sweepstakes," in which opposing parties use claims of offense as cudgels. In the process, the bar for what we consider unacceptable speech is lowered further and further.

Since 2013, new pressure from the federal government has reinforced this trend. Federal antidiscrimination statutes regulate on-campus harassment and unequal treatment based on sex, race, religion, and national origin. Until recently, the Department of Education's Office for Civil Rights acknowledged that speech must be "objectively offensive" before it could be deemed actionable as sexual harassment—it would have to pass the "reasonable person" test. To be prohibited, the office wrote in 2003, allegedly harassing speech would have to go "beyond the mere expression of views, words, symbols or thoughts that some person finds offensive."

But in 2013, the Departments of Justice and Education greatly broadened the definition of sexual harassment to include verbal conduct that is simply "unwelcome." Out of fear of federal investigations, universities are now applying that standard—defining unwelcome speech as harassment—not just to sex, but to race, religion, and veteran status as well. Everyone is supposed to rely upon his or her own subjective feelings to decide whether a comment by a professor or a fellow student is unwelcome, and therefore grounds for a harassment claim. Emotional reasoning is now accepted as evidence.

If our universities are teaching students that their emotions can be used effectively as weapons—or at least as evidence in administrative proceedings—then they are teaching students to nurture a kind of hypersensitivity that will lead them into countless drawn-out conflicts in college and beyond. Schools may be training students in thinking styles that will damage their careers and friendships, along with their mental health.

FORTUNE-TELLING AND TRIGGER WARNINGS

Burns defines *fortune-telling* as "anticipat[ing] that things will turn out badly" and feeling "convinced that your prediction is an already-established fact." Leahy, Holland, and McGinn define it as "predict[ing] the future negatively" or seeing potential danger in an everyday situation. The recent spread of demands for trigger warnings on reading assignments with provocative content is an example of fortune-telling.

The idea that words (or smells or any sensory input) can trigger searing memories of past trauma—and intense fear that it may be repeated—has been around at least since World War I, when psychiatrists began treating soldiers for what is now called post-traumatic stress disorder. But explicit trigger warnings are believed to have originated much more recently, on message boards in the early days of the Internet. Trigger warnings became particularly prevalent in self-help and feminist forums, where they allowed readers who had suffered from traumatic events like sexual assault to avoid graphic content that might trigger flashbacks or panic attacks. Search-engine trends indicate that the phrase broke into mainstream use online around 2011, spiked in 2014, and reached an all-time high in 2015. The use of trigger warnings on campus appears to have followed a similar trajectory; seemingly overnight, students at universities across the country have begun demanding that their professors issue warnings before covering material that might evoke a negative emotional response.

In 2013, a task force composed of administrators, students, recent alumni, and one faculty member at Oberlin College, in Ohio, released an online resource guide for faculty (subsequently retracted in the face of faculty pushback) that included a list of topics warranting trigger warnings. These topics included classism and privilege, among many others. The task force recommended that materials that might trigger negative reactions among students be avoided altogether unless they "contribute directly" to course goals, and suggested that works that were "too important to avoid" be made optional.

It's hard to imagine how novels illustrating classism and privilege could provoke or reactivate the kind of terror that is typically implicated in PTSD. Rather, trigger warnings are sometimes demanded for a long list of ideas and attitudes that some students find politically offensive, in the name of preventing other students from being harmed. This is an example of what psychologists call "motivated reasoning"—we spontaneously generate arguments for conclusions we want to support. Once *you* find something hateful, it is easy to argue that exposure to the hateful thing could traumatize some *other* people. You believe that you know how others will react, and that their reaction could be devastating. Preventing that devastation becomes a moral obligation for the whole community. Books for which students have called publicly for trigger warnings within the past couple of years include Virginia Woolf's *Mrs. Dalloway* (at Rutgers, for "suicidal inclinations") and Ovid's *Metamorphoses* (at Columbia, for sexual assault).

Jeannie Suk's *New Yorker* essay described the difficulties of teaching rape law in the age of trigger warnings. Some students, she wrote, have pressured their professors to avoid teaching the subject in order to protect themselves and their classmates from potential distress. Suk compares this to trying to teach "a medical student who is training to be a surgeon but who fears that he'll become distressed if he sees or handles blood."

However, there is a deeper problem with trigger warnings. According to the most-basic tenets of psychology, the very idea of helping people with anxiety disorders avoid the things they fear is misguided. A person who is trapped in an elevator during a power outage may panic and think she is going to die. That frightening experience can change neural connections in her amygdala, leading to an elevator phobia. If you want this woman to retain her fear for life, you should help her avoid elevators.

But if you want to help her return to normalcy, you should take your cues from Ivan Pavlov and guide her through a process known as exposure therapy. You might start by asking the woman to merely look at an elevator from a distance—standing in a building lobby, perhaps—until her apprehension begins to subside. If nothing bad happens while she's standing in the lobby—if the fear is not "reinforced"—then she will begin to learn a new association: elevators are not dangerous. (This reduction in fear during exposure is called habituation.) Then, on subsequent days, you might ask her to get closer, and on later days to push the call button, and eventually to step in and go up one floor. This is how the amygdala can get rewired again to associate a previously feared situation with safety or normalcy.

Students who call for trigger warnings may be correct that some of their peers are harboring memories of trauma that could be reactivated by course readings. But they are wrong to try to prevent such reactivations. Students with PTSD should of course get treatment, but they should not try to avoid normal life, with its many opportunities for habituation. Classroom discussions are safe places to be exposed to incidental reminders of trauma (such as the word *violate*). A discussion of violence is unlikely to be followed by actual violence, so it is a good way to help students change the associations that are causing them discomfort. And they'd better get their habituation done in college, because the world beyond college will be far less willing to accommodate requests for trigger warnings and opt-outs.

The expansive use of trigger warnings may also foster unhealthy mental habits in the vastly larger group of students who do not suffer from PTSD or other anxiety disorders. People acquire their fears not just from their own past experiences, but from social learning as well. If everyone around you acts as though something is dangerous—elevators, certain neighborhoods, novels depicting racism—then you are at risk of acquiring that fear too. The psychiatrist Sarah Roff pointed this out last year in an online article for *The Chronicle of Higher Education*. "One of my biggest concerns about trigger warnings," Roff wrote, "is that they will apply not just to those who have experienced trauma, but to all students, creating an atmosphere in which they are encouraged to believe that there is something dangerous or damaging about discussing difficult aspects of our history."

In an article published last year by *Inside Higher Ed*, seven humanities professors wrote that the trigger-warning movement was "already having a chilling effect on [their] teaching and pedagogy." They reported their colleagues' receiving "phone calls from deans and other administrators investigating student complaints that they have included 'triggering' material in their courses, with or without warnings." A trigger warning, they wrote, "serves as a guarantee that students will not experience unexpected discomfort and implies that if they do, a contract has been broken." When students come to *expect* trigger warnings for any material that makes them uncomfortable, the easiest way for faculty to stay out of trouble is to avoid material that might upset the most sensitive student in the class.

MENTAL FILTERING AND DISINVITATION SEASON

As Burns defines it, *mental filtering* is "pick[ing] out a negative detail in any situation and dwell[ing] on it exclusively, thus perceiving that the whole situation is negative." Leahy, Holland, and McGinn refer to this as "negative filtering," which they define as "focus[ing] almost exclusively on the negatives and seldom notic[ing] the positives." When applied to campus life, mental filtering allows for simpleminded demonization.

Students and faculty members in large numbers modeled this cognitive distortion during 2014's "disinvitation season." That's the time of year—usually early spring—when commencement speakers are announced and when students and professors demand that some of those speakers be disinvited because of things they have said or done. According to data compiled by the Foundation for Individual Rights in Education, since 2000, at least 240 campaigns have been launched at U.S. universities to prevent public figures from appearing at campus events; most of them have occurred since 2009.

Consider two of the most prominent disinvitation targets of 2014: former U.S. Secretary of State Condoleezza Rice and the International Monetary Fund's managing director, Christine Lagarde. Rice was the first black female secretary of state; Lagarde was the first woman to become finance minister of a G8 country and the first female head of the IMF. Both speakers could have been seen as highly successful role models for female students, and Rice for minority students as well. But the critics, in effect, discounted any possibility of something positive coming from those speeches.

Members of an academic community should of course be free to raise questions about Rice's role in the Iraq War or to look skeptically at the IMF's policies. But should dislike of *part* of a person's record disqualify her altogether from sharing her perspectives?

If campus culture conveys the idea that visitors must be pure, with résumés that never offend generally left-leaning campus sensibilities, then higher education will have taken a further step toward intellectual homogeneity and the creation of an environment in which students rarely encounter diverse viewpoints. And universities will have reinforced the belief that it's okay to filter out the positive. If students graduate believing that they can learn nothing from people they dislike or from those with whom they disagree, we will have done them a great intellectual disservice.

WHAT CAN WE DO NOW?

Attempts to shield students from words, ideas, and people that might cause them emotional discomfort are bad for the students. They are bad for the workplace, which will be mired in unending litigation if student expectations of safety are carried forward. And they are bad for American democracy, which is already paralyzed by worsening partisanship. When the ideas, values, and speech of the other side are seen not just as wrong but as willfully aggressive toward innocent victims, it is hard to imagine the kind of mutual respect, negotiation, and compromise that are needed to make politics a positive-sum game.

Rather than trying to protect students from words and ideas that they will inevitably encounter, colleges should do all they can to equip students to thrive in a world full of words and ideas that they cannot control. One of the great truths taught by Buddhism (and Stoicism, Hinduism, and many other traditions) is that you can never achieve happiness by making the world conform to your desires. But you can master your desires and habits of thought. This, of course, is the goal of cognitive behavioral therapy. With this in mind, here are some steps that might help reverse the tide of bad thinking on campus.

The biggest single step in the right direction does not involve faculty or university administrators, but rather the federal government, which should release universities from their fear of unreasonable investigation and sanctions by the Department of Education. Congress should define peer-on-peer harassment according to the Supreme Court's definition in the 1999 case *Davis v. Monroe County Board of Education*. The *Davis* standard holds that a single comment or thoughtless remark by a student does not equal harassment; harassment requires a pattern of objectively offensive behavior by one student that interferes with another student's access to education. Establishing the *Davis* standard would help eliminate universities' impulse to police their students' speech so carefully.

Universities themselves should try to raise consciousness about the need to balance freedom of speech with the need to make all students feel welcome. Talking openly about such conflicting but important values is just the sort of challenging exercise that any diverse but tolerant community must learn to do. Restrictive speech codes should be abandoned.

Universities should also officially and strongly discourage trigger warnings. They should endorse the American Association of University Professors' report on these warnings, which notes, "The presumption that students need to be protected rather than challenged in a classroom is at once infantilizing and anti-intellectual." Professors should be free to use trigger warnings if they choose to do so, but by explicitly discouraging the practice, universities would help fortify the faculty against student requests for such warnings.

Finally, universities should rethink the skills and values they most want to impart to their incoming students. At present, many freshman-orientation programs try to raise student sensitivity to a nearly impossible level. Teaching students to avoid giving unintentional offense is a worthy goal, especially when the students come from many different cultural backgrounds. But students should also be taught how to live in a world full of potential offenses. Why not teach incoming students how to practice cognitive behavioral therapy? Given high and rising rates of mental illness, this simple step would be among the most humane and supportive things a university could do. The cost and time commitment could be kept low: a few group training sessions could be supplemented by Web sites or apps. But the outcome could pay dividends in many ways. For example, a shared vocabulary about reasoning, common distortions, and the appropriate use of evidence to draw conclusions would facilitate critical thinking and real debate. It would also tone down the perpetual state of outrage that seems to engulf some colleges these days, allowing students' minds to open more widely to new ideas and new people. A greater commitment to formal, public debate on campus—and to the assembly of a more politically diverse faculty—would further serve that goal.

Thomas Jefferson, upon founding the University of Virginia, said: 52

> This institution will be based on the illimitable freedom of the human mind. For here we are not afraid to follow truth wherever it may lead, nor to tolerate any error so long as reason is left free to combat it.

We believe that this is still—and will always be—the best attitude for American universities. Faculty, administrators, students, and the federal government all have a role to play in restoring universities to their historic mission.

Thinking Critically about the Text

What are your views on free speech? Have you ever felt that your rights were being infringed upon? Have you ever felt oppressed by the speech of someone else? How do you think colleges and universities can create safe environments where difficult ideas can be addressed?

Examining the Issue

1. Which two terms do the authors identify as quickly gaining ground on college campuses?
2. How do the authors define "vindictive protectiveness"?
3. Why do the authors reference Socrates? What does this add to their argument?
4. What is "cognitive behavioral therapy," as defined by Lukianoff and Haidt?
5. What point are the authors making by sharing the "so-called water-buffalo incident" (paragraph 24)? How does it support their thesis? (Glossary: *Thesis*)
6. The authors identify multiple cognitive distortions. Identify one of them and explain what it means in your own words.
7. Why do the authors believe that trigger warnings are bad for students? Do you agree or disagree?

MAKING CONNECTIONS

Writing and Discussion Suggestions on Getting an Education

1. Do you regard trigger warnings as necessary, problematic, or both at the same time? In answering, consider these additional questions: What is the nature of free speech? What is the nature of political correctness? How have they evolved over the years? Is it possible for both to exist simultaneously?

When forming your answer, you might want to consult additional articles in your library or on the Web.

2. Do employee praise programs benefit employers? How do they help companies? How do they hurt them? What sort of feedback do employees need to reach their full potential?

3. Are there benefits to being uncomfortable? Is it a necessary step in learning? Starting a new job or attending a new school can be stressful and overwhelming. Are there steps that can be taken to ease these transitions? Is stress a necessary part of growth?

4. Suppose that you have children who are going away to college. You have received a letter from a school administrator detailing the "Campus Speech Codes." One of them specifies that no microaggressions will be tolerated. Write a letter to the college, explaining whether or not you support its decision to ban microaggressions and why. Include whether you think the ban will be successful and suggest steps the college might take to address microaggressions (whether or not they are banned). For ideas, revisit Lukianoff and Haidt's essay, "The Coddling of the American Mind" on page 610 and Derald Wing Sue's essay, "Racial Microaggressions in Everyday Life: Is Subtle Bias Harmful?" on page 588.

5. **Writing with Sources.** Do some research into the office cultures of major companies (for instance, Google, *Slate* magazine). Is the culture of each company casual or more formal? What sort of encouragement or benefits does the company provide for its employees? Are you more drawn to a company that prioritizes the happiness of its employees or that prioritizes employees' success? Do any of the organizations you looked at seem to have the perfect balance of happiness and success? Write an essay evaluating two or three of the businesses from your research. For models of and advice on integrating sources in your essay, see Chapters 14 and 15.

6. **Writing with Sources.** Look into the work of other cognitive scientists. Do you find any who disagree with Lukianoff and Haidt and support trigger warnings and speech codes? What are the central points of their arguments? Do you find others whose research agrees with Lukianoff and Haidt? After you finish your research, write a synthesis paper explaining the dominant perspective and citing important points the experts have raised.

7. Siobhan Crowley argues that the classroom could be one of the safest places to encounter triggering experiences. As she is a teaching assistant, some might find her comments insightful and philosophic, while others might argue that her views are self-serving. From your perspective as a student, how convincing do you find her argument? Write an essay in which you argue for a set of priorities that should be used to create campus guidelines on free or protected speech.

8. The central problem in this cluster is that feelings — both those of accomplishment and those of offense — are subjective. While one person may be "completely averse to confetti," another person may flourish with a more colorful style of encouragement. The authors in these readings provide examples of a number of extremes, but guidelines usually try to find the average perspective and uphold it. How might a business or college find a workable compromise? Are there situations where the extreme opinion should be given greater weight, or is it always important to find the elusive "happy medium"?

9. What is the ideal environment for learning? Do you prefer quiet or working in groups? Write a proposal for a flexible workspace (either professional or academic) that would meet the needs of a variety of learning styles. Feel free to get creative in your features for the space (movable walls? encouragement stations? controversy zones?). Include arguments for what each feature will contribute to the space.

WRITING SUGGESTIONS FOR ARGUMENTATION

1. Think of a product that you like and want to use even though it has an annoying feature. Write a letter of complaint, in which you attempt to persuade the manufacturer to improve the product. Your letter should include the following points:
   a. a statement concerning the nature of the problem
   b. evidence supporting or explaining your complaint
   c. suggestions for improving the product

2. Select one of the position statements that follow and write an argumentative essay in which you defend that statement.
   a. Living in a dormitory is (or is not) as desirable as living off campus.
   b. Student government shows (or does not show) that the democratic process is effective.
   c. America should (or should not) be a refuge for the oppressed.
   d. Interest in religion is (or is not) increasing in the United States.
   e. We have (or have not) brought air pollution under control in the United States.
   f. The need to develop alternative energy sources is (or is not) serious.
   g. America's great cities are (or are not) thriving.
   h. Fraternities and sororities do (or do not) build character.
   i. We have (or have not) found effective means to dispose of nuclear or chemical wastes.
   j. Fair play is (or is not) a thing of the past.
   k. Human life is (or is not) valued in a technological society.
   l. The consumer does (or does not) need to be protected.
   m. America should (or should not) feel a commitment to the starving peoples of the world.
   n. Money is (or is not) the path to happiness.
   o. Animals do (or do not) have rights.

3. Think of something on your campus or in your community that you would like to see changed. Write a persuasive argument that explains what is wrong and how you think it ought to be changed. Make sure you incorporate other writing strategies into your essay — for example, description, narration, or illustration — to increase the effectiveness of your persuasive argument. (Glossary: *Description; Illustration; Narration*)

4. Read some articles in the editorial section of today's paper (in print or online) and pick one with which you agree or disagree. Write a letter to the editor that presents your point of view. Use a logical argument to support or refute the editorial's assertions. Depending on the editorial, you might choose to use different rhetorical strategies to reach your audience. (Glossary: *Audience*) You might use cause and effect, for example, to show the correct (or incorrect) connections made by the editorial. (Glossary: *Cause and Effect Analysis*)

5. **Writing with Sources.** Working with a partner, choose a controversial topic like the legalization of medical marijuana or any of the topics in writing suggestion 2. Each partner should argue one side of the issue. Decide who is going to write on which side of the issue and keep in mind that there are often more than two sides to an issue. Then each of you should write an essay, trying to convince your partner that your position is the most logical and correct.

   You'll both need to do research online or in the library to find support for your position. For models of and advice on integrating sources in your essay, see Chapters 14 and 15.

6. **Working with Sources.** Visit the World Wildlife Foundation online to learn more about the wildlife protection campaign that prompted this chapter's opening image (see worldwildlife.org/pages/stop-wildlife-crime). Once you have a good understanding of the site's message and goals, write an essay in which you analyze whether this chapter's opening image works, carefully explaining your reasoning in the context of the campaign's audience and mission. What argument is at the core of the campaign? How did the campaign use visuals — both in print and online — to give its message impact? What other types of images might the foundation have used, and would those have been effective? Online, the foundation encourages visitors to share the ads via social media. Is this something you would e-mail to your friends or post on Facebook or Twitter? Why or why not? For models of and advice on integrating sources in your essay, see Chapters 14 and 15.

7. Take a close look at the public service advertisement at the top of the next page. What kind of an argument does it represent? Is it effective, in your opinion? Why or why not? If you were going to create an ad responding to this one — or an ad similarly warning against violence — what would it look like?

8. **Writing in the Workplace.** You're a summer intern at a midsized news Web site. A freelance journalist sends you the final draft of his commissioned article so that you can correct any grammar mistakes before it's read by your boss. As you read it, you realize that a few sentences stand out for their distinct, different style. You run those sentences through a search engine and, sure enough, the freelancer plagiarized them from an independent, personally run

Copyright © Bill Aron / PhotoEdit — All rights reserved.

blog. Write a thorough, professional e-mail to your boss, explaining the situation and why the plagiarism is a concern. Can you run the piece? How would doing so affect the credibility and reputation of the journalist? To what extent must freelancers produce original content? How might the freelancer defend his actions? Would that defense matter? Since you're on a deadline, propose a solution to your boss. What next steps can your organization take to accurately and ethically report on the story?

Courtesy of Adbusters Media Foundation

CHAPTER **13**

Combining Strategies

WHAT DOES IT MEAN TO COMBINE STRATEGIES?

EACH OF THE PRECEDING CHAPTERS OF *SUBJECT & STRATEGY* EMPHAsizes a particular writing strategy: narration, description, illustration, process analysis, and so forth. The essays and selections within each of these chapters use the given strategy as the dominant method of development. It is important to remember, however, that the *dominant* strategy is rarely the *only* one used to develop a piece of writing. To fully explore their topics, writers often use other strategies in combination with the dominant strategy.

To highlight and reinforce this point, we focus on the use of multiple strategies in the Questions on Strategy section following each professional selection. In this chapter on combining strategies, we offer a collection of essays that make notable use of several different strategies. You will encounter such combinations of strategies in the reading and writing you do in other college courses. Beyond the classroom, you might write a business proposal using both description and cause and effect to make an argument for a new marketing plan, or you might use narration, description, and illustration to write a news story for a company blog or a letter to the editor of your local newspaper.

For an example of a visual text that combines strategies, see the advertisement on the opposite page. Few ad campaigns have been more successful than the California Milk Processor Board's "Got Milk?" promotion initiated in 1993. That campaign's use of celebrities, serial format, striking visuals, and pared-down, direct language made it instantly recognizable, and, inevitably, widely imitated. Among its many imitators is this Adbusters parody ad, "Why Milk?" which seeks to promote soy milk as a healthier alternative to cow's milk. While the Adbusters ad is primarily an argument for drinking soy milk and avoiding cow's milk, the ad copy and image of the soy-milk lover also implicitly rely for their impact on the strategies of narration, illustration, comparison and contrast, and cause and effect analysis.

COMBINING STRATEGIES IN WRITTEN TEXTS

The following essay by Sydney Harris reveals how several strategies can be used effectively, even in a brief piece of writing. Although primarily a work of definition, notice how "A Jerk" also uses illustration and personal narrative to engage the reader and achieve Harris's purpose.

A JERK

I don't know whether history repeats itself, but biography certainly does. The other day, Michael came in and asked me what a "jerk" was—the same question Carolyn put to me a dozen years ago.

At that time, I fluffed her off with some inane answer, such as "A jerk isn't a very nice person," but both of us knew it was an unsatisfactory reply. When she went to bed, I began trying to work up a suitable definition.

It is a marvelously apt word, of course. Until it was coined, not more than twenty-five years ago, there was really no single word in English to describe the kind of person who is a jerk—"boob" and "simp" were too old hat, and besides they really didn't fit, for they could be lovable, and a jerk never is.

Thinking it over, I decided that a jerk is basically a person without insight. He is not necessarily a fool or a dope, because some extremely clever persons can be jerks. In fact, it has little to do with intelligence as we commonly think of it; it is, rather, a kind of subtle but persuasive aroma emanating from the inner part of the personality.

I know a college president who can be described only as a jerk. He is not an unintelligent man, nor unlearned, nor even unschooled in the social amenities. Yet he is a jerk cum laude, because of a fatal flaw in his nature—he is totally incapable of looking into the mirror of his soul and shuddering at what he sees there.

A jerk, then, is a man (or woman) who is utterly unable to see himself as he appears to others. He has no grace, he is tactless without meaning to be, he is a bore even to his best friends, he is an egotist without charm. All of us are egotists to some extent, but most of us—unlike the jerk—are perfectly and horribly aware of it when we make asses of ourselves. The jerk never knows.

Essays that employ thoughtful combinations of rhetorical strategies have some obvious advantages for the writer and the reader. By reading the work of professional writers, you can learn how multiple strategies can be used to your advantage—how a paragraph of narration, a vivid description, a clarifying instance of comparison and contrast, or a clear definition can help convey your purpose and thesis.

For example, let's suppose you wanted to write an essay on the slang you hear on campus. You might find it helpful to use a variety of strategies:

Definition—to explain what slang is

Illustration—to give examples of slang

Comparison and contrast—to differentiate slang from other types of speech, such as idioms or technical language

Division and classification—to categorize different types of slang or different topics that slang terms are used for, such as courses, students, food, grades

Or let's say you wanted to write a paper on the Japanese Americans who were sent to internment camps during World War II while the United States was at war with Japan. The following strategies would be available to you:

Illustration—to illustrate several particular cases of families that were sent to internment camps

Narration—to tell the stories of former camp residents, including their first reaction to their internment and their actual experiences in the camps

Cause and effect—to examine the reasons the United States government interned Japanese Americans and the long-term effects of this policy

When you rely on a single mode or approach to an essay, you lose the opportunity to come at your subject from a number of different angles, all of which complete the picture and any one of which might be the most insightful or engaging and, therefore, the most memorable for the reader. This is particularly the case with essays that attempt to persuade or argue. The task of changing readers' beliefs and thoughts is so difficult that writers look for any combination of strategies that will make their arguments more convincing.

SAMPLE STUDENT ESSAY USING SUBJECTS AND STRATEGIES

During her senior year, while working as an undergraduate researcher in a developmental biology lab at Syracuse University, Ria Foye-Edwards wrote the following essay to explore a new technology solution that would provide environmentally friendly meat and keep up with consumer demand. Her essay, written under the guidance of her science writing mentor, Brian Howard, naturally incorporates several rhetorical modes working in combination as she analyzes the new process, describes and illustrates the benefits and pitfalls of the plan, and speculates on the response from consumers.

The "Steaks" Are High: *In Vitro* Meat Moves
from the Petri Dish to the Palate
Ria Foye-Edwards

Over the past century and a half the world has witnessed some of the most innovative ideas come to life; some of these ideas were stumbled upon by accident and others arose from pure inquiry. Take, for instance, the creation of the potato chip and the discovery of the antibiotic, penicillin. These inventions have proven successful over time and are still being produced for the public today.

However, great creations are seldom the result of trickery and accident (as were the potato chip and penicillin), but instead the outcome of years of hard work done by researchers who aim to fix worldwide problems.

One issue that has attracted much concern is the rapid use of Earth's natural resources and the strain that humans are inflicting on the environment in order to support a growing population. As a result, the world's population of 7 billion people requires and uses massive amounts of energy and land—resources which are not easily replenished.

For millennia, farming livestock for meat has proven a dependable method of providing food for many. In recent years, however, as researchers from around the globe become more aware of the changing climate, livestock have been determined as one of the main sources of methane, a major greenhouse gas.

One of the most creative attempts to reinvent a food system that is environmentally friendly and capable of keeping up with rising demand is the use of a tissue engineering method to create *in vitro* meat.

Producing *in vitro* meat involves extracting muscle cells from an animal, putting them into a growth medium, and letting the cells proliferate and develop into muscle tissue—which is the main component of meat we consume. This method, if performed on a large scale, could supplement increasing meat demands and use fewer animals, supporters say.

Dr. Mark Post, a researcher at Maastricht University in the Netherlands, is currently at the forefront of research to produce *in vitro* beef, also called cultured beef. Post first became involved with the idea back in 2008 when he taught tissue engineering at Eindhoven University of Technology.

"I coincidentally came across people who were interested in the idea and specifically an older gentleman in Amsterdam who had been obsessed with the notion of creating meat from stem cells through cell culture," Post recalls.

Process analysis: how in vitro meat is made

It wasn't by coincidence, but rather hard work that six years later Post and his team have successfully made the first *in vitro* hamburger. "It's a traditional cell culture method so you use culture medium containing amino acids, sugars, minerals and vitamins with the addition of fetal bovine serum to grow the cells . . . it takes about eight to nine weeks and is pretty intensive, for one hamburger you typically grow about twenty billion cells," exclaims Post.

Description: how the first sample turned out

The cultured burger has been sampled and the tasters agreed that it had a texture similar to a farmed beef burger, but that it lacked the fat that is responsible for additional flavor and fatty acids. As a result, research is currently being undertaken by Post to culture fat cells. "Currently we are culturing fat cells separately," he says. "We could co-culture them with muscle cells; however, it's more complex, and that would be the next phase."

Post and his team are experimenting with new ideas in order to enhance the burger's appearance and taste. "Another thing we are working on is trying to boost the expression of myoglobin, which is a protein in the muscle that carries iron and oxygen . . . I have a feeling that the iron contributes to the taste and definitely adds to the color of the meat through its oxygen carrying. We hope that helps recreate the taste," Post adds.

Analysis: current cost

With the current method, this process remains rather time consuming and production must be scaled up in order to reduce the price of the product (which is currently £250,000, that's $400,145!) and make it readily available to the public. However, there is much concern from researchers and those advocating for *in vitro* meat about general acceptance. Post says, "Are people generally going to accept this as an alternative for meat? As for the vegan and vegetarian communities some are very receptive and welcome this idea while others are more skeptical and feel it's still an animal-derived product."

Illustration: reasons animal activists support the project

Alanna Wagy, a College Campaign Assistant for PETA, shared several reasons why PETA is among those in the vegan/vegetarian community who are supportive of *in vitro* meat. In fact, PETA is offering a one million dollar reward for the first researcher to create *in vitro* chicken. "Since we announced the contest, which actually ended on the fourth of May, more research than ever has been done in terms of *in vitro* meat in the U.S. and internationally," shares Wagy. But, unlike Dr. Post's motive for securing the welfare of the environment, PETA has concerns rooted more strongly in the protection of the animals that are being used for food sources.

Cause and effect: the reason for PETA's involvement

Wagy claims, "We decided to get involved because of the number of chickens that are killed. Roughly one million chickens are killed in an hour in the U.S and we realized that, while it's somewhat easy to transition to a vegan diet and live plant based, there are always going to be people who are set in their dietary habits. We wanted to explore every possible alternative to stop animal cruelty at the source."

Cause and effect: impact on livestock farms and meat manufacturers

This attempt to stop animal cruelty at its root could possibly cause livestock farms and meat manufacturing companies to dwindle. That is, if ever *in vitro* meat becomes the dominant form of meat production, this could spell trouble for existing producers. However, these companies could perhaps transition to new methods that will keep their businesses thriving. But how would *in vitro* meat impact local farmers? Would they be able to transition and produce *in vitro* meat like larger livestock manufacturers? Dr. Post describes such a scenario:

Narration: a scenario in which *in vitro* meat would be useful

> There might be incentives to doing this [producing *in vitro* meat] on a smaller scale. Take, for instance, a small town with a farm with a few animals where local townsmen feed them, tend to them and even give them names—and once in a while you take a sample from them for the stem cells and, in a building adjacent to the farm, you grow the meat for the entire community. Then you won't have a lot of transport issues, people realize where their meat is coming from, and it would become more idealistic.

If *in vitro* meat catches on, it will likely take some time before seeing it in the "beef" aisle at the grocery store. But what's clear is that much progress has been made since the idea was first introduced. With researchers like Dr. Post and organizations like PETA promoting a more sustainable and animal friendly alternative, who knows if researchers will invent even more foods *in vitro*.

> **Conclusion**   That being said, there is still plenty of time for the public to form its opinion and either accept or reject this new form of meat production. But for those working towards an *in vitro* food system they can only hope for one thing: for society to remain open to this alternative method.

16

Analyzing Ria Foye-Edwards Essay: Questions for Discussion

1. What is Foye-Edwards's thesis?
2. What would be the benefits of *in vitro* meat? What are the concerns?
3. Why does Foye-Edwards anticipate that *in vitro* meat will be supported by PETA and other animal rights organizations?
4. Does *in vitro* meat seem like a viable solution to the environmental issues Foye-Edwards raises in the third and fourth paragraphs?

SUGGESTIONS FOR USING A COMBINATION OF STRATEGIES IN AN ESSAY

As you plan, write, and revise your essay using a combination of strategies, be mindful of the writing process guidelines described in Chapter 2. Pay particular attention to the basic requirements and essential ingredients of each writing strategy you choose.

▶ Planning Your Combined Strategies Essay

Planning is an essential part of writing any good essay. You can save yourself a great deal of trouble by taking the time to think about the key building blocks of your essay before you actually begin to write. Before you can start combining strategies in your writing, it's essential that you have a firm understanding of the purposes and workings of each strategy. Once you become familiar with how the strategies work, you should be able to recognize ways to use and combine them in your writing.

Sometimes you will find yourself using a particular strategy almost intuitively. When you encounter a difficult or abstract term or concept — *liberal*, for example — you will define it almost as a matter of course. If you become perplexed because you are having trouble getting your readers to appreciate the severity of a problem, a quick review of the strategies will remind you that you could also use description and illustration.

Knowledge of the individual strategies is crucial because there are no formulas or prescriptions for combining strategies. The more you write and the more aware you are of the options available to you, the more skillful you will become at thinking critically about your topic, developing your ideas, and conveying your thoughts to your readers.

DETERMINE YOUR PURPOSE. The most common purposes in nonfiction writing are (1) to express your thoughts and feelings about a life experience, (2) to inform your readers by explaining something about the world around them, and (3) to persuade readers to embrace some belief or action. Your purpose will determine the dominant strategy you use in your essay.

If your major purpose is to tell a story of a river-rafting trip, you will primarily use narration. If you wish to re-create the experience of seeing a famous landmark for the first time, you may find description most helpful. If you wish to inform your readers, you may find definition, cause and effect, process analysis, comparison and contrast, and/or division and classification to be best suited to your needs. If you wish to convince your readers of a certain belief or course of action, argumentation is an obvious choice.

FORMULATE A THESIS STATEMENT. Regardless of the purpose you have set for yourself in writing an essay, it is essential that you commit to a thesis statement, usually a one- or two-sentence statement giving the main point of your essay.

> Party primaries are an indispensable part of the American political process.

> Antibiotic use must be curtailed. Antibiotics have been overprescribed and are not nearly as effective as they once were at combating infections among humans.

A question is not a thesis statement. If you find yourself writing a thesis statement that asks a question, answer the question first and then turn your answer into a thesis statement. A thesis statement can be presented anywhere in an essay, but usually it is presented at the beginning of a composition, sometimes after a few introductory sentences that set a context for it.

▶ Organizing Your Combined Strategies Essay

DETERMINE YOUR DOMINANT STRATEGY. Depending on your purpose for writing, your thesis statement, and the kinds of information you have gathered in preparing to write your essay, you may use any of the following strategies as the dominant strategy for your essay: narration, description, illustration, process analysis, comparison and contrast, division and classification, definition, cause and effect analysis, or argumentation.

DETERMINE YOUR SUPPORTING STRATEGIES. The questions listed below—organized by rhetorical strategy—will help you decide which strategies will be most helpful to you in the service of the dominant strategy you have chosen for your essay and in achieving your overall purpose.

Narration. Are you trying to report or recount an anecdote, an experience, or an event? Does any part of your essay include the telling of a story (something that happened to you or to a person you include in your essay)?

Description. Does a person, a place, or an object play a prominent role in your essay? Would the tone, pacing, or overall purpose of your essay benefit from sensory details?

Illustration. Are there examples—facts, statistics, cases in point, personal experiences, interview quotations—that you could add to help achieve the purpose of your essay?

Process analysis. Would any part of your essay be clearer if you included concrete directions about a certain process? Are there processes that readers would like to understand better? Are you evaluating any processes?

Comparison and contrast. Does your essay contain two or more related subjects? Are you evaluating or analyzing two or more people, places, processes, events, or things? Do you need to establish the similarities and differences between two or more elements?

Division and classification. Are you trying to explain a broad and complicated subject? Would it benefit your essay to reduce this subject to more manageable parts to focus your discussion?

Definition. Who is your audience? Does your essay focus on any abstract, specialized, or new terms that need further explanation so readers understand your point? Does any important word in your essay have many meanings and need to be clarified?

Cause and effect analysis. Are you examining past events or their outcomes? Is your purpose to inform, speculate, or argue about why an identifiable fact happens the way it does?

Argumentation. Are you trying to explain aspects of a particular subject, and are you trying to advocate a specific opinion on this subject or issue in your essay?

▸ Revising and Editing Your Combined Strategies Essay

LISTEN TO WHAT YOUR CLASSMATES HAVE TO SAY. The importance of student peer conferences cannot be stressed enough, particularly as you revise and edit your essay. Others in your class will often see, for example, that the basis for your classification needs adjustment or that there are inconsistencies in your division categories that can easily be corrected—problems that you may not be able to see yourself because you are too close to your essay. To maximize the effectiveness of working with your classmates, use the guidelines on page 36. Take advantage of suggestions when you know them to be valid and make revisions accordingly.

QUESTION YOUR OWN WORK WHILE REVISING AND EDITING. Revision is best done by asking yourself key questions about what you have written. Begin by reading, preferably aloud, what you have written. Reading aloud forces you to pay attention to every single word, and you are more likely to catch lapses in the logical flow of thought. After you have read your paper through, answer the following questions for revising and editing and make the necessary changes.

For help with twelve common writing problems, see Chapter 16.

> **Questions for Revising and Editing: Combining Strategies**
>
> 1. Do I have a purpose for my essay?
> 2. Is my thesis statement clear?
> 3. Does my dominant strategy reflect my purpose and my thesis statement?
> 4. Do my subordinate strategies effectively support the dominant strategy of my essay?
> 5. Are my subordinate strategies woven into my essay in a natural manner?
> 6. Have I revised and edited my essay to avoid wordiness?
> 7. Have I used a variety of sentences to enliven my writing?
> 8. Have I avoided errors in grammar, punctuation, and mechanics?

On Dumpster Diving

LARS EIGHNER

Born in Corpus Christi, Texas, in 1948, Lars Eighner grew up in Houston and attended the University of Texas–Austin. After graduation, he wrote essays and fiction, and several of his articles were published in magazines like *Threepenny Review*, the *Guide*, and *Inches*. A volume of short stories, *Bayou Boy and Other Stories*, was published in 1985. Eighner became homeless in 1988 when he left his job as an attendant at a mental hospital. The following piece, which appeared in the *Utne Reader*, is an abridged version of an essay that first appeared in *Threepenny Review*. The piece eventually became part of Eighner's startling account of the three years he spent with his dog as a homeless person, *Travels with Lizbeth* (1993). His publications include the novel *Pawn to Queen Four* (1995), the short-story collection *Whispered in the Dark* (1996), and the nonfiction book of essays *Gay Cosmos* (1995).

Eighner uses a number of rhetorical strategies in "On Dumpster Diving," but pay particular attention to how his process analysis of the "stages that a person goes through in learning to scavenge" contributes to the success of the essay as a whole.

By permission of Lars Eighner

Preparing to Read

Are you a pack rat, or do you get rid of what is not immediately useful to you? Outside of the usual kitchen garbage and empty toothpaste tubes, how do you make the decision to throw something away?

1. I began Dumpster diving about a year before I became homeless.

2. I prefer the term *scavenging*. I have heard people, evidently meaning to be polite, use the word *foraging*, but I prefer to reserve that word for gathering nuts and berries and such, which I also do, according to the season and opportunity.

3. I like the frankness of the word *scavenging*. I live from the refuse of others. I am a scavenger. I think it a sound and honorable niche, although if I could I would naturally prefer to live the comfortable consumer life, perhaps — and only perhaps — as a slightly less wasteful consumer owing to what I have learned as a scavenger.

4. Except for jeans, all my clothes come from Dumpsters. Boom boxes, candles, bedding, toilet paper, medicine, books, a typewriter, a virgin male love doll, coins sometimes amounting to many dollars: All came from Dumpsters. And, yes, I eat from Dumpsters, too.

There is a predictable series of stages that a person goes through in learning to scavenge. At first the new scavenger is filled with disgust and self-loathing. He is ashamed of being seen.

This stage passes with experience. The scavenger finds a pair of running shoes that fit and look and smell brand-new. He finds a pocket calculator in perfect working order. He finds pristine ice cream, still frozen, more than he can eat or keep. He begins to understand: People do throw away perfectly good stuff, a lot of perfectly good stuff.

At this stage he may become lost and never recover: All the Dumpster divers I have known come to the point of trying to acquire everything they touch. Why not take it, they reason, it is all free. This is, of course, hopeless, and most divers come to realize that they must restrict themselves to items of relatively immediate utility.

I live from the refuse of others. I am a scavenger.

The finding of objects is becoming something of an urban art. Even respectable, employed people will sometimes find something tempting sticking out of a Dumpster or standing beside one. Quite a number of people, not all of them of the bohemian type, are willing to brag that they found this or that piece in the trash.

But eating from Dumpsters is the thing that separates the dilettanti from the professionals. Eating safely involves three principles: using the senses and common sense to evaluate the condition of the found materials; knowing the Dumpsters of a given area and checking them regularly; and seeking always to answer the question "Why was this discarded?"

Yet perfectly good food can be found in Dumpsters. Canned goods, for example, turn up fairly often in the Dumpsters I frequent. I also have few qualms about dry foods such as crackers, cookies, cereal, chips, and pasta if they are free of visible contaminants and still dry and crisp. Raw fruits and vegetables with intact skins seem perfectly safe to me, excluding, of course, the obviously rotten. Many are discarded for minor imperfections that can be pared away.

A typical discard is a half jar of peanut butter—though nonorganic peanut butter does not require refrigeration and is unlikely to spoil in any reasonable time. One of my favorite finds is yogurt—often discarded, still sealed, when the expiration date has passed—because it will keep for several days, even in warm weather.

No matter how careful I am I still get dysentery at least once a month, oftener in warm weather. I do not want to paint too romantic a picture. Dumpster diving has serious drawbacks as a way of life.

I find from the experience of scavenging two rather deep lessons. The first is to take what I can use and let the rest go. I have come to think that there is no value in the abstract. A thing I cannot use or make useful, perhaps by trading, has no value, however fine or rare it may be.

The second lesson is the transience of material being. I do not suppose that ideas are immortal, but certainly they are longer-lived than material objects.

The things I find in Dumpsters, the love letters and rag dolls of so many lives, remind me of this lesson. Now I hardly pick up a thing without envisioning the time I will cast it away. This, I think, is a healthy state of mind. Almost everything I have now has already been cast out at least once, proving that what I own is valueless to someone.

I find that my desire to grab for the gaudy bauble has been largely sated. I think this is an attitude I share with the very wealthy—we both know there is plenty more where whatever we have came from. Between us are the rat-race millions who have confounded their selves with the objects they grasp and who nightly scavenge the cable channels for they know not what.

I am sorry for them.

Thinking Critically about the Text

In paragraph 15, Eighner writes, "I hardly pick up a thing without envisioning the time I will cast it away. This, I think, is a healthy state of mind." React to this statement. Do you think such an attitude is healthy or defeatist? If many people thought this way, what impact would it have on our consumer society?

Questions on Subject

1. What stages do beginning Dumpster divers go through before they become what Eighner terms "professionals" (paragraph 9)? What examples does Eighner use to illustrate the passage through these stages? (Glossary: *Illustration*)

2. What three principles does one need to follow in order to eat safely from Dumpsters? What foods are best to eat from Dumpsters? What are the risks?

3. What two lessons has Eighner learned from his Dumpster diving experiences? Why are they significant to him?

4. Dumpster diving has had a profound effect on Eighner and the way he lives. How do his explanations of choices he makes, such as deciding which items to keep, enhance his presentation of the practical art of Dumpster diving?

5. How do you respond to Eighner's Dumpster-diving practices? Are you shocked? Bemused? Accepting? Challenged?

Questions on Strategy

1. Eighner's essay deals with both the immediate, physical aspects of Dumpster diving, such as what can be found in a typical Dumpster and the physical price one pays for eating out of them, and the larger, abstract issues that

Dumpster diving raises, such as materialism and the transience of material objects. (Glossary: *Concrete/Abstract*) Why does he describe the concrete things before he discusses the abstract issues raised by their presence in Dumpsters? What does he achieve by using both types of elements?

2. Eighner's account of Dumpster diving focuses primarily on the odd appeal and interest inherent in the activity. Paragraph 12 is his one disclaimer, in which he states, "I do not want to paint too romantic a picture." Why does Eighner include this disclaimer? How does it add to the effectiveness of his piece? Why do you think it is so brief and abrupt?

3. Eighner uses many rhetorical techniques in his essay, but its core is a fairly complete process analysis of how to Dumpster dive. (Glossary: *Process Analysis*) Summarize this process analysis. Why do you think Eighner did not title the essay "How to Dumpster Dive"?

4. Discuss how Eighner uses illustration to bring the world of Dumpster diving to life. (Glossary: *Illustration*) What characterizes the examples he uses?

5. Writers often use process analysis in conjunction with other strategies, especially argument, to try to improve the way a process is carried out. (Glossary: *Argument; Process Analysis*) In this essay, Eighner uses a full process analysis to lay out his views on American values and materialism. How is this an effective way to combine strategies? Think of other arguments that could be strengthened if they included elements of process analysis.

Questions on Diction and Vocabulary

1. Eighner says he prefers the word *scavenging* to *Dumpster diving* or *foraging*. What do those three terms mean to him? Why do you think he finds the discussion of the terms important enough to include it at the beginning of his essay? (Glossary: *Diction*)

2. According to Eighner, "eating from Dumpsters is the thing that separates the dilettanti from the professionals" (paragraph 9). What do the words *dilettante* and *professional* connote to you? (Glossary: *Connotation/Denotation*) Why does Eighner choose to use them instead of the more straightforward *casual* and *serious*?

3. Eighner says, "The finding of objects is becoming something of an urban art" (paragraph 8). What does this sentence mean to you? Based on the essay, do you find his use of the word *art* appropriate when discussing any aspect of Dumpster diving? Why or why not?

Combining Strategies in Action

As a class, discuss the strategies that Eighner uses in his essay: narration, process analysis, cause and effect, illustration, and definition, for example. Where in the essay has he used each strategy and to what end? Has he used any other strategies not mentioned above? Explain.

Writing Suggestions

1. Write a process analysis in which you relate how you acquire a consumer item of some importance or expense to you. (Glossary: *Process Analysis*) Do you compare brands, store prices, and so on? (Glossary: *Comparison and Contrast*) What are your priorities — must the item be stylish or durable, offer good overall value, give high performance? How do you decide to spend your money? In other words, what determines which items are worth the sacrifice?

2. In paragraph 3, Eighner states that he "live[s] from the refuse of others." How does his confession affect you? Do you think that we have become a throw-away society? If so, how? How do Eighner's accounts of homelessness and Dumpster diving make you feel about your own consumerism and trash habits? Write an essay in which you examine the things you throw away in a single day. What items did you get rid of? Why? Could those items be used by someone else? Have you ever felt guilty about throwing something away? If so, what was it and why did you feel guilty?

3. One person's treasure is another person's trash. In the photograph below, young adults in their early twenties explore what's available inside a Dumpster near a supermarket in Charlotte, North Carolina. Stephanie Braun, in plaid, hands a fruit to Kaitlyn Tokay, pictured in front. Choose a theme derived from the photograph and Eighner's essay — for example, the treasure/trash statement above or whether this sort of Dumpster diving is the purest form of recycling — and write an essay that includes at least three different strategies used in combination.

Gary O'Brien/Charlotte Observer/MCT via Getty Images

How to Reengineer Crops for the 21st Century

MICHAEL WHITE

Systems biologist Michael White was born in Providence, Rhode Island, in 1974. He received his B.A. in music performance from Brigham Young University in 2000. White confesses that "I entered college with the desire to perform, teach, and write about music but struggled to put in the necessary hours of piano practice — too many other interesting subjects, like science, competed for my attention." No surprise then that he went on to get a Ph.D. in biochemistry from the University of Rochester School of Medicine in 2006. He is an assistant professor of genetics at Washington University School of Medicine in St. Louis, Missouri. White has written extensively in peer-reviewed journals, including *Genomics* and *Molecular Systems Biology*, and he has also blogged for the *Huffington Post* and written an online science column for *Pacific Standard*. While he now spends most of his time in the lab, White recognizes that "writing is a critical part of my job. As a science writer, my goal is to be accurate, yet understandable and interesting to someone who is not a scientist. More importantly, I don't want to simply explain the latest research to passive, uncritical readers; I want to push readers to ask questions and form opinions about issues that may be highly technical, but which have a big impact on the world we share." White's research goal is "to solve important biomedical problems by discovering new functional relationships in genomic data."

Jonni Cook Sergi

The essay below first appeared in August 2015 in *Pacific Standard*, a magazine aimed at changing "private behavior and public policy" by raising important issues and shining a spotlight on potential problem solvers. As you read White's essay, notice how he uses a combination of strategies to advance his argument.

Preparing to Read

How do you view genetically modified food? Have you encountered the concept before? Do you worry about the effects genetic modification will have on health and the environment or see it as an important solution to addressing world hunger? After reading, consider whether this article alters or supports your current view.

Though we don't always find what we want at the grocery store, in the United States, we don't worry that the store will run out of food. The world, however, can run out—and there is a good chance that it will, unless we make major upgrades to crop production. By 2050, the global demand for food crops will likely double, as the world's population grows by more than 30 percent, and as the citizens of developing nations emerge from poverty and can afford to eat more and better foods. Unless we increase the world's capacity to grow food, the demand for food will outstrip supply in the next few decades.

> Unless we increase the world's capacity to grow food, the demand for food will outstrip supply in the next few decades.

This is a tall order, because we can't meet our needs by simply clearing more land for agriculture—important ecosystems would be damaged and the emission of greenhouse gases would be accelerated. Compounding the problem, demand for non-food crops that make up raw materials for biofuels is growing; these crops are now competing with food crops for available land. If we're going to meet the growing global demand for crops in a sustainable way, we will need to increase yields from the cultivated land that we already have.

To meet this challenge, an international group of academic, government, and industry scientists has come up with an unusual solution: re-designing photosynthesis, the fundamental biological process by which plants use sunlight to convert water and carbon dioxide in the atmosphere into something that we can eat. The group of scientists—led by Donald Ort, a plant biologist at the University of Illinois and a research leader at the United States Department of Agriculture—has just published a proposal that lays out several ambitious ideas on how to improve photosynthesis in crop plants. Despite being one of nature's most fundamental and widespread biological processes, photosynthesis is not especially efficient in crop plants as they grow in the unnatural setting of a farm field. The inefficiency of photosynthesis presents an untapped opportunity to improve crop yields, Ort and his colleagues argue, because "photosynthesis is the only determinant [of yields] that is not close to its biological limits." Using biotechnology, they claim, scientists can re-design the process to produce crop plants with higher yields, and move closer to solving our "looming agricultural crisis."

The notion of re-designing the extremely complex process at the core of a plant's biology might sound like fantasy—biologists struggle to re-design even simple biological systems, and all existing genetically modified crops were created through alterations that are minor compared to those it would take to re-design photosynthesis. Yet, the researchers argue, the rapid pace of innovation in biotechnology over the past several decades has often made bold ideas that seem overly ambitious become feasible much sooner than expected. "Creative and radically new ideas for redesigning photosynthesis are therefore worth pursuing because even strategies that presently seem fanciful may inspire new thinking in unimagined directions," the team writes. And, in fact, some ideas for re-designing photosynthesis are already being developed in the lab. Ort and one of his co-authors, Stephen Long, direct a project at the University of Illinois called Realizing Increased Photosynthetic Efficiency, which is funded by a $25 million grant from the Bill & Melinda Gates foundation and focused on improving photosynthesis in several important food crops.

In their proposal, the researchers discuss several key aspects of photosynthesis that could be improved. For example, photosynthesis is not particularly efficient in full sunlight, because crop plants absorb more light than they can actually use, and therefore they waste energy dealing with harmful byproducts created by the extra photons. Another inefficiency is caused by the increased levels of carbon dioxide in our atmosphere: Too much carbon dioxide leads to a metabolic bottleneck at a key step in photosynthesis, which slows down the overall process. Interestingly, other organisms have evaded some of the inefficiencies of photosynthesis found in crop plants. The simplest way to re-design photosynthesis in crop plants is to swap in more efficient components from these other photosynthesizing organisms, like algae and certain bacteria. Ort and his colleagues point out that, technologically, swapping these components is not quite feasible yet, but likely will be soon.

Another intriguing idea is developing what the researchers term a "smart canopy," by planting different versions of the same crop together. Taller plants would photosynthesize better in full sunlight, while shorter plants, shaded by the taller ones, would do best in low light. As the researchers write, "An optimized canopy would have lighter green upright leaves at the top of the canopy and dark green horizontal leaves at the base." This is the opposite of how most crop plants grow. The dramatic crop re-design necessary for a smart canopy is also not yet feasible, since it would require extensive genetic modifications that are prohibitively difficult with current technology.

In fact, few of the ideas proposed by Ort and his colleagues are feasible with current technology, but that's the point: The researchers are urging us to think about the long game, and to begin developing the technology we'll need to upgrade crops in the future. The world's population will grow from seven billion now to up to 12 billion by the end of the century, and climate change will have an increasingly negative effect on our crops. "Overcoming these challenges," the researchers argue, "will require major investments in long-term research programs, which are presently not being made, at least not in the public sector." It's not clear how many of these investments would yield results on the time scale we need, but some of them might if we begin making them now.

Genetically engineering crops to increase their yield isn't the only proposed approach to expanding the world's agricultural capacity, but, whether we like it or not, genetic engineering will certainly have to be part of the conversation. It's true that we can get more out of the crops we already have by closing what's called the yield gap, the difference between how much a crop could yield per acre with enough water and nutrients, and how much we're actually harvesting. (One recently published study estimated that by closing yield gaps, crop output could increase by as much as 80 percent in some cases.) However, this is not easy, and in many areas around the world, major staple crop yields are stagnating or even declining, rather than improving.

To solve the world's looming food shortage in a way that's environmentally sustainable, we can't just rely on closing the yield gaps of existing crops — we also need crops that yield more. A public commitment to make such crops would require not only more investment in the necessary research, but also a critical mechanism that we currently lack: a modernized regulatory process for evaluating GMO crops that is both scientifically sound and publicly transparent. As the proposals by Ort and his colleagues demonstrate, genetic engineering is a potentially powerful tool for addressing the world's food problem; as a society, we need to decide quickly whether to use it.

Thinking Critically about the Text

White says that genetically engineered plants "will certainly have to be part of the conversation" for solving world hunger. Do you agree? Are there social or political problems that could be addressed to end hunger? Are those solutions equally feasible?

Questions on Subject

1. What is photosynthesis, and why do White and other scientists want to "re-design" it?
2. Why does White believe that it will become necessary to use genetic engineering to grow additional food?
3. How would a "smart canopy" work? How would it be beneficial?
4. Why does White seem unconcerned that "few of the ideas proposed by Ort and his colleagues are feasible with current technology" (paragraph 7)?
5. What call to action does White use to close his essay? Do you find it convincing? (Glossary: *Beginnings/Endings*)

Questions on Strategy

1. In paragraph 6, White describes a growth system called "smart canopy," briefly detailing the process by which plants would grow together to maximize photosynthesis. (Glossary: *Process Analysis*) What does this explanation contribute? How is it simplified for a general audience? (Glossary: *Audience*)

2. Along with his analysis of the proposal from Ort and his team, White includes specific examples and quotations to illustrate some important points the scientists made. (Glossary: *Illustration*) In paragraph 6 he incorporates direct quotation. Where else does he bring in information from this source? Besides quotation, what other techniques does he use?
3. White begins and ends his piece with warnings about an impending global food crisis. How does this make the rest of his argument more convincing?

Questions on Diction and Vocabulary

1. Although White is writing for the more general audience in *Pacific Standard*, he is discussing a technical scientific topic. Find examples of scientific jargon he uses throughout the essay. (Glossary: *Jargon*) Do these terms make sense in context, or do you need to look them up?
2. Using a dictionary, look up any of the following words you don't know: *capacity* (paragraph 1), *ecosystems* (2), *emission* (2), *biofuels* (2), *photosynthesis* (3), *determinant* (3), *feasible* (4), *byproducts* (5), *metabolic* (5), *stagnating* (8), *regulatory* (9).

Combining Strategies in Action

White's essay is essentially a close reading of the proposal from Donald Ort and his team of scientists. As a class, do a close reading of your own, highlighting and annotating "How to Reengineer Crops for the 21st Century." Be sure to refer to the box on page 7 for a reminder of what to annotate in a text and pages 8–10 for a sample annotated essay.

Writing Suggestions

1. Advances in science can be exciting and hopeful, but they can also be concerning from ethical or environmental standpoints. Consider the potential dangers of some of the changes that White and the other scientists proposed. Then write an essay explaining why food should not be genetically modified or, conversely, why the benefits of genetic modification outweigh the risks.
2. **Writing with Sources.** White addresses the issue of world hunger in his essay. Select another important global issue (for instance, climate change or violence against members of a specific race, religion, or gender) and do some research in your school library or on the Web to see what scientists and other experts are proposing as solutions. Write a paper analyzing one of the proposed solutions and explaining why you think that it is an important option to consider. For models of and advice on integrating sources in your essay, see Chapters 14 and 15.

Language Chauvinism: The Ugly American Revisited

COOPER THOMPSON

Cooper Thompson was born in 1950 and grew up in suburban New Jersey. He began his career working in construction before pursuing work providing counseling and promoting diversity. He has been writing for more than thirty years, sharing his reflections on oppression, race, and gender from his privileged position as a "white, middle class, heterosexual man." Following his relocation to Nurnberg, Germany, in 2003, Thompson also began writing on issues related to language and immigration, drawing on his own experiences. A frequent contributor to *The Diversity Factor,* an online journal, Thompson has published in both English and German. He is the co-author of *White Men Challenging Racism: 35 Personal Stories* (2003) and also works as a personal coach and counselor.

In the following essay, which appeared in Volume 16 of *The Diversity Factor* in 2008, Thompson shares his observations about American tourists and their lack of cultural sensitivity when traveling abroad.

Preparing to Read

Have you ever travelled outside of the United States? Did you encounter any problems understanding what others were saying or difficulties in making yourself understood? If you were born in another country, what were your experiences like upon visiting the United States for the first time? Can you relate to any of Thompson's concerns?

It happened again the other day. As I was walking through Nurnberg, Germany, a couple of tourists from the U.S. asked me, in English, for directions to the Christmas Market. I was happy to help and showed them the way. But it would have been nice if they had first asked me, "Do you speak English?" instead of simply assuming that I did.

I also come from the U.S. and my first language is also English. Maybe these tourists thought that I was one of them—something about the way I walk, or my face, or my clothing perhaps? I was wearing a pair of pants I bought in the U.S. (and made in Romania) but my coat was a German brand. No, I suspect that they simply assumed that everyone here speaks English.

In my experience, this is not an isolated event. Last year, on a Lufthansa flight leaving from Frankfurt and going to the U.S., a man sitting behind me asked, in English, when the flight was expected to arrive in Boston. I don't believe I had said anything or done anything to suggest that I spoke English. And it was a German airline. I was in a bad mood that day, and instead of simply answering him, I asked him in a not-so-friendly voice. "Why do you assume that I speak English?" In response, he challenged me on my "bad" attitude. "Don't take out your frustrations on me," he said. "I was just asking a question." I chose to apologize for having said what I did, because I had taken out frustrations on him. He could have reciprocated, and it could have opened up a dialogue. But he didn't.

> No, I suspect they simply assumed that everyone here speaks English.

Another example, this time from an experience I had in France recently. I was sitting in a restaurant outside of Paris, at a table by myself, reading a German book and eating dinner. A father and son from the U.S. sat next to me; I suspected that they were from the east coast based on their accent. Without first saying "hello" or even, "Can I ask you question," the son suddenly asked me in English, "What's that you're eating?" I paused, took a breath, remembered my last experience on the Lufthansa flight, and this time, simply answered him.

A little later, as they were finishing dinner and ordering dessert, I had another opportunity to hold my tongue. The father wanted a big cup of coffee, exactly like he could get in the US. Trouble is, he had been at a Starbucks in Paris and got his tall filtered coffee just the way he wanted it. He thought he could get the same thing in this small, local restaurant. In an increasingly angry tone of voice, he told the French speaking waitress that the espresso she had served him wasn't what he wanted.

As I listened to him, I thought, "She's not going to understand him." He was talking in circles, in run-on sentences, using slang, speaking faster—and louder—as he got more frustrated. Finally, his son intervened and explained to him that he wasn't going to get his coffee here the way that he was used to in the US. Astoundingly, the father didn't understand that: if he could get his coffee at Starbucks, why not here? After all, there's a Starbucks in Paris. "Ah," I thought sarcastically, "one more reason to boycott Starbucks." They're helping to export a cherished U.S. value: "I want what I want when I want it."

I sometimes wonder if there's another value being exported, this one from the folks who don't want other languages spoken in the U.S.: "English Only." Recently, on a local train departing from the main station in Nurnberg, a young U.S. soldier in civilian clothes asked me and a couple of other passengers if we knew the train schedule. I guess I really hadn't learned my lesson from the Lufthansa flight, so I decided to challenge him. He got defensive, too, and told me, "I've lived here for a couple of years, and they understand what I'm saying. Everyone here speaks English." He was headed to a village near a U.S. army base. I know this village. There are other U.S. citizens living there, and they certainly speak English all the time. But in my experience, the locals speak dialect most of the time, and it's likely that some of them, and maybe many of them, don't speak English very well.

I live in Germany now, married to a German, and have made the decision to learn and use German when I'm in public places and in most social settings. My German isn't great—I make mistakes all the time, and sometimes it takes a little patience to understand me. And as a 58-year-old, it hasn't been easy to learn a new language in the last couple of years. I'm told by Germans that it's rare to find a U.S. citizen who speaks German. I've met U.S. (and British) citizens, some of whom have lived here for over a decade, who have told me, "I'm not going to learn German. I don't need to. At work, we speak English, and when I go shopping, people understand me." I'm sure that there are enclaves of U.S. and British citizens living around the world and who don't try to speak the local languages.

I'm not surprised that so many U.S. citizens make the assumption that everyone outside the U.S. speaks English. It is a dominant language in multinational corporations, and many young people in Europe study English in school. Here in Germany, many Germans and non-U.S. immigrants understand some English and can speak a few words. But not everyone; about 50% of the people here claim that they speak some English, which means that at least 50% don't. My in-laws, for example, are in the second category; my mother- and father-in-law don't even speak the high German that I'm learning. They speak a dialect that I can barely understand. Even among those Germans who have taken English in school, many are nervous about speaking English, for fear that they will mispronounce something.

So I am troubled when U.S. citizens immediately use English here, without first checking out if the listener can, or wants to, use English. I see this assumption of English fluency as a reflection of the privilege that comes from being a U.S. citizen and having English as a mother tongue. This may sound harsh, but to me, when U.S. citizens behave this way, it comes off as, "We're from the U.S. We don't have to think about how to communicate with others. They need to adjust to us." I call that arrogance. It's indicative of the arrogance of too many people from the U.S. It's indicative of U.S. economic and political policy towards the rest of the world. "We're from the U.S. We'll call the shots. We'll decide how others are to behave."

The next day after the restaurant experience with the father and son, I was boarding an Air France flight to the U.S. The man sitting next to me—from his accent, I assumed that he was a native French speaker—wanted to know if I was willing to change seats with his friend a couple of rows back, so that they could sit together. But before he asked me that, we exchanged a few words in both French and English, to decide which language we could and would use. We ended up using both. In my experience, this is a frequent occurrence in Europe: negotiating the language we'll use in a given situation. And sometimes, two or more languages are used simultaneously, each person choosing the one that they want to use, either for comfort or for practice. For someone listening in to the conversation, it may sound strange, but it works just fine.

I don't expect tourists from the U.S. and England visiting Nurnberg for the Christmas Market to learn German. I do expect them to be aware of language differences and to negotiate in some small way when communicating with non-native English speakers. So, my request is a simple one: first ask, "Do you speak English?" It would be nice if they also learned a few basic words in German, like "hello, thank you, and goodbye." "Sprechen Sie English?" would get them bonus points. Using a little German, and demonstrating their awareness that not everyone does or wants to speak English, would be interpreted by me as an act of humility.

I'm aware that there is nothing new in my comments here. When I shared these incidents with someone recently, she said, "Yup, the Ugly American." I don't expect that a small gesture like asking, "Sprechen Sie English?" or "Parlez-vous Anglais?" will lessen the level of arrogance projected by U.S. citizens onto the rest of the worlds' citizens. It will take strong leadership and radical change in values in the U.S. for that to change. But in the short term, I'd appreciate a simple "Do you speak English?" It would be a step in the right direction.

Thinking Critically about the Text

What events prompted Thompson to write this essay? What "cherished U.S. value" does he object to finding in France? How does Thompson's discussion of language apply to other aspects of culture?

Questions on Subject

1. Several times throughout the essay, Thompson refers to his experience on the Lufthansa flight. What happened on that flight? Why did it make such an impact on Thompson?
2. Does Thompson state his thesis explicitly? If so, where? What is his thesis?
3. Why is Thompson offended by the man from the United States who wanted a different kind of coffee?

4. In paragraph 12, Thompson says that he doesn't "expect tourists from the U.S. and England visiting Nurnberg for the Christmas Market to learn German." Does this statement undermine his argument? Why or why not?

5. Why would Thompson be satisfied if visitors asked, "Do you speak English?" before speaking to him in that language? To Thompson, what does this question imply about the person who is asking it?

Questions on Strategy

1. The first sentence of this piece is "It happened again the other day." Did not knowing what "It" was make you want to keep reading to find out? Why might this be a risky way for Thompson to begin his essay? (Glossary: *Beginnings/Endings*)

2. How does Thompson's use of dialogue contribute to his *ethos* as a writer? (Glossary: *Ethos*) Why might he have felt it was important to let readers hear the tourists speaking in their own words?

3. Thompson argues his point through a series of personal narrative examples, recounting memorable experiences. (Glossary: *Narration*) How well do these examples support his point? Does the fact that he, another native English speaker, is relating them give them more or less impact?

4. Thompson himself is a native English speaker, one who "make[s] mistakes all the time" when trying to speak German (paragraph 8). How does he contrast himself with the U.S. tourists he encounters? (Glossary: *Comparison and Contrast*)

5. Why does Thompson bring up the nervousness some Germans feel about speaking English and mention that his in-laws cannot understand even his German?

Questions on Diction and Vocabulary

1. The writer of this essay uses the first person and narrates many personal encounters. How would the tone of the essay change if it were written in the third person? (Glossary: *Tone*) Would the author be as convincing if he were relating someone else's experiences rather than his own?

2. Why does Thompson say that "I want what I want when I want it" is a "cherished U.S. value" (paragraph 6)? Is he being sincere here? (Glossary: *Irony*)

Combining Strategies in Action

In this essay, Thompson is comparing American tourists to the citizens of other countries and contrasting Americans' expectations with the realities of their visits. Visit a local supermarket and find the international foods aisle. If you were visiting from another country, do you think you could find all your familiar favorites? Compare and contrast the selection in this aisle with the broad range of foods you would find in one of the countries represented. Then use this comparison to make an argument for why foreign travel is important and why travelers should try to find experiences (edible or otherwise) that are not available to them in their home countries.

Writing Suggestions

1. In paragraph 3, Thompson says, "He could have reciprocated, and it could have opened up a dialogue. But he didn't." How would opening a dialogue have helped in this situation? Have you ever been in a situation in which you wanted to address an issue and the other person shut you down? How about a situation where you were able to resolve a minor (or major) conflict by talking it out? Write an essay recounting your experience.

2. Thompson expresses his frustration with the assumption that he speaks English. What assumptions have people made about you or someone you know? Do any of them bother you? Write an essay proposing, as Thompson has done, some ways to address the assumptions that were made about you or someone you know. Explain, briefly, the reasons the assumptions are being made and remember to be courteous to other viewpoints as you assert your own.

Me Talk Pretty One Day

DAVID SEDARIS

David Sedaris was born in 1956 in New York, the second of six children. He came to prominence after reading his essay "Santaland Diaries" on National Public Radio in December 1992. This essay, describing his experiences as an elf in a department store during the holidays, launched his career as a humorist. Since then, Sedaris has published numerous books, including the bestselling essay collections *Dress Your Family in Corduroy and Denim* (2004) and *Let's Explore Diabetes with Owls* (2013). His writing regularly appears in *The New Yorker*, and he has been nominated for three Grammy Awards.

Frederic SOULOY/ Gamma-Rapho via Getty Images

The selection below comes from Sedaris's book *Me Talk Pretty One Day* (2000), a collection of autobiographical essays, many of which recount his experiences living in Normandy, France, with his partner, Hugh. In this essay, Sedaris shares his attempts to learn French, finding humor in the egalitarian cruelty of his instructor.

Preparing to Read

Do you tend to struggle learning new things, or do they come easily to you? How might you respond to a difficult teacher? Would that teacher inspire you to work harder or make you feel discouraged?

At the age of forty-one, I am returning to school and have to think of myself as what my French textbook calls "a true debutant." After paying my tuition, I was issued a student ID, which allows me a discounted entry fee at movie theaters, puppet shows, and Festyland, a far-flung amusement park that advertises with billboards picturing a cartoon stegosaurus sitting in a canoe and eating what appears to be a ham sandwich.

I've moved to Paris with hopes of learning the language. My school is an easy ten-minute walk from my apartment, and on the first day of class I arrived early, watching as the returning students greeted one another in the school lobby. Vacations were recounted, and questions were raised concerning mutual friends with names like Kang and Vlatnya. Regardless of their nationalities, everyone spoke what sounded to me like excellent French. Some accents were better than others, but the students exhibited an ease and confidence that I found intimidating. As an added discomfort, they were all young, attractive, and well-dressed, causing me to feel not unlike Pa Kettle trapped backstage after a fashion show.

The first day of class was nerve-racking because I knew I'd be expected to perform. That's the way they do it here—it's everybody into the language pool, sink or swim. The teacher marched in, deeply tanned from a recent vacation, and proceeded to rattle off a series of administrative announcements. I've spent quite a few summers in Normandy, and I took a monthlong French class before leaving New York. I'm not completely in the dark, yet I understood only half of what this woman was saying.

> That's the way they do it here — it's everybody into the language pool, sink or swim.

"If you have not *meimslsxp* or *lgpdmurct* by this time, then you should not be in this room. Has everyone *apzkiubjxow*? Everyone? Good, we shall begin." She spread out her lesson plan and sighed, saying, "All right, then, who knows the alphabet?"

It was startling because (a) I hadn't been asked that question in a while and (b) I realized, while laughing, that I myself did not know the alphabet. They're the same letters, but in France they're pronounced differently. I know the shape of the alphabet but had no idea what it actually sounded like.

"*Ahh.*" The teacher went to the board and sketched the letter *a*. "Do we have anyone in the room whose first name commences with an *ahh*?"

Two Polish Annas raised their hands, and the teacher instructed them to present themselves by stating their names, nationalities, occupations, and a brief list of things they liked and disliked in this world. The first Anna hailed from an industrial town outside of Warsaw and had front teeth the size of tombstones. She worked as a seamstress, enjoyed quiet times with friends, and hated the mosquito.

"Oh, really," the teacher said. "How very interesting. I thought that everyone loved the mosquito, but here, in front of all the world, you claim to detest him. How is it that we've been blessed with someone as unique and original as you? Tell us, please."

The seamstress did not understand what was being said but knew that this was an occasion for shame. Her rabbity mouth huffed for breath, and she stared down at her lap as though the appropriate comeback were stitched somewhere alongside the zipper of her slacks.

The second Anna learned from the first and claimed to love sunshine and detest lies. It sounded like a translation of one of those Playmate of the Month data sheets, the answers always written in the same loopy handwriting: "Turn-ons: Mom's famous five-alarm chili! Turn offs: insecurity and guys who come on too strong!!!!"

The two Polish Annas surely had clear notions of what they loved and hated, but like the rest of us, they were limited in terms of vocabulary, and this made them appear less than sophisticated. The teacher forged on, and we learned that Carlos, the Argentine bandonion player, loved wine, music, and, in his words, "making sex with the womans of the world." Next came a beautiful young Yugoslav who identified herself as an optimist, saying that she loved everything that life had to offer.

The teacher licked her lips, revealing a hint of the saucebox we would later come to know. She crouched low for her attack, placed her hands on the young woman's desk, and leaned close, saying, "Oh yeah? And do you love your little war?"

While the optimist struggled to defend herself, I scrambled to think of an answer to what had obviously become a trick question. How often is one asked what he loves in this world? More to the point, how often is one asked and then publicly ridiculed for his answer? I recalled my mother, flushed with wine, pounding the table top one night, saying, "Love? I love a good steak cooked rare. I love my cat, and I love . . ." My sisters and I leaned forward, waiting to hear our names. "Tums," our mother said. "I love Tums."

The teacher killed some time accusing the Yugoslavian girl of masterminding a program of genocide, and I jotted frantic notes in the margins of my pad. While I can honestly say that I love leafing through medical textbooks devoted to severe dermatological conditions, the hobby is beyond the reach of my French vocabulary, and acting it out would only have invited controversy.

When called upon, I delivered an effortless list of things that I detest: blood sausage, intestinal pâtés, brain pudding. I'd learned these words the hard way. Having given it some thought, I then declared my love for IBM typewriters, the French word for *bruise*, and my electric floor waxer. It was a short list, but still I managed to mispronounce IBM and assign the wrong gender to both the floor waxer and the typewriter. The teacher's reaction led me to believe that these mistakes were capital crimes in the country of France.

"Were you always this *palicmkrexis*?" she asked. "Even a *fiuscrzsa ticiwelmun* knows that a typewriter is feminine."

I absorbed as much of her abuse as I could understand, thinking, but not saying, that I find it ridiculous to assign a gender to an inanimate object which is incapable of disrobing and making an occasional fool of itself. Why refer to Lady Crack Pipe or Good Sir Dishrag when these things could never live up to all that their sex implied?

The teacher proceeded to belittle everyone from German Eva, who hated laziness, to Japanese Yukari, who loved paintbrushes and soap. Italian, Thai, Dutch, Korean, and Chinese—we all left class foolishly believing that the worst was over. She'd shaken us up a little, but surely that was just an act designed to weed out the deadweight. We didn't know it then, but the coming months would teach us what it was like to spend time in the presence of a wild animal, something completely unpredictable. Her temperament was not based on a series of good and bad days but, rather, good and bad moments. We soon learned to dodge chalk and protect our heads and stomachs whenever she approached us with a question.

She hadn't yet punched anyone, but it seemed wise to protect ourselves against the inevitable.

Though we were forbidden to speak anything but French, the teacher would occasionally use us to practice any of her five fluent languages.

"I hate you," she said to me one afternoon. Her English was flawless. "I really, really hate you." Call me sensitive, but I couldn't help but take it personally.

After being singled out as a lazy *kfdtinvfm*, I took to spending four hours a night on my homework, putting in even more time whenever we were assigned an essay. I suppose I could have gotten by with less, but I was determined to create some sort of identity for myself: David, the hardworker, David the cut-up. We'd have one of those "complete this sentence" exercises, and I'd fool with the thing for hours, invariably settling on something like, "A quick run around the lake? I'd love to! Just give me a moment while I strap on my wooden leg." The teacher, through word and action, conveyed the message that if this was my idea of an identity, she wanted nothing to do with it.

My fear and discomfort crept beyond the borders of the classroom and accompanied me out onto the wide boulevards. Stopping for a coffee, asking directions, depositing money in my bank account: these things were out of the question, as they involved having to speak. Before beginning school, there'd been no shutting me up, but now I was convinced that everything I said was wrong. When the phone rang, I ignored it. If someone asked me a question, I pretended to be deaf. I knew my fear was getting the best of me when I started wondering why they don't sell cuts of meat in vending machines.

My only comfort was the knowledge that I was not alone. Huddled in the hallways and making the most of our pathetic French, my fellow students and I engaged in the sort of conversation commonly overheard in refugee camps.

"Sometimes me cry alone at night."

"That be common for I, also, but be more strong, you. Much work and someday you talk pretty. People start love you soon. Maybe tomorrow, okay."

Unlike the French class I had taken in New York, here there was no sense of competition. When the teacher poked a shy Korean in the eyelid with a freshly sharpened pencil, we took no comfort in the fact that, unlike Hyeyoon Cho, we all know the irregular past tense of the verb *to defeat*. In all fairness, the teacher hadn't meant to stab the girl, but neither did she spend much time apologizing, saying only, "Well, you should have been *vkkdyo* more *kdeynfulh*."

Over time it became impossible to believe that any of us would ever improve. Fall arrived and it rained every day, meaning we would now be scolded for the water dripping from our coats and umbrellas. It was mid-October when the teacher singled me out, saying, "Every day spent with you is like having a cesarean section." And it struck me that, for the first time since arriving in France, I could understand every word that someone was saying.

Understanding doesn't mean that you can suddenly speak the language. Far from it. It's a small step, nothing more, yet its rewards are intoxicating and deceptive. The teacher continued her diatribe and I settled back, bathing in the subtle beauty of each new curse and insult.

"You exhaust me with your foolishness and reward my efforts with nothing but pain, do you understand me?"

The world opened up, and it was with great joy that I responded, "I know the thing that you speak exact now. Talk me more, you, plus, please, plus."

Thinking Critically about the Text

Sedaris catalogues his attempt to learn a foreign language, and the essay ends with him discovering that he can understand French. Has he accomplished his goal of "talking pretty"? How did the behavior of his instructor impact Sedaris's satisfaction with his accomplishment?

Questions on Subject

1. Why does the instructor mock her students when they share their likes and dislikes?
2. Why is the comparison between the French teacher and "a wild animal" appropriate? Can you think of a comparison that would be more fitting?
3. How does Sedaris respond to the persistent criticism of his French teacher?
4. How did Sedaris's attitude toward speaking French outside the classroom change after he began to take classes?
5. Why, at the end of the essay, does Sedaris bathe in "the subtle beauty of each new curse and insult"?

Questions on Strategy

1. Sedaris refers to his classmates primarily by their nationalities. How does this help you to visualize the class? What other descriptive details could Sedaris have included instead? (Glossary: *Description*)
2. Despite noting that he and his classmates knew only simple words in French, Sedaris declares his love for "IBM typewriters" and his "electric floor waxer" on the first day of class (paragraph 15). Why might he have chosen these words, ones that don't typically come up in a beginner's language class? What other out-of-place words does he use?
3. In paragraph 13, Sedaris includes a brief flashback to his mother. Why might he have included it in his narrative? What does it contribute to the author's sense of the ridiculous? To his sense of meaningless oppression? (Glossary: *Organization*)

4. Why does Sedaris feel that assigning genders to words is silly? Is his reasoning convincing?

5. What is the effect of the final sentence? Why is it a perfect ending to the piece? (Glossary: *Beginnings/Endings*)

Questions on Diction and Vocabulary

1. Sedaris uses random collections of letters instead of actual French words in his essay (for example, *meimslsxp* in paragraph 4). Why do you think he chose to do so? What does it contribute to the comedy of the piece?

2. Throughout the essay, Sedaris uses very poor grammar in English to illustrate the poor grammar he was using in French. How is this nonstandard English more effective in communicating his struggle than standard English would have been? (Glossary: *Strategy*)

Combining Strategies in Action

Examine the following conversation (documented by Ursula Bellugi in 1970) between Eve, a twenty-four-month-old child, and her mother:

Eve: Have that?

Mother: No, you may not have it.

Eve: Mom, where my tapioca?

Mother: It's getting cool. You'll have it in just a minute.

Eve: Let me have it.

Mother: Would you like to have your lunch right now?

Eve: Yeah. My tapioca cool?

Mother: Yes, it's cool.

Eve: You gonna watch me eat my lunch?

Mother: Yeah, I'm gonna watch you eat your lunch.

Eve: I eating it.

Mother: I know you are.

Eve: It time Sarah take a nap.

Mother: It's time for Sarah to have some milk, yeah. And then she's gonna take a nap and you're gonna take a nap.

Eve: And you?

Mother: And me too, yeah.

Compare the grammar of Eve's speech with that of her mother. What grammatical features are systematically missing from Eve's speech? Now look at a conversation between Eve and her mother recorded only three months later:

Mother: Come and sit over here.

Eve: You can sit down by me. That will make me happy. Ready to turn it.

Mother: We're not quite ready to turn the page.

Eve: Yep, we are.

Mother: Shut the door, we won't hear her then.

Eve: Then Fraser won't hear her too. Where he's going? Did you make a great big hole there?

Mother: Yes, we made a great big hole in here; we have to get a new one.

Eve: Could I get some other piece of paper?

Mother: You ask Fraser.

Eve: Could I use this one?

Mother: I suppose so.

Eve: Is Fraser goin take his pencil home when he goes?

Mother: Yes he is.

When you compare Eve's speech at twenty-four months to her speech at twenty-seven months, what changes do you notice? Try to describe the grammatical understanding or rules Eve seems to have acquired. What parts of her speech provide evidence for the grammar she has learned? Using these conversations and your comparisons of Eve's grammatical constructions, discuss how learning a foreign language is similar to a young child learning to speak for the first time.

Writing Suggestions

1. Think of a misadventure of your own and brainstorm details of what went wrong and why. Then write a comedic narrative, incorporating vivid descriptive language and examples to engage readers.

2. As a native speaker of a language, you have several basic language competencies. For example, you can determine whether an utterance is a grammatical sentence. Other competencies include the ability to tell when two or more sentences are synonymous, recognize ambiguity in a sentence, and interpret completely novel utterances. Discuss these competencies, suggesting examples from your own speech to illustrate each one of the skills.

3. Write an essay in which you explore your experiences learning a second language. Did you grow up in a household in which two or more languages were spoken? If so, were you encouraged to be bilingual or monolingual? At what grade level was a second language introduced in school? For you, what were the greatest stumbling blocks in learning a second language, and what did you do to overcome them? Based on your own experiences with languages, what are the advantages and disadvantages of being bilingual?

WRITING SUGGESTIONS FOR COMBINING STRATEGIES

1. Select a piece you have written for this class in which you used one primary writing strategy and rewrite it using another strategy. For example, choose a description you wrote and redraft it as a process analysis. Remember that the choice of a writing strategy influences the writer's "voice"; a descriptive piece might be lyrical, while a process analysis might be straightforward. How does your voice change along with the strategy? Does your assumed audience change as well? (Glossary: *Audience*)

    If time allows, exchange a piece of writing with a partner and rewrite your partner's piece using a different strategy. Discuss the choices you each made.

2. Select an essay you have written this semester, either for this class or for another class. What was the primary writing strategy you used? Build on this essay by integrating another strategy. For example, if you wrote an argument paper for a political science class, you might try using narrative to give some historical background to the paper. (Glossary: *Argument; Narration*) For a paper in the natural sciences, you could use subjective description to open the paper up to nonscientists. (Glossary: *Objective/Subjective*) When you're finished, ask yourself: How did use of the new strategy affect your paper?

3. The choice of a writing strategy reflects an author's voice — the persona he or she assumes in relation to the reader. Read back through any personal writing you've done this semester — a journal, letters to friends, e-mail. Can you identify the strategies you use outside formal academic writing, as part of your natural writing voice? Write a few pages analyzing these strategies and your writing voice, using one of the rhetorical strategies studied this term. For example, you could compare and contrast your e-mail postings to your letters home. (Glossary: *Comparison and Contrast*) Or you could do a cause and effect analysis of how being at college has changed the tone or style of your journal writing. (Glossary: *Cause and Effect Analysis*)

4. **Writing with Sources.** Review the "Why Milk?" ad that opens this chapter (page 630). Write an essay in which you discuss the ad and the issues that underlie it. As you work, consider these questions: What are the potentially harmful effects of producing milk by using hormones and antibiotics? Of drinking such milk? If you agree that change is needed, explain what you would change and how. If you disagree with the ad, respond to the implicit claims of those who *do* call for change. Consider placing your argument in the context of economic, social, scientific, ethical, or ideological discussions of

modern agriculture, the environment, health, diet, capitalism, advertising, political correctness, or another related topic that interests you.

You will need to do some research to bolster your claims. For models of and advice on integrating sources in your essay, see Chapters 14 and 15.

5. **Writing in the Workplace.** Find a local newspaper editorial dealing with a controversial social or educational problem. Outline the issues involved and the strategies that the editorial writer used to present his or her argument. Then assume that you — a concerned citizen — are given equal space in the newspaper to present an opposing viewpoint. Make notes for a rebuttal argument and for the development strategies you might use to support your argument, considering, for example, narration, process analysis, comparison and contrast, and/or illustration. Finally, write your response to the editorial and submit a copy to the newspaper that published the original piece.

Joel Robison/Trevillion Images

CHAPTER **14**

Writing with Sources

WHAT DOES IT MEAN TO WRITE WITH SOURCES?

MANY OF YOUR COLLEGE ASSIGNMENTS WILL CALL UPON YOU TO DO research and write using information from sources. To do this effectively, you will have to learn some basic research practices—locating and evaluating print and online sources, taking notes from those sources, and documenting those sources. (For help with research and documentation, see Chapter 15, pages 716–38.) Even more fundamental than this, however, is to understand what it *means* to do research and to write with sources.

Your purpose in writing with sources is not to present a collection of quotations that report what others have said about your topic. Rather, your goal is to *analyze*, *evaluate*, and *synthesize* the materials you have researched so that you become a full-fledged participant in the conversation about your topic. To enter into this conversation with authority, you will have to learn how to use sources ethically and effectively. To help you on your way, this chapter provides advice on summarizing, paraphrasing, and quoting sources; integrating sources; and avoiding plagiarism. In addition, two student papers and two professional essays model different ways of engaging meaningfully with sources and of reflecting that engagement in writing.

On the opposite page, note how Joel Robison's surreal photograph plays with the idea of writing with sources. Using books and other sources as his literal foundation, his writing transforms from mere words on a page into elegant, butterfly-like origami structures with identities of their own.

WRITING WITH SOURCES

Outside sources can be used to:

- Support your thesis and points with statements from noted authorities
- Offer memorable wording of key terms or ideas
- Extend your ideas by introducing new information
- Articulate opposing positions for you to argue against

Consider Sharon Begley's use of an outside source in the following paragraph from her *Newsweek* essay "Praise the Humble Dung Beetle":

> Of all creatures great and small, it is the charismatic megafauna—tigers and rhinos and gorillas and pandas and other soulful-eyed, warm, and fuzzy animals—that personify endangered species. That's both a shame and a dangerous bias. "Plants and invertebrates are the silent majority which feed the entire planet, stabilize the soil, and make all life possible," says Kiernan Suckling, cofounder of the Center for Biological Diversity. They pollinate crops and decompose carcasses, filter water and, lacking weapons like teeth and claws, brew up molecules to defend themselves that turn out to be remarkably potent medicines: The breast-cancer compound taxol comes from a yew tree, and a leukemia drug from the rosy periwinkle. Those are tricks that, Suckling dryly notes, "polar bears and blue whales haven't mastered yet."

Here Begley quotes Kiernan Suckling, a biologist specializing in biodiversity, to support her contention that it's "both a shame and a dangerous bias" to have tigers, polar bears, and other photogenic mammals be the headliners for all endangered species.

Sometimes source material is too long and detailed to be quoted directly in its entirety. In such cases, a writer will choose to summarize or paraphrase the material in his or her own words before introducing it in an essay. For example, notice how Judith Newman summarizes two lengthy sleep studies for use in her essay "What's Really Going On Inside Your Teen's Head," which appeared in the November 28, 2010, issue of *Parade* magazine:

> In a pair of related studies published in 1993 and 1997 by Mary Carskadon, a professor of psychiatry at Brown University and director of the Sleep Research program at Bradley Hospital in Rhode Island, Carskadon and colleagues found that more physically mature girls preferred activities later in the day than did less-mature girls and that the sleep-promoting hormone melatonin rises later in teenagers than in children and adults. Translation: Teenagers are physically programmed to stay up later and sleep later.

Here, Newman introduces her summary with an extensive signal phrase highlighting Mary Carskadon's academic credentials, and she concludes with a pointed statement of the researchers' conclusion, information that is needed to broaden her discussion.

In the following passage from "Blaming the Family for Economic Decline," Stephanie Coontz uses outside sources to present the position that she will argue against:

> The fallback position for those in denial about the socioeconomic transformation we are experiencing is to admit that many families are in economic stress but to blame their plight on divorce and unwed motherhood. Lawrence Mead of New York University argues that economic

inequalities stemming from differences in wages and employment patterns "are now trivial in comparison to those stemming from family structure." David Blankenhorn claims that the "primary fault line" dividing privileged and nonprivileged Americans is no longer "race, religion, class, education, or gender" but family structure. Every major newspaper in the country has published editorials and opinion pieces along these lines. This "new consensus" produces a delightfully simple, inexpensive solution to the economic ills of America's families. From Republican Dan Quayle to the Democratic Party's Progressive Policy Institute, we hear the same words: "Marriage is the best antipoverty program for children."

Now I am as horrified as anyone by irresponsible parents who yield to the temptations of our winner-take-all society and abandon their family obligations. But we are kidding ourselves if we think the solution to the economic difficulties of America's children lies in getting their parents back together. Single-parent families, it is true, are five to six times more likely to be poor than two-parent ones. But correlations are not the same as causes. The association between poverty and single parenthood has several different sources, suggesting that the battle to end child poverty needs to be fought on a number of different fronts.

By letting the opposition articulate their own position, Coontz reduces the possibility of being criticized for misrepresenting her opponents; at the same time, she sets herself up to give strong voice to her thesis.

LEARNING TO SUMMARIZE, PARAPHRASE, AND QUOTE FROM YOUR SOURCES

When taking notes from your sources, you must decide whether to summarize, paraphrase, or quote directly. The approach you take largely depends on the content of the source passage and the way you envision using it in your paper. Be aware, however, that making use of all three of these techniques — rather than relying on only one or two — will keep your text varied and interesting.

Learning to summarize, paraphrase, and quote effectively and correctly is essential for the writing you'll do in school, at work, and in everyday life. The following sections will help you understand how the three techniques differ, when to use these techniques, and how to make them work within the context of your writing.

▶ Summarizing

When you *summarize* material from one of your sources, you use your own words to capture in condensed form the essential idea of a passage, an article, or an entire chapter. Summaries are particularly useful when you are working with lengthy, detailed arguments or long passages of narrative or descriptive background information not germane to the overall thrust of your paper. You simply want to capture the essence of the passage while dispensing with the details because you are confident that your readers will readily understand the point being made or will not need to be convinced about the validity of the point. Because you are distilling information, a summary is always shorter than the original; often a chapter or more can be reduced to a paragraph, or several paragraphs to a sentence or two. Remember, in writing a summary you should use your own words.

Consider the following paragraphs in which Richard Lederer compares big words with small words:

> When you speak and write, there is no law that says you have to use big words. Short words are as good as long ones, and short, old words—like *sun* and *grass* and *home*—are best of all. A lot of small words, more than you might think, can meet your needs with a strength, grace, and charm that large words do not have.
>
> Big words can make the way dark for those who read what you write and hear what you say. Small words cast their clear light on big things—night and day, love and hate, war and peace, and life and death. Big words at times seem strange to the eye and the ear and the mind and the heart. Small words are the ones we seem to have known from the time we were born, like the hearth fire that warms the home.
>
> —RICHARD LEDERER,
> "The Case for Short Words," pages 558–59

A student wishing to capture the gist of Lederer's point without repeating his detail wrote the following summary:

> Lederer favors short words for their clarity, familiarity, durability, and overall usefulness (558–59).

▶ Paraphrasing

When you *paraphrase* a source, you restate the information in your own words instead of quoting directly. Unlike a summary, which gives a brief overview of the essential information in the original, a paraphrase seeks to maintain the same level of detail as the original to aid readers in understanding or believing the information presented. A summary, then, condenses the original material, while a paraphrase presents the original information in approximately the same number of words as the original.

Paraphrase can be thought of as a sort of middle ground between summary and quotation, but beware: While a paraphrase should closely parallel the presentation of ideas in the original, it should not use the same words or sentence structure as the original. Even though you are using your own words in a paraphrase, it's important to remember that you are borrowing ideas and therefore must acknowledge the source of these ideas with a citation.

How would you paraphrase the following passage from a speech by Martin Luther King, Jr.?

> But one hundred years later [after the Emancipation Proclamation], we must face the tragic fact that the Negro is still not free. One hundred years later, the life of the Negro is still sadly crippled by the manacles of segregation and the chains of discrimination. One hundred years later, the Negro lives on a lonely island of poverty in the midst of a vast ocean of material prosperity. One hundred years later, the Negro is still languishing in the corners of American society and finds himself an exile in his own land.
>
> —Martin Luther King Jr., "I Have a Dream"

One student paraphrased the passage from King's speech as follows:

> Speaking on the one hundredth anniversary of the Emancipation Proclamation, King observed that African Americans still found themselves a marginalized people. He contended that African Americans did not experience the freedom that other Americans did—in a land of opportunity and plenty, racism and poverty affected the way they lived their lives, separating them from mainstream society (par. 3).

In most cases, it is better to summarize or paraphrase materials—which by definition means using your own words—instead of quoting verbatim (word for word). Capturing an idea in your own words ensures that you have thought about and understood what your source is saying.

▶ Using Direct Quotation

You should reserve direct quotation for important ideas stated memorably, for especially clear explanations by authorities, and for arguments by proponents of a particular position. Consider the following direct quotation that one student chose. The student quotes a passage from Malcolm Jones's article "Who Was More Important: Lincoln or Darwin?" that appeared in *Newsweek* on July 14, 2008. Notice how Jones captures Charles Darwin's mixed emotions upon realizing the impact his theory of evolution would have on the world:

> "As delighted as he was with his discovery, Darwin was equally horrified, because he understood the consequences of his theory. Mankind was no longer the culmination of life but merely part of it; creation was mechanistic and purposeless. In a letter to a fellow scientist, Darwin wrote that confiding his theory was 'like confessing a murder.' Small wonder that instead of rushing to publish his theory, he sat on it — for twenty years."

The skillful prose Jones uses to describe Darwin's state of mind makes this passage well worth quoting in full rather than summarizing or paraphrasing.

▶ Using Direct Quotation with Summary or Paraphrase

On occasion, you'll find a useful passage with some memorable phrases in it. Avoid the temptation to quote the whole passage; instead, you can combine summary or paraphrase with direct quotation. Consider, for example, the following paragraph from Rosalind Wiseman's essay on schoolgirls' roles in cliques:

> Information about other people is currency in Girl World — whoever has the most information has the most power. I call that girl the "Banker." She creates chaos by banking information about girls in her social sphere and dispensing it at strategic intervals.
>
> For instance, if a girl has said something negative about another girl, the Banker will casually mention it to someone in conversation because she knows it's going to cause a conflict and strengthen her status as someone in the know. She can get girls to trust her because when she pumps them for information it doesn't seem like gossip; instead, she does it in an innocent, "I'm trying to be there for you" kind of way.
>
> — Rosalind Wiseman, "The Queen Bee and Her Court," page 358

Note how one student cited this passage using paraphrase *and* quotation:

> In Wiseman's schema, the most dangerous character in the clique is the Banker, who "creates chaos by banking information about girls in her social sphere and dispensing it at strategic intervals" (358). The Banker spreads gossip freely in order to cement her position as someone "'in the know'" (358).

Be sure that when you directly quote a source, you copy the words *exactly* and put quotation marks around them. Check and double-check your copy for accuracy, whether it's handwritten, transcribed, or copied and pasted from the original source.

▶ Integrating Borrowed Material into Your Text

Whenever you use borrowed material, be it a quotation, paraphrase, or summary, your goal is to integrate it smoothly and logically to avoid disrupting the flow of your paper or confusing your readers. It is best to introduce such material with a *signal phrase* that alerts readers that borrowed information is about to be presented. A signal phrase minimally consists of the author's name and a verb (e.g., *Michael Pollan contends*).

How well you integrate a quote, paraphrase, or summary into your paper depends partly on varying your signal phrases and, in particular, choosing verbs for these signal phrases that accurately convey the tone and intent of the writers you are citing. Signal phrases help readers better follow your train of thought. If a writer is arguing, use the verb *argues* (or *asserts*, *claims*, or *contends*); if the writer is contesting a particular position or fact, use the verb *contests* (or *denies*, *disputes*, *refutes*, or *rejects*). In using verbs that are specific to the situation in your paper, you bring your readers into the intellectual debate as well as avoid the monotony of repeating such all-purpose verbs as *says* or *writes*.

The following are just a few examples of how you can vary signal phrases to add interest to your paper:

Malcolm X confesses that . . .

As professor of linguistics at Georgetown University, Deborah Tannen has observed . . .

Bruce Catton, noted Civil War historian, emphasizes . . .

Rosalind Wiseman rejects the widely held belief that . . .

Robert Ramírez enriches our understanding of . . .

Jane Shaw, formerly a senior fellow at the Property and Environment Research Center, contends . . .

Here are other verbs that you might use when constructing signal phrases:

acknowledges	declares	points out
adds	endorses	reasons
admits	grants	reports
believes	implies	responds
compares	insists	suggests
confirms		

Signal phrases also let your reader know exactly where your ideas end and someone else's begin. Never confuse your reader by inserting a quotation that appears suddenly without introduction in your paper. Unannounced quotations leave your reader wondering how the quoted material relates to the point you are trying to make.

Unannounced Quotation

> It's no secret that digital technology is having profound effects on American society, often shaping our very attitudes about the world. We're living at a time when this technology makes it not only possible, but also surprisingly easy for us to copy and share software, music, and video. Is this a good situation? Software and music companies see such copying as theft or a violation of copyright law. "[M]any of my students see matters differently. They freely copy and share music. And they copy and share software, even though such copying is often illegal" (417).

In the following revision, the student integrated the quotation from Gorry's essay "Steal This MP3 File: What Is Theft?" by giving the name of the writer being quoted, referring to his authority on the subject, noting that the writer is speaking from experience, and using the verb *counters*.

Integrated Quotation

> It's no secret that digital technology is having profound effects on American society, often shaping our very attitudes about the world. We're living at a time when this technology makes it not only possible, but also surprisingly easy for us to copy and share software, music, and video. Is this a good situation? Software and music companies see such copying as theft or a violation of copyright law. "[M]any of my students see matters differently," counters information technology specialist and Rice University professor G. Anthony Gorry. "They freely copy and share music. And they copy and share software, even though such copying is often illegal" (417).

▶ Synthesizing Several Sources to Deepen Your Discussion

Synthesis enables you to weave your ideas with the ideas of others in a single paragraph, deepening your discussion and often helping you arrive at a new interpretation or conclusion. By learning how to synthesize the results of your research from your own perspective, you can arrive at an informed opinion of your topic.

When you synthesize several sources in your writing, you get your sources to "talk" with one another. You literally create a conversation in which you take an active role. Sometimes you will find yourself discussing two or three sources together to show a range of views regarding a particular topic or issue—this is called *informational* or *explanatory synthesis*. At other times, you will have opportunities to play your sources off against one another so as to delineate the opposing positions—this is called *persuasive* or *argument synthesis*.

In the following example from her essay "The Qualities of Good Teachers," student Marah Britto uses informational synthesis to combine her own thoughts about good teachers with the thoughts of three other writers. In doing so, she explains the range of attributes that distinguish good teachers from their peers:

> We have all experienced a teacher who in some way stands out from all the others we have had, a teacher who has made an important difference in each of our lives. While most of us can agree on some of the character traits—dedication, love for students, patience, passion for his/her subject—that such teachers have in common, we cannot agree on that special something that sets them apart, the something that distinguishes them from the crowd. For me, it was my sixth-grade teacher Mrs. Engstrom, a teacher who motivated with her example. She never asked me to do anything that she was not willing to do herself. How many teachers show their love of ornithology by taking a student out for a bird walk at 5:30 in the morning, on a school day no less? For Thomas L. Friedman, it was his high school journalism teacher Hattie M. Steinberg. In "My Favorite Teacher," he relates how her insistence upon the importance of "fundamentals" made a lifelong impression on him, so much so that he never had to take another journalism course (12). For Carl Rowan, it was his high school English, history, and civics teacher Miss Bessie Taylor Gwynn, whose influence he captures in "Unforgettable Miss Bessie." Miss Bessie taught Rowan to hold himself to high standards, to refuse "to lower [his] standards to those of the crowd" (87). And for Joanne Lipman, it was Mr. Jerry Kupchynsky, her childhood music teacher. She remembers how tough and demanding he was on his students, how he made his students "better than we had any right to be." Ironically, Lipman muses, "I doubt any of us realized how much we loved him for it." Interestingly, isn't it mutual respect and love that is at the heart of any memorable student–teacher bond?
>
> Sources
>
> Friedman, Thomas L. "My Favorite Teacher." *Subject & Strategy*. Edited by Paul Eschholz and Alfred Rosa, 14th ed, Bedford/St. Martin's, 2017, pp. 12–14.

> Lipman, Joanne. "And the Orchestra Played On." *New York Times*, 28 Feb. 2010, www.nytimes.com/2010/02/28/opinion/28lipman.html?_r=0.
> Rowan, Carl T. "Unforgettable Miss Bessie." *Reader's Digest*, Mar. 1985, pp. 87–91.

The second example is taken from student Bonnie Sherman's essay "Should Shame Be Used as Punishment?" Here she uses argument synthesis deftly to combine Hawthorne's use of shame in *The Scarlet Letter* with two opposing essays about shame as punishment, both of which appeared together in the *Boston Globe*. Notice how Sherman uses her own reading of *The Scarlet Letter* as evidence to ultimately side with Professor Kahan's position:

> Shame has long been used as an alternative punishment to more traditional sentences of corporeal punishment, jail time, or community service. American colonists used the stocks to publically humiliate citizens for their transgressions. In *The Scarlet Letter*, author Nathaniel Hawthorne recounts the story of how the community of Boston punished Hester Prynne for her adulterous affair by having her wear a scarlet letter "A" on her breast as a badge of shame. Such punishments were controversial then and continue to spark heated debate in today's world of criminal justice. Like June Tangney, psychology professor at George Mason University, many believe that shaming punishments—those designed to humiliate offenders—are unusually cruel and should be abandoned. In her article "Condemn the Crime, Not the Person," she argues that "shame serves to escalate the very destructive patterns of behavior we aim to curb" (34). Interestingly, Hester Prynne's post-punishment life of community service and charitable work does not seem to bear out Tangney's claim. In contrast, Yale Law School professor Dan M. Kahan believes that Tangney's "anxieties about shame . . . seem overstated," and he persuasively supports this position in his essay "Shame Is Worth a Try" by citing a study showing that the threat of public humiliation generates more compliance than does the threat of jail time (34).
>
> Sources
> Hawthorne, Nathaniel. *The Scarlet Letter*. Bantam Books, 1981.
> Kahan, Dan M. "Shame Is Worth a Try." *Boston Globe*, 5 Aug. 2001, p. A34.
> Tangney, June. "Condemn the Crime, Not the Person." *Boston Globe*, 5 Aug. 2001, p. A34.

In your essay, instead of simply presenting your sources with a quotation here and a summary there, look for opportunities to use synthesis, to go beyond an individual source by relating several of your sources to one another and to your own thesis. Use the following checklist to help you with synthesis in your writing.

> **Checklist for Writing a Synthesis**
>
> 1. Start by writing a brief summary of each source that you will refer to in your synthesis.
> 2. Explain in your own words how your sources are related to one another and to your own ideas. For example, what assumptions do your sources share? Do your sources present opposing views? Do your sources illustrate a range or diversity of opinions? Do your sources support or challenge your ideas?
> 3. Have a clear idea or topic sentence for your paragraph before starting to write.
> 4. Combine information from two or more sources with your own ideas to support or illustrate your main idea.
> 5. Use signal phrases and parenthetical citations to show your readers the source of your borrowed materials.
> 6. Have fresh interpretations or conclusions as a goal each time you synthesize sources.

AVOIDING PLAGIARISM

The importance of honesty and accuracy in doing library research can't be stressed enough. Any material borrowed word for word must be placed within quotation marks and properly cited; any idea, explanation, or argument you have paraphrased or summarized must be documented, and it must be clear where the paraphrased material begins and ends. In short, to use someone else's ideas, whether in their original form or in an altered form, without proper acknowledgment is to be guilty of plagiarism.

You must acknowledge and document the source of your information whenever you do any of the following:

- Quote a source word for word
- Refer to information and ideas from another source that you present in your own words, as either a paraphrase or a summary
- Cite statistics, tables, charts, graphs, or other visuals

You do not need to document the following types of information:

- Your own observations, experiences, ideas, and opinions
- Factual information available in a number of sources (information known as "common knowledge")
- Proverbs, sayings, or familiar quotations

For a discussion of MLA-style in-text documentation, see pages 728–30.

The Council of Writing Program Administrators offers the following helpful definition of *plagiarism* in academic settings for administrators, faculty, and students: "In an instructional setting, plagiarism occurs when a writer deliberately uses someone else's language, ideas, or other (not common knowledge) material without acknowledging its source." Note, however, that accusations of plagiarism can be substantiated even if plagiarism is accidental. A little attention and effort at the note-taking stage can go a long way toward eliminating the possibility of such inadvertent plagiarism. While taking notes, check all direct quotations against the wording of the original and double-check your paraphrases to be sure that you have not used the writer's wording or sentence structure. It is easy to forget to put quotation marks around material taken verbatim or to use the same sentence structure and most of the same words—substituting a synonym here and there—and record it as a paraphrase. In working closely with the ideas and words of others, intellectual honesty demands that you distinguish between what you borrow—and therefore acknowledge in a citation—and what is your own.

While writing your paper, be careful whenever you incorporate one of your notes into your paper: Make sure that you put quotation marks around material taken verbatim and double-check your text against your notes—or, better yet, against the original if you have it on hand—to make sure that your quotations are accurate and that all paraphrases and summaries are really in your own words.

Using Quotation Marks for Language Borrowed Directly

Whenever you use another person's exact words or sentences, you must enclose the borrowed language in quotation marks. Without quotation marks, you give your reader the impression that the wording is your own. Even if you cite the source, you are guilty of plagiarism if you fail to use quotation marks. The following example demonstrates both plagiarism and a correct citation for a direct quotation.

Original Source

> On my father's side, I figured, high cheekbones and almond eyes probably showed evidence of native-Andean blood. The aquiline profiles and curly hair on my mother's side, on the other hand, are common on Mediterranean shores. My best guess: I was mostly European, a bit of native South American, and perhaps a dash of Middle Eastern.
>
> —Carolina A. Miranda,
> "Diving into the Gene Pool,"
> *Time* magazine, 20 Aug. 2006, page 64

Plagiarism

On my father's side, I figured, high cheekbones and almond eyes probably showed evidence of native-Andean blood, confesses Carolina A. Miranda. The aquiline profiles and curly hair on my mother's side, on the other hand, are common on Mediterranean shores. My best guess: I was mostly European, a bit of native South American, and perhaps a dash of Middle Eastern (64).

Correct Citation of Borrowed Words in Quotation Marks

"On my father's side, I figured, high cheekbones and almond eyes probably showed evidence of native-Andean blood," confesses Carolina A. Miranda. "The aquiline profiles and curly hair on my mother's side, on the other hand, are common on Mediterranean shores. My best guess: I was mostly European, a bit of native South American, and perhaps a dash of Middle Eastern" (64).

▶ Using Your Own Words and Word Order When Summarizing and Paraphrasing

When summarizing or paraphrasing a source, you need to use your own language. Pay particular attention to word choice and word order, especially if you are paraphrasing. Remember, it is not enough simply to use a synonym here or there and think you have paraphrased the source; you *must* restate the idea from the original in your own words, using your own style and sentence structure. In the following example, notice how plagiarism can occur when care is not taken in the wording or sentence structure of a paraphrase. Notice that in the acceptable paraphrase, the student writer uses her own language and sentence structure.

Original Source

Stereotypes are a kind of gossip about the world, a gossip that makes us prejudge people before we ever lay eyes on them. Hence it is not surprising that stereotypes have something to do with the dark world of prejudice. Explore most prejudices (note that the word means prejudgment) and you will find a cruel stereotype at the core of each one.

—Robert L. Heilbroner,
"Don't Let Stereotypes Warp Your Judgments,"
Think magazine, June 1961, page 43

Unacceptably Close Wording

According to Heilbroner, we prejudge other people even before we have seen them when we think in stereotypes. That stereotypes are related to the ugly world of prejudice should not surprise anyone. If you explore the heart of most prejudices, beliefs that literally prejudge, you will discover a mean stereotype lurking (43).

Unacceptably Close Sentence Structure

Heilbroner believes that stereotypes are images of people, images that enable people to prejudge other people before they have seen them. Therefore, no one should find it surprising that stereotypes are somehow related to the ugly world of prejudice. Examine most prejudices (the word literally means prejudgment) and you will uncover a vicious stereotype at the center of each (43).

Acceptable Paraphrase

Heilbroner believes that there is a link between stereotypes and the hurtful practice of prejudice. Stereotypes make for easy conversation, a kind of shorthand that enables us to find fault with people before ever meeting them. If you were to dissect most human prejudices, you would likely discover an ugly stereotype lurking somewhere inside it (43).

> ## Preventing Plagiarism
>
> ### Questions to Ask about Direct Quotations
>
> - Do quotation marks clearly indicate the language that I borrowed verbatim?
> - Is the language of the quotation accurate, with no missing or misquoted words or phrases?
> - Do brackets or ellipsis marks clearly indicate any changes or omissions I have introduced?
> - Does a signal phrase naming the author introduce each quotation? Does the verb in the signal phrase help establish a context for each quotation?
> - Does a parenthetical page citation follow each quotation?
>
> ### Questions to Ask about Summaries and Paraphrases
>
> - Is each summary and paraphrase written in my own words and style?
> - Does each summary and paraphrase accurately represent the opinion, position, or reasoning of the original writer?
> - Does each summary and paraphrase start with a signal phrase so that readers know where my borrowed material begins?
> - Does each summary and paraphrase conclude with a parenthetical page citation?
>
> ### Questions to Ask about Facts and Statistics
>
> - Do I use a signal phrase or some other marker to introduce each fact or statistic that is not common knowledge so that readers know where the borrowed material begins?
> - Is each fact or statistic that is not common knowledge clearly documented with a parenthetical page citation?

Finally, as you proofread your final draft, check all your citations one last time. If at any time while you are taking notes or writing your paper you have a question about plagiarism, consult your instructor for clarification and guidance before proceeding.

SAMPLE STUDENT ESSAY USING LIBRARY AND INTERNET SOURCES

Courtney Sypher wrote the following essay following a unit on the uses and abuses of social media in one of her psychology courses. At about the same time, the news was full of sordid stories about how students were using social media and the Internet to bully their peers. Sypher decided to explore the world of cyberbullying, especially as it manifested itself on college campuses.

Sypher began by brainstorming about her topic, listing recent news stories that had received a great deal of attention. She then went to her college library and searched the Internet, where she located additional information about these stories and about current research on cyberbullying from a number of credible sources. After carefully reading her sources and taking notes, she decided to organize her essay around two central examples of cyberbullying on college campuses.

Sypher's essay is annotated so that you can readily see how she has effectively integrated sources into her paper and has used them to establish, explore, and support her key points. Sypher uses MLA-style documentation.

From Computer Cruelty to Campus Crime:
Cyberbullying at College
Courtney Sypher

Does anyone really believe that "sticks and stones may break your bones, but names will never hurt you?" Words hurt, especially now that they come in through every laptop, tablet, and phone we own. And today, this *cyberbullying* doesn't just stop with words, but can also include compromising images or videos that are stolen or coerced. Cyberbullying has only been possible in the past decade, and yet it's everywhere, affecting students from grade school through college. Distressingly, not everyone sees it as a true cultural problem. Some people believe that bullying is a natural part of growing up, and the Facebook page "Cyberbullying is a Joke" has more than five hundred "likes." Rightly, many more people disagree, as evidenced by a more popular page titled "Stop Cyberbullying," which has tens of thousands of fans. Such numbers suggest that, on the whole, awareness and prevention movements are popular, but the newness of cyberbullying means that we understand very little about it. This is especially troubling when we look at college campuses, where students' independence and lack of parental supervision (and protection) have led to deadly consequences.

Ongoing research in the fields of psychology, sociology, and education is working not only to define what cyberbullying is, but also to understand its effects. In some ways cyberbullying is simply a new type of bully behavior. In their book *Cyber Bullying: Bullying in the Digital Age*, psychologists Robin M. Kowalski, Susan P. Limber, and Patricia W. Agatston call the phenomenon a "recent variant of the traditional bullying process, in which individuals use electronic communication as a medium to harass, degrade, embarrass, and deliberately hurt others" (23). Other research studies identify several distinguishing features that make cyberbullying seem more dangerous than what had been seen with traditional bullying. In their 2006 study entitled "Bullies Move Beyond the Schoolyard," criminal justice professors Justin W. Patchin and Sameer Hinduja suggest that cyberbullying's "perceived anonymity" and ability to "exten[d] into the home environment via personal computers or cell phones" can make it seem "more volatile" and more invasive than typical afterschool banter (qtd. in Dempsey et al. 963). And in a 2012 study, Allison G. Dempsey and her colleagues noted that

SAMPLE STUDENT ESSAY USING LIBRARY AND INTERNET SOURCES | **683**

<table>
<tr>
<td>Sypher synthesizes sources to arrive at a definition of cyberbullying</td>
<td>because of the far-reaching, always-on nature of our devices, "cyber aggressors have the opportunity to victimize a greater number of people and in front of a larger audience than in traditional peer victimization" (963). Ultimately, cyberbullying means *non-stop* harassment by *more bullies* against *more victims*.</td>
</tr>
<tr>
<td>Sypher introduces a "hybrid" case of cyberbullying with a signal phrase and marks the end with a parenthetical citation of author's name</td>
<td>At least one college campus recently documented a sort of hybrid case: a traditional bullying tactic possibly emboldened by the perceived anonymity of cyberbullying. ABC News reported that on October 8, 2012, at Miami University of Ohio (MU), a typed flier titled "Top Ten Ways to Get Away with Rape" was found hanging in the men's bathroom of a coed dormitory. The flier included tips "encouraging men to have sex with unconscious women because it 'doesn't count,' drugging women with 'roofies,' and slitting women's throats if they recognized their attackers" (Curry). While some may</td>
</tr>
<tr>
<td>Sypher then analyzes and interprets the meaning of the MU Ohio example</td>
<td>dismiss the flier as a vague example of traditional harassment, the anonymity of its typed print and its display in a busy public space are similar to—and perhaps even inspired by—a public Facebook post. In fact, social media enabled news of the flier to spread rapidly, with a mix of consequences. As more students found out about it, more students (especially women) felt threatened and victimized. Yet, that attention also helped the MU campus to alert the national press, which put pressure on the university to conduct a stronger investigation. Technology's ability to instantaneously spread information both exacerbated and helped to resolve the situation.</td>
</tr>
<tr>
<td>Sypher transitions to discussion of cyberbullying in the digital realm; she uses a quote to support her point about the large number of incidents on college campuses</td>
<td>More typically, when we talk about cyberbullying, we refer to behavior that's exclusively in the digital realm. For some, cyberbullying may be personal, harassing name calling via text messages, while for others that name calling may occur in a social media forum that encourages others to participate, resulting in a wall full of slams. For others still, cyberbullying may be even more invasive, involving private, often revealing, videos or photos that bullies repost to public sites. This broad range of possible activities could be a driving force in the large number of college students who report being victims of cyberbullying tactics. Research by two Indiana State University counseling and school psychology professors Bridget Roberts-Pittman and Christine MacDonald reported that "almost 22 percent of college students reported being cyberbullied," an appalling statistic that suggests as many as 1 in 5 college students has been a victim (Sicking).</td>
</tr>
</table>

3

4

> Rutgers University student Tyler Clementi's cyber victimization and resultant suicide in 2010 is perhaps the most notorious case of cyberbullying on a college campus. As reported by PCMag.com, on September 19, 2010, Clementi's roommate and bully, Dharun Ravi, used his computer to film Clementi having an "intimate encounter with another man." Ravi streamed the live video to another computer and then tweeted about it, ultimately "outing the 18-year-old Clementi as gay" (Poeter). Clementi, who only recently came out to his parents, committed suicide three days later in the wake of Ravi's very public invasion of his privacy. Mainstream media coverage of the case led to bullying-awareness and prevention campaigns that focused on exposing and ending the harassment faced by LGTBQ teens and young adults, but it also raised a number of questions about the responsibilities of the community at large.
>
> Ravi's behavior raises important questions about how to appropriately punish adult perpetrators of cyberbullying. ABC News reported that Ravi and another student were charged with "invasion of privacy" and fined. Ravi was also "convicted of a hate crime for using a webcam to spy on Clementi" and served twenty days of a thirty-day jail sentence. For many people—including the prosecution who sought a more substantial prison term—this punishment seemed insufficient (Koenigs et al.). Even the MU Ohio rape flier creators could face serious charges (Curry). As many researchers, including the U.S. Department of Education, are noting, college bullying occurs among adults, which makes "the legal framework very, very different." In college, the consequences for bullying are often much more stringent, which may be a reason behaviors most would consider "bullying" elsewhere are swept instead into the broader, more lenient category of campus "hazing" (U.S. Dept. of Ed. Higher Ed. Center). A link between bullying and hazing and between hazing and sorority/fraternity life—or simply among freshman students—is unsurprising. According to one developmental psychologist, making friends is often a primary student goal, and bullies often have, or are at least perceived to have, more friends and power (Marshall).
>
> The rocky transition from the support systems of high school to the often radical aloneness of college may explain the appeal of bullying and of the more anonymous practice of cyberbullying in particular. For largely friendless first-year students, new media may help maintain old support

systems, but it may also become a space for asserting themselves to new "friends." Classmates often become cyber friends first, using social media to bond over common interests and antagonisms. It is not difficult, then, to imagine that the two young men believed responsible for the MU Ohio rape flier may have built a friendship over the flier's creation, or that Ravi bonded with the others involved in his bullying of Clementi.

Perhaps our loosely defined attention to college hazing allows us to skip over a serious conversation about the prevalence and harm of bullying, a conversation that maybe we're scared to have. Incidents like those at MU and Rutgers, however, reinforce the importance of having these conversations on campus, of increasing cyberbullying awareness, and of focusing discussion not on the ills of hazing, but on the crime of being an adult aggressor, both in person and online.

Sypher calls for action: increase awareness by holding more public educational events and discussions on college campuses

Works Cited

MLA style used for list of works cited: entries are presented in alphabetical order by authors' last names; first line of each entry begins at the left margin and subsequent lines are indented

Curry, Colleen. "'Top Ten Ways to Get Away With Rape' Flier Posted at Miami University in Ohio." *ABC News*, 5 Oct. 2012, abcnews.go.com/US/miami-university-student-posts-top-ten-ways-rape/story?id=17481607.

Dempsey, Allison G., et al. "Differences Between Peer Victimization in Cyber and Physical Settings and Associated Psychosocial Adjustment in Early Adolescence." *Psychology in the Schools*, vol. 46, no. 10, 2009, pp. 962–72.

Koenigs, Michael, et al. "Rutgers Trial: Dharun Ravi Sentenced to 30 Days in Jail." *ABC News*, 21 May 2012, abcnews.go.com/US/rutgers-trial-dharun-ravi-sentenced-30-days-jail/story?id=16394014.

Kowalski, Robin M., et al. *Cyber Bullying: Bullying in the Digital Age.* Wiley-Blackwell, 2007.

Marshall, Jessica. "Why Do People Bully?" *Discovery News*. 1 Apr. 2010, news.discovery.com/human/psychology/bullying-phoebe-prince-teens.htm.

The correct MLA forms for other kinds of publications are given on pages 716-38

Poeter, Damon. "Mystery Witness Testifies in Rutgers Cyberbullying Trial." *PC Magazine*, 2 Mar. 2012, www.pcmag.com/article2/0,2817,2401095,00.asp.

Sicking, Jennifer. "ISU Study: Nearly 40 Percent of College Students Report Being Bullied." *Indiana Statesman*, 24 Oct. 2011.

U.S. Department of Education's Higher Education Center. "Bullying and Cyberbullying at Colleges and Universities." Jan. 2012, safesupportivelearning.ed.gov/sites/default/files/sssta/20130315_january2012.pdf.

Analyzing Courtney Sypher's Source-Based Essay

1. What is Sypher's thesis? Does she support it adequately? Are there any places where you think she needs additional evidence to support her claims?
2. What is Sypher's purpose in writing this essay? Is she more interested in persuading us to adopt a certain position or in informing us about cyberbullying?
3. What kinds of sources does Sypher use? Are they credible? Are they appropriately current? Do they represent a wide enough range of sources?
4. Do you agree with Sypher's conclusion? Why or why not?
5. Generally speaking, how could Sypher make her essay even stronger? If you had the opportunity to talk with her, what questions would you ask her? What recommendations for revision would you make?

Bees: Why Are They Dying?

WAYNE ELLWOOD

Wayne Ellwood was born in Canada and is the author of several books: *The No-Nonsense Guide to Globalization* (2010), *The No-Nonsense Guide to Degrowth and Sustainability* (2014), and *NoNonsense Globalization: Buying and Selling the World* (2015). He is the former editor of the *New Internationalist*, a Canadian magazine focusing on "people, ideas, and action for global justice."

In this essay, first published in the September 2009 edition of *New Internationalist*, he looks for clues as to why honeybees, so necessary for pollinating the plants we eat, are dying off in large numbers. He finds three contributing factors and calls for changes in our current agricultural systems.

New Internationalist

Preparing to Read

Have you ever been stung by a bee? Why, in spite of their occasional annoyance, do you think bees are important? Besides pollinating food, what other important contributions do bees make?

It's safe to say that the late John Muir would not recognize California's vast Central Valley were he to visit today. When the intrepid Scots-American naturalist and founder of the Sierra Club travelled by foot through the region in the 1860s and 1870s he was astounded by the richness and diversity of the plants and flowers which carpeted the valley bottom and surged up the mountain slopes. In rapturous prose he described what he called the "bee pastures":

> *When California was wild, it was one sweet bee-garden throughout its entire length, north and south, and all the way across from the snowy Sierra to the ocean . . . The Great Central Plain, during the months of March, April and May was one smooth, continuous bed of honey-bloom, so marvellously rich that, in walking from one end of it to the other, a distance of more than 400 miles, your foot would press about a hundred flowers at every step. Mints, gilias, nemophilas, castilleias, and innumerable compositoe were so crowded together that, had 99 per cent of them been taken away, the plain would still have seemed to any but Californians extravagantly flowery. The radiant, honeyful corollas, touching and overlapping, and rising above one another, glowed in the living light like a sunset sky . . .* [1]

---

[1] Excerpted from *The Mountains of California* by John Muir, available at www.sierraclub.org

Fast forward a century and a half and you're presented with a very different scene. Twelve-lane super highways weave through valley bottoms edged by suburban sprawl. Houses in serried ranks march up the hill sides. In the areas left untouched by strip malls and industrial parks, thousands of acres of tomatoes, peppers, beans, strawberries, and lettuce are tended by Mexican workers in irrigated fields drenched with pesticides, herbicides, and fungicides.

> Where there is no nectar or pollen there are no bees.

But in the unique micro-climate of the San Joaquin and Sacramento valleys, fruits and vegetables give way to another cash crop—almonds. John Muir's "bee pastures" have been extirpated, replaced by 700,000 acres of almond trees. Eighty per cent of the world's almonds are grown here. The state exports more than a billion dollars' worth a year; the nuts are twice as big a money-spinner as the vaunted California wine industry. In February, a canopy of white blossoms extends to the horizon. The irony is that almond trees still need to be pollinated to produce fruit. But the crop is so large and so intensively cultivated that the few wild bees that remain can't do the job. Apart from a few weeks of almond blossoms, the area is a floral desert. Where there is no nectar or pollen there are no bees.

Instead, growers rent honeybees from commercial beekeepers for a fee of $150-$200 per hive. The massive almond mono-forest requires nearly two million hives, which are trucked in from other parts of the US. Bees are stacked on pallets, hauled thousands of miles from more than 38 states, unloaded by forklift and scattered through the almond groves. Big beekeepers now make more from selling "pollination services" than from honey. Of the three million commercial bee colonies in the US, more than two-thirds travel for pollination every year.[2]

It is one long tour of duty covering the entire growing season. And it happens across North America. Honeybees are the migrant farm workers of the insect world. They're critically important for almond growers—there would be no crop without them. And it's good business for the beekeepers. But for the bees it's another matter. They keep dying and no one knows exactly why.

News of a mass die-off of bees first broke in 2006. Dave Hackenberg is one of Pennsylvania's biggest beekeepers. He makes most of his income from renting out his bees. In October 2006 he trucked a batch of his hives to Florida to feed on Brazilian pepper (a widespread imported "exotic" that now blankets much of the state) after they'd worked the blueberries

---

[2]*Robbing the bees*, Holly Bishop, p. 133

and pumpkins up north. When he checked the bees a month later he was stunned. Most of the hives were ghost towns: honeycomb, a few nurse bees and the occasional queen remained, but little else. Hackenberg had 400 hives on the site and all but 32 had collapsed. And the puzzling thing was there were no dead bees in sight. It was like they had simply disappeared, vanished. Not only that, but opportunistic raiders (moths and beetles) that usually invade a hive after it's in trouble refused to go near the dead zones. The syndrome was quickly given a new name: colony collapse disorder (CCD).[3]

It wasn't long before other beekeepers across the US were reporting similar losses. By the spring of 2007 it was clear that CCD was widespread. A quarter of all US beekeepers had suffered losses and more than 30 per cent of all bee colonies in the country were completely wiped out. Eerie reports of huge die-offs also came from Australia, Canada, Brazil, China, Europe and other regions. In Britain, losses averaged more than 30 per cent over 2007-08. But nowhere did they approach those in the US and nowhere else was the term CCD applied.

BEES IN ONE BASKET

It's not unusual for bees to die in large numbers. Cold weather, deadly mites, bacteria, viruses, parasites, pesticide poisoning and fungal infections are common. Northern beekeepers often lose 10 per cent of their bees over the winter. So, you might be wondering, what's the big deal? There are still lots of bees around, beekeepers can rebuild their hives—and maybe it's not such a bad idea if some of those almond orchards are converted back to pasture. Unfortunately, it's not so simple. *Apis mellifera*, also known as the European honeybee, accounts for nearly all the bees managed by beekeepers in Europe, the Americas, Asia, Australia and New Zealand/Aotearoa. They are the one true global bee and they've become essential to modern industrial agriculture. It's as if we've put all our bees in one basket.

Honeybees are generalists. They'll feed on just about anything that's blooming. According to the International Bee Research Association, a third of our diet comes from flowering crops and honeybees are responsible for pollinating about 80 per cent of them. They are essential in the production of at least 90 commercially grown foods. Apples, pears, apricots, melons, broccoli, garlic, onions, peppers, tomatoes and coffee—they all rely on bees for pollination. Trying to put a dollar value on "pollination services" is a bit like trying to put a price on fresh air or clean water.

---

[3] For the full story of Hackenberg's discovery see *Fruitless Fall* by Rowan Jacobsen, pp. 57–66

Pollinators are more important than that. Bee-pollinated forage and hay crops like alfalfa and clover are also used to feed the animals that supply meat, milk and cheese. It doesn't matter whether you're a vegetarian or a meat-eater. Bees put food on the table. A report by the National Research Council in Washington hit the nail on the head: "Pollinator decline is one form of global change that actually does have credible potential to alter the shape of the terrestrial world."[4]

Pollinators, especially bees, are what pioneering environmentalist Rachel Carson called a keystone species, at the very centre of the entire food web. Remove the keystone and the whole collapses.

To complicate matters, there is mounting evidence that native bees (bumblebees, alkali bees, mason bees, carpenter bees, sweat bees, etc) and other pollinators like moths, butterflies, bats and humming birds are also in steep decline. In Britain, more than half the native bumblebees have become extinct or will face extinction in the next few decades. In some parts of Holland, bee diversity has declined by 80 per cent over the past 25 years. In Canada, researcher Sheila Colla found that three species of bumblebee formerly common in southern Ontario and the northeastern US have disappeared since the 1970s. And in the US, the Oregon-based Xerces Society for Invertebrate Conservation has placed four bumblebees, including the rusty-patched bumblebee and the Franklin's bumblebee, on its list of most endangered insects.

Disease is the main suspect in the decline of the North American bumblebees. Dr. Laurence Packer, a world expert in wild bees at York University in Toronto, believes US greenhouse growers are the most likely culprit. Bumblebees are widely used for "buzz pollination" of greenhouse crops like tomatoes and peppers. In the 1980s growers sent bees to Europe to perfect breeding techniques. The bees returned infected with *nosema ceranae*, a single-celled protozoa originally from southeast Asia, which destroys the bees' digestive tract. Before long the disease had spread to wild bumblebees.

The globalization of the bee industry has helped spread pathogens around the world—mites, bacteria, fungi, parasites and a whole host of deadly viruses. But there is consensus among scientists that habitat loss, the intensification of agriculture and the routine use of agro-chemicals are also playing havoc with bee populations and opening the door to disease. Bees need a varied diet to thrive. No single pollen source contains the vitamins, proteins, minerals and fats necessary for good nutrition. That's exactly what they're not getting with today's massive mono-crops and suburbanization.

---

[4] "The Status of Pollinators in North America,' National Research Council, Washington, www.nap.edu

Many cash crops—like blueberries and sunflowers—have low-protein pollens. Farmers plough fields to the margins, hedges are grubbed out, verges mown and wildflowers (aka "weeds") doused with herbicides. Meadows, prairies and wetlands have been paved and drained. In England, for example, flower-rich grasslands have declined by 97 per cent in the last 60 years. This loss of ecological diversity has a knock-on effect in the insect world. When bees can't get the nutrients they need they're malnourished, weakened and more prone to disease.

Pesticides are another danger, especially a new group of insecticides called *neonicotinoids*—a synthetic form of nicotine which is soaked up by the plant's leaves, stems and roots. Bugs take a bite and these deadly neurotoxins do their work. Imidacloprid, the biggest seller of the "neonics" is approved for use on 140 crops in more than 100 countries, a bonanza for the German chemical giant, Bayer.[5]

These chemicals are not supposed to form lethal concentrations in pollen or nectar, but the French are taking no chances. The country banned their use on sunflowers in 1999 shortly after they were introduced and honeybees began to die en masse. Bee populations gradually increased again after the ban. Since then "neonics" have been withdrawn in Germany, Italy and Slovenia.

Elsewhere the pesticides are still in wide use even as researchers continue to study them. So far two things are clear. At high levels "neonics" can disrupt the bees' nervous system causing disorientation and eventually death. And second, the chemicals have been found at "sub-lethal" amounts in pollen, the bees' main protein source. The real question is how many sub-lethal doses does it take to become lethal? No-one knows. The other unknown is how the hundreds of agro-chemicals now in use combine in the environment to become toxic. The chemical companies don't test for the interaction of different chemicals and governments don't demand they do. A recent study of CCD-afflicted colonies found more than 170 different chemicals in bees from the affected hives, including fluvalinate and coumaphos, commonly used by beekeepers to combat varroa mites.[6] It seems the lessons of Rachel Carson's classic work on pesticide poisoning, *Silent Spring*, have been slow to filter through.

NO SMOKING GUN

All of these factors can lead to what University of Guelph pollination biologist Peter Kevan calls unnatural "stress" on the bees. Combine this with long distance travel and you've got a problem, says Dr. Kevan, a member of

[5]*Fruitless Fall*, pp. 84–99
[6]'Solving the mystery of the vanishing bees,' *Scientific American*, March 31/09

the US National Academy of Science's Committee on Status of Pollinators in North America.

"The bees are bounced from one end of the country to the other, usually from east to west in the winter, which means they're also getting cold and heat shock en route. Transport is part and parcel of commercial beekeeping in the US. And pollination services are dictated largely by huge scale mono-cropping. Once the bees get there they have no food except what they can get from the crop for three or four weeks. It isn't surprising that there's a lot of stress on these bees. Good lord, if you put me through that I'd certainly be pretty susceptible to a cold or the flu or whatever might be going around."

A lot of ink has been spilled on "the mystery of the disappearing bees" and scientists have been unleashed to find the cause of CCD. So far no single culprit has been found; there is no smoking gun. In fact, it's turned out to be a lot more complicated. The closest human parallel seems to be HIV. Bees suffering from CCD are riddled with all manner of diseases. It's like there has been a general collapse in the bees' immune system and opportunistic invaders have jumped in, much like the way pneumonia might kill someone with AIDS. A consensus is building that multiple factors interact to weaken the hives, making them susceptible to a range of pathogens and viruses.

Others are beginning to ask more fundamental questions about the nature of modern farming. Could it be that the high-tech, chemically dependent system we have created over the last 50 years, first in the West and now globally, is the source of the problem? The small-scale diversity of the family farm has been replaced by an industrial agricultural model on the narrow notion of economic efficiency and growth at all costs. Our food system is so dependent on cheap oil—for fertilizers, pesticides, powering farm machinery and transporting crops to market—that we have backed ourselves into a dangerous corner.

As Vermont beekeeper Ross Conrad writes: "One of the guiding principles of the industrial model . . . is the desire to maximize production and thus profits. When applied to agriculture this typically results in the drive to push biological organisms to the limits of their capacity."[7]

We can now produce mountains of cheap food with minimal labour. But in the process we've levelled biodiversity and become less resilient. Writer and activist Chip Ward argues that we reduce the resilience of natural systems at our peril: "There is little resilience in a manmade system of food production that relies on healthy populations of commercial bee colonies to pollinate crops and too little resilience left in the natural world for

---

[7]'Natural Beekeeping,' Ross Conrad, *Bee Culture*, Jan 01/09. www.beeculture.com

bees to recover quickly from whatever is wiping them out . . . The cult of efficiency," Ward says, threatens more than the bees. "How futile it is in the long run to impose narrow notions of efficiency on natural systems that are profoundly dynamic and inherently unpredictable."[8]

CCD is a wake-up call, a signal that our modern agricultural system is in deep crisis. People rightly worry about the loss of the big showcase mammals: the polar bear, the tiger, the wolf, the elephant. But the insect world may be a better indicator of the health of our natural systems. It's not just the bees that are in trouble. It's us.

[8]'Diesel-driven bee slums and impotent turkeys: the case for resilience,' Chip Ward, www.tomdispatch.com

Thinking Critically about the Text

Why does Ellwood conclude that agriculture is to blame for the loss of so many bees? Does he cite sufficient evidence to prove his claim? What natural "shocks" are compounding the chemical stresses faced by the bees?

Questions on Subject

1. What is CCD syndrome?
2. What, according to Rachel Carson, is a keystone species?
3. What is Ellwood's thesis? Where in this selection do you find it?
4. Name all the possible causes of bee death the article mentions. Does Ellwood suggest some causes are more destructive than others, and if so, which ones?

Questions on Strategy

1. How does Ellwood use cause and effect in this essay? Cite several examples. (Glossary: *Cause and Effect*)
2. What is the purpose of the long quote Ellwood includes in his first paragraph? Has he integrated this source successfully? Why or why not?
3. Ellwood provides many examples in this essay. Are all his examples effective? Are there any you would drop? Which resonate most with you? Are there other types of evidence that might have made his essay stronger? (Glossary: *Evidence*)
4. In paragraph 14, Ellwood writes that on commercial farms, "hedges are grubbed out, verges mown, and wildflowers (aka 'weeds') doused with herbicides." Do you know exactly what the first two phrases mean? What can you figure out from the overall context? What does this terminology suggest about who Ellwood imagines as his audience?

5. Identify the signal phrases that Ellwood uses to introduce his sources. How do these signal phrases help you as a reader? Besides giving the name of each source, what other information does Ellwood provide?

6. Ellwood writes that "honeybees are the migrant farm workers of the insect world" (paragraph 5). Is this analogy successful? Explain. (Glossary: *Analogy*)

Questions on Diction and Vocabulary

1. How would you describe Ellwood's diction in this essay? What words and phrases lead you to this conclusion?

2. Ellwood begins paragraph 5: "It is one long tour of duty covering the entire growing season." Who is doing this "tour of duty" and why do you think Ellwood used this metaphor?

3. Refer to a dictionary to determine the meanings of the following words as Ellwood uses them in this selection: *intrepid* (paragraph 1), *extirpated* (3), *pallets* (4), *terrestrial* (9), *edifice* (10), *pathogens* (13), *consensus* (13), *havoc* (13), *rampant* (13), *prone* (14), *en masse* (16), *susceptible* (20), *legions* (20), *premised* (21), *resilience* (23).

Writing with Sources in Action

Break into small groups and select a topic of immediate environmental concern. Each person in the group should find a single quotation on the subject. Then, as a class, incorporate each quotation into a paragraph on the topic. Remember that some quotations may be used to address opposing claims.

Writing Suggestions

1. **Writing from Sources.** Bees are not the only species that is frequently harmed by pesticides and other chemicals associated with agriculture. Do some research into another species experiencing difficulties and write a cause and effect essay explaining how that species is being harmed. Feel free to also suggest potential solutions. For models of and advice on integrating sources in your essay, see this chapter and Chapter 15.

2. **Writing in the Workplace.** Pretend that you work for a major agricultural conglomerate. You are writing a proposal for your supervisor and the board of directors to suggest changes in the company's fertilizing and pesticide practices. Make a case for why each change will benefit the long-term success of the company, as well as the environment. Use this reading and any additional research necessary to support your position.

How Social Media Is Changing Hollywood

NICOLA FREEDMAN

Nicola Freedman majored in film studies and history at the University of Sydney in Australia. She graduated in 2015 and hopes to pursue a career in film or television. Her essay appeared in issue 6 of *Digital America*, an online journal about digital culture and its impact on American life.

In this piece, Freedman argues that social media has changed not just how we respond to new films but which films are actually being made. She suggests that social media has become such a decisive factor in the success or failure of films that studios are beginning to select only those films with a clear digital marketing campaign.

Preparing to Read

What types of movies do you enjoy? Do you get your recommendations from social media or some other outlet? If you hear negative reviews about a movie, how likely are you to see it anyway?

The advent of the digital age has significantly changed the strategies of filmmakers and—in particular—Hollywood. The marketing process, as well as the very window a film has to succeed, has been transformed and shortened. More so than ever, the importance of delivering a big opening box office weekend for a film has become paramount to its success. Films that fail to live up to initial projections and expectations are declared "dead on arrival" after only a few crucial days of exposure. The technological advances underlying the growth and widespread acceptance of social media have been the decisive factor in expediting this shift. These social media sites provide spontaneous reactions from a wide and diverse pool of individuals and have therefore ensured that word of mouth now flies instantly across the digital universe rather than being restricted to a limited circle of friends. Social media has also become an essential channel in creating the buzz needed to fill those opening night seats. The films that end up being green-lit are almost inevitably those that most easily lend themselves to this type of promotion, delivering less of a risk of not realizing those crucial opening numbers. Using a few key case studies of successful and unsuccessful Hollywood blockbusters, this essay will argue that the advent and inexorable rise of social media has made word of mouth much more of a decisive factor than ever before. Moreover, it now provides the primary route for grabbing the attention of Hollywood's target audience in the time prior to the given film's release. As a result, there is a growing scarcity of original stories coming from Hollywood as low-risk cinematic formulas have proven to be more attractive given the types of investments driving these blockbusters.

Technology has changed the basic economics of the film industry. In the digitized world, the traditional model of Hollywood is crumbling. Media theorist, Mark Poster attributes this shift in part to the fact that in the digital age consumers are now also producers. Subsequently, he notes that, "In the past decade, each major industry has faced a threat to its existence from the digitization of cultural objects and the transformation of consumer into creator/user" (245). In other words, it is now easier for would-be creators of entertainment to reach an audience without depending solely on the acceptance by a few gatekeepers that dominated a limited number of media channels.

> In the digitized world, the traditional model of Hollywood is crumbling.

Moreover, as Warner Bros. chairman Kevin Tsujihara notes, "There's incredible competition with television and with video games. And that's not even considering the Internet content that you're now seeing out there" (McClintock and Masters). Grabbing the attention then of a prime film-going audience (18–29) with a notoriously short attention span provides a very limited time in which a studio can hope to focus enough of these individuals during that crucial initial weekend. In this sense, sources of entertainment have become less of a scarce resource. Filmmakers can no longer depend on bored teenagers in search of amusement to bankroll their efforts. As copyright expert and lawyer Lawrence Lessig astutely observes, "This narrowing has an effect on what is produced. The product of such large and concentrated networks is increasingly homogenous. Increasingly safe. Increasingly sterile" (166). For instance, while in 1981 seven of the top-earning films were original, three decades later not one is an original film. That twenty-nine superhero adventures have been released since 2008 when "Iron Man" grossed more than $300 million at the box office is telling of the lack of originality and risk-taking in Hollywood (Smith). The sequel or formula film is hardly new in Hollywood. The difference is the increased dominance in determining cinematic productions. It is still the case that as Hollywood goes, so goes cinema, since "The top ten film studios receive 99 per cent of all film revenue" (Lessig 163).

While word of mouth moved at a slower pace even as little as a decade ago, today a film can be almost surgically destroyed on its opening night, indeed before its first showing is completed. The advent of social media in the 21st century has been largely responsible for this shift. These sites have enabled information, both positive and negative, to be spread much more quickly today than ever before, reaching larger audiences. As danah boyd and Alice E. Marwick note, "Tweets can be posted and read on the web, through SMS, or via third-party clients written for desktop computers, smartphones, and other devices. These different access methods allow for instant postings of photos, on-the-ground reports, and quick replies to other users" (116). Word of mouth has essentially become digitized through such sites as Twitter and Facebook. Everyone has in essence become a critic with crowd views evaluating everything from restaurants to books to movies. As a study conducted by Penn Schoen Berland for *The Hollywood Reporter* reveals, "72% [of moviegoers] post about movies on social networking sites after watching a film, while 20% post before and 8% during" (Godley). This de-professionalization of critical response has made the initial results at the box office much more important in determining a film's financial success. In turn, any chance of a film's success developing over a longer period of time has become increasingly unlikely. Moreover, this de-professionalization has also removed the protections that would prevent a lackluster film from instantly flopping. As Michael Cieply observes, the film industry's " . . . hits routinely score more than 40 percent of their sales within days of opening." Films seldom recover from an initial widespread pan, which means that one avenue that allows a studio a hedge against bombing is an initial substantial opening. Achieving that result will help mitigate any subsequent drop in box office results. In this digital age of instant judgment when big budget films are open country wide at multiple screens, there is no time for a fan base to slowly build. Thus a weak opening spells the end of any hopes a studio might have invested in these special-effects blockbusters. If the social media buzz is mixed, fewer people are likely to be eager to see it and they certainly won't see it again. The fact remains that the way people think about a film is often heavily influenced by this consensus. This causes individuals to reassess any initial views of a given film. Since multiple viewings serve to transform a film into a huge box office success, these days a social media hype necessarily translates into bottom-line profits. Thus it has become more difficult to reproduce the *Titanic* formula, with some fans viewing it 8-10 times.

THE LONE RANGER: DOA

The role of social media in determining a film's success is underscored by examining the negative case, namely the poor performance of *The Lone Ranger* (2013). The film combined ignorance of the film's target audience with a real lack of understanding of how to manipulate social media. Billed as an epic adventure western, the film — on paper — had everything going

5

for it. It had a big-name producer, a huge Hollywood name in Johnny Depp and a lot of financial backing from a major Hollywood studio. Nevertheless, the film bombed in its opening weekend at the box office. It took in a total of $29.4 million over the crucial three-day weekend, ultimately failing to recuperate its budget of $225 million (Cunningham). While critics panned the film, its demise owed largely to the lack of positive social media buzz. "Fizziology's metrics tracked 21,156 tweets, Facebook comments or blog posts being made about the movie a week prior to its release, which only sounds like a lot until you look at Robert Downey Jr.'s latest outing as Tony Stark, which had 1,639,691 by comparison" (McMillan). Failure to create the right buzz beforehand meant less anticipation and ultimately fewer ticket purchases. With negative first-night responses, the film essentially never made it out of the starting gate. As Vice President and Chief Analyst of BoxOffice.com Phil Contrino stated, "The marketing campaign hasn't connected in a significant way . . . It's not something that people are really that excited about compared to how 'Despicable Me 2' is doing on Facebook and Twitter" (qtd in Acuna). However, in the past, it would have taken far longer for the viewing public to come to such conclusions about a film. Moreover, the film would not have faced such fierce competition for the attention of the viewer, as marketing was largely restricted to television and radio ads as well as press releases. Even had the pre-release marketing been savvier, the vehicle itself, *The Lone Ranger,* was unlikely to lend itself easily to the digital world of social media. The story potentially struck sparks with the baby-boomer generation growing up on 1950s television fare, but the chords that needed to be struck were with the target digital generation. For them, such a theme exerted no immediate resonance. Even proven movie stars require the appropriate vehicle. In effect, the film highlights why Hollywood studios generally churn out productions that resemble cookie-cutter assemblages that mostly compete in terms of special effects.

Due to the need to create anticipation and buzz before it opens to achieve the requisite initial box office success, social media has changed the very nature of the films produced. While smaller, narrative driven films were once a mainstay, the majority of green-lit studio films are now specifically made to have a big initial box office performance in order to hedge against the risks posed by any ensuing negative social media. To draw people into the cinema, studios have therefore devoted more time and money into visual spectacles, namely special-effects-driven films. While such blockbuster films have been fixtures in Hollywood since their inception in the 1980s, today the digitization of technology and the ability to achieve visualizations that stretch the imagination means that an ever-greater proportion of Hollywood films fall into this genre. Many blockbusters as a result appear to be script-light but effects-heavy. Certainly the ultra-successful *Transformers* series fits nicely into this category.

TRANSFORMERS: EFFECTS TO THE RESCUE

Special effects are utilized as both a novelty and attraction, a device that is much more effective on a large screen as opposed to a home viewing. Aimed at a demographic (18–29) that has proven to be a more reliable cinema-going audience, films now increasingly stress a few key elements that are more likely to appeal to this target audience. Moreover, the past few years in particular have witnessed the rise of the franchise and comic book films. In other words, studios risking hundreds of millions in production costs (let alone marketing expenses) will always choose to hedge their bets by opting to film the familiar, especially the familiar that lends itself to widescreen special effects, such as comic book franchises. In line with this argument, of those surveyed it was the men that preferred to see the larger-budget, blockbuster films. For instance, Joe (20) noted, " . . . if I am going to spend my money on a movie ticket when I could easily see it free online in a few weeks, I want a real movie experience that can only be experienced at the cinema." Brendan (20) echoed these sentiments, stating that he went to see, "Mostly high budget films that make use of sound, and grand visuals the most. I watch most films outside the cinema, so when I go to see a film, the cinematic setting should contribute substantially to the experience of viewing said film." These responses reflect a growing trend. As a result of Hollywood's desire to target this core demographic and thus reap dependable financial gains, they are producing identikit films. As Paramount chairman and CEO Brad Grey affirms, "We're in the franchise game—whether it's *Transformers* or whether it's creating a new franchise with *Teenage Mutant Ninja Turtles* . . . , we'll continue to do that, and we'll do it to the point where we're making four or five of those franchises per year" (qtd. in McClintock and Masters). It is unsurprising given that these films combine key elements of special effects and target the studio's core demographic. By doing so, the studios circumvent the risk of social media killing their film's chances before it even has an opportunity to succeed. These are also the type of films that lend themselves to a cleverly manipulated social media buzz prior to release.

GUARDIANS OF THE GALAXY: SOMETHING DIFFERENT

Moreover, Hollywood studios have had to adjust their marketing techniques to be more social-media friendly. In an attempt to reduce the risk attached to these expensive projects by having them gutted by negative social media, the studios have both bolstered and adjusted their marketing strategies. Greater emphasis has been placed on social media in the hopes of generating the right buzz that will serve to build anticipation, pushing the film into a "must-see" status. Given the increased importance of that initial box office take, creating a stampede to the local cinema has become a categorical imperative. As Jon Penn asserts, "It's [social media] a tactical tool that can allow studios to improve your marketing campaign in real time" (qtd. in Lang). The effectiveness of this tool is exemplified by the success of *Guardians of the Galaxy* (2014). For instance, prior to release, the film successfully built product recognition and favorable responses on social media. The trailer went viral, and subsequently attracted " . . . 88,000 mentions across Twitter, Facebook and various blogs in a 12-hour period between 11 p.m. EST until 11 a.m. EST" (Lang). Moreover, the cast and director were heavily promoted, featuring in livestream chats and extensive Q&As with Yahoo! and Tumblr, as well as Twitter by employing the hashtag #AsktheGuardians. The objective was to transform obscure characters into ones far more familiar and likable. As Ben Carlson, president and co-creator of social media tracking site Fizziology notes, "I think a lot of people didn't know how the film was going to work . . . But they nailed the tone. It was light and fun and full of action and you see that reflected in the social media reaction" (qtd. in Lang). It again reveals how significant social media is, because even a less familiar idea, if it gets the right buzz and anticipation (and generates a big initial weekend), can be a huge success. It is still possible to start with unfamiliar characters, but only if they can properly be transformed through the magic of social media. Risks then are more apparent than real. Given the constraints imposed by social media, Hollywood does not dare to alter the familiar factors and structures of these films (*Guardians* coming off the ensemble, superhero group of *The Avengers*). Thus, as projecting the right social media buzz has become more critical, getting that strategy wrong has become even more costly. It might be argued that there is no longer room for anything resembling failure at this stage. When comparing a film like *Guardians of the Galaxy* to *The Lone Ranger* these disparate outcomes reveal that while marketing has become more important, at the same time it is less reliable because it can be harder to control and manipulate. Social media simply requires that too many elements be deftly coordinated. Viral advertising is thus extremely important given the potentially massive exposure successful viral media can provide.

In addition, the determinative role of social media has also seen an increase in the need for an actor's online presence. While actors have always been required to promote their films, it was generally resigned to scheduled television appearances and magazine interviews, these being the only effective promotion channels. However, although there is still a reliance on the more traditional media to launch films, in the digital age new venues to do so have now multiplied at an alarming rate. An actor's social media presence—whether it is on Facebook, Instagram or Twitter—can therefore have a significant impact in garnering buzz for their film. Hollywood actress Chloe Moretz observed this shift, stating, "Instead of being asked how you want to approach [the role], they tell you that if you don't Instagram or Tweet your movies then they aren't going to succeed" (qtd. in Nealey). A film can get a worldwide boost from an actor tweeting out to their thousands or millions of followers to go and see it. For instance, actor Vin Diesel bolstered online buzz for *Guardians of the Galaxy*, given both his active presence on a variety of social media sites and his large following on them. With more than 80 million connected fans across two networks (Facebook and Twitter), his posted updates often get over 2 million reactions. His ability to reach such an enormous audience in only a matter of seconds allows for waves of widespread promotion over those crucial pre-release weeks. Moreover, the new, technology-driven actions that the film industry is taking are imitated around the world. In Bollywood for instance, " . . . actors now change their display names on social networking site Twitter to their reel names in order to promote their films and make their fans familiar with their on-screen avatars. Stars also change their profile picture to the look they don in the films" (Singh). That the industry is reshaping its practices underscores the crucial role that the digitization of word of mouth has had. This is another indication that Hollywood recognizes social media as a key factor in determining a film's success.

Ultimately, it is evident that digitization has altered the very nature of the Hollywood film industry. Specifically, social media has become a decisive factor in determining a film's box office success. The studios' attempts to adapt to this change are revealed in the types of films they choose to produce and the manner in which they have amped up their marketing efforts to generate buzz.

Works Cited

Acuna, Kirsten. "'The Lone Ranger' Is Lining Up To Be Disney's Next 'John Carter' Bust." *Business Insider*, 3 July 2013, www.businessinsider.com/the-lone-ranger-looks-like-it-bomb-2013-7.

Cieply, Michael. "A Last Hurrah for 'Night at the Museum' Franchise, and for Robin Williams." *The New York Times*, 30 Nov. 2014, www.nytimes.com/2014/12/01/business/media/a-last-hurrah-for-night-at-the-museum-franchise-and-for-robin-williams.html?_r=0.

Cunningham, Todd. "Johnny Depp Can't Save 'Lone Ranger' From Being 'John Carter'-Sized Bomb for Disney." *The Wrap*, 7 July 2013, www.thewrap.com/just-48m-5-day-holiday-weekend-lone-ranger-john-carter-sized-bomb-101526/.

Dodes, Rachel. "Twitter Goes to the Movies." *The Wall Street Journal*, 3 Aug. 2012, www.wsj.com/articles/SB10000872396390443343704577553270169103822.

Godley, Chris. "THR's Social Media Poll: How Facebook and Twitter Impact the Entertainment Industry." *The Hollywood Reporter*, 21 Mar. 2012, www.hollywoodreporter.com/gallery/facebook-twitter-social-media-study-302273/1-social-media-as-entertainment.

Guardians of the Galaxy. Directed by Gore Verbinski, performances by Chris Pratt and Zoe Saldana, Marvel Studios, 2014.

Lang, Brent. "'Guardians of the Galaxy' Trailer a Social Media Smash, Bigger Than 'Man of Steel.'" *TheWrap*, 19 Feb. 2014, www.thewrap.com/guardians-galaxy-trailer-social-media-smash-bigger-man-steel/.

Lessig, Lawrence. *Free Culture*, Penguin Press, 2004.

The Lone Ranger. Directed by James Gunn. Performances by Johnny Depp and Armie Hammer, Walt Disney Pictures, 2013.

Marwick, Alice E., and d. boyd. "I Tweet Honestly, I Tweet Passionately: Twitter Users, Context Collapse, and the Imagined Audience." *New Media & Society*, vol. 13, no. 1, July 7, 2010, pp. 114-33. Sage Publishing, doi:10.1177/1461444810365313.

McClintock, Pamela, and Kim Masters. "Executive Roundtable: 6 Studio Heads on China Plans, Superhero Overload, WB Layoffs, 'Fast & Furious' Future." *The Hollywood Reporter*, 13 Nov. 2014, www.hollywoodreporter.com/news/executive-roundtable-6-studio-heads-748102.

McMillan, Graeme. "Why Aren't More People Talking About 'The Lone Ranger'?" *The Hollywood Reporter*, 2 July 2013, www.hollywoodreporter.com/heat-vision/johnny-depps-lone-ranger-why-578731.

Nealey, Joshua. "Vin Diesel Cast in 'Guardians of the Galaxy' Due to Social Media?" *Hypable*, 27 Aug. 2014, www.hypable.com/marvel-guardians-of-the-galaxy-social-media-casting/.

Poster, Mark. *Information Please: Culture and Politics in the Age of Digital Machines*. Duke UP, 2006.

Singh, Apurva. "Bollywood's Latest Trend: Actors Change Names on Twitter to Promote Upcoming Movies." *The Indian Express*, 19 Aug. 2014, indianexpress.com/article/entertainment/bollywood/bollywoods-latest-trend-actors-change-names-on-twitter-to-promote-upcoming-movies/.

Smith, Elliott. "Why Are Superhero Movies So Popular?" *University of Phoenix*, 6 Feb. 2014, www.phoenix.edu/forward/perspectives/2014/02/why-are-superhero-movies-so-popular.html.

Thinking Critically about the Text

Has Freedman changed your mind in any way about how social media is impacting the film industry? Can you think of any other industries that might be similarly impacted by social media?

Questions on Subject

1. Why does Freedman think that social media has shortened "the very window a film has to succeed" (paragraph 1)?
2. What competition is the film industry facing? What impact does this competition have on the films that get made, according to Freedman?
3. How does Freedman claim that special effects saved the *Transformers*?
4. What are "viral advertising" and "viral media" (8)? What role do they play in making a movie successful?
5. How has Freedman seen the role of an actor change due to social media? What problems might this cause?

Questions on Strategy

1. Freedman begins her essay with an overview of the film industry before providing specific examples of how it has changed and why. How is this organization effective? (Glossary: *Organization*) How does it contribute to a reader's understanding?
2. What is Freedman's thesis? Where does she state it? (Glossary: *Thesis*)
3. Why do you think Freedman selected the movies she chose to use as examples? (Glossary: *Examples*) What other films might fit the categories she presents?
4. Identify three or four of the transitions that Freedman uses in this essay. How do they help to link her ideas and build unity? (Glossary: *Unity*)

Questions on Diction and Vocabulary

1. Examine the signal phrases Freedman uses to introduce quotes from her sources. How do they add context to the material she is quoting?
2. Freedman uses a metonym, Hollywood, to stand in for the entire film industry. (Glossary: *Figurative Language*) How does this device simplify her essay, making it easier for readers to follow?
3. Film-industry jargon such as "green-lit" (paragraph 1) and "formula film" (3) appears throughout Freedman's essay. What does this jargon tell you about Freedman's intended audience? Explain.

Writing with Sources in Action

Using the examples on pages 671 and 679–80 as a model, write a *paraphrase* for each of the following paragraphs — that is, restate the original ideas in your own words, using your own sentence structure.

> The history of life on earth has been a history of interaction between living things and their surroundings. To a large extent, the physical form and the habits of the earth's vegetation and its animal life have been molded by the environment. Considering the whole span of earthly time, the opposite effect, in which life actually modifies its surroundings, has been relatively slight. Only within the moment of time represented by the present century has one species — man — acquired significant power to alter the nature of his world.
> — Rachel Carson,
> "The Obligation to Endure," *Silent Spring*

> Extroverts are energized by people, and wilt or fade when alone. They often seem bored by themselves, in both senses of the expression. Leave an extrovert alone for two minutes and he will reach for his cell phone. In contrast, after an hour or two of being socially "on," we introverts need to turn off and recharge. My own formula is roughly two hours alone for every hour of socializing. This isn't antisocial. It isn't a sign of depression. It does not call for medication. For introverts, to be alone with our thoughts is as restorative as sleeping, as nourishing as eating. Our motto: "I'm okay, you're okay — in small doses."
> — Jonathan Rauch,
> "Caring for Your Introvert"

> No, the romance and beauty were all gone from the river. All the value any feature of it had for me now was the amount of usefulness it could furnish toward compassing the safe piloting of a steamboat. Since those days, I have pitied doctors from my heart. What does the lovely flush in a beauty's cheek mean to a doctor but a "break" that ripples above some deadly disease? Are not all her visible charms sown thick with what are to him the signs and symbols of hidden decay? Does he ever see her beauty at all, or doesn't he simply view her professionally and comment upon her unwholesome condition all to himself? And doesn't he sometimes wonder whether he has gained most or lost most by learning his trade?
> — Mark Twain,
> *Life on the Mississippi*

Writing Suggestions

1. **Writing with Sources.** Look up some movie reviews for one of the films Freedman discusses in her essay. Then, compose a brief essay explaining how the reviews contributed to the success or the failure of the movie. Don't forget to use signal phrases and remember to review this chapter for advice on smoothly integrating and synthesizing your sources.

2. **Writing with Sources**. The American Film Institute (www.afi.com) keeps a list of past awards dating back to 2000. Review some of the award winners for previous years. Would those films have been made using Freedman's criteria? Write an essay explaining why films that might not go viral still need to be made. Use the AFI's list of winners as well as other sources to support your claim. For models of and advice on integrating sources in your essay, see this chapter and Chapter 15.

The English-Only Movement
Can America Proscribe Language with a Clear Conscience?

JAKE JAMIESON

An eighth-generation Vermonter, Jake Jamieson was born in the town of Berlin and grew up in nearby Waterbury, home of Ben & Jerry's Ice Cream. He graduated from the University of Vermont with a degree in elementary education and a focus in English. After graduation Jamieson "bounced around" California and

Courtesy of Jake Jamieson

Colorado before landing in the Boston area, where he directed the product innovation and training department for iProspect, a search-engine marketing company. Currently, he is living in Montpelier and works out of his house for an online marketing company with some freelancing on the side.

Jamieson wrote the following essay while he was a college student and has updated it for inclusion in this book. As one who believes in the old axiom "If it isn't broken, don't fix it," Jamieson is intrigued by the official-English movement, which advocates fixing a system that seems to be working just fine. In this essay he tackles the issue of legislating English as the official language for the United States. As you read, notice how he uses outside sources to set out the various pieces of the English-only position and then uses his own thinking and examples, as well as experts who support his side, to undercut that position. Throughout his essay, Jamieson uses MLA-style in-text citations together with a list of works cited.

Preparing to Read

It is now possible to go many places in the world and get along pretty well using English, no matter what other languages are spoken in the host country. If you were to emigrate, how hard would you work to learn the predominant language of your chosen country? What advantages would there be in learning that language, even if you could get by with English? How would you feel if the country had a law that forced you to learn and use its language as quickly as possible? Write down your thoughts about these questions.

Jake Jamieson
Professor Rosa
Composition 101
May 10, 2010

The English-Only Movement:
Can America Proscribe Language with a
Clear Conscience?

Many people think of the United States as a giant cultural "melting pot" where people from other countries come together and bathe in the warm waters of assimilation. In this scenario the newly arrived immigrants readily adopt American cultural ways and learn to speak English. For others, however, this serene picture of the melting pot does not ring true. These people see the melting pot as a giant cauldron into which immigrants are tossed; here their cultures, values, and backgrounds are boiled away in the scalding waters of discrimination. At the center of the discussion about immigrants and assimilation is language: Should immigrants be required to learn English or should accommodations be made so they can continue to use their native languages?

Those who argue that the melting-pot analogy is valid believe that immigrants who come to America do so willingly and should be expected to become a part of its culture instead of hanging on to their past. For them, the expectation that immigrants will celebrate this country's holidays, dress as Americans dress, embrace American values, and most importantly, speak English is not unreasonable. They believe that assimilation offers the only way for everyone in this country to live together in harmony and the only way to dissipate the tensions that inevitably arise when cultures clash.

A major problem with this argument, however, is that there is no agreement on what exactly constitutes the "American way" of doing things. Not everyone in America is of the same religious persuasion or has the same set of values, and different people affect vastly different styles of dress. There are so many sets of variables that it would be hard to defend the argument that there is only one culture in the United States.

Currently, the one common denominator in America is that the majority of us speak English, and because of this a major movement is being staged in favor of making English the country's "official" language while it is still the country's national and common language. Making English America's official language would change the ground rules and expectations surrounding immigrant assimilation. According to the columnist and social commentator Charles

Krauthammer, making English the official language has important implications:

> "Official" means the language of the government and its institutions. "Official" makes clear our expectations of acculturation. "Official" means that every citizen, upon entering America's most sacred political space, the voting booth, should minimally be able to identify the words president and vice president and county commissioner and judge. The immigrant, of course, has the right to speak whatever he wants. But he must understand that when he comes to the United States, swears allegiance, and accepts its bounty, he undertakes to join its civic culture. In English. (521)

Many reasons are given to support the notion that making English the official language of the land is a good idea and that it is exactly what this country needs, especially in the face of the growing diversity of languages in metropolitan areas. Indeed, the National Center for Education Statistics reports that in 2008, 21 percent of children ages 5-17 spoke a language other than English at home (Sec. 1).

Supporters of English-only contend that all government communication must be in English. Because communication is absolutely necessary for democracy to survive, they believe that the only way to ensure the existence of our nation is to make sure a common language exists. Making English official would ensure that all government business, from ballots to official forms to judicial hearings, would have to be conducted in English. According to former senator and presidential candidate Bob Dole, "Promoting English as our national language is not an act of hostility but a welcoming act of inclusion." He goes on to state that while immigrants are encouraged to continue speaking their native languages, "thousands of children [are] failing to learn the language, English, that is the ticket to the 'American Dream'" (qtd. in Donegan 51). Political and cultural commentator Greg Lewis echoes Dole's sentiments when he boldly states, "to succeed in America . . . it's important to speak, read, and understand English as most Americans speak it. There's nothing cruel or unfair in that; it's just the way it is" (par. 5).

For those who do not subscribe to this way of thinking, however, this type of legislation is anything but the "welcoming act of

Jamieson 3

inclusion" that it is described to be. Many of them, like Myriam Marquez, readily acknowledge the importance of English but fear that "talking in Spanish—or any other language, for that matter—is some sort of litmus test used to gauge American patriotism" ("Why and When" A12). Others suggest that anyone attempting to regulate language is treading dangerously close to the First Amendment and must have a hidden agenda of some type. Why, it is asked, make a language official when it is already firmly entrenched and widely used in this country without legislation to mandate it?

According to language diversity advocate James Crawford, the answer is plain and simple: "discrimination." He states that "it is certainly more respectable to discriminate by language than by race" or ethnicity. He points out that "most people are not sensitive to language discrimination in this nation, so it is easy to argue that you're doing someone a favor by making them speak English" (qtd. in Donegan 51). English-only legislation has been criticized as bigoted, anti-immigrant, mean-spirited, and steeped in nativism by those who oppose it, and some go so far as to say that this type of legislation will not foster better communication, as is the claim, but will instead encourage a "fear of being subsumed by a growing 'foreignness' in our midst" (Underwood 65).

For example, when a judge in Texas ruled that a mother was abusing her five-year-old girl by speaking to her only in Spanish, an uproar ensued. This ruling was accompanied by the statement that by talking to her daughter in a language other than English, the mother was "abusing that child and . . . relegating her to the position of housemaid." The National Association for Bilingual Education (NABE) condemned this statement for "labeling the Spanish language as abuse." The judge, Samuel C. Kiser, subsequently apologized to the housekeepers of the country, adding that he held them "in the highest esteem," but stood firm on his ruling (qtd. in Donegan 51). One might notice that he went out of his way to apologize to the housekeepers he might have offended but saw no need to apologize to the millions of Spanish speakers whose language had just been belittled in a nationally publicized case.

This tendency of official-English proponents to put down other languages is one that shows up again and again, even though they maintain that they have nothing against other languages or the people who speak them. If there is no malice intended toward other languages, why is the use of any language other than English so

Jamieson 4

often portrayed by them as tantamount to lunacy? In a listing of the "New Year's Resolutions" of various conservative organizations, a group called U.S. English, Inc., stated that the U.S. government was not doing its job of convincing immigrants that they "must learn English to succeed in this country." Instead, according to Stephen Moore and his associates, "in a bewildering display of irrationality, the U.S. government makes it possible to vote, file a tax return, get married, obtain a driver's license, and become a U.S. citizen in many languages" (46).

Now, according to this mind-set, speaking any language other than English is "abusive," "irrational," and "bewildering." What is this world coming to when people want to speak and make transactions in their native language? Why do they refuse to change and become more like us? Why can't immigrants see that speaking English is quite simply the right way to go? These and many other questions like them are implied by official-English proponents when they discuss the issue.

Conservative attorney David Price argues that official-English legislation is a good idea because most English-speaking Americans prefer "out of pride and convenience to speak their native language on the job" (A13). Not only does this statement imply that the pride and convenience of non-English-speaking Americans is unimportant but also that their native tongues are not as important as English. The scariest prospect of all is that this opinion is quickly gaining popularity all around the country. It appears to be most prevalent in areas with high concentrations of Spanish-speaking residents.

To date a number of official-English bills and one amendment to the Constitution have been proposed in the House and Senate. There are more than twenty-seven states—including Missouri, North Dakota, Florida, Massachusetts, California, Virginia, and New Hampshire—that have made English their official language, and more are debating the issue every day. An especially disturbing fact about this debate—and it was front and center in 2007 during the discussions and protests about what to do with America's 12.5 million illegal immigrants—is that official-English laws always seem to be linked to anti-immigration legislation, such as proposals to limit immigration or to restrict government benefits to immigrants.

Although official-English proponents maintain that their bid for language legislation is in the best interest of immigrants, the facts tend to show otherwise. University of Texas professor Robert D. King strongly believes that "language does not threaten American unity." He recommends that "we relax and luxuriate in our linguistic richness and our traditional tolerance of language differences" (531). A decision has to be made in this country about what kind of message we will send to the rest of the world. Do we plan to allow everyone in this country the freedom of speech that we profess to cherish, or will we decide to reserve it only for those who speak English? Will we hold firm to our belief that everyone is deserving of life, liberty, and the pursuit of happiness in this country? Or will we show the world that we believe in these things only when they pertain to us and people like us? "The irony," as columnist Myriam Marquez observes, "is that English-only laws directed at government have done little to change the inevitable multicultural flavor of America" ("English-Only Laws").

Jamieson 6

Works Cited

Donegan, Craig. "Debate over Bilingualism: Should English Be the Nation's Official Language?" *CQ Researcher*, 19 Jan. 1996, pp. 51-71.

King, Robert D. "Should English Be the Law?" *Subject & Strategy*. Edited by Alfred Rosa and Paul Eschholz, 11th ed., Bedford/St. Martin's, 2008, pp. 522-31.

Krauthammer, Charles. "In Plain English: Let's Make It Official." *Subject & Strategy*. Edited by Alfred Rosa and Paul Eschholz, 11th ed., Bedford/St. Martin's, pp. 519-21.

Lewis, Greg. "An Open Letter to Diversity's Victims." *Washington Dispatch*, 12 Aug. 2003, www.washingtondispatch.com/open-letter-to-victims/.

Marquez, Myriam. "English-Only Laws Serve to Appease Those Who Fear the Inevitable." *Orlando Sentinel*, 10 July 2000, p. A10.

---. "Why and When We Speak Spanish Among Ourselves in Public." *Orlando Sentinel*, 28 June 1998, p. A12.

Moore, Stephen, et al. "New Year's Resolutions." *National Review*, 29 Jan. 1996, pp. 46-48.

Price, David. "English-Only Rules: EEOC Has Gone Too Far." *USA Today*, 28 Mar. 1996, Final ed., p. A13.

Underwood, Robert L. "At Issue: Should English Be the Official Language of the United States?" *CQ Researcher*, 19 Jan. 1996, p. 65.

United States. Dept. of Educ. Inst. of Educ. Sciences. Natl. Center for Educ. Statistics. *The Condition of Education 2010*. NCES, 2010, nces.ed.gov/pubs2010/2010028.pdf.

Thinking Critically about the Text

Jamieson claims that "there are so many sets of variables that it would be hard to defend the argument that there is only one culture in the United States" (paragraph 3). Do you agree with him, or do you see a dominant "American culture" with many regional variations? Explain.

Questions on Subject

1. What question does Jamieson seek to answer in his paper? How does he answer that question?
2. How does Jamieson counter the argument that the melting-pot analogy is valid? Do you agree with his counterargument?
3. Former senator Bob Dole believes that English "is the ticket to the 'American Dream'" (paragraph 6). In what ways can it be considered a "ticket"?
4. James Crawford believes that official-English legislation is motivated by "discrimination" (paragraph 8). What exactly do you think he means? Do you think Crawford would consider Bob Dole's remarks in paragraph 6 discriminatory? Explain.
5. In his concluding paragraph, Jamieson leaves his readers with three important questions. How do you think he would answer each one? How would you answer them?

Questions on Strategy

1. What is Jamieson's thesis, and where does he present it? (Glossary: *Thesis*)
2. How has Jamieson organized his argument? (Glossary: *Organization*)
3. Jamieson is careful to use signal phrases to introduce each of his quotations and paraphrases. How do these signal phrases help readers follow the flow of the argument in his essay? (Glossary: *Signal Phrase*)
4. For what purpose does Jamieson quote Greg Lewis in paragraph 6? What would have been lost had he dropped the Lewis quotation? Explain.
5. In paragraph 9, Jamieson presents the example of the Texas judge who ruled that speaking to a child only in Spanish constituted abuse. What point does this example help Jamieson make?

Questions on Diction and Vocabulary

1. What for you constitutes the "'American way' of doing things" (paragraph 3)? Do you think the meaning of "American way" has changed in the past decade or two? Explain.
2. What are the connotations of the words *official* and *English-only*? In your opinion, do these connotations help or hinder the English-only position? What are

the connotations of the word *immigrant*? What insights into America's language debate do these connotations give you? (Glossary: *Connotation/Denotation*)

3. Consult a dictionary to determine the meanings of the following words as Jamieson uses them in this selection: *assimilation* (paragraph 1), *dissipate* (2), *implications* (4), *nativism* (8), *malice* (10).

Writing with Sources in Action

For each of the following quotations, write an acceptable paraphrase and then a paraphrase including a partial quotation that avoids plagiarism (see pages 671–73 and 678–80). Pay particular attention to the word choice and the sentence structure of the original.

> A truly equal world would be one where women ran half of our countries and companies and men ran half of our homes. The laws of economics and many studies of diversity tell us that if we tapped the entire pool of human resources and talent, our performance would improve. — SHERYL SANDBERG,
> *Lean In*

> Astronauts from over twenty nations have gone into space and they all come back, amazingly enough, saying the very same thing: The earth is a small, blue place of profound beauty that we must take care of. For each, the journey into space, whatever its original intents and purposes, became above all a spiritual one.
> — AL REINHERT,
> *For All Mankind*

> One of the unusual things about education in mathematics in the United States is its relatively impoverished vocabulary. Whereas the student completing elementary school will already have a vocabulary for most disciplines of many hundreds, even thousands of words, the typical student will have a mathematics vocabulary of only a couple of dozen words. — MARVIN MINSKY,
> *The Society of Mind*

Writing Suggestions

1. **Writing with Sources.** While it's no secret that English is the common language of the United States, few of us know that our country has been extremely cautious about promoting a government-mandated "official language." Why do you suppose the federal government has chosen to take a hands-off position on the language issue? If it has not been necessary to mandate it in the past, why do you think that people now feel a need to declare English the "official language" of the United States? Do you think that this need is real? Write an essay articulating your position on the English-only issue. Support your position with your own experiences and observations as well as several outside sources. For models of and advice on integrating sources in your essay, see this chapter and Chapter 15.

2. **Writing with Sources.** In preparation for writing an essay about assimilating non-English-speaking immigrants into American society, consider the following three statements:
   a. At this time, it is highly unlikely that Congress will legislate that English is the official language of the United States.
   b. Immigrants should learn English as quickly as possible after arriving in the United States.
   c. The cultures and languages of immigrants should be respected and valued so that bitterness and resentment will not be fostered, even as immigrants are assimilated into American society.

   In your opinion, what is the best way to assimilate non-English-speaking immigrants into our society? After doing some research on the issue, write an essay in which you propose how the United States, as a nation, can make the two latter statements a reality without resorting to an English-only solution. How can we effectively transition immigrants to speaking English without provoking ill will? For models of and advice on integrating sources in your essay, see this chapter and Chapter 15.

3. **Writing with Sources.** Is the English-only debate a political issue, a social issue, an economic issue, or some combination of the three? In this context, what do you see as the relationship between language and power? After doing some research on the topic, write an essay in which you explore the relationship between language and power as it pertains to the non-English-speaking immigrants trying to live and function within the dominant English-speaking culture. For models of and advice on integrating sources in your essay, see this chapter and Chapter 15.

© AfriPics.com/Alamy Stock Photo

CHAPTER **15**

A Brief Guide to Researching and Documenting Essays

IN THIS CHAPTER, YOU WILL LEARN SOME VALUABLE RESEARCH techniques:

- How to establish a realistic schedule for your research project
- How to conduct research online using directory and keyword searches
- How to evaluate sources
- How to analyze sources
- How to develop a working bibliography
- How to take useful notes
- How to acknowledge your sources using Modern Language Association (MLA) style in-text citations and a list of works cited

ESTABLISHING A REALISTIC SCHEDULE

A research project easily spans several weeks. So as not to lose track of time and find yourself facing an impossible deadline at the last moment, establish a realistic schedule for completing key tasks. By thinking of the research paper as a multistaged process, you avoid becoming overwhelmed by the size of the whole undertaking.

Your schedule should allow at least a few days to accommodate unforeseen needs and delays. Use the following template, which lists the essential steps in writing a research paper, to plan your own research schedule:

Research Paper Schedule

Task	Completion Date
1. Choose a research topic and pose a worthwhile question.	___/___/___
2. Locate print and electronic sources.	___/___/___
3. Develop a working bibliography.	___/___/___
4. Evaluate your sources.	___/___/___
5. Read your sources, taking complete and accurate notes.	___/___/___
6. Develop a preliminary thesis and make a working outline.	___/___/___
7. Write a draft of your paper, integrating sources you have summarized, paraphrased, and quoted.	___/___/___
8. Visit your college writing center for help with your revision.	___/___/___
9. Decide on a final thesis and modify your outline.	___/___/___
10. Revise your paper and properly cite all borrowed materials.	___/___/___
11. Prepare a list of works cited.	___/___/___
12. Prepare the final manuscript and proofread.	___/___/___
13. Submit your research paper.	___/___/___

FINDING AND USING SOURCES

You should use materials found through a search of your school library's holdings—including books, newspapers, journals, magazines, encyclopedias, pamphlets, brochures, and government documents—as your primary tools for research. These sources, unlike many open-Internet sources,[*] are reviewed by experts in the field before they are published, generally

---

[*] By "open-Internet," we mean the vast array of resources, ranging from Library of Congress holdings to pictures of a stranger's summer vacation, available to anyone using a search engine. Because anyone with a computer and Internet access can post information online, sources found on the open Internet should be scrutinized more carefully for relevance and reliability than those found through a search of academic databases or library holdings.

overseen by a reputable publishing company or organization, and examined by editors and fact checkers for accuracy and reliability.

The best place to start your search, in most cases, is your college library's home page (see figure below). Here you will find links to the library's computerized catalog of hard-copy holdings, online reference works, periodical databases, electronic journals, and a list of full-text databases. Most libraries also provide links to other helpful materials, including subject study guides and guides to research.

To get started, decide on some likely search terms and try them out. You might have to try a number of different terms related to your topic in order to generate the best results. (For tips on refining your searches, see pages 720–22.) Your goal is to create a preliminary listing of books, magazine and newspaper articles, public documents and reports, and other sources that may be helpful in exploring your topic. At this early stage, it is better to err on the side of listing too many sources. Then, later on, you will not have to backtrack to find sources you discarded too hastily.

You will likely find some open-Internet sources to be informative and valuable additions to your research. The Internet is especially useful in

Courtesy of the Bankier Library, Brookdale Community College providing recent data, stories, and reports. For example, you might find a just-published article from a university laboratory or a news story in your local newspaper's online archives. Generally, however, open-Internet sources should be used alongside other sources and not as a replacement for them. The Internet offers a vast number of useful and carefully maintained resources, but it also contains much unreliable information. It is your responsibility to determine whether a given Internet source should be trusted. (For advice on evaluating sources, see pages 722–24.)

▶ Conducting Keyword Searches

When searching for sources about your topic in an electronic database, in the library's computerized catalog, or on the Internet, you should start with a keyword search. To make the most efficient use of your time, you will want to know how to conduct a keyword search that is likely to yield solid sources and leads for your research project. As obvious or simple as it may sound, the key to a successful keyword search is the quality of the keywords you generate about your topic. You might find it helpful to start a list of potential keywords as you begin your research and add to it as your work proceeds. Often you will discover combinations of keywords that will lead you right to the sources you need.

Databases and library catalogs index sources by author, title, and year of publication, as well as by subject headings assigned by a cataloger who

```
Database Name: University of Vermont Libraries
Search Request: Title = apes, language
Search Results: Displaying 1 of 1 entries
                                            ◀ Previous    Next ▶

                                            Long View    MARC View

                    Apes, language, and the human mind / Sue Savage-Rumbaugh, Stuart G....

      Main Author: Savage-Rumbaugh, E. Sue, 1946-
            Title: Apes, language, and the human mind / Sue Savage-Rumbaugh, Stuart G. Shanker, Talbot J. Taylor.
        Published: New York : Oxford University Press, 1998.
      Description: x, 244 p. : ill. ; 24 cm.
       Subject(s): Bonobo --Psychology.
                   Kanzi (Bonobo)
                   Human-animal communication.
                   Language acquisition.
                   Neurolinguistics.

       Collection: Bailey/Howe Books (3rd Floor)
      Call Number: QL737.P96 S254 1998
   Number of Items: 1
           Status: Not Charged Check Shelf
```

Computer Catalog Screen: Complete Record for a Book
Courtesy of University of Vermont Libraries

has previewed the source. In order to generate results, the keywords you use will have to match words found in one or more of these categories. Once you begin to locate sources that are on your topic, be sure to note the subject headings listed for each source. You can use these subject headings as keywords to lead you to additional book sources or, later, to articles in periodicals cataloged by full-text databases like *InfoTrac*, *LexisNexis*, *Expanded Academic ASAP*, or *JSTOR* to which your library subscribes. The figure on page 720 shows a typical book entry in a computer catalog. Notice the subject headings, all of which can be used as possible keywords.

The keyword search process is somewhat different—more wide open—when you are searching on the Web. It is always a good idea to look for search tips on the help screens or advanced search instructions for the search engine you are using before initiating a keyword search. When you type in a keyword in the "Search" box on a search engine's home page, the search engine electronically scans Web sites, looking for matches to your keywords. On the Web, the quality of the keywords used determines the relevance of the hits on the first page or two that come up. While it is not uncommon for a search on the Internet to yield between 500,000 and 1,000,000 hits, the search engine's algorithm puts the best sources up front. If after scanning the first couple of pages of results you determine that these sites seem off topic, you need to refine your terms to either narrow or broaden your search.

Refining Keyword Searches on the Web

While some variation in command terms and characters exists among databases and popular search engines, the following functions are almost universally accepted. If you have a particular question about refining your keyword search, seek assistance by clicking on "Help" or "Advanced Search."

- Use quotation marks or parentheses to indicate that you are searching for words in exact sequence — e.g., "whooping cough"; (Supreme Court).
- Use AND or a plus sign (+) between words to narrow your search by specifying that all words need to appear in a document — e.g., tobacco AND cancer; Shakespeare + sonnet.
- Use NOT or a minus sign (−) between words to narrow your search by eliminating unwanted words — e.g., monopoly NOT game, cowboys−Dallas.
- Use OR to broaden your search by requiring that only one of the words need appear — e.g., buffalo OR bison.
- Use an asterisk (*) to indicate that you will accept variations of a term — e.g., "food label*" for food labels, food labeling, and so forth.

Using Subject Directories to Define and Develop Your Research Topic

If you are undecided about your exact topic, general search engines might not yield the credible depth of information you need for initial research and brainstorming. Instead, explore subject directories—collections of sites and online resources organized and edited by human experts. Search *subject directories* online or try popular options like INFOMINE: *Scholarly Internet Resource Collections* and the Best of the Web Directory. Subject directories can also help if you simply want to see if there is enough material to supplement your print-source research. Once you choose a directory's subject area, you can select more specialized subcategories and eventually arrive at a list of sites closely related to your topic.

The most common question students have at this stage of a Web search is, "How can I tell if I'm looking in the right place?" There is no straight answer; if more than one subject area sounds plausible, you will have to dig more deeply into each of their subcategories, using logic and the process of elimination to determine which one is likely to produce the best leads for your topic. In most cases, it doesn't take long—usually just one or two clicks—to figure out whether you're searching in the right subject area. If you click on a subject area and none of the topics listed in its subcategories seems to pertain even remotely to your research topic, try a different subject area. As you browse through various subject directories, keep a running list of keywords associated with your topic that you can use in subsequent keyword searches.

EVALUATING YOUR SOURCES

You do not have to spend long in the library to realize that you do not have time to read every print and online source that appears relevant. Given the abundance of print and Internet sources, the key to successful research is identifying those books, articles, Web sites, and other online sources that will help you most. You must evaluate your potential sources to determine which materials you will read, which you will skim, and which you will simply eliminate. Here are some evaluation strategies and questions to assist you in identifying your most promising sources.

Strategies for Evaluating Print and Online Sources

Evaluating a Book
- Read the back or inside cover copy for insights into the book's coverage and currency as well as the author's expertise.
- Scan the table of contents and identify any promising chapters.

- Read the author's preface, looking for his or her thesis and purpose.
- Check the index for key words or key phrases related to your research topic.
- Read the opening and concluding paragraphs of any promising chapter; if you are unsure about its usefulness, skim the whole chapter.
- Ask yourself: Does the author have a discernible bias? If so, you must be aware that this bias will color his or her claims and evidence. (See Analyzing Your Sources, pages 724–25.)

Evaluating an Article

- Ask yourself what you know about the journal or magazine publishing the article:
  - Is the publication scholarly or popular? Scholarly journals (*American Economic Review*, *Journal of Marriage and Family*, the *Wilson Quarterly*) publish articles representing original research written by authorities in the field. Such articles always cite their sources in footnotes or bibliographies, which means you can check their accuracy and delve deeper into the topic by locating these sources. Popular news and general interest magazines (*National Geographic*, *Smithsonian*, *Time*, *Ebony*), on the other hand, publish informative, entertaining, and easy-to-read articles written by editorial staff or freelance writers. Popular essays sometimes cite sources but often do not, making them somewhat less authoritative and less helpful in terms of extending your own research.
  - What is the reputation of the journal or magazine? Determine the publisher or sponsor. Is it an academic institution or a commercial enterprise or individual? Does the publisher or publication have a reputation for accuracy and objectivity?
  - Who are the readers of this journal or magazine?
- Try to determine the author's credentials. Is he or she an expert?
- Consider the title or headline of the article as well as the opening paragraph or two and the conclusion. Does the source appear to be too general or too technical for your needs and audience?
- For articles in journals, read the abstract (a summary of the main points) if there is one. Examine any photographs, charts, graphs, or other illustrations that accompany the article and determine how useful they might be for your research purposes.

Evaluating a Web Site or Document Found on the Open Internet

- Consider the original location of the document or site. Often the URL, especially the top-level domain name, can give you a clue about the kinds of information provided and the type of organization behind the site. Common suffixes include:

  .com — business/commercial/personal

  .edu — educational institution

(continued on next page)

(continued from previous page)

    .gov — government sponsored

    .net — various types of networks

    .org — nonprofit organization, but also some commercial or personal

(Be advised that *.org* is not regulated like *.edu* and *.gov*, for example. Most nonprofits use *.org*, but many commercial and personal sites do as well.)

- Examine the home page of the site:
    - Does the content appear to be related to your research topic?
    - Is the home page well maintained and professional in appearance?
    - Is there an "About" link on the home page that takes you to background information on the site's sponsor? Is there a mission statement, history, or statement of philosophy? Can you verify whether the site is official — actually sanctioned by the organization or company?
- Identify the author of the document or site. What are the author's qualifications for writing on this subject?
- Determine whether a print equivalent is available. If so, is the Web version identical to the print version, or is it altered in some way?
- Determine when the site was last updated. Is the content current enough for your purposes?

You can also find sources on the Internet itself that offer useful guidelines for evaluating electronic sources. One excellent example was created by reference librarians at the Wolfgram Memorial Library of Widener University. Type *Wolfgram evaluate web pages* into a search engine to access that site.

On the basis of your evaluation, select the most promising books, articles, and Web sites to pursue in depth for your research project.

ANALYZING YOUR SOURCES

Before you begin to take notes, it is essential that you read critically and carefully analyze your sources for their theses, overall arguments, amount and credibility of evidence, bias, and reliability in helping you explore your research topic. Look for the writers' main ideas, key examples, strongest arguments, and conclusions. While it is easy to become absorbed in sources that support your own beliefs, always seek out several sources with opposing viewpoints, if only to test your own position. Look for information about the authors themselves — information that will help you determine their authority and where they position themselves in the broader conversation on the issue. You should also know the reputation and special interests of book publishers and magazines because you are likely to get different views—conservative, liberal, international, feminist—on the same topic depending on the publication you read. Use the following checklist to assist in analyzing your print and online sources.

> **Checklist for Analyzing Print and Online Sources**
> - What is the writer's thesis or claim?
> - How does the writer support this thesis? Does the evidence seem fact based, or is it mainly anecdotal?
> - Does the writer consider opposing viewpoints?
> - Does the writer have any obvious political or religious biases? Is the writer associated with any special-interest groups, such as Planned Parenthood, Greenpeace, Amnesty International, or the National Rifle Association?
> - Is the writer an expert on the subject? Do other writers mention this author in their work?
> - Is important information documented through footnotes or links so that it can be verified or corroborated in other sources?
> - What is the author's purpose — to inform, to argue for a particular position or action, something else?
> - Do the writer's thesis and purpose clearly relate to your research topic?
> - Does the source reflect current thinking and research in the field?

DEVELOPING A WORKING BIBLIOGRAPHY FOR YOUR SOURCES

As you discover books, journal and magazine articles, newspaper stories, and Web sites that you think might be helpful, you need to start maintaining a record of important information about each source. This record, called a working bibliography, will enable you to know where sources are located as well as what they are when it comes time to consult them or acknowledge them in your list of works cited or final bibliography. In all likelihood, your working bibliography will contain more sources than you actually consult and include in your list of works cited.

Some people make separate bibliography cards, using a 3- by 5-inch index card, for each work that might be helpful to their research. By using a separate card for each book, article, or Web site, you can continually edit your working bibliography, dropping sources that do not prove helpful for one reason or another and adding new ones.

With the digitization of most library resources, you now have the option to copy and paste bibliographic information from the library computer catalog and periodical indexes or from the Internet into a document on your computer that you can edit throughout the research process. You can also track your project online with a citation manager like Zotero, Mendeley, or EndNote. One advantage of the copy/paste option over the index card method is accuracy, especially in punctuation, spelling, and capitalization—details that are essential in accessing Internet sites.

Checklist for a Working Bibliography of Print and Online Sources

For Books

- Library call number
- Names of all authors, editors, and translators
- Title and subtitle
- Publication data:
    - Place of publication (city and state)
    - Publisher's name
    - Date of publication
- Edition (if not the first) and volume number (if applicable)

For Periodical Articles

- Names of all authors
- Name and subtitle of article
- Title of journal, magazine, or newspaper
- Publication data:
    - Volume number and issue number
    - Date of issue
    - Page numbers

For Internet Sources

- Names of all authors and/or editors
- Title and subtitle of the document
- Title of the longer work to which the document belongs (if applicable)
- Title of the site or discussion list
- Name of company or organization that owns the Web site
- Date of release, online posting, or latest revision
- Format of online source (Web page, .pdf, podcast, etc.)
- Date you accessed the site
- Electronic address (URL) or Digital Object Identifier (DOI)

> **For Other Sources**
> - Name of author, government agency, organization, company, recording artist, personality, etc.
> - Title of the work
> - Format (pamphlet, unpublished diary, interview, television broadcast, etc.)
> - Publication or production data:
>   Name of publisher or producer
>   Date of publication, production, or release
>   Identifying codes or numbers (if applicable)

TAKING NOTES

As you read, take notes. You're looking for ideas, facts, opinions, statistics, examples, and evidence that you think will be useful in writing your paper. As you work through the articles, look for recurring themes and mark the places where the writers are in agreement and where they differ in their views. Try to remember that the effectiveness of your paper is largely determined by the quality—not necessarily the quantity—of your notes. The purpose of a research paper is not to present a collection of quotes that show you've read all the material and can report what others have said about your topic. Your goal is to analyze, evaluate, and synthesize the information you collect—in other words, to enter into the discussion of the issues and thereby take ownership of your topic. You want to view the results of your research from your own perspective and arrive at an informed opinion of your topic. (For more on Writing with Sources, see Chapter 14.)

Now for some practical advice on taking notes: First, be systematic. If you use note cards, write one note on a card and use cards of uniform size, preferably 4- by 6-inch cards because they are large enough to accommodate even a long note on a single card and yet small enough to be easily handled and carried. If you keep notes electronically, consider creating a separate file for each topic or source or use a digital research application like those mentioned previously (Zotero, Mendeley, or EndNote). If you keep your notes organized, when you get to the planning and writing stage, you will be able to sequence your notes according to the plan you have envisioned for your paper. Furthermore, if you decide to alter your organizational plan, you can easily reorder your notes to reflect those revisions.

Second, try not to take too many notes. One good way to help decide whether to take a note is to ask yourself, "How exactly does this material help prove or disprove my thesis?" You might even try envisioning where in your paper you could use the information. If it does not seem relevant to your thesis, don't bother to take a note.

Once you decide to take a note, you must decide whether to summarize, paraphrase, or quote directly. The approach that you take is largely determined by the content of the passage and the way you envision using it in your paper. For detailed advice on summary, paraphrase, and quotation, see Chapter 14, pages 669–77.

DOCUMENTING SOURCES

When you summarize, paraphrase, or quote a person's thoughts and ideas, and when you use facts or statistics that are not commonly known or believed, you must properly acknowledge the source of your information. You must document the source of your information when you:

- Quote a source word for word
- Refer to information and ideas from another source that you present in your own words as either a paraphrase or a summary
- Cite statistics, tables, charts, or graphs

You do not need to document:

- Your own observations, experiences, and ideas
- Factual information available in a number of reference works (known as "common knowledge")
- Proverbs, sayings, and familiar quotations

A reference to the source of your borrowed information is called a *citation*. There are many systems for making citations, and your citations must consistently follow one of these systems. The documentation style recommended by the Modern Language Association (MLA) is commonly used in English and the humanities and is the style used for student papers throughout this book. Another common system is American Psychological Association (APA) style, which is used in the social sciences. In general, your instructor will tell you which system to use. For more information on documentation styles, consult the appropriate manual or handbook. For MLA style, consult the *MLA Handbook*, 8th ed. (MLA, 2016).

There are two components of documentation in a research paper: the *in-text citation*, placed in the body of your paper, and the *list of works cited*, which provides complete publication data on your sources and is placed at the end of your paper.

▶ In-Text Citations

Most in-text citations, also known as parenthetical citations, consist of only the author's last name and a page reference. Usually, the author's name is given in an introductory or signal phrase (see pages 673–74) at the beginning of the borrowed material, and the page reference is given in parentheses at the end. If the author's name is not given at the beginning, it belongs in the parentheses along with the page reference. The parenthetical reference signals the end of the borrowed material and directs your readers to the list of works cited should they want to pursue a source.

Consider the following examples of in-text citations from a student paper on the debate over whether to make English America's official language.

In-Text Citations (MLA Style)

Diaz 4

Many people are surprised to discover that English is not the official language of the United States. Today, even as English literacy becomes a necessity for people in many parts of the world, some people in the United States believe its primacy is being threatened right at home. Much of the current controversy focuses on Hispanic communities with large Spanish-speaking populations who may feel little or no pressure to learn English. Columnist and cultural critic Charles Krauthammer believes English should be America's official language. He notes that this country has been "blessed ... with a linguistic unity that brings a critically needed cohesion to a nation as diverse, multiracial and multiethnic as America" and that communities such as these threaten the bond created by a common language (112). There are others, however, who think that "language does not threaten American unity. Benign neglect is a good policy for any country when it comes to language, and it's a good policy for America" (King 64).

Citation with author's name in the signal phrase

Citation with author's name in parentheses

Diaz 5

Works Cited

King, Robert D. "Should English Be the Law?" *Atlantic Monthly*, Apr. 1997, pp. 55-64.

Krauthammer, Charles. "In Plain English: Let's Make It Official." *Time*, 12 June 2006, p. 112.

In the preceding example, the student followed MLA guidelines for documentation. The following sections provide MLA guidelines for documenting a variety of common sources. For advice on documenting additional, less frequently cited sources, consult the *MLA Handbook* 8th ed. (MLA, 2016).

LIST OF WORKS CITED

In this section, you will find general guidelines for creating a list of works cited, followed by sample entries designed to cover the citations you will use most often.

Guidelines for Constructing Your Works Cited Page

1. Begin the list on a new page following the last page of text.
2. Center the title *Works Cited* at the top of the page.
3. Double-space both within and between entries on your list.
4. Alphabetize your sources by the authors' last names. If you have two or more authors with the same last name, alphabetize by first names.
5. If you have two or more works by the same author, alphabetize by the first word of the titles, not counting *A*, *An*, or *The*. Use the author's name in the first entry and three unspaced hyphens followed by a period in subsequent entries:

    Twitchell, James B. *Branded Nation: The Marketing of Megachurch, College Inc., and Museumworld*. Simon & Schuster, 2005.

    ---. "The Branding of Higher Ed." *Forbes*, 25 Nov. 2002, p. 50.

    ---. *Look Away, Dixieland: A Carpetbagger's Great-Grandson Travels Highway 84*. Louisiana State UP, 2011.

6. If no author is known, alphabetize by title.
7. Begin each entry at the left margin. If the entry is longer than one line, indent the second and subsequent lines one-half inch.
8. Italicize the titles of books, journals, magazines, and newspapers. Use quotation marks for titles of periodical articles, chapters and essays within books, short stories, and poems.

▶ Periodical Print Publications: Journals, Magazines, and Newspapers

> **Standard Information for Periodical Print Publications**
>
> 1. Name of the author of the work; for anonymous works, begin entry with the title of the work
> 2. Title of the work, in quotation marks
> 3. Name of the periodical, italicized
> 4. Series number or name, if relevant
> 5. Volume number (for scholarly journals that use volume numbers)
> 6. Issue number (if available, for scholarly journals)
> 7. Date of publication (for scholarly journals, year; for other periodicals, day, month, and year, as available)
> 8. Page numbers

Scholarly Journal Article

For all scholarly journals—whether paginated continuously throughout a given year or not—provide the volume number (if one is given), the issue number, the year, and the page numbers. Separate the volume number and the issue number with a comma.

> Ercolino, Stefano. "The Maximalist Novel." *Comparative Literature*, vol. 64, no. 3, Summer 2012, p. 56.

Magazine Article

When citing a weekly or biweekly magazine, give the complete date (day, month, year).

> Grossman, Lev. "A Star Is Born." *Time*, 2 Nov. 2015, pp. 30–39.
>
> Kunzig, Robert. "The Will to Change." *National Geographic*, Nov. 2015, pp. 32–63.

When citing a magazine published every month or every two months, provide the month or months and year. If an article in a magazine is not printed on consecutive pages—for example, an article might begin on page 45, then skip to 48—include only the first page followed by a plus sign.

> Mascarelli, Amanda Leigh. "Fall Guys." *Audubon* Nov.–Dec. 2009:44+.

Newspaper Article

> Bellafante, Ginia. "When the Law Says a Parent Isn't a Parent." *New York Times*. 3 Feb. 2013, natl. ed.: 27.

Review (Film or Book)

> Lane, Anthony. "Human Bondage." Review of *Spectre*, directed by Sam Mendes, *The New Yorker*, 16 Nov. 2015, pp. 96–97.

> Walton, James. "Noble, Embattled Souls." Review of *The Bone Clocks* and *Slade House*, by David Mitchell, *The New York Review of Books*, 3 Dec. 2015, pp. 55–58.

If the review has no title, simply begin with *Review* after the author's name. If there is neither a title nor an author, begin with *Review* and alphabetize by the title of the book or film being reviewed.

Anonymous Article

When no author's name is given, begin the entry with the title.

> "Pompeii: Will the City Go from Dust to Dust?" *Newsweek*, 1 Sept. 1997, p. 8.

Editorial (Unsigned/Signed)

> "Policing Ohio's Online Courses." *Plain Dealer* [Cleveland], 9 Oct. 2012, p. A5. Editorial.

> Stengel, Richard. "In Drones We Trust." *Time*, 11 Feb. 2013, p. 2. Editorial.

Letter to the Editor

> Lyon, Ruth Henriquez. "A Word to the Editor." *Audubon*, Jan.–Feb. 2013, p. 10. Letter.

▸ Nonperiodical Print Publications: Books, Brochures, and Pamphlets

---

Standard Information for Nonperiodical Print Publications

---

1. Name of the author, editor, compiler, or translator of the work; for anonymous works, begin entry with the title
2. Title of the work, italicized
3. Edition
4. Volume number
5. Name of the publisher and year of publication

Book by a Single Author

> Al-Maria, Sophia. *The Girl Who Fell to Earth*. Harper, 2012.

When writing the publisher's name, omit business words such as *Co.* or *Company*, but do include shortened versions for university presses (e.g., *Cambridge UP* for Cambridge University Press).

Anthology

> Marcus, Ben, editor. *New American Stories*. Vintage Books, 2015.

Book by Two or More Authors

For a book by two authors, list the authors in the order in which they appear on the title page.

> O'Reilly, Bill, and Martin Dugard. *Killing Kennedy*. Henry Holt, 2012.

For a book by three or more authors, list the first author in the same way as for a single-author book, followed by a comma and the abbreviation *et al.* ("and others").

> Cunningham, Stewart, et al. *Media Economics*. Palgrave Macmillan, 2015.

Book by Corporate Author

> Human Rights Watch. *World Report of 2015: Events of 2014*. Seven Stories Press, 2015.

Work in Anthology

Include the page numbers of the selection after the anthology's year of publication.

> Sayrafiezadeh, Saïd. "Paranoia." *New American Stories*, edited by Ben Marcus, Vintage Books, 2015, pp. 3–29.

Article in Reference Book

> Anagnost, George T. "Sandra Day O'Connor." *The Oxford Companion to the Supreme Court of the United States*. 2nd ed., 2005.

If an article is unsigned, begin with the title.

> "Ball's in Your Court, The." *The American Heritage Dictionary of Idioms*. 2nd ed., Houghton Mifflin Harcourt, 2013.

Note that widely used reference works do not require a publisher's name. Also note that page numbers are not necessary if entries in a reference work are arranged alphabetically.

Introduction, Preface, Foreword, or Afterword to Book

> Sullivan, John Jeremiah. "The Ill-Defined Plot." Introduction. *The Best American Essays 2014*, edited by John J. Sullivan and Robert Atwan, Houghton Mifflin Harcourt, 2014, pp. xvii–xxvi.

Translation

> Ullmann, Regina. *The Country Road: Stories*. Translated by Kurt Beals, New Directions Publishing, 2015.

Illustrated Book or Graphic Novel

> Moore, Alan. *V for Vendetta*. Illustrated by David Lloyd, DC Comics, 2008.

Book Published in Second or Subsequent Edition

Eagleton, Terry. *Literary Theory: An Introduction.* 3rd ed., U of Minnesota P, 2008.

Brochure or Pamphlet

The Legendary Sleepy Hollow Cemetery. Friends of Sleepy Hollow Cemetery, 2008.

Government Publication

Canada, Minister of Aboriginal Affairs and Northern Development. 2015–16 *Report on Plans and Priorities.* Minister of Public Works and Government Services Canada, 2015.

List the government, the agency, and the title.

▶ Web Publications

The following guidelines and models for citing information retrieved from the World Wide Web have been adapted from the most recent advice of the MLA — as detailed in the *MLA Handbook*, 8th ed. (2016) — and from the "MLA Style" section on MLA's Web site (www.mla.org). You will notice that citations of Web publications have some features in common with both print publications and reprinted works, broadcasts, and live performances.

Standard Information for Web Publications

1. Name of the author, editor, or compiler of the work

    (For works with more than one author, a corporate author, or an unnamed author, apply the guidelines for print sources; for anonymous works, begin entry with the title.)

2. Title of the work, italicized, unless it is part of a larger work, in which case put it in quotation marks

3. Title of the overall Web site, italicized (if distinct from item 2 above)

4. Publisher or sponsor of the site

5. Date of publication (day, month, and year)

6. Date of access (day, month, and year) if the date of publication is not listed

7. Location

Although MLA does not absolutely require URLs in works cited entries, it does recommend that you include URLs in your works-cited list. Even though URLs can become obsolete in a matter of months and can give a cluttered feel to your works-cited list, they are useful in the short run because they help readers locate your source quickly, especially if your paper is in digital format and the URLs are clickable. Some publishers assign a digital object identifier—a DOI—to each online publication. Because a DOI remains with an article even when a URL changes, you should cite a DOI instead of a URL whenever possible. Insert the DOI or the URL as the last item in an entry, immediately after the date of publication. The DOI or URL is followed by a period. The following example illustrates an entry with the DOI included:

> Young, Michelle D., and Frank Perrone. "How Are Standards Used, by Whom, and to What End?" *Journal of Research on Leadership Education*, vol. 11, no. 1, 2016, doi: 10.1177/1942775116647511.

If a DOI or URL extends over more than one line, break the DOI or URL after a slash, hyphen, or period. Do *not* add spaces, hyphens, or any other punctuation to indicate the break.

ONLINE SCHOLARLY JOURNALS. To cite an article, a review, an editorial, or a letter to the editor in a scholarly journal existing only in electronic form on the Web, provide the author, the title of the article, the title of the journal, the volume and issue, and the date of issue, followed by the page numbers (if available), and the DOI or URL.

Article in Online Scholarly Journal

> Bryson, Devin. "The Rise of a New Senegalese Cultural Philosophy?" *African Studies Quarterly*, vol. 14, no. 3, Mar. 2014, pp. 33–56, asq.africa.ufl.edu/files/ Volume-14-Issue-3-Bryson.pdf.

PERIODICAL PUBLICATIONS IN ONLINE DATABASES

Journal Article from Online Database or Subscription Service

> Spychalski, John C. Review of *American Railroads—Decline and Renaissance in the Twentieth Century*, by Robert E. Gallamore and John R. Meyer. *Transportation Journal*, vol. 54, no. 4, Fall 2015, pp. 535–38. *JSTOR*, doi:10.5325/ transportationj.54.4.0535.

Magazine Article from Online Database or Subscription Service

> Rosenbaum, Ron. "The Last Renaissance Man." *Smithsonian*, Nov. 2012, pp. 39–44. *OmniFile Full Text Select*, web.b.ebscohost.com.ezproxy.bpl.org/.

Newspaper Article from Online Database or Subscription Service

> "The Road toward Peace." *The New York Times*, 15 Feb. 1945, p. 18. Editorial. *ProQuest Historical Newspapers: The New York Times*, search.proquest.com/ hnpnewyorktimes.

NONPERIODICAL WEB PUBLICATIONS. This category of Web publication includes all Web-delivered content that does not fit into one of the previous two categories (online scholarly journal publications and periodical publications from an online database).

Online Magazine Article

Leonard, Andrew. "The Surveillance State High School." *Salon*, 27 Nov. 2012, www.salon.com/2012/11/27/the_surveillance_state_high_school/.

Online Newspaper Article

Crowell, Maddy. "How Computers Are Getting Better at Detecting Liars." *The Christian Science Monitor*, 12 Dec. 2015, www.csmonitor.com/Science/Science-Notebook/2015/1212/How-computers-are-getting-better-at-detecting-liars.

Humphrey, Tom. "Politics Outweigh Arguments about School Vouchers." *Knoxville News Sentinel*, 24 Jan. 2016, www.knoxnews.com/opinion/columnists/tom-humphrey/tom-humphrey-politics-outweigh-arguments-about-school-vouchers-29c77b33-9963-0ef8-e053-0100007fcba4-366300461.html.

Book or Part of Book Accessed Online

For a book available online, provide the author, the title, the editor (if any), original publication information, the name of the database or Web site, and the URL.

Piketty, Thomas. *Capital in the Twenty-First Century*. Translated by Arthur Goldhammer, Harvard UP, 2014. *Google Books*, books.google.com/books?isbn=0674369556.

If you are citing only part of an online book, include the title or name of the part directly after the author's name.

Woolf, Virginia. "Kew Gardens." *Monday or Tuesday*. Harcourt, 1921, *Bartleby.com: Great Books Online*, www.bartleby.com/85/7.html.

Online Speech, Essay, Poem, or Short Story

Milton, John. *Paradise Lost: Book I. Poetry Foundation*, 2014, www.poetryfoundation.org/poem/174987.

Online Encyclopedia or Other Reference Work

Hall, Mark. "Facebook (American Company)." *The Enyclopaedia Britannica*, 2 Jul. 2014, www.britannica.com/topic/Facebook.

"House Music." *Wikipedia*, 16 Nov. 2015, en.wikipedia.org/wiki/House_music.

Online Artwork, Photographs, Maps, Charts, and Other Images

Clough, Charles. *January Twenty-First*. 1988–89, Joslyn Art Museum, Omaha, www.joslyn.org/collections-and-exhibitions/permanent-collections/modern-and-contemporary/charles-clough-january-twenty-first/.

Online Government Publication

United States, Department of Agriculture, Food and Nutrition Service, Child Nutrition Programs. *Eligibility Manual for School Meals: Determining and Verifying Eligibility*. National School Lunch Program, July 2015, www.fns.usda.gov/sites/default/files/cn/SP40_CACFP18_SFSP20-2015a1.pdf.

Blog Posting

Kiuchi, Tatsuro. *Tatsuro Kiuchi: News & Blog*, tatsurokiuchi.com. Accessed 3 Mar. 2016.

Online Video Recording

Nayar, Vineet. "Employees First, Customers Second." *YouTube*, 9 Jun. 2015, www.youtube.com/watch?v=cCdu67s_C5E.

▶ Additional Common Sources

Television or Radio Broadcast

"Federal Role in Support of Autism." *Washington Journal*, narrated by Robb Harleston, C-SPAN, 1 Dec. 2012.

Sound Recording

Bizet, Georges. *Carmen*. Performances by Jennifer Larmore, Thomas Moser, Angela Gheorghiu, and Samuel Ramey, Bavarian State Orchestra and Chorus, conducted by Giuseppe Sinopoli, Warner, 1996.

Film or Video Recording

Scott, Ridley, director. *The Martian*. Performances by Matt Damon, Jessica Chastain, Kristen Wiig, and Kate Mara, Twentieth Century Fox, 2015.

Work of Visual Art

Bradford, Mark. *Let's Walk to the Middle of the Ocean*. 2015, Museum of Modern Art, New York.

If you use a reproduction of a piece of visual art, give the institution and city as well as the complete publication information for the source.

O'Keeffe, Georgia. *Black and Purple Petunias*. 1925, private collection. *Two Lives: A Conversation in Paintings and Photographs*, edited by Alexandra Arrowsmith and Thomas West, HarperCollins, 1992, p. 67.

Interview

Weddington, Sarah. "Sarah Weddington: Still Arguing for *Roe*." Interview by Michele Kort, *Ms.*, Winter 2013, pp. 32–35.

For interviews that you conduct, provide the name of the person interviewed, the type of interview (personal, telephone, e-mail), and the date.

Proulx, E. Annie. Telephone interview. 27 Jan. 2013.

Cartoon or Comic Strip

Zyglis, Adam. "City of Light." *Buffalo News*, 8 Nov. 2015, adamzyglis.buffalonews.com/2015/11/08/city-of-light/. Cartoon.

Advertisement

AT&T. *National Geographic*, Dec. 2015, p. 14. Advertisement.

Lecture, Speech, Address, or Reading

Smith, Anna Deavere. "On the Road: A Search for American Character." National Endowment for the Humanities, John F. Kennedy Center for the Performing Arts, Washington, 6 Apr. 2015. Address.

Letter, Memo, or E-Mail Message

Thornbrugh, Caitlin. "Coates Lecture." Received by Rita Anderson, 20 Oct. 2015.

Smithson 5

Did Dr. Bryant want anything else in the header?

experiment with new things and break free from your parents. Both lectures infuriated me. As a studious only child who ~~had grown up~~ *grew up* surrounded by adults, I shared none of these sentiments and felt patronized ~~and condescended to~~. I considered myself ~~a rather~~ *an* intelligent, mature person who ~~consequently~~ *consequently* not only sought approval of adults, but *also* set high academic and moral expectations for myself. Common assumptions of the contrary made me ~~blow up~~ *lose my temper* with my parents and *diminished* my respect for Dr. Wolf, at *whom* I pouted and fumed, making a scene. Every time I argued, however, my parents ~~would respond~~ with a nudge to the parent*s* sitting beside them, See. This is why we are here. The stereotype ~~entangled and stuck~~ *had trapped* ~~with me~~. Whether through reverting to childhood or jumping ahead to adulthood, I knew I had no other choice but to avoid this *teenage* development stage altogether if I wanted to be respected. I had to convince my parents that though I was a teen ~~chronologically~~ *by age*, I was not and never would be a teen at heart. Fed up with the bad reputation society ~~has given~~ *gave* them, Poole claims, they decide it is easier to fulfil low expectations than to conquer

Unfortunately,
Many teens do not take this approach ~~to those seven years of life~~.

them ~~all~~, and they succumb to their parents' justifications that experimentation and rebellion are "just part of growing up". ~~They just do what they think people expect them to.~~ Others, like Tracy, *embody* the stereotype because they ~~have~~ observed their parents doing the same. The assumptions made supporting the

It's often more about parents that their children: to say teenage delinquency is inevitable reflects parents' own feelings of inadequacy

~~theory that teenage delinquency is inevitable is a reflection of parents' feelings of inadequacy, whether~~
~~they are poor role models or not.~~ By diverting the root of teen issues from parental responsibility and instead attributing it to chronology, parents boost their own self-esteem, *oblivious* ~~to the fact that they are~~ tearing down the self-esteem of their child. The stereotype, when *im*~~posed~~ on unruly and obedient teens alike, becomes not only an inaccurate assumption but *also* a self-fulfilling prophesy for parents and authoritative figures ~~with a~~ *they don't realize the* harmful impact *they can have* on the adolescents they target, evoking fear in thirteen year olds like myself of becoming a dreaded, awful teenager.

Is it "of" or "to"?

⋆ *Remember to include Poole and Doyle in Works Cited*

CHAPTER **16**

Editing for Grammar, Punctuation, and Sentence Style

ONCE YOU HAVE REVISED YOUR ESSAY AND YOU ARE CONFIDENT THAT you have said what you wanted to say, you are ready to begin editing your essay. During the editing stage of the writing process, you identify and correct errors in grammar, punctuation, and sentence style. You don't want a series of small errors to detract from your paper: Such errors can cause confusion in some cases, and they can also cause readers to have second thoughts about your credibility as an author.

This chapter addresses twelve common writing problems that instructors from around the country told us trouble their students most. For more guidance with these or other editing concerns, be sure to refer to a writer's handbook or ask your instructor for help.

1 Run-ons: Fused Sentences and Comma Splices

Writers can become so absorbed in getting their ideas down on paper that they sometimes incorrectly combine two independent clauses—word groups that could stand on their own as complete sentences—creating a *run-on sentence*. A run-on sentence fails to show where one thought ends and another begins, and it can confuse readers. There are two types of run-on sentences: the fused sentence and the comma splice.

A *fused sentence* occurs when a writer joins two independent clauses with no punctuation and no coordinating conjunction.

> **fused sentence** The delegates at the state political convention could not decide on a leader they were beginning to show their frustration.

741

A *comma splice* occurs when a writer uses only a comma to join two or more independent clauses.

comma splice The delegates at the state political convention could not decide on a leader, they were beginning to show their frustration.

There are five ways to fix run-on sentences.

1. **Create two separate sentences with a period.**

   edited The delegates at the state political convention could not decide on a leader ~~they~~ .They were beginning to show their frustration.

2. **Use a comma and a coordinating conjunction to join the two sentences.**

   edited The delegates at the state political convention could not decide on a leader , and they were beginning to show their frustration.

3. **Use a semicolon to separate the two clauses.**

   edited The delegates at the state political convention could not decide on a leader ; they were beginning to show their frustration.

4. **Use a semicolon followed by a transitional word or expression and a comma to join the two clauses.**

   edited The delegates at the state political convention could not decide on a leader ; consequently, they were beginning to show their frustration.

5. **Subordinate one clause to the other, using a subordinate conjunction or a relative pronoun.**

   edited ~~The~~ When the delegates at the state political convention could not decide on a leader, they were beginning to show their frustration.

   edited The delegates at the state political convention could not decide on a leader , who were beginning to show their frustration, ~~they were beginning to show their frustration.~~

2 Sentence Fragments

A *sentence fragment* is a part of a sentence presented as if it were a complete sentence. Even if a word group begins with a capital letter and ends with a period, a question mark, or an exclamation point, it is not a sentence unless it has a subject (the person, place, or thing the sentence is about) and a verb (a word that tells what the subject does) and expresses a complete thought.

> sentence fragment My music group decided to study the early works of Mozart. *The child prodigy from Austria.*

Word groups that do not express complete thoughts are often freestanding subordinate clauses beginning with a subordinating conjunction such as *although, because, since, so, that,* or *unless.*

> sentence fragment The company president met with the management team every single week. *So that problems were rarely ignored.*

You can correct sentence fragments in one of two ways.

1. **Integrate the fragment into a nearby sentence.**

   > edited My music group decided to study the early works of Mozart~~.~~ , the ~~The~~ child prodigy from Austria.

   > edited The company president met with the management team every single week~~.~~, ~~So~~ so that problems were rarely ignored.

2. **Develop the fragment into a complete sentence by adding a subject or a verb.**

   > edited My music group decided to study the early works of Mozart. The child prodigy ˄was from Austria.

   > edited The company president met with the management team every single week. ~~So that problems~~ Problems were rarely ignored.

Sentence fragments are not always incorrect. In fact, if used deliberately, a sentence fragment can add useful stylistic emphasis. In narratives, deliberate sentence fragments are most commonly used in dialogue and in descriptive passages that set a mood or tone. In the following passage taken from "Not Close Enough for Comfort" (pages 104–06), David P. Bardeen uses fragments to convey the awkwardness of the lunch meeting he had with his brother Will:

> I asked him about his recent trip. He asked me about work. Short questions. One-word answers. Then an awkward pause.

3 Comma Faults

Commas help communicate meaning by eliminating possible misreadings. Consider this sentence:

> After visiting William Alan Lee went to French class.

Depending upon where you put the comma, it could be Lee, Alan Lee, or William Alan Lee who goes to French class.

> edited   After visiting William Alan, Lee went to French class.
>
> edited   After visiting William, Alan Lee went to French class.
>
> edited   After visiting, William Alan Lee went to French class.

The comma, of all the marks of punctuation, has the greatest variety of uses, which can make its proper use seem difficult. It might help to think of the comma's role this way: In every case, the comma functions in one of two basic ways—to *separate* or to *enclose* elements in a sentence. By learning a few basic rules based on these two functions, you will be able to identify and correct common comma errors.

1. **Use a comma to separate two independent clauses joined by a coordinating conjunction.**

   > incorrect   Tolstoy wrote many popular short stories but he is perhaps best known for his novels.
   >
   > edited   Tolstoy wrote many popular short stories, but he is perhaps best known for his novels.

2. **Use a comma to separate an introductory phrase or clause from the main clause of a sentence.**

   > incorrect   In his book *Life on the Mississippi* Mark Twain describes his days as a riverboat pilot.
   >
   > edited   In his book *Life on the Mississippi*, Mark Twain describes his days as a riverboat pilot.
   >
   > incorrect   When the former Soviet Union collapsed residents of Moscow had to struggle just to survive.
   >
   > edited   When the former Soviet Union collapsed, residents of Moscow had to struggle just to survive.

3. **Use commas to enclose nonrestrictive elements.** When an adjective phrase or clause adds information that is essential to the meaning of a sentence, it is said to be *restrictive* and should not be set off with commas.

   The woman wearing the beige linen suit works with Homeland Security.

The adjective phrase "wearing the beige linen suit" is essential and thus should not be set off with commas; without this information, we have no way of identifying which woman works with Homeland Security.

When an adjective phrase or clause does not add information that is essential to the meaning of the sentence, it is said to be *nonrestrictive* and should be enclosed with commas.

> incorrect Utopian literature which was popular during the late nineteenth century seems to emerge at times of economic and political unrest.

> edited Utopian literature,which was popular during the late nineteenth century,seems to emerge at times of economic and political unrest.

4. **Use commas to separate items in a series.**

> incorrect The three staples of the diet in Thailand are rice fish and fruit.

> edited The three staples of the diet in Thailand are rice, fish, and fruit.

4 Subject-Verb Agreement

Subjects and verbs must agree in number—that is, a singular subject (one person, place, or thing) must take a singular verb, and a plural subject (more than one person, place, or thing) must take a plural verb. While most native speakers of English use proper subject-verb agreement in their writing without thinking about it, some sentence constructions can be troublesome to native and non-native speakers alike.

INTERVENING PREPOSITIONAL PHRASES

When the relationship between the subject and the verb in a sentence is not clear, the culprit is usually an intervening prepositional phrase (a phrase that begins with a preposition such as *on*, *of*, *in*, *at*, or *between*). To make sure the subject agrees with its verb in a sentence with an intervening prepositional phrase, mentally cross out the phrase (*of the term* in the following example) to isolate the subject and the verb and determine if they agree.

> incorrect The first one hundred days of the term has passed quickly.

> edited The first one hundred days of the term ~~has~~ have passed quickly.

COMPOUND SUBJECTS

Writers often have difficulty with subject-verb agreement in sentences with compound subjects (two or more subjects joined together with the word *and*). As a general rule, compound subjects take plural verbs.

> incorrect My iPod, computer, and television was stolen.
>
> edited My iPod, computer, and television ~~was~~ *were* stolen.

However, in sentences with subjects joined by *either . . . or, neither . . . nor,* or *not only . . . but also,* the verb must agree with the subject closest to it.

> incorrect Neither the students nor the professor are satisfied with the lab equipment.
>
> edited Neither the students nor the professor ~~are~~ *is* satisfied with the lab equipment.

5 Unclear Pronoun References

The noun to which a pronoun refers is called its *antecedent* or *referent*. Be sure to place a pronoun as close to its antecedent as possible so that the relationship between them is clear. The more words that intervene between the antecedent and the pronoun, the more chance there is for confusion. When the relationship between a pronoun and its antecedent is unclear, the sentence becomes inaccurate or ambiguous. While editing your writing, look for and correct ambiguous, vague, or implied pronoun references.

AMBIGUOUS REFERENCES

Make sure all your pronouns clearly refer to specific antecedents. If a pronoun can refer to more than one antecedent, the sentence is ambiguous.

> ambiguous Adler sought to convince the reader to mark up *his* book.

In this sentence, the antecedent of the pronoun *his* could be either *Adler* or *reader*. Does Adler want his particular book marked up, or does he want the reader to mark up his or her own book? To make an ambiguous antecedent clear, either repeat the correct antecedent or rewrite the sentence.

> edited Adler sought to convince the reader to mark up ~~his~~ *Adler's* book.
>
> edited Adler sought to convince the reader to mark up ~~his~~ *his or her* book.

VAGUE REFERENCES

Whenever you use *it, they, you, this, that,* or *which* to refer to a general idea in a preceding clause or sentence, be sure that the connection between the pronoun and the general idea is clear. When these pronouns lack a specific antecedent, you give readers an impression of vagueness and carelessness.

To correct the problem, either substitute a noun for the pronoun or provide an antecedent to which the pronoun can clearly refer.

> vague The tornadoes damaged many of the homes in the area, but it has not yet been determined.
>
> edited The tornadoes damaged many of the homes in the area, but ~~it~~ *the extent of the damage* has not yet been determined.
>
> vague In the book, they wrote that Samantha had an addictive personality.
>
> edited In the book, ~~they wrote that~~ Samantha had an addictive personality.

Whenever the connection between the general idea and the pronoun is simple and clear, no confusion results. Consider the following example:

> The stock market rose for a third consecutive week, and this lifted most investors' spirits.

IMPLIED REFERENCES

Make every pronoun refer to a stated, not an implied, antecedent. Every time you use a pronoun in a sentence, you should be able to identify its noun equivalent. If you cannot, use a noun instead.

> implied After all of the editing and formatting, it was finished.
>
> edited After all of the editing and formatting, ~~it~~ *the research report* was finished.

Sometimes a modifier or possessive that implies a noun is mistaken for an antecedent.

> implied In G. Anthony Gorry's "Steal This MP3 File: What Is Theft?" he shows how technology might be shaping the attitudes of today's youth.
>
> edited In ~~G. Anthony Gorry's~~ "Steal This MP3 File: What Is Theft?" ~~he~~ *G. Anthony Gorry* shows how technology might be shaping the attitudes of today's youth.

6 Pronoun-Antecedent Agreement

Personal pronouns must agree with their antecedents in *person*, *number*, and *gender*.

AGREEMENT IN PERSON

There are three types of personal pronouns: first person (*I* and *we*), second person (*you*), and third person (*he*, *she*, *it*, and *they*). To agree in person, first-person pronouns must refer to first-person antecedents, second-person pronouns to second-person antecedents, and third-person pronouns to third-person antecedents.

> **incorrect** A scientist should consider all the data carefully before you draw a conclusion.

> **edited** A scientist should consider all the data carefully before ~~you draw~~ *he or she draws* a conclusion.

AGREEMENT IN NUMBER

To agree in number, a singular pronoun must refer to a singular antecedent, and a plural pronoun must refer to a plural antecedent. When two or more antecedents are joined by the word *and*, the pronoun must be plural.

> **incorrect** Karen, Rachel, and Sofia took her electives in history.

> **edited** Karen, Rachel, and Sofia took ~~her~~ *their* electives in history.

When the subject of a sentence is an indefinite pronoun such as *everyone, each, everybody, anyone, anybody, everything, either, one, neither, someone,* or *something*, use a singular pronoun to refer to it or recast the sentence to eliminate the agreement problem.

> **incorrect** Each of the women submitted their résumé.

> **edited** Each of the women submitted ~~their~~ *her* résumé.

> **edited** ~~Each~~ *Both* of the women submitted their ~~résumé~~ *résumés*.

If a collective noun (*army, community, team, herd, committee, association*) is understood as a unit, it takes a singular pronoun; if it is understood in terms of its individual members, it takes a plural pronoun.

> **as a unit** The class presented its annual spring musical.

> **as individual members** The class agreed to pay for their own art supplies.

AGREEMENT IN GENDER

Traditionally, a masculine, singular pronoun has been used for indefinite antecedents (such as *anyone, someone,* and *everyone*) and to refer to generic antecedents (such as *employee, student, athlete, secretary, doctor,* and *computer specialist*). But *anyone* can be female or male, and women are employees (or students, athletes, secretaries, doctors, and computer specialists), too. The use of masculine pronouns to refer to both females and males is considered sexist; that is, such usage leaves out women as a segment of society or diminishes their presence. Instead, use *he or she, his or her,* or, in an extended piece of writing, alternate in a balanced way the use of *he* and *she* throughout. Sometimes the best solution is to rewrite the sentence to put it in the plural or to avoid the problem altogether.

> **sexist** If any student wants to attend the opening performance of *King Lear,* he will have to purchase a ticket by Wednesday.
>
> **edited** If any student wants to attend the opening performance of *King Lear,* ^(he or she) ~~he~~ will have to purchase a ticket by Wednesday.
>
> **edited** If any ^(students) ~~student~~ wants to attend the opening performance of *King Lear,* ^(they) ~~he~~ will have to purchase ~~a ticket~~ ^(tickets) by Wednesday.
>
> **edited** ^(All tickets for) ~~If any student wants to attend~~ the opening performance of *King Lear,* ~~he will have to purchase a ticket~~ ^(must be purchased) by Wednesday.

7 Dangling and Misplaced Modifiers

A *modifier* is a word or group of words that describes or gives additional information about other words in a sentence. The words, phrases, and clauses that function as modifiers in a sentence can usually be moved around freely, so place them carefully to avoid unintentionally confusing—or amusing—your reader. As a rule, place modifiers as close as possible to the words you want to modify. Two common problems arise with modifiers: the misplaced modifier and the dangling modifier.

MISPLACED MODIFIERS

A *misplaced modifier* unintentionally modifies the wrong word in a sentence because it is placed incorrectly.

> **misplaced** The waiter brought a steak to the man covered with onions.
>
> **edited** The waiter brought a steak ^(covered with onions) to the man ~~covered with onions~~.

DANGLING MODIFIERS

A *dangling modifier* usually appears at the beginning of a sentence and does not logically relate to the main clause of the sentence. The dangling modifier wants to modify a word—often an unstated subject—that does not appear in the sentence. To eliminate a dangling modifier, give the dangling phrase a subject.

dangling   Staring into the distance, large rain clouds form.

edited   Staring into the distance, ^Jon saw large rain clouds form.

dangling   Walking on the ceiling, he noticed a beautiful luna moth.

edited   ^He ~~Walking on the ceiling, he~~ noticed a beautiful luna moth^, walking on the ceiling.

8 Faulty Parallelism

Parallelism is the repetition of word order or grammatical form either within a single sentence or in several sentences that develop the same central idea. As a rhetorical device, parallel structure can aid coherence and add emphasis. Franklin Roosevelt's famous Depression-era statement "I see one-third of a nation *ill-housed, ill-clad,* and *ill-nourished*" illustrates effective parallelism. Use parallel grammatical structures to emphasize the similarities and differences between the items being compared. Look for opportunities to use parallel constructions with paired items or items in a series, paired items using correlative conjunctions, and comparisons using *than* or *as*.

PAIRED ITEMS OR ITEMS IN A SERIES

Parallel structures can be used to balance a word with a word, a phrase with a phrase, or a clause with a clause whenever you use paired items or items in a series—as in the Roosevelt example above.

1. **Balance a word with a word.**

    faulty   Like the hunter, the photographer has to understand the animal's patterns, characteristics, and where it lives.

    edited   Like the hunter, the photographer has to understand the animal's patterns, characteristics, and ~~where it lives~~ ^habitat.

2. **Balance a phrase with a phrase.**

    faulty   The hunter carries a handgun and two rifles, different kinds of ammunition, and a variety of sights and telescopes to increase his chances of success.

    edited   The hunter carries ~~a handgun and two rifles~~ ^several types of guns, different kinds of ammunition, and a variety of sights and telescopes to increase his chances of success.

3. **Balance a clause with a clause.**

> faulty Shooting is highly aggressive, photography is passive; shooting eliminates forever, photography preserves.
>
> edited Shooting is ~~highly~~ aggressive, photography is passive; shooting eliminates ~~forever~~, photography preserves.

PAIRED ITEMS USING CORRELATIVE CONJUNCTIONS

When linking paired items with a correlative conjunction (*either/or, neither/nor, not only/but also, both/and, whether/or*) in a sentence, make sure that the elements being connected are parallel in form. Delete any unnecessary or repeated words.

> incorrect The lecture was both enjoyable and it was a form of education.
>
> edited The lecture was both enjoyable and ~~it was a form of education~~ educational.

COMPARISONS USING *THAN* OR *AS*

Make sure that the elements of the comparison are parallel in form. Delete any unnecessary or repeated words.

> incorrect It would be better to study now than waiting until the night before the exam.
>
> edited It would be better to study now than ~~waiting~~ to wait until the night before the exam.

9 Weak Nouns and Verbs

The essence of a sentence is its subject and its verb. The subject—usually a noun or pronoun—identifies who or what the sentence is about, and the verb captures the subject's action or state of being. Sentences often lose their vitality and liveliness when the subject and the verb are lost in weak language or buried.

WEAK NOUNS

Always opt for specific nouns when you can; they make your writing more visual. While general words like *people, animal,* or *dessert* name groups or classes of objects, qualities, or actions, specific words like *Samantha, camel,* and *pecan pie* appeal to readers more because they name individual objects, qualities, or actions within a group. Think about it—don't you prefer reading about specifics rather than generalities?

weak noun   The flowers stretched toward the bright light of the sun.

                           tulips
edited   The ~~flowers~~ stretched toward the bright light of the sun.

STRONG VERBS

Strong verbs energize your writing by giving it a sense of action. Verbs like *gallop, scramble, snicker, tweak, fling, exhaust, smash, tear, smear, wrangle,* and *flog* provide readers with a vivid picture of specific actions. As you reread what you have written, be on the lookout for weak verbs like *is, are, have, deal with, make, give, do, use, get, add, become, go, appear,* and *seem*. When you encounter one of these verbs or others like them, seize the opportunity to substitute a strong action verb for a weak one.

weak verb   Local Boys and Girls Clubs in America assist in the promotion of self-esteem, individual achievement, and teamwork.

                                                promote
edited   Local Boys and Girls Clubs in America ~~assist in the promotion of~~ self-esteem, individual achievement, and teamwork.

While editing your essay, look for opportunities to replace weak nouns and verbs with strong nouns and action verbs. The more specific and strong you make your nouns and verbs, the more lively, descriptive, and concise your writing will be.

When you have difficulty thinking of strong, specific nouns and verbs, reach for a dictionary or a thesaurus—but only if you are sure you can discern the best word for your purpose. Thesauruses are available free online and in inexpensive paperback editions; most word processing programs include a thesaurus as well.

10 Shifts in Verb Tense, Mood, and Voice

SHIFTS IN TENSE

A verb's tense indicates when an action takes place—sometime in the past, right now, or in the future. Using verb tense correctly helps your readers understand time changes in your writing. Shifts in tense—using different verb tenses within a sentence without a logical reason—confuse readers. Unnecessary shifts in verb tense are especially noticeable in narration and process analysis writing, which are sequence and time oriented. Generally, you should write in the present or past tense and maintain that tense throughout your sentence.

incorrect   The painter studied the scene and pulls a fan brush decisively from her cup.

                                             pulled
edited   The painter studied the scene and ~~pulls~~ a fan brush decisively from her cup.

SHIFTS IN MOOD

Verbs in English have three moods: *indicative*, *imperative*, and *subjunctive*. Problems with inconsistency usually occur with the imperative mood.

> incorrect In learning a second language, arm yourself with basic vocabulary, and it is also important to practice speaking aloud daily.
>
> edited In learning a second language, arm yourself with basic vocabulary and ~~it is also important to~~ practice speaking aloud daily.

SHIFTS IN VOICE

Shifts in voice—from active voice to passive voice—usually go hand in hand with inconsistencies in the subject of a sentence.

> incorrect The archeologists could see the effects of vandalism as the Mayan tomb was entered.
>
> edited The archeologists could see the effects of vandalism as they entered the Mayan tomb ~~was entered~~.

11 Wordiness

Wordiness occurs in a sentence that contains words that do not contribute to the sentence's meaning. Wordiness can be eliminated by (1) using the active voice, (2) avoiding "there is" and "it is," (3) eliminating redundancies, (4) deleting empty words and phrases, and (5) simplifying inflated expressions.

1. **Use the active voice rather than the passive voice.** The active voice emphasizes the doer of an action rather than the receiver of an action. Not only is the active voice more concise than the passive voice, it is a much more vigorous form of expression.

   > passive *The inhabitants of Londonderry were overwhelmed* by the burgeoning rodent population.
   >
   > active *The burgeoning rodent population overwhelmed* the inhabitants of Londonderry.

   In the active sentence, *The burgeoning rodent population* is made the subject of the sentence and is moved to the beginning of the sentence—a position of importance—while the verb *overwhelmed* is made an active verb.

2. **Avoid "There is" and "It is."** "There is" and "It is" are expletives—words or phrases that do not contribute any meaning but are added only to fill out a sentence. They may be necessary with references to time and weather, but they should be avoided in other circumstances.

> wordy   There were many acts of heroism following the earthquake.
>
> edited   ~~There were many~~ **Many** acts of heroism ~~following~~ **followed** the earthquake.

Notice how the edited sentence eliminates the expletive and reveals a specific subject—*acts*—and an action verb—*followed*.

3. **Eliminate redundancies.** Unnecessary repetition often creeps into our writing and should be eliminated. For example, how often have you written expressions such as *large in size, completely filled, academic scholar,* or *I thought in my mind*? Edit such expressions by deleting the unnecessary words or using synonyms.

Sometimes our intent is to add emphasis, but the net effect is extra words that contribute little or nothing to a sentence's meaning.

> redundant   A big huge cloud was advancing on the crowded stadium.
>
> edited   A ~~big~~ huge cloud was advancing on the crowded stadium.
>
> redundant   After studying all night, he knew the basic and fundamental principles of geometry.
>
> edited   After studying all night, he knew the basic ~~and fundamental~~ principles of geometry.

4. **Delete empty words and phrases.** Look for words and phrases we use every day that carry no meaning—words that should be eliminated from your writing during the editing process.

> empty   One commentator believes that America is for all intents and purposes a materialistic society.
>
> edited   One commentator believes that America is ~~for all intents and purposes~~ a materialistic society.

Following are examples of some other words and expressions that most often can be eliminated.

basically	I think/I feel/I believe	surely	very
essentially	it seems to me	severely	quite
extremely	kind of/sort of	tend to	
generally	really	truly	

5. **Simplify inflated expressions.** Sometimes we use expressions we think sound authoritative in hopes of seeming knowledgeable. We write *at this point in time* (instead of *now*) or *in the event that* (instead of *if*). However, it is best to write directly and forcefully and to use clear language. Edit inflated or pompous language to its core meaning.

inflated   The law office hired two people who have a complete knowledge of environmental policy.

edited   The law office hired two people who ~~have a complete knowledge of~~ *are experts.* environmental policy.

inflated   The president was late on account of the fact that her helicopter would not start.

edited   The president was late ~~on account of the fact that~~ *because* her helicopter would not start.

12 Sentence Variety

While editing your essays, you can add interest and readability to your writing with more sentence variety. You should, however, seek variety in sentence structure not as an end in itself but as a more accurate means of reflecting your thoughts and giving emphasis where emphasis is needed. Look for opportunities to achieve sentence variety by combining short choppy sentences, varying sentence openings, and reducing the number of compound sentences.

SHORT CHOPPY SENTENCES

To make your writing more interesting, use one of the following four methods to combine short choppy sentences into one longer sentence.

1. **Use subordinating and coordinating conjunctions to relate and connect ideas.**   The coordinating conjunctions *and, but, or, nor, for, so,* and *yet* can be used to connect two or more simple sentences. A subordinating conjunction, on the other hand, introduces a subordinate clause and connects it to a main clause. Common subordinating conjunctions include:

after	before	so	when
although	even if	than	where
as	if	that	whereas
as if	in order that	though	wherever
as though	rather than	unless	whether
because	since	until	while

short and choppy   Short words are as good as long ones. Short, old words—like *sun* and *grass* and *home*—are best of all.

combined   Short words are as good as long ones*, and short,* ~~short,~~ old words—like *sun* and *grass* and *home*—are best of all.

—Richard Lederer,
"The Case for Short Words," page 558

2. **Use modifiers effectively.** Instead of writing a separate descriptive sentence, combine an adjective modifier to convey a more graphic picture in a single sentence.

   short and choppy — The people who breed German shepherds in Appleton, Wisconsin, are also farmers. And they are wonderful farmers.

   combined — The people who breed German shepherds in Appleton, Wisconsin, are also *wonderful* farmers. ~~And they are wonderful farmers.~~

3. **Use a semicolon or colon to link closely related ideas.**

   short and choppy — Pollution from carbon emissions remains a serious environmental problem. In some respects it is the most serious problem.

   combined — Pollution from carbon emissions remains a serious environmental problem*; in* ~~. In~~ some respects it is the most serious problem.

4. **Use parallel constructions.** Parallel constructions use repeated word order or repeated grammatical form to highlight and develop a central idea. As a rhetorical device, parallelism can aid coherence and add emphasis.

   short and choppy — The school busing issue is not about comfort. It concerns fairness.

   combined — The school busing issue is not about comfort *but about* ~~. It concerns~~ fairness.

SENTENCE OPENINGS

More than half of all sentences in English begin with the subject of the sentence followed by the verb and any objects. The following sentences all illustrate this basic pattern:

   Martha plays the saxophone.

   The president vetoed the tax bill before leaving Washington for the holidays.

   The upcoming lecture series will formally launch the fund-raising campaign for a new civic center.

If all the sentences in a particular passage in your essay begin this way, the effect on your readers is monotony. With a little practice, you will discover just how flexible the English language is. Consider the different ways in which one sentence can be rewritten so as to vary its beginning and add interest.

original   Candidates debated the issue of military service for women in the auditorium and did not know that a demonstration was going on outside.

varied openings   *Debating the issue of military service for women,* the candidates in the auditorium did not know that a demonstration was going on outside.

In the auditorium, the candidates debated the issue of military service for women, not knowing that a demonstration was going on outside.

As they debated the issue of military service for women, the candidates in the auditorium did not know that a demonstration was going on outside.

Another way of changing the usual subject–verb–object order of sentences is to invert—or reverse—the normal order. Do not, however, sacrifice proper emphasis to gain variety.

USUAL ORDER	INVERTED ORDER
The crowd stormed out.	Out stormed the crowd.
The enemy would never accept that.	That the enemy would never accept.
They could be friendly and civil.	Friendly and civil they could be.

COMPOUND SENTENCES

Like a series of short, simple sentences, too many compound sentences—two or more sentences joined by coordinating conjunctions—give the impression of haste and thoughtlessness. As you edit your paper, watch for the word *and* used as a coordinating conjunction. If you discover that you have overused *and,* try one of the following four methods to remedy the situation, giving important ideas more emphasis and making it easier for your reader to follow your thought.

1. **Change a compound sentence into a simple sentence with a modifier or an appositive.**

    compound   Richard Lederer is a linguist, and he is humorous, and he has a weekly radio program about language.

    appositive   Richard Lederer ~~is a~~ linguist, ~~and he is humorous, and he~~ has a weekly radio program about language.
                         , a humorous

2. **Change a compound sentence into a simple sentence with a compound predicate.**

   compound   Martin Luther King, Jr. chastises America for not honoring its obligations to people of color, and he dreams of a day when racism will no longer exist.

   compound predicate   Martin Luther King, Jr. chastises America for not honoring its obligations to people of color/and ~~he~~ dreams of a day when racism will no longer exist.

3. **Change a compound sentence into a simple sentence with a phrase or phrases.**

   compound   Women have a number of options in the military, and the responsibilities are significant.

   with a phrase   Women have a number of options in the military_with significant responsibilities_, ~~and the responsibilities are significant~~.

4. **Change a compound sentence into a complex sentence.**

   compound   Farmers are using new technologies, and agriculture is becoming completely industrialized.

   complex   _Because farmers_ ~~Farmers~~ are using new technologies, ~~and~~ agriculture is becoming completely industrialized.

APPENDIX

Thematic Writing Assignments

GREAT WRITING BEGINS WITH THE IDEAS WE FORM AS WE READ.

When we read, we follow the logic of people with different backgrounds and beliefs. We reach conclusions that challenge us to reflect on the world and our experiences in new ways. We spend time wandering through someone else's mind, discovering insights we love and outlooks that strike us as odd—sometimes at the same time. Just as visiting a new place forms lasting memories, reading shapes our perception. When we sit back down to write, we discover that we have important things to say. Things that we *must* say.

This appendix helps you practice the leap from reading to writing, using visuals and readings that are already part of the book. Each cross-chapter cluster reveals multiple aspects of engaging topics and shows how different writing strategies and a range of ideas work together to bring a single subject to life. Specific assignments help you articulate your reaction and enter into the conversation.

Whether your instructor uses these thematic writing assignments in class discussion, for weekly assignments, or as a reference for your final paper, this appendix is your concrete guide for practicing reading as a writer.

Note: For a complete, alternative thematic table of contents, see pages xxxi–xxxviii.

Education

Mortimer Adler, How to Mark a Book   235
Russell Baker, Discovering the Power of My Words   50
Thomas L. Friedman, My Favorite Teacher   12
Nikki Giovanni, Campus Racism 101   268
Stephen King, Reading to Write   67

Paul Roberts, *How to Say Nothing in 500 Words* 242

David Sedaris, *Me Talk Pretty One Day* 657

Write a brief essay identifying and defining three to five principles that you believe are the foundation of a strong education system. Consider: What environments were most conducive to your personal learning? What other factors contributed to the success of those experiences? Did you have an instructor or a mentor, or did you teach yourself? Should students always have complete access to information, or are there advantages to limiting content? How important is it for students to enjoy what they learn? How does Adler's discussion of how to mark up a text translate into electronic books or documents? How might it need to be adapted?

Women and Men

David P. Bardeen, *Not Close Enough for Comfort* 104

Jon Katz, *How Boys Become Men* 455

Deborah M. Roffman, *What Does "Boys Will Be Boys" Really Mean?* 420

Deborah Tannen, *But What Do You Mean?* 344

Deborah Tannen, *How to Give Orders Like a Man* 202

Sojourner Truth, *Ain't I a Woman?* 525

Write an essay about your experience with the gendered cultural expectations discussed by the authors above. Do such expectations help people find themselves, or are they too quick to gloss over our human vulnerabilities? Do you feel pressure to conform to gender stereotypes, or have you ever pressured others to do so? How might these stereotypes have contributed to Bardeen's hesitations and Tannen's mishaps?

The Natural World

Alicia Ault, *How Do Spiders Make Their Webs?* 263

Barbara Bowman, *Guns and Cameras* (student essay) 287

Deborah Cramer, *A Bird Whose Life Depends on a Crab* 481

Wayne Ellwood, *Bees: Why Are They Dying?* 687

Helen MacDonald, *Hiding from Animals* 148

Cherokee Paul McDonald, *A View from the Bridge* 5

Michael Pollan, *Eating Industrial Meat* 256

Jim Tassé, *Trailcheck* (student essay) 129

Michael White, *How to Reengineer Crops for the 21st Century* 646

Write a journal entry in which you explore how technology, urbanization, and modern life shape the way that humans experience nature. Compare MacDonald's idyllic time in nature to Barbara Bowman's thoughts on hunting. What threatens Cramer's birds and Ellwood's bees? What drives scientists to learn more about nature? How does science endanger the natural world, and how might it protect that world? What should be our relationship to nature?

Inequality, Economics, and Society

Lars Eighner, *On Dumpster Diving*   641

Emilia Klimiuk, *Where Did All the Money Go?* (infographic)   440

Jo Goodwin Parker, *What Is Poverty?*   407

Jeannette Walls, *A Woman on the Street*   136

Poverty is part of a chain of consumption, habits, and economic forces often outside an individual's control. Write an essay in which you define poverty and economic inequality. To what extent are your answers influenced by the country in which you were born? Have you ever participated in philanthropy or volunteered to assist the disadvantaged? Do you feel any responsibility to do so? In what ways do these selections prompt you to rethink your purchasing habits?

Justice, Ethics, and Crime

G. Anthony Gorry, *Steal This MP3 File: What Is Theft?*   414

Henry David Thoreau, *Resistance to Civil Government*   528

Andrew Vachss, *The Difference between "Sick" and "Evil"*   312

Barry Winston, *Stranger Than True*   110

Write an editorial on why it is difficult to form absolute judgments about criminal situations. Consider the following: What complexities must we address in a thoughtful discussion of a crime? What might Vachss or Winston—both lawyers—say about the importance of the law? Thoreau raises the question of whether the law is the same as justice and how a moral person might respond. Are his thoughts still relevant today? To what extent do you believe that the current legal system is fair and just?

Power of Language

Russell Baker, *Discovering the Power of My Words*   50

Keith Eldred, *Secular Mantras* (student essay)   41

Jake Jamieson, *The English-Only Movement: Can America Proscribe Language with a Clear Conscience?* (MLA model)   706

Derald Wing Sue, *Racial Microaggressions in Everyday Life: Is Subtle Bias Harmful?* 588

Deborah Tannen, *But What Do You Mean?* 344

Cooper Thompson, *Language Chauvinism: The Ugly American Revisited* 651

Malcolm X, *Coming to an Awareness of Language* 92

What affects how we construct our sentences, our tone, and our message? Are the factors psychological, sociological, biological, or a combination of those types? Write a reflection comparing how Malcolm X or Tannen might respond. What advice might Tannen share with Malcolm X about motivating his readers? To what extent is precision important in our word choice, even when discussing a simple thing like coffee? How important is such precision when discussing more abstract ideas? How can thoughtless words be harmful? How might Malcolm X respond to Derald Wing Sue?

Technology in Modern Life

Nicola Freedman, *How Social Media Is Changing Hollywood* 695

Grant Snider, *Life in the Woods (cartoon)* 78

Andrew Sullivan, *iPod World: The End of Society?* 460

Courtney Sypher, *From Computer Cruelty to Campus Crime: Cyberbullying at College* (student essay) 682

Technology fosters social connections, but it also disconnects us from real-life surroundings. With so many apps, networks, and social sites, social media and technology are not just reflecting society but reshaping it. Write an essay about what we gain—and perhaps lose—when we focus on our devices instead of what's around us. Brainstorm a list of ways that technology impacts your life on a daily basis. Is there anything you couldn't do without technology? Is there anything that would be better without technology? How has technology affected the ways you interact with family, friends, and acquaintances? Why are we obsessed with our screens? How has your perspective evolved over time? How important is it to form impressions and make decisions without influence from social media? Is that even possible in today's media landscape?

Sense of Place

Kevin Cunningham, *Gentrification* (student essay) 447

Plato, *The Allegory of the Cave* 509

Robert Ramírez, *The Barrio* 141

How does place affect who we are? Write an editorial for your local or college newspaper about how the geography of your community contributes to its identity. Imitate the ways in which Ramírez and Cunningham describe their emotional, nostalgic connections to specific elements of their hometowns. Consider how perception plays a role in your understanding of a community, as an insider or an outsider, particularly keeping in mind the issues Plato raises on the nature of perception. Address how large-scale trends like increased population, demographic shifts, and urbanization could affect your community in thirty or fifty years.

Glossary of Rhetorical Terms

Abstract See *Concrete/Abstract*.

Allusion An allusion is a passing reference to a familiar person, place, or thing drawn from history, the Bible, mythology, or literature. An allusion is an economical way for a writer to capture the essence of an idea, atmosphere, emotion, or historical era, as in "The scandal was his Watergate," or "He saw himself as a modern Job," or "Everyone there held those truths to be self-evident." An allusion should be familiar to the reader; if it is not, it will add nothing to the meaning.

Analogy Analogy is a special form of comparison in which the writer explains something unfamiliar by comparing it to something familiar: "A transmission line is simply a pipeline for electricity. In the case of a water pipeline, more water will flow through the pipe as water pressure increases. The same is true of a transmission line for electricity." See also the discussion of analogy on pages 283–84.

Analytical Reading Reading analytically means reading actively, paying close attention to both the content and the structure of the text. Analytical reading often involves answering several basic questions about the piece of writing under consideration:

1. What does the author want to say? What is his or her main point?
2. Why does the author want to say it? What is his or her purpose?
3. What strategy or strategies does the author use?
4. Why and how does the author's writing strategy suit both the subject and the purpose?
5. What is special about the way the author uses the strategy?
6. How effective is the essay? Why?

For a detailed example of analytical reading, see Chapter 1.

Appropriateness See *Diction*.

Argument Argument is one of the four basic types of prose. (Narration, description, and exposition are the other three.) To argue is to attempt to convince the reader to agree with a point of view, to make a given decision, or to pursue a particular course of action. Logical argument is based on reasonable explanations and appeals to the reader's intelligence. See Chapter 12 for further discussion of argumentation. See also *Logical Fallacies; Persuasion*.

Assertion An assertion is the thesis or proposition that a writer puts forward in an argument.

Assumption An assumption is a belief or principle, stated or implied, that is taken for granted.

Attitude A writer's attitude reflects his or her opinion on a subject. For example, a writer can think very positively or very negatively about a subject. In most cases, the writer's attitude falls somewhere between these two extremes. See also *Tone*.

Audience An audience is the intended readership for a piece of writing. For example, the readers of a national weekly newsmagazine come from all walks of life and have diverse opinions, attitudes, and educational experiences. In contrast, the readership for an organic chemistry journal is made up of people whose interests and educational backgrounds are quite similar. The essays in this book are intended for general readers—intelligent people who may lack specific information about the subject being discussed.

Beginnings/Endings A *beginning* is the sentence, group of sentences, or section that introduces an essay. Good beginnings usually identify the thesis or controlling idea, attempt to interest the reader, and establish a tone. Some effective ways in which writers begin essays include (1) telling an anecdote that illustrates the thesis, (2) providing a controversial statement or opinion that engages the reader's interest, (3) presenting startling statistics or facts, (4) defining a term that is central to the discussion that follows, (5) asking thought-provoking questions, (6) providing a quotation that illustrates the thesis, (7) referring to a current event that helps establish the thesis, or (8) showing the significance of the subject or stressing its importance to the reader.

An *ending* is the sentence or group of sentences that brings an essay to closure. Good endings are purposeful and well planned. Endings satisfy readers when they are the natural outgrowths of the essays themselves and convey a sense of finality or completion. Good essays do not simply stop; they conclude.

Cause and Effect Analysis Cause and effect analysis is one of the types of exposition. (Process analysis, definition, division and classification, illustration, and comparison and contrast are the others.) Cause and effect analysis answers the question *why?* It explains the reasons for an occurrence or the consequences of an action. See Chapter 11 for a detailed discussion of cause and effect analysis. See also *Exposition*.

Claim A claim is the thesis or proposition put forth in an argument.

Classification Classification, along with division, is one of the types of exposition. (Process analysis, definition, comparison and contrast, illustration, and cause and effect analysis are the others.) When classifying, the writer arranges and sorts people, places, or things into categories according to their differing characteristics, thus making them more manageable for the writer and more understandable for the reader. See Chapter 9 for a detailed discussion of classification. See also *Division; Exposition*.

Cliché A cliché is an expression that has become ineffective through overuse. Expressions such as *quick as a flash, dry as dust, jump for joy,* and *slow as molasses* are all clichés. Good writers normally avoid such trite expressions and seek instead to express themselves in fresh and forceful language.

Coherence Coherence is a quality of good writing that results when all sentences, paragraphs, and longer divisions of an essay are naturally connected. Coherent writing is achieved through (1) a logical sequence of ideas (arranged in chronological order, spatial order, order of importance, or some other appropriate order), (2) the thoughtful repetition of key words and ideas, (3) a pace suitable for your topic and reader, and (4) the use of transitional words and expressions. Coherence should not be confused with unity. See *Unity*. See also *Transitions*.

Colloquial Expressions A colloquial expression is characteristic of or appropriate to spoken language, or to writing that seeks its effect. Colloquial expressions are informal, as *chem, gym, come up with, be at loose ends, won't,* and *photo* illustrate. Thus, colloquial expressions are acceptable in formal writing only if they are used purposefully.

Comparison and Contrast Comparison and contrast is one of the types of exposition. (Process analysis, definition, division and classification, illustration, and cause and effect analysis are the others.) In comparison and contrast, the writer points out the similarities and differences between two or more subjects in the same class or category. The function of any comparison and contrast is to clarify—to reach some conclusion about the items being compared and contrasted. See Chapter 8 for a detailed discussion of comparison and contrast. See also *Exposition*.

Conclusions See *Beginnings/Endings*.

Concrete/Abstract A *concrete* word names a specific object, person, place, or action that can be directly perceived by the senses: *car, bread, building, book, Abraham Lincoln, Chicago,* or *hiking*. An *abstract* word, in contrast, refers to general qualities, conditions, ideas, actions, or relationships that cannot be directly perceived by the senses: *bravery, dedication, excellence, anxiety, stress, thinking,* or *hatred*.

Although writers must use both concrete and abstract language, good writers avoid using too many abstract words. Instead, they rely on concrete words to define and illustrate abstractions. Because concrete words affect the senses, they are easily comprehended by the reader.

Connotation/Denotation Both connotation and denotation refer to the meanings of words. *Denotation* is the dictionary meaning of a word, the literal meaning. *Connotation*, on the other hand, is the implied or suggested meaning of a word. For example, the denotation of *lamb* is "a young sheep." The connotations of *lamb* are numerous: *gentle, docile, weak, peaceful, blessed, sacrificial, blood, spring, frisky, pure, innocent,* and so on. Good writers are sensitive to both the denotations and the connotations of words, and they use these meanings to their advantage in their writing. See also *Slanting*.

Controlling Idea See *Thesis*.

Deduction Deduction is the process of reasoning from a stated premise to a necessary conclusion. This form of reasoning moves from the general to the specific. See Chapter 12 for a discussion of deductive reasoning and its relation to argumentative writing. See also *Induction; Syllogism*.

Definition Definition is one of the types of exposition. (Process analysis, division and classification, comparison and contrast, illustration, and cause and effect analysis are the others.) Definition is a statement of the meaning of a word. A definition may be either brief or extended, part of an essay or an entire essay itself. See Chapter 10 for a detailed discussion of definition. See also *Exposition*.

Denotation See *Connotation/Denotation*.

Description Description is one of the four basic types of prose. (Narration, exposition, and argument are the other three.) Description tells how a person, place, or thing is perceived by the five senses. Objective description reports these sensory qualities factually, whereas subjective description gives the writer's interpretation of them. See Chapter 5 for a detailed discussion of description.

Dialogue Dialogue is conversation that is recorded in a piece of writing. Through dialogue writers reveal important aspects of characters' personalities as well as events in the narrative.

Diction Diction refers to a writer's choice and use of words. Good diction is precise and appropriate—the words mean exactly what the writer intends, and the words are well suited to the writer's subject, intended audience, and purpose in writing. The word-conscious writer knows that there are differences among *aged*, *old*, and *elderly*; *blue*, *navy*, and *azure*; and *disturbed*, *angry*, and *irritated*. Furthermore, this writer knows in which situation to use each word. See also *Connotation/Denotation*.

Division Like comparison and contrast, division and classification are separate yet closely related mental operations. Division involves breaking down a single large unit into smaller subunits or breaking down a large group of items into discrete categories. For example, the student body at your college or university can be divided into categories according to different criteria (by class, by home state or country, by sex, and so on). See also *Classification*.

Dominant Impression A dominant impression is the single mood, atmosphere, or quality a writer emphasizes in a piece of descriptive writing. The dominant impression is created through the careful selection of details and is, of course, influenced by the writer's subject, audience, and purpose. See also the discussion on pages 127–28 in Chapter 5.

Draft A draft is a version of a piece of writing at a particular stage in the writing process. The first version produced is usually called the *rough draft* or *first draft* and is a writer's beginning attempt to give overall shape to his or her ideas. Subsequent versions are called *revised drafts*. The copy presented for publication is the *final draft*.

Editing During the editing stage of the writing process, the writer makes his or her prose conform to the conventions of the language. This includes making final improvements in sentence structure and diction, and proofreading for wordiness and errors in grammar, usage, spelling, and punctuation. After editing, the writer is ready to prepare a final copy.

Emphasis Emphasis is the placement of important ideas and words within sentences and longer units of writing so that they have the greatest impact. In general, the end has the most impact, and the beginning nearly as much; the middle has the least. See also *Organization*.

Endings See *Beginnings/Endings*.

Essay An essay is a relatively short piece of nonfiction in which the writer attempts to make one or more closely related points. A good essay is purposeful, informative, and well organized.

Ethos *Ethos* is a type of argumentative proof having to do with the ethics of the arguer: honesty, trustworthiness, and even morals.

Evaluation An evaluation of a piece of writing is an assessment of its effectiveness or merit. In evaluating a piece of writing, you should ask the following questions: What is the writer's purpose? Is it a worthwhile purpose? Does the writer achieve the purpose? Is the writer's information sufficient and accurate? What are the strengths of the essay? What are its weaknesses? Depending on the type of writing and the purpose, more specific questions can also be asked. For example, with an argument you could ask: Does the writer follow the principles of logical thinking? Is the writer's evidence convincing?

Evidence Evidence is the data on which a judgment or an argument is based or by which proof or probability is established. Evidence usually takes the form of statistics, facts, names, examples or illustrations, and opinions of authorities.

Examples Examples illustrate a larger idea or represent something of which they are a part. An example is a basic means of developing or clarifying an idea. Furthermore, examples enable writers to show and not simply tell readers what they mean. The terms *example* and *illustration* are sometimes used interchangeably. See also the discussion of illustration on pages 173–86 in Chapter 6.

Exposition Exposition is one of the four basic types of prose. (Narration, description, and argument are the other three.) The purpose of exposition is to clarify, explain, and inform. The methods of exposition presented in this text are process analysis, definition, division and classification, comparison and contrast, illustration, and cause and effect analysis. For a detailed discussion of each of these methods of exposition, see the appropriate chapter.

Fact A fact is a piece of information presented as having a verifiable certainty or reality.

Fallacy See *Logical Fallacies*.

Figures of Speech Figures of speech are brief, imaginative comparisons that highlight the similarities between things that are basically dissimilar. They make writing vivid and interesting and therefore more memorable. The most common figures of speech are these:

Simile—An implicit comparison introduced by *like* or *as*: "The fighter's hands were *like* stone."

Metaphor—An implied comparison that uses one thing as the equivalent of another: "All the world's a stage."

Personification—A special kind of simile or metaphor in which human traits are assigned to an inanimate object: "The engine coughed and then stopped."

Focus Focus is the limitation that a writer gives his or her subject. The writer's task is to select a manageable topic given the constraints of time, space, and purpose. For example, within the general subject of sports, a writer could focus on government support of amateur athletes or narrow the focus further to government support of Olympic athletes.

General See *Specific/General*.

Idiom An idiom is a word or phrase that is used habitually with a particular meaning in a language. The meaning of an idiom is not always readily apparent to nonnative speakers of that language. For example, *catch cold, hold a job, make up your mind,* and *give them a hand* are all idioms in English.

Illustration Illustration is a type of exposition. (Definition, division and classification, comparison and contrast, cause and effect analysis, and process analysis are the others.) With illustration the writer uses examples—specific facts, opinions, samples, and anecdotes or stories—to support a generalization and to make it more vivid, understandable, and persuasive. See Chapter 6 for a detailed discussion of illustration. See also *Examples*.

Induction Induction is the process of reasoning to a conclusion about all members of a class through an examination of only a few members of the class. This form of reasoning moves from the particular to the general. See Chapter 12 for a discussion of inductive reasoning and its relation to argumentative writing. Also see *Deduction*.

Introductions See *Beginnings/Endings*.

Irony Irony is the use of words to suggest something different from their literal meaning. For example, when Jonathan Swift proposes in "A Modest Proposal" that Ireland's problems could be solved if the people of Ireland fattened their babies and sold them to the English landlords for food, he meant that almost any other solution would be preferable. A writer can use irony to establish a special relationship with the reader and to add an extra dimension or twist to the meaning of a word or phrase.

Jargon See *Technical Language*.

Logical Fallacies A logical fallacy is an error in reasoning that renders an argument invalid. Some of the more common logical fallacies are these:

Oversimplification—The tendency to provide simple solutions to complex problems: "The reason we have inflation today is that OPEC has unreasonably raised the price of oil."

Non sequitur ("it does not follow")—An inference or conclusion that does not follow from established premises or evidence: "It was the best movie I saw this year, and it should get an Academy Award."

Post hoc, ergo propter hoc ("after this, therefore because of this")—Confusing chance or coincidence with causation. Because one event comes after another one, it does not necessarily mean that the first event caused the second: "I won't say I caught a cold at the hockey game, but I certainly didn't have it before I went there."

Begging the question—Assuming in a premise that which needs to be proven: "If American autoworkers built a better product, foreign auto sales would not be so high."

False analogy—Making a misleading analogy between logically unconnected ideas: "He was a brilliant basketball player; therefore, there's no question in my mind that he will be a fine coach."

Either/or thinking—The tendency to see an issue as having only two sides: "Used car salespeople are either honest or crooked."

See also Chapter 12.

Logical Reasoning See *Deduction; Induction*.

Logos *Logos* is a type of argumentative proof having to do with the logical qualities of an argument: data, evidence, and factual information.

Metaphor See *Figures of Speech*.

Narration Narration is one of the four basic types of prose. (Description, exposition, and argument are the other three.) To narrate is to tell a story, to tell what happened. Although narration is most often used in fiction, it is also important in nonfiction, either by itself or in conjunction with other types of prose. See Chapter 4 for a detailed discussion of narration.

Objective/Subjective *Objective* writing is factual and impersonal, whereas *subjective* writing, sometimes called *impressionistic* writing, relies heavily on personal interpretation. For a discussion of objective description and subjective description, see Chapter 5.

Opinion An opinion is a belief or conclusion not substantiated by positive knowledge or proof. An opinion reveals personal feelings or attitudes or states a position. Opinion should not be confused with argument.

Organization In writing, organization is the thoughtful arrangement and presentation of one's points or ideas. Narration is often organized chronologically. Exposition may be organized from simplest to most complex or from most familiar to least familiar. Argument may be organized from least important to most important. There is no single correct pattern of organization for a given piece of writing, but good writers are careful to discover an order of presentation suitable for their audience and their purpose.

Paradox A paradox is a seemingly contradictory statement that may nonetheless be true. For example, "We little know what we have until we lose it" is a paradoxical statement.

Paragraph The paragraph, the single most important unit of thought in an essay, is a series of closely related sentences. These sentences adequately develop the central or controlling idea of the paragraph. This central or controlling idea, usually stated in a topic sentence, is necessarily related to the purpose of the whole composition. A well-written paragraph has several distinguishing characteristics: a clearly stated or implied topic sentence, adequate development, unity, coherence, and an appropriate organizational strategy.

Parallelism Parallel structure is the repetition of word order or form either within a single sentence or in several sentences that develop the same central idea. As a rhetorical device, parallelism can aid coherence and add emphasis. Roosevelt's statement, "I see one third of a nation ill-housed, ill-clad, ill-nourished," illustrates effective parallelism.

Pathos A type of argumentative proof having to do with audience: emotional language, connotative diction, and appeals to certain values.

Personification See *Figures of Speech*.

Persuasion Persuasion, or persuasive argument, is an attempt to convince readers to agree with a point of view, to make a given decision, or to pursue a particular course of action. Persuasion appeals heavily to the emotions, whereas logical argument does not. For the distinction between logical argument and persuasive argument, see Chapter 12.

Point of View Point of view refers to the grammatical person of the speaker in an essay. For example, a first-person point of view uses the pronoun *I* and is commonly found in autobiography and the personal essay; a third-person point of view uses the pronouns *he*, *she*, or *it* and is commonly found in objective writing. See Chapter 4 for a discussion of point of view in narration.

Prewriting Prewriting encompasses all the activities that take place before a writer actually starts a rough draft. During the prewriting stage of the writing process, the writer selects a subject area, focuses on a particular topic, collects information and makes notes, brainstorms for ideas, discovers connections between pieces of information, determines a thesis and purpose, rehearses portions of the writing in his or her mind or on paper, and makes a scratch outline. For some suggestions about prewriting, see Chapter 2, pages 24–31.

Process Analysis Process analysis is a type of exposition. (Definition, division and classification, comparison and contrast, illustration, and cause and effect analysis are the others.) Process analysis answers the question *how?* and explains how something works or gives step-by-step directions for doing something. See Chapter 7 for a detailed discussion of process analysis. See also *Exposition*.

Publication In the publication stage of the writing process, the writer shares his or her writing with the intended audience. Publication can take the form of a typed or an oral presentation, a photocopy, or a commercially printed rendition. What's important is that the writer's words are read in what amounts to their final form.

Purpose Purpose is what the writer wants to accomplish in a particular piece of writing. Purposeful writing seeks to *relate* (narration), to *describe* (description), to *explain* (process analysis, definition, division and classification, comparison and contrast, illustration, and cause and effect analysis), or to *convince* (argument).

Revision During the revision stage of the writing process, the writer determines what in the draft needs to be developed or clarified so that the essay says what the writer intends it to say. Often the writer needs to revise several times before the essay is "right." Comments from peer evaluators can be invaluable in helping writers determine what sorts of changes need to be made. Such changes can include adding material, deleting material, changing the order of presentation, and substituting new material for old.

Rhetorical Question A rhetorical question is a question that is asked but requires no answer from the reader. "When will nuclear proliferation end?" is such a question. Writers use rhetorical questions to introduce topics they plan to discuss or to emphasize important points.

Rough Draft See *Draft*.

Sequence Sequence refers to the order in which a writer presents information. Writers commonly select chronological order, spatial order, order of importance, or order of complexity to arrange their points. See also *Organization*.

Signal Phrase A signal phrase introduces borrowed material — a summary, paraphrase, or quotation — in a researched paper and usually consists of the author's name and a verb (for example, *Daphna Oyserman contends*). Signal phrases let readers know who is speaking and, in the case of summaries and paraphrases, exactly where the writer's ideas end and the borrowed material begins. For suggestions on using signal phrases, see Chapter 14, pages 673–74.

Simile See *Figures of Speech*.

Slang Slang is the unconventional, very informal language of particular subgroups of a culture. Slang, such as *bummed, coke, split, hurt, dis, blow off,* and *cool,* is acceptable in formal writing only if it is used purposefully.

Slanting Slanting is the use of certain words or information that results in a biased viewpoint.

Specific/General *General* words name groups or classes of objects, qualities, or actions. *Specific* words, in contrast, name individual objects, qualities, or actions within a class or group. To some extent, the terms *general* and *specific* are relative. For example, *dessert* is a class of things. *Pie*, however, is more specific than *dessert* but more general than *pecan pie* or *chocolate cream pie*.

Good writing judiciously balances the general with the specific. Writing with too many general words is likely to be dull and lifeless. General words do not create vivid responses in the reader's mind as concrete, specific words can. However, writing that relies exclusively on specific words may lack focus and direction — the control that more general statements provide.

Strategy A strategy is a means by which a writer achieves his or her purpose. Strategy includes the many rhetorical decisions that the writer makes about organization, paragraph structure, syntax, and diction. In terms of the whole essay, strategy refers to the principal rhetorical mode that the writer uses. If, for example, a writer wishes to show how to make chocolate chip cookies, the most effective strategy would be process analysis. If it is the writer's purpose to show why sales of American cars have declined in recent years, the most effective strategy would be cause and effect analysis.

Style Style is the individual manner in which a writer expresses ideas. Style is created by the author's particular selection of words, construction of sentences, and arrangement of ideas.

Subject The subject of an essay is its content, what the essay is about. Depending on the author's purpose and the constraints of space, a subject may range from one that is broadly conceived to one that is narrowly defined.

Subjective See *Objective/Subjective*.

Supporting Evidence See *Evidence*.

Syllogism A syllogism is an argument that utilizes deductive reasoning and consists of a major premise, a minor premise, and a conclusion. For example:

All trees that lose leaves are deciduous. (*Major premise*)

Maple trees lose their leaves. (*Minor premise*)

Therefore, maple trees are deciduous. (*Conclusion*)

See also *Deduction*.

Symbol A symbol is a person, place, or thing that represents something beyond itself. For example, the eagle is a symbol of the United States, and the bear is a symbol of Russia.

Syntax Syntax refers to the way in which words are arranged to form phrases, clauses, and sentences as well as to the grammatical relationship among the words themselves.

Technical Language Technical language, or jargon, is the special vocabulary of a trade or profession. Writers who use technical language do so with an awareness of their audience. If the audience is a group of peers, technical language may be used freely. If the audience is a more general one, technical language should be used sparingly and carefully so as not to sacrifice clarity. See also *Diction*.

Thesis A thesis is a statement of the main idea of an essay. Also known as the *controlling idea*, a thesis may sometimes be implied rather than stated directly.

Title A title is a word or phrase set off at the beginning of an essay to identify the subject, to capture the main idea of the essay, or to attract the reader's attention. A title may be explicit or suggestive. A subtitle, when used, extends or restricts the meaning of the main title.

Tone Tone is the manner in which a writer relates to an audience — the "tone of voice" used to address readers. Tone may be described as friendly, serious, distant, angry, cheerful, bitter, cynical, enthusiastic, morbid, resentful, warm, playful, and so forth. A particular tone results from a writer's diction, sentence structure, purpose, and attitude toward the subject. See also *Attitude*.

Topic Sentence The topic sentence states the central idea of a paragraph and thus limits and controls the subject of the paragraph. Although the topic sentence most often appears at the beginning of the paragraph, it may appear at any other point, particularly if the writer is trying to create a special effect. Also see *Paragraph*.

Transitions Transitions are words or phrases that link sentences, paragraphs, and larger units of a composition to achieve coherence. These devices include parallelism, pronoun references, conjunctions, and the repetition of key ideas, as well as the many conventional transitional expressions, such as *moreover, on the other hand, in addition, in contrast,* and *therefore*. Also see *Coherence*.

Unity Unity is achieved in an essay when all the words, sentences, and paragraphs contribute to its thesis. The elements of a unified essay do not distract the reader. Instead, they all harmoniously support a single idea or purpose.

Verb Verbs can be classified as either strong verbs (*scream, pierce, gush, ravage,* and *amble*) or weak verbs (*be, has, get,* and *do*). Writers prefer to use strong verbs to make their writing more specific, more descriptive, and more action filled.

Voice Verbs can be classified as being in either the active or the passive voice. In the active voice, the doer of the action is the grammatical subject. In the passive voice, the receiver of the action is the subject:

Active: Glenda questioned all the children.

Passive: All the children were questioned by Glenda.

Also, voice refers to the way an author "talks" or "sounds" in a particular work as opposed to a style that characterizes an author's total output. Voice is generally considered to be made up of a combination of such elements as pacing or sense of timing, word choice, sentence and paragraph length, or the way characters sound in a written composition.

Writing Process The writing process consists of five major stages: prewriting, writing drafts, revision, editing, and publication. The process is not inflexible, but there is no mistaking the fact that most writers follow some version of it most of the time. Although orderly in its basic components and sequence of activities, the writing process is nonetheless continuous, creative, and unique to each individual writer. See Chapter 2 for a detailed discussion of the writing process. See also *Draft; Editing; Prewriting; Publication; Revision.*

Acknowledgements (continued from page ii)

Mortimer Adler, "How to Mark a Book." Originally published in *Saturday Review of Literature,* July 6, 1940. Reprinted by permission.

Mitch Albom, "If You Had One Day with Someone Who's Gone," originally appeared in the September 17, 2006, issue of *Parade.* Copyright © 2006 ASOP, Inc. Reprinted by permission of the author.

Isabel Allende, "Writing Is an Act of Hope." © Isabel Allende, 1989. Reprinted by permission.

Nancy Amour, "James Harrison is Right, You Shouldn't Get a Prize for Showing Up," *USA Today,* August 18, 2015. © 2015 USA Today. All rights reserved. Used by permission and protected by the Copyright Laws of the United States. The printing, copying, redistribution, or retransmission of this Content without express written permission is prohibited.

Maya Angelou, "Chapter 15" from I KNOW WHY THE CAGED BIRD SINGS by Maya Angelou, copyright © 1969 and renewed 1997 by Maya Angelou. Used by permission of Random House, an imprint and division of Penguin Random House LLC. All rights reserved.

Alicia Ault, "How Do Spiders Make Their Webs" from *The Smithsonian Magazine.* Copyright 2015 SMITHSONIAN INSTITUTION. Reprinted with permission from Smithsonian Enterprises. All rights reserved. Reproduction in any medium is strictly prohibited without permission from Smithsonian Institution.

Russell Baker, "Discovering the Power of My Words." Copyright © 1982 by Russell Baker. Reprinted by permission of Don Congdon Associates, Inc.

David Bardeen, "Not Close Enough for Comfort," from *The New York Times,* February 29, 2004. Reprinted by permission of David Bardeen.

Suzanne Britt, "Neat People Vs. Sloppy People." Reprinted by permission of the author.

Bruce Catton, "Grant and Lee: A Study in Contrasts," originally published in *The American Story,* edited by Earl Schneck Miers, 1956. Copyright © 1956 U.S. Capitol Historical Society. Reprinted by permission. All rights reserved.

Roger Cohen, "The Organic Fable," *The New York Times,* September 7, 2012. © 2012 The New York Times. All rights reserved. Used by permission and protected by the Copyright Laws of the United States. The printing, copying, redistribution, or retransmission of this Content without express written permission is prohibited.

Deborah Cramer, "A Bird Whose Life Depends on a Crab," *The New York Times,* November 27, 2013. © 2013 The New York Times. All rights reserved. Used by permission and protected by the Copyright Laws of the United States. The printing, copying, redistribution, or retransmission of this Content without express written permission is prohibited.

Brent Crane, "For a More Creative Brain, Travel," *The Atlantic Magazine,* March 31, 2015. © 2015 The Atlantic Media Co., as first published in The Atlantic Magazine. All rights reserved. Distributed by Tribune Content Agency, LLC

Juno Díaz, "Fear," *The New York Times,* June 28, 2015. © 2015 The New York Times. All rights reserved. Used by permission and protected by the Copyright Laws of the United States. The printing, copying, redistribution, or retransmission of this Content without express written permission is prohibited.

Jeremy Dowsett, "What My Bike Has Taught Me about White Privilege." Copyright © Jeremy D. Dowsett. Reprinted by permission.

Barbara Ehrenreich, "The Selfish Side of Gratitude," *The New York Times,* January 3, 2016. © 2016 The New York Times. All rights reserved. Used by permission and protected by the Copyright Laws of the United States. The printing, copying, redistribution, or retransmission of this Content without express written permission is prohibited.

Lars Eighner, "On Dumpster Diving," from *Travels with Lizbeth: Three Years on the Road and on the Streets.* Copyright © 1993 by Lars Eighner. Reprinted by permission of St. Martin's Press, LLC. All right reserved.

Wayne Ellwood, "Bees: Why Are They Dying?" *The New Internationalist Magazine,* Issue 425, September 1, 2009. © 2009 The New Internationalist. Reprinted by permission.

ACKNOWLEDGEMENTS

Linda Flower, "Writing for an Audience," from *Problem-Solving Strategies for Writing*, Fourth Edition. Copyright © 1993 Harcourt College Publishing. Reprinted by permission of the author.

Nicola Freedman, "How Social Media Is Changing Hollywood," *Digital America*, Issue No. 7. Copyright © Nicola Freedman. Used by permission.

Thomas Friedman, "My Favorite Teacher," *The New York Times*, January 9, 2001. Copyright © 2001 The New York Times. All rights reserved. Used by permission and protected by the Copyright Laws of the United States. The printing, copying, redistribution, or retransmission of this Content without express written permission is prohibited.

William Galston, "Telling Americans to Vote, Or Else," *The New York Times*, November 6, 2011. © 2011 The New York Times. All rights reserved. Used by permission and protected by the Copyright Laws of the United States. The printing, copying, redistribution, or retransmission of this Content without express written permission is prohibited.

Nikki Giovanni, "Campus Racism 101," from *Racism 101*. Copyright © 1994 by Nikki Giovanni. Reprinted by permission of HarperCollins Publishers.

Natalie Goldberg, "Be Specific," from *Writing Down the Bones: Freeing the Writer Within*. Copyright © 1986 by Natalie Goldberg. Reprinted by arrangement with The Permissions Company, Inc., on behalf of Shambhala Publications, Inc., Boulder, Colorado. www.shambhala.com.

Ellen Goodman, "The Company Man." Reprinted with the permission of Simon & Schuster, Inc. from CLOSE TO HOME by Ellen Goodman. Copyright © 1979 The Washington Post Company. All rights reserved.

G. Anthony Gorry, "Steal This MP3 File: What Is Theft?" Reprinted by permission of the author.

James Hamblin, "Buy Experiences, Not Things," *The Atlantic Magazine*, October 7, 2014. © 2014 The Atlantic Media Co., as first published in *The Atlantic Magazine*. All rights reserved. Distributed by Tribune Content Agency, LLC

Michael Jonas, "The Downside of Diversity," *The New York Times*, August 5, 2007. © 2007 The New York Times. All rights reserved. Used by permission and protected by the Copyright Laws of the United States. The printing, copying, redistribution, or retransmission of this Content without express written permission is prohibited.

Mindy Kaling, excerpt(s) from IS EVERYONE HANGING OUT WITHOUT ME? (AND OTHER CONCERNS) by Mindy Kaling, copyright © 2011 by Mindy Kaling. Used by permission of Crown Archetype, an imprint of the Crown Publishing Group, a division of Penguin Random House LLC. All rights reserved.

Jon Katz, "How Boys Become Men," from *Glamour Magazine*. Copyright © 1993 by Jon Katz. Reprinted with permission of International Creative Management, Inc.

Martin Luther King, Jr., "The Ways of Meeting Oppression." Reprinted by arrangement with The Heirs to the Estate of Martin Luther King Jr., c/o Writers House as agent for the proprietor, New York, NY. Copyright © 1958, 1963 Martin Luther King Jr. Copyright © renewed 1991 Coretta Scott King.

Stephen King, "Reading and Writing," from *On Writing: A Memoir of the Craft*. Copyright © 2000 by Stephen King. Reprinted by permission of Scribner, a division of Simon & Schuster, Inc.

Phyllis Korkki, "The attachment that still makes noise," *The New York Times*, March 23, 2013. © 2013 The New York Times. All rights reserved. Used by permission and protected by the Copyright Laws of the United States. The printing, copying, redistribution, or retransmission of this Content without express written permission is prohibited.

Tim Krieder, "The Busy Trap," *The New York Times*, July 1, 2012. © 2012 The New York Times. All rights reserved. Used by permission and protected by the Copyright Laws of the United States. The printing, copying, redistribution, or retransmission of this Content without express written permission is prohibited.

Anne Lamott, "Shitty First Drafts" from BIRD BY BIRD: SOME INSTRUCTIONS ON WRITING AND LIFE by Anne Lamott, copyright © 1994 by Anne Lamott. Used by permission of Pantheon Books, an imprint of the Knopf Doubleday Publishing Group, a division of Penguin Random House LLC. All rights reserved.

Richard Lederer, "The Case for Short Words," from *The Miracle of Language*. Copyright © 1991 by Richard Lederer. All rights reserved. Reprinted by permission of Atria Publishing Group.

ACKNOWLEDGEMENTS | 777

Greg Lukianoff and Jonathan Haidt, "The Coddling of the American Mind," *The Atlantic Magazine,* September 1, 2015. © 2015 The Atlantic Media Co., as first published in *The Atlantic Magazine.* All rights reserved. Distributed by Tribune Content Agency, LLC.

Helen MacDonald, "Hiding from Animals," *The New York Times,* July 19, 2015. © 2015 The New York Times. All rights reserved. Used by permission and protected by the Copyright Laws of the United States. The printing, copying, redistribution, or retransmission of this Content without express written permission is prohibited.

Cherokee Paul McDonald, "A View from the Bridge," originally published in the *Sun Sentinel, Sunshine Magazine* (Fort Lauderdale, FL). Copyright © 1989 by Cherokee Paul McDonald. Reprinted by permission.

John Metta, "I, Racist." Copyright © John Metta. Reprinted by permission.

Bharati Mukherjee, "Two Ways to Belong in America," originally published in *The New York Times,* September 22, 1996. Copyright © 1996 by Bharati Mukherjee. Reprinted by permission of the author.

Anahad O'Connor, "Coca-Cola Funds Scientists Who Shift Blame for Obesity Away From Bad Diets," *The New York Times,* as it appeared in *The Dallas Morning News,* August 9, 2015. Copyright © 2015 The New York Times. All rights reserved. Used by permission and protected by the Copyright Laws of the United States. The printing, copying, redistribution, or retransmission of this content without express written permission is prohibited.

Susan Orlean, "On Voice," from *Telling True Stories,* ed. by Mark Kramer and Wendy Cal, Plune 2007. Reprinted by permission of Susan Orlean.

Jo Goodwin Parker, "What Is Poverty?" from *America's Other Children: Public Schools Outside Suburbia* by George Henderson. Copyright © 1971. Reprinted by permission of University of Oklahoma Press.

Michael Pollan, "The Feedlot: Making Meat," from THE OMNIVORE'S DILEMMA: A NATURAL HISTORY OF FOUR MEALS by Michael Pollan, copyright © 2006 by Michael Pollan. Used by permission of Penguin Press, an imprint of Penguin Publishing Group, a division of Penguin Random House LLC.

Robert Ramirez, "The Barrio." *Thanks to learning about Bahá'u'lláh, Founder of the Bahá'í Faith, I now know "the earth is but one country," or one big barrio.* Reprinted by permission of the author.

Paul Roberts, "How to Say Nothing in Five Hundred Words," from *Understanding English,* 1st Edition, © 1958. Reprinted by permission of Pearson Education, Inc., Old Tappan, NJ.

Deborah M. Roffman, MS, "What Does 'Boys Will Be Boys' Really Mean?" Reprinted by permission of the author.

David Sedaris, "Me Talk Pretty One Day," by David Sedaris. Copyright © 1999 by David Sedaris. First published in *Esquire* and reprinted by permission of Little, Brown and Company and Don Congdon Associates, Inc. All rights reserved.

Derald Wing Sue, "Racial Microaggressions in Everyday Life: Is Subtle Bias Harmful?" *Psychology Today,* October 5, 2010. Reprinted by permission from the author.

Andrew Sullivan, "iPod World: The End of Society?" from *The Sunday Times of London,* February 20, 2005. Copyright © 2005 by The Sunday Times of London. Reprinted by permission of News International Syndication Limited.

Amy Tan, "Mother Tongue." Copyright © 1990 by Amy Tan. First appeared in THE THREEPENNY REVIEW. Reprinted by permission of the author and the Sandra Dijkstra Literary Agency.

Deborah Tannen, "But What Do You Mean?" *Redbook,* 183, October 1994. Copyright Deborah Tannen. Reprinted with permission.

Deborah Tannen, "How to Give Orders Like a Man," *New York Times Magazine,* August 8, 1994. Adapted from *Talking 9 to 5: Women and Men at Work,* HarperCollins. Reprinted with permission.

Cooper Thompson, "Language Chauvinism: The Ugly American Revisited." Copyright © Cooper Thompson. Reprinted by permission.

Andrew Vachss, "Difference Between 'Sick' and 'Evil,'" originally published in *Parade,* July 14, 2002. Copyright © Andrew Vachss. All rights reserved. Reprinted by permission of the Andrew Vachss. For more information, see http://www.vachss.com.

Judith Viorst, "The Truth About Lying." Originally appeared in *Redbook.* Copyright © 1981 by Judith Viorst. Reprinted by permission of Don Congdon Associates, Inc.

Jeannette Walls, "A Woman on the Street," from *The Glass Castle: A Memoir.* Copyright © 2005 Jeannette Walls. All rights reserved. Reprinted with permission of Scribner, a Division of Simon & Schuster, Inc.

Michael White, "How to Reengineer Crops for the 21st Century," *Pacific Standard,* August 12, 2015. Copyright © 2015 Pacific Standard, Republished with permission conveyed through Copyright Clearance Center, Inc.

Barry Winston, "Stranger Than True," *Harper's Magazine,* December 1986. Copyright © 1986 by Harper's Magazine. All rights reserved. Reprinted from the December issue by special permission.

Rosalind Wiseman, excerpt(s) from QUEEN BEES AND WANNABES, 3rd EDITION: HELPING YOUR DAUGHTER SURVIVE CLIQUES, GOSSIP, BOYS, AND THE NEW REALITIES OF GIRL WORLD by Rosalind Wiseman, copyright © 2002, 2009, 2016 by Rosalind Wiseman. Used by permission of Harmony Books, an imprint of the Crown Publishing Group, a division of Penguin Random House LLC. All rights reserved.

Malcolm X, "Coming to an Awareness of Language," from THE AUTOBIOGRAPHY OF MALCOLM X by Malcolm X as told to Alex Haley, copyright © 1964 by Alex Haley and Malcolm X. Copyright © 1965 by Alex Haley and Betty Shabazz. Used by permission of Ballantine Books, an imprint of Random House, a division of Penguin Random House LLC. All rights reserved.

Jeffrey Zaslow, "The Most-Praised Generation Goes to Work," *The Wall Street Journal,* April 20, 2007. Copyright © 2007 Dow Jones. Republished with permission of Dow Jones; permission conveyed through Copyright Clearance Center, Inc.

Index

Abstract words, 405
Academic disciplines, writing strategies across, 33–34. *See also under* specific writing strategy
Accept/except, 404
Action-oriented argument, 491–92
Active verbs, 232–33, 752
Active voice, 232–33, 753, 758
Adler, Mortimer, "How to Mark a Book," 225, 235–39
Affect/effect, 404
Agreement
　pronoun-antecedent, 747–49
　subject-verb, 745–46
"Ain't I a Woman?" (Truth), 525–26
Albom, Mitch, "If You Had One Day with Someone Who's Gone," 196–99
"Allegory of the Cave, The" (Plato), 509–15
Allende, Isabel, "Writing as an Act of Hope," 73–77
American Psychological Association (APA) documentation system, 728
Analogy
　in comparison and contrast essay, 283–84
　false, 507
Analytical reading. *See* Reading process
Analyze, as a direction word, 24
Anecdote/antidote, 404
Angeles, Katie, "The Forgotten Personality Type," 336–39
Angelou, Maya, "Sister Flowers," 154–59
Annotation of reading selection, 7–10
Antecedents (referents), 746–47
Antidote/anecdote, 404
APA (American Psychological Association) documentation system, 728
Appeals, classical, 493–94
Appositives in compound sentences, 757
Argue, as a direction word, 24

Argumentation (essay)
　in academic disciplines, 497–98
　audience for, 494, 504
　classical appeals in, 493–94
　combining strategies with, 639
　definition of, 26, 489
　inductive and deductive reasoning, 495
　as organizational strategy, 31
　organizing and writing of, 505–06
　other rhetorical strategies in, 494–97, 506
　planning of, 503–05
　refutations to, 505
　revising/editing of, 406–508
　student essay as example of, 499–502, 588–92
　types of, 490–92
　as writing strategy, 492–97
　in written texts, 489–90
Argumentation (readings)
　"Ain't I a Woman?" (Truth), 525–26
　"The Allegory of the Cave" (Plato), 509–15
　"The Case for Short Words" (Lederer), 558–61
　"Celebrity Obsession: Is It Healthy Behavior?" (Suarez), 499–502
　"The Coddling of the American Mind" (Lukianoff and Haidt), 610–23
　"The Compliment Complex" (Zaslow), 602–07
　"The Declaration of Independence" (Jefferson), 518–21
　"I, Racist" (Metta), 581–87
　"A Modest Proposal" (Swift), 548–55
　"On the Subject of Trigger Warnings" (Crowley), 608–09
　"The Organic Fable" (Cohen), 574–76
　"Racial Microaggressions in Everyday Life: Is Subtle Bias Harmful?" (student essay) (Sue), 588–92

Argumentation (readings) *(continued)*
  "Resistance to Civil Government" (Thoreau), 528–45
  "Telling Americans to Vote, or Else" (Galston), 568–71
  "What My Bike Has Taught Me about White Privilege" (Dowsett), 594–97
  "You Shouldn't Get a Prize for Showing Up" (Armour), 564–66
Argumentative writing, 26
Argument (persuasive) synthesis, 675
Aristotle, 493
Armour, Nancy, "You Shouldn't Get a Prize for Showing Up," 491, 564–66
Articles
  citation of, 731–32
  evaluation of, 722–23
  working bibliography for, 726
As, comparisons with, 751
"Attachment that Still Makes Noise, The" (Korkki), 161–65
Audience, 26–28. *See also* "Writing for an Audience" (Flower)
  for argumentation, 494, 504
  for definition essay, 402
Ault, Alicia, "How Do Spiders Make Their Webs?", 263–65

Baker, Russell, "Discovering the Power of My Words," 50–54
Balanced tone, 452–53
Bambara, Toni Cade, "The Lesson," 332–33
Bardeen, David P., "Not Close Enough for Comfort," 104–06, 743
"Barrio, The" (Ramírez), 141–44
Bechdel, Alison, 22, 24
"Bees: Why Are They Dying?" (Ellwood), 687–93
Begging the question, 507
Beginnings of essays, 38
Begley, Sharon, "Praise the Humble Dung Beetle," 668
"Be Specific" (Goldberg), 187–88
"Best Friends" (student essay) (Solomon), 396–99
Bibliography, working, 725–27. *See also* Works Cited list
  of online sources, 726–27
  of print sources, 726–27
Big Drink, The: The Story of Coca-Cola (Kahn), 80
"Bird Whose Life Depends on a Crab, A" (Cramer), 481–83
"Blaming the Family for Economic Decline" (Coontz), 668–69

Block comparison, 282, 283
Block organization, 291–92
Books
  citation of, 732–34
  evaluation of, 722–23
  working bibliography for, 726
Borrowed material, 673–74
Both/and, paired items with, 751
Bowman, Barbara, "Guns and Cameras" (student essay), 287–88
Brainstorming, 28
Britt, Suzanne, "Neat People vs. Sloppy People," 294–96
Britto, Marah, "The Qualities of Good Teachers," 675–76
Brooks, John, *Telephone,* 442
" 'Busy' Trap, The" (Kreider), 213–16
"But What Do You Mean?" (Tannen), 344–50
"Buy Experiences, Not Things" (Hamblin), 299–303

"Campus Racism 101" (Giovanni), 268–71
"Case for Short Words, The" (Lederer), 490, 558–61, 670, 755
Categorize, as a direction word, 24
Catton, Bruce, "Grant and Lee: A Study in Contrasts," 319–23
Causal chain, 442–44
Cause and effect analysis
  in academic disciplines, 445–46
  combining strategies with, 639
  definition of, 441
  as organizational strategy, 31
  organizing and writing of, 451–52
  planning of, 449–51
  revising/editing of, 452–54
  student essay as example of, 446–49
  as writing strategy, 444–45
  in written texts, 441–44
Cause and effect analysis (readings)
  "A Bird Whose Life Depends on a Crab" (Cramer), 481–83
  "Coca-Cola Funds Scientists Who Shift Blame for Obesity Away from Bad Diets" (O'Connor), 474–77
  "The Downside of Diversity" (Jonas), 465–71
  "Gentrification" (student essay) (Cunningham), 447–49
  "How Boys Become Men" (Katz), 455–57
  "iPod World: The End of Society?" (Sullivan), 460–63
  "Celebrity Obsession: Is It Healthy Behavior?" (Suarez), 499–502

Chronological organization, 88
Cicero, 493
Citations
    definition of, 728
    in-text, 728–30
    systems for making, 728
Classical argumentation, 493–94
Classification. *See* Division and classification (essay)
Clauses, punctuating, 742, 744
Clustering, 29
Coarse/course, 404
"Coca-Cola Funds Scientists Who Shift Blame for Obesity Away from Bad Diets" (O'Connor), 474–77
"Coddling of the American Mind, The" (Lukianoff and Haidt), 610–23
Cohen, Roger, "The Organic Fable," 574–76
Colons, 756
Combined strategies (essay)
    definition of, 631
    organizing of, 638–39
    planning of, 637–38
    revising/editing of, 639–40
    student essay as example of, 633–37
    in written texts, 632–33
Combined strategies (readings)
    "How to Reengineer Crops for the 21st Century" (White), 646–49
    "Language Chauvinism: The Ugly American Revisited" (Thompson), 651–54
    "Me Talk Pretty One Day" (Sedaris), 657–61
    "On Dumpster Diving" (Eighner), 641–43
    "The 'Steaks' Are High: In Vitro Meat Moves from the Petri Dish to the Palate" (student essay) (Foye-Edwards), 633–37
"Coming to an Awareness of Language" (Malcolm X), 92–94
Commas, 743–45
Comma splices, 742
Commoner, Barry, *The Politics of Energy,* 442–43
"Company Man, The" (Goodman), 427–29
Compare, as a direction word, 24
Comparison, 283
    block, 282, 283
    point-by-point, 282–83
    points of, 290–91
Comparison and contrast (essay)
    in academic disciplines, 285–86
    analogy in, 283–84
    combining strategies with, 639
    definition of, 281
    as organizational strategy, 31
    organizing and writing of, 291–93
    planning of, 289–91
    student essay as example of, 286–88
    as writing strategy, 284–85, 289–93
    in written texts, 281–84
Comparison and contrast (readings)
    "Buy Experiences, Not Things" (Hamblin), 299–303
    "The Difference between 'Sick' and 'Evil'," (Vachss), 312–15
    "Grant and Lee: A Study in Contrasts" (Catton), 319–23
    "Guns and Cameras" (student essay) (Bowman), 286–88
    "Neat People vs. Sloppy People" (Britt), 294–96
    "Two Ways to Belong in America" (Mukherjee), 306–09
"Compliment Complex, The" (Zaslow), 602–07
Compound sentences, 757–58
Compound subjects and subject-verb agreement, 745–46
Conjunctions
    correlative, 751
    subordinating and coordinating, 755
Connotations, 405
Context (setting) in narration essay, 80
Contrast, as a direction word, 24
Coontz, Stephanie, "Blaming the Family for Economic Decline," 668–69
Correlative conjunctions, paired items using, 751
Course/coarse, 404
Cramer, Deborah, "A Bird Whose Life Depends on a Crab," 481–83
Crane, Brent, "For a More Creative Brain, Travel," 191–93
Critique, as a direction word, 24
Critiques, peer, 36–37
Crowley, Siobhan, "On the Subject of Trigger Warnings," 608–09
Cunningham, Kevin, 446–49

Dangling modifiers, 749–50
Databases, keyword searches in, 720–21
"Declaration of Independence, The" (Jefferson), 518–21
Deductive reasoning, 495
Define, as a direction word, 24

Definition (essay)
  in academic disciplines, 395–96
  audience for, 402
  combining strategies with, 639
  definition of, 391
  as organizational strategy, 31
  organizing and writing of, 403–04
  planning of, 400–403
  revising/editing of, 404–06
  student essay as example of, 396–99
  types of, 392–94
  as a writing strategy, 394–95
  in written texts, 391–94
Definition (readings)
  "Best Friends" (student essay) (Solomon), 396–99
  "The Company Man" (Goodman), 427–29
  "The Selfish Side of Gratitude" (Ehrenreich), 432–35
  "Steal This MP3 File: What Is Theft?" (Gorry), 414–17
  "What Does 'Boys Will Be Boys' Really Mean?" (Roffman), 420–24
  "What Is Poverty?" (Parker), 405–11
Del Rey, Lester, *The Mysterious Sky,* 284
Description (essay)
  in academic disciplines, 128–29
  definition of, 125
  objective, 127
  organization of, 133–34
  planning of, 132–33
  revising/editing of, 135
  student essay as example of, 129–32
  subjective, 127
  as writing strategy, 126–28
  in written texts, 125–26
Description (readings)
  "The Attachment that Still Makes Noise" (Korkki), 161–65
  "The Barrio" (Ramírez), 141–44
  "Hiding from Animals" (Macdonald), 148–51
  "Sister Flowers" (Angelou), 154–59
  "Trailcheck" (student essay) (Tassé), 129–32
  "A Woman on the Street" (Walls), 135–39
Details in narration essay, 80
Devoe, Alan, *Lives Abroad,* 225–26
Díaz, Junot, "The Terror," 98–101
"Difference between 'Sick' and 'Evil', The" (Vachss), 312–15
Directional process analysis, 224–25
Direction words and phrases, 24–25
Direct quotations, 671–73, 678–79

Disciplines, writing strategies across academic, 33–34
"Discovering the Power of My Words" (Baker), 50–54
"Discrimination Is a Virtue" (Miller), 391–92
Disinterested/uninterested, 405
"Diving into the Gene Pool" (Miranda), 678–79
Division and classification (essay)
  in academic disciplines, 334–35
  combining strategies with, 639
  definition of, 331
  as organizational strategy, 31
  organizing and writing of, 341–43
  planning of, 339–41
  revising/editing of, 343
  student essay as example of, 335–39
  as writing strategy, 334
  in written texts, 331–33
Division and classification (readings)
  "But What Do You Mean" (Tannen), 344–50
  "The Forgotten Personality Type" (student essay) (Angeles), 335–39
  "Mother Tongue" (Tan), 379–84
  "The Queen Bee and Her Court" (Wiseman), 353–64
  "The Truth about Lying" (Viorst), 367–71
  "The Ways of Meeting Oppression" (King), 340–41, 374–76
Documentation, 728–30
Dominant impression, 127
"Don't Let Stereotypes Warp Your Judgments" (Heilbroner), 679–80
"Don't Peak in High School" (Kaling), 116–18
"Downside of Diversity, The" (Jonas), 465–71
Dowsett, J., "What My Bike Has Taught Me about White Privilege," 594–97
Draft. *See* First draft
"Draft: Why the Country Needs It, The" (Fallows), 496–97

"Eating Industrial Meat" (Pollan), 256–60
Editing, 39–40. *See also* specific writing strategies, revising/editing of
  for grammar, punctuation, and style, 741–58
Effect/affect, 404
Ehrenreich, Barbara, 432–35
Eighner, Lars, "On Dumpster Diving," 641–43

Either/or
    paired items with, 751
    subject-verb agreement with, 746
Either/or thinking, 507
Eldred, Keith, "Secular Mantras: Magic Words," (student essay), 40–47
Ellwood, Wayne, "Bees: Why Are they Dying?", 687–93
Eminent/immanent/imminent, 405
Endings of essays, 38
"English-Only Movement, The" (Jamieson), 706–12
Ethos in classical appeals, 493, 504
Etymological definition, 392
Etymology, 392
Evaluate, as a direction word, 24
Evaluation of sources, 722–24
Except/accept, 404
Explain, as a direction word, 24
Explanatory (informational) synthesis, 674–75
Exploratory (informational) argument, 491
Expressions, inflated, 754–55
Expressive writing, 26
Extended definition, 392, 393–94

Fallows, James, "The Draft: Why the Country Needs It," 496–97
False analogy, 507
Faulty parallelism, 750–51
Faulty reasoning. *See* Logic, errors of
Feedback. *See* Peer critiques
First draft
    organizing and writing, 31–35
    revision of, 35–39
Flashback, in narration essay, 88
Flower, Linda S., "Writing for an Audience," 60–63
Focused argument, 491
"For a More Creative Brain, Travel" (Crane), 191–93
"Forgotten Personality Type, The" (Angeles), 336–39
Formal definition, 392
Formal writing vs. informal writing, 27
Foye-Edwards, Ria, "The 'Steaks' Are High: In Vitro Meat Moves from the Petri Dish to the Palate" (student essay), 632–37
Freedman, Nicola, "How Social Media Is Changing Hollywood," 695–703
Friedman, Thomas L., "My Favorite Teacher," 12–14, 675–76
Friedrich, Otto, 283

"From Computer Cruelty to Campus Crime: Cyber-bullying at College" (student essay) (Sypher), 681–86
Fused sentences, 741

Galston, William, "Telling Americans to Vote, or Else," 568–71
Gender, pronoun-antecedent agreement in, 748–49
General words, 405
"Gentrification" (Cunningham), 447–49
Giovanni, Nikki, "Campus Racism," 268–71
Gladstone, Bernard, 223–24
Goldberg, Natalie, "Be Specific," 187–88
Goodman, Ellen, "The Company Man," 427–29
Gorry, Anthony, "Steal This MP3 File: What Is Theft?", 414–17
Grammar, editing for, 741–58
"Grant and Lee: A Study in Contrasts" (Catton), 319–23
"Guns and Cameras" (student essay) (Bowman), 287–88

Haidt, Jonathan, "The Coddling of the American Mind," 610–23
Hamblin, James, "Buy Experiences, Not Things," 299–303
Harris, Sydney, "A Jerk," 632
Hasty generalization, 507
Heilbroner, Robert L., "Don't Let Stereotypes Warp Your Judgments," 679–80
Heinrich, Bernd, 134
    One Man's Owl, 125–26, 127
Here Is New York (White), 331–32
"Hiding from Animals" (Macdonald), 148–51
"How Boys Become Men" (Katz), 455–57
"How Do Spiders Make Their Webs?" (Ault), 263–65
"How Social Media Is Changing Hollywood" (Freedman), 695–703
"How to Give Orders Like a Man" (Tannen), 202–10
"How to Mark a Book" (Adler), 225, 235–39
"How to Reengineer Crops for the 21st Century" (White), 646–49
"How to Say Nothing in 500 Words" (Roberts), 242–53

"I, Racist" (Metta), 581–87
Ideas, gathering, 28–30
"If You Had One Day with Someone Who's Gone" (Albom), 196–99
Illustrate, as a direction word, 24

Illustration
  in academic disciplines, 175–76
  combining strategies with, 639
  definition of, 173
  as organizational strategy, 31
  organization of, 185–86
  planning of, 183–85
  revising/editing of, 186
  student essay as example of, 176–82
  as writing strategy, 175–76
  in written texts, 173–74
Illustration (readings)
  "Be Specific" (Goldberg), 187–88
  "The 'Busy' Trap" (Kreider), 213–16
  "For a More Creative Brain, Travel" (Crane), 191–93
  "How to Give Orders Like a Man" (Tannen), 202–10
  "If You Had One Day with Someone Who's Gone" (Albom), 196–99
  "Weight Management: More Than a Matter of Good Looks" (student essay) (Kersch), 176–82
Immanent/imminent/eminent, 405
Immediate cause, 444
Imminent/eminent/immanent, 405
Impressionistic description, 127
Inductive reasoning, 495
Inflated language, 754–55
Informal writing vs. formal writing, 27
Informational (explanatory) synthesis, 674–75
Informational (exploratory) argument, 491
Informational process analysis, 225–26
Informative writing, 26
Integrated quotations, 674
Internet. *See* Online sources
Interpret, as a direction word, 24
In-text citations, 728–30
"iPod World: The End of Society?" (Sullivan), 460–63
It is, avoiding, 753–54

Jamieson, Jake, "The English-Only Movement," 706–12
Jefferson, Thomas, "The Declaration of Independence," 518–21
"Jerk, A" (Harris), 632
Jonas, Michael, "The Downside of Diversity," 465–71
Jones, Malcolm, "Who Was More Important: Lincoln or Darwin?", 671–72
"Juggling is Easier Than You Think" (Peterson), 227–30

Kahn, E. J., Jr. *The Big Drink: The Story of Coca-Cola,* 80
Kaling, Mindy, "Don't Peak in High School," 116–18
Katz, Jon, "How Boys Become Men," 455–57
Kersch, Paula, "Weight Management: More Than a Matter of Good Looks" (student essay), 176–82
Keyword searches, 720–21
King, Martin Luther, Jr.,
  "The Ways of Meeting Oppression," 340–41, 374–76
King, Stephen "Reading to Write," 67–72
Korkki, Phyllis, "The Attachment that Still Makes Noise," 161–65
Kreider, Tim, "The 'Busy' Trap," 213–16

Lamott, Anne, "Shitty First Drafts," 55–59
Language, inflated, 754–55
"Language Chauvinism: The Ugly American Revisited" (Thompson), 651–54
LaPierre, Laura, "Why Are You Here?" (student essay), 83–85
Lederer, Richard, 26
  "The Case for Short Words," 490, 558–61, 670, 755
"Lesson, The" (Bambara), 332–33
"Life in the Woods" (Snider), 78–79
List, as a direction word, 25
List of Works Cited. *See* Works Cited list
Lives Around Us (Devoe), 225–26
Logic, errors of
  in cause and effect analysis, 451–52
  types of, 507
Logical argument, 490–91
Logos in classical appeals, 493–94
Lukianoff, Greg, "The Coddling of the American Mind," 610–23

Macdonald, Helen, "Hiding from Animals," 148–51
Main idea. *See* Thesis statement; Topic
Malcolm X, "Coming to an Awareness of Language," 92–94
McCullough, David, *Truman,* 282–83
McDonald, Cherokee Paul, "A View from the Bridge," 5, 8–10, 132
"Me Talk Pretty One Day" (Sedaris), 657–61
Metta, John, "I, Racist," 581–87
Miller, Robert Keith, "Discrimination Is a Virtue," 391–92
Miranda, Carolina A., "Diving into the Gene Pool," 678–79
Misplaced modifiers, 749

Modern Language Association (MLA)
  documentation system, 728
  in-text citations, 728–30
  Works Cited list, 730–38
"Modest Proposal, A" (Swift), 548–55
Modifiers
  in compound sentences, 757
  dangling, 749–50
  definition of, 749
  misplaced, 749
  for sentence variety, 756
Mood shifts, 753
"Mother Tongue" (Tan), 379–84
Mukherjee, Bharati, "Two Ways to Belong in America," 306–09
"My Favorite Teacher" (Friedman), 12–14, 675–76
Mysterious Sky, The (Del Rey), 284

Name-calling, 507
Narration (essay)
  in academic disciplines, 81–82
  combining strategies with, 639
  context (setting), 86–87
  definition of, 79
  as organizational strategy, 31
  organization of, 88
  planning of, 85–87
  revising/editing of, 90–91
  student essay example of, 82–85
  writing of, 88–90
  as writing strategy, 81
  in written texts, 79–80
Narration (readings)
  "Coming to an Awareness of Language" (Malcolm X), 92–94
  "Don't Peak in High School" (Kaling), 116–18
  "Not Close Enough for Comfort" (Bardeen), 104–06
  "Stranger Than True" (Winston), 110–13
  "The Terror" (Díaz), 98–101
  "Why Are You Here?" (student essay) (LaPierre), 82–85
"Neat People vs. Sloppy People" (Britt), 294–96
Negative definition, 393
Neither/nor
  paired items with, 751
  subject-verb agreement with, 746
Newman, Judith, "What's Really Going On Inside Your Teen's Head," 668
Nonrestrictive phrases or clauses, 745
Non sequitur (it does not follow), 507

"Not Close Enough for Comfort" (Bardeen), 104–06, 743
Note-taking, 727–28
Not only . . . but also
  paired items with, 751
  subject-verb agreement with, 746
Nouns
  strong vs. weak, 751–52
Number, pronoun-antecedent agreement in, 748

Objective description, 127
O'Connor, Andrew, "Coca-Cola Funds Scientists Who Shift Blame for Obesity Away from Bad Diets," 474–77
"On Dumpster Diving" (Eighner), 641–43
One Man's Owl (Heinrich), 125–26
Online sources
  bibliography for, 725–27
  citation of, 734–37
  evaluation of, 723–24
  working bibliography for, 726
"On the Subject of Trigger Warnings" (Crowley), 608–09
"On Voice" (Orlean), 64–66
Open-Internet sources, 718–20
"Organic Fable, The" (Cohen), 574–76
Organizational (writing) strategies
  for argumentation essay, 492–93, 505
  determination of, 32–34
  types of, 31
Organization in narration essay, 80, 88
Orlean, Susan "On Voice," 64–66
Outline
  for comparison and contrast, 291–92
  for description essay, 134
  for narration essay, 88
Outline, as a direction word, 25
Oversimplification
  in argumentation, 507
  in cause and effect analysis, 451

Parallel construction
  for emphasis, 292
  faulty, 750–51
  sentence variety and, 756
Paraphrasing, 670–71, 679–80
Parker, Jo Goodwin, "What Is Poverty?", 405–11
Passive voice, 753
Pathos in classical appeals, 494, 504
Peer critiques, 36–37. *See also* individual strategies, revising/editing of
Person, pronoun-antecedent agreement in, 747–49

Persuasive argument, 490–91
Persuasive (argument) synthesis, 675
Peterson, William, "Juggling Is Easier Than You Think" (student essay), 227–30
Plagiarism
    avoiding, 677–81
    definition of, 678
Plato, "The Allegory of the Cave," 509–15
Point-by-point comparison, 282–83
Point-by-point organization, 291–92
Point of view in narration essay, 80, 87
Points of comparison, 290–91
Politics of Energy, The (Commoner), 442–43
Pollan, Michael, "Eating Industrial Meat," 256–60
Pompous language, 754–55
Post hoc, ergo propter hoc (after this, therefore because of this), 451–52, 507
"Praise the Humble Dung Beetle" (Begley), 668
Prepositional phrases and subject-verb agreement, 745
Principal/principle, 405
Print sources
    evaluation of, 722–23
Process analysis (essay)
    in academic disciplines, 232–33
    combining strategies with, 639
    definition of, 223
    directional, 224–25
    informational, 225–26
    as organizational strategy, 31
    organizing and writing of, 231–32
    planning of, 231
    revising/editing of, 232–34
    student essay as example of, 227–30
    as writing strategy, 224–26
    in written texts, 223–24
Process analysis (readings)
    "Campus Racism 101" (Giovanni), 268–71
    "Eating Industrial Meat" (Pollan), 256–60
    "How Do Spiders Make Their Webs?" (Ault), 263–65
    "How to Mark a Book" (Adler), 235–39
    "How to Say Nothing in 500 Words" (Roberts), 242–53
    "Juggling is Easier Than You Think" (student essay) (Peterson), 227–30
Pronouns
    pronoun-antecedent agreement, 747–49
    unclear references, 746–47
Proofreading, 39–40. *See also* specific writing strategies, revising/editing of
Prove, as a direction word, 25

Purpose, 26
Purpose for writing. *See* specific writing strategy

"Qualities of Good Teachers, The" (Britto), 675–76
"Queen Bee and Her Court, The" (Wiseman), 353–64, 672
Quiet (subtle) argument, 492
Quotation marks, for language borrowed directly, 678–79
Quotations
    direct, 671–73, 678–79
    integrated, 674
    unannounced, 674

"Racial Microaggressions in Everyday Life: Is Subtle Bias Harmful?" (Sue), 588–92
Ramírez, Robert, "The Barrio," 141–44
Reading process
    developing effective, 3–11
    practice with ("My Favorite Teacher"), 12–15
    as writer, 20–21
"Reading to Write" (King), 67–72
Reconciliation argument, 492
Redundancies, eliminating, 754
Referents (antecedents), 746–47
Remote cause, 444
Research, 29. *See also* Sources, finding and using
Research papers. *See also* Sources
    note-taking for, 727–728
    schedule for, 717–18
"Resistance to Civil Government" (Thoreau), 528–45
Restrictive phrases or clauses, 744–45
Review, as a direction word, 25
Roberts, Paul, "How to Say Nothing in 500 Words," 242–53
Roffman, Deborah M., "What Does 'Boys Will Be Boys' Really Mean?", 420–24
Run-on sentences, 741–42
Russell, Bill, *Second Wind,* 174

Search engines, subject directories of, 722
Second Wind (Russell), 174
"Secular Mantras: Magic Words" (student essay) (Eldred), 40–47
Sedaris, David, "Me Talk Pretty One Day," 657–61
"Selfish Side of Gratitude, The" (Ehrenreich), 432–35
Semicolons, 742, 756

Sentence fragments, 742–43
Sentences
  compound, 757–58
  fused, 741–42
  punctuation in, 742, 743–45
  run-on, 741–42
Sentence variety, 755–58
Setting (context) in narration essay, 80
Sherman, Bonnie, "Should Shame Be Used as Punishment?" (Sherman), 676
"Shitty First Drafts" (Lamott), 55–59
"Should Shame Be Used as Punishment?" (Sherman), 676
Signal phrases, 673
"Sister Flowers" (Angelou), 154–59
Snider, Grant "Life in the Woods," 78–79
Solomon, Howard, Jr., "Best Friends" (student essay), 396–99, 403
Sources. *See* Online sources; Print sources; Works Cited list; Writing with Sources
Specific words, 405
"Steal This MP3 File: What Is Theft?" (Gorry), 414–17
Stipulative definition, 393
"Stranger Than True" (Winston), 110–13
Strong verbs. *See* Active verbs
Student essays
  "Best Friends" (Solomon), 396–99
  "Celebrity Obsession: Is It Healthy Behavior?" (Suarez), 499–502
  "From Computer Cruelty to Campus Crime: Cyberbullying at College" (Sypher), 681–86
  "The Forgotten Personality Type" (Angeles), 336–39
  "Gentrification" (Cunningham), 447–49
  "Guns and Cameras" (Bowman), 287–88
  "Juggling is Easier Than You Think" (Peterson), 227–30
  "Secular Mantras: Magic Words" (Eldred), 40–47
  "The 'Steaks' Are High: In Vitro Meat Moves from the Petri Dish to the Palate" (Foye-Edwards), 633–37
  "Trailcheck" (Tassé), 129–32
  "Weight Management: More Than a Matter of Good Looks" (Kersch), 176–82
  "Why Are You Here?" (LaPierre), 83–85
Suarez, Kate, "Celebrity Obsession: Is It Healthy Behavior?", 499–502
Subject directories of search engines, 722
Subjective description, 127
Subject-verb agreement, 745–46
Subtle (quiet) argument, 492

Sue, Derald Wing, "Racial Microaggressions in Everyday Life: Is Subtle Bias Harmful?" (student essay), 588–92
Sullivan, Andrew, "iPod World: The End of Society?", 460–63
Summary
  plagiarism and, 679–81
  of source material, 669–70
Swift, Jonathan, "A Modest Proposal," 548–55
Syllogisms, 495–96
Synonymous definition, 392–93
Synthesis of sources, 674–77
Synthesize, as a direction word, 25
Sypher, Courtney, "From Computer Cruelty to Campus Crime: Cyberbullying at College" (student essay), 681–86

Tan, Amy, "Mother Tongue," 379–84
Tannen, Deborah
  "But What Do You Mean?", 344–50
  "How to Give Orders Like a Man," 202–10
Tassé, Jim, "Trailcheck" (student essay), 129–32
Telephone (Brooks), 442
"Telling Americans to Vote, or Else" (Galston), 568–71
Tense. *See* Verb tense
"Terror, The" (Díaz), 98–101
Than, comparisons with, 751
Than/then, 405
There is, avoiding, 753–54
Thesis statement
  in argumentation essay, 504
  in cause and effect analysis, 450–51
  in combined strategies essay, 638
  in comparison and contrast essay, 290
  in definition essay, 401–02
  in division and classification essay, 341
  formulation of, 30–31
Thompson, Cooper, "Language Chauvinism: The Ugly American Revisited," 651–54
Thoreau, Henry David, 5
  "Resistance to Civil Government," 528–45
Topic
  gathering ideas on, 28–30
  selection of, 25, 85
Trace, as a direction word, 25
"Trailcheck" (student essay) (Tassé), 129–32
Transitional words. *See also* Words
  in illustrative essay, 186
  in narration essay, 89
  in process analysis, 232

Truman (McCullough), 282–83
Truth, Sojourner, "Ain't I a Woman?", 525–26
"Truth about Lying, The" (Viorst), 367–71
"Two Ways to Belong in America" (Mukherjee), 306–09

Unannounced quotations, 674
Uninterested/disinterested, 405

Vachss, Andrew, "The Difference between 'Sick' and 'Evil'," 312–15
Verbs
  in signal phrases, 673
  strong (action) vs. weak, 751–52
Verb tense
  consistency of, 88–89, 233–34
  in narration essay, 88–89
  in process analysis, 233–34
  shifts in, 742
"View from the Bridge, A" (McDonald), 5, 8–10, 132
Viorst, Judith, "The Truth about Lying," 367–71
Visual texts, analysis of, 15–19
Voice. *See also* "On Voice" (Orlean)
  active and passive, 753
  shifts in, 753

Walls, Jeannette, "A Woman on the Street," 127, 135–39
"Ways of Meeting Oppression, The" (King), 340–41, 374–76
Web sites, evaluation of, 723–24. *See also* Online sources
"Weight Management: More Than a Matter of Good Looks" (student essay) (Kersch), 176–82
"What Does 'Boys Will Be Boys' Really Mean?" (Roffman), 420–24
"What Is Poverty?" (Parker), 405–6, 405–11
"What My Bike Has Taught Me about White Privilege" (Dowsett), 594–97
"What's Really Going On Inside Your Teen's Head" (Newman), 668
Whether/or, paired items with, 751
White, E. B.
  definition of democracy, 394–95
  Here Is New York, 331–32
White, Michael, "How to Reengineer Crops for the 21st Century," 646–49
"Who Was More Important: Lincoln or Darwin?" (Jones), 671–72

"Why Are You Here?" (student essay) (LaPierre), 82–85
Winston, Barry, "Stranger Than True," 110–13
Wiseman, Rosalind, "The Queen Bee and Her Court," 353–64, 672
"Woman on the Street, A" (Walls), 127, 135–39
Wordiness, 753–55
Words. *See also* Transitional words
  abstract, 405
  for balanced tone, 452–53
  connotation of, 405
  denotation of, 404–5
  empty, 754
  general, 405
  specific and concrete, 132–33, 405–6
Works Cited list, 730–38. *See also* Bibliography, working
  guidelines, 730
  MLA documentation style for, 730–38
  nonperiodical print publications, 732–34
  other common sources, 737–39
  periodical print publications, 731–32
  Web publications, 734–37
World Wide Web. *See* Online sources
Writing
  formal vs. informal, 27
  importance of, 23
  types of, 26
"Writing as an Act of Hope" (Allende), 73–77
"Writing for an Audience" (Flower), 60–63
Writing process
  audience, 26–28
  direction words for assignment, 24–25
  gathering of ideas, 28–30
  purpose, 26
  subject area and topic, 25
  thesis, 30–31
Writing strategies. *See* Organizational (writing) strategies; specific strategy
Writing with sources (essays)
  analyzing, 724–25
  avoiding plagiarism of, 677–81
  bibliography for, 725–27
  borrowed material from, 673–74
  direct quotations from, 671–73
  documentation of, 728–30
  evaluating, 722–24
  finding and using, 718–22
  paraphrasing, 670–71

student essay with, 681–86
summarizing, 669–70
synthesizing, 674–77
Writing with sources (readings)
"Bees: Why Are They Dying?" (Ellwood), 687–93
"From Computer Cruelty to Campus Crime: Cycberbullying at College" (student essay) (Sypher), 681–86
"The English-Only Movement" (Jamieson), 706–12
"How Social Media Is Changing Hollywood" (Freedman), 695–703

X, Malcolm, "Coming to an Awareness of Language," 92–94

"You Shouldn't Get a Prize for Showing Up" (Armour), 491, 564–66

Zaslow, Jeffrey, "The Compliment Complex," 602–07

INSTRUCTOR'S MANUAL

SUBJECT & STRATEGY

A Writer's Reader

14TH EDITION

With 2016 MLA

PAUL ESCHHOLZ   ALFRED ROSA

Cover image: Andy Roberts/Getty Images

Instructor's Manual

Subject & Strategy
A Writer's Reader

FOURTEENTH EDITION

Paul Eschholz
University of Vermont

Alfred Rosa
University of Vermont

bedford/st.martin's
Macmillan Learning

Boston | New York

Copyright © 2017, 2014, 2011, 2008 by Bedford/St. Martin's. All rights reserved.

Instructors who have adopted *Subject & Strategy*, Fourteenth Edition, as a textbook for a course are authorized to duplicate portions of this manual for their students.

Manufactured in the United States of America.

1 0 9 8 7 6
f e d c b a

For information, write: Bedford/St. Martin's, 75 Arlington Street, Boston, MA 02116   (617-399-4000)

ISBN: 978-1-319-07823-2

Cover image: Andy Roberts/Getty Images

Preface

The purpose of this instructor's manual is to suggest responses to the questions and prompts that accompany each selection in *Subject & Strategy*. Naturally, there are no substitutes for your own experience with each essay and for common sense about what will challenge and engage your students. Our intent in writing this manual is to save you time, not to dictate answers. On occasion, you may disagree with our interpretation or emphasis, but we trust that the suggested responses will be useful at least as starting points for class discussion.

Planning Your Course

Many instructors who use *Subject & Strategy* begin the course by having their students read the first two chapters of the text: "Reading" and "Writing." There, students will find guidelines for reading analytically and for using reading in the process of writing. Of particular interest in Chapter 1 are Cherokee Paul McDonald's "A View from the Bridge" (pages 5–10), which provides a step-by-step model of active reading, and Thomas L. Friedman's "My Favorite Teacher" (pages 12–15), which invites students to apply what they have learned. This Instructor's Manual includes additional study questions and possible responses for these Chapter 1 readings. In Chapter 2, students are encouraged to develop an effective writing process, in part by examining a case study of a student paper in progress. Many instructors choose then to assign Chapter 3, "Writers on Writing," which features essays in which well-known writers, including Anne Lamott and Stephen King, express both the joy and hard work of writing.

The arrangement of this book suggests one possible sequence for teaching Chapters 4–12: the movement from narration through the subsequent rhetorical strategies, culminating with argumentation, where those strategies are all brought to bear. Each chapter is self-contained, however, so that you may follow any sequence you prefer, omitting or emphasizing a chapter, according to the needs of your students.

Chapter 13, "Writing Essays Using Subjects and Strategies," and Chapter 14, "Writing with Sources," are typically introduced in the latter weeks of a course, once students have mastered some of the basic rhetorical strategies and are ready to move on to more advanced work. In Chapter 13, students learn how to use more than one strategy to achieve their purpose; a sample student essay and four professional essays demonstrate the possibilities. Chapter 14 offers sound, detailed advice on effectively integrating sources through quotation, summary, synthesis, and paraphrase and on avoiding plagiarism. This chapter features four essays that integrate outside sources, and it provides questions and prompts that direct students' attention to those integration techniques. Chapter 15, which is especially useful in courses that require students to do independent research, offers advice on finding and evaluating sources and on the mechanics of documentation. This chapter includes up-to-date guidelines for the Modern Language Association's documentation style.

Several sections in the book may be particularly helpful as you plan your course. In addition to the complete **Contents** on page xiii, you may enjoy the alternative **Thematic Contents** on page xxxi. This edition also includes an **Appendix of Thematic Writing Assignments** on page 760, offering a structured and useful way of connecting the book's readings and visuals through topical questions that resonate with students.

Using the Material Accompanying the Readings

This edition includes **chapter-opening images** for every chapter, increasing the opportunities for discussing and studying how visual rhetoric works. The chapter-opening images in each rhetorical modes chapter (Chapters 4–13) are particularly useful for underlining the importance and ubiquity of the strategies. A brief discussion of the image opens each rhetorical chapter, and a writing prompt related to the image appears among the end-of-chapter writing assignments.

The introductions to the strategy chapters explain the strategy and then model it with an annotated student essay that uses the strategy. We have found that model student essays like these can be especially helpful in introducing novice writers to the various rhetorical strategies and establishing realistic expectations for their own work.

We also have a **Using** [the strategy] **across the Disciplines section** in each chapter to show students how rhetorical strategies are used outside the composition classroom—whether in the humanities, the natural sciences, or the social sciences.

Suggestions for Using [the strategy] **as a Writing Strategy** offer advice for every stage of the writing process, with special emphasis on revising. You may wish to encourage students to consult Chapter 16, "Editing for Grammar, Punctuation, and Sentence Style," during the final stages of revising and proofreading a piece.

The **headnotes**, **prompts**, and **questions** that accompany each professional selection focus on different aspects of the essays:

- The *headnotes* offer biographical and publication information, as well as some insight into the selection's content and how the reading employs the mode under discussion.
- The *Preparing to Read* prompts are prereading exercises—often used by instructors as journal prompts—that encourage students to explore what they already know about the topic of the essay.
- The *Thinking Critically about the Text* prompts are intended to engage students with an issue, a concern, or an idea raised in the selection they have just read.
- *Questions on Subject* are designed to focus students' attention on the author's purpose and on the major points of the essay, as well as to promote class discussions of the selection. In addition, they provide a convenient means of checking comprehension. If you desire, these questions might be used as the basis for content quizzes.
- *Questions on Strategy* focus students' attention on analyzing the various strategies the authors have used in composing their essays. In answering these questions, students are encouraged to put themselves in the author's place and understand how they may use the same strategies in their own writing. Through this analysis, students come to a better understanding of the principles of good writing. There are also questions that ask students to examine passages in each selection where the writer has used *multiple* strategies in support of the dominant pattern of development. These questions illustrate and reinforce the points made in Chapter 13, "Writing Essays Using Subjects and Strategies."
- *Questions on Diction and Vocabulary* emphasize the importance of each author's diction, his or her choice of appropriate words and phrases. In every question, we have tried to stress the importance of the verbal context in which such choices are made.
- *Strategy in Action* activities follow each reading and encourage students to explore both the practical and the academic uses of the various rhetorical strategies. Many of these activities are visually based; all of them can be used as icebreakers to launch class discussion of a particular reading.

- *Writing Suggestions* can be found at the end of each selection and at the end of each chapter. To encourage student competency in researching and documenting students' work, many prompts are specifically labeled as Writing with Sources. In this edition, we've included new Writing in the Workplace prompts to help students envision how to carry the strategies into their professional careers.

We are very interested in hearing from anyone who has constructive ideas about either *Subject & Strategy* or this manual. We are always receptive to thoughts on how our book might be made even more useful for teachers and students. We can be reached at the Department of English, 400 Old Mill, The University of Vermont, Burlington, VT 05405-4030, or via our editors at Bedford/St. Martin's, at composition@macmillanlearning.com.

Paul Eschholz
Alfred Rosa

Contents

Preface iv

1 Reading 1
CHEROKEE PAUL MCDONALD, *A View from the Bridge* 1
THOMAS L. FRIEDMAN, *My Favorite Teacher* 4

2 Writing 8
Sample Worksheets for Peer Review 8

3 Writers on Writing 10
RUSSELL BAKER, *Discovering the Power of My Words* 10
ANNE LAMOTT, *Shitty First Drafts* 11
LINDA S. FLOWER, *Writing for an Audience* 12
SUSAN ORLEAN, *On Voice* 13
STEPHEN KING, *Reading to Write* 14
ISABEL ALLENDE, *Writing as an Act of Hope* 16

4 Narration 17
MALCOLM X, *Coming to an Awareness of Language* 17
JUNOT DÍAZ, *The Terror* 19
DAVID P. BARDEEN, *Not Close Enough for Comfort* 21
BARRY WINSTON, *Stranger Than True* 22
MINDY KALING, *Don't Peak in High School* 25

5 Description 27
JEANNETTE WALLS, *A Woman on the Street* 27
ROBERT RAMÍREZ, *The Barrio* 29
HELEN MACDONALD, *Hiding from Animals* 31
MAYA ANGELOU, *Sister Flowers* 33
PHYLLIS KORKKI, *The Attachment that Still Makes Noise* 35

6 Illustration 37
NATALIE GOLDBERG, *Be Specific* 37
BRENT CRANE, *For a More Creative Brain, Travel* 38
MITCH ALBOM, *If You Had One Day with Someone Who's Gone* 40
DEBORAH TANNEN, *How to Give Orders Like a Man* 42
TIM KREIDER, *The "Busy" Trap* 43

7 Process Analysis 46
MORTIMER ADLER, *How to Mark a Book* 46
PAUL ROBERTS, *How to Say Nothing in 500 Words* 48
MICHAEL POLLAN, *Eating Industrial Meat* 49
ALYSSA AULT, *How Do Spiders Make Their Webs?* 51
NIKKI GIOVANNI, *Campus Racism 101* 53

8 Comparison and Contrast 56
SUZANNE BRITT, *Neat People vs. Sloppy People* 56
JAMES HAMBLIN, *Buy Experiences, Not Things* 57
BHARATI MUKHERJEE, *Two Ways to Belong in America* 59
ANDREW VACHSS, *The Difference between "Sick" and "Evil"* 62
BRUCE CATTON, *Grant and Lee: A Study in Contrasts* 64

9 Division and Classification 67
DEBORAH TANNEN, *But What Do You Mean?* 67
ROSALIND WISEMAN, *The Queen Bee and Her Court* 69
JUDITH VIORST, *The Truth about Lying* 71
MARTIN LUTHER KING, JR., *The Ways of Meeting Oppression* 72
AMY TAN, *Mother Tongue* 74

10 Definition 77
JO GOODWIN PARKER, *What Is Poverty?* 77
G. ANTHONY GORRY, *Steal This MP3 File: What Is Theft?* 78
DEBORAH M. ROFFMAN, *What Does "Boys Will Be Boys" Really Mean?* 80
ELLEN GOODMAN, *The Company Man* 82
BARBARA EHRENREICH, *The Selfish Side of Gratitude* 85

11 Cause and Effect Analysis 87
JON KATZ, *How Boys Become Men* 87
ANDREW SULLIVAN, *iPod World: The End of Society?* 88
MICHAEL JONAS, *The Downside of Diversity* 90
ANAHAD O'CONNOR, *Coca-Cola Funds Scientists Who Shift Blame for Obesity Away from Bad Diets* 92
DEBORAH CRAMER, *A Bird Whose Life Depends on a Crab* 94

12 Argumentation 96
CLASSIC ARGUMENTS
PLATO, *The Allegory of the Cave* 96
THOMAS JEFFERSON, *The Declaration of Independence* 98
SOJOURNER TRUTH, *Ain't I a Woman?* 99
HENRY DAVID THOREAU, *Resistance to Civil Government* 101
JONATHAN SWIFT, *A Modest Proposal* 103

CONTEMPORARY ARGUMENTS 105
  RICHARD LEDERER, *The Case for Short Words* 105
  NANCY ARMOUR, *You Shouldn't Get a Prize for Showing Up* 106
  WILLIAM GALSTON, *Telling Americans to Vote, or Else* 108
  ROGER COHEN, *The Organic Fable* 109
ARGUMENT CLUSTER: Race and Privilege: How to Address a System of Bias? 111
  JOHN METTA, *I, Racist* 111
  DERALD WING SUE, *Racial Microaggressions in Everyday Life: Is Subtle Bias Harmful?* 112
  J. DOWSETT, *What My Bike Has Taught Me about White Privilege* 113
ARGUMENT CLUSTER: Getting an Education: What's the Line between Comfort and Learning? 114
  JEFFREY ZASLOW, *The Compliment Complex* 114
  SIOBHAN CROWLEY, *On the Subject of Trigger Warnings* 115
  GREG LUKIANOFF AND JONATHAN HAIDT, *The Coddling of the American Mind* 116

13 Writing Essays Using Subjects and Strategies 118
  LARS EIGHNER, *On Dumpster Diving* 118
  MICHAEL WHITE, *How to Reengineer Crops for the 21st Century* 120
  COOPER THOMPSON, *Language Chauvinism: The Ugly American Revisited* 121
  DAVID SEDARIS, *Me Talk Pretty One Day* 123

14 Writing with Sources 125
  WAYNE ELLWOOD, *Bees: Why Are They Dying?* 125
  NICOLA FREEDMAN, *How Social Media Is Changing Hollywood* 126
  JAKE JAMIESON, *The English-Only Movement: Can America Proscribe Language with a Clear Conscience?* 128

CHAPTER 1 Reading

A View from the Bridge
CHEROKEE PAUL MCDONALD

ASSIGNMENT QUESTIONS

Preparing to Read (p. 5)

The great American philosopher and naturalist Henry David Thoreau has written: "The question is not what you look at, but what you see." We've all had the experience of becoming numb to sights or experiences that once struck us with wonderment; sometimes, however, with luck, something happens to renew our appreciation. Think of an example from your own experience. What are some ways we can retain or recover our appreciation of the remarkable things we have come to take for granted?

▪ Thinking Critically about the Text (IM Only)

The jogger and the kid are very different from each other, but they share an interest in fishing. What role does the tarpon play in this story? What can a shared interest do for a relationship between two people?

▪ Questions on Subject (IM Only)

1. Why is the narrator angry with the kid at the beginning of the story?
2. What clues lead up to the revelation that the kid is blind? Why does it take the narrator so long to realize it?
3. "Why don't you get yourself some decent equipment?" the narrator asks the kid (paragraph 19). Why does McDonald include this question? Speculate about the answer.
4. Near the end of the story, why does the narrator say to the kid, "No, my friend, thank you for letting me see that fish" (paragraph 43)?
5. The boy boasts that one day he will catch big sport fish, too. Why does the narrator say he "wished [he] could be there when it happened" (paragraph 48)?

▪ Questions on Strategy (IM Only)

1. Notice the way the narrator chooses and actually adjusts some of the words he uses to describe the fish to the kid. Why does he do this? What is McDonald's desired effect?
2. By the end of the essay, we know much more about the kid than the fact that he is blind, but, after the initial description, McDonald characterizes him only indirectly. As the essay unfolds, what do we learn about the kid, and by what techniques does the author convey this knowledge?
3. Reread the description of the kid (paragraphs 2 and 3). Which details gain significance as events unfold over the course of the essay?
4. McDonald is able to move his story along rather quickly by being selective about what he tells the reader. For example, examine paragraphs 9–13 and explain how the author moves the action forward.

5. This essay, descriptive in theme and intent, is structured as a narrative. (Glossary: *Narration*) What makes the combination of story and description effective? Suppose McDonald had started his essay with a statement like this: "If you really want to see something clearly, try describing it to a blind child." How would such an opening change the impact of the essay? Which other rhetorical strategies might McDonald have used along with the new opening?

- **Questions on Diction and Vocabulary (IM Only)**
  1. What is the metaphor in paragraph 24? Why is it apt? How does this metaphor enhance McDonald's description? (Glossary: *Figures of Speech*)
  2. What is the connotation of the word *view* in the title? Of the word *bridge*? (Glossary: *Connotation/Denotation*)
  3. You may be unfamiliar with some of the fishing-related vocabulary in this essay. What sort of fish is a tarpon? In the context of fishing, define *drag* (paragraph 16), *pilings* (23), *seawall* (26), *leader* (27).

RESPONSES

Preparing to Read (p. 5)
Something happens in this essay: McDonald tells the story of an event that helped revive his narrator's sense of wonder and appreciation. This assignment asks students to remember and describe a similar event in their own lives. It is designed to elicit both narrative and description, the strategies McDonald uses. It also asks students to consider the cause and effect of apathy, a question that is central to McDonald's essay but one with which he deals only indirectly.

Thinking Critically about the Text (IM Only)
The tarpon is something of value to both the narrator and the kid, but because they perceive the fish in profoundly different ways, each can add to the other's ability to appreciate it. Each enriches the other's understanding and enjoyment of something they both like. A shared interest (in this case, the tarpon) allows a connection to occur between two people who otherwise would pass each other by. At the end of their encounter, the narrator is better able to see and appreciate both the fish and the kid.

Questions on Subject (IM Only)
1. There are two aspects to the narrator's frustration. The first aspect is that he is exercising and doesn't want to break stride and interrupt his workout. The second is that the kid's demand at first seemed unreasonably simplistic, and thus selfish.
2. The kid wore wrap-around sunglasses (paragraph 3); he was "fumbling" with his rod and reel (4); he could not see the shrimp by his foot (10); his fingers "felt" for the drag setting (16); he thought he had lost the fish when the line went slack (20); and he asked the narrator to tell him what the fish looked like (29). The narrator does not realize the kid is blind because he is preoccupied with his jogging and because the kid is a competent angler whose behavior does not arouse suspicion.
3. The narrator has developed enough admiration for the kid's skill to notice with regret the inadequacy of his equipment. Because he cannot see it, though, the kid is probably unaware that his gear is not "decent."

4. The narrator is both acknowledging the kid's thanks and reciprocating them. As he describes the tarpon carefully to please the kid, the narrator comes to his own renewed sense of wonder and appreciation for the beauty of the fish.
5. The narrator and kid have developed a symbiotic relationship that allows them both to see events in a new way: the kid sees the fish for the first time through the narrator's description, and the narrator appreciates the details of things that he once took for granted, like fishing technique and what a tarpon looks like. Catching a sport fish would not only be a huge victory for the kid, and the narrator would love to share in that victory, but being there would also give the narrator another chance to experience the heightened appreciation of detail.

Questions on Strategy (IM Only)

1. The narrator seeks to use words and phrases that are familiar to a child. He also looks for words that appeal to a sense other than sight (e.g., he starts to say that the fish is three feet long, but he then changes to the more concrete and sensory phrase, "as long as one of your arms" [33]). The effect is a description both accessible and vivid.
2. We learn that the kid is courteous; he says "please" (paragraphs 5 and 8) and "thanks" (12 and 42). He is, against all odds, a capable, determined fisherman (15, 24, and 47). Both the act of fishing and the fish itself give him tremendous delight. We see his joy in hooking and playing the fish (15 and 22), his pleasure in the narrator's description, and his desire to set the fish free (37). McDonald uses dialogue and telling details to convey this knowledge to us.
3. The sailfish patch on his cap foreshadows the kid's ambition to be a big game fisherman; the dark glasses foreshadow his blindness.
4. There are several things to notice here. First, McDonald omits any description or flourish and concentrates on describing the events efficiently. Second, in paragraph 10, McDonald leaves out the customary "I said," phrase, instead incorporating it into the next paragraph. Third, McDonald uses two complex sentences (9 and 11) that contain a lot of information and read more quickly and smoothly than several short sentences would.
5. The narrative structure is effective because it adds suspense to the piece. The reader does not realize that the kid is blind until paragraph 31, and this revelation adds great impact to the narrator's description of the fish. Also, the narrative includes dialogue, which McDonald uses to great effect. McDonald's point is made indirectly, by illustration, in the narrative essay; to open the essay with a thesis statement would require a shift of strategy from story to argument. Students will have various ideas about how McDonald might have supported a different opening; some possibilities are illustration, exemplification, description, and cause and effect.

Questions on Diction and Vocabulary (IM Only)

1. The fish is compared to a silver missile. This comparison is apt because the words imply not just beauty but speed and power, yet the kid remains in control. These words also anticipate the dramatic way the narrator describes the fish to the kid.
2. A view is not just what is seen but it is also a perspective, a way of seeing. The bridge spans the water, but it also represents the connection of respect and understanding that develops between the narrator and the kid.
3. *Tarpon* (paragraph 14): large game fish of tropical Atlantic waters. *Drag* (16): a device that retards by friction the unreeling of the fishing line. *Pilings* (23): a structure of long, slender columns driven vertically into the ground or ocean floor. *Seawall* (26): breakwater. *Leader* (27): a short length of material for attaching the end of a fishing line to a lure or hook.

My Favorite Teacher
THOMAS L. FRIEDMAN

ASSIGNMENT QUESTIONS

Preparing to Read (p. 12)

If you had to name your three favorite teachers of all time, who would they be? Why do you consider each one a favorite? Which one, if any, are you likely to remember twenty-five years from now? Why?

■ Thinking Critically about the Text (IM Only)

What do you think Friedman means when he states, "The Internet can make you smarter, but it can't make you smart" (paragraph 11)? What, according to Friedman, is missing on the Internet? Do you agree?

■ Questions on Subject (IM Only)

1. Hattie M. Steinberg taught her students the fundamentals of journalism—"not simply how to write a lead or accurately transcribe a quote, but, more important, how to comport yourself in a professional way and to always do quality work" (paragraph 3). According to Friedman, what other fundamentals did she introduce to her students? Why do you think Friedman values these fundamentals so much?
2. Why do you think Friedman tells us three times that Hattie's classroom was number 313 at St. Louis Park High School?
3. According to Friedman, what went wrong when the "huge dot-com-Internet-globalization bubble" (10) of the late 1990s burst? Do you agree?
4. Why did Steinberg have her students read the *New York Times* first thing every morning?

■ Questions on Strategy (IM Only)

1. Friedman claims that his high school journalism teacher, Hattie M. Steinberg, was "someone who made the most important difference in my life" (1). What descriptive details does Friedman use to support this thesis? (Glossary: *Thesis*)
2. Friedman punctuates his description of Steinberg's teaching with short, pithy sentences. For example, he ends paragraph 2 with the sentence "She was that good" and paragraph 3 with "She wanted to teach us about consequences." Identify several other short sentences Friedman uses. What do these sentences have in common? How do short sentences like these affect you as a reader? Explain.
3. What details in Friedman's portrait of his teacher stand out for you? Why do you suppose Friedman chose the details that he did? What dominant impression of Hattie M. Steinberg do they collectively create? (Glossary: *Dominant Impression*)
4. In paragraph 7, Friedman quotes Steinberg directly. What does he gain by having her speak for herself?

> ■ **Questions on Diction and Vocabulary (IM Only)**
> 1. In paragraph 2, Friedman calls his teacher "the legendary journalism teacher at St. Louis Park High School." Why do you suppose he chose the word *legendary* instead of say *excellent*, *well-known*, or *influential*? In paragraph 4, he calls her "the toughest teacher I ever had." What does the word *toughest* connote for you? (Glossary: *Connotation/Denotation*)
> 2. Friedman credits Steinberg with teaching her students the "fundamentals." Do you think that the word *fundamentals* is both appropriate and effective as he uses it? What other words could he have used instead of *fundamentals*?
> 3. Identify the metaphor and the simile in paragraph 5. (Glossary: *Figures of Speech*) How do they work to help readers envision Hattie and her classroom?

RESPONSES

Preparing to Read (p. 12)
You might want to remind students that these do not have to be schoolteachers. Their favorite teacher could be a person who taught them how to tie their shoes, play piano or soccer, or use their computer. Teachers can be found everywhere.

Thinking Critically about the Text (IM Only)
Students may have varying interpretations of what Friedman means by this statement. Many will probably mention that the Internet provides information, but it does not teach the user how to use or interpret the information, nor does it help the user to develop character when applying or borrowing the information.

Questions on Subject (IM Only)
1. At the end of paragraph 10, Friedman presents characteristics that represent Steinberg's understanding of fundamentals: "reading, writing, arithmetic; church, synagogue, and mosque; the rule of law; and good governance." Friedman uses this series of items to illustrate how the principles and aspects of journalism that Steinberg taught her students also applied to larger concerns of life.
2. Friedman's repeated references to Room 313 reflect the deep impression that the activities within that room made on him and the amount of time he spent there during high school. Now when he thinks of his teacher and the experiences he had with her, he thinks of Room 313.
3. Friedman believes that, in the rush to make a lot of money quickly, the dot-coms "forgot the fundamentals of how to build a profitable company." Students may or may not agree with Friedman's statement. Ask students whether they believe that the same thing happened in the nation's housing, banking, and financial markets in recent years.
4. Steinberg had her students read the *New York Times* every morning because that's how "real journalists start their day" (paragraph 9). Specifically, Anthony Lewis and James Reston start their day reading the paper. Of course, it was also a way to expose students to well-thought-out, well-written models of journalism and analysis. Ask students how reading models of good writing can improve one's own writing, a method they'll use as they encounter the student and professional selections in *Subject & Strategy*.

Questions on Strategy (IM Only)

1. Friedman's examples point out key aspects of his own career in journalism, thereby establishing the important role Hattie Steinberg played in his life. One example, his interview with an advertising executive for his high school newspaper—during which the advertising executive used a four-letter word that Friedman and Steinberg decided to print—taught Friedman about the consequences of one's behavior. He also describes his first published story for the school paper, for which he covered a lecture by and then interviewed Ariel Sharon. This event indicates the direction his career followed, focusing on issues in the Middle East. Friedman says that the *New York Times* was delivered every morning to Room 313, emphasizing how the paper exerted an enormous influence over his approach to journalism, beginning the professional path that led him from being Steinberg's student to a successful columnist for the *Times*. Finally, Friedman's example about the "dot-com-Internet-globalization bubble" that burst impresses upon readers the real secret to success that Steinberg passed on to him: fundamentals that transferred across different industries, jobs, and areas of life.

2. Examples of short sentences in Friedman's essay include the following:

    "She wanted to teach us about consequences." (paragraph 3)

    "Competition was fierce." (4)

    "His name was Ariel Sharon. First story I ever got published." (4)

    "She was a woman of clarity in an age of uncertainty." (5)

    "These fundamentals cannot be downloaded." (11)

    In each case, the short sentence emphasizes the key point developed in the paragraph in which it appears. Students' opinions about how the sentences affect them as readers may vary, but most will probably acknowledge the way in which the sentences dramatically emphasize the main ideas presented throughout the essay or the manner in which they create a sense of rhythm and fluency in the prose by varying sentence length and structure.

3. Students' opinions about which examples stand out for them and why Friedman chose those examples may vary. Whichever details they select, however, the general idea or dominant impression conveyed should reflect Friedman's emphasis on Steinberg's stern but principled and committed behavior toward her students.

4. By letting Steinberg speak for herself, Friedman is able to "show" what his teacher was really like. Her words are direct, deliberate, and stern, which supports his description of her. The quote thus increases Friedman's credibility with readers. Also, the quote varies the writing style, piquing reader interest and keeping their attention through to the end of the piece.

Questions on Diction and Vocabulary (IM Only)

1. *Legendary* connotes something timeless and memorable. Lots of things are *excellent*, like a good meal or a great movie, but we often forget those sorts of things as soon as we are done. Something *legendary* is not soon forgotten; it is remembered through the ages and held in high esteem, even by those who did not know the person or have the experience. Steinberg had become *legendary* in this way. *Toughest* has different connotations for different students. Some will say it means not being able to slip through with merely adequate work or that the teacher had very high standards. Tough teachers often have high expectations and rarely accept excuses.

2. Student reactions will vary. Most know that the term *fundamentals* refers to *basic tools*, *basic knowledge*, or *foundational knowledge* (all other phrases he might have used) one can then build on. Steinberg offered her students not just the fundamentals of writing

but also "how to comport yourself in a professional way and to always do good quality work." These are fundamentals because they are transferrable skills and can apply to all aspects of living, not just writing. Friedman says he never needed another journalism class, suggesting he was able to build on the foundation Steinberg helped her students build for themselves.

3. Friedman uses the following simile in paragraph 5: "we hung around her classroom like it was a malt shop and she was Wolfman Jack." Many students will not be familiar with Wolfman Jack, a famous disc jockey in the 1960s and 1970s. Still, they will understand the idea that spending time in her classroom was tantamount to hanging out with friends after school. She had a kind of star quality that drew kids to her and even made her cool, despite her status as a teacher in her sixties.

CHAPTER 2 Writing

Sample Worksheets for Peer Review

In a typical peer critique session, a student reads her or his paper aloud to one or two students. The students then discuss the paper, and the reviewers take notes that the author can use during revision. A few different worksheets are often helpful, and we've provided two models below.

The reviewer should record the author's responses to specific questions.

Author Name:
Paper Title:
Reviewer Name:

Peer Critique Worksheet: Answers from the Author

(Reviewer asks questions, author answers verbally, and reviewer records responses.)

1. Have you focused your **topic**?

2. Does your **thesis statement** clearly identify your topic and make an assertion about it?

3. Is the **writing strategy** you have chosen the best one for your purpose?

4. Are your **paragraphs** adequately developed, and does each support your thesis?

5. Is your **beginning** effective in capturing the reader's interest and introducing the topic?

6. Is your **conclusion** effective? Does it grow naturally from what you've said in the rest of your essay?

7. Have you accomplished your **purpose**?

(Return this filled-out questionnaire to the author.)

Each peer reviewer should also complete an evaluation reflecting his or her thoughts about the paper, which may differ from those of the author.

Author Name:
Paper Title:
Reviewer Name:

Peer Critique Worksheet: Answers from the Reviewer

1. What is the **purpose** in this essay?

2. What is the **thesis**? Where is it stated?

3. Is the **thesis statement** sufficiently focused?

4. Does each **paragraph** support the thesis? If not, what can the author do to correct the problem?

5. Is the **organization** of the essay the best one for the material?

6. What is the **strongest part** of the essay? What can the author do to build on that aspect of the essay?

7. What is the **weakest part** of the essay? What can the author do to correct any problems?

8. What might the author add to the draft?

(Return this filled-out questionnaire to the author.)

The first two chapters and the glossary in *Subject & Strategy* may be especially useful to students as they complete these two worksheets.

CHAPTER 3 Writers on Writing

Discovering the Power of My Words
RUSSELL BAKER

Preparing to Read (p. 50)
Since few students will have had specific "writing teachers," most will probably write about an English teacher or a history teacher who gave them assignments. These questions encourage students to think about the kinds of writing instruction they have received, their personal reactions to that instruction, and the long-term benefits. The questions prepare them to relate to Baker's personal experience.

Thinking Critically about the Text (p. 53)
Most students will be able to relate to the expository essay format to which Baker refers; such essays include the five-paragraph essay (introduction, three body paragraphs, and conclusion). Students write these essays about plays or classic literature, usually quoting the text or citing cases to prove a point about a theme—for example, loss, gender, irony, or a character's true nature (good/evil). Unlike "The Art of Eating Spaghetti," these traditional essays do not ask students to bring forth their own personal experiences, write in the first person, or convey a story for its own sake. Traditional expository essays teach structure and how to build a case, use evidence, and find themes.

   Most students will expect that Baker would understand just the kind of writing assignments that the cartoon is depicting: assignments that make the mind "numb" (paragraph 6). Baker came to prim Mr. Fleagle's class believing, "Of all forms of writing, none seemed so boring as the essay" (6). Students will probably believe that Baker would find it ironic that writing for the teacher does not produce the kind of piece that instructors find really exemplary, whereas writing about something personally meaningful found in an assignment, as Baker did in "The Art of Eating Spaghetti," produces material more likely to be "the very essence of the essay" (12).

Discussing the Craft of Writing (p. 54)
1. Baker describes Mr. Fleagle as having a "dullness and inability to inspire. He was said to be stuffy, dull, and hopelessly out of date" (paragraph 2). He looked roughly seventy years old and prim, wearing "severe" eyeglasses and sporting primly cut hair. His clothes included vested suits, neckties, and starched shirts. His facial features matched his style; he had a pointed jaw, straight nose, and a way of speaking with grammatical accuracy and acuity. He appeared to be a "comic antique." Baker creates the dominant impression of Mr. Fleagle as someone from an earlier era by juxtaposing him with a younger and free-spirited person.
   You may want to ask students to describe Baker based on the picture of him at the beginning of this essay. He too has a formal appearance and seems about the age of Mr. Fleagle. What insight can they gain from this?
2. Because writing requires the author's intelligence and general life experience, choice enables a writer to find a hook or something inspiring. This inspiration, in turn, gives the writing momentum and infuses the reader with the author's own passion, something that Baker thought Mr. Fleagle seemed unable to do.

3. Baker describes the experience of seeing the topic as "produc[ing] an extraordinary sequence of mental images. Surging up from the depths of memory came a vivid recollection of a night in Belleville . . ." (7). Baker has a visceral response to the title: The night reminds him of the joy of being with his family, of laughter, and of everyone's inability to feel adequate when eating this new food. Like writing, nobody knew how to eat spaghetti primly and properly, so they laughed about their awkwardness. They had to throw "what was proper" out the window and just slop through themselves. This is exactly what Baker does when he writes the essay.

4. Whereas Baker believed that writing what came to him and not writing in a controlled manner would cause him to fail the assignment, his passion and ability to write about something true and meaningful captured the power of the personal essay.

5. Baker felt touched that someone would be moved by his words rather than by his analysis. In expository essays, writers quote from the text and rarely speak in the first person. In his spaghetti essay, Baker felt he used his voice and his true self. In addition, Baker's words infected the class with the kind of passion and inspiration he experienced when he wrote the essay and when he ate the meal. He communicated something important and personally meaningful through words. Others wanted to hear his words, too. Despite his distaste for the prim and proper approach, he found writing has something to offer.

6. Mr. Fleagle does not necessarily need to inspire students; he needs to help his students find inspiration in themselves. The narrative offers several insights into writing. First, a writing teacher should not be judged by his or her mannerisms, but rather by his or her ability to help students find their own words. Writing can be many things: a way to describe a play and to communicate with others. Writing can be a powerful way to communicate a personal experience to others who care about what you have to say. It is important not to give up on writing even if the topics do not appeal. When inspired, even the most reluctant English student has something to say.

Shitty First Drafts
ANNE LAMOTT

Preparing to Read (p. 55)
Students will most likely view writing first drafts as a chore. They may say that they have a pattern of frustration, false starts, and procrastination. Some will even say they have written first drafts and turned them in as is.

Thinking Critically about the Text (p. 59)
Some students may find Lamott's use of the word *shitty* offensive or even unprofessional. However, they should see that the word is in keeping with Lamott's light-hearted tone and the frustration writers often feel. Another word might not have captured her feelings as acutely.

Discussing the Craft of Writing (p. 59)
1. Lamott means that nonwriters have a romantic view of the writer's life and process — that words flow freely from the writer's mind to the page. In reality, writing is difficult, and writers often find themselves blocked or doubtful of their abilities.
2. By "more or less," Lamott means that while in the thick of the process, it's hard to have perspective on how effective the process is or how well one is using it. Her sentiments are personal, but they do reflect a predicament many writers face.

3. Lamott suggests that first drafts are more about psychology than content and that the real hurdle is believing in oneself enough to get ideas down on paper. Content is something that can be refined in subsequent drafts, when the writer has gained confidence from surmounting the most difficult part of the process: the first draft.
4. Lamott's thesis statement is located in paragraph 3: "For me and most of the other writers I know, writing is not rapturous. In fact, the only way I can get anything written at all is to write really, really shitty first drafts."
5. Lamott infuses her essay with black humor: "All right, one of them does, but we do not like her very much" (paragraph 1); "One might hope for bad things to rain down on a person like this" (2); "Some readers took umbrage at my comparing mounds of vegetable puree with various ex-presidents' brains" (5); "I'd obsess about getting creamed by a car before I could write a decent second draft" (7). Her use of humor mirrors some of the negative thoughts writers often have. Most students will appreciate and identify with Lamott's candor and sense of humor.
6. Lamott discusses her difficulties so that readers can better understand how much work writing truly entails. Students will find this information reassuring because it shows them that even professional writers have difficulties.

Writing for an Audience
LINDA S. FLOWER

Preparing to Read (p. 60)
Student responses will vary. This prompt is designed to get students thinking about audience — how their diction and tone can differ according to the audience. The truthfulness of students' accounts will probably vary as well.

Thinking Critically about the Text (p. 63)
According to Flower, "the real purpose of a paper may be for you to make connections between two historical periods, to discover for yourself the principle behind a laboratory experiment, or to develop and support your own interpretation of a novel. A good college paper doesn't just rehash the facts; it demonstrates what your reader, as a teacher, needs to know — that you are learning the thinking skills his or her course is trying to teach" (paragraph 9).

Discussing the Craft of Writing (p. 63)
1. A competent writer will look at the distance between him- or herself and the audience, a distance created by differences such as age or background, knowledge about the topic, attitudes toward it, and personal or professional needs. The writer must analyze those needs, clarify what the reader needs to know, and adapt that knowledge to the reader.
2. Flower defines *knowledge* as a "conscious awareness of explicit facts and clearly defined concepts" that "can be easily written down or told to someone else." *Attitude*, on the other hand, is an "image" or "a loose cluster of associations" (paragraph 4). The distinction is important because "a reader's image of a subject is often the source of attitudes and feelings that are unexpected and, at times, impervious to mere facts" (5). Once aware of this, writers can bridge the distance between themselves and the reader through word choice and examples.

3. Students can begin by defining *connotation*: word associations derived from personal experience, reading, and the influence of others, as opposed to *denotation*, the literal meaning of a word. Flower uses the word *lakes* to illustrate the clusters of associations that are connected with a word. Engage students in a discussion of the examples; for example, ask them how *home* differs from *house*.

4. Students' responses may vary, though Flower seems to make conscious attempts to direct her diction and examples at a college audience. The second paragraph asks students to imagine themselves writing to their parents about a wilderness survival expedition they would like to join. The writers must bridge the gap between themselves and their New York City parents by communicating their desire to join this expedition in language their parents can understand. In her discussion of needs, for instance, Flower focuses on writing done on a job and in college courses—both examples of the kinds of writing that concern college students.

5. When the language used is too technical for the reader, he or she tunes out. Writers use definitions, meaningful examples, description, comparison and contrast, and tone to bridge the gap between themselves and the reader. When readers ask classmates, friends, or parents to help, the answers will vary depending on the education and background of these people.

On Voice
SUSAN ORLEAN

Preparing to Read (p. 64)
Reading aloud can reveal whether what someone has written is similar or dissimilar to his or her voice. This might be a new way of thinking for students. Orlean promotes a style of writing that is "natural, intuitive, and instinctive," but before reading her essay, students might not have had that same goal in mind. They might have been proud of writing with wit or sarcasm, even if it lacked the authenticity of their own natural speaking voice. Reading-aloud experiences might also reveal to writers their own uncertainty and hesitancy in writing. They can see how much more they mute themselves in writing than in speaking with friends. Some students may have little or no experience reading their own writing aloud.

Thinking Critically about the Text (p. 66)
Orlean explains the children's painting analogy in the following way: Children's artwork can be wonderful, but they eventually reach an age when others critique their work, pointing out the ways in which it does not represent reality (e.g., "houses don't look like that"). This, she claims, causes people to lose their visual creativity and emotional authenticity. The same happens in writing. Many students will find this analogy successful because most remember when they felt free to paint as they wished. Most will have lived through the transition of freely creating art to having to master some aspect of art. Those students may easily draw the comparison to writing. International students or students who have no recollection of creating art in their childhood might not relate to this analogy.

Discussing the Craft of Writing (p. 66)
1. Orlean describes voice as "the way the writer *talks*." Students may describe voice as being yourself; writing with honesty, authenticity, or truthfulness; or writing in a way that is not about pleasing others. Voice is foundational to uniqueness in writing, which in turn is

often a foundation of great, strong writing. As Orlean notes, being clever for its own sake is rarely as powerful as just being yourself. Students may also say that a piece without voice will not have as great an impact on the reader.

2. Self-analysis, or understanding who one is, allows a writer to be powerful, distinct, and real. In other words, you must know who you are and why you are writing to have a powerful voice. Self-analysis also helps identify the writer's purpose for writing. Strong purpose has power. Students may cite an example of a piece of writing that felt really authentic — perhaps an application essay, like one for college entrance, that required them to reveal themselves.

3. Orlean believes reading aloud offers the writer the opportunity to see how closely writing style matches speaking style. Writers can see and hear how *real* their writing sounds and whether the writing differs too much from how they might tell the same story to friends or family. She wants us to see if our writing sounds like our speaking, and reading to ourselves will not be able to reveal any discrepancies.

4. Pacing determines mood and also whether an attempt at humor will be successful. Orlean says that writers change the pace of a piece by using shorter or longer sentences. Students may note that persuasive pieces tend to move "faster" than reflective pieces. When trying to convince a reader of something, a writer may want to push her or his audience forward, whereas an essay that prompts reflecting on a poem or rethinking an older idea might take more time.

5. Orlean's editor meant that by using "bananas" as an analogy for the basketball players' feet, she was taking her readers' focus off the basketball court and introducing a new set of connotations: warm weather, palm trees, and hot beaches, all of which would distract her readers. Sending readers' focus away from her subject was not desirable; it didn't contribute to the cohesion of her writing.

6. There are differences between voice and style. Style is the total way that someone might describe your writing. This has to do with sentence structures, that is, the way the person puts words together on a written page. Voice is the natural personality or core of the writer. Voice is what you hear when you read. However, students might point out there are some elements of overlap. Voice could rightly be considered a *part* of style.

7. By describing herself as more than a writer — a gardener, a parent, and even humorously as a *doodler* — Orlean reminds readers that we are not one-dimensional. We are complex people, needing to express this complexity and our multifaceted nature through our writing. It would be a pity not to allow our written voice to be as rich as our lives.

Reading to Write
STEPHEN KING

Preparing to Read (p. 67)
Most students will see a connection between reading and writing. At a very basic level, reading can offer something to write about. Students may also say that, when they read, they get more exposure to the written word, providing them with an understanding of how good writing is supposed to look and on a deeper level, even unconsciously, an understanding of the structure and sound (voice) of good writing, all of which can help them when they write. Some students, however, might say that reading and writing are not connected. These

students might struggle with reading but like writing. For these individuals, writing can lead back into reading: The more they write, the more they begin to appreciate what others have written. It is possible that a few students may say that they don't want to be influenced by others' writing or that when they read a lot they have trouble getting started with their own writing. In these cases, the reading might either intimidate the students or overwhelm the students' ideas or voice. Ask students what they hope to get from reading. (Pleasure? Knowledge?) Do they prefer some types of writing over others? What might they learn from those preferences? How might their reading lead to writing, and how might their writing also lead to reading?

Thinking Critically about the Text (p. 71)
When King says that "quite often the bad books have more to teach than the good ones" (paragraph 2), he means that one learns what not to do as much as what to do as a writer when reading poor writing. Bad prose may be more instructive because it is easier to avoid the pitfalls of bad writing than it is to achieve the grace of great writing. Some writers might despair when reading remarkable works like *The Grapes of Wrath*, feeling they will never write anything as good. But there is inspiration in exemplary work, too. One can't achieve great heights in writing unless she or he has been "swept away" (6) by such.

Discussing the Craft of Writing (pp. 71–72)
1. King seems to find the word *zestful* artificial (and thus a mark of bad writing). He emphasizes that he doesn't think he's ever used *zestful* because for him it became synonymous with artless writing after he read that "terrible" story where Leinster "had fallen in love with the word" (paragraph 3). It was like a "vaccination" against using words that don't feel natural (and repeating them dully). King learned what to avoid in his writing by reading terrible fiction.
2. Examples of different styles that King experienced through reading include not only the bad prose of Leinster, *Valley of the Dolls*, *Flowers in the Attic*, and *The Bridges of Madison County*, but also the "green and wonderous" work of Ray Bradbury, the "clipped . . . stripped, and hardboiled" James M. Cain, and the "luxurious and Byzantine" Lovecraft (paragraph 8). King states that developing a writing style doesn't "occur in a vacuum" (8). He learned by imitating a variety of styles he admired. According to King, "[y]ou have to read widely," try on different styles, and thereby develop the tools you need to write well (8).
3. King believes it is impossible to be both a writer and a member of polite society because writers who write "truthfully" (paragraph 10) can't be concerned with whether or not they are perceived as rude or offensive in their work (and they likely will be).
4. King does not like TV because an aspiring writer does not have enough time both to read widely and to watch TV. "Reading takes time," and writers need time "to do some serious turning inward toward the life of the imagination" (paragraph 11).
5. King points out that not everyone gets joy out of a pursuit like writing, using for an example the dilemma of his son Owen, who "fell in love with Bruce Springsteen's E Street Band, particularly with Clarence Clemons, the band's burly sax player" (paragraph 13). But when Owen practiced on his saxophone, there was "no joy in it" (15). King says playing a musical instrument is the same as reading and writing. You need to find pleasure in it so it will not feel like a "rehearsal." The importance of reading, even for those who don't love writing, is that "[t]he more you read, the less apt you are to make a fool of yourself with your pen or word processor" (17).

Writing as an Act of Hope
ISABEL ALLENDE

Thinking Critically about the Text (p. 77)
Students will have different exposure to and knowledge of Latin America. Some may have origins there, others may have travelled for pleasure and others may know the region only through story and media. Many students may admit ignorance regarding the extent of corruption and the extremes of poverty, violence, lack of leadership, drugs, and tyranny. The fragility of life and governmental structures may be new to those peering in. To demonstrate the poverty, Allende contrasts the world of the rich, with their purebred "elegant dogs" and servants, with the slums where children play naked with famished mutts.

Preparing to Read (p. 73)
Many students will say that they only write for school assignments, but push them to consider the text messages they send, to-do lists they keep, or even the notes they write in birthday cards. Ask them to consider what each type of writing helps them to accomplish.

Discussing the Craft of Writing (p. 77)
1. Allende says she writes for several reasons — sometimes she writes simply because she feels compelled to do so, not knowing the reason or intended final product. She wrote one piece as a letter to a dying family member. She also writes to record history — to tell what ought not to be forgotten. Finally, the reason most elaborated in the piece is her desire to write in order to communicate. Latin American writers, she says, do not have the luxury of writing separated from the complexities that surround them. Powerless to end the corruption, drugs, crime, and poverty, they grasp onto their words; they write, "as an act of hope, a sort of communion with other men" (paragraph 14).
2. Students may interpret the line differently. Not speaking can feel like a form of exile. When not writing, Allende may have felt on the outside pulling away from, rather than leaning into, the complexities of her world. Her rich and complicated region required engagement. Perhaps silence was a way of trying to protect herself. Exiled people have no legitimate voice in the home country. They are outcasts. Therefore, it is by speaking (writing) that she found her way back in. She brought voice to where she felt she had none.
3. Student answers will vary. They will likely write about some larger social or political issue rather than a personal one, although a personal memory is a perfectly legitimate answer.
4. Writing can be something that wells up in you. Or writing may be something you feel called to do as a response to a certain political or social situation. Writing also can be something that enables you to connect with other people; in Allende's case, a dying family member. The title "Writing as an Act of Hope" speaks to her belief that, across all these forms of writing, something good can come of words.
5. This single-sentence paragraph enables Allende to shift the tone of the piece and change the direction. She had been talking about her grandfather and needed to pivot the piece to her writing, which served as a political and social commentary on Latin America. She also uses the sentences to bring the readers back to the theme of the essay, which is *why she writes*.
6. In the case of Latin America, the *dark corners* and *shadows* likely refer to the corruption; imperialist intentions; performative versus committed democracy; and the seemingly unending cycles of violence, crime, and poverty. In these shadows are the forgotten children and the corrupt politicians. These dark corners are where militaries train to protect money and power rather than individuals. You may want to ask students what *shadows* and *dark corners* they see in their own communities.

CHAPTER 4   Narration

Coming to an Awareness of Language
MALCOLM X

Preparing to Read (p. 92)
To prepare the students for this prompt, start by introducing some concepts of language — speech and vocabulary. Malcolm X explains that it is language that has empowered him. Another angle to try would be to consider why we admire people who use language in a fresh or an eloquent way.

Thinking Critically about the Text (p. 95)
Because Malcolm X was able to improve his language skills, his life changed. Is that all it takes? Even though Malcolm X communicates more effectively, there are passages in this essay where he recounts times when language escapes him. Most notable is the time when Malcolm X tries to emulate Bimbi, only to find that the words he sees in books might as well be in another language (paragraph 10). Any of these instances is a point where the class can stop and discuss what makes for effective communication. Have students talk about vocabulary or spelling lessons they had in school. Ask them if they believe reading helps improve language skills.

Questions on Subject (p. 95)
1. Malcolm X refers to himself as "the most articulate hustler" (paragraph 8) but acknowledges that his fluency in street language was not enough to make his words "functional." There is a basic difference between the spoken ("articulate hustler") and the written ("functional"), and there is an awareness that one does not naturally guarantee the other. It can be said that the difference between "functional" and "articulate" is something like the difference between "form" (functional) and "content" (articulate). Language can be said to function if it follows the prescribed order and use of nouns, verbs, and adjectives. However, articulate speech goes further; through the use of precise language and imagery, it communicates and inspires emotions and new ideas — it commands attention (8). This attempt to write meaningfully rather than merely functionally is the essential struggle faced by any serious writer. It is a valid distinction, if the reader or writer realizes that both components are necessary for successful writing.
2. The implied reason for the warden's keeping track of prisoners' conversion attempts is reasonable; any self-organization among the prison populace would be construed as a threat to authority and discipline. This reason seems relatively valid to the reader because a nongoverned prison population is seen to be at constant risk of violence and uprisings. Prison is for punishment; therefore the warden is within his rights to monitor any situation he may deem potentially harmful. The stated reason — that the warden's real concern is his own guilt for being "the devil" (paragraph 5) — is disturbing to readers (especially white readers) unfamiliar with the concept and timbre of Afrocentric rhetoric of the time. The statement reveals Malcolm X's own deep anger toward — and perhaps hatred of — whites. A reader may be confused by the disparity between the two assertions, but it will become apparent that these words represent a doctrine and, as such, will arouse either wholehearted agreement or complete disagreement, depending on the individual reader.

3. Malcolm X refers to the fact that even though he is institutionalized, he has never been freer in his life (paragraph 17). Yet the nature of this freedom is a mitigated one, dependent on a tenuous relationship between the freedom that books and knowledge have given him and the freedom of returning to society. In this sense, the language and education that the books in prison provide are liberating. They have liberated his mind from the confines of the penitentiary, enabling him to forget that his body remains confined to a cell.

Questions on Strategy (p. 95)

1. Because Malcolm X was the leader of an entire sociopolitical movement for African Americans, it is important that his words be taken directly from him and not recycled second- or thirdhand. The power of his message can be felt more strongly through the use of "I"; the reader is actually getting the benefit of direct communication with Malcolm X.
2. Responses will vary according to the levels of understanding of the students. Worth noting are the facts that Malcolm X took great care and effort to copy the dictionary and to expand his horizons and that he took pride in his postprison activism.
3. Malcolm X is quick to suggest that his experience with language was liberating. He speaks of having "written words that [he] never knew were in the world" (paragraph 15). His vocabulary marks a man who has taught himself to speak in a form of Standard English. One of Malcolm X's goals is to share his struggles with the English language. He accomplishes this goal by excluding multisyllabic or hard-to-spell words, in exchange for clear prose that makes his feelings accessible to a wide variety of readers, from children to adults.
4. Malcolm implies that knowledge is power and education is freedom. Before undertaking his homemade education, Malcolm X believed that he "not only wasn't articulate, [he] wasn't even functional" (paragraph 8). By the end he had power and felt "truly free" (17). Malcolm X learned that he needed to become the person he wanted to be.
5. The events of Malcolm X's narrative could be diagrammed into a causal chain similar to this: Dictionary > Inadequacy > Literacy > Freedom. The story is told with an emphasis on the causal links in the narrative. Emphasizing these links brings the reader along the same personal growth path as that of Malcolm X. When the reader participates in this causal chain, the powerful realization that Malcolm X comes to (education and literacy create freedom) is not just read about but experienced.

Questions on Diction and Vocabulary (pp. 95–96)

1. Examples of Malcolm X's street-savvy voice include "the hustling world" (paragraph 1); "slick, sharp-looking hustlers" (2); "trying some hype to shake up the warden's office" (3); and "Look, daddy, let me pull your coat about a cat" (8).
2. Responses will vary according to students' ways of learning. Some strategies that might come up in discussion are appealing to authority (dictionary, parents, teachers), listening to how others use words (learning by example), or guessing at the meaning (trial and error). Each strategy can lead to finding meaning. You may want to discuss the pros or cons of each approach.
3. *Hustler* (paragraph 2): one who uses fraudulent or unscrupulous methods to obtain money; a swindler. *Slick* (2): sly; shrewdly adroit. *Hype* (3): a swindle, deception, or trick. *Frustrated* (8): disappointed; helplessly dismayed. *Emulate* (10): to attempt to imitate so as to equal or surpass. *Riffling* (12): flipping hastily with the fingers. *Inevitable* (17): sure to occur, happen, or come.

The Terror
JUNOT DÍAZ

Preparing to Read (p. 98)
Not all students are avid readers. If students struggle to find responses, prompt them to share the books (or poems or plays) they read for class while in middle school and ask whether any of the material made an impact on them. Remind students that the impact can be either positive or negative.

Thinking Critically about the Text (p. 101)
Students may share stories about being bullied. If they do not, you can ask them to share a story about someone they know who was bullied or if they remember bullying someone else.

Questions on Subject (p. 101)
1. Díaz attributes the name-calling he experienced to "white middle-class bigotry." There must have been stories circulating that people from the Dominican Republic ate dogs. They called him a "sand nigger" likely because he was a darker-skinned man from an island country.
2. Díaz most likely told his brother that he was having a great time because he was ashamed of the bullying and because his brother — who was sick with leukemia — had his own struggles. Díaz may not have wanted to burden his brother. He likely believed his sick brother could do little to help him.
3. "Being afraid" suggests a more constant state of being whereas "fear" suggests a momentary emotion. People living in war-torn countries, for example, are *afraid*. They live "in" fear. Fear is a more momentary experience, like when we lose control of our car in a snow storm. We experience fear in that moment, but we do not necessarily say that we are afraid of driving. Díaz's fear became constant — immutable like his brown skin. This constant fear made him afraid.
4. Díaz attributed his safety to his vigilant efforts to avoid the brothers. If he changed the game, even very slightly, he feared disturbing the universe's delicate balance. It is possible, however, that the brothers lost interest in him immediately after the fight. But Díaz had to gather the courage to test their disinterest in him. He had to challenge his belief that he was safe only if he hid. In doing so, he freed himself.

Questions on Strategy (pp. 101–102)
1. By providing the context first, the reader sees the narrator as even more vulnerable. Many readers appreciate the tenderness of that life stage and may be touched by his brother's sickness. This causes readers to feel sympathy for the narrator even before he takes his beating. By the time he is beaten, readers jump to his defense. If he had described the beating in the first paragraph, readers may not have felt as close to him. Díaz's structure creates the possibility that the reader, along with Díaz, feels personally attacked.
2. First-person point of view creates a greater sense of intimacy between the narrator and the reader. Third person creates a kind of distance. We can separate ourselves from our vulnerability, as can the author. In first person, we dive in together. Anything that happens to the narrator happens to us. Our destinies are united during the reading of the piece, which can increase reader engagement.

3. Díaz offers these details about his brother, "40 pounds lighter and barely able to piss under his own power, looking as if he were one bad cold away from the grave" (paragraph 3). The details show the brother's proximity to death. The details are fresh and reflect the sensibilities of an adolescent, not an adult. The phrase, "barely able to piss under his own power" may shock some readers. Because it is an uncommon way to describe leukemia, the statement may increase reader alertness. The observation might be something that stands out to an adolescent.

4. By shifting tenses, Díaz brings the readers into the action. Successful writing carries writers through a variety of emotions at varying tempos. Shifting tenses brings readers into the fight, making it hard for the reader to turn away.

5. In paragraph 2, Díaz places himself in the seventh grade. In paragraph 3, Díaz lets us know his father left the year prior. After the family fell into poverty, his brother was diagnosed with leukemia. In paragraph 5, we learn the "beat-down" occurred after his brother was already in the hospital. In paragraph 6, we learn Díaz goes home to an empty house and returns to school the next day with a black eye. Díaz exists in a state of fear from the beat-down until sophomore year in high school (13). As a sophomore, he faces his fears and presumably lives the rest of his days feeling much less afraid. The sequence of events tells readers the age of the author, the context in which he was living, and the duration of the fear.

6. The fragments show the fragmented thinking of a child still in development. They also reflect the nature of inner thoughts, which are rarely fully formed — they are more notions and impressions than fully formed ideas. The fragments also show a child who lived largely in his own mind. He did not live in full sentences. He lived in books and had few friends around. He seemed to live in bursts and retractions — going out into the world to attend school but then quickly retreating to the safety of his home and his own mind.

Questions on Diction and Vocabulary (p. 102)

1. By "deep in the vulnerability matrix," Díaz means that he is already experiencing a sense of defenselessness. He had no father, he had a brother who was on the verge of death, he attended a new school filled with bigoted students, and he was in the middle of the already awkward phase of adolescence.

2. In paragraph 6, Díaz uses a more formal phrase: "I didn't actually lose any teeth or break any limbs or misplace an eye." He also uses the more informal phrase, "no one noticed that I had gotten stomped." The formal/informal mix demonstrates Díaz's skillful ability to narrate the event from the perspective of an adult. The informal phrases show us that he can zoom right back into the mind of his younger self. In this way, we live the events through both perspectives. We can relate to the adult and also to the child. The contrast also highlights the vulnerability of the child who, at the time, did not have access to this older, wiser, less fearful self.

3. *Bigotry* (paragraph 2): prejudice or intolerance for one different from oneself. *Leukemia* (3): cancer of the blood cells. *Hypervigilant* (10): very aware of one's surroundings. *Remission* (13): when there is no longer evidence of cancer in the body. It can be complete or partial.

Not Close Enough for Comfort
DAVID P. BARDEEN

Preparing to Read (p. 104)
Students will have a variety of stories about people keeping secrets from them. This prompt is an opportunity for students to reflect on how secrets have affected their relationships. You may want to ask students if they think keeping secrets from people can be a good thing or a hurtful thing.

Thinking Critically about the Text (p. 106)
Will once questioned David about his sexual orientation, so he probably was not totally surprised by David's revelation. When David came out, Will asked several questions, perhaps suggesting a lack of surprise. However, Will's calmness could be a reflection of the distance that had grown between the twins. Knowing his brother had kept a secret from him may have also made Will feel betrayed and not trusted. For Will, David's sexual orientation could be further proof that they had more differences than similarities, making closeness even more challenging. Some students might suggest that Will distanced himself from David out of a fear that he too might be gay or be labeled gay.

Questions on Subject (pp. 106–107)
1. Bardeen probably had many reasons for not telling his brother sooner. As a teenager Bardeen seemed afraid of his sexual orientation and withdrew from most relationships (paragraph 11). Later, he probably feared being rejected by his brother and losing their close relationship. Maybe he thought Will would push him away, fearing that he too might be gay or be labeled gay.
2. It is often said that twins feel closer to each other than to any other person in the world and that twins share an almost psychic bond. However, twins are individuals who have their own feelings, thoughts, and desires; like non-twins, they keep secrets from each other. The word *romantic* refers to the idealized but impractical belief that the relationship between twins is different from that between any other two siblings. In fact, an individual can hardly ever truly be known by another, even if a twin.
3. Bardeen apologizes to his brother for keeping such a large secret from him. Will's response to David is, "No I think it's great" (paragraph 17), which can be read as Will thinking that David apologized for being gay.
4. Bardeen probably hoped that coming out would bring him and his brother closer together, or at least explain some of the distance they felt. Students may think this hope was unrealistic because the gulf between the brothers seemed so wide. At the same time, the revelation might offer the brothers some insight into why their relationship waned.
5. Bardeen's secret had created a gulf between him and his brother (paragraph 14). Students will have different ideas about what will be necessary to heal the relationship. If Bardeen could say to Will everything he writes in his essay, the brothers would have a good chance of healing their relationship.

Questions on Strategy (p. 107)
1. Bardeen uses first-person point of view because coming-out is telling one's own story in one's own voice. Third-person point of view would create the sense that Bardeen was hiding himself and not being honest to himself or his audience about his secret.

2. Bardeen bookends his coming-out to others (paragraphs 3–6) with his conversation with his brother, contrasting how "easy" it was to confide in people who didn't know him with how difficult it was to confide in someone with whom he was once extremely close. Paragraphs 3 through 6 explain how Bardeen built up the courage to talk to David and the process he went through to come out to other people in his life. Had Bardeen begun his narrative with paragraphs 3 through 6, the gravity of his discussion with David—the deliberation and thoughts he was having as they talked—would not have been expressed with the same urgency or emotion.
3. The dialogue shows the nature of the brothers' relationship and how hard it has become for them, despite the closeness they once shared, to talk to each other. The clipped dialogue captures the tension of the conversation.
4. Bardeen uses short sentences and sentence fragments to reflect his fear and hesitation about coming out to his brother. The clipped sentences illustrate how difficult it is for the brothers to communicate now that they have grown apart.
5. The title suggests that too much distance can be more uncomfortable than too much closeness. Students will differ in how well they think the title captures the essence of the brothers' relationship. The brothers' conversations, and their inability to stay abreast of each other's lives, suggest that for both brothers the distance has become uncomfortable.
6. Students will have different opinions about whether the similarities or the differences were more interesting and revealing. Many students may find the similarities in paragraph 6 unusual and remarkable: The brothers went to college together, had similar friends, and lived in the same city. Students may find the differences in paragraph 11 sad and revealing: As teenagers, Will became engaged with the world; David withdrew. David's sullenness enables the reader to understand that he withdrew from many people, not just from Will. These differences, rather than the similarities, shed more light on the brothers' growing distance.

Questions on Diction and Vocabulary (pp. 107–108)

1. Students may find Bardeen's voice apologetic and wistful—apologetic for lying to his brother, and wistful about the relationship he wants to rebuild. Bardeen's diction tells the reader that he values the closeness he once had with his brother and that he will dedicate time and energy to bridging the gap that has emerged between them.
2. Bardeen uses the word *fraud* because it reflects his feelings of guilt for misleading people. He says "in an unforgiving sense" (paragraph 4) to temper the harsh feelings he has about himself for not coming out to the important people in his life. Students might suggest terms such as *hiding*, *pretending*, or *protecting* as replacements for *fraud*.
3. *Baffled* (paragraph 6): perplexed. *Melancholy* (11): depression; rejection; gloom. *Demeanor* (11): conduct. *Sullen* (11): gloomily silent; morose. *Intimacy* (19): familiarity; something of a deeply personal or private nature.

Stranger Than True
BARRY WINSTON

Preparing to Read (p. 110)
Students are likely to have many different opinions about this issue, especially in light of the media attention that has been given to celebrity cases. When evidence is made public and seems to point to a person's guilt, many would like simply to convict the person and

dispense with the trial. But they must remember that the right to a trial is at the heart of our judicial process and that we need to let the process play itself out for the system to work. Trials ensure that the accused get their day in court and that the public does not rush to judgment.

Thinking Critically about the Text (p. 113)
Students have told us that Winston's story shows how the "system" can protect innocent people even when all the evidence appears to be stacked against them. In other cases, they believe that lawyers are needed to make sure that "guilty" clients are accorded all their rights. You might even try asking students how they would feel if they were accused of something they had not done and were not allowed a lawyer themselves.

Questions on Subject (pp. 113–114)
1. As the D.A. says in paragraph 10, "[I]n a case like this, I gotta put on witnesses. Weird Wally is on the bench. If I try to go without witnesses, he might throw me out." The D.A.'s decision is ironic because without the witnesses the plea bargain might have gone through and the truth might never have been known.
2. Holloway was reluctant to talk with Winston because he was scared. After telling Trooper Johnson what he thought had happened the night of the accident, he realizes that he told him "wrong, and I was scared and I didn't know what to do, and that's why . . . why I wouldn't talk to you [Winston]" (paragraph 15). Holloway might have been afraid that it would appear he had lied to the trooper.
3. Holloway decides to speak up because his conscience is bothering him—he knows that he cannot let the young man plead guilty when he is not guilty. Winston apparently believed that it would be worse "to piss off the judge by objecting" than to "listen to a lecture on the evils of drink from this jerk Holloway" (paragraph 14). His snap decision not to object turns out to be right even if Winston himself cannot articulate his reasons for resisting his instincts to object.
4. In the words of Yogi Berra, Winston's point seems to be "It ain't over 'til it's over." In letting our legal system work the way it was intended to work, justice prevails and even lawyers can be surprised. In the end, if only one innocent person whom everybody believes is guilty is exonerated, then lawyers can feel justified in defending clients when they "know" they are guilty.

Questions on Strategy (p. 114)
1. To establish the context of the story, Winston tells the reader that it is a true story and the reader can verify the facts. He goes on to explain how he got the law case, what the "kid" tells him, in essence all the details of how his client came to attend the party, how much he drank, at what intervals he drank the beers, and how he came to be in the hospital. The kid tells him all that he can remember but also that he cannot remember events from a certain time forward.
2. Winston includes only those details he knows, thus keeping readers guessing as he himself is guessing. Of course, one would like to have had the testimony of the victim in the crash, but she has died. If she were alive or her brother could remember who was driving the car, the case would never have gone to trial. When students suggest information that Winston omitted, have them explain what it would contribute to the story.
3. The first paragraph sets the pace of Winston's narrative. The sentences are short and punchy, and they come fast—just as you might imagine him to speak. He is rather

excitable and he is all business. He also wants his story to convey a sense of events moving quickly and routinely, possibly to make all the more dramatic the sudden twist the story takes in paragraph 15.

4. Winston alerts us to the bizarre nature of his story by being ironic. He says, in effect: This story is so bizarre it has got to be true and you can check for yourself. Such a statement also establishes his credibility as a narrator.

5. Winston uses dialogue more in the courtroom scene than elsewhere in the story to give a sense of immediacy and drama to the way the story concludes. Winston would rather create the scene at this critical juncture than be so obviously a narrator—he would rather show than tell. Earlier the situation was not so critical, and he needed merely to give background quickly and accurately.

6. Winston is not so much concerned with drawing fine distinctions when it comes to Mr. and Mrs. Thorne or Trooper Johnson. They are pretty much ordinary characters, two innocent bystanders and a police officer doing his duty. The author is concerned, instead, with what he feels is the strange behavior of Mr. Holloway, and his presumptions about him are not good. So Winston paints a picture of him as a wimp and a moralizer and someone who does not understand what is going on—and someone who is also afraid of getting involved. Well, he is, but not for the reasons that Winston believes and not for the reasons he leads the reader to believe. Holloway is afraid because, in his mind, he has done wrong. Consequently, Holloway is presented as more interesting than the other witnesses to the accident. The story rides on his character.

Questions on Diction and Vocabulary (p. 114)

1. Winston is all business, pretty much an average, what-you-see-is-what-you-get kind of guy. His voice is established through his sometimes rather rough diction: for example, "striped-ass ape" (paragraph 5); "what the hell can he do" (6); "Why the hell have you got all those people here?" (9); "That jerk Holloway" (9); "piss off the judge" (14).

2. Winston does not have high hopes for the kid, and yet he puts his faith in the fact that he is trying to do the best he can for him legally. His tone reveals that he believes he should defend his client to the best of his ability and see where the case takes them both. He lets us know in no uncertain terms how annoyed he is with himself for not being more in control and decisive about whether he should challenge Mr. Holloway's request to make a statement: "All my bells are ringing at once, and my gut is screaming at me, Object! Object! I'm trying to decide in three quarters of a second whether it'll be worse to listen to a lecture on the evils of drink from this jerk Holloway or piss off the judge by objecting" (paragraph 14). In the end, Winston is as incredulous as anyone else yet falls back on his legal training with the following smug pronouncement: "And that's why I can stand to represent somebody when I know he's guilty" (16). That statement, of course, is meant to get us all thinking about prejudging, not just in legal situations but everywhere else in life as well.

3. *Felony* (paragraph 1): any of several crimes such as murder, rape, or burglary that are thought to be more serious than a misdemeanor. *Agitated* (7): upset or disturbed. *Misdemeanor* (8): an offense of lesser gravity than a felony for which the punishment may be a fine or imprisonment in a minimum rather than a higher security facility. *Probation* (8): the action of suspending the sentence of one convicted of a minor offense and the granting of freedom on the promise of good behavior. *Bolt* (9): to move or spring forward suddenly.

Don't Peak in High School
MINDY KALING

Preparing to Read (p. 116)
Students will have widely varied high school experiences, and some may have the sort of experience that Kaling advises against. If that is the case, try to keep the focus on how the disparate high school experiences can all translate into a successful college career.

Thinking Critically about the Text (p. 119)
Most students (at least in the United States) will not have received the message that being quiet and observant was an admirable quality for a teenager. Teenagers are encouraged to play leading roles in sports, theater, social groups, and classes. Advertising encourages young people to buy products that will make them shine and become even more noticeable. These products suggest that their use will bring more friends, more notoriety, and — perhaps most important — desirable boyfriends or girlfriends. Kaling's essay challenges the messages coming from the media and movies. She uses the essay to support the less told, but probably much healthier, storylines.

Questions on Subject (p. 119)
1. Kaling describes her childhood as controlled and isolated from much of the stereotypical school experience. In paragraph 3, she talks about her ignorance about drugs due, in part, to the lack of parties she attended. Her parents controlled the amount of television she watched and had her focus on acing her PSATs and participating in clubs. She does not seem to resent her parents for this kind of control. In fact, in paragraph 9, she says, "in high school, I had fun in my academic clubs, watching movies with my girlfriends, learning Latin . . .," and she also enjoyed time with her family.
2. The numbers may not match for a number of reasons. First, the mismatch suggests that there are more than two ways to find success. There are limitless ways. The mismatching numbers makes a humorous case for pursuing education. Being able to count is important. How successful could one be without an education? Last, the mismatch tests the reader's alertness.
3. She means *overlooked* in many senses: overlooked by peers that did not invite her to parties; overlooked by older men who did not return her affection or admiration; and, more generally, overlooked by media, movies, and songs that did not find her storyline worthy of retelling. Her story shines a light on that *overlooked* child who now seems to be quite the opposite. You may want to ask students to consider if her feeling of being overlooked might be what compels her now to stay in the spotlight.
4. The thesis is in the title, "Don't Peak in High School" and in paragraph 1, her number three way to get where she is "stay in school and be a respectful and hardworking wallflower, and go to an accredited non-online university."

Questions on Strategy (p. 119)
1. In paragraph 2, Kaling broadens the discussion to include teenage girls worrying about being popular in high school.
2. Kaling starts the essay by introducing the topic and her thesis, *don't peak in high school.* Then she talks a bit about her experience, the cultural messages about what teenage life is supposed to be like (paragraphs 4–6). She then offers an alternative narrative to the

iconic song "Jack and Diane" (7–8). She concludes saying how satisfying she found her quieter experience and reminds teenagers that life extends beyond high school. Speaking less about herself helps her focus on larger cultural narratives. Her personal story can inspire individuals, but by speaking broadly and offering alternative models for admirable teenage behavior, she can begin to shift the culture.

3. Kaling's references to songs and television shows help the reader become consciously aware of where she might have picked up some of her stories about the ideal way to be. By pointing out these widely known names, she helps readers wake up within the culturally constructed dream. When identified and critiqued, young people are less likely to be driven by these stories. Students may note that these shows and songs may be less recognizable to today's teenagers who do not know *21 Jump Street*.

4. Kaling describes, for example, under what conditions she could watch television and what she could watch. Noting that she learned that pot and marijuana were the same thing on *21 Jump Street* demonstrates that she did not hang out with people using or talking about drugs. These details are useful because they might help students recognize themselves. They can feel less ashamed by their own ignorance of certain things. If they have or had similar experiences, she helps them stop feeling bad about them.

Questions on Diction and Vocabulary (pp. 119–120)

1. The combination of tones helps Kaling both connect with teenagers and demonstrate what her education made possible. Had she only spoken like a teenager, she could appear less educated and even less wise. Using a solely sophisticated tone could make her sound too removed from the teenage experience to be seen as a role model. Or she might simply feel too inaccessible to readers. Readers might feel that if someone who they can relate to has become so successful, then maybe they could be successful too.

2. By addressing teenage girls, Kaling indicates to the readers the intended audience of her essay. Even adult women and men can likely relate, however. More mature women may still harbor some shame about their teenage years. Men also had their own pressures. Her final line to John Cougar Mellencamp challenges one of the creators of larger cultural storylines. She pushes those who are writing songs, stories, television shows, and movies to tell a better story.

3. Using the words *guess* and *a little* performs at least two functions. First, such use contributes to the informal tone of the essay. These words also soften the reader's resistance to Kaling's opinion. The song is well loved by many and a direct attack might put off some readers. This way she can softly and gently present an alternative response to the song.

4. *Gleaned* (paragraph 3): gathered material bit by bit. *Anthem* (5): a stirring popular song that speaks to a particular group, subculture, viewpoint, or age group. *Loitering* (8): to hang out in an area without a particular purpose. *Franchised* (9): legal arrangement for the purchased right to a business and its branding from the corporate or governmental owner. *Unrequited* (10): not reciprocated.

CHAPTER 5 Description

A Woman on the Street
JEANNETTE WALLS

Preparing to Read (p. 136)
Most students will probably see the homeless as a kind of "other," people with whom they have little in common and maybe even fear. There is a tendency to think of the homeless as a unified group rather than as individuals that share a single attribute: They have no fixed roof over their head. It might be different if they have known someone homeless, been homeless themselves, or worked with the homeless.

Thinking Critically about the Text (p. 139)
Seeing her mother helps Walls see herself. For most readers, seeing someone who is homeless won't prompt this reflection because someone who is homeless will seem very different from themselves. Walls cannot so easily discount the differences because the homeless person she saw was her mother. When Walls walks back into her own home, she sees it through her mother's eyes. Nice furnishings and a comfortable existence are a stark contrast to her mother's Dumpster diving.

Questions on Subject (p. 139)
1. From Walls's presentation of her dialogue with her mother, her mother *seems* happy. She does not complain or bemoan her situation. Yet the state of her body and her lack of self-care might suggest otherwise. We cannot know from the essay how truly happy her mother is, although she seems less perturbed than her daughter regarding their differences in lifestyles.
2. Walls seems more disturbed than her mother about their different lifestyles and her attitudes about those differences. We cannot tell how happy Walls is overall in her life, although we see that, in regard to her parents, she feels no peace. In fact, she says that she cannot truly enjoy her life knowing how her parents have chosen to live. She is also pained by her embarrassment of them.
3. Walls's mother tells Walls that she thinks people are too wasteful, but she has also asked for perfume in the past, so we do not really know whether she is against all material possessions as an absolute principle, or if she feels she just does not need them for herself. It seems she doesn't approve of her daughter's values, but we do not know to what extent this has to do with material possessions.
4. Walls's mother might not like to see her daughter's apartment because, in seeing it, she herself might have to face the painful difference in their life circumstances. It might be easier to judge her daughter's lifestyle in an abstract way rather than face it literally. Just as it was difficult for Walls to see her mother dig through the trash, perhaps it would have been as difficult for her mother to see Walls's apartment.
5. Her mother is trying to make Walls see how uncomfortable she is with herself. She wants Walls to see the importance of self-acceptance. She believes her daughter focuses on the wrong things in life. We do not know whether this means her choice of career, her choice of husband, or how she values and uses money. Her mother's criticism is broad. Presumably, readers will share more of Walls's values than her mother's, so students will

have to reflect on their own values to answer this question. Does valuing creature comforts mean that one's values are confused? Student answers will vary.

Questions on Strategy (p. 139)

1. Walls describes her mother with "long hair streaked with gray, tangled and matted, and her eyes had sunk deep into their sockets" (paragraph 2). She seems to enjoy her life, "rooting happily through a Dumpster" (5). Her mother was also someone who used to be active (cliff diving) and artistic (painting in the desert) and in fact still values commenting on the arts (a recent Picasso exhibit). She seems articulate and educated. She is also a married woman with a husband who seems to share her values.
2. Walls describes herself as someone living on Park Avenue, well-dressed (wearing heels) with an active social life (she was headed to a party when she saw her mother). She is someone who has invested time in designing a home that feels comfortable and appealing to her. She has spent time framing artwork and creating a cozy atmosphere. She has a husband who works late, presumably with a good and high-paying job. Walls tells the reader and her mother that she is embarrassed by her parents' lifestyle. We know that she has offered to help them multiple times, and they have refused.
3. The whole excerpt is a contrast between the life choices made by Walls and her mother. They seem to share only a love of art and a love of each other. Otherwise, their values are quite different. The chapter opens with Walls dressed for a party and heading out in a cab, a stark contrast to her mother digging through a Dumpster. The difference is also in their attitudes, with her mother seemingly acting "happily" while Walls felt ashamed and ran home. Her mother seemed to have no shame about her own life.
4. The article was arranged using induction. Induction is about reasoning toward a conclusion. It moves from the particular to the general. We learned about each woman's lifestyle choices by hearing about the details. This helped us to understand Walls's experiences and feelings. The essay did not start with some general declaration that Walls then had to prove.
5. Walls appears to be a reliable narrator because she does not hide her own shame (admitting she hid from her mother) or her own inner conflicts (feeling uncomfortable living in her nice home while her parents lived in the streets). This builds the reader's trust. She does not try too hard to make herself look good. She tells readers that she has tried to help her family, but they refused. When she meets her mother at the Chinese restaurant, we see firsthand this refusal to accept help.
6. The single sentence in paragraph 4 encapsulates very clearly Walls's shame (hiding in the seat) and the difference in their lifestyles (she lives on Park Avenue and takes taxis around the city). Its brevity draws attention to these issues, emphasizing their importance to the piece.

Questions on Diction and Vocabulary (pp. 139–140)

1. Words representing Walls's life include *Park Avenue, overdressed, elevator man, polished wood floor, Vivaldi, Persian rugs,* and *overstuffed leather armchair*. Words representing her mother's life include *Dumpster, trash, childish glee, tangled, matted, grime,* and *bulky*. These terms highlight the difference in their lives. Walls is living a stereotypical highbrow lifestyle in New York City, surrounded by the expensive objects in her home, classical music, and fashionable clothes. Her mother is living with seemingly more glee, but she does not groom and survives on the scraps others leave behind.
2. Her mother seems to be ironic when she asks for the electrolysis treatment. She is mocking the notion that a woman needs such treatment to feel good about herself as a woman.

She's showing her daughter that she can feel good about herself without all those modern-day trappings.
3. Student answers will vary. The title highlights three important points. First, "a woman on the street" is not just a stand-alone stranger but a person who is someone's mother or daughter. She has an identity that connects her to society and to humanity. Second, the title reminds readers that being "a woman" is something Walls and her mother share. Their experiences are vastly different, and yet fundamental parts of their existence are the same. Third, the title emphasizes the moment of Walls's wishful thinking, wanting to pretend that the "woman on the street" is a random stranger she can justify ignoring, when in reality the woman is so much more. Students may have a variety of ideas for alternate titles. If you ask them to focus on the themes, they might suggest "My Mother on the Street," "My Family Secret," or "Lessons from My Mother."

The Barrio
ROBERT RAMÍREZ

Preparing to Read (p. 141)
Students always find something to write about when describing a neighborhood in which they've lived. They often focus on their house or apartment, school, places they frequented, family, or friends. We like to ask how many students have lived in a single town or city or at the same address their whole lives, live in an ethnic neighborhood, or live in the same town or city as their grandparents or other relatives. Students who come from older, more established neighborhoods often have different stories to tell about their sense of community than do students from the suburbs. A sense of community can grow out of a shared history and feelings of connection to a place. Students cite ethnicity and extended families as factors contributing to a sense of community.

Thinking Critically about the Text (p. 144)
Most students have mixed feelings about wanting to visit or live in the barrio. Many are curious enough to want to visit, but few are willing to commit to live there. Invariably they start by pointing to the positive qualities of life in the barrio, especially the strong feelings of family. However, they always come back to the negative elements—the severe overcrowding, the feelings of being trapped, and the perpetuation of the past at the expense of a future.

Questions on Subject (pp. 144–145)
1. *Barrio* is a Spanish word that refers to a chiefly Spanish-speaking neighborhood, typically in a city in the southwestern United States. Ramírez generally describes barrios as isolated communities "fenced off by railroads, canals, and expressways" (paragraph 2). The train image transports readers into the barrio in the opening paragraphs and out at the end. The train tracks are a reminder of the boundary between the barrio and the outside world.
2. One way that the barrios of the Southwest are paradoxical is that they are traditional communities hemmed in by signs of progress (railroads and highways). In addition, while the barrio is enclosed, once inside, the boundaries become quite fluid, so that "[m]embers of the barrio describe the entire area as their home" (paragraph 4).
3. For the residents of the barrio, it is "a refuge from the harshness and the coldness of the Anglo world" (paragraph 4); as a result, most members of the barrio have no desire to

leave. Rejected by the outside world, these castoffs have banded together in the barrio where all their needs—material as well as emotional and spiritual—are met.

4. In paragraph 13, Ramírez explains how the bright neon colors of the houses catch viewers' eyes and stimulate their curiosity. The "orange, chartreuse, lime-green, yellow, and mixtures of these and other hues" highlight the individuality of each home (paragraph 13). The outside world stands in sharp contrast. While the barrio is refreshing, the Anglo suburb is "narcotizing like revolting rows of similar houses, which neither offend nor please" (13).

5. The owners of the *tortillería, panadería*, corner grocery, barbershop, pool hall, and *cantina* appear to be financially independent. As Ramírez explains, "Many lower-income families of the barrio manage to maintain a comfortable standard of living through the communal action of family members who contribute their wages to the head of the family" (paragraph 16). For those poor families who have not achieved financial security, life is miserable. They "remain trapped in the nineteenth century and survive as best they can" (18).

Questions on Strategy (p. 145)

1. Ramírez compares the fences in the barrio with the walls of the Anglo community to symbolize the easy interaction among the people of his culture compared with the isolation and separation within the Anglo world.

2. Metaphors appear in a number of places throughout Ramírez's essay:
Paragraph 1: "this pulsing light . . . beats slower, like a weary heartbeat"
4: "from the angry seeds of rejection grow the flowers of closeness between outcasts, not the thorns of bitterness"
5: "the warmth of the tortilla factory is a wool *sarape*"
17: "Their houses, aged and bent, oozing children, are fissures in the horn of plenty."
These metaphors compare things common to the barrio with other things that are relevant to it. The wool sarape is as common as the factory. The horn of plenty, broken and empty, is also a metaphor for the people of the barrio.

3. Had Ramírez begun his description of the barrio with the negative aspects of life there, he would have risked having readers misunderstand the intent of his essay. Ramírez wants us to understand that life in the barrio is satisfying and necessary. He saves the sadder aspects of life there until the end, so that readers do not confuse his desire for our understanding with a desire for pity.

4. The shopkeeper extends credit to those unable to pay (paragraph 7). The young men perform rituals of manhood for the approval or disapproval of the old men who only watch (10). Families—extended, large, inclusive of neighbors—maintain the sense of belonging, order, and tradition that keeps the people of the barrio here. Even the poor of the barrio serve as a visual reminder of the attitudes and isolation of the Anglo community outside its borders (11 and 12).

5. In paragraph 12, Ramírez talks about the barrio as "closeness." He says, "The feeling of family, a rare and treasurable sentiment, pervades and accounts for the inability of the people to leave. The barrio is this attitude manifested on the countenances of the people, on the faces of their homes, and in the gaiety of their gardens" (12). In paragraphs 17 and 18, however, Ramírez presents the darker side of the barrio. This is the barrio of the families who have not achieved a sense of financial security. These "poorer barrio families remain trapped in the nineteenth century and survive as best they can" (18). One gets the impression from Ramírez that change is occurring in the rest of the world and that the outside world is leaving the barrio behind. Change "eludes their reach, in their own backyards, and the people, unable and unwilling to see the future, or even touch the present, perpetuate the past" (2).

Questions on Diction and Vocabulary (p. 145)

1. The Spanish phrases, spoken as if the reader understands them, lend an aura of authenticity and color to Ramírez's essay. These words allow us to hear the people of the barrio. The other words—*home, refuge, family,* and *closeness*—connote warmth, community, intimacy, and friendliness. They are meant to emphasize the positive feelings of life in the barrio that are known only to its inhabitants.

2. In this essay, the word *leprous* connotes disease, ugliness, contagiousness, and isolation. Like lepers, the Chicano residents of the barrio have been shunned by the Anglo world and relegated to their isolated section of town. Ramírez's use of this strong language hammers home the harsh reality of life in the barrio and serves to remind readers that barrio inhabitants essentially are seen and treated as outsiders and outcasts in the larger society.

3. In the first paragraph alone, students will find several examples of personification: A streetlight "beats slower, like a weary heartbeat" and "the barrio is deep asleep." The class might debate whether in "metal wheels squealing" and "the train shudders" Ramírez uses personification or simple description.

Hiding from Animals
HELEN MACDONALD

Preparing to Read (p. 148)

In additional to describing the emotions they associate with nature, students might also describe a specific place or a general location (mountains, ocean) which appeals to them. You might want to discuss the lure (or turnoff) of such places and invite students to consider what makes the outdoors so appealing to some while repelling others.

Thinking Critically about the Text (p. 151)

Macdonald's purpose in writing the essay is to introduce readers to the interesting tensions involved in wildlife observation. Hides, used to observe animals, paradoxically connect and separate wildlife observers from the very landscape that is the source of their wonder. She engages non-naturalist readers by not assuming any background knowledge about hides. She describes in detail the look, smell, and feel of the hide and what it allows and prohibits. This piques the curiosity of readers not familiar with this form of wildlife observation.

Questions on Subject (p. 151)

1. A hide is a building whose purpose is to make humans invisible so they can observe wildlife. Photographic blinds are earlier versions of the hide that were presumably designed specifically for photographers. Both are for observation. Other earlier versions were used to conceal hunters.

2. Macdonald is disappearing from the gaze of animals. She is making herself invisible to the animal kingdom.

3. By comparing the hide window to a television screen, Macdonald is pointing out the passivity and separation from the world one observes. One is not an actor either on TV or in the hide — one simply observes the behavior of others.

4. The unspoken rules in hides are be silent (or speak in a murmur), and do not make or take phone calls, slam the door, extend hands out the windows, or — at least in Great Britain — correct others if they misidentify an animal. These rules are in place to help make humans invisible to the animals.
5. You can hide to take a picture, witness a rare animal, hunt, experience the meditative patience required, separate oneself from the landscape, become an observer, or witness "true reality."

Questions on Strategy (p. 152)
1. The first-person perspective works well for this piece because many readers may be unfamiliar with hides and their complexities. By maintaining the first-person perspective, Macdonald allows the reader to journey along with her and also experience a bit of the hide. The first-person point of view allows the reader almost to smell the wood, see the otters, and feel the uncomfortable tensions when too many individuals come to the hide.
2. In paragraph 4, Macdonald says that "turning yourself into a pair of eyes in a darkened box distances you from the all-encompassing landscape around the hide, reinforcing a divide between human and natural worlds, encouraging us to think that animals and plants should be looked at but not interacted with . . ."
3. Macdonald narrates in paragraph 2. This narration gives readers a sense of what it can feel like in the hide. In paragraph 9, she narrates about a hide with a group of people restraining themselves from correcting the incorrect identification of a large brown rat. This narration invites the reader into the uncomfortable social situations that can exist. Readers can feel, and even laugh a bit, at the tensions that Macdonald introduces them to in the essay.
4. Macdonald compares observing hides with hunting hides in paragraph 3. This helps readers understand the distinction between observing out of interest and reverence compared to observing for food or sport. She compares the window to a TV screen in paragraph 4 to highlight the disconnected and passive feeling one can experience in a hide. She also compares solo hide experiences with social hide experiences. This comparison highlights how the presence of other humans affects the experience.
5. By beginning with the tension, Macdonald draws readers into the drama. Tension propels a narrative; description simply sets the scene. Readers might not have continued reading for beauty alone. They may wish to read on simply to find the resolution to the tension.

Questions on Diction and Vocabulary (p. 152)
1. The impression is that these hides act as some kind of disappearing cloak. One assumes the vantage point of a ghost, angel, or spirit of some sort. This can be a kind of etheric experience. One is almost disembodied and removed from the physical world in order to observe and understand it better.
2. Macdonald presents photographers as pressed for time. They experience an urgency that seems antithetical to the simple observer. Their equipment seems to put an even greater barrier between them and nature. Not just their humanness, but technology also divides them. They seem almost like bumbling, nervous, desperate chasers.
3. This might be an opportune moment to discuss how to use context clues to discern the meaning of unfamiliar words. Ask for suggestions of words that are unfamiliar to students and work as a class to find moments in the text that give clues to their meaning.

Sister Flowers
MAYA ANGELOU

Preparing to Read (p. 154)
Students may also refer to a song, an author, an instrument, or a sport that gave them comfort during a time of struggle. Encourage them to consider these options. Mrs. Flowers thought that reading was good, but incomplete, for Marguerite. Are music, books, and sports sometimes enough, or do we need people at these times? What are the downsides of relying on just one thing? You might ask students to consider how a person can enrich a song, a book, or an instrument.

Thinking Critically about the Text (p. 159)
Marguerite had recently been raped and, as such, was sought out as a body, not for her mind or as a person. She needed to be validated as a whole person, as something greater than what had happened to her. Everyone needs to be seen as something greater than what is happening in their lives. Being liked by others takes people beyond their immediate surroundings and gives them hope and perspective.

Questions on Subject (p. 159)
1. Angelou's main point is that Sister Flowers carried herself with respect. Sister Flowers was able to show grace in all weather, hot or cold, and gave Marguerite an example of how to carry herself despite the storm in her life. Marguerite says, "[S]he made me proud to be Negro, just by being herself" (paragraph 11).
2. Sister Flowers always seemed to keep a slight distance from others. She wore gloves, remained proper, and was not sloppy in her communications. She did not encourage dropping one's guard and letting others make her vulnerable. She carried herself with grace and strength first and foremost and then with kindness.
3. For Marguerite, reading became an escape, a wonderful way to develop her mind, but reading alone could not reconnect her with people and teach her how to reach out to others. Too much reading without speaking could make her too internal and could cause her to withdraw from the world.
4. Angelou makes a powerful statement in paragraph 13: "It was fortunate that I never saw her in the company of powhitefolks. For since they tend to think of their whiteness as an evenizer, I'm certain that I would have had to hear her spoken to commonly as Bertha . . ." For Marguerite, Sister Flowers's image within the black community as a leader and role model would not have necessarily been acknowledged by the white community. Sister Flowers's power extended within and not necessarily beyond the black community.
5. If Sister Flowers liked Marguerite, Marguerite too could like herself. Sister Flowers's love for her gave her permission to love herself. Sister Flowers was a respected figure and her attention gave Marguerite a sense of self-worth.

Questions on Strategy (p. 159)
1. Angelou creates the dominant impression of a woman who respected herself and others. Sister Flowers wore gloves, nice dresses, and hats. She was independent of the church yet did not rebuff others. She spoke well and was educated, but she did not look down on people with less education. Angelou creates this impression by remarking on her dress and describing her interactions with the less educated, such as Marguerite's mother.

2. Angelou incorporates numerous visual descriptions of Mrs. Flowers: "She had the grace of control" (paragraph 2), "thin without the taut look of wiry people" (2), "[h]er skin was a rich black that would have peeled like a plum if snagged" (3). Angelou also describes her hats, clothing, and ways of walking, noting that Mrs. Flowers would "drift off the road" (9) or "continue her easy gait up the hill" (8). In contrast, Marguerite's mother is described as "shelling peas" (8). Angelou also uses sound to bring the reader close to Mrs. Flowers, describing her as "soft-voiced" (10). She begins describing the house with reference to its scents, "the sweet scent of vanilla had met us as she opened the door" (29), and continues with visual imagery: "I looked around the room that I had never in my wildest fantasies imagined I would see. Browned photographs leered or threatened from the walls . . . I wanted to gobble up the room entire . . ." (32).

3. Angelou gives clues that the mother might have asked Sister Flowers to give her daughter "a little talking to" in two instances: in paragraph 9, when her mother tells Marguerite to run and play while she talks with Sister Flowers; and in paragraph 15, when Sister Flowers says, "I've been meaning to talk to her, anyway." Momma knew that Marguerite would respect and respond to Sister Flowers; everyone did. She also knew that she was not able to assist her daughter. She put pride aside and accepted that someone else might be able to help. While Marguerite's mother was not highly educated, she demonstrated her love for her daughter and had the ability to identify someone who could help.

4. By having Marguerite imagine the conversations, Angelou helps readers get insight into her perspective and feelings of shame and helps them better understand Mrs. Flowers's strength and Marguerite's desperate need for reassurance.

5. Angelou's reference to subject-verb agreement in paragraph 10 illustrates Marguerite's aspiration and her insecurity. She is already better educated than Momma, and we know because we are reading this essay that this is the beginning of Angelou's interest in language and literature and that she will become a writer. Marguerite is ashamed of her grandmother's ungrammatical speech. However, the vernacular Momma uses is perfectly acceptable to the most revered woman in Marguerite's young world, Sister Flowers. It also gives the impression of Momma's warmth—as if it is a private, intimate language—and of her humble upbringing.

Questions on Diction and Vocabulary (p. 160)

1. Angelou uses the figures of speech "like an old biscuit, dirty and inedible" (paragraph 1) and "[h]er skin was a rich black that would have peeled like a plum if snagged" (3) to create a contrast between the two women. The young girl is dried and hard, whereas the older woman has a lusciousness and softness. It is the transfer of some of this sweet plum that Angelou writes about. Mrs. Flowers brought the life and richness back to Marguerite.

2. Momma speaks in an uneducated manner, conjugating verbs incorrectly. Mrs. Flowers speaks with precision. Sister Flowers seems unbothered by Marguerite's mother. She later explains to Marguerite, "[A]lways be intolerant of ignorance but understanding of illiteracy. That some people, unable to go to school, were more educated and even more intelligent than college professors" (35). Mrs. Flowers does not judge intelligence based on literacy. This is another good lesson for Marguerite because it means that literacy alone is not necessarily intelligence, that escaping into books is not necessarily everything.

3. Just as Marguerite describes herself as a dirty biscuit and Sister Flowers like a rich plum, people are more than their skin. It is their inner lives that give them a glow. The same holds true for words; the passion that one infuses into the words and the meaning one conveys are what give words life. You may want to ask students to consider how two

people singing the same song can produce an entirely different experience. If one loves the song and another does not understand the song, the beauty will be conveyed differently if at all. When Marguerite has to speak words, she has to put herself in them and she has to bring them and herself back into the world. She wants to be whole and perhaps needs to first use others' words before she can find her own voice. Mrs. Flowers does not want her to stop speaking.

The Attachment that Still Makes Noise
PHYLLIS KORKKI

Preparing to Read (p. 161)
Most students will likely fall into the second category, of those who have never given staplers a great deal of thought. Ask students whether they would miss having staplers around if they were suddenly gone, and what other small, useful items they rarely consider but wouldn't want to lose.

Thinking Critically about the Text (p. 165)
Many students may believe that paper receipts will disappear. They may even find themselves using paper money less frequently. Between credit cards, online shopping, and now purchasing with smartphones, the need for paper money continues to diminish. Coins may also decrease in usage. People can pay for parking meters with smartphones and for tolls with electronic passes. Tickets for events may also soon all be predominantly online. Paper clips might also start disappearing along with staplers. Once technology companies figure out how we can charge our devices without cords, many power cords may disappear. Students will respond differently to these and other changes. Something is lost and gained as a result of many of these shifts. Examples of what could be lost include paper tickets from a World Series game that cannot be framed if they were available only online; the sound of change in one's pocket, money jars; kids sitting and counting their pennies for candy or toys.

Questions on Subject (p. 166)
1. Students will have different responses to the sound of the stapler. Some may associate it with the sounds of the Industrial Revolution. It sounds a bit like a factory noise as compared to a more contemporary BING! that comes with the arrival of a text message. Students may say it has an aggressive sound or the sound of certainty.
2. Students will resonate differently with the idea that staplers mean getting work done. Some may also associate the sound of printing a final draft as the sound of work being done. Others might suggest the sound of a laptop closing or the computer powering down, which might mean they finished a day's work. Or, the click of the "send" or "submit" button after having finished a paper or an application.
3. The seemingly simple apparatus of the stapler, Korkki claims, is more sophisticated than it seems. The staples must be pushed forward after each staple is forced down by a blade then the anvil needs to provide the base to help close the staple. The stapler has triumphed by being able to reset after each staple is expelled. It must be strong enough to force the metal through the paper and then be able to close the staple around the paper and hold it into place. They have triumphed over physics.
4. The people who have grown up with staplers are dying. The younger generations do not associate a complete office as requiring a stapler. Furthermore, the notion of office space

is changing more generally. People work from coffee shops, airports, etc. and do not bring staplers with them to these locations. Work is increasingly paperless: more is done via e-mail – attachments are simply attached to messages. While the industry can look abroad to countries without as many technological advancements, eventually, they will adopt these tools. As Internet access and laptops increase, the need for staplers will likely decrease.

Questions on Strategy (p. 166)

1. Opening with a question to which most readers can respond affirmatively engages a wide audience. Readers recognize themselves as someone to whom the article applies. Yes, I own a stapler! This article is about me! Even something so common has a uniting effect; we are the people with staplers. It creates community from the outset.

2. Students may or may not be familiar with the movie, yet Korkki contextualizes them sufficiently so that those who have not seen the movie can understand her point. Furthermore, the fact that many readers may not know *The Man in the Grey Flannel Suit* speaks to her point that some things in our culture become extinct. Someday the stapler might be as forgotten or as unfamiliar as these films are to some readers.

3. Staplers are similar to guns, claims Korkki, because "they contain magazines meant to be filled with metal objects that you load and release." (paragraph 18) Unlike guns, of course, staplers are not produced to inflict harm. They are used in the office, not on the battlefield. Staplers help complete projects. Guns often complete lives. Some students may enjoy the comparison not having considered the mechanistic similarities between the two devices. Others may consider the comparison as overreaching — of course these objects are produced for entirely different purposes.

4. In paragraph 5, Korkki names the major stapler companies. In paragraph 6, she introduces Acco, the company that owns Swingline — the world's best-selling stapler. In paragraph 7, she introduces the Parrot Speed Fastener Company that first produced the Swingline. In paragraph 12, she talks about the sale of Swingline to American Brands. In paragraph 24, she talks about the profits of Industrywide — a company that sells staplers. These companies show the genealogy of the stapler, how many companies have been involved, and the size of the industry. We rarely think about how the daily objects in our lives come to be a part of our experience and the numbers of people involved in producing them.

Questions on Diction and Vocabulary (p. 166)

1. These statements show how dependent people can become on their staplers and their strength. Without staplers, certain work just cannot be done. There is no replacement for the stapler. They also may symbolize the most solid material in the building. They can withstand fire. They make the world of technology almost look fragile in comparison. These two phrases suggest that the stapler might be around a lot longer than we think.

2. *Conglomerate:* a group of smaller individual companies brought together under one company. *Pedigree:* distinguished ancestry/history. *Quarry;* referring to the way machines grip stone in an excavation site. The stapler dives down into the rich source of paper to grab and hold it. *Philanthropist:* a wealthy person who gives money and/or time to assist others in need. Those they help may be poor, ill, or in some other way disenfranchised. *Parody:* a story that mocks — for the amusement of others — some aspect of life, a place or kind of person, *Melding:* combination of. *Heft:* weight. *Tensile:* the amount something can bend without breaking. *Robust;* strongly built. *Entrenched:* solidly established. *Modular:* designed with standardized dimensions to serve a variety of uses.

CHAPTER 6 Illustration

Be Specific
NATALIE GOLDBERG

Preparing to Read (p. 187)

This exercise puts into practice the advice Goldberg gives in the first three sentences of her essay: "Be specific. Don't say 'fruit.' Tell what kind of fruit—'It is a pomegranate.'" The term *woods* is general; *redwood forest* is specific. Because nearly all students will at some time have walked in a woods of some sort but very few will have seen an actual redwood forest, it might be interesting to ask whether the second part of their response to the exercise is more detailed and precise than the first—and, if so, why. Explore the possibility that words can sometimes be more evocative than memory.

Thinking Critically about the Text (p. 189)

Students are asked to examine and expand their specific knowledge of aspects of their own environment. Goldberg says that we might gain by this activity because knowing the names of things grounds us, clears the mind, and makes us more awake and "more friendly toward the environment" (paragraph 3). It surprises her that so few people are able to name the plants and trees in their own yards; it is cheating to ask others because they can provide only unreliable, secondhand knowledge. Besides, it is important to know with certainty for oneself.

Questions on Subject (p. 189)

1. To know the name of something "connects us to the earth"; it makes us more awake and friendly toward the environment (paragraph 3). It allows us to "[penetrate] more deeply" into what is in front of us and to learn from it (5); it grounds us and makes us more attentive in a group (6).
2. A writer needs to know not only the name of a particular thing but also the month, day, and moment of the context in which it is important (paragraph 4). Precision in time is as important as precision in identity in making a subject real and immediate to the reader.

Questions on Strategy (p. 189)

1. Williams grounds his poetry in precise, concrete descriptions of familiar objects, starting with their names. It is his belief that intimate knowledge of the things closest to us leads to a broad understanding of the world and our important ideas about it. The comments and lines of poetry quoted by Goldberg support her thesis that it is important to "be specific" in order to learn and know.
2. The lists help define the term *specific* because each is made up of particular members of a general category. They forcefully show that names do, in fact, convey very precise images; each name on the list removes a particular object from its category by bringing to mind a picture of that object in a setting furnished by the reader's imagination.
3. Goldberg is addressing writers. In paragraph 4 she quotes William Carlos Williams: "Write what's in front of your nose." She mentions writing groups (paragraph 6) and gives advice to "a writer" (7).

4. Goldberg's illustrations of naming help define her central concept that knowing the names of things helps both writers and readers achieve an appreciation and understanding of their world. Definitions are abstract; examples of any kind make them more specific and concrete for the reader.

Questions on Diction and Vocabulary (p. 189)
1. According to Goldberg's example (i.e., addressing a girl by her name rather than by "girl"), people—and by extension, things—are dignified when they are recognized by name as specific individuals instead of as members of a general class. The term *integrity* implies uniqueness, wholeness, and self-worth.
2. *Beingness* is a term coined by Goldberg to emphasize the manner in which a name brings to mind specific qualities of an object and thereby evokes the reality of the object.
3. "Dayseye" recalls both the appearance of the daisy itself—a round golden eye with petals for lashes—and the season of long, sunny summer days during which it blooms. In the context of paragraph 4, it helps the reader "hone . . . awareness: to the name, to the month, to the day, and finally to the moment." In the context of the essay, the example of the "dayseye" emphasizes various ways in which a name creates a specific image, including the object itself and its setting of time and place.
4. *Pomegranate* (paragraph 1): a thick-skinned, reddish fruit with many seeds. *Integrity* (4): a firm adherence to a code of moral or artistic values.

For a More Creative Brain, Travel
BRENT CRANE

Preparing to Read (p. 191)
You will likely have students with a variety of travel experiences. Some may have traveled abroad extensively, while others might never have left their home state, including to go to college. Emphasize that travel in this context is more about experiencing new things rather than geographical distance. Ask if students have ever been to a multicultural event, or if they have been on a camping trip, and invite them to share the barrage of emotions associated with new experiences.

Thinking Critically about the Text (p. 193)
Student responses will vary. International students may feel reassured that the struggles of assimilation will pay off in ways they had not considered. Those who have not traveled may consider its advantages. You may want to discuss the differences between study abroad and going to live in a country. Study abroad programs tend to be fairly insular and protected unless students live with local people. Students may also ponder the kind of creativity that travel inspires. Is it all creativity? Does travel inspire creativity in science, math, art, cooking, and music as well as in writing? Crane does not make this distinction between areas of creativity. Perhaps no one has studied whether the impact is greater in one creative pursuit than in another.

Questions on Subject (p. 194)
1. Crane does not define creativity directly. A definition can be gleamed from the text itself. In paragraph 6, he quotes expert Adam Galinsky, who says that creativity has to do with the ability to jump between different ideas. The more different ideas someone has been exposed to on a deep level, the more ideas she or he can draw from.

2. Immersion means engaging with the local culture and environment. It means leaving one's cultural bubble to interact with different peoples and styles of living. We do not really absorb the experience or build new neural pathways if we simply visit a place without interacting with it. A creative boost requires separating from one's habitual way of operating in the world.
3. By "cultural bubbles," Crane means existing only within the framework to which we are accustomed. These pockets, which are isolated from the rest of the world, tend to be self-contained and self-referential. They operate only according to their own norms and tend not to expand beyond certain confines. You can travel in cultural bubbles if you take a cruise or go to a resort that has only a limited or very constructed presentation of the local population. Students may describe their cultural bubbles by the kinds of people within them, the music, food, rules of behavior, laws, and so on. You can ask students to imagine an actual bubble that contains people, food, music, clothes, and ways of behaving that travel with people.
4. Student reactions to Galinsky's assertion will vary. Some will say that the increase in travel does not seem to have reduced the amount of violent conflict on the planet. They also may note that a number of jihadists have been living in the United States or Europe and still decided to incite terror attacks. Others may say that they have noticed a shift in their ability to appreciate difference since having traveled.

Questions on Strategy (p. 194)
1. In paragraph 2, Crane states his thesis that living abroad can increase creativity.
2. Most students will have heard of these writers. Crane likely uses them as examples because most readers will have heard of them. Readers might also be surprised to learn that these writers traveled so extensively. Sometimes we think of writers as always at their desks, giving birth to ideas out of the ether.
3. Crane talks about the impact of travel on the fashion industry. Students may like to hear more examples of creativity in business, math, science, or other areas.
4. Crane opens with the topic and his thesis, providing several examples of creative people who traveled. Then he provides examples of the science behind the claim that travel increases creativity. After making his case, he looks at nuances within the science, such as the optimal number of countries, the distance of the culture from one's own, and the kind of travel that works best. He ends by broadening the argument, saying that creativity is not just good for us, it is good for humanity.
5. He starts one paragraph with, "In Galinsky's latest study," which alerts readers that new information is coming. Another paragraph starts with "the researchers also found," which also alerts readers about new information. The paragraph that starts with "traveling might have other brain benefits too" tells us that we will still be learning about the benefits of travel, but now in new ways.

Questions on Diction and Vocabulary (p. 194)
1. Crane uses words that are accessible to a wide range of readers. When he introduces scientific words like *neuroplasticity*, he takes care to define the words. He does not use complicated words unless they add to his argument. Talking about neuroplasticity in the beginning of the essay may intimidate some readers, but it also has the advantage of letting readers know he has done his research. The reference to science helps establish his authoritative voice. Otherwise, readers might think that this claim that travel helps creativity is something he thought of on his own. Scientific language adds credibility. Making sure he defines the terms ensures that he does not lose or disinterest readers.

2. *Anecdotally* (paragraph 4): based on reports or observations. *Neural* (4): of or relating to the brain. *Synapses* (4): where the message travels from one nerve cell to the other. *Cognitive* (5): of or relating to mental activities. *Disparate* (5): distinct in character; separate from one another. *Correlation* (6): relationship between things that happen or change together. *Hypothesized* (7): suggested an idea or theory. *Acculturated* (9): merging of cultures. *Categorical* (11): operating according to categories. *Hamper* (11): slows progress.

If You Had One Day with Someone Who's Gone
MITCH ALBOM

Preparing to Read (p. 196)
The questions prepare students for Albom's question, "What would you do if you had one more day?" This question helps them first identify the person with whom they would like to share that day. When reading the essay, students will already have someone in mind and will have a chance to answer before learning Albom's and his friends' perspectives.

Thinking Critically about the Text (p. 199)
His mother is shocked to the point of disbelief and denial when learning of her father's death. "Dead? How could he be dead? Hadn't she seen him the night before, when she kissed him goodnight?" (paragraph 2). Her response to the news: "'You're a liar'" (3). Rabbi Wolpe still thinks about the sudden loss of his father: "[a]t some moment every day, he is an eleven-year-old boy who lost his dad to a sudden heart attack in 1938" (16). The shock of losing someone suddenly seems to have made these losses harder. They could not say goodbye. People regret not being able to change their last interaction with the person. Maury De Young just sat under a tree and cried after his son was killed in a car accident. With a death from old age, people have time to say good-bye, talk about the past, heal any wounds, and tell the person they love them. Because they can just slowly start to let go, there may be less denial than in cases of sudden loss.

Questions on Subject (p. 199)
1. Albom's mother cried because she too wanted to have several more minutes with her lost loved one.
2. They all responded by saying they would do normal activities together. See the answer for the section Thinking Critically about the Text. Most of them wanted just to express their love and appreciate the simple pleasure of the other person's company. The life lesson Albom draws is that the simple day-to-day things are precious and we should cherish them. This is reminiscent of the John Lennon lyrics, "Life is what happens when we're busy making other plans."
3. Rabbi Wolpe meant that his father is trapped in the time and way that he remembers him. Because he can no longer interact with his father, Wolpe's memories are all that exist of him.
4. She did not want to let her father down. He had high expectations for his daughter and believed she could do something important, which is why he invested in her learning. We later learn that he encouraged her to become a doctor. She remembers her last assignment and perhaps feels guilty that she did not live up to his hopes. She wanted to complete her last assignment. It represents how, at times when something happens suddenly, time slows and we remember everything in great detail. The essence of her relationship with him was his desire for her to excel and her desire not to disappoint.

Questions on Strategy (pp. 199–200)

1. Answers will vary. By opening with his mother's story, Albom brings his own life into the story. Although he does not relate a firsthand experience, he shares with the reader a sense of his family and their experience, setting an intimate tone for the story. Albom also ends the essay with his mother's experience and how it made him appreciate the present moment even more. Her experience of loss taught him what is important in his own life in the present.

2. Albom asks this question of each of the people featured in the essay, and their answers structure the essay. By asking the rhetorical question, he brings readers closer to the subject and makes them part of the discussion he leads. He wants readers to realize that they too desire the simple experiences, not just the wild ones. The question may also prompt students to think of a breakup or loss of a friendship. Loss of a relationship can feel like a death.

3. In paragraph 10, Albom says, "I began to pose this scenario to other people—friends, colleagues, readers. How would they spend a day with a departed loved one?" The answers come from people around the country, two of whom held religious positions, as a pastor and as a rabbi. Despite their titles, they had to face sudden loss. It equalized them all. They all support his findings that most people want to relive the simple things together. They want them to know how much they were loved and for the living and dead to forgive themselves for everything that happened. For example, Wolpe wanted his father to stop thinking he caused his brother's blindness. No one would focus on the death itself.

4. In paragraphs 3 and 4, Albom repeats the concept of a "lie," the initial denying of a sudden loss. "'You're a liar,' my mother said." The next paragraph begins, "But it wasn't a lie." He challenges the reality in his mother's head. It's another voice to counteract hers. He uses a similar technique between paragraphs 14 and 15. He writes, "Some might say, 'That's such an ordinary day.'" Then the next paragraph starts with "Maybe that's the point." This reasserts that, in fact, the ordinary is the extraordinary. It is okay to repeat it, both in an essay and in life.

5. One-sentence paragraphs show readers the importance of the ideas they contain. It took Albom a long time to realize that he wanted to ask the question of his mother, not just of the people he interviewed. The one-sentence paragraph is almost like a sigh, an epiphany that would have become lost and tangled with other sentences in a longer paragraph.

Questions on Diction and Vocabulary (p. 200)

1. By letting people speak for themselves, Albom adds more voices to the essay. Rather than just his voice, he builds his case by enabling others to make the same point, that the simple is important. The point of the essay is to have each person answer the question and for the reader to answer the question for him- or herself.

2. Albom writes clearly and plainly. He seems unaffected by pretense, and his simplicity in style reinforces his thesis. He uses writing to communicate what is important, not to bring the exotic or fantastic to life.

3. *Scenario* (paragraph 10): an imagined or projected sequence of events. *Vaudevillian* (17): someone who performed in light or amusing theatrical works; these works often included singing and dancing. *Lament* (20): a formal display of sorrow or grief. *Wistfully* (22): reflectively or forlornly. *Giddy* (27): light-hearted, frivolous. *Detrimental* (29): causing detriment or harm. *Inculcate* (29): to instill by repetition or admonition.

How to Give Orders Like a Man
DEBORAH TANNEN

Preparing to Read (p. 202)
Whether we like to admit it or not, the act of communication is not as simple as the diagram of speaker > message > receiver > action. Although Tannen focuses on how gender influences communication, there are numerous other factors that determine whether a message is received or an order is carried out. Factors such as age, gender, class, or relationship to the speaker can influence how and why communication happens. With this prompt, students are asked how the situation and their relationship with the speaker determine how they listen or obey.

Thinking Critically about the Text (p. 210)
In Western culture people believe that communication must be direct. In stating the opposite, Tannen is challenging this view and offering students another way to look at human communication. She is also pointing out that communication is not necessarily a verbal action. One point of departure from this question might be a discussion of the many forms of nonverbal communication in human interaction.

Questions on Subject (p. 210)
1. Tannen defines indirect speech in paragraph 16, where she states, "everyone is indirect, meaning more than is put into words and deriving meaning from words that are never actually said." The built-in liability of indirect speech, Tannen continues, "is a risk that the other will either miss or choose to ignore your meaning." Direct speech can be misinterpreted as a power play or as an indication that the speaker has low regard for the person(s) to whom he or she is speaking.
2. Culturally and socially, fathers are sometimes seen as the bosses or dominant figures in the family. Thus, it follows that the "superior" person would have the choice and opportunity to use both direct and indirect speech to those considered "inferior"—the children.
3. In her exploration of bosses "who issue bald commands" (paragraph 11), Tannen urges her readers to consider the reasons for direct speech, pointing out, "Considering the many influences on conversational style, individuals have a wide range of ways of getting things done and expressing their emotional states" (12). [*Note:* This response should also be considered in conjunction with that of question 2.]
4. Japanese speakers typically let their sentences trail off because "expressing ideas before knowing how they will be received seems intrusive" (34). This reflects the Japanese value called *omoiyari*, or "empathy."

Questions on Strategy (pp. 210–211)
1. Tannen's thesis, presented in paragraph 4, is that indirect speech is a result of culture, circumstance, and socioeconomic situations, not of personality, and should not be seen as lesser than—or preferable to—direct speech.
2. Just as fathers are perceived as the "superiors" in the family unit, it is generally believed that the male—particularly in business—occupies a higher position within a corporate structure and thus uses both direct and indirect speech. This is highlighted by the author's focusing on men as examples.

3. Tannen's primary audience is working women, "middle-to-upper-management," who daily encounter situations similar to the examples given. This is the reason for the focus on indirect speech—it is much more likely to be used by women in a work situation.
4. The seeming incongruity can be explained by understanding that variances in sensitivity to indirect meaning and indirect speech account for how well or how poorly members of a team will work together and understand each other. An intuitive understanding of one's colleagues would appear to make for a more successful working environment. These examples work to support Tannen's thesis that indirect speech patterns are not linked to personality—even men in subordinate positions use them.
5. Comparison and contrast are used to illustrate the cultural differences between American and Japanese people. Indirectness is much more prevalent—and highly regarded—in Japan, whereas direct, straight-to-the-point communication is favored in the United States. In showing the expectations and the demeanor of the speakers and listeners to be different, Tannen is furthering her argument that indirect speech depends on many factors, especially culture. Yet she does not assert this point; instead, she lets her cross-cultural examples speak for her. In effect, these examples work through indirect communication, by implying rather than telling.

Questions on Diction and Vocabulary (p. 211)
1. There is a tendency to associate the military and things termed militaristic with direct speech, especially commands. Tannen shows, however, that much of the military's training is accomplished by using indirect speech, citing examples from a boot camp and the Pentagon (paragraph 15)—thus the irony.
2. Responses will vary. Paragraph 11 marks a point where Tannen's voice becomes both more formal and more technical ("A subordinate addressing a superior"). This question draws attention to the fact that Tannen is a professor of linguistics and is not entirely able to escape the discourse of the academy. If this fact is brought to light, students will be able to consider themselves as participants in a discourse community. To extend this discussion, you might ask your students: "What are the differences between the ways students talk in class and out of class?"
3. *Admonishing* (3): reprimanding. *Self-deprecating* (3): excessively modest. *Manipulative* (5): managed deviously or for one's own advantage. *Prerogative* (7): right or privilege. *Subservience* (8): the state of being inferior and therefore servile. *Cheeky* (10): cleverly rude; impish. *Deferential* (11): courteously respectful; humbled. *Imperious* (13): overbearing; domineering. *Liability* (16): something disadvantageous. *Mitigated* (28): moderated. *Broached* (28): introduced as a subject. *Gleaned* (32): inferred. *Relief* (33): sharpness of outline due to contrast. *Empathy* (34): identification with the feelings, thoughts, and so on, of another.

The "Busy" Trap
TIM KREIDER

Preparing to Read (p. 213)
College students are notoriously busy, skimping on sleep to meet competing academic and social demands. This can be a good opportunity to bring the classroom discussion around to time management and to set realistic expectations regarding the time it takes to research, write, and revise.

Thinking Critically about the Text (p. 216)

Student opinions will vary. Some who define success as career accomplishments may believe that being busy is necessary. They may believe that we are here in life to engage in activities and that busyness is a sign that one is living a full life. In the Jewish tradition, for example, life accomplishments are seen as the purpose of life. Some might note the cost on relationships, creativity, and joy. Students may note that people who provide for others (children or aging parents) might need to be busy to bring in enough income.

Questions on Subject (p. 217)

1. Kreider does not say so directly, but readers can imply that people might have to face a feeling of emptiness without all that busyness. They might also question some of their decisions and their relationships. He does suggest that people might have to face that their activities are not ultimately all that important or meaningful.

2. From reading the *World Book Encyclopedia* Kreider likely acquired knowledge, developed a love of learning, and nurtured his sense of wonder. By creating animated films, he developed his creativity and had a vehicle for self-expression. Playing in the woods with friends, he developed a connection to nature, skills of working with others, and maybe — because the game was a form of combat — a sense of competition.

3. By "real writing," Kreider likely means writing that feels solid, is authentic, and represents his true voice. He was not just producing words but writing in a way that he felt connected to them. Constant interruptions and other obligations have kept him away from "real writing." He is suggesting that we lose quality when we are overcommitted. We cannot be really present to the work at hand if we are exhausted and hurrying off to the next activity. He would likely consider this essay "real writing" because he is talking about something that matters in a way that is clear and purposeful. It is an essay that could change behavior and how people live their lives. Real writing has that power.

4. Kreider uses "bad influence" ironically. Those who believe in busyness will advocate for more work and less play. They would consider people like Kreider distractions. In this playful line, he helps readers see the absurdity of all this commitment. His essay asks subtly, "Why are we so afraid of play?"

Questions on Strategy (p. 217)

1. Kreider compares people who are busy to people who are exhausted. Exhausted people, he says, are those committed to back-to-back shifts in the intensive care unit (ICU) or people commuting long distances to multiple minimum-wage jobs. Busy people are those, he says, with self-imposed obligations such as activities and classes. Through the comparison, he makes the distinction that not everyone who has a full schedule is running away from downtime. In doing so, he speaks to potential critics who will want to say, "Hey, there are people who are legitimately busy." The comparison also helps readers to identify the two types in themselves. We are rarely all one way or another. Some of our commitments are legitimate and others are to elevate self-importance or run from the quiet.

2. In paragraph 6, Kreider says, "[I]f your job wasn't performed by a cat or a boa constrictor in a Richard Scarry book, I'm not sure it's necessary." In paragraph 7, he says, "I feel like a reprobate who does not deserve to live on any day that I do not write." In paragraph 10, he says that idleness is as important to the brain as "vitamin D is to the body and deprived of it we suffer a mental affliction as disfiguring as rickets." Students may identify other examples as well.

3. Kreider's audience seems clearly to be people who are busy (but perhaps *not* people who are exhausted). He is writing to others he believes are caught up in the "busy trap" as a way to encourage them to free themselves from what he believes he himself has escaped.

4. Krieder does not actually consider himself a bad influence. He believes that his article might be an important wake-up call to those who embrace busyness in their lives.

Questions on Diction and Vocabulary (pp. 217–218)

1. In paragraph 2, Kreider compares people who are exhausted (i.e., those who are busy by necessity) with those whom he believes are busy by choice (i.e., those who are taking classes or participating in other voluntary obligations). This comparison allows Kreider to deflect criticism that some, such as doctors or those struggling to make ends meet, are not simply choosing to be busy. Because Kreider anticipates and acknowledges this exception, he is able to make a stronger argument.

2. *Unmolested* is a much stronger term than *bothered* or *interrupted*. It implies that some actual harm — molestation — is being prevented. The obligations Kreider mentions seem to be (according to paragraph 8) e-mails and other professional obligations.

3. By *obligations,* Kreider means anything he has to do for someone else. Obligations could be meetings he has to attend, forms he must complete, writing, or any other task assigned to him. By using the word *unmolested,* he suggests that asking people do to things is a kind of personal violation. Students may add a critique here saying that humans live communally and in relation to one another. Kreider seems to live a very isolated life in which he reports to no one but also seems to have no one, or few people, in his life.

4. *Acquiescence* (paragraph 5): tacit acceptance. *Existential* (6): reaffirming of existence. *Obviated* (6): to make something no longer necessary (obsolete). *Histrionic* (6): too emotional or dramatic. *Reprobate* (7): condemned strongly as unworthy or even evil. *Insidiously* (8): causing harm in a gradual way that is not noticed. *Rickets* (10): a disease (often in children) that comes from a vitamin D deficiency; it causes a softening of the bones. *Indolence* (12): inclination toward laziness. *Frenetic* (12): wild or frantic. *Resolute* (12): committed or determined.

CHAPTER 7 Process Analysis

How to Mark a Book
MORTIMER ADLER

Preparing to Read (p. 235)
Answers will vary according to what works for the individual student. Students may answer with some of the strategies they will read about (taking notes, writing in the margins). You might begin discussion for this prompt by asking what kinds of texts students have problems reading or for what purposes they read.

Thinking Critically about the Text (p. 239)
Answers will vary according to students' answers to the Preparing to Read prompt. Have students discuss what they learned and how they might modify their own reading strategies.

Questions on Subject (pp. 239–240)
1. The first kind of book owner "has all the standard sets and best-sellers—unread, untouched" (paragraph 6). The second has many books—some read—"but all of them as clean and shiny as the day they were bought" (paragraph 6). And the third has books that are "dog-eared and dilapidated, shaken and loosened by continual use, marked and scribbled in from front to back" (6). In Adler's eyes the third type is the only one who "owns" books because these books have been actively devoured by the owner.
2. Adler claims that writing in the book you are reading keeps you awake, helps you think a book through, and helps you remember your thoughts and the author's (paragraph 9). Most students readily agree with Adler's points.
3. The soul of the book, meaning the information the book contains, can be separated from the body of the book in the sense that its information can be transmitted to the reader. The separation of the soul of the book from the physical book is a good thing because it allows us to interact with the book. Also, seeing the book as a tool, rather than as a sacred or collectible object, means that readers are more likely to be skeptical and critical when they read.
4. In Adler's schema, the conversation should be a series of questions or remarks to a person who is not present (the author). Marking a book carries on the conversation by attempting to engage the reader and author in a dialogue. It is an expression of difference between the reader and the writer, the result of questioning oneself and the "teacher."
5. Answers will vary.

Questions on Strategy (p. 240)
1. Adler assumes throughout the essay that he is talking to nonbelievers, so he addresses the unspoken objections of his readers. However, in addressing his readers as nonbelievers, his argument could alienate those who do believe what he says or make the nonbelievers even more resistant to his ideas.
2. "You shouldn't mark up a book which isn't yours" (paragraph 3). This sentence lets the reader know that marking up books can be done only once they are bought or owned.

"There are two ways in which one can own a book" (4). Building on the idea of ownership introduced in paragraph 3, this sentence clarifies the direction of paragraph 4 by distinguishing the two ways in which books can be owned (by payment and by writing in them). The phrase "[c]onfusion about what it means to *own* a book" (5)—suggesting that there is a confusion in the term *ownership*—unifies the rest of paragraph 5 by setting up another explanation for ownership. "There are three kinds of book owners" (6). Moving from the concept of ownership to that of owners, this sentence provides a schema for the types of people who own books.

3. These verbal cues indicate that Adler's process analysis is directional. In the first fourteen paragraphs he is describing not *how* to do something but *why*. He begins with his thesis, and then he supports his argument with several points. It is not until the second half of the essay that he explains how to go about marking books. This method is necessary to Adler's purpose. He assumes that his readers have been told all their lives, under threat of punishment, not to write in books or simply that to write in a book is to deface it.

4. The summary of Adler's process analysis will vary from student to student, but it should include these basic steps: (1) underlining, (2) inserting numbers in the margin, (3) circling keywords, and (4) writing questions in the margin. With statements like "Unless you do [write between the lines], you are not likely to do the most efficient kind of reading" (1) and "the physical act of writing . . . brings words and sentences more sharply before your mind and preserves them better in your memory" (12), Adler is implicitly arguing that his way is the better way to read.

5. Throughout his process analysis explanation, Adler explicates three main ideas using cause and effect reasoning: that writing in the book you are reading keeps you awake, that writing in the book helps you think a book through, and that writing in the book helps you remember your thoughts and the author's. In this sense, his description of reading has an effect on the reader's interest and understanding. The cause of this effect is Adler's method of reading. In taking the time to explain the benefits (effects) of each step in his process (causes), he persuades his readers that they should try his method.

Questions on Diction and Vocabulary (p. 240)

1. The analogy works in reference to Adler's idea that to own a book requires time and effort, as does friendship (unlike acquaintances, which require simply knowing a name and a face). This analogy is important to Adler's overall argument because his way of reading is much slower than the traditional way of reading. If he is to persuade his readers to read by marking, he must concede this fact and argue that the traditional way only provides a superficial understanding of a book.

2. The "I" voice that Adler uses in the essay could help his explanation by showing the reader that he has experience with his way of reading. It gives the essay a more casual, conversational feel that might appeal to some readers. It shows that he still uses his own method, even as an adult and as a professional educator. The "I" voice might also hinder the explanation for some readers by exposing Adler's bias toward his own way of reading.

3. Adler uses the phrase "active reading" to refer to all of the physical things he does to maintain his conversation with the book—underlining, starring, writing comments, and the like.

How to Say Nothing in 500 Words
PAUL ROBERTS

Preparing to Read (p. 242)
The prompt elicits a subjective response, so answers will vary. Students are asked to consider their writing histories and attitudes prior to reading a piece that is exclusively about writing. Keep in mind that not everyone views writing as a positive experience.

Thinking Critically about the Text (p. 253)
Roberts's essay works by pointing to features that exemplify bad writing or good writing. Yet he never asks readers to look at their own work. This prompt asks the students to consider their writing using Roberts's criteria. You might start the discussion by analyzing a sample of your own work on an overhead transparency.

Questions on Subject (p. 253)
1. Answers will vary.
2. According to Roberts, the job of the writer is to "find the argument, the approach, the angle, the wording that will take the reader with him" (paragraph 7). This is especially difficult for college students because they are assigned subjects that have been much discussed and written about; it is hard for them to find a fresh approach. As your students if this is a valid statement.
3. Roberts offers the following techniques of good writing: (a) find a fresh approach, (b) take an unpopular or seldom used side of a subject, (c) avoid the obvious content, (d) be specific rather than abstract, (e) use colorful words but avoid overly fancy or potentially biased words, (f) avoid euphemisms, and (g) use pat expressions sparingly or not at all. Ask your students which of these techniques they use most often, which are easiest to use, and which they ignore, and why.
4. By taking an unusual approach, a writer can reach a set word goal. A less-used angle or fresh stance provides the opportunity for a student to write a full-length essay, as does using specific examples instead of abstract statements.
5. Modern psychology has made it more difficult to write well because the jargon used is complicated and inflated. As Roberts notes, modern psychology "contributes many polysyllables in which we can wrap our thoughts and blunt their force" (paragraph 27).

Questions on Strategy (p. 254)
1. Roberts's thesis remains unstated, so answers will vary. However, the successful answer will find a unifying thread that runs through all sections of this essay; for example, "This essay exposes the most important mistakes that college writers make and tells you how to avoid them."
2. Much like the strategy being studied, Roberts does not just tell students how to do something; he shows them how to do it. Have your students write scratch outlines by themselves, with a partner, or in small groups during class. Then put the finished product of each pair or group on the board. Follow the text for specifics.
3. In keeping with his wry humor, Roberts's title is a come-on, much like the promise of something for nothing from a sweepstakes offer. He draws the reader in by saying that he will show him or her a way to say nothing in 500 words and winds up doing exactly the opposite — teaching the reader how to write an effective, legitimate 500-word essay. This

catchy title serves its purpose by capturing readers' interest. The title "How to Write a 500-Word Essay" — while accurate — probably would not capture the attention of many readers.

4. Roberts's main point, that good writing is not a simple act of inserting colorful words or avoiding pat expressions, is supported by his own writing style (Roberts's style displays a model of good writing). By illustrating points that he wishes to make, such as the plight of the pitiful Alfy Simkins, Roberts gives his subject life and relevance. There is substance to material supported by good descriptions, illustrations, and definitions.

5. Roberts's style is light, accessible, and humorous. He has a wry sense of humor that he combines with well-chosen words to which students can relate. A particular example of this is the almost absurdist way in which he gives an example of writing about modern music: "Whenever I hear Gerber Spinklittle play 'Mississippi Man' on the trombone, my socks creep up my ankles" (paragraph 19). The narrated description of the pathetic football player Alfred Simkins is also vividly and comically detailed. There are many such examples in this selection, which enhance Roberts's process analysis by elaborating each step in the process.

Questions on Diction and Vocabulary (p. 254)

1. Is it not so much a question of what is in the essay that dates it as what is not in the essay. Current college problems are much more serious than football and fraternities: Students today are worried about violence, sexually transmitted infections (STIs), drugs, terrorism, and economic conditions. Also, Roberts refers to "the portable typewriter" (paragraph 3); these days he would no doubt talk about a laptop or a tablet. Finally, there is Roberts's exclusive use of male pronouns, indicating that this selection was written a while ago.

2. Color words "are calculated to produce a picture or induce an emotion." Colored words have powerful connotations that may undermine an argument or create a distraction. Colorless words are vague or unimaginative.

3. Roberts's sarcastic and dry tone is captured in the first words of the essay — the title — in which he presents the idea that he is going to teach the reader how to say nothing. Students may have different reactions to Roberts's tongue-in-cheek style. Allow room for a number of options.

Eating Industrial Meat
MICHAEL POLLAN

Preparing to Read (p. 256)

Students may come to this essay from several different perspectives: Some may never have considered where their food comes from; some may have read related books, such as Eric Schlosser's *Fast Food Nation*; some may be aware of controversies over irradiation of and hormones in food; some may be vegetarian or vegan; some may have gardened, raised animals, fished, or hunted and eaten what they raised, caught, or killed. Ask students how they perceive the food they buy in the store. Do they connect it to live animals or crops? Do any students have opinions about what it means to buy organic food or "free-range chicken" or "grass-fed beef"? Ask students how they might feel if they grew their own food or raised their own cattle or chickens and ate only what they themselves had grown. How would such an experience make them feel about how we feed ourselves and the world?

Thinking Critically about the Text (p. 261)

Pollan's first impression of the feedlot—"Not a bad little piece of real estate"—is quickly undermined by a closer look at the pond. Several times over the course of the essay something that looks just fine at first glance turns out, upon closer examination, to be either problematic or sinister: The "pond" is a "manure lagoon" (paragraph 1); the manure, in other contexts useful as a fertilizer, is so toxic it would kill crops (1); steer 534 is large and healthy-looking, but his eyes are red from "feedlot dust," which is "fecal dust" (4); and his apparent health is complicated by the very corn that is being used to fatten him up (8–11).

Questions on Subject (p. 261)

1. Farmers don't want the liquefied manure from the feedlot because it is so different from purely natural steer manure that, rather than nourishing plants, it would kill them. As it is, when the manure from concentrated animal feeding operations (CAFOs) ends up in waterways, it appears to mutate fish and amphibians; Pollan describes it as "toxic waste" (paragraph 1). Pollan suggests that industrialized beef is toxic.

2. Although butchers might look at 534 as an array of cuts of meat, feedlot managers might consider him "a most impressive machine for turning number 2 field corn into cuts of beef" (paragraph 6). Steer 534 is also a "link in a food chain," whose health is "inextricably linked to our own" (7–8). "We inhabit the same microbial ecosystem as the animals we eat" (8), so a microbiologist might see 534 as a potential carrier of deadly bacteria (9). A taxpayer might see 534 as the product of farm subsidies and "a barrel of oil" (13–14).

3. It was discovered that changing a cow's diet in the days before it is slaughtered—from corn to grass—reverses the acidification of its rumen and kills off as much as 80 percent of the *E. coli* bacteria resident in its gut. The process works by mimicking the cow's natural diet, returning its rumen to a neutral pH.

4. The cattle industry and the U.S. Department of Agriculture (USDA) find feeding grass to cattle impractical because a corn diet allows a steer to gain four pounds per day, such that cattle get bigger faster, in a way that cannot be replicated with a grass diet. If a steer is switched from corn to grass a few days before slaughter, it could mean a potential loss of more than ten pounds per steer, not an insignificant figure when beef sells by the pound. Instead, the cattle industry chooses to irradiate the meat in the hope that all the bacteria will be killed.

5. The ostensibly cheap corn fed to cows turns out to have hidden costs—for one, it creates antibiotic-resistant *E. coli* strains by providing an unnaturally acidic environment in the rumen of cattle whose diets are supplemented by antibiotics. In addition, the corn is grown with petroleum-based fertilizers and transported using yet more petroleum, depleting a nonrenewable resource. The manure of the corn-fed steers is also an environmental toxin.

Questions on Strategy (p. 261)

1. Pollan organizes his essay around the narrative of his visit to steer 534. While relaying the anecdote, he leaves the story to explain something that he has seen or to describe a consequence of an event or circumstance. For example, he notes that 534 has bloodshot eyes and then talks about why that might be: "Dr. Metzin had told me that some animals are irritated by feedlot dust. . . . [T]he dirt in a feedyard is not ordinary dirt; no, this is fecal dust" (paragraph 4). This allows him not only to describe his experience at the feedlot but also to give readers enough background information to interpret what he sees.

2. The process by which bacteria enter cattle and end up in the hamburgers we eat begins with the natural bacteria cattle have in their digestive systems. Corn-fed cattle that are given antibiotics breed antibiotic-resistant bacteria in their guts that can be particularly

dangerous for humans. They pass the bacteria in their manure, but since the feces is in a confined feedlot where the cattle live, it ends up in the dust and caked on steers' hides. Cattle are slaughtered at such rapid rates that some of the manure ends up in the meat during the process.

3. A natural barrier to infection is diminished by feeding corn to cows because corn changes the neutral pH in the guts of the cattle. Corn-fed cattle have acidic rumen, so the bacteria in their guts is often able to survive human stomach acid, leaving the deadly bacteria to inhabit the digestive systems of people who consume such beef. When the bacteria that inhabit grass-fed cattle are consumed by humans, on the other hand, strong stomach acids in the human digestive tract kill those bacteria.

4. Pollan uses transitions to move from paragraph to paragraph so that he can either expand on an idea from the previous paragraph—". . . I would not say he looked happy. / He's clearly eating well, though" (paragraphs 4, 5)—or look at a different aspect of the same broader issue: "We inhabit the same microbial ecosystem as the animals we eat, and whatever happens in it also happens to us. / Then there's the deep pile of manure on which I stand, in which 534 sleeps" (8, 9). He is able, through transitions (such as "follow the fertilizer. . . all the way to the oil fields of the Persian Gulf. / I don't have a sufficiently vivid imagination to look at my steer and see a barrel of oil" [13, 14]) to step back from a statement he has made and look at the bigger picture and then step back again from the bigger picture to consider an even larger reality.

5. Pollan connects what's happening to 534 to the oil fields of the Persian Gulf through 534's consumption of corn that is fertilized with petroleum-based fertilizers and transported to the cattle by trucks run on petroleum; the lifestyle of steers like 534 is petroleum-costly and leads directly to greater oil consumption by the United States.

Questions on Diction and Vocabulary (p. 261)
1. "Marbling" in this context refers to the patterns of fat through the muscle of the steers' meat.
2. Pollan ends paragraph 5 with an ironic "(Shucks)" in response to the feedlot manager's personification of 534 as "a handsome looking beef." The word "handsome," in this context, struck Pollan as a sentimentalization of the steer and the ugly feedlot process of fattening cattle for slaughter.
3. When Pollan says in paragraph 7, "Yet metaphors of the factory and the machine obscure as much as they reveal about the creature standing before me," he means that while the cattle are in a sense meat machines—factories that turn corn into beef—they are also living creatures; thinking of them exclusively as mechanical contraptions obscures the fact that they are animals that have to sleep in their own feces. While Pollan focuses on the problems with the feedlot that most influence human consumers (bacteria, petroleum), he is careful to note also that "[he] would not say [534] looked happy" (paragraph 4).

How Do Spiders Make Their Webs?
ALYSSA AULT

Preparing to Read (p. 263)
You might ask students to break into pairs or small groups to discuss their writing processes rather than trying to share these as a class. Expect a wide range of responses, and encourage students to discuss not just the process itself but why it is so intriguing and what they would like to learn about it that they do not already know.

Thinking Critically about the Text (p. 265)

Because spider web fibers are stronger than steel, we could use these fibers to replace the use of steel in bridges, railways, and building materials. Spider web fibers could also be used for safety belts or used to drill or for any number of other purposes.

Questions on Subject (p. 266)

1. In paragraph 5, Ault quotes an expert who says that spiders use webs offensively and defensively. Vibrations in the strands alert spiders to predators. Webs also trap prey.
2. In paragraph 2, Ault describes spider silk by saying that it is "stronger than steel and has impressive tensile strength . . ." Spider silk is known, therefore, for both its strength and elasticity. Scientists find it valuable because no human-made substance has that combination. Because spider silk cannot yet be fully replicated, scientists have only just begun to discover its possible uses.
3. Spiders also use web-building to create defensive systems that can alert them when prey is nearby.
4. The fact that spiders build their webs at night adds a bit of mystique to these already curiously powerful animals. Building at night makes them seem secretive and strategic as well as powerful.

Questions on Strategy (p. 266)

1. Ault's purpose, as stated in the article, is to pique our interest in spiders as powerful engineers and planners. This helps us both appreciate spiders and consider what might be possible for us if we could produce what they do. Paragraph 1 hooks readers and piques their curiosity about these creatures. She speaks of them in such a positive light, describing them as "skilled engineers with amazing planning skills. . . ." Without saying so directly, she asks readers not to pass them off as useless creatures or be afraid of them. She might save the lives of a few spiders. Readers may hesitate to kill them after reading this essay of appreciation.
2. Ault's audience is people who likely have spiders in their daily lives but do not know much about them. We know this because she shares basic information about their webs and web construction that any expert would already know. She points out the kind of spider the average American would have seen — the orb weaver spider. This suggests that she is looking to educate a broad audience.
3. Ault creates the impression that webs are very sophisticated creations made of some of the world's finest materials. She begins the essay by talking about the quality of the material and then describes in paragraphs 10 to 15 how the orb weaver spider makes its web. This description helps readers appreciate the amount of strategy and work that goes into the average web. She describes how the spider pulls the silk from its glands (paragraph 11), then how the web "balloon" soars to make its first connection (12), how the spider selects the best attachment points (12), and then how the spider constructs the interior of the web. The fact that spiders of the same species have the same process demonstrates that the process it not haphazard but is hard wired.
4. At night, a spider, once it has picked a location, begins the process of setting up the web's primary structure. Pulling silk from the glands in its legs, it establishes seven primary points of attachment by attaching twenty dry strands to different points. Once the seven best are established, the spider disconnects the other thirteen and then begins the process (from the outside in) of constructing the interior. Going in a circle, it attaches each sticky thread to the seven main attachments. This stickiness in the web allows the spider to trap prey.

5. Ault quotes only Jonathan Coddington, the director of the Global Genome Initiative and senior scientist at the Smithsonian's National Museum of Natural History. Students might say that an expert on spiders would be a good addition to the essay. Also, they might point out that, since this publication was in the *Smithsonian* magazine, perhaps it would have added more credibility to also include experts *not* part of that institution.
6. The essay begins by introducing the topic and the purpose of the essay — to increase the appreciation for spider web materials as well as spiders' planning skills. Ault begins by talking about the spider web materials (paragraphs 2–7). She then describes the process of building a web (8–14). She then talks about how the web is used to capture prey. The essay concludes with a list of companies investing in spider silk. In paragraph 5, the question "why build webs?" alerts readers to a shift in topic. Paragraph 12 begins with the word *eventually*, which tells the readers that Ault is lapsing time in order to show them the next part of the process. Paragraph 13 starts with the phrase "the spider then," which tells readers she is moving on to the next part of the process. Paragraph 14 begins with the word *then*, telling us that she is still describing the process.

Questions on Diction and Vocabulary (p. 266)

1. Ault's tone is conversational and authoritative. She wants to attract readers to the topic, so she must tread lightly. She does not want to challenge their beliefs about spiders but simply inform them about their admirable attributes. She uses simple words so that readers do not have to struggle with technical vocabulary, but she quotes enough facts so that readers can trust her. Students may also say that they can sense her genuine appreciation of these creatures. By calling them skillful, gifted, and rigorous in paragraph 1, readers know quickly that she is a fan.
2. The simile "like an angler with a fish on the line" creates the image of the spider casting silk the way a fisherman casts a line. We can visualize the line gliding through the air and then — with a tug — indicating to the spider or fisherman on the other end that the goal has been achieved. This reinforces the notion that the spider, like the fisherman, is skilled and strategic.
3. *Lustrous* (paragraph 1): reflecting light; glittering; sparkling. *Taxonomy* (5): scientific classification. *Replenish* (6): to fill up again. *Soluble* (7): able to be dissolved in a liquid. *Planar* (10): lying in a plane. *Solipsistic* (13): describing a philosophy that only your existence is real. *Concentric* (14): having the same center. *Depletes* (14): to lessen the principal substance. *Coup de grace* (15): an action that finally destroys something that has been getting weaker.

Campus Racism 101
NIKKI GIOVANNI

Preparing to Read (p. 268)

You may want students to consider whether race relations on their campus are typical. Does it matter whether the campus is in an urban or a rural environment, on the East or West Coast, in the North or South, or religious or secular? Encourage students to cite specific examples in support of their views.

Students may notice that Giovanni teaches at Virginia Tech University. Although this article was published before the April 2007 shooting incident at Virginia Tech, you may want students to consider how a massacre like that equalizes all races. The killer did not care about the race of his victims; his pathological behavior was the result of numerous factors, including a general hatred toward people and an untreated mental illness. How did his race play into people's conception of the shootings?

Thinking Critically about the Text (p. 272)

Students may have fiscal responsibilities to pay for college or food. Students want college to be a social environment as well: They may participate in theater, the newspaper, or sports, all of which can take substantial amounts of time and energy. In addition, students have friends, go to parties, and fall in and out of love. All of this goes on while they are living together in dorms or off-campus housing. Students have many new experiences, in a new environment, that demand their attention. Each student will have different priorities, and his or her academic interest and capabilities will have a great effect on classroom successes. Students may argue that much of their education comes from their out-of-class activities. Their education goals may include participating in all of the wonderful activities college has to offer.

Questions on Subject (p. 272)

1. Giovanni's audience is predominantly black college students. The first paragraph does not identify the race of the young people in the postcards. By the third paragraph, where Giovanni writes "You're going to interact," we know for sure that her intended readers are black students.
2. Giovanni dismisses the notion that it is hard to be a black student in a predominantly white college in paragraph 3. She then goes on to illustrate that many experiences are far worse than being in a white college: such as being in jail, not being educated, or joining the military because of limited opportunities. In addition, she dismisses the notion by pointing out that black students will have to interact with a white world anyway. She wants to instill the idea that being in college is an opportunity.
3. Giovanni wants black students to see themselves as typical students because the keys to success are the same for everyone. They should not alienate themselves from the white world; there is only one world, and they can handle it.
4. Giovanni uses the questions and answers starting in paragraph 14 to show black students how to respond to ignorant and "stupid questions" from white students. She encourages her readers to choose self-control and empowerment over victimization.
5. Unlike educational progress, which is a "national concern" (paragraph 34), for students the focus on education must remain personal: They attend college to educate themselves, not the world. In particular, she warns black students that spending too much time educating white people can become a distraction that slows them down and holds them back.

Questions on Strategy (p. 272)

1. Giovanni argues for black students to take control of their own futures and to find ways to achieve academic success. Her thesis is stated in paragraph 4: "There are discomforts attached to attending predominantly white colleges, though no more so than living in a racist world."
2. At the start of her essay, Giovanni wants to give readers a sampling of the attitudes young people have about education. The short sentences reflect the quick or rash decisions that some students make about their education.
3. Her personal narrative offers an example of how she handled living in a white world, which in turn gives her authority to write about the subject. Because Giovanni has succeeded in a white world, she has the authority to advise others.

4. These Q&A examples, in line with her title, "Campus Racism 101," provide a manual for dealing with racism. The article gives black students both keys to success and concrete ways to deal with the kinds of racism she knows they will face.
5. Giovanni means that the larger goal of educational progress needs to be handled by society. The students' goal is to become educated. She wants her readers to focus on that reason for attending college. Her purpose is to help black students succeed by encouraging them to stay focused on that goal, while letting others work on the larger problem.

Questions on Diction and Vocabulary (p. 273)
1. Students' reactions to the title will vary. "Campus Racism 101" suggests that the article will offer a detailed discussion of racism or a how-to manual on being racist. Some students will be surprised to discover that the article is actually about how to handle and overcome racism.
2. Giovanni shows that ignorance and stupidity can even come from educated people and that being "smart" in the real world has more to do with one's background. White people who go to school can also be really "stupid" in their behavior. She wants everyone to pay more attention to their behavior and think about what they are saying. Had she used the word *thoughtless*, she would have separated the white students from those less educated. She's trying to get the reader to realize the point made in *Forrest Gump*: "Stupid is as stupid does." Stupidity knows no racial or educational boundaries. She does want to insult the white students enough to make them be more thoughtful and to avoid assuming that their race or education protects them from being ignorant.
3. Giovanni's tone is both impassioned and instructional. She converts her anger and frustration into productive advice, just as she has done in her personal life. Her anger at ignorance and the kinds of statements people make is here transformed into a productive how-to-succeed guide for students.

CHAPTER 8 Comparison and Contrast

Neat People vs. Sloppy People
SUZANNE BRITT

Preparing to Read (p. 294)
This prompt functions on the assumption that we all fall prey to the trap of stereotyping. You might prepare for this prompt by asking for a list from the class about the kinds of stereotypes they have seen or experienced.

Thinking Critically about the Text (p. 296)
Britt breaks her distinction between neat and sloppy people along moral lines. She claims that neat people are lazy, mean, and immoral; sloppy people are planning, caring, and loving. Chances are students will know about exceptions to Britt's categories. You might begin a discussion by asking why Britt's categories are too reductive.

Questions on Subject (pp. 296–297)
1. Referring to the distinction between neat and sloppy people as a "moral" one is pure irony. With this sarcastic reference, Britt may well be making fun of all other socioeconomic and political debates in which superior morality is claimed by both sides of a decidedly nonmoral debate. The use of a pseudomoralistic tone helps Britt make her point.
2. The "heavenly vision" and "precise plan" held dear by sloppy people is the concept of "someday": someday they will accomplish everything. Of course, because "someday" is always somewhere in the future, it never arrives. As a result, sloppy people remain sloppy.
3. Sloppy people tend to be packrats—people who collect things and never throw anything away—whereas neat people clear everything away, often while still in use. Basic truisms like this one provide the foundation from which Britt takes off in exaggeration. Ask your students to give some well-known characteristics of neat and sloppy people, then discuss whether each one has merit or is just an unwarranted stereotype.

Questions on Strategy (p. 297)
1. Britt starts almost every paragraph repeating the type of person she will discuss further, "neat" or "sloppy." The reader can never get lost and can follow the singsong tone of the essay. Between paragraphs 5 and 6, she makes a smooth transition from her discussion of sloppy to neat people. She begins paragraph 5 with "Sloppy people can't bear to part with anything," and the last sentence in the paragraph smoothes the transition to neat people: "A neat person would just bulldoze the desk." She starts paragraph 6 with "Neat people are bums." Most students will find this essay delightfully easy to follow.
2. Describing sloppy people as those who "save everything, planning someday to file, order, and straighten out the world" (paragraph 4) and who "give loving attention to every detail" (5), while writing of neat people as being "lazier" (1) than sloppy people, being "bums and clods at heart" (6) and having "cavalier attitudes toward possessions" (6), neatly reverses the assumed roles of neat and sloppy people. Britt also makes the sloppy person appear saintly and generous, whereas the neat person is portrayed as being mean, nasty, and selfish. These exaggerations help make Britt's basic point that the labels "good" and "bad" or "right" and "wrong" are highly subjective and frequently misused.

3. Because this is an exaggerated, humorous essay, it would be to Britt's disadvantage to point out the similarities between the two types of people she is trying to show at opposite ends of the spectrum. Similarities are inherent; answers will vary depending on each student's particular viewpoint. This will make for a lively class discussion, and the variety of examples given will ensure that students understand the strategy being discussed.

4. In this essay the block system of contrast is actually an extended version of point-by-point contrast; Britt presents an idea, backs it up with outrageous details, and then goes on to contrast it with its counterpart. If simple point-by-point contrast had been used, much of the entertaining hyperbole would have been lost and the essay would have been dull.

5. Britt's use of examples in this essay is effective only because she goes to such absurd lengths to exaggerate her purpose and point. In paragraph 4, Britt writes the following about sloppy people: "the books spill from the shelves onto the floor, the clothes pile up in the hamper and closet, the family mementos accumulate in every drawer." Compare these examples to what she writes in paragraph 6 about neat people: "They have cavalier attitudes toward possessions, including family heirlooms. Everything is just another dustcatcher to them. If anything collects dust, it's got to go and that's that." Britt's statements of comparison and contrast need examples like these to make clear the comparison between the moral sloppy person and the immoral neat person. The comparisons or contrasts remain plain statements without support if Britt does not use examples.

Questions on Diction and Vocabulary (p. 297)

1. Britt is reverential when referring to sloppy people, using phrases and words like "extreme moral rectitude" (paragraph 2), "all these noble reasons and more" (4), "give loving attention to every detail" (5), and "meticulously creating" (5). She is disapproving and disdainful when describing neat people, referring to those "bums and clods" (6) who are "vicious" (9) with mail, who "bulldoze" (5), and who are "incredibly wasteful" (10) as well as "so insensitive" (12).

2. For the most part, Britt uses straightforward, clearly stated prose. It is easy to read and understand her word choices. Britt's use of simple language indicates that she is addressing a wide audience, from adolescents to adults. Student opinions will vary about the particular places where Britt uses precise words to good effect. You might ask the students what makes some words better than others (e.g., why is the expression "bums and clods at heart" better than "bad"?).

3. *Rectitude* (2): integrity; moral standards. *Tentative* (3): hesitant; not final or complete. *Meticulously* (5): painstakingly; extremely carefully; with great attention to detail. *Heirlooms* (6): valuable or sentimental property passed from one, usually familial, generation to another. *Salvaging* (9): saving from loss, decay, or destruction. *Swath* (12): a path made when mowing.

Buy Experiences, Not Things
JAMES HAMBLIN

Preparing to Read (p. 299)

Expect a great deal of diversity in student responses. Food and friends will likely come up. Given the likely ages of your students, partying or sports are also likely candidates. Focus on the question of whether there are multiple types of happiness. As a class, see if the students can agree on several central categories. Then discuss whether the initial student responses seem to fit within these categories.

Thinking Critically about the Text (p. 303)

Student answers will vary. Hamblin notes how individuals respond differently to the question when vacation time was used instead of money. You may want to ask if students feel the same ways about titles or even Twitter followers, for example.

Questions on Subject (p. 303)

1. This statistic will surprise most readers. This wandering, Hamblin claims, often makes us unhappy. We are happiest when engaged in moment-to-moment experiences. This supports his point that experiences, not objects, make us happy. If we are happiest in the moment, then it follows that it is worth our time constructing better and better moments.

2. In paragraph 3, Hamblin states his thesis, "experiences bring people more happiness than do possessions."

3. When anticipating something, we are starting to live into the experience. We imagine how something might be. Anticipation *is* part of the experience of whatever we are thinking about. If experience makes us happy and anticipation is part of the experience, then anticipation itself can contribute to our happiness.

4. Impatience is a disgruntled sentiment. We are not satisfied where we are or with what is happening, so we become irritable. When feeling impatient, we are not creating an experience in our mind; we are focused on what is wrong with the moment. Anticipation is a much more creative exercise. When we anticipate, we simulate experiences in the mind.

Questions on Strategy (p. 304)

1. Hamblin wants readers to consider that their material possessions contribute little to their overall happiness. He wants to encourage them, as the title says, to buy experiences rather than objects. This will save readers money and enhance their experience of life.

2. Hamblin's essay is primarily organized with a point-by-point comparison. In many paragraphs he describes the differences between material objects and experiences in their ability to make us happy. He keeps the comparisons close rather than describing the impact of objects on our happiness and then turning to the impact of experiences. He could have described the impact of each and then let the readers see clearly how experiences add so much more to our lives.

3. The graph makes visually clear how material objects and experiences differ in their overall ability to contribute to our happiness, excitement, and pleasantness. Readers can see these factors related to one another as well as consider whether — in light of this visual evidence — pursuing material objects really makes sense.

4. The dialogue helps demonstrate how differently we feel about experiences and objects. In dialogue we can see that it is almost absurd to think that objects can bring us joy. Hamblin also makes clear in the dialogue that experiences have a better warranty. If they turn out to be not so great, then at least we have a great story. He shows that we cannot do this as easily with objects. Dialogue shows the absurd and also adds some humor (as in the case of Vampire Weekend).

5. Hamblin uses a variety of examples, which helps him reach a wide range of readers who may be attracted to different experiences or material possessions. Some readers may want to discredit his argument by saying that a certain object or experience does not appeal to them. Showing how the argument holds up regardless of the specific object or experience strengthens Hamblin's argument.

Questions on Diction and Vocabulary (p. 304)

1. Hamblin wants to reach a sophisticated, affluent, and educated audience, likely one with material wealth. Writing to poor people that they should want experiences might actually be insulting. The article does not make this distinction, but it is likely that material objects matter at least to a point. If you have no bed, you might prefer it to a nice day at the park. Because he does not even address this point, we can assume he is writing to an audience whose members are meeting a certain amount of their basic needs. In the first paragraph, he cites a statistic, mentions Harvard, and quotes the very prestigious journal *Science*. This will tell readers that he is drawing on the most respected sources, which helps him reach an educated audience that respects these sources. Because he keeps the rest of the language simple, we can infer that the piece is not meant to be a scholarly argument. He uses basic examples to make his points. In paragraph 4, for example, he writes, "Experiential purchases like trips, concerts, movies . . . " He does not assume people know what he means by experiential purchases. He appeals to educated readers and keeps the writing simple.

2. "And, yes, it does" is a much more informal expression and begins to shift the reader from the scientific tone of the essay's introduction to the more conversational style of the rest of the article. Hamblin likely placed the science and quotations at the beginning to earn readers' trust. Once he did so, he could shift and connect with them less formally. In this more intimate style, he can connect with readers more intimately.

3. *Intrinsically* (paragraph 2): part of the essential nature of the thing. *Nostalgic* (2): pleasure and sadness that comes from remembering the past and wishing to experience it again. *Whimsical* (2): playful or amusing. *Accrues* (3): increases in value gradually. *Elicits* (5): gets a response from. *Metric* (5): standard of measurement. *Fraught* (5): stressed or worried. *Dilemma* (6): situation in which you have to make a difficult choice. *Hedonic* (7): of or relating to pleasure. *Nidus* (15): a place where something originates. *Hypothesis* (20): an idea or theory not proven. *Squandered* (21): use something in a foolish way.

Two Ways to Belong in America
BHARATI MUKHERJEE

Preparing to Read (p. 306)

Views will likely be influenced by whether or not students are themselves immigrants (particularly those who are in the United States to go to college) or whether their parents, grandparents, or close family members were immigrants. It may be useful to ask students to react to the phrase "We are a nation of immigrants." The current American political debate may have galvanized student views as "for" or "against" immigration. Ask students how black-and-white pro/con arguments might oversimplify an issue—regardless of where they themselves fall on the debate. It may be productive to allow a debate on these issues, or it may be more useful to create a neutral climate in the classroom. Issues in the news that are likely to come up: Is Donald Trump's 2016 campaign proposal to build a wall between the United States and Mexico unconstitutional and biased or a necessary step toward a "secure" border? What groups are more likely to feel that immigrants "take our jobs" or are "criminals"? What groups are more likely to believe recent immigrants do work "that no one else will do," like farm labor or housecleaning? Does media coverage inflame or simply inform us about the immigration debate? Mukherjee's essay helps students think about immigration from the perspective of the immigrant. You might ask students why an immigrant would want to be an American citizen and why an immigrant would want to stay a citizen of a parent country.

Thinking Critically about the Text (p. 309)

When Mukherjee's sister says in paragraph 10, "'If America wants to play the manipulative game, I'll play it too,'" she means her sister plans to subvert the intention of the law by working within the letter of it. For students, the sister's plan can be an important reminder that policies that restrict the rights of U.S. immigrants, whether here legally or illegally, feel like personal attacks; immigrants are personally affected by laws that are largely theoretical for most Americans. Student responses will range from sympathy to accusations of hypocrisy. It might be helpful to ask students what they would do if they were wearing the immigrants' shoes.

Questions on Subject (p. 310)

1. There might be disagreement on the thesis of Mukherjee's essay. It could be argued that her thesis is implied and concerns the contributions of immigrants to America or the injustice of American immigration laws. However, the most powerful point on the subject is personal and supports Mukherjee's thesis as: "The price that the immigrant willingly pays, and that the exile avoids, is the trauma of self-transformation" (paragraph 15). She presents this statement directly at the end of the essay, after spending some pages describing that very phenomenon. It might be useful to ask students if they agree or disagree that this is the thesis of the essay.

2. Mukherjee's arguments in favor of citizenship grow out of her personal preferences: "I need to feel like a part of the community I have adopted. . . . I need to put roots down, to vote and make the difference that I can" (paragraph 15). Her sister's arguments for retaining her Indian citizenship are similarly personal; she feels like an Indian, and she wants to retire to India (4).

3. Mukherjee's sister feels "used" by attempts to change American laws regarding benefits for noncitizens because she believes there was an implied contract she entered into when she began working in America and that she has kept her end of the bargain: "For over thirty years, I've invested my creativity and professional skills into the improvement of *this* country's preschool system. I've obeyed all the rules, I've paid my taxes" (paragraph 8). She feels that the contract is being violated by changing the rules without any warning. She has done nothing wrong, yet she is losing some of her rights.

4. At the end of paragraph 11, Mukherjee asks, "Which of us is the freak?" Student responses will vary. Note, however, that Mukherjee goes on to imply that neither sister is a freak; they simply have different priorities, and their actions can be traced back to those priorities. Mukherjee's sister's decision seems more surprising, yet if you understand her reasoning, it seems entirely rational.

5. When Mukherjee says in paragraph 15, "The price that the immigrant willingly pays, and that the exile avoids, is the trauma of self-transformation," she means that when a person emigrates from a homeland and becomes a citizen of a new country, her or his identity is deeply changed. Mukherjee rejected "three thousand years" of family tradition when she chose her own husband and decided not to return to India (paragraph 5). She went from being an Indian woman to being an American woman of Indian ancestry; her sister, on the other hand, is "here to maintain an identity, not to transform it" (9).

6. Student responses will vary as to which sister made the right decision. Some may feel that if they, as Americans, were to live in another country, they would want to retain their citizenship. They might also hope to return to the United States one day. Those students might think that Mukherjee's sister, Mira, made the right decision. Others may feel as Bharati Mukherjee does or even that it is wrong to accept the benefits of living in a

country and not the responsibility of citizenship. The fact that Mukherjee embraces "transformation" (paragraph 15), however, suggests that the decision to become a citizen has personal motivations above and beyond the abstract idea of obligations to the country where one lives.

Questions on Strategy (p. 310)

1. Mukherjee's essay is a combination of block and point-by-point organization: She considers both sides of one issue, she takes a longer space to consider one experience or point of view, and then she returns to the dialogue.

2. This pattern of organization is appropriate because it allows Mukherjee to present the complexities of her subject; a simple point-by-point analysis of the pros and cons of citizenship would minimize the ambiguities inherent in her decision to become a citizen and her sister's decision to remain an alien.

3. Mukherjee chooses to let Mira speak for herself in this essay, allowing her to make arguments with which Mukherjee herself disagrees. If Mukherjee had merely summarized her sister's words, Mira's reasoning wouldn't have been as clear and her persuasive points would have been muted. Allowing Mira to speak for herself shows respect for her views.

Questions on Diction and Vocabulary (p. 310)

1. Mukherjee uses the word "mongrelization" (in quotation marks) to refer to the end of ethnic and cultural purity. She turns this negative racist word upside down to celebrate what it means to her to marry outside one's race: "fluidity, self-invention, blue jeans and T-shirts, and renouncing three thousand years (at least) of caste-observant, 'pure culture' marriage" (paragraph 5).

2. Mukherjee's use of quotation marks around "quota" (paragraph 5), "pure culture" (5, 11), "aliens" (7), "illegal" (12), and "nontraditional" (13), among other words, distances her from the way these words are used in society and invites readers to consider their meanings and the assumptions behind those meanings. For example, what does it mean for a person to be "illegal"?

3. Mukherjee says that her sister's anger "sounded like the description of a long-enduring, comfortable yet loveless marriage, without risk or recklessness" (paragraph 9). She uses "marriage" to depict both the legal and the emotional relationship immigrants have with the country in which they live. Her sister's sense of betrayal arises from a desire "that we be loved" (9). By contrast, when America spoke to Mukherjee, "[she] married it . . . surrendering those thousands of years of 'pure culture'" (11) to embrace something about America and a new "transformed" identity she had there that appealed to her.

4. "By choosing a husband who was not my father's selection, I was opting for fluidity, self-invention, blue jeans and T-shirts, and renouncing three thousand years (at least) of caste-observant, 'pure culture' marriage in the Mukherjee family" (paragraph 5). *Caste* (5): one of the hereditary social classes in Hinduism that restricts the occupation of its members and their association with the members of other castes; a division of society based on differences of wealth, inherited rank or privilege, profession, occupation, or race. *Ethics* (6): a system by which acts are judged within their contexts instead of by categorical principles. *Scapegoating* (7): unmerited blaming of a representative person or group. *Subtext* (9): the implicit or metaphorical meaning. *Expatriate* (15): someone who leaves his or her native country to live elsewhere; someone who renounces allegiance to her or his native country.

The Difference between "Sick" and "Evil"
ANDREW VACHSS

Preparing to Read (p. 312)
Students may define evil in various ways, offering simple or complex descriptions. Some may say evil is simply purposefully harming another. Others may talk about actions and attitudes that lack compassion or caring for others. Some students may associate evil with more extreme cases, such as genocide, school shootings, or even villains such as The Joker from the *Batman* series. A discussion of fictional villains may also be useful because these characters are often less complicated than real figures, making it easier to pinpoint what makes them evil. For example, the question of whether every Nazi was evil is more complicated than determining Lex Luthor's evilness. Much scholarship has been dedicated to understanding, locating, and reflecting on evil. Remind students that the topic is an open one.

Thinking Critically about the Text (p. 316)
Student answers will vary as they speculate about why "our society distrusts the term *evil*." Maybe, in part, it's because *evil* has biblical and comic book overtones. It has an inhuman, otherworldly quality to it that we do not often want to see or acknowledge as existing in the world in which we find ourselves. The concept of evil can be difficult to deal with and understand for several reasons. If evil exists, we actually might see ourselves as called on to take action. We have in our culture what Vachss feels is confusion between "sick" and "evil." Vachss believes we have a tendency to excuse behavior for this reason: We allow the topic to be confusing so we do not have to face the truth or the tough decisions.

Questions on Subject (p. 316)
1. In the first paragraph, Vachss asks, "Are those who abuse their positions of trust to prey upon children . . . sick . . . or are they evil?" How we answer this question will determine how we react to the actions of these people. If we see them as sick, we in effect see them as blameless and treat them as victims. This takes the focus away from the children and the evil inflicted upon them. Perpetrators are not held responsible for their behavior in the same way if we label them as sick.
2. The difference is that "sick is a condition" (paragraph 9) whereas "evil is a behavior" (10). "Evil is always a matter of choice" (11). Vachss believes that, as long as the public continues to muddy the waters on this debate, "we will continue to give aid and comfort to our most pernicious of enemies" (13). Public confusion leads to incorrect action or not enough action.
3. Vachss believes psychology's approach and euphemisms result in allowing us "to absolve the predator of responsibility for his behavior" (paragraph 19). We do not hold people accountable if we call them sick.
4. If a perpetrator claims sickness only *after* he or she has been caught, we understandably question whether this claim is simply a ploy to reduce a sentence rather than a cry for help. Had the person wanted to heal and change, he or she would have asked for help *before* finding him- or herself charged with an offense.
5. Vachss believes we are so quick to declare predators as sick because "sickness not only offers the possibility of finding a cure but also assures us that the predator didn't really mean it. After all, it is human nature to try to understand inhuman conduct" (paragraph 25). In doing this, we do not hold people accountable, he believes. We cannot fight evil if we do not acknowledge it for what it is.

6. Vachss wants his readers to work toward amending the laws. Students might consider writing their state legislatures and asking that members of the religious community be required to report child abuse when they suspect it. In 2002 (when this article was written), members of religious communities were not required to report abuses, allowing much abuse to occur. Students may or may not find Vachss's argument convincing, though they might respect how he asked for very direct action.

Questions on Strategy (p. 316)

1. Vachss's thesis is in the second paragraph when he says, "we need to answer that fundamental question. Because without the truth, we cannot act. And until we act, nothing will change." In his mind, the distinction between "sick" and "evil" must be made clear so that we can address wrongs and protect our children.

2. In the article, Vachss tells the reader that his life's work has been the protection of children and that he has conducted this work in a wide variety of settings. His commitment and breadth of experience count as his expertise. In the introduction to the essay, readers learn more about him. He has been the director of a maximum-security prison, worked as a lawyer to protect children, and has written extensively on crime. All these experiences contribute to his expertise and authority as a writer.

3. The purpose in writing this essay is to make a distinction between "sick" and "evil" in a way that will resonate with readers, perhaps encouraging readers to get involved in the political process of reforming how we as a society handle heinous crimes. Vachss wants readers not to be seduced by the idea that all offenders are simply in need of healing. He wants evil to be stopped and believes that in being clear about what evil is, we can actually work to eradicate its effects, if not its very origin.

4. In paragraphs 6 to 14, Vachss works to make very clear the difference between "sick" and "evil" so that readers will agree that a clear and important distinction exists that is "beyond dispute." He uses a powerful and graphic "sick" example—a woman putting her baby in the oven to eradicate the devil—and an equally powerful "evil" example—the renting of a baby to pornographers. He then, using one-sentence paragraphs, aims to clarify even further how they are different: "sickness is a condition" (9) and "evil is a behavior" (10). In paragraph 14, he provides an example to clarify this distinction. Fantasizing about child abuse is sick, whereas actually acting on the idea is evil. Students will then discuss how they responded to the examples.

5. Student responses will vary. This absurd example highlights Vachss's point that every action could be considered a sickness. We must draw the line somewhere. Some students will find the extreme nature of the example very illustrative of his point. Some might find it too bizarre an example to be convincing.

6. Vachss most likely dedicates space to discussing the concept of "evil" so that his readers will recognize it when they see it. With a clear distinction in their minds, readers might be more likely to take strong action in the face of evil rather than make excuses for predatory behavior. This is Vachss's hope.

Questions on Diction and Vocabulary (pp. 316–317)

1. *Must* in the phrase "evil must be fought" (paragraph 13) has power because it is unequivocal. Vachss is very clear about what he espouses. *Cure* (16) is a strong verb because it has finality to it. The idea that one can be cured from acting in evil ways has very important sociopolitical consequences. *Contort* (25) is a descriptive verb demonstrating the kind of mental acrobatics he believes society undertakes to avoid facing the truth.

2. Student responses will vary. Some may be so accustomed to this notion of predators being called "sick" that they will not have recognized the oxymoron as such. Vachss believes this notion is inherently wrong because it distracts us from the focus of "protecting our children."
3. *Revulsion* (paragraph 1): a strong feeling of distaste or dislike. *Venue* (3): location. *Mandate* (5): an authoritative order or command. *Facile* (6): easy or complacent. *Pernicious* (13): causing insidious harm or ruin. *Sociopathy* (15): the condition of being sociopathic, a person lacking in the ability to feel empathy. *Insinuate* (21): to suggest subtly. *Propensities* (24): natural tendencies or inclinations.

Grant and Lee: A Study in Contrasts
BRUCE CATTON

Preparing to Read (p. 319)
This question prepares students to consider how little they actually know about the personalities and contributions of Civil War generals. You may want to ask students to do a quick online search on the two generals to place them historically.

Thinking Critically about the Text (p. 323)
Catton prepares readers for this claim by discussing first the strong differences between these two men and the commitment to their cause. Each had inner resolve and a passionate army behind them. It surprised everyone that men with such differences and such passion could let go of war and come together. These Civil War generals represent the competing ideologies of the country: tradition and privilege versus individual fate and democracy, commitment to one's past versus commitment to the future of the nation. Lee's surrender meant letting go of tradition in exchange for a unified nation; the ruling class would have to struggle for its status, and individual accomplishment would trump birthright.

Questions on Subject (p. 324)
1. Grant supported growth and change and felt his destiny was tied to the larger nation; Lee held on to tradition, believing change threatened his way of life. Lee saw his future tied to the region rather than the nation as a whole. "And that, perhaps, is where the contrast between Grant and Lee becomes most striking. The Virginia aristocrat, inevitably, saw himself in relation to his own region. He lived in a static society which could endure almost anything except change. . . . The Westerner, on the other hand, would fight with equal tenacity for the broader concept of society" (paragraphs 10 and 11).
2. Both were "marvelous fighters" (paragraph 13); demonstrated tenacity, fidelity, and "[d]aring . . . resourcefulness" (15); could "think faster and move faster than the enemy" (15); and "at the end [could] turn quickly from war to peace" (16). These similarities are important because they show that Grant and Lee were great at their roles and, in the end, were able to let the war go so the country could reunite. Had one been unable to let go of the battle, the country would have had a harder time coming back together. These men were so revered that their agreement to end the war set an example.
3. As in the age of chivalry, tidewater Virginia operated on a belief in "pronounced inequality in the social structure" (paragraph 5): Land was the key source of wealth, and an enduring class of men ruled. There were those who worked the land (previously serfs)

and those who ruled and profited from it (previously the nobles). Lee believed in noblesse oblige—that is, the rich were obligated to rule society with the perspective of one who does not work the land.

4. Grant relished the notion that each man could determine his own destiny rather than remain dependent on class structure for success. He believed in industry, creation, and growth—elements of American culture we take for granted today. It could be argued that his ideas are now dated, as businesses become increasingly reliant on their own success. In the global economy, success is tied to the health and prosperity of the planet, not just the nation.

Questions on Strategy (p. 324)

1. If Catton had looked at the similarities, he would have lost the buildup to his last statement: "Appomattox was one of the great moments of American history" (paragraph 16). The differences, in contrast, make the coming together of these great leaders so astonishing. Had Catton started with the similarities, readers would have seen the coming together of the generals and the nation as natural progressions. By pointing out their different ideologies, he helps readers better understand the dramatic ending of the Civil War.

2. Catton talks about both men, then goes into each individually, then does one point-by-point contrast, then compares them together. Paragraph 3: both Lee and Grant; paragraphs 4–6: Lee; paragraphs 7–9: Grant; paragraph 10: Lee; paragraph 11: Grant; paragraphs 12 and 13: both.

3. Catton uses a number of transitional devices, including restatement and comparison and contrast. Paragraph 3 begins with a comparison: "They were two strong men." Paragraph 9 presents a contrast: "Yet along with this feeling. . . ." Paragraph 10 also uses contrast: "And that, perhaps is where the contrast. . . ." Paragraph 12 uses cause and effect/restatement/contrast: "So Grant and Lee were in complete contrast. . . ." A comparison appears in paragraph 13, "Yet it was not all contrast . . . ," and a sequence in paragraphs 14 and 16, "to begin with" and "Lastly."

4. Catton takes great care to describe the attitudes of both men. Cause and effect analysis shows how their upbringings informed their beliefs. The description of how each man viewed entitlement and rule sharpens their differences: Lee was the "aristocratic ideal" (paragraph 6), whereas Grant was "self-reliant" (7). Cause and effect analysis shows us that Lee wanted to hold on to his background of culture and tradition and that Grant's hard upbringing caused him to value what he had earned on his own and to be rewarded for that personal accomplishment. Grant believed in the power of the individual because he experienced it growing up; Lee experienced the benefits and privileges of a noble upbringing and wanted to perpetuate those values. Describing each man separately, then relative to one another, enables the reader to see just how deeply the differences between them ran.

Questions on Diction and Vocabulary (p. 324)

1. "[T]wo conflicting currents" (paragraph 3): evokes the image of two very strong bodies of water going in different directions and furthers Catton's point that both men were essentially of the same matter, simply flowing apart from one another. It also reinforces the enormous challenges of bringing these two opposing currents into one direction or one strong river. "[S]inewy fiber" (7): demonstrates that Grant's men came from a background in which they themselves were as strong as the men who worked the land. Grant and the North valued their strength and connection to the land, not the soft hands of aristocracy, as an entitlement to power. "As its horizons expanded, so did his" (9): The

borders grew but the horizons did not literally expand. Grant saw his own destiny tied up with the growth of the country; this further contrasts with Lee, who tied his destiny to his region, not to any far-off horizon.
2. *Poignant* (2): heartfelt. *Chivalry* (5): rules and customs of medieval knighthood, including the values of honor, courtesy, generosity, and valor. *Sanctified* (6): made holy or sacred. *Sinewy* (7): tough, firm, braided, resilient. *Obeisance* (7): deference or homage. *Tidewater* (8): water affected by the flow and ebb of the tide. *Tenacity* (11): toughness. *Aspiration* (13): strong desire, aim, longing, or ambition.

CHAPTER 9 Division and Classification

But What Do You Mean?
DEBORAH TANNEN

Preparing to Read (p. 344)
Although communication styles can be very personal, you might tell your class that they are also influenced by outside social factors, such as region or cultural background. A student's family members may consider him or her to be a fairly relaxed communicator, but someone from a different background may find his or her style to be more formal. Invite students to consider their own styles in a larger social context.

Thinking Critically about the Text (p. 350)
Student answers will vary. Some may say that all language is culturally prescribed. Others may say that there are some universal standards. They may identify "thank you" or "please" as examples. Tannen complicates "thank you" quite effectively, however, saying that, while the words can be translated from one language to the next, they can convey many different meanings. You may want to draw a parallel with universal human rights. Are there certain ways of speaking, just as many believe there are certain human rights we all share? Or is it too easy to assume that the right way is *our* way, especially for U.S. citizens, who live in a country whose values are so widely broadcast they tend to pressure much of the rest of the world to conform?

Questions on Subject (p. 350)
1. In paragraph 2, Tannen introduces her thesis: "unfortunately, women and men often have different ideas about what's appropriate, different ways of speaking."
2. Tannen looks at the following categories of communication: apologies, criticism, thank yous, fighting, praise, complaints, jokes. Students may propose different categories. She could have added a category on "requests" to consider how men and woman make requests differently. "Greetings and departures" could be another category. Do men and women greet one another differently? One area where she could make a distinction is between how people operate at work versus in romantic relationships. Or how men and women are perceived when they are public figures. What happens when a woman becomes famous versus a man: Are people's perceptions of each different? There could be a category called "public communication."
3. Students will respond differently to Tannen's interpretation. The woman may have thought *she* originally forgot to give Tannen her number. Or maybe she was apologizing that she did not follow up and confirm that Tannen still had it. Perhaps she forgot she gave Tannen her card to begin with and was apologizing for the oversight.
4. Relating is an important part of the human experience. Not all talking is used to convey information. Some talking is simply part of feeling the connection with others. Relating well is enjoyable and helps us get things done. Conversational rituals help us connect with each other even if there is nothing particular we need to say.

Questions on Strategy (p. 351)

1. In paragraph 2, Tannen tells us that she wants to help correct the miscommunication in language between men and women. She is especially concerned when these language differences put women at a disadvantage.

2. Using a question as the title highlights the confusion that Tannen is trying to help smooth out between the sexes. It shows uncertainty and encourages us to become curious, rather than judgmental, about the differences. We are invited to explore with her exactly what it is that we all mean to say.

3. Throughout the essay, Tannen compares how men and women communicate. In the Apologies section, we learn that women apologize as a way of relating and men avoid it, fearing they will be viewed in the "one down" position. This highlights some confusion that can occur. Women are not necessarily apologizing for making a mistake, but men can use it subconsciously as a way to keep women down. When women understand these differences, they can keep themselves from being subjugated by the differences. In the Criticism section, Tannen notes the differences between forms of feedback between men and women. Women can be more tentative. She uses this comparison to encourage women not to be put off by the communication style of men. Men's style of giving feedback does not necessarily mean that the women did a bad job. Students may also pull examples from any of the other communication categories.

4. Students will share which examples resonated with them and which did not. They may provide examples from their own lives that would have worked. Students may say that citing some academic studies could have strengthened Tannen's argument. For example, she could have said that a study was done with company CEOs and found that apologizing turned them off and made them tentative about promotions. Or maybe she could have cited other studies that supported her thesis. Many of her points come from more anecdotal experiences.

5. Tannen organizes her essay according to areas of communication. Most students will likely find this organization very clear. It leaves out certain differences—intimate communication versus professional communication, but the structure keeps the discussion focused and accessible.

Questions on Diction and Vocabulary (p. 351)

1. Tannen's diction is colloquial. She is talking about how we speak in daily interactions. Her diction matches our daily exchanges. She is talking about everyday language and therefore uses everyday language. This gives the piece coherence. She uses conjunctions, for example, *they're, she's,* and so on. She also uses the verb *to be* (*is, are, was*) quite often. Conjunctions and the verb *to be* are used less often with formal diction. She uses simple words to describe her point: *concerned, thinking, reassuring.* Her words are understood by all readers. There is no confusing vocabulary.

2. *Self-deprecating* (paragraph 4): positioning oneself or one's activities as unimportant. *Convention* (11): a widely accepted way of doing things. *Tentativeness* (11): done with hesitancy. *Intrinsically* (12): inherently. *Reciprocate* (14): to do something for someone that is similar to what was done for you. *Adrenaline* (17): substance produced by the body when one experiences a strong emotion; it increases the heart rate. *Rebuttal* (20): an argument that proves something false using evidence. *Soliciting* (24): making a request for. *Rapport* (25): a friendly relationship. *Malcontent* (27): a person who is always angry or upset about something.

The Queen Bee and Her Court
ROSALIND WISEMAN

Preparing to Read (p. 353)

This prompt prepares students to think about the roles they play in social structures as well as how those structures influence students' behavior and perceptions of themselves. Students will have different experiences with cliques—some positive, some negative. For the most part, students will refer to their elementary school cliques as having been determined by factors such as a shared homeroom, reading group, bus stop, or neighborhood. Students might say that high school cliques, in contrast, are sophisticated and political and determined not by proximity but by shared interests and experiences such as musical taste, sports, grades, parents' wealth, fashion, drug use, or even sexual activity.

Thinking Critically about the Text (p. 364)

Students' personal experiences will affect how accurate they find Wiseman's classification system to be. Students may say that they played different roles at different ages or feel that no one role suits them perfectly. Consider asking those young men who do agree with Wiseman's classifications if they had sisters or lots of female friends. Some young men who have not had exposure to girls in groups may not recognize these traits because they tend to be expressed most markedly among girls themselves.

Questions on Subject (p. 364)

1. The Queen Bee is controlling, intimidating, exclusive, persuasive, charming, strategically affectionate, powerful, and vengeful. "Through a combination of charisma, force, money, looks, will, and manipulation, this girl reigns supreme over the other girls" (paragraph 2). Students will agree or disagree with Wiseman's assessment on the basis of their own experiences.

2. Most students will enjoy the quotes from young girls. They provide support for Wiseman's classification system and also suggest that Wiseman consulted girls when forming her categories, making her more authoritative on the subject. Some students may say the quotes enable them to think more about their own experiences and how the roles are fluid.

3. Wiseman uses a formula of expressing benefits and drawbacks to demonstrate that each of the positions in the clique comes with a price—for example, being a Queen Bee has drawbacks, and being a Target has advantages. The formula illustrates that a certain balance of pros and cons exists for each role and that parents should accentuate the positive but be mindful of the negative when considering their daughters' positions in cliques.

4. Students will be split on this question. Some may agree with Wiseman that each role has benefits, something to be learned; for Targets, their experience at the bottom of the social totem pole teaches them about the necessity for empathy and objectivity. Every role teaches a social survival skill. Some students may disagree with Wiseman, saying that members of certain categories—specifically Targets—do not benefit from their role in the social structure because they serve only to uphold the power of those above them.

5. According to Wiseman, cliques form because students become frightened and overwhelmed when they leave the secure world of their small elementary schools. "We put our girls in this strange new environment [of junior, middle, and high school] at exactly the same time that they're obsessively microanalyzing social cues, rules, and regulations and therefore are their most insecure" (paragraph 55). Cliques provide rules and regulations in a large and often overwhelming environment.

Questions on Strategy (pp. 364–365)

1. Wiseman means that cliques are more than just a pecking order or superficial structure; in fact, they serve a purpose, have an effect on members' lives, and deserve to be examined thoughtfully. Most students will agree this is Wiseman's thesis because it states the purpose of her essay and establishes its structure.

2. Wiseman's audience is parents of teenage girls, and her subject is cliques and self-esteem. Her statement is designed for parents to broach the subject with sensitivity and to gain their daughters' trust by having the teen girls validate their own experiences by talking about them within the context of Wiseman's classification. She doesn't want parents to lecture their daughters; she wants them to have an open, honest dialogue. Wiseman believes girls' social structures are immensely complex, and she warns parents against oversimplifying the issues.

3. Wiseman divides girls into the following groups: Queen Bee, Sidekick, Banker, Floater, Torn Bystander, Pleaser/Wannabe/Messenger, and Target.

4. Wiseman uses a top-to-bottom organization: She starts with the most powerful member of a clique (the Queen Bee, who sits atop the social totem pole) and then progresses downward (to the Target, a clique's least powerful member). Most students will find this organization effective because it illustrates the Queen Bee's power and the effects of that power on the other members of the clique. The organization also reinforces the idea that a clique is defined by the Queen Bee; without her to rule it, the clique would not exist. Some students may feel that girls' roles are more amorphous, overlapping, and not as clearly defined; therefore, they will feel that Wiseman's organization is too linear.

5. Definition enables Wiseman to explain why she chose each category's name and what the person in each role gains and loses by occupying that position in the clique. Illustration brings breadth to the definitions and builds confidence in Wiseman as an authority on the topic. Comparison and contrast elucidates the differences among categories, keeping the distinctions clear while also illustrating how roles within the group can shift. By comparing and contrasting roles, Wiseman shows how each is defined by the others—how each needs the others in order to exist.

Questions on Diction and Vocabulary (p. 365)

1. Most students will agree that Wiseman's title is effective because it accurately and creatively encapsulates the categories within a structure—a royal court—that describes the members' positions in relation to their leader, the Queen Bee. Some students may suggest alternate, more overlapping classifications such as Leader, Follower, Outsider, Talker, Listener, and Loser.

2. Wiseman's attitude toward cliques is serious and measured. She states, "Our best politicians and diplomats couldn't do better than a teen girl does in understanding the social intrigue and political landscape that lead to power" (paragraph 1). She is somewhat disdainful of Queen Bees, stating, "If your daughter's the Queen Bee and you could spy on her, you would (or should) be mortified by how she treats other girls" (2).

3. *Cliques* (paragraph 1): small exclusive groups of people. *Omnipotent* (2): having unlimited authority or influence. *Mortified* (2): deeply humiliated or embarrassed. *Anointed* (3): consecrated; made or declared sacred. *Cynical* (10): expressing jaded or scornful skepticism or negativity. *Agenda* (11): a list of things to be done. *Utilitarian* (21): devoted to mere material interests. *Oust* (22): to eject; expel. *Rationalize* (30): to justify. *Perimeter* (35): the outer limits of an area. *Precarious* (36): dangerously insecure; unstable.

The Truth about Lying
JUDITH VIORST

Preparing to Read (p. 367)

The prompt will elicit a subjective response (allow room for a variety of views). You might ask students about the times they have lied—whether it was to conceal or to avoid hurting feelings. Discuss these personal experiences before you have students try to define and then classify types of lies.

Thinking Critically about the Text (p. 372)

Lying has always been understood as a negative social practice, but Viorst offers a number of examples of lies that can protect or keep trust. These sections promote another understanding of lying. Answers will vary on the necessity of these lies. Have students discuss whether telling the truth is the better alternative.

Questions on Subject (p. 372)

1. Viorst is wary of giving advice on lying because "too many people would promptly disagree" (paragraph 1).
2. There are contradictions inherent in both the "protective" and "peace-keeping" categories of lies. The very fact that these lies are rationalized as being for the "good" of oneself or others is contradictory: If lying is bad, how can some lies be good?
3. In telling a protective lie, one would make the assumption that the truth would be too damaging to the listener. Students will likely disagree with this assumption. Discuss it.
4. A peace-keeping lie is told primarily to prevent the teller from having to experience discord resulting from the truth; protective lies are told to spare the feelings of others from a damaging truth. Thus the basic difference between the two categories is that peace-keeping lies are told to protect the teller whereas protective lies are told to protect the listener.

Questions on Strategy (p. 372)

1. Viorst categorizes lies as social lies, peace-keeping lies, protective lies, and trust-keeping lies. This is an adequate division for the writer; other people may have other categorizations. Ask your students if they can think of any additional categories.
2. Viorst accommodates those with steadfast views on lying by first assuring the reader that she "can't present any ultimate conclusions" (paragraph 1) and then by showing within each section circumstances that could justify the lie or not, depending on the individual view of the reader. She challenges her audience by posing direct questions—such as "What about you?"—at the end of each section.
3. The liar and the listener have varying significance from one category of lies to another. In peace-keeping and some social lies, for example, the lie is being told for the good of the liar, whereas with protective and some other social lies, the lie is for the benefit of the listener. Ask your students whom the other categories benefit.
4. This question demands individual responses from students. While on the subject of social lies, for example, Viorst gives readers opportunities to respond to specific situations. See paragraphs 3 through 6.
5. Beginning in paragraph 45, Viorst opens her essay to the thoughts of others. In this way, the readers are given a cross-section of people who lie and a variety of reasons they do—a

clever way for Viorst to reinforce her point without direct claims. At the end, the reader is unsure if he or she has been lied to throughout this essay—a very effective way to conclude a selection on lying.

6. The examples used by students in this response will depend on each individual. Viorst's use of examples strengthens her classification of lies. She gives the reader categories, and then provides examples of her distinctions about lies. In paragraph 3, after classifying social lies, she writes, "Will you say to people, when it simply isn't true, 'I like your new hairdo,' 'You're looking much better,' 'It's so nice to see you,' 'I had a wonderful time'?" Viorst shows and tells at the same time. As a result, the reader gets a complete picture of what she is talking about.

Questions on Diction and Vocabulary (pp. 372–373)

1. Viorst keeps her diction simple, familiar, and accessible. This keeps the readers interested and also helps the author avoid sounding preachy. Some word choice examples that illustrate this are "simply isn't true" (paragraph 3); "do you have the courage—or is it the cruelty?" (13); and "do you find yourself ready, willing and able to lie?" (15).

2. *Mellifluous* (paragraph 7): flowing in a smooth or sweet manner. *Supersede* (18): to replace; to displace; to supplant. *Dissemble* (32): to give a false or misleading appearance to; to conceal the real nature of.

The Ways of Meeting Oppression
MARTIN LUTHER KING, JR.

Preparing to Read (p. 374)
It will be useful to learn just how much students know about the civil rights movement—and how they interpret what they know—before they read this selection. Martin Luther King, Jr. and the work he did must now be placed in a historical perspective, and many students may be unfamiliar with the tactics he used and the context in which he used them. They may not know that the goals of the civil rights movement were to outlaw racial discrimination and enfranchise African Americans. The two pieces of legislation that accomplished these goals were the Civil Rights Act (1964), which outlawed racial discrimination, and the National Voting Rights Act (1965). You may wish to have a class discussion on the civil rights movement before having the students read the essay, so that the history and issues of the movement are clear. Additional information about the civil rights movement is included in the headnote to that selection.

Thinking Critically about the Text (p. 376)
This question is meant to encourage students to stop and think about the meaning of oppression—and the manner in which it can be inflicted—and the conditions faced by African Americans in the South when Martin Luther King, Jr. began his protest movement. Discuss what has changed in the past fifty or so years. Have students discuss whether they believe that people are still being oppressed today. Make sure they understand the distinction between prejudice and oppression and are ready to defend their answers based on their observations of modern society. Key definitions include: Oppress, to subjugate or persecute by unjust use of force or authority; to weigh heavily upon and thus depress the mind or spirits. Prejudice, irrational suspicion or hatred of a particular group, race, or religion.

Questions on Subject (p. 377)

1. The "freedom of exhaustion" (paragraph 2) is the sense of relief that can be found in giving up, in accepting or ignoring injustice so that one no longer struggles against it. King views such acceptance as siding with the oppressors. By failing to resist injustice, people are communicating that the situation is morally acceptable, and they become as evil as those oppressing them.
2. King says, "Religion reminds every man that he is his brother's keeper. To accept injustice or segregation passively is to say to the oppressor that his actions are morally right" (paragraph 3). Religion demands that we speak up.
3. Violence, says King, is "impractical and immoral" (paragraph 5). It seeks to destroy rather than build, and "it thrives on hatred rather than love" (5). In achieving a victory based on violence, the victors create an imbalance in which they are likely to become brutal and their fallen enemies terribly embittered. History has shown that this system does not last.
4. In King's view, nonviolent resistance can make the racial struggle — and, one can presume, any other struggle — transcend its specific context to become an issue of injustice versus justice. There are no enemies, just a system that is flawed and is being resisted.

Questions on Strategy (p. 377)

1. King's purpose is to present the three ways with which oppression can be met and to argue that one of them, nonviolent resistance, is the best way to meet it. The paragraphs can be divided into three groups. After one sentence that presents King's opinion about the existence of three ways to deal with oppression, paragraphs 1 through 3 present the first way, acquiescence, and why King disapproves of it. Paragraphs 4 through 6 present the second way, violence, and, in much the same manner as before, why King disapproves of it as a response. Paragraphs 7 through 10 present the third way, nonviolent resistance, and King's argument that this is by far the best way to meet oppression. King organizes his essay in a very simple fashion, as described here, but it works very well. He presents the two methods he wishes to criticize first, effectively removing them as viable options before he presents the method he wishes to promote. He then provides a powerful argument in favor of nonviolent resistance so that the reader is left with a positive understanding of it, further negating the first two options in the reader's mind.
2. King is trying to deflect anger and resentment from the individuals who administer the system and direct it toward the system itself. Hatred of people too easily leads to violence and bitterness, which, he argues, are not solutions for those searching for a healthy society. Hating the system makes it easier to persuade people to resist nonviolently because those who administer the system are in many ways as much victims of it as are those oppressed by the system.
3. King's intended audience is obviously well read and intelligent. They are those who will lead others in the movement, who will explain how it is to be done and why it is to be done in a certain way. King probably intends some of those involved in the system of oppression to read the essay as well, and his eloquent style and learned, reasoned approach to the situation are meant to make such people stop and think about what they are doing.
4. King makes effective use of illustration, although he does not provide specific examples when he feels it to be unnecessary. His direct biblical reference to Moses and the slaves who did not embrace freedom supports a point that some readers may not believe — that some of those who are oppressed welcome the oppression. In places where he feels his point is more obvious, he uses a simple reference, such as "History is cluttered with the wreckage of nations that failed to follow this command" (paragraph 5). King uses

figurative language and oratory techniques to help present his argument. He also presents cause and effect sequences for each of his three responses to oppression, with nonviolent resistance providing the only positive effect. Division and classification help King sort out three clear responses to oppression and argue in favor of the response he prefers—nonviolent resistance.

Questions on Diction and Vocabulary (pp. 377–378)

1. King became famous for his stirring oration and eloquence. The "desolate night of bitterness" (paragraph 6) is a striking image, one that is meant to defuse the imagery of those who were advocating violence. It emphasizes that the thrill of victory is short and that what follows is usually just as bad as what preceded the violence and will worsen the lives of children and grandchildren. Such a powerful image is much more compelling than a more prosaic statement would have been, and by appealing to his readers' concern for their children, it undercuts the tempting scenario of a quick, violent victory over the oppressors.

2. Falsehood and malice are not mentioned in King's arguments against physical violence, so they add a new dimension to his discussion. Although not involving physical violence, using falsehood to end oppression will create an unstable system upon which a dialogue can be based, like a violent overthrow. It is therefore an analogous tactic to be avoided. Malice will also create enmity, which will undermine the process of reconciliation in any new system created through its use. Hate has been mentioned as a by-product of violence and something that makes it an immoral tactic. Hatred makes nonviolent resistance difficult, and it turns a struggle for justice into one for victory and annihilation of the hated party or parties. Destruction is also a by-product of violence, a sign of brutality on the part of the victors and a reason for the defeated to be bitter in their defeat. Again, King is arguing that the system of oppression needs to be opposed and that the opposition must appeal to everyone's conscience, not simply promote the cause of the oppressed.

3. *Acquiescence* (paragraph 1): acceptance; consent. *Tacitly* (1): implicitly; by nature. *Yoke* (2): shackle; harness. *Perpetrators* (8): those who commit crimes. *Glib* (9): slick; silver-tongued. *Sublime* (9): inspiring; noble.

Mother Tongue
AMY TAN

Preparing to Read (p. 379)
After students have discussed how their speaking might change in different contexts, move the conversation into a discussion of how different writing situations also affect language. You might point out that a text or a social media post invites a very different style of writing than an academic essay or a professional cover letter.

Thinking Critically about the Text (p. 384)
Students may respond differently to the idea that someone would find their writing "easy to read." Some may consider it a compliment, whereas others may consider it an indicator that the piece was not academic or professional enough. It might depend on the audience for whom it was intended. If a piece is not able to communicate its ideas to an intended audience, however, then it has failed its task. Why would we ever want to write a piece that is purposefully hard to read? To prove our own intelligence?

Questions on Subject (p. 385)

1. In paragraph 3, Tan introduces the main idea of the essay: "Recently, I was made keenly aware of the different Englishes I do use." We know she will talk about the use of different kinds of English in her experience.

2. In paragraph 3, Tan introduces the standard English she learned in school. She offers the following phrase as an example of this English, "the intersection of memory upon imagination." She describes this kind of English as having "carefully wrought grammatical phrases . . . normalized forms, past perfect tenses, conditional phrases . . ." In paragraph 4, she talks about the kind of English she uses with her mother. She calls this "the language of intimacy" and "family talk." In paragraph 6, she provides an example. Tan experiences this family English as "vivid, direct, full of observation and imagery" (7). To those not familiar with this type of English, the communication would be seen as filled with errors. The verbs are incorrectly conjugated and sometimes missing altogether. Articles and direct objects are also often missing.

3. Tan felt ashamed as a child because she considered her mother's English "broken," "fractured," and "limited" (8). Now she considers her mother's English "simple" (21) but still full of imagery and containing the passion, intent, and unique manner of the speaker. It is full and complete even if it is neither wholly English nor wholly Chinese.

4. Students will respond differently to this question. Some may argue there are correct answers on many English tests. There are rules of grammar and there are relations between words that can be identified. Many may agree that, while these rules exist, English and the humanities — because they are often about interpretation — have more possible answers than math and science.

Questions on Strategy (p. 385)

1. Tan's purpose in this essay is to show how she came to see English not as one static language that could be spoken correctly or incorrectly but rather as a form of communication that can have many iterations. In paragraphs 2 and 3, she tells readers that she sees the forms of English she uses as variations. Then she tells how she came to see them that way rather than one as broken and the other as correct.

2. She begins the essay with a negative definition, "I am not a scholar of English or literature." She defines herself as a "writer" and a lover of languages. She defines herself as one who thinks often about language.

3. Student responses to the examples will vary. Some may have a hard time following the transcription of her mother's story. The idea is to show its structure rather than communicate the content, but some readers might struggle to glean the meaning. They may find this struggle distracting.

4. Some students may struggle with the example and appreciate Tan's explanation. In paragraph 6, Tan chooses to show versus tell. Something would have been lost had she just tried to describe the language. Readers would have had an incomplete picture. Actually quoting her mother helps readers see the differences between the two Englishes introduced in the essay.

5. The limitations of her mother's English are only limitations when compared to standard English taught in school. Tan realized over time that the simple English her mother used still communicated a great deal. Her mother's English may have been wrong grammatically but it did not lack in meaning and effectiveness. This shows us that language does not have to be correct to be powerful and understood. This seeming contradiction works to encourage readers to be less judgmental about what they perceive to be "broken English."

6. Readers of Tan's essay are somewhere in-between her mother and her academic audience. We know this because she uses an English far less abstract than the English used during her lecture and one more complex than the one used by her mother. She uses standard American spoken English, which is used in magazines, television, and conversation. Her English is grammatically correct (unlike her mother's) but not abstract. Her first-person narrative helps keep the piece simple and accessible.

Questions on Diction and Vocabulary (p. 385)

1. Tan's diction is personable and welcoming. She reveals herself by using first-person narration. She shares her personal thoughts and personal growth with the reader. Using "I" and talking about what made her "ashamed" and what she later "realized" makes readers feel close: We are welcomed into her inner experience.

2. *Normalized* (paragraph 4): converting another part of speech into a noun (as in *legalize* into *legalization*). *Belies* (7): to show something as false or wrong. *Empirical* (9): based on testing or experience. *Guise* (10): a way of seeming that is untrue (related to *disguise*). *Insular* (15): separated from other people or cultures. *Semantic* (16): relating to the meaning of words and phrases. *Associative* (17): related to one another. *Quandary* (20): confusing situation. *Nascent* (20): recently formed or developed.

CHAPTER 10 Definition

What Is Poverty?
JO GOODWIN PARKER

Preparing to Read (p. 407)
Students will have various responses to the prompt because *poor* is an ambiguous term that will lead to many interpretations. You might prepare for this prompt by asking about the multiple meanings of the word *poor*. Keep in mind that Parker's poverty encompasses more than economics.

Thinking Critically about the Text (p. 411)
Much of Parker's essay works by attempting to create empathy in the reader. She tries to place the reader in her conditions and times. Students' responses to the prompt will vary; take time to discuss a few of the responses. Discuss how personal experience affects one's opinion on a subject.

Questions on Subject (p. 411)
1. Parker could not have the operation that was recommended for her because she could not afford it, she was afraid of it, and she did not have the time or resources to take care of her children during the time it would take her to recover (paragraph 3). She quit her job because she was spending more on day care than she possibly could afford and still be able to feed her family (3).
2. Parker claims that asking for help is humiliating and shameful and results in getting the runaround. The only reason that she is compelled to seek help in spite of all of this is for the sake of her children (paragraph 6).
3. Readers are not given a precise reason for the husband's departure; they are merely told by Parker that she purposely "destroyed" her marriage (8). She claims that she hopes her husband has been able to better himself because "[h]e never could hope with us to drag him down" (8).
4. Parker is implying that those without money are taken advantage of in insidious, humiliating ways. The neighbor obviously expects sexual favors as payment for a ride.
5. Depending on the personal outlook of the reader, the dreams described are either within reach or completely out of the question. Parker would probably regard these dreams as unrealistic.

Questions on Strategy (pp. 411–412)
1. Parker wants to make people aware of the plight of the poor. She drives home—very forcefully—the misery and squalor of poverty by using extended definition. The reader is placed in Parker's scene.
2. Parker uses narrative, description, some negative and some synonymous definitions in this essay. There are no statistics or quotations from other sources. Parker leaves such information out because she does not want her definition of poverty to become impersonal.
3. Eight of the fifteen paragraphs of this essay begin with "Poverty is . . ."; two others begin with "But you say to me . . ."—an indication that Parker has tried many times (and

failed) to make others understand her dire predicament. Also, the words *tired*, *dirt*, and *smell* are repeated throughout the selection, again to hammer home the horrific circumstances that poverty causes.

4. The most striking details Parker uses are those that were obviously meant to be the most disturbing, such as an infant's skin peeling off with an old diaper, insects everywhere, and the stench of poverty: "watching gnats and flies devour your baby's tears when he cries" (paragraph 5); "insects in your food, in your nose, in your eyes, and crawling over you when you sleep" (5). The emotional impact comes from the realization of the terrible toll that poverty exacts on children, especially babies. Most readers can identify with the basic needs of food and shelter; when they are faced with the images of children deprived of even these basic needs they respond emotionally. By using description and examples, Parker's definition of poverty is not read about but felt (almost experienced).

Questions on Diction and Vocabulary (p. 412)

1. "Poverty is an acid that drips on pride until all pride is worn away" (paragraph 13) and "Poverty is a chisel that chips on honor until honor is worn away" (13) describe the corrosive destruction of poverty and mirror—through repetition—the drudgery that must be endured by those being systematically eaten away and destroyed by poverty. The metaphoric imprisonment reflected in the phrase "the bars of my poverty" (10) reinforces the feelings of being trapped, helpless, and desperate. The reader responds to the raw force and emotion of these phrases as much as to the plain, simple words and phrases used elsewhere.

2. Parker uses the bar metaphor and the paradox of freedom in alcohol and drugs to show her children's future. The poverty has already determined their fate—they are behind bars. The freedom of alcohol and drugs is not a freedom but another type of bar, as it allows for only a temporary escape—one always comes back to the real problem.

3. The tone of this essay is angry and defensive, and very blunt; Parker wants her descriptions to shock and horrify readers so that they will have an inkling about the true nature of poverty. This is shown in phrases such as "Listen without pity. I cannot use your pity" (paragraph 1); "You say in your clean clothes coming from your clean house, 'Anybody can be clean.' Let me explain about housekeeping with no money" (4); "the red cloud of shame and the rising black cloud of despair" (7); "Your children won't play with my boys" (10). With the pronoun *you*, she speaks to her audience directly. She seems to be addressing an audience unfamiliar with poverty, however. What risks does she take by making such assumptions about this audience?

4. *Chronic* (paragraph 3): constantly recurring. *Anemia* (3): medical condition in which the blood is low in iron, resulting in fatigue and pallor. *Grits* (4): porridge of cooked ground hominy. *Oleo* (4): margarine. *Antihistamines* (5): medicines used to stop symptoms of colds, flu, and allergies.

Steal This MP3 File: What Is Theft?
G. ANTHONY GORRY

Preparing to Read (p. 414)

This prompt asks students to consider their definition of and experiences with theft. Ask students if they have ever had anything stolen. What was stolen? How did they feel? Students' answers will enable them to reflect on Gorry's idea that technology has changed the way young people think about theft.

Thinking Critically about the Text (p. 418)

Students' answers will differ based on their experience with file sharing. Students might think that the amount of music they copy determines the morality of their actions. Some students may say that copying music for profit rather than for personal use is the sole distinction between sharing and stealing.

Questions on Subject (p. 418)

1. Intellectual property is a commercially valuable product of the creative mind: music, literature, films, and the like. Intellectual property is ideas and content; other types of property are physical. For example, a story in a book is intellectual property—the ideas remain the property of the author. However, the physical, printed book belongs to whoever purchases it.
2. The music industry has filed "legal actions against companies that provide the infrastructure for file sharing" (paragraph 3), as well as against individuals who post large amounts of pirated music online. The music industry has also sought "to create media that cannot be copied or can be copied only in prescribed circumstances" (5). Gorry states that "the industry's multifaceted defense has failed" (6).
3. Most students will agree that the football player was guilty of stealing because he took a book he did not purchase. Ask students to discuss the question, "Does giving in to temptation equal entrapment?"
4. Gorry means that the easier it is to copy something, the less likely people are to feel that the copying itself is theft. The level of "awkwardness of the copying aligns [people's] actions with moral guidelines and legal standards" (paragraph 11). Gorry suggests that people believe photocopying a few pages from a book does not constitute theft because it is fast and easy; photocopying an entire book does constitute theft because it is time consuming and probably more expensive than simply buying the book itself.
5. Gorry states, "Treating customers like thieves is a certain recipe for failure" (paragraph 15). Instead of litigation, he feels that the music industry should embrace music downloads and file sharing and "perhaps [offer its own] repositories of digital music for downloading . . . gaining revenue from the scope and quality of its holdings" (15). Students' opinions of this solution will vary.

Questions on Strategy (p. 418)

1. Gorry's thesis appears in paragraph 15: "The lesson from my classroom is that digital technology has unalterably changed the way a growing number of customers think about recorded music."
2. Students may differ as to how effectively Gorry achieves his purpose. Students will agree with Gorry's statement that "had we had the same digital technology when we were young, we probably would have engaged in the same copying and sharing of software, digital music, and video that are so common among students today. We should not confuse lack of tools with righteousness" (paragraph 13).
3. Gorry juxtaposes the MP3 file on his laptop in 2003 with the story of the football player stealing a book in the 1960s. He also uses the example of photocopying a few pages from a book versus photocopying a whole book. These examples show how perceptions of theft have become tied to ease of the method employed. Gorry suggests that students do not think copying is theft: "where the material is disconnected from the physical moorings of conventional stores and copying is so easy, many of my students see matters differently" (paragraph 12).

4. Gorry is a professor of computer science at Baylor University. He teaches a course in which "students ... explore the effects of information technology on society," including "discussion of intellectual property in the information age" (paragraph 2).
5. Ask students if they are familiar with *Bye Bye Birdie* and whether that familiarity is essential to understanding the quotations. The quotations illustrate how Gorry comes to understand that "had we had the same digital technology when we were young, we probably would have engaged in the same copying and sharing" (paragraph 13).
6. Gorry uses another question/answer transition in paragraphs 9 and 10. He also uses repetition of key ideas: paragraphs 2 and 3 and 3 and 4; transitional expressions: paragraph 13; parallelism: paragraph 10; and conjunctions: paragraph 12.

Questions on Diction and Vocabulary (p. 419)
1. Gorry's essay first appeared in the *Chronicle of Higher Education*; his audience is fellow professors. The pronoun *we* in paragraph 13 refers to Gorry's peers—professors who came of age before the era of music downloads. He quotes a song from *Bye Bye Birdie*, a story about growing up in the 1950s. Most young people today will not be familiar with the musical. He says, "I remember that the 'kids' in my class are children of the information age" (paragraph 1). If he were writing to students or younger people, he likely would have written "*you* are children of the information age."
2. Gorry's diction is conversational and professional. He refers to the course he teaches, explaining for his audience of fellow professors how the topic of intellectual property and file sharing comes up in class. Some of Gorry's terms are elevated or technical, but they are appropriate for his audience. For example, he writes, "The readings for the class amply demonstrated the complexity of the legal, technical, and economic issues surrounding intellectual property in the information age" (paragraph 10).
3. *Disseminate* (3): to spread. *Encoded* (3): having undergone standardized formatting of electronic data. *Emporium* (4): a large retail store or place of business. *Infringements* (4): violations; transgressions. *Repositories* (15): places where things are stored; warehouses.

What Does "Boys Will Be Boys" Really Mean?
DEBORAH M. ROFFMAN

Preparing to Read (p. 420)
The expression "boys will be boys" will likely bring to mind stereotypes of crude, sexual, and possibly violent behavior. This expression implies that it is natural for boys to, for example, enjoy rough physical play, be quick to anger, bully or worse, be interested in sports, have an aversion to domestic labor, pursue casual sex, and behave irresponsibly in a relationship. The expression also implies that there is an inherent and socially acceptable quality to these characteristics and behaviors.

Thinking Critically about the Text (p. 424)
Roffman asks her readers to think about what the expression "boys will be boys" really means because she wants her readers to understand how "astonishingly negative" (paragraph 9) and insulting the expression is about boys. Instead of finding the "messy ... selfish ... insensitive" (9) depiction of boys accurate, Roffman finds it an implicit condemnation of boys as "animals" (10). Roffman believes that "[w]e need to explain why the notion that 'boys will be boys' embodies a bogus and ultimately corrupting set of

expectations that are unacceptable" (22) because accepting such a pervasive cultural stereotype allows boys to take advantage of their relationships with adults and girls (19), while at the same time it hurts their self-respect and confidence (20, 24).

Questions on Subject (pp. 424–425)

1. Roffman's students suggested that she did not want to view the episode of *Family Guy* in class because of: "The language? The women dressed like 'bimbos'? The implied sexual acts? The mistreatment of the mother?" (paragraph 4). She responds to these questions by informing the students that it is "the less obvious images and messages that got [her] attention" (5). Instead, she objected to the "underlying assumption in the show, and often in our society, that boys, by nature, are bad" (5).

2. When Roffman revealed her reason for not viewing the show in class, some of the boys reacted to the show with indignation and anger. According to Roffman, "It was a good moment: Recognizing for the first time the irony that maybe it was they who were really being demeaned . . ." (paragraph 6).

3. Roffman finds the infamous Janet Jackson and Justin Timberlake "wardrobe malfunction" at the 2004 Super Bowl halftime festivities to be a "twisted kind of compliment to women and a hidden and powerful indictment of men" (paragraph 7). It is evidence of "this long-standing folk 'wisdom' about boys" that allows society to ignore insensitive male behavior. Roffman continues that Jackson was "excoriated," while Timberlake "got a free pass" (7). Roffman believes it is demeaning to men to assume they aren't capable of being responsible for their actions, that only the female should be held accountable for such behavior (7, 8).

4. Roffman objects to the advertising and entertainment industry practice of glorifying and sexualizing women's bodies because it inherently assumes that the man looking at the ad is "just another low-life guy who lives and breathes to ogle and grab every large-breasted woman he sees" (paragraph 18). Roffman finds the adult responses to these images and messages to be disturbing because they "aren't nearly as clued in about how destructive these ubiquitous images and messages can be for boys" (14).

5. Roffman sees the source of the "boys will be bad" stereotype in the "time when men were the exclusively entitled gender," as "[m]any did behave badly, simply because they could" (paragraph 15). She suggests that such gender myths have staying power because "as stereotypes go, they can be remarkably invisible" (16).

Questions on Strategy (p. 425)

1. Roffman opens her essay with an anecdote about her seventh graders' asking to view and discuss an episode of *Family Guy* in their human sexuality class, which effectively allows her to draw in and surprise her readers with what is really offensive in the intentionally offensive farce: American popular culture is a purveyor of destructive and pervasive stereotypes about men (paragraph 5). Some fans of the show might suggest that being offensive is part of the show's humor and that the male stereotypes are no different from the other lampoons of American life. Others will find it particularly effective because it shows just how pervasive the stereotype is.

2. Roffman's purpose in writing this essay is to show that "no matter how demeaning today's culture may seem toward girls and women," it may be "fundamentally more disrespectful of boys and men" (paragraph 8).

3. The series of questions Roffman asks in paragraph 10 functions to solidify her argument that the "boys will be boys" stereotype is disrespectful to men and harmful to society. The questions imply that when we think about boys more seriously we will not accept a

superficial and one-dimensional view of them as "animals." "Is it possible ... we really think ..." is a rhetorical construction that does not need an answer. Therefore, these questions allow her to build her case for what is problematic about the stereotype.

4. Roffman's analogy is intended to explain how a boy in today's society is unable to tell how he is being manipulated by these stereotypes. By presenting the boy as a fish in water, Roffman clearly explains how pervasive these stereotypes are.

Questions on Diction and Vocabulary (p. 425)

1. Roffman's intended audience is adults who might see nothing wrong with the "boys will be boys" stereotype. In paragraph 7, the pronoun *you* refers to the reader and in paragraph 8 the pronouns *us* and *we* refer to society as a whole. Boys and children are referred to but not addressed, as if they are not the intended audience, and adults are referred to as part of the discussion.

2. In paragraph 9, Roffman lists the negative traits and characteristics of boys suggested by the expression "boys will be boys." The connotations associated with Roffman's list of negative traits and characteristics associated with boys range from harmless and possibly funny to dangerous and harmful. She clearly starts with adjectives with light connotations such as "messy" and "immature" and drives the point forward by using increasingly unacceptable traits such as "violent, predatory, and animal-like."

3. "It centers on Stewie, a sexist, foul-mouthed preschooler who hates his mother, fantasizes killing her off in violent ways, and wants to prevent his parents from making a new baby—until he realizes that he might get to have a sibling as nasty as he is" (paragraph 3). *Sibling* (3): a brother or sister. *Expletive* (3): an interjectory word or expression, frequently profane; an exclamatory oath. *Farce* (4): a comedy based on unlikely situations and exaggerated effects. *Irony* (6): the use of words to convey a meaning that is the opposite of the words' literal meaning. *Excoriated* (7): denounced or berated severely. *Paradoxically* (7): seemingly contradictory or absurdly true. *Bandy* (11): to pass from one to another or back and forth; trade; exchange. *Cesspool* (12): a place for the sediment of a drain or for receiving the sewage from a house. *Ubiquitous* (14): existing or being everywhere, especially at the same time; omnipresent. *Insidious* (14): intended to entrap or beguile.

The Company Man
ELLEN GOODMAN

Preparing to Read (p. 427)
Students will have a variety of career paths in mind. Encourage students to discuss the expectations of those diverging paths. Are there any expectations or sacrifices that are similar for the majority of the paths? Are there expectations that students consider unfair but will submit to anyway?

Thinking Critically about the Text (p. 429)
Goodman adds these details because many readers may make similarly false assumptions. They assume they are healthy because they do not engage in the riskiest behaviors. The details help her correct this false assumption. Phil's employer supported and encouraged his long hours. The end of the essay shows us that the employer is looking for someone like Phil

who will sacrifice health for work. The entire work environment and the demands of the job supported or encouraged his lifestyle choices, leading to his untimely death.

Questions on Subject (p. 429)

1. Goodman mentions the concept of Type A personality in paragraph 2. She defines it as a "workaholic."
2. Phil invested all of his emotional, mental, and physical energy in his work. There was nothing left for his wife, his children, or himself. The stress of the job and his singular focus on his work, she claims, killed him. He died of exhaustion and ill health from too much stress. She does not mean that the job killed him in the sense that the ceiling collapsed on him. His body collapsed under the weight of the job itself.
3. Goodman suggests that Phil worked as hard as he did in order to become president one day (paragraph 3). He may have also worked this hard to hide from his life, himself, and his family. He may have had fears of intimacy that made work feel more comfortable than home. Also, as time went on, he had developed no other interests and therefore had no reason not to work. He was not a very fully developed person. Students may offer other explanations.
4. Not including the specific profession in the essay has several advantages. First, more readers can identify with Phil. They might be an executive or know executives. In addition, not mentioning the exact profession stresses the point that it did not matter what Phil was doing. He was not, Goodman suggests, committed to the mission of his career or company. He was driven by stress and ambition.

Questions on Strategy (pp. 429–430)

1. Goodman's purpose in this essay is to help readers check themselves and their loved ones to see if they are working themselves to death. Or, if not to death, to consider how obsession with work might rob people of rich, happy, and healthy lives. In paragraph 2, she emphasizes the short reflection period of those attending the funeral. They knew why Phil died and thought briefly about their own choices. Her essay expands and develops this period of reflection. She presents him as a man who did not live, who emotionally abandoned his wife and died young. She paints a tragic picture of Phil and encourages readers not to make the same mistake.
2. Waiting until paragraph 3 helps readers project their own experiences first. They can imagine themselves or someone they love dying that way. This pulls readers in and helps them connect emotionally with the content.
3. To support her point, Goodman provides a series of details about Phil and about the type of person who dies by overwork. We know in paragraph 3 that he was one of six vice presidents vying for the president's position when he retired. So we know he is in a competitive situation. And we know that he had no extracurricular interests, always ate the same meal, and wore the same outfits (paragraph 5). We learn in paragraph 6 that he is responsible for about sixty people—some of whom would try to replace him. This detail and the detail in paragraph 3 about his competition creates the image of a conveyor belt of nameless employees all fighting for each other's jobs. They are all faceless, nameless executives trying to get to the top of something we are not sure has any meaning. We learn in paragraph 7 that he had limited personal relations with his family. In paragraph 13, we learn of the resentment that his wife had about Phil's obsession with work. The prior two paragraphs list the impact on his family. We see from this picture that not only did Phil suffer physically but his choices had a very real impact on those who loved him. We see a

man who invests everything in a company that will easily replace him and little in the family that could not.

4. *Extracurricular* is a word associated with school-age people, not adults. By choosing this expression, Goodman helps us see Phil a bit more sympathetically. It also positions him as a dry person. High school students with no outside activities are seen as rather boring and unexpressed. They are of no interest to top schools because the top schools want more well-rounded people. *Survivors* is also a curious term and suggests that his family survived the tragedy of Phil. They survived his hard work while it killed him. The term is often used after someone dies, but putting it in quotes in this context highlights the tragedy of his loss and the brutal impact of his choices on others. "Dearly beloved" is in quotes to highlight that he did not treat his children as dearly beloved. It is used ironically.

5. Goodman's tone is a bit acerbic and harsh. She wants to drive home the point that Phil's overwork and choices destroyed his body and hurt his family—and benefitted no one. She wants to shock readers and help them wake up. Therefore, she does not treat Phil too tenderly or sympathetically. In paragraph 4, she writes about him thinking he was fit because he did not smoke. This phrase comes off as a bit snarky: We can almost hear under her words that Phil was being an idiot. In paragraph 6, Goodman tells us that the obituary did not mention that three people working under him were vying for his job. Again, she points out that the sweet obituary told only part of the story. Her deconstruction of the words used in the obituary in the next few paragraphs also shows the contrast between how Phil lived and how he was being portrayed. "Dearly beloved" is in contrast with the fact that he did not take time to love. Those who "survived" Phil really survived his absence during his life as well as his death. This essay does not coddle Phil or the reader.

6. The numbers referring to the company give the impression of nameless employees all competing against and then replacing one another. Phil's age shows us how young he was when he died and the youth of his wife. Forty-eight is young to be a widow. Fifty-one is young to die especially when one is affluent and has access to health care. The numbers help paint the picture of Phil's life without having to say literally that he died young or that the company had many employees to replace one another.

Questions on Diction and Vocabulary (p. 430)

1. Goodman repeats "Type A" in paragraph 1 and paragraph 3. Once she has defined the term, she can use it as shorthand. Many people associate Type A with having strong, positive attributes. Her use of the term in this context helps readers associate it with possible early death. She repeats "dearly beloved" in paragraph 9 to highlight the contrast between the phrase and how Phil treated his family. By repeating that he was overweight in paragraphs 4 and 14, she reminds readers that being overweight may be a sign that one is making choices similar to Phil's.

2. Goodman's diction is informal. Many short sentences give the piece an informal feel and replicate how we speak more than how we write. Using conjunctions like *didn't* in paragraph 6 contribute to the informal feel. Her phrase "you could have picked him out in a minute from a lineup" (14) creates the image of Phil as a criminal. She has criminalized him for working too hard. Associating Phil with crime would less likely occur in a formal piece. The phrase "no one was really surprised" in paragraph 15 gives readers the impression that they are just hanging out with and thinking about regular folks.

3. *Thrombosis* (paragraph 2): blood clots blocking blood vessels. *Conceivably* (3): possibly. *Discreetly* (16): not likely to be seen by many people.

The Selfish Side of Gratitude
BARBARA EHRENREICH

Preparing to Read (p. 432)
You could keep this a broad discussion about positivity or turn it into a more directed discussion about how to deal with academic pressure. If you teach this essay toward the end of the year, it might be a useful moment to bring up strategies for coping with end-of-term stress.

Thinking Critically about the Text (p. 435)
Students will define gratitude for themselves. You may want to ask if students think there is a difference between gratitude and appreciation. Gratitude may suggest a kind of struggle, whereas appreciation is much lighter. Given how hard life is, we must be grateful, which is in contrast to simply appreciating a beautiful day because it is beautiful.

Questions on Subject (p. 435)
1. According to the article, the benefits of gratitude include giving us greater happiness; better health; and a warm, comforting glow. The health benefits include a stronger immune system and lower blood pressure. It augments happiness by giving us more joy and pleasure. The article suggests, but does not state directly, that expressing gratitude can enhance some relationships. The article also suggests that gratitude can help those who have so much to appreciate all that they *do* have.
2. In paragraph 2, Ehrenreich says that gratitude is expressing our thanks.
3. Ehrenreich suggests that people who are being exploited are probably not the ones who need to express gratitude. Those benefitting from their exploitation ought to start appreciating them verbally and materially—by providing for them.
4. Compared to other self-improvement approaches, gratitude is both about other people and often expressed to other people. Thus, it is prosocial. Ehrenreich says that there is a moral reason for expressing this gratitude. We do owe it. To her, the health benefits seem secondary. If not done correctly, this self-improvement approach may simply replicate the cycles of inequity that exist.
5. At the end of the essay, Ehrenreich suggests that we need to figure out how to express our debt to those who serve us and from whose work we benefit. By gratitude, she means materially improving their conditions and paying them better.

Questions on Strategy (p. 435)
1. Both seem a bit forced, constructed, and trendy. Pumpkin items are here for a season and often have an overly sweet taste. This shows that Ehrenreich thinks this enthusiasm for gratitude may wane: It might be here only for a proverbial season. It also might be a bit decorative, symbolizing something and trying to capitalize on a trend. We become entranced with the allure of both.
2. Ehrenreich's purpose is to challenge the national obsession with gratitude. She pushes back, saying that it ought to be expressed materially and not just internally. Self-improvement is very individually focused; gratitude makes us think of others. She likes this but thinks we need to go further by moving into action. In paragraph 3, she challenges the narcissism of focusing on gratitude. She reinforces her point in the final paragraph, urging readers into action.

3. In paragraphs 2 and 4, Ehrenreich provides examples of the kinds of people touting the health benefits of gratitude. She illustrates how the financial crisis of 2008 made people realize that they could not live on positive thoughts alone. Eventually they would have to pay the mortgage. She offers a nice juxtaposition between the success of the book *The Secret* and the 2008 crash to illustrate the gap between thinking positively and living positively. She illustrates the limitations of gratitude when discussing the lives of Walmart employees. She shows the gap between the CEO's salary and an employee's salary. This example illustrates how the obsession with gratitude can be a way to keep the poor in poverty. Telling them to be grateful for having less is morally egregious. Students may provide other examples, but they need to describe how effective those examples were for them. Other interesting illustrations could have been finding a study to see if the health benefits of gratitude are the same for the rich as well as the poor.
4. Ehrenreich organizes her essay by giving a mini-history about gratitude as a tool of self-improvement in paragraphs 4 to 6. Then she bounces between experts who call for displays of gratitude and examples of why those expressions might be problematic.
5. Through her quotes, Ehrenreich questions the validity of these terms. Is this really a science or just a way to focus more on ourselves? She is challenging the obsession with and institutionalization of these concepts.

Questions on Diction and Vocabulary (p. 436)

1. Ehrenreich's tone is rather skeptical of this obsession with gratitude. In paragraph 3, she makes a somewhat snarky comment that points to the self-focus of gratitude. She asks, "Is gratitude always appropriate?" She cites people who challenge as well as support the gratitude craze. Students may provide other examples, such as the almost mockery of the yoga instructor quoted on CNN. They may also consider her tone dismissive of the gratitude craze.
2. *Exhortations* (paragraph 2): attempts to influence someone. *Cultivate* (2): foster the growth of. *Speculative* (6): based on guesses or ideas. *Stances* (6): publically stated opinions. *Resilience* (6): the ability to be strong and successful again after something bad happens. *Fiat* (8): command or order. *Hypothetical* (8): based on a guess with no evidence. *Initiative* (9): ability to start something. *Affirmation* (11): the act of saying something in a positive way. *Hoopla* (14): excitement about something. *Onanism* (14): self-gratification. *Tenuous* (15): not strong or definite. *Solidarity* (16): feeling of unity that comes from people sharing the same ideas.

CHAPTER 11   Cause and Effect Analysis

How Boys Become Men
JON KATZ

Preparing to Read (p. 455)
Katz's essay closely explores some of the more painful rituals through which boys in mainstream American culture establish gender identity. This prompt asks students to recall and evaluate related childhood experiences of their own. It might be interesting for students to discuss the differences between the experiences cited by girls and those recalled by boys. Discussion might also reveal interesting differences and similarities between Katz and students of varied cultural backgrounds.

Thinking Critically about the Text (p. 458)
Students' responses will vary. Their answers will reveal significant assumptions that stem from their personal backgrounds. Note that Katz does not attempt to tell where "Boy Justice" comes from; therefore, students will have to support their answers with illustrations from their own experience and reading.

Questions on Subject (p. 458)
1. According to Katz, women see men this way because they do not understand the boyhood "Code of Conduct," which is often carried into adulthood. The perceptive student might detect the circular logic in this argument—that women don't understand men because they don't understand male culture. Follow-up questions might include "What is the origin of this Code of Conduct?" and "Do boys learn it from men or culture, or is it somehow innate?"
2. Answers will vary.
3. "More than anything else, boys are supposed to learn how to handle themselves" (paragraph 7). Students' answers about what girls are supposed to learn will vary; some believe they need to learn how to handle themselves as well, how to act modestly or in a "ladylike" way.
4. "Frontier Justice," as it appears in western stories and John Wayne movies, glorifies the manly strength and independence of heroic individuals acting to achieve justice outside the boundaries of the law. As Katz sees it, "Boy Justice" follows the same sort of pattern, but it is even more arbitrary and less forgiving.
5. Men gain sensitivity "when they lose their jobs, their wives, or their lovers. Others learn it through a strong marriage, or through their own children" (paragraph 19). Students will identify various other factors that might promote male sensitivity. It might be interesting to discuss their reasons for considering those other factors.

Questions on Strategy (p. 458)
1. Katz addresses young women specifically as "you" in paragraph 4. Also, the "you" in paragraph 18 may be assumed to be young women.
2. Katz begins his essay by referring to men as "we" and follows with a long example in which the chief male character is "I." Men do not appear as the abstract "them" until paragraph 15. The change shifts the emphasis away from a narrative account of boyhood experience to a generalization of how men behave in American culture.

3. The location of the quotes in paragraphs 16 and 17 makes the transition from an emphasis on the personal and anecdotal experiences of boys to a general and objective analysis of the behavior of men.
4. Katz's first anecdote, which tells about the boy who refuses to be chicken, opens the essay (paragraphs 1 and 2) and illustrates his argument that boys are acculturated to accept pain rather than show fear. His second anecdote (7 through 14) centers the essay. It recounts his personal memory of telling on a tormentor and suffering for it. Katz's final narrative (20 through 23) ends the essay with an account of a bullying episode he witnesses as an adult, showing that the youthful male behavior he deplores (both the bullying and its acceptance by the victim) is still prevalent in our society. In the paragraphs between narratives (3 through 6 and 15 through 19), Katz analyzes how the characteristics of men in our society are rooted in their behavior as boys.
5. The irony expressed in the statement "fine" is that the boy really was not fine. Other boys challenged and attacked him. He was "fine" in the sense that he has learned how boys behave with one another. He chose not to admit fear, pain, frustration, or disappointment. He had learned to become a man.

Questions on Diction and Vocabulary (p. 458)
1. An "ethic" involves a moral choice; a "rule" is a principle or a customary practice. The choice to experience pain rather than show fear is based on deeply rooted values.
2. *Chicken*, for most readers, connotes someone too afraid to perform a dare or action requested by peers. It is most often used only between young children or with older adults who have a childlike tendency to accept dares. *Weird* connotes someone who acts differently from others or whom others perceive to be different.
3. While the word may be used less today than it was in Katz's childhood, most readers will say that the word *rat* connotes someone who tattles on other children. In addition, a slang definition of *rat* connotes "scoundrel." As a verb, it can mean to betray one's associates by giving information. The boys who picked on Katz could hardly be viewed as associates. Regardless, tattling on anyone, according to Katz, is against the code of conduct among boys.

iPod World: The End of Society?
ANDREW SULLIVAN

Preparing to Read (p. 460)
Sullivan's article focuses on the downside of having an iPod. Most students will write about the positive side, and any negatives will relate to the machine's design rather than its social effects.

Thinking Critically about the Text (p. 463)
In paragraph 5, Sullivan says that the iPod has left us isolated and atomized. He says the device is the death of culture and the birth of infinite subculture. The question remains: Will people stop hearing new ideas and stop seeking shared experiences? Many students may argue that the advent of the Internet and iTunes has actually exposed them to more music and opinions than ever before. How often did students read each other's written opinions

before blogs? iTunes recommends all sorts of songs that you have not heard. Friends still pass each other new songs through the computer.

Questions on Subject (p. 463)

1. The iPod has changed the way people move through the world; Sullivan wonders if something is lost when people tune out the world around them and tune in to their music.
2. He can listen to anything from his music collection; it has a sleek design and fits in his pocket. On the downside, the iPod has become an addiction for him and others, causing them to tune out their surroundings, miss social cues, and go on autopilot. He says iPod people's eyes glaze over; they become "Stepford commuters" (paragraph 4).
3. Sullivan means that people identify with smaller and smaller groups, united by common tastes and beliefs. People tune in to worlds that appeal to them, identifying with those who share favorite teams, music genres, or political beliefs. You may want to ask students if they think the Internet has actually allowed for the opposite.
4. He suggests that we put the iPod down and reconnect with the noises and smells of the world in order to feel more connected. Students' opinions will vary. The conclusion provides a solution to the problems he sees when he travels. In addition, the conclusion comes from his personal experience of having forgotten his iPod. He learned something and wants to pass this revelation on to readers.

Questions on Strategy (p. 463)

1. The size of the iPod makes it easy to carry around and to fit and rearrange one's whole music collection. The earplugs are small and discreet. These features turn regular commuters into zombies, traveling to their own soundtrack.
2. Students' answers will vary. Not everyone will have been to one of the huge Apple stores or own an iPod, for that matter. The stores are filled with identical-looking iPods; one store is even open twenty-four hours. He associates both iPods and cults with glazed eyes. Sullivan draws similarities between cult leaders and the Apple staff, portraying them as indoctrinators eager to add more folks to their tribe, all dressed in cultic white garb. His analogy is tongue in cheek, of course, with some funny comparisons.
3. He contrasts the past by saying that people did remove themselves from the world, just not while they were still in it. In the present world, people can isolate themselves from others even in a crowd. You may want to ask students the difference between listening to an iPod and reading a book while waiting for a train or plane. Is an iPod really more distancing? Sullivan contrasts how music was listened to in the past versus the present. In the past people listened in their homes or in concert halls, but usually together. Now they can listen anywhere but can choose to do so alone.
4. In paragraphs 2 and 9, he says that we are missing all of the sounds around us. In other words, even though we are listening to more, we are hearing less: "It's strange to be among so many people and hear so little. Except that each one is hearing so much" (2). Ironically, tuning in to our music tunes us out. In paragraph 1, the city is getting quieter because everyone is listening to their iPods, but they are really hearing little of the silence, instead cramming their music in their heads. On the subways, commuters are all together and yet "all sealed off from each other" (4). He uses irony to help readers see themselves; they are sealing themselves off from their own lives when trying to be the stars of their own music videos. They think they are connecting with themselves by listening to their music when in fact they are contributing to their isolation.
5. Sullivan panics. The effect is that he again starts to listen to the world around him.

Questions on Diction and Vocabulary (pp. 463–464)

1. He uses British slang words such as *bloke* (paragraph 7).
2. Atoms are the smallest particle of a chemical element. By using words like "atomization" (paragraph 5) and "atomized" (7), Sullivan implies that technology in general and iPods in particular reduce us to separate particles. In order to change the elements of an atom, it must undergo nuclear fission or fusion, a difficult process that takes huge amounts of energy. Sullivan uses these ideas to underscore his point that iPods do not stimulate people to change opinions or gain new outlooks; instead, they make it more difficult for people to experience something new or random. He worries that "Americans are beginning to narrowcast their own lives. . . . Technology has given us finally a universe entirely for ourselves—where the serendipity of . . . opinion[s] that might actually force us to change our mind about something are all effectively banished" (5). His terms work well as metaphors, demonstrating the isolating power of technology as well as the lack of change or growth that he worries it may produce. Students may disagree that iPods have this effect. People share music, and the iTunes Web site encourages users to listen to new music.
3. Sullivan writes in an informal style, referring to his personal experience, his "panic" (paragraph 10), and to colloquialisms like "bloke" (7) and "cabby" (10). He also writes in the second person, infusing the essay with a chatty, rather than an academic, tone. He uses humor to describe iPod users as "hermit crabs" (6), "surgically attached" (6), "Stepford commuters" (4), which makes the essay witty and light instead of heavy-handed or didactic.

The Downside of Diversity
MICHAEL JONAS

Preparing to Read (p. 465)
Students may believe that people who live in ethnically diverse communities demonstrate stronger civic engagement and interconnectedness than people who live in homogeneous communities because they are exposed to wider and more diverse ideas. They may believe that lack of exposure to diversity breeds passivity in homogeneous communities.

Thinking Critically about the Text (p. 471)
Despite Putnam's findings that ethnic diversity might be a liability, he argues that it can be "ultimately valuable and enriching" (paragraph 37). This seeming contradiction is explained when he writes, "Experience shows that social divisions can eventually give way to 'more encompassing identities' that create a 'new, more capacious sense of "we"'" (34).

Questions on Subject (p. 471)
1. The effects of greater social diversity include "tension and discord" and a loss of civic engagement (paragraph 20). However, "the creative tensions unleashed by those differences in the workplace may vault those same places to the cutting edge of the economy and of creative culture" (31). Putnam believes the losses are significant enough that efforts should be made to mitigate them, and he has done work to promote "efforts . . . to increase civic connections in communities" (39).
2. "Social capital," a term coined by Putnam, refers to the "social networks—whether friendships or religious congregations or neighborhood associations—that he says are key indicators of civic well-being" (paragraph 13).

3. Putnam worried that his findings would subject him to "liberal attacks" (paragraph 15), but his "worst fears" were "about how his results could be used" by conservatives and even racists (33) at a time of "intense political debate, from immigration to race-based admissions to schools" (4).

4. Evidence that runs counter to Putnam's research on ethnic diversity yielding a "civic malaise" (paragraph 21) is found in "the vigor often associated with urban centers, where ethnic diversity is greatest" (29). "[A] parallel line of emerging research suggests [diversity] can be a big asset when it comes to driving productivity and innovation" (29). "'[B]y hanging out with people different than you, you're likely to get more insights. Diverse teams tend to be more productive'" (30). Political scientist Scott Page calls it "the diversity paradox" (32).

5. For increasing social capital within diverse ethnic communities, Putnam suggests expanding "support for English-language instruction and investing in community centers and other places that allow for 'meaningful interaction across ethnic lines'" (paragraph 37).

Questions on Strategy (p. 471)

1. Jonas's essay reports the research findings that indicate ethnic diversity causes diminishment of social capital. Other causes were considered, such as "greater income ranges, higher crime rates, and more mobility among their residents" (paragraph 16), but "the connection remained strong" (18). The effects of diversity on members of a community were "distrust," withdrawal, disaffection, and isolation (18).

2. Conservative think-tank fellow John Leo criticizes Putnam's presentation of his findings because Leo says social scientists are supposed to be objective and neutral. Leo says, "You're just supposed to tell your peers what you found" (paragraph 38). Instead Putnam frets about his findings and suggests that, despite the ill effects of diversity in the short term, in the long term diversity could create new ties that expand the definition of "we" (34) and suggests programs for creating more community ties in diverse neighborhoods (37). Leo's criticisms are answered by John Wolfe when he says, "'Social scientists are both scientists and citizens'" and that he "sees nothing wrong in Putnam's efforts to affect some of the phenomena he studies" (40).

3. Jonas uses a number of short one- or two-sentence paragraphs to emphasize certain points, including "'The extent of the effect is shocking. . . .'" (paragraph 3); "'Diversity, at least in the short run,' he writes, 'seems to bring out the turtle in all of us'" (22); "'It's an important addition to a growing body of evidence on the challenges created by diversity,' says Harvard economist Edward Glaeser." (24); "So how to explain New York, London, Rio de Janeiro, Los Angeles—the great melting-pot cities that drive the world's creative and financial economies?" (28). While these passages could have been combined with other paragraphs, letting them stand alone allows a reader to pause and give more attention to the points made. They function as an outline of the information in the essay.

4. In his essay, Jonas quotes from numerous expert sources but none so much as John Putnam. He depicts the controversy over Putnam's findings through the reactions of other experts, such as Scott Page, John Leo, and John Wolfe. This technique separates the findings from the controversy and gives Putnam's research more credibility as evidence in the essay.

5. Jonas appears objective in his treatment of Putnam's work. He explores the implications for immigration and other issues, goes into detail about contradictory evidence in relation to big cities, and brings in views that oppose Putnam's. This builds credibility for the information in the essay. Jonas may possibly be tipping his hand that he supports diversity by his sympathetic portrayal of Putnam's advocacy and fears about how his research might be used by conservatives.

Questions on Diction and Vocabulary (p. 472)

1. In *Bowling Alone*, John Putnam studied how bowling changed from a very social activity to one primarily enjoyed by solitary individuals. "Bowling alone" is a good metaphor for loss of social capital, including decreased communication, social withdrawal, and the general "turtle" effect (paragraph 22) that occurs even among people of the same culture.
2. Putnam's quotation uses the simile "People . . . pull in like a turtle" (paragraph 19). He compares those who live in diverse neighborhoods to turtles to underscore how they withdraw into their homes instead of engage civically with friends, with neighbors, and in politics.

Coca-Cola Funds Scientists Who Shift Blame for Obesity Away from Bad Diets
ANAHAD O'CONNOR

Preparing to Read (p. 474)

Weight and health can be very sensitive topics. If you have concerns over discussing these issues in class, consider asking students to journal on the topic, or steer the conversation to depictions of weight (and weight gain/loss) in the media.

Thinking Critically about the Text (p. 478)

Students will likely have a different feeling about how the medical advice is being used *after* reading the article. You might want to ask if they can imagine how they thought of this advice *before* reading.

Questions on Subject (p. 478)

1. Coke has been promoting the medical advice that, in order to stay fit, people need to balance calories taken in with calories burned. Their message is suggesting to people that, if they find themselves overweight, it is because they are not moving enough, not because soda is unhealthy. The title prepares the readers for an argument about the true cause of obesity and the potential effects of Coca-Cola's marketing.
2. O'Connor believes that a combination of lack of exercise and ingesting too many calories causes obesity.
3. The Global Energy Balance Network is a group that "promotes the argument that weight-conscious Americans are overly fixated on how much they eat and drink while not paying enough attention to exercise" (paragraph 2). Coca-Cola's support of this network includes a great deal of funding for this calorie balance approach to health. The network, with Coca-Cola's support, may promote the idea that if you work out more, you can eat more. The soda company loves this idea because it can continue to promote sports and its soda together. It makes it look like a health-conscious company when, in fact, it is not.
4. This clash would seem to be the contention by some scientists that exercise is a more important focus in weight loss and the contention by others that a focus on healthy eating is paramount.
5. Coke supports the idea that health involves balancing the calories eaten with the calories burned. By creating opportunities for exercise, Coke would seem to be removing barriers from people buying more of their product.

Questions on Strategy (p. 478)

1. The entire article hinges around two important questions of cause-and-effect. The first is whether or not poor eating is a major contributor to obesity (paragraphs 17, 20, 21, 23). The second is whether or not the funding from Coke is likely to influence the findings of the Global Energy Balance Network (4, 6, 12, 16).

2. O'Connor writes to a general audience which has likely been exposed to Coca-Cola's messaging and who are likely not aware that major corporations such as Coke often sponsor medical research. If O'Connor's audience were aware of this fact, he would not go to such length to explain that it is common, that it can have a negative impact on findings, and why the lapses in acknowledging Coke's support are so meaningful. The fact that he takes such care to do so means that he wants to educate readers who may have not been exposed to this knowledge. Given that O'Connor is writing for the *New York Times* Health and Wellness blog, we can assume that his readers already have an interest in the topic of personal health and fitness.

3. O'Connor would likely say that it does not make them corrupt, but it does make them suspect. You can tell that O'Connor is skeptical of Blair's defense because his bracketed note includes the phrase "allegedly by accident" and he follows the quote with a paragraph noting that studies suggest that corporate funding often biases scientific findings. Stylistically, we feel that Blair and O'Connor are in conversation with each other, with Blair offering a statement that O'Connor then refutes.

4. If people believe that sugary drinks like Coca-Cola have a serious impact on their health, they may stop buying them and sales will drop off, making Coke lose money. Also, proposed tax increases on sugary drinks (meant to encourage people to buy healthier alternatives) will impact how often consumers purchase soda. Paragraphs 4 to 6 provide evidence for these views.

5. Quotations will vary. The reasoning behind the sources may include presenting an opposing argument in order to refute it and presenting evidence in support of the central claim.

6. O'Connor's citations are somewhat spotty. Sometimes he includes direct quotes from specific sources (Steven N. Blair, Michele Simon, James O. Hill) while other times he simply cites "Health experts" (paragraph 4) or includes a fact without citation ("consumption of full-calorie sodas by the average American has dropped by 25 percent" in paragraph 5).

Questions about Diction and Vocabulary (p. 479)

1. Responses will vary, but students should note O'Connor's use of single quotes around 'science-based,' as well as the juxtaposition of Coca-Cola's identity as a sugary beverage producer with their purported identity as a solver of the obesity crisis.

2. *Fixated* (paragraph 2): to be focused on something to the exclusion of other things. *Misleading* (4): to indicate something that is false. *Deflect* (4): to block something from its intended target. *Backlash* (6): a negative response. *Transparent* (11, 12): to be see-through. *Omitted* (13): left out. *Oversight* (13): a mistake. *Corrupt* (14): to be dishonest or without morals. *Bias* (15): to have an interest in one side of an argument over another. *Glycemic* (22): having glucose in your blood. *Philanthropy* (24): the practice of doing good things for others.

3. Student responses will vary, but they should identify that this string of words relates to things that are not included. They contribute to the main idea of the paragraph by underscoring the information (namely, Coke's financial support) that was left out of publicity information by the Global Energy Balance Network. This paragraph contributes to O'Connor's overall point that corporate sponsorship of this sort can make scientific results suspect.

A Bird Whose Life Depends on a Crab
DEBORAH CRAMER

Preparing to Read (p. 481)
You might ask students to do some additional research on this topic, exploring animals and plants that have gone extinct and why, or looking into how public views of extinction have changed since conservation agencies began labeling animals as "endangered." Some students may be surprised by the number of plants (and fungi) that have also gone extinct, largely through rapidly shifting ecosystems. Ask them to keep this chain of interconnectedness in mind when reading Cramer's essay.

Thinking Critically about the Text (p. 483)
Cramer's article argues that the red knots are endangered because the horseshoe crabs (their food source) is endangered. While climate change seems to have killed many crabs, Cramer lists some other very convincing factors contributing to their demise. These crabs are in danger because of their use as bait for other creatures, the biomedical uses of their blood, the inability of the biomedical industry to ensure their survival after blood extraction, and overfishing. Students might think these other reasons could be even stronger contributors to their demise than climate change.

Questions on Subject (p. 483)
1. In paragraph 3, Cramer tells us that "the number of horseshoe crabs has declined over the years."
2. Horseshoe crabs are intrinsically valuable because of their 475-million-year history. They are instrumental to the survival of the red knot bird, who relies on the crabs for food. Because of the crabs' sensitivity to bacterial toxins, their blood has a number of important biomedical uses for humans. It can be used for vaccines, intravenous medicines, heart stents, and artificial hips (paragraph 4).
3. The Western Atlantic flyway is the 9,300-mile area between Tierra del Fuego and the Canadian Artic through which the birds migrate. This can be inferred from the second sentence in paragraph 2.
4. Both are facing extinction. The red knot is most threatened by the threats to the horseshoe crab.

Questions on Strategy (pp. 483–484)
1. In paragraph 3, Cramer states her purpose. She wants to let us know that the crabs are declining, which hurts the red knot birds and us. She states her call to action most clearly in the last paragraph: "We need to address threats to the red knots before another storm or a bad spawning season for crabs pushes the birds closer to extinction."
2. Cramer is writing for a general audience. We know because she does not assume any knowledge about either species and uses minimal technical vocabulary.
3. Most student will say that Cramer uses little technical language. She uses technical terms like "bacterial toxins" (paragraph 4) but then explains how these toxins enabled the crabs to survive. She also explains the kind of medical uses that most readers can understand, such as artificial hips. She does not choose examples that would be confusing for nonscientists. In paragraph 10, she mentions the increase in acid levels in water and how that affects other species, but she does not provide a technical explanation of why acid

hurts animals. It is not necessary for her overall point. She focuses on the mortality of animals, not the exact biological processes killing them.

4. Cramer cites evidence from the United States Fish and Wildlife Service that the red knot is near extinction (paragraph 5). She provides evidence in the form of statistics and offers estimated numbers of crabs dying each year from the use of their blood (paragraph 8). She cites a statistic that crabs will be used increasingly for their blood—an 85% increase since 2004. In paragraph 11, she claims that 70% of the best horseshoe crab spawning beaches were wiped out in Hurricane Sandy. Students will likely find this information convincing. Quotes from experts citing her same position might also be helpful.

5. Cramer has a balanced tone. Her use of evidence prevents her from exaggerating claims. She avoids word like *always* and *never*. She uses words like *crucial* (paragraph 2) when actually true. The birds do indeed require the food at that location to finish their migration.

6. The numbers add to Cramer's credibility and strengthen her argument. The numbers tell a story. We can see the mortality rates and the impact of human activity on these species.

Questions on Diction and Vocabulary (p. 484)

1. Cramer uses the verb "depend" (paragraph 4) to emphasize how much humans need crabs. She uses "demand" (5) to emphasize the intensity with which the crabs are sought. In paragraph 8, the use of "extracts" provides a visceral sense of the kind of process crabs undergo to serve humanity. In paragraph 10, she refers to how we "pump" carbon dioxide into the atmosphere, which increases the acidity of the water. The image of us "pumping" gas emphasizes our complicity and irresponsibility.

2. *Spawn* (paragraph 1): to produce or layer eggs in water. *Russet* (2): reddish-brown color. *Abundance* (2): a large amount. *Converge* (2): to come together. *Exquisitely* (4): extremely. *Toxins* (4): poisonous substances for living things. *Intravenous* (4): entering the body through a vein. *Dwindled* (5): gradually became smaller. *Whelk* (6): a kind of large marine snail. *Moratorium* (7): a time when an activity is not allowed. *Mortality* (8): death rate. *Migratory* (12): moving from one place to another at different times of the year.

CHAPTER 12   Argumentation

CLASSIC ARGUMENTS

The Allegory of the Cave
PLATO

Preparing to Read (p. 509)
Plato can be difficult reading for undergraduates. Consider bringing in items such as scented candles or cotton balls that appeal to the various senses. These items might later serve as useful, concrete objects for discussing the nature of reality and how a person's senses can have an impact on his or her understanding of it.

Thinking Critically about the Text (p. 515)
Using an allegory helps readers imagine the dynamic without overly considering their place within the landscape. They can consider it abstractly first and then consider how it relates to themselves. This decreases resistance to the new idea. In addition, Plato can show the phenomena even to people who he believes are trapped in his proverbial cave. People with little education could imagine people living in a cave forced to look at shadows more easily than they could recognize their own ignorance. Readers would also likely become defensive were Plato to tell them directly he believed that most of them were blind. Without the allegory, it also might be hard to understand Plato's point. We cannot see as easily the dynamics operating in the world in which we find ourselves. Everything looks "normal." However, had Plato described his theory in plain language, it might have helped readers who found the cave allegory confusing or distracting. It might be easy to forget that this idea of people chained with their heads facing shadows is a metaphor for human enlightenment.

Questions on Subject (pp. 515–516)
1. Students' responses will differ regarding whether they believe Plato has succeeded in showing how far human nature is enlightened. He makes clear that he believes the majority of people live in ignorance and highlights the challenges of moving between the different states of consciousness. Students will also say whether they believe, in the context of the piece, that human nature is enlightened.
2. Plato set the allegory in a prison to emphasize that ignorance is a kind of cage. Freedom can be found only through enlightenment and true knowledge. The intended impact is that readers will be motivated to try to free themselves from their own prison of ignorance. The other message is that it positions the enlightened as having the job of liberating others.
3. The prison represents what we see, not what we know. In the prison we respond only to the images flashing before us and we understand little about how they came to be or what they mean. The sun represents the source of knowledge and natural cycles (plants, day/night, etc.). Ascending out of the cave, an individual finds him- or herself cast into the intellectual world. This intellectual world is not easy to see, especially for one who has lived in the cave. To see beyond representational images requires effort, whereas watching and commenting upon shadows does not. Once the gaze is fixed on reason and truth instead of false representations, it must remain there always.

4. Plato believes that when people understand that most of the world lives in ignorance, responding only to shadows of reality, then the responsibility lies with those who have the knowledge to liberate and guide the others. These must be the rulers, the political leaders. He says that once the best minds become refined and solidly good, they must not remain in the upper world but descend again and learn to adjust their eyes to see the world the way the prisoners see it. Then, knowing the true nature of things, they can guide the nation-state better. With a clear philosophy on how the world works, one can determine what kind of political structure makes sense. Note that every political system has a philosophy about the nature of people, even if not expressly stated. Plato starts with the philosophy and then expounds on what kind of system makes sense given the state of human enlightenment.

5. Student opinions will vary. They may challenge the concept that there is such as a thing as a "true" philosopher but see value in thinking philosophically about the world. Some may say that the pursuit of true knowledge is, indeed, a very worthy aspiration.

Questions on Strategy (p. 516)

1. Plato opens with the claim that most of humanity is unenlightened, that is, chained by ignorance (paragraph 1). After making his case for the state of humankind, he then proposes a political system in which only the wise and virtuous rule. To do this, the enlightened must return to the dark and guide the others in terms they can understand. This will uplift the whole state because the ruleres are motivated by truth, not ambition (65–66).

2. Plato cites Homer, who lived a few hundred years earlier, because he was a respected thinker. Homer may have been visually impaired, but his access to the world of knowledge made him a great seer of things. Homer was not a prisoner in the way that Plato sees those imprisoned by ignorance. Students may have had other reactions to the Homer reference.

3. Process analysis is also used to show how prisoners ascend to knowledge and to describe how enlightened rulers must lead. Plato also uses cause and effect; the effect of ignorance is poor leadership. The effect of philosopher-led states is great statehood. Students may note others.

4. Plato's dialogue with his brother slows down the pace of the argument. This allows readers to consider each point along with Glaucon. The dialogue format also enables Plato to provide affirmative confirmation of his ideas. Glaucon agrees with Plato and this encourages the reader to do the same. Glaucon also can pose questions that the readers may have, providing Plato the opportunity to elaborate and clarify his points. Most students will likely enjoy the dialogue format.

5. In paragraph 59, Plato explains that those enlightened enough to be legislators are not ruling just to make themselves happy. For the State to function, legislators must hold the entire State together through persuasion and necessity. All people must benefit from the State *and* each other; otherwise, the State would cease to exist. In paragraph 61, Plato argues that, because the enlightened have received so much knowledge, they are morally obliged to use it to guide the ignorant and create a great State.

Questions on Diction and Vocabulary (p. 516)

1. Some students may enjoy this format. Glaucon's enthusiasm and confirmation encourages readers to do the same. Others might find it too self-congratulatory and would prefer to have Plato let them — without this constructed audience — decide whether the ideas ring true. You might draw the comparison to laugh tracks used in television comedy shows.

Producers add laughter to accentuate the humor. It somehow makes the show seem funnier to have other people laughing.

2. The meaning has not changed much. The term is thought to come from Pythagoras in Ancient Greek; it meant "lover of wisdom" or "friend of wisdom." According to the Oxford English Dictionary, today the word *philosopher* means "A lover of wisdom; an expert in or student of philosophy (in various senses); a person skilled or engaged in philosophical inquiry." The word appeared in English around 1300. Today, philosophers engage in a wide range of subfields, including epistemology, logic, metaphysics, ethics, ontology, and aesthetics.

The Declaration of Independence
THOMAS JEFFERSON

Preparing to Read (p. 518)
The term *democracy* will elicit any number of responses from students. This prompt works on the assumption that most Americans get their ideas of democracy from the Declaration without really knowing it. Try to find the link between students' responses and the Declaration of Independence.

Thinking Critically about the Text (p. 521)
Because of its foundational status in American government and law, the Declaration of Independence maintains a continual presence in American life and culture. You might foster a discussion along the lines of how it specifically remains in our consciousness. The other questions in the prompt are purely subjective (leave room for interpretations).

Questions on Subject (pp. 521–522)
1. Rulers get their authority, according to Jefferson, from those they rule, from "the consent of the governed" (paragraph 2). Governments are instituted to safeguard the rights and freedom of the people "to secure these rights" (2).
2. According to Jefferson, "when a long train of abuses and usurpations pursuing invariably the same Object evinces a design to reduce them under absolute Despotism, it is their right, it is their duty, to throw off such government" (paragraph 2). Injustice is grounds for overthrowing an unacceptable government, with the assumption that those being oppressed could rule themselves much more fairly and effectively.
3. The question prompts students to examine each of the "injuries and usurpations" (paragraph 2), but ask them about the rhetorical strategy of listing so many. Does Jefferson consider them all equally injurious, or is the strength of his argument in the accrual of these outrages? If students feel that certain of these usurpations are more "just cause" for revolution than others, ask them if it is Jefferson's language that leads them to this conclusion.
4. The colonists petitioned repeatedly, "warned," "reminded," and "appealed" the English king, but to no avail (paragraph 31).
5. Jefferson specifically declares independence from the British Crown. He also declares the right to "levy War, conclude Peace, contract Alliances, establish Commerce" (paragraph 32).

Questions on Strategy (p. 522)

1. *Major premise*: "[A]ll men are created equal" and are entitled to "unalienable Rights," including freedom and self-rule (paragraph 2). *Minor premise*: The colonists are being oppressed (2). Conclusion: The colonies are entitled to freedom and self-rule (2).
2. The "self-evident" truths are that "all men are created equal, that they are endowed by their Creator with certain unalienable Rights, that among these are Life, Liberty and the pursuit of Happiness" (paragraph 2). As the major premise of the argument, these truths—when proven to be violated by the king—are the proof that independence is needed.
3. According to the syllogism in question 1, the major premise is supported by the first paragraph of the Declaration. Because the major premise is more ethereal than concrete, the "evidence" offered is more emotional than factual.
4. The pattern in the list of grievances in paragraphs 3 through 29 goes from least harmful to most harmful. The king's transgressions can be categorized as (a) active transgressions (3 through 7), (b) passive transgressions (8 and 9), (c) transgressions affecting the individual (10 through 14), and (d) transgressions affecting society (15 through 29). Ask your students to come up with different categories and examples.
5. Because of the injustices inflicted and endured (cause), the colonists have the right to declare their independence (effect). Jefferson's argumentation is supported by this cause and effect reasoning.

Questions on Diction and Vocabulary (p. 522)

1. Jefferson is addressing both his fellow colonists and his oppressors. His defiant tone is appropriate for this document.
2. The language ranges from coolly reasonable—"it becomes necessary for one people to dissolve the political bands which have connected them with another" (paragraph 1)—to deeply emotional—"He is at this time transporting large Armies of foreign Mercenaries to compleat works of death, desolation and tyranny already begun with circumstances of Cruelty & perfidy scarcely paralleled in the most barbarous ages, and totally unworthy the Head of a civilized nation" (27).
3. A paraphrase would be the following: "They did not listen to us and they treated us badly, so we shall break away and rule ourselves with the fairness and kindness that we deserve. We shall fight them if we must, but we are willing to make a peaceable alliance." Jefferson's tone in the original sentences is defiant and determined.

Ain't I a Woman?
SOJOURNER TRUTH

Preparing to Read (p. 525)

Many students might respond that they have never attended a rally but have heard speeches on television. Others will recall a speaker who spoke at their high school or gave the graduation address. Ask students how they might react to a speech by Barack Obama, Stephen Colbert, Glenn Beck, Nelson Mandela, Hillary Rodham Clinton, Sonia Sotomayor, Jennifer Lopez, or Kanye West. Which speakers would they be likely to trust or view skeptically?

Thinking Critically about the Text (p. 526)

We've had success having a student read Truth's speech aloud to the class before starting the discussion. In this way Truth's down-home idiomatic images come to life. While students find different things memorable about the speech, most agree that her claims for the importance of women and her positioning of Christ's mother in Christianity are memorable. Most students can't believe that a black woman was speaking this way in the 1800s prior to the Civil War.

Questions on Subject (p. 526)

1. When Truth says, "Where there is so much racket there must be something out of kilter" (paragraph 1), she means that if women of the North and the Negroes of the South are making a lot of noise about their rights, something must be unequal. She believes that white men are going to find themselves in a "fix" (1) because they will cease to dominate the rights of each group.
2. Truth's credentials as a woman are that she is as strong as a man, she has plowed and planted, she has borne the lash, she has eaten as much as a man, and she has had thirteen children.
3. Truth counters the argument that "women can't have as much rights as men, 'cause Christ wasn't a woman" (paragraph 4) by saying that Christ came from God and a woman and that "Man had nothing to do with Him" (4).

Questions on Strategy (pp. 526–527)

1. Truth's purpose is to point out how strong women are and that they don't need to be "helped into carriages, and lifted over ditches, and to have the best place everywhere" (paragraph 2). She sets herself up as a strong example and role model for her white audience. It's important for her to define a woman in the terms that she does because the men in the audience don't see women in the same way.
2. Truth's comments regarding "[t]hat man over there" (paragraph 2) and "that little man in black" (4) let her audience know that she isn't defined by what men say. She thinks for herself.
3. By repeating "And ain't I a woman?" four times in paragraph 2, Truth tries to convince the audience that she's for real. She believes what she says. She also asks the audience to speculate on what the fuss is all about (paragraph 1), what "this thing in the head" (intellect) is (3) and why this has anything to do with women's or Negroes' rights. She lets the audience stop and consider her questions and draw their own conclusions. She then asks, "Where did your Christ come from?" (4). Here she makes it very clear that Christ came from God and a woman, that "[m]an had nothing to do with Him" (4). Truth presents this answer as a fact. Because she does not expect the "little man in black" (4) to answer her question, she answers for him.
4. Truth's tone is forceful, defiant, passionate, and convincing. Answers will vary, but most students point to phrases and clauses like "Ain't I a woman?" (paragraph 2), "Look at me!" (2), "Look at my arm!" (2), "no man could head me" (2), "little man in black" (4), "Where did your Christ come from?" (4), and "the men better let them" (5).
5. Truth compares men's view of women with her own opinion. She believes that she is as strong as men while "[t]hat man over there" (paragraph 2) thinks that women need help. She can "bear the lash as well" as a man and she has "borne thirteen children," who were "most all sold off to slavery" (2).

Questions on Diction and Vocabulary (p. 527)
1. Truth's diction is filled with slang and uneducated jargon. She tells what she thinks in simple, straightforward, idiomatic language. She appears to be a person who isn't afraid of work, who is confident, and who is worldly wise in spite of her lack of formal education.
2. *Kilter* (paragraph 1): good working order. *Ditches* (2): narrow trenches used to hold or carry off water or serve as boundaries. *Intellect* (3): the mind's power of reasoning and acquiring knowledge. *Obliged* (6): gratified by performing a small service.

Resistance to Civil Government
HENRY DAVID THOREAU

Preparing to Read (p. 528)
To jump-start discussion, consider beginning with a class brainstorming session on the pros and cons of a central government. Some pros may include support programs, highways, and national parks. Some cons may include unwanted interference and taxes.

Thinking Critically about the Text (pp. 545–546)
Thoreau says that he pays his highway tax because his goal is not to be a nuisance to his neighbors but to live congruently within himself. He makes clear that he is not against any particular item for which his taxes pay and that he is refusing allegiance to the State more generally. Regarding education, he does not actually say he paid taxes for schools. He says that he is working to educate his fellow man by living as he does and writing this essay on resistance.

Questions on Subject (p. 546)
1. To Thoreau, the State is a machine largely run by men acting like machines or operating with their minds but *not* with their conscience. He says that the State treats itself as superior to the individual when the opposite ought to be true. He says the individual must be seen as a higher and independent power than the State. The State ought to derive its power through this and in service to this. Thoreau said that presently he felt the opposite was true. The individual was being treated as inferior to the State and in service to it. Individuals must serve the State with their conscience—their only job is to do at any moment what they believe is right. They must make known the kind of government they wish to have. The State ought to abide by these requests.
2. Thoreau says that if ten or even one honest man in the State of Massachusetts ceased to hold slaves, withdrew his support from slavery, and was willing to be locked up for it, this action could change the country. Student reactions to this claim will vary. It supports Thoreau's point that the actions of the individual matter. No one can assume his voice does not matter or that he cannot change the nation through the exercise of his moral conscience.
3. Thoreau may include these details about his neighbors to make several points. First, he wants to show how uncomfortable other people are with resistance and how little they understand the freedom of living according to their conscience. They wanted to save him from the discomfort of speaking up and even though they are well meaning, they partially robbed him from seeing the true workings of the State. He had powerful insights in and when he emerged from prison. He shows how people pull each other back into

compliance, allowing the State to rule them all. He might also be subtly suggesting that it would have been better had they joined him in prison than tried to bail him out.

4. He says that the State never "confronts a man's sense, intellectual or moral . . ." (paragraph 27) because it lacks superior wit or honesty to do so. It must rely on brute strength because that is how it rules. The government says to him, "[Y]our money or your life" (27). This does not appeal to any higher sense of truth. It is a threat issued by the State because it has the power — if not the moral right — to take both.

5. An enlightened State would be in service to the moral individual who accepted the responsibility of doing what he believed was right. An enlightened State would treat the individual as a neighbor, not as a subject, and work in service to that neighbor. This State must recognize the individual as a higher and independent power.

Questions on Strategy (p. 546)

1. Student answers will vary. Most will likely say that the first-person narrative brings the points closer. The point is that Thoreau lived what he spoke. This is what made him so powerful. In the third person, we would likely lose the connection to the individual — both within Thoreau and the individual within ourselves. Because individual thinking and action is the focus of this essay, much would be lost through distance and abstraction.

2. Thoreau's problem is with the whole machine of government. Tweaking a particular branch or office would not be enough to upend what he sees as an entirely repressive system.

3. The works of Shakespeare and the Bible are texts that convey messages that ring true throughout centuries. Thoreau likely hoped (and he was correct) that his work would do the same. Mentioning them also gives him borrowed credibility. Referencing them allows him to borrow some of the respect that these works have earned. Relating to the Bible, he says that the New Testament has great messages, but no person has been able to use it effectively to improve our legislation.

4. Thoreau makes the distinction between "those who call themselves abolitionists" and those who "are" abolitionists. Those who want to be authentic, and to be more than the name itself, must take action — he recommends immediately withdrawing support from the Massachusetts State government.

5. Thoreau is making a distinction between those who are actually abolitionists, and those who simply call themselves abolitionists. This distinction is important because Thoreaua is using it to challenge those who would like to be thought of as abolitionists, but who do not want to take any action to support abolition.

Questions on Diction and Vocabulary (pp. 546–547)

1. Students will offer many examples. In paragraph 19, for example, Thoreau uses italics. He writes that "because [the individual] cannot do *every thing,* it is not necessary that he should do *something* wrong." His use of italics emphasizes his understanding that it is impossible to do *every thing* and that he believes that the inability to act in all ways does not give individuals the permission to make grave moral errors. He uses italics to help readers see how they might be justifying wrongdoing by using the excuse that they cannot solve all the world's ills.

2. An example is in paragraph 23, when Thoreau writes, "Absolutely speaking, the more money, the less virtue; for money comes between a man and his objects, and obtains them for him; it was certainly no great virtue to obtain it." The simple clauses keep the reader focused, and the semicolons give the sentences a kind of pace and momentum. Thoreau keeps the

reader with him, close at hand, and the semicolons keep the reader from veering too far off in his own reverie. He leads the reader through a whole argument in one phrase. Some students might find this cumbersome. Some may say they enjoy the rhythm and pacing.

A Modest Proposal
JONATHAN SWIFT

Preparing to Read (p. 548)
Students can visit Web sites such as cagle.msnbc.com/politicalcartoons/ and www.cartoonstock.com to see examples of satirical cartoons and have some fun.

Thinking Critically about the Text (p. 556)
Students will catch on to the satire at different points. In paragraph 2, Swift writes, "a fair, cheap, and easy method of making these children sound, useful members of the commonwealth." Our culture is not used to thinking of children as useful or sound. They just are. This might tip some students off. In paragraph 9, Swift reveals his plan for eating children. All students will probably catch on here.

Questions on Subject (p. 556)
1. Swift addresses the problem of the countless homeless children and the parents who cannot support them. He estimates that only 30,000 of the 200,000 women bearing children can afford to care for their children. He proposes selling these children when they are one year old, to families and individuals who will eat them. He sees many advantages: the poor would get money for their children, many people would be fed, men who would normally be unhappy about their wives' babies will now see them as economic assets rather than liabilities, taverns would have a new ingredient for their recipes, and Dublin could increase exported beef products to assist the nation's economy.
2. Swift dismisses several expedients; in doing so, he proposes them in earnest. Because eating children is absurd, these dismissed "expedients" are really proposed solutions: taxing people who leave Dublin for Spain or Barbados, only using Irish-made products, banning importation, rejecting the notion of foreign luxury, discouraging women from fanning the flames of pride and vanity that make them want foreign goods, teaching people to love their country and each other, maintaining integrity, and asking shopkeepers to buy only local goods.
3. The "author" of the proposal sells himself as a concerned, selfless countryman. He presents his proposal as a pragmatic response to a problem that he has "turned [his] thoughts [to] for many years" (paragraph 4). His true voice comes through when he "dismisses" other solutions (see answer to Question 2 above). These are his true solutions to the problem.
4. The title sets the tone and helps disguise the satirical nature of the essay. The title encourages readers to think of the author as an earnest person who is trying to propose a solution. It is also ironic; what could be less "modest" than proposing to eat children?
5. The statement is ironic because people do not see children as needing to contribute to society. Usually society contributes to children. So the idea that they can give back is ironic. The title is ironic (see answer to Question 4 above). In paragraph 5, Swift refers to abortions as "sacrificing poor innocent babes." His solution, which is meant to prevent abortions, ironically calls for the sacrifice of innocent babies.

Questions on Strategy (p. 556)

1. Swift wants to persuade his readers to think of real solutions, to take responsibility for the problems of the country, and to lead themselves out of the absurd. He wants people to get upset at his solution and start to value their country's economy. He wants them to react against becoming a despicable culture that would eat its own children. Students will probably feel angry when hearing about the eating of one-year-olds and the suggestion that twelve- to-fourteen-year-olds are good or bad meat. When Swift discusses the benefits of the meat to tavern menus, many readers will be laughing. Once they understand the essay is satirical, the absurdity becomes enjoyable.

2. Swift begins his essay by defining the problem he wishes to solve. He describes the women and the children who go hungry. He sets up the problem to which he can provide his sickening solution.

3. The narrator sounds like an authority because he can describe the problem so clearly and has numbers to back it up. He can reference the 170,000 women who cannot support their children. This makes him sound like he has done research. Early in the essay, he also discusses that he has put a great deal of thought into the proposal. The benefits he delineates also show that he has thought this through, giving him even greater authority. If this absurd persona can create a sense of authority, then anyone can propose a better solution. Anyone can fight him and stand up for what is right. He wants to shock the reader, challenging him or her to make a better proposal.

4. The narrator makes a logical case. He presents a problem, describes how his solution addresses multiple aspects, and offers tremendous benefits to almost everyone. The calculations in paragraph 6 add to the logical strength of his argument. He calculates the benefit, establishing his authority.

5. Swift uses *cause and effect*: Poor women have too many babies, which results in poverty and starvation; eating the babies would improve the economy and health of the nation. He uses *illustration* to describe the problem in paragraph 1. He uses *division* and *classification* to explain the various benefits of eating babies, including the economic, social, and gastronomical advantages.

Questions on Diction and Vocabulary (pp. 556–557)

1. The tone is overly sincere and galvanizing. The term *modest proposal* positions the narrator as an earnest person looking to make a case. His language is especially effective in his description of the problem and in the list of benefits of eating children in paragraphs 20 through 27. When he uses phrases like "in the sincerity of my heart" (paragraph 33), he sounds false in his sincerity. He uses a similar phrase in paragraph 8: "I shall now therefore humbly propose . . ." Constantly restating his humility makes him suspect. Students may say he sounds subdued, patriotic, or passionate.

2. By using the term *modest*, Swift can more stealthily introduce his gut-wrenching proposal. This term encourages readers to let down their defenses and be carried by Swift's writing. Had he used an expression like "the only proposal," readers might have felt more on the defensive, fighting the writer's tone rather than accepting his satirical solution.

3. He uses the word *breeders* (paragraph 6) to reduce people to their most basic, animalistic, and functional traits: Babies are for food and women are for breeding. In dehumanizing the culture, Swift hopes to incense readers enough to claim back their humanity and use their higher selves to adopt solutions. Other words that suggest Irish origins include *shillings*, *pound*, *babes* (instead of "babies"), *popish*, *shambles*, *groat*, and *Pretender*.

CONTEMPORARY ARGUMENTS

The Case for Short Words
RICHARD LEDERER

Preparing to Read (p. 558)
Many people can identify books or other pieces of writing that they like without having to think a lot about it. When asked to identify why they like a particular piece of writing or what it is about it that they like, however, few can provide a quick answer. Before reading the Lederer essay, students should identify why they like a certain piece of writing and think hard about what they like in the writing itself. Their answers will vary. Students should be ready to discuss their choices and their reasons for liking them. Have them discuss what their preferences say about their other tastes and personality traits.

Thinking Critically about the Text (p. 561)
Lederer's essay will have more influence on how students view their own writing if they use his premise to analyze something they wrote in the recent past. Many students equate ponderous sentence structure and inappropriately arcane vocabulary choices with eloquent writing, and Lederer's essay will clearly debunk that association. For those who do tend to use long words in their papers, the answer to the last part of the question should be interesting. How successful was Lederer in converting students to his way of thinking? Students may wish to discuss in which situations using many long words and demonstrating a large vocabulary are appropriate.

Questions on Subject (p. 561)
1. Lederer contends that short words should be "the spine and the heart of what you speak and write" (paragraph 4). He demonstrates the feasibility of his argument by writing the title and first four paragraphs of his essay using only one-syllable words.
2. As already stated, students — and anyone else trying to impress or appear learned — tend to use an inappropriately elaborate vocabulary when producing writing that will be evaluated by others. Therefore, Lederer's argument is important. His essay will be most valuable to students because it will help them with their writing now and in the future.
3. Lederer's students react with "obligatory moans and groans" (paragraph 10). Their essays, as demonstrated by the two examples, usually turn out very well. The assignment teaches the students that writing well does not demand a large, complex vocabulary. Sometimes the simplest way to state something is the best way.
4. Because Lederer does not name the source of this pressure to "produce high-sounding polysyllables" (paragraph 10), student responses should explore how they personally got the impression that large words make for good writing. Then they can analyze why this myth is perpetuated.
5. Answers will vary.

Questions on Strategy (p. 562)
1. Answers will vary, but if students are being honest, most will probably say that they were surprised. Most students should also find the first four paragraphs to be an effective demonstration of the utility of small words.
2. Lederer's purpose is not to argue that small words should be used to the exclusion of all others. Indeed, he states outright in his single-syllable exercise: "If a long word says just what you want to say, do not fear to use it" (paragraph 4).

3. Lederer shows that small words can be used to great effect by both famous authors and his own students. To support his argument, he first quotes great orators and writers who used them well. He then includes essays written by his fourteen-year-old students. The student essays are both well written and very powerful.
4. Students' answers will vary, but be sure they are defended well. In selecting examples from their own reading, each student's choice of writing need not be entirely monosyllabic, but it needs to demonstrate clearly the validity of Lederer's argument.
5. Some students may argue that the ending is too corny to be effective, while others will note that the informal language reinforces one of the themes of the piece: that proper writing does not have to be stiff or highfalutin. Students should also note that this essay's ending is effective because it is a clear call to action.

Questions on Diction and Vocabulary (p. 562)
1. Paragraphs 3 and 4 contain several such similes. Some are a little poetic, so students' reactions to their effectiveness will probably vary. Make sure students clearly present why they find them effective or not.
2. The quotes Lederer uses in paragraph 9 are from familiar sources and, given the respect accorded them, have probably earned such ringing endorsements. "Mighty" and "ringing monosyllables" (9) may strike students as odd phrasing, but because Churchill's speech is considered so powerful and memorable in history, it is not overstatement. Lederer probably includes the descriptions to emphasize just how much impact small words can have if they are used well.
3. Almost all the verbs the students use in the two essays are active verbs. In such an exercise, no one "is dreaming"—one "wants" or "dreams" or "basked" (paragraph 10). The exercise is a very good way to encourage the use of active verbs instead of the passive voice, which is a trap into which many students fall. The results are apparent from the essays themselves. Strong action verbs energize writing, conveying more meaning in fewer words.

You Shouldn't Get a Prize for Showing Up
NANCY ARMOUR

Preparing to Read (p. 564)
Consider taking an informal poll of your students and ask them if they remember participation awards as being particularly meaningful or meaningless. Compare your results to Armour's statement that most children do not find such awards to be of value.

Thinking Critically about the Text (p. 566)
Armour says that Harrison's other behavior ought not distract from the strength of his message about participation trophies. This inclusion has the added benefit of reminding readers not to reject all of someone's comments because they have made mistakes in some areas of life. Student opinions will vary.

Questions on Subject (p. 566)
1. Participation trophies give young people a distorted view of life. Later, they may be shocked at "the harsh realities of life . . ." (paragraph 5). Also, not having to work for anything seems to be contributing to a larger sense of depression and even increased stress (5). Armour's thesis is in paragraph 3: "someone had the misguided notion that kids should live in la-la land where everything is perfect, there are no hardships or heartbreaks, and you get a shiny trophy or a pretty blue ribbon just for being you."

2. In paragraph 9, Armour explains the rationality of "everybody-gets-a-trophy" proponents. They say that these trophies encourage children always to try their best and persevere. She also says in paragraph 11 that the participation trophies are designed to protect children.

3. Students will have varying opinions. Some may say that Armour does not cite enough statistics or proof to convince all readers that they are really more depressed *because* of participation trophies. They might be stressed out because of the pressure of technology or because of unavailable parents, or because they are in a culture of emotionally unavailable people, and so on. In other words, she does not sufficiently prove that participation trophies are the *cause* of this depression or show us how widespread this depression and stress actually are.

4. Armour believes that adults give these trophies as an "affirmation that our kids are as wonderful as we think they are. It's also a way to fool ourselves into thinking that we are sheltering them, at least temporarily, from the cold, cruel world" (paragraph 14). Adults can think they are being good protectors of ideal children.

Questions on Strategy (pp. 566–567)

1. Armour wants to startle readers and provide a bit of a wake-up call for them. This is a similar lesson she wants children to learn. She thinks that losing may teach them that life is not always fair. Students may note that not winning is not necessarily teaching children that life is not fair but that it actually *is* fair. You win a prize if you win. The old adage "life isn't fair" applies to this argument only if children are losing because the judges are biased. This may occasionally be the case, but in most instances children lose because someone else is stronger. In any event, the opening phrase creates the emotional jolt in the reader, which is similar to the one she wants to create for children.

2. Armour means that children are told a lie when they receive these participation trophies. She says that they are taught incorrect lessons about the world and that the trophies decrease the value of their true wins. Awards mean more when earned. Children will be taught lessons of real value when they are allowed to win *and* lose.

3. Merryman's quote shows there might be a real long-term benefit to holding back on these participation trophies. Her comment suggests that we might better serve children's overall success if we delay their rewards. Let them be disappointed and learn how the game of life really works. If we can allow ourselves to do this, they might have real wins later on, wins that are far bigger than we could have imagined. The quote suggests that being a great parent might mean letting children struggle a bit.

4. Leaving the word to stand on its own adds emphasis and allows the reader to reflect on the previous thought for a moment without moving on.

5. Saying that children do not value the trophies suggests that we are not really giving them anything by giving them these false prizes. They do not have the meaning suggested by many people that "everybody gets a trophy." This claim also supports the idea that the trophies are for the parents, not the children.

Questions on Diction and Vocabulary (p. 567)

1. Students will respond differently. Some might like his slightly irreverent way of speaking. It makes him sound like an average person. This use of slang may make some readers feel closer to him; others may discount his comment because he seems to be a bit flippant in his presentation style.

2. Armour's readers rarely come to her for academic analysis so her tone is appropriate for this piece. To make it academic, she would need to remove terms like "amen" and

colloquial phrases like "a punch to the gut" (paragraph 5) or "if you've taken a peek at any 9-year-old's room" (13).
3. *Proponents* (9): advocates. *Incentive* (9): something that encourages someone to work harder. *Affirmation* (14): confirmation. *Resilience* (17): the ability to become strong, successful, and happy after a challenging event.

Telling Americans to Vote, or Else
WILLIAM GALSTON

Preparing to Read (p. 568)
If students do not seem engaged in the topic, you might ask whether they have encountered any politicians whom they do not approve of or any they particularly like. Once they are engaged in having opinions about the results, it will be easier for students to see why voting matters.

Thinking Critically about the Text (p. 571)
Galston does not believe that democracy can function properly when a majority of the population does not vote. Students might consider Galston's argument *focused* and/or *logical*. It is a focused argument because it has only one objective: to convince readers to make voting mandatory. It is a logical argument because he substantiates his claims about the importance of voting.

You could add a class discussion that points to a significant and dangerous hole in Galston's argument. Many people *not* voting face barriers to doing so. For example, they may not have child care or transportation. They may be on drugs or have an undiagnosed mental illness because they do not have health care. Or they may have trouble with the language. The fine imposed on people who can barely pay their electricity or other basic bills could be devastating and demoralizing. What, if anything, does Galston offer about helping people overcome the barriers that make it hard to vote? He suggests that people do not vote because of laziness, but people in lower socioeconomic groups face real challenges. Enforcing this practice without exploring and addressing why people do not vote can further subjugate them financially and morally.

Questions on Subject (p. 571)
1. He means that U.S. citizens talk about and the U.S. government grants people lots of rights (freedom, clean water, education, representation), but the government does not ask for much action in return.
2. Argument one: "[A] democracy cannot be strong if its citizenship is weak" (paragraph 5). Argument two: Democracy is not democratic if large groups of people are underrepresented. Viewpoints will be missing (6). Argument three: Low voter turnout polarizes the country. Elections end up being dominated by "hard-core partisans" (9).
3. In paragraph 8, Galston acknowledges that enforcing voting would "impose greater burdens on those with fewer resources." He says that this will make it *more* likely that these people will vote. They have more to lose by paying the fine. In paragraph 13, he acknowledges that there is no guarantee that the mandatory voting policy in Australia would work in the United States. He also acknowledges that the idea of mandatory voting contradicts the freedoms stated in the U.S. Constitution. He suggests that a handful of states with varying civil traditions try mandatory voting to see how well it works. He encourages a variety of people to monitor and consider the consequences. Students will offer additional rebuttals to the counterarguments Galston advances.

4. The argument is still relevant because there are elections for Congress every two years and there are also local city and town elections happening regularly.
5. Those with fewer resources often do not vote. As a result, their needs are less well articulated. Participation in voting would help them feel a "sense of participation in national politics" (paragraph 7).

Questions on Strategy (pp. 571–572)

1. The title uses a more shocking tone than the article itself. The title grabs readers' attention with drama, but the article aims to win them over with logical argument. The title helps Galston attract a wide audience; the logical argument style within the article helps him retain that audience.
2. The jury duty comparison at the start of the article helps diffuse dissent immediately. All readers can recognize the argument that 'Hey, you're right, we do have to go to jury duty. How is this different?' By drawing a comparison to a requirement that already exists, Galston can show that his idea is not anti-American but rather an extension of an existing tradition.
3. The Australian comparison is strong because the country has many similarities to the United States and because it had great success with mandatory voting laws. Students may note that Australia has nowhere near the diversity of the United States (economically or ethically) and this might have a big impact on the program's success anywhere else.
4. The clear argumentation style helps Galston maintain close contact with readers. They cannot drift off or get lost. To make the structure even more clear, he could have added headings with the name of each argument.

Questions on Diction and Vocabulary (p. 572)

1. Galston wants to appeal to the general, educated, and probably Anglo-Saxon public. He uses slightly sophisticated language: *intense partisan polarization* (paragraph 1), *enforcement mechanism,* (2), and *attenuated* (5). He also relies on statistics and references to American values that could be hard to understand for less-educated people and/or immigrants. Therefore, he is largely speaking to readers that already identify with American values and see themselves as resembling Australia. Immigrants might be less likely to recognize the similarities of these countries or to be as easily persuaded by them.
2. *Prevalence* (paragraph 3): the quality of being common or widespread. *Libertarian* (3): a member of a political party espousing free will above all else. *Attenuated* (5): reduced in force. *Reciprocity* (5): situation in which a person or groups do something similar for each other. *Disparities* (7): differences. *Mobilization* (7): moving people into action. *Quadrennial* (10): happening every four years. *Biennial* (10): happening every two years. *Electorate* (10): all people who are eligible to vote in an election. *Asymmetry* (11): having two parts that are not the same or are unequal.

The Organic Fable
ROGER COHEN

Preparing to Read (p. 574)
Do most students eat on campus or off? Students on meal plans have very different concerns than those who prepare their own food, but all should be able to offer opinions about what matters to them and why.

Thinking Critically about the Text (p. 576)

Students will say whether they are convinced by Cohen's argument. Many have likely read materials in support of organics, and Cohen's singular essay might not be enough to change their opinions. If he could prove that there really was no difference for *all* foods, then maybe people would stop buying them. There's a list called the "dirty dozen" that talks about the 12 foods where it matters most to buy organics. Cohen does not talk about these 12 foods. Perhaps in these foods it really does make a difference. He says that the long-term impact could be that we will not be able to feed the planet if we use only organic farming processes. Cohen does not address the argument that part of the reason we cannot feed the planet is actually the large consumption of beef. You may want to ask students to research how much land and water cattle require and the pressure this places on the planet. Population increase is another important factor. Then, with the whole class, discuss whether the consumption of bovine products (especially in the United States and China) has a greater or smaller impact than organic farming on our future ability to feed the planet.

Questions on Subject (pp. 576–577)

1. Cohen is making a logical argument. We know because he cites sources to back his claims. He wants to persuade readers but through logic rather than through manipulative language.
2. By "class-driven decision" (paragraph 4) Cohen means a decision that serves a particular class of people rather than the whole planet.
3. Cohen means that "organic" is more a designation used to sell products at a higher price than to provide meaningful value and nutrition. He cites the Stanford University study as an example; this study found that organic fruits and vegetables provided no additional benefits.
4. Cohen says that the organic movement will not support genetically modified foods because "that would go against the ideology and romance of a movement which says: We are for nature, everyone else is against nature" (paragraph 12). He believes that, in order to feed a growing planet and reduce our dependency on pesticides, we will need to rely on genetic modification.
5. Cohen means that he values people above the planet. For him there is an either/or choice to be made. Likely one does not have to choose, but he makes this shocking statement to push back on the cultural proclivity toward organics. He is trying to show people that buying organics might not necessarily be more loving than advocating for processes that will feed more people. This statement could possibly offend readers who think of themselves as caring *because* they buy organics.

Questions on Strategy (p. 577)

1. Cohen's thesis is the entire second paragraph. Using a long sentence as a full paragraph, he can both challenge the obsession with organics as a concept and demonstrate what he believes is the potential impact of moving to a solely organic way of farming on the growing population on earth.
2. In paragraph 3, Cohen cites the Organic Trade Association to highlight the amount of money spent on organic foods. He uses this statistic to support his point that many people are becoming increasingly obsessed with organics. In paragraph 5, he cites the Stanford University study to support his claim that organics are not actually better. In paragraph 8, he cites the requirements of the Department of Agriculture for foods labeled organic in order to support his point that organic labeling at least has some restrictions—unlike terms like *natural*.

3. The use of O instead of the word *organic* supports Cohen's claim that the word is largely meaningless. He does not give it the dignity of its full name. He also shows how its repetition makes it almost meaningless. Organic seems to be used as frequently on a menu as the letter O.
4. By saying three positive details about organics, Cohen shows that he is educated on the subject and tries to bring back readers he may have offended with his earlier claims and who may be shocked by the Stanford University study. These positive details could help proponents to feel less betrayed by the results of the study.
5. Cohen focuses more on the fact that organics are not as healthy—likely because he wants to pull people away from buying the products. Most people buy organics for their own health, not the planet's health. If he wants to change their minds, he must speak to their primary concerns. This was an important strategic decision. He connects the ideas by suggesting that, if you think you are saving the world by eating organic, think again. He makes the claim that nonorganic might actually be the more humanitarian choice.

Questions on Diction and Vocabulary (p. 577)
1. This term is used as a kind of mockery. In most of the essay, Cohen uses facts to make his claim, but in this instance he uses a phrase that sounds kind of flippant. He does this in part to say that the term itself is really a kind of meaningless slang. He jolts the readers, making the point that the term *organic* is as silly as the phrase "organic, schmorganic."
2. In the context of this essay, *pseudoscientific* is an apt term because it describes science that is used to promote something without any basis on accepted methodology.
3. The term *high yield* applies to crops that have big harvests compared to the amount of land cultivated. Low-yield crops produce less food on the same amount of land.

ARGUMENT CLUSTER
Race and Privilege: How to Address a Sysytem of Bias?

I, Racist
JOHN METTA

Thinking Critically (p. 587)
Student responses will vary. You may want to ask them if there were certain people or environments that helped them better understand the race issues around them or that they themselves faced.

Examining the Issue (p. 587)
1. The topic is race. Metta does not want to discuss it because he thinks people around him, even those who love him, will say he is overreacting or being too sensitive. He also says that people will point out how much better things are today than they were forty years ago. He keeps his mouth shut because it is part of an unspoken agreement in the culture that nice liberal friends ought to be kept comfortable.

2. Student answers will vary. It might be beneficial to discuss the following question in class: If someone is a member of a minority group, does that mean that person cannot be racist? There can be the assumption that only white privileged people can be racist.
3. Students' answers will vary. Metta's claim that the discourse works to protect white feelings does ring true. You may want to ask whether they think the Black Lives Matter campaign works to protect white feelings.
4. "Tone police" refers to the ways in which people angry about racism are shushed back into silence. Those operating in the institutions that perpetuate racism often try to control the angry expressions of those pointing out instances of racism.
5. Student answers will vary based on experience.
6. Metta quotes his sister, who defines how people in the North and South deal with race: "down here, at least people are honest about being racist." Throughout the essay, he is alluding to and pointing to what could be considered "racist"—that even white, liberal people can be racists. He also indirectly defines what racism is, such as moving out of a black neighborhood for "better schools." He says that racism is not slavery and avoids using certain racial slurs or the term *segregated public spaces*. He says that racism is really about cops attacking and killing an innocent man, the death of a 12-year-old from playing with a toy gun, or making movies with only white people. He also defines a racist system as one that allows upward mobility only for some.
7. Metta means that prosperity and opportunity are correlated with being white not black. Moving away from black people for a "better life" is a way of further separating the races and perpetuating the oppression of black people.
8. Metta believes racism exists to keep white people in power.

Racial Microaggressions in Everyday Life: Is Subtle Bias Harmful?
DERALD WING SUE

Thinking Critically about the Text (p. 593)
Students may think awareness is enough to interrupt the pattern of these microaggressions. Others may advocate for more robust changes such as policy changes or consequences for such aggressions. You may want to ask how interrupting microaggressions could violate free speech rights. When is biased allowed? When is it not?

Examining the Issue (p. 593)
1. In paragraph 6, Sue says that microaggressions are comments that, "on the surface, appear like a compliment or seem quite innocent and harmless, but nevertheless, they contain what we call demeaning meta-communications or hidden messages." He finds these messages concerning because those receiving such communications can experience "an erosion of their mental health, job performance, classroom learning, the quality of social experience and ultimately their standard of living" (paragraph 10).
2. Reiterating that the aggressions are unconscious has at least two purposes. First, it tells the reader that Sue is not blaming people for being purposefully hurtful. This keeps readers from being defensive. Labeling the behavior unconscious also encourages readers not to absolve themselves just because they may not be consciously aware of their actions. He encourages everyone to look a little deeper. This strengthens Sue's argument because

it supports his claim that there is a subcategory of aggression that is not overt. Students may say that it weakens his argument because they believe aggression requires consciousness.
3. Sue introduces the term *microassaults*, which are uttered consciously and intentionally either with words or with the use of symbols. *Microinsults* are verbal and nonverbal but more subtly convey a diminishing attitude toward another culture or heritage. Microinsults can be unconscious. Symbols, like flags, would be less likely to be part of this category, but you can discuss with the class the confederate flag debate and whether the use of the confederate flag would be considered a microassault or microinsult. The third category is *microinvalidations*. This category dismisses the thoughts or feelings of another race. It creates an exclusionary atmosphere. The major differences have to do with the consciousness level of the speaker and the subtly of the message.
4. In paragraph 12, Sue says that "our research suggests that microinsults and microinvalidations are potentially more harmful because of their invisibility, which puts people of color in a psychological bind: while people of color might be insulted, they are often uncertain why, and perpetrators are unaware that anything has happened and are not aware they have been offensive." People of color are punished for speaking up or psychologically hurt by not speaking up, Sue claims.
5. The personal story tells the reader that Sue is a person of color. The narration quickly draws the reader into the dynamic that the article will examine. Most readers can easily visualize the situation. The narration acts to hook readers and even cause them to consider if they have ever been victims or perpetrators of a similar act.
6. To introduce the term in context before defining it.
7. Sue calls them "brief" and "everyday" to highlight the subtle nature of such dynamics. They are not big demonstrations of racism. This encourages readers to be on the lookout for the ways these microaggressions are evident around them. The reference to the terms also suggests how such insults build up over time, adding a little more pain every day. Over time this can contribute to the erosion of a person's self-esteem.

What My Bike Has Taught Me about White Privilege
J. DOWSETT

Thinking Critically about the Text (p. 598)
The a ha! moment that Dowsett describes is when people have their privilege exposed. They feel uncomfortable when they begin to see the ways in which their privilege operates and how others lack that same access. Students will say whether they have had such an a ha! moment.

Examining the Issue (p. 598)
1. In paragraph 3, Dowsett says that white privilege talk is not intended to make a moral assessment or a moral claim about privilege; it is intended to talk about systemic imbalance.
2. White privilege means having systemic advantages because of a racism that has grown out of historical injustices. It does not mean that someone is bad for being white, just that they have significant advantages because they are white.

3. Drivers yell at him to get on the sidewalk. "People in cars think it is funny to roll down their window and yell something right when they get beside me. Or to splash me on purpose..." (paragraph 7).
4. Well-intentioned people put him in danger because they "see the road from the privileged perspective of a car" (paragraph 10). Car drivers do not change lanes for bikes the way they do for other cars. People drive too close to cyclists, not realizing how scary that is for the bike riders. Car drivers also do not realize the danger of broken bottles and potholes for bike riders.
5. The semi truck driver can be more careless in the road without worry. He can think good thoughts, be a good person, and still cause damage to others without hurting himself. He does not have to be hyperaware.
6. In paragraph 12, Dowsett draws the connection between privilege and bike riding. He says, "[L]ike drivers, nice, non-aggressive white people can move in the world without thinking about the 'potholes' or the 'gravel' that people of color have to navigate, or how things that they do—not intending to hurt or endanger anyone—might actually be making life more difficult or more dangerous for a person of color."
7. By "p-word" (paragraph 17), Dowsett means "privilege."
8. Dowsett's analogy works for almost any type of privilege. For instance, those with college educations might appear to be semi-drivers to those who do not have access to a college education. Those living in first-world countries can easily make uninformed choices—such as purchasing certain brands or visiting certain tourist locations—that might make those in third-world countries feel that they have been sideswiped.

ARGUMENT CLUSTER
Getting an Education: What's the Line between Comfort and Learning?

The Compliment Complex
JEFFREY ZASLOW

Thinking Critically about the Text (p. 607)
By showing the two extremes, Zaslow subtly encourages readers to think about what a middle ground might look like. By showing the old version of almost no compliments, he also validates some of the compliment movement, showing that he is not totally averse to acknowledgment. He just wants to encourage more of a middle ground.

Examining the Issue (p. 607)
1. In paragraph 3, Zaslow says, "Bosses, professors and mates are feeling the need to lavish praise on young adults, particularly twenty-somethings, or else see them wither under an unfamiliar compliment deficit."
2. Students will comment on the effectiveness of Zaslow's examples. He illustrates his point that companies are going crazy with compliments. He offers the examples of Lands' End and Bank of America hiring consultants to help managers learn how to compliment

(paragraph 4). He also presents the examples of Scooter Store Inc., which has a "celebrations assistant," and the Container Store, which offers compliments to staff members every 20 seconds. In paragraph 7, he refers to a study by Jean Twenge who studied the narcissism of students to illustrate what he claims was a significant increase since the 1980s. In paragraph 10, Zaslow cites Judy Neary, who says that the downside of all these compliments is people stop believing them.
3. In paragraph 13, Zaslow discusses the compliment complex as a generational issue. He cites Bob Nelson, a consultant for companies on how to increase praise. He claims that people over 60 like formal, public recognition. Paychecks also feel like recognition to them. Nelson says that baby boomers respond to free massages and high-tech gadgets. He says that employees under the age of 40 want trendy merchandise and also nearly constant feedback on how well they are doing.
4. Zaslow does not agree that people should be acknowledged just for showing up. It creates such low expectations and ultimately makes people dependent on outside praise for accomplishment.
5. This compliment craze creates pressure because if people do not feel like they are praised at every moment, they feel like a failure. Zaslow does not state this directly, but the craze also discourages people from developing an internal gage for their performance. They are entirely dependent on external feedback, which may or may not be forthcoming. It also creates a lot of pressure for managers who are afraid that if people do not get the praise they need they will leave their jobs.
6. The academic pressure is that professors need to receive great student evaluations in order to receive tenure, but if they create higher standards or do not give praise so easily, they might not get these great evaluations. Thus, the compliment complex pressures professors to give praise where it may not really be due.
7. The celebration consultant is responsible for showering confetti on other employees, but she does not want it for herself. This is ironic because you would think that, if she uses it to make others feel good, she believes that it works. Her response, however, suggests that the compliment it is supposed to communicate might be as trivial as the little pieces of paper that shower employees. Even she, maybe, thinks that the confetti is a little much.

On the Subject of Trigger Warnings
SIOBHAN CROWLEY

Thinking Critically about the Text (p. 609)
The author's teaching experience is relevant in that she has spent a great deal of time in the classroom. However, students might also argue that she has some bias because she may not want to alter her curriculum to incorporate trigger warnings. Ask students to find textual support for their position.

Examining the Issue (p. 609)
1. The thesis is the idea that trigger warnings might end up robbing students of the opportunity to face their fears. Her thesis can be found in the last three lines of her argument.
2. The first is that students will not be professionally qualified (paragraph 3). The second is that student will be unprepared to face triggering content after graduation (5).

3. Crowley makes her argument on the basis of her authority as both an instructor and as a student. Students will share whether they find her position convincing.
4. In paragraph 4, Crowley notes that it would not hurt someone majoring outside of the humanities to miss out on the content of *Othello*. This is a concession to her argument in paragraph 3 that a student or instructor would have "glaring blind spots" if they skipped over certain triggering topics each time they appeared in the canon.
5. Students will have a variety of opinions, but it is likely that Crowley means that facing difficult issues can give someone a firmer foundation for encountering them in the future.
6. Students will list the majors they feel might be particularly triggering, or not triggering at all. Some majors unlikely to have triggering content include math, biology, physics, and music. Majors more likely to address difficult topics are history, literature, psychology, and law.
7. Student opinions will vary.

The Coddling of the American Mind
GREG LUKIANOFF AND JONATHAN HAIDT

Thinking Critically about the Text (p. 623)
Students will share their experiences and reflections on free speech. They might highlight the tension between safe spaces and free speech, saying whether they find the two incompatible.

Examining the Issue (p. 623)
1. *Microaggressions* and *trigger warnings*.
2. *Vindictive protectiveness* is the phenomenon of silencing various ideas and uses of language in order to turn campuses into "safe spaces" to protect students from potential psychological harm.
3. Socrates taught people how to think, not what to think. The authors use this fact to defend their argument that schools ought not indoctrinate students with safe ideas but rather teach them how to reason through ideas.
4. Cognitive behavioral therapy is "the most extensively studied non-pharmaceutical treatment of mental illness and is used widely to treat depression, anxiety disorders, eating disorders and addiction" (paragraph 17).
5. The "water buffalo incident" in paragraph 24 points to how inane some of these accusations are. The accused student was actually using a term referring to rowdy people and found himself in danger of expulsion. The authors use this story to show how the "safe spaces" campaign has gone too far.
6. Cognitive distortions include overgeneralizing, discounting positives, and emotional reasoning. Overgeneralizing means taking one incident or moment and applying it to a larger whole. For example, being rejected from one college does not mean that one is always rejected. Or a sarcastic comment from a friend does not mean that the friend is always sarcastic. Discounting positives is when we tend to focus only on the bad and we do not note or appreciate the good in our lives or even about ourselves. Emotional reasoning is when we allow our emotional response to something to impact how we see a situation or a person. For example, we may be hurt and make up stories about why someone did something. We cannot think clearly in this state.

7. Trigger warnings affect what can be said in the classroom. This limits what can be taught in class. This also makes many people vulnerable to attack for not heeding these ever-changing but increasingly restrictive rules. Such warnings teach students to be scared of ideas and to avoid subjects that might be sensitive, and they ultimately prevent them from learning how to think.

CHAPTER 13 Writing Essays Using Subjects and Strategies

On Dumpster Diving
LARS EIGHNER

Preparing to Read (p. 641)
In this age of conservation and recycling, many students may have thought very hard about how they use things and how they choose to discard them. This question asks them to analyze not only what they do with waste but how and why they do it. The class may also wish to discuss how the thought of ultimately disposing of goods influences their decisions when they are buying them, which will lead into the Thinking Critically about the Text question.

Thinking Critically about the Text (p. 643)
Eighner's essay underscores how wasteful we are and emphasizes that everything we buy ultimately ends up somewhere. Yet, as a society, we are always urged to buy more and acquire more. In the Preparing to Read prompt, students were asked to discuss personal experience. Here they must ponder the question in the context of Eighner's essay and the potential effect personal beliefs may have on society as a whole.

Questions on Subject (p. 643)
1. There is the stage of shame and self-loathing; the stage of discovery, where the scavenger discovers the wealth to be found in Dumpsters; and the stage of professionalism, when the diver is willing and able to eat from Dumpsters. Eighner provides vivid examples of the goods to be found in the Dumpsters that move scavengers through their period of shame. Such items as a working calculator and still-frozen ice cream indicate the thoughtlessness with which people throw things away (paragraph 6). The discussion of food to be found and consumed in Dumpsters is more prosaic, but Eighner again provides specific examples.
2. Eating from Dumpsters requires scavengers to use their senses and common sense to evaluate the food, to know Dumpsters in an area and check them regularly, and to always question why something may have been discarded (paragraph 9). Canned food, dry food, raw fruits and vegetables, peanut butter, and yogurt are good things to eat from Dumpsters (10 and 11). Dysentery is a hazard that Eighner mentions, but it can be inferred that there must be others (12).
3. Eighner has learned to take what he can use and let the rest go (paragraph 13) and that material being is transient (14). He has learned not to grab for objects just for the sake of having them, and he has found a peace that he believes eludes the "rat-race millions," confounded as they are by their consumer society (16).
4. Because a novice diver is often tempted to take whatever he or she can carry, the ability to find something of true value is indeed an art. One must know where to find it and how to identify a worthy find. Eighner shows the reader, one item at a time, how much thought goes into selecting each find.
5. Students will have different reactions to Dumpster diving. Some may find it sad, while others may empathize, having sorted through thrift shops or furniture left at the curb.

One could even make the case that shopping is Dumpster diving with money. There is an art to shopping: knowing what is worth acquiring, with or without money.

Questions on Strategy (pp. 643–644)

1. Eighner discusses the concrete aspects of Dumpster diving to teach readers what it is like—what can be found in Dumpsters, how scavenging affects its practitioners, what makes it a potential hazard, and so on. It is only from this base of knowledge that he can then discuss the abstract, particularly the transience of material objects. For those who have never found such things as new running shoes or working calculators in Dumpsters, a discussion of transience may have little meaning. Eighner's concrete experiences give his abstract lessons credence.

2. Eighner's discussion of just how much good material can be found in Dumpsters does make scavenging sound almost attractive, but most readers will still be repelled by the idea of it—particularly when it comes to eating. By mentioning the grim reality of how regularly one struggles with disease when eating out of Dumpsters, Eighner maintains credibility in the eyes of the average reader and acknowledges the opinion most readers will have that "Dumpster diving has serious drawbacks as a way of life" (paragraph 12). The mention is brief, though, because the drawbacks to scavenging do not contribute to Eighner's purpose for writing the essay, which is to communicate what he has learned from all the good stuff he has found in Dumpsters.

3. Students should be able to provide a brief process analysis. Eighner's choice of title reflects his desire to communicate what he has learned from the process of Dumpster diving, not to present how to do it.

4. Students should identify many of the examples previously discussed. They will probably give various answers to the second part of the question, but students should touch on one of the following three characteristics: The examples are surprising, in terms of what can be found in Dumpsters; they are presented with candor and frankness, especially when Eighner discusses food; and they are presented quickly but effectively, so that it is very easy to picture the objects and to understand their implications.

5. Dumpster diving is a process. If the reader is able to understand how it is done, including its inherent challenges, problems, and rewards, it is then far easier to understand any lessons that may be learned from it. It is therefore a very effective strategy for Eighner to provide readers with a process analysis of Dumpster diving before presenting his conclusions or arguments regarding what he has learned from it. Students will provide various answers to the second part of the question, but they should explain why it is important to present the process they choose before presenting a related conclusion or argument. Ask students to discuss why it is important to present exactly what happens or how to do something before proposing an argument based on the process.

Questions on Diction and Vocabulary (p. 644)

1. Eighner says that he likes "the frankness of the word *scavenging*" (paragraph 3). It does not mislead in the way "foraging" does—it does not imply a gathering of natural goods; it implies living directly from refuse. He considers it a valid niche in society. A definition of scavenging is important enough for Eighner to include at the beginning because it establishes his view of his subject and because it establishes the frank tone maintained throughout the rest of the essay.

2. Students will have different connotations for *dilettanti* and *professional*, but they should indicate that there is a strong contrast between the two. Eighner establishes just how big

a step it is to eat from Dumpsters by using these terms. Also, the word *professional* should imply that the person makes his or her living from it—he or she is very good at it, and it is how he or she survives. Eighner's choice of these two words elevates the level of his discussion. He wants to make several serious points about society; calling himself a professional gives him more authority.

3. Eighner's statement emphasizes just how many good things—or how much good "stuff"—is thrown away. He implies that it has become acceptable to scavenge for certain objects, that the finder is savvy and skillful. Opinions will differ on the use of the word *art*. The choice of the word is a little odd—*recreation* or *skill* might have been chosen more readily—but it communicates Eighner's appreciation for the validity of the activity.

How to Reengineer Crops for the 21st Century
MICHAEL WHITE

Preparing to Read (p. 646)
It is entirely possible that students will not have considered the matter of genetically engineered food before. If this is true for your students, ask them for their opinions about organic or locally sourced foods instead. This conversation will serve as a useful counterpoint after they have read White's essay.

Thinking Critically about the Text (p. 649)
Students will weigh in on whether they agree that genetically engineered crops must be part of the conversation. The increasing world population is a huge part of the problem. If the population stopped increasing, then there may be less need to panic. Students might also point out how the increasing consumption of meat is leading toward the looming crisis. Pesticides and other farming procedures also deplete the land. These factors have an impact on food production. Students may also speak of climate change or poorer countries destroying their land with toxic chemicals.

Questions on Subject (p. 649)
1. Photosynthesis is "the fundamental biological process by which plants use sunlight to convert water and carbon dioxide in the atmosphere into something we can eat" (paragraph 3). Some scientists want to redesign photosynthesis to make it more efficient in order for crops to produce higher yields.
2. White believes that it will be necessary to engineer food genetically in order to meet the food needs of a growing number of people. The world's population, he says, will grow from 7 billion up to 12 billion by the end of the century.
3. A "smart canopy" is created when farmers plant crops of differing heights together. Taller plants that like direct sunlight could be placed next to those that do better with low light. This allows farmers to increase the yields of both plants, making better use of the space.
4. White is not concerned about the present design limitations because he says that the genetically modified crops already existing required alterations far more advanced than what would be required to modify photosynthesis.

5. White wants readers to embrace this approach to increasing yields and to politically support the funding needed to conduct further research. Students will say whether they find these calls to action convincing.

Questions on Strategy (pp. 649–650)
1. This explanation helps readers envision a farming strategy that seems like a logical approach to increasing yields. This simplified explanation helps allay the fears of readers who may be concerned with genetic modifications to foods. Instead, farmers are simply getting smarter about how to use sunlight. The impact is that the approach seems logical and uncontestable.
2. In paragraph 7, White quotes the proposal to encourage readers to support long-term research in this area. In addition to quotations, White cites in paragraph 8 an unnamed study that says that this kind of modification can increase yields by 80%.
3. Noting the impending crisis gives White's article urgency and encourages readers to pay attention. Fear motivates readers.

Questions on Diction and Vocabulary (p. 650)
1. White refers to greenhouse gases and biofuels in paragraph 2. He refers to photosynthesis (3), which he defines. Most students will say that the terms make sense in context.
2. *Capacity* (paragraph 1): the largest amount that could be held. *Ecosystems* (2): everything that exists in a particular environment. *Emissions* (2): In this case, the expulsion of greenhouses gases into the atmosphere. *Biofuels* (2): fuels composed or produced from biological material. *Photosynthesis* (3): the process by which a plant turns water and carbon dioxide into food when the plant is exposed to light. *Determinant* A factor or element that determines the outcome of a situation. *Feasible* (4): possible to do. *Byproducts* (5): anything produced as a result of some other process. *Metabolic* (5): pertaining to the chemical processes by which a plant or animal uses food, water, and so on, to make energy or to heal. *Stagnating* (8): to stop developing or progressing. *Regulatory* (9): pertaining to rules that control something.

Language Chauvinism: The Ugly American Revisited
COOPER THOMPSON

Preparing to Read (p. 651)
For students who have not traveled outside the United States, you might ask about regional accents or cultures if they have visited other cities or states. You might also suggest that students think of some quirks in their own hometowns that might be confusing for visitors.

Thinking Critically about the Text (p. 654)
The events in this essay all involved strangers assuming that Thompson spoke English in non-English-speaking countries. He starts with a Christmas market in Germany, then talks about the German flight from Frankfurt, and then his experience in France. The cherished U.S. value is getting what Americans want when they want it.

Questions on Subject (pp. 654–655)

1. In paragraph 3, Thompson writes about a Lufthansa flight leaving from Frankfurt going to the United States. The man sitting behind him asked him in English when the flight would arrive in Boston. He was frustrated and quipped back, "Why do you assume that I speak English?" He then apologized. He said that, had the man apologized, there would have been an opportunity to discuss the issue more fully. It was an example that was representative of his point and also represented a missed opportunity for more complete communication.
2. Thompson states his thesis most clearly in the title and at the beginning of paragraph 6: "I sometimes wonder if there's another value being exported, this one from folks who don't want other languages spoken in the U.S.: 'English Only.'"
3. Thompson was frustrated that the man could not understand that some things are done differently in other places and that not everything has to be a replica of the United States or Starbucks.
4. This does not undermine Thompson's argument. He is not arguing that people must learn the language of the place they are visiting; he simply wants people not to assume that everyone speaks English.
5. Asking whether someone speaks English mitigates the problem of language chauvinism. By asking this question, Americans can show that they do not assume that the world depends on their language. It conveys modesty and respect.

Questions on Strategy (p. 655)

1. Some readers might be drawn in by the unexplained word "it." The risk is that other readers may think that they missed something, they may be confused, or they may be turned off by the assumption that they know what Thompson is talking about.
2. In the dialogue we can experience the upset that the author feels. We can feel with him how he is triggered by the assumptions and maybe even see ourselves in one of the parties. He wants readers to recognize themselves in the tourist voices; he hopes this will lessen the chances that they themselves behave this way.
3. Readers will react to Thompson's use of personal narratives. Many may say it draws them closer to the points he is making. They can imagine similar situations. The fact that he is a native English speaker might cause some readers to find that his point makes less of an impact.
4. Thompson does not assume that people speak English and he tries to speak the local language.
5. Thompson wants to highlight that it is not easy to speak another language. To assume someone speaks English puts them in the awkward position of having to try to speak it, and they might not feel comfortable doing so. This also encourages readers to be kinder when they hear mistakes in conversation.

Questions on Diction and Vocabulary (p. 655)

1. If the essay were told in the third person, it might come off as preachy. The personal narrative brings us closer to the incidents and lets us see our own reflections more clearly.
2. Americans have a reputation for being demanding in their requests. Thompson is overexaggerating a bit, but he is highlighting the reputation Americans have around the world for being this way.

Me Talk Pretty One Day
DAVID SEDARIS

Preparing to Read (p. 657)
If you teach this essay near the end of the term, it might be a useful moment for students to reflect on their successes and struggles in your classroom, and how they might move forward with their knowledge, as Sedaris does at the end of his essay.

Thinking Critically about the Text (p. 661)
Sedaris's essay does not end with him "talking pretty" but at least he is talking. He made some small improvements, mostly in comprehension. The instructor's feedback made the students feel like they would never improve. She was most discouraging and insulting. Yet her high standards helped make even his small accomplishments feel significant.

Questions on Subject (p. 661)
1. Readers have to guess why the instructor insulted the likes and dislikes of the students. It seemed like a way to belittle the students and terrorize them a bit, either because she did not like teaching or thought this would be an effective means of motivating them.
2. Sedaris says that she was like a wild animal because she was unpredictable, changing not from day to day but from moment to moment (paragraph 18). Other analogies could include a temperamental toddler or someone who is hallucinating.
3. "I absorbed as much of her abuse as I could understand" (paragraph 17). He took her direct comment of "I hate you" personally (20). But the instructor's abuse did make Sedaris work harder. He spent four hours a night working on his homework.
4. Sedaris became more nervous about speaking outside the classroom once he started the class. He became more aware of errors. By the end, however, his comprehension had improved and this made him more eager to engage in the language.
5. Sedaris basked because he was just so happy he could understand what she was saying.

Questions on Strategy (pp. 661–662)
1. Readers can visualize the class as a very diverse, international group. This also helps portray the teacher as someone who berated all people learning French, not just the Americans. Sedaris could have included the reasons why people were learning French or the languages they grew up speaking.
2. Sedaris wanted to startle the teacher and maybe impress her with his vocabulary. He was also partly making fun of her. She taunted others. He then used the question as an opportunity to taunt her. *Blood sausage* and *intestinal patés* are items he also discussed that were peculiar for a beginners' class.
3. The irony is in getting all stirred up and almost agitated about things we love. Loving something tends to evoke very different emotions — softer ones. The idea of pounding out what we love and being ridiculed for things we appreciate seems absurd.
4. Sedaris writes, "I find it ridiculous to assign a gender to an inanimate object which is incapable of disrobing and making an occasional fool of itself" (paragraph 17). He uses this as a form of mockery; it is not a real critique. Languages develop the way they do often without logic. His reasoning is not supposed to be convincing; it is supposed to be funny.

5. Sedaris's last line shows us that his speaking ability did not improve, but his enthusiasm was strong and his comprehension was growing. It gives language learners permission to make mistakes and keep going. Progress can be made and the language can be enjoyed even without perfection.

Questions on Diction and Vocabulary (p. 662)

1. The use of a random collection of letters helps readers appreciate how the words sounded to Sedaris. Had he just used the French words, those who speak French would have understood the meaning; others could have guessed. By using nonsense words, he could connect with all readers—at one time or another we have all heard words that made no sense to us. Readers could laugh at themselves and laugh together.
2. Sedaris uses a "show, don't tell" method in this essay. He shows the bad grammar versus explaining it. This helps readers imagine how Sedaris sounds speaking in French and even how they might sound speaking another language.

CHAPTER 14 Writing with Sources

Bees: Why Are They Dying?
WAYNE ELLWOOD

Preparing to Read (p. 687)
Students may have read articles in the news about bees dying off in large numbers, or this might be the first time they have encountered the concern of scientists over the bee population. Many students may find this to be a difficult topic to care about, which is a great place to begin discussion. Ask students why, in the face of wars and poverty, or even smaller personal concerns, should we care about the bees? If you do not get any responses, consider the impact on global hunger if bees are not able to pollinate food sources as a starting point.

Thinking Critically about the Text (p. 693)
Pastures have been replaced by cash crops. Farms producing single crops offer less diversity of plants for bees to enjoy. These crops also only blossom at certain times, creating floral deserts the rest of the year. Farming also brings pesticides, which hurts the bees, and the long distances they travel create additional shocks. Students will say whether they believe Ellwood cited sufficient evidence for this claim.

Questions on Subject (p. 693)
1. CCD stands for "colony collapse disorder." Hundreds of agrochemicals are poisoning the bees and causing CCD syndrome, which manifests like HIV in bees. It causes all kinds of diseases in bees, which eventually kills whole colonies.
2. Keystone species, according to Carson, are at the very center of the entire food web. Remove this species and the whole food chain collapses.
3. In paragraph 5, Ellwood offers his thesis — bees are crucial and they are dying for reasons that are not yet clear.
4. Causes of death for bees include floral deserts, which are fields that have only short seasons of blossoms for the bees. Monocropping severally challenges the health of bees. Farms that use every inch of land prevent bees from even pollinating small hedges. Disease is the main cause of death for North American bees. CCD is a deadly condition that seems to be caused by chemicals used in farming. The condition kills bees in a variety of ways.

Questions on Strategy (pp. 693–694)
1. Chemicals cause CCD syndrome, which kills bees. Monocropping causes floral deserts. The lack of bees has caused the birth of a new industry: pollinating services.
2. The quote in paragraph 1 helps readers imagine the richness and diversity of plants that used to exist and helps them imagine how that diversity could exist again. Ellwood is showing what is possible. Students will say whether they see this quote as integrated.
3. Students will select examples they found powerful or less convincing. The discussion of the almond industry and the busing in of pollinating bees creates a powerful visual. It helps when Ellwood describes a specific situation rather than creating a list of diseases or

problems. He strengthens his argument by offering examples of the problem in other countries. This shows that he has done his research and that the problem is worldwide and not restricted to the United States. Students' opinions will vary.

4. Whether or not students understand the exact meaning, they will likely understand that hedges are important, some fields need to be left unmowed, and herbicides hurt bees. The terminology suggests that Ellwood's audience is fairly savvy about farming techniques.

5. Students will say whether or not they find Ellwood's analogy convincing. It seems that it will be increasingly true.

Questions on Diction and Vocabulary (p. 694)

1. Ellwood's diction amplifies the problem to the reader interested in the details of the growing problem with bees. Expressions like "cash crop" highlight the monetization of farming, which contributes to the loss of bee populations (paragraph 3). The phrase "intensively cultivated" points to the pressure that current farming techniques place on the bees (3). Students will offer other examples. Ellwood also reiterates his main point using simple words such as "bees put food on the table" (9).

2. The phrase "long tour of duty" in paragraph 5 highlights how we have enlisted bees to do our work for us. Like soldiers they offer their lives for ours. Ellwood's lists in paragraph 8 highlight a variety of problems for bees: cold weather, deadly mites, bacteria, viruses, parasites, pesticide poisoning, and fungal infections. Each of these terms point to death for bees.

3. *Intrepid* (1): feeling no fear; bold or brave. *Extirpated* (3): destroyed or removed completely. *Pallets* (4): straw-filled, temporary beds. *Terrestrial* (9): of or relating to the earth. *Edifice* (10): a large structure. *Pathogens* (13): organisms that cause disease. *Consensus* (13): a general agreement. *Havoc* (13): a situation of much destruction or confusion. *Rampant* (13): growing quickly in a way that is hard to control. *Prone* (14): likely to have, do, or suffer from. *En masse* (16): a single group all together. *Susceptible* (20): easy to affect or influence. *Legions* (20): large groups of soldiers. *Premised* (21): based on. *Resilience* (23): the ability to become strong and healthy after a hard time.

How Social Media Is Changing Hollywood
NICOLA FREEDMAN

Preparing to Read (p. 695)
Along with discussing how social media recommendations may change what a student wants to see, you might discuss how various media companies are also changing how students view movies. Netflix, Amazon Prime, and Red Box have all created tidal shifts in the movie-viewing market. Some of these trends might prove useful in adding complexity to your class discussion of Freedman's essay.

Thinking Critically about the Text (p. 703)
Readers will likely say that they learned something about the impact of social media on film from the article. Few have likely heard about the impact from the filmmakers and film producers' perspective. Television and the music industries likely have similar problems, as do video game producers.

Questions on Subject (p. 703)

1. If people do not support a film immediately or, worse, if they pan the film, the box office results will reflect this quickly. Word of mouth now happens more quickly than ever before. If the film is great, everyone knows. If it is not, they now know almost instantly.
2. The film industry is facing competition from video games and consumers producing their own content. It is harder for films to attract people's attention.
3. Special effects bring people into the theaters. They can see something in the cinema that has less of an impact when they watch at home.
4. Viral advertising and media refers to content being passed from consumer to consumer. A concept, video, or tweet moves around and around. This is difficult to predict, although content can be designed so that it can go viral more easily. Consumers can spread positive reviews about a movie. They can also spread negative impressions of the movie.
5. Actors must now promote their movies on their social media outlets, including Instagram and Twitter. If they do not promote their own movies, the movies are often not seen. If an actor does not participate in social media, it can really hurt the box office results for his or her movie.

Questions on Strategy (pp. 703–704)

1. This background information helps situate the argument and informs readers how the industry works. Adding social media to the mix now makes more sense because we can see a period of change.
2. In paragraph 1, Freedman says, "[U]sing a few key case studies of successful and unsuccessful Hollywood blockbusters, this essay will argue that the advent and inexorable rise of social media has made word of mouth much more of a decisive factor than ever before."
3. Freedman selected movies that many readers would recognize. Even if they had not seen them they would likely have heard of them. In the case of *The Lone Ranger*, they would at least have recognized the actor Johnny Depp. Other superhero movies (*Batman*, *Superman*, *X-Men*) would have been good examples. For cult films and original stories, Freedman could have listed *Dirty Dancing* or *Back to the Future*. For flops, she could list any number of films no one has likely seen.
4. Freedman starts paragraph 3 with "Moreover," which continues the argument and idea without having to write an overly long paragraph. She starts paragraph 4 with "while word of mouth . . ." to set up her point about the importance of word of mouth in the age of social media. She also uses headings that help with transitions and direct the reader.

Questions on Diction and Vocabulary (p. 704)

1. Freedman often uses soft signal phrases like "he notes," which make the signal phrase almost unnoticeable. This keeps a smooth flow. She emphasizes a point in paragraph 3 when she says, "lawyer Lawrence Lessig astutely observes . . ." She is adding her approval to his words.
2. There are so many subdivisions in the film industry, and social media might be affecting each slightly differently. But rather than focus on these nuances, Freedman is able to keep the gaze fixed on Hollywood more generally and the blockbuster films known to most readers.
3. Freedman expects her audience to know something about films. She wrote the essay for a magazine called *Digital America*, which likely has a sophisticated readership when it comes to film. For readers who are not film buffs, this makes the article feel like an insider piece, which can add to the excitement.

The English-Only Movement: Can America Proscribe Language with a Clear Conscience?

JAKE JAMIESON

Preparing to Read (p. 706)

For some students, English will not be their first language, and they will have experiences to share about learning English in the United States. Although most students are likely to say that they would work hard to learn the predominant language of a chosen country, it might be useful to talk about how difficult that might be for some people. You might ask students if they've tried to learn another language before, and if so, how easy or hard it was for them. You might ask students whether they have visited a country where English was not the predominant language and what their experience was like. Were they grateful to find people who could speak English? If they moved to that country, would they feel similarly grateful to have the opportunity to speak English? Responses will vary on how students would feel if laws forced them to learn and use the predominant language as quickly as possible. Would they feel welcome?

Thinking Critically about the Text (p. 713)

Responses will vary regarding whether students agree with Jamieson's claim that "[t]here are so many sets of variables that it would be hard to defend the argument that there is only one culture in the United States" (paragraph 3). The mainstream cultural idea of a two-parent house-in-the-suburbs family does have many variations, but traditionally the white middle class (Anglo-Saxon descent) has been considered the dominant American culture. Students might be asked how they fit into that "mainstream" and whether the prevalence of that idea of mainstream has the cultural power to still be considered "the norm."

Questions on Subject (p. 713)

1. The question that Jamieson wants to answer in his essay is: "Should immigrants be required to learn English or should accommodations be made so they can continue to use their native languages?" (paragraph 1). Jamieson notes that the melting-pot idea of assimilation is in reality "a giant cauldron" where differences "are boiled away in the scalding waters of discrimination" (1) and quotes language diversity advocate James Crawford that discrimination is behind the English-only laws (8). He goes on to point out that English-only laws have been linked to anti-immigration laws (12) and that the English-only sentiment is concentrated in areas with large Spanish-speaking populations (12). Jamieson sees the official-English requirement as a form of discrimination that violates the constitutional right of citizens not only to freedom of speech (7, 14) but also to "life, liberty, and the pursuit of happiness" (14). In his last paragraph, he quotes columnist Myriam Marquez's assertion that whatever language is spoken, a more multiethnic American cultural landscape is inevitable.

2. Jamieson counters the people who argue that the melting-pot analogy is valid by indicating that the kind of harmonious assimilation the analogy alludes to is a myth, that in fact the melting pot is "a giant cauldron" where differences "are boiled away in the scalding waters of discrimination" (paragraph 1). Jamieson counters the melting-pot myth of "harmony and the only way to dissipate the tensions that inevitably arise when cultures clash" by asserting that immigrants have not always come to this country because they wanted to "embrace American values" (2) and, further, that there's no consensus on what the "'American way' of doing things" is (3). His evidence: "Not everyone in America is of the

same religious persuasion or has the same set of values, and different people affect vastly different styles of dress" (3). Student responses to whether this is a persuasive counterargument will vary. Some may add to the counterargument from their own experience of "variables" (3); others may indicate that Jamieson's evidence of cultural variation is weak.

3. In paragraph 6, former senator Bob Dole is quoted as saying that English "is the ticket to the 'American Dream'" and Greg Lewis's quotation shows what he means: To "succeed in America" a person needs to be fluent in the dominant language of the country. While few would disagree with this statement, some—like language diversity advocate James Crawford—might argue that success could occur in occupations that service a group that doesn't have English as the dominant language. Some might say that when political commentator Greg Lewis supports Dole's position by saying, "it's just the way it is," Dole's position is revealed to allow for, accept, and in this way promote discrimination.

4. Language diversity advocate James Crawford sees the issue as "plain and simple: 'discrimination'" (paragraph 7), by which he means English-only sentiment is veiled racial bigotry. It is against the law to discriminate based on race, but English-only advocates can skirt the issue by saying their subject is language, not ethnicity (8). Others like Myriam Marquez are also concerned that speaking a language other than English can be used as a "litmus test . . . to gauge American patriotism" (7), which would justify discrimination. Crawford would lump Dole's comments in with the English-only advocates as being "bigoted, anti-immigrant, mean-spirited, and steeped in nativism" (8) because Dole accepts (and thereby promotes) the use of a dominant language as a means of de facto discrimination.

5. In his concluding paragraph, Jamieson leaves his readers with three important questions:
   - "Do we plan to allow everyone in this country the freedom of speech that we profess to cherish, or will we decide to reserve it only for those who speak English?"
   - "Will we hold firm to our belief that everyone is deserving of life, liberty, and the pursuit of happiness in this country?"
   - "Or will we show the world that we believe in these things only when they pertain to us and people like us?"

Jamieson aligns himself with those who find English-only legislation in violation of the constitutional rights invoked in the first two questions. The third question is a rhetorical chastisement directed at those who would use English-only rules to violate the Constitution. Student responses are likely to vary as to whether they agree or not with Jamieson.

Questions on Strategy (p. 713)

1. Jamieson's thesis is found in the question in the first paragraph: "At the center of the discussion about immigrants and assimilation is language: Should immigrants be required to learn English or should accommodations be made so they can continue to use their native languages?" While not a statement, the essay is organized as an answer to this question. The implied thesis is that English-only legislation constitutes discrimination.

2. Jamieson's focused argument is organized in a linear fashion, from an implied assertion to evidence to conclusion, including proof and counterproof and a classical appeal to ethical behavior. Opposing viewpoints are included to show their inadequacies and thereby strengthen Jamieson's own position. His goal is to change the reader's mind about a controversial issue. He presents his thesis, then explains his points: First he defines the issue in the form of a question. Then he presents his evidence through his own reason supported by the expert testimony from Clarkson and Marquez that English-only laws are a form of discrimination. He includes quotations from Dole and Krauthammer to represent the opposite point of view so that he can argue against it, moving back and forth

between these authorities to compare and contrast views. He concludes with an ethical appeal not to discriminate but to uphold the constitutional rights of those who are not fluent English speakers.

3. Signal phrases that introduce quotations in Jamieson's essay include the following: "According to former senator and presidential candidate Bob Dole . . ." (paragraph 6), "Many of them, like Myriam Marquez, readily acknowledge . . . but fear that . . ." (7), and "According to language diversity advocate James Crawford . . ." (8). He brings in point and counterpoint with these quotes, which allows him to argue against Dole's position with the support of Marquez and Crawford.

4. In paragraph 6, Jamieson includes a quotation from political commentator Greg Lewis to reinforce Dole's point: " 'to succeed in America . . . it's important to speak, read, and understand English as most Americans speak it. There's nothing cruel or unfair in that; it's just the way it is' " (6). Without the Lewis quotation, the essay would lose the idea that the English-only advocates accept discrimination (" 'it's just the way it is' "). Jamieson uses these quotations to argue against the position that the English-only point of view is "welcoming" (6) or nondiscriminatory.

5. Jamieson supports Crawford's assertion that English-only advocates are "bigoted, anti-immigrant, mean-spirited, and steeped in nativism" (paragraph 8) with an example in paragraph 9 of a Texas judge who ruled that a mother's speaking only Spanish to her child constituted abuse: " 'relegating her to the position of housemaid.' " He stood firm on this ruling, even though he later apologized to housekeepers. With this example, Jamieson shows how English-only beliefs rely on the notion that languages other than English are not only associated with lower socioeconomic groups but are also deemed inferior, with second-class discriminatory status.

Questions on Diction and Vocabulary (pp. 713–714)

1. Responses will vary. To help students think about how perceptions of the "American way" might have changed over the past decades, consider asking them how their parents or other older adults talk about it, and/or how the "American way" is portrayed in older films and television shows.

2. The word *official* connotes legality, formality, the public sphere, rule-boundedness, and so on, with which students might have either negative or positive associations. "English-only" might imply intolerance to some, and a (negative) desire to homogenize a country that has always been known for its diversity; to others, it might connote an (appropriate) insistence on order and adherence to rules. Some students might (negatively) associate the word *immigrant* with being an outsider, alien, or "noob"—connotations that might be considered to reveal a nativistic American attitude. Others might positively associate *immigrant* with such qualities as resourcefulness, independence, and cultural "authenticity."

3. *Assimilation* (paragraph 1): the act of making similar or of absorbing into a culture or population. *Dissipate* (2): to break up and vanish. *Implications* (4): meanings that are suggested rather than explicitly stated. *Nativism* (8): the favoring of inhabitants born to a particular locale over immigrants or newcomers. *Malice* (10): a desire to cause pain, injury, or distress.

Bedford/St. Martin's is here for you.

At Bedford, providing support to teachers and their students who choose our books and digital tools is our first priority. For a complete list of resources, visit **macmillanlearning.com/subjectandstrategy /catalog.**

Download your Instructor Resources. Available from our online catalog, the *Instructor's Manual for Subject & Strategy* features answers to questions and suggestions for class discussions.

Join Our Community! The Macmillan English Community is now Bedford/St. Martin's home for professional resources, featuring Bedford Bits, our popular blog site offering new ideas for the composition classroom and composition teachers. Connect and converse with a growing team of Bedford authors and top scholars who blog on Bits: Andrea Lunsford, Nancy Sommers, Steve Bernhardt, Traci Gardner, Barclay Barrios, Jack Solomon, Susan Bernstein, Elizabeth Wardle, Doug Downs, Liz Losh, Jonathan Alexander, and Donna Winchell.

In addition, you'll find an expanding collection of additional resources that support your teaching.

- Sign up for webinars
- Download resources from our professional resource series that support your teaching
- Start a discussion
- Ask a question
- Follow your favorite members
- Review projects in the pipeline

Visit community.macmillan.com to join the conversation with your fellow teachers.

Save trees. If you do not need this evaluation copy, please pass it on to an interested colleague or return it by printing a label from **macmillanlearning.com/examcopy**.